The
Castles
of
Scotland

The
Castles
of
Scotland

a comprehensive reference and
gazetteer to more than 2700 castles
and fortified sites

THIRD EDITION

Martin Coventry

GOBLINSHEAD

Musselburgh

First Published 1995
Second edition 1997
Third Edition 2001
© Martin Coventry 1995/1997/2001

Published by GOBLINSHEAD
130B Inveresk Road, Musselburgh EH21 7AY, Scotland
Tel: +44 (0)131 665 2894   Fax: +44 (0)131 653 6566
Email: goblinshead@sol.co.uk

British Library Cataloguing in Publication Data
A catalogue record for this book is available from the British Library.

hardback ISBN 1 899874 27 5
paperback ISBN 1899874 26 7

Typeset by GOBLINSHEAD from electronic Castles database
using Desktop Publishing
Printed by Polestar-AUP Aberdeen
Written, published and printed in Scotland

Third Edition
Photographs and maps by Martin Coventry
except Castle Tioram and Neidpath Castle (Janine Hunter), Invergarry Castle
(Eileen Barrie), Cramond Tower (Joyce Miller), Brochel Castle (Georgi
Coventry), Ackergill Tower (Ackergill)Glamis Castle (Glamis), Winton
House (Winton), Dalhousie Castle (Dalhousie)
Colour section (hardback only) by Martin Coventry except Castle Tioram
(Janine Hunter), Brochel Castle (Georgi Coventry), Traquair House (Anna
Coventry) and Dairsie Castle (Alasdair Anderson)
Other illustrations from collections of Grace Ellis and Martin Coventry
Line illustrations from McGibbon and Ross: *Castellated and Domestic
Architecture of Scotland*
Drawings by Laura Ferguson and Alasdair Anderson
Architectural diagrams by Lindsay Blair
Special thanks to Gordon Mason, Helen Fraser, Andrew Kerr, Alasdair
Anderson, Janine Hunter, Georgi Coventry and Grace Ellis

Contents

List of Illustrations
Preface
How to Use the Book

Introduction   1

The Development of the Castle in Scotland   3
Glossary of Terms   8
Place-Name Elements   11

Maps   15

Maps locating every castle in the book
Main Map / 1 Dumfries & Galloway / 2 Borders / 3 Ayr,
Renfrew & Lanarkshire / 4 Lothians /5 Argyll &
Dunbarton / 6 Stirling & Falkirk /
7 Fife / 8 Perth & Angus / 9 Highland, South /
10 Aberdeen & Moray/ 11 Western Isles, Orkney &
Shetland / 12 Sutherland & Caithness

Castles   41

A to Z guide

Indexes   419

Ghosts and Bogles Index   419
Family Names Index   420

Further Reading   436

List *of* Illustrations

Kildrummy Castle (MC) frnt cover
Dunnottar Castle (MC) back cover
Crathes Castle (MC)   back cover
Corgarff Castle (MC)   back cover
Drum Castle (MC)   back cover
Kilchurn Castle (MC)   frontispiece
Dun Carloway (MC) 3
Duffus Castle (MC) 4
Castle Sween (MC) 4
Dunnottar Castle (MC) 4
Diagram of L-plan tower (LB) 5
Plan of a keep (LB) 6
Alloa Tower (MC) 6
Plan of a tower (LB) 6
Plan of a L-plan tower (LB) 6
Greenknowe Tower (M&R) 6
Plan of a Z-plan tower (LB) 7
Claypotts Castle (MC) 7
Armadale Castle (1920?) 7
The Main Map (MC) 17
Dumfries & Gall Map (MC) 18
Borders Map (MC) 20
Ayr, Renfrew & Lanark (MC) 22
Lothians Map (MC) 24
Argyll & Dunbarton Map (MC) 26
Stirling & Falkirk Map (MC) 28
Fife Map (MC) 30
Perth & Angus Map (MC) 32
Highland South Map (MC) 34
Aberdeen & Moray Map (MC) 36
Western Isles, Ork & Shet (MC) 38
Sutherland & Caith Map (MC) 39
Abbot House (M&R) 43
Aberdour Castle (MC) 44
Abergeldie Castle (1920?) 44
Aberuchill Castle (M&R) 45
Aboyne Castle (1910?) 45
Ackergill Tower (Ackergill) 46
Affleck Castle (M&R) 47
Aldbar Castle (1910?) 49
Aldie Castle (M&R) 50
Allanton House (1916?) 51
Allardice Castle (M&R) 51
Alloa Tower (MC) 52
Almond Castle (M&R) 52
Amisfield Tower (MC) 53
Ardblair Castle (1910?) 54
Ardchattan Priory (MC) 54
Ardrossan Castle (MC) 56
Argyll's Lodging (M&R) 58
Arnage Castle (M&R) 58
Aros Castle (MC) 59
Ashintully Castle (M&R) 60
Auchindoun Castle (M&R) 63
Balbegno Castle (M&R) 67
Balbithan House (M&R) 68
Balgonie Castle (M&R) 70
Ballindalloch Castle (MC) 72
Ballone Castle (M&R) 73
Balnagown Castle (1910?) 74
Balvaird Castle (M&R) 76
Balvenie Castle (MC) 76
Barcaldine Castle (MC) 78
Barra Castle (M&R) 81
Beaufort Castle (1910?) 83
Bedlay Castle (M&R) 83
Benholm Castle (M&R) 85

Bishop's House, Elgin (MC) 87
Blackness Castle (MC) 90
Blair Castle (1910?) 91
Borthwick Castle (MC) 95
Bothwell Castle (MC) 96
Braemar Castle (MC) 98
Braikie Castle (AA) 99
Brochel Castle (GC) 101
Brodick Castle (MC) 102
Brodie Castle (MC) 102
Brotherton Castle (1912?) 103
Broughty Castle (1907?) 104
Brunstane House (M&R) 105
Bruntsfield House (M&R) 105
Buchanan Castle (1914?) 106
Burleigh Castle (M&R) 107
Busbie Tower (M&R) 108
Caerlaverock Castle (1905?) 110
Cairnbulg Castle (1910?) 110
Callendar House (1905?) 114
Carleton Castle (M&R) 118
Carnasserie Castle (MC) 119
Carrick Castle (M&R) 120
Cassillis House (1905?) 122
Castle Campbell (MC) 123
Castle Fraser (MC) 124
Castle Gogar (M&R) 125
Castle Grant (M&R) 125
Castle Huntly (M&R) 127
Castle Leod (M&R) 127
Castle Menzies (M&R) 128
Castle of Mey (1910?) 130
Castle Stuart (M&R) 132
Castle Sween (MC) 133
Castle Tioram (JH) 134
Cathcart Castle (1905?) 136
Cawdor Castle (MC) 137
Cessford Castle (MC) 137
Cessnock Castle (1910?) 137
Clackmannan Tower (M&R) 139
Claypotts Castle (MC) 140
Colliston Castle (1910?) 144
Comlongon Castle (M&R) 145
Corgarff Castle (MC) 147
Cortachy Castle (1905?) 148
Coxton Tower (MC) 151
Craig Castle (1905?) 151
Craigcrook Castle (M&R) 152
Craighall (1920?) 153
Craigievar Castle (MC) 154
Craigmillar Castle (1910?) 155
Craigneil Castle (1910?) 155
Craignethan Castle (MC) 156
Cramond Tower (JM) 157
Cranshaws Tower (1908?) 158
Crathes Castle (MC 158
Crichton Castle (MC) 159
Crookston Castle (M&R) 160
Culcreuch Castle (LF) 162
Culross Palace (MC) 163
Dalhousie Castle (Dalhousie) 165
Dalquharran Castle (M&R) 167
Dalzell House (M&R) 168
Darnaway Castle (1920?) 169
Dean Castle (M&R) 170
Delgatie Castle (MC) 171
Dirleton Castle (JM) 173

Douglas Castle (1910?) 175
Doune Castle (LF) 175
Drochil Castle (M&R) 177
Drum Castle (MC) 178
Drumlanrig Castle (M&R) 179
Duart Castle (MC) 181
Duff House (MC) 183
Dumbarton Castle (1910?) 183
Dun Beag (MC) 185
Dun Carloway (MC) 185
Dunbar Castle (1919?) 188
Dundas Castle (M&R) 189
Dunderave Castle (1910?) 190
Dundonald Castle (1905?) 190
Dunfermline Palace (M&R) 191
Dunnottar Castle (MC) 192
Dunrobin Castle (1910?) 194
Dunskey Castle (MC) 194
Dunstaffnage Castle (MC) 195
Duntrune Castle (1910?) 196
Duntulm Castle (MC) 196
Dunvegan Castle (MC) 197
Easter Greenock Castle (M&R) 200
Edinample Castle (LF) 201
Edinburgh Castle (1905?) 202
Edzell Castle (M&R 203
Eilean Donan Castle (1905?) 204
Elcho Castle (MC) 205
Elie Castle (1910?) 206
Ellon Castle (1910?) 207
Elphinstone Tower (M&R) 207
Ethie Castle (M&R) 209
Falkland Palace (M&R) 210
Falside Castle (M&R) 211
Farnell Castle (1910?) 211
Fenton Tower (MC) 213
Fernie Castle (M&R) 213
Ferniehirst Castle (1905?) 214
Fetteresso Castle (1910?) 214
Findlater Castle (1910?) 215
Flemington Tower (M&R) 219
Fort George (MC) 222
Galdenoch Castle (M&R) 223
Gardyne Castle (M&R) 224
Garleton Castle (1905?) 224
Gartshore House (M&R) 226
Girnigoe Castle (1920?) 228
Glamis Castle (Glamis) 229
Glenbuchat Castle (M&R) 231
Gordon Castle (1910?) 234
Grandtully Castle (1905?) 235
Grange House (M&R) 235
Granton Castle (M&R) 236
Greenan Castle (1905?) 236
Greenknowe Tower (M&R) 236
Hailes Castle (M&R) 239
Hallforest Castle (M&R) 240
Hamilton Palace (1910?) 241
Hatton Castle (M&R) 243
Hawthornden Castle (1905?) 244
Hermitage Castle (M&R) 245
Hillslap Tower (M&R) 247
Hoddom Castle (1911?) 247
Holyrood Palace (MC) 248
Huntingtower Castle (MC) 251
Huntly Castle (MC) 252

Illieston House (M&R) 253
Inglismaldie Castle (M&R) 255
Innerpeffray Castle (LF) 256
Innes House (M&R) 256
Innerwick Castle (M&R) 256
Inveraray Castle (1910?) 257
Invergarry Castle (EB) 259
Invergordon Castle (1920?) 259
Inverlochy Castle (MC) 260
Inverquharity Castle (1910?) 261
Inverugie Castle (1910?) 262
Jerviston (M&R) 264
Keiss Castle (1910?) 266
Kelburn Castle (M&R) 266
Kellie Castle (MC) 267
Kellie Castle (M&R) 267
Kilbryde Castle (M&R) 270
Kilchurn Castle (MC) 270
Kildrummy Castle (MC) 271
Killochan Castle (M&R) 273
Kilmartin Castle (M&R) 274
Kilravock Castle (M&R) 275
Kinfauns Castle (1905?) 276
Kinnaird Castle (1910?) 278
Kinnaird Castle (M&R) 279
Kinnaird Head Castle (MC) 279
Kinnairdy Castle (1910?) 280
Kinneil House (M&R) 280
Kirkhope Tower (M&R) 282
Kisimul Castle (MC) 284
Knockdolian Castle (1910?) 285
Lamb's House (MC) 287
Lauriston Castle (MC) 290
Law Castle (1910?) 290
Leith Hall (MC) 291
Lennoxlove (MC) 292
Liberton Tower (M&R) 294
Linlithgow Palace (M&R) 295
Loch an Eilean Castle (1905?) 297
Loch Doon Castle (M&R) 298
Lochindorb Castle (M&R) 300
Lochleven Castle (MC) 301
Lochmaben Castle (1910?) 301
Lochnaw Castle (1930?) 302
Lochranza Castle (MC) 303
Lordscairnie Castle (M&R) 305
Loudoun Castle (1904?) 305
Luffness House (M&R) 306
Macduff's Castle (M&R) 308
MacLellan's Castle (LF) 308
Mains Castle (Lan) (1905?) 309
Mains Castle (Angus) (1910?) 310
Mauchline Castle (1910?) 313
Maybole Castle (M&R) 313
Meggernie Castle (1910?) 314
Merchiston Castle (M&R) 317
Methven Castle (M&R) 317
Midhope Castle (1910?) 318
Midmar Castle (M&R) 318
Mingary Castle (M&R) 319
Monkland House (M&R) 321
Monzie Castle (1903?) 322
Moy Castle (MC) 325
Muchalls Castle (M&R) 326
Neidpath Castle (JH) 329
Newark Castle (Bor) (M&R) 330
Newark Castle (Fife) (1920?) 331

Newark Castle (Ren) (1905?) 331
Niddry Castle (MC) 334
Noltland Castle (1910?) 334
Old Place of Mochrum (1910?) 339
Orchardton Tower (MC) 340
Otterston Tower (M&R) 342
Peel Ring of Lumphanan (MC) 345
Pilrig House (M&R) 347
Pinkie House (M&R) 347
Pitfirrane Castle (M&R) 349
Pitsligo Castle (1910?) 351
Pittheavlis Castle (M&R) 352
Pollok Castle (M&R) 354
Portencross Castle (1910?) 355
Preston Tower (MC) 356
Queen Mary's House (MC) 358
Rait Castle (MC) 360
Ravenscraig Castle (MC) 362
Red Castle (R&C) (M&R) 362
Red Castle (Angus) (1924?) 363
Redhouse Castle (M&R) 363
Rosslyn Castle (1934?) 367
Rosyth Castle (M&R) 368
Rothesay Castle (MC) 368
Rothiemay Castle (1920?) 369
Rowallan Castle (1917?) 370
Roxburgh Castle (1917?) 370
Ruthven Barracks (M&R) 371
Saddell Castle (M&R) 372
Sanquhar Castle (1910?) 373
Sauchie Tower (M&R) 373
Seton House (1920?) 375
Skelmorlie Castle (1910?) 377
Slains Castle (MC) 378
Smailholm Tower (MC) 379
Spedlins Tower (M&R) 380
Spynie Palace (MC) 381
Stair (M&R) 382
Stenhouse (M&R) 383
Stirling Castle (M&R) 384
Strathaven Castle (MC) 387
Strome Castle (MC) 388
Thurso Castle (1903?) 395
Tantallon Castle (MC) 390
Tarbert Castle (Argyll) 391
Thirlestane Castle (M&R) 394
Threave Castle (M&R) 395
Thurso Castle (1903?) 395
Tilquhillie Castle (1910?) 397
Tolquhon Castle (MC) 398
Torphichen Preceptory (M&R) 399
Torwood Castle (M&R) 400
Traquair House (MC) 402
Tulliallan Castle (1906?) 403
Tullibole Castle (M&R) 404
Urquhart Castle (M&R) 406
Wedderlie House (M&R) 409
Wemyss Castle (1903?) 409
Whitekirk (MC) 413
Winton House (Winton) 415
Woolmet House (M&R) 416
Yester Castle (M&R) 417

Colour section (hbk only) by
Martin Coventry except Tioram (J.
Hunter), Brochel (G. Coventry),
Traquair (A. Coventry) and Dairsie
(A. Anderson)

Preface

THIS BOOK was conceived on a cold and sunny day in September at the sprawling ruins of Slains Castle, once the magnificent mansion of the Hay Earls of Errol. Now in its third edition, and some ten years in the making, the intention is still the same: a comprehensive source of information on all the castles and fortified houses of Scotland. There are around 600 'new' castles in this edition, as well as mansions and other historic buildings which were never fortified and are not castles in any sense. The word 'castle' in a name of a building does not necessarily mean it was ever fortified, and this sometimes seems to surprise people. Alternatively, there has also been some debate about what actually constitutes a castle: that many do not deserve the term, or others are 'chateaux'. In this book buildings which were fortified and the homes of landowners are taken to be castles.

Some buildings are in a dangerously ruined condition and should only be explored if at all with great caution. Many are accessible with care at most times but some landowners, as of old, need to be asked before invading their property: after all you would not want your head removed and tied to a peat-spade. Although some castles are within towns and accessible by public transport, many others require a car to visit.

The information in this book has been checked as far as possible. Different sources, however, do conflict (such as the use of Mons Meg at the siege of Threave Castle) and there are substantial gaps. No doubt there are more sites waiting to be discovered.

Where a site is believed to be open this has been indicated. We have tried, where possible, to check this information with the properties or with their advertising material. Ruins not in the care of Historic Scotland or the NTS are usually on private ground, and access to them is unclear.

My own favourite castles are based on three qualities: the castle's history and any grim, grisly and ghostly stories attached to it; how good it is to explore; and the beauty of the location and building,

be it ruined or complete. However, I have not visited (and have no wish to do so) all the sites recorded in this book. Some are too ruined, are mounds or just sites, some are baronial mansions with no more than a vestige of a fortress, some are simply too plain, and others are fenced off. There is also simply not time.

The history of a castle is as important as the physical remains. Some strongholds have a long and fascinating past yet no more than a vestige of their former strength survives, such as the castles at Inverness, Roxburgh or Dunbar. Alas that in all the histories of all the castles in all the wide lands of Scotland not one mentions a Coventry. There are, however, Coventrys buried in the graveyard of St Bridget's Church near Aberdour Castle, which is about as near as my family ever came. Incidentally 'Coventry' is an old Scottish name, and there have been Coventrys in Scotland since the 13th century. So hoots mon to the individual who wanted to know why an English man was writing a book about Scottish castles.

There are many ghost stories in this book. These have been included as they are an integral part of castles tradition. The number and variety are fascinating, but should – in most cases – only be taken as stories: there is certainly no intention to imply that the owners believe these tales. Many completely refute the stories, and some are hostile to the idea. Although perhaps extra care should be taken when visiting the toilets at Craignethan ...

My favourite castle remains Dirleton Castle: all it needs is a dragon to be the perfect romantic fortress. Others worth mentioning are Tantallon; Blackness; Dunnottar; Crathes; Slains; Craigievar; Tolquhon; Cessford; Braemar; Delgatie; Fyvie; Cawdor; Kildrummy; Neidpath; Traquair; Caerlaverock; Stirling; Crichton; Craignethan; Claypotts; Balvaird; Duffus; Elcho; Edzell; Huntingtower; Glamis; Blair; Dunrobin; Kilchurn; Duart; Duntulm; Dun an Sticar; and so so many more. And last but not least, Moy Castle because little compares to a cold sunny day in April at Lochbuie.

In a book of this size and complexity there are many many people to thank. Particular thanks go to Gordon W. Mason, who provided invaluable information, especially on the Glasgow area and Lanarkshire, more of which can be found in his own book 'Castles of Glasgow and the Clyde'. I would also like to say a thank you to Helen Fraser, Andrew Kerr, who both supplied invaluable information, to Grace Ellis, for many of the illustrations, to Graham Coe and to Hilary Horrocks at the NTS. Hullo or thanks also (in no particular order) to John Britten, John Scott Durbin, Phil Plevey, Reinold Gayre, Kathlyn Fforde, Janine Hunter, James H. Lindsay, N. S. F. Cram-Sinclair, Charles Henderson, Robert Parry, Jim Kelly, R. A. Gordon Stuart, Ronald J. Cumming, Keith Jepson, Eleanor and Clyde Moore, Ian Wright, Colin Stirling, Elizabeth Hepburn, R. R. Duff, Stuart Morris of Balgonie, Richard Lewis, Lawrence Hunter, David Hamilton, David Hunter, Alasdair and Margie Anderson, Stewart Walker, Professor Archie Duncan, and mostly to Joyce Miller, for all her help and support, practical and emotional. A general thank you to all those castle owners and administrators who returned proofs in such a short time.

MC, Musselburgh, 2000

If you have any comment about the book or know of corrections or additions – please contact:

Martin Coventry
GOBLINSHEAD
130B Inveresk Road
Musselburgh EH21 7AY, Scotland

If you would like further copies of this book, and are finding it difficult to purchase from your local bookshop, or would like more information about GOBLINSHEAD products as they become available, please contact the publishers at the address below.

GOBLINSHEAD
130B Inveresk Road
Musselburgh EH21 7AY, Scotland

GOBLINSHEAD

Other published titles in Scottish history
Wee Guide to Scottish History (1996)
Wee Guide to Mary, Queen of Scots (1996)
Wee Guide to Robert the Bruce (1996)
Wee Guide to the Haunted Castles of Scotland (1996)
Wee Guide to William Wallace (1997)
Wee Guide to Robert Burns (1997)
Wee Guide to the Churches and Abbeys of Scotland (1997)
Wee Guide to the Picts (1998)
Wee Guide to the Jacobites (1998)
Wee Guide to Castles and Mansions of Scotland (1998)
Haunted Places of Scotland (1999)
Wee Guide to Prehistoric Scotland (1999)
Wee Guide to Macbeth and Early Scotland (1999)
Wee Guide to Whisky (1999)
William Wallace – Champion of Scotland (1999)
The Hebrides (1999)
Castles of Glasgow and the Clyde (2000)
Myth and Magic (2000)
Wee Guide to Scottish Ghosts and Bogles (2000)
Wee Guide to Rob Roy MacGregor (2000)
Planned for 2001
Tales from the Pit (2001)
Wee Guide to Scotland (2001)
Wee Guide to Flora MacDonald (2001)
Scots Wha Hae:
a romp through Scotland's history (2001)
Scottish Witches and Wizards (2001)

Warning

Many castles are sited in inaccessible and dangerous locations, and other sites are dangerously ruined. Many sites should not be visited, and great care should be taken, particularly with children, when visiting any site.

The inclusion of a castle, or other site, in this book – in the map section or in the text – is no indication whatsoever as to whether access is available or that the building or site is open to the public.

Where the information was available, the castles or sites which are open to the public are marked in the text and have been checked for 2001. The text, at the end of the entry, gives opening and facilities – but this should be used for guidance only.

How *to* Use *the* Book

This book is quite self-explanatory and easy to use. This section, however, explains its format and what the entries contain; how the grading system and map references work, and how the information can be found. Please also refer to the diagram on the following page.

Introduction

The reference sections at the beginning of the book cover the development of the castle as a fortified structure, as well as the general historical background. *The Development of the Castle* starts with brochs and duns, through motte and bailey and stone castles of enclosure, to simple, then complex, stone keeps or towers and castellated mansion houses. The *Glossary of Terms* explains the most commonly used architectural words associated with castles, their structure and features. The *Place-Name Elements* section is included to provide some explanation about the development and origin of names.

Maps

This section includes a main map showing the areas covered by the maps on the subsequent pages of that section. The key includes the new unitary authorities, which came into being in 1996. The other 12 maps are divided by areas which are similar to the pre-1996 regions, with division of the bigger regions. Strathclyde has been divided into Ayr, Renfrew and Lanarkshire (Strathclyde, South); and Argyll and Dunbartonshire; while Highland has been divided into Sutherland and Caithness; and Highland, South.

Each map includes a list of castles on the opposite page, and their number on the map.

Castles

The entries are alphabetical, but those castles which have several names, or where alternative names are recorded, are cross-referenced. The spelling of names, both family and castle, has tended to vary throughout the years, so these have been standardised to simplify usage (such as 'Stewart' and not 'Stuart'). The author makes no judgement on the correctness or otherwise of the versions used in this book.

The main section of the book is an alphabetical listing of over 2700 fortified sites, and each entry follows a standardised form (also see over). Please note that a 'space' is sorted before 'a' ie Castle Duff, Castle Eocha, Castle of Constantine, Castle Patrick, Castleindulf, Castlemalcolm.

The status of the site has been categorised as follows:

- Ruin or site – the ruin or site is usually on private property
- Historic Scotland
- National Trust for Scotland
- Private – the building is privately owned, and unless otherwise stated is NOT open to the public.

The Ordnance grid reference and Landranger sheet follows. Where a grid reference may be approximate it is followed by [?].

The stars reflect the completeness and interest of the site as a stronghold and castle, and do not reflect the architectural merit of the building or its interest as a visitor attraction.

> * = nothing or virtually nothing remains of the original castle.
>
> ** = part of the castle survives, although it is quite ruinous or what remains is incorporated into another building.
>
> *** = substantial part of the castle survives, either as a ruin, or altered, incorporated into, or part of another building.
>
> **** = most of the original castle survives and/or it is particularly large, interesting or representative.
>
> ***** = as above, but where there are other features, such as fine interiors, gardens, location, contents, other special interest, pub handy.

The map reference given refers to the map and castle number for the maps in the book.

The opening details have been checked either with the owners themselves or against their individual advertising materials for 2001. However, although every care has been taken to provide accurate information, access should be confirmed with the individual sites as details may differ from those included. Inclusion in the book is no indication that the site is open to the public or that it should be visited. Many sites, particularly ruins, are potentially dangerous and great care should be taken: the publisher and author cannot accept any responsibility for damage or injury caused during any visit.

Admission charges are as follows:

- £ = standard entrance is less than £3.50
- ££ = standard entrance is between £3.50 and £5.00
- £££ = standard entrance is more than £5.00

Indexes

Indexes follow the alphabetical section:

- Ghosts and Bogles – castles which have ghost stories associated with them. These are just stories, however, recorded in various sources, and many owners absolutely refute them.
- Family names – sorted alphabetically by surname, listing all sites associated with that family.

Further Reading

Further reading concludes the book, listing books containing more information on Scottish castles or history.

Castle Entry (also see previous page)

Name of site ───────── **●Cawdor Castle**

Inverness & Nairn: About 5 miles south-west of Nairn, on B9090 off A96, at Cawdor, just east of Allt Dearg, at Cawdor Castle.

Location ─────────

Quality of site as a stronghold

●Private● NH 847499●OS: 27 *****●Map: 9, no: 129●

Status ─────────

Castles of Scotland map and number

One of the most magnificent and well-preserved strongholds in Scotland, Cawdor Castle incorporates a tall plain keep, dating from the 14th century, although the parapet and upper works were added in 1454. The castle has a deep ditch, and is reached by a drawbridge. Mainly three-storey ranges, gabled and crowned with bartizans and corbelled-out chambers, were built on all sides of the keep in the 16th and 17th centuries. There is a pit prison.

Ordnance Survey Grid Reference ─────────

Exterior Description

Across the drawbridge defending the entrance is a massive iron yett, which was brought here from Lochindorb Castle after 1455. The keep rises to four storeys and a garret within a flush parapet, and has very thick walls pierced by small windows. There are bartizans at each of the corners, as well as machiolated projections.

Ordnance Survey Landranger Sheet ─────────

The entrance is now in the basement, but was originally at first floor level. Both the basement and the third floor are vaulted. A straight stair, in the thickness of one wall, leads up to the hall on the first floor – although this would formerly have been a stair down to the cellars. A turnpike stair climbs to the upper floors.

Interior Description

In the later ranges, there is an iron yett postern gate to the moat, some fine 17th-century fireplaces; and there are many portraits, furnishings and a collection of tapestries.

The title 'Thane of Cawdor' is associated with Macbeth, but Duncan was not murdered here, as the castle is not nearly old enough, and he was killed in battle near Spynie. The Calders had an earlier stronghold near here [NH 858512], but nothing remains.

The 1st Thane of Cawdor took the name of Calder when granted the lands by Alexander II in 1236, although one story is that the family were descended from a brother of Macbeth. The 3rd Thane was murdered by Sir Alexander Rait of nearby Rait Castle.

The 5th Thane built much of the present castle. The method of selecting the site for Cawdor Castle was unusual as it was chosen by a donkey allowed to roam at will until it came to a suitable spot. Cawdor is also built over a tree, the remains of which are in the vaulted basement. It was believed to be a hawthorn, but in fact it proved to be a holly tree and it died in about 1372, when the castle was built.

History and families

The Campbells obtained Cawdor by kidnapping the girl heiress, Muriel Calder, and marrying her at the age of 12 to the Earl of Argyll's son, Sir John Campbell, in 1511. Campbell of Inverliver led the kidnapping, and lost all six of his sons.

The Campbells of Cawdor, her descendants, remained at the castle. They gave refuge to Simon, Lord Lovat, during his flight from Hanoverian troops in 1746 during the Jacobite Rising, and hid him in a secret room in the roof. Fraser was eventually caught and executed. Bonnie Prince Charlie had visited the same year.

A ghost in a blue velvet dress has reputedly been seen here, as has an apparition of John Campbell 1st Lord Cawdor.

Hauntings

OPEN: Open May-mid-Oct, daily 10.00-17.30; last admission 17.00.

Opening

Fine collections of portraits, furnishings and tapestries. Explanatory displays. Three shops: gift shop, wool and book shop. Licensed restaurant and snack bar. Gardens, grounds and nature trails. Golf course and putting. Disabled access to grounds; some of castle. Car and coach parking. Group concessions. Conferences. £££.

Visitor Facilities and Features

Tel: 01667 404615 Fax: 01667 404674
Email: info@cawdorcastle.com Web: www.cawdorcastle.com

Tel, Fax, Email, Web

Introduction

Development *of the* Castle 3

Glossary *of* Terms 8

Place-Name Elements 11

Development of the Castle

THE MAIN FUNCTION of the castle was defensive, to protect the laird and his family from their enemies, in as comfortable surroundings as possible; but the castle also served as the centre of administration of the laird's lands, where tenure, economy and trade were controlled, where law was dispensed, wrong-doers punished, and taxes collected. The design of castles depended very much on the social organization, political climate, expense and building fashions of the time – but it was always a show of the lord's wealth, prestige and power, and a symbol of his authority. Most, however, were never intended as strategic fortresses and were fortified houses: strong enough to see off a raid or foray but vulnerable to attack by a determined army, especially with the increased use of effective artillery. Some do not feel that such buildings merit the term 'castle', although using 'chateau' hardly seems more accurate.

Introduction

The earliest fortified sites consist of hill forts, brochs and duns, dating from before recorded history. Some of these were occupied as late as the 17th century – and the sites of many others were reused for later fortresses. Hill forts are found all over Scotland, but brochs and duns tend to be concentrated in the north and west.

Motte and bailey castles were introduced to Scotland along with feudalism – although they are unevenly distributed, being particularly numerous in Galloway, where there was unrest among the native population in the 12th century, but with few surviving examples in Lothian. This form of defence was not used for long. Stone castles were already being used in Orkney and Norse controlled areas from the 12th century, and brochs and duns were modified or reused.

By the 13th century castles of enclosure (enceinte) were being built, where a site was surrounded by a strong stone wall encircling timber or stone buildings. These developed, in some cases, into large castles with strong keeps, gatehouses and towers.

Large stone castles were expensive to build and maintain, and in the late 14th and 15th centuries simple keeps were built, usually with a barmkin or courtyard. The keep evolved into the tower house, which was not as strong but more complex, and had more regard to comfort. Hundreds of these towers were built in the 16th century. During the later 16th and 17th centuries the simple rectangular tower house developed into L- and Z-plan tower houses, which provided more accommodation, comfort as well as covering fire.

At the same time as nobles built and developed keeps and tower houses, the kings of Scots built or refurbished ornate royal palaces. These were often developed out of older strongholds, but during the 15th and 16th centuries were remodelled in the Renaissance style to become comfortable residences.

As the need for defence decreased, many castles and tower houses were developed into mansion houses.

There is a great deal of overlap between the different types of stronghold, and often a new castle was built on the site of a previous one, and reused materials from the original or simply built around, or out of, the existing building. There are also definite regional differences. In areas such as the Borders, feuds, reiving and warfare and land ownership contributed to the building of a large number of simple tower houses, peel towers and bastles, although few of these survive intact. Whereas in Aberdeenshire there are a large number of 17th-century Z-plan tower houses. The topography of particular areas influenced the position and style of building: an island in a marsh was as good a site as a rocky promontory.

Hill Forts, Brochs and Duns

Hill forts may date from as early as the Neolithic period to about 500BC, and some were used until medieval times. Ramparts of earth and stone walls, often laced with timber, or wooden palisades protected hilltops or other defensible sites. Some hill forts enclosed whole villages within their ramparts.

Brochs and duns date from about 100BC, and a few were occupied into the 17th century.

Brochs are round hollow towers, built of dry-stone masonry, with very thick walls. These walls were formed from two shells of masonry with a gallery running up inside the wall. The entrance was extremely narrow, allowing only one person at a time to enter, and a small guard chamber defended the entrance. There were often many buildings around the broch, with outer ditches and ramparts to defend the settlement. Brochs appear to have been concentrated in Orkney and Shetland, Caithness and Sutherland, and the Western Isles, but there are also examples in other parts of the country, including Lothian and Dumfries and Galloway.

The best remaining examples of brochs are Mousa and Clickhimin (Shetland), Dun Carloway (Lewis), Midhowe and Gurness (Orkney), Dun Dornigail (Sutherland) the Glen Elg brochs (Lochaber) and Dun Beag (Skye).

Duns are also most widely distributed in the north and west. Dun

Dun Carloway – an Iron Age broch

means hill or fortified place in Gaelic, and is used for both duns and brochs in Gaelic-speaking areas.

The general distribution of duns is similar to that of brochs, but duns are usually irregular in plan, following the contours of a rock, and can vary in size from a small homestead to a hill fort. The building style was sometimes very similar to brochs, and they could have had galleried walls and small cells within the walls. Dun an Sticar and Dun Ban on North Uist are good examples of duns, although both were occupied into medieval times, as were Dun Carloway, Dun Beag and many others.

It is hard to see how it has been possible for authorities to distinguish between the two types of structures, when existing remains of both are so fragmentary, confused and overbuilt. It is also not clear who they were built to defend against, although it may have been Roman slave ships.

Motte and Bailey Castles (12th century)
During the 12th century motte and bailey castles were introduced into Scotland along with feudalism, mostly into lowland areas, where the style was adopted and adapted by native lords. Motte and bailey castles are mostly concentrated in Clydesdale, Galloway and Grampian. There appear to have been few in central Scotland, Lothians, the north-west and the Highlands.

Motte and bailey castles consisted of an earthen mound, known as a motte, and a courtyard, or bailey, enclosed by a wooden palisade and defended by a ditch. The plan of the motte was usually round, but some were also oval or rectangular and used existing defensive features such as ravines, spits of land between rivers, or cliff tops. At the base of the motte was a dry or wet ditch or moat.

A wooden tower was built on the motte, where the lord and his followers could shelter if attacked. The bailey contained many buildings, such as the hall, chapel, kitchen, bakehouse and stables. The motte and bailey were linked by a removable bridge which spanned the ditch.

Often all that remains today is evidence of the earthworks, some

Duffus Castle – a motte and bailey castle

good examples of these being Motte of Urr (Galloway), Peel Ring of Lumphanan and Doune of Invernochty (both Gordon). Duffus Castle (Moray) and Rothesay Castle (Bute) are two of the few examples where a stone keep was added – as the earthen motte was often not strong enough to take a stone building. Other mottes and their surrounding earthworks were reused by later castle builders.

Wooden castles were not used for long, as they could be set alight, but had the advantage of being easy and quick to build. Most of the

castles built by Edward I of England to control Scotland were built of wood; after his costly Welsh campaigns, which included the building of such massive castles as Caernarvon, he could afford little else.

Stone Castles of Enclosure or Enceinte (12th/13th century)
Stone began to be used as a building material, because it was less vulnerable to attack by fire and because it was easily obtainable. Stone castles of enclosure were built as early as the 11th or 12th century, but the majority appeared in the 13th century. The simplest form was a wall enclosing a two-storey hall block of wood or stone. The entrance to the hall block was on the first floor, and reached by a ladder, which could be removed easily during attack. The wall was usually surrounded by a ditch and rampart.

Castle Sween – originally a simple castle of enclosure

There are good examples of castles of enclosure on the western side of Scotland, including Castle Sween (Argyll), Castle Tioram (Morvern) and Mingary Castle (Ardnamurchan).

By the 13th century, walls were heightened and strengthened, enclosing a courtyard which contained both the hall and lord's chamber, as well as kitchens, bakeries, brewhouses, stables and storerooms. Corner towers were added to defend the castle. The walls were pierced by slits through which crossbows could be fired.

The weakest part of these castles was the entrance through the wall, and strong gatehouses were added with portcullises, drawbridges, iron-studded doors, and murder-holes. The curtain walls were given battlements for archers to shelter behind.

By the 14th century, large stone castles such as Bothwell Castle (Lanarkshire), Caerlaverock Castle (Dumfries) and Kildrummy Castle (Gram-

Dunnottar Castle – a large and spectacular fortress

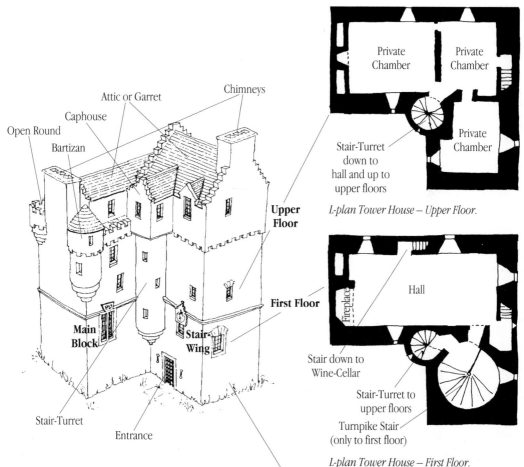

Private Chamber

Private Chamber

Stair-Turret down to hall and up to upper floors

Private Chamber

L-plan Tower House – Upper Floor.

Upper Floor

Attic or Garret

Chimneys

Caphouse

Open Round

Bartizan

First Floor

Hall

Fireplace

Stair down to Wine-Cellar

Stair-Turret to upper floors

Turnpike Stair (only to first floor)

L-plan Tower House – First Floor.

Main Block

Stair-Wing

Stair-Turret

Entrance

Basement

Diagram of L-plan tower house, showing the three main floors.
The basement contained the entrance, at the foot of the stair-wing, and was occupied by a kitchen, wine-cellar, and food-cellar. The main turnpike stair only climbed to the first-floor hall, while the upper floors were reached by a turnpike stair in the turret in the re-entrant angle. The lord's private chamber was on the floor above the hall, although there was little privacy for the rest of the household, as each room opened from the last. The upper floors and garret or attic housed guests or servants. The turret stair rose up to the parapet, and was crowned by a caphouse and watch-chamber.

The tower would have had a walled courtyard, or barmkin, enclosing ranges of buildings, including stabling, workshops, a brewhouse and more accommodation.

The walls of the tower were usually harled and whitewashed. The heraldic panel showed the arms of the lord and his wife, who used her own family name, and the date of building or alteration.

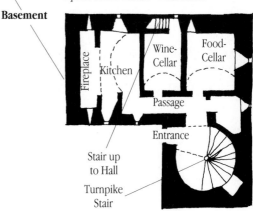

Wine-Cellar

Food-Cellar

Fireplace

Kitchen

Passage

Entrance

Stair up to Hall

Turnpike Stair

L-plan Tower House – Basement.

pian) had been built. These castles had a keep — a large strong tower separate from the rest of the castle — as well as a gatehouse. The keep had a hall and chambers for the lord. These castles also had thick curtain walls with round or square corner towers.

There are relatively few large castles left in Scotland, partly due to the expense of constructing and maintaining such large buildings, and partly because many were destroyed by the Scots, during the Wars of Independence, so that they could not be reused by the English. However, some strong royal castles were maintained, including those at Edinburgh, Stirling, Roxburgh, Dumbarton and Dunbar, and a few of the most powerful families could also afford massive fortresses such as the Douglas strongholds of Tantallon (Lothian) and Threave (Galloway) and the Keith stronghold of Dunnottar (Grampian).

Simple Keeps (14th/15th century)

These consisted of a simple square or rectangular tower, usually with

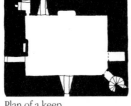

an adjoining courtyard. The walls of the keep were thick, and normally rose to at least three storeys to a flush crenellated parapet with a projecting wooden gallery. The basement and first floor were vaulted to increase the strength of the building. The size of the keep depended on the wealth of the builder.

Plan of a keep

The basement contained a cellar, often with no connection to the floor above. The hall was on the first floor, with a private chamber for the lord on the floor above, and a garret storey above this. The thick walls contained many mural chambers, either small bedrooms or garderobes. The entrance was at first-floor level, and was reached by an external timber stair, which could be removed during an attack. Stairs led up, within the walls, to each floor. The keep was roofed with stone slates, or slabs, to protect the keep against attack by fire.

Alloa Tower – now a simple keep

The courtyard enclosed buildings such as a kitchen, stables, chapel, brewhouse, and was surrounded by a wall often with a ditch and drawbridge.

Royal Palaces (15th/16th century)

The Stewart kings spent much of their energy acquiring wealth, usually by forfeiting unpopular subjects. They built or remodelled royal palaces in the Renaissance style at Stirling, Holyrood (Edinburgh), Linlithgow (West Lothian) and Falkland (Fife) with elaborate ornamentation, larger windows and classical and religious carvings.

Tower Houses (16th century)

In 1535 an Act of Parliament declared that every landed man that had land valued at £100 (Scots) was to build a castle to defend his lands.

Although there is no clear divide, tower houses evolved from keeps.

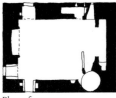

The walls became less thick, and the entrance was moved to the basement. Parapets were corbelled-out so that they would overhang the wall and missiles dropped on attackers below. The corners had open rounds, and the stair was crowned by a caphouse and watch-chamber. Gunloops and shot-holes

Plan of a tower

replaced arrowslits. The walls were harled and often whitewashed to weatherproof the building. This would, however, make the castle stand out from – rather than blend into – the landscape.

Tower houses also underwent change and adaption in the 16th century. After the Reformation, with the increased wealth of Protestant landowners, and the increased availability of land, which had previously belonged to the Church, many examples of more comfortable tower houses were built. These were mostly in the north-east, the central belt and the south, including the Borders and Galloway.

The reduction in the need for defensive features meant that these later tower houses were more spacious and comfortable. The structures were still built vertically, and most continued to have one room on each floor. However, wings or towers were either incorporated into or added to the design. Good examples of tower houses can be found at Smailholm Tower (Borders), Crathes Castle (Grampian) and Amisfield Tower (Dumfries & Galloway).

L-plan Tower Houses (from mid 16th century)

The L-plan tower house had a stair-wing added to the main block. The stair was usually turnpike and climbed only to the hall on the first floor. The upper floors were reached by a turnpike stair in a small stair-turret corbelled out, above first-floor level, in the re-entrant angle. This stair was crowned by a caphouse and watch-chamber. In some cases, the wing contained a stair which climbed to all floors, and sometimes a separate stair-tower stood within the re-entrant angle, and the wing contained chambers. Greenknowe Tower (Borders) is a fine ruined L-plan tower house while Craigievar (Grampian) is complete.

Plan of an L-plan tower

The defensive features became less obvious. Larger windows were still protected by iron yetts or grills, and gunloops became ornamental. Open rounds were replaced by bartizans, with conical roofs, and parapets were

Greenknowe Tower – an L-plan tower

covered. Decorative features, as well as heraldic panels, inscribed lintels, tempera painting and modelled plaster work were introduced. These design features showed French and Italian influences. The tower usually had a courtyard with ranges of buildings, including a brewhouse, stabling and more accommodation. There were formal and walled gardens, as well as orchards and parks.

The basement was vaulted and contained a kitchen with a large fireplace, a wine-cellar with a small stair to the hall above, and other cellars. The hall was on the first floor of the main block with private chambers, on the floors above, and within the garret or attic storey.

Z-plan Tower Houses (late 16th century)

A variation of the L-plan, a Z-plan tower house consisted of a main block, with two towers at diagonally opposite corners. One of the towers usually housed a stair, while the other provided more accommodation.

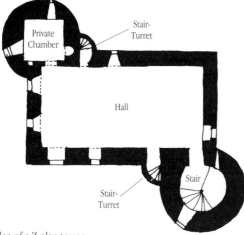

Plan of a Z-plan tower

Often further wings or ranges were added to the tower making it E-plan.

Glenbuchat Castle (Grampian) is a fine example of a ruined Z-plan tower house, as is Drochil Castle (Borders), while Claypotts Castle (Angus) is still roofed.

Forts (16th/17th/18th century)

With the advent of more sophisticated artillery, the castle became increasingly redundant as a major defensive structure. As early as the 1540s, forts were being built to withstand attack by cannon. The English constructed forts, during the invasion of Scotland in 1547-50, including those at Roxburgh (Borders), Eyemouth (Borders) and Haddington (Lothian), which consisted of ramparts and bastions of earth rather than high walls. In the 1650s Cromwell built forts known as Citadels such as those at Ayr, Leith (Lothian), Perth, Inverlochy (Highland) and Aberdeen. The Hanoverian Government built forts, barracks and roads after the Jacobite Risings of 1715 and 1745, including those at Fort George, Fort William, Fort Augustus and Ruthven Barracks (all Highland). Other castles such as Corgarff and Braemar (Grampian) were given artillery bastions, and were used as bases for campaigns against illicit whisky distilling in the late 18th century.

Castellated Mansion Houses

Even before the Jacobite Risings, most houses had ceased to be fortified. By the mid 18th century, most new houses were built in a classical, palladian or symmetrical style, designed by architects such as William Adam and his son Robert. Many castles were abandoned at this time, because they were uncomfortable and unfashionable as dwellings – many landowners wishing to forget their unruly and barbaric past.

In the 19th century, baronial mansions came into fashion, incorporating or recreating mock castellated features such as towers and turrets, corbelling and machiolations. In many cases these were called castles, although they were certainly never fortified.

Castles, themselves, were reused, restored and reoccupied. Architects such as William Burn, James Gillespie Graham and David Bryce in the 19th century, and Sir Robert Lorimer in the 20th century, designed these castellated mansions. Many of these large country houses did not survive use by the government in World War II, while some others have been used as hotels, schools and youth hostels. Others still remain the centre of estates, some still owned by the original families.

The fashion for restoring and living in many of the smaller towers and fortified houses has greatly increased in recent years. It has to be said, however, that some of these 'restorations' are less than perfect and leave the building looking a complete mess.

Armadale Castle – a castellated mansion

Claypotts Castle – a Z-plan tower house

Glossary *of* Terms

Item	Definition
Arcade	A series of arches supported by piers or columns. A blind arcade is built against a wall
Arch	A self-supporting structure capable of carrying a superimposed load over an opening
Architrave	A moulding surrounding, or framing, a doorway or window opening
Ashlar	Masonry of worked stone blocks with even faces and squared edges
Astragal	A bar in a window, often wooden, between the panes
Attic	The top storey entirely within a gabled roof
Aumbry	Originally almry, 'a place for alms'. A cupboard, usually in a stone wall, originally to hold sacred vessels for the Mass, but later for domestic use
Bailey	A defensible area enclosed by a wall or palisade and a ditch
Balustrade	Ornamental parapet of posts and railings
Barbican	A building or enclosure, usually of modest size and defensive strength, to protect an entrance or gateway
Barmkin	A walled courtyard, often of modest size and defensive strength
Bartizan	A turret, corbelled out from a wall, usually crowning corners of a building
Basement	The lowest storey of a building, sometimes below ground level
Bastle House	Small tower house with a living room over a byre
Batter	A slight inward inclination or tilt of a wall from its base upwards, either to add strength or to make tunnelling by attacking forces more difficult
Battlement	A crenellated parapet to shoot between the solid sections, or merlons – the crenel being the space
Bay	A section or compartment of a building
Bay window	A window projecting from a building at ground level, either rectangular or polygonal, of one or more storeys. If it is corbelled out above ground level, it is an oriel window
Boss	A knob or projection to cover the intersection of ribs in a vault
Bow window	As bay window; but bow windows are curved in plan
Brattice *(Scots: bretasche)*	A projection from a wall-head, normally built of wood, providing machicolations
Broch *(Scots)*	A round tower-like structure, open in the middle, the double wall of dry-stone masonry being linked by slabs to form internal galleries at varying levels. Found in north and west Scotland, most probably dating from the 1st century AD although some were in use until the 17th century.
Buttress	A vertical member projecting from a wall to stabilise it, or to resist the lateral thrust of an arch, roof or vault. A flying buttress transmits the thrust to a heavy abutment by an arch or half-arch
Cable moulding	A Norman moulding carved like a length of rope
Caphouse	A small watch-chamber at the top of a turnpike stair, often opening into the parapet walk and sometimes rising from within the parapet
Caponier	A covered passage across a ditch of a castle to defend the bottom of the ditch from attack
Castle	A fortified house or stronghold, residence of a nobleman
Castellations	Battlements and turrets
Chevron	A Norman zigzag decorative design based on an inverted V
Classic	Revival of classical architectural styles used by the Greeks and Romans, characterized by columns, pediments and symmetrical designs
Close *(Scots)*	A courtyard or passage giving access to a number of buildings
Colonnade	Range of evenly spaced columns
Corbiestepped *(Scots)*	Squared stones forming steps upon a gable
Corbel	A projecting bracket supporting other stonework or timbers
Courtyard castle	Usually a castle of some size and importance built around a central courtyard, normally with a tower or keep, gatehouse, and ranges of buildings such as a kitchen, bakehouse, stable and chapel
Crenellations	Battlements made up of crenels and merlons
Crowstepped	Squared stones forming steps upon a gable (corbiestepped)
Curtain Wall	A high enclosing stone wall around a bailey
Donjon	The keep or central fortress in a castle
Doocot *(Scots)*	A dovecot
Dormer Window	A window standing up vertically from a slope of a roof
Dressings	Features such as quoins or string-courses made from smoothly-worked stone
Drystane *(Scots)*	Dry-stone construction without mortar
Dun, Dum	An Iron Age fortified enclosure, built of dry-stone, often with galleried walls, dating from the 1st century although some were occupied until the 16th century. Can be similar to brochs but not always round in plan
E-plan tower house	Tower house with a main block and at least two wings at right angles, dating from the 16th and 17th centuries
Eaves	The overhanging edge of a roof
Embrasure	A small splayed opening in the wall or battlement of a fortified building
Enceinte	The line of the wall encircling a fortress
Entresol	A low storey within two high ones (mezzanine)
Fore	Structure protecting an entrance, as in forestair, forework
Fortalice *(Scots)*	A medium-sized fortified building
Fosse	A ditch
Fresco	A painting done on wet plaster
Frieze	A horizontal band of ornament
Gable	A vertical wall or other vertical surface, frequently triangular, at the end of a pitched roof, often with a chimney. In Scotland often corbiestepped (crowstepped)
Gallery	A balcony or passage, often with seats, usually overlooking a great hall or garden
Garderobe	A medieval privy, usually built into the wall of a castle
Garret	The top storey of a building within the roof
Gothic	Non-classical medieval architecture, distinguished by high-pitched roofs, sharp-pointed arches, and narrow windows, which progressively became less severe. Revived in its various forms by the Victorians
Groin	The line of intersection of two vaults
Gunloop	An opening for shooting firearms through with an external splay. See also shot-hole
Hall House	Defensible two-storey building containing a hall above a basement
Hammer-beam	An elaborate type of roof used in Gothic and Tudor buildings. To avoid tie-beams across an imposing hall, short timber cantilevers (or hammer-beams) were used

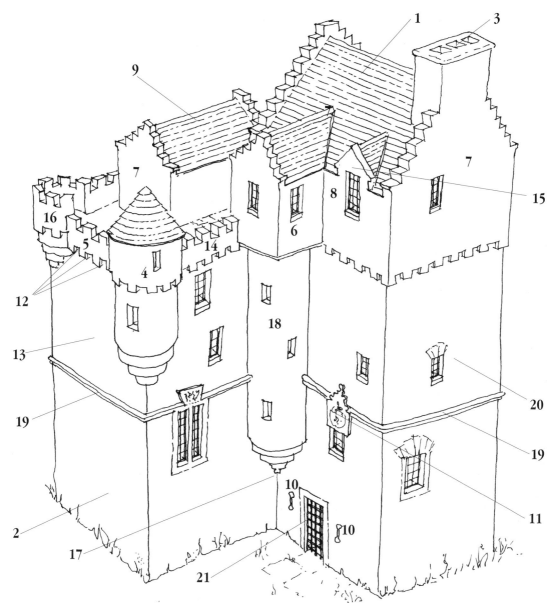

L-plan tower house showing common elements.

ITEMS

1. **Attic**
2. **Basement**
3. **Chimney**
4. **Bartizan** (with conical roof, corbelled out)
5. **Battlement**
6. **Square caphouse**
7. **Corbiestepped gable**
8. **Dormer window**
9. **Garret**
10. **Gunloops**
11. **Heraldic panel**
12. **Machiolations**
13. **Main Block**
14. **Parapet**
15. **Pediment** (triangular)
16. **Round** (open)
17. **Re-entrant angle**
18. **Stair-turret** (corbelled out)
19. **String-course**
20. **Stair-wing**
21. **Yett** (protecting entrance)

Harling *(Scots)* Wet dash, or roughcasting, hurled or dashed onto a rubble wall of a castle or house to give additional protection against the weather

Heraldic panel A stone panel where the arms and initials of a noble and his wife were recorded. Often records the date, referring usually to the construction or modification of a building

Hill fort Fortified site often on summit of a hill or coastal promontory, usually with series of ditches and ramparts, many with stone walls. Although most of these settlements were small, others were large towns. Dates from Iron Age. Many later castles were built within these fortifications.

House A castle, tower or fortalice, especially where these have been extended or modified; also mansion etc

Jamb The side of a doorway, window, or other opening

Keep Strong stone tower. A citadel or ultimate strong point, normally with a vaulted basement, hall and additional storeys. Often with very thick walls, a flush parapet, and mural chambers. Dates from the 14th and 15th centuries. Originally called a donjon

L-plan tower house Distinctive Scottish form of the tower house in which a wing was added at right angles to the main tower block, thereby affording greater protection by covering fire and providing more accommodation. Dates between 1540–1680

Lancet window A slender pointed arch window

Lintel A horizontal beam of stone, bridging an opening

Loggia Covered open arcade

Loop A small opening to admit light or for the firing of weapons

Machiolation A slot for dropping stones or shooting missiles

Main Block Principal part of a castle, usually containing the hall and lord's chamber

Merlon One of the solid tooth-like projections of a battlement

Mezzanine A low storey between two higher ones (entresol)

Moat A ditch, water filled or dry, around an enclosure

Motte A steeply sided flat-topped mound

Motte and bailey A defence system, Roman in origin, consisting of an earth motte (mound) carrying a wooden tower with a bailey (open court) with an enclosing ditch and palisade

Moulding An ornament of continuous section

Mullion A vertical dividing beam in a window

Murder-holes Openings in the roofs of passages, especially entrances, through which attackers could be ambushed

Newel The centre post in a turnpike or winding stair

Niche A vertical recess in a wall, often to take a statue

Ogee A double curve, bending one way then the other

Oratory A small private domestic chapel

Oriel A bay window projecting out from a wall above ground level

Palace An old Scottish term for a two-storey hall block

Pantile A roof-tile of curved S-shape section

Parapet A wall for protection at any sudden drop but defensive in a castle

Pediment A small gable over a doorway or window, especially a dormer

Peel Originally a palisaded court. Later a stone tower house

Pend *(Scots)* An open-ended passage through a building, at ground level

Pendant A suspended feature of a vault or ceiling, usually ending in a boss

Pepperpot turret A bartizan with conical or pyramidal roof

Pinnacle Small slender turret or spire

Piscina A basin with a drain for washing the Communion or Mass vessels, usually set in, or against, a wall

Pit-Prison A dark prison only reached by a hatch in a vault

Pleasaunce, Pleasance A walled garden

Plinth The projecting base of a wall. It may be battered or stepped

Pointing Exposed mortar joints of masonry or brickwork

Portcullis A wooden and/or iron gate designed to rise and fall in vertical grooves

Postern A secondary gateway or doorway; a back entrance

Quatrefoil Like a four-petalled flower or leaf

Quoin Dressed (ie carefully shaped) stone at a corner of a building

Rampart A stone or earth wall surrounding a castle

Re-entrant angle Inside corner where two wings of a building meet when at right angles

Renaissance Rebirth; the rediscovery of classical architecture in Italy about 1420, which then spread throughout Europe, coming to Scotland somewhat later

Rib-Vault A vault supported by ribs or decorated with them

Roll-and-hollow moulding Simple round edging formed at outside vertical corner of hewn stone at the side of door or window

Roll moulding Moulding of near-circular or semi-circular pattern

Romanesque (or Norman) Pre-Gothic style of medieval architecture characterised by round-headed arches

Round *(Scots)* A roofless bartizan

Roundel Round open turret

Royal castle A castle held by a keeper or constable for the monarch

Scale-and-platt Stair with short straight flights and turnings at landings

Screen A wall, wooden or stone, to divide an adjoining kitchen from the hall in a castle

Segmented Broken into segments of a circle

Sill The horizontal projection at the bottom of a window

Skew *(Scots)* Sloping or sloped stones finishing a gable higher than the roof

Shot-Hole A small round hole in a wall through which weapons were fired

Slight To destroy a castle's defences to a greater or lesser extent

Solar *(Literally, sun-room)* Upper living-room of the lord in a medieval dwelling

Spring Level at which a vault or an arch rises

Squinch A small arch built obliquely across each internal angle of a square tower or other structure to carry a turret or tower

Steading *(Scots)* A group of farm buildings

Stoup A vessel for holy water

String-Course Intermediate course, or moulding, projecting from the surface of a wall

Tempera Form of wall painting directly on plaster or wood

Tower House Self-contained house with the main rooms stacked vertically usually with a hall over a vaulted basement with further storeys above. Normally in a small courtyard, or barmkin. Dating from 1540 to about 1680

T-plan House or tower where the main (long) block has a wing or tower (usually for the stair) in the centre of one front

Transom Horizontal dividing beam in a window

Trefoil Like a three-petalled flower or leaf

Turnpike stair Spiral stair around a newel or central post

Turret A small tower usually attached to a building

Vault An arched ceiling of stone. Tunnel- or barrel-vaulting, the simplest kind, is, in effect, a continuous arch. Pointed tunnel-vaults are found occasionally in Scottish buildings. Groin-vaults have four curving triangular surfaces created by the intersection of two tunnel-vaults at right-angles. Also see Rib-vault

Yett A strong hinged gate made of interwoven iron bars

Wall-Walk A walkway on top of a wall, protected by a parapet

Walled Enclosure A simple castle, normally where a wall encloses a rock or island with a wooden hall and buildings. Dates from the 12th and 13th centuries (castle of enceinte, castle of enclosure)

Ward A defensive enclosure with a stone wall

Z-plan Distinctive Scottish form of the tower house whereby two corner towers were added to the main tower block at diagonally opposite corners, thereby affording greater protection by covering fire and providing more accommodation. Dates from the 16th and 17th centuries

Place-Name Elements

BRITTONIC is the first identifiable language used in Scotland. It was the language of the Britons of Strathclyde, and is closely related to Welsh. A similar language may have been spoken by the Picts, as place-name elements used in Brittonic Gaelic occur in Fife and Grampian where the Picts predominated.

Gaelic came to dominate in most parts of Scotland, after the 9th century, with the influx of Scots from Ireland, and is still spoken in the Hebrides and some parts of the mainland.

Norse was the language brought by Norse invaders to Orkney, Shetland, the Western Isles, and large parts of the mainland, including Caithness and Sutherland.

English was spoken from about the 5th century in Lothian, and by the 12th century dominated lowland areas, including the south of Scotland, Fife, and Grampian, although Gaelic predominated in the Highlands and Islands until the middle of the 18th century. The nobles, many of Norman descent, spoke French in medieval times, but this has left little impression in place names.

Scots, although derived from English, became increasingly different, with its own unique words and grammar, from the 14th century. It predominated, even being used by the kings and queens, until the 17th century when the Crowns of Scotland and England were united.

Element	Origin	Original	Definition
A			
a	Norse	a	river
a Deas	Gaelic	a Deas	to the south
an Ear	Gaelic	an Ear	to the east
an Iar	Gaelic	an Iar	to the west
a Tuath	Gaelic	a Tuath	to the north
aber	Brittonic	aber	confluence, river mouth
abhainn	Gaelic	abhainn	river
ach	Gaelic	achadh	field
–aig	Norse	vik	bay
aird	Gaelic	aird	height
ald, alt	Gaelic	allt	stream
annat, annet	Gaelic	annaid	church, mother church
ard	Gaelic	ard	high, tall, promontory
ardan, arden	Gaelic	ardan	a point of land, promontory of field
auch	Gaelic	achadh	field
auchan, auchen	Gaelic	achadh	field of
auchter, ochter	Gaelic	uachdar	top, high place, upper part
auld, ault	Gaelic	allt	stream
avon	Gaelic	abhainn	river
–ay	Norse	–ey	an island
B			
bal, balla, bally	Gaelic	baile	farm, village
balloch	Gaelic	bealach	pass
bally	Gaelic	baile	farm, village
ban, bane	Gaelic	ban	white, light-coloured, fair
barr	Gaelic	barr	top, summit
beg	Gaelic	beag	small
belloch	Gaelic	bealach	pass
ben	Gaelic	beinn	hill, mountain

–bie	Norse	byr	farm, village, dwelling place
–bister	Norse	bolstadr	farm, village, dwelling place
blair	Gaelic	blar	field, battlefield
–busta	Norse	bolstadr	farm, village, dwelling place
–boll	Norse	bolstadr	farm, village, dwelling place
brae	Gaelic	brae	slope
breck	Gaelic	breac	speckled, a trout
–bster	Norse	bolstadr	farm, village, dwelling place
bun	Gaelic	bun	foot, rivermouth
–busta	Norse	bolstadr	farm, village, dwelling place
–burgh	Norse	burg	fort, settlement
buidhe	Gaelic	buidhe	yellow
–by	Norse	byr	farm, village, dwelling place
C			
caer	Brittonic	caer	fort, hill
cairn	Gaelic	carn	cairn, heap of stones
caisteal	Gaelic	caisteal	castle
calder	Brittonic	calder	hard water
cambus	Gaelic	camas	bay
car	Brittonic	caer	fort, hill
car	Gaelic	*several*	cairn, town, fort, rock ledge
carrick	Gaelic	carraig	rock
carse	Scots	carse	low-lying land around a river
cladach	Gaelic	cladach	rocky beach
clash	Gaelic	clais	furrow, groove, ditch
cleish	Gaelic	clais	furrow, groove, ditch
cleugh	Scots	cleugh (*klooch*)	gorge, ravine
coll, collie, colly	Gaelic	coille	wood, forest
cool	Gaelic	cul	the back, back of hill
corrie	Gaelic	coire	a hollow in mountain or hill
cors, corse	Scots	corse	cross
coul	Gaelic	cul	the back
craig, craik	Gaelic	creag	crag, hill
craig, craik	Brittonic	carreg	crag, hill
cro, croe	Gaelic	crodh	cattle
D			
dail, dal	Gaelic	dail	field, valley, river meadow
dail, dal(l)	Brittonic	dal	field, valley, river meadow
–dal(l)	Norse	–dalr	valley
–dale	Norse	–dalr	valley
damh	Gaelic	damh	stag
darrach, darroch	Gaelic	darach	oak timber
dauch, davach	Gaelic	dabhach	vat, tub
dearg	Gaelic	dearg	red
deas	Gaelic	deas	south
dhu	Gaelic	dubh	black
din	Gaelic	dun	fort
doch	Gaelic	dabhach	vat, tub
dol	Gaelic	dail	field, valley
doon	Gaelic	dun	fort
donn	Gaelic	donn	brown
dorch	Gaelic	dorch	dark
doun	Gaelic	dun	fort

11

drochit	Gaelic	drochaid	bridge
drom, drum	Gaelic	druim	back, ridge
dubh	Gaelic	dubh	black
duin	Gaelic	dun	fortress, fort, hill
dul	Brittonic	dal	river meadow
dum, dun	Gaelic	dum	fortress, fort, hill

E

ear	Gaelic	ear	east
eccles	Gaelic	eaglais	church
edin	Gaelic	aodann	face
eglis	Gaelic	eaglais	church
enach, enoch	Gaelic	aonach	hill, slope, green plain
ess	Gaelic	eas	waterfall
–ey	Norse	ey	island, islet

F

fal(l)	Scots	faw	variegated, different colours
fas	Gaelic	fas	level place, place to stop
fauld	Scots	fauld	fold, pen
fell	Norse	fell, fjall	hill, mountain
ferin	Gaelic	fearann	land, estate, farm
fern	Gaelic	fearn	alder tree
fetter	Gaelic	leitir	slope
fin(n)	Gaelic	fionn	white, pale coloured; blessed
firth	Scots	firth	sea inlet, estuary
four	Brittonic	four	pasture

G

gare, gair	Gaelic	gearr	short
gart	Brittonic	garth	field
gart, garth	Norse	gardr	garden, yard, enclosure
garv	Gaelic	garbh	rough, thick
gate	Scots	get, geit	way, road, path
geal	Gaelic	geal	white
gil(le)	Gaelic	gille	boy, servant
glac(k)	Gaelic	glac, glaic	hollow
glas(s)	Gaelic	glas	grey, green, greeny-grey
glen	Gaelic	gleann	narrow valley, valley, glen
gorm	Gaelic	gorm	blue
gour, gower	Galeic	gabhar	she-goat

H

hal(ly)	Scots	haly	holy
haugh	Scots	hauch, haugh	river-meadowland
heugh	Scots	heuch	cliff, precipice, steep bank
hop(e)	Norse	hop	bay
hope	Scots	hope	upland valley
how(e)	Scots	howe	hollow, basin of land

I

–i, i	Norse	ey	island, islet
iar	Gaelic	iar	west
inch	Gaelic	innis	island
inner	Gaelic	inbhir	rivermouth
innis, ins(c)h	Gaelic	innis	island
inver	Gaelic	inbhir	confluence, rivermouth

K

ken	Gaelic	ceann	head, headland
ker	Gaelic	cearthramh	fourth part, quarter
ker	Norse	kjarr	brushwood, thicket
kerse	Scots	carse	low-lying land around a river

kil	Gaelic	cill(e)	chapel, church, burial ground
kin	Gaelic	ceann	head, at the head
knock	Gaelic	cnoc	knoll, small hillock
know(e)	Scots	knoll	lump, small hill
kirk	Scots	kirk	church
kyle	Gaelic	caolas	straight, narrows

L

lag	Gaelic	lag	hollow
laggan	Gaelic	laggan	small hollow
laid(e)	Gaelic	leathad	slope, hillside, brae
lairig	Gaelic	lairig	pass
land	Scots	lan(d)	land, building on land
law	Scots	law	rounded, conical hill
lax	Norse	lax	salmon
lecl	Gaelic	leac	flat stone, slab
led	Gaelic	leathad	slope, hillside, brae
les	Gaelic	lios	garden, enclosure
letter	Gaelic	leitir	steep slope, hillside
liath	Gaelic	liath	grey, grey-blue
links	Scots	links	stretch of sandy land
lin, linn	Gaelic	linne	lake, pool, waterfall
lis	Gaelic	lios	garden, enclosure
loan	Scots	loan	grassy (cattle) track
loan, lon(e)	Gaelic	lon	meadow, marsh, pool
loch	Gaelic	loch	loch
lui	Gaelic	laoigh	of the calf
lu(i)b	Gaelic	lub	bend, curve

M

machar	Gaelic	machair	low-lying fertile sandy ground
maddy	Gaelic	madach	dog, of the dog family
mains	Scots	mains	home farm of estate
mam	Gaelic	mam	round hill
march	Scots	march, merch	boundary
mell(an), mell(on)	Gaelic	meall(on)	rounded hill (of the)
merse	Scots	merse, mers	border
miln–	Scots	mill, miln	mill
mon(i)	Gaelic	monadh	hill, moor
mo(u)nt	English	mount	hill
mo(u)nt, mo(u)nth	Gaelic	monadh	hill, moor
more, mor	Gaelic	mor	big
moss	Scots	moss, mos	boggy ground, marsh
muck	Gaelic	muc	pig

N

ness	Norse	ness	headland, promontory
nether	English	nether	lower of two
–nis(h)	Gaelic	nis	headland, promontory
nock	Gaelic	cnoc	hill
nor	Scots	norat/nor	north

O

ob	Gaelic	ob	creek, bay
ochter	Gaelic	uachdar	upper part, top
ord	Gaelic	ord	hammer, round hill
our	Gaelic	odhar	dun, fawn coloured

P

pen	Brittonic	pen	head
pend	Scots	pen	arched passageway
penny, pin	Scots	pennyland	measure of land
per, pit	Brittonic	pit, pett	share, portion of farm land

pol(l), pool	Gaelic	poll	pool, pit
–poll, –pool	Norse	bolstadr	farm, village, dwelling place
pres(s)	Gaelic	preas	bush, thicket, clump

Q

quarrel	Scots	quarrel	stone-quarry

R

rannich, rannoch	Gaelic	raineach	fern, bracken
ree	Gaelic	righ	king
ree	Gaelic	ruighe	shieling, slope for cattle
ree	Gaelic	frith	deer forest
rhu	Gaelic	rubha	headland, promontory
rig(g)	Scots	rig	ridge, strip of ploughed land
ros, ross	Gaelic	ros	promontory, wood
roy, ruadh	Gaelic	ruadh	red, brown, reddish-brown

S

sauchie	Scots	sauch, saugh	willows, willow-land
scaur	Scots	scaur	steep, sheer rock
–set(t), –setter	Norse	setr	dwelling, house
sgor(r)	Gaelic	sgor	sharp rock, rocky peak
–shader	Norse	setr	dwelling, house
shee	Gaelic	sidh	fairy knoll, hillock
shen	Gaelic	sean	old
siar	Gaelic	iar	west
sker(ry)	Norse	sker	sea rock
slack	Norse	slakki	hollow between hills
slew	Gaelic	sliabh	mountain, hill
sloc(k)	Gaelic	sloc(hd)	pit, hollow
spidal, spit(t)al(l)	English	spittal	charity hospital, shelter
spittle	English	spittal	charity hospital, shelter
sgur(r)	Gaelic	sgor	sharp rock, rocky peak
–sta	Norse	stadr	dwelling, farm
stane	Scots	stane	stone
–ster	Norse	setr	dwelling, house
stob	Gaelic	stob	point
strath	Gaelic	srath	open valley, river valley
stron(e)	Gaelic	sron	nose, point
stuc(k)	Gaelic	stuc	small jutting hill, peak

T

tar	Gaelic	tar	over
tarbat, tarbe(r)t	Gaelic	tairbeart	isthmus
tarf(f)	Gaelic	tarbh	bull
tay, tee	Gaelic	taigh	house
temple	English	temple	land owned by Knights Templar
tibber	Gaelic	tobar	well
tillie	Gaelic	tulach	smallish hill, hillock
tipper	Gaelic	tobar	well
tir(e)	Gaelic	tir	land
tober	Gaelic	tobar	well
tod	Scots	tod	fox
tol(l)	Gaelic	toll	hole, hollow
tom	Gaelic	tom	hillock
–ton, –toun	English	tun	farm
tor(r), tore, tra	Gaelic	torr	mound, heap, castle
–toul	Gaelic	(an) t-sahbail	of the barn
train	Gaelic	train	third
traigh	Gaelic	traigh	sandy beach
trav	Gaelic	tarbh	bull
tuath	Gaelic	tuath	north

tullie, tullich, tulloch	Gaelic	tulach	smallish hill
ty	Gaelic	taigh	house
tyre	Gaelic	tir	land

U

uaine	Gaelic	uaine	green

V

–vaig	Norse	vik	bay
–val	Norse	fjall	hill, mountain
vane	Gaelic	bhan	fair
vat	Norse	vatn	water, lake
vennel	Scots	vennel, venal	narrow alley
–vi(k), –vig	Norse	vik	bay
voe	Norse	vik	bay

W

–wall, –way	Norse	vagr	bay
weem	Gaelic	uamh	natural cave, cavity
–wick	Norse	vik	bay
wynd	Scots	wynd	narrow winding street

Y

yett	Scots	yett/yate	gate, door, hill pass

Maps

Index 16
Main Map 17
1 Dumfries & Galloway 18-19
2 Borders 20-21
3 Ayr, Renfrew & Lanarkshire 22-23
4 Lothians 24-25
5 Argyll & Dunbarton 26-27
6 Stirling & Falkirk 28-29
7 Fife 30-31
8 Perth & Angus 32-33
9 Highland, South 34-35
10 Aberdeen & Moray 36-37
11 Western Isles, Orkney & Shetland 38
12 Sutherland & Caithness 39

Main Map – Index

Index *by* Region *(1974-96)*

Argyll & Dunbarton	26-27
Borders	20-21
Central *(see* Stirling & Falkirk*)*	28-29
Dumfries & Galloway	18-19
Fife	30-31
Grampian *(see* Aberdeen & Moray*)*	36-37
Highland, South	34-35
Highland, North *(see* Sutherland & Caithness*)*	39
Lothians	24-25
Strathclyde, North *(see* Argyll & Dunbarton*)*	26-27
Strathclyde, South *(see* Ayr, Renfrew & Lanarkshire*)*	18-19
Sutherland & Caithness	39
Tayside *(see* Perth & Angus*)*	32-33
Western Isles, Orkney & Shetland	38

Index *by* County *(pre-1974)*

Aberdeen *(see* 10 Aberdeen & Moray*)*	36-37
Angus *(see* 8 Perth & Angus*)*	32-33
Argyll *(see* 5 Argyll & Dunbarton*)*	26-27
Ayrshire *(see* 3 Ayr, Renfrew & Lanark*)*	22-23
Banff *(see* 10 Aberdeen & Moray*)*	36-37
Berwick *(see* 2 Borders*)*	20-21
Caithness *(see* 12 Sutherland & Caithness*)*	39
Clackmannan *(see* 6 Stirling & Falkirk*)*	28-29
Dumfries *(see* 1 Dumfries & Galloway*)*	18-19
Dunbartonshire *(see* 5 Argyll & Dunbarton*)*	26-27
East Lothian *(see* 4 Lothians*)*	24-25
Fife *(see* 7 Fife*)*	30-31
Inverness *(see* 9 Highland, South*)*	34-35
Kincardine *(see* 10 Aberdeen & Moray*)*	36-37
Kinross *(see* 8 Perth & Angus*)*	32-33
Kirkcudbright *(see* 1 Dumfries & Galloway*)*	18-19
Lanarkshire *(see* 3 Ayr, Renfrew & Lanarkshire*)*	22-23
Midlothian *(see* 4 Lothians*)*	24-25
Moray *(see* 10 Aberdeen & Moray*)*	36-37
Nairn *(see* 9 Highland, South*)*	34-35
Orkney *(see* 11 Western Isles etc*)*	38
Peebles *(see* 2 Borders*)*	20-21
Perth *(see* 8 Perth & Angus*)*	32-33
Renfrew *(see* 3 Ayr, Renfrew & Lanark*)*	22-23
Ross & Cromarty *(see* 9 Highland, South*)*	34-35
Roxburgh *(see* 2 Borders*)*	20-21
Selkirk *(see* 2 Borders*)*	20-21
Shetland *(see* 11 Western Isles etc*)*	38
Stirling *(see* 6 Stirling & Falkirk*)*	28-29
Sutherland *(see* 12 Sutherland & Caithness*)*	39
Western Isles *(see* 11 Western Isles, etc*)*	38
West Lothian *(see* 4 Lothians*)*	24-25
Wigtown *(see* 1 Dumfries & Galloway*)*	18-19

Index *by* Local Authorities *(Apr 96)*

District (1974-96)	New Authority (1996-)	Map & Page no
Angus	Angus	8 Perth & Angus (32-33)
Annandale & Eskdale	Dumfries & Galloway	1 Dumfries & Gall. (18-19)
Argyll & Bute	Argyll & Bute	5 Argyll & Dunb. (26-27)
Badenoch & Strathspey	Highland	9 Highland, South (34-35)
Banff & Buchan	Aberdeen	10 Aberdeen & Moray (36-37)
Bearsden & Milngavie	East Dunbartonshire	3 Ayr, Lanark & Ren. (22-23)
Berwickshire	Scottish Borders	2 Borders (20-21)
Caithness	Highland	12 Sutherland & Caith. (39)
City of Aberdeen	City of Aberdeen	10 Aberdeen & Moray (36-37)
Clackmannan	Clackmannan	6 Stirling & Falkirk (28-29)
Clydebank	West Dunbartonshire	3 Ayr, Lanark & Ren. (22-23)
Clydesdale	South Lanarkshire	3 Ayr, Lanark & Ren. (22-23)
Cumbernauld & Kilsyth	North Lanarkshire	3 Ayr, Lanark & Ren. (22-23)
Cumnock & Doon Valley	East Ayrshire	3 Ayr, Lanark & Ren. (22-23)
Cunningham	North Ayrshire	3 Ayr, Lanark & Ren. (22-23)
Dunbarton	West Dunbartonshire	5 Argyll & Dunb. (26-27)
Dundee	Dundee	8 Perth & Angus (32-33)
Dunfermline	Fife	7 Fife (30-31)
East Kilbride	South Lanarkshire	3 Ayr, Lanark & Ren. (22-23)
East Lothian	East Lothian	4 Lothians (24-25)
Eastwood	East Renfrewshire	3 Ayr, Lanark & Ren. (22-23)
Edinburgh	Edinburgh	4 Lothians (24-25)
Ettrick & Lauderdale	Scottish Borders	2 Borders (20-21)
Falkirk	Falkirk	6 Stirling & Falkirk (28-29)
Glasgow	Glasgow	3 Ayr, Lanark & Ren. (22-23)
Gordon	Aberdeenshire	10 Aberdeen & Moray (36-37)
Hamilton	South Lanarkshire	3 Ayr, Lanark & Ren. (22-23)
Inverclyde	Inverclyde	3 Ayr, Lanark & Ren. (22-23)
Inverness	Highland	9 Highland, South (34-35)
Kilmarnock & Loudon	East Ayrshire	3 Ayr, Lanark & Ren. (22-23)
Kincardine & Deeside	Aberdeenshire	10 Aberdeen & Moray (36-37)
Kirkcaldy	Fife	7 Fife (30-31)
Kyle & Carrick	East Ayrshire	3 Ayr, Lanark & Ren. (22-23)
Lochaber	Highland	9 Highland, South (34-35)
Midlothian	Midlothian	4 Lothians (24-25)
Monklands	North Lanarkshire	3 Ayr, Lanark & Ren. (22-23)
Moray	Moray	10 Aberdeen & Moray (36-37)
Motherwell	North Lanarkshire	3 Ayr, Lanark & Ren. (22-23)
Nairn	Highland	9 Highland, South (34-35)
North East Fife	Fife	7 Fife (30-31)
Orkney	Orkney	11 W. Isles, Ork. & Shet. (38)
Perth & Kinross	Perth & Kinross	8 Perth & Angus (32-33)
Renfrew	Renfrewshire	3 Ayr, Lanark & Ren. (22-23)
Roxburgh	Scottish Borders	2 Borders (20-21)
Ross & Cromarty	Highland	9 Highland, South (34-35)
Shetland	Shetland	11 W. Isles, Ork. & Shet. (38)
Skye & Lochalsh	Highland	9 Highland, South (34-35)
Stewartry	Dumfries & Galloway	1 Dumfries & Gall. (18-19)
Stirling	Stirling	6 Stirling & Falkirk (28-29)
Strathkelvin	East Dunbartonshire	3 Ayr, Lanark & Ren. (22-23)
Sutherland	Highland	9 Highland, South (34-35)
Tweeddale	Scottish Borders	2 Borders (20-21)
West Lothian	West Lothian	4 Lothians (24-25)
Western Isles	Western Isles	11 W. Isles, Ork. & Shet. (38)
Wigtown	Dumfries & Galloway	1 Dumfries & Gall. (18-19)

Main Map

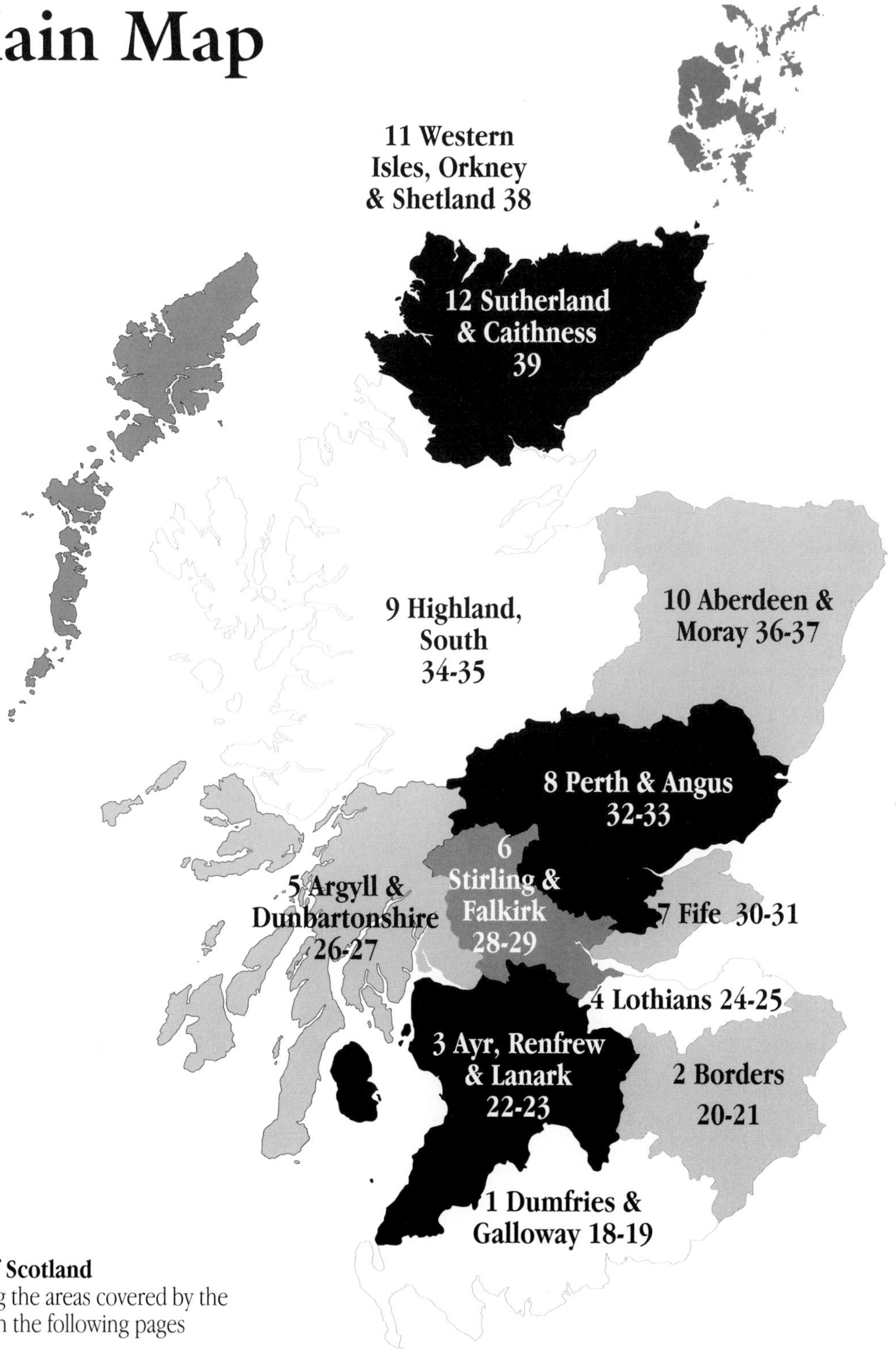

11 Western Isles, Orkney & Shetland 38

12 Sutherland & Caithness 39

9 Highland, South 34-35

10 Aberdeen & Moray 36-37

8 Perth & Angus 32-33

6 Stirling & Falkirk 28-29

5 Argyll & Dunbartonshire 26-27

7 Fife 30-31

4 Lothians 24-25

3 Ayr, Renfrew & Lanark 22-23

2 Borders 20-21

1 Dumfries & Galloway 18-19

Map of Scotland
showing the areas covered by the
maps on the following pages

1 Dumfries & Galloway

1.4 cms = 10 kms, 1 inch = 11.25 miles

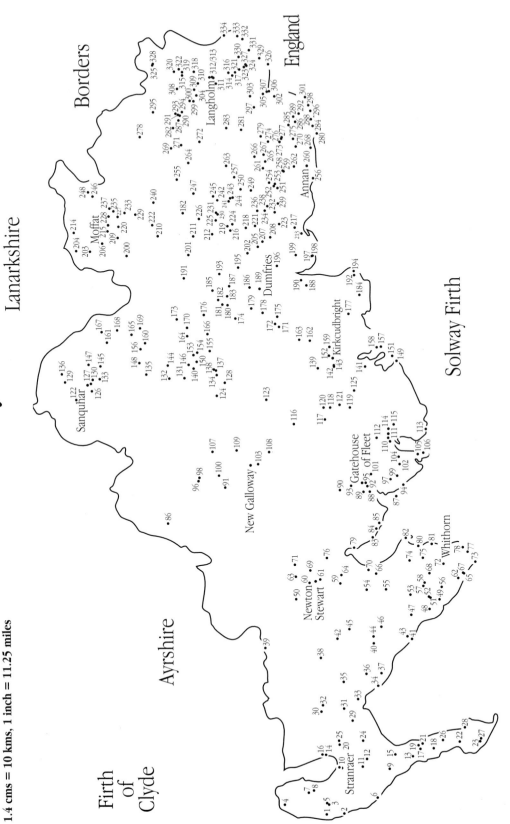

Lanarkshire

Borders

England

Ayrshire

Firth
of
Clyde

Solway Firth

Sanquhar

Moffat

Dumfries

Kirkcudbright

New Galloway

Gatehouse
of Fleet

Newton
Stewart

Whithorn

Stranraer

Annan

Langholm 312/313

18

Map 1:
List of Castles

1 Galdenoch Castle
2 Kemp's Walk Fort
3 Lochnaw Castle
4 Corsewall Castle
5 Lochnaw Castle
6 Dunskey Castle
7 Craigoch Castle
8 Balwherrie
9 Kildonan
10 Stranraer Castle
11 Kilhilt
12 Garthland Castle
13 Low Ardwell
14 Innermessan Castle
15 Balgreggan
16 Craigcaffie Tower
17 Killaser Castle
18 Logan House
19 Ardwell House
20 Inch Crindil
21 Auchness Castle
22 Clanyard Castle
23 Auchneight
24 Freugh Tower
25 Castle Kennedy
26 Killumpha Tower
27 Broadwall
28 Drummore Castle
29 Dunragit House
30 Larg Castle
31 Old Halls of Craig
32 Balneil
33 Castle of Park
34 Sinniness Castle
35 Carscreugh Castle
36 Craigneveoch Castle
37 Auchenmaig
38 Loch Ronald
39 Loch Maberry Castle
40 Castle Loch Castle
41 Craigoch
42 Craighlaw Castle
43 Aryolland
44 Old Place of Mochrum
45 Mindork Castle
46 Crailloch
47 Druchtag Motte
48 Myrton Castle
49 Barmeal Castle
50 Castle Stewart

51 Dowies
52 Moure Castle
53 Longcastle
54 Torhouse Castle
55 Barnbarroch Castle
56 Craigdhu
57 Drumgin Castle
58 Ravenstone Castle
59 Bishop's Palace, Penninghame
60 Minnigaff Motte
61 Machermore Castle
62 Glasserton House
63 Garlies Castle
64 Clachary
65 Port Castle
66 Baldoon Castle
67 Physgill House
68 Castlewigg
69 Larg Tower
70 Wigtown Castle
71 Old Risk
72 Castle Hill, Whithorn
73 Castle Feather
74 Sorbie Castle
75 Old Place of Broughton
76 Muirfad Castle
77 Cutreoch
78 Isle of Whithorn Castle
79 Cassencarie House
80 Galloway House
81 Cruggleton Castle
82 Eggerness Castle
83 Carsluith Castle
84 Kirkdale Tower
85 Barholm Castle
86 Banck Castle
87 Ardwall Island
88 Ardwall
89 Buck o' Bield
90 Rusko Castle
91 Barskeoch
92 Cardoness Castle
93 Pulcree
94 Castle Haven
95 Cally Castle
96 Dundeugh Castle
97 Plunton Castle
98 Glenhoul
99 Barmagachan
100 Earlstoun Castle
101 Enrick
102 Borgue
103 Kenmure Castle
104 Nunton Castle

105 Balmangan Tower
106 Manor Castle
107 Lochinvar Castle
108 Shirmers Castle
109 Barscobe Castle
110 Kirkcudbright Castle
111 MacLellan's Castle
112 Cumstoun Castle
113 Raeberry Castle
114 Lochfergus
115 Bombie Castle
116 Parton Place
117 Balmaghie
118 Threave Castle
119 Auchlane Castle
120 Greenlaw Tower
121 Threave Garden and Estate
122 Tower
123 Corsock Castle
124 Rough Island
125 Gelston Castle
126 Kemps Castle
127 Sanquhar Castle
128 Lettrick Castle
129 Carco Castle
130 Ryehill Castle
131 Crawfordton Tower
132 Killiewarren
133 Eliock House
134 Brockloch
135 Arkland Tower
136 Castle Robert
137 Sundaywell Tower
138 Bogrie Tower
139 Motte of Urr
140 Old Crawfordton
141 Orchardton Tower
142 Buittle Place
143 Buittle Castle
144 Tynron Doon
145 Dalpeddar
146 Maxwelton House
147 Gilmour Castle
148 Auchengassel Castle
149 Balcary Tower
150 Stewarton
151 Heston Island
152 Edingham Castle
153 Breckonside Tower
154 Auchenfedrick
155 Place of Snade
156 Drumlanrig Castle
157 Castlehill of Barcloy
158 West Barcloy

159 Barclosh Castle
160 Tibbers Castle
161 Coshogle Castle
162 Corra Castle
163 Drumcoltran Tower
164 Barjarg Tower
165 Enoch Castle
166 Lagg Tower
167 Dalveen Castle
168 Durisdeer Castle
169 Morton Castle
170 Dinning
171 Auchenfranco Castle
172 Loch Rutton
173 Closeburn Castle
174 Fourmerkland Tower
175 Hills Tower
176 Auldgirth
177 Auchenskeoch Castle
178 Cullochan Castle
179 Terregles Castle
180 Isle Tower
181 Portrack Castle
182 Dalswinton Castle
183 Cowhill Tower
184 Wreaths Tower
185 Newlands
186 Lincluden Collegiate Church
187 Carzeid
188 Abbot's Tower
189 Dumfries Castle
190 Kirkconnel House
191 Glenae Tower
192 Arbigland House
193 Amisfield Tower
194 McCulloch's Castle
195 Tinwald Place
196 Craigs
197 Caerlaverock Castle
198 Caerlaverock
199 Isle Tower
200 Kinnelhead Tower
201 Wreaths Tower
202 Torthorwald Castle
203 Mellingshaw Tower
204 Raecleugh Tower
205 Bucklerhole
206 Blacklaw Tower
207 Rockhall
208 Mouswald Tower
209 Auchen Castle
210 Boreland Tower
211 Ross Castle
212 Elshieshields Tower

213 Cockpool Castle
214 Corehead
215 Chapel
216 Cockie's Field
217 Comlongon Castle
218 Rammerscales House
219 Lochmaben Castle
220 Lochmaben Castle
221 Holmains Castle
222 Lochwood Tower
223 Raffles Tower
224 Lochmaben Castle
225 Bridgemuir
226 Spedlins Tower
227 Duncrieff
228 Frenchland Tower
229 Poldean
230 Applegarth
231 Dinwoodie
232 Denbie
233 Breconside Tower
234 Dormont
235 Cornal Tower
236 Daltonhook
237 Craigieburn
238 Kirkwood
239 Moss Castle
240 Wamphray Tower
241 Muirhead
242 Kirkton Tower
243 Lockerbie Tower
244 Netherplace
245 Old Walls
246 Runstonfoote
247 Hewke
248 Boadsbeck Castle
249 Castlemilk
250 Mallscastle
251 Repentance Tower
252 Hoddom Castle
253 Hallguards Castle
254 Knockhill
255 Gillesbie Tower
256 Newbie Castle
257 Tundergarth Castle
258 Brydekirk Tower
259 Luce
260 Annan Castle
261 Kirkconnel Tower
262 Warmanbie
263 Lunelly Tower
264 Carterton
265 Nucke
266 Scotsbrig

267 Birrens
268 Dornock
269 Black Esk Tower
270 Stapleton Tower
271 Tanlawhill Tower
272 Crossdykes
273 Bonshaw Tower
274 Blacket House
275 Albie
276 Robgill Tower
277 Woodhouse Tower
278 Raeburnfoot
279 Kirkconnel Tower
280 Torduff
281 Limbridgeford
282 Bankburnfoot
283 Kirtlehead
284 Westhills
285 Kirkpatrick Tower
286 Calvertsholm
287 Shiel
288 Baurch
289 Redhall Castle
290 Bogle Walls, Enzieholm
291 Westerkirk
292 Stonehouse Tower
293 Crooks Castle
294 Knock
295 Glendinning Castle
296 Redkirk
297 Auchinbetrig
298 Old Graitney
299 Bombie
300 Westerhall Tower
301 Sarkbridge
302 Greenwrae
303 Barnglies
304 Carlesgill
305 Sark Tower
306 Cowholm
307 Croftsike
308 Calfield Tower
309 Craig
310 Barntalloch Tower
311 Wauchope Castle
312 Langholm Tower
313 Langholm Tower
314 Irvine Tower
315 Kirkton Tower
316 Broomholm Tower
317 Auchenrivock Tower
318 Flask Tower
319 Glendivan
320 Bush

321 Mumbiehirst Tower
322 Arkleton Tower
323 Hollows Tower
324 Gilnockie Tower
325 Glenvorann
326 Woodslee Tower
327 Thorniewhats
328 Burnfoot
329 Hallgreen
330 Outer Woodhead
331 Archerbeck
332 Harelaw Tower
333 Whitlawside
334 Muirburnhead

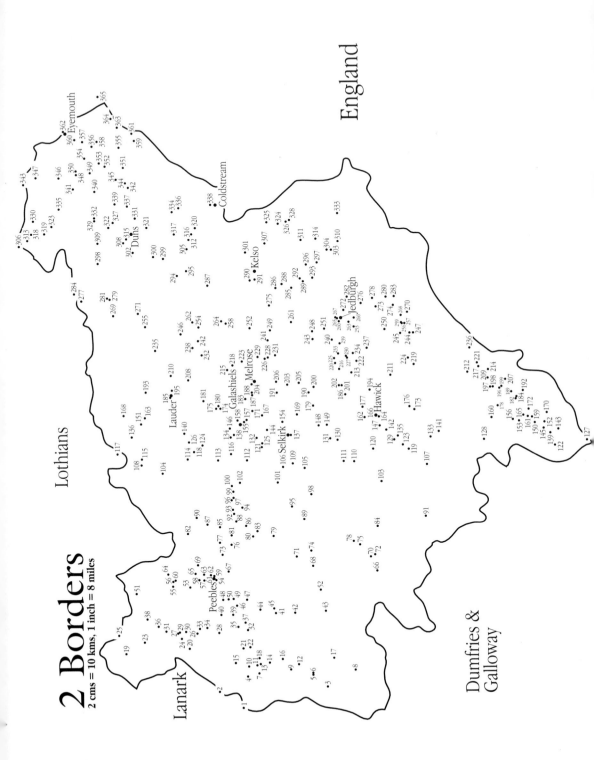

2 Borders

2 cms = 10 kms, 1 inch = 8 miles

Lothians

Lanark

England

Coldstream

Eyemouth

Duns

Kelso

Galashiels

Lauder

Melrose

Selkirk

Jedburgh

Hawick

Peebles

Dumfries & Galloway

Map 2:
List of Castles

1 Hartree Tower
2 Skirling Castle
3 Hawkshaw Castle
4 Kilbucho Place
5 Oliver Castle
6 Bield Tower
7 Quarter House
8 Fruid Castle
9 Kingledores
10 Whitslade Tower
11 Kittlehall
12 Polmood
13 Wrae Tower
14 Mossfennan
15 Broughton Place
16 Stanhope Tower
17 Talla
18 Drumelzier Castle
19 Baddingsgill House
20 Kirkurd
21 Dreva Castle
22 Tinnis Castle
23 West Linton
24 Callands House
25 Carlops
26 Drochil Castle
27 Grahams Walls
28 Harrow Hope
29 Whiteside Tower
30 Flemington Tower
31 Romanno Tower
32 Dawyck House
33 Stevenson
34 Wester Happrew
35 Halmyre House
36 Lour Tower
37 Macbiehill
38 Posso Tower
39 Easter Dawyck
40 Easter Happrew
41 Kirkhope Tower
42 Manorhead Tower
43 Cramalt Tower
44 Langhaugh Tower
45 Langhaugh Tower
46 Woodhouse Hill
47 Castlehill Tower
48 Barns Tower
49 Hallyards

50 Caverhill Tower
51 Easter Deans
52 Cockburn's Tower
53 Cringletie House
54 Neidpath Castle
55 Black Barony Castle
56 Moredun House
57 Chapelhill
58 Winkston Tower
59 Peebles Castle
60 Hopeton Castle
61 County Hotel, Peebles
62 Smithfield Castle
63 Hutchinfield Tower
64 Boreland Tower
65 Foulitch Tower
66 Ettrick House
67 Haystoun
68 Dryhope Tower
69 Shieldgreen Tower
70 Thirlestane Tower
71 Blackhouse Tower
72 Gameshcleuch Tower
73 Horsburgh Tower
74 Craig Douglas Castle
75 Tushielaw Tower
76 Cardrona Tower
77 Nether Horsburgh Castle
78 Eldinhope Tower
79 Cow Peel
80 Grieston Tower
81 Ormiston Tower
82 Woolandslee Tower
83 Shillinglaw Castle
84 Buccleuch Castle
85 Lee Tower
86 Traquair House
87 Colquhar Tower
88 Pirn
89 Catslack Tower
90 Glentress Tower
91 Old Howpasley
92 Kirnie Tower
93 Purvishill Tower
94 Plora Tower
95 Deuchar Tower
96 Caberston Tower
97 Bold
98 Kirkhope Tower
99 Scrogbank
100 Holylee
101 Hangingshaw
102 Elibank Castle

103 Alemoor Tower
104 Howliston Tower
105 Alkwood Tower
106 Newark Castle
107 Slaidhills Tower
108 Crookston Old House
109 Bowhill
110 Whitslade Tower
111 Todrig Tower
112 Ashiesteel House
113 Windydoors Tower
114 Ewes Castle
115 Hoppringle Castle
116 Whytbank Tower
117 Gilston Peel
118 Lugate Castle
119 Broadhaugh
120 Harden
121 Yair House
122 Puddingburn Tower
123 Allanmouth Tower
124 Torsance Castle
125 Fairnilee
126 Stow
127 Greena Tower
128 Gorrenberry Tower
129 Branxholme Castle
130 Salenside Castle
131 Woll
132 Calfshaw
133 Brugh
134 Torwoodlee Tower
135 Whitchesters
136 Hartside Castle
137 Selkirk Castle
138 Blindlee Tower
139 Syde Tower
140 Muirhouse Tower
141 Grey Coat Peel
142 Goldielands Tower
143 Mangerton Tower
144 Sunderland Hall
145 Copshaw Tower
146 Buckholm Tower
147 Crumhaugh Tower
148 North Synton
149 Synton
150 Roan Tower
151 Overhowden
152 Whithaugh Tower
153 Foulshiels Tower
154 Greenhead Tower
155 Old Gala House

156 Hartsgarth Tower
157 Hunter's Hall, Galashiels
158 Ladhope Tower
159 Westburnflat Tower
160 Hermitage Castle
161 Redheugh Castle
162 Stirches
163 Collielaw
164 Lovells' Castle, Hawick
165 Parck
166 Drumlanrig's Tower, Hawick
167 Castle of Faldonside
168 Carfrae Peel
169 Whitmuir Hall
170 Hillhouse Tower
171 Abbotsford
172 Liddel Castle
173 Stobs Castle
174 Hillslap Tower
175 Colmslie Tower
176 Adderston
177 Burnhead Tower
178 Baholm Tower
179 Riddell Tower
180 Langshaw Tower
181 Cocklaw Castle
182 Brighouse Tower
183 Westhouses
184 Dinlabyre
185 Lauder Tower
186 Horsleyhill
187 Darnick Tower
188 Darnick
189 Kellyly
190 Lilliesleaf Tower
191 Castle of Holydean
192 Clintwood Castle
193 Burncastle
194 Cavers House
195 Thirlestane Castle
196 Coldsyde
197 Breaken Tower
198 Riccarton Tower
199 Haggishaugh
200 Chapel
201 Monk's Tower
202 Hassendean Castle
203 Kippilaw House
204 Melrose Abbey
205 Cavers Carre
206 Bowden
207 Larriston Tower
208 Whitslaid Tower

209 Faseyside Tower
210 Old Thirlestane Castle
211 Hawthornside
212 Byrsted Tower
213 Denholm
214 Thorlieshope Tower
215 Rhymer's Tower
216 Minto House
217 Hudshouse Tower
218 Cowdenknowes
219 Wauchope Tower
220 Fatlips Castle
221 Copshaws Tower
222 Spittal Tower
223 Redpath
224 Wolflee
225 Barnhills Tower
226 Mantle House
227 Fast Castle
228 Dryburgh Abbey
229 Bemersyde House
230 Hallrule
231 Lessudden House
232 Morriston Tower
233 Newton Tower
234 Bedrule Castle
235 Spottiswoode House
236 Peel Tower
237 Fulton Tower
238 Corsbie Tower
239 Rue Castle
240 Lanton Tower
241 Mertoun House and Garden
242 Huntly
243 Ancrum House
244 Slacks Peel
245 Chesters
246 Bassendean House
247 Dykeraw Tower
248 Maltan Walls
249 Littledean Tower
250 Kilnsike Peel
251 Timpendean Tower
252 Smailholm Tower
253 Grey Peel
254 Greenknowe Tower
255 Wedderlie House
256 Hindhaughead
257 Clessley Peel
258 Whiteside Peel
259 Longslack Sike
260 Hundalee House
261 Fairnington House

262 Gordon Castle
263 Jedburgh Castle
264 Mellerstain
265 Queen Mary's Hse, Jedburgh
266 Ferniehirst Castle
267 Stone Hill, Jedburgh
268 Roughlee
269 Scarlaw Peel
270 Northbank Peel
271 Evelaw Tower
272 Hunthill
273 Old Jeddart
274 Mervinslaw Pele
275 Makerstoun House
276 Mossburnford Castle
277 Cranshaws Castle
278 Dolphinston Tower
279 Peelhill
280 Overton Tower
281 Longformacus
282 Crag Tower
283 Eggerston Castle
284 Harehead Castle
285 Ormiston Tower
286 Wallace's Tower
287 Hume Castle
288 Sunlaws House
289 Eckford Tower
290 Floors Castle
291 Roxburgh Castle
292 Moss Tower
293 Wooden Hill
294 Greenlaw Castle
295 Old Greenlaw Castle
296 Marlfield House
297 Cessford Castle
298 Windshiel
299 Redbraes Castle
300 Polwarth Castle
301 Sprouston
302 Langton Castle
303 Heatherlands Tower
304 Whitton Tower
305 Purves Hall
306 Dunglass Castle
307 Lurdenlaw Tower
308 Borthwick Castle
309 Cockburn Tower
310 Chesterhouse Tower
311 Linton Tower
312 Mersington Tower
313 Cockburnspath House
314 Corbet Tower

315 Duns Castle
316 Leitholm Peel
317 Bite-About Pele
318 Cockburnspath Castle
319 Bowshiel Tower
320 Belchester
321 Nisbet House
322 Preston
323 Kilspindie Castle
324 Graden Tower
325 Hoselaw Tower
326 Thirlestane Tower
327 Broom House
328 Lochtower
329 Bunkle Castle
330 Old Cambus
331 Wedderburn Castle
332 Manderston
333 Mowhaugh Tower
334 Swinton
335 Renton Peel
336 Little Swinton
337 Kelloe Bastle
338 The Hirsel
339 Blanerne Castle
340 Billie Castle
341 Houndwood House
342 Blackadder Castle
343 Fast Castle
344 Allanbank House
345 Chirnside
346 Press Castle
347 Lumsdaine
348 Heugh Head
349 Ferney Castle
350 Reston
351 Hutton Castle
352 Edington Bastle
353 Edington Castle
354 East Reston Tower
355 Foulden Bastle
356 Peelwalls
357 Ayton Castle
358 Bastleridge
359 Paxton House
360 Linthill House
361 Edrington Castle
362 Eyemouth
363 Mordington House
364 Lamberton
365 Berwick Castle

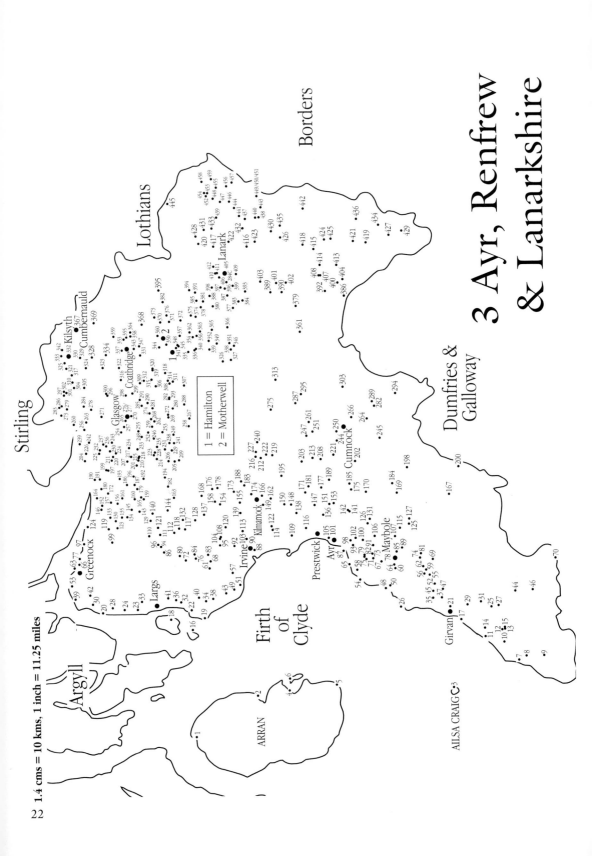

3 Ayr, Renfrew & Lanarkshire

1.4 cms = 10 kms, 1 inch = 11.25 miles

22

1 = Hamilton
2 = Motherwell

Stirling
Lothians
Borders
Dumfries & Galloway
Argyll
Firth of Clyde
ARRAN
AILSA CRAIG

Greenock
Largs
Glasgow
Kilsyth
Cumbernauld
Coatbridge
Lanark
Kilmarnock
Irvine
Prestwick
Ayr
Maybole
Cumnock
Girvan

Map 3: List of Castles

1 Lochranza Castle
2 Brodick Castle
3 Ailsa Craig Castle
4 Whitehouse
5 Kildonan Castle
6 Holy Island
7 Ardstinchar Castle
8 Glenapp Castle
9 Carlock
10 Knockdolian Castle
11 Carleton Castle
12 Kirkhill Castle
13 Craigneil Castle
14 Knockdaw Castle
15 Bardrochat
16 Little Cumbrae Cas.
17 Ardmillan Castle
18 Ballikillet Castle
19 Portencross Castle
20 Castle Wemyss
21 Ballochtoul Castle
22 Hunterston Castle
23 Knock Castle
24 Skelmorlie Castle
25 Daljarroch
26 Turnberry Castle
27 Pinwherry Castle
28 Kelly House
29 Dinvin Motte
30 Inverkip Castle
31 Pinmore
32 Southannan Castle
33 Brisbane House
34 Law Castle
35 Trochrague
36 Fairlie Castle
37 Camregan Castle
38 Tarbet Castle
39 Castle Levan
40 Crosbie Castle
41 Kelburn Castle
42 Dunrod Castle
43 Montfode Castle
44 Kildonan
45 Killochan Castle
46 Dochroyle
47 Penkill Castle
48 Culzean Castle

49 Ardrossan Castle
50 Thomaston Castle
51 Saltcoats
52 Bargany Castle
53 Goutock Castle
54 Dunure Castle
55 Brunston Castle
56 Lochmodie Castle
57 Kerelaw Castle
58 Dunduff Castle
59 Dalquharran Castle
60 Crossraguel Abbey
61 Tower
62 Drummochreen
63 Greenock Castle
64 Baltersan Castle
65 Glenays Castle
66 Cartsdyke
67 Brockloch Castle
68 Monk Castle
69 Kilkerran Castle
70 Dornal Castle
71 Beoch
72 Swinlees
73 Garryhorn
74 Drummellan Castle
75 Craigskean
76 Pitcon
77 Easter Greenock Cas.
78 Maybole Castle
79 Sauchie Castle
80 Kilbirnie House
81 Barclanachan
82 Knockdon Castle
83 Blair Castle
84 Kersland
85 Kilhenzie Castle
86 Glengarnock Castle
87 Greenan Castle
88 Fullarton Castle
89 Dalduff Castle
90 Seagate Castle
91 Smithston Castle
92 Eglinton Castle
93 Newark Castle
94 Ladyland Castle
95 Monkredding House
96 Larabank Castle
97 Newark Castle
98 Brigend Castle
99 Duchal Castle
100 Auchendrane Castle
101 Ayr Castle
102 Nether Auchendrane

103 Stane Castle
104 Clonbeith Castle
105 Newton Castle
106 Cassillis House
107 Kirkmichael House
108 Montgreenan Castle
109 Crosbie House
110 Cloak Castle
111 Barr Castle
112 Woodside House
113 Perceton House
114 Auchans
115 Cloncaird Castle
116 Monkton House
117 Broadstone Castle
118 Hill of Beith
119 Kilmacolm Castle
120 Auchenharvie Castle
121 Belltrees Peel
122 Dundonald Castle
123 Dennistoun Castle
124 Finlaystone House
125 Blairquhan
126 Barbieston
127 Milton
128 Giffen Castle
129 Castle Semple
130 Grymm's Castle
131 Skeldon Castle
132 Hessilhead Castle
133 Kilallan House
134 Ranfurly Castle
135 Gryffe Castle
136 Auchencruive Castle
137 Aiket Castle
138 Underwood Castle
139 Bushie Tower
140 Elliston Castle
141 Martnaham Castle
142 Fergus Loch
143 Auchinames Castle
144 Auchenbathie Castle
145 Penwold
146 Parkglen Wood
147 Templehouse
148 Barnweill Castle
149 Caprington Castle
150 Craigie Castle
151 Gadgirth House
152 Park
153 Sundrum Castle
154 Lainshaw Castle
155 Kilmaurs Place
156 Houston House

157 Barochan House
158 Corsehill Castle
159 Cochrane Castle
160 Milliken
161 Craigends House
162 Treesbanks
163 Caldwell Tower
164 Bishopton House
165 Johnstone Castle
166 Riccarton Castle
167 Bradan Castle
168 Dunlop House
169 Keirs Castle
170 Kerse Castle
171 Tarbolton Motte
172 Dargavel House
173 Rowallan Castle
174 Dean Castle
175 Drumsoy Castle
176 Robertland Castle
177 Stair
178 Pokelly
179 Wallace's Buildings
180 Rossland
181 Coilsfield Castle
182 Banklug Castle
183 Auchinloss
184 Laight Castle
185 Drongan Castle
186 Middleton
187 Ridford
188 Craufurdland Castle
189 Trabboch Castle
190 Erskine Castle
191 Bar Castle
192 Stanely Castle
193 Walkinshaw
194 Cowden Hall
195 Carnell
196 Ferguslie Castle
197 Northbar
198 Dalmellington Castle
199 Inchinnan Castle
200 Loch Doon Castle
201 Blackhall Manor
202 Auchencloigh Castle
203 Mauchline Castle
204 Cochno Castle
205 Fingalton
206 Glanderston Castle
207 Gallowhill
208 Auchinleck Castle
209 Langton
210 Hawkhead Castle

211 Renfield
212 Barr Castle
213 Kingencleugh Castle
214 Arthurlie House
215 Whiteford Tower
216 Loudoun Castle
217 Ralston
218 Hawkhead Castle
219 Sorhill
220 Renfrew Castle
221 Ochiltree Castle
222 Cessnock Castle
223 Tower Rais
224 Inch Castle
225 Drumry Castle
226 Law Tower
227 Loudoun
228 Dubs
229 Netherplace
230 Blawarthill
231 Pollok Castle
232 Garscadden Castle
233 Crookston Castle
234 Cardonald Castle
235 Darnley Castle
236 Knightswood Castle
237 Cloberhill
238 Newton Mearns
239 Mains Castle
240 Newmilns Tower
241 Langrig
242 Gartconner Castle
243 Jordanhill
244 Ward of Lochnorris
245 Waterhead Castle
246 Corslie Castle
247 Sorn Castle
248 Pollok House
249 Mearns Castle
250 Terringzean Castle
251 Gilmilnscroft
252 Auldhouse
253 Druid's Temple Hill
254 Partick Castle
255 Haggs Castle
256 Douglaston House
257 Stobcross
258 Eaglesham Castle
259 Bogton Castle
260 Craigmaddie Castle
261 Daldilling
262 Lee Castle
263 Bardowie Castle
264 Old Hall Auchincross

265 Anderston
266 Boreland Castle
267 Polnoon Castle
268 Cathcart Castle
269 Castle Hill, Busby
270 Baronial Hall, Gorbals
271 Possil
272 The Peel, Busby
273 Craigharnet Castle
274 Aitkenhead Castle
275 Main Castle
276 Glasgow Castle
277 Provand's Lordship, Glasgow
278 Cadder Castle
279 Woodhead Castle
280 Rough Hill
281 Castlemilk
282 Knockshinnoch
283 Ballanreoch Castle
284 Broken Tower
285 Rutherglen Castle
286 Balcorrach Castle
287 Whitehaugh Castle
288 Lickprivick Castle
289 Black Bog Castle
290 Stonelaw Tower
291 Farme Castle
292 Mains Castle
293 Comyn's Castle
294 Blackcraig Castle
295 Chapelhouse
296 Robroyston House
297 Bencloich Castle
298 Carntyne
299 Tollcross
300 Cardarroch House
301 Glorat House
302 Maiden Castle
303 Kyle Castle
304 Kincaid House
305 Kirkintilloch Peel
306 Gilbertfield Castle
307 Torrance Castle
308 Calderwood Castle
309 Kenmuir
310 Antermony Castle
311 Craigneith Castle
312 Newton House
313 Wellwood House
314 Crossbasket Castle
315 Drumsargad Castle
316 Provan Hall

317 Auchenreoch Castle
318 Old Place, Blantyre
319 Blantyre Priory
320 Bothwell Castle
321 Old Place
322 Bishop's House, Lochwood
323 Bedlay Castle
324 Gartshore House
325 Balcastle
326 Strathaven Castle
327 Gillbank House
328 Bademheath Castle
329 Board
330 Auchinvole House
331 Tannochside House
332 Kilsyth Castle
333 Dovecotwood Castle
334 Inchnock Castle
335 Eddlewood Castle
336 Hamilton Palace
337 Gartsherrie House
338 Tweedie Castle
339 Glassford
340 Darngaber Castle
341 Barncluith Castle
342 Colzium Castle
343 Monkland House
344 Orbiston House
345 Cadzow Castle
346 Castle Brocket
347 Carnbroe House
348 Chatelherault
349 Cot Castle
350 Ross House
351 Plotcock Castle
352 Holm Castle
353 Airdrie House
354 Broomhill Castle
355 Rochsolloch
356 Patrickholm
357 Dalzell House
358 Cairnhill House
359 Rochsoles House
360 Jerviston
361 Parisholm
362 Raploch Castle
363 Ringsdale Castle
364 Gartlea
365 Cander
366 Blackwood House
367 Cumbernauld Castle
368 Lauchope House
369 Palacerigg

370 Cleland Castle
371 Wishaw House
372 Castlehill, Cambusnethan
373 Knownoble
374 Auldton
375 Garrion Tower
376 Coltness Castle
377 Glenane
378 Wallans
379 Hazelside Castle
380 Craignethan Castle
381 Waygateshaw House
382 Murdostoun Castle
383 Auchtyfardle Castle
384 Duntervy Castle
385 Hallcraig House
386 Glenrae Castle
387 Stonebyres House
388 Hallbar Tower
389 Poneil
390 Douglas Castle
391 Kirkton of Carluke
392 Moss Castle
393 Moat, Lesmahagow
394 Belstane Castle
395 Allanton House
396 Cairnie Castle
397 Nemphlar
398 The Lee
399 Dowane
400 Snar Castle
401 Parkhall
402 Thornil Castle
403 Folkerton Castle
404 Glendorch Castle
405 Lanark Castle
406 Craiglockhart Castle
407 Boghouse Castle
408 Crawfordjohn Castle
409 Corehouse Castle
410 Castlehill, Lanark
411 Jerviswood House
412 Cleghorn House
413 Glengonnar Castle
414 Gilkerscleugh House
415 Nether Abingdon
416 Carmichael House
417 Carstairs Castle
418 Moat
419 Glenochar Castle
420 Westshield
421 Glengeith
422 Westraw

423 Eastend
424 Bower of Wandel
425 Crawford Castle
426 Wiston Place
427 Smithwood
428 Eastshield Tower
429 Kirkhope Tower
430 Fatlips Tower
431 Couthalley Castle
432 Covington Castle
433 Carnwath House
434 Wintercleuch Castle
435 Lamington Tower
436 Little Clyde
437 Quothquan
438 Annieston Castle
439 Carnwath Mill
440 Cormiston Towers
441 Shieldhill
442 Windgate House
443 Coulter Motte
444 White Castle
445 Torbrex Castle
446 Gladstone Castle
447 Ogs Castle
448 Todholes Castle
449 Boghall Castle
450 Biggar Kirk
451 Biggar Castle
452 Weston
453 Westhall Tower
454 Hills Tower
455 Walston
456 Elsrickle
457 Edmonston Castle
458 Dunsyre Castle
459 Dolphinton

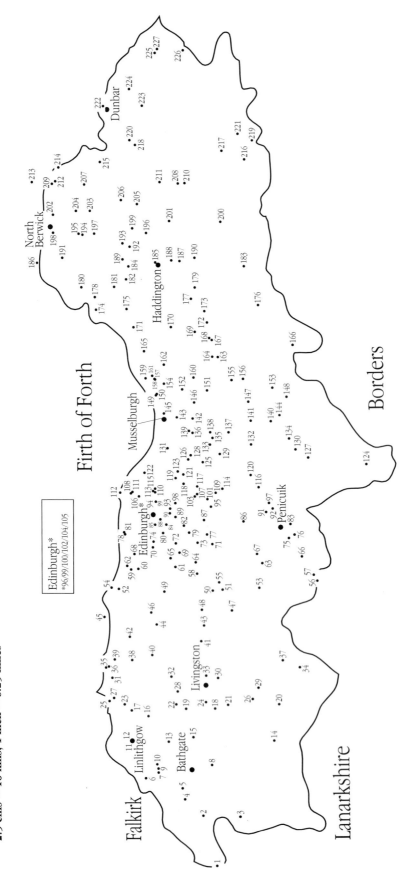

4 Lothians

2.5 cms = 10 kms, 1 inch = 6.25 miles

Firth of Forth

Borders

Lanarkshire

Falkirk

Edinburgh*
*96/99/100/102/104/105

Linlithgow

Bathgate

Livingston

Edinburgh*

Musselburgh

North Berwick

Dunbar

Haddington

Penicuik

24

Map 4:
List of Castles

1 Bedlormie
2 Polkemmet House
3 Ogilface Castle
4 Bridge Castle
5 Couston Castle
6 Carriber Castle
7 Torphichen Preceptory
8 Lochcote Tower
9 Bathgate Castle
10 Kipps Castle
11 West Port House, Linlithgow
12 Linlithgow Palace
13 Tartraven Castle
14 Baads Castle
15 Illieston House
16 Ochiltree Castle
17 Kingscavil
18 Livingston Peel
19 Dechmont House
20 Harburn Castle
21 Alderstone House
22 Strathbrock Castle
23 Pardovan Castle
24 Newyearfield
25 Mannerston
26 Murieston Castle
27 The Binns
28 Houston House
29 Linnhouse
30 Calder House
31 Midhope Castle
32 Kirkhill House
33 Pumpherston
34 Easter Colzium
35 Abercorn Castle
36 Hopetoun House
37 Cairns Tower
38 Duntarvie Castle
39 Staneyhill Tower
40 Niddry Castle
41 Bonnington House
42 Dundas Castle
43 Hatton House
44 Hallyards

45 Inchgarvie
46 Carlowrie Castle
47 Cockburn House
48 Dalmahoy
49 Castle Gogar
50 Curriehill Castle
51 Malleny House
52 Dalmeny House
53 Bavelaw Castle
54 Barnbougle Castle
55 Lennox Castle
56 Newhall Castle
57 Coaltown Tower
58 Riccarton
59 Whitehouse
60 Barnton Tower
61 Redhall Castle
62 Cramond Tower
63 Howlet's House
64 Baberton House
65 Corstorphine Castle
66 Brunstane Castle
67 Logan House
68 Lauriston Castle
69 Saughton House
70 Craigcrook Castle
71 Bonaly Tower
72 Stenhouse
73 Colinton Castle
74 Ravelston House
75 Penicuik Tower
76 Ravensneuk Castle
77 Dreghorn Castle
78 Granton Castle
79 Craiglockhart Castle
80 Roseburn House
81 Caroline Park House
82 Craighouse
83 Uttershill Castle
84 Dalry House, Edinburgh
85 Dean House
86 Fulford Tower
87 Comiston House
88 East Coates House
89 Merchiston Castle
90 Wrychtishousis
91 Greenlaw House
92 Auchendinny House

93 Bruntsfield House
94 Edinburgh Castle
95 Morton House
96 Gladstone's Land, Edinburgh
97 Old Woodhouselee Castle
98 Grange House
99 Dingwall Castle, Edinburgh
100 Kirk o' Field
101 Mortonhall
102 John Knox House, Edinburgh
103 Liberton Tower
104 Canongate Tolbooth
105 Huntly House, Edinburgh
106 Pilrig House
107 Liberton House
108 Leith
109 Broomhill House
110 Holyroodhouse
111 Lamb's House, Leith
112 Martello Tower, Leith
113 Croft an Righ House
114 Straiton
115 Lochend House
116 Rosslyn Castle
117 MacBeth's Castle, Liberton
118 Inch House
119 Peffermill House
120 Hawthornden Castle
121 Craigmillar Castle
122 Craigentinny House
123 Niddrie Marischal
124 Hirendean Castle
125 Drum House
126 Edmonstone Castle
127 Rosebery House
128 Woolmet House
129 Melville Castle
130 Temple Preceptory
131 Brunstane House
132 Dalhousie Castle
133 Sheriffhall
134 Arniston House
135 Lugton
136 Newton
137 Newbattle Abbey
138 Dalkeith House

139 Monkton House
140 Newbyres Tower
141 Masterton House
142 Smeaton Castle
143 Inveresk Lodge
144 Catcune Tower
145 Pinkie House
146 Carberry Tower
147 Southsyde Castle
148 Borthwick Castle
149 Morrison's Haven Fort
150 Prestongrange House
151 Cousland Tower
152 Falside Castle
153 Crichton Castle
154 Dolphingstone Castle
155 Oxenfoord Castle
156 Ford House
157 Hamilton House
158 Northfield House
159 Harlawhill
160 Elphinstone Tower
161 Preston Tower
162 Tranent Tower
163 Cakemuir Castle
164 Ormiston Castle
165 Seton House
166 Fala Luggie Tower
167 Penkaet Castle
168 Woodhall
169 Winton House
170 Penston
171 Longniddry House
172 Keith Marischal
173 Saltoun Hall
174 Kilspindie Castle
175 Redhouse Castle
176 Humbie Old Place
177 Herdmanston
178 Luffness House
179 Pilmuir House
180 Saltcoats Castle
181 Ballencrieff House
182 Byres
183 Kidlaw
184 Garleton Castle
185 Haddington Castle
186 Fidra

187 Colstoun House
188 Lennoxlove
189 Kilduff House
190 Eaglescairnie
191 Dirleton Castle
192 Barnes Castle
193 Athelstaneford
194 Sydserf
195 Fenton Tower
196 Stevenson House
197 Congalton
198 North Berwick Priory
199 Beanston
200 Yester Castle
201 Morham Castle
202 Castle Hill, North Berwick
203 Waughton Castle
204 Balgone House
205 Hailes Castle
206 Markle
207 Whitekirk
208 Stoneypath Tower
209 Tantallon Castle
210 Nunraw Castle
211 Whittinghame Castle
212 Auldhame
213 Bass Rock
214 Seacliff Tower
215 Tyninghame House
216 Mayshiel
217 Johnscleugh
218 Biel
219 Penshiel Grange
220 Belton House
221 Gamelshiel Castle
222 Dunbar Castle
223 Spott House
224 Broxmouth House
225 Innerwick Castle
226 Black Castle
227 Thornton Tower

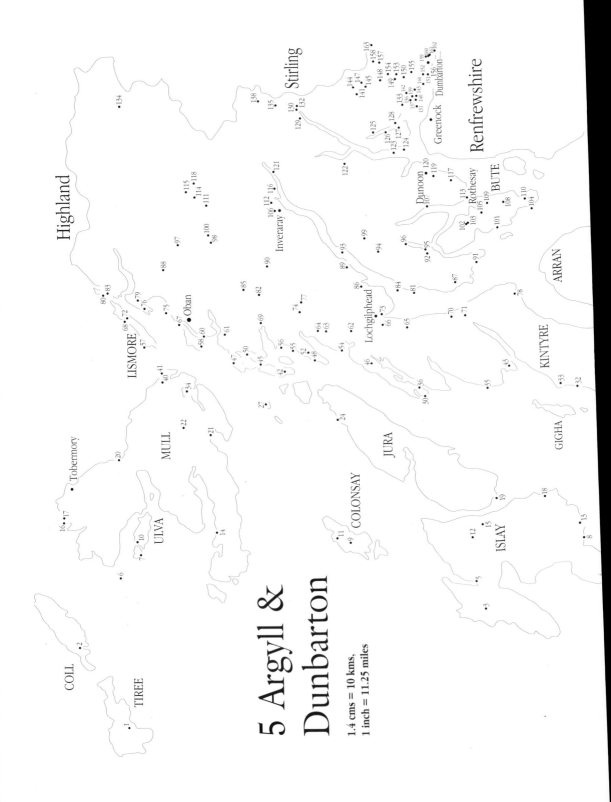

5 Argyll & Dunbarton

1.4 cms = 10 kms,
1 inch = 11.25 miles

Highland

Stirling

Renfrewshire

Greenock

Dumbarton

Dunoon

Rothesay

BUTE

ARRAN

KINTYRE

GIGHA

Inveraray

Lochgilphead

Oban

LISMORE

MULL

Tobermory

ULVA

COLONSAY

JURA

ISLAY

COLL

TIREE

Map 5:
List of Castles

1 Castle Loch Heylipol	45 Caisteal nan Con	93 Castle Lachlan	123 Knockderry Castle	153 Balloch Castle
2 Breachacha Castle	46 Eilean na Circe	94 Achanelid	124 Craigrownie Castle	154 Boturich Castle
3 Gorm Castle	47 Ardfad Castle	95 Eilean Dearg Castle	125 Faslane Castle	155 Place of Bonhill
4 Dun Athad	48 Craignish Castle	96 Auchenbreck Castle	126 Blairvadach Castle	156 Dumbarton Castle
5 A' Chrannog	49 Kildonan Dun	97 Inverawe House	127 Rosneath Castle	157 Ardoch
6 Cairnburgh Castle	50 Ardmaddy Castle	98 Caisteal Suidhe Cheannaidh	128 Ardincaple Castle	158 Ross Priory
7 Dun Eiphinn, Gometra	51 Saddell Castle	99 Garvie Castle	129 Arrochar House	159 Overtoun Castle
8 The Ard, Port Ellen	52 Corranmore	100 Loch Tromlee	130 Tighvechtichan	160 Barnhill House
9 Dun Eibhinn	53 Torrisdale Castle	101 Kilmory Castle	131 Ardmore	161 Tresmass
10 Dun Ban, Ulva	54 Duntrune Castle	102 Wester Kames Castle	132 Tarbet Castle	162 Dunglass Castle
11 Loch an Sgoltaire Castle	55 Lunga	103 Kames Castle	133 Camis Eskan	163 Kilmaronock Castle
12 Finlaggan	56 Dun an Garbh-Sroine	104 Dunagoil	134 Achallader Castle	
13 Dunyvaig Castle	57 Achadun Castle	105 Rothesay Castle	135 Inveruglas Castle	
14 Dun na Muirgheidh	58 Gylen Castle	106 Inveraray Castle	136 Keppoch House	
15 Dun Bhoraraic	59 Airds Castle	107 Balliemeanoch	137 Ardardan Castle	
16 Dun Ara	60 Gallanach Castle	108 Mount Stuart House	138 Eilean Vhow Castle	
17 Glengorm Castle	61 Rarey	109 Ascog House	139 Blairrhenechan Tower	
18 Dun Trudernish	62 Dunadd	110 Kelspoke Castle	140 Geilston House	
19 Claig Castle	63 Kilmartin Castle	111 Fraoch Eilean Castle	141 Bannachra Castle	
20 Aros Castle	64 Carnasserie Castle	112 Dubh Loch Castle	142 Darleith House	
21 Moy Castle	65 Achnakeil	113 Toward Castle	143 Kilmahew Castle	
22 Loch Sguabain Castle	66 Glendarroch	114 Kilchurn Castle	144 Camstraddan Castle	
23 Lossit House	67 Dunollie Castle	115 Glenstrae Castle	145 Rossdhu Castle	
24 Aros Castle	68 Castle Coeffin	116 Dunderave Castle	146 Ardoch Tower	
25 Tirfergus	69 Loch a' Phearsain	117 Knockamillie Castle	147 Inchgalbraith Castle	
26 Glenbarr Abbey	70 Stonefield Castle	118 Stronmilchan	148 Inchmurrin Castle	
27 Dun Chonnuill	71 Tarbert Castle	119 Kilmun Church	149 Cameron House	
28 Dunaverty Castle	72 Tirefour Broch	120 Dunoon Castle	150 Tullichewan Castle	
29 Kilchrist Castle	73 Kilmory Castle	121 Ardkinglas House	151 Cardross Manor House	
30 Caisteal Nighinn Ruaidh, Danna	74 Torran	122 Carrick Castle	152 Dalmoak Castle	
31 Tangy Loch	75 Dunstaffnage Castle			
32 Dundonald Castle	76 Lochnell House			
33 Largie Castle	77 Fincharn Castle			
34 Eilean Amalaig Castle	78 Skipness Castle			
35 Kilberry Castle	79 Barcaldine Castle			
36 Castle Sween	80 Castle Shuna			
37 Lochhead Castle	81 Castle Ewen			
38 Moil Castle	82 Caisteal na Nighinn Ruaidhe			
39 Kilkerran Castle	83 Castle Stalker			
40 Torosay Castle	84 Ballimore			
41 Duart Castle	85 Loch na Sreinge			
42 Leccamore Dun	86 Asknish House			
43 Ardpatrick Castle	87 Asgog Castle			
44 Island Muller Castle	88 Ardchattan Priory			
	89 Minard Castle			
	90 Innis Chonnel Castle			
	91 Ardlamont House			
	92 Glen Caladh Castle			

27

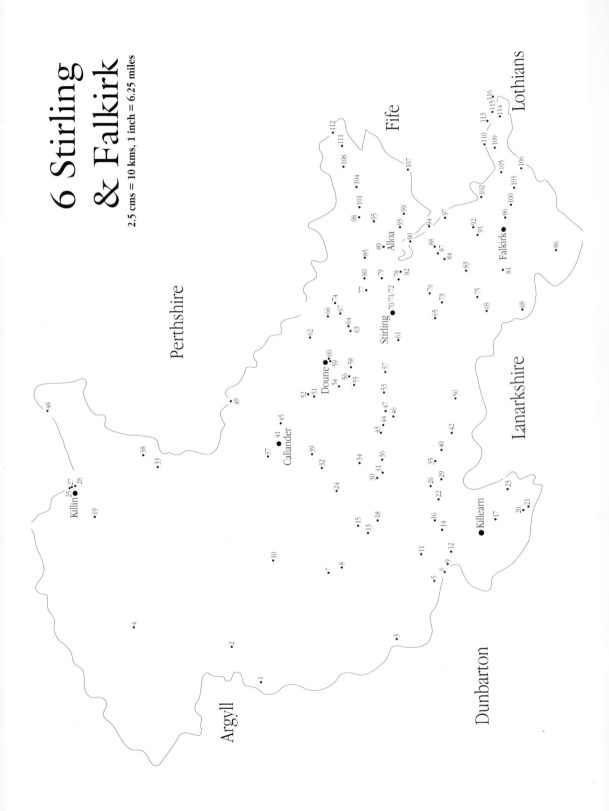

6 Stirling & Falkirk

2.5 cms = 10 kms, 1 inch = 6.25 miles

Argyll

Perthshire

Fife

Lothians

Lanarkshire

Dunbarton

Killin

Callander

Doune

Stirling

Alloa

Falkirk

Killearn

28

Map 6:
List of Castles

1 Inversnaid
2 Glengyle Castle
3 Strathcashell
4 Loch Dochart Castle
5 Buchanan Castle
6 Catter Castle
7 Duke Murdoch's Castle
8 Duchray Castle
9 Drumquhassle Castle
10 Eilean Molach
11 Craigievern Castle
12 Gartness Castle
13 Peel of Claggans
14 Carbeth House
15 Gartartan Castle
16 Ballindalloch Castle
17 Duntreath Castle
18 Peel of Gartfarran
19 Bovain
20 Craigend Castle
21 Mugdock Castle
22 Old Ballikinrain
23 Ballagan Castle
24 Inchtalla Castle
25 Finlarig Castle
26 Edinbellie Castle
27 Eilean Ran Castle
28 Kinnell House
29 Balglass Castle
30 Arnfinlay Castle
31 Tower of Garden
32 Rednock Castle
33 Edinample Castle

34 Cardross House
35 Balgair Castle
36 Arnprior Castle
37 Leny House
38 Ardveich Castle
39 Rusky Castle
40 Culcreuch Castle
41 Callander Castle
42 Fintry Castle
43 Broich House
44 Castlehill, Kippen
45 Auchleshie
46 Boquhan Castle
47 Glentirran
48 Mains Castle
49 Craigton
50 Graham's Castle
51 Lanrick Castle
52 Colliechat Castle
53 Old Leckie House
54 Gartincaber House
55 Coldoch
56 Burnbank
57 Gargunnock House
58 Kincardine Castle
59 Doune Castle
60 Newton Castle
61 Touch House
62 Kilbryde Castle
63 Arnhall Castle
64 Keir House
65 Old Sauchie
66 Bishop's Palace, Dunblane
67 Old Kippencross
68 Castle Cary
69 Rankine Castle

70 Stirling Castle
71 Argyll's Lodging
72 Mar's Work, Stirling
73 Auchenbowie House
74 Glassingall
75 Herbertshire Castle
76 Bannockburn House
77 Airthrey Castle
78 Steuarthall
79 Manor Castle
80 Blairlogie Castle
81 Rough Castle
82 Polmaise Castle
83 Torwood Castle
84 Plean Castle
85 Menstrie Castle
86 Castle Hill, Slamannan
87 Bruce's Castle
88 Carnock House
89 Tullibody
90 Kersie
91 Stenhouse
92 Skaithmore Tower
93 Alloa Tower
94 Airth Tower
95 Sauchie Tower
96 Callendar House
97 Airth Castle
98 Alva Castle
99 Clackmannan Tower
100 Westquarter
101 Tillicoultry Castle
102 Carse Castle
103 Polmont House
104 Harviestoun Castle
105 Inveravon Castle

106 Almond Castle
107 Hartshaw Tower
108 Castle Campbell
109 Kinneil House
110 Karig Lion Castle
111 Cowden Castle
112 Muckhart Castle
113 Grange House
114 Bonhard House
115 Carriden House
116 Blackness Castle

29

7 Fife

2.5 cms = 10 kms, 1 inch = 6.25 miles

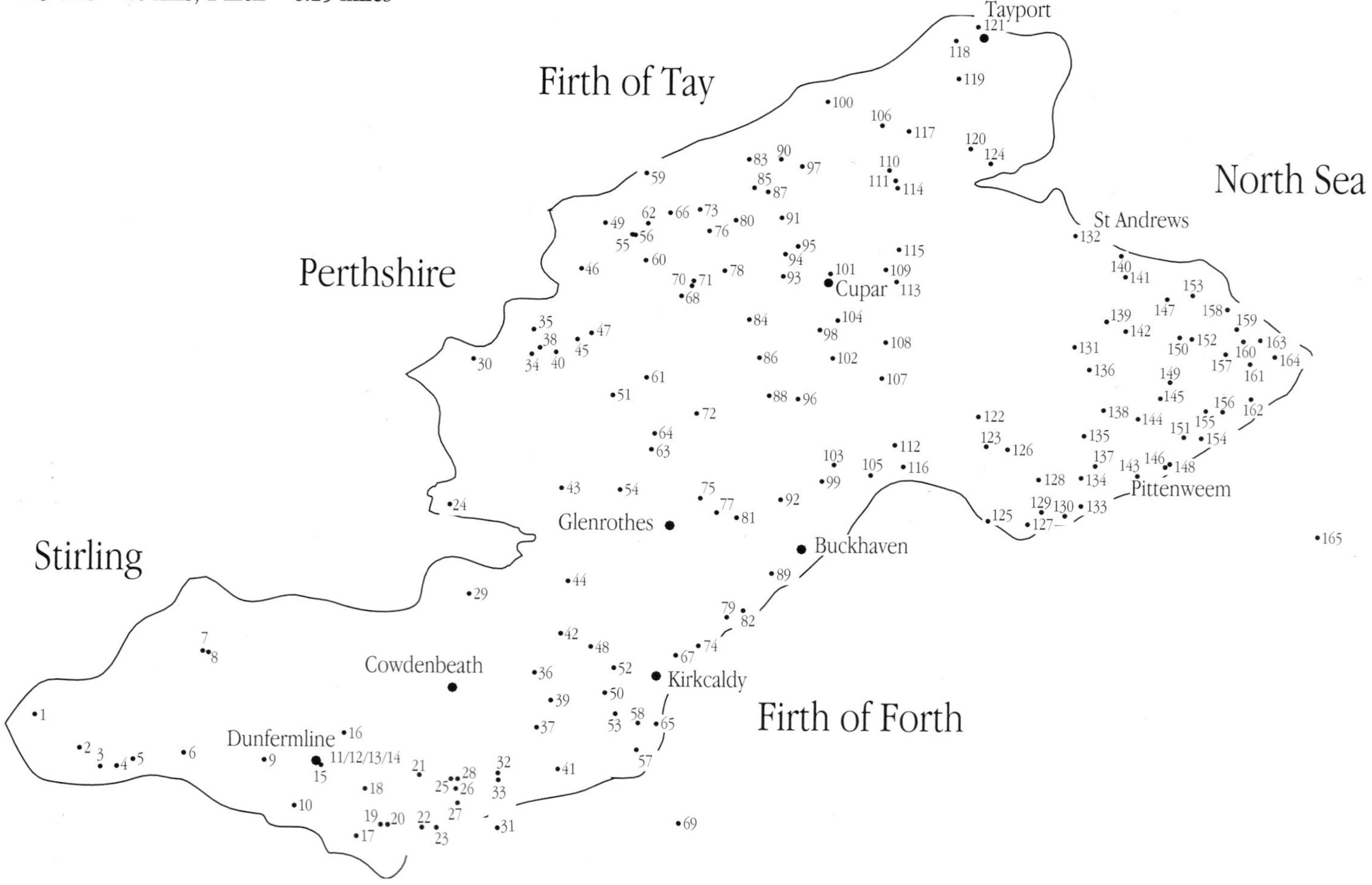

North Sea

Firth of Tay

Firth of Forth

Perthshire

Stirling

Tayport

St Andrews

Pittenweem

Buckhaven

Kirkcaldy

Glenrothes

Cowdenbeath

Dunfermline

Cupar

Map 7:
List of Castles

1 Tulliallan Castle
2 Bordie Castle
3 Blair Castle
4 Dunimarle Castle
5 Culross Palace
6 Torrie Castle
7 Kirklands Tower
8 Killernie Castle
9 Pitfirrane Castle
10 Broomhall
11 Pittencrieff House
12 Malcolm's Tower
13 Dunfermline Abbey and Palace
14 Abbot House, Dunfermline
15 Hill House
16 Garvock Hill
17 Rosyth Castle
18 Pitreavie Castle
19 Selvage
20 Inverkeithing
21 Fordell Castle
22 St David's Castle
23 Donibristle Castle
24 Balcanquhal Tower
25 Otterston Tower
26 Couston Castle
27 Dalgety
28 Cockairnie
29 Lochore Castle
30 Pitlochie Castle
31 Inchcolm Abbey
32 Hillside
33 Aberdour Castle
34 Corston Tower
35 Pitlour
36 Hallyards Castle

37 Knockdavie Castle
38 Cairneyflappet Castle
39 Balmuto Tower
40 Cash Tower
41 Rossend Castle
42 Carden Tower
43 Strathendry Castle
44 Ballfield
45 Reedie
46 Pitcairlie House
47 Myres Castle
48 Torbain Tower
49 Denmylne Castle
50 Balwearie Castle
51 Falkland Palace
52 Raith Tower
53 Pitteadie Castle
54 Leslie House
55 Old Lindores Castle
56 Lindores Castle
57 Kinghorn Castle
58 Grange
59 Ballinbreich Castle
60 Woodmill House
61 Lathrisk House
62 Kinnaird House
63 Bandon Tower
64 Pittillock House
65 Seafield Tower
66 Dunbog Castle
67 Ravenscraig Castle
68 Halhill Tower
69 Inchkeith
70 Melville House
71 Monimail Tower
72 Forthar Tower
73 Ayton
74 St Serf's Church, Dysart
75 Barnslee
76 Collairnie Castle

77 Balgonie Castle
78 Fernie Castle
79 West Wemyss
80 Parbroath Castle
81 Balfour House
82 Wemyss Castle
83 Creich Castle
84 Rankeilour Castle
85 Luthrie
86 Pitlessie Castle
87 Colluthie House
88 Downfield
89 MacDuff's Castle
90 Mountquhanie Castle
91 Lordscairnie Castle
92 Maiden Castle
93 Carslogie House
94 Balgarvie Castle
95 Kilmaron Castle
96 Clatto Castle
97 Rathillet House
98 Scotstarvit Tower
99 Durie House
100 Naughton Castle
101 Cupar Castle
102 Struthers Castle
103 Aithernie Castle
104 Hill of Tarvit Mansion House
105 Lundin Tower
106 Easter Kinnear Castle
107 Castle of Tacis
108 Craighall
109 Rumgally House
110 Logie House
111 Airdit House
112 Pitcruvie Castle
113 Dura House
114 Pitcullo Castle
115 Dairsie Castle
116 Largo Castle

117 Cruvie Castle
118 Scotscraig
119 Kirkton
120 Leuchars Castle
121 Tayport Castle
122 Lathallan Castle
123 Rires Castle
124 Earlshall
125 Kincraig Castle
126 Balcarres House
127 Elie Castle
128 Kilconquhar Castle
129 Elie House
130 Ardross Castle
131 Kinaldy Castle
132 St Andrews Castle
133 Newark Castle
134 Abercrombie Castle
135 Kellie Castle
136 Pittarthie Castle
137 Balcaskie House
138 Carnbee
139 Stravithie Castle
140 Kinkell
141 Kingask
142 Dunino Den
143 Pittenweem Priory
144 Balhouffie
145 Chesterhill
146 Dreel Castle
147 Inchmurtach
148 Old Manse
149 Airdrie House
150 Draffan Castle
151 Innergellie House
152 Kippo
153 Pitmilly House
154 Capelochy Castle
155 Thirdpart House
156 Barns

157 Newhall Tower
158 Kingsbarns Castle
159 Cambo House
160 Randerston
161 Wormiston House
162 Crail Castle
163 Randolphstoun Castle
164 Balcomie Castle
165 Isle of May

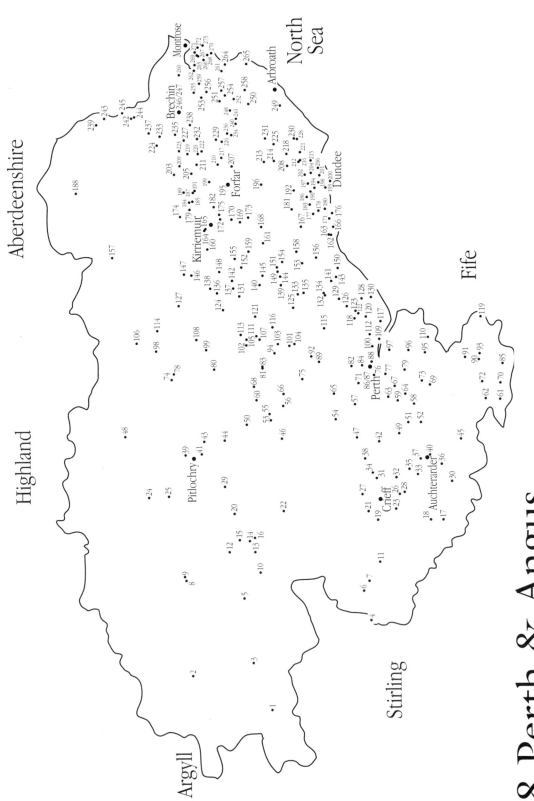

North Sea

Aberdeenshire

Highland

Argyll

Stirling

Fife

Montrose

Brechin

Arbroath

Kirriemuir

Forfar

Dundee

Pitlochry

Crieff

Auchterarder

Perth

8 Perth & Angus

1.4 cms = 10 kms, 1 inch = 11.25 miles

Map 8: List of Castles

1 Caisteal an Duibhe	45 Glendevon Castle	93 Lochleven Castle	141 Baledgarno Castle	189 Coull	237 Kilgarie
2 Eilean nam Faoileag	46 Trochrie Castle	94 Tower of Lethendy	142 Inverquiech Castle	190 Ballumbie Castle	238 Aldbar Castle
3 Meggernie Castle	47 Keillour Castle	95 Easter Fordel	143 Moncur Castle	191 Inshewan	239 Shanno
4 Ardvorlich	48 Bothan an Lochain	96 Balmanno Castle	144 Kinpurnie Castle	192 Gagie House	240 Gardyne Castle
5 Carnbane Castle	49 Gascon Hall	97 Moredun Hall	145 Belmont Castle	193 Claypotts Castle	241 Middleton House
6 Loch Earn Castle	50 Rotmell	98 Dalnaglar Castle	146 Newton	194 Pitkerro House	242 Edzell Castle
7 Dundurn	51 Duncrub	99 Kingseat	147 Balintore Castle	195 Forfar Castle	243 Auchmull Castle
8 Dunalastair	52 Keltie Castle	100 Kinfauns Castle	148 Airlie Castle	196 Fotheringham Castle	244 Dunlappie
9 Palace an Righ	53 Bishop's Palace, Dunkeld	101 Meikleour House	149 Bannatyne House	197 Murroes Castle	245 Dalbog Castle
10 Fearnan	54 Logie-Almond House	102 Glasclune Castle	150 Castle Huntly	198 Linlathen House	246 Brechin Castle
11 Aberuchill Castle	55 Dunkeld House	103 Castle Hill, Cargill	151 Hatton Castle	199 Carse Gray	247 Bishop's Palace, Brechin
12 Garth Castle	56 Rohallion Castle	104 Kinclaven Castle	152 Ruthven Castle	200 Broughty Castle	248 Kinnell Castle
13 Kenmore Castle	57 Methven Castle	105 Drumlochy Castle	153 Lundie Castle	201 Balmossie	249 Kellie Castle
14 Taymouth Castle	58 Ha' Tower	106 Loch Beanie	154 Balcraig Castle	202 Kingennie	250 Colliston Castle
15 Comrie Castle	59 Forteviot	107 Ardblair Castle	155 Baikie Castle	203 Brandy Den	251 Bolshan Castle
16 Braes of Taymouth	60 Cardney House	108 Corb Castle	156 Fowlis Castle	204 Ethiebeaton	252 Boysack
17 Feddal	61 Aldie Castle	109 Elcho Castle	157 Clova Castle	205 Barnyards	253 Farnell Castle
18 Braco Castle	62 Tullibole Castle	110 Balvaird Castle	158 Auchterhouse	206 Grange of Monifieth	254 Braikie Castle
19 Tom a' Chaisteal, Trowan	63 Dupplin Castle	111 Newton Castle	159 Castleton of Eassie	207 Dod	255 Kinnaird Castle
20 Castle Menzies	64 Invermay Tower	112 Balthayock Castle	160 Balfour Castle	208 Affleck Castle	256 Fithie
21 Cluggy Castle	65 Kinvaid Castle	113 Craighall	161 Denoon Castle	209 Vayne Castle	257 Easter Braikie Castle
22 Wester Shian	66 Murthly Castle	114 Forter Castle	162 Invergowrie House	210 Wemyss Castle	258 Kinblethmont
23 Drummond Castle	67 Condie	115 Newhall	163 Invergowrie Castle	211 Finavon Castle	259 Bonnyton Castle
24 Blair Castle	68 Bishop Sinclair's Tower	116 Stormont	164 Kinnordy	212 Pitairlie Castle	260 House of Dun
25 Fincastle House	69 Struie Castle	117 Pitfour Castle	165 Kinnordy	213 Kirkbuddo	261 Courthill
26 John the Bangster's House	70 Cleish Castle	118 Evelick Castle	166 Blackness Manor House	214 Hynd Castle	262 Old Montrose Castle
27 Monzie Castle	71 Huntingtower Castle	119 Arnot Castle	167 Strathmartine Castle	215 Ardestie Castle	263 Maryton
28 Muthill	72 Hall Yard	120 Glendoick House	168 Claverhouse Castle	216 Downieken Castle	264 Red Castle
29 Grandtully Castle	73 Rossie Ochil	121 Rattray Castle	169 Glamis Castle	217 Rescobie Castle	265 Ethie Castle
30 Ogilvie Castle	74 Whitefield Castle	122 Pitroddie	170 Cossans Castle	218 Monikie Castle	266 Dysart
31 Inchbrackie Castle	75 Stewart Tower	123 Kilspindie Castle	171 Dudhope Castle	219 Markshouse	267 Rossie Castle
32 Innerpeffray Castle	76 Pitheavlis Castle	124 Bamff House	172 Logie House	220 Woodrae Castle	268 Dunninald Castle
33 Tullibardine Castle	77 Mailer	125 Lintrose House	173 Thornton Castle	221 Old Downie	269 Craig House
34 Abercairny	78 Ashintully Castle	126 Fingask Castle	174 Cortachy Castle	222 Flemington Tower	270 Black Jack's Castle
35 Strathallan Castle	79 Ecclesiamagirdle House	127 Newton Castle	175 Fletcherfield Castle	223 Careston Castle	271 Montrose Castle
36 Gleneagles Castle	80 Blackcraig Castle	128 Megginch Castle	176 Dundee Castle	224 Menmuir	272 Inchbrayock House
37 Auchterarder Castle	81 Clunie Castle	129 Kinnaird Castle	177 Claverhouse Castle	225 Carnegie Castle	273 Usan House
38 Castleton	82 Scone Palace	130 Errol Park	178 Mains Castle	226 Balgavies Castle	
39 Black Castle of Moulin	83 Clunie Castle	131 Alyth Castle	179 Inverquharity Castle	227 Furdstone Castle	
40 Kincardine Castle	84 Balhousie Castle	132 Pitkindie House	180 Carbet Castle	228 Balmachie	
41 Dunfallandy	85 Dowhill Castle	133 Pitcur Castle	181 Tealing House	229 Turin House	
42 Williamston	86 Perth Castle	134 Ballairdie Castle	182 Ballinshoe Tower	230 Panmure Castle	
43 Pitcastle	87 Gowrie House, Perth	135 Dores Castle	183 Powrie Castle	231 Carmyllie Castle	
44 Logierait Castle	88 Kinnoull Castle	136 Craig Castle	184 Quiech Castle	232 Melgund Castle	
	89 Inchbervie Castle	137 Balloch Castle	185 Shielhill	233 Balnamoon	
	90 Kinross House	138 Peel of Lintrathen	186 Wedderburn Castle	234 Auchtermeggities	
	91 Burleigh Castle	139 Keillor Castle	187 Auchleuchrie	235 Findrowie Castle	
	92 Stobhall	140 Kinloch	188 Invermark Castle	236 Guthrie Castle	

9 Highland, South
(excluding Sutherland & Caithness)

Sutherland

Aberdeen-
shire

Perthshire

Argyll

Dornoch

Tain

Cromarty

Nairn

Grantown on Spey

Kingussie

Ullapool

Gairloch

Kyle of Lochalsh

RAASAY

Portree

SKYE

CANNA

RUM

EIGG

MUCK

Mallaig

Fort William

1 = Inverness
91/92/94

34

Map 9:
List of Castles

1 Dun Channa
2 Dunvegan Castle
3 Coroghon Castle
4 Dun Beag
5 Caisteal Uisdein
6 Duntulm Castle
7 Caisteal an Duin Bhain
8 Caisteal Dubh nan Cliar
9 Mingary Castle
10 Dun Grugaig
11 Raasay House
12 Drimnin Castle
13 Dun Ringill
14 Caisteal nan Con
15 Brochel Castle
16 Dun Sgathaich
17 Glenborrodale Castle
18 Armadale Castle
19 Castle Tioram
20 Caisteal Camus
21 Ardtornish Castle
22 Kinlochaline Castle
23 Caisteal Maol
24 Inverie
25 Flowerdale
26 Bernera Barracks
27 Caisteal Mhicleod
28 Glensanda Castle
29 Dun Telve
30 Dun Troddan
31 Dun Grugaig
32 Strome Castle
33 Caisteal Grugaig
34 Eilean Donan Castle
35 Isle Maree
36 Eilean Ghruididh
37 Eilean nan Craobh
38 Fort William
39 Inverlochy Castle
40 Caisteal Mhic Cneacall
41 Tor Castle
42 Dun Lagaidh
43 Balloan Castle
44 Achnacarry
45 Eilean Darroch
46 Keppoch Castle
47 Invergarry Castle
48 Ardachy
49 Fort Augustus
50 Erchless Castle
51 Coul House
52 Fairburn Tower
53 Loch Kinellan
54 Castle Leod
55 Loch Laggan Castle
56 Beaufort Castle
57 Brahan Castle
58 Ord House
59 Belladrum
60 Dochmaluag Castle
61 Urquhart Castle
62 Docharty
63 Lovat Castle
64 Castle Spynie
65 Tulloch Castle
66 Moniack Castle
67 Tarradale Castle
68 Dingwall Castle
69 Muir of Clunes
70 Kinkell Castle
71 Newton House
72 Kilcoy Castle
73 Dun da Lamh
74 Red Castle
75 Foulis Castle
76 Aldourie Castle

77 Castle Spioradain
78 Tom a' Chaisteal, Kirkton
79 Ardross Castle
80 Novar House
81 Spittal Castle
82 Fyrish House
83 Bunchrew House
84 Balconie Castle
85 Dunain
86 Castle Craig
87 Kinbeachie Castle
88 Contullich Castle
89 Cluny Castle
90 Ness Castle
91 Balnain House
92 Inverness Castle
93 Achnacloich Castle
94 Macbeth's Castle
95 Tordarroch Castle
96 Castle Heather
97 Leys Castle
98 Newmore Castle
99 Meikle Daan
100 Inshes House
101 Arkendeith Tower
102 Ormond Castle
103 Braelangwell
104 Castlehill
105 Invergordon Castle
106 Poyntzfield
107 Inverbreakie
108 Edderton Castle
109 Culloden House
110 Chanonry
111 Daviot Castle
112 Delny Castle
113 Castle Stuart
114 Castletown
115 Halhill Castle
116 Fort George

117 Balnagown Castle
118 Ruthven Barracks
119 Tarbat House
120 Moy Castle
121 Dalcross Castle
122 Tain Castle
123 Cromarty Castle
124 Dunskeath Castle
125 Pitcalnie
126 Kilravock Castle
127 Allan
128 Dunachton Castle
129 Cawdor Castle
130 Loch Slin Castle
131 Shandwick Castle
132 Inverlaidnan
133 Balblair
134 Cadboll Castle
135 Rothiemurchus
136 Nairn Castle
137 Red Castle
138 Rait Castle
139 Geanies Castle
140 Loch an Eilean Castle
141 Meikle Tarrel
142 Corbet
143 Little Tarrel
144 Auldearn Castle
145 Haven
146 Lochloy Castle
147 Ballone Castle
148 Penick Castle
149 Inshoch Castle
150 Lethen House
151 Tom Pitlac
152 Moyness Castle
153 Ardclach Bell Tower
154 Lochindorb Castle
155 Muckrach Castle
156 Castle Roy

157 Inverallan
158 Castle Grant
159 Lethendry Castle

35

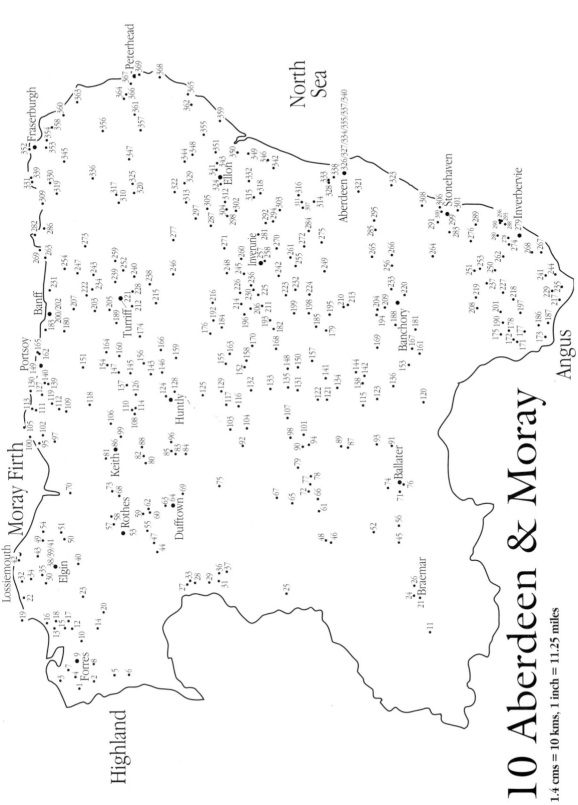

10 Aberdeen & Moray

1.4 cms = 10 kms, 1 inch = 11.25 miles

North Sea

Highland

Moray Firth

Angus

36

Map 10:
List of Castles

1 Brodie Castle
2 Darnaway Castle
3 Culbin
4 Dalvey Castle
5 Logie House
6 Dunphail Castle
7 Moy House
8 Altyre House
9 Forres Castle
10 Blervie Castle
11 Inverey Castle
12 Burgie Castle
13 Milton Brodie House
14 Craigmill
15 Kilbulack Castle
16 Hempriggs Castle
17 Asliesk Castle
18 Earnside Castle
19 Burghead
20 Tor Castle
21 Kindrochit Castle
22 Invergie Castle
23 Castle Hill, Pluscarden
24 Braemar Castle
25 Delnabo
26 Invercauld House
27 Balindalloch Castle
28 Tullochcarron Castle
29 Kilmaichlie House
30 Quarrelwood Castle
31 Drumin Castle
32 Gordonstoun
33 Castle Stripe
34 Duffus Castle
35 Findrassie Castle
36 Deskie Castle
37 Blairfindy Castle
38 Elgin Castle
39 Thunderton House, Elgin
40 Castle Hill, Birnie
41 Bishop's House, Elgin
42 Kinneddar Castle
43 Spynie Palace
44 Craigneach Castle
45 Balmoral Castle
46 Corgarff Castle
47 Wester Elchies
48 Allargue House
49 Leuchars House
50 Coxton Tower
51 Lhanbryde
52 Rineten
53 Rothes Castle
54 Innes House
55 Easter Elchies
56 Abergeldie Castle
57 Aikenway Castle
58 Dundurcus Castle
59 Gauldwell Castle
60 Buchromb
61 Skellater House
62 Kininvie House
63 Balvenie Castle
64 Mortlach
65 Auchernach
66 Candacraig
67 Bademyon Castle
68 Balnabreich
69 Auchindoun Castle
70 Gordon Castle
71 Knock Castle
72 Doune of Invermochty
73 Mains of Mulben
74 Abergairn Castle
75 King's Haugh
76 Brackley Castle
77 Colquhonnie Castle
78 Castle Newe
79 Glenbuchat Castle
80 Drummuir
81 Killiesmont
82 Davidston House
83 Edinglassie Castle
84 Beldorney Castle
85 Invermarkie Castle
86 Milton Keith Tower
87 Coldstone
88 Pitlurg Castle
89 Migvie Castle
90 Glenkindie House
91 Dee Castle
92 Hall of Tolophin
93 Loch Kinord Castle
94 Towie Castle
95 Rathven
96 Aswanley House
97 Letterfourie
98 Kildrummy Castle
99 Auchoynanie
100 Findochty Castle
101 Peel of Fichlie
102 Rannas Castle
103 Lesmoir Castle
104 Craig Castle

105 Trochach Castle
106 Davoch of Grange
107 Brux Castle
108 Auchanachie Castle
109 House of Skeith
110 Daugh
111 Cullen House
112 Deskford Castle
113 Cullen Castle
114 Ruthven
115 Couil Castle
116 Druminnor Castle
117 Castlehill, Druminnor
118 Edingight House
119 Inaltrie Castle
120 Birse Castle
121 Hallhead
122 Cushnie Castle
123 Aboyne Castle
124 Huntly Castle
125 Gartly Castle
126 Avochie Castle
127 Birkenbog House
128 Carvichen
129 Leith Hall
130 Findlater Castle
131 Asloun Castle
132 Knockespock House
133 Terpersie Castle
134 Corse Castle
135 Breda
136 Mains of Balfour
137 Rothiemay Castle
138 Auchenhove Castle
139 Fordyce Castle
140 Glassaugh House
141 Craigievar Castle
142 Auchlossan House
143 Cobairdy
144 Peel Ring of Lumphanan
145 Mains of Mayen
146 Lessendrum House
147 Tillydown
148 Haughton House
149 Portsoy Castle
150 Balfluig Castle
151 Park
152 Castle Croft
153 Finzean House
154 Crombie Castle
155 Wardhouse
156 Conzie Castle
157 Lynturk Castle
158 Leslie Castle

159 Drumdollo Castle
160 Kinnairdy Castle
161 Easter Clune Castle
162 Boyne Castle
163 Dunnideer Castle
164 Auchintoul
165 Craig of Boyne Castle
166 Frendraught Castle
167 Tillyfruskie
168 Castle Forbes
169 Castle Maud
170 Licklerhead Castle
171 Finella's Castle
172 Balbegno Castle
173 Inglismaldie Castle
174 Auchenhamper
175 Fasque
176 Culsalmond
177 Eslie
178 Fettercairn House
179 Shiels
180 Inchdrewer Castle
181 Strachan
182 Place of Tillyfour
183 Buchragie House
184 Newton House
185 Tillycairn Castle
186 Caddam Castle
187 Balmakewan Castle
188 Blackhall Castle
189 Carnousie Castle
190 Kincardine Castle
191 Westhall
192 Freefield House
193 Pitfichie Castle
194 Cluny Crichton Castle
195 Corsindae House
196 Harthill Castle
197 Thornton Castle
198 Cluny Castle
199 Monymusk Castle
200 Banff Castle
201 Auchcairnie
202 Duff House, Banff
203 Balravie Castle
204 Raemoir
205 Forglen House
206 Pittodrie House
207 Eden Castle
208 Drumtochty Castle
209 Loch of Leys
210 Cunningar
211 Tullos House
212 Dorlaithers Castle
213 Midmar Castle
214 Logie House
215 Hatton Manor
216 Warthill House
217 Morphie Castle
218 Haulkerton Castle
219 Glenfarquhar Castle
220 Tilquhillie Castle
221 Turriff Castle
222 Castle of King Edward
223 Fetternear House
224 Castle Fraser
225 Blairbowie Castle
226 Pitcaple Castle
227 Pittarrow Castle
228 Gask House
229 Snadon
230 Balquhain Castle
231 Castle of Cullen of Buchan
232 Kemnay House
233 Crathes Castle
234 Garnieston Castle
235 Kirkside Castle
236 Inveramsay
237 Monboddo House
238 Towie Barclay Castle
239 Delgatie Castle
240 Lauriston Castle
241 Lauriston Castle
242 Thainstone House
243 Craigston Castle
244 Kaim of Mathers Castle
245 Lethenty Castle
246 Fyvie Castle
247 Fisherie
248 Mounie Castle
249 Skene House
250 Kair House
251 Glenbervie House
252 Idoch Castle
253 Mondynes Castle
254 Pitgair Castle
255 Hallforest Castle
256 Dores Castle
257 Bass of Inverurie
258 Keith Hall
259 Auchry Castle
260 Barra Castle
261 Kintore Castle
262 Arbuthnott House
263 Findon Castle
264 House of Mergie
265 Drum Castle
266 Durris House

267 Brotherton Castle
268 Benholm Castle
269 Lichnet Castle
270 Balbithan House
271 Meldrum House
272 Kinellar House
273 Byth House
274 Allardice Castle
275 Tertowie House
276 Castle of Fiddes
277 Gight Castle
278 Pitcarry
279 Hallgreen Castle
280 Largie Castle
281 Old Kendal
282 Castle of Troup
283 Fetteresso Castle
284 Binghill Castle
285 Maryculter House
286 Auchmeddan Castle
287 Tillyhilt Castle
288 Kinneff Castle
289 Barras Castle
290 Cadden Castle
291 Urie House
292 Straloch House
293 Whistleberry Castle
294 Disblair House
295 Kingcausie
296 Adam's Castle
297 Haddo House
298 Tolquhon Castle
299 Tolbooth Museum, Stonehaven
300 Cowie House
301 Dunnottar Castle
302 Udny Castle
303 Elrick House
304 Pitmedden House
305 Shethin
306 Cowie Castle
307 Mains of Dyce
308 Muchalls Castle
309 Dundarg Castle
310 Fedderate Castle
311 Parkhill House
312 Dumbreck Castle
313 House of Schivas
314 Grandhome House
315 Tillycorthie Castle
316 Bishop's Palace, Loch Goul
317 Brucklay Castle
318 Tillery
319 Boyndlie House
320 Old Maud
321 Pitfodels Castle
322 Savoch Castle
323 Portlethen Castle
324 Castle of Esslemont
325 Clacknach Castle
326 Provost Ross's House, Aberdeen
327 Dub Castle
328 Benholm's Lodging
329 Arnage Castle
330 House of Tyrie
331 Pitsligo Castle
332 Fiddes Castle
333 Bishop's Palace, Old Aberdeen
334 Provost Skene's House, Aberdeen
335 Aberdeen Castle
336 Strichen
337 Pitfodel's Lodging
338 Mar's Castle, Aberdeen
339 Pitrulie Castle
340 Aberdeen Tolbooth
341 Ellon Castle
342 Orrock House
343 Waterton Castle
344 Dudwick Castle
345 House of Auchiries
346 Menie House
347 Aden House
348 Kinmuck Castle
349 Foveran Castle
350 Knockhall Castle
351 Auchmacoy House
352 Kinnaird Head Castle
353 Philorth Castle
354 Cairnbulg Castle
355 Leask House
356 Kininmonth House
357 Ludquharn
358 Inverallochy Castle
359 Old Slains Castle
360 Lonmay Castle
361 Faichfield House
362 Ardendraught
363 Rattray Castle
364 Ravenscraig Castle
365 Slains Castle
366 Inverugie Castle
367 Castle of Inverugie
368 Boddam Castle
369 Keith Inch Tower

11 The Western Isles, Orkney & Shetland

UNST

FETLAR

YELL

MAINLAND

Shetland

Lerwick

Scalloway

SANDAY

EDAY

STRONSAY

WESTRAY

ROUSAY

SHAPINSAY

Gairsay

Wyre

Kirkwall

MAINLAND

Stromness

Orkney

HOY

SOUTH
RONALDSAY

LEWIS

Stornoway

HARRIS

Tarbert

Western
Isles

BENBECULA

Lochmaddy

Lochboisdale

NORTH
UIST

SOUTH
UIST

BARRA

Castlebay

Map 11: List of Castles
1 Castle Sinclair
2 Kiessimul Castle
3 Dun Vulan
4 Ormaclett Castle
5 Dun a' Ghallian
6 Caisteal Bheagram
7 Loch nan Clachan Dun
8 Borve Castle
9 Dun Raouill
10 Weaver's Castle
11 Dun Buidhe
12 Caisteal Calvay
13 Dun Ban, Loch Caravat
14 Dun Torcuill
15 Dun Aonais
16 Dun an Sticar
17 Gunnery of MacLeod
18 Dun Mhic Laitheann

19 Stac Dhomhnuill Chaim
20 Amhuinnsuidhe Castle
21 Bearasay
22 Dun Carloway
23 Borrowston
24 Stac a' Chaisteal
25 Dun Bragar
26 Lews Castle
27 Stornoway Castle
28 MacLeod's Castle
29 Dun Airnistean
30 Caisteal a' Mhorair

31 Skaill House
32 Castle of Snusgar
33 Brough of Birsay
34 Earl's Palace, Birsay
35 Castle Bloody
36 Cairston Castle
37 Burn of Lushan
38 Martello Towers
39 Midhowe Broch
40 The Wirk
41 Gurness Broch
42 Ellibister
43 Damsay
44 Noltland Castle

45 Langskaill House
46 Cubbie Roo's Castle
47 Tankerness House, Kirkwall
48 Kirkwall Castle
49 Earl's Palace, Kirkwall
50 Bishop's Palace, Kirkwall
51 Halcro
52 Castle Grimness
53 Balfour Castle
54 Sealskerry Bay
55 Castle of Stackel Brae
56 Carrick House

57 Busta House
58 Ness of Burgi Fort
59 Strom Castle
60 Jarlshof
61 Scalloway Castle
62 Mousa Broch
63 Clickhimin Broch
64 Fort Charlotte
65 Muness Castle

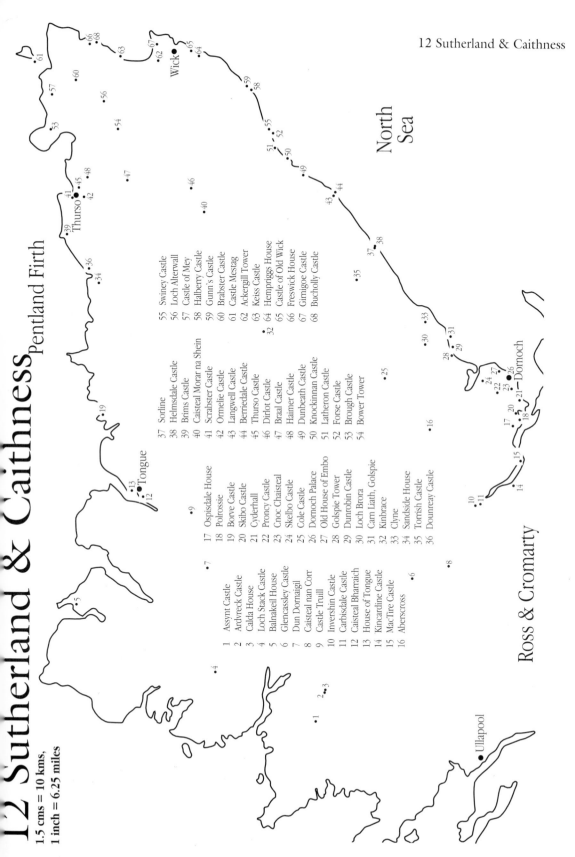

12 Sutherland & Caithness
Pentland Firth

1.5 cms = 10 kms,
1 inch = 6.25 miles

North Sea

Ross & Cromarty

Wick

Thurso

Tongue

Dornoch

Ullapool

1 Assynt Castle
2 Ardvreck Castle
3 Calda House
4 Loch Stack Castle
5 Balnakeil House
6 Glencassley Castle
7 Dun Dornaigil
8 Caisteal nan Corr
9 Castle Truill
10 Invershin Castle
11 Carbisdale Castle
12 Caisteal Bharraich
13 House of Tongue
14 Kincardine Castle
15 MacTire Castle
16 Aberscross

17 Ospisdale House
18 Polrossie
19 Borve Castle
20 Skibo Castle
21 Cyderhall
22 Proncy Castle
23 Cnoc Chaisteal
24 Skelbo Castle
25 Cole Castle
26 Dornoch Palace
27 Old House of Embo
28 Golspie Tower
29 Dunrobin Castle
30 Loch Brora
31 Carn Liath, Golspie
32 Kinbrace
33 Clyne
34 Sandside House
35 Torrish Castle
36 Dounreay Castle

37 Sorline
38 Helmsdale Castle
39 Brims Castle
40 Caisteal Morar na Shein
41 Scrabster Castle
42 Ormelie Castle
43 Langwell Castle
44 Berriedale Castle
45 Thurso Castle
46 Dirlot Castle
47 Braal Castle
48 Haimer Castle
49 Dunbeath Castle
50 Knockinnan Castle
51 Latheron Castle
52 Forse Castle
53 Brough Castle
54 Bower Tower

55 Swiney Castle
56 Loch Alterwall
57 Castle of Mey
58 Halberry Castle
59 Gunn's Castle
60 Brabster Castle
61 Castle Mestag
62 Ackergill Tower
63 Keiss Castle
64 Hempriggs House
65 Castle of Old Wick
66 Freswick House
67 Girnigoe Castle
68 Bucholly Castle

39

Castles
(A-Z)

Castle Entry *(also see previous page)*

Name of site ——— ● **Cawdor Castle**

Inverness & Nairn: About 5 miles south-west of Nairn, on B9090 off A96, at
Cawdor, just east of Allt Dearg, at Cawdor Castle.

Location ———

Status ———

Ordnance Survey
Grid Reference

Ordnance Survey
Landranger Sheet

● **Private** ● NH 847499 ● OS: 27   ***** ● **Map: 9, no: 129** ●

Quality of site
as a stronghold

Castles of Scotland
map and number

Exterior
Description

Interior
Description

History and
families

Hauntings

Opening

Visitor Facilities
and Features

Tel, Fax, Email, Web

One of the most magnificent and well-preserved strongholds in Scotland,
Cawdor Castle incorporates a tall plain keep, dating from the 14th century,
although the parapet and upper works were added in 1454. The castle has a
deep ditch, and is reached by a drawbridge. Mainly three-storey ranges, gabled
and crowned with bartizans and corbelled-out chambers, were built on all
sides of the keep in the 16th and 17th centuries. There is a pit prison.

Across the drawbridge defending the entrance is a massive iron yett, which
was brought here from Lochindorb Castle after 1455. The keep rises to four
storeys and a garret within a flush parapet, and has very thick walls pierced by
small windows. There are bartizans at each of the corners, as well as
machiolated projections.

The entrance is now in the basement, but was originally at first floor level.
Both the basement and the third floor are vaulted. A straight stair, in the
thickness of one wall, leads up to the hall on the first floor – although this
would formerly have been a stair down to the cellars. A turnpike stair climbs
to the upper floors.

In the later ranges, there is an iron yett postern gate to the moat, some fine
17th-century fireplaces; and there are many portraits, furnishings and a
collection of tapestries.

The title 'Thane of Cawdor' is associated with Macbeth, but Duncan was not
murdered here, as the castle is not nearly old enough, and he was killed in
battle near Spynie. The Calders had an earlier stronghold near here [NH
858512], but nothing remains.

The 1st Thane of Cawdor took the name of Calder when granted the lands by
Alexander II in 1236, although one story is that the family were descended
from a brother of Macbeth. The 3rd Thane was murdered by Sir Alexander
Rait of nearby Rait Castle.

The 5th Thane built much of the present castle. The method of selecting the
site for Cawdor Castle was unusual as it was chosen by a donkey allowed to
roam at will until it came to a suitable spot. Cawdor is also built over a tree,
the remains of which are in the vaulted basement. It was believed to be a
hawthorn, but in fact it proved to be a holly tree and it died in about 1372,
when the castle was built.

The Campbells obtained Cawdor by kidnapping the girl heiress, Muriel
Calder, and marrying her at the age of 12 to the Earl of Argyll's son, Sir John
Campbell, in 1511. Campbell of Inverliver led the kidnapping, and lost all six
of his sons.

The Campbells of Cawdor, her descendants, remained at the castle. They
gave refuge to Simon, Lord Lovat, during his flight from Hanoverian troops in
1746 during the Jacobite Rising, and hid him in a secret room in the roof.
Fraser was eventually caught and executed. Bonnie Prince Charlie had visited
the same year.

A ghost in a blue velvet dress has reputedly been seen here, as has an
apparition of John Campbell 1st Lord Cawdor.

**OPEN: Open May-mid-Oct, daily 10.00-17.30; last
admission 17.00.**

*Fine collections of portraits, furnishings and tapestries. Explanatory displays. Three
shops: gift shop, wool and book shop. Licensed restaurant and snack bar. Gardens,
grounds and nature trails. Golf course and putting. Disabled access to grounds; some
of castle. Car and coach parking. Group concessions. Conferences. £££.*
Tel: 01667 404615   Fax: 01667 404674
Email: info@cawdorcastle.com   Web: www.cawdorcastle.com

A

Abbot House, Dunfermline

Fife: Short distance north of Dunfermline Abbey, south of A994, in the Maygate.
Private NT 089875 [?] OS: 65 ** Map: 7, no: 14
Abbot House is a 16th-century house, built after the Reformation for the Commendator of Dunfermline Abbey. It consists of the remains of a substantial town house, with two projecting stair-towers and an extension.

The lands were originally a property of the Abbey, but were acquired by Robert

Pitcairn, who probably built the house. The property passed to Captain James Stewart, Earl of Arran, while other owners included the Master of Gray, the Gordon Earl of Huntly, and Anne of Denmark, wife of James VI.

The house is now a heritage centre, and has displays about the house and Dunfermline.
OPEN: Open all year, daily 10.00-17.00, except closed Christmas Day and New Year's Day.
Guided tours. Explanatory displays. Gift shop. Restaurant with outside seating in garden. Garden. WC. Disabled access to ground floor and WC. Disabled parking only; public carparks within 600 yards. Group concessions. £ (Upstairs exhib only).
Tel: 01383 733266 Fax: 01383 624908
Email: dht@abbothouse.fs.net.co.uk Web: www.abbothouse.co.uk

Abbot Hunter's Tower *see* Mauchline Castle

Abbots Hall, Burntisland *see* Rossend Castle

Abbotsford

Scottish Borders: About 2 miles west of Melrose, just west of B6360, east of River Tweed, at Abbotsford.
Private NT 508343 OS: 73 * Map: 2, no: 171
Sir Walter Scott, the famous Scottish writer and historian, bought Cartley Hole farmhouse, by the Tweed, in 1812, which he renamed Abbotsford. He had the old house demolished in 1822, and it was replaced by the main block of Abbotsford as it is today to form a large baronial mansion with turrets, battlements and corbiestepped gables. Scott collected many historic artefacts, such as a crucifix which belonged to Mary Queen of Scots, and there is an impressive collection of armour and weapons at the house, including Rob Roy MacGregor's gun, Claverhouse's pistol and the Marquis of Montrose's sword. Access to study, library, drawing room, entrance hall and armouries, as well as the dining room, where Scott died in 1832. His library of more than 9000 rare volumes is preserved at the house. There are also extensive gardens and grounds, and a private chapel which was added after Scott's death.

The ghost of Sir Walter Scott is said to haunt the dining room, where he died in 1832 after exhausting himself trying to pay off a huge debt. Sightings of his appari-

tion have been reported in recent times. Another ghost, said to have been witnessed here, is the spirit of George Bullock, who died in 1818 and was in charge of the rebuilding of Abbotsford. The sounds of furniture being dragged across the floor were reportedly heard.
Other refs: Cartley Hole
OPEN: Open daily: 3rd Monday in Mar-Oct, Mon-Sat 10.00-17.00, Sun 14.00-17.00; Jun-Sep, daily including Sun 10.00-17.00; other dates by appt.
Guided tours. Gift shop. Tearoom. Extensive gardens and grounds. WCs. Disabled access by private entrance. Car and coach parking. Group concessions. ££.
Tel: 01896 752043 Fax: 01896 752916
Email: abbotsford@melrose.bordernet.co.uk

Abbot's Tower

Dumfriesshire: About 6 miles south of Dumfries, on minor roads east of A710, about 0.5 miles north-east of Sweetheart Abbey, north of New Abbey Row.
Private NX 972667 OS: 84 * Map: 1, no: 188**
Abbot's Tower is a 16th-century L-plan tower house of three storeys and a garret. The stair-wing is crowned by a caphouse, there is a stair-turret corbelled-out in the re-entrant angle, and there were bartizans at each of the other corners. The tower has had a courtyard.

The basement was vaulted, and the hall, on the first floor, has a fireplace.

The tower was built by John Brown, second last abbot of Sweetheart Abbey. It has been restored.
Other refs: Lasonn

Abbot's Tower *see* Crossraguel Abbey

Abercairny

Perth & Kinross: About 3 miles north-east of Crieff, on minor roads south of A85, at Abercairny.
Private NN 913226 OS: 58 * Map: 8, no: 34
Site of castle, demolished in the 19th century and replaced by a large 19th-century mansion – once a splendid Gothic edifice – itself demolished in the 20th century to build a smaller house.

It was a property of the Murrays of Abercairny from around 1299, when John Murray of Drumsagard married Mary, heir of Malise, Earl of Strathearn. The Murrays still own the modern house.

Abercorn Castle

Lothians: About 3 miles west and north of South Queensferry, on footpath west of Hopetoun House, near the shore of the Firth of Forth, north of Abercorn.
Ruin or site NT 083794 OS: 65 * Map: 4, no: 35
Site of castle, nothing of which remains except a landscaped mound which covers the very ruinous remains of two buildings.

A castle here, dating from the 12th century, was a property of the Avenel family. It passed by marriage to the Grahams in the mid 13th century, then, again by marriage, to the Mures in the early 14th century. By 1400, the Douglas Earls of Douglas held the castle, and James the Gross, 6th Earl, died here in 1443. The castle was destroyed, after a month-long siege, by James II in 1455, during his campaign against the Black Douglases. Many of the garrison were hanged. The lands then passed to the Setons, and the castle site was excavated in 1963.

Abercrombie Castle

Fife: About 1 mile north-east of St Monace, on minor road just south of B942 or north of A917, at or near Abercrombie.
Ruin or site NO 518028 [?] OS: 59 * Map: 7, no: 134
Site of castle of the Abercrombie family, who held the property from 1260.

Aberdeen Castle

Aberdeen & Gordon: About 0.5 miles north-east of Aberdeen railway station, on minor roads near A956, north of the harbours, south-east of new cathedral.
Ruin or site NJ 944063 OS: 38 * Map: 10, no: 335
Nothing remains of a 13th-century castle.

The castle was held for the English during the Wars of Independence, and visited by Edward I of England in 1296. It was recaptured, then destroyed by the Scots in 1308, and probably never rebuilt. A chapel, dedicated to St Ninian, was built here. Cromwell constructed a fort in the 1650s, but only a fragment remains, and a barracks was also built in the 18th century. The site of the castle is now occupied by two tower blocks.

There is said to have been a royal palace in Aberdeen [NJ 942060], a property of Malcolm Canmore in the 11th century and given to the Trinitarian friary in the city. There are apparently some medieval remains at the site.

There was also a blockhouse and watch-tower at the harbour.

Aberdeen Tolbooth

Aberdeen & Gordon: Castle Street (continuation of Union Street), Aberdeen.
Private NJ 950065 OS: 38 *** Map: 10, no: 340
The 17th-century tolbooth, which is vaulted and has turnpike stairs, houses Aberdeen's museum of civic history. The museum charts the history of local government and crime and punishment. The old cells can be visited, Jacobite prisoners were held here in 1746, and there are interactive displays.
Other refs: Tolbooth, Aberdeen
OPEN: Open Apr-Sep, Tue-Sat 10.00-17.00, Sun 14.00-17.00.
Guided tours. Explanatory displays. Disabled access. Parking Nearby.
Tel: 01224 621167

Aberdour Castle

Fife: In Aberdour, south of A921, north of Aberdour harbour, just south of Aberdour railway station.
His Scot NT 193854 OS: 66 **** Map: 7, no: 33
Aberdour Castle is a ruined E-plan tower house, consisting of a 14th-century keep and later wings and extensions, some of which are complete. Buildings including a bakehouse and brewhouse block were added in the 16th century, and about 1630 the castle was extended by a block occupied by a long gallery. The castle had a walled courtyard, of which a round turret survives. A terraced garden has been restored, and there is also a fine walled garden.

It was a property of the Mortimer family, one of whom gave his name to 'Mortimer's Deep', the stretch of water between Inchcolm and Aberdour, after his coffin was cast overboard there. Aberdour was a possession of Thomas Randolph, friend and captain of Robert the Bruce, by 1325, but in 1342 the property passed to the Douglases, who were made Earls of Morton about 1456. James Douglas, 4th Earl of Morton, was Regent Morton for the young James VI in 1572, although in 1581 he was executed for his part in the murder of Darnley, the second husband of Mary, Queen of Scots. Much of the castle had been abandoned by 1725 when the family moved to nearby Aberdour House, which was formerly known as Cuttlehill, although one wing of the old castle may have been occupied by Robert Watson of Muirhouse until his death in 1791. Part of the castle had been burned out in 1715, and much of the keep collapsed in 1844 and 1919. One range was used as a barracks, school room, masonic hall and dwelling until 1924 when the castle was put into the care of State. Aberdour House was held by the Douglases until the 20th century, but recently divided into flats.

The nearby chapel of St Fillans, which later became the parish church, dates from the 12th century, although it was much altered in the 17th. It became ruinous, but was restored in the 19th century. The burial ground has interesting memorials, including a now fallen stone commemorating many of the Coventry family.
Other refs: Cuttlehill
OPEN: Open all year: Apr-Sep, daily 9.30-18.30; Oct-Mar, Mon-Wed and Sat, 9.30-16.30, Thu 9.30-12.00, Sun 14.00-16.30, closed Fri; closed 25/26 Dec and 1/2 Jan.
Explanatory displays. Tearoom. Gift shop. Disabled access and WC. Parking. £.
Tel: 01383 860519 Fax: 0131 668 8888
Email: hs.explore@scotland.gov.uk Web: www.historic-scotland.gov.uk

Abergairn Castle

Kincardine & Deeside: About 1 mile north of Ballater, on minor road and foot north of B972 in Pass of Ballater, south-west of Balmenach, east of Abergairn.
Ruin or site NO 358974 OS: 44 * Map: 10, no: 74
Abergairn Castle is a very ruined 17th-century tower house, little of which remains except the basement. It consisted of a main block with a round tower at one corner. It was held by the Farquharsons.
Other refs: Glencairn Castle

Abergeldie Castle

Kincardine & Deeside: About 5 miles west of Ballater, on minor road north of B976, just south of River Dee, 2 miles east of Balmoral Castle, just north of Mains of Abergeldie.
Private NO 287953 OS: 44 *** Map: 10, no: 56
Abergeldie Castle is a 16th-century tower house of three storeys and an attic. It has corbiestepped gables and a turret crowns one corner. A semi-circular stair-tower is corbelled out to square, and topped by a balustraded parapet. A large adjoining mansion has been demolished.

The basement is vaulted, as is the hall on the first floor.

Abergeldie was a property of the Gordons from 1482. James Gordon of Abergeldie

was killed at the Battle of Pinkie in 1547. During a feud with the Forbeses over land, the seven sons of a Gordon laird were murdered by Forbes of Strathgirnock. They had been out digging peat, and their severed heads were spiked on the ends of their peat spades. Forbes was summarily executed for the deed in his own house by Gordon of Abergeldie.

In 1592 the castle was attacked and torched by the Mackenzies. Bonnie Dundee used it as a mustering place for Jacobites in 1689. Abergeldie was captured for William and Mary by General Mackay the same year, but then nearly seized by the Farquharsons for the Jacobites in 1690. The castle was leased to Queen Victoria in the 19th century for housing guests. The later additions have been demolished, and the castle is occupied by the Gordons.

The castle is reputedly haunted by the spirit of a French maid, Catherine Frankie, known as 'Kittie Rankie', who is said to have been accused of witchcraft at the end of the 16th century. The story goes that the unfortunate Catherine was asked by the wife of the house why her husband was delayed aboard ship. When Catherine told her that he was dallying with other women, the wife had Catherine imprisoned in the castle dungeon and accused of witchcraft – a similar story is told of the

Aberuchill Castle

Brahan seer. Catherine was then burned at the stake, and her ghost has reputedly been seen in the castle, most often in the tall clock-tower. Other disturbances include mysterious noises, and the ringing of a bell when misfortune is about to strike the family.

Aberlady Castle *see* Luffness House

Aberscross

Sutherland & Caithness: About 8 miles north-west of Dornoch, to north of A839, 3 miles north and west of Rogart Statuin, at or near Aberscross.
Ruin or site NC 705050 [?] OS: 16 * Map: 12, no: 16
Site of castle, built by the de Moravia family when they moved to Sutherland at the end of the 12th century. There are no remains, and the location is not certain.

Aberuchill Castle

Perth & Kinross: About 2 miles west and south of Comrie, on minor roads south of A85 at Comrie or Dalchonzie, south of the River Earn, at Aberuchill.
Private NN 745212 OS: 51 * Map: 8, no: 11**
Aberuchill Castle consists of a 17th-century L-plan tower house, crowned by bartizans, with a round stair-tower in the re-entrant angle. The tower rises to three storeys and an attic, and the walls are harled and whitewashed. The house is dated 1607. The house has been much altered, with extensions by John Bryce, and a two-storey wing, which was added around 1805.
   The lands were originally a property of the MacGregors, but acquired by the Campbells in 1596, who built the castle soon afterwards. The MacGregors, however, continued to extort money from the Campbells. The castle was damaged by the Jacobites under Bonnie Dundee in 1689, but after the 1715 Jacobite Rising, when the MacGregors were on the losing side, the Campbell laird decided to stop paying blackmail. However, when Rob Roy MacGregor, with a band of clansman, appeared during a dinner party the Campbells quickly found the money. The house was occupied until gutted by a recent fire.

Aboyne Castle *see* Coull Castle

Aboyne Castle

Kincardine & Deeside: About 0.5 miles north of Aboyne, on minor road east of B9094 or north of A93 in Aboyne, 1 mile north of the Dee, west of Loch of Aboyne.
Private NO 526995 OS: 44 ** Map: 10, no: 123
Once a strong fortress, Aboyne Castle is a tall 17th-century tower house, rectangular in plan, of five storeys and a garret. It has a six-storey round stair-tower, which is corbelled out to square and was crowned by a watch-chamber.

It was originally a property of the Bissets. Walter Bisset of Aboyne was defeated by the Earl of Atholl in an tournament in 1242. As a result and in a fit of anger, Bisset murdered the Earl and set fire to his lodging. This started a feud, and many of the Bissets fled to Ireland. The castle passed in 1242 to the Knights Templars, then to the Frasers, then in 1355 to the Keiths. In 1307 Edward I of England had ordered that the castle was to be reinforced. By the early 15th century it had been acquired by the Gordons of Huntly, with whose descendants it remains. The family were made Viscounts Aboyne in 1632, and Earls of Aboyne in 1660.
   The Campbell Earl of Argyll captured the castle for the Covenanters, and used it as his headquarters in 1640. It was altered in 1801, 1869, and extensively rebuilt in the 1970s. It is still occupied.
   Highland games are held in September on the village green.

Achadun Castle

Argyll & Dunbartonshire: On island of Lismore, about 7 miles north-west of Oban, on minor road and foot west of B8045 at Baligrundle, 0.5 miles west of Achaduin.

Ruin or site   NM 804392   OS: 49   **   Map: 5, no: 57

Sited on the top of a ridge, Achadun is a ruinous 13th-century castle of enclosure, which had a square hall block on one side and another less substantial range along another. There were two entrances, one of which gave access to a stair to the parapet walk.

It was held by the Bishops of Argyll until about 1510, when they moved to Saddell in Kintyre, and part of their cathedral, the Cathedral of St Moluag, now considerably altered, is still used as a parish church.

Other refs: Achanduin Castle; Auchindown Castle

Achallader Castle

Argyll & Dunbartonshire: About 3.5 miles north and east of Bridge of Orchy, on minor road east of A82, 1 mile north-east of end of Loch Tulla, at Achallader.

Ruin or site   NN 322442   OS: 50   **   Map: 5, no: 134

Not much remains of a 16th-century tower house, except two walls. It formerly rose to three storeys and a garret, and there were many shot-holes.

It was originally held by the Fletcher family, but most of the existing building was constructed by Sir Duncan Campbell of Glenorchy. Campbell is said to have acquired the property around 1590. He tricked the then laird into killing an English soldier who was grazing his horses in the laird's cornfield. The laird fled, and Campbell took his lands. The castle was torched in 1603 by the MacGregors, and in 1689 by Jacobites, and not restored. The castle ruin was the scene of a conference in 1691 between the Campbell 1st Earl of Breadalbane and Jacobite Highland chiefs, who agreed to an armistice in exchange for Hanoverian gold.

Achananchie *see* Auchanachie Castle

Achanduin Castle *see* Achadun Castle

Achanelid

Argyll & Dunbartonshire: About 2 miles north of Clachan of Glendaruel, on minor road and foot west of A886, on west bank of River Ruel, about 0.3 miles south of Achanelid.

Ruin or site   NS 006874   OS: 55   **   Map: 5, no: 94

Achanelid consists of a rectangular motte, surrounded by ditch, with the foundations of two buildings on the summit.

Achastle *see* Langwell Castle

Achastle *see* Swiney Castle

Achastle *see* Forse Castle

Acheson's Haven Fort *see* Morrison's Haven Fort

Achincass *see* Auchen Castle

Achlouchrie *see* Auchleuchrie

Achnabreac Castle *see* Auchenbreck Castle

Achnacarry

South Highland: About 9 miles north-east of Fort William, on minor roads west of B8005, south of River Arkaig, at Achnacarry.

Private   NN 175878   OS: 41   *   Map: 9, no: 44

The ruins remain of a 17th-century house of the Camerons, destroyed by Hanoverian troops after the Jacobite Rising of 1745. The Camerons had moved here from Tor Castle in 1665, but were forfeited for their part in the Jacobite Rising, under Cameron of Lochiel, although they recovered the property in 1784.

The modern Achnacarry House dates from 1802, and was designed by James Gillespie Graham. It is still occupied by the Camerons of Lochiel, but not open to the public.

A museum, housed in a converted cottage, charts the history of the Camerons, their involvement in the Jacobite Risings, and subsequent resurgence. There are also displays on the Queen's Own Cameron Highlanders, and the Commandos who trained here during World War II.

Other refs: Clan Cameron Museum, Achnacarry

OPEN: House not open. Museum open Apr-mid Oct, daily 13.30-17.00; Jul & Aug, daily 11.00-17.00 .

Guided tours on request. Explanatory displays. Gift shop. Garden. WC. Disabled access. Car and coach parking. Group concessions. £.

Tel: 01397 712090

Email: museum@achnacarry.fsnet.co.uk   Web: www.clan-cameron.org

Achnacloich Castle

Ross & Cromarty: About 3 miles north of Alness, on minor roads east of A836, east of Loch Achnacloich, south-east of Easter Achnacloich.

Ruin or site   NH 670734 [?]   OS: 21   *   Map: 9, no: 93

Site of castle, nothing of which apparently remains.

Achnakeil

Argyll & Dunbartonshire: About 5 miles south of Lochgilphead, near B8024, at or near Achnakeil.

Ruin or site   NR 841814 [?]   OS: 55   *   Map: 5, no: 65

Possible site of castle.

Ackergill Tower

Sutherland & Caithness: About 2.5 miles north of Wick, on minor roads north of A9, on southern side of Sinclair's Bay, at Ackergill Tower.

Private   ND 352547   OS: 12   ****   Map: 12, no: 62

Ackergill Tower is a strong 15th-century keep of five storeys, the upper works of which, including a flush parapet and rounds, are 19th century. There are modern extensions, and it was formerly surrounded by a ditch, said to be 12 feet wide and deep.

The arched entrance leads to a passage to a straight mural stair, which climbs to the first floor. The basement is vaulted. The hall, on the first floor, is also vaulted and has a minstrels gallery, which is reached by a mural stair. Turnpike stairs lead up to the upper floors and parapet.

The lands were a property of the Cheynes, but passed by marriage to the Keith Earls Marischal about 1350. In 1518 Keith of Ackergill and his son were ambushed and slain by the Gunns. Alexander Keith of Ackergill was kidnapped by the Sinclair

Earl of Caithness, and in 1556 the castle was besieged by the Sinclairs. It was sold to the Sinclairs in 1612, and garrisoned for Cromwell in the 1650s. It was later acquired by the Oliphants, then in 1699 by the Dunbars of Hempriggs, who owned it until the 1980s. The castle was remodelled by David Bryce in 1851, and is still occupied, now being used as a conference/hospitality centre.

Helen Gunn, the 'Beauty of Braemore' was already betrothed to a man she loved when she was seized and carried off to Ackergill by Dugald Keith, who desired her for himself. The poor girl was imprisoned in an upstairs chamber, but rather than yield to Dugald, threw herself from the tower and was killed – a stone is said to mark the spot where she hit the ground. Her ghost, a 'Green Lady', is said to have been seen in the castle, and a rowan tree 'Fair Ellen's Tree' still grows at Braemore.

OPEN: Open all year.

Offers totally exclusive use. Accommodation: 25 bedrooms, including 17 in castle, all with private facilities. Fine Scottish kitchen. Conferences and meetings. Opera house. Angling and golf. Garden. Parking.

Tel: 01955 603556 Fax: 01955 602140
Email: www.ackergill-tower.co.uk Web: AckergillTower@compuserve.com

Adam's Castle

Kincardine & Deeside: About 2.5 miles north-east of Inverbervie, on minor road and foot east of A92, on cliffs, 0.25 miles north-east of Whistleberry Castle, Rouen Bay.

Ruin or site NO 864757 OS: 45 * Map: 10, no: 296
Site of castle located on a promontory.

Adderston

Borders: About 3.5 miles south of Hawick, on minor roads and foot east of B6399, east of Slitrig Water, 0.5 miles north-east of Stobs Castle, near Adderston Shiels.

Ruin or site NT 514092 OS: 79 * Map: 2, no: 176
Site of tower house of the Croziers, nothing of which remains. It was also known as Cleary or Cleerie.

Other refs: Edderstoun; Cleerie Castle

Aden House

Banff & Buchan: About 10 miles east of Peterhead, on minor roads off A950, Mintlaw.

Private NJ 981479 OS: 30 * Map: 10, no: 347**
Site of castle, which was replaced by a mansion of 1832, itself now a shell. The lands were a property of the Keiths in 1324, but passed to the Russells of Montcoffer in 1758. The grounds of the estate are now a country park, covering some 230 acres of woodland, lake and farmland.

Other refs: Alneden

OPEN: Open all year: May-Sep daily 11.00-16.30; Apr and Oct wknds only, 12.00-16.30; last admission 30 mins before closing.

Guided tours. Gift shop. Tearoom. Picnic and BBQ area. WC. Nature trail. Aberdeenshire Farming Museum. Wildlife centre. Sensory garden. Disabled access. Car and coach parking.

Tel: 01771 622857 Fax: 01771 622884

Affleck Castle

Angus & Dundee: About 4 miles north of Monifieth, on minor roads east of B978 and west of B962, about 0.25 miles west of Monikie, at Affleck.

Private NO 493389 OS: 54 ** Map: 8, no: 208**
Standing on high ground, Affleck Castle is a tall L-plan 15th-century keep, of four storeys and a garret within the parapet. The parapet has open rounds, a machiolated projection over the entrance, and a square caphouse over the stair-tower. The walls are pierced by gunloops.

The basement is vaulted to support the stone-flagged floor of the hall above. The hall has a fine fireplace, windows with stone seats, and there are many mural chambers. A vaulted oratory, on the floor above, has a holy-water stoup, piscina and aumbry, with stone candle holders at either side of the altar.

The Auchinlecks, or Afflecks, held the lands from 1471 until the mid 17th century, when it passed to the Reid family. The family was forfeited in 1746 for their part in

the Jacobite Rising. On seeing government troops coming to take the castle, the lady of the house escaped to Dundee with many of the castle's valuables, and eventually joined her husband in France. The castle was abandoned around 1760, and a new modern house built nearby. The tower was taken into State care, but this was relinquished because of problems of access.

Other refs: Auchenleck

Aikenhead Castle *see* Aitkenhead Castle

Aikenway Castle

Moray: About 5 miles north of Charlestown of Aberlour, on minor roads north of A95 at Craigellachie, south of loop in River Spey, north of Aikenway.

Ruin or site NJ 291509 OS: 28 * Map: 10, no: 57
There are some remains of a castle, built on a steep promontory above a loop of the river. It was a property of the Leslies around the middle of the 15th century.

Aiket Castle

Ayrshire: About 4 miles south-east of Beith, on minor road between B706 and B778, just north of the Glazert Burn, two miles south-west of Dunlop.

Private NS 388488 OS: 63 ** Map: 3, no: 137
Aiket Castle is a 16th-century tower house of four storeys, to which later extensions have been added. There is a stair-tower, corbelled-out at first-floor level, at one corner, with a conical roof. The tower has corbiestepped gables, but does not appear to have had a parapet. The walls are harled and whitewashed.

The lands were owned by the Cunninghams from the end of the 15th century or earlier. One of the family, Alexander Cunningham, took part in the murder of Hugh Montgomery, Earl of Eglinton, in 1586. Cunningham was himself shot dead near Aiket soon afterwards by Montgomery's kinsmen. The property passed to the Dunlops at the beginning of the 18th century, and was later used to house farm labourers until burned down in the 1960s. It was restored in 1979.

Aikwood Tower

Borders: About 4 miles west and south of Selkirk, just south of B7009, east of the Ettrick Water.

Private   NT 420260   OS: 73   ***   Map: 2, no: 105

Aikwood Tower is a rectangular 16th-century tower house of four storeys and an attic without a parapet. Two corbelled-out bartizans crown the tower, and the steeply pitched roof has corbiestepped gables.

The old entrance, at ground level but no longer in use, has an iron-studded door. It opened into a lobby, which leads into the vaulted basement, and to a wide turnpike stair. The hall, on the first floor, has an elaborate fireplace, and there is also a small 'laird's room'. The upper floors are occupied by private chambers.

The tower was a property of the Scotts of Harden in the 17th century, and is said to have been the residence of the 13th-century wizard, Michael Scott. Little is known of his life, but he is said to have studied at Oxford, Paris and Padua, and in Toledo in 1217. He translated works of Aristotle, and was tutor to Emperor Frederick – as well as reputedly being a wizard. The tower was derelict in the 19th century, but has been restored by and is now home to Sir David Steel, Presiding Officer of the Scottish Parliament.

There is an exhibition about James Hogg, the 'Ettrick Shepherd', the well-known Scottish writer and poet, and temporary exhibitions of art and sculpture.

Other refs: Oakwood Tower

OPEN: Open May-Sep, Tue, Thu and Sun 14.00-17.00 until end 2002.

Permanent exhibition: James Hogg, the Ettrick Shepherd; medieval-style garden. Temporary art exhibitions. Car parking. £.

Tel: 01750 52253   Fax: 01750 52261

Email: steel@aikwoodscottishborders.com

Web: www.aikwoodscottishborders.com

Ailsa Craig Castle

Ayrshire: On south-east side of island of Ailsa Craig, in the Firth of Clyde about 10 miles east of Girvan.

Private   NX 023995   OS: 76   **   Map: 3, no: 3

On an island in the Firth of Clyde, Ailsa Craig Castle is a ruined plain 16th-century tower house. It is rectangular in plan, and rose to at least four storeys.

The partly subterranean basement, due to the slope of the ground, is vaulted, as is the ground floor. The hall, on the first floor, has a wide fireplace. The lower floors are connected by a straight stair, while the upper floors were reached by a turnpike stair. There are traces of a small courtyard.

It was a property of Crossraguel Abbey from 1404 until the 16th century, when it passed to the Kennedys of Culzean and Cassillis, who built the castle. In 1597 Ailsa Craig was captured by Hugh Barclay of Ladyland and held for the Spanish.

The island, which rises to 1114 feet, is Britain's fourth largest gannetry, and also has colonies of guillemots and other sea birds. Marble from the island was used to make curling stones.

OPEN: The island can be visited: contact Lighthouse Attendant (tel: 01465 713219).

Ainrick *see* Enrick

Airdit House

Fife: About 2.5 miles east and south of Leuchars, on minor roads west of A92, 1 mile south-west of Balmullo, at Airdit.

Ruin or site   NO 412200   OS: 59   *   Map: 7, no: 111

Site of castle and mansion.

The lands were a property of the MacDuff Earls of Fife from the 13th century or earlier. They passed to the Stewart Dukes of Albany who held them until 1425 when Murdoch, the then Duke, was forfeited and executed.

Other refs: Ardit

Airdrie House

Fife: About 3 miles west of Crail, on minor road north of B9171, at Airdrie.

Private   NO 567084   OS: 59   **   Map: 7, no: 149

Airdrie House is a 16th-century tower house. It consists of a rectangular main block and a square wing, which rises a storey higher. A corbelled-out turret, in the re-entrant angle, is crowned by a square caphouse. The tower is dated 1586, but has been altered and windows enlarged.

The lands belonged to the Dundemore family, one of whom was Regent during the minority of Alexander III, and they fought for the Scots in the Wars of Independence. Airdrie passed to the Lumsdens in the 15th century, one of whom was Sir John Lumsden, president of the Court of Session. The property was sold to the Turnbulls of Pittencrieff in 1602, then passed through several families including the Prestons around the turn of the 17th century, Anstruthers in 1674, then the Erskine Earls of Kellie. The house is in good condition and still occupied.

Airdrie House

Lanarkshire & Glasgow: To west of Airdrie, on minor roads north of A8010, at Monklands General Hospital.

Ruin or site   NS 749654 [?]   OS: 64   *   Map: 3, no: 353

Site of castle, which was replaced by Airdrie House, a baronial mansion which may have incorporated some of the earlier building.

The lands were a property of the Cleland family, but passed to the Hamiltons in 1490. William Wallace is said to have marshalled his forces near the house before the disastrous Battle of Falkirk in 1298. The Cleland laird of the time is thought to have been his brother-in-law. One of the family was killed at the Battle of Flodden in 1513. The Hamiltons of Airdrie were Covenanters and fought at the Battle of Drumclog in 1679, and the house was captured and garrisoned for Charles II.

The property passed to the Elphinstones, then the Aitchisons, Alexanders, then the Wilsons. The house was then used as the local maternity hospital until demolished in 1964 when Monklands General Hospital was built.

Airds Castle

Argyll & Dunbartonshire: Just south of Carradale, on minor roads and foot south of B879 in Carradale, north of Port Righ Bay, east coast of Kintyre, at Airds.

Ruin or site   NR 820383   OS: 68   *   Map: 5, no: 59

Airds is a very ruined castle of enclosure. It was a property of the MacDonald Lord of the Isles, but passed to the Crown on their forfeiture, then to Sir Adam Reid of Barskimming in 1498. It had been recovered by the MacDonalds of Dunyvaig, although by 1605 they had returned it to the Reids.

Airlie Castle

Angus & Dundee: About 4 miles north-east of Alyth, on minor roads north of A926, just east of meeting of River Isla and Melgam Water, 0.25 miles north of Mains of Airlie.

Private   NO 293522   OS: 53   **   Map: 8, no: 148

Once a fortress of great strength, Airlie Castle consisted of a 15th-century keep and courtyard. A deep ditch cut off an angle of land between two rivers, and beyond this was a massive curtain wall with a strong gatehouse. The gatehouse, which had a portcullis, was altered in the 16th century with the addition of a conical-roofed caphouse. Little else of the old castle remains.

The castle was built in 1432 by the Ogilvies, and visited by Mary, Queen of Scots. Although it had previously withstood sieges, in 1640 it was captured and sacked by the Earl of Argyll with 4000 troops – James Ogilvie, 1st Earl of Airlie, had fled Scotland rather than sign the National Covenant. The ballad 'The Bonnie House o' Airlie' tells how the pregnant wife of Ogilvie was turned out of doors – probably at Forter Castle rather than Airlie – by Argyll after the castle had been taken, pillaged and partly demolished. Argyll himself is supposed to have taken a hand in the destruction with a hammer.

Ogilvie joined the Marquis of Montrose, and was captured at the defeat of Philiphaugh in 1645, although he later managed to escape. The 4th Earl fought in the Jacobite Rising of 1745, but had to flee Scotland. He was pardoned in 1778, but the title not recovered until 1826. The castle was never rebuilt, then replaced by a mansion in 1793, which incorporates some of the earlier building. This house was restored in the 20th century, and is still occupied.

A ram, the 'Doom of Airlie Castle', is said to circle the castle when one of the family is near death or bad fortune about to strike.

Other refs: Errolly

Airnistean *see* Dun Airnistean

Airntully Castle *see* Stewart Tower

Airth Castle

Stirlingshire & Clackmannan: About 4 miles north of Falkirk, on minor road west of A905, south of Airth, about 0.5 miles from River Forth, north of the Pow Burn.

Private   NS 900869   OS: 65   ***   Map: 6, no: 97

Airth Castle consists of a squat 14th-century keep, now known as Wallace's Tower, of three storeys and an attic within a crenellated parapet. The east wing, which has two turrets of different sizes, probably also dates from the 13th or 14th century. The corbiestepped gabled roof probably dates from when the castle was extended by a wing with dormer windows in the 16th century, and a new wing was also added in 1581. The castle was greatly altered in the 19th century, with a new castellated and towered front, obscuring much of the older work.

A stronghold here was held by a Fergus de Erth (Airth) in 1309. The castle saw action in the Wars of Independence when William Wallace rescued his uncle, the Priest of Dunipace, from Airth after he had been imprisoned by the English. Around 1470 the property passed by marriage to the Bruces, and in 1488 the castle was attacked and burned by James III. Airth was restored with compensation from James IV, son of James III, who had led the rebel forces at the battle.

It passed by marriage to the Elphinstones in 1642: several of the family are buried in the Airth aisle of the nearby ruinous Old Airth Church. In 1717 the property was acquired by the Grahams, whose descendants owned it until 1920. Since 1971 Airth has been used as a hotel and country club.

One room of the castle is said to be haunted by the ghost of a 17th-century housekeeper. The story goes that she neglected two children in her care, and still searches the building for them after they were killed in a fire.

Other refs: Wallace's Tower; Erth

OPEN: Hotel – open all year.

122 rooms, of which 23 are located in the 14th-century castle. Dining restaurant and a cocktail bar. Conservatory. Restaurant and the stables bar, health centre, gymnasium, sauna and sunbed. Extensive conference and banquet facilities.

Tel: 01324 831411   Fax: 01324 831419   Web: www.radisson.com

Airth Tower

Stirlingshire & Clackmannan: About 6 miles north of Falkirk, on minor road south of A905, at Dunmore, about 1.5 miles north west of Airth, just north of 'The Pineapple'.

Private   NS 890889   OS: 65   ***   Map: 6, no: 94

Airth Tower is a simple 15th-century tower or keep, rectangular in plan, of four storeys. The parapet had open rounds and a conical-roofed caphouse, although these were from the 19th century. The tower is now quite ruinous, but had also been altered when most of the windows were enlarged.

The lands passed by marriage to the Elphinstones before 1340, but the present tower was probably built about 1508 by Sir John Elphinstone. His son, Alexander, was killed at the Battle of Flodden in 1513, and another of the family, Alexander, was slain at Pinkie in 1547. Yet another Alexander was made a judge of the Supreme Court of Scotland in 1599, and later Lord High Treasurer. In 1754 the property was sold to the Murray Earls of Dunmore.

The basement has been the burial vault of the Earls of Dunmore since 1820, but was broken into and despoiled in the early 1990s.

Other refs: Dunmore Tower; Elphinstone Tower

Airthrey Castle

Stirlingshire & Clackmannan: About 2.5 miles north-east of Stirling Castle, on minor roads north of B998 just west of junction with A91, in campus of Stirling University, at Airthrey.

Private   NS 813967   OS: 57   *   Map: 6, no: 77

Airthrey Castle, now part of the University of Stirling, is a much-altered castellated mansion. The original house was designed by Robert Adam, and started about 1791 for the Haldane family, who never occupied it. It passed to the Abercrombies, who held it until 1890.

Airyolland

Galloway: About 4 miles north-west of Port William, on minor roads north of A747, 1 mile west of Elrig, at or near Airyolland.

Ruin or site   NX 308475   OS: 82   *   Map: 1, no: 43

There are some remains of a castle or old house, which probably dated from the

16th or 17th century. It was a property of the Dunbars, but passed to the Vaux family in 1583.

Aithernie Castle

Fife: About 1.5 miles north of Leven, west of B927, just north of turn-off (east) for Bankhead Farm.

Ruin or site   NO 379035   OS: 59   *   Map: 7, no: 103

Little remains of a 17th-century tower house except one upstand of masonry. It was in good condition around 1710, but a ruin by 1803.

The property belonged to the Lundin family in the 13th century, but passed to the Carmichaels, then the Inglises. It was acquired by the Riggs family, who probably built the castle, then sold to the Watsons in 1670.

Aitkenhead Castle

Lanarkshire & Glasgow: In Glasgow, 0.5 miles east of B766, in King's Park, Carmunnock Road, Aitkenhead House.

Ruin or site   NS 596603   OS: 64   *   Map: 3, no: 274

Site of castle, which was replaced by a mansion. The lands were a property of the Stewarts, but passed to the Maxwells in the 14th century, then later to the Hamiltons, then the Gordons.

The present mansion dates from 1806, and was extended in 1823

Other refs: Aikenhead Castle

Albie

Dumfriesshire: About 3 miles north-east of Ecclefechan, on minor road east of B722 just south of junction with B725, south of Waterbeck, at or near Albie.

Ruin or site   NY 247772 [?]   OS: 85   *   Map: 1, no: 275

Site of tower house, a property of the Bells.

Aldbar Castle

Angus & Dundee: About 3 miles west and south of Brechin, on minor roads south of B9134, about 0.5 miles south of River South Esk, at Mains of Aldbar.

Ruin or site   NO 572577   OS: 54   *   Map: 8, no: 238

Aldbar Castle consisted of a 16th-century castle, to which had been added large 19th-century extensions. It rose to four storeys and a garret, with a stair-tower,

rising a storey higher, in the re-entrant angle. Bartizans crowned the corners. Some windows had iron yetts, and the walls were pierced by gunloops. The castle was completely demolished in 1965.

It originally belonged to the Crammond family, but in 1577 was sold to the Lyon Lord Glamis. A member of the family, Thomas Lyon, was one of those who kidnapped the young James VI and held him in Ruthven Castle (Huntingtower) in what became known as the 'Ruthven Raid'. It was he who told his king: 'Better bairnis grete than grown men' when James was having a bit of a blubber. Aldbar was sold to the Sinclairs, then passed to the Youngs, then to the Chalmers of Balnacraig, who remained in possession until the 20th century.

Other refs: Auldbar Castle

Aldcambus *see* Old Cambus

Alderstone House

Lothians: About 1.5 miles south-west of Livingston, on minor road between A71 and B7015, south of the River Almond.

Private   NT 044662   OS: 65   **   Map: 4, no: 21

Alderstone House is a plain altered 16th-century tower house of three storeys, rectangular in plan. It was extended in the 17th century, and there is a also later wing. Many of the windows have been enlarged.

The basement is vaulted, and contained the kitchen with a wide fireplace. The tower has been very altered inside.

It was built by the Kinlochs, but in 1656 was acquired by the Sandilands Lord Torphichen, who sold it to John Mitchell of Todhaugh in 1692. It is currently used as company offices.

Aldie Castle

Perth & Kinross: About 2 miles south and east of Crook of Devon, on minor roads south of A977, north of A823, north of the Pow Burn.

Private   NT 052977   OS: 58   *   Map: 8, no: 61**

Aldie Castle is a 16th-century tower house of three storeys and an attic, to which

was added a two-storey wing. A three-storey unvaulted range was built parallel to the main tower, and then a linking range was added. Bartizans, with gunloops and conical roofs, crown three corners, while a small watch-chamber tops the stair.

The original entrance was at the foot of the stair-tower. The basement is vaulted, and the hall is on the first floor.

The property belonged to the Mercers of Aldie from the mid 14th century, but later passed to the Murray Lord Nairne. The house was partly ruinous until restored in the 1950s, and is occupied.

Aldinhope *see* Eldinhope Tower

Aldourie Castle

Inverness & Nairn: About 8 miles south-west of Inverness, on minor roads west of B862, on east side of northern tip of Loch Ness, at Aldourie Castle.

Private   NH 601372   OS: 26   **   Map: 9, no: 76

Aldourie Castle, a mansion of 1853 which was restored about 1900, incorporates a 17th-century castle with a round tower and parapet. It was a property of the Frasers, then the Grants, but passed to the Mackintoshes in the 18th century.

The castle is said to be haunted by a 'Grey Lady', and her apparition reputedly walks from a bedroom in the ancient part of the castle to the old hall.

Alemoor Tower

Borders: About 6.5 miles west of Hawick, near minor road north of B711, near Alemoor Loch.

Ruin or site   NT 404157   OS: 79   *   Map: 2, no: 103

Site of tower house, which was completely destroyed when a road was built. The lands were a property of the Hepburn Earls of Bothwell from 1511.

Other refs: Wester Alemoor

Allan

Ross & Cromarty: About 3.5 miles south-east of Tain, on minor roads south of B9165 or north of B9175, 1.5 miles west of Fearn, at Allan.

Ruin or site   NH 815771   OS: 21   *   Map: 9, no: 127

Site of castle of the Munros.

Allanbank House

Borders: About 4.5 miles east of Duns, at or near B6437 in Allanton, near the meeting of the Blackadder and Whiteadder Waters.

Ruin or site   NT 864546   OS: 74   *   Map: 2, no: 344

Allanbank House, a small mansion designed by David Bryce in 1848, was completely demolished in 1969. The mansion replaced an earlier house, dating from the 17th century or earlier, which was a property of the Stewart family. The property later passed to the Kirkpatrick Sharpe family.

Robert Stewart of Allanbank, made a baronet of Nova Scotia in 1687, met a pretty Italian or French girl, Jean, in Paris and they became lovers. Stewart, however, seems to have tired of her or his parents disapproved: whatever, he planned to return to Allanbank. On his day of departure, Jean tried to stop him leaving, but was thrown under Stewart's carriage and trampled to death under the horse's hooves.

The ghost, 'Pearlin Jean', is said then to have followed Stewart back to Allanbank and began to haunt the grounds and house. Her apparition was seen, doors would open and close by themselves, and ghostly feet and the rustling of her gown were heard round the passages. The room in which the ghost was most commonly seen was abandoned. The old house was demolished in 1849, and a new mansion built, but the disturbances appear to have continued, occurrences being reported as late as the turn of the century. The newer mansion, however, was itself demolished in 1969.

Allanfauld Castle *see* Kilsyth Castle

Allanhaugh *see* Allanmouth Tower

Allanhaugh *see* Westhouses

Allanmouth Tower

Borders: About 3.5 miles south-west of Hawick, on minor road south of A7, south of the River Teviot, south of the Allan Water, near Newmill.

Ruin or site   NT 455102   OS: 79   *   Map: 2, no: 123

Little remains of a 16th-century tower house, rectangular in plan, except the ruins of the vaulted basement. The tower stands within an earthwork, and was a property of the Scotts, who had another tower nearby at Broadhaugh. The tower was in ruins by 1663.

Other refs: Raesknowe; Allanhaugh

Allanton House

Lanarkshire & Glasgow area: About 1.5 miles east and north of Newmains, south of South Calder Water, at or near village of Allanton.

Ruin or site   NS 850580 [?]   OS: 72   *   Map: 3, no: 395

Site of castle, which had been incorporated into a large mansion, designed by James Gillespie Graham, with a fine large park and picturesque lake. The mansion was completely demolished in the 20th century.

It was originally a property of Arbroath Abbey, but passed to the Stewarts, who were descended from Alexander Stewart, 4th High Steward of Scotland. Allanton was visited by Cromwell in 1650, and later held by the Seton-Stewarts of Allanton and Touch, possibly until 1930.

Allanton House – see previous page

Allardice Castle

Kincardine & Deeside: About 1.5 miles north-west of Inverbervie, on minor roads south of B967, just north of Bervie Water, south of Mains of Allardice, at Allardice Castle.

Private   NO 818739   OS: 45   *   Map: 10, no: 274**

Built in the early 17th century and extended in 1695, Allardice Castle consists of ranges of buildings and a curtain wall enclosing a courtyard. The courtyard is entered by a pend through the basement of the oldest part. The whitewashed walls of the old part rise to four storeys and an attic, and there is fine corbelling.

   The basement is vaulted and contained the kitchen, with the hall and private chambers on the floors above. A stair-turret is corbelled out to form a watch-chamber.

   Robert the Bruce gave the lands to the Allardice family, who held the property for many centuries, before it passed by marriage to the Barclays of Urie in the 18th century.

   The house was later used as a farmhouse, and, although burned out in the 1970s, has been restored and reoccupied.

Other refs: Castle of Allardice; Allardyce Castle

Allargue House

Aberdeen & Gordon: About 7 miles west and south of Strathdon, on minor road east of A939, north of River Don, 0.5 miles north of Corgarff, at or near Allargue House.

Private   NJ 259095 [?]   OS: 37   *   Map: 10, no: 48

Site of castle or old house.

Alloa Tower

Stirlingshire & Clackmannan: In Alloa, on minor roads south of A907, about 0.25 miles north of the River Forth.

NTS   NS 889925   OS: 58   *   Map: 6, no: 93**

Alloa Tower is an altered 15th-century keep, although it may incorporate older work. The rectangular keep rises to four storeys and a garret within a flush parapet. The parapet has open rounds at the corners, and a machiolation over the entrance. A caphouse, with a conical roof, crowns a turnpike stair. The walls are very thick. There was a large courtyard with ranges of buildings, and there were extensive gardens.

   The basement is vaulted, as is the second floor, and the hall was on the first floor. The keep has been altered inside, including the addition of a large turnpike stair in 1710. The top floor has a fine and rare medieval timber roof.

   The property was given to Sir Robert Erskine, Great Chamberlain of Scotland, in 1360, and has remained with his descendants, the Earls of Mar. Mary, Queen of Scots, was reconciled with Henry Stewart, Lord Darnley, here in 1565, and made the family Earls of Mar. James VI visited the castle.

   One of the Erskine family was 'Bobbing John', the 6th (or 11th) Earl of Mar, leader of the Jacobites in the 1715 Jacobite Rising. He was so-called because of his ability to change sides between the Hanoverians and Jacobites. A large mansion adjoining the castle was destroyed by a fire in 1800, and a portrait of Mary, Queen of Scots, as well as many other treasures, were burned.

   The nearby classical mansion of the 1830s, later remodelled and castellated, was demolished in 1959. The tower has been restored.

OPEN: Open Apr-Sep, daily 13.30-17.30; Oct, Sat-Sun only 13.30-17.30; last admission 17.00.

Explanatory displays. Collection of portraits of the Erskine family. WC. Disabled WC and access to ground floor only. Parking nearby. Group concessions. £.

Tel: 01259 211701   Email: information@nts.org.uk   Web: www.nts.org.uk

Allardice Castle

Alloa Tower – see previous page

Almond Castle

Stirlingshire & Clackmannan: About 3 miles west of Linlithgow, on minor roads east and north of A801, just north of the Union Canal, within the grounds of a factory.

Private   NS 956773   OS: 65   *   Map: 6, no: 106**

Almond Castle, also known as Haining Castle or The Haining, consists of a ruined altered 15th-century keep, now L-plan. A courtyard, with a wall and ditch, formerly enclosed the remains of ranges of buildings, added in the 16th century.

The basement is vaulted, and the hall was on the first floor, with the kitchen in the wing. The upper floors were reached by a turnpike stair.

It was a property of the Crawfords from 1425, who built the castle about 1470, but passed to the Livingstones in 1540. They changed the name from Haining to Al-

mond in 1633, when James, 3rd son of the Earl of Linlithgow, was created Baron Livingstone of Almond. It was forfeited by the Livingstone Earl of Callendar in 1716, after the Jacobite Rising, and the castle abandoned in the 1750s.

Other refs: Haining Castle; Vellore

Alneden *see* Aden House

Alterwall *see* Loch Alterwall

Altyre House

Moray: About 2.5 miles south of Forres, on minor roads east of A940, about 0.5 miles east of Findhorn River, south of Loch of Blairs, at Altyre House.

Private   NJ 027550   OS: 27   *   Map: 10, no: 8

Altyre House, much remodelled and extended in the late 19th century, was demolished in 1962.

The lands were a property of the Cummings, or Comyns, of Altyre from 1492. The family were descended from the once great and powerful family of Comyn, who backed the wrong side in the Wars of Independence and were destroyed by Robert the Bruce.

Alva Castle

Stirlingshire & Clackmannan: About 1 mile east of Alva, on minor roads north of A91, in woodland park.

Ruin or site   NS 901975   OS: 58   *   Map: 6, no: 98

Site of tower house, which is mentioned in 1542. It was incorporated into a mansion of 1636, itself one wing of Alva House. The mansion was set in fine wooded grounds.

Alva was a property of the Stirlings, then the Menteiths, but passed to the Erskines in 1620. This branch of the family were related to the Earls of Mar, and Sir John Erskine found a rich vein of silver in a nearby glen in 1710 – the proceeds helped to buy him a pardon after being involved in the Jacobite Rising of 1715. The property was sold to the Johnstones of Westerhall in 1775, and remained with their descendants until 1929. The lands had to be sold because of debt, while the house deteriorated and was used for target practice in World War II. It has since been completely demolished.

Alyth Castle

Perth & Kinross: In Alyth, 5 miles east of Blairgowrie and Rattray, near B952 north of A926, near the Alyth Burn, at or near the town of Alyth.

Ruin or site   NO 247485   OS: 53   *   Map: 8, no: 131

Not much remains of a castle near Alyth, except a large fallen wall and some ramparts.

Guinevere, wife of King Arthur, was reputedly imprisoned here by the Picts. Alyth was made a burgh of barony for the Ogilvie Earl of Airlie in 1488, but was a property of the Lindsay Earls of Crawford from 1303 until 1620.

OPEN: Access to cross-slab at all reasonable times.

Am Fraoch Eilean Castle *see* Claig Castle

Amhuinnsuidhe Castle

Western Isles: About 8 miles north-west of Tarbert on the island of Harris, near B887, on Loch Leosavay, on north shore of West Loch Tarbert, at Amhuinnsuidhe.

Private   NB 045085   OS: 13   *   Map: 11, no: 20

Amhuinnsuidhe Castle, which was designed by David Bryce, is a modern mansion. It was a property of the Murray Earls of Dunmore, then Lord Leverhume, who died in 1925.

Other refs: Fincastle

Amisfield Tower

Dumfriesshire: About 5.5 miles north of Dumfries, on minor roads 1 mile north of A701 at Amisfield village, at Amisfield Tower.

Private   NX 992838   OS: 78   ***   Map: 1, no: 193**

One of the most impressive and well-preserved of all Border castles, Amisfield Tower is a 16th-century tower house, square in plan, of four storeys and an attic and gar-

'Fair Maiden Lilliard lies under this stane,
Little was her stature, but great was her fame,
Upon the English loons she laid many thumps,
And when her legs were cuttid off, she fought upon her stumps.'

Anderston

Lanarkshire & Glasgow: About 1.5 miles west of Glasgow Cathedral, east of M8, Bishop Street, Anderston.
Ruin or site NS 582653 OS: 64 * Map: 3, no: 265
Probable site of manor of the Bishops of Glasgow.

Annan Castle

Dumfriesshire: In Annan, on minor road west of B722, north of B723, just east of the River Annan.
Ruin or site NY 192668 OS: 85 * Map: 1, no: 260
Sites of castle.
Nothing remains of a castle of the Bruce family, who rose to be Kings of Scots. It was built about 1124 and used as late as 1570.
The church tower was regarded as a secondary stronghold in the town and stocked with arms by Edward I of England in 1299. It was destroyed during an attack in 1547. In the 1560s the Maxwell Lord Herries built a large new tower in the town but this has also been demolished.

Annieston Castle

Lanarkshire & Glasgow area: About 3 miles west of Biggar, on minor road north of A72, south of River Clyde, 1 mile north of Symington, at Annieston.
Ruin or site NS 997366 OS: 72 * Map: 3, no: 438
Little remains of a tower house, except some of the formally vaulted basement and part of a turnpike stair.

Anstruther Castle *see* Dreel Castle

Antermony Castle

Lanarkshire & Glasgow area: About 1 mile east of Milton of Campsie, on minor road north of A891, just south of Antermony Loch, at Antermony.
Ruin or site NS 662765 [?] OS: 64 * Map: 3, no: 310
Site of tower house of the Flemings, who held the lands from 1424. The property passed to the Lennox family. The castle was demolished in the 18th century, and replaced by a mansion, Antermony House, itself now also demolished. The property passed to the Bells.

Applegarth

Dumfriesshire: About 2 miles north-west of Lockerbie, on minor roads north of A709 or east of B7020, east of River Annan, at or near Applegarthtown.
Ruin or site NY 105840 OS: 78 * Map: 1, no: 230
Possible site of tower house.

Appletreeleaves Tower *see* Ladhope Tower

Arbigland *see* McCulloch's Castle

Arbigland House

Dumfriesshire: About 2 miles east of Kirkbean, on minor roads east of A710, west of sea, at Arbigland House.
Private NX 989574 OS: 84 ** Map: 1, no: 192
Site of castle, known as Arbigland Hall, the site now a sunken Rose garden. Arbigland House is a fine classical mansion, with a main block and pavilions, built by William Craik in 1755 and replaced the older building.
The property was held by the MacCullochs, then the Murrays, then the Carnegie Earl of Southesk, but was sold to the Craik family in 1679, then to the Blacketts in 1852. John Paul Jones, founder of the American Navy, was born at nearby Kirkbean and worked on the estate as a gardener.
The grounds around the house are said to be haunted by the daughter of one of the Craik owners, the 'Ghost of the Three Crossroads'. She is said to have fallen for

---

ret, with a profusion of corbelling and turrets. The roof is steeply pitched. A round stair-tower projects, above first-floor level, and is corbelled out to square at the parapet. A gabled watch-tower crowns one corner, while the other three corners have bartizans with conical roofs. A machiolation defends the entrance.

The basement is vaulted. The hall, on the first floor, has three windows and a garderobe. A turnpike stair, in one corner, leads to the floors above, which have fine fireplaces and traces of tempera wall-painting.

The Charteris family held the lands from the 13th century, one of the family being Chancellor to Alexander II, and they built the tower, although there was probably a stronghold here from the 12th century. The family feuded with the Kilpatricks of Kirkmichael, and Roger Kilpatrick was murdered in 1526. Sir Robert Charteris of Amisfield fought a duel with Sir James Douglas of Drumlanrig in 1530. In 1636 the property passed to John Dalziel of Newton. The Dalziels were active Royalists during the Civil War, and Captain Alexander Dalziel was executed in 1650. A 19th-century mansion was built nearby. The tower is in an excellent state of repair, and still occupied.
Other refs: Hempisfield Tower

An Eilean Castle *see* Loch an Eilean Castle

Ancrum House

Borders: About 3 miles north-west of Jedburgh, near B6400, south of the Ale Water, in or near Ancrum.
Private NT 625245 [?] OS: 74 * Map: 2, no: 243
Ancrum House, a 19th-century baronial mansion, was built on the site of a castle dating from 1558 and built by Robert Kerr of Ferniehirst. The castle was destroyed by fire in 1873, restored, then burned again in 1885. It was later rebuilt, but was demolished in 1970.
It was originally a property of the Bishops of Glasgow, but passed to the Kerrs, who were made Earls of Ancram, then to the Scotts.
The Battle of Ancrum Moor was fought nearby in 1545. An English army of 5000 men raided the area, but was routed by a Scottish force. Lilliard, a girl of Teviotdale, fought in the Scottish army, her lover having been murdered by the English. After receiving many wounds, she was herself slain, the event recorded in 'Lilliard's Edge', by a monument near the A68, and by some terrible verse.

a groom called Dunn, but her parents thought the lad beneath her station. Dunn disappeared: he may have been murdered by the girl's brothers, and she reportedly fled the house, and was not seen again. Whatever end she came to, her apparition is said to have been seen in the grounds, and occasionally in the house. Dunn's ghost, on a phantom horse, has also been reported near the main gates.

Arboll *see* Red Castle

Arbuthnott House

Kincardine & Deeside: About 5.5 miles north-east of Laurencekirk, on minor roads south of B967 at village of Arbuthnott, just north of Bervie Water, at Arbuthnott.
Private NO 795750 OS: 45 ** Map: 10, no: 262
Arbuthnott House, originally a 13th- or 14th-century castle, dates from the 15th century. A further range was built in the 17th century, and some fine ceilings were added about 1685. In the 1750s the gateway side of the courtyard was replaced, and the house remodelled to create a symmetrical mansion.

It is a property of the Arbuthnotts, who have held the lands from the 12th century and built the castle. In 1420 Hugh Arbuthnott was implicated for the murder of John Melville of Glenbervie – by throwing him in a cauldron of boiling water, then drinking the resultant broth. In 1641 the family head was made Viscount, and the family still live at the house. The gardens are open all year, as is the house on specified occasions.
OPEN: Gardens open all year, daily 9.00-17.00. House open certain days and by arrangement: tel to check.
Guided tours only. WC. Disabled access to ground floor. Parking. £.
Tel: 01561 320417/361226 Fax: 01561 320476
Email: keith@arbuthnott.co.uk Web: www.arbuthnott.co.uk

Archerbeck

Dumfriesshire: About 1.5 miles north-east of Canonbie, on minor road north of B6357, at or near Archerbeck,
Ruin or site NY 416778 OS: 85 * Map: 1, no: 331
Probable site of tower house.

Ardachy

South Highland: About 1 mile south of Fort Augustus, on minor roads south of A82, east of River Tarff, at Ardachy Lodge.
Private NH 380075 OS: 34 ** Map: 9, no: 48
Ardachy, a modern mansion, stood on lands which were originally held by the Frasers of Lovat from the 15th century. The property was sold to the MacEwans in 1952, and is said to have been haunted by the apparition of a previous owner, a Mrs Brewin. The house was later sold, and is said to have been demolished.
Other refs: Ardochy

Ardardan *see* Ardmore

Ardardan Castle

Argyll & Dunbartonshire: About 1 mile north-west of Cardross, on minor road south of A814, 1 mile east of Ardmore, at or near Ardardan.
Private NS 331785 OS: 63 * Map: 5, no: 137
Site of tower house of the Noble family.

Ardblair Castle

Perth & Kinross: About 0.75 miles west of Blairgowrie, on minor road just south of A923, about 0.25 miles east of Rae Loch, at Ardblair.
Private NO 164445 OS: 53 *** Map: 8, no: 107
Ardblair Castle consists of an L-plan 16th-century tower house of three storeys and an attic, to which has been added a later wing. A stair-turret, corbelled out above first-floor level in the re-entrant angle, is capped by a conical roof. Later wings enclose a courtyard, where a wall, with a central arched gateway, is dated 1668. The castle was defended by a loch, which has been mostly drained.

The basement of the tower is vaulted, and the hall was on the first floor.

The property passed to the Blairs of Balthayock in 1399, and there was probably an earlier stronghold here. In 1554 they were tried for the murder of George Drum-

mond of Ledcrieff and his son, and Patrick Blair of Ardblair was beheaded. The property passed by marriage to the Oliphants of Gask in 1792, and the Blair Oliphant family own the castle. The Oliphants were Jacobites, and when they sold Gask in the 20th century, many Jacobite mementoes were brought to Ardblair. Laurence Oliphant was an aide-de-camp to Bonnie Prince Charlie, and Caroline Oliphant, using the pen-name Mrs Bogan of Bogan, wrote many ballads, including 'Charlie is my Darling' and 'Will ye no come back again?' The house is still occupied.

The castle is reputedly haunted by a 'Green Lady', dressed in green silk, who searches through the chambers of the castle. She is reputed to be the ghost of Lady Jean Drummond of nearby Newton, who had fallen in love with one of the Blairs of Ardblair. The families feuded, and Lady Jean seems to have died of a broken heart, drowned in a local marsh.
OPEN: Open by appointment only.
Tel: 01250 873155 Fax: 01250 873155

Ardcastle *see* Asknish House

Ardchattan Priory

Argyll & Dunbartonshire: About 6.5 miles north-east of Oban, on minor road between A828 and B845, on north side of Loch Etive, at Ardchattan.
His Scot NM 971349 OS: 49 *** Map: 5, no: 88
Set in a peaceful location, Ardchattan Priory, a Valliscaulian establishment dedicated to St Modan, was founded in 1231 by Duncan MacDougall. Robert the Bruce held a parliament here in 1309, and the lands passed to the Campbells of Cawdor in 1602. The buildings were torched in 1644 by Alasdair Colkitto MacDonald, and again in 1654 by Cromwell's forces. Colin Campbell of Glenure, murdered in 1752, is buried here – the events surrounding his death feature in the novel 'Kidnapped' by Robert Louis Stevenson.

Part of the church, used by the parish until 1731 but now ruinous, is in the care of Historic Scotland and houses 16th-century carved grave slabs and an early Christian carved wheel cross. Other priory buildings were incorporated into a mansion,

which was altered and enlarged in the 1840s, and is still occupied by the Campbells. A fine four-acre garden features herbaceous borders, roses, sorbus and many varieties of hebe.

The priory ruins are said to be haunted by the ghost of a nun. She is said to have been the lover of one of the monks. She hid beneath the floor so that she could visit her lover at night, but the prior found her and had her buried alive.

OPEN: Ruins of priory open all reasonable times; house NOT open; gardens open Apr-Oct, daily 9.00-18.00.

Facilities as gardens. Guidebook. WC. Disabled access. Car and limited coach parking. £ (gardens).

Tel: 01631 750274 Fax: 01631 750238

Ardchonnel Castle *see* Innis Chonnel Castle

Ardclach Bell Tower

South Highland: About 8.5 miles south-east of Nairn, on minor roads off A939, Ardclach.

His Scot NH 953453 OS: 27 ** Map: 9, no: 153

Ardclach Bell Tower is a small two-storey fortified bell tower, harled and with corbie-stepped gables. It was built in 1655 to summon worshippers to the nearby church and warn if there was any danger.

OPEN: Access at all reasonable times – apply to key holder (tel: 0131 668 8800)

Tel: 0131 668 8800 Fax: 0131 668 8888

Email: hs.explore@scotland.gov.uk Web: www.historic-scotland.gov.uk

Ardencaple Castle *see* Ardincaple Castle

Ardendraught

Banff & Buchan: About 1 mile south of Cruden Bay, on minor roads and foot east of A975, on Bay of Cruden, east of Aulton of Ardendraught.

Ruin or site NK 082349 OS: 30 * Map: 10, no: 362

Site of castle. The location is not certain, and another possibility is at Aulton of Ardendraught [NK 077354].

Ardestie Castle

Angus & Dundee: About 1 mile north-east of Monifieth, on minor road south-west of junction of A92 and B962, at Mains of Ardestie.

Ruin or site NO 505342 OS: 54 * Map: 8, no: 215

Little or nothing remains of a castle of the Maule Earls of Panmure.

The castle may have been at Ashbank [NO 506336].

Ardfad Castle

Argyll & Dunbartonshire: On island of Seil, about 4 miles south-west of Kilninver, on minor roads and foot west of B844, on Ardfad point, just north of Ardfad.

Ruin or site NM 769194 OS: 55 ** Map: 5, no: 47

The remains of a 16th-century Z-plan castle and courtyard, standing on a rock on the island of Seil. The tower consisted of a main block and two round towers, one of which survives. The building was said to be well preserved in 1915.

It was a property of the MacDougalls of Ardincaple.

Ardgith Castle *see* Ellon Castle

Ardgowan Castle *see* Inverkip Castle

Ardiherald *see* Old Kendal

Ardincaple Castle

Argyll & Dunbartonshire: West side of Helensburgh, on minor roads north of A814, just east of the shore of the Gareloch, at or near Ardencaple.

Private NS 282830 OS: 56 * Map: 5, no: 128

Ardincaple Castle, formerly a large castellated mansion, incorporated part of a castle of the MacAulays, but was mostly demolished in 1957. It was said to incorporate

work from the 12th century, but much was built by the 11th laird in the 16th century. The castle had a moat, traces of which were still visible in the 1930s.

The MacAulays held land here from at least the 13th century. The castle was abandoned as a roofless ruin, and sold to the Campbells in 1767. The building was rebuilt and remodelled in 1764 and 1772, passed to the Colquhouns of Luss by 1890, but was demolished in 1957 except for a square tower of four storeys to make way for a naval housing estate.

The old castle is said to have had a brownie.

Other refs: Ardencaple Castle

Ardit *see* Airdit House

Ardkinglas House

Argyll & Dunbartonshire: About 5 miles east of Inveraray, signposted off A83 Loch Lomond to Inveraray Road, south bank of Loch Fyne at northern tip, in village of Cairndow, at Ardkinglas.

Private NN 175104 OS: 56 * Map: 5, no: 121

Site of castle of enclosure of the Campbells, which was demolished before 1798, but a vestige of which survived in the 19th century. It is known to have been repaired in 1586, and had three towers in a courtyard surrounded by a wall.

It was replaced by a house, itself replaced by a mansion which was destroyed by fire in 1840. The present Ardkinglas House was built in 1906 and designed by Sir Robert Lorimer for Sir Andrew Noble, who held the property in 1905. It is still occupied by the Noble family.

The woodland garden has a fine collection of rhododendrons and conifers.

OPEN: Ardkinglas Woodland Garden open, daily dawn to dusk; Ardkinglas House open strictly for groups by appt only.

Guided tours for groups by appt. Picnic area. Plant and craft sales and refreshments available from Tree Shop nearby. WC. £.

Tel: 01499 600261/263 Fax: 01499 600241

Email: ardkinglas@btinternet.com Web: www.ardkinglas.com

Ardlamont House

Argyll & Dunbartonshire: About 4.5 miles south of Tighnabruaich, on minor roads 3 miles south of B8000, on Cowal, on Ardlamont Point, at Ardlamont House.

Private NR 981659 OS: 62 * Map: 5, no: 91

Site of castle of the Lamonts, part of which may be incorporated into Ardlamont House.

The name Lamont derives from the Norse word for 'lawman' and occurs as a first name in the 13th century, and as a surname in the 15th. The family were powerful in Cowal until massacred by the Campbells in 1646, their castles of Toward and Asgog both being sacked. Ardlamont then became their chief house until sold in 1893.

Ardmaddy Castle

Argyll & Dunbartonshire: About 5 miles south and west of Kilninver, on minor road south of B844, on the east shore of the Sound of Seil, north of Ardmaddy Bay, at Ardmaddy.

Private NM 788164 OS: 55 * Map: 5, no: 50

Ardmaddy Castle, a mansion dating from 1737, incorporates the basement of a 15th-century castle. It was extended by James Gillespie Graham in 1838, then again in 1862 by David Bryce.

It was a property of the MacDougalls, who built the castle, but passed to the Campbells. The castle was burned down in 1620, but was enlarged by Neil Campbell, who was executed by Charles II in 1685. In 1692 it passed to the Campbell Earls, then Marquises, of Breadalbane.

The fine walled garden features rhododendrons, azaleas and climbing plants, shrubs and herbaceous perennials. There are woodland walks, with fine views, as well as a water garden.

OPEN: Gardens open all year, daily dawn to dusk; castle not open.

Plant sales. Walled garden, water features and woodland walks. Parking. £.

Tel: 01852 300353 Fax: 01852 300353

Email: c.m.struthers@lineone.net

Ardmillan Castle

Ayrshire: About 2 miles south of Girvan, on minor road south of A77, about 0.25 miles south of the shore of the Firth of Clyde, at Ardmillan.
Private NX 169945 OS: 76 ** Map: 3, no: 17
Ardmillan Castle is a ruined altered 16th-century tower house. It consists of a rectangular main block with projecting round towers – although one of the towers has been demolished. The castle was much added to and altered in following centuries.

The main block of three storeys and a garret is crowned, at the gables only, by a corbelled-out parapet with open rounds. The remaining round tower is corbelled out to square and crowned by a caphouse. The castle has been surrounded by a courtyard.

It was a property of the Kennedys of Bargany from at least 1476, but passed by marriage to the Crawfords of Baidland in 1658. It had been visited by Mary, Queen of Scots, in 1563. James Crawford of Ardmillan became Lord Ardmillan, the well-known Scottish judge and Lord of Session, in 1855. The castle was burned out in the 20th century, and remains a shell.

Ardmore

Argyll & Dunbartonshire: About 2 miles west of Cardross, on minor road south of A814, on Ardmore Point on the north shore of the Firth of Clyde, at Ardmore.
Private OS: ** Map: 5, no: 131
Site of castle or old house, rebuilt or replaced in 1654, and remodelled and enlarged as a mansion, with a battlemented central tower, in 1806. Three towers, dating from the 16th or 17th century, survive, including one with gunloops.

It was held by the Geils family at the end of the 18th century. The grounds are managed by the Scottish Wildlife Trust, and there is a nature trail.
Other refs: Hill of Ardmore; Ardardan

Ardneil *see* Portencross Castle

Ardoch

Argyll & Dunbartonshire: About 4 miles north of Balloch, on minor road and foot north of A811, south side of Loch Lomond, about 0.3 miles west of Ardoch.
Ruin or site NS 412864 OS: 56 * Map: 5, no: 157
Site of castle or old mansion. The present remains may not be from this building, as the use of Place and the marking of 'Airdoch' on Blaeu's map suggests a grander house. Ardoch was a property of the Findlays.
Other refs: Old Place of Ardoch

Ardoch *see* Poyntzfield

Ardoch Tower

Argyll & Dunbartonshire: About 1.5 miles south-east of Cardross, on minor road north of Ardoch on north shore of River Clyde, at Ardochmore.
Private NS 364768 OS: 63 * Map: 5, no: 146
Site of tower house of the Bontines, near Ardochmore Farm, which was replaced by a house, itself demolished.

The property passed by marriage to the Grahams of Gartmore, who built Ardoch House, a small mansion dating from 1870 with a round tower at one corner. One of its occupants was Robert Bontine Cunningham Graham, who became the first president of the Scottish Labour Party in 1888, then the president of the National Party of Scotland in 1928.
Other refs: Tower of Ardoch

Ardochy *see* Ardachy

Ardpatrick Castle

Argyll & Dunbartonshire: About 9.5 miles south-west of Tarbert on Knapdale, on minor roads south of B8024, on Ardpatrick Point on north-west side of West Loch Tarbert.
Private NR 753593 [?] OS: 62 * Map: 5, no: 43
Site of castle, probably of the Campbells.
St Patrick is said to have landed here.

Ardross Castle

Fife: About 1 mile north east of Elie, at Ardross south of the A917 near the sea.
Ruin or site NO 509006 OS: 59 * Map: 7, no: 130
Little remains of an altered 14th- or 15th-century keep and castle, except the basement and the ruins of a later block.

It was built by the Dishington family, but sold to Sir William Scott of Elie in 1607, and passed to Sir William Anstruther towards the end of the 17th century.

Ardross Castle

South Highland: About 4.5 miles north and west of Alness, on minor roads west of A836, north of River Averon, south of Ardross, at Ardross House.
Private NH 611741 OS: 21 * Map: 9, no: 79
Ardross Castle is a fine castellated mansion with a profusion of turrets, bartizans and corbiesteps. It was remodelled and extended in 1880-1, and incorporates an older building.

Ardross was a property of the Munros, but had passed to the Mathiesons, then in 1880 to the Perrins family, who rebuilt the mansion. Charles William Dyson Perrins was the manager and owner of the famous Lea and Perrins company, makers of Worcester Sauce.

Ardrossan Castle

Ayrshire: In Ardrossan, south of the A78 and north and east of A738, north of railway line to harbour.
Ruin or site NS 233424 OS: 63 ** Map: 3, no: 49
Standing on a ridge above the town and defended by a ditch, Ardrossan Castle consists of a ruined 15th-century keep, modified from the original gatehouse, and a vaulted range with a kitchen and cellars. A deep passageway down stairs leads to a well. Part of the keep survives to the corbels of the parapet, but the rest of the castle is very ruinous.

An earlier castle here was a property of the Barclays, but by the 13th century had

passed to the Ardrossan family. William Wallace captured the castle, and had it dismantled, having the murdered garrison thrown into the dungeon. This event was afterwards known as 'Wallace's Larder'. The castle was acquired and remodelled by Sir John Montgomery, who fought at the battles of Otterburn in 1388, capturing Harry 'Hotspur' Percy, and Homildon Hill in 1402. His son was created Lord Montgomery around 1445, and his grandson became the 1st Earl of Eglinton in 1508. The family sheltered here in 1528 when their castle at Eglinton was sacked and burned by the Cunninghams, but Ardrossan was afterwards little used. In the 1650s Cromwell had stone taken from the castle to build a Citadel at Ayr, and in 1911 the local council had the site cleared and consolidated.

The ruin is in a dangerous condition.

The castle is said to be haunted by the ghost of William Wallace, which is only reputedly seen on stormy nights.
OPEN: Access at all reasonable times – view from exterior.
Parking Nearby

Ardstinchar Castle

Ayrshire: Just east of Ballantrae, north of junction of A77 with B7044, just north of the River Stinchar, at Ardstinchar.

Ruin or site NX 086824 OS: 76 ** Map: 3, no: 7

Little survives of Ardstinchar Castle, except one side of a 15th-century keep and foundations of a hall and other ranges. They stood within an irregular courtyard, which had outbuildings and at least one other square tower. The castle was defended by a ditch.

The castle was built by the Kennedys about 1450. It was visited by Mary, Queen of Scots, in 1563. In 1601 Gilbert Kennedy, 16th baron of Bargany and Ardstinchar, was slain by his kinsman the Kennedy Earl of Cassillis over a claim to the lands of Crossraguel Abbey. Much of the castle was demolished about 1770 and the materials used to build the bridge over the river.

Ardtornish Castle

South Highland: About 1.5 miles south-east of Lochaline, on minor road and foot 4 miles east of A884, on Ardtornish Point, on north side of Sound of Mull.

Ruin or site NM 692426 OS: 49 ** Map: 9, no: 21

Not much remains of Ardtornish Castle, a simple 13th- or 14th-century hall house of the MacDonalds, built on a rocky crag. There are foundations of other buildings.

The laird of MacInnes and five of his sons were murdered here about 1319. It was here that John MacDonald, Lord of the Isles and Earl of Ross, signed the treaty of Westminster-Ardtornish in 1461 – by which he, the Earl of Douglas, and Edward IV of England agreed to divide Scotland between them. The plan came to nothing, and James IV had destroyed the Lordship of the Isles by 1493. The castle then passed to the MacLeans, but was abandoned towards the end of the 17th century. The castle was consolidated at the beginning of the 20th century.

Ardtornish House [NM 703475] is a mansion of 1856-66, and was a property of the Smiths in the 19th century. Ardtornish Estate is a 35,000 acres Highland estate with 24 acres of established gardens around the house.

Accommodation is available on the estate (tel 01967 421288 or www.ardtornish.co.uk).

Ardveich Castle

Stirlingshire & Clackmannan: About 2 miles east of Lochearnhead, just north of A85 on the north bank of Loch Earn, on the west side of Beich Burn, east of Dalveich.

Ruin or site NN 615244 OS: 51 * Map: 6, no: 38

Site of castle, apparently a Z-plan tower house with a narrow main block and round towers, although little or nothing remains.

Other refs: Dalveich Castle

Ardverikie *see* Loch Laggan Castle

Ardvorlich

Perth & Kinross: About 4 miles west of St Fillans, on minor road west of A85, on the southern side of Loch Tay, at the head of Glen Vorlich, at Ardvorlich.

Ruin or site NN 633229 OS: 51 * Map: 8, no: 4

Site of castle of the Stewarts.

Ardvreck Castle

Sutherland & Caithness: About 1.5 miles north-west of Inchnadamph, on foot west of A837, on promontory on north side of Loch Assynt, at Ardvreck Castle.

Ruin or site NC 240236 OS: 15 ** Map: 12, no: 2

Standing on a peninsula into Loch Assynt, Ardvreck Castle consists of a ruined square keep of three storeys, with a round stair-turret corbelled out to square. The basement was vaulted, and the walls are pierced with shot-holes. The castle was much altered in the 16th century, and there was a walled garden. A rampart cut off the peninsula.

It was a property of the MacLeods of Assynt, who built the castle. It was where James Graham, Marquis of Montrose, took refuge after losing the Battle of Carbisdale in 1650. Montrose was betrayed to the Covenanters, and subsequently executed in Edinburgh, his body dismembered and displayed in public. The castle was sacked in 1672 by the Mackenzies, and replaced by Calda House [NC 254234],

south-east of Ardvreck by the main road, itself burned out by the MacRaes in 1760 and never restored. The property had passed to the Mackenzies, but they were forfeited after the Jacobite Rising, and it was sold to the Earl of Sutherland in 1758.

The castle is said to be haunted by the weeping ghost of one of the daughters of a MacLeod chief, who threw herself out of one of the windows; as well as the ghost of a tall grey-clad man.

OPEN: Access at all reasonable times – view from exterior.

Parking Nearby.

Ardwall

Galloway: About 1.5 miles south-west of Gatehouse of Fleet, on minor road east of A75, on west side of Water of Fleet, at or near Ardwall.

Ruin or site NX 581547 OS: 83 * Map: 1, no: 88

The mansion, which dates from 1762 and was altered and extended in the 19th century, may stand on the site of a castle. The mansion was a property of the MacCullochs of Ardwall.

Ardwall Island

Galloway: About 5 miles south of Gatehouse of Fleet, on minor roads and boat west of B727.

Ruin or site NX 573496 OS: 83 * Map: 1, no: 87

Site of hall house or castle, which dated from the 13th or 14th century.

There was an earlier chapel here, and probably an early Christian community. Many burials were found during excavation, dating from the 5th to 11th centuries. Several cross-slabs and stones carved with crosses, dating from the 8th to the 11th century, were also discovered and are now in Dumfries Museum. The island can be reached at low tide.

Ardwell House

Galloway: About 9.5 miles south of Stranraer, on minor road west of A716 at Ardwell village, near Ardwell House.

Private NX 103455 [?] OS: 82 * Map: 1, no: 19

Site of a castle with a moat of the MacCullochs, which stood near Ardwell House, an 18th-century mansion. There are country house gardens and grounds with flowering shrubs and woodland walks.

OPEN: House not open; garden and grounds open Mar-Oct, 10.00-18.00; walled garden and green house close 15.00.

Plant centre and gift shop. Picnic area. Partial disabled access and WC. Car and coach parking. £.

Tel: 01776 860227 Fax: 01776 860288

Argyll's Lodging

Stirling & Clackmannanshire: In Stirling at the top of Castle Wynd, on minor roads west of A9, near Stirling Castle.

His Scot NS 793938 OS: 57 *** Map: 6, no: 71

Argyll's Lodging is a fine and well-preserved 17th-century town house. Gabled blocks with dormer windows surround a courtyard, while one side is enclosed by a wall. Many of the rooms within the lodging have recently been restored and furnished in 17th-century style.

The Lodging was built by Sir William Alexander of Menstrie, but passed to the Campbell Earls of Argyll. The 9th Earl, who was executed for treason in 1685 after leading a rising against James VII, stayed at the Lodging.

OPEN: Open all year: Apr-Sep, daily 9.00-17.15 (last ticket sold); Oct-Mar, daily 9.30-16.15 (last ticket sold); closed Christmas and New Year.

Visitor centre with explanatory displays. Gift shop. WC. Disabled access. Car and coach parking. £ (Joint ticket available with Stirling Castle).

Tel: 01786 461146/450000 Fax: 01786 448194

Arkendeith Tower

Ross & Cromarty: About 2.5 miles west of Fortrose on the Black Isle, on minor roads north of A832, 0.5 miles north-west of Avoch, at Arkendeith.

Ruin or site NH 695561 OS: 26 * Map: 9, no: 101

Little remains of a tower house, except a vaulted basement. It formed part of a castellated mansion dating from the 17th century, and was a property of the Bruces of Kinloss.

Argyll's Lodging, Stirling – see previous page

Arkland Tower

Dumfriesshire: About 3.5 miles west and north of Moniaive, on minor roads
north of A702 at Penpoint, west of Scar Water, at Arkland.
Ruin or site NX 803980 OS: 78 * Map: 1, no: 135
Site of tower house, located in the garden of Arkland House.

Arkleton Tower

Dumfriesshire: About 4 miles north of Langholm, on minor road east of A7, east
of Ewes Water, just to north of Arkleton.
Ruin or site NY 380914 [?] OS: 79 * Map: 1, no: 322
Site of tower house, some remains of which survived in the 19th century.
 The property was apparently held by the Maxwells, but given to the Armstrongs in
1537. By 1671 it was a property of the Elliots. Arkleton House replaced the tower,
and the last vestiges were removed in the 19th century.

Armadale Castle

South Highland: At Armadale on the island of Skye, on the south-east coast of
Sleat, on A851, at Armadale Castle.
Private NG 640047 OS: 32 * Map: 9, no: 18
A mansion rather than a fortress, Armadale Castle was built in 1815 by James Gillespie
Graham for Lord MacDonald of Sleat, and extended with a block designed by David
Bryce in 1855. The previous MacDonald residences of Duntulm Castle [NG 410743]
and Monkstadt House [NG 380675] both having been abandoned. Dr Johnson
visited Armadale in 1773. In 1925 the MacDonalds moved to Ostaig. Armadale Cas-
tle, burned out and ruined, now houses the Museum of the Isles in some of the
outbuildings.
Other refs: Museum of the Isles, Armadale Castle
**OPEN: Open Apr-Oct, daily 9.30-17.30, last entry 17.00; gardens open
all year.**
*Guided tours. Explanatory displays. Gift shops. Licensed restaurant. Tea room. Picnic
area. WC. Disabled access. Car and coach parking. Self-catering accommodation
available all year. Group concessions. ££.*
Tel: 01471 844305/227 Fax: 01471 844275
Email: office@cland.demon.co.uk Web: www.cland.demon.co.uk

Arnage Castle

Aberdeen & Gordon: About 4.5 miles north of Ellon, on roads west of A948, east
of Ebrie Burn, about 1 mile north of Mains of Arnage, at Arnage Castle.
Private NJ 936370 OS: 30 * Map: 10, no: 329**
Arnage Castle is a 16th-century Z-plan tower house of three storeys, to which has
been added a mansion. The main block has a projecting stair-wing, and two stair-
turrets, in the re-entrant angles, are corbelled out above first-floor level. The walls
are pierced by shot-holes, but many of the windows have been enlarged. All that
remains of a courtyard is a well.
 The original entrance, now sealed, was at the foot of the projecting stair-wing.
The basement is vaulted, the hall was on the first floor, and private chambers occupied the floors above.
 The property passed by marriage to the Cheyne family in the 14th century. In
1643 it was sold to the Sibbalds, then in 1702 to John Ross, who was later Provost of
Aberdeen. It was restored in the 1930s, and is still occupied.

Arnfinlay Castle

Stirlingshire & Clackmannan: About 5 miles south-east of Aberfoyle, on minor
roads north of the A811, south of the River Forth, near Gartentruach.
Ruin or site NS 587955 [?] OS: 57 * Map: 6, no: 30
Site of castle, also known as Arnfindlay, nothing of which survives.
Other refs: Castle of Arnfinlay

Arngomery House *see* Broich House

Arnhall Castle

Stirlingshire & Clackmannan: About 4 miles north and west of Stirling, on minor
roads south of B824, 0.5 miles north of River Teith, about 0.5 mile south-west of
Kier House.
Ruin or site NS 764986 OS: 57 ** Map: 6, no: 63
Arnhall Castle is a very ruined 17th-century L-plan tower house of three storeys,
which formerly had round bartizans. It had a courtyard. It belonged to the Dow
family.

Arniston House

Lothians: About 2 miles south-west of Gorebridge, on minor roads north off
B6372, just east of River South Esk, at Arniston.
Private NT 326595 OS: 66 * Map: 4, no: 134
Site of old house or castle, with a vaulted basement, known latterly as 'Old Arniston
House'. Dating from before 1592, the old house was demolished when the present
mansion was built.
   It was a property of Sir James Dundas, who was knighted by James VI, and many of
the family were lawyers and statesmen. The present Arniston is a symmetrical clas-
sical mansion, built for Robert Dundas of Arniston by William Adam in 1726. The
house was altered in 1754 and 1877. A section was gutted because of dry rot, and
is undergoing restoration. The house retains fine plasterwork.
Other refs: Old Arniston House
**OPEN: Open Apr-Jun: guided tours on each Tue starting at 14.00 and
15.30; Jul-mid Sep, Tue, Thu and Sun 14.00-17.00; private groups of
10-50 accepted all year by prior arrangement.**
Guided tours. WC. Disabled WC. Car and coach parking. ££ (house).
Tel: 01875 830230/515 Fax: 01875 830515

Arnot Castle

Perth & Kinross: About 4 miles north of Cardenden, on minor road just north of
the A911, about 0.25 miles south of the Arnot Reservoir, at Arnot.
Ruin or site NO 207016 OS: 58 ** Map: 8, no: 119
Arnot Castle is a ruined rectangular 16th-century tower house of four storeys, although it may incorporate earlier work. It has a vaulted basement, and there was a
courtyard with later outbuildings. It was a property of the Arnot family.

Arnprior Castle

Stirlingshire & Clackmannan: In Arnprior, near the meeting of the A811 and
B8034, about 0.5 miles south of the River Forth.
Ruin or site NS 613949 OS: 57 * Map: 6, no: 36
Nothing remains of Arnprior Castle, although the ruins could be traced at the end
of the 18th century.
   The lands were held by the Menzies family around the turn of the 16th century,
but passed to the Buchanans. The laird was visited by James V and his retinue after
Buchanan had thieved a wagon of the king's goods. He seems to have been for-
given, being invited back to Stirling still wearing his head. Buchanan of Arnprior
was killed at the Battle of Pinkie in 1547.

Aros Castle

Argyll & Dunbartonshire: On north of Jura, at Glengarrisdale.
Private NR 645968 [?] OS: 61 * Map: 5, no: 24
Aros Castle was a property of the MacLeans, who held the north of Jura, although
the exact location is not certain. In 1620 the Campbells, to whom the southern part
of the island had passed from the MacDonalds, complained that they were being

harassed by the MacLeans. This came to battle in 1647, and at Glengarrisdale a
force of Campbells surprised the MacLeans, slaying many of them.
Other refs: Glengarrisdale Castle

Aros Castle

Argyll & Dunbartonshire: On island of Mull, about 8 miles south-east of
Tobermory, on minor road east of A848, west side of the Sound of Mull, just
south-east of Aros Mains.
Ruin or site NM 563450 OS: 47 ** Map: 5, no: 20
Once one of the most important sites on Mull, Aros Castle consists of a ruined
13th-century hall house, the ground floor of which is choked with fallen masonry,
and an overgrown courtyard, which contained several buildings. The castle was
protected by a steep drop to the beach, and a ditch and wall on the landward side,
with a drawbridge.
   It was built by the MacDougalls, but at the beginning of the 14th century passed to
the MacDonald Lords of the Isles. Three charters were issued from the castle by the

Lords in 1410, 1469 and 1492. After the forfeiture of the Lord of the Isles in 1493, it
was acquired by the MacLeans of Duart. On the orders of James VI in 1608, Lord
Ochiltree lured many unruly island chiefs onto his ship, where they were imprisoned and sent to Edinburgh for punishment. The lands later passed to the Campbells, but Aros lost importance to Tobermory in the 18th century. The lands around
Aros and castle were put up for sale in 1996.
Other refs: Dounarwyse

Arrochar House

Argyll & Dunbartonshire: In Arrochar, off A83, at the northern most end of Loch
Long, at the Cobbler Hotel.
Ruin or site NN 297039 OS: 56 * Map: 5, no: 129
Arrochar House was a residence or castle of the MacFarlanes, who had several
strongholds around Arrochar and Loch Lomond. It was their seat in 1697, and the
Cobbler Hotel incorporates foundations from this building.
   The MacFarlanes held lands around Arrochar from the end of the 12th century,
and fought for Robert the Bruce at the Battle of Bannockburn in 1314. The chief
was slain at Flodden in 1513, another at Pinkie in 1547, and they sacked Boturich
Castle in the early 16th century. They were on the winning side when the forces of
Mary, Queen of Scots, were defeated at Langside in 1568, and at the Battle of Inverlochy in 1645. Their castle at Inveruglas was burned by Cromwell in the 1650s. The
clan did not come out for the Jacobites, however, and the lands were sold in 1767,
and passed to the Colquhouns of Luss, the MacFarlanes' former rivals and enemies.
   MacFarlane's Lantern was a full moon, a good night for thieving cattle.
   The present building is said to be haunted. The young daughter of one of the
chiefs fell in love with a member of the Colquhouns of Luss. Her father heard of the
relationship, and ordered it to stop. She ignored his warnings, and an example was
made of the poor girl. She was locked in one of the chambers of Arrochar House

with no food or water. The poor lass died, and it is said that her apparition, a 'Green Lady', wanders the present building.
Other refs: Cobbler Hotel, Arrochar; Inveriach House
OPEN: Hotel – open all year and to non-residents.
109 rooms with ensuite facilities. Refreshments and dinners. Car and coach parking. Themed tours. User friendly for less well-abled guests.
Tel: 01301 702238/747 Fax: 01301 702353

Arthurlie House

Renfrewshire: To north of Barrhead, on minor roads south of A736, south of Levern Water, off Arthurlie Street, at Arthurlie.
Private NS 504588 OS: 64 * Map: 3, no: 214
Arthurlie House, a mansion built about 1810 and now part of St Mary's Convent, is built on the site of a series of older houses.
 The lands were held by the Pollocks from 1372. In 1439 the family lost the property, and it was divided into Arthurlie and West Arthurlie. The property was held by the Rosses of Hawkhead and the Stewarts of Castlemilk.
Other refs: Nether Arthurlie; East Arthurlie

Ascog Castle *see* Asgog Castle

Ascog House

Argyll & Dunbartonshire: On island of Bute about 1.5 miles south-east of Rothesay, near A844 on the eastern side of Bute, just west of the sea, at Ascog.
Private NS 105633 [?] OS: 63 ** Map: 5, no: 109
Ascog House is an L-plan tower house, probably built in the 16th century. A dormer is dated 1687.
 The original entrance, now sealed, was in the re-entrant angle, and there is a corbelled-out watch-chamber.
 The lands may have been a property of the Glass family from the 15th century. They later passed to the Fairlies, but were acquired in 1587 by the Stewarts, who held the property until the middle of the 18th century.
OPEN: Can be rented through the Landmark Trust.
Tel: 01628 825925

Asgog Castle

Argyll & Dunbartonshire: About 2.5 miles south-west of Tighnabruaich, on track west of B8000, west of Asgog loch, on Cowal peninsula, east of Cnoc a' Chaisteal, at Asgog.
Ruin or site NR 946705 OS: 62 ** Map: 5, no: 87
Asgog Castle is a very ruined 15th-century stronghold with a keep and courtyard. The basement was vaulted, and there were at least two further storeys. A stair led up from the basement.
 Not to be confused with Ascog Castle on Bute, this was the Lamont stronghold which was torched and destroyed, with much treachery and murder, by the Campbells in 1646 after a long siege. The Lamonts were Royalists, and had been raiding Campbell lands, but had been promised that their people would go free if they surrendered the castle. The Campbell Marquis of Argyll had over 200 men, women and children slaughtered, although he himself was later executed in 1661 for treason.
 The building is in a dangerous condition.
Other refs: Ascog Castle; Castle Ascog

Ashiesteel House

Borders: About 3 miles west of Galashiels, on minor road south from A72 about 1.5 smile south-west of Colvenfords, south of the River Tweed.
Private NT 432351 [?] OS: 73 ** Map: 2, no: 112
Standing in the grounds of a former hospital, Ashiesteel House incorporates a rectangular 17th-century tower house. The house was enlarged and altered on at least four occasions, the last in Victorian times when it was given corbiestepped gables and dormers.
 It was a property of the Russells, but was later the home of Sir Walter Scott from 1804-12. It was here that he wrote 'The Lay of the Last Minstrel', 'The Lady of the Lake', 'Marmion', and part of Waverley novels.

Ashintully Castle

Perth & Kinross: About 2 miles north-east of Kirkmichael, on minor road north of B950, at Ashintully.
Private NO 101613 OS: 43 * Map: 8, no: 78**
Ashintully Castle is a 16th-century L-plan tower house of four storeys and a garret, to which a large wing was added in the 17th century. It was remodelled in the late

18th and 19th century after becoming ruinous. The walls are pierced by gunloops and shot-holes. The castle is dated 1583.
 The basement has been vaulted, but the interior has been modernised. A straight stair leads to the hall, and a turnpike stair climbs to the floors above.
 It was a property of the Spaldings. In 1587 Andro Spalding was besieged in the castle, then badly treated by a band of Stewarts and Blairs. The property passed to the Rutherfords in 1750. It is still occupied.
 The castle is said to be haunted by the ghost of 'Green Jean', who held the castle in her own right. She was murdered – along with her servant, who was stuffed up the chimney – by her uncle so that the castle and lands passed to him. Her ghost is reputedly seen at the family burial ground and in the castle. Two other ghosts are said to haunt the grounds: one a messenger wrongly murdered for not having delivered a message; the other 'Crooked Davie', a tinker hanged for trespassing.

Asknish House

Argyll & Dunbartonshire: About 5 miles north-east of Lochgilphead, on minor road south of A83, 1 mile north-east of village of Lochgair, north side of Loch Gair, at Asknish House.
Private NR 930913 [?] OS: 55 * Map: 5, no: 86
Site of castle, which was replaced by a mansion.
 It was a property of the Campbells of Auchinbreck in 1583, but sacked in 1685 because the family had supported the Earl of Argyll's rebellion against James VII. The property was held by the Campbells until 1745. The castle was demolished about 1780, and replaced by Asknish House [NM 928915].
Other refs: Lochraig; Ardcastle

Asliesk Castle

Moray: About 7 miles west of Elgin, on minor roads south of A96, south of Alves Wood, north-west of Monaughty Wood, at Asliesk.
Ruin or site NJ 108598 OS: 28 * Map: 10, no: 17
Little remains of a 16th-century L-plan tower house, with a corbelled out stair-tower and bartizans. It was a property of the Innes or Brodie family.

Asloun Castle

Aberdeen & Gordon: About 2 miles south and west of Alford, on minor road west of A980, just north of the Strow Burn, just east of Castleton of Asloun, at Asloun.

Ruin or site NJ 543149 OS: 37 ** Map: 10, no: 131

Little remains of a 16th-century Z-plan tower house, except one round tower and walling from the main block. The basement was vaulted, and the wall pierced by gunloops.

It was built by the Calder family, and later held by the Forbeses. The Marquis of Montrose spent the night here before defeating the Covenanters, led by General Baillie, at the Battle of Alford in 1645.

Other refs: Castle of Asloun

Assynt Castle

Sutherland & Caithness: About 4 miles north-west of Inchnadamph, on track and foot east of A837 at Little Assynt, on island, Eilean Assynt, near the south shore of Loch Assynt.

Ruin or site NC 189251 OS: 15 * Map: 12, no: 1

Very little remains of a 14th-century keep and castle on an island, a property of the MacLeods of Assynt. Their later stronghold was at Ardvreck Castle. The island was besieged in 1585 by the Mackays of Strathnaver, although the siege was raised by the Earl of Sutherland, then again in 1646 by the Mackenzies. Eilean Assynt may have been used as a prison.

Other refs: Eilean Assynt

Aswanley House

Aberdeen & Gordon: About 7 miles west of Huntly, on minor roads south of A920, just south of River Deveron, 1.5 miles east of Haugh of Glass, at Mains of Aswanley.

Private NJ 445397 OS: 28 ** Map: 10, no: 96

Aswanley consists of a long low L-plan building of two storeys and a garret, with a round stair-tower projecting from the main block. It was formerly enclosed by a courtyard, the arched entrance for which still survives. The building has been greatly altered, and the roofline lowered. The walls are harled and yellow-washed.

Aswanley was a possession of the Cruickshanks, but passed to the Gordons, then in 1440 to the Calders. The property was sold because of debt to the Duffs of Braco in 1768. The house is still occupied.

Athelstaneford

Lothians: About 2.5 miles north-east of Haddington, near B1343, at Athelstaneford.

Ruin or site NT 533774 [?] OS: 66 * Map: 4, no: 193

Site of 16th-century castle of the Hepburns, of which only the doocot remains, dated 1563. It was a property of Sir John Hepburn, Marshal of France, and companion-in-arms to Gustavus Adolphus.

The 16th-century doocot has been restored. It houses an unmanned audio-visual display on the battle in 832 at which the Picts and Scots defeated the Northumbrian King Athelstane. A white diagonal cross of clouds floated across the blue sky, giving the army of Picts and Scots the courage to defeat the larger Northumbrian force. The St Andrews Cross, the Saltire, was then adopted as the flag of Scotland – or so the story goes.

OPEN: Heritage centre: open daily, Apr-Sep 10.00-17.00.
Explanatory displays. Disabled access. Car and coach parking.
Tel: 01620 880378

Auchanachie Castle

Aberdeen & Gordon: About 4.5 miles north-west of Huntly, on minor roads east of A96, west of B9022, 0.5 miles west of Ruthven, north of the Cairnie Burn, at Auchanachie.

Private NJ 498469 OS: 29 ** Map: 10, no: 108

Auchanachie Castle consists of a 16th-century tower house of three storeys and a large round stair-tower, as well as many later and lower additions. The walls are harled and pierced by shot-holes, and many of the windows are small. There is a panel with the words 'From Our Enemies Defend Us O Christ' – probably from the Forbeses – and the date 1594.

The basement of the tower is vaulted, and has three stone bosses carved with the arms of Gordon, Fraser and Campbell. The turnpike stair is very steep, and the tiny hall on the first floor is also vaulted.

Auchanachie was a Gordon property, and held by the oldest sons of Avochie – the castle of which itself is now only a fragmentary ruin. This family took an active part in the fighting during the reigns of Mary, Queen of Scots, and James VI. The castle is still occupied.

There was another stronghold called Ruthven nearby [NJ 510468].

Other refs: Achananchie

Auchans

Ayrshire: About 3 miles north-east of Troon, on minor road south of A759, about 0.5 miles west of Dundonald.

Ruin or site NS 355346 OS: 70 ** Map: 3, no: 114

Auchans incorporates a much-altered 15th-century keep in an L-plan house. It consists of a long main block of three storeys and an attic and a lower wing. A square stair-tower stands in the re-entrant angle, while a round stair-tower is capped by a square corbelled-out watch-chamber.

Apart from the vaulted kitchens, the floors have all collapsed.

Auchans was a property of the Wallaces. One of the family, Colonel James Wallace, was a Covenanter, and led the Pentland Rising of 1666. The property was sold to the Cochranes of Coldoun, who altered and extended the house by demolishing much of Dundonald Castle. Sir William Cochrane suffered during the Civil War of the 1650s for supporting the Royalists, but was rewarded by being made Earl of Dundonald in 1669. The property passed to the Montgomery Earls of Eglinton, and was the home of the beautiful Susanna Kennedy of Culzean, widow of the 9th Earl. She remained a staunch Jacobite until her death in 1780 at the age of 91. The poet Allan Ramsay dedicated his work 'The Gentle Shepherd' to her. According to tradition, in her old age she trained rats which would summon to dine with her. The house was later divided into workers flats, fell into disrepair, and is ruinous.

Auchavoulin *see* Toward Castle

Auchaynanie *see* Auchoynanie

Auchcairnie

Kincardine & Deeside: About 3 miles north-east of Fettercairn, on minor road just north of B966, at or near Auchcairnie.

Ruin or site NO 690755 OS: 45 * Map: 10, no: 201

Site of castle.

Other refs: Castle of Auchcairnie

Auchen Castle

Dumfriesshire: About 2 miles south-west of Moffat, on minor roads west of M74, about 0.25 miles west of Evan Water, south of Lawesknowe.

Ruin or site NT 063035 OS: 78 * Map: 1, no: 209

Auchen Castle is a 13th-century castle of enclosure. It consists of a very thick, but ruinous, curtain wall, which encloses a courtyard, in which there do not appear to have been any stone buildings. The gateway was protected by a barbican, and the corners had solid towers.

It may have been built by Thomas Randolph, Earl of Moray, and was held by the Dunbar Earls of Moray in the 14th century, then the Douglases of Morton, then the Maitlands in the 15th century. A new house, also called Auchen Castle, 'a structure of considerable extent', was built nearby, after the property passed to the Youngers.

Other refs: Auchencass Castle; Achincass

Auchenames *see* Auchinames Castle

Auchenbathie Castle

Renfrewshire: About 3.5 miles north-east of Beith, near the B776 junction with minor road to east, just west of the Barcraig Reservoir.

Ruin or site NS 397565 OS: 63 ** Map: 3, no: 144

Little remains of a small 14th-century keep, and there is a motte nearby.

It was held by the Wallaces of Elderslie, and it is related – by Blind Harry – that the lands were a property of Malcolm, William Wallace's father. Auchenbothie House, built in 1898, is a rambling harled mansion, with towers, turrets, corbiestepped gables and dormer windows.

Other refs: Barcraig Castle

Auchenbowie House

Stirlingshire & Clackmannan: About 3.5 miles south of Stirling, on minor road west of A872, west of the M80, at Auchenbowie.

Private NS 798874 OS: 57 ** Map: 6, no: 73

Auchenbowie House, a three-storey mansion of 1666, incorporates an altered 16th-century L-plan tower house of three storeys and an attic. A semi-hexagonal stair-tower stands in the re-entrant angle. No defensive features remain. The house was extended in 1768 and in the 19th century.

The lands belonged to the Cunninghams of Polmaise, but were bought by Robert Bruce, who was Provost of Stirling in 1555. One of the family, Captain William Bruce, killed a Charles Elphinstone in a duel at the end of the 17th century. In 1708 Auchenbowie passed by marriage to the Munros. The house is in good condition, and still occupied.

Auchenbreck Castle

Argyll & Dunbartonshire: About 11 miles north of Rothesay, on minor road just east of A886, just south of Auchenbreck Burn, 0.5 mile east of Loch Riddon, at Auchenbreck.

Ruin or site NS 020813 [?] OS: 63 * Map: 5, no: 96

Site of castle of enclosure of the Campbells of Auchenbreck, who had held the lands from about 1500. The castle was still occupied in the 18th century, but by 1870 had been demolished, and there are few remains.

Other refs: Achnabreac Castle

Auchencass Castle *see* Auchen Castle

Auchencloigh Castle

Ayrshire: About 3 miles east and south of Drongan, on minor road south of B7046, just east of Auchencloigh.

Ruin or site NS 495166 OS: 70 ** Map: 3, no: 202

Not much survives of a 15th-century castle.

Other refs: Auchincloigh

Auchencruive Castle

Ayrshire: About 3 miles east and north of Ayr, on minor roads south of B743, north of River Ayr, at or near Auchencruive.

Private NS 387235 OS: 70 * Map: 3, no: 136

Site of castle, on which stands Auchencruive House, now called Oswald Hall, an Adam mansion of 1767. The house was later extended, and built for the Oswald family, hence the name change. It has been owned by the Scottish Agricultural College since 1927.

The lands were held by the Wallaces, but in 1374 passed to the Cathcarts. The Cathcarts had their principal seat here from the 15th century. Alan Cathcart was a Protestant, and fought against Mary, Queen of Scots, at the Battle of Langside in 1568. The family were Hanoverians, and opposed the Jacobites at Sheriffmuir in 1715 and Culloden in 1746. The property passed to the Murrays in 1758, then the Oswalds from 1764 until 1925.

Other refs: Auchincruive Castle

Auchendinny House

Lothians: About 1 mile north-east of Penicuik, on minor road just east of B7026, south of River North Esk, south of Auchendinny village, at Auchendinny House.

Private NT 252613 OS: 66 ** Map: 4, no: 92

The small mansion with flanking pavilions, designed by Sir William Bruce and dating from about 1705, incorporates two vaulted chambers from an earlier house. The present house is in good repair, and still occupied.

Other refs: Auchindinny

Auchendrane Castle

Ayrshire: About 5 miles south of Ayr, on minor road east of A77, just west of the River Doon, at or near Auchendrane.

Ruin or site NS 335152 OS: 70 * Map: 3, no: 100

Site of castle, which consisted of a high tower, outbuildings, orchards, gardens and parks. It became ruinous in the 18th century, but some remains survived in 1837, and the foundations were apparently traceable later in the century. It was cleared away and replaced by Blairstone House, a castellated mansion which dated from the 18th century or earlier but was extended in 1880-1.

Mure of Auchendrane murdered Sir Thomas Kennedy of Culzean, younger son of Gilbert, 3rd Earl of Cassillis. This deed was revenge for the murder by the Earl of Mure's son-in-law, Kennedy of Bargany. The Earl had managed to escape punishment for his crime. Mure and his son were caught, tried and executed. This inspired Sir Walter Scott's play 'Auchendrane', or 'The Ayrshire Tragedy', which is apparently not one of his better pieces of work.

The property passed by marriage to the Cathcarts in 1793, and was sold to the Coats in 1868.

Other refs: Blairstone House

Auchendrane House *see* Nether Auchendrane

Auchenfedrick *see* Breckonside Tower

Auchenfedrick

Dumfriesshire: About 4 miles east and south of Moniaive, on minor road north of B729, about 0.25 miles north-west of Wallacetown, west of Bankhead, at Auchenfedrick.

Ruin or site NX 843882 OS: 78 * Map: 1, no: 154

Not much remains of two towers, which stand some 230 yards apart, with the remains of outbuildings. These may have replaced an earlier hall house.

Auchenfranco Castle

Galloway: About 5 miles south-west of Dumfries, on minor roads north of A711, just south of Lochrutton, about 0.5 miles south of Lochfoot, at Auchenfranco.

Ruin or site NX 893724 OS: 84 * Map: 1, no: 171

Site of a formerly strong castle with earthworks. There were some remains about 1825.

Auchengassel Castle

Dumfriesshire: About 4 miles north-west of Thornhill, on minor roads 2 miles west of A76, about 1.5 miles west of Drumlanrig Castle, at or near Auchengassel.

Ruin or site NX 826994 [?] OS: 78 * Map: 1, no: 148

Site of castle.

Auchengower *see* Craigoch Castle

Auchenhamper

Aberdeen & Gordon: About 6.5 miles south-west of Turriff, on minor roads north of B9024, at or near Auchenhamper.

Ruin or site NJ 645458 [?] OS: 29 * Map: 10, no: 174

Site of castle.

Auchenharvie Castle

Ayrshire: About 4.5 miles north-east of Irvine, on minor roads east of A736 at Torranyard, just north of Laigh Auchenharvie, in a quarry.

Ruin or site NS 363443 OS: 70 ** Map: 3, no: 120

Auchenharvie is a 15th-century keep, with a corbelled-out parapet and open rounds. The basement and hall were vaulted, and a turnpike stair, in one corner, climbed to all floors and to the parapet.

It was owned by the Cunninghams of Kilmaurs, but abandoned when Seabank House, at Stevenson, was built. The Cunninghams of Auchenharvie were active industrialists and extracted coal from their lands as well as running a brewery.

Auchenhove Castle

Kincardine & Deeside: About 3.5 miles north-east of Aboyne, on minor roads north of A93, east of Mill Farm, at Auchenhove.

Ruin or site NJ 555024 OS: 37 * Map: 10, no: 138

Little remains of a 16th-century castle with a courtyard. It was held by the Duguid family from about the middle of the 15th century, and burned by Cumberland's forces during the Jacobite Rising in 1746.

Auchenleck *see* Affleck Castle

Auchenmaig

Galloway: About 4 miles south-east of Glenluce, on minor road north of A747 at Glen of Luce, about 0.5 miles north of Luce Bay, at or near Auchenmaig.

Ruin or site NX 239525 [?] OS: 82 * Map: 1, no: 37

Site of tower house.

Auchenreoch Castle

Lanarkshire & Glasgow area: About 3 miles west and south of Kilsyth, south of A803 near junction with A891, at Auchinreoch Mains.

Ruin or site NS 678767 OS: 64 * Map: 3, no: 317

Site of 16th-century tower house of the Kincaid family, which later passed to the Buchanans.

Other refs: Auchinreoch

Auchenrivock Tower

Dumfriesshire: About 3 miles south of Langholm, on minor road just west of A7, just west of the River Esk, at Auchenrivock.

Ruin or site NY 373805 OS: 79 * Map: 1, no: 317

Not much remains of a tower house of the Irvines or (Irvings). It was burned by the English under Sir Christopher Dacre in 1513.

Other refs: Stakeheugh Tower

Auchenskeoch Castle

Galloway: About 6 miles east of Dalbeattie, on minor road just north of B793, about 1 mile north of Caulkerbush, at Castle Farm.

Ruin or site NX 917588 OS: 84 ** Map: 1, no: 177

Little survives of Auchenskeoch Castle, a ruined 16th-century Z-plan tower house, except two chambers with gunloops. It was held by the Lindsays, then the Crichtons, but later passed to the Mackenzies.

Auchenvole *see* Auchinvole House

Auchernach

Aberdeen & Gordon: About 2.5 miles north of Strathdon, on minor roads north of A944, north of Water of Nochty, at or near Auchernach.

Ruin or site NJ 330159 [?] OS: 37 * Map: 10, no: 65

Site of castle or old house. There was a mansion dating from 1809, which is often described as 'long reputed the best in the district', on the site of an older house. The mansion was demolished in 1945. There were vaulted chambers, and a walled garden and a doocot.

Auchernach was a property of the Forbeses. Charles Forbes of Auchernach was master of the barracks of Corgarff Castle towards the end of the 18th century. His son made his fortune in India, becoming a Lieutenant General.

Auchinames Castle

Renfrewshire: About 2 miles south of Bridge of Weir, on minor roads south of A761, about 0.5 miles south-west of Kilbarchan, at Auchenames.

Ruin or site NS 395625 OS: 63 * Map: 3, no: 143

Site of a 14th-century castle, which consisted of a very high keep or tower. The castle had been demolished by the end of the 18th century, although a vestige survived until 1825. It was a property of the Crawfords of Auchinames, who had been given the lands by Robert the Bruce in 1320. The lands were only sold by the Crawfords in the 20th century.

Other refs: Auchenames

Auchinbetrig

Dumfriesshire: About 5 miles west of Canonbie, on minor roads north of B6537 or east of B722, south of Woodside Burn, at or near Solwaybank.

Ruin or site NY 307769 [?] OS: 85 * Map: 1, no: 297

Site of tower house 'of reasonable strength', which was attacked by the English in 1596.

Other refs: Solwaybank

Auchincloigh *see* Auchencloigh Castle

Auchincross *see* Old Hall of Auchincross

Auchincruive Castle *see* Auchencruive Castle

Auchindinny *see* Auchendinny House

Auchindoun Castle

Moray: About 2.5 miles south and east of Dufftown, on minor road east of A941, just west of River Fiddich, north of Ben Main, at Auchindoun.

Ruin or site NJ 348374 OS: 28 *** Map: 10, no: 69

Auchindoun Castle is a ruined L-plan tower house of three storeys and probably formerly a garret, incorporating work from the 15th century. The walls are pierced by gunloops. A courtyard, with a round tower, encloses the tower, and ruined ranges of buildings housed a kitchen and brewhouse.

The basement of the tower was vaulted, and contained cellars, including the wine-cellar with a small stair to the floor above. A turnpike stair, in one corner, led up to

the vaulted hall on the first floor. There were private chambers in the wing and on the floors above.

The existing castle was built for John, Earl of Mar, who was murdered by his brother, James III, at Craigmillar Castle. It passed to Robert Cochrane, a master mason, one of James III's favourites. In 1482 he was hanged from Lauder Bridge by nobles led by Archibald 'Bell the Cat' Douglas, Earl of Angus.

The castle was acquired by the Ogilvies, but by 1535 had passed to the Gordons. In 1571 a party of Gordons, led by Adam Gordon of Auchindoun, besieged Corgarff Castle during a feud with the Forbeses. Corgarff was burned, killing Margaret Campbell, wife of the Master of Forbes, and her family and retainers, totalling 27 folk as told in the old ballad 'Edom o' Gordon'. Auchindoun may have been torched itself, either in 1544 or 1671 depending on the story, the tale told in the old ballad 'Fair Helen of Auchindoun'. It is a relief to know that those of us not blessed with fair face or bonnie looks or golden hair rarely get slain in old ballads.

Auchindoun, itself, was sacked again and torched in 1591 by the Mackintoshes in revenge for the murder of the Bonnie Earl o' Moray at Donibristle by the Marquis of

Huntly and Sir Patrick Gordon of Auchindoun. Gordon was later killed at the Battle of Glenlivet in 1594. The castle was restored, but by 1725 had been partly demolished for materials.

The castle has recently been consolidated, and is in the care of Historic Scotland – although a sign on the approach road warns of bulls.

OPEN: Not currently accessible to the public.

Auchindown Castle *see* Achadun Castle

Auchinleck Castle

Ayrshire: About 2 miles south-west of Catrine, on minor roads south of A76 and north of A70, about 0.5 miles west of Auchinleck House, above the Lugar Water.
Ruin or site   NS 501232   OS: 70   *   Map: 3, no: 208
Built on a rock, little remains of Auchinleck Castle, a 16th-century L-plan tower house, formerly with a moat and drawbridge. The basement was vaulted, and the site is overgrown.

The remains of an earlier castle, probably 14th century, L-shaped in plan, stand nearby to the west [NS 500232].

The lands originally belonged to the Auchinlecks, but in 1504 passed by marriage to the Boswells of Balmuto. The castle was abandoned about 1760 when the family moved to nearby Auchinleck House. One of the family was Alexander Boswell, Lord Auchinleck, a judge of the Court of Session; another was James Boswell, who accompanied Doctor Johnson on his tour of the Highlands in 1773. Sir Alexander Boswell of Auchinleck was slain in 1822 by James Stewart of Dunearn after Boswell had caricatured Stewart.

The newer house was, in turn, replaced by a late 18th-century classical mansion, after the Adams, which was restored in the 1980s.
Other refs: Old Place of Auchinleck; Auchinleck Old House

Auchinleck Old House *see* Auchinleck Castle

Auchinloss

Ayrshire: About 2 miles north-east of Kilmarnock, on minor roads east of B7038, north of the Craufurdland Water, near or at Assloss.
Ruin or site   NS 447401 [?]   OS: 70   *   Map: 3, no: 183
Site of 16th-century tower house.

Auchinreoch *see* Auchenreoch Castle

Auchintoul

Banff & Buchan: About 1 mile west of Aberchirder, on minor roads north of A97 or south of B9023, east of Burn of Auchintoul, at Auchintoul.
Private   NJ 615524 [?]   OS: 29   **   Map: 10, no: 164
Auchintoul is a 17th-century castle of the Gordons. It was formerly U-plan, before demolition, but now consists of a three-storey block with a massive round tower. The walls of the tower are pierced by shot-holes. There is a walled garden.

Patrick Gordon of Auchintoul was one of the most eminent commanders of Peter the Great in Russia. His son, Alexander Gordon of Auchintoul, was also a general in the Russian army, but returned to Scotland in 1711 and commanded part of the Jacobite army in 1715. He later wrote a biography of Peter the Great.

Auchintoul was held by the Duff Dukes of Fife in the 1890s.

Auchinvole House

Lanarkshire & Glasgow area: About 0.5 miles south of Kilsyth, on minor road west of B802 or north of B8023, just south of the Kelvin River, at Auchinvole.
Private   NS 714769   OS: 64   **   Map: 3, no: 330
Auchinvole House consisted of a plain altered 16th-century L-plan tower house. A very small stair-turret, above third-floor level, led to a small watch-chamber. A bartizan crowned one corner. The tower had been altered and extended, but has been demolished except for a doocot tower and walling, probably from a garden.

The basement was vaulted and contained a kitchen with a wide-arched fireplace. A turnpike stair climbed to second-floor level, the upper floors being reached by the stair-turret.

The house was probably built by the Stark family, and may have later been held by the Wallaces.

The house was said to be have been haunted. The ghost of a woman reportedly sat at a window, looking to the spot where her treacherously murdered lover was buried.
Other refs: Auchenvole

Auchlane Castle

Galloway: About 2.5 miles south-west of Castle Douglas, on minor roads south of A75, just south of the Auchlane Burn, at or near Auchlane.
Ruin or site   NX 741584   OS: 84   *   Map: 1, no: 119
Very little survives of a castle, materials from which were used to build Auchlane Farm. It was a property of the MacLellans in the 14th century.

Auchleshie

Stirlingshire & Clackmannan: About 1 mile south-east of Callander, on minor road north of A84 at Dalvorich, east of the Keltie Water, at or near Dalvey.
Ruin or site   NN 654072   OS: 57   *   Map: 6, no: 45
Site of castle of the Buchanan family.

Auchleuchrie

Angus & Dundee: About 4 miles north-east of Kirriemuir, on minor roads and foot north of B957, on north bank of River South Esk, 0.5 miles south-east of Auchleuchrie.
Ruin or site   NO 443573   OS: 54   **   Map: 8, no: 187
Site of castle, standing over a deep gorge in the river, of which only part of the ditch remains.
Other refs: Castle Hill, Auchleuchrie; Achlouchrie

Auchlossan House

Kincardine & Deeside: About 4 miles north-east of Aboyne, on minor roads north of A93 or south of A980, about 2 miles south of Lumphanan, at Auchlossan.
Private   NJ 571021   OS: 37   **   Map: 10, no: 142
Auchlossan is a greatly altered and extended 17th-century house of the Ross family, but still has shot-holes defending the entrance. It is still occupied.

Auchmacoy House

Aberdeen & Gordon: About 2.5 miles east of Ellon, on minor roads east of A92, north of River Ythan, at Auchmacoy.
Private   NJ 992308   OS: 30   *   Map: 10, no: 351
Auchmacoy House, a mansion dating from 1835, stands on the site of a castle. There is a fine garden and a doocot which dates from the 17th century.

It was a property of the Buchans of Auchmacoy from 1318, who still live at the 19th-century house. One of the family was General Buchan, a Jacobite who was defeated at the Battle of Cromdale by the forces of William and Mary in 1690.

Auchmeddan Castle

Banff & Buchan: About 9 miles west of Fraserburgh, near B9031, about 1 mile south-east of Pennan, 1 mile south of sea at Pennan Head, at or near Mains of Auchmeddan.
Ruin or site   NJ 850647 [?]   OS: 30   *   Map: 10, no: 286
Site of 16th-century castle, demolished in the late 18th century.

It was a property of the Bairds of Auchmeddan from 1568, but passed about 1750 to the Gordon Earls of Aberdeen. One of Thomas the Rhymer's prophecies was that 'there shall be an eagle in the craig while there is a Baird in Auchmeddan'. A pair of eagles, which had nested in a crag near the castle, are supposed to have left the area at the same time as the Bairds.

The property, however, was sold to another family of Bairds in 1858.

Auchmull Castle

Angus & Dundee: About 4 miles north and east of Edzell, on minor roads 3.5 miles north of B966 at Edzell, north of River North Esk, at or near Auchmull.
Ruin or site   NO 585748 [?]   OS: 44   *   Map: 8, no: 243
Site of a castle of the Lindsays of Edzell, built early in the 16th century and demolished in 1773. There were still remains in 1875, but nothing now remains except a stone with the date 1601.

It was apparently built by Sir David Lindsay, Lord Edzell, as a refuge for his son who was implicated in the murder of his uncle, Lord Spynie.

Auchneight

Galloway: About 18 miles south of Stranraer, on minor roads west of B7041 at Damnaglaur, at or near Auchneight.
Ruin or site   NX 110334   OS: 82   *   Map: 1, no: 23
Possible site of castle, a hunting lodge of the MacCullochs.

Auchness Castle

Galloway: About 9 miles south of Stranraer, on minor road west of A716, about 0.5 miles west of Luce Bay, about 1 mile south of Ardwell, at Auchness.
Private   NX 106447   OS: 82   **   Map: 1, no: 21
Auchness Castle is a very altered and extended 16th-century tower house of three storeys and a garret. The roof is steeply pitched, and has corbiestepped gables.
  It was a property of the MacDowall family, and is still occupied as a farmhouse.

Auchoynanie

Moray: About 2 miles east of Keith, on minor roads east of A96 or south of A95, west of Balloch Wood, at or near Mains of Auchoynanie.
Ruin or site   NJ 455495 [?]   OS: 28   *   Map: 10, no: 99
Nothing remains of a castle of the Gordons, although some traces survived until 1910.
Other refs: Auchaynanie

Auchry Castle

Banff & Buchan: About 4 miles east of Turriff, on minor road just north of B9170, 1 mile west of Cuminestown, at Castle of Auchry.
Ruin or site   NJ 788507   OS: 29   *   Map: 10, no: 259
Site of castle of the Cumming, or Comyn, family. An old mansion here was a property of the Lumsdens in the 19th century.
Other refs: Castle of Auchry

Auchterarder Castle

Perth & Kinross: About 0.5 miles north of Auchterarder, on minor road north of A824, at or near Castleton.
Ruin or site   NN 936133   OS: 58   *   Map: 8, no: 37
Little remains of Auchterarder Castle, except walls with gunloops and some earthworks.
  Malcolm Canmore probably had a hunting seat here in the 11th century, but the first reference is in 1277. Edward I of England stayed at Auchterarder in 1296. It was a property of the Grahams, but passed by marriage to the Drummonds. In 1559 a treaty was signed here between Mary of Guise as Regent and the Protestant Lords which secured freedom of worship for some time. During the Jacobite Rising in 1716, the Earl of Mar ordered the town to be burned to prevent the Campbell Duke of Argyll and his troops taking shelter.

Auchterhouse

Angus & Dundee: About 7 miles north-east of Dundee, on minor road just south of B954, at Auchterhouse.
Private   NO 332373   OS: 53   **   Map: 8, no: 158
The Old Mansion House incorporates part of a 16th-century castle of Auchterhouse, which was remodelled in the 17th century, and again when the roofline was altered. Some excellent plasterwork survives, and part of the basement is vaulted.
  Nearby is the vaulted basement of the Wallace Tower, a 15th-century keep.
  The lands were held by the Ramsays in the 13th century, but the keep was built by the Stewart Earls of Buchan, who held the lands from at least 1497. The property passed to James Stewart, Earl of Moray, then around 1660 to Patrick Maule, Earl of Panmure, before passing to the Ogilvie Earl of Airlie. The house is now a hotel.
  William Wallace is said to have visited the old castle.
Other refs: Wallace Tower; Old Mansion House, Auchterhouse
OPEN: Hotel.
Tel: 01382 320366   Fax: 01382 320400
Email: oldmansionhouse@netscapeonline.co.uk
Web: visitscotland.com/oldmansionhouse

Auchterlony *see* Kellie Castle

Auchtermeggities

Angus & Dundee: About 1.5 miles north-east of Letham, on minor roads south of A932, at or near Balmadies House
Ruin or site   NO 553497   OS: 54   *   Map: 8, no: 234
Site of castle, probably of the Piersons.
Other refs: Balmadies House

Auchtyfardle Castle

Lanarkshire & Glasgow: About 1 mile north-east of Lesmahagow, on minor road south of B7018, at or near Bogside.
Ruin or site   NS 826409 [?]   OS: 71   *   Map: 3, no: 383
Probable site of castle.
  The lands were a property of Lesmahagow Priory, and granted to the Dowane family, later passing to the Weirs and the Kennedys.

Auld Hill, Portencross *see* Portencross Castle

Auld Hoose, Old Graitney *see* Old Graitney

Auld Machan Castle *see* Broomhill Castle

Auldbar Castle *see* Aldbar Castle

Auldearn Castle

Inverness & Nairn: About 2.5 miles east and south of Nairn, on minor roads just south of A96 or north of B9111, to north-west of village of Auldearn.
NTS   NH 917557   OS: 27   *   Map: 9, no: 144
Not much remains of a 12th-century castle except a motte. It was a royal castle, built by William the Lyon. Auldearn was a royal burgh by 1180s, and the lands passed to Dunbar of Cumnock in 1511.
  Just to the south of Auldearn is the site of the battle in 1645 when the Marquis of Montrose defeated an army of Covenanters, led by General Hurry (or Urie) – a battle plan is on display. A 17th-century doocot in the earthworks was presented to The National Trust for Scotland in 1947 and is open to the public.
  Nearby Boath House, a three-storey mansion of 1830, may incorporate part of an older house or tower. It was built for the Dunbars, and is still occupied.
Other refs: Boath House
OPEN: Access at all reasonable times.
Explanatory board. Parking nearby. £

Auldgirth

Dumfriesshire: About 6 miles south and east of Thornhill, near A76 at Auldgirth, east of the River Nith.
Ruin or site   NX 915868   OS: 78   *   Map: 1, no: 176
Site of castle, which consisted of a small keep or tower house with a vaulted basement. The remains of the castle were demolished in 1927.
Other refs: Low Auldgirth

Auldhall, Boquhan *see* Boquhan Castle

Auldhame

Lothians: About 3 miles east of North Berwick, north of A198 at Auldhame, less than 0.5 miles east of Tantallon Castle, north of Seacliff beach, on a wooded ridge.
Ruin or site   NT 602847   OS: 67   **   Map: 4, no: 212
Auldhame is a 16th-century L-plan tower house. It consists of a main block of three storeys and a projecting stair-tower. The courtyard side is mostly ruined, but the beach side is complete to the wallhead.
  The basement is vaulted, part of it surviving, with a wide arched fireplace and domed bread-oven. Little remains of a courtyard.
  The lands originally belonged to the church, but were acquired by Sir Adam Otterburn of Reidhall, King's Advocate and Provost of Edinburgh, before the Reforma-

tion, and he probably built the house. The village of Auldhame was near the house, but the parish was united with Whitekirk in the 17th century, and the church demolished in 1770. There are no obvious signs of either church or village today.

One of the three corpses of St Baldred is said to have been buried here in 756, the other burial sites being Preston and Tyninghame.

Auldhouse

Lanarkshire & Glasgow: About 3 miles east of Barrhead, on minor roads west of B769, at Auldhouse.

Private   NS 557605   OS: 64   **   Map: 3, no: 252

Auldhouse is an L-plan tower house of three storeys, dating from the 17th century or earlier, but much altered in following centuries. There is a stair-tower in the re-entrant angle, and part of the building has corbiestepped gables. Many windows have been enlarged, while others have been sealed.

It was a property of the Maxwells from about 1450 until early in the 17th century. George Maxwell was involved in a witch trial at Gourock in 1676, and later fell ill with a 'hot and fiery distemper'. Dolls apparently representing him, which were stuck with pins, were found in the house of a widow, and the poor woman and her family were accused of witchcraft and burned at Paisley. The house is in good condition, and still occupied.

Auldton

Lanarkshire & Glasgow area: About 2 miles east of Wishaw, on minor roads south of A72, about 0.25 miles east of Ashgill.

Private   NS 795502   OS: 64   **   Map: 3, no: 374

Auldton, although once fortified, retains no defensive features. The house is dated 1610.

It was a property of the Hamiltons of Dalserf, then used as a farm and became ruinous. It has been restored and reoccupied.

Avoch Castle *see* Ormond Castle

Avochie Castle

Aberdeen & Gordon: About 4.5 miles north of Huntly, on minor roads south of B9118 at Milltown of Rothiemay, east of River Deveron, just east of Avochie House.

Ruin or site   NJ 536466   OS: 29   *   Map: 10, no: 126

Avochie Castle is very ruined 16th-century tower house. Only the gable ends, with a corbelled-out bartizan at one corner, survive.

It was a property of the Gordons of Avochie, who took an active part in the fighting of the reigns of Mary, Queen of Scots, and James VI. The modern Avochie House is nearby [NJ 533466].

Avondale Castle *see* Strathaven Castle

Ayr Castle

Ayrshire: In Ayr, on minor roads west of A77, on the south bank of the River Ayr, about 0.25 miles east of the harbour.

Ruin or site   NS 335222 [?]   OS: 70   *   Map: 3, no: 101

Site of castle.

William the Lyon built a castle here early around the turn of the 13th century. The castle was torched by Robert the Bruce in 1298, captured by the English in 1306, and retaken by Bruce in 1314. It was apparently garrisoned by French forces after the death of James V in 1542. The castle was ruined by 1650 and the remains were demolished when Cromwell had a Citadel built in Ayr. The Citadel was a six-sided fort with bartizans at the corners, and part survives. The old church of St John, within the fort, was used to store weapons; and the restored tower survives with a corbelled-out crenellated parapet. The Citadel was given to the Montgomerys of Eglinton .

Wallace Tower or Auld Tower [NS 338218] was a two-storey building with very thick walls. It was a property of the Cathcarts of Corbieston, but passed to the Ritchies, then in 1673 to the town. It was demolished and replaced by the present building in 1832.

There were several other old houses in Ayr, including a three-storey mansion of the Osborne family on the north side of the High Street. It was demolished in 1881.

There was also a large turreted house nearby, a property of the Blairs of Adamton, then the Chalmers of Gadgirth, but this is also gone. William Wallace is said to have escaped from the tolbooth in Ayr, but this has also been demolished.

Lady Cathcart's House [NS 336220], which dates from the 17th century, survives at 22 Sandgate, as does Loudoun Hall [NS 337221] on New Bridge Street. This latter building dates from the beginning of the 16th century, and has a vaulted basement. It was built by James Tait, a burgess of Ayr, but sold to the Campbells of Loudoun around 1530.

Other refs: Wallace Tower, Ayr

Ayton

Fife: About 5 miles north-west of Cupar, on minor road just north of A913, just south of Denmuir, at or near Ayton.

Ruin or site   NO 302183   OS: 59   *   Map: 7, no: 73

Site of 15th- or early 16th-century castle. Andrew Ayton, 'Master of the Works', built a castle here after the lands had been given to him by James IV.

Other refs: Denmuir

Ayton Castle

Borders: About 2.5 miles south-west of Eyemouth, on minor road just south of B9635, about 0.5 miles east of Ayton, north of the Eye Water.

Private   NT 929614   OS: 67   *   Map: 2, no: 357

Pronounced 'Eye-ton' after the Eye Water, Ayton Castle, a rambling 19th-century castellated mansion with a profusion of turrets, battlements and towers, stands on the site of an old castle.

Ayton was originally a property of the Aiton or Ayton family, although the castle was built by a Norman called de Vescie, but passed by marriage to the Homes. The castle was seized and slighted by the English in 1448, then besieged by the English in 1497-8 when it was believed to be one of the strongest castles between Berwick and Edinburgh. It was held by the English during the invasion of Scotland in 1547-50. The Homes were forfeited after their part in the Jacobite rising of 1715, and by 1765 the Fordyce family had acquired the property.

By 1834 the old castle had been replaced by a classical mansion, which was burned to the ground that year, and a new Baronial mansion, designed by James Gillespie Graham, was built in the 1840s for William Mitchell-Innes, then extended by the architect David Bryce in 1860. It passed to the Liddel-Grainger family, whose descendants still occupy it.

Two other towers are believed to have been near Ayton: one known as Huildie's Tower [NT 928618], held by a family called Huildie; the other Wall Tower [NT 928613], which was held by the Orkney family.

Other refs: Huildie's Tower; Wall Tower

OPEN: Open May-Sep, Sun 14.00-17.00 or by appt at any time.

Guided tours. Woodlands. Disabled access. Car and coach parking. £.

Tel: 01890 781212/781550

A' Chrannog

Argyll & Dunbartonshire: About 4.5 miles north-west of Bridgend, by minor roads and foot north of B8017, south-east tip of Loch Gruinart, north-west of Craigens.

Ruin or site   NR 294674   OS: 60   *   Map: 5, no: 5

An earthwork on a promontory is probably the remains of a fortification built by Sir James MacDonald in 1615 when his family were trying to recover their lands on Islay.

B

Baads Castle

Lothians: About 1.5 miles south-west of West Calder, on minor roads east of A704 or A71, south-west of Cairnview Mains, at or near Baads Mains.
Ruin or site NT 006614 [?] OS: 65 * Map: 4, no: 14
Probable site of castle, a property of the Douglases in the 16th century and burned in 1736.
Other refs: Badds Castle

Baberton House

Lothians: About 4 miles south west of Edinburgh castle, on minor road north of A70, near Baberton Mains.
Private NT 195696 [?] OS: 66 ** Map: 4, no: 64
Baberton House incorporates a much-altered 17th-century tower house.
It was built by Sir James Murray of Kilbaberton, Master of Works to the Crown.

Baddingsgill House

Borders: About 2.5 miles north-west of West Linton, on minor roads 2.5 miles north of A702 at West Linton, east of Lyne Water, at Baddingsgill House.
Private NT 131549 OS: 72 ** Map: 2, no: 19
Baddingsgill House, a later mansion, incorporates vaults from a tower house of the Lawsons.
Other refs: Cairnmuir

Badds Castle *see* Baads Castle

Badenheath Castle

Lanarkshire & Glasgow area: About 3.5 miles south-west of Cumbernauld, on minor roads north of A80, about 0.25 miles north of the Luggie Water, at or near Badenheath.
Ruin or site NS 713724 OS: 64 * Map: 3, no: 328
Site of a large 15th-century castle. Although part was still habitable about 1900 and there were also remains of a keep, the castle was completely demolished in 1953.
It was a property of the Boyds of Kilmarnock. Robert Boyd of Badenheath was one of Queen Mary's bodyguard at Langside in 1568, and exiled by Regent Moray as a result. The castle may have been held by the Coupers in the late 17th century, then by the Keiths from 1708.

Badenyon Castle

Aberdeen & Gordon: About 7.5 miles west of Kildrummy, on minor roads 4.5 miles north of A97 at Glenbuchat, north of Coulins Burn, at or near Badenyon.
Ruin or site NJ 340190 [?] OS: 37 * Map: 10, no: 67
Site of 13th-century castle which had a tower and ditch.
It was held by John o' Badenyon in the 13th century, but passed to the Gordons of Glenbuchat. It was abandoned about 1590, and the family moved to Glenbuchat Castle.
Other refs: Glenbuchat Castle

Badhindrocht *see* Broken Tower

Baholm Tower

Borders: About 4 miles north of Newcastleton, on east of B6399 and Hermitage Water, not far from Steele Road.
Ruin or site NY 515950 [?] OS: 79 * Map: 2, no: 178
Nothing remains of a 16th-century tower house of the Elliots.
Other refs: Barholm Tower; Bowholm Tower

Baikie Castle

Angus & Dundee: About 4.5 miles east of Alyth, on minor road south of A926 just west of Airlie, about 0.5 miles south of Airlie, at or near Baikie.
Ruin or site NO 319492 OS: 53 * Map: 8, no: 155
Site of 13th-century castle, probably on an island in the now drained Baikie Loch. The castle consisted of ranges around a courtyard with a strong wall, moat and drawbridge. There were some remains in the 19th century.
It was a property of the Fentons in the 13th century, but passed to the Lyons of Glamis around 1450.

Balachtowyrl *see* Ballochtoul Castle

Balantradoch *see* Temple Preceptory

Balbegno Castle

Kincardine & Deeside: About 0.5 miles south-west of Fettercairn, on minor roads north of B966, south-east of the Wood of Barna, at Balbegno.
Private NO 639730 OS: 45 ** Map: 10, no: 172**
Balbegno is a fine altered 16th-century L-plan tower house, to which has been added a small late 18th-century mansion. The main block of the tower rises to four storeys and a garret, but the stair-wing rises a storey higher to be crowned by a corbelled-out square watch-chamber, with corbiestepped gables. The tower is dated 1569. Fine carved figures decorate a dummy window.
The original entrance was in the re-entrant angle at the foot of the wing. It led to

a straight stair up to the hall on the first floor. A turnpike stair led to the upper floors. The vaulted basement contained the old kitchen and cellars. The hall is groined and vaulted, and the vault rests on grotesquely carved heads. There are tempera painted coats of arms of the nobility on the groin vaulting.
The Woods acquired the lands in 1488, and built the original castle. In 1687 Balbegno was sold to the Middletons, later passed to the Ogilvies, then by the 19th century to the Ramsays. It is not currently occupied.

Balbithan House

Aberdeen & Gordon: About 3.5 miles south-east of Inverurie, on minor roads south of B993 or north of B977, 2 miles north of River Don at Kintore.
Private NJ 812189 OS: 38 **** Map: 10, no: 270
Balbithan is a fine 16th-century L-plan tower house of three storeys. It has a wide stair-tower in the re-entrant angle, the upper part of which was reached by a turret stair. Bartizans crown the gables, the walls are harled, and the roof line has been altered. There are later extensions.

The main entrance is at the foot of the stair-tower. The ground floor is not vaulted, and the main stair is straight. The hall, now the library and billiard room, on the first floor, has a small turnpike to the former kitchen below and up to the second floor.

Private chambers occupied the floors above. Traces of tempera wall painting were uncovered during restoration.

The lands had belonged to the Abbey of Lindores, but were held by the Chalmers family from 1490. They moved from their previous castle at Old Balbithan [NJ 797174?] because, 'tis said, a cannon ball fired from the tower of Hallforest, a stronghold of the Keiths, landed in the courtyard of their old castle. Balbithan was sacked by Covenanters in 1640, and the Marquis of Montrose made the castle a rendezvous during the wars with the Covenanters in the 1640s. It provided a refuge for Jacobites after the Battle of Culloden in 1746. The house had passed to the Hay family in 1690, but was acquired by the Gordons early in the 18th century, then the Keith Earls of Kintore in 1859. It is in good condition, and still occupied.
Other refs: Old Balbithan

Balblair

Inverness & Nairn: About 1 mile south-west of Nairn, on minor road north of B9091, just south of railway line, at Balblair.
Private NH 873553 OS: 27 * Map: 9, no: 133
Balblair incorporates work from the late 17th century. It was held by the Rose family, who had their main stronghold at Kilravock. A party of Cummings are said to have been murdered here by the Mackintoshes in the 16th century. The castle housed some of the men of the Hanoverian army of the Duke of Cumberland in 1746, but is now used as an old people's home.

Balcanquhal Tower

Fife: About 5 miles west and south of Auchtermuchty, on minor road west of A912, at or near Balcanquhal.
Ruin or site NO 163010 OS: 58 * Map: 7, no: 24
Nothing remains of a late 15th-century castle of the Balcanquhal family, which was mentioned in 1527 and 1581.

Balcarres House

Fife: About 3 miles north of Elie, on minor road north of B942 to B941, west of the Den Burn, at Balcarres.
Private NO 476044 OS: 59 *** Map: 7, no: 126
Balcarres House, a large more modern mansion, incorporates a 16th-century Z-plan tower house, dating from 1595. Good oak panelling, carving and plasterwork

survive in the house. There is an extensive garden, and a ruined chapel from 1635 serves as the family burial ground.

The basement is vaulted, and the hall is on the first floor of the main block.

It was a property of the Lindsay Lords Menmuir from 1587, and the family became Lord Balcarres in 1633, then Earls of Balcarres in 1651. Charles II visited the same year. Colin, the 3rd Earl, fought for James VII, and had to flee to Holland between 1693 and 1700. He returned and joined the Jacobites in 1715, but was confined to Balcarres for the rest of his life as punishment. Alexander Lindsay, 6th Earl of Balcarres, also became the Earl of Crawford in 1808. The castle was much altered in 1838-43 by William Burn, and in the mid 19th century by David Bryce. The Lindsays still occupy the house.

Balcary Tower

Galloway: About 6.5 miles south of Dalbeattie, on minor roads east of A711, on west shore of Auchencairn Bay, at Balcary Tower.
Private NX 827495 OS: 84 ** Map: 1, no: 149
The old mansion may incorporate part of a castle.

Balcaskie House

Fife: About 1.5 miles north-west of Pittenweem, on minor road east of B942 at West Lodge, just east of the Dreet Burn, 1 mile north of St Monace.
Private NO 526035 [?] OS: 59 ** Map: 7, no: 137
Balcaskie, a U-plan symmetrical mansion altered and extended in 1665, 1750 and 1830, incorporates a 16th-century L-plan tower house. The original formal garden survives.

It was a property of the Strangs from before 1466, although there was probably a castle here in the 13th century, held by an Ivor Cook. John Strang of Balcaskie was slain at the Battle of Pinkie in 1547. The property was sold in 1615, and passed to the Moncrieffes, who extended the house. New service ranges were added after it was sold to Sir William Bruce in 1665. Much of Bruce's original interior remains, including painted ceilings by De Witt and plaster by Dunsterfield. The house passed to the Stewarts of Grandtully, then the Nicholsons of Kemnay, then to the Anstruthers in 1698, and is still occupied by them.

Balcastle

Lanarkshire & Glasgow area: About 0.75 miles west of Kilsyth, on minor roads north of A803, just south-east of Balcastle Farm.
Ruin or site NS 702782 OS: 64 * Map: 3, no: 325
Site of castle on motte.

It was a property of the Earls of Lennox, but passed to the Callendar family, then by marriage to the Livingstones. The family had several castles, including their stronghold at Kilsyth.
Other refs: Ba' Castle

Balcomie Castle

Fife: About 1.5 miles north and east of Crail, on minor roads east of Crail to Fifeness from A917, about 0.5 miles east of Fifeness.
Private NO 626099 OS: 59 *** Map: 7, no: 164
Balcomie Castle is a 16th-century L-plan tower house of five storeys and a garret, to which has been added an 18th-century house. It consists of a main block and offset square wing, which only joins the main block at one corner. A small stair-tower is corbelled out in one re-entrant angle, linking the first and second floors. Two two-storey bartizans, both with shot-holes, crown the wing's gable. The small gatehouse also survives. There is a walled garden.

The fine plaster ceilings from here were taken to Dean Castle, near Kilmarnock.

The lands were held by John de Balcomie in 1375, although nothing of the surviving castle is earlier than 16th century. The property passed in 1526 to the Learmonths of Clatto. Mary of Guise stayed at Balcomie after landing at Fifeness on her way to marry James V. Sir James Learmonth of Balcomie was one of the Fife Adventurers who in 1598 tried to take land on Lewis and was slain for his pains. In 1705 Balcomie passed to the Hopes, then later to the Scotts of Scotstarvit, then the Erskine Earls of Kellie. The castle is now used as a farmhouse.

The building is said to be haunted by the spirit of a young man. The lad was starved to death because he would not stop whistling – which seems a little harsh.

Balconie Castle

Ross & Cromarty: About 3.5 miles south-west of Alness, on minor roads south of
A9, south of the river Glass, on the north shore of the Cromarty Firth, on
Balconie Point.
Ruin or site NH 625652 OS: 21 * Map: 9, no: 84
Site of 12th- or 13th-century castle, a property of the Earls of Ross. Balconie House,
built in the 19th century, incorporated part of the castle, but was demolished in the
1960s or 70s.

Balcorrach Castle

Lanarkshire & Glasgow area: About 5 miles north-east of Milngavie, just north of
A891, about 1 mile west of Lennoxtown, at or near Balcorrach.
Ruin or site NS 614789 [?] OS: 64 * Map: 3, no: 286
Site of 15th-century castle of the Lennox family. The castle may have been some
distance to the north [NS 613797]. This branch of the family was descended from
Donald, son of Duncan, the 8th Earl of Lennox. They lived at the castle from 1421
until they moved to Woodhead around 1570.

Balcraig Castle

Angus & Dundee: About 7 miles south-east of Alyth, south-east of B954 about 1
mile east of Newtyle, in Glack of Newtyle, at or near Millhole.
Ruin or site NO 312400 [?] OS: 53 * Map: 8, no: 154
Site of castle, south of the ruined Hatton Castle, some remains of which survived in
the 19th century.

Balcruvie Castle *see* Pitcruvie Castle

Baldoon Castle

Galloway: About 1.5 miles south and west of Wigtown, on minor roads east of
A746, just south of the River Bladnoch, at Baldoon Mains
Ruin or site NX 426536 OS: 83 * Map: 1, no: 66
Little remains of Baldoon Castle, a property of the Dunbars of Westfield from 1530
until about 1800.

The castle is said to be haunted. In 1669 Janet Dalrymple of Carscreugh was in
love with Archibald Rutherford, son of Lord Rutherford, but he was poor and her
parents were against the marriage. They chose Sir David Dunbar of Baldoon, and
persuaded Janet to marry him. All was not well, however, although there are different versions of what happened next. Janet was either murdered on her wedding
night, after having tried to slay her new husband, or died insane soon afterwards.
Her ghost is said to be seen here on the anniversary of her death, 12 September. Sir
Walter Scott's 'Bride of Lammermuir' (and then Donizetti's opera) were inspired
by the events here.

Dunbar recovered sufficiently to marry a daughter of the Montgomery Earl of
Eglinton.

Baledgarno Castle

Perth & Kinross: About 2.5 miles west of Longforgan, on minor roads east of
B953 at Baledgarno, at or near Castlehill.
Ruin or site NO 276304 [?] OS: 53 * Map: 8, no: 141
Site of early 12th-century castle of King Edgar of Scots, although it was held by the
Cameron or Cambo family until 1365 or later. Baledgarno was visited by Edward I
of England in 1296 during the Wars of Independence. The site of the castle may be
at Castlehill.
Other refs: Balledgarno

Balfluig Castle

Aberdeen & Gordon: About 1 mile south-east of Alford, on minor roads south of
A944, in the Howe of Alford, at Balfluig.
Private NJ 586150 OS: 37 * Map: 10, no: 150**
Balfluig Castle is a plain 16th-century L-plan tower house. It consists of a main
block of three storeys and a garret with an offset wing. The offset wing joins at the
corner, and rises a storey higher to be crowned by a watch-chamber. A semi-circular stair-tower stands in one re-entrant angle, and slit windows, and there is a courtyard.

The entrance, in the main re-entrant angle within the courtyard, is defended by

gunloops. The basement is vaulted and contains the kitchen, with a wide fireplace;
and the wine-cellar, with a small stair to the hall above. A vaulted guardroom occupies the base of the wing, and there is a small pit prison. The hall, on the first floor,
has an adjoining vaulted private chamber.

Balfluig was held by the Forbes family. It was burned after the Battle of Alford in
1645 when the Marquis of Montrose defeated a Covenanter army. The property
was sold to Farquharson of Haughton in 1753. The castle was later used as a farmhouse, but derelict by the 1960s. It has been restored and reoccupied.

Another tower, probably at Little Endovie [NJ 583146], was so close to Balfluig
that the respective lairds could take shots at each other from within the walls. It is
said that the laird of Little Endovie was so wounded and slain.
Other refs: Little Endovie; Endovie
OPEN: By written appt only.
Accommodation occasionally available for holidays.
Tel: 020 7624 3200

Balfour *see* Mains of Balfour

Balfour Castle

Orkney: On south-west side of island of Shapinsay, Orkney, on minor roads west
of B9059 at Balfour, at Balfour Castle.
Private HY 475165 OS: 6 * Map: 11, no: 53
Balfour Castle, a castellated mansion, was begun in 1847 for David Balfour, and
designed by the architect David Bryce. The Balfours sold the property in 1961, and
the castle is now run as a small private hotel. There is a large walled garden.

A 17th-century house at Sound, also on Shapinsay, was held by the Buchanans,
and burned to the ground in 1746 by Hanoverian soldiers.
Other refs: Sound
**OPEN: Hotel – private guests only. Castle and garden open May-Sep,
Wed – buy ticket from tourist information office (£15.00 including
boat).**
*Guided tours. Gift shop. Afternoon tea (incl in price). Picnic area. Garden. WC. Car and
coach parking. £££.*
Tel: 01856 711282 Fax: 01856 711283
Email: balfourcastle@btinternet.com Web: www.balfourcastle.co.uk

Balfour Castle

Angus & Dundee: About 3 miles west of Kirriemuir, on minor road south of B951
at Kirkton of Kingoldrum, just north of the Cromie Burn, at Balfour Mains.
Private NO 337546 OS: 53 ** Map: 8, no: 160
Although once a strong fortress, not much remains of Balfour castle except a substantial round tower of six storeys, adjoining a more modern farmhouse. The tower
appears to have stood at one corner of a courtyard castle, other traces of which still
remain. The walls are pierced by gunloops, and there is a lean-to roof.

The basement is vaulted, and was originally reached from the courtyard, but a
new entrance has been opened.

The castle may have been built by Cardinal Beaton for Marion Ogilvie, his favourite mistress (or wife), and their many children, but it is more likely to have been
built by Marion's brother, Walter Ogilvie. It later passed to the Fotheringhams,
then the Farquharsons. The castle was reduced in size when the farmhouse was
added about 1838.

Balfour House

Fife: About 4 miles east of Glenrothes, on minor roads south of the A911, south
of the River Leven near Milton of Balgonie.
Ruin or site NO 324003 OS: 59 * Map: 7, no: 81
Balfour House, although now very ruined, incorporated the vaulted basement of a
strong 16th-century L-plan tower house, with a 17th-century wing. It was remodelled into a large castellated mansion by David Bryce in 1853, but blown up in the
1960s by the then owners of the estate. Nothing survives except a mound of rubble.

The lands were owned by the Balfours, but in 1360 passed by marriage to the
Bethunes or Beatons, who held the property at least until the end of the 19th
century. One of the family was Cardinal David Beaton, who was murdered at St
Andrews in 1546, and this is another of the places he was said to haunt. Mary,
Queen of Scots, is believed to have visited Balfour with Henry Stewart, Lord Darnley.

Balgair Castle

Stirlingshire & Clackmannan: About 1 mile west of Fintry, on minor road west of B822, north of Endrick Water, south of Overglinns farm.

Ruin or site NS 607884 OS: 57 * Map: 6, no: 35

Site of tower house, probably dating from the 16th century.

Balgair was a property of the Cunninghams of Glengarnock from 1467, but passed to the Galbraiths of Culcreuch in 1563, then the Buchanans in 1605. It may have been held by the Napiers of Gartness at one time.

Other refs: Overglinns; Old Place of Balgair

Balgarvie Castle

Fife: About 1 mile north-west of Cupar, on minor roads west of A913, at Balgarvie.

Ruin or site NO 354157 OS: 59 * Map: 7, no: 94

Site of a strong castle, said to have been taken and completely destroyed by the English during the Wars of Independence at the beginning of the 14th century – at the same time as Cupar Castle was being besieged. The lands were held by the Balfours from the 15th century or earlier.

Balgavies Castle

Angus & Dundee: About 2 miles north and east of Letham, on minor roads north of A932 and south of B9113, just east of Mains of Balgavies, at Balgavies House.

Ruin or site NO 540516 OS: 54 * Map: 8, no: 226

Little remains of a 16th-century castle, except vaulted cellars. It formerly had a moat.

Balgavies may have been held by the Ochterlony family, then the Guthries, but by 1543 it had passed to the Prestons. It was later a property of the Lindsays, but was destroyed by James VI in 1594 after the family had sheltered Jesuits. The castle was never rebuilt.

Balgillo *see* Broughty Castle

Balglass Castle

Stirlingshire & Clackmannan: About 4 miles east of Killearn, on minor roads south of the B818, near Place of Balglass.

Ruin or site NS 585876 [?] OS: 57 * Map: 6, no: 29

Only earthworks remain of Balglass Castle or 'Baron's Place', once a strong 13th-century castle. The site may have been at NS 581868.

William Wallace is said to have sheltered here during the Wars of Independence. Balglass was a property of the Stirlings of Craigbarnet from 1486, but passed to the Bontines in the 17th century. In 1648 one of the family murdered the Reverend John Collins, Presbyterian minister of Campsie, on his way home from a presbytery meeting.

Other refs: Baron's Place

Balgone House

Lothians: About 2 miles south and east of North Berwick, on minor roads south of A198 and north of B1377, at Balgone.

Private NT 567825 OS: 67 ** Map: 4, no: 204

Balgone House is an early 17th-century L-plan tower house, to which has been added a later mansion. The tower rises to three storeys and an attic within corbiestepped gables

The kitchen was in the basement, and has a wide arched fireplace. A turnpike stair led to the upper floors.

It was a property of the Rosses of Hawkhead, but passed to the Semples, then by marriage to the Sutties of Addiston in 1680.

Balgonie Castle

Fife: About 3.5 miles east of Glenrothes, on minor road south of A911 from Milton of Balgonie, on the south bank of the River Leven.

Private NO 313007 OS: 59 *** Map: 7, no: 77

Balgonie Castle is a fine 14th-century keep of five storeys and a garret within a crenellated parapet. The keep stands in a courtyard, which encloses ranges of buildings, some of them ruined, dating from the 14th to 18th centuries.

One range, mostly from 1496, incorporates a 14th-century tower and chapel. This block contains a hall, and was originally only connected to the keep by a bridge. A joining block, with a scale and platt stair, was added in 1666.

Another 15th- or 16th-century range was remodelled between 1635 and 1641, and again in 1702. The gatehouse, mostly from the 15th century, has two guardrooms and a prison with a privy.

The basement and first floor of the keep are both vaulted, and originally had separate entrances. A turnpike stair climbs from the first floor to the parapets.

The castle was built by the Sibbalds, who held the property from before 1246, but passed by marriage to Sir Robert Lundie, later Lord High Treasurer, who extended the castle about 1496. James IV visited Balgonie in 1496, as did Mary, Queen of Scots, in 1565. It was sold in 1635 to Alexander Leslie, who fought for Gustavus Adolphus of Sweden during the 30 Years War and was made a Field Marshal. Leslie was captured at Alyth in Angus after the Battle of Dunbar in 1650, while on the losing side against Cromwell, and imprisoned in the Tower of London, only the intervention of the Queen of Sweden saving his life. He died at Balgonie in 1661. The castle was captured and plundered by Rob Roy MacGregor and 200 clansmen in 1716. It was sold in 1824 to the Balfours of Whittinghame.

Balgonie is believed to be haunted, and ghostly voices and apparitions have been witnessed in the Great Hall. A skeleton was found buried under the floor in 1912.

A 'Green Lady', Green Jeanie, thought to be the spirit of one of the Lundies, has been seen in recent times, and was recorded in 1842 as being a 'well-known ghost'. Other ghosts include a 17th-century soldier, the sounds of a spectral dog, a hooded figure and a medieval apparition.

It has recently been restored and is occupied. The castle is open to the public every day, all year, and many weddings are held here.

OPEN: Open all year, daily 10.00–17.00, unless hired for a private function, including Christmas & New Year.

Guided tours. Picnic area. Disabled access to ground floor. Car and coach parking. Weddings. £.

Tel: 01592 750119 Fax: 01592 753103

Balgreggan

Galloway: About 6 miles south of Stranraer, on minor roads off B7042, 2 miles south of Stoneykirk, at or near Balgraggan.

Ruin or site NX 089500 [?] OS: 82 * Map: 1, no: 15

Site of castle of the MacDowalls, which stood near the now demolished Balgreggan House, itself a property of the Maitlands in the 19th century. There is a large motte nearby with a ditch [NX 095505], and the castle may have been nearer here.

Balhaggardie *see* Pittodrie House

Balhouffie

Fife: About 2.5 miles north of Anstruther, just north of B9171, at or near Balhouffie.

Ruin or site NO 553062 [?] OS: 59 * Map: 7, no: 144

Site of castle or old house.

The lands are mentioned in the 15th century, and were sold in 1642 to the Gibsons. A mansion was in ruins by 1802.

Balhousie Castle

Perth & Kinross: About 0.75 miles north of Perth railway station, on minor roads east of A912, about 0.25 miles west of River Tay, at North Inch, at Balhousie.

Private NO 115244 OS: 58 ** Map: 8, no: 84

Balhousie Castle, a large castellated mansion of 1860 designed by David Smart, incorporates a 16th-century L-plan tower house. One wall is dated 1631.

Balhousie was held by the Eviot family until 1478 when it was sold to the Mercers, then passed in 1625 to the Hay Earls of Kinnoul. It was taken over by the army after World War II, and in 1962 became the regimental headquarters and museum of the Black Watch.

The museum features pictures, medals, uniforms and other military mementoes, telling the story of the Black Watch from its founding in 1739 to the present day.

OPEN: Open May-Sep Mon-Sat 10.00-16.30; Oct-Apr, Mon-Fri 10.00-15.30; closed 23 Dec-4 Jan; closed last Sat of Jun; other times by appt.

Explanatory displays. Audiotours. Gift shop. WC. Car parking.
Tel: 0131 310 8530 Fax: 01738 643245 Email: bw.rhq@btclick.com

Balintore Castle

Angus & Dundee: About 5 miles north-west of Kirriemuir, on minor roads north of B951, east of Balintore, at Balintore Castle.

Private NO 290590 OS: 53 * Map: 8, no: 147

Balintore Castle, a 19th-century castellated mansion, was built for David Lyon in 1865 by David Bryce, but later held by the Chirnside family. The house was abandoned in the 1960s.

Ballagan Castle

Stirlingshire & Clackmannan: About 3.5 miles north of Milngavie, on minor road just north of the A891, at Ballagan House, about 0.5 miles south of Spout of Ballagan.

Ruin or site NS 572796 OS: 64 * Map: 6, no: 23

Site of a large 12th-century castle. It was surrounded by two courtyards, and had a moat with a drawbridge. It was known as Campsie Castle, then from 1390 Strathblane, then from 1425 Ballagan.

It was a property of the Earls of Lennox, then the Stirlings of Ballagan from 1522 until 1756. The castle was occupied until around 1760 when nearby Ballagan House, itself much altered in 1896, was built using materials from the old stronghold.

There is a fine waterfall, Spout of Ballagan, nearby.

Other refs: Campsie Castle; Strathblane Castle

Ballairdie Castle

Perthshire: About 3 miles north and west of Inchture, near B953, 0.5 miles northwest of Abernyte, at or near Ballairdie.

Ruin or site NO 253319 OS: 53 * Map: 8, no: 134

Site of castle.

Other refs: Castle of Ballairdie; Carqubannan Castle

Ballanreoch Castle

Lanarkshire & Glasgow area: About 1.5 miles north-west of Lennoxtown, on minor roads just north of A891, east of Finglen Burn, at Clachan of Campsie, at former Campsie Glen Hotel.

Ruin or site NS 610794 OS: 64 * Map: 3, no: 283

Site of castle. The property was held by the Grahams, but passed to the Brisbanes of Bishopton in 1423, and they built the castle. The property was sold in 1652 to the MacFarlanes of Keighton, and they built or rebuilt the house, possibly incorporating part of the old building. The MacFarlanes sold the property in 1921, and the building became the Campsie Glen Hotel. This building was burned out in the 1980s, but has been renovated for another use.

Other refs: Kirkton Hall; Ballencleroch

Balledgarno *see* Baledgarno Castle

Balledmond *see* Kirkton

Ballekillet *see* Ballikillet Castle

Ballencleroch *see* Ballanreoch Castle

Ballencrieff House

Lothians: About 3 miles north of Haddington, on minor road south of B1377, east of junction with A6137, at Ballencrieff.

Ruin or site NT 487783 OS: 66 *** Map: 4, no: 181

Ballencrieff House, ruinous since a fire in 1868, has recently been restored and incorporates a 16th-century castle. The walls of the main block are pierced by gun-loops. The building was remodelled in 1730.

The basement contains two cellars and a kitchen, while the hall and a private chamber occupy the first floor.

It was built by John Murray, 1st Lord Elibank, around 1586. Dr Johnson visited in 1773.

Balleshan Castle *see* Bolshan Castle

Ballfield

Fife: About 3 miles north-east of Lochgelly, by minor roads and foot south of B921, west of Dogton Stone, east of Balgreggie Farm, at Ballfield Plantation.

Ruin or site NT 230967 OS: 58 * Map: 7, no: 44

Possible site of castle.

Balliemeanoch

Argyll & Dunbartonshire: About 1 mile south of Strachur on Cowal, near junction with minor roads just west of A815, just west of River Cur, 0.5 miles south-west of Balliemeanoch.

Ruin or site NS 102999 OS: 56 ** Map: 5, no: 107

Balliemeanoch consists of a rectangular motte, with the remains of a medieval building. Another motte stands nearer Balliemeanoch [NN 108010].

Ballikillet Castle

Ayrshire: About 0.5 miles north of Millport on Great Cumbrae island, on minor road just west of B899, at Ballikillet.

Ruin or site NS 172560 [?] OS: 63 * Map: 3, no: 18

Site of castle or mansion, some remains of which survive.

It was a property of the Montgomerys, who owned much of the island until the early 18th century.

Other refs: Billikellet; Ballekillet

Ballikinrain *see* Old Ballikinrain

Ballimore

Argyll & Dunbartonshire: About 3 miles north of Kilfinan, on minor roads west of B8000, 1 mile south of Otter Ferry, east coast of Loch Fyne, south-west of Ballimore House.

Ruin or site NR 922833 OS: 55 * Map: 5, no: 84

Site of castle, on a steep-sided motte, of the MacEwans of Otter. The property passed to the Campbells in the 15th century, and the MacEwans became a broken clan, who survived by thievery. The summit of the mound has two burial enclosures of the Campbells of Otter, dating from the 19th century.

Other refs: Cnoc Mhic Eoghainn

Ballinbreich *see* Balnabreich

Ballinbreich Castle

Fife: About 2.5 miles north-east of Newburgh, on minor roads and foot north of the A913, near the south shore of the Firth of Tay, at Ballinbreich.

Ruin or site NO 271204 OS: 59 *** Map: 7, no: 59

Still an impressive ruin, Ballinbreich Castle is a 15th-century courtyard castle, which was altered and extended in the 16th century. It consists of an L-plan range, with a stair-tower in the re-entrant angle. A curtain wall encloses a rectangular courtyard.

The original entrance has been engulfed by later work, and the new entrance is defended by a round tower with gunloops. The vaulted ground floor of the range contains the kitchen. A ruined chapel has a sedilia and piscina.

The Leslies acquired the property about 1312, and began to build the castle soon afterwards, although it was rebuilt and extended in the 16th century. They were made Earls of Rothes in 1457, then Dukes of Rothes in 1680. The castle had been visited by Mary, Queen of Scots, in 1565. The property was sold to the Dundases of Kerse in the 19th century, and they were made Earls of Zetland (Shetland) in 1838, then Marquises in 1873.
Other refs: Balmbreich; Bambreich

Ballindalloch *see* Tullochcarron Castle

Ballindalloch Castle

Moray: About 7.5 miles south-west of Charlestown of Aberlour, on A95, 0.5 miles north of B9008, just east of River Avon, at Ballindalloch.
Private   NJ 178365   OS: 28   *   Map: 10, no: 27**
Ballindalloch Castle incorporates a 16th-century Z-plan tower house, which was extended and altered in 1845. The old part consists of a main block with towers projecting at opposite corners. A round stair-tower in the middle of one front, which rises a storey higher than the main block, is crowned by a square watch-chamber. A lower wing was added in the 18th century, and in the 19th century the house was extended again. The walls of the tower are pierced by shot-holes and small windows.
   The tower has been greatly altered inside, but the basement is vaulted, and the

hall would have been on the first floor, with private chambers occupying the floors above and in the towers. One fireplace is dated 1546.
   The lands originally belonged to the Ballindalloch family, but had passed to the Grants by 1499. There was an earlier castle, known as Castle Stripe [NJ 185361]. The present castle was captured and sacked by the Gordons during a feud, and was burned by the Marquis of Montrose after the Battle of Inverlochy in 1645. In the 18th century it passed by marriage to the Macphersons. The house is still occupied by the Macpherson-Grants.
   A 'Green Lady' has reputedly been seen in the dining room, and reports of a 'Pink Lady' are also recorded. Another ghost is said to be that of General James Grant, who died in 1806. Grant was very proud of the improvements he had made to the estate, and his phantom is said to ride around the lands every night to survey his achievement. He is then said to go into the wine cellar.
OPEN: Open Easter–Sep, Sun-Fri 10.30-17.00, closed Sat; other times by appt throughout the year.
Many rooms. Large collection of 17th-century Spanish paintings. Audio-visual presentation. Shop. Tea room. WC. Gardens and grounds. Rock garden. Rose garden. River walks. Famous breed of Aberdeen Angus cattle. Disabled access to ground floor and grounds. £££.
Tel: 01807 500206   Fax: 01807 500210
Email: enquiries@ballindallochcastle.co.uk
  Web: www.ballindallochcastle.co.uk

Ballindalloch Castle

Stirlingshire & Clackmannan: About 1 mile west of Balfron, on minor roads west of A875, north of Endrick Water, at Ballindalloch.
Ruin or site   NS 535885   OS: 57   *   Map: 6, no: 16
Site of castle, which is occupied by a large 19th-century mansion. A 17th-century sundial survives.
   The castle was a property of the Cunningham Earls of Glencairn, but by the 18th century the lands had passed to the Dunmores, and by the 19th to the Coopers.
Other refs: Balnadalloch

Ballindalloch Old Castle *see* Castle Stripe

Ballingray *see* Moure Castle

Ballinshoe Tower

Angus & Dundee: About 2 miles south-east of Kirriemuir, on minor roads east of A94 or west of A929, just east of Ballinshoe.
Ruin or site   NO 417532   OS: 54   **   Map: 8, no: 182
Ballinshoe is a small ruined 16th-century tower house, rectangular in plan, of two storeys and an attic. One corner is crowned by a bartizan, and there was a stair-tower, now gone, at one corner.
   The basement was not vaulted, there was one chamber on each floor, and the walls are pierced by shot-holes.
   It was a property of the Lindsay family, but passed to the Fletchers in the middle of the 17th century.

Balliol's Castle *see* Loch Doon Castle

Balloan Castle

Ross & Cromarty: About 8 miles south of Ullapool, on minor roads west of A835, at southern tip of Loch Broom, near Lochbroom Church.
Ruin or site   NH 160830 [?]   OS: 20   *   Map: 9, no: 43
Site of castle, which is said to have dated from the 13th century and was a property of the Earls of Ross. It may have later passed to the MacDonnels or the MacDonalds, or the Mackenzies.
   Inverbroom House [NH 182837] was formerly known as Balloan House, and this may be the site of the castle as there were earlier buildings here.
Other refs: Inverbroom House; Castle of Balloan

Balloch Castle

Argyll & Dunbartonshire: In Balloch, east of the A82, west of A811, at the southern end of Loch Lomond, in Balloch Castle Country Park.
Ruin or site   NS 386826   OS: 56   *   Map: 5, no: 153
Little remains of Balloch Castle, a 13th-century stronghold with a ditch, except earthworks. It was probably abandoned by the beginning of the 16th century for Inchmurrin Castle.
   It was a property of the Earls of Lennox until their forfeiture in 1425 when it passed to the Stewarts of Darnley, who were then made Earls of Lennox. The property was sold to the Colquhouns of Luss in 1652. The existing Balloch Castle, a castellated mansion dating from 1808, incorporates some materials from the old stronghold, and now houses a visitor centre. It stands in a country park.
OPEN: Country park open all year, dawn to dusk; visitor centre open Easter-Oct, daily 10.00-17.50.
Visitor centre. Country park with varying habitats and many trails. Walled garden. Gift shop. WC. Disabled limited access and WC. Car and limited coach parking.
Tel: 01389 758216   Fax: 01389 755721 Head Office

Balloch Castle

Perth & Kinross: About 1 mile east and north of Alyth, just east of B954, at Balloch.
Ruin or site   NO 263495   OS: 53   *   Map: 8, no: 137
Site of castle, on or near which a later farm was built. It was a property of the Rollo family.
   Barry Hill, about 0.5 miles to the north, is an impressive hill fort.

Ballone Castle – see below

Balloch Castle *see* Taymouth Castle

Balloch Castle *see* Inverquiech Castle

Ballochtoul Castle

Ayrshire: On east side of Girvan, on minor roads east of A714, at Ballochtoul.
Ruin or site   NX 192976   OS: 76   *   Map: 3, no: 21
Site of castle, formerly of five storeys. It was apparently a property of the Grahams of Knockdolian, but passed to Boyd of Penbrill.
Other refs: Balachtowyrl

Ballogie Castle *see* Midmar Castle

Ballone Castle

Ross & Cromarty: About 10 miles east of Tain, on minor roads and foot east of B9165, just west of sea, 0.5 miles north of Rockfield, at Ballone Castle.
Ruin or site   NH 929838   OS: 21   *   Map: 9, no: 147**
Ballone Castle is a large late 16th-century Z-plan tower house. It consists of a main block of three storeys and a garret, and a round tower and square stair-tower projecting from opposite corners. There are two ruined stair-turrets. Corbelled-out bartizans crown the corners, and have shot-holes and stone roofs. A courtyard enclosed ranges of buildings, including a bakehouse.
   The arched entrance, at the foot of one stair-tower, leads to the main turnpike stair, which climbs only to the first floor. The upper floors are reached by the turret stairs. In the square tower is a guardroom and small adjoining vaulted prison. The main block basement is vaulted and contains the kitchen, which had an arched fireplace; and wine-cellar, with a small stair up to the hall above. The hall, on the first floor, had a private chamber off the main block.
   The lands were a property of the Earls of Ross, but passed to the Dunbars of Tarbat in 1507, then to the Mackenzies in 1623, who were made Earls of Cromartie in 1703 and changed the name to Castlehaven. It was abandoned in favour of Tarbat House, a three-storey classical mansion, in the late 17th century, and was ruined by 1680. Although long unroofed, the castle is being restored.
Other refs: Tarbat Castle; Castlehaven

Ballumbie Castle

Angus & Dundee: About 4 miles north-east of Dundee, on minor roads north of B961 and west of B978, on Ballumbie Road, near ruined Ballumbie House.
Ruin or site   NO 445344   OS: 54   **   Map: 8, no: 190
Ballumbie is a ruined 14th-century courtyard castle, two round towers and part of the courtyard wall of which were incorporated into the ruinous stables of the unroofed Ballumbie House. The castle was ruinous by 1682.
   It was a property of the Lovells until the 17th century. Henry Lovell of Ballumbie was so unruly in the 1560s that James Durham of Pitkerro fled his house in terror, and the minister of Monifieth had his manse torched.

Balmachie

Angus & Dundee: About 2 miles north-west of Carnoustie, on minor road north of A92, at or near Balmachie.
Ruin or site   NO 545370 [?]   OS: 54   *   Map: 8, no: 228
Site of castle or old house.

Balmadies House *see* Auchtermeggities

Balmaghie

Galloway: About 3 miles west of Castle Douglas, on minor roads south of B795, about 1 mile west of River Dee, at or near Balmaghie House.
Ruin or site   NX 718633 [?]   OS: 84   *   Map: 1, no: 117
Site of castle of the MacGie family, who held the property from the 16th century or earlier.

Balmain *see* Fasque

Balmakewan Castle

Kincardine & Deeside: About 5.5 miles north-east of Brechin, on minor roads south of B974, just north of River North Esk, at Balmakewan.
Ruin or site   NO 667663   OS: 45   *   Map: 10, no: 187
Little or nothing remains of a castle, except one wall and a fireplace. There is a modern mansion nearby.

Balmangan Tower

Galloway: About 4 miles south-west of Kirkcudbright, on minor road south from B727, about 0.25 miles from the west side of Kirkcudbright Bay, at Balmangan.
Ruin or site NX 651456 OS: 83 ** Map: 1, no: 105
Little remains of Balmangan Tower, a 16th-century tower house, except the vaulted basement and some of the hall on the first floor. There was a stair in one corner.
Other refs: Tower of Balmangan

Balmanno Castle

Perth & Kinross: About 2 miles south of Bridge of Earn, on minor roads south of A912, about 0.25 miles south-east of Dron, 0.25 miles west of Newbigging, at Balmanno.
Private NO 144156 OS: 58 * Map: 8, no: 96**
Balmanno Castle is a 16th-century L-plan tower house, with a square tower in the re-entrant angle, to which was added new wings in the 20th century. The walls are harled and whitewashed. The castle was surrounded by a wet moat, part of which has been filled in.
   The basement has been vaulted, and the hall was on the first floor, but the interior has been completely remodelled.
   The lands originally belonged to the Balmanno family, but were sold to the Auchinlecks, or Afflecks, about 1570, who built the castle. By the late 17th century, Balmanno had passed to the Murrays of Glendoick, and in 1752 to the Belshes of Invermay. After being used as a farmhouse, it was restored and modified by Sir Robert Lorimer in 1916-21. It is still occupied.

Balmbreich *see* Ballinbreich Castle

Balmoral Castle

Kincardine & Deeside: About 7 miles west of Ballater, between Ballater and Braemar on A93, on south bank of the Dee, at Balmoral.
Private NO 255952 OS: 44 * Map: 10, no: 45
Site of 16th-century tower house, replaced by Balmoral Castle, a large castellated mansion dominated by a tall turreted and battlemented tower, which became the holiday home of Queen Victoria and Prince Albert. The old castle consisted of a tower, square in plan, with bartizans at three of the corners, as well as a walled courtyard and later additions.
   Robert II had a hunting seat here, but in 1390 the Drummonds built a stone castle. The property was acquired by the Gordon Earls of Huntly, but passed to the Farquharsons of Inverey in 1662. The Farquharsons got into debt, and had to sell the lands in 1798, probably back to the Gordons who owned it until 1852. That year it was sold to Prince Albert, husband of Queen Victoria, and in 1855 he had the present castle built. It is still often used by the royal family.
OPEN: Gardens, grounds and exhibitions open mid Apr-Jul , daily 10.00-17.00 (check opening); last recommended admission 15.30.
Display of carriages. Exhibition of paintings, works of art and Royal Tartans in the Castle Ballroom. Pony trekking and pony cart rides. Gift shop. Cafe. WC. Disabled access to exhibition, shops, cafe, gardens and WC. Car and coach parking. ££.
Tel: 01339 742334 Fax: 01339 742034
Email: info@balmoralcastle.com Web: www.balmoralcastle.com

Balmossie

Angus & Dundee: About 1 mile north-east of Broughty Ferry, on minor roads north of A930, just north of the Dighty Water, at Balmossie Mill.
Ruin or site NO 476326 [?] OS: 54 * Map: 8, no: 201
Site of 16th-century castle, probably of the Maule Earls of Panmure.

Balmuto Tower

Fife: About 2.5 miles north of Burntisland, on minor roads north of the B9157, north of Meadowfield, at Balmuto.
Private NT 221898 OS: 66 ** Map: 7, no: 39
Balmuto Castle, although much altered, incorporates a strong square 15th-century keep, with later ornamental windows, as well as two 16th-century extensions. It was originally part of a larger house, but much of this has been demolished. The corbelled-out crenellated parapet was added about 1797. The keep is dated 1594.

The basement of the keep and most of the early extensions are vaulted, and there is a mural stair.
   It was a property of the Glens, but passed to the Boswells. Sir Alexander Boswell of Balmuto was killed at the Battle of Flodden in 1513. The castle was destroyed in the 1560s or 70s, although it was later restored, and Sir John Boswell was a favourite of James VI. The tower was restored between 1974 and 1984.

Balnabreich

Moray: About 5 miles west of Keith, on minor roads north of A95, at or near Balnabreich.
Ruin or site NJ 345500 [?] OS: 28 * Map: 10, no: 68
Site of castle of the Grants.
Other refs: Ballinbreich; Castle of Balnabreich

Balnabreich Castle *see* Fuirdstone Castle

Balnadalloch *see* Ballindalloch Castle

Balnagown Castle

Ross & Cromarty: About 8 miles north-east of Alness, on minor roads north of A9 at Milton, west of Balnagown River, at Balnagown Castle.
Private NH 763752 OS: 21 * Map: 9, no: 117**
Balnagown Castle is a much-altered tower house, which dates in part from the 14th century but was remodelled in the 17th century. The old part consists of a tall

gabled block of four storeys and a garret, with two slender towers at two corners. These towers and the battlements are probably later additions. It was been much altered and added to in the late 18th and early 19th centuries by James Gillespie Graham. Many of the windows have been enlarged. One gable is dated 1672.
   The basement is vaulted. The interior of the castle is richly furnished, and the hall, on the first floor, has a fine chimney piece from 1700.
   The castle was built by the Ross family about 1375. The 8th laird, Alexander, terrorised the neighbouring properties, and was imprisoned in Tantallon Castle. He died in 1592, but his son, George, was also a wicked fellow, and held John Ross in Balnagown Castle after seizing him in Edinburgh. George was also accused of much murder, and with aiding the fugitive Earl of Bothwell. His sister, Katherine – wife of Robert Munro of Foulis – was charged with being a witch, but although some of her friends were burned, she managed to escape prosecution by getting her own people onto the jury at her trial – a sensible precaution. The property remained with the Ross family until 1978.
   'Black' Andrew Munro was a man believed guilty of many dastardly deeds. He was finally brought to account in 1522, and hanged from one of the windows off the Red Corridor of the castle. His ghost is said to haunt Balnagown, and to manifest itself to women, who he had liked to abuse in life: his female servants were made to thresh corn naked. Sounds of footsteps from unoccupied areas have also been recorded.
   The castle is also thought to be haunted by a 'Grey Lady', the ghost of a young

woman, clad in a grey dress with auburn hair and green eyes: a murdered 'Scottish princess'. Her apparition is said to have appeared in the dining room, then walked to the drawing room, and there vanished.

Both ghosts are recorded as having been witnessed in the 20th century.

Balnain House

South Highland: 40 Huntly Street, Inverness, Highland.
Private NH 663445 OS: 26 *** Map: 9, no: 91
The fine Georgian building, standing on the banks of the River Ness, was used as a field hospital by Hanoverian troops after the Battle of Culloden in 1746. It features an audio-visual exhibition about Scotland's musical heritage from prehistory until present times.
OPEN: Open all year, daily 10.00-17.00; Jul-Aug, Mon-Fri 10.00-20.00.
Explanatory displays. Gift shop. Licensed cafe bar. WC. Disabled access. Car parking nearby. Group concessions. £.
Tel: 01463 715757 Fax: 01463 713611
Email: music@balnain.com Web: www.balnain.com

Balnakeil House

Sutherland & Caithness: About 1 mile north-west of Durness, on minor road north of A838 at Durness, on Balnakeil Bay, east of sea, at Balnakeil.
Private NC 391687 OS: 9 ** Map: 12, no: 5
Balnakeil House is an altered and extended 18th-century house of three storeys and a garret, which may incorporate older work. It is now E-plan, consisting of a main block and wings projecting at either end. The walls are harled and whitewashed, and many of the windows are small.

The basement is occupied by a series of vaulted chambers at different levels. The hall, on the first floor of the main block, has a moulded fireplace.

Balnakeil was a property of the Bishops of Caithness, and they had a residence here. By 1611 it had passed to the Mackay family, then later to the Mackay Lords Reay. It is still occupied.

Balnamoon

Angus & Dundee: About 3.5 miles north-west of Brechin, on minor roads 3 miles north of A94, 0.5 miles north of the Cruick Water, at Balnamoon.
Private NO 552638 OS: 44 ** Map: 8, no: 233
Balnamoon is an altered 15th-century castle of the Collace family, to which has been added a mansion of about 1830. The property was later held by the Carnegies.

Balneil

Galloway: About 5.5 miles north of Glenluce, on minor roads north of A75, east of Water of Luce, 0.3 miles south-east of New Luce, at or near Balneil.
Ruin or site NX 179639 OS: 82 * Map: 1, no: 32
Site of castle.

The lands were a property of Glenluce Abbey, but passed to the Kennedy Earls of Cassillis, then to the Vauxs of Barnbarroch, then in the 17th century to the Rosses. In 1643 it passed by marriage to the Dalrymples of Stair, and was probably abandoned around 1668 when the mansion at Carscreugh was completed.
Other refs: Old Place of Balneil

Balnespick *see* Castle Hill, Whithorn

Balquhain Castle

Aberdeen & Gordon: About 3 miles north-west of Inverurie, on minor roads west of A96 at Drimmies, 1 miles east of Chapel of Garioch, just south of Balquhain Mains.
Ruin or site NJ 732236 OS: 38 ** Map: 10, no: 230
Balquhain Castle is a ruined 15th-century keep, rectangular in plan, of four storeys. Only one side of the keep survives. Traces of a courtyard remain, including the foundations of a round tower.

The basement, and probably the hall, were vaulted.

Balquhain was a Leslie property from 1340, but torched in 1526 during a feud with the Forbes family. Mary, Queen of Scots, spent the night here before the Battle of

Corrichie in 1562, when her forces defeated the Gordon 4th Earl of Huntly. In 1746 the castle was burned by the forces of the Duke of Cumberland, and probably never restored.
Other refs: Castle of Balquhain

Balquhollie Castle *see* Hatton Castle

Balranald *see* Clyne

Balravie Castle

Banff & Buchan: About 3 miles north and west of Turriff, on minor roads east of B9121, west of River Deveron, at or near Mountblairy.
Ruin or site NJ 694546 OS: 29 * Map: 10, no: 203
Site of castle, a property of the Stewart Earls of Buchan.
Other refs: Mountblairy

Balrossie *see* Polrossie

Baltersan Castle

Ayrshire: About 1 mile south-west of Maybole, just south of the A77 at Baltersan Mains, about 0.5 miles north-east of Crossraguel Abbey.
Ruin or site NS 282087 OS: 70 *** Map: 3, no: 64
Baltersan Castle is a 16th-century L-plan tower of three storeys, an attic and a garret. A square stair-wing is crowned by a corbelled-out watch-chamber with a projecting square oriel window. There are bartizans at two of the corners with shot-holes. The castle was begun in 1584.

The entrance, in the wing in the re-entrant angle, leads to the vaulted basement, containing the kitchen and cellars. The main turnpike stair leads to the first-floor hall, then on to the second floor. The upper floors are reached by a small turnpike stair corbelled-out in the re-entrant angle. The hall has been a fine chamber.

The castle once had gardens, orchards and parks.

The castle was built by David Kennedy of Pennyglen. The 4th Earl of Cassillis had obtained the lands in 1574 from the Commendator of Crossraguel Abbey, Allan Stewart, by boiling him in sop at Dunure Castle until he signed them over. The property passed to the Kennedys of Culzean in 1656. The building is in a dangerously ruined condition, but may have been, or is about to be, restored.

Balthayock Castle

Perth & Kinross: About 3.5 miles east of Perth, on minor road north of A85, about 0.5 miles north-east of Kinfauns, at mouth of Glen Carse, at Balthayock.
Ruin or site NO 174230 OS: 58 *** Map: 8, no: 112
Balthayock Castle is a massive, strong 14th-century keep, rectangular in plan, altered in the 16th century with the remodelling of the upper part of the building, and again around 1870 when the windows were enlarged. The entrance, at first floor level, is reached by an external stone stair, but a doorway has also been opened into the basement through a narrow window. The keep is dated 1578.

The basement and the hall, on the first floor, are vaulted and were originally connected only by a straight stair. A turnpike stair led to the upper floors.

It was a property of the Blairs of Balthayock from around the turn of the 13th century, although it is said that it was held by the Knights Templar at one time. In the 19th century it was a property of the Lawsons.

Balvaird Castle

Perth & Kinross: About 4 miles south of Bridge of Earn, on minor road and foot east of A912, about 1 mile south of Glen Farg, about 0.25 miles south-west of Balvaird.
His Scot NO 169118 OS: 58 **** Map: 8, no: 110
Balvaird Castle is a fine L-plan tower house, incorporating work from the 15th century, with the remains of outbuildings in a courtyard. The massive tower has a main block of three storeys and an attic, the wing rising a storey higher. A square stair-tower, in the re-entrant angle, is crowned by a caphouse and watch-chamber. The roof has corbiestepped gables, and the parapet projects on corbelling.

The entrance is in the foot of the stair-tower. The basement is vaulted, and contains the kitchen in the wing, with a pit-prison in the thickness of the walls. The

hall, on the first floor, has a fine fireplace.

The courtyard has had ranges of buildings, but these are mostly ruined, apart from the two-storey gatehouse. The second storey is corbelled out and contains a chapel.

Balvaird was a Barclay property, but passed by marriage to the Murrays of Tullibardine in 1500, who built the castle. The family were made Viscounts Stormont and Earls of Mansfield, and moved to Scone Palace [NO 114267]. The castle is still owned by the Murrays, but now in the care of the State.

OPEN: Open Jul-Sep, Sat-Sun 9.30-18.30; other times view from exterior.
Car and coach parking (when open). £.
Tel: 0131 668 8800   Fax: 0131 668 8888
Email: hs.explore@scotland.gov.uk   Web: www.historic-scotland.gov.uk

Balvenie Castle

Moray: About 0.5 miles north of Dufftown, on minor road south of B975 just east of junction with A941, west of River Fiddich, at Balvenie.
His Scot NJ 326409 OS: 28 **** Map: 10, no: 63
In a pleasant location, Balvenie Castle consists of a large ruinous courtyard castle, with a 13th-century curtain wall and surrounding ditch, a 16th-century L-plan tower house at one corner, and other 15th-century ruined ranges within the courtyard. The walls are pierced by gunloops.

The entrance, still with the original yett, is flanked by a projecting round tower.

The early work contains a massive vaulted cellar and bakery on the ground floor, and a great hall with a pointed vault above. The upper floors are ruined.

The 16th-century L-plan tower rises to four storeys. It has two stair-towers, the larger of which is crowned by a corbelled-out watch-chamber. The windows are small.

There are three barrel-vaulted cellars, and another in adjoining tower, which has a fine chamber on the first floor over the entrance pend.

The Comyns built the first castle, but it was destroyed or reduced by the forces of Robert the Bruce in 1308 after having been visited by Edward I in 1304. Balvenie passed to the Douglases, who rebuilt the castle. It was granted to John Stewart, Earl of Atholl, by James II following the fall of the Black Douglases in 1455. Mary, Queen of Scots, probably visited in 1562.

In 1614 Balvenie was sold to Robert Innes of Innermarkie. The castle was used by the Marquis of Montrose during his campaign against the Covenanters in 1644-5. It was nearby that a Covenanter force, led by Alexander Leslie, defeated a Royalist army in 1649, taking 900 prisoners. The Innes family suffered much by supporting the Royalist side in the Civil War, and had to sell the property to the Duffs of Braco in 1687. Balvenie was garrisoned by Jacobites in 1689, but in 1715 was held against them by the Duffs. It was not occupied after William Duff committed suicide here in 1718, and was unroofed by 1724 – although a Hanoverian force, under the Duke of Cumberland, briefly held it in 1746. The ruins were put into the care of the State in 1929.

The castle is said to be haunted by a 'White Lady', as well as a groom and two horses and other disturbances.
Other refs: Mortlach
OPEN: Open Apr-Sep, daily 9.30-18.30, last ticket sold 18.00.
Explanatory boards. Gift shop. Picnic area. WC. Car parking. Group concession. £.
Tel: 01340 820121   Fax: 0131 668 8888
Email: hs.explore@scotland.gov.uk   Web: www.historic-scotland.gov.uk

Balwearie Castle

Fife: About 2.5 miles south and west of Kirkcaldy, on minor road south of B925, north of the Tiel Burn, at Balwearie.
Ruin or site NT 251903 OS: 59 ** Map: 7, no: 50
Balwearie Castle is a ruined altered 15th-century keep, one half of which has collapsed while the other rises to about four storeys. The basement was vaulted, and there are traces of a courtyard.

Balwearie was a property of the Scotts from the 13th century, although the present remains date from after 1463. It may have been the home of the 13th-century Michael Scott, thought to have been born at Aikwood in the Borders, who was a scholar and studied at Oxford, Toledo and Padua, and is sometimes known as 'the Wizard' because of his reputed supernatural powers. He is said to have died about 1250, and is also associated with Glenluce Abbey. A later Michael, or perhaps the same, was a member of the party that went to Norway to bring Princess Margaret, the Maid of Norway, back to Scotland after the death of Alexander III in 1286. The Scotts held the property until the end of the 17th century, when it passed to the Melville Earl of Melville.

Thomas Scott of Balwearie, justice clerk, died in 1539, and his apparition, with a company of devils, is said to have appeared to James V at Linlithgow on the night of his death. Scott told the king that he was damned for serving him.

Balwherrie

Galloway: About 4.5 miles north-west of Stranraer, on minor roads east of B798 or west of A716, at or near Balwherrie.
Ruin or site NX 018658 OS: 82 * Map: 1, no: 8
Site of castle or old house. The lands of Balwherrie are mentioned in 1459 and later.

Balzieland Tower *see* Logan House

Bambreich *see* Ballinbreich Castle

Bamff House

Perth & Kinross: About 3 miles north-west of Alyth, on minor roads north of B952 at Alyth, or west of B954, or just south of Incheoch, at Bamff.
Private NO 222515 OS: 53 ** Map: 8, no: 124
Bamff House incorporates a 16th-century tower house of three storeys and an attic with corbiestepped gables. To this has been added a large mansion of 1828 and 1844, designed by William Burn. The walls are pierced by gunloops, and the windows have originally been protected with iron yetts.

The Ramsays held the property from 1232 or before, when Neis de Ramsay was physician to Alexander II. Alexander Ramsay served as physician to James VI and Charles I, and in 1666 Charles II created Gilbert Ramsay a baronet after bravery at the Battle of Rullion Green.

Banck Castle

Galloway: About 0.5 miles north-west of Carsphairn, on minor road just east of A713, east of Water of Deugh, at or near Lagwyne.
Ruin or site   NX 558939 [?]   OS: 77   *   Map: 1, no: 86
Probable site of castle, a property of the MacAdams of Waterhead. It was destroyed by fire.
Other refs: Lagwine Castle; Lagwyne Castle

Bandon Tower

Fife: About 2 miles north of Glenrothes, on minor road west of A92, about 0.5 mile east and north of Court Reservoir, at Bandon.
Ruin or site   NO 276043   OS: 59   *   Map: 7, no: 63
Bandon is a ruined 16th-century tower house of three storeys with the remains of a round turret. Most of the building has collapsed.
   It was a property of the Balfours of Balbirnie from 1498 or earlier, but then passed to the Beaton family, one of whom was Cardinal David Beaton. The Balfours, however, held Bandon between 1580 and 1630.

Banff Castle

Banff & Buchan: To east side of Banff, west of High Shore, on minor roads east of A97, just west of sea at Banff Bay, west of River Deveron, in Banff.
Ruin or site   NJ 689642   OS: 29   **   Map: 10, no: 200
Not much remains of a 12th-century castle of enclosure, except sections of the substantial curtain walls, with wide ditches and ramparts.
   It was built by the Comyn Earls of Buchan. The castle was visited by Edward I of England in 1296, who had it garrisoned, but recaptured by the Scots about 1310. The property was sold to the Sharps, and was the birthplace of Archbishop James Sharp in 1618. He was brutally murdered at Magus Muir in 1679. The castle was in ruins before 1746, and a more modern house, an Adam mansion of around 1750, is built within the walls.

Bankburnfoot

Dumfriesshire: About 6.5 miles north-west of Langholm, on minor road west of B709, north of Black Esk, at or near Bankburnfoot.
Ruin or site   NY 268925   OS: 79   *   Map: 1, no: 282
Site of tower house.

Bankend Castle *see* Isle Tower

Banklug Castle

Renfrewshire: About 5 miles south-west of Barrhead, on minor roads north of A736, 2.5 miles west of Neilston, at or near Banklug.
Ruin or site   NS 446564   OS: 64   *   Map: 3, no: 182
Site of tower house.
Other refs: Lugbank

Bannachra Castle

Argyll & Dunbartonshire: About 3 miles east and north of Helensburgh, on minor roads south of B832, just south of Fruin Water, about 1 mile west of Arden, at Bannachra.
Ruin or site   NS 343843   OS: 56   **   Map: 5, no: 141
Bannachra Castle is a ruined 16th-century tower house of three storeys, rectangular in plan, with corbiestepped gables and shot-holes under the windows.
   The lands belonged to the Galbraiths, but passed to the Colquhouns, who built the tower about 1512. Sir Humphrey Colquhoun was murdered here by the MacGregors or MacFarlanes in 1592. He was shot by an arrow through a window, on his way to bed, having been illuminated and betrayed by a treacherous servant. Bannachra may have then been sacked, and does not appear to have been used afterwards.
   This and other events led to bad blood between the MacGregors and Colquhouns,

which came to battle at Glen Fruin in 1603. The Colquhouns were defeated and slaughtered, but the MacGregors were proscribed by James VI, and their chief executed.

Bannatyne House

Angus & Dundee: About 5.5 miles south-east of Alyth, on minor road west of B954, to west of town of Newtyle, at Kirkton, at Bannatyne House.
Private   NO 294410   OS: 53   *   Map: 8, no: 149**
Bannatyne House is a late 16th-century L-plan tower house of three storeys, with extensive additions of the 18th century. The house is harled and whitewashed, and there is a bartizan, with shot-holes, crowning one corner.
   The interior has been much altered. The basement is no longer vaulted, but the kitchen has a wide arched fireplace with a massive chimney stack. The hall is on the first floor.
   It was a property of the Bannatynes. George Bannatyne compiled a unique collection of the works of authors, including Dunbar and Henryson. He began the collection in 1568 at Bannatyne, while avoiding an outbreak of plague in Edinburgh.

Bannockburn House

Stirlingshire & Clackmannan: About 2.5 miles south of Stirling, on minor roads just south of A99 just north-east of junction with M9, at Bannockburn House.
Private   NS 809889   OS: 57   **   Map: 6, no: 76
Bannockburn House, although much altered and extended, consists of a 17th-century block, with dormer windows and corbiestepped gables, and later additions.
   It was built by the Rollo family, but passed to the Pattersons. The family's Jacobite sympathies led to both the forfeiture of the lands after the 1715 Jacobite Rising, and to an invitation to Bonnie Prince Charlie to stay in the house during the 1745 Rising. It was during this visit that Bonnie Prince Charlie met Clementina Walkinshaw, who became his mistress. She followed him into exile, and they had a daughter, Charlotte, in 1753. The house is still occupied.

Bar Castle

Renfrewshire: To north of Erskine, on minor roads west of A726, west of Rashielee.
Ruin or site   NS 463709   OS: 64   *   Map: 3, no: 191
Site of castle, a property of the Stewarts of Barscube from 1490 until 1673.
Other refs: Old Bar Castle; Barscube Castle

Barbieston

Ayrshire: About 5 miles north-east of Maybole, on minor roads south of B7034, south-east Dalrymple, north of River Doon, at Barbieston.
Ruin or site   NS 368142   OS: 70   *   Map: 3, no: 126
Site of castle or fortified house, which dated from the 14th century or earlier, incorporated into a later mansion. The building was demolished in the middle of the 19th century.
   Barbieston originally belonged to the Dalrymple family, from whom the Earls of Stair are descended. It passed in the late 14th century to the Kennedys, who later became Earls of Cassillis.

Barcaldine Castle

Argyll & Dunbartonshire: About 4 miles north of Connel, on minor west of A828 at Ferlochan, 0.5 miles west of Loch Creran, 3.5 miles west of Barcaldine village.
Private   NM 907405   OS: 49   **   Map: 5, no: 79**
Formerly known as the Black Castle of Barcaldine, Barcaldine is a fine 16th-century L-plan tower house of three storeys and an attic. The two blocks of the L are slightly offset. A round stair-tower stands in the re-entrant angle and four large bartizans crown the corners of the tower. The walls are harled and whitewashed, and pierced by many gunloops and shot-holes.
   The entrance, at the foot of the stair-tower, still has a heavy iron yett behind an oak door. The basement is vaulted, and contains a kitchen and cellars. A small straight stair climbs from the wine-cellar to the hall on the first floor.
   It was built by Sir Duncan Campbell of Glenorchy, who also had castles at Kilchurn, Achallader, Loch Dochart, Finlarig, Balloch – now called Taymouth – and Edinample. The castle was garrisoned in 1645 and in 1687. In the 1680s the Campbells of Barcaldine invaded Caithness in an attempt to seize the Sinclair Earldom

(they had acquired the considerable debts of the last Earl). Although they ultimately failed, they were compensated by being created Earls of Breadalbane, and
knowing that the number of Sinclairs in the world had been greatly reduced.

The Barcaldine family were involved in the murder of Sir Colin Campbell of Glenure, the Red Fox, in 1752 which features in Robert Louis Stevenson's 'Kidnapped'.
John Campbell of Barcaldine, half brother of the Red Fox, tried James Stewart for
the murder and had him hanged, although 12 of the 15 members of the jury were
Campbells. By 1842 the castle had become ruinous, and the property was sold.

It was bought back by the Campbells in 1896, and restored. The sister of the then
owner, Harriet, died in the castle. Her apparition a 'Blue Lady' has reputedly been
seen, and it is said that on windy nights a piano can sometimes be heard.

The castle is still occupied by the Campbells of Barcaldine. Bed and breakfast
accommodation is available in July and August, although there is restricted access
to bedrooms during public opening.
Other refs: Black Castle of Barcaldine
**OPEN: Open mid Jul-mid Aug, daily 11.00-17.30; other times by appt.
Accommodation available Jul-Aug. Restricted access to bedrooms
during public opening Jul-Aug.**
*Explanatory displays. Secret stairs. Bottle dungeon. Tearoom. Gifts. Garden. Car
parking. £. B&B accommodation: 1 double ensuite room and 1 family bedroom with
shower room.*
Tel: 01631 720598 Fax: 01631 720598
Email: barcaldine.castle@tesco.net Web: www.oban.org.uk

Barclanachan *see* Kilkerran Castle

Barclanachan

Ayrshire: About 4 miles south of Maybole, on minor road south of B741, 2 miles
east and north of Dailly, south of Girvan Water, at Kilkerran.
Ruin or site NS 305030 OS: 76 * Map: 3, no: 81
Kilkerran, a classical mansion, dates from 1730, but was remodelled by William
Adam, then extended or altered in 1818 by James Gillespie Graham, in 1854 by
David Bryce, and in 1873. It may incorporate or stand on the site of the old tower of
Barclanachan

The Ferguson Lord Kilkerran moved from the old castle of Kilkerran [NS 293005]
about 1730.
Other refs: Kilkerran

Barclosh Castle

Galloway: About 2 miles north-east of Dalbeattie, on minor road east from A793,
about 0.25 miles west of Loch Fern, at Barclosh.
Ruin or site NX 855624 OS: 84 ** Map: 1, no: 159
Little remains of Barclosh Castle, a small 16th-century tower house, except a few
upstands of masonry.

It was a property of the Maxwell, Lord Herries, who helped Mary, Queen of Scots,
flee to England after the Battle of Langside in 1568.

Barcloy *see* West Barcloy

Barcloy Castle *see* Castlehill of Barcloy

Barcraig Castle *see* Auchenbathie Castle

Bardowie Castle

Lanarkshire & Glasgow area: About 1.5 miles east and south of Milngavie, on
minor roads north of the A807, north side of Bardowie Loch, at Bardowie.
Private NS 580738 OS: 64 * Map: 3, no: 263**
Bardowie Castle is a 16th-century tower house, rectangular in plan, of three storeys
and a garret within a parapet. The upper storey was later altered to provide a second hall, the crenellations becoming the windows. In the late 17th century a two-
storey wing was added, and the building was remodelled in the 18th century.

The entrance to the tower, by an arched doorway, led to a vaulted basement and
to a straight mural stair leading to the vaulted first-floor hall. A second straight
mural stair led upwards from the hall. Two small stairs, one straight and one turnpike, at opposite corners of the hall, lead to the now covered parapet.

Bardowie was a property of the Galbraiths of Baldernock, but in the 14th century
passed by marriage to the Hamiltons of Cadzow, who moved here from Craigmaddie. The family were involved in feuding, and in 1526 John Hamilton of Bardowie
was killed by the Logans of Balvie, his son was slain by the Campbells of Auchenbowie, and in 1591 they quarrelled with the Grahams of Dougalston.

In 1707 Mary Hamilton, sister of John Hamilton of Bardowie, married Gregor 'Black
Knee' MacGregor, Rob Roy's nephew and chief of the clan. The castle later passed
by marriage to the Buchanans of Leny and Spittal.

Bardrochat

Ayrshire: About 8 miles south of Girvan, on minor road south of A765, south of
River Stinchar, at Bardrochat.
Private NX 153853 OS: 76 * Map: 3, no: 15
Bardrochat was built in 1893 by the architect George M. Watson for Robert McE-
wen, then extended in 1906-8 by the architect Sir Robert Lorimer. Robert McEwen
was a noted philanthropist, and the same family still live at the house.
OPEN: Open Apr-Sep, Mon-Fri 9.00-17.00.
Partial disabled access. Accommodation available. Parking. £.
Tel: 01465 881242 Fax: 01465 881330

Bargany Castle

Ayrshire: About 4 miles east and north of Girvan, on minor road south of B741
and minor road east of B734, just south of the Water of Girvan, at Bargany.
Ruin or site NS 244003 OS: 76 * Map: 3, no: 52
Nothing remains of Bargany Castle, a property of the Kennedys. It consisted of a
tower house enclosed by a courtyard with four-storey corner towers.

Kennedy of Bargany was murdered by the Kennedy Earl of Cassillis in 1601 during
a dispute over land. The castle was demolished to build the 17th-century mansion
of Bargany, itself incorporating a fortified house, for the Dalrymple Earls of Stair.
The house became derelict, but was recently renovated, and is still held by the
same family.
OPEN: Garden: open Mar-Oct, daily 10.00-19.00.
Disabled access. Parking. £ (contributions box).
Tel: 01465 871249 Fax: 01465 871282

Barholm Castle

Galloway: About 5 miles south-west of Gatehouse of Fleet, on minor roads north of A75, just south of Barholm, about 0.25 miles from the shore of Wigtown Bay.
Ruin or site NX 521529 OS: 83 * Map: 1, no: 85**
Barholm Castle is a fine 16th-century L-plan tower house of three storeys. It consists of a main block and a small, but higher wing, which is crowned by a caphouse. The windows and doorway have fine mouldings.

The entrance leads to the vaulted basement, and to a wide turnpike stair, which rises to parapet level.

It was a property of the MacCullochs. John Knox used Barholm as a place of refuge before fleeing to the continent. In 1579 John Brown of Carsluith was called to account for the murder of MacCulloch of Barholm. The MacCullochs were ardent Covenanters. Major John MacCulloch of Barholm was executed for his part in the Pentland Rising and Battle of Rullion Green in 1666. The castle is still occupied.

Barholm Tower *see* Baholm Tower

Barjarg Tower

Dumfriesshire: About 3.5 miles south of Thornhill, on minor road 3.5 miles south of A702 at Penpoint, about 0.5 miles west of the River Nith, at Barjarg.
Private NX 876901 OS: 78 * Map: 1, no: 164**
Barjarg Tower is a 16th-century L-plan tower house of four storeys and an attic within a crenellated parapet. To this has been added a large 19th-century mansion. Bartizans, with conical roofs, crown two corners of the tower, and an open round crowns another. A later round stair-tower projects from the tower.

The entrance, in the wing, still has an iron yett and leads to the vaulted basement and the original stair.

The property was held by the Douglas Earls of Morton in the 16th century, but the tower was built by the Griersons who had been given the property in 1587. It passed by marriage in the 19th century to the Erskine Lord Tinwald, then to the Hunters.

Barmagachan

Galloway: About 5 miles south-west of Kirkcudbright, on minor road west of B727 at Borgue, about 1 mile north-west of Borgue, at Barmagachan.
Private NX 613494 OS: 83 * Map: 1, no: 99
Barmagachan is a small rectangular 17th-century house of two storeys and a garret. The gables are steeply pitched, and the thick walls are whitewashed.

The house has been much altered inside, and there is no vaulting. There may have been a small courtyard.

It was a property of the Keiths, but passed by marriage to the Muirs in 1459. It was sold to the MacLellan family in 1511. Robert MacLellan of Barmagachan, an ardent Covenanter, was forfeited for his part in the Pentland Rising of 1666. He escaped, however, with banishment to America; others were less lucky. The property was sold by the family in 1737.

Barmeal Castle

Galloway: About 3.5 miles west of Whithorn, on minor road north of A747, south-east of the Fell of Barhullion, at or near Barmeal.
Ruin or site NX 378412 OS: 83 * Map: 1, no: 49
Site of tower house, apparently once a place of some strength, some traces of which survive.

Barnbarroch Castle

Galloway: About 3 miles south-west of Wigtown, on minor road west of A714, east of B7052, at or near Barnbarroch.
Ruin or site NX 398516 [?] OS: 83 * Map: 1, no: 55
Site of much-modified castle of the Vaux family.

The lands passed by marriage to the Vaux family about 1384. Sir Patrick Vaux of Barnbarroch was made ambassador to Denmark in 1587, and a Lord of Session. The house was greatly altered in the 19th century, gutted by fire in 1941, and remains a ruin.

Barnbougle Castle

Lothians: Around 2.5 miles east of South Queensferry, on minor road east of B924, north of Dalmeny House, on southern shore of Firth of Forth.
Private NT 169785 OS: 65 ** Map: 4, no: 54
Barnbougle Castle, mostly dating from 1881, incorporates cellars from a castle of the 16th and 17th centuries. It stands in the grounds of Dalmeny House.

Barnbougle was held by the Mowbrays of Barnbougle from the 12th century until sold to the Hamilton Earl of Haddington in 1615, who in turn sold it to the Primrose family in 1662. The ruins were 'restored' around 1880 by Archibald Philip Primrose, 5th Earl of Rosebery, who was Foreign Secretary in 1886 and 1892-4, and Prime Minister from 1894-5. He supported Scottish Home Rule, and wrote many historical works.

A ghostly hound is said to haunt the grounds of Barnbougle, and appears howling shortly before the Laird of Barnbougle is to die, a story dating from the time of the Crusades. This is reputedly the origin of the name of 'Hound Point', just to the north-west of Barnbougle, and now a tanker berth.

Barncluith Castle

Lanarkshire & Glasgow area: About 1.5 miles south-east of Hamilton, on minor road south of A72, west of the Water of Avon, at Barncluith.
Private NS 729545 OS: 64 ** Map: 3, no: 341
Barncluith is a plain 16th-century tower house, rectangular in plan, of three storeys and a garret within a steeply pitched roof.

The basement is semi-subterranean, owing to the falling away of the ground. The lower floors were altered completely to house a heating system for the nearby mansion, but the upper floors are more or less original and the windows are small. It is in a good state of repair.

Barncluith – 'Baron's Cleugh' – was built in 1583 by John Hamilton, whose descendants were made Lords Belhaven. Graham of Claverhouse, Bonnie Dundee, spent the night here before the Battle of Bothwell Brig in 1679, when the Covenanters were defeated by the Duke of Monmouth.

The castle had a 16th-century terraced garden, Dutch in style.
Other refs: Baron's Cleugh

Barnes Castle

Lothians: About 2 miles north-east of Haddington, south of minor road between B1347 and Barney Mains, about 0.5 miles south-west of Athelstaneford.
Ruin or site NT 529766 OS: 66 ** Map: 4, no: 192
Barnes Castle was planned as a strong castle with six square towers around a courtyard, which enclosed ranges of buildings. It was never completed, and not built above the vaults. The entrance, in the middle of one wall, was flanked by square towers.

Sir John Seton of Barnes built the castle, but died before it was finished. He spent much of his life as a diplomat at the court of Philip II of Spain. James VI recalled him, and made him Treasurer of the Household.
Other refs: The Vaults

Barngleish *see* Barnglies

Barnglies

Dumfriesshire: About 4 miles west of Canonbie, on minor roads north of B6357, east of River Sark, at Barnglies.
Ruin or site NY 329776 OS: 85 * Map: 1, no: 303
Site of castle, which is apparently occupied by a farmhouse.
Other refs: Barngleish

Barnhill House

Argyll & Dunbartonshire: About 1.5 miles east of Dumbarton, on minor roads north of A82 at Milton, north of Loch Bowie, at Barnhill House.
Private NS 425756 OS: 64 ** Map: 5, no: 160
Barnhill House, a two-storey house mostly from the 19th century, incorporates part of a 16th-century castle.

It was a property of the Colquhouns of Milton, who moved here from Tresmass in 1543.

Barnhills Tower

Borders: About 4.5 mile west of Jedburgh, on minor roads north of B6405, north of the River Teviot, about 0.3 miles south-west of Barnhills Farm.
Ruin or site NT 589212 OS: 74 ** Map: 2, no: 225
Little remains of Barnhills, a 16th-century rectangular tower house, except the vaulted basement with traces of a stair in one corner. The basement has gunloops.
   It was a property of the Turnbulls, but was torched by the English under the Earl of Hertford in 1545.

Barns

Fife: About 1 mile west and south of Crail, on minor road north of A917, north of dismantled railway, at Old Barns.
Ruin or site NO 597068 OS: 59 ** Map: 7, no: 156
Site of castle, which belonged to the Cunninghams, but then passed through several families to the Anstruthers. It would appear to have also been known as West Barns.
   Drummond of Hawthornden stayed here in 1620. His intended bride, Mary Cunningham of Barns, was burned to death on the eve of their wedding, and Drummond was heartbroken became a learned recluse. It was apparently inhabited by farm labourers, but has been demolished.
Other refs: West Barns

Barns Tower

Borders: About 3.5 miles west and south of Peebles, on minor roads south of A72, on south bank of River Tweed, at Barns.
Ruin or site NT 215391 OS: 73 *** Map: 2, no: 48
Barns Tower is rectangular 15th-century tower house of three storeys and an attic. The tower has lost its parapet, and has a later roof and gables.
   The entrance, still with an iron yett, leads through the lobby to the vaulted basement. A narrow mural stair rises to the first floor, the upper floors reached by a modern wooden stair.
   It was a property of the Burnets of Burntisland, and built about 1498. The tower was probably abandoned when the nearby mansion was built in 1773. One of John Buchan's early novels is called 'John Burnett of Barns'.

Barnsdale Castle *see* Rescobie Castle

Barnslee

Fife: About 0.5 miles east of Markinch, on minor roads north of A911 or B9130, north of River Leven, at Barnslee.
Ruin or site NO 304015 [?] OS: 59 * Map: 7, no: 75
Site of castle of the MacDuff Thanes of Fife. The site is probably occupied by a small mansion. One story is that an underground passage goes from here to Maiden Castle, which is about three miles away.
Other refs: Dalginch; Brunton

Barntalloch Tower

Dumfriesshire: About 2 miles north of Langholm, on minor roads west of A7 and east of B709, just north of the River Esk, just south-west of Potholm.
Ruin or site NY 353878 OS: 79 * Map: 1, no: 310
Little remains of Barntalloch Tower, a tower house standing on a 12th-century rocky motte with a large bailey. The site was protected by steep slopes, while a ditch cut off the other approach. There was a burgh of barony here, which had a great annual fair, long since transferred to Langholm.
   The motte was built by the Coningsburgh family, but passed to the Lindsays in 1285.
Other refs: Staplegordon

Barnton Tower

Lothians: About 4 miles west of Edinburgh Castle, north of A90, in the Barnton area of Edinburgh.
Ruin or site NT 188758 OS: 66 * Map: 4, no: 60
Site of castle. A hunting lodge here, called 'Cramond Regis', was used by the kings of Scots. A castle was owned by Sir George Crichton, Admiral of Scotland and Sher-iff of Linlithgow, but was destroyed in August 1444 by a force led by Sir John Forrester of Corstorphine on behalf of the King. Barnton House may have been built on the site, and was a property of the Elphinstone Lord Balmerino in 1623. It was held by the Ramsays of Barnton until 1885. The house has been completely demolished.

Barnweill Castle

Ayrshire: About 3 miles north-west of Tarbolton, on minor roads south and west of B730, just west of Barnweill, east of Underhills.
Ruin or site NS 407302 OS: 70 * Map: 3, no: 148
Site of castle on motte, called 'Old Castle of Barnwyil' on Blaeu's Atlas Novus map of Kyle. A ruinous 17th-century church lies to the south. Barnweill House, dating from the 18th century, is used as a farmhouse.
   On story is that the name 'Barnweill' comes from William Wallace's torching of the Barns of Ayr, when the reputedly said 'the Barns of Ayr burn weel'. Well, it might be true.
Other ref: Old Castle of Barnwyil

Barnyards

Angus & Dundee: About 4.5 miles north of Forfar, on or near B957, just north of River South Esk, at or near Barnyards.
Ruin or site NO 479576 [?] OS: 54 * Map: 8, no: 205
Site of castle, the ruins of which were used to build the farm. Vaults and the remains of walls survived at the end of the 18th century. It was a property of the Lindsays.

Barochan House

Renfrewshire: About 2 miles north-east of Bridge of Weir, on minor roads east of the B789, at Barochan.
Private NS 415686 OS: 64 * Map: 3, no: 157
Barochan House, a 19th-century mansion, incorporates part of a much-altered 16th-century tower house. The existing building is almost all modern, the old part of the house being demolished in 1947 because of dry rot. An older castle stood on the nearby Castlehill, but it was burned down in the 16th century and replaced by the new building.
   It was a property of the Flemings from the 13th century, and seven of the family were slain at the Battle of Flodden in 1513. It passed to the Semple family in the 16th century, who held the property until 1863. The estate was subsequently divided.
   The Barochan Cross, a sculptured cross with warriors and human figures, may date from as early as the 8th century. The cross was moved from the original site here to Paisley Abbey.

Baronial Hall, Gorbals

Lanarkshire & Glasgow: To south of Glasgow, 100 yards south of Gorbals Cross, Gorbals Street, at or near The Citizens' Theatre.
Ruin or site NS 592641 [?] OS: 64 * Map: 3, no: 270
Site of a tower house which formed part of a C-plan mansion and dated from the 16th century.
   The property was held by the Bishops of Glasgow, but by 1512 had passed to the Elphinstones. George Elphinstone was knighted by James VI in 1594, and Provost of Glasgow in 1600. The property was sold to Viscount Belhaven (?) in 1634 because of debt, and the mansion extended. It was acquired by the city in 1661, and used as a town hall, school and jail, but had been completely demolished by 1870.
   There was a leper hospital and chapel here, dedicated to St Ninian, but these have also gone. Gorbals, which was formerly known as Bridgend, was well known for producing good swords and small firearms in medieval times.
Other refs: Elphinstone Tower

Baron's Cleugh *see* Barncluith Castle

Baron's Place *see* Balglass Castle

Barr Castle

Renfrewshire: About 0.5 miles west and south of Lochwinnoch, just south of the A760, about 0.25 miles north of Barr Loch.

Ruin or site   NS 347582   OS: 63   **   Map: 3, no: 111**

Barr Castle is a well-preserved 15th-century keep of four storeys and a garret, modified in the 16th century and later. A plain corbelled-out parapet has four open rounds. The walls are pierced by gunloops and other slits. The gables have collapsed except for the chimney stack, and little survives of a courtyard.

The basement contained the kitchen and a cellar. A turnpike stair led up to the hall, on the first floor, which had a large fireplace. Each of the upper floors contained two private chambers, reached by a turnpike stair.

Barr was built by the Glen family, but in the 17th century passed to the Hamiltons of Ferguslie. They abandoned the castle in the 18th century for a new house, itself replaced in the 19th century by a mansion.

Barr Castle

Ayrshire: In Galston, on minor roads south of A719 junction with B7037, on back streets on south-east side of village.

Ruin or site   NS 502365   OS: 70   *   Map: 3, no: 212**

Built on a rocky outcrop, Barr Castle is a massive 15th-century keep of five storeys. Only the corbels, for a parapet and open rounds or bartizans, survive the addition of a later roof. The windows are very small and some still have iron yetts. Nothing remains of the courtyard.

Barr was a property of the Lockharts. William Wallace is said to have taken refuge here during the Wars of Independence, but if he did it must have been in an earlier stronghold. John Lockhart of Barr was a zealous Protestant and had George Wishart, who was later martyred, preach here in 1545, and John Knox do the same in 1556. The 9th Lord sold Barr to Campbells of Cessnock in 1670. It is now a masonic hall.

Barra Castle

Aberdeen & Gordon: About 3 miles north-east of Inverurie, just west of B9170, 1.5 miles south-west of Oldmeldrum, at Barra Castle.

Private   NJ 792258   OS: 38   **   Map: 10, no: 260**

Barra Castle is a 17th-century L-plan tower house of three storeys and a garret, incorporating older work and altered and extended in the 18th century. It consists of a main block and an offset projecting wing, with a round stair-tower in one of the re-entrant angles. The stair-tower is corbelled out to square, and crowned by a watch-chamber. Two round towers, with conical roofs, project at the corner of the main block and the corner of the wing. The 18th-century addition extends from the end of the main block to form three sides of a courtyard, a curtain wall completing the last side. The house is dated 1614 and 1618.

The entrance, in the re-entrant angle within the courtyard, leads into the vaulted basement, which contains a kitchen and cellars. A wide turnpike stair leads to the hall on the first floor. The hall has been subdivided, at an early date, to form two rooms. The floors above are occupied by many private chambers.

The King family held the property from the mid 13th century. It was nearby that Robert the Bruce defeated the Comyn Earl of Buchan during the Wars of Independence in 1308. The Kings of Barra feuded with the Setons of Meldrum, one of the Kings having slain a Seton in 1530. Despite this, the property was sold to the Setons, who sold it to the Reids in 1658, then to the Ramsay family in 1750, who

Barra Castle

built the extension in 1755. Although used as a farmhouse from around 1766 to 1909, the house was restored when it passed by marriage to the Irvines in the 20th century. It is still occupied.

Barras Castle

Kincardine & Deeside: About 3.5 miles south of Stonehaven, on minor roads west of A92, at or near East Mains of Barras.
Ruin or site   NO 856804   OS: 45   *   Map: 10, no: 289
Not much remains of a castle or old house of the Ogilvies of Barras, which was demolished in 1862.
Other refs: Place of Barras; Old House of Barras

Barrogill Castle *see* Castle of Mey

Barscobe Castle

Galloway: About 2 miles north-east of New Galloway, on minor road north of A712 0.5 miles east of Balmaclellan, west of Barscobe Hill, at Barscobe.
Private   NX 660806   OS: 77   *   Map: 1, no: 109**
Barscobe Castle is a plain 17th-century L-plan tower house of three storeys and a garret. It consists of a main block and a higher wing, which is crowned by a watch-chamber. Many of the windows are small. The castle is dated 1648.
   The basement has been vaulted, although this has been removed, but a turnpike stair remains.
   Barscobe was built by MacLellans, who were ardent Covenanters, and was occupied by them until 1779. Although abandoned after use as a farmhouse, it has been restored and reoccupied.

Barscube Castle *see* Bar Castle

Barskeoch

Galloway: About 2.5 miles north-west of St John's Town of Dalry, on minor roads west of A762, , north of Garroch Burn, at or near Over Barskeoch.
Ruin or site   NX 589829   OS: 77   *   Map: 1, no: 91
Possible site of tower, although it may have been located at Barskeoch Mains [NX 608833]. Barskeoch is marked on Blaeu's Atlas at the first site.

Bass Castle *see* Bass Rock

Bass of Inverurie

Aberdeen & Gordon: To the south-east of Inverurie, just north of B993, south of meeting of River Urie and River Don, east of Port Elphinstone, at The Bass.
Ruin or site   NJ 782206   OS: 38   *   Map: 10, no: 257
Bass of Inverurie or Inverurie Castle consists of a large 12th-century motte and bailey of David, Earl of Garioch and Huntingdon. It was used by Robert the Bruce in 1307-8, and it was nearby that he defeated an army led by John Comyn, Earl of Buchan, which led to the destruction by Bruce of most of Buchan.
Other refs: Inverurie

Bass Rock

Lothians: A rock in the Firth of Forth, just over 1 mile north of Tantallon Castle, about 3 miles north-east of North Berwick, south-west of Rock.
Ruin or site   NT 602873   OS: 67   **   Map: 4, no: 213
The Bass, a huge rock in the Firth of Forth, was the hermitage of St Baldred, a saint who died here in 756. There are some remains of a chapel dedicated to the saint.
   It was a property of the Lauder family from 1318. A curtain wall of the 16th century and later, developed for artillery, was built near the only landing place. In 1567 it was a possession of Lauder of the Bass, who supported Mary, Queen of Scots, at the Battle of Carberry Hill – where she was effectively defeated. In the 1650s The Bass was used to harry Cromwell's supply ships. It was sold to the Crown in 1671, and used as a prison for Covenanters. In 1691 four imprisoned Jacobite officers captured the rock, and held it for the exiled James VII for nearly three years. The

castle was dismantled in 1701, but repaired when a lighthouse was built on the site of the Governor's House in 1902.
Other refs: The Bass; Bass Castle
OPEN: Boat trips from North Berwick go around Bass Rock – tel 01620 892838 (boat trips) or 01620 892197 (tourist information office).
Car parking.
Tel: 01620 892838

Bassendean House

Borders: About 2 miles north-west of Gordon, on minor road north of A6089, north of Eden Water, at Bassendean.
Private   NT 628458   OS: 74   *   Map: 2, no: 246
Bassendean incorporates part of an altered and extended 16th-century tower house. It has bartizans and corbiestepped gables. Many new windows have been inserted and old ones enlarged.
   It has been greatly altered inside.
   The Homes were granted the property in 1577. George Home of Bassendean had to flee to Holland because of his opposition to James VII. He helped to mastermind the Revolution of 1689, which brought William and Mary to the throne. The house is still occupied.

Bastleridge

Borders: About 3 miles south of Eyemouth, on minor roads east of B6355 or north of A6105, 1 mile east of Prenderguest, at or near Bastleridge.
Ruin or site   NT 933591 [?]   OS: 67   *   Map: 2, no: 358
Site of bastle or tower, long a property of the Homes.
Other refs: Peelwalls

Bathgate Castle

Lothians: To south of Bathgate, to south or near A89, south of railway line and station, at golf course.
Ruin or site   NS 981680   OS: 65   *   Map: 4, no: 9
Little remains of Bathgate Castle, except some earthworks.
   The lands were given by Robert the Bruce to his daughter, Marjorie, who married Walter, the High Steward, and founded the royal house of Stewart. Walter died here in 1328. The castle was dismantled in the 14th century, and the property acquired by the Marjoribanks in the 18th century.

Baturich Castle *see* Boturich Castle

Baurch

Dumfriesshire: About 2 miles east of Gretna, on minor roads south of B721, north of north coast of Solway Firth, at or near Baurch.
Ruin or site   NY 285658   OS: 85   *   Map: 1, no: 288
Site of tower house.

Bavelaw Castle

Lothians: About 2.5 miles south of Balerno outside Edinburgh, on minor road south of A70, just south of Threipmuir Reservoir.
Private   NT 168628   OS: 65   *   Map: 4, no: 53**
Bavelaw Castle is a 16th-century L-plan tower house of three storeys and an attic, extended and altered in later centuries. A small round tower projects at one corner of the main block; and the thick walls are pierced by small windows and many gunloops.
   The entrance leads into the vaulted basement, which contains cellars and a kitchen in the wing, and to the turnpike stair.
   The property was owned by the Braids, but passed by marriage to the Forresters of Niddry, then to the Mowbrays of Barnbougle, then in the 16th century to the Dundas family, who may have built the castle. Mary, Queen of Scots, is said to have stayed here (there is a Queen Mary's chamber), as well as James VI. In 1628 Bavelaw passed to the Scotts of Harperigg, but was abandoned and became ruinous. It was restored by Sir Robert Lorimer around 1900, and is still occupied.

The Castles *of* Scotland

Ba' Castle *see* Balcastle

Beanston

Lothians: About 3 miles east and north of Haddington, on minor roads north of A1 or east of B1347, at Beanston.

Private NT 549763 OS: 66 ** Map: 4, no: 199

Beanston, a much-altered house of 1621, was a property of the Hepburns of Beanston.

Bearasay

Western Isles: About 5 miles north and west of Breaclete, by minor roads and boat north of B8059, about 2 miles north and west off the north-west tip of Great Bernera, Bearasay.

Ruin or site NB 121425 OS: 13 * Map: 11, no: 21

There are ruins of buildings on the island.

Bearasay was the stronghold of Neil MacLeod about 1610. He was only captured when his wife and children were left on a skerry to drown, and was executed in 1613.

Beaton's Tower *see* Monimail Tower

Beaufort Castle

Inverness & Nairn: About 2.5 miles south and west of Beauly, on minor roads west of A833 or south of A831, just south of River Beauly, at Beaufort Castle.

Private NH 507430 OS: 26 * Map: 9, no: 56

Beaufort Castle is a modern mansion and was built about 1880, but there was an earlier stronghold, called Castle Dounie, here. It was destroyed and razed to the ground by the Duke of Cumberland after the Jacobite Rising of 1745.

The lands were originally a property of the Bissets, but passed to the Frasers of Lovat towards the end of the 13th century. The castle was besieged by the English in 1303. The Frasers feuded with the MacDonalds of Clan Ranald, which came to battle in 1544 at 'the field of shirts'. The Frasers were defeated, and Lord Lovat and

his son were both slain. The castle was damaged and captured by Cromwell in 1650.

Simon, Lord Lovat, who was active for Bonnie Prince Charlie during the Jacobite Rising of 1745, was condemned to death in 1747. However, just before he was to be executed, seating holding spectators waiting for his hanging collapsed, and killed many of them – which seems to have afforded him some grim amusement.

The castle was destroyed, and the family forfeited, but the Frasers recovered the property, and built a new house in 1882. The castle had to be sold by the family in the 1990s because of debt.

One of the Brahan Seer's prophesies was that a fox will rear a litter of cubs in the hearth at the castle – which may well have happened.

Other refs: Castle Dounie; Dounie Castle

Bedlay Castle

Lanarkshire & Glasgow area: About 3 miles south and east of Kirkintilloch, on minor roads north of A80, just north east of Muirhead, at Bedlay.

Private NS 692701 OS: 64 * Map: 3, no: 323**

Bedlay Castle is a 16th-century L-plan tower house. It consists of a main block of two storeys and projecting stair-wing, which rises a storey higher. To this has been added a later range, with two round towers, of three storeys and a garret. A small turret-stair is corbelled out in the re-entrant angle. Many of the windows have been enlarged.

The entrance, in the foot of the stair-tower, leads to the vaulted basement. The basement contains a cellar and the old kitchen. The main turnpike stair leads to the first floor.

The property belonged to the Bishops of Glasgow, but the original castle was built by the Boyds of Kilmarnock, who acquired the lands at the Reformation. In 1642 it was sold to the Robertson Lord Bedlay, who extended the building. It was sold again in 1786, and in 1805 purchased by the Campbells of Petershill. It later

passed to the Christies, is in good condition and still occupied.

The castle is said to be haunted by the ghost of Bishop Cameron, who died in suspicious circumstances about 1350. Hauntings in the house, including an apparition of a large bearded man, were recorded in the 1970s.

Another story is that at dusk on a summer's evening, on the old Glasgow-Stirling road, a coach and horses could be heard. As it approached the rear gate from the garden, the apparition of a young girl would appear and step into the road. A distant scream was then heard, followed by total silence.

During the time when it was held by Campbells, they built a mausoleum in the garden. Following the construction, there were tales of spectral appearances in the grounds. In the 18th century, they had the mausoleum moved to Lambhill cemetery – the ghosts are said to have followed.

Bedlormie

Lothians: About 4 miles west of Armadale, on minor road north of A89 at Entryfoot, about 1 mile east of Blackridge, at Bedlormie.

Private NS 874675 OS: 65 * Map: 4, no: 1

Bedlormie is a 17th-century L-plan tower house. It consists of a main block and projecting wing, with a stair-tower in the re-entrant angle.

The house does not appear to have been vaulted, although it has been greatly altered inside, only the turnpike stair remaining.

The lands were held by the Forresters of Corstorphine until the 16th century, when they passed to the Livingstone Earls of Linlithgow. The property remained with them until 1853.

Bedrule Castle

Borders: About 2 miles east of Denholm, on minor roads south of B6358, near Rule Water, near hamlet of Bedrule.

Ruin or site   NT 598180 [?]   OS: 80   *   Map: 2, no: 234

Little remains of Bedrule, a 13th-century oval castle of enclosure with five round towers and a strong gatehouse.

It was held by the Comyns, and visited by Edward I in 1298. The property passed to the Douglases in the early 14th century, then to the Turnbulls the following century. In about 1494, two hundred of the Turnbull family were brought before James IV 'with halters round their necks and naked swords in their hands'.

Beeltoun *see* Belton House

Beil *see* Biel

Belchester

Borders: About 3.5 miles north-west of Coldstream, on minor roads south of B6461 or east of A697, about 0.5 miles south of Leitholm, at Belchester.

Private   NT 794433   OS: 74   **   Map: 2, no: 320

Belchester, a mansion of about 1800 which was extended again in the late 19th century, incorporates a much-altered tower house.

Beldorney Castle

Aberdeen & Gordon: About 8.5 miles south of Keith, on minor roads south of A920, just west of River Deveron. 1.5 miles south of Haugh of Glass, at Beldorney.

Private   NJ 424369   OS: 28   *   Map: 10, no: 84**

Beldorney is a large 16th-century Z-plan tower house, which has been much extended in later centuries. It consists of a main block of three storeys, with a square tower and a large round tower at opposite corners. A slender stair-turret, in the re-entrant angle between the main block and round tower, is crowned by a watch-chamber. A later and lower wing has been added to form one side of the small courtyard, and there is an adjoining modern house. A Renaissance gateway survives, as does a courtyard wall of 1673.

The original entrance is from the courtyard in the foot of the stair-tower. The basement is vaulted, and has contained the kitchen. A stair climbs from one of the cellars to the hall above.

Beldorney belonged to the Ogilvies, but passed to the Gordons around 1500, who built the house. It was acquired by John Lyon, when the Gordons got into debt, but he was unpopular and murdered by his tenants. In 1689 the castle was pillaged by Jacobites. Beldorney was sold to the Buchans, then to the Grants. The building was restored in the 1960s, and during this restoration early wall paintings were discovered. It was restored again in the 1980s, and is occupied.

Belladrum

South Highland: About 3.5 miles south of Beauly, on minor roads east of A833, east of Belladrum Burn, at or near Belladrum.

Ruin or site   NH 518417   OS: 26   *   Map: 9, no: 59

Site of castle. Belladrum House, a modern mansion, was a property of the Merrys at the end of the 19th century.

Belltrees Peel

Renfrewshire: About 0.5 miles east of Lochwinnoch, west of A737, on spit of land in Castle Semple Loch.

Ruin or site   NS 363587   OS: 63   *   Map: 3, no: 121

Built on what was an island, Belltrees Peel is a low 16th-century tower house, built between 1547 and 1572. It is said to have been in the shape of an irregular pentagon.

It was held by the Stewarts in the 15th century, but was later a property of the Semple family. Sir James Semple of Belltrees was educated with James VI, and became ambassador to France in 1601.

Other refs: The Peel, Lochwinnoch; Beltrees

Bell's Tower *see* Kirkconnel Tower

Belmont Castle

Perth & Kinross: About 6.5 miles east of Blairgowrie, on minor roads west of B954 at Meigle, about 0.5 miles south-west of Meigle, at Belmont Castle.

Private   NO 286439   OS: 53   **   Map: 8, no: 145

Belmont Castle, a large modern castellated mansion, surrounds a tower house of three storeys and a garret within a parapet. The walls are harled. A square clock-turret has been added to the tower.

The interior has been completely altered.

The lands originally belonged to the Bishop of Dunkeld, but passed to the Nairns of Dunsinane. In the 17th century Belmont was acquired by the advocate Sir George Mackenzie of Rosehaugh – who earned the name 'Bluidy Mackenzie' for his ruthless persecution of Covenanters. The property passed by marriage to the Wharn-cliffe family, then to Sir Henry Campbell-Bannerman, Prime Minister in 1905 as leader of the Liberal Party. He was the son of a Glasgow draper, who became Lord Provost of Glasgow. He inherited a fortune from an uncle, was MP for Stirling burghs from 1868, and knighted in 1895.

The house is now a Church of Scotland Eventide home.

Other refs: Kirklands Tower; Kirkhill of Meigle

Belstane Castle

Lanarkshire & Glasgow area: About 1.5 miles north of Carluke, on minor road east of A73, at Belstane.

Ruin or site   NS 850515 [?]   OS: 72   *   Map: 3, no: 394

Site of 16th-century tower house, which was demolished in 1840 for a kale yard.

The property was owned by the Livingstones, but later passed to the Lindsays, the Maxwells, then the Douglases.

Belton House

Lothians: About 2.5 miles south west of Dunbar, on minor roads east of B6370, at Old Belton.

Ruin or site   NT 644766   OS: 67   **   Map: 4, no: 220

The remains of a 16th-century tower house, including three barrel-vaulted chambers of the basement, survive in the now ruinous house, which was itself remodelled in 1865. The house stood 'in a beautiful winding glen, embosomed among stately trees'.

The property was held by Cunninghams of Belton, but passed by marriage in 1468 to the Hays of Yester. In 1687 it was granted to David Hay, second son of the Marquis of Tweeddale.

Other refs: Beeltoun; Place of Belton

Beltrees *see* Belltrees Peel

Bemersyde House

Borders: About 3 miles east of Melrose, on minor road west of B6356, east of the River Tweed.

Private   NT 592334   OS: 73   *   Map: 2, no: 229**

Standing on a rocky knoll beside the river, Bemersyde House is an altered 16th-century tower house of six storeys, to which a mansion was added in 1761 and 1796 on both sides of the tower. The parapet of the tower has corbelled-out open rounds, and there are corbiestepped gables.

The main entrance leads into a vaulted basement with an entresol floor. The hall is on the main first floor. A turnpike stair in one corner climbs to the upper floors.

The Haigs built the castle after 1535, although they had held lands here since the 12th century. One of True Thomas's prophecies is regarding the family: 'Tide, tide, whate'er betide, There's aye be the Haigs of Bemersyde'. Gilbert Haig of Bemersyde was one of the leaders of a Scottish force who defeated the English at the Battle of Sark in 1449, and another of the family, William Haig, died at Flodden in 1513. The tower was torched by the English in 1545.

In 1854 the family died out, and the house passed to a distant relation, but in 1921 it was presented to Field-Marshal Earl Haig for his part in 'winning' World War I, and it is still held by the Haigs.

Bencloich Castle

Lanarkshire & Glasgow area: About 3.5 miles north and west of Kirkintilloch, on minor road north of A891, just north of Lennoxtown, at or near Bencloich Mains.
Ruin or site NS 635785 [?] OS: 64 * Map: 3, no: 297
Site of a castle, nothing of which survives.

The Lennox family had a castle here in the 15th century, having acquired the lands in 1421. A later house, dating from 1659, was built by the Livingstones of Kilsyth. The building, described as a tower, was almost entire in 1804, but then demolished to build cottages and farms.

Bendochty *see* Rattray Castle

Benholm Castle

Kincardine & Deeside: About 2 miles south-west of Inverbervie, on minor roads west of A92, 1.5 miles west of Gourdon, just south of Mains of Benholm.
Ruin or site NO 804705 OS: 45 ** Map: 10, no: 268
Standing above a deep ravine, Benholm Castle consists of a ruined 15th-century keep, square in plan, of four storeys with a more modern mansion attached. The keep had a crenellated corbelled-out parapet with open rounds at three corners. The stair was crowned by a square caphouse and watch-chamber.

The entrance led to two vaulted chambers in the basement. The hall, on the first floor, had a large fireplace, and windows with stone seats.

Benholm was a property of the Lundie family, who built the castle, but later passed to the Ogilvies, then the Keith Earls Marischal. It was from here that in 1623 the 5th Earl's widow stole money and jewels 'to a great amount'. The property was sold to the Scots in 1659, who added a large mansion. The house was used as a hospital by Polish troops during World War II, but was abandoned and became ruinous. It was about to be restored when a storm in 1992 brought down half the keep.

The castle is said to be haunted.
Other refs: Tower of Benholm

Benholm's Lodging

Aberdeen & Gordon: About 2 miles north of Aberdeen railway station, on minor roads north of A956, just south of River Don, in Tillydrone suburb.
Private NJ 936089 OS: 38 * Map: 10, no: 328**
Benholm's Lodging is an altered small early 17th-century Z-plan tower house. It consists of a main block of three storeys and two round towers at opposite corners.

The gables of the main block are corbiestepped, and the round towers have conical roofs.

The tower originally stood near the Nethergate, in Aberdeen, and was built by Sir Robert Keith of Benholm, brother to the 5th Earl Marischal. There was a dispute in the family over property, and Sir Robert seized and garrisoned Deer Abbey, and besieged his brother's castle of Ackergill in Caithness. The Lodging was later occupied by Dr Patrick Dun, principal of Marischal College, then the Hays of Balbithan, then various merchants. It was acquired by Aberdeen City in 1918. It was neglected, but then moved stone by stone from the centre of the city to Tillydrone, near St Machar's Cathedral, to make way for offices. It is in a good state of repair.

Wallace Tower, another name for the lodging, is said to come from Wellhouse Tower.
Other refs: Wallace Tower

Beoch

Ayrshire: About 3 miles north of Maybole, on minor roads west of B7024, at Beoch.
Ruin or site NS 295145 OS: 70 * Map: 3, no: 71
Site of castle, some remains of which survived in the 19th century. The present building is modern.
Other refs: Buyack

Bernera Barracks

South Highland: About 0.3 miles north of Glenelg, on minor roads west of A87 at Shiel Bridge, on east side of Glenelg Bay, at mouth of Glen More, at Bernera.
Ruin or site NG 815197 OS: 33 ** Map: 9, no: 26
Built to control the crossing to Skye, Bernera Barracks, which dates from the 1720s, consists of ruined ranges of buildings around a courtyard, and had accommodation for over 200 men. The garrison was reduced after the failure of the Jacobite rising in 1746, and abandoned about 1800. The road to Glenelg mostly follows the course of an old military way.

There was a castle nearby [NG 816202], known as Caisteal Mhicleod on the high ground to the north of the river. It was a property of the MacLeods of Dunvegan.

There are three fine brochs or duns – Dun Telve [NG 829172], Dun Troddan [NG 833172] and Dun Grugaig [NG 851159] – in Glenelg.
Other refs: Glenelg

Berriedale Castle

Sutherland & Caithness: About 5 miles south-west of Dunbeath, by track and foot east of A9, south of mouth of Berriedale Water at sea, just south of Berriedale grave yard.
Ruin or site ND 121224 OS: 17 * Map: 12, no: 44
Not very much remains of a 15th-century keep and courtyard, except for fragments of the curtain wall and foundations of ranges of buildings and a gatehouse.

It was held by the Cheynes in the 14th century, then passed by marriage to the Sutherlands, then to the Oliphants by 1526. It was sold to the Sinclair Earls of Caithness in 1606.

This is said to be the site of Beruvik in the Orkneyinga Saga.

Bervie *see* Hallgreen Castle

Berwick Castle

Borders: In Berwick-upon-Tweed, on minor road south of A1, site at Berwick railway station.
Ruin or site NT 999590 [?] OS: 75 ** Map: 2, no: 365
Although now in England, Berwick was a Scottish burgh by 1120 and had its own castle. It was taken and sacked in 1296 by Edward I of England, and reputedly 16,000 of its inhabitants were slaughtered. It was at the castle that the 'Ragman Roll' was signed, the lists of names of the many Scots who did homage to Edward I. The burgh and castle were recovered by the Scots in 1318, but then changed hands many times until 1482 when they finally fell to the English for the last time. It was at the castle that Isabella Duff, Countess of Buchan, was imprisoned for four years in a cage hung from the walls, as punishment for crowning Robert the Bruce.

The castle survived this only to be destroyed when the railway was built, and a station constructed on the site. Parts of the walls still exist.

Bheagram Castle *see* Caisteal Bheagram

Biel

Lothians: About 3.5 miles west and south of Dunbar, on minor roads south of A1, just north of the Biel Water, at Biel.
Private NT 637759 OS: 67 ** Map: 4, no: 218
Biel was a fortified house with vaulted cellars said to date from the 13th century. This was incorporated into a castellated mansion, reputedly the longest house in Europe, in the first half of the 19th century. It was much reduced to its present form in 1950-1.

The property was sold to John Hamilton, 1st Lord Belhaven, in 1647 (or 1641), and remained with the family until 1958 when sold to the present owner Charles Spence. The 2nd Lord Belhaven made a famous speech in the old Scottish parliament in 1706 against the Union of Parliaments. There is a stone plaque on the house bearing the inscription in Latin: 'The first year of the betrayal of Scotland'.

There is a tradition that the well-being of the property is dependent on the good repair of 'The Cardinal's Hat' [NT 624744] on top of the rood well at Stenton.

'The White Lady of Biel', reputedly an apparition of Anne Bruce of Earlshall, is said to have been seen in the grounds. She was wife of the 3rd Lord Belhaven, who himself died in 1721.
Other ref: Beil
OPEN: By appt only.
Contribution to charity.
Tel: 01620 860355

Bield Tower

Borders: At Tweedsmuir, on A701, west of River Tweed, at Bield.
Ruin or site NT 100248 OS: 72 * Map: 2, no: 6
The present house, which is a two-storey L-plan building, dates from the 18th century and was formerly used as a coaching inn. It is said to stand on the site of an tower house, which was occupied in 1696. This is very close to the site of Oliver Castle, however, and this may be the same site.

Over Oliver was a 16th-century tower house of the Tweedies, while Nether Oliver passed from the Flemings to the Hays.

Biggar Castle

Lanarkshire & Glasgow area: Near Biggar, on High Street, near A702 junction with B7016, east of the River Clyde.
Ruin or site NT 043378 OS: 72 * Map: 3, no: 451
Site of a once impressive 13th-century castle of the Flemings, who were descended from Baldwin, a Fleming who settled here in the 12th century. The family moved to nearby Boghall in the 14th century. The castle site passed to a Reverend Livingston in 1659, and the site was subsequently occupied by an inn, slaughter house, a school, and now a house.

William Wallace won a battle against the English at Biggar in 1297, although the size of the English army – said to number 60,000 men, according to Blind Harry – seems a little large even for Wallace to manage.

The town of Biggar retains its medieval plan with a wide main street and narrow strips of land behind each property.

Biggar Kirk

Lanarkshire & Glasgow: Off A72 or A702, Manse, High Street, Biggar, Lanarkshire.
Private NT 042378 OS: 72 * Map: 3, no: 450**
The impressive 16th-century church, dedicated to St Mary, has a crenellated tower with gunloops, and is still used as a parish church. The kirk was a collegiate establishment, founded by Malcolm Lord Fleming in 1545, although it probably incorporates older work. It was restored in the 1870s and again in the 1930s, and there are good examples of modern stained glass.
OPEN: Open during summer months.
Explanatory displays. Sales area. Induction loop for church services. Car parking.
Tel: 01899 211050

Bigla Cumming's Castle *see* Tom Pitlac

Billie Castle

Borders: About 3 miles north and west of Chirnside, on minor roads and footpath west of B6437, just north of Billiemains.
Ruin or site NT 851596 OS: 67 * Map: 2, no: 340
Billie Castle is a very ruined 15th-century keep and courtyard with a gatehouse, of which only earth works and the base of the massive keep survive. There was a stone stair in one corner, and a ditch protected the castle on three sides.

It was a property of the Dunbars from the beginning of the 13th century, then the Douglas Earl of Angus from 1435. Archibald Douglas, Earl of Angus, sheltered here in 1528 while James V was unsuccessfully besieging Tantallon Castle. In 1540 the castle was forfeited to the Crown, and Billie was granted to the Rentons, but in 1544 it was one of the many Border castles destroyed by the English under the Earl of Hertford. There is a verse associated with the castle:
'Bunkle, Billie and Blanerne,
Three castles strong as airn;
Built when Davy was a bairn;
They'll all gang doon
Wi' Scotland's croon
And ilka ane shall be a cairn.'
This could, however, be said of many other Scottish castles and towers.

Billikellet *see* Ballikillet Castle

Binghill Castle

Aberdeen & Gordon: About 3 miles west of Dyce, on minor roads north of A96 or east of B979, 1 mile east of Blackburn, at or near Tyrebagger Hill.
Ruin or site NJ 844127 [?] OS: 38 * Map: 10, no: 284
Site of castle.

Binns, The *see* The Binns

Birkenbog House

Banff & Buchan: About 2 miles south-east of Cullen, on minor roads south of A98 or east of B9018, south of Kilnhillock, at Birkenbog.
Private NJ 536651 OS: 29 * Map: 10, no: 127
Birkenbog House, an early 18th-century house, incorporates an older round tower, and there was an E-plan tower house here around 1590.

It was a property of the Abercrombies of Birkenbog. The house was abandoned about 1770 for Glasshaugh House, a three-storey symmetrical mansion, which is itself now derelict.

Birnie *see* Castle Hill, Birnie

Birrens

Dumfriesshire: About 6 miles south-east of Lockerbie, on minor roads south of B725 or north of B722, 0.5 miles south-east of Middlebie, north of Mein Water, at Birrens.
Ruin or site NY 219751 OS: 85 ** Map: 1, no: 267
There was a Roman fort here, of which well-preserved ditches survive, and there have been many finds recovered from the site. Within the earthworks was a small tower house of the Carlyles, dating from the 15th century or earlier, and possibly occupied until the middle of the 18th century.

Birsay Palace *see* Earl's Palace, Birsay

Birse Castle

Kincardine & Deeside: About 5 miles south of Aboyne, on minor roads 6 miles west of B976 or 5 miles south of B976 on Fungle Road, west of Ballochan, at Birse.
Private NO 520905 OS: 44 * Map: 10, no: 120**
Birse Castle, a sizeable L-plan mansion, incorporates a simple 16th-century tower house, square in plan, of three storeys. It has a round tower, corbelled out to square, at one corner.

It was a property of the Bishops of Aberdeen, but later passed to the Gordons of

Cluny. The castle was apparently torched about 1640 by local people as they felt the Gordons were encroaching on their lands. The castle was abandoned and was very ruined by 1887, but was rebuilt in 1930 and extended. It is still occupied.

Bishop Sinclair's Tower

Perth & Kinross: About 4 miles north-east of Dunkeld, on minor road just north of A923, 1 mile north-east of Loch of Butterstone, just south-east of Laighwood Farm.

Ruin or site   NO 077457   OS: 53   *   Map: 8, no: 68

Nothing remains of Bishop Sinclair's Tower, which may have dated from the late 13th century. In the 1790s two vaults and the fragments of other buildings still survived. The castle was defended by wet ditches and had a drawbridge.

It was probably built by William Sinclair, who was Bishop of Dunkeld from 1309. He was active on behalf of Robert the Bruce, and is known as the 'fighting bishop' as in 1317 he rallied the Scots against an English attack on Dunfermline. He crowned Edward Balliol in 1333, and died in 1337.

Other refs: Laighwood

Bishopton House

Renfrewshire: About 3.5 miles north-east of Bridge of Weir, on minor roads south of the A8, about 0.5 miles west of Bishopton.

Private   NS 422717   OS: 64   **   Map: 3, no: 164

Bishopton House consists of a tall 17th-century L-plan tower house, which probably incorporates earlier work. The main block rises to three storeys and a garret, and has a projecting wing with a scale-and-platt stair. The tower was extended by a lower wing and later work. The building has been considerably altered inside and out after being remodelled in 1916-20.

The original entrance, in the wing, leads to the stair and to a passage which opens into the vaulted basement. The basement contains a kitchen with a wide fireplace.

Bishopton was a property of the Brisbane family from 1332 or earlier until about 1671, and they built the castle. It passed to the Walkinshaws, Dunlops, Semples, then the Maxwells of Pollok. In the 19th century the property was held by the Stewart Lord Blantyre. The castle was used as a farmhouse, but is now part of the Convent of the Good Shepherd.

Other refs: Old Bishopton

Bishop's Castle, Glasgow *see* Glasgow Castle

Bishop's Castle, Partick *see* Partick Castle

Bishop's Castle, Scrabster *see* Scrabster Castle

Bishop's House, Elgin

Moray: In Elgin, on minor roads north of A96, south of the River Lossie, just west of the cathedral at top North College Street, at edge of Cooper Park.

His Scot   NJ 221631   OS: 28   *   Map: 10, no: 41**

A residence of the Bishops of Moray, Bishop's House is an altered 15th-century L-plan building. In the 16th century a new wing was added to the stair-tower and this, with the tall arched gateway piercing it, is the part that survives. The walls rise to three storeys, while the stair-tower rises a storey higher to be crowned by a gabled watch-chamber. The windows are small, except for a fine oriel.

The basement is vaulted, and the main block contained a kitchen and two cellars. The wing, within the tall archway, has a standing-place for horses, with an adjoining cellar. The hall, on the first floor, formerly had fresco paintings.

The house was built a few years after the town and cathedral had been torched by Alexander Stewart, the Wolf of Badenoch. After the Reformation it passed to the Setons. The house was complete until the end of the 18th century, when it was unroofed. In 1851 the Grant Earl of Seafield started to demolish it, but was stopped by protests, and the building was gifted to Elgin and later restored.

The L-plan North College was probably built as the Deanery in 1520. It is a fairly substantial building with good mouldings, corbels and pedimented dormer windows. In 1858 it was transformed into an elegant modernised house.

South College probably incorporates part of the 16th-century Archdeacon's house,

and still has some of its boundary wall. Both these buildings were possibly fortified.

The Tower Hotel, in the High Street, may incorporate a 17th-century fortified lodging of the Leslies.

Other refs: Elgin

OPEN: Open all year – view from exterior.

Bishop's House, Lochwood

Lanarkshire & Glasgow area: About 3.5 miles north-west of Coatbridge, on minor roads west of A752, south of Bishop Loch, at or near Lochwood.

Ruin or site   NS 692666   OS: 64   *   Map: 3, no: 322

Site of hunting lodge of the Bishops of Glasgow, some remains of which survived in the 19th century. They are said to have linked the Molendinar burn, Hogganfield, Frankfield and Bishops lochs with a canal system so that they could sail here by barge from Glasgow Castle. The property passed to the Main family after the Reformation.

Other refs: Lochwood

Bishop's Palace, Birnie *see* Castle Hill, Birnie

Bishop's Palace, Brechin

Angus & Dundee: To west of Brechin, on minor roads south of A935 or east of B9134, just north of River South Esk, near Brechin Cathedral.

Ruin or site   NO 597601   OS: 54   Map: 8, no: 247

Little remains of the Bishop's Palace, built by Bishop Carnock between 1429 and 1450, except one fragment of wall of the gateway. The ruins of the palace and the canons' houses survived at the end of the 17th century, but there are now no remains.

Other refs: Carnock's Tower, Brechin; Brechin, Bishop's Palace

Bishop's Palace, Dornoch *see* Dornoch Palace

Bishop's Palace, Dunblane

Stirlingshire & Clackmannan: In Dunblane, on minor roads west of B8033, east of Allan Water, south-west of Cathedral.

Ruin or site   NN 782014 [?]   OS: 57   *   Map: 6, no: 66

Not much survives of the Bishop's Palace, dating from the 13th century, except the remains of four vaulted ranges. The palace appears to have consisted of ranges of buildings around a courtyard.

There may have been a church from the 7th century, founded by Saint Blane, but the Cathedral dates from the 13th century, except for the 11th-century tower. The nave became ruined after the Reformation, while the choir was used as the parish church. The church was restored from 1889, and there is fine wood carving dating from the 15th century.

Margaret Drummond, who was poisoned along with her two sisters at Drummond Castle, is buried in the choir. She is believed to have been murdered to free James IV to marry Margaret Tudor, sister of Henry VIII of England.

Other refs: Dunblane, Bishop's Palace

Bishop's Palace, Dunkeld

Perth & Kinross: To south-west of Dunkeld, on minor roads west of A923, north of River Tay, to the south-west of the Cathedral.

Ruin or site   NO 013424   OS: 53   *   Map: 8, no: 53

Site of castle, the Episcopal palace for the cathedral here, which was built in 1408 by Bishop Cardney, although nothing now remains. It consisted of a keep with a later wing and chapel, added by Bishop Brown. Dunkeld was besieged by Jacobites in 1689, and the palace may not have survived the burning of the town.

Dunkeld was a Christian centre from early times, and Kenneth MacAlpin had relics brought from Iona to here to protect them from Norse raids.

The cathedral is a fine building dating from the 13th century, the choir of which is used as a parish church, while the nave is ruined. Alexander Stewart, the Wolf of Badenoch, is buried here.

Other refs: Dunkeld Castle

Bishop's Palace, Dunoon *see* Dunoon Castle

Bishop's Palace, Fetternear *see* Fetternear House

Bishop's Palace, Kinneddar *see* Kinneddar Castle

Bishop's Palace, Kirkwall

Orkney: To west of Kirkwall on Orkney, on minor road just south of A960, across road from cathedral, off Palace Road, next to Earl's Palace.

His Scot   HY 449108   OS: 6   *   Map: 11, no: 50**

The Bishop's Palace consists of a hall block of three storeys and an attic, with a large four-storey round tower at one end. The building incorporates work from the 12th century, although it was much altered in the 16th century. The round tower had a corbelled-out parapet and a garret of two storeys. The palace was altered again at the end of the 16th century, with the addition of an arched loggia and corbelled-out turrets. A courtyard wall probably joined it to the nearby Earl's Palace.

The basement was vaulted, for which the walls of the hall block were thickened. The basement of the round tower was also vaulted and the upper floors contained square chambers. A turnpike stair in the round tower led to the upper floors.

The palace was the residence of the Bishops of Orkney from the 12th century, when Orkney was held by the Norsemen. King Haakon Haakonson died here in 1263 after his defeat at the Battle of Largs.

In 1568 Robert Stewart, an illegitimate son of James V, acquired the lands of the Bishopric of Orkney, as well as the Earldom in 1581. He was followed by his son, Patrick Stewart, in 1593, who had the Bishop's Palace remodelled and built the Earl's Palace, which was completed about 1600. He was executed in 1615 along with his father, Robert, after Patrick had led a rising in the islands, which had to be put down by the Sinclair Earl of Caithness.

The palace returned to the Bishops of Orkney, who occupied it until 1688. It is now in the care of Historic Scotland.

OPEN: Open Apr-Sep, daily 9.30-18.30; last ticket 30 mins before closing.

Explanatory displays. Parking nearby. £. Joint entry ticket for all Orkney monuments available.

Tel: 01856 875461   Fax: 0131 668 8800

Email: hs.explore@scotland.gov.uk   Web: www.historic-scotland.gov.uk

Bishop's Palace, Loch Goul

Aberdeen & Gordon: About 2 miles north-east of Dyce, just north of B997 at Locheye, to south of Bishops' Loch (Loch Goul).

Ruin or site   NJ 911142   OS: 38   *   Map: 10, no: 316

Little or nothing remains of a palace of the Bishops of Aberdeen, dating from the 13th century. The site is to be cleared of undergrowth and surveyed. The palace is said to have consisted of a hall, two other blocks, and a small chapel or oratory.

Bishop Hugh de Benholm was burned to death here in the palace in 1282. It may not have been reused after the Bishop's Palace in Old Aberdeen was built in the 14th century.

Other refs: Loch Goul, Bishop's Palace

Bishop's Palace, Lower Kenly *see* Inchmurtach

Bishop's Palace, Old Aberdeen

Aberdeen & Gordon: To north of Aberdeen, on minor roads west of A956, east of St Machar's Cathedral, New Aberdeen.

Ruin or site   NJ 940088 [?]   OS: 38   *   Map: 10, no: 333

Site of bishop's palace for St Machar's Cathedral. It was destroyed in 1336, but had been rebuilt by the middle of the 15th century. It was demolished in the 1650s and the materials removed to built Cromwell's Citadel in Aberdeen.

There was a Christian community here from 580, and the nearby cathedral [NJ 939088] is dedicated to St Machar, a disciple of St Columba, who was active among the Picts and founded a church here. It became the cathedral of the Bishops of Aberdeen in 1140, but the present building dates mostly from 1350-1520. The nave and twin towers remain in use, while the transepts are ruinous and chancel is gone – the central tower collapsed in 1688. There is an impressive heraldic ceiling of panelled oak dating from 1520, which is decorated with the coats of arms of many noble families; and impressive stained-glass windows. There are many interesting memorials in the burial ground.

Other refs: Old Aberdeen, Bishop's Palace

Bishop's Palace, Penninghame

Galloway: About 3 miles south of Newton Stewart, on minor roads west of A714, just north of Bishop Burn, south-east of Mains of Penninghame.

Ruin or site   NX 409605   OS: 83   *   Map: 1, no: 59

Site of palace or castle defended by a moat of the Bishops of Galloway, perhaps dating from the 13th century. It may have been superseded by a residence at Clachary.

Other refs: Penninghame Hall

Bishop's Palace, Stow *see* Stow

Bishop's Tower, Cramond *see* Cramond Tower

Bite-About Pele

Borders: About 4.5 miles south of Duns, on minor roads south of B6460, about 0.3 miles north-east of West Printonan.

Ruin or site   NT 784467   OS: 74   *   Map: 2, no: 317

Bite-About Pele is a very ruined L-plan tower house, dating from the 16th century, the wing of the L probably housing a stair. The name is said to be derived from when the tower was being besieged by the English. The garrison was low in provisions, and had to share their food, each taking a 'bite about'.

Other refs: West Printonan; Printonan

Black Barony Castle

Borders: About 4 miles north of Peebles, on minor road west of A703 at Eddleston, near the meeting of the Fairydean Burn and the Eddleston Water.

Private NT 236472 OS: 73 * Map: 2, no: 55

Black Barony, a symmetrical house of about 1700-15, incorporates a 16th-century L-plan tower house, although parts may be older.

   The lands were held from 1412 by the Murrays of Haltoun, Darnhall or Blackbarony, and they built the castle. Sir John Murray of Darnhall was knighted by James VI, and enclosed his lands, earning the nickname 'The Dyker'. The property passed from the Murrays, was used as a hotel, but is now a training college for the ambulance service.

Other refs: Darnhall Castle; Blackbarony Castle

Black Bog Castle

Ayrshire: West of New Cumnock, on minor road and foot west of the A76, south of the River Nith, just north of old church.

Ruin or site NS 618137 OS: 71 * Map: 3, no: 289

Nothing remains of Black Bog Castle, a 13th-century castle of the Cospatrick Earls of Dunbar and March. It passed to the Dunbars of Cumnock, then to Crichton of Sanquhar in 1622. It was ruinous in 1580, but had apparently been rebuilt by 1650. The last vestiges were removed towards the end of the 18th century.

   This site is noted as also being called Blackcraig by the RCAHMS, but this refers to another castle [NS 634082] some miles south of Cumnock.

Other refs: Cumnock Castle; New Cumnock

Black Castle

Lothians: About 2.5 miles west of Cockburnspath, on minor roads west of A1, to west of Oldhamstocks, near Oldhamstocks Burn.

Ruin or site NT 738707 OS: 67 * Map: 4, no: 226

Site of castle, some remains of which survived about 1800. It was a property of the Hepburns.

Black Castle *see* Cakemuir Castle

Black Castle of Barcaldine *see* Barcaldine Castle

Black Castle of Moulin

Perth & Kinross: About 0.5 miles north-east of Pitlochry railway station, on minor road and foot south of A924, outskirts of Pitlochry, just south-east of Moulin.

Ruin or site NN 946589 OS: 52 ** Map: 8, no: 39

Originally on a strong site on an island in a loch, little remains of the Black Castle of Moulin except the traces of two round corner towers and some of an enclosing wall. There was a landing place for boats as well as a causeway. The loch was drained in the 18th century.

   The castle was built in 1320s – on the site of an older castle of the 11th or 12th century – by Sir John Campbell of Lochow, nephew of Robert the Bruce, later created Earl of Atholl by David II. The castle may have been occupied as late as the 16th century, and abandoned and torched because of plague.

Other refs: Caisteal Dubh Mhaothlinne; Moulin Castle

Black Craig *see* Dun da Lamh

Black Esk Tower

Dumfriesshire: About 8.5 miles north-west of Langholm, on minor roads and tracks west of B709, east of Black Esk, at or near Westside.

Ruin or site NY 231929 OS: 79 * Map: 1, no: 269

Site of tower, nothing of which remains, a property of the Beatties.

Other refs: Westside Tower

Black Hall *see* Blackhall Castle

Black Jack's Castle

Angus & Dundee: About 3 miles south of Montrose, on minor roads east of A92, just north of the sea, 0.5 miles south of Dunninald Castle, near Boddin, at Black Jack.

Ruin or site NO 708535 OS: 54 * Map: 8, no: 270

Little or nothing remains of Black Jack's Castle, a 15th-century stronghold of the Grays, the name coming from either the rock the castle was built on, or one of the family. It was held by Andrew Gray when, in 1579, 1580 and 1581, the family attacked and eventually sacked nearby Red Castle, with a force of Protestants, to remove the Episcopal minister.

   The old castle had been abandoned by the end of the 17th century when a new castle was built nearby [NO 704543], itself replaced in 1824 when Dunninald Castle, a mansion designed by James Gillespie Graham, was built.

Other refs: Dunninald

Black Tower of Drumlanrig *see* Drumlanrig's Tower, Hawick

Blackadder Castle

Borders: About 4 miles east of Duns, on minor roads north of B6460, south of Blackadder Water, 1 mile north-east of Blackadder Mains.

Ruin or site NT 856540 OS: 74 * Map: 2, no: 342

Site of Blackadder Castle, parts of which were probably incorporated into the 18th-century Blackadder House, which was itself demolished around 1925.

   The property originally belonged to the Blackadder family. The Homes, however, murdered the male heirs to the lands, then forced the remaining daughters to marry sons of Home of Wedderburn, after besieging them in the castle here. In 1514 Alexander, 3rd Lord Home, sheltered here during his conflict with John, Duke of Albany, and Albany had the castle slighted the following year. Home was executed in 1516. By 1836 the property had passed to the Houston-Boswells.

Blackbarony Castle *see* Black Barony Castle

Blackcraig Castle

Perth & Kinross: About 7 miles north and west of Blairgowrie, on minor road west of A924, just west of the River Ardle, at Blackcraig Castle.

Private NO 108534 OS: 53 ** Map: 8, no: 80

Blackcraig Castle consists of a late 16th-century tower of three storeys, with a stair-tower, to which a mansion was added in 1856.

   Blackcraig was probably a property of the Maxwells from 1550 or earlier.

Blackcraig Castle

Ayrshire: About 3.5 miles south of New Cumnock, on minor roads south of A76 at junction with B741, east of Afton Water, at or near Blackcraig.

Ruin or site NS 634082 OS: 71 * Map: 3, no: 294

Site of castle.

Blacket House

Dumfriesshire: About 3 miles east of Ecclefechan, on minor road east of B722 at Eaglesfield, north of the Kirtle Water at Blacket House.

Ruin or site NY 243743 OS: 85 ** Map: 1, no: 274

Blacket House is a ruined 16th-century L-plan tower house. The stair-wing survives, but little remains of the main block except a basement with shot-holes. It is mentioned in 1584, and there is a stone with the date 1663.

   It was a property of the Bells, one of whom was the rejected suitor and murderer of 'Fair Helen of Kirkconnel Lee' as related in the old ballad. He tried to shoot Helen's lover, Adam Fleming, but she took the bullet and was slain. The tower was sacked by the English in 1547.

Other refs: Blackwood

Blackhall Castle

Kincardine & Deeside: About 2 miles west of Banchory, on minor roads west of B974, south of River Dee, at or near Blackhall.

Ruin or site   NO 670961   OS: 45   *   Map: 10, no: 188

Site of castle, said to have been a keep with turrets, which was replaced by or incorporated into a mansion in 1771, itself demolished about 1947.

Other refs: Black Hall

Blackhall Manor

Renfrewshire: About 0.25 miles south of Paisley Abbey, north of A726, just south of the Cart Water, at Blackhall.

Private   NS 490630   OS: 64   **   Map: 3, no: 201

Blackhall Manor is an altered 16th-century house of two storeys and an attic. A projecting tower contains a turnpike stair. The walls are pierced by shot-holes.

The vaulted basement contained cellars and a kitchen. The hall and a private chamber occupied the first floor.

The lands were granted to Sir John Stewart by Robert III in 1396, although Blackhall is mentioned in the 13th century. Much of the present house was built by Stewart of Ardgowan in the 16th century. It was used as a farmhouse after 1710, was roofless and ruined by the end of the 19th century, but restored in the 1980s, and is occupied.

Blackhouse Tower

Borders: About 4 miles north-east of Cappercleuch, on minor road north of A708 at Craig Douglas, just east of the Douglas Burn, at Blackhouse.

Ruin or site   NT 281273   OS: 73   *   Map: 2, no: 71

Blackhouse is a very ruined rectangular 16th-century tower house, with a round stair-tower, near the entrance, at one corner.

The property probably belonged to the Douglases from the 13th century or earlier, and an older castle here may have been used by Sir James Douglas, friend of Robert the Bruce.

The tower is traditionally associated with the tragedy related in the old ballad 'The Dowie Dens of Yarrow'. Seven large stones near the tower are said to mark the spot where seven brothers of the lady in the ballad, Margaret, were slain by her lover, although he too died.

The property was held by the Pringles in 1509, but had passed to the Stewarts of Traquair by the end of the 16th century.

Blacklaw Tower

Dumfriesshire: About 2.5 miles north-west of Moffat, on minor road and foot north of A701, south side of Blacklaw Hill, east of Evan Water, just east of A74.

Ruin or site   NT 052067   OS: 78   *   Map: 1, no: 206

Little remains of Blacklaw Tower, a 16th-century tower house, except the vaulted basement and foundations of a courtyard with ranges.

Blacklaw was a property of the Lindsays around 1315, but passed to the Herries of Terregles, then in 1510 to the Maxwells. By 1592 the lands were held by the Johnstones, but later passed to the Douglases of Fingland, one of whom wrote the song 'Annie Laurie', about one of the Lauries of Maxwelton, around 1700.

Blackness Castle

Stirlingshire & Clackmannan: About 4 miles east of Bo'ness, on the south shore of the Firth of Forth from the B903 or B9109 at the village of Blackness.

His Scot   NT 056803   OS: 65   ***   Map: 6, no: 116**

Standing on an outcrop of rock on a promontory in the Firth of Forth, Blackness is a grim and impressive courtyard castle, which was used as the state prison. It was built in the 15th century, but was much modified in later centuries for artillery.

The main entrance has an iron yett of 1693, and is protected by a spur with caponier and gun platforms. It leads into the courtyard, the curtain wall dating partly from the 15th century, although it was massively strengthened for artillery in the 16th and 17th centuries.

The oldest part is the central square 15th-century keep of four storeys, heightened in 1553, and altered again with the addition of a projecting round stair-tower. It was used as a prison for nobles, each chamber having a fireplace and latrine.

The landward tower is probably the site of the 15th-century hall, but the present building, dating mostly from 1540, housed the main residential accommodation for the castle.

The sea tower served as an artillery platform, and as a secondary prison, a hatch giving access to a pit-prison, which was open to the sea at high tide.

In medieval times Blackness was an important port for the royal burgh of Linlithgow. The castle is first mentioned in 1449 as a prison. The Viponts had held the lands since before 1200, but in the 15th century Blackness was acquired by George Crichton, brother of the Chancellor of Scotland. During the reign of James II in 1444, the Douglases seized and sacked the castle, but it was quickly recovered by the Crichtons. In 1453 Sir George Crichton stopped his son, James, inheriting the property. James captured Blackness Castle, and imprisoned his father until forced to surrender by the King.

The castle was burned by an English fleet in 1481, and was the meeting place between James III and rebellious nobles in 1488.

From 1537, under Sir James Hamilton of Finnart – builder of Craignethan Castle – work began to turn the castle into an artillery fort, making it one of the most formidable fortresses in Scotland at that time. In 1543 Cardinal David Beaton was imprisoned here, and in 1544 the Douglas Earl of Angus. When Mary, Queen of Scots, fled to England in 1568 the castle held out for her until 1573. About 1600 the captaincy passed from the Stewarts to the Livingstones.

The castle was captured by General Monck in 1650 during Cromwell's invasion of Scotland, being bombarded by land and sea, but most damage was done by a battery placed on the high ground on the landward side. The castle was not repaired until 1660, when it was used as a prison again.

In the 19th century, Blackness was greatly altered to hold powder and stores, and became the central ammunition depot for Scotland. In 1912 the castle was handed over to the care of the State, and a major programme of restoration and repair was carried out between 1926 and 1935.

OPEN: Open all year: Apr-Sep, daily 9.30-18.30; Oct-Mar, Mon-Wed

and Sat 9.30-16.30, Thu 9.00-12.00, Sun 14.00-16.30, closed Fri; closed 25/26 Dec and 1/2 Jan.
Gift shop. WC. Parking. Group concessions (over 11). £.
Tel: 01506 834807   Fax: 0131 668 8888
Email: hs.explore@scotland.gov.uk   Web: www.historic-scotland.gov.uk

Blackness Manor House
Angus & Dundee: About 2 miles west of Dundee, on minor roads north of A85, west of Ninewells Hospital, 0.5 miles north of the Firth of Tay, at Blackness.
Ruin or site   NO 370300   OS: 54   *   Map: 8, no: 166
Blackness Manor was a long house of two storeys and an attic, with a projecting round stair-tower. The basement contained a kitchen and cellars. The house is marked on a map by Thomas Pont of around 1592, and was demolished in 1939.

Blackwood *see* Blacket House

Blackwood House
Lanarkshire & Glasgow: About 4 miles north-west of Lesmahagow, on minor road north of A726 or west of B7078, 1.5 miles west of Blackwood, at Blackwood House.
Ruin or site   NS 773433   OS: 71   *   Map: 3, no: 366
Site of castle or old house. It was replaced by a mansion.
The lands were a property of the Weirs of Blackwood. James Weir of Blackwood was one of the supporters of Mary, Queen of Scots, and one of those accused of the murder of Darnley. The property passed to the Lawries, and at the end of the 19th century was held by the Hope Veres.

Blair Castle
Fife: About 3 miles east and south of Kincardine, north of the B9037, about 1 mile east of Longannet Power Station, just north of the sea.
Private   NS 968858   OS: 65   *   Map: 7, no: 3
Blair Castle, an early 19th-century mansion and now a convalescent home for miners, was built on the site of an earlier castle or mansion, itself built by Archbishop Hamilton of St Andrews in the second half of the 16th century.

Blair Castle
Ayrshire: About 3.5 miles north of Kilwinning, on minor roads east and south of A737 at Dalry and B707, about 1 mile south-east of Dalry.
Private   NS 305480   OS: 63   **   Map: 3, no: 83
In wooded and landscaped grounds, Blair Castle incorporates a much-altered 16th-century L-plan tower house, which was extended by a long 17th-century wing. A square stair-tower in the re-entrant angle was also added in the 17th century, and the whole house was remodelled and extended again in 1893. The earliest part of the building, a strong keep, may date from the 13th or 14th century.
The entrance, in the square stair-tower, leads to a vaulted basement and to a turnpike stair, although little else of the original building survives. The walls of the tower are up to 14 feet thick.
The Blair family held the property from 1165. Sir Bryce Blair is named in Blind Harry's epic poem 'The Wallace' and in John Barbour's 'The Brus' because of the dubious honour of being hanged, although as a patriot, at Ayr along with William Wallace's uncle. William Blair fought with the Covenanters, but was captured by John Graham of Claverhouse, although he later escaped. Robert Burns visited the castle, and it is still owned by descendants of the original family.
OPEN: Gardens open all year – donation welcome.

Blair Castle
Perth & Kinross: About 7 miles north of Pitlochry, 1 mile north-west of Blair Atholl, on minor roads north of B8079 from A9, at Blair Castle.
Private   NN 867662   OS: 43   *   Map: 8, no: 24**
Blair Castle, a much altered and extended rambling white-washed castellated mansion, incorporates the 13th-century Comyn's Tower, of which only the lower part survives. The building was then added to through the centuries, but completely remodelled in the 18th century, with the removal of its upper storeys, to turn it into a plain mansion. The Duke of Atholl had the architect David Bryce restore the look of the mansion back to the original in 1872.

In 1263 the Comyns built a castle here on lands actually owned by David Strathbogie, Earl of Atholl. Edward III of England stayed at the castle in 1336. James V visited in 1529, as did Mary, Queen of Scots, in 1564. The property had passed to the Stewart Earls of Atholl, but in 1629 was granted to John Murray, Master of Tullibardine.
Montrose used it as a mustering point before the Battle of Tippermuir, and in 1653 the castle was besieged, captured and partly destroyed with powder by Colonel Daniel, one of Cromwell's commanders. However, it was complete enough for the young Earl of Atholl to try to recapture it in 1654.
The castle was garrisoned by Bonnie Dundee, John Graham of Claverhouse, in 1689, and it was here that his body was brought after the Battle of Killiecrankie. The Earls of Atholl were made Marquises, then Dukes of Atholl in 1703.
Bonnie Prince Charlie stayed here in 1745, during the Rising. The following year the castle was held by Hanoverian forces, and attacked and damaged by Lord George Murray, Bonnie Prince Charlie's general and the Duke's brother. It is the last castle in Britain to have been besieged. Robert Burns visited in 1787.
Blair Castle is home of the Atholl Highlanders, Britain's only remaining private regiment.
OPEN: Open Apr-Oct, daily 10.00-18.00; last admission 17.00.
Some 30 interesting rooms. Collections of paintings, tapestries, arms, armour, china, costumes and Jacobite mementoes. Fine Georgian plasterwork. Guided tours for groups. Gift shop. Licensed restaurant. Tearoom. Walled garden. Picnic area. Deer park. Disabled access & facilities. Car and coach parking. Group concessions. ££.
Tel: 01796 481207   Fax: 01796 481487
Email: office@blair-castle.co.uk   Web: www.great-houses-scotland.co.uk/blair

Blair, The *see* Blairlogie Castle

Blairbowie Castle
Aberdeen & Gordon: About 3.5 miles west of Inverurie, on minor roads west of A96, 1 mile south-east of Chapel of Garioch, south-west of Blairbowie.
Ruin or site   NJ 724226 [?]   OS: 38   *   Map: 10, no: 225
Site of castle, the last remains of which were removed about 1850.

Blairfindy Castle
Moray: About 6.5 miles north of Tomintoul, on minor roads west of B9008, west of River Livet, at Castleton of Blairfindy.
Ruin or site   NJ 199286   OS: 36   *   Map: 10, no: 37**
Blairfindy Castle is a ruined 16th-century L-plan tower house, which is complete to the wallhead. It consists of a main block and projecting stair-wing, offset to provide two re-entrant angles. A very narrow stair-turret rises above first-floor level in the main re-entrant angle. One corner is crowned by the remains of a corbelled-out bartizan. The walls are pierced with small windows and many shot-holes.
The basement is vaulted and contains the kitchen with a wide arched fireplace and oven. A wine-cellar has a small stair to the hall above in the thickness of the walling. The hall, on the first floor, has a fireplace. The upper floors were reached by the turret stair in the re-entrant angle.

The lands were held by the Grants, but passed to the Gordons of Huntly, who built the castle. In 1594 the Battle of Glenlivet was fought nearby. The Gordon Earl of Huntly and Hay Earl of Errol defeated an army, led by the Earl of Argyll, with the slaughter of over 700 of Argyll's men, including MacLean of Duart. The building is derelict.
Other refs: Castle of Blairfindy

Blairhenechan Tower

Argyll & Dunbartonshire: About 1.5 miles north-west of Cardross, on minor roads north of A814, at or near Drumhead.
Ruin or site   NS 338792   OS: 63   *   Map: 5, no: 139
Site of tower house, which is mentioned in the 16th century. Drumhead, which dates from the 18th and 19th century, may be built on the site. Blaeu's Atlas of The Lennox, however, has Blairhenechan virtually on the coast.
Other refs: Drumhead Tower

Blairlogie Castle

Stirlingshire & Clackmannan: About 3 miles north-east of Stirling, on minor road just north of the A91, west of Blairlogie.
Private   NS 827969   OS: 57   *   Map: 6, no: 80**
Standing in a strong position in the Ochils, Blairlogie Castle is a small rectangular tower, said to date from 1513, of two storeys and an attic. To this was added a stair-wing in 1582, making it L-plan. It has corbiestepped gables, and was later extended and altered.
   The basement of the original tower is vaulted, and the hall occupied the first floor.
   Blairlogie was a possession of the Spittal family from the late 15th century until 1767, when it passed by marriage to the Dundases of Blair. The castle was used as a farmhouse, and is occupied.
Other refs: The Blair; Blair, The

Blairquhan

Ayrshire: About 7 miles south-east of Maybole, signposted off A77, on minor road north of B741, just south of the Water of Girvan, just north of Straiton.
Private   NS 367055   OS: 70   *   Map: 3, no: 125
Blairquhan, a large castellated mansion designed by William Burn in 1821-4, replaced a castle incorporating the 14th-century McWhurter's Tower and a range from 1573. There is a walled garden.
   It was a property of the MacWhurters, but passed to the Kennedys in the 15th century, then to the Whitefoords in 1623. Charles Whitefoord of Blairquhan fought for the Hanoverians at the Battle of Culloden in 1746. In 1790 the property passed to the Hunter Blairs, and is still held by the same family.
Other refs: McWhurter's Tower
OPEN: Open mid Jul-mid Aug, daily 13.30-17.00, closed Mon; last admission 16.15; grounds open until 18.00; open at all other times by appt.
Good collection of furniture and pictures, including Scottish Colourists. Self-guided tours – guided tours by arrangement. Gift shop. Tea room. WC. Walled garden. Picnic area. Partial disabled access and WC. Car and coach parking. ££.
Tel: 01655 770239   Fax: 01655 770278
Email: enquiries@blairquhan.co.uk   Web: blairquhan.co.uk

Blairstone *see* Nether Auchendrane

Blairstone House *see* Auchendrane Castle

Blairvadach Castle

Argyll & Dunbartonshire: About 1 mile north and west of Rhu, on minor roads east of A814, east side of Gare Loch, at or near Blairvadach.
Ruin or site   NS 263853 [?]   OS: 56   *   Map: 5, no: 126
Site of 16th-century tower house, also recorded as Blairvadic and Blairvaddick. The present mansion is modern.
   The lands were held by the MacAulays of Ardincaple, but were sold to Andrew Buchanan, a Glasgow merchant, around the end of the 18th century.

Blanerne Castle

Borders: About 3 miles east and north of Duns, on minor road between A6105 and B6355, north of the Whiteadder Water, behind Blanerne House.
Ruin or site   NT 832564   OS: 67   *   Map: 2, no: 339
Little remains of Blanerne Castle, a 16th-century L-plan castle, except the ruined wing and a two-storey range with an oven at one end.
   It was owned by the Lumsdens of Blanerne, although there was probably an earlier castle on the site.
   'Bunkle, Billie and Blanerne,
   Three castles strong as airn;
   Built when Davy was a bairn;
   They'll all gang doon
   Wi' Scotland's croon
   And ilka ane shall be a cairn.'
Other refs: Lumsden Castle

Blantyre Castle *see* Old Place, Blantyre

Blantyre Priory

Lanarkshire & Glasgow: About 3 miles north of Hamilton, on foot east of B758, on west bank of River Clyde, 1.5 miles north of Blantyre, 0.25 miles north-east of Craigknowe.
Private   NS 686594   OS: 64   *   Map: 3, no: 319
Perched on a steep bank of the Clyde opposite Bothwell Castle, little remains of the Augustinian priory, founded around 1240 by Patrick, Earl of Dunbar, and dedicated to the Holy Rood. The property passed after the Reformation to Walter Stewart of Minto in 1599, the family having been Commendators. The Stewarts were made Lords Blantyre in 1606.
   The Stewarts lived in the priory, but in 1606 Lady Blantyre left with her daughters for Cardonald, leaving Lord Blantyre in the building. The reason given was the ghostly activities and unexplained noises that plagued the household at night. One of the family was Frances Stewart, Duchess of Richmond and Lennox, who was the model for Britannia on British coins. She was responsible for having the name of Lethington Castle changed to Lennoxlove.

Blastwood *see* Westhills

Blawarthill

Lanarkshire & Glasgow area: About 2.5 miles east and south of Clydebank, on minor roads north of A814, at or near Blawarthill Hospital.
Ruin or site   NS 520687 [?]   OS: 64   *   Map: 3, no: 230
Site of 15th-century castle, a property of the Maxwells in the 17th century.

Blervie Castle

Moray: About 2.5 miles south-east of Forres, on minor roads east of B9010, about 1 mile north-east of Rafford, east of Mains of Blervie, at Blervie Castle.
Ruin or site   NJ 071573   OS: 27   *   Map: 10, no: 10**
Blervie Castle is a ruined 16th-century Z-plan tower house, of which only one of the projecting towers survive. The surviving part is a five-storey square tower, with a round stair-tower in what was the re-entrant angle. It has a parapet with open rounds. Not much remains of the main block, and there is nothing at all of the matching tower at the opposite corner. The walls are pierced by gunloops and shot-holes.
   The basement of the tower is vaulted, as is the first and top storey.
   The property was originally held by the Comyns, and there appears to have been a royal castle here in the 13th century. The present castle was built after it had passed to the Dunbars. Blervie was sold to the Mackintoshes, at the beginning of the 18th century, who in turn sold it to the Duffs of Braco, Earls of Fife. The castle was partly demolished about 1776 to build nearby Blervie Mains.

Blindlee Tower

Borders: About 2 miles north-west of Galashiels, on minor road and foot south of A72, south of Balnakiel House, north side of Meigle Hill, at Blindlee.
Ruin or site   NT 471373 [?]   OS: 73   *   Map: 2, no: 138
Site of tower house, a vestige of which survived in the 19th century.

Blochairn House *see* Provan Hall

Blythswood *see* Renfield

Boadsbeck Castle

Dumfriesshire: About 5 miles north-east of Moffat, on minor roads east of A708, to south of Moffat Water, at or near Bodesbeck.
Ruin or site   NT 148093   OS: 78   *   Map: 1, no: 248
Site of tower house.
Other refs: Bodesbeck

Board

Lanarkshire & Glasgow: About 1.5 miles south of Kilsyth, on minor roads north of B8048 or west of B802, at or near Board.
Ruin or site   NS 713750   OS: 64   *   Map: 3, no: 329
Site of castle.
  The lands were a property of the Erskines until 1339 when they were exchanged for Garscadden with the Flemings of Cumbernauld.

Boath House *see* Auldearn Castle

Boddam Castle

Banff & Buchan: About 3 miles south of Peterhead, on minor roads east of A952, to the south of Boddam just west of the sea, at Boddam Castle.
Ruin or site   NK 133419   OS: 30   **   Map: 10, no: 368
On a headland surrounded by cliffs, Boddam Castle is a very ruined 16th-century courtyard castle with ranges of buildings including a chapel, of which only foundations remain. The gateway survives.
  It was built by the Keiths of Ludquharn, who were later made Baronets of Nova Scotia.

Bodesbeck *see* Boadsbeck Castle

Bog o' Gight Castle *see* Gordon Castle

Boghall Castle

Lanarkshire & Glasgow area: About 0.25 miles south of Biggar, on minor roads and foot south of A702, just south east of Boghall Farm.
Ruin or site   NT 041370   OS: 72   **   Map: 3, no: 449
Taking its name from its flat marshy site, the ruined remains of Boghall Castle date mostly from the 16th century, although they may incorporate a much earlier stronghold. Two D-shaped towers survive, one of two storeys. The walls are pierced by gunloops. Other fragments of buildings surround a roughly rectangular courtyard.
  The property passed by marriage to the Flemings in the late 13th century, who were descended from Baldwin, a Fleming, who settled at Biggar in the 12th century. Edward II stayed at Boghall in 1310. The Flemings were made Earls of Wigtown in 1341, although this title was sold to the Douglases in 1372. In 1458 the family were made Lords Fleming of Cumbernauld. Mary, Queen of Scots, visited in 1565, but in 1568 after the Battle of Langside, Boghall was surrendered to the Regent Moray following a siege. In 1605 the Flemings were again made Earls of Wigtown, but a Cromwellian force occupied the castle in 1650. The 6th and last Earl died in 1747. The castle was abandoned soon afterwards, and although a substantial and picturesque ruin early in the 19th century, was robbed of stone and little now remains.

Boghouse *see* Druchtag Motte

Boghouse *see* Crawfordjohn Castle

Boghouse Castle

Lanarkshire & Glasgow: Just south of Crawfordjohn, just east of B740, 3 miles south-west of junction with A74.
Ruin or site   NS 878236   OS: 71   *   Map: 3, no: 407
Site of castle, of which there were some remains in 1836, but nothing now remains.

It was probably built in the 16th century by Sir James Hamilton of Finnart using materials from Crawfordjohn Castle [NS 879238]. James V entertained his mistress, Catherine Carmichael here, and the property was exchanged by Hamilton for the barony of Kilmarnock with James V in 1535. Hamilton was executed for treason in 1540, although the property eventually returned to the Hamiltons.
Other refs: Crawfordjohn

Bogle Walls, Enzieholm

Dumfriesshire: About 5.5 miles north-west of Langholm, just south of B709, south of River Esk, at Enzieholm.
Ruin or site   NY 292912   OS: 79   *   Map: 1, no: 290
The earthworks of an Iron Age fort appear to have been reused in medieval times.
Other refs: Enzieholm

Bognie Castle *see* Conzie Castle

Bogrie Tower

Dumfriesshire: About 4 miles south of Moniaive, on minor roads about 3.5 miles west of B729 from Dunscore, north of the Glenesslin Burn, at Bogrie.
Ruin or site   NX 812849   OS: 78   *   Map: 1, no: 138
Bogrie Tower is a ruined two-storey tower house, which was partly demolished in 1680. The castle had been used as a place of refuge by Covenanters.
  It was owned by the Kirk family in the 1630s, but later passed by marriage to the Gordons of Lochinvar.

Bogton Castle

Renfrewshire: About 2 miles south-west of Rutherglen, just west of B767, in Muirend just south-east of railway station, at Bogton.
Ruin or site   NS 575596   OS: 64   *   Map: 3, no: 259
Site of tower house, probably replaced by a mansion, itself demolished, and nothing remains.
  It was a property of the Blairs from 1543, who built the castle.

Boharm Castle *see* Gauldwell Castle

Bold

Borders: About 3 miles east of Innerleithen, on minor road south of A72, on south bank of the Tweed, at or near Bold.
Ruin or site   NT 374374 [?]   OS: 73   *   Map: 2, no: 97
Site of tower house.

Bolshan Castle

Angus & Dundee: About 2 miles north-east of Friockheim, on minor roads south of A934 or east of A933, at Bolshan.
Ruin or site   NO 617521   OS: 54   *   Map: 8, no: 251
Site of castle.
  It was a property of Arbroath Abbey, but passed to the Ogilvies of Lintrathen in the 15th century, who probably built the castle. It was sold to the Carnegie Earl of Southesk in 1634, but passed to the Crown in 1716 on their forfeiture for their part in the Jacobite Rising, then in 1720 to the York Buildings Company. It was sold in 1764 to the Carnegies of Pittarrow, and the family recovered the Earldom of Southesk in 1855. A mansion stood on the estate, but was demolished in the 18th century.
Other refs: Balleshan Castle

Bombie

Dumfriesshire: About 4 miles north-west of Langholm, on minor road west of B709, west of River Esk, north-west of Hopsrig, at or near Bombie.
Ruin or site   NY 319886   OS: 79   *   Map: 1, no: 299
Site of tower house.
Other refs: Hopsrig

Bombie Castle

Galloway: About 1.5 miles east of Kirkcudbright, on minor roads south of B727, just east of the Balgredan Burn, just west of Bombie.
Ruin or site   NX 708501   OS: 83   *   Map: 1, no: 115
Bombie Castle is a moated site, with no remains of what was a large castle.

It was a property of the MacLellans. The MacLellans feuded with the Douglases, and in 1452 Sir Patrick MacLellan was murdered by beheading at Threave Castle by the Earl of Douglas. The MacLellans had their revenge by helping to besiege Threave after the fall of the Black Douglases in 1455. William MacLellan of Bombie was killed at the Battle of Flodden in 1513. A MacLellan of Bombie was murdered in Edinburgh's High Street in 1527 by a Gordon of Lochinvar. In 1569 Sir Thomas MacLellan of Bombie, Provost of Kirkcudbright, acquired the lands and buildings of the Franciscan Greyfriars Monastery in Kirkcudbright, and later those of the old royal castle. In 1582 he completed a new tower house in the burgh, MacLellan's Castle, abandoning Bombie.

Bona Ferry *see* Castle Spioradain

Bonaly Tower

Lothians: About 4 miles south-west of Edinburgh Castle, on minor roads south of B701, east of Torduff Reservoir, north of Bonaly Country Park, at Bonaly Tower.
Private   NT 214678   OS: 66   *   Map: 4, no: 71
The present small mansion, dating mostly from 1836, remodelled in 1866 by David Bryce, and extended again in 1888, incorporates an older house.

The property was bought from Gillespie's Hospital in 1811 by the well-known judge Lord Cockburn, then changed hands through many families. The house has been divided, and is still occupied.

Bonhard House

Stirlingshire & Clackmannan: About 1.5 miles south-east of Bo'ness, on minor road south of A904, about 0.25 miles north of East Bonhard Farm.
Ruin or site   NT 020799 [?]   OS: 65   *   Map: 6, no: 114
Once standing in a commanding position on high ground, Bonhard House was burned out, and then demolished. It consisted of an altered 16th-century L-plan tower house of three storeys and a garret. A semi-octagonal stair-tower stood in the re-entrant angle.

The original entrance was in the foot of the stair-tower. The basement was not vaulted, and contained a kitchen. The hall was on the first floor.

It was owned by the Cornwalls of Bonhard.
Other refs: Springfield; Polkmyl Tower

Bonhill *see* Place of Bonhill

Bonnington House

Lothians: About 2 miles south-west of Ratho on minor roads west of B7030 at Bonnington or north of B7015. 0.5 miles north-west of Wilkieston, at Bonnington House.
Private   NT 111691   OS: 65   **   Map: 4, no: 41
The two-storey harled house dates from 1622, although it was remodelled in the 19th century. There is a walled garden.

The lands were a property of the Erskine family, but by the middle of the 17th century had passed to the Foulis Lord Colinton, then successively to the Durhams, Cunninghams and the Wilkies of Ormiston.

Bonnyton Castle

Angus & Dundee: About 3.5 miles south-west of Montrose, just south of A934, at Bonnyton.
Ruin or site   NO 657559 [?]   OS: 54   *   Map: 8, no: 259
Nothing remains of Bonnyton Castle, although there were some remains in the 19th century. There is a doocot nearby. Two heraldic stones are built into farm buildings, one dated 1601.

It was held by the Woods of Bonnyton, who held lands here from 1493 until the beginning of the 18th century.

Bonshaw Tower

Dumfriesshire: About 5 miles north-east of Annan, on minor road south of A74 at Kirtlebridge, just south of Kirtlebridge, west of Kirtle Water at Bonshaw.
Private   NY 243720   OS: 85   **   Map: 1, no: 273**
Bonshaw is a 16th-century rectangular tower house of three storeys and a garret within the corbelled-out parapet. The walls are pierced with gunloops, but the pitch of the roof has been altered.

The entrance leads to a mural passageway into the vaulted basement and to the turnpike stair. There is a cramped pit-prison within the thickness of one wall. The hall, on the first floor, has a wide fireplace.

Bonshaw was the seat of the Irvine or Irving family. William de Irwin or Irvine was armour bearer to Robert the Bruce, and granted Drum in Aberdeenshire as reward for long service. Bonshaw was sacked in 1544 by the English, but twice successfully withstood sieges by Lord Maxwell in 1585. The Georgian house adjacent to the tower is also in the ownership of the Irvings.
OPEN: Visitors are welcome, but by appt only.
Tel: 01461 500256   Email: bruceirving@sol.co.uk

Boquhan Castle

Stirlingshire & Clackmannan: About 1.5 miles south-east of Kippen, on minor roads south of A811, east of Boquhan Burn, at or near Auldhall.
Ruin or site   NS 661935 [?]   OS: 57   *   Map: 6, no: 46
Site of castle, the last remains of which were removed about 1760. Auldhall, an 18th-century house of two storeys, may be built on or near the site.

The old castle 'witnessed some sharp collisions of the clans'. It was a property of the Grahams, although it is also recorded as being held by the Bason family.

A site at Boquhan [NS 670946] has also been suggested.
Other refs: Auldhall, Boquhan

Bordie Castle

Fife: About 1.5 miles east of Kincardine, about 1 mile north of the Longannet Power Station, just south of the A985 at Bordie.
Ruin or site   NS 956869   OS: 65   *   Map: 7, no: 2
Bordie Castle apparently consists of part of an L-plan tower, formerly of three storeys. It is not clear whether the building was ever completed.

Boreland Castle

Ayrshire: About 2 miles south-east of Cumnock, on A76, at Borland.
Ruin or site   NS 586174   OS: 71   *   Map: 3, no: 266
Site of castle of old house, some remains of which survived in the 19th century.
Other refs: Borland Castle

Boreland Tower

Dumfriesshire: About 6 miles south and west of Moffat, on minor road west of A701, just west of the Kinnel Water, at Boreland.
Ruin or site   NY 065958   OS: 78   **   Map: 1, no: 210
Not much remains of Boreland Tower, a 16th-century tower house, except the ruined vaulted basement.

Boreland Tower

Borders: About 5 miles north of Peebles, on minor roads east of A703, north-west of Boreland, on the west side of Milky Law.
Ruin or site   NT 255480   OS: 73   *   Map: 2, no: 64
Site of 16th-century tower house, to the north-west of the farmhouse. It was a property of the Andersons and Gibsons. It was held jointly by both families until 1620, then by the Gibsons to the middle of the 19th century.

Borgue

Galloway: About 4 miles south-west of Kirkcudbright, just south of B727, just north of Borgue House.
Ruin or site   NX 633483   OS: 83   **   Map: 1, no: 102
Borgue Old House, which was replaced by Borgue House, is ruinous.

There was probably a stronghold here in the 12th century, a property of the Hugh de Morville. It is likely that it was destroyed by the men of Galloway in the 1170s during a rising against the king of Scots. Borgue Old House was a property of the Blairs.

There was a 12th-century church at Borgue.

Other refs: Borgue Old House

Borgue Castle *see* Castle Haven

Borgue Old House *see* Borgue

Borland Castle *see* Boreland Castle

Borrowston

Western Isles: About 5 miles north of Callanish, on minor roads west of A858, 1.5 miles west of Carloway, north side of Loch Carloway, Borrowston, Lewis.

Ruin or site   NB 193422   OS: 8   *   Map: 11, no: 23

An old castle is said to have been demolished when a pier was built here, but it is more likely it was an Iron Age dun – which may have been used into medieval times.

Borthwick Castle

Borders: About 1 mile north-west of Duns, on minor road to quarry, north of A6105.

Ruin or site   NT 770544   OS: 67   *   Map: 2, no: 308

Site of 16th-century L-plan tower house with a corbelled-out stair-turret in the re-entrant angle. A courtyard enclosed 16th-century ranges of buildings.

The basement was vaulted, and had a scale-and-platt stair to the first floor. A later house was built within the courtyard.

It was a property of the Cockburns, and was excavated before being destroyed by quarrying – a commemorative stone stands near the site.

Borthwick Castle

Lothians: About 2 miles south-east of Gorebridge, on minor road between north of A7 and south of B6372, south of Gore Water, just east of Borthwick village.

Private   NT 370597   OS: 66   *****   Map: 4, no: 148

One of the most impressive castles in Scotland, Borthwick Castle is a magnificent U-plan keep of five storeys with projecting wings of seven and eight storeys, separated by a deep narrow recess. The walls are massively thick, but there are no gunloops. A corbelled-out machiolated parapet has open rounds, and the castle is roofed with stone flags. It stands in a courtyard, formerly with a curtain wall and strong round towers at the corners, only one of which remains.

The main entrance, on the first floor, is reached by a bridge from the curtain wall. A guardroom opens off one side of the entrance. The basement is vaulted, and has its own entrance, a turnpike stair leading to the first floor through the guardroom.

The vaulted hall is on the first floor of the main block, and has a minstrels gallery, reached by a small stair. There is a massive fireplace, and the windows are deeply recessed because of the thickness of the walls. The kitchen, on the same floor, has a huge wide fireplace. There are three further storeys above the hall, one of the chambers having an oratory with piscina and aumbry.

The wings contain private chambers, reached by stairs in the thickness of the walls.

The property was held by the Borthwicks. One of the family had accompanied the heart of Robert the Bruce to Granada in Spain on crusade along with the Black Douglas and other Scottish nobles. Although the crusade was a disaster for the Scots, and many were slain, Borthwick distinguished himself by killing a Moorish chief and sticking his severed head on a pike. The castle was built by Sir William Borthwick in 1430 on the site of an earlier stronghold. The tomb of Borthwick is in nearby Borthwick Church – which is open to the public.

The 4th Lord Borthwick was slain at the Battle of Flodden in 1513. James Hepburn, Earl of Bothwell, and Mary, Queen of Scots, visited the castle in 1567 after their marriage and were besieged here, Mary only escaping disguised as a man. Cromwell besieged the castle, but it only took a few cannon balls to get the castle to surrender – the damage done to the parapet never being repaired. The Borthwick family abandoned the castle in the 17th century, and the castle became derelict, although it was restored in 1890. During World War II, Registrar records were

stored here, along with paintings from the National Gallery. The castle was leased as a conference centre, but is now a hotel.

There is a sad and gruesome ghost story. A local girl, called Ann Grant, was apparently made pregnant by one of the Borthwick lords. The poor young woman, heavy with child, was seized, slashed across the abdomen with a sword, and then left to die in what is now the haunted room. A modern visitor to the castle reported how he had seen a vision of the murder, as did a previous owner.

Guests in the haunted room, the Red Room, experienced several manifestations. The temperature in the chamber would suddenly drop, and scratchings were heard on the inside of the door. Footsteps were often heard on the turnpike stair from the room, around 1.30 am, when nobody was apparently about. A heavy fire door opened by itself one night, and during a business conference weeping and wailing was heard even although there was nobody in that part of the castle. A tale reports that one of the previous owners had the haunted room exorcised, but apparently to no effect.

Other refs: Lochorwart; Mote of Lochorwart

OPEN: Hotel: open mid-Mar to 2 Jan and to non-residents. Borthwick Church open all year, daily.

10 rooms with ensuite facilities. Castle may be booked for exclusive use. Conferences, weddings, banquets and meetings. Not suitable for disabled. Garden.

Tel: 01875 820514   Fax: 01875 821702

Borve Castle

Western Isles: About 3.5 miles south of Balivanich on Benbecula, on foot just north of B892 at Borve, about 0.5 miles north of sea, south of Cnoc-na Monadh, at Borve.

Ruin or site   NF 774506   OS: 22   **   Map: 11, no: 8

Borve Castle is a strong ruined 14th-century keep or hall house of three storeys, which was built by the MacDonalds. It stood on lands of John MacDonald of Islay, and was occupied until at least 1625. It was burned down in the late 18th century.

Other refs: Caisteal Borve; Castle Wearie

Borve Castle

Sutherland & Caithness: About 2 miles north-east of Bettyhill, on minor road and foot 0.5 miles north-east of Farr, east side Farr Point, west of sea, at Borve Castle.
Ruin or site NC 725642 OS: 10 * Map: 12, no: 19
Some ruined remains survive of a tower house and courtyard of the Mackays, built on a superb location on a promontory. It was still occupied in 1630, but was besieged with cannon and captured in 1655. The castle is also said to have been captured and destroyed by the Earl of Sutherland in 1554 or 1565.
  The original stronghold is thought to have been built by a Norseman called Torquil.
Other refs: Farr Castle

Botel Castle *see* Buittle Castle

Botel Place *see* Buittle Place

Bothan an Lochain

Perthshire: About 10 miles north and east of Blair Atholl, on minor roads and track 10 miles north and east of B8079, east of River Tilt and north of An Lochain
Ruin or site NN 982781 OS: 43 * Map: 8, no: 48
Site of palace or residence of the Stewart Earls of Atholl, where James V was entertained and which burned down afterwards. The area around Glen Tilt was used for hunting by Scottish monarchs, including Mary, Queen of Scots.

Bothan na Dige, Stronmilchan *see* Stronmilchan

Bothwell Castle

Lanarkshire & Glasgow area: About 3 miles north and west of Hamilton, on minor roads west of the B7071, east bank of the River Clyde, about 0.5 miles south of Uddingston.
His Scot NS 688594 OS: 64 ** Map: 3, no: 320**
Bothwell Castle is one of the largest and finest stone castles in Scotland, with what has been a magnificent moated round keep within a courtyard.
  The courtyard is enclosed by a strong thick curtain wall, in some places rising to 60 feet high, defended by towers. Within the walls are the ruins of many buildings, including a hall and chapel. Only the foundations of a large tower, at one corner, survive, but another tower is complete to the corbelled wallhead, and the prison tower and adjacent wall, which date from the 13th century, also remain.
  The magnificent round keep has a surrounding ditch partly hewn out of rock, 25 feet wide and 15 feet deep. The entrance to the keep is through a fine pointed doorway, originally reached by a drawbridge across the ditch. The entrance, through a portcullis, led into a passage to the hall. There is a turnpike stair to the basement with a well. Half of the keep was destroyed in the 14th century.
  Due to its position, size and strength, Bothwell Castle was of major importance during the Wars of Independence. It was held by the English in 1298-9, but was besieged by Scots and eventually taken after 14 months. In 1301 Edward I recap-

tured the castle, and it became the headquarters of Aymer de Valence, Earl of Pembroke, Edward I's Warden of Scotland. It was surrendered to the Scots in 1314, and the keep was partly demolished at this time.
  In 1336 the castle was taken and rebuilt by the English, and Edward III made Bothwell his headquarters, but it was demolished again after recapture by the Scots, led by Andrew Moray, around 1337.
  In 1362 it was acquired by Archibald the Grim, 3rd Earl of Douglas and Lord of Galloway, and he rebuilt much of the castle. After the forfeiture of the Black Douglases in 1455, it was given to the Crichtons, but after their forfeiture in turn, it passed to Sir John Ramsay of Balmain; then to Patrick Hepburn, Lord Hailes, later Earl of Bothwell, who exchanged it for Hermitage Castle with the Douglases in 1492.
  In the 17th century Archibald Douglas, 1st Earl of Forfar, built a Palladian mansion – demolished in 1926 – near the castle, dismantling part of the castle for materials. In the 19th century the castle passed to the Homes, and in 1935 was placed in the care of the State, and has since been repaired, with the rebuilding of part of the curtain wall.
Other refs: Valence Castle
OPEN: Open all year: Apr-Sep, daily 9.30-18.30; Oct-Mar, Mon-Wed and Sat 9.30-16.30, Thu 9.30-12.00, Sun 14.00-16.30, closed Fri; closed 25/26 Dec and 1/2 Jan.
Explanatory boards. Gift shop. WC. Car and coach parking. £.
Tel: 01698 816894 Fax: 0131 668 8888
Email: hs.explore@scotland.gov.uk Web: www.historic-scotland.gov.uk

Boturich Castle

Argyll & Dunbartonshire: About 1.5 miles north of Balloch, on minor roads west of the A811, near the southern end of Loch Lomond.
Private NS 387845 OS: 56 * Map: 5, no: 154
Boturich Castle, a castellated mansion dating mostly from 1830 and designed by Robert Lugar, incorporates some of a 15th-century L-plan castle. The old castle was ruinous in 1830, and the mansion was extended in 1854. Part of the basement is vaulted.
  The castle may have been built by the Earls of Lennox, but on their forfeiture passed to the Haldanes of Gleneagles in 1425. John Haldane of Gleneagles was killed at the Battle of Flodden in 1513. The castle was sacked by the MacFarlanes of Arrochar, but passed to the Buchanans of Ardoch in 1792, then in the 1850s to the Findlays.
Other refs: Baturich Castle

Bovain

Stirlingshire & Clackmannan: About 3 miles south-west of Killin, on minor road west of A827 at Monemore or north of A85 at Ledcharrie, just north of River Dochart, at Bovain.
Ruin or site NN 541306 [?] OS: 51 * Map: 6, no: 19
Site of castle of the MacNabs.

Bowden

Borders: About 1.5 miles south of Melrose, on B6398, north of Bowden Burn, Bowden.
Ruin or site NT 554305 OS: 73 * Map: 2, no: 206
There were several tower houses or bastles in the village of Bowden, of which there were some remains at the end of the 19th century.
  Part of the present church probably dates from the 15th century or earlier, while most is from the 17th century, although it was founded in 1128. The church was remodelled in 1794 and again in 1909. There are interesting burial monuments, including vaults of the Kerrs of Roxburghe, latterly Dukes, and a memorial to Lady Grizel Baillie, as well as other grave markers.

Bower of Wandel

Lanarkshire & Glasgow area: About 3.5 miles north of Abington, just west of A73 about 1.5 miles north of junction with A74, just east of River Clyde, at Bower of Wandel.
Ruin or site NS 952228 OS: 72 * Map: 3, no: 424
Crowning a rocky eminence surrounded on three sides by the Clyde, Bower of

Wandel consists of a very ruined 15th-century castle. Only part of the basement, which was vaulted with gunloops, survives.

It was a property of the Jardines from the 12th until the 17th century, and there was an earlier stronghold here. Bower is said to have been a favourite hunting place of James V.

Other refs: Wandel Tower

Bower Tower

Sutherland & Caithness: About 5 miles south-east of Castleton, on minor roads south of B876, Bowertower, at or near Mains.

Ruin or site   ND 230619   OS: 12   *   Map: 12, no: 54

Site of tower house, which is mentioned in 1628.

Bowhill

Borders: About 3 miles west of Selkirk, on minor roads south of A708, south of the Yarrow Water, Bowhill.

Private   NT 426278   OS: 73   *   Map: 2, no: 109**

Home of the Duke and Duchess of Buccleuch, Bowhill is an extensive rambling mansion, dating mainly from 1812, although part may date from 1708. The house was remodelled in 1831-2 by the architect William Burn. The ruins of Newark Castle are in grounds.

OPEN: Park open Easter-end Aug, daily 12.00-17.00, except closed Fri, also open Fri in Jul, 12.00-17.00; house open Jul, daily 13.00-16.30; other times by appt for educational groups.

Fine collections of paintings and artefacts, including the Duke of Monmouth's saddle and execution shirt. Audio-visual presentation. Restored Victorian kitchen and fire engine display. Sales area (gift shop Jul). Restaurant. WC. Garden and country park. Disabled facilities; wheelchair visitors free. Ruins of Newark Castle in grounds. Car and coach parking. ££.

Tel: 01750 22204   Fax: 01750 22204

Email: bht@buccleuch.com   Web: www.heritageontheweb.co.uk

Bowholm Tower *see* Baholm Tower

Bowness *see* Slains Castle

Bowshiel Tower

Borders: About 2.5 miles north and west of Granthouse, on minor road west of A1, north of the Pease Burn.

Ruin or site   NT 786677 [?]   OS: 67   **   Map: 2, no: 319

Site of 16th-century tower.

Boyndlie House

Banff & Buchan: About 6 miles south-west of Fraserburgh, on minor roads west of A98, at or near Boyndlie House.

Private   NJ 915620   OS: 30   *   Map: 10, no: 319

The present house was remodelled in 1814, but incorporates 17th-century work. It was a property of the Forbeses from the 16th century.

Other refs: House of Boyndlie

Boyne Castle

Banff & Buchan: About 1.5 miles east of Portsoy, on minor roads and foot north of B9139, west of Burn of Boyne, 0.5 miles south of the sea at Boyne Bay, at Boyne.

Ruin or site   NJ 612657   OS: 29   **   Map: 10, no: 162

Boyne Castle consists of a very ruinous and overgrown 16th-century courtyard castle, with four round corner towers and a twin-turreted gatehouse. There is a ditch, and the entrance is by a raised and walled causeway. Ranges of buildings were enclosed within the courtyard. It was once a fine place, and there were gardens and orchards.

The lands were held by Thomas Randolph, Earl of Moray, about 1320, but passed to the Edmonstones, then by marriage to the Ogilvies. The castle was built by Sir George Ogilvie of Dunlugas after 1575. It was still occupied in 1723, and there are remains of two walled gardens.

Boysack

Angus & Dundee: About 2 miles east of Friockheim, on minor roads north of B965, south of Lunan Water, at or near Boysack.

Ruin or site   NO 621491   OS: 54   *   Map: 8, no: 252

Site of castle, which was a property of the Carnegies in the 17th century. The family moved to Kinblethmont House in 1678 and the building was allowed to fall into ruin. Part may be built into one gable of the present house.

Braal Castle

Sutherland & Caithness: About 5 miles south of Thurso, on minor roads east of B874, north of Halkirk, just north of River Thurso, east of Braal Castle school.

Ruin or site   ND 139601   OS: 12   *   Map: 12, no: 47**

Braal Castle is a ruined 13th- or 14th- century keep, with thick walls and a ditch. Another building may have been a hall-block, but less of it remains.

The basement was not vaulted, and the hall was on the first floor.

This may have been a stronghold of Harold, Earl of Caithness, who died in 1206. It was a property of the Stewarts by 1375, but passed to the Crichtons in the middle of the 15th century, then to the Sinclair Earls of Caithness by 1547, then the Sinclairs of Ulbster. They built the nearby castellated mansion in the 19th century, which was used as a school, but is now divided into flats.

Other refs: Brawl Castle

Brabster Castle

Sutherland & Caithness: About 7 miles east of Castletown, on minor roads south of A836, near Brabstermire House.

Ruin or site   ND 316695   OS: 12   **   Map: 12, no: 60

Not much survives of Brabster Castle, a 17th-century tower house, except one gable wall incorporated into a kiln. It was a property of the Sinclairs of Brabster, and was replaced by Brabstermire House, a two-storey 18th-century building.

Brackley Castle

Kincardine & Deeside: About 0.5 miles south of Ballater, on minor roads south of B976, south of River Dee meeting with River Muick, at House of Glenmuick.

Private   NO 365945 [?]   OS: 44   *   Map: 10, no: 76

House of Glenmuick, a 19th-century mansion, stands on the site of a castle.

It was a property of the Gordons. John Gordon of Brackley was murdered by John Farquharson of Inverey in 1666, as told in the old ballad 'The Baron of Brackley'. The castle may have been attacked in the 1689-90 Jacobite Rising, as well as in the later rebellions.

Other refs: Braichlie

Braco Castle

Perth & Kinross: About 6 miles north of Dunblane, on minor roads north of B8033 just west of A822, west of River Knaik, 2 miles north-west of Braco, at Braco Castle.

Private   NN 824113   OS: 57   **   Map: 8, no: 18

Braco Castle consists of a plain 16th-century tower house of four storeys, to which a projecting tower was added. In the middle of the 17th century the building was extended, enclosing the stair-tower, and further additions were made in the 18th, and then again in the 19th century.

The original entrance was at the foot of the projecting wing, and part of the basement is vaulted.

Braco was a property of the Graham Earls of Montrose, one of whom was created a baronet of Braco in 1625. In 1715 Braco was garrisoned by Jacobite forces during the Rising. The last of the Grahams to live here died in 1790, and the property later passed to the Smythes.

The castle is said to be haunted.

Bradan Castle

Ayrshire: About 7 miles south and west of Dalmellington, on minor roads, foot and boat south of B741 at Straiton, in Loch Bradan.

Ruin or site   NX 428970   OS: 77   *   Map: 3, no: 167

Site of castle on an island in the loch. The level of the water of the loch, which is a reservoir, has been raised, and the island is submerged.

Other refs: Loch Bradan Castle

Braelangwell

South Highland: About 7 miles west and south of Cromarty, on minor roads west of B9160, east of Allt Dubhach, at or near Braelangwell.

Ruin or site   NH 696645 [?]   OS: 21   *   Map: 9, no: 103

Possible site of castle. Braelangwell is a two-storey classical mansion, dating from the late 18th century although remodelled in 1839-44.

Braelangwell was a property of the Urquharts from the end of the 17th century or earlier, but in 1839 was sold to the Frasers.

Braemar Castle

Kincardine & Deeside: About 0.5 miles north-east of Braemar, on A93, south of River Dee.

Private   NO 156924   OS: 43   **   Map: 10, no: 24**

Set in a rugged area of Scotland, Braemar Castle is an altered 17th-century L-plan tower house, with a round stair-tower in the re-entrant angle, and bartizans crowning the corners. The tower is surrounded by 18th-century star-shaped artillery defences. There is an unventilated pit-prison, and the original iron yett.

The basement is vaulted, but much of the rest of the interior has been altered, as has the parapet and upper part of the tower.

The castle was built in 1628 by John Erskine, 2nd Earl of Mar. The Earls of Mar supported William and Mary when the Stewart James VII was deposed in 1689. As a

result the castle was captured and torched out by John Farquharson of Inverey, the 'Black Colonel', who was a staunch Jacobite. It was left a ruin until 1748.

Although the family had resisted the Jacobites, John Erskine, 6th Earl of Mar, led the 1715 Jacobite Rising. He was more of a politician than a soldier, however, and the rebellion fizzled out. Mar fled abroad and was stripped of his lands. The property passed to the Farquharsons of Invercauld, and after the 1745-6 Jacobite Rising was taken over by the government, refurbished, and turned into a barracks, some of the walls bearing the scribblings of the garrison. The troops left in 1797, the castle was restored, and Queen Victoria visited when she attended the Braemar

gathering. The castle was reoccupied in the early 19th century.

One story is that Braemar is haunted the ghost of a young blonde-haired woman. A couple on their honeymoon were staying in the castle in the second half of the 19th century. Early in the morning the husband left to go hunting, but his wife woke later, and, not knowing about the hunting, believed she had been abandoned. In despair, the poor woman threw herself from the battlements. Her ghost is said to haunt the castle, searching for her husband. Her apparition reputedly was sighted in 1987, and it is thought that she only appears to those who have recently been married. Ghostly footsteps, the light tread of a woman, have also been reported.

Another spirit said to haunt the castle is that of John Farquharson of Inverey, also known as the 'Black Colonel', reportedly leaving behind a burning candle.

Other refs: Old Mar

OPEN: Open Apr-Oct, daily 10.00-18.00, last entry 17.30, closed Fri; also open Fri in Jul and Aug.

Many interesting rooms. Guided tours. Explanatory sheets. Gift shop. WC. Picnic area. Car and coach parking. Group concessions. £.

Tel: 01339 741219   Fax: 01339 741219   Email: invercauld@aol.com

Braes of Taymouth

Perthshire: About 5 miles west and south of Aberfeldy, on minor road east of A827, 1 mile east of Kenmore, at Braes of Taymouth.

Private   NN 791456   OS: 52   **   Map: 8, no: 16

Braes of Taymouth is listed as a tower house, and consists of a tower of three storeys with a wing. It is still occupied.

Brahan Castle

Ross & Cromarty: About 3.5 miles south-west of Dingwall, on minor roads south of A835, about 2.5 miles west of Conon Bridge, at or near Brahan House.

Ruin or site   NH 513549 [?]   OS: 26   *   Map: 9, no: 57

Site of castle, dating from the early 17th century but later remodelled. It latterly consisted of a main block and wings around a walled courtyard. By 1965 it had been demolished except for one wall.

It was a property of the Mackenzies of Brahan, Earls of Seaforth. The family eventually lost everything as foretold by the Brahan Seer, Coinneach Odhar (Kenneth Mackenzie), so called because the Mackenzies of Brahan were his patrons. Isabella, 3rd Countess of Seaforth, demanded to know from Coinneach why her husband remained in Paris, and was so angered when she was told that he had been dallying with a French lady that she ordered Coinneach's death by burning in a barrel of tar on Chanonry Point. The dates given for these events are around 1670.

Before he died, Coinneach prophesied that the last clan chief would follow his sons to the grave, deaf and dumb, and that one of his daughters would kill the other. The last chief became deaf through illness and finally too weak to speak after seeing his four sons die. His eldest daughter succeeded him, but a carriage she was driving, near Brahan, overturned and killed her sister. This seems a very detailed and full prophecy: for her own peace of mind the Countess of Seaforth might have been advised not have patiently heard him out.

A nearby stretch of the Conon River is said to have been haunted by a water sprite.

Braichlie *see* Brackley Castle

Braidwood Castle *see* Hallbar Tower

Braikie Castle

Angus & Dundee: About 6 miles south of Brechin, on minor roads south and east of A934 or north of B965, 1.5 miles east of Friockheim, at Braikie Castle.

Ruin or site   NO 628509   OS: 54   *   Map: 8, no: 254**

Braikie Castle is a 16th-century L-plan tower house of four storeys. A stair-turret is corbelled-out above first-floor level in the re-entrant angle and crowned by a roofless bartizan on one gable. There are shot-holes below most windows. The tower is dated 1581.

The entrance, in the re-entrant angle, has an iron yett and leads into the basement and to the main stair which climbs to the first-floor hall. The basement contains the wine-cellar with a small stair to the hall above. Original daub-and-wattle wall partitions survive.

It was a property of the Frasers of Oliver, but passed to the Grays about 1750, then

to the Ogilvies. The tower is derelict, and some of the roof has collapsed.

There was another tower house at Easter Braikie [NO 637515].
Other refs: Wester Braikie

Brakenside *see* Breconside Tower

Brandy Den

Angus & Dundee: About 7 miles west of Brechin, on minor roads north of A90, east of Noranside and 0.5 miles south-west of Fern, Brandy Den.
Ruin or site NO 478610 OS: 44 * Map: 8, no: 203
Site of castle, some remains of which survived in the 19th century. The castle was abandoned for Vayne [NO 493599].

It was a property of the Mowats of Fern from around the turn of the 13th century until about 1450. The property passed to the Lindsay Earls of Crawford, then the Carnegies.
Other refs: Fern

Branxholme Castle

Borders: About 3 miles south-west of Hawick, on minor road north of A7 at Branxholme, north of the River Teviot.
Private NT 464116 OS: 79 ** Map: 2, no: 129
Branxholme Castle consists of an altered 16th-century tower house of five storeys, possibly Z-plan, incorporated into a later mansion of 1790 and later. It was built on the site of an older castle. Vaulted chambers survive in the basement, along with a newel stair, but the building has been very altered inside.

The lands were acquired by the Scotts in 1420, and the castle is still owned by them. The old castle was burned by the Earl of Northumberland in 1532, but held against the English during the invasion of 1547. It was slighted by the Scotts themselves in 1570, the work being completed by the English, under the Earl of Essex, with gunpowder. It was rebuilt in the 1570s by Sir Walter Scott of Buccleuch.

The Scotts were often Wardens of the Scottish Middle March, and were involved in the raiding and feuding in the Borders. Sir Walter Scott of Buccleuch led the raid that rescued William Armstrong of Kinmont (Kinmont Willie in the old ballad) from imprisonment in Carlisle Castle in 1596.

The family became Lords in 1606, Earls in 1612, and finally Dukes of Buccleuch in 1663. The castle was largely remodelled by William Burn in 1837 for the 5th Duke.

Brawl Castle *see* Braal Castle

Breachacha Castle

Argyll & Dunbartonshire: About 5 miles south-west of Arinagour on island of Coll, on minor road south of B8070, near modern Breachacha Castle.
Private NM 159539 OS: 46 **** Map: 5, no: 2
On the edge of the bay, Breachacha Castle, built in the 14th century, consists of a square keep of four storeys and a gabled garret within a later parapet. It stands at one corner of a courtyard enclosed by a curtain wall, with a round tower at one corner and a range of buildings. A machiolation defends the entrance, and there is an artillery fortification.

The hall, on the first floor of the keep, did not have a fireplace. A turnpike stair is topped by a caphouse. In the 17th century a three-storey block was added beside the round tower. The kitchen lay outside the walls.

Breachacha was given by Robert the Bruce to Angus Og MacDonald of the Isles, but changed hands between the MacDonalds, MacNeils and MacLeans. In 1431 it was seized by the MacLeans of Coll, but they feuded with the MacLeans of Duart, who captured the castle in 1578. Donald MacLean of Coll garrisoned it against the Campbell Earl of Argyll in 1679. A new mansion was built nearby in 1750, and the castle became ruinous. Dr Johnson and Boswell visited in 1773. The property passed to the Stewarts of Glenbuchie in 1856, but the castle was bought and restored by a descendant of the MacLeans in 1965. The keep has been reroofed and the timber floors replaced, and the castle has been reoccupied.
Other refs: Breachahcadh Castle

Breachahcadh Castle *see* Breachacha Castle

Breaken Tower

Borders: About 6.5 miles north and east of Newcastleton, on minor roads south of B6357, just north of Liddel Water, just south of Larriston.
Ruin or site NY 544942 [?] OS: 79 * Map: 2, no: 197
Site of tower house of the Elliots, the last vestiges of which were removed for building dykes in 1792. This is said to be the same tower as Prinkinghaugh, although Pont locates this latter site to the north of the Liddel Water.
Other refs: Prinkinghaugh Tower; Pickeringshaw Tower

Brechin Castle

Angus & Dundee: To west of Brechin, on minor roads south of A935 or east of B9134, just north of River South Esk, at Brechin Castle.
Private NO 597599 OS: 54 ** Map: 8, no: 246
Brechin Castle incorporates some cellars from a 16th-century L-plan tower house, but is mostly a mansion from the 17th and 18th centuries. There is a walled garden.

It was at Brechin, and possibly at an earlier castle, that John Balliol, Toom Tabard, was forced to abdicate as King of Scots by Edward I of England in 1296. Sir Thomas Maule defended the castle for three weeks in 1303, against the English, until slain by a missile from a catapult. The castle was owned by the Maules, but passed to the Erskine Earl of Mar, until sold to the Maule Earl of Panmure in 1646. They built the existing mansion in 1711. The family were forfeited for their part in the 1715 Jacobite Rising, but the property was bought back by a relation and the title restored. It later passed to the Ramsays of Dalhousie, and the house is still occupied by the Earl of Dalhousie.

The nearby cathedral is mainly 13th century although the adjoining round tower may date from the 10th century when the site was occupied by Culdees.

In 1452 at Brechin a royal army under Alexander Seton, 1st Earl of Huntly, defeated a force under Alexander Lindsay, 4th Earl of Crawford.

Brechin Castle Centre is part of the Dalhousie Estates, and features Scottish breeds of domestic animals, pets corner and pheasantry, farm buildings and displays of traditional agricultural machinery and implements. Pictavia, which houses exhibits and information about the Picts, is also located here.

OPEN: Castle not open. Brechin Castle Centre open summer, Mon-Sat 9.00-18.00; winter, Mon-Sat 9.00-17.00, Sun 10.00-17.00; closed Christmas and New Year.

Guided tours by prior arrangement. Gift shop. Restaurant. Picnic area. Play area for under fives and main play area in country park. WC. Car and coach parking. Group concessions. £.
Tel: 01356 626813 Fax: 01356 626814
Email: Dalhousieestates@btinternet.com

Brechin, Bishop's Palace *see* Bishop's Palace, Brechin

Breckonside Tower *see* **Breconside Tower**

Breckonside Tower

Dumfriesshire: About 4 miles south-east of Moniaive, on minor road north of B729, at Breconside, about 1 mile north of the Cairn Water, west of The Mull, west of Breconside.
Ruin or site NX 840889 OS: 78 ** Map: 1, no: 153
Little remains of a tower house and range of outbuildings of the Maxwells. A Maxwell of Breckonside is mentioned in 1552.
Other refs: Auchenfedrick

Breconside Tower

Dumfriesshire: About 2.5 miles south of Moffat, on minor roads south of A708 and east of A701 at south junction with A74, west of the Breconside Burn.
Private NT 109022 OS: 78 ** Map: 1, no: 233
Breconside Tower consists of a small rectangular 16th-century tower house of three storeys and a garret, with 17th-century alterations and extensions. Corbiestepped gables have been added, and the windows enlarged.
  The original entrance led to the turnpike stair, which has been replaced by an octagonal stair-turret added in the middle of one side. The basement is vaulted, but the first-floor hall is now subdivided. Some 17th-century panelling survives.
  The property was owned by the Johnstones, but is now a farmhouse.
Other refs: Breckonside Tower; Brakenside

Breda

Aberdeen & Gordon: About 1.5 miles west and north of Alford, on minor roads north of A980, south of River Don, at or near Breda House.
Private NJ 549167 [?] OS: 37 * Map: 10, no: 135
Site of castle or old house. The present mansion is a baronial pile, dating from the end of the 19th century. The adjoining Broadhaugh House was demolished in 1963.
Other refs: Broadhaugh House

Bridge Castle

Lothians: About 1.5 miles north of Armadale, west of B8084, near junction with A801, just west of the Barbauchlaw Water, at Bridge Castle.
Private NS 944709 OS: 65 * Map: 4, no: 4**
Standing on a rocky outcrop, Bridge Castle consists of a substantial 14th-century keep of three storeys and an attic, within a parapet, which was later altered to L-plan. To this was added a tall 17th-century wing of four storeys and an attic, and then 19th-century extensions. The corbelled-out parapet dates from the 17th century, and has open rounds at the corners, but does not extend to the additions.
  The building has been altered inside, but the basement of the old part is vaulted and contained a kitchen. The hall was on the first floor, and private chambers occupied the floors above. A turnpike stair, which rose in the wing of the L, has been removed, and replaced by a modern stair in the later work. The basement and first floors of the 17th-century wing are both vaulted.
  The lands were sold by the Stewarts to William, Lord Livingstone, in the 1580s, who extended the castle. Bridge Castle was in the barony of Ogilface – which had a castle, now completely ruinous. The Livingstone family became Earls of Linlithgow, but were forfeited for their part in the Jacobite Rising of 1715, and the property passed to the Hopes. The castle was remodelled and enlarged in 1871, and is still occupied.
Other refs: Ogilface; Little Brighouse

Bridgehouse *see* **Brighouse Tower**

Bridgemuir

Dumfriesshire: About 1.5 miles north-east of Lochmaben, on minor roads east of B7020, east of Kinnel Water, at or near Bridgemuir.
Ruin or site NY 093845 OS: 78 ** Map: 1, no: 225
Site of tower house.

Bridgend of Tay *see* **Kinnoull Castle**

Brigend Castle

Ayrshire: About 3 miles south of Ayr, near B7024, to the south of Alloway, on the south bank of the River Doon, just south of the Old Brig of Doon.
Ruin or site NS 334177 OS: 70 ** Map: 3, no: 98
Not much remains of Brigend Castle, a ruinous 16th-century tower house, except the vaulted basement.
  It was a property of the Montgomerys of Brigend.
Other refs: Doonside Castle

Brighouse Tower

Borders: About 4 miles north and east of Newcastleton, on minor roads and foot north of B6357, north of Liddel Water, 0.3 miles north of Dinlabyre, at Brighouse.
Ruin or site NY 526921 OS: 79 * Map: 2, no: 182
Site of tower house of the Croziers.
  There may have been another tower house at Brighousecleughhead [NY 526933]
Other refs: Bridgehouse; Brighousecleughhead

Brighousecleughhead *see* **Brighouse Tower**

Brims Castle

Sutherland & Caithness: About 5 miles west and north of Thurso, on minor road north of A836, just south of sea at Port of Brims, at Brims Castle.
Ruin or site ND 043710 OS: 12 * Map: 12, no: 39**
Brims Castle is a 16th-century L-plan tower house of three storeys and a garret, consisting of a main block and square stair-wing. An open turret crowns one corner above the entrance, and the gables are corbiestepped. The original windows are small. A walled courtyard, with a moulded gateway, encloses ranges of later buildings.
  The entrance, at first-floor level in the wing, is reached by a modern external stair. The basement is vaulted, and reached by a small stair from the hall on the first floor. Private chambers occupied the upper floors.
  Brims was a property of the Sinclairs of Dunbeath, occupied until the 20th century, but is now derelict and roofless.

Brisbane House

Ayrshire: About 2 miles north of Largs, on minor road north from A78 in Largs, just west of the Noddsdale Water, at Brisbane Mains.
Ruin or site NS 209622 OS: 63 * Map: 3, no: 33
Brisbane House, a four-storey symmetrical mansion dating from the 17th century, was built on the site of an earlier castle, but was demolished in the 20th century. Only part of one of the later wings survives.
  The lands, called Kelsoland, had belonged to the Kelso family from the 13th century, but were sold to the Shaws of Greenock in 1624, and they built the house in 1634. In 1650 Robert Kelso bought the property back, but the name was changed to Brisbane after it was sold to James Brisbane of Bishopton in 1671. Sir Thomas Brisbane, who was born in the house, served as a soldier, but was very interested in astronomy. He built observatories at Makerstoun in Scotland, and near Sydney in Australia, where he was Governor of New South Wales from 1821-25. It was held by the Brisbanes until the 20th century. It was unroofed around 1938, then mostly demolished.
Other refs: Kelsoland; Killincraig

Broadhaugh

Borders: About 3.5 miles south-west of Hawick, on minor road east of A7, east side of River Teviot, at or near Broadhaugh.
Ruin or site NT 449093 [?] OS: 79 * Map: 2, no: 119
Site of tower house, a property of the Scotts of Allanhaugh.
Other refs: Ringwodhay

Broadhaugh House *see* **Breda**

Broadstone Castle

Ayrshire: About 1 mile south-east of Beith, on minor roads east of B706 or south of B777, at Broadstonehall.

Ruin or site   NS 359528 [?]   OS: 63   *   Map: 3, no: 117

Site of castle, the last remains of which were removed around the end of the 18th century when the present farm of Broadstonehall was built.

The lands were a property of the Liddles in 1452, but apparently passed to the Montgomerys, then in 1650 were sold to the Greenock family. The castle was still used until around 1700.

Broadwall

Galloway: About 18 miles south of Stranraer, just of B7041, 3 miles south of Drummore, at or near Broadwall.

Ruin or site   NX 130333   OS: 82   *   Map: 1, no: 27

Probable site of castle.

Broch of Gurness *see* Gurness Broch

Broch of Midhowe *see* Midhowe Broch

Broch of Mousa *see* Mousa Broch

Broch of Tirefour *see* Tirefour Broch

Brochel Castle

South Highland: On north-east side of island of Raasay, about 8 miles north of East Suinish pier, on minor road 6.5 miles north of Clachan, at Brochel.

Ruin or site   NG 585463   OS: 24   **   Map: 9, no: 15

Perched on a high rock in a spectacular location, Brochel Castle is a small ruined fortress, built early in the 16th century by the MacLeods of Raasay. Stumps of walls surround an uneven courtyard, contouring the rock, with several towers. It was entered by a steep stair, leading to a passageway through the gatehouse.

The last chief resident at Brochel was probably Iain Garbh around 1648, after

which the family moved to Clachan, at Kilmaluag, further south on Raasay, although this later tower house has gone.

The ruin is in a dangerous condition, but can be easily viewed from the exterior.

Brockloch

Dumfriesshire: About 4 miles south and east of Moniaive, on minor road west of B729 at Dunscore, 0.25 miles west of Sundaywell, at Brockloch.

Ruin or site   NX 802844   OS: 78   *   Map: 1, no: 134

Not much remains except foundations of a tower house with the scant remains of other buildings from a farm.

Brockloch Castle

Ayrshire: About 1 mile north west of Maybole, on minor roads north of B7023 and west of B7024, at or near Brockloch.

Ruin or site   NS 289113 [?]   OS: 70   *   Map: 3, no: 67

Site of 16th-century L-plan tower house, probably of the Kennedys, a vestige of which remained in the 19th century.

It was nearby that the Kennedy Earl of Cassillis ambushed and mortally wounded Kennedy of Bargany in 1602. The two had feuded over land.

Brodick Castle

Ayrshire: About 2 miles north of Brodick on Isle of Arran, on minor road west of A841, on north side of Brodick Bay, at Brodick Castle.

NTS   NS 016378   OS: 69   *   Map: 3, no: 2**

Occupying a magnificent site overlooking Brodick Bay, Brodick Castle incorporates a 15th-century keep at one end, the lower part of which may date from the 13th century. Extensive additions were made in the 19th century.

The old part rises to three storeys and an attic within a corbelled-out crenellated parapet. There are two stair towers, one with the parapet continuing around it, and the other crowned by a caphouse. An adjacent artillery battery was built in the 1650s.

The basement of the old part is vaulted, and contained the original kitchen. The tower has been much altered inside, but turnpike stairs lead to the upper storeys.

Arran was held by the Norsemen until driven out by Somerled in the 12th century, although the property only passed to the Scottish Crown in 1266. The Stewarts of Menteith built the original castle, but it was held by the English during the Wars of Independence until 1307 when recaptured by the Scots. It was damaged by English ships in 1406, and by the MacDonald Lord of the Isles about 1455. Arran passed to the Boyds in 1467, then to the Hamiltons in 1503. The 1st Hamilton Earl of Arran rebuilt the castle about 1510, but it was damaged in a raid in 1528 between feuding Campbells and MacLeans, and again in 1544 by the Earl of Lennox for Henry VIII of England.

It was extended and remodelled by the Regent Arran in the 1550s, but was captured by the Campbells in 1639 to be retaken by the Hamiltons. In the 1650s the castle was occupied by Cromwell's troops.

Extensive additions were made in 1844 by James Gillespie Graham for the marriage of Princess Marie of Baden to the 11th Duke of Hamilton, and in 1958 Brodick was taken over by The National Trust for Scotland.

A 'Grey Lady' is said to haunt the older part of the castle, her spirit possibly that of one of three women starved to death in the dungeons because they had plague. Two other ghosts associated with the castle are that of a sitting man, which has reportedly been seen in the library; and that of a White Deer, apparently only seen when one of the chiefs of the Hamiltons is near death.

OPEN: Castle open daily, Apr-Oct 11.00-16.30, last admission 16.00; Jul-Aug, daily 11.00-17.00, last admission 16.30; reception centre and shop, 10.00-17.00, also Nov-Dec, Sat-Sun 11.00-15.00; restaurant as reception centre except Apr-Oct 11.00-17.00; walled garden open all year, daily 9.30-17.00; country park open all year, 9.30-sunset; Goatfell open all year – weather permitting.

Collections of furniture, porcelain, pictures and silver. Gift shop. Licensed restaurant. WC. Gardens and country park, ice house, summer house and adventure playground. Nature trail and access to Goatfell. Disabled WC and access. Car and coach parking. £££.

Tel: 01770 302202   Fax: 01770 302312
Email: information@nts.org.uk   Web: nts.org.uk

Brodick Castle – see previous page

Brodie Castle

Moray: About 4 miles west of Forres, on minor roads just north of A96, west of Muckle Burn, 0.5 miles south-west of Dyke, at Brodie Castle.

NTS NH 980578 OS: 27 **** Map: 10, no: 1

A large and impressive building, Brodie Castle was mostly built in the 16th and 17th centuries, but may date in part from the 12th century, although this is disputed. The castle consists of a large 16th-century Z-plan tower house, with extensive additions, which was further enlarged in the 19th century by the architect William Burn.

The old tower rises to four storeys and a garret within a corbelled-out parapet. A wide stair-turret, crowned by a conical roof, is corbelled out in the re-entrant angle.

The basement contains five vaulted chambers, including a kitchen with a great fireplace and bread oven. The only windows are slits and gunloops. The hall, on the first floor, is also vaulted.

The property was owned by the Brodies from 1160. It was torched in 1645 by Lord Lewis Gordon, because the Brodies were Covenanters, although much of the internal work survived. The house was renovated in 1980 after passing to The National Trust for Scotland, although it is still occupied by the Brodies.

An apparition of a woman is said to have been witnessed in the nursery room in 1992.

A fine Pictish cross-slab, known as Rodney's Stone, stands in the avenue up to the castle, and was found in the burial ground of the old church of Dyke and Moy.

OPEN: Open daily, Apr-Sep, Mon-Sat 11.00-17.30, Sun 13.30-17.30; Oct, Sat 11.00-17.30, Sun 13.30-17.30; last admission 16.30; other times by appt; tearoom closes 16.30; grounds open all year, 9.30-sunset.

Collection of paintings and furniture. Guided tours available. Explanatory displays. Gift shop. Tearoom. WC. Picnic area. Garden and adventure playground. Disabled facilities including Braille guides. Car and coach parking. Group concessions. £££.

Tel: 01309 641371 Fax: 01309 641600
Email: information@nts.org.uk Web: nts.org.uk

Broich House

Stirling & Clackmannanshire: About 0.5 miles north-west of Kippen, on minor roads south of B8037, near Arngomery House.

Ruin or site NS 641951 OS: 57 * Map: 6, no: 43

Broich House, which was demolished in 1852, appears to have been defended by a ditch and rampart. Arngomery House is a 19th-century mansion.

Other refs: Arngomery House

Broken Tower

Lanarkshire & Glasgow: About 3 miles west of Kirkintilloch, on minor roads north of A807 or west of B822, west of Torrance, at or near Tower.

Ruin or site NS 613741 OS: 64 * Map: 3, no: 284

Site of tower house, a vestige of which survived in 1860 although nothing now remains.

Other refs: Tower, Torrance; Badhindrocht

Broom House

Borders: About 1.5 miles north-east of Duns, on minor roads east of A6112, south of Whiteadder Water, at or near Broom House.
Ruin or site NT 803567 OS: 74 * Map: 2, no: 327
Site of castle, on which was built Broom House in 1813, although this later house has also been demolished.

Broomhall *see* Corstorphine Castle

Broomhall

Fife: About 3 miles south-west of Dunfermline, on minor roads south of A985, just north of Limekilns on the north shore of the Firth of Forth, at Broomhall.
Private NT 077837 OS: 65 * Map: 7, no: 10
Broomhall, a long three-storey classical mansion of 1796-7, stands on the site of an earlier house, dating from 1580. It was altered several times including in 1705 and 1796.

It was a property of Dunfermline Abbey, but purchased by the Richardson family after the Reformation. It was sold to Sir George Bruce at the beginning of the 17th century, and the name was changed to Broomhall. The family were made Earls of Elgin in 1633, then Earls of Kincardine in 1647, and they still occupy the house.

Broomhall is said to house the helmet and two-handed sword of Robert the Bruce, the latter having been used to 'knight' Robert Burns at Clackmannan Tower, as well as a bed slept in by Charles I.
Other refs: Gedeleth; West Gellet

Broomhill Castle

Lanarkshire & Glasgow area: About 0.5 miles west of Larkhall, on minor roads west of B7078, just east of Avon Water, south of Millheugh, at Broomhill.
Ruin or site NS 754508 OS: 64 * Map: 3, no: 354
Site of castle, which once rose to four storeys and had bartizans. It was altered and extended in later centuries.

The lands were a property of the Hamiltons from 1473. The family supported Mary, Queen of Scots. Sir John Hamilton died of wounds received at Langside, and the castle was torched by Sir William Drurie in 1572. It was rebuilt in 1585, and extended and remodelled in later centuries. The property passed to the Birnies, but the house was demolished after a fire in 1943, except for cellars.

Broomhill was reputedly haunted by a 'Black Lady', seen in both the house and in the area. The story goes that a beautiful Indian woman, either a servant or princess, disappeared about 1900, and may have been murdered. She was believed to be the mistress of Captain Henry McNeil-Hamilton, who died in 1924.
Other refs: Auld Machan Castle; Machan

Broomhill House

Lothians: About 4 miles south of Edinburgh Castle, on minor roads south of B701, south of Kaimes, just north of Burdiehouse, north of Swanston Burn, at Broomhills.
Ruin or site NT 269674 [?] OS: 66 * Map: 4, no: 109
Site of keep with a wet moat and drawbridge. The castle was ruined by 1792, and the mansion was built on the site, itself demolished in the 20th century.

It was a property of the Hendersons of Fordel from 1508. In 1648, one of the sisters of Sir John Henderson was imprisoned in the Tolbooth of Edinburgh, having been accused of witchcraft. She apparently poisoned herself the night before she was due to be executed: strangled then burned at the stake.

In 1709 the property was sold to the Bairds of Newbyth, then in 1827 to the Trotters of Mortonhall.

Broomholm Tower

Dumfriesshire: About 2 miles south of Langholm, on minor road west of B6318, east of River Esk, at or near Broomholm.
Ruin or site NY 372817 OS: 79 * Map: 1, no: 316
Site of tower house, which was demolished about 1745 and replaced by a mansion.

Brotherton Castle

Kincardine & Deeside: About 6 miles south-east of Laurencekirk, on minor roads east of A92, west of the sea, about 0.5 miles north of Johnshaven, at Lathallen School.
Private NO 803676 OS: 45 * Map: 10, no: 267
Site of castle. Brotherton House, baronial mansion built in 1866, stands on the site and now used as a school: it is called Lathallen.

The property was held by the Brotherton family, who built the castle, but in the 17th century passed to the Scotts who still held it in the 20th century.
Other refs: Lathallen

Brough Castle

Sutherland & Caithness: About 4.5 miles north-east of Castletown, on minor roads and foot north of A836, east of B855, north of village of Brough, just south of sea.
Ruin or site ND 228741 OS: 12 * Map: 12, no: 53
Little or nothing remains of a castle of enclosure, on a promontory, except the ditch.
Other refs: Castle of Braigh

Brough of Birsay

Orkney: About 18 miles north-west of Kirkwall, on minor road and foot north of A966, on Brough of Birsay (tidal island).
His Scot HY 239285 OS: 6 * Map: 11, no: 33**
On a tidal island is the Brough of Birsay, an early Christian settlement, which was later used by Norsemen, and became an important centre. Thorfinn the Mighty, Earl of Orkney had a house here, and there was a substantial 12th-century church, consisting of a rectangular nave, smaller chancel and an apse. There are also the foundations of an enclosure wall, and several other buildings. A fine Pictish sculptured stone decorated with figures was found here, the original is now in the Museum of Scotland, while there is a replica on the islet. The island is reached by a causeway, which floods at high tide.
OPEN: Open all year: tel 0131 668 8800 for details – check tides as causeway floods.
Parking nearby. £. Combined ticket available for all Orkney monuments.
Tel: 0131 668 8800 Fax: 0131 668 8888
Email: hs.explore@scotland.gov.uk Web: www.historic-scotland.gov.uk

Broughton *see* Old Place of Broughton

Broughton Place

Borders: About 5 miles east of Biggar, on minor road east of A701, just north of Broughton village, south of Hollows Burn, at Broughton Place.
Private NT 117372 OS: 72 * Map: 2, no: 15
Although Broughton Place appears to be a tower house, it was built in 1938 by the architect Sir Basil Spence. However, a house which burned down here in 1773 incorporated work from an old tower house.

It was owned by the Murrays, one of whom, John Murray of Broughton, was Secretary to Bonnie Prince Charlie. After the failure of the Jacobite Rising of 1745, he remained in Scotland to guard the Loch Arkaig treasure, 40,000 Louis d'Ors, which has never been found. He was captured but escaped punishment by denouncing Simon Fraser, Lord Lovat, who was less lucky and executed. The property was sold to Robert MacQueen, Lord Braxfield, about 1755.

The drawing room and hall are open to the public, and paintings and crafts by living British artists are for sale. The gardens are open and have fine views of the Tweeddale hills. There are also national collections of Thalictrum and Tropaeolum.
Other refs: Little Hope
OPEN: Gallery open Apr-mid Oct and mid Nov-Christmas.
Gift shop. Garden. Garden centre. WC. Disabled access. Car and coach parking.
Tel: 01899 830234

Broughty Castle

Angus & Dundee: To south of Broughty Ferry, on minor roads south of A930, just north of shore of Firth of Tay, east of harbour, at Broughty Castle.
Private NO 465304 OS: 54 * Map: 8, no: 200**
Broughty Castle consists of a tall 15th-century keep of five storeys and a garret within a later machiolated parapet. It has been much altered, and was given artillery emplacements in the 19th century, the wing dating from this time.

A stair climbs in the thickness of the walls in one corner, and is crowned by a gabled caphouse.

The Grays built the original castle in the 1490s. During the English invasion of Scotland in 1547-50, Patrick, 4th Lord Gray, a treacherous fellow, delivered up

Broughty Castle to the English. From here, and the fort on Balgillo Hill, they harried Dundee. The castle was stormed by the Scots with French help in 1550, and partly demolished. It was complete enough, however, to be held for Mary, Queen of Scots, by the Hamilton Duke of Chatelherault until 1571. It was taken by General Monck for Cromwell in 1651.

By 1821, it was a roofless ruin, but was eventually bought by the War Office in 1851, radically enlarged and altered internally, and given gun emplacements. The castle is now a museum of whaling and fishery, arms and armour, a branch of Dundee museums. There are fine views of the Tay.
Other refs: Balgillo; Burgh Tay Castle
OPEN: Open Apr-Sep, Mon-Sat 10.00-16.00, Sun 12.30-16.00; Oct-Mar, Tue-Sat 10.00-16.00, Sun 12.30-16.00, closed Mon.
Explanatory displays. Sales area. Parking.
Tel: 01382 436916 Fax: 01382 436951
Email: Broughty@dundeecity.gov.uk Web: www.dundeecity.gov.uk

Brounston *see* Brunston Castle

Broxmouth House

Lothians: About 1 mile south-east of Dunbar, on minor roads east of A1087, west of Spott Burn, north-east of Broxburn, at Broxmouth.
Private NT 696766 OS: 67 * Map: 4, no: 224
The present mansion appears to date from no earlier than the end of the 18th century. An earlier building on the site is marked on Blaeu's Atlas Novus map of Lothian within a park, and Cromwell garrisoned the house and used it as his headquarters in 1650 during the Battle of Dunbar. Cromwell is said to have watched the

battle from a hillock near the house now known as Cromwell's Mount.

Broxmouth was a property of the Homes, but later passed to the Kerr Dukes of Roxburgh. It is still occupied.

Bruce's Castle

Stirlingshire & Clackmannan: About 5 miles north and west of Falkirk, on minor roads north and foot of B9124, south-west of Carnock House, just south of Castleton.
Ruin or site NS 857878 OS: 65 ** Map: 6, no: 87
Bruce's Castle, which was earlier known as Carnock Tower, is a ruinous 15th-century keep or tower. The remains consist of the vaulted basement, part of the vaulted hall, and the beginning of a stair in the basement.

It was built by the Airths of Plean in the 15th century, but about 1480 passed to the Hepburns, and was damaged and slighted in a family quarrel around 1489. It was acquired by the Bruces of Auchenbowie in the early 16th century, but in 1608 passed to the Drummonds of Carnock. They changed the name to distinguish it from Carnock House.
Other refs: Carnock Tower; Tower of Carnock

Brucklaw Castle *see* Brucklay Castle

Brucklay Castle

Aberdeen & Gordon: About 2.5 miles north-east of New Deer, on minor roads east of A981 or west of A950, at Brucklay Castle.
Private NJ 913502 OS: 30 ** Map: 10, no: 317
Brucklay Castle, although greatly altered and now ruined, was originally a 16th-century tower, extended in the 17th century, again in 1765, and finally in 1849. The basement was vaulted.

It was a property of the Fordyce family in the 19th century, and is now ruinous.
Other refs: Brucklaw Castle

Brugh

Borders: About 5.5 miles south and west of Hawick, on minor roads and foot east of A7, east of Allan Water, about 0.3 miles west of Dod, at Burgh Hill.
Ruin or site NT 467058 OS: 79 * Map: 2, no: 133
Site of tower house, rising to two storeys and dating from the 16th century. The castle had been demolished by the end of the 18th century to build dykes.

The property was held by the Scotts of Allanhaugh in 1560, but by 1595 had passed to the Elliots, then by 1632 to the Scotts of Buccleuch.
Other refs: Burgh Hill

Brunstane Castle

Lothians: About 2 miles south west of Penicuik, on minor road south of A766, on the north bank of the river North Esk.
Ruin or site NT 201582 OS: 66 * Map: 4, no: 66**
Brunstane Castle is a ruined 16th-century L-plan tower house of three storeys, with a square stair-tower in the re-entrant angle. The stair-tower is crowned by a corbelled-out caphouse. There are gunloops under the windows. Part of the courtyard survives with a square tower. The tower is dated 1568.

The basement contained the kitchen with a large fireplace. The hall was on the first floor.

The property belonged to the Crichtons. In 1546 George Wishart, the Protestant martyr, who had been sheltering in the tower, was seized and taken to St Andrews (via Elphinstone Tower and Ormiston) to be burned as a heretic. The laird of Brunstane was subsequently found guilty of plotting with the English, and the castle was torched in 1547. John, Lord Maitland, acquired the property in 1632, and he extended the castle.
Other refs: Brunston

Brunstane House

Lothians: About 4.5 miles east of Edinburgh Castle, in the Brunstane area of Edinburgh, on minor road south of the A1, in Brunstane Road South.
Private NT 316725 OS: 66 ** Map: 4, no: 131
Brunstane House is an altered 16th-century L-plan tower house, which probably incorporates parts of an older castle. It was greatly remodelled and extended in the

1630s, in 1672-4 by Sir William Bruce, in 1735-44 when William Adam rebuilt the south range, and in the 1850s.

The original castle was destroyed after the Battle of Pinkie in 1547, but was apparently rebuilt about 1565. The property was held by the Crichtons of Brunstane, but in 1632 was acquired by John Dundas, Viscount Maitland, who was later Duke of Lauderdale, a very powerful man in Scotland. It was sold in 1733 to Lord Milton, who had William Adam extend the house. The house is still occupied, although it has been divided.

Other refs: Gilberton

Brunston *see* Brunstane Castle

Brunston Castle

Ayrshire: About 5 miles north and east of Girvan, on minor road west and foot of B741 just west of Dailly, on the north bank of the Water of Girvan.

Ruin or site NS 261012 OS: 76 ** Map: 3, no: 55

Not much remains of Brunston Castle, a 17th-century T-plan tower house of at least three storeys, except the vaulted basement and a stair-turret.

It was built in 1620 by the Kennedys. 'Black Bessie' Kennedy lived here after the death of her third husband, William Baillie of Carrick. Her relatives Kennedy of Bargany and Kennedy Earl of Cassillis had a long and bitter quarrel over the possession of Bessie and her lands, which ended with the murder of Bargany.

Other refs: Brounston

Bruntisfield House *see* Bruntsfield House

Brunton *see* Barnslee

Bruntsfield House – see above

Bruntsfield House

Lothians: In Edinburgh, on minor roads east of A702, in the Bruntsfield area of Edinburgh, just south of Bruntsfield Links, as part of Gillespie's School.

Private NT 252723 [?] OS: 66 ** Map: 4, no: 93

Bruntsfield House is a much-altered 16th-century Z-plan tower house of three storeys and an attic, although parts may date from the 15th century and the site itself is older. It consists of a main block, projecting towers at opposite corners, and an addition of 1605. The house has been much remodelled, except for one side. A round stair-tower is corbelled out in one re-entrant angle.

The basement has been vaulted, and a straight stair leads to the first floor, the upper floors reached by turnpike stairs. The interior has been much altered, but there is fine panelling and fireplaces. A secret room was found in the early 19th century.

Bruntsfield takes its name from Richard Browne, ['Browne's Field'] King's Sergeant of the Muir, but passed to the Lauders in 1381, and was held by them until the beginning of the 17th century. Sir Alexander Lauder was Provost of Edinburgh, as was his son, another Alexander, who was killed at the Battle of Flodden in 1513. In 1603 the property was sold to the Fairlies of Braid, who altered the house in the following years, but in 1695 it passed to the Warrenders. In 1880 the house was surrounded by 75 acres of grass parks, but in 1935 it was sold to the city of Edinburgh, and is now part of James Gillespie's school.

Other refs: Bruntisfield House

Brux Castle

Aberdeen & Gordon: About 1.5 miles east of Kildrummy, on minor roads south of A944 at Brux, south of the Don, at or near Mains of Brux.

Ruin or site NJ 490169 OS: 37 * Map: 10, no: 107

Site of tower house of the Forbeses of Brux. Parts may be built into the derelict Mains of Brux. Jonathan Forbes of Brux was a Jacobite, and hid in the laird's lug at Craigievar to escape capture.

Brydekirk Tower

Dumfriesshire: About 3 miles north of Annan, on minor roads east of B723, north of village of Brydekirk, west of the River Annan, at or near Brydekirk Mains.

Ruin or site NY 187711 [?] OS: 85 * Map: 1, no: 258

Site of 16th-century tower house, part of a gable of which is built into Brydekirk Mains.

Bu of Cairston *see* Cairston Castle

Buccleuch Castle

Borders: About 3.5 miles east of Ettrick, on minor road south of B711, near the Rankle Burn, at Buccleuch.

Ruin or site NT 328143 OS: 79 * Map: 2, no: 84

Site of 16th-century castle of the Scotts, on the site of earlier stronghold.

Sir Michael Scott of Buccleuch fought at the Battle of Halidon Hill in 1333, but was killed at the Battle of Durham in 1346. The castle was burned in 1544 by the English under the Earl of Hertford. The Scotts killed several of the Kerrs of Cessford in 1526 during a feud, and Walter Scott of Buccleuch was murdered by the Kerrs in the High Street of Edinburgh in 1552. Walter Scott of Buccleuch rescued 'Kinmont' Willie Armstrong from Carlisle Castle in 1596. The Lordship of Buccleuch was created in 1606 for Sir Walter Scott of Buccleuch. The 2nd Lord was created Earl in 1612 and a Dukedom was created in 1663 for James, Duke of Monmouth, on his marriage to Anna, Countess of Buccleuch. He was executed for leading a rebellion in 1685, and she was made Duchess in her own right. She died in 1732. The foundations were unearthed with the building of the farmhouse in 1832, but there are now no remains.

Other refs: East Buccleuch

Buchanan Castle

Stirlingshire & Clackmannan: About 0.5 miles west of Drymen, on minor roads south of B807, west of A809, about 0.5 miles north west of Kilmaronock Castle, at Buchanan.

Private NS 463886 OS: 57 ** Map: 6, no: 5

Buchanan Castle, a huge castellated ruin, incorporates an L-plan tower house. The

ruin is crowned with the remains of many turrets, bartizans and towers. The main block of two storeys and an attic has towers, at either end, and a three-storey turreted entrance block.

The old castle was the seat of the Buchanans, but in 1682 was sold to the Graham Marquises of Montrose because of financial difficulties. They were made Dukes in 1707, and the 1st Duke spent much of his time trying to track down Rob Roy MacGregor. It was burned down in 1850, and a new house built in 1854 and designed by William Burn. The gardens were modelled by Capability Brown, but have been replaced by a golf course. Rudolf Hess, Hitler's deputy, was imprisoned here after flying to Scotland. The castle is ruined but consolidated.

The castle is reputed to be haunted.

There was an earlier castle, Buchanan Pele, to the south of the present building [NS 457886], the site of which is now a golf course. It apparently consisted of 'an old tower and a great many other buildings'. It was demolished before 1724.

Other refs: Peel of Buchanan

Bucharin Castle *see* Gauldwell Castle

Bucholly Castle

Sutherland & Caithness: About 10 miles north of Wick, on foot east of A9, about 1 mile south of Freswick House, on cliffs west of sea, at Castle Geo.
Ruin or site ND 382658 OS: 12 ** Map: 12, no: 68
Standing on a narrow rocky promontory above the sea, Bucholly Castle is a ruined 12th- or 13th-century castle and courtyard, to which a keep and gatehouse were later added. Part of the gatehouse and sunken entrance passage survives, but the rest of the castle is very ruined.

According the Orkneyinga Saga, Svein Aliefson, a Norse pirate, is said to have had a stronghold here in the 12th century. The present castle was built by the Mowats of Bucholly in the 13th century, who held lands in Aberdeenshire, but in 1616 was sold to the Sinclairs of Rattar. The castle was probably abandoned at the beginning of the 17th century for Freswick House.

The castle is in a dangerous state, and should be approached – if at all – with great care.

Bucholly was said to be 'strongly expressive of the jealous and wretched condition of the tyrant owners'.

Other refs: Freswick Castle

Buchragie House

Banff & Buchan: About 2 miles west of Banff, on foot north of A98 or south of B9139
Ruin or site NJ 659644 OS: 29 * Map: 10, no: 183
Little remains of a castle or old house of the Ogilvies except traces of masonry.

Buchromb

Moray: About 3 miles north of Dufftown, on minor road north of A941, west of River Fiddich, at or near Buchromb.
Private NJ 313439 OS: 28 * Map: 10, no: 60
Site of castle. The castellated mansion of 1873 has been demolished, but incorporated part of an earlier building.

Buck o' Bield

Galloway: About 1.5 miles west and south of Gatehouse of Fleet, on minor road north of A75, south of Anwoth, at Bushybield.
Ruin or site NX 581559 OS: 83 * Map: 1, no: 89
Site of castle or old house, said to be baronial in character, but demolished in 1827.

It was a property of the Rutherfords around 1630, and occupied by Samuel Rutherford, the Covenanting minister of Anwoth. It was held by the Gordons by the end of the 17th century, and in 1690 William Gordon of Buck o' Bield was shot and killed by Godfrey MacCulloch. MacCulloch was beheaded in 1697 by the Maiden, an early Scottish guillotine, which is preserved in the Museum of Scotland in Edinburgh.

Other refs: Bush o' Bield; Bushybield

Buckholm Tower

Borders: About 1 mile north and west of Galashiels, on minor roads east and south of A7 at Buckholm, west of Buckholm Hill.
Ruin or site NT 482379 OS: 73 ** Map: 2, no: 146
Buckholm Tower is a ruined 16th-century L-plan tower house of three storeys, and stands beside a later house. A small stair-tower projects from the main block. Only a section of the courtyard wall survives.

The basement is vaulted, but did not connect with the hall on the first floor – a separate entrance was reached by an external stair.

The lands of Buckholm were held by Melrose Abbey, but passed to the Pringles or Hoppringles. They were accused of treason, and their tower was burned in 1547. The tower is derelict and the roof has fallen in.

The ruins are reputedly haunted by one of the 17th-century Pringle Lairds. He was a cruel man and spent his time persecuting Covenanters, sadistically murdering folk in his dungeon. He was cursed by the wife of one of his victims, and afterwards lived in great terror, as if pursued by ghostly hounds. Pringle's ghost can reputedly be seen running from a pack of dogs on the anniversary of his death, and screams and cries heard from the dungeon of the tower.

Bucklerhole

Dumfriesshire: About 3 miles east of Dumfries, by minor roads and foot north of A75, 1.5 miles south and east of Torthorwald, at or near Bucklerhole.
Ruin or site NY 044762 [?] OS: 84 * Map: 1, no: 205
Site of tower house, some remains of which survived in the second half of the 19th century.

Buittle Castle

Galloway: About 1 mile north-west of Dalbeattie, on minor road north of A745, just west of the Urr Water, about 200 yards east of Buittle Place.
Ruin or site NX 819616 OS: 84 * Map: 1, no: 143
Standing on a site which was occupied in prehistoric times, Buittle Castle is a large ruined and overgrown courtyard castle with a surrounding ditch, dating from the 13th century. Foundations and fragments of a gatehouse survive with the remains of a drawbridge pit. Excavation uncovered foundations of stone buildings, within the courtyard, one of which may have been occupied in the 15th century. Evidence of two square timber towers and a palisade, which had been burned down, were also unearthed.

Devorgilla of Galloway, heiress of Allan, Lord of Galloway, and her husband, John Balliol, built the castle in the 1240s. Their son, John Balliol, was born here in 1249. With her husband, Devorgilla started Balliol College in Oxford, and after his death, she founded Sweetheart Abbey, where his heart is buried. She died in 1290. Her son, who succeeded in 1267, was chosen to be John I, King of Scots, by Edward I of England in 1292. The castle was occupied by English forces after Balliol was deposed in 1296; but the Scots captured the castle in 1313 and it was slighted. The lands were given to Sir James Douglas. John Balliol died in exile in France, but his son, Edward Balliol reoccupied the site when he was king, probably after 1346.

Occupation dates back to prehistoric times and there was a royal burgh here in 1324, although little remains. A 16th-century tower house, called Buittle Place, was built nearby.

Other refs: Botel Castle

Buittle Place

Galloway: About 1 mile west of Dalbeattie, on minor road north of A745, short distance west of the Water of Urr, near 13th-century Buittle Castle.

Private   NX 817616   OS: 84   *   Map: 1, no: 142**

Buittle Place is a late 16th-century L-plan tower house, probably largely built from masonry from the nearby 13th-century castle. The roof has been lowered, and nothing remains of bartizans but corbelling. A round stair-turret rises in the re-entrant angle.

The original entrance, in the wing, led to a stair, which has been removed, up to the hall on the first floor, and to the basement of the wing. The vaulted basement, of the main block, is reached by a modern doorway. The house has been extensively altered. The first floor is now reached by an external stairway.

From the 13th century the lands of Buittle were held by the Balliol family, who were based at nearby Buittle Castle. The property passed to the Douglas family, and in the 16th century to the Maxwells. In 1790 the tower was a roofless ruin, but it has been restored and is now occupied.

Other refs: Botel Place

Bunchrew House

Inverness & Nairn: About 3 miles west of Inverness, on minor roads north of A862, on south shore of Beauly Firth, east of Bunchrew Burn, at Bunchrew House.

Private   NH 621459   OS: 26   **   Map: 9, no: 83

Bunchrew House, dating mostly from the 18th and 19th centuries, incorporates a 17th-century castle or house.

It was a property of the Forbeses of Culloden, one of whom, Duncan Forbes, was Lord President of the Court of Session and died in 1747. Bunchrew later passed to the Frasers.

Bunkle Castle

Borders: About 2 miles north and east of Preston, just south of B6438, 1 mile north-east of junction with A6112.

Ruin or site   NT 805596   OS: 67   *   Map: 2, no: 329

Little remains of the large 12th-century castle of Bunkle, except some fragments of masonry.

Bunkle passed by marriage from the Bonkyl family to John Stewart in 1288. He was the son of Alexander the High Steward, and killed at the Battle of Falkirk in 1298. His sons, however, went on to great things: Alexander was Earl of Angus; Alan Earl of Lennox; Walter the progenitor of the Earls of Galloway; and James the progenitor of the Earls of Atholl, Buchan and Traquair, as well as the lords of Lorn and Innermeath. The castle passed to the Douglas Earls of Angus, then to the Homes.

'Bunkle, Billie and Blanerne,
Three castles strong as airn;
Built when Davy was a bairn;
They'll all gang doon
Wi' Scotland's croon
And ilka ane shall be a cairn.'

Burgh Hill *see* Brugh

Burgh Muir Castle *see* Wrychtishousis

Burgh Tay Castle *see* Broughty Castle

Burghead

Moray: About 8 miles north-west of Elgin, on minor roads off B9089, on promontory on the south side of the Moray Firth, at Burghead.

Ruin or site   NJ 110690   OS: 28   *   Map: 10, no: 19**

Burghead was a major stronghold of the Picts, although it had been used since prehistoric times. Although much damaged when a village was built on most of the site, this was an outstanding example of a Pictish fortification.

Eighteenth-century illustrations show the fort consisting of three 800-feet long ramparts in an arrowhead arrangement. Only the central ridge now remains. The fort was built between the 4th and 6th centuries, and was destroyed some time

about 9th-10th century. Many fine Pictish carvings were found here, which can now been seen on display in the Burghead Library, Elgin Museum, the Museum of Scotland in Edinburgh and the British Museum in London. The fort was sufficiently intact for Thorfinn the Mighty, Earl of Orkney, to use it as a base. It was nearby that Duncan (of Macbeth fame) was defeated by Thorfinn in 1040; then Duncan was also defeated by Macbeth in battle, and died of his wounds at Spynie.

The well, rediscovered in 1809, is thought to be early Christian and consists of a rock-hewn chamber, reached down stone steps. It has been identified by some as being associated with the local cult of St Ethan, and has a deep tank of water surrounded by a platform, with a basin and pedestal in opposite corners. St Ethan, Aethen or Ethernanus was a disciple of St Columba and founded several churches on the eastern side of Scotland. There was another well [NJ 121691], dedicated to St Ethan, although this is apparently now overgrown and disused.

OPEN: Rock-cut well: access at all reasonable times; contact info is for well.

Parking nearby.

Tel: 0131 668 8800   Fax: 0131 668 8888
Email: hs.explore@scotland.gov.uk   Web: www.historic-scotland.gov.uk

Burgie Castle

Moray: About 3.5 miles east of Forres, on minor roads south of A96, south of distillery, south-east of Burgie House, at Burgie Castle.

Ruin or site   NJ 094593   OS: 27   *   Map: 10, no: 12**

Burgie Castle now only consists of one tower from a large 17th-century Z-plan tower house. The tower rises to six storeys, and has a parapet with open rounds. A tall stair-turret, in the former re-entrant angle with the demolished main block, is crowned by a caphouse. The walls are pierced by gunloops and shot-holes, and iron yetts bar some of the windows. The castle was extended in 1702.

The entrance to the basement still has an iron yett. The basement is vaulted as is the 5th and 6th floor.

Not much of the main block remains. The castle stands within a pleasance wall with a well, in what has been the courtyard.

Burgie passed from the Abbey of Kinloss in 1566 to the Dunbars, who built the castle. Dunbar of Burgie fought against the Marquis of Montrose in 1645, but bankrupted himself paying for supplies for Charles II's army in 1650 and had to sell the property to his kinsman Thomas Dunbar of Grange. Most of the castle was demolished in 1802 to build the Burgie House, itself rebuilt in 1912 as a plain two-storey mansion.

Burleigh Castle

Perth & Kinross: About 1.5 miles north of Kinross, just north of A911 at Burleigh, east of Milnathort, about 0.5 miles north of Loch Leven.

His Scot   NO 130046   OS: 58   *   Map: 8, no: 91**

Although once a large and imposing castle, Burleigh Castle now consists of a ruined 15th-century keep of four storeys. It is joined by a surviving section of court-

yard wall, with a gate, to a corner tower. The corner tower is round at the base, but corbelled out and crowned with a square chamber. The walls are pierced by shot-holes.

The rectangular keep had a corbelled-out parapet and garret storey, but these are gone except for the remains of open rounds.

The entrance led, through a lobby, to a turnpike stair, which climbed to all storeys and was crowned by a caphouse. The basement is vaulted, and the hall was on the first floor.

It was a property of the Balfours of Burleigh from 1446, who built the castle, and visited by James IV.

In 1707 the Master of Burleigh fell in love with a young servant girl and was sent abroad to forget her. On leaving, he swore if she married, he would return and kill her husband. She married Henry Stenhouse, the schoolmaster of Inverkeithing, and the Master duly returned and shot and killed the poor man. Burleigh fled, but was captured, tried and sentenced to death by beheading. However, he managed to escape by changing clothes with his sister, and fled to the continent. He returned and fought for the Jacobites in the 1715 Rising, after which the family were forfeited. Burleigh died unmarried in 1757.

The lands passed to the Irwins, then to Graham of Kinross.

OPEN: Access at all reasonable times – key holder at 16 Burleigh Road, Milnathort (tel: 01577 862408).
Parking nearby.
Tel: 0131 668 8800 Fax: 0131 668 8888
Email: hs.explore@scotland.gov.uk Web: www.historic-scotland.gov.uk

Burn Castle *see* Burncastle

Burn of Lushan

Orkney: About 6.5 miles north and west of Finstown, on foot east of B905, northeast of Click Mill, near Burn of Lushan.
Ruin or site HY 332231 [?] OS: 6 * Map: 11, no: 37
Probable site of castle.

Nearby [HY 325228] is an Orcadian horizontal mill, which is in working condition.

Burnbank

Stirling & Clackmannanshire: About 2.5 miles south and west of Doune, on minor road just north of A873, south side of Burnbank Cottage, east of Mains of Burnbank.
Ruin or site NS 710988 OS: 57 * Map: 6, no: 56
Site of castle, a property of the Muschetts of Burnbank or Tolgarth.

Burncastle

Borders: About 2 miles north of Lauder, on minor road east of A697, west of Earnscleugh Water, at Burncastle.
Ruin or site NT 538514 OS: 73 * Map: 2, no: 193
Site of tower house, a property of the Logans of Restalrig from the early 16th century.
Other refs: Burn Castle

Burnfoot

Dumfriesshire: About 6.5 miles north of Langholm, on minor roads east of A7, near meeting of Eweslees and Carewoodrig Burns, at or near Burnfoot.
Ruin or site NY 390964 [?] OS: 79 * Map: 1, no: 328
Site of tower house, a property of Archie (Armstrong?) of Whithaugh.

Burnhead Tower

Borders: About 1.5 miles north-east of Hawick, on minor road just south of B6359 near junction with A7.
Private NT 514166 OS: 79 ** Map: 2, no: 177
Burnhead Tower is a 16th-century tower house, formerly of three storeys and a garret, within the remains of an incomplete parapet, to which has been added a modern house.

The original windows are very small, and there is a gunloop in one wall.

The basement houses two vaulted chambers, and a stair is reached via a vaulted lobby from the entrance.

It was owned by the Scotts or the Elliots, and Hobbie Elliot of Burnhead was accused of engaging in a foray in 1584. The tower and house are in good condition and occupied.

Busbie Tower

Ayrshire: About 4 miles north-west of Kilmarnock, on minor roads north of B751 and south of B769, at or near Busbie Mains.
Ruin or site NS 392409 OS: 70 * Map: 3, no: 139
Site of 17th-century tower house of four storeys and a garret. The walls were pierced by gunloops. The tower was crowned at the corners by a gabled caphouse, over the turnpike stair, and by bartizans with stone roofs and shot-holes.

The entrance was in the basement, and led to two vaulted cellars and to a turnpike stair, in one corner, up to the hall on the first floor. A further stair from one of the cellars also led up to the first floor. The upper storeys were divided, and contained private chambers

It was built by the Mowats, who owned the property until the early part of the 17th century. The castle was ruined by the 19th century, but was demolished in the 1950s. A later mansion was built at Cunninghamhead.
Other refs: Cunninghamhead

Busby Peel *see* The Peel, Busby

Bush

Dumfriesshire: About 4.5 miles north of Langholm, on minor road west of A7, west of Ewes Water, at or near Bush.
Ruin or site NY 375923 [?] OS: 79 * Map: 1, no: 320
Probable site of tower house, possibly of the Armstrongs.

Bush o' Bield *see* Buck o' Bield

Bushybield *see* Buck o' Bield

Busta House

Shetland: About 22 miles north-west of Lerwick, on minor roads west of A910, at
Busta House.
Private   HU 344670   OS: 3   ***   Map: 11, no: 57
Busta (pronounced 'Boosta') House is a tall, harled and white-washed mansion,
which is believed to date from 1588. It was remodelled and extended in 1714, and
then again in 1984. It is now a comfortable and fine hotel, set in its own ground and
with a harbour.

Busta was a property of the Giffords of Busta, who held much property on Shetland having made their fortunes as merchants. The four sons of the laird were
drowned in 1748 and the only male heir was Gideon, child of a local maid Barbara
Pitcairn with one of the sons. Although she was apparently married to the son,
Barbara was thrown out, and it is said that her sad ghost haunts the building, searching for her son. Gideon had no direct heirs, and the resulting lawsuits from who
should inherit the property left the estate impoverished.

There have also been several sightings of an apparition in the Linga room. The
ghost is said to be a grey-haired woman, in a brown dress and lace cap. It may be
Elizabeth Mitchell, wife of Thomas Gifford.

Other manifestations include the sound of heavy footsteps coming from the Foula
Room when unoccupied. Lights and other electrical equipment have also turned
themselves off and on.
OPEN: Hotel – open all year.
*Accommodation with ensuite facilities. Refreshments and fine food. Ideal location for
touring, wildlife, archaeology and history and walking. Parking.*
Tel: 01806 522506   Fax: 01806 522588
Email: busta@mes.co.uk   Web: www.mes.co.uk/busta

Buyack *see* Beoch

Byres

Lothians: About 2 miles north of Haddington, on minor road east of A6137,
about 1 mile west of Camptoun, at Byres.
Private   NT 495770   OS: 66   *   Map: 4, no: 182
Byres consists of the remains of a tower house or keep, rising to two storeys with a
vaulted basement.

It was originally a property of the Byres family, but passed to the Lindsays of the
Byres. Patrick Lindsay, 6th Lord Lindsay of Byres, supported the Reformation, and
was involved in the plot to murder Rizzio. He took a leading part in compelling
Mary, Queen of Scots, to abdicate, and was a party in the Ruthven Raid. John Lind-
say, 10th Lord Lindsay of Byres, was made Earl of Lindsay in 1633. He joined the
Covenanters, and fought at Marston Moor in 1644 against Charles I.
Other refs: The Byres

Byrsted Tower

Borders: About 8 miles north and east of Newcastleton, on west of B6357, north
and east of Saughtree.
Ruin or site   NY 568999 [?]   OS: 80   *   Map: 2, no: 212
Site of 16th-century tower house.

Byth House

Banff & Buchan: About 7 miles north-east of Turriff, on minor roads north of A98,
2 miles north of New Byth, at or near Byth House.
Ruin or site   NJ 816565 [?]   OS: 29   *   Map: 10, no: 273
Virtually nothing survives of a castle built by Deacon Forbes of Byth in 1593, which
was superseded by a large house in 1693, in turn replaced by a new house in 1932.
Other refs: House of Byth

Caberston Tower

Borders: About 2.5 miles east and north of Innerleithen, on minor road north of
A72, about 0.5 miles east of Walkerburn, north of the River Tweed.
Ruin or site   NT 369376   OS: 73   *   Map: 2, no: 96
Site of tower, which was square in plan and latterly rose to two storeys. It was
incorporated into a later farmhouse, but the whole buildings has been demolished.

It was a property of the Stewarts of Caberston in 1563.
Other refs: Old Caberston

Cadboll Castle

Ross & Cromarty: About 7 miles east and south of Tain, on minor roads south of
B9165 or north of B9166, 1 mile north of Hilton of Cadboll, at Cadboll.
Ruin or site   NH 879776   OS: 21   **   Map: 9, no: 134
Cadboll Castle is a ruined strongly built L-plan tower house. It consists of a main
block and wing, part of which has been demolished. It was built in the 14th century, but much modified in the 16th and 17th centuries. A roofless bartizan crowns
one corner of the main block. The walls are pierced by shot-holes and gunloops,
and the original windows are very small.

The basement was vaulted as are three first-floor chambers. The entrance, at first-
floor level, is reached by an external stone stair.

It was a property of the MacLeods of Cadboll, but passed to the Sinclairs. The
building was apparently destroyed by Alexander Ross of Balnagown as he was ordered to repair the damage in 1572-4. Cadboll was abandoned for the nearby house
in the early 18th century. Part of the old castle is used as a farm store.
Other refs: Catboll Castle

Caddam Castle

Kincardine & Deeside: About 6.5 miles north-east of Brechin, on minor roads
west of B974, south-west of Luthermuir, south of the Luther Water, at Caldhame.
Ruin or site   NO 665682 [?]   OS: 45   *   Map: 10, no: 186
Nothing survives of 16th-century Caddam Castle, which was a property of the Bar-
clays.
Other refs: Caldhame Castle

Cadden Castle

Kincardine & Deeside: About 2 miles north-east of Inverbervie, on minor roads
east of A92, east of Kinneff on coast.
Ruin or site   NO 859748   OS: 45   *   Map: 10, no: 290
Site of castle, standing on a rock, which was defended by a ditch and drawbridge.
Other refs: Castle of Cadden

Cadder Castle

Lanarkshire & Glasgow area: About 3 miles west and south of Kirkintilloch, north
of A803, south of the River Kelvin.
Ruin or site   NS 605728   OS: 64   *   Map: 3, no: 278
Site of castle of the Stirlings of Cadder or Calder. Sir John Stirling of Cadder was
killed at the Battle of Halidon Hill in 1333. John Knox is said to have preached here.

Cadder House, now a golf clubhouse, stands on or near the site of the castle, and
dates in part from 1624 or earlier. In 1814 a hoard of some 350 gold coins, which
had been hidden after 1438, was found near the front lawn of the house. Some of
the coins are in the Museum of Scotland.

There is also a motte [NS 605724], close to Cadder Kirk, to the south-east.
Other refs: Calder Castle; Cawder Castle

Caddroun Burn Tower *see* Copshaws Tower

Caddroun Burn Tower *see* Hudshouse Tower

Cadzow Castle

Lanarkshire & Glasgow area: About 1.5 miles south-east of Hamilton, on minor roads south of A72, on the south bank of the Avon Water.

His Scot NS 734538 OS: 64 * Map: 3, no: 345**

Cadzow Castle dates from the 12th century, but most of the present ruin is of a tower house of 1540, with outbuildings and a courtyard. It is an early example of a castle built to withstand artillery. The ruins consist of a strong keep with round towers at two corners, one very ruinous.

An earlier castle may have stood at Castlehill [NS 729548], although the site is now occupied by a housing scheme.

The castle was used by the kings of Scots, including David I, but passed to the Comyns, then on their forfeiture to the Hamiltons in the early part of the 14th century. The Hamiltons came from Homildon in Northumberland, hence their name. They were made Dukes of Chatelherault in France – a title granted by Henri II. Mary, Queen of Scots, visited the castle in 1568 after escaping from Lochleven Castle. The castle was besieged in 1570 by troops supporting the Earl of Lennox in his fight against the Hamiltons, and the castle surrendered after two days. In 1579 the castle was captured by the Regent Morton's forces, and dismantled to be left as a ruin.

It stands in Chatelherault park, which is open to the public, although the castle is currently being consolidated by Historic Scotland.

OPEN: Park open to the public except Christmas and New Year – castle: view from exterior.

See Chatelherault Hunting Lodge.

Tel: 01698 426213 Fax: 01698 421537

Email: hs.explore@scotland.gov.uk Web: www.historic-scotland.gov.uk

Caerlaverock

Dumfriesshire: About 8 miles south-east of Dumfries, on minor road south of B725, about 0.5 mile north of the Solway Firth, near Caerlaverock Castle.

Ruin or site NY 027655 OS: 84 * Map: 1, no: 198

Near the famous Caerlaverock Castle are the late 12th-century foundations of a rectangular castle which stood on a mound.

Caerlaverock Castle

Dumfriesshire: About 7 miles south and east of Dumfries, on minor road south of B725, about 0.5 miles north of the Solway Firth, at Caerlaverock.

His Scot NY 026656 OS: 84 ** Map: 1, no: 197**

Once a formidable fortress and still a magnificent ruin, Caerlaverock Castle consists of a triangular courtyard with a gatehouse at one corner, round towers at the others, and ranges of buildings between, all still surrounded by a wet moat.

The gatehouse has two tall round towers, pierced by many gunloops, flanking the entrance, and was reached by a drawbridge over the moat. It was given heavy machiolations in the late 15th century. The basement is vaulted, and a tall late 15th-century stair-tower has been added. A fine vaulted hall occupied the first floor.

One of the round towers, Murdoch's Tower – so called because Murdoch, Duke of Albany was imprisoned here before execution in 1425 – remains to its full height,

but the other was demolished to foundations. The curtain wall, on this side, was also dismantled.

There were ranges of buildings on each side of the courtyard. Little remains of one side, but the other ranges survive to the wallhead. A fine Renaissance range, the Nithsdale Apartments, built in 1634, has two large chambers on the first floor over barrel-vaulted cellars. The windows are large, and are surmounted with carvings.

The castle was built in the 13th century by the Maxwells, and has a long eventful history. It was captured by the English in 1300, after a siege by Edward I of England, the event being commemorated in a poem in medieval French 'Le Siege de Kalavreock'. The castle was held by the English until 1312, when the keeper Sir Eustace Maxwell joined the Scots. He successfully resisted an English attack, but afterwards slighted the castle.

In the 1330s the castle was repaired. Herbert Maxwell submitted to Edward III of England in 1347, and in 1357 Roger Kirkpatrick captured the castle for the Scots, although Kirkpatrick was later murdered here. In 1425 Murdoch, Duke of Albany, was imprisoned in one of the towers. There was further rebuilding in 1452-88 by Robert, 2nd Lord Maxwell. He added the machiolated parapets to the towers, and remodelled the gatehouse.

James V visited the castle prior to defeat at Solway Moss in 1542. The castle was surrendered to the English in 1545, as part of the negotiated settlement, but was later recaptured by the Scots, only to be taken and slighted by an English force led by the Earl of Sussex in 1570. It was remodelled again in 1634.

In 1640, the Earl and his garrison of 200 men surrendered the castle to a force of Covenanters after a siege of 13 weeks. It was then reduced by demolishing much of the curtain wall and one corner tower, and unroofing the rest. The Maxwells moved to Terregles, then to Traquair House. By the late 18th century the ruin was already popular with visitors, and the Duke of Norfolk transferred it to the care of the State for consolidation in 1946.

OPEN: Open all year: Apr-Sep, daily 9.30-18.30; Oct-Mar, Mon-Sat 9.30-16.30, Sun 14.00-16.30; last ticket 30 mins before closing; closed 25/26 Dec and 1/2 Jan.

Visitor centre, children's park and nature trail to old castle. Tea room. Picnic area. Explanatory panels. Replica siege engine. Reasonable disabled access and WC. Car and coach parking. Group concessions. £.

Tel: 01387 770244 Fax: 0131 668 8800

Email: hs.explore@scotland.gov.uk Web: www.historic-scotland.gov.uk

Cairn Shuin *see* Kinbrace

Cairnbulg Castle

Banff & Buchan: About 2.5 miles south-east of Fraserburgh, on minor roads south of B9033, 1 mile south of sea, just east of Water of Philorth, at Cairnbulg.

Private NK 016640 OS: 30 ** Map: 10, no: 354**

A large and impressive stronghold, Cairnbulg Castle consists of a 14th-century massive altered keep of four storeys and a garret, within a corbelled-out parapet with open rounds. It was altered in 15th and 16th centuries, when lower ranges, and a strong round tower of three storeys were added. The walls are harled.

The basement is vaulted. The hall, on the first floor, has windows, with stone seats and a large fireplace. A pit-prison survives in the thickness of the walling.

The round tower has a vaulted basement, with gunloops, and the chamber above

is octagonal. The lower work linking it to the main keep is a modern reconstruction of a 16th-century hall range.

The property was held by the Comyns, but was given to the Earl of Ross by Robert the Bruce in 1316. It passed to the Frasers in 1375, and remained with them until 1666, when they had to sell the castle to pay off debts. They moved to Philorth House. The castle was abandoned in 1799, and became derelict, part of it being demolished. It was rebuilt and restored in 1899 when it was held by the Gordons.

Philorth House was burned down in 1915, and the Frasers bought back Cairnbulg in 1934. It is still occupied.

Cairnburgh Castle

Argyll & Dunbartonshire: Two of the Treshnish Isles, 2 miles from the Island of Mull at Rubh' a' Chaoil, on Cairn na Burgh Beg and Cairn na Burgh Mor to the north of the group of isles.

Ruin or site   NM 308450   OS: 47   **   Map: 5, no: 6

The castle was built on two islands. Cairnburghbeg consists of a walled courtyard from at least as early as 1249, with other work of a later date. A barrack here was 'tolerably entire' in the 1890s.

Cairnburghmore [NM 305447] also consists of a walled courtyard.

It was a property of the MacDougalls of Lorn until 1309, after which it was kept for the Crown by the MacDonald Lord of the Isles, then the MacLeans of Duart. MacLean of Duart had the chief of the MacLaines of Moy imprisoned here to prevent him producing an heir. MacLaines's only female companion was an old ugly woman, whom he made pregnant. MacLaine himself was murdered, but the woman managed to escape and produced a son, who eventually recovered the property. James IV had the castle besieged in 1504 when held by the rebellious Lachlan MacLean. It was surrendered to the Covenanter General David Leslie in 1647, and many of the books and records rescued from Iona were destroyed in a siege by Cromwell's forces in the 1650s. Although the castle held out against the Campbells in 1679, it was again surrendered in 1692. The castle was garrisoned during both the 1715 and 1745 Jacobite Risings.

Cairncross Tower *see* Redpath

Cairneyflappet Castle

Fife: About 1.5 miles south-west of Auchtermuchty, near A912, to east of Strathmiglo, near Mansfield.

Ruin or site   NO 220102   OS: 58   *   Map: 7, no: 38

Site of castle, which had a large moat and was mentioned in 1420 and 1509, but demolished in 1734. There are no remains. It is believed to have been quickly and poorly built, and 'Cairneyflappet' was a nickname given to it by James V.

The lands were a property of the Earls of Fife in the 12th century, but had passed to the Scotts of Balwearie by the 16th century. The laird is said to have built, or presumably rebuilt, the castle here so that he could entertain James V. The town hall steeple was built from the remains. The property passed to the Balfours of Burleigh about 1600, then in the 18th century to the Skenes of Hallyards.

Other refs: Strathmiglo Castle; Cairnie

Cairnhill *see* Carnell

Cairnhill House

Lanarkshire & Glasgow: About 1 mile south of Airdrie, on minor roads west of B802, Cairnhill Road, at Cairnhill.

Ruin or site   NS 756641   OS: 64   *   Map: 3, no: 358

Probable site of castle. Cairnhill House was a picturesque mansion of 1841, which incorporated an 18th-century building. The mansion was demolished in 1991, except for the stables and doocot.

Cairnhill was a property of the Nisbets at the end of the 19th century.

Cairnie *see* Cairneyflappet Castle

Cairnie Castle

Lanarkshire & Glasgow: About 1.5 miles west of Lanark, near A72, west of River Clyde, at or near Linnmill.

Ruin or site   NS 853438 [?]   OS: 71   *   Map: 3, no: 396

Site of castle, of which there were some remains at the end of the 18th century.

Cairnmuir *see* Baddingsgill House

Cairns Tower

Lothians: About 6.5 miles west and south of Balerno, on minor road just south of the A70, at south-west end of the Harperigg Reservoir, near Cairns House.

Ruin or site   NT 091604   OS: 65   **   Map: 4, no: 37

Cairns Castle is a ruined altered 15th-century keep of at least three storeys, with an adjoining wing.

The basement is vaulted, the kitchen is on the ground floor, with a hall above. A turnpike stair, in the corner between the main block and the wing, led to all floors.

It was a property of the Crichtons, but may have passed to the Tennants. This castle may also have been known as 'East Cairns Castle', although this may refer to another stronghold nearby.

Other refs: East Cairns Castle

Cairston Castle

Orkney: About 1.5 miles east of Stromness on Orkney, on minor roads east of A965, on west shore of Bay of Ireland, near Bu of Cairston.

Ruin or site   HY 273096   OS: 6   *   Map: 11, no: 36

Not much remains of a 16th-century courtyard castle, with a round corner turret, which enclosed ranges of buildings. It may incorporate or be on the site of a 12th-century stronghold mentioned in the Orkneyinga Saga.

The castle was built by William Gordon who was granted Cairston by Robert Stewart, Earl of Orkney, in 1587. Cairston House, which stands nearby, is a modern mansion.

Other refs: Bu of Cairston

Caisteal a' Cuilean Curta *see* Garth Castle

Caisteal an Duibhe

Perth & Kinross: In Glen Lyon, on minor road 20 miles west of B846 at Keltney Burn, north of River Lyon, east of Pubil.

Ruin or site   NN 466423 [?]   OS: 51   *   Map: 8, no: 1

Site of castle, little or nothing of which remains.

Other refs: Pubil Tower

Caisteal an Duin Bhain

South Highland: Off unlisted road, 0.5 miles south of Port, Caisteal an Duin Bhain, Muck.

Ruin or site   NM 422787   OS: 39   **   Map: 9, no: 7

A wall encloses the top of a rocky stack on the south-east coast of the island. The wall survives to a height of four feet, and there are the ruins of a later rectangular building within the wall. Further walls have been added between the stack and the sea. The fort may have been occupied in medieval times.

Caisteal an Ime *see* Kinlochaline Castle

Caisteal a' Bhrebider *see* Weaver's Castle

Caisteal a' Mhorair

Western Isles: About 1.5 miles north of North Tolsta, on minor road and foot north of B895, Traigh Geiraha, on coast, Lewis.

Ruin or site   NB 537497   OS: 8   **   Map: 11, no: 30

The remains of a castle or dun on a virtually inaccessible stack of rock, consisting of a ruinous wall on the summit and the foundations of a rectangular building.

Caisteal Bharraich

Sutherland & Caithness: About 1 mile west of Tongue, on minor roads and foot
south of A838 in Tongue, on east side of Kyle of Tongue south of Rhian Burn, at
Caisteal Bharraich.
Ruin or site   NC 581567   OS: 10   **   Map: 12, no: 12
Caisteal Bharraich, built on a promontory, is a two-storey ruined tower house of
the Bishops of Caithness.
Other refs: Castle Varrich; Varrich
OPEN: Access at all reasonable times – care should be taken.
Parking nearby.

Caisteal Bheagram

Western Isles: About 13 miles north of Lochboisdale on South Uist, on minor
road (and boat) west of A865 at Drimsdale, on islet in Loch an Eilean, at Caisteal
Bheagram.
Ruin or site   NF 761371   OS: 22   **   Map: 11, no: 6
Standing on an islet in Loch an Eilean, Caisteal Bheagram is a ruined 17th-century
tower house, although the site was occupied by a dun or earlier castle before this.
The tower has two shot-holes. The perimeter of the island was surrounded by
another wall, and within were several other buildings and a garden, all now re-
duced to foundations. There was apparently a causeway out to the island.
   It was held by Ranald Alanson of Ylandbigrim, a MacDonald, who also held Dun
Sgathaich in Sleat in 1505.
Other refs: Bheagram Castle

Caisteal Borve *see* Borve Castle

Caisteal Calvay

Western Isles: About 2 miles south-east of Lochboisdale, by boat south-east of
A865, on rock on north coast of island of Calvay at mouth of Loch Boisdale, at
Calvay.
Ruin or site   NF 817182   OS: 31   *   Map: 11, no: 12
Caisteal Calvay is a very ruined stronghold with a square tower and two ranges of
buildings within a courtyard. It stands on a tidal islet, and was formerly reached by
a causeway.
   The lands were held by the MacNeils until around 1600. The castle was already
ruined when Bonnie Prince Charlie sheltered here in 1746 after the defeat of his
forces at the Battle of Culloden.
Other refs: Calvay Castle

Caisteal Camus

South Highland: About 3.5 miles north of Armadale on island of Skye, on east
coast of Sleat, on foot east of A851, south of Cnoc Uaine, east side of Knock Bay.
Ruin or site   NG 671087   OS: 32   **   Map: 9, no: 20
Standing on a steep headland with a ditch cutting off the promontory, Caisteal
Camus, sometimes Caisteal Chamius, consists of a very ruined 15th-century keep,
of which one part, with a window, remains to some height. There are traces of later
buildings.
   The site was originally occupied by a dun. The castle was owned by the MacLeods
in the 15th century, but was captured during an attack on Sleat by the MacDonalds
along with Dun Sgathaich. In 1431 the castle was taken by royal forces during the
struggles between James I and the Lords of the Isles. In an attempt to resurrect the
Lordship, the castle was besieged by Alastair Crotach MacLeod, who had already
seized Dun Sgathaich, but eventually he had to withdraw.
   The castle was extended, then remodelled in 1596 when the MacDonalds owned
the property. It was still occupied in 1632, but by 1689 the castle had been abandoned and was decaying, much of the stone being used for nearby buildings. Beware of packs of dogs.
   The castle is said to be haunted by a 'Green Lady', a gruagach, a ghost associated
with the fortunes of the family who occupied the castle. If good news was to come,
the ghost would appear happy, but if there was bad news she would weep. The
castle is also said to have had a glastaig, a spirit particularly concerned with looking
after livestock.
Other refs: Knock Castle; Dun Horavaig

Caisteal Chonil *see* Dun Grugaig

Caisteal Dubh Mhaothlinne *see* Black Castle of Moulin

Caisteal Dubh nan Cliar

South Highland: About 1 mile south-west of Kilchoan, on minor roads and foot
west of B8007, on south coast of Ardnamurchan, on shore near Ormsaigbeg.
Ruin or site   NM 473631   OS: 47   **   Map: 9, no: 8
Not much remains of a very small tower, probably built as an outpost of Mingary
Castle to protect Kilroan Bay. It may have risen to two storeys, and dates from the
16th or 17th century. The names means the 'black castle of the minstrels'.

Caisteal Eoghainn a' Chinn Bhig *see* Loch Sguabain Castle

Caisteal Grugaig

South Highland: About 6 miles north-west of Shiel Bridge, on minor roads and
track west of A87 at Shiel Bridge, 0.5 miles west of Totaig, opposite Eilean Donan
Castle, at Dun Grugaig.
Ruin or site   NG 867251   OS: 33   **   Map: 9, no: 33
Set in a picturesque location, Caisteal Grugaig consists of the impressive remains of
a broch. The wall survives to a height of 13 feet, and there are mural chambers, a
door check and the remains of a stair. A massive triangular lintel is still in place
above the entrance passageway.
Other refs: Dun Totaig

Caisteal Maol

South Highland: About 0.5 miles east of Kyleakin on island of Skye, on minor
road and foot south of A850 in Kyleakin, on the east side of the harbour.
Ruin or site   NG 758264   OS: 33   **   Map: 9, no: 23
Overlooking the ferry crossing between Skye and the mainland at Kyle of Lochalsh,
Caisteal Maol, 'bare castle', is a very ruined 15th-century keep, of which only two
walls remain to second-floor level. Large parts collapsed in 1949 and 1989.
   According to tradition, the castle was built by a Norse princess called 'Saucy Mary'
who was married to a MacKinnon chief. Their main income was from tolls on ships
sailing through the Kyle. It is said that she was buried beneath a large cairn on the
top of Beinn na Caillaich ('mountain of the old woman').
   In the middle ages the castle was known as Dunakin, and a stronghold of the
MacKinnons. In 1513 after James IV's defeat and death at Flodden, a great meeting
of Highland chiefs was held here in an attempt to restore the Lordship of the Isles,
but the attempt failed. The castle was probably abandoned sometime around the
middle of the 17th century when the MacKinnons moved to Kilmarie.
   The MacKinnons fought for the Marquis of Montrose at both Auldearn and Inverlochy in 1645, a MacKinnon regiment fought for Charles II at Worcester, and they
were Jacobites, fighting at the Battle of Sheriffmuir in 1715 and Glenshiel in 1719.
The Chief of MacKinnon sheltered Bonnie Prince Charlie after his defeat at the
Battle of Culloden in 1746, for which he was given the recipe for Drambuie, a whisky
liqueur, although the original recipe apparently used cognac.
   In 1951 a hoard of coins was found hidden in a chink of masonry on the outer face
of one of the walls. Although very ruined, the remains have now been secured –
rather too late as with many of the castles in the Islands.
Other refs: Dunakin
OPEN: Access at all reasonable times.

Caisteal Mearn *see* Caisteal nan Corr

Caisteal Mernaig *see* Glensanda Castle

Caisteal Mhic Cneacall

Ross & Cromarty: To west of Ullapool, on minor roads west of A835, on
promontory on east side of Loch Broom, on Ullapool Point.
Ruin or site   NH 124943   OS: 19   *   Map: 9, no: 40
Site of castle, some remains of which survived about 1900. It may have been a

property of the MacDonnels or MacDonalds, although the name means 'Mac Nicholson's Castle'.

Caisteal Mhic Eoghainn *see* Castle Ewen

Caisteal MhicLeod

South Highland: About 7 miles west of Shiel Bridge, on minor road west of A87 at Shiel Bridge, near Galltair, Glenelg.

Ruin or site NG 816202 OS: 33 ** Map: 9, no: 27

The ruined Iron Age dun consists of the remains of a massive semi-circular wall and outworks. It was still in use in the 16th century, and is associated with Alastair Crotach MacLeod. It is said that a careless nursemaid dropped a baby from one of the windows.

Caisteal Morar na Shein

Sutherland & Caithness: About 11 miles south-west of Watten, on minor roads south of B870 at Westerdale, to north of Loch More, at or near Lochmore Cottage.

Ruin or site ND 084461 [?] OS: 12 * Map: 12, no: 40

Site of castle, nothing of which remains.

It was a property of the Cheynes from around 1340, but ruinous by 1769.

Other refs: Morac

Caisteal na Coire *see* Caisteal nan Corr

Caisteal na Gruagaich *see* Glensanda Castle

Caisteal na Nighinn Ruaidhe

Argyll & Dunbartonshire: About 15 miles south-east of Oban, on minor road 4.5 miles east of A816 at Kilmelford, on small island at west end of Loch Avich.

Ruin or site NM 916137 OS: 55 * Map: 5, no: 82

Little survives of Caisteal na Nighinn Ruaidhe ('castle of the red-haired girls'), a 13th-century castle of enclosure and hall house of the Campbells.

Other refs: Loch Avich; Caisteal na Thighinn Ruaidhe

Caisteal na Thighinn Ruaidhe *see* Caisteal na Nighinn Ruaidhe

Caisteal nan Con

South Highland: About 7.5 miles north-west of Lochaline, on foot south of B849, on point on east side of Sound of Mull, south of Killundine, at Caisteal nan Con.

Ruin or site NM 584487 OS: 47 ** Map: 9, no: 14

Caisteal nan Con, 'castle of dogs', is a simple ruined hall house or tower house, formerly of three storeys, and is built within a prehistoric fort. It has been ascribed to the middle or end of the 17th century, but this seems too late.

It was a property of the MacLeans of Duart, and is said to have been used as a hunting lodge by the occupants of Aros Castle.

Other refs: Killundine Castle

Caisteal nan Con

Argyll & Dunbartonshire: On north-east of island of Torsa, about 6.5 miles south of Kilninver, by boat and foot south of B8003 at Cuan on south tip of Seil, at Caisteal nan Con.

Ruin or site NM 765136 OS: 55 ** Map: 5, no: 45

On a rocky crag on the small island of Torsa, Caisteal nan Con – 'castle of dogs' – consists of the ruins of a simple keep on the summit of the rock. There is a rectangular lower courtyard with a round tower in one corner. It was built in the 15th century. Near the stronghold is an inlet which may have been used as a slipway for boats.

It was a property of the Campbells, then MacDougalls of Rarey, but later passed to the MacLeans.

Other refs: Torsa Castle

Caisteal nan Corr

Sutherland & Caithness: About 8 miles west and south of Lairg, on minor road and foot south of A837 west of Invercassley, just north of River Oykel, at Caisteal nan Corr.

Ruin or site NC 466012 OS: 16 ** Map: 12, no: 8

Not much remains of a tower house, except the basement and earthworks.

Other refs: Caisteal na Coire; Caisteal Mearn

Caisteal Nighinn Ruaidh, Danna

Argyll & Dunbartonshire: About 5 miles south of Tayvallich, on minor roads south of B8025, on island of Danna just off the coast of Knapdale, at or near Danna na Cloiche.

Ruin or site NR 694778 OS: 61 * Map: 5, no: 30

Caisteal Nighinn Ruaidh, 'castle of the red-haired girls', is said to have stood at or near Danna na Cloiche. The building was reported as being tall and rising to three storeys, and it was apparently demolished about 1890.

Caisteal Suidhe Cheannaidh

Argyll & Dunbartonshire: About 1.5 miles north and west of Kilchrenan, on minor road and foot west of B845, 0.3 miles north-west of Achnacraobh, at Caisteal Suidhe Cheannaidh.

Ruin or site NN 029242 OS: 50 * Map: 5, no: 98

The well-preserved remains of a round dun, defended on three sides by the steepness of the ground. The walls now survive to about 6.5 feet high, although it is recorded that, before being used for building materials, they survived to a height of 20 feet.

Caisteal Uisdein

South Highland: About 4 miles south of Uig on Skye, on east side of Loch Snizort Beag, on minor road and foot 0.75 miles west of A856, at Caisteal Uisdein.

Ruin or site NG 381583 OS: 23 ** Map: 9, no: 5

Caisteal Uisdean, Hugh's Castle, is a ruined rectangular 16th-century tower of just two storeys, but it may have had a garret floor within a parapet. There is a stair, in the thickness of the wall, and the hall, on the first floor, had a fireplace.

Hugh MacDonald, the builder, was outlawed for piracy, his exploits extending even to the fishermen of Fife, although he was later pardoned and made steward of Trotternish. However, about 1602 he plotted to overthrow his MacDonald kin by slaughtering them at Castle Uisdean, but the plot was discovered, and he was eventually caught after fleeing to Dun an Sticar on North Uist and imprisoned in Duntulm Castle. He was given salted beef and no water, and when the pit where he had been buried was finally opened his skeleton was found with a broken pewter jug, which he had destroyed with his teeth. His skull and thigh bones were kept in a window of the parish church until buried in 1827.

Other refs: Uisdean

Cakemuir Castle

Lothians: About 4.5 miles east and south of Gorebridge, on minor road south of B6458 half way between A7 and A68, just south of Cakemuir Burn.

Private NT 413591 OS: 66 ** Map: 4, no: 163**

Cakemuir Castle is a mid 16th-century square tower of four storeys and a garret within a parapet. It has a projecting stair-tower, crowned by a square watch-chamber; and was extended by a long three-storey block. The walls are pierced by shot-holes.

The castle was built by Adam Wauchope, an advocate who defended James Hepburn, Earl of Bothwell, against the charge of murdering Darnley, the second husband of Mary, Queen of Scots. The hall is known as Queen Mary's room, as it was here she arrived in 1567, disguised as a man, after escaping from a besieging force at Bothwell Castle. Extensions were made in 1701, and the last Wauchope to own Cakemuir died in 1794. It was altered again in the late 19th century, 1926, and in the 1950s, and is still occupied.

The castle is said to have replaced an earlier stronghold, known as Black Castle [NT 404595?].

Other refs: Black Castle

Caladh Castle *see* Glen Caladh Castle

Calcruchie *see* Castle Stewart

Calda House

Sutherland & Caithness: About 1.5 miles north and west of Inchnadamph, just west of A837, on north side of Loch Assynt, at Calda House.
Ruin or site NC 244234 OS: 15 ** Map: 12, no: 3
Calda House consists of a large and substantial ruinous mansion, and replaced Ardvreck Castle [NC 240236]. The lands were a property of the MacLeods of Assynt, but passed to the Mackenzies who built the house about 1660. The family were said to have held riotous parties, and soon became short of money. The house was plundered and torched in 1737. The Mackenzies were forfeited after the Jacobite Rising, and the house was sold to the Earl of Sutherland in 1758, then burned out by the MacRaes in 1760, and never restored.
Other refs: Eddercalda House; White House, Calda

Caldenoch Castle *see* Galdenoch Castle

Calder Castle *see* Cadder Castle

Calder House

Lothians: About 2 miles east of Livingston, at Mid Calder, on minor road south of B7015, south of the River Almond.
Private NT 073673 OS: 65 ** Map: 4, no: 30
Calder House is a 16th-century L-plan tower house of three storeys and a garret. The walls are very thick, and the basement is vaulted and contained a kitchen.
  It was a property of the Douglas family, but passed to the Sandilands in the 14th century. John Sandilands of Calder and his uncle were assassinated by the Douglases because of their support for James II in the 1450s. Sir James Sandilands was Preceptor of the powerful religious-military Order of the Knights of St John, whose headquarters were at the Preceptory of Torphichen. After the Reformation he was made Lord Torphichen, acquiring much of their lands. John Knox held a service here in 1556. The family still occupy the house.

Calderwood Castle

Lanarkshire & Glasgow area: About 1 mile north-east of East Kilbride, on minor roads south of A725, east of the River Calder.
Private NS 658560 OS: 64 * Map: 3, no: 308
Site of castle, with a large keep which collapsed in 1773. Some of the outbuildings were incorporated into a mansion, which was greatly extended in 1840.
  Calderwood was a property of the Maxwells of Calderwood for 500 years from 1363, the family being a branch of the Maxwells of Pollok. The castle may have been built or rebuilt by Sir James Hamilton of Finnart, although there was certainly an older building on the site.
Other refs: East Kilbride

Caldhame Castle *see* Caddam Castle

Caldsyde *see* Coldsyde

Caldwell Tower

Renfrewshire: About 4 miles west of Neilston, just north of B776, 0.3 miles west of junction with A736, about 0.5 miles west of Uplawmoor, west of Lugton Water.
Private NS 422551 OS: 64 ** Map: 3, no: 163
Caldwell Tower is a small square 16th-century tower house of three storeys and a corbelled-out parapet. It may incorporate parts of an earlier castle, although the roof is modern. The walls are pierced by shot-holes, below the windows, and there have been gunloops, now sealed. The castle had a courtyard.
  The basement is vaulted, as is the hall on the first floor.
  Caldwell was held by the Mure family. William Mure was involved with the Covenanters in the Pentland Rising, which ended in defeat in 1666 at Rullion Green. He fled abroad and his lands were forfeited and given to the Dalziels. The castle fell into disrepair, and, although the Mure family recovered the property, the castle

never seems to have been reoccupied, although it was restored in the 17th century. The family moved to Hall of Caldwell in the 18th century, then to Caldwell House, designed by Robert Adam, in 1773.
Other refs: Tower of Caldwell

Calfhill Tower *see* Hillslap Tower

Calfield Tower

Dumfriesshire: About 1.5 miles west of Langholm, on minor roads north of B7068, at or near Calfield.
Ruin or site NY 341845 [?] OS: 79 * Map: 1, no: 308
Site of tower house. There were two more towers nearby, or at least in the parish, known as Nease (Naze?) and Hill.
  Calfield was a property of the Armstrongs.
Other refs: Nease Tower; Hill Tower

Calfshaw

Borders: About 2 miles south-west of Galashiels, on minor roads north of A707 or B7060, south of Hoghill, east of Calfshaw.
Ruin or site NT 466336 OS: 73 * Map: 2, no: 132
Probable site of tower house.

Callander Castle

Stirlingshire & Clackmannan: Just south of Callander, just north of A81 at junction with A892, south of the River Teith.
Ruin or site NN 629076 OS: 57 * Map: 6, no: 41
Only earthworks and a single fragment of masonry survive from a 15th- or 16th-century castle of the Livingstones, later Earls of Callander, who held the property from the 15th century. It had a tower, square in plan, of considerable height.

Callands House

Borders: About 1 mile south of Romannobridge, on minor roads west of B7059 or east of A701, west of Lyne Water, at or near Callands House.
Private NT 155459 [?] OS: 72 * Map: 2, no: 24
Site of tower house. The present house, which was renovated in 1840, may be built on the site, and was held by the Murrays in the 19th century.
Other refs: Callends

Callendar House

Stirlingshire & Clackmannan: In Falkirk, on minor roads south of A803, in Callendar Park.
Private NS 898794 OS: 65 ** Map: 6, no: 96
Callendar House, a large ornate mansion with towers and turrets, incorporates a 15th-century castle. The castle once had a deep ditch and courtyard, and still has very thick walls. The building was greatly altered and extended in later centuries.
  It was held by the Callendar family from 1244, but the family was forfeited in 1345, and the property passed to the Livingstones (or Livingstons). Mary, Queen of Scots, stayed here several times in the 1560s; and the family were made Earls of Callendar in 1641, then of Linlithgow. The castle was stormed and captured by Cromwell in 1651. The Livingstones were forfeited for their part in the 1715 Jacobite Rising, and

the house was leased by the Boyd Earl of Kilmarnock, although he was himself beheaded for his part in the 1745 Rising. Bonnie Prince Charlie stayed here in 1745; and General Hawley and a Hanoverian army camped near here before going on to defeat at the nearby Battle of Falkirk the next year. The house passed to William Forbes, a copper merchant, and he and his descendants remodelled and extended the house and held it until the 20th century. It is now in the care of the local council.

OPEN: Open all year: Mon-Sat 10.00-17.00; also Apr-Sep, Sun 14.00-17.00; open most public hols.

Permanent displays. Temporary exhibitions. Restored 1820s kitchen with costumed interpretation. History research centre. Contemporary art gallery. Gift shop. Tea room. Garden. Park with boating, pitch and putt. Woodland walks. Children's play area. WC. Disabled access. Car and coach parking. Group concessions. £.

Tel: 01324 503770 Fax: 01324 503771
Email: callendarhouse@falkirkmuseums.demon.co.uk
Web: www.falkirkmuseumsdemon.co.uk

Callends *see* Callands House

Cally Castle

Galloway: About 0.5 miles south of Gatehouse of Fleet, on minor road north of A75, just north of Cally Palace Hotel, to west of Cally Loch.
Ruin or site NX 598554 OS: 83 * Map: 1, no: 95
Only one wall survives of a 16th-century tower house, formerly of four storeys. The basement was vaulted, and the castle was defended by a moat.

The lands were held by the Stewarts in the 13th century, but later passed to the Murrays, then the Lennoxes.

Cally House, now the Cally Palace Hotel, replaced the castle in 1763, and was designed by Robert Milne. It was extended in 1835 and later, held by the Murray-Stewarts of Broughton, and is now a hotel.
Other refs: Kelly; Kally

Calvay Castle *see* Caisteal Calvay

Calvertsholm

Dumfriesshire: About 2.5 miles west and north of Gretna, on minor roads south of B6357, south of Kirtle Water, at or near Calvertsholm.
Ruin or site NY 281689 OS: 85 * Map: 1, no: 286
Site of tower house.

Cambo House

Fife: About 1 mile south of Kingsbarns, on minor roads east of A917, on East Neuk of Fife, just west of sea, at Cambo.
Private NO 604115 OS: 59 * Map: 7, no: 159
Site of castle. The present classical mansion was rebuilt after a fire in 1878.

The property was held by a Norman De Cambo, but had passed by 1364 to the Myrtoun, or Morton, family. It was sold in 1688 to the Erskine family, who still own the property.

Set about the Cambo Burn, the walled garden features snowdrops and bulbs in spring, fine herbaceous borders, an extensive rose collection of 200 varieties and ornamental potager. There is a September border and a colchicum meadow in autumn. Woodland walks follow the burn to a secluded sandy beach.

OPEN: Garden: open all year, daily 10.00-dusk; house not open.
Guided tours can be arranged. Picnics allowed. Victorian walled garden. Woodland walks. Golf course. Disabled access. Car and coach parking. £. Self-catering and b&b accommodation available.
Tel: 01333 450313 Fax: 01333 450987
Email: cambohouse@compuserve.com Web: www.camboestate.com

Cambusnethan House *see* Castlehill, Cambusnethan

Cameron House

Argyll & Dunbartonshire: About 2 miles north and west of Alexandria, on minor roads east of A82, on west side of Loch Lomond, at Cameron.
Private NS 376831 OS: 56 * Map: 5, no: 149**
Site of castle.

Set in a picturesque position on the banks of Loch Lomond, Cameron House is a castellated mansion. The present building dates mostly from 1830 and, following a fire, was remodelled in 1865 by the architect William Spence. It may incorporate a 14th-century castle, itself remodelled into a fine house in the 17th century, and extensive alterations were also made in 1806.

The lands were originally held by the Lennox family, but were sold to the Smolletts in 1763. Dr Johnson and Boswell visited in 1772. The house is now a hotel and leisure centre.

One of the room is said to be haunted, and objects appear which in fact do not exist.

OPEN: Hotel & leisure centre – open all year.
96 rooms with ensuite facilities. Restaurants. Conferences, weddings and banquets. Leisure facilities, including indoor pools. Marina. 9 hole golf course.
Tel: 01389 755565 Fax: 01389 759522

Camilla *see* Hallyards Castle

Camis Eskan

Argyll & Dunbartonshire: About 3 miles north-west of Cardross, on minor roads north of A814, about 0.5 miles east of Craigendoran, outskirts of Helensburgh, at Camis Eskan.
Private NS 321815 OS: 63 * Map: 5, no: 133
Site of castle, replaced by a house of 1648, which was then remodelled and extended in 1840 and 1915. The oldest part has a vaulted basement.

It was a property of the Dennistouns of Colgrain from the 14th century, but was acquired by the Campbells of Breadalbane in 1836 and held by them until the 20th century. The house was later used as a TB hospital, but has been subdivided into luxury flats.

There may have been another castle or old house at Colgrain [NS 324801], which may have been more important than Camis Eskan, although on Blaeu's map of The Lennox, Colgrain is further west of Camis Eskan rather than east.
Other refs: Camus Eskan; Colgrain House

Campbell Castle *see* Castle Campbell

Campbeltown *see* Kilkerran Castle

Campbeltown *see* Moil Castle

Campbeltown *see* Lochhead Castle

Campsie Castle *see* Ballagan Castle

Camregan Castle

Ayrshire: About 2 miles east and north of Girvan, just south of B734, just south of Camregan, on the north side of Camregan Hill.
Ruin or site NX 215987 OS: 76 * Map: 3, no: 37
Little remains of a castle, which had a courtyard and was defended by a ditch. It was a property of the Cathcarts from the 13th century.

Camstraddan Castle

Argyll & Dunbartonshire: About 7 miles north-east of Helensburgh, on minor roads east of A82, on western shore of Loch Lomond, 0.5 miles south of Luss, at Camstraddan House.
Ruin or site NS 359922 OS: 56 * Map: 5, no: 144
Site of castle, formerly on an island in the bay, also spelt Camstradden.

It was a property of the Colquhouns of Luss from 1395. The 6th Laird of Camstraddan fought at the Battle of Pinkie in 1547. The castle was replaced by Camstraddan House, which was built in 1739.
Other refs: Castle of Camstraddan

Camus Eskan *see* Camis Eskan

Candacraig

Aberdeen & Gordon: About 10 miles north of Ballater, on minor roads south of A944, north of River Don, 0.5 miles south of Rough Park at Candacraig.

Ruin or site NJ 339111 OS: 37 * Map: 10, no: 66

Site of castle of the Andersons. Candacraig House may incorporate part of this building, although it mostly dates from 1835 and was built by John Smith for the Wallaces. It was extended in 1900, and altered again in 1956 after a fire. There is a walled garden, dating from the 1820s, featuring specialist hardy plants, some from the Himalayas and the Far East.

OPEN: House not open. Garden open May-Sep, daily 10.00-18.00.

Explanatory displays. Gift shop. Plant centre. WC. Disabled access. Car parking. Coach parking by arrangement only. £ (donation). Accommodation available.

Tel: 01975 651226 Fax: 01975 651391

Candecaill *see* Dee Castle

Cander

Lanarkshire & Glasgow: About 2 miles south of Larkhall, on minor roads south of A71, east of Stonehouse, on east side of Cander Water.

Ruin or site NS 768468 [?] OS: 64 * Map: 3, no: 365

Site of castle, which 'seems to have been in decay in 1700'. Kand is marked on Blaeu's Atlas Novus map of North Clydesdale.

Other refs: Kand

Canna Castle *see* Coroghon Castle

Canongate Tolbooth

Lothians: Canongate (Royal Mile), Edinburgh.

Private NT 265738 OS: 66 * Map: 4, no: 104**

Canongate Tolbooth, dating from 1591, houses the People's Story, a museum which charts the lives of the ordinary folk of Edinburgh from the late 18th century to the present day. There are reconstructions, including a prison cell, 1930's pub, and 1940's kitchen, as well as photographs, displays, sounds, smells and an audio-visual presentation.

OPEN: Open all year: Jun-Sep, Mon-Sat 10.00-18.00; Oct-May, Mon-Sat 10.00-17.00; also open Sun 14.00-17.00 during Festival.

Explanatory displays. Audio-visual presentation. Gift shop. WC. Disabled access and WC. Parking nearby.

Tel: 0131 225 2424 x4057 Fax: 0131 557 3346

Capelochy Castle

Fife: About 1 mile north-east of Anstruther Easter, 0.5 miles east of Kilrenny, on minor road south of A917, south-west of Caiplie, near shore.

Ruin or site NO 585051 OS: 59 * Map: 7, no: 154

Probable site of castle.

Caprington Castle

Ayrshire: About 2 miles south-west of Kilmarnock, on minor roads north of B7038 and east of A759, just south of the River Irvine.

Private NS 407363 OS: 70 ** Map: 3, no: 149

Caprington Castle consists of a massive 15th-century, or earlier, keep with a small stair-wing and a substantial later wing – which were all encased in a castellated mansion of about 1829, with a large tower over the entrance.

The property was owned by the Wallaces of Sundrum, who were descended from William Wallace, from 1385; but in 1400 passed by marriage to the Cunninghams. The Cunninghams were baronets of Nova Scotia from 1669 to 1829. The castle is still occupied.

Caraldston *see* Careston Castle

Carberry Tower

Lothians: About 2 miles north-east of Dalkeith, on minor road east of A6124, just west of Queen Mary's Mount.

Private NT 364697 OS: 66 * Map: 4, no: 146**

Carberry Tower is a small square 16th-century tower house of four storeys within a massive corbelled-out parapet. A caphouse crowns the stair at the one corner. The walls are pierced by gunloops. The tower was extended by a large mansion in 1819.

The lands were held by the Abbey of Dunfermline, but the tower was built by Hugh Rigg about 1543, near the site of the Battle of Carberry Hill, where, in 1567, Mary, Queen of Scots was defeated. The property passed to the Blairs in 1659, then the Dicksons of Inveresk in 1689, then the Fullertons, then by marriage to the Elphinstone family – whose original tower, Elphinstone Tower, is nearby. The adjoining mansion was added in 1819, and there are later alterations and extensions. It is still occupied.

The corbiestepped gable of the original castle were apparently over-decorated with cherubim:

'Auld Hugh Rigg was very very big,
But a bigger man than he,
When his cherubs chirped,
Upon his new house of Carberee!'

Carbet Castle

Angus & Dundee: About 3 miles east of Dundee, on minor roads north of A929, 0.5 miles north-east of Broughty Ferry, at No 7 Camphill Road.

Ruin or site NO 413316 OS: 54 * Map: 8, no: 180

An earlier house here was extended by the Grimond family in the 19th century, but was completely demolished, except for the gate lodge, because of dry rot.

Carbeth House

Stirlingshire & Clackmannan: About 1 mile north of Killearn, on minor roads north of A875 junction with B818, south of Endrick Water, at Carbeth House.

Private NS 524876 OS: 57 * Map: 6, no: 14

Site of 15th-century castle. The present mansion, Carbeth House, dates partly from the 17th century, and may incorporate part of the castle. The house was remodelled as a castellated mansion in 1840, and was altered again in 1879.

The lands were a property of the Grahams, but passed to the Buchanan family in 1476, and they built the castle. The house is still occupied.

Carbisdale Castle

Sutherland & Caithness: About 3.5 miles north-west of Bonar Bridge, on minor roads north of A9, south of Kyle of Sutherland, north of Culrain, in Carbisdale.

Private NH 575955 OS: 21 * Map: 12, no: 11

Carbisdale Castle, dating mostly from 1910-11, was built on the site of Culrain Lodge for Duchess Blair, second wife of the 3rd Duke of Sutherland. The Duchess and her husband's family did not get on, and she had to build the mansion outwith the Dukes of Sutherland's area of control. It is now a youth hostel.

It was near here that the Marquis of Montrose was defeated by Covenanters in 1650.

Other refs: Culrain Lodge

Carco Castle

Dumfriesshire: About 2.5 miles north of Sanquhar, near B740, north of Crawick Water, at or near Carco.

Ruin or site NS 789141 OS: 71 * Map: 1, no: 129

Site of tower house, a property of the Crichtons of Carco. The family are said to have abandoned the tower towards the end of the 16th century, and moved to another building at Orchard [NS 781127].

Other refs: Chapel Hill; Orchard

Cardarroch House

Lanarkshire & Glasgow: About 1 mile east of Bishopbriggs, on minor roads south of B812, 0.5 miles east of Robroyston Mains, at Cardarroch.

Ruin or site NS 638695 OS: 64 * Map: 3, no: 300

Nothing remains of T-plan house with corbiestepped gables. It consisted of a main block of 1625, extended in 1718, with a small projecting stair-tower, making the building T-plan. The house rose to two storeys and a garret.

Carden Tower

Fife: About 1 mile south and east of Cardenden, on minor roads south of A92, north and east of Shawsmill.

Ruin or site NT 226937 OS: 58 ** Map: 7, no: 42

Once a castle of some importance, Carden Tower is a very ruined 16th-century L-plan tower house.

It was a property of the Martin family from 1482 or earlier, and they built the tower. The castle passed through various hands, until becoming derelict by the 1720s. Although the site was almost lost to open-cast mining, it was rescued, conserved, and cleared.

Parking is available, and the site is signposted.

OPEN: Access at all reasonable times.

Cardney House

Perth & Kinross: About 2 miles north and east of Dunkeld, on minor road north of A923, west of Loch of Butterstone, at Cardney House.

Private NO 050453 OS: 52 * Map: 8, no: 60

Possible site of castle.

The property was held by the Stewarts. Marion of Cardney was a mistress of Robert II in the second half of the 14th century, and it was from her that the Stewarts of Airntully, Dalguise and Murthly were descended. Marion was a sister of Robert, Bishop of Dunkeld, who was later one of the hostages for the return of James I.

Cardon *see* Quarter House

Cardonald Castle

Lanarkshire & Glasgow area: In Cardonald area of Glasgow, on minor roads south of A8, 0.75 miles north of Crookston Castle, at Cardonald.

Private NS 526645 OS: 64 * Map: 3, no: 234

Site of castle.

The property was held by the Stewarts of Darnley from the early 15th century, and in 1565 they built a large castle here, known as Cardonald Castle or Place. The property passed to the Stewarts of Blantyre in 1584, but the castle was demolished in 1848, and replaced by a farm house, which is now owned by the local council. A date stone of 1565 from the castle is preserved in the house

Cardoness Castle

Galloway: About 0.75 miles south-west of Gatehouse of Fleet, just west of B796 north of junction with A75, west of the Water of Fleet.

His Scot NX 591552 OS: 83 * Map: 1, no: 92**

Standing on a rocky mound, Cardoness Castle is a late 15th-century rectangular keep of four storeys and formerly a garret within a flush parapet. Remains of outbuildings survive in the ruined courtyard.

The entrance leads through a mural lobby to a guardroom and to a turnpike stair. The basement is vaulted and consists of two rooms, and there is a pit-prison. The hall, on the first floor, has a wide moulded fireplace. A straight stair, from the turnpike stair, leads to the second floor, which has two rooms, also with fine fireplaces.

Cardoness passed to the MacCullochs by marriage around 1450. They were an unruly lot, the 2nd MacCulloch laird being outlawed in 1471 and again in 1480. His successor, Ninian, robbed the widow of the 2nd laird of all her goods. Thomas MacCulloch, his son, besieged the Adairs of Dunskey in 1489, and soon after plundered the castle of his kinsman, MacCulloch of Adair. Thomas died at the Battle of Flodden in 1513. The last of the family was Sir Godfrey MacCulloch, who shot William Gordon of Buck (or Bush) o' Bield in 1690, fled abroad, returned and was spotted in a church in Edinburgh. He was beheaded in 1697 by the Maiden, an

early Scottish guillotine preserved in the Museum of Scotland in Edinburgh.

Cardoness had passed to the Gordons in 1629, and was later held by the Maxwells.

OPEN: Open Apr-Sep, Mon-Sat 9.30-18.30; open Oct-Mar wknds only, Sat 9.30-16.30, Sun 14.00-16.30; last ticket 30 mins before closing; closed 25/26 Dec and 1/2 Jan.

Visitor centre. WC. Car and coach parking. Group concessions. £.

Tel: 01557 814427 Fax: 0131 668 8888

Email: hs.explore@historic-scotland.gov.uk Web: www.historic-scotland.gov.uk

Cardrona Tower

Borders: About 3.5 miles east and south of Peebles, on minor roads south of B7062, in Cardrona Forest, west of Cardrona Burn.

Ruin or site NT 300378 OS: 73 * Map: 2, no: 76**

Cardrona Tower is a small 16th-century L-plan tower, formerly of three storeys and a garret, with a parapet on one side of the main block. All traces of the courtyard have gone.

The entrance, at the foot of the small wing, leads to a turnpike stair – which turns anti-clockwise – and to the vaulted basement. The hall, on the first floor, has a fireplace.

The Govans held Cardrona from 1358 until 1685, when the tower passed to the Williamsons. It was abandoned in 1685, but still almost entire in 1794.

Cardross Castle *see* Cardross Manor House

Cardross House

Stirlingshire & Clackmannan: About 2.5 miles south of Port of Menteith, on minor road east of B8034, west of Flanders Moss, at Cardross.

Private NS 605976 OS: 57 ** Map: 6, no: 34**

Cardross House consists of a small early 16th-century L-plan tower house, with a round stair-tower in the re-entrant angle. To this has been added a long three-storey extension with double gables. The original tower was remodelled with bartizans to match the new work. In the 18th century a new front was added, together with further extensions.

The original entrance was in the stair-tower, the stair leading to the hall on the first floor and the upper storeys. The basement is vaulted, and contains a prison, in the thickness of the walling, and a kitchen in the wing. The hall, on the first floor, has a fine fireplace and windows with stone seats.

The first extension contains some fine plaster ceilings of the 16th or 17th century. More good plasterwork was added in the mid 18th century.

The property was originally held by the Priory of Inchmahome, but passed to the Erskines of Cardross about 1590. Cromwell is said to have garrisoned the castle in the 1650s. The house is still occupied.

Cardross Manor House

Argyll & Dunbartonshire: To west of Dumbarton, west of A812 or north of A814, about 3 miles east of village of Cardross, near Brucehill, on Castlehill.

NTS NS 385757 [?] OS: 63 * Map: 5, no: 151

Site of a 14th-century castle or fortified manor house, which does not appear to have been used after 1329. The site is believed to have been at Castlehill.

The property was held by the Grahams, but was exchanged by them for Old Montrose with Robert the Bruce. The Grahams later became Earls, Marquises and Dukes of Montrose. The castle or manor was built by Robert the Bruce, King Robert I of Scots, in the 1320s. Although there is some debate as to whether it was fortified, it seems unlikely that Robert the Bruce would leave his security to chance in such uncertain times. Bruce died here on 7 June 1329, and his heart was taken from his body and taken on pilgrimage to Granada by Sir James Douglas. Douglas, and others of the Scots nobility who had joined him, were killed by Moors in Spain, but Bruce's heart was returned to Scotland and buried in Melrose Abbey, while the rest of his remains are interred in Dunfermline Abbey.

There are some remains of the old parish church in Levengrove Park.

Other refs: Cardross Castle; Castlehill, Cardross

OPEN: Access at all reasonable times.

Careston Castle

Angus & Dundee: About 4.5 miles west of Brechin, on minor road north of A94, 0.75 miles east of Noran Water, just west of Mains of Careston, at Careston Castle.
Private NO 530599 OS: 54 * Map: 8, no: 223**
Careston Castle is a 17th-century Z-plan tower house of four storeys and a garret which incorporates part of a 15th-century castle. It has been much altered and extended in later centuries by a two-storey main block and stair-turret. The stair-turret has been engulfed by a corbiestepped extension, joining at right angles. Bartizans, crowning the castle, have had their original conical roofs replaced by crenellations. The house was remodelled in the 18th century and given a symmetrical front with tall gabled corner towers and an arcaded basement storey.
The Dempsters owned the property. One of the family fought with the Bishop of Brechin over land, and stole cattle and horses and was involved in the kidnapping of monks. The property passed to the Lindsays, who extended the castle, then to the Carnegies. It was sold to the Stewarts of Grandtully in 1707, and remodelled in 1714. It is still occupied.
Other refs: Carvaldstan Castle; Caraldston

Carfrae Peel

Borders: About 5 miles north of Lauder, on minor roads north of A68, near Hillhouse.
Ruin or site NT 502551 OS: 73 ** Map: 2, no: 168
Carfrae Peel is a small ruined tower house, with a round stair-tower and vaulted basement, but little remains above this level. It was a property of the Sinclairs.

Cargill Castle *see* Castle Hill, Cargill

Carlesgill

Dumfriesshire: About 3.5 miles north-west of Langholm, on minor road south of B709, south of River Esk, at or near Carlesgill.
Ruin or site NY 330880 OS: 79 * Map: 1, no: 304
Site of tower house.

Carleton Castle

Ayrshire: About 6 miles south of Girvan, on minor roads east of A77, at Carleton.
Ruin or site NX 133895 OS: 76 ** Map: 3, no: 11
Carleton Castle is a ruined rectangular 15th-century keep, formerly of five storeys, with a destroyed corner. There was a small courtyard with apparently had corner towers.
The basement, which probably contained the kitchen, and the hall were both vaulted.

It was a property of the Cathcart family.
The ghost of Sir John Cathcart is said to haunt the building. He married several women in turn, after having murdered the last. However, his last wife, May Kennedy of Culzean, realising what was going to happen, managed to kill Cathcart by pushing him to his death, thereby saved herself. It is said that ghostly cries and screams have been heard from the castle.
OPEN: Access at all reasonable times – care should be taken.
Parking nearby.

Carlinghoups *see* Carlops

Carlock

Ayrshire: About 3.5 miles south and east of Ballantrae, on minor road east of A77, west of Water of App, in Glen App, at or near Carlock House.
Private NX 095770 [?] OS: 76 * Map: 3, no: 9
Site of castle.
Other refs: Karlock

Carlops

Borders: In or near Carlops, near A702.
Ruin or site NT 161560 [?] OS: 72 * Map: 2, no: 25
Site of tower house.
The present village of Carlops was founded in 1784 for cotton-weaving and then woollen manufacturing.
Other refs: Carlinghoups; Karlinghoups

Carlowrie Castle

Lothians: About 1 mile east of Kirkliston, on minor roads east of A8000 or B800, north of River Almond at Boathouse Bridge, at Carlowrie.
Ruin or site NT 142744 [?] OS: 66 * Map: 4, no: 46
Site of mansion, which apparently had no fortified origins.
In the 19th century the property was held by the Hutchinsons.

Carluke *see* Kirkton of Carluke

Carmichael House

Ayrshire: About 5 miles south-east of Lanark, on minor roads west of A73, north of Cleuch Burn, at Carmichael.
Private NS 938391 OS: 72 * Map: 3, no: 416
Site of 14th-century castle. The present house, dating from 1734, was never completed and consists of two wings and a joining corridor.
The Carmichaels held the lands from the 1370s or earlier. One of the family, John Carmichael, slew the Duke of Clarence, brother of Henry V of England, at the Battle of Bauge in 1421 – and the family's crest is a broken spear. The head of the family fought against Charles I at the Battle of Marston Moor in 1644, and against the Marquis of Montrose at the Battle of Philiphaugh in 1645, although two of his brothers were Royalists. In 1701 the family were made Earls of Hyndford, and John Carmichael, 3rd Earl, was a British envoy to Prussia and Russia. The family were Hanoverians.
The lands and titles passed to the Anstruthers, and who changed their name to the Carmichael-Anstruthers, then to Carmichael. The house is still occupied by the same family.
Carmichael Heritage Centre is nearby [NS 948388] which features information on the Carmichaels and other lowland Scottish families.

Carmunnock *see* Castlemilk

Carmyllie Castle

Angus & Dundee: About 4 miles south of Letham, on minor roads west of B961 or east of B9128, 0.5 miles east of Greystone, at Carmyllie.
Ruin or site NO 546432 OS: 54 * Map: 8, no: 231
Site of castle, nothing of which survives.
Carmyllie was a property of Arbroath Abbey, then passed through several families after the Reformation, until it was held in 1640 by the Maules of Panmure.

Carn Liath, Golspie

Sutherland & Caithness: On A9, 3 miles E of Golspie, Sutherland.
His Scot   NC 870013   OS: 17   **   Map: 12, no: 31
Carn Liath consists of the fine remains of a broch and surrounding settlement. A silver brooch was found here, dating from the 4th or 5th century, suggesting the settlement was used by the Picts. The brooch is now held at the Museum of Scotland in Edinburgh.
OPEN: Access at all reasonable times.
Parking.
Tel: 0131 668 8800   Fax: 0131 668 8888
Email: hs.explore@scotland.gov.uk   Web: www.historic-scotland.gov.uk

Carnasserie Castle

Argyll & Dunbartonshire: About 8.5 miles north of Lochgilphead, on minor road west of A816, west of the Kilmartin Burn, 3 miles from the south end of Loch Awe, at Carnasserie.
His Scot   NM 837009   OS: 55   *   Map: 5, no: 64**
Carnasserie Castle consists of a ruined 16th-century tower house, of five storeys and a garret, and lower hall-block. The parapet has open rounds at three of the corners, and a corbelled-out bartizan at the other. The walls are pierced by many gunloops and shot-holes. A courtyard has an arch dated 1681.
The entrance, in one corner of the wing, is surmounted by a Gaelic inscription

urging faith in God. The entrance to the vaulted basement leads, through a long narrow passage, to a wine-cellar, a kitchen with a fireplace and stone sink, and other cellars.
The hall, on the first floor of the block adjoining the tower, has an ornamental fireplace. Private chambers occupied the floors above.
The castle was built by John Carswell, who published the first ever book in Gaelic in 1567, the Gaelic version of the Book of Common Order. He also had a castle at Kilmartin, and was Chancellor of the Chapel-Royal at Stirling. He was made Bishop of the Isles in 1566 by Mary, Queen of Scots. On his death in 1572 the property passed to the Campbells of Auchinbreck. It was captured and sacked by the MacLeans and MacLachlans during the Earl of Argyll's rebellion in 1685.
OPEN: Access at all reasonable times.
Picnic area. Car and coach parking.
Tel: 0131 668 8800   Fax: 0131 668 8888
Email: hs.explore@scotland.gov.uk   Web: www.historic-scotland.gov.uk

Carnbane Castle

Perth & Kinross: About 7 miles west and north of Kenmore, on minor road 7 miles west of B846 at Keltney Burn, just north of River Lyon, at Carnbane.
Private   NN 677478   OS: 51   *   Map: 8, no: 5
All that remains of Carnbane Castle is the vaulted basement of a 16th-century tower house with gunloops on either side of a gateway passage. A small courtyard enclosed ranges of buildings, only the foundations of which remain.

The hall was on the first floor of the tower house.
It was built by Red Duncan Campbell the Hospitable – which does not explain the gunloops.

Carnbee

Fife: About 3 miles north of Pittenweem, on minor road north of B9171, at or near Carnbee.
Ruin or site   NO 530067   OS: 59   *   Map: 7, no: 138
Site of castle. A date stone of 1638 survives built into a house at Carnbee.
The lands are mentioned in 1309, and in the 16th century. The castle or later house was demolished in 1813. Carnbee House was built in 1819-20.

Carnbroe House

Lanarkshire & Glasgow area: About 2 miles south of Coatbridge, east of junction of B7070 with A725, south bank of the North Calder Water, just west of Carnbroe Mains Farm.
Ruin or site   NS 735623 [?]   OS: 64   *   Map: 3, no: 347
Carnbroe House, a much-altered 16th-century L-plan tower house of three storeys and a garret, was demolished in the middle of the 20th century. Two round towers projected from the main block.
The basement contained three vaulted chambers and the hall was on the first floor. The building had been greatly altered internally.
Carnbroe was held by the Baillies, but passed to the Hamiltons.

Carnegie Castle

Angus & Dundee: About 4 miles north-west of Carnoustie, on minor road south of B9127 or north of B961, north of Crombie Country Park, at Carnegie.
Ruin or site   NO 535415   OS: 54   *   Map: 8, no: 225
Site of castle of the Carnegie family, who held the property from 1358 until the 18th century. The family later became Earls of both Southesk and Northesk.

Carnell

Ayrshire: About 4 miles south-east of Kilmarnock, on minor road east of A719 and west of A76, at Carnell, just south of the Cessnock Water.
Private   NS 467323   OS: 70   **   Map: 3, no: 195
Carnell consists of a rectangular plain 15th-century keep, to which a large 19th-century mansion, extended in 1871, has been added. The keep rises to three storeys and a garret within a remodelled corbelled-out parapet. A gabled stair-tower, probably of the late 16th century, is crowned by a caphouse.
The entrance is modern. The basement is vaulted, and has a wide kitchen fireplace, which is dated 1569.
Carnell was a property of the Wallaces. William Wallace of Carnell was killed at the Battle of Flodden in 1513. The lands passed to the Cathcarts in the 17th century, but the Wallaces recovered them and retained them until the 19th century. In 1843 Colonel John Ferrier Hamilton had William Burn remodel the older buildings, and added an L-plan Jacobean mansion. The house is still occupied.
Other refs: Cairnhill

Carnock House

Stirlingshire & Clackmannan: About 2.5 miles west of Airth, on minor road north of B9124 at Powdrake, at Carnock House.
Private   NS 865882   OS: 65   **   Map: 6, no: 88
Site of tower house, a long three-storey house with two projecting stair-towers and corbiestepped gables, dormer windows, and a parapet, which was demolished in 1941. It had fine plaster ceilings, fragments of which are said to be preserved at Kinneil House.
The lands were a property of the Somervilles, but passed to the Bruces of Auchenbowie in the early 16th century, then in 1608 to the Drummonds of Carnock, who built the house. It replaced nearby Bruce's Castle, originally known as the Tower of Carnock. Carnock was acquired by the Nicholsons in 1634, then the Shaws of Greenock in the 18th century, who held it until the 20th century.

Carnock Tower *see* Bruce's Castle

Carnock's Tower, Brechin *see* Bishop's Palace, Brechin

Carnousie Castle

Banff & Buchan: About 3.5 miles west of Turriff, on minor roads south of B9025, about 1 mile north of River Deveron, just east of Mains of Carnousie.

Private NJ 670504 OS: 29 *** Map: 10, no: 189

Carnousie Castle is a late 16th-century Z-plan tower house of three storeys and a garret. It consists of a main block and a square gabled tower, crowned by a watch-chamber, and a round tower, with a conical roof, at opposite corners. A small turret is corbelled out in the main re-entrant angle above second-floor level. In 1740 William Adam added a long wing, but in recent years this has been demolished.

The entrance, at the foot of the square tower, leads to a scale-and-platt stair which climbs only to the first floor. A vaulted basement contains cellars and a kitchen.

Carnousie was a property of the Ogilvies. Their lands were wasted in the 1640s, the Ogilvies were ruined, and in 1683 had to sell the property to the Gordons. It then passed through several families until the 20th century when it was abandoned, for a while being used as a piggery. It has been restored in recent years, and is occupied.

Other refs: Old House of Carnousie

Carntyne

Lanarkshire & Glasgow: About 2 miles east of Glasgow Cathedral, on minor roads south of A8, just south of Carntyne Road, at Carntyne Square.

Private NS 636651 [?] OS: 64 * Map: 3, no: 298

Site of castle, hall or old house. It was replaced by Carntyne House in 1802.

The lands were a property of the Grays of Carntyne from the Reformation.

Carnwath House

Lanarkshire & Glasgow area: In or near Carnwath, near junction of A70 with A721 and B7016 with A70.

Private NS 975465 OS: 72 * Map: 3, no: 433

Carnwath House, a plain mansion of two storeys, incorporated work from a tower house of the 16th or 17th century. The building was demolished in 1970 when a new club house was built for Carnwath Golf Club.

An early castle was situated on the motte at the west end of the village [NS 975467] on an impressive motte, and was constructed by Sir John Somerville of Carnwath and Linton. The motte is particularly steep, and access to a blockhouse was by a tunnel, through the base, then a stairwell to the centre.

Carnwath was a property of the Somervilles from 1140, but passed to Lockhart of the Lee in the 17th century. In 1639 Robert Dalziel was made Earl of Carnwath. The Dalziels were Jacobites, and were forfeited after the 1715 Jacobite Rising.

Carnwath Mill

Lanarkshire & Glasgow: About 1 mile south-east of Carnwath, on minor roads south of A721, west of North Medwin (burn), south of Kaimend, at Carnwath Mill.

Private NS 997454 OS: 72 ** Map: 3, no: 439

The farmhouse incorporates a much altered tower or bastle house. A stone, carved with the date 1611, survives on an adjacent wall.

Caroline Park House

Lothians: About 3 miles north of Edinburgh Castle, on minor roads west of A901, south of the shore of the Firth of Forth, at Caroline Park in Granton.

Private NT 227773 OS: 66 ** Map: 4, no: 81

Caroline Park, although much modified and extended, incorporates a tower house built by Andrew Logan in 1585. In 1683 it was acquired by Sir George Mackenzie of Tarbat, who added new ranges to create a courtyard mansion. It was sold to the Campbell Duke of Argyll in 1739, who changed the name to Caroline Park after his daughter, or alternatively after George II's queen. It passed by marriage to the Scott Dukes of Buccleuch. Alterations were made in the 1740s, and later, and there are some fine interiors. The house is still occupied and in good condition.

A 'Green Lady', the apparition of Lady Royston, wife of Sir James Mackenzie, younger son of Lord Tarbat, is said to haunt the house. On certain days, her phantom is reported to appear at midnight from an old well, and go to the entrance of the house, where she vanishes. She is said to then reappear in the small courtyard and ring an old bell.

A ghostly cannon ball is also said to have been witnessed several times smashing through the window of the Aurora Room. This is recorded as being a relatively common occurrence in the 1850s.

Other refs: House of Royston; Royston Castle

Carquhannan Castle *see* Ballairdie Castle

Carriber Castle

Lothians: About 2.5 miles south west of Linlithgow, north of A706, south of the River Avon, near Muiravonside Country Park, west of Easter Carriber.

Ruin or site NS 966751 OS: 65 ** Map: 4, no: 6

Little remains of Carriber Castle or Tower, a 16th-century tower house, except one gable and foundations.

It was built by Rob Gibb, who had been jester to James V and married Margaret Shaw, a royal mistress.

Other ref: Easter Carriber

Carrick Castle

Argyll & Dunbartonshire: About 4.5 miles south of Lochgoilhead, on minor road 4.5 miles south of B839 at Lochgoilhead, west shore of Loch Goil, at Carrick Castle.

Ruin or site NS 194944 OS: 56 *** Map: 5, no: 122

Standing on a rock jutting into Loch Goil, Carrick Castle is a 15th-century keep, although there may have been a stronghold here from the 13th century. The castle rises to three storeys and a garret within a flush parapet. The windows are arched,

and a small courtyard occupied a higher part of the rock, but little remains of ranges of buildings within the walls. There was formerly a ditch and drawbridge on the landward side.

There are two entrances, both from the courtyard, one in the basement, one above to the first floor, the two floors having no connecting stair. The basement is not vaulted and the hall, on the first floor, was once a fine apartment, and had windows with stone seats. Two straight stairs lead off on either side of the entrance, one climbing only to the second storey, the other to the parapet.

An earlier castle here may have been a hunting seat of the kings of Scots. It was originally a Lamont stronghold, but passed in 1368 to the Campbell Earls of Argyll. Mary, Queen of Scots, stayed here in 1563. In 1685 the lands were pillaged, and the castle burned during Argyll's rebellion. The property later passed to the Murray Earls of Dunmore.

It is currently being restored, and a pit-prison has been discovered.

Other refs: Castle of Carrick

Carrick House

Orkney: To the north of the island of Eday in Orkney, on minor roads west of B9063, just west of the shore of Calf Sound, at Carrick.

Private HY 567384 OS: 5 ** Map: 11, no: 56

Carrick House, a 17th-century house of three storeys with corbiestepped gables, incorporates part of an older building. An arched entrance to the courtyard is dated 1633.

It was a property of John Stewart, Lord Kinclaven, but passed on his death to the Buchanans, then to James Fea of Clestrain, who captured the pirate John Gow in 1725. Gow, born in Stromness in Orkney, was not a very good pirate and managed to run his ship aground on the Calf of Eday. He was caught and executed. The island passed to the Laings, then in 1848 to the Hebden family who still occupy Carrick House.

OPEN: Open Jun-Sep, Sun 14.00 onwards – tel to check; other times by arrangement.

Guided tours. Picnic area. WC. Limited disabled access. Car parking. £.

Tel: 01857 622260 Fax: 01857 622260

Carriden House

Stirlingshire & Clackmannan: About 1.5 miles east of Bo'ness, on minor road east from A904, near the shore of the Firth of Forth, near site of Roman Fort.

Private NT 026808 OS: 65 * Map: 6, no: 115**

Carriden House consists of a much-altered 16th-century tower house of five storeys, to which a large modern mansion has been added. Bartizans, with gunloops, crown the corners, but the roof pitch has been lowered. Most of the windows have been enlarged, but over a first-floor window is the date 1602.

The basement is vaulted.

The lands were held by the Cockburn family from 1358 until 1541, when they passed to the Abercrombies. In 1601 the property was sold to Sir John Hamilton of Letterick, who was made Lord Bargany, and he built most of the remaining house. It was then sold to the Setons, passed through many families, including the Cornwalls of Bonhard, to the Hopes, two of whom were distinguished admirals. It is still occupied.

Carronglen *see* Durisdeer Castle

Carryill *see* Carzeid

Carscreugh Castle

Galloway: About 2 miles north-east of Glenluce, on minor road north of A75, south side of Carscreugh Fell, just west of Carscreugh.

Ruin or site NX 223599 OS: 82 ** Map: 1, no: 35

Carscreugh Castle, a ruined late 17th-century mansion, incorporates a 17th-century tower house, with later square wings.

It passed from the Vaux family to Ross of Balneil, and then by marriage to James Dalrymple, Lord Stair, who built the mansion. It was probably abandoned by 1695.

Janet Dalrymple of Carscreugh was forced to marry Sir David Dunbar of Baldoon, although in love with another man. Janet died at Baldoon on her wedding night, although the circumstances surrounding her death are unclear. Her ghost, in a blooded wedding dress, is said to haunt the ruins of Baldoon.

Carse *see* Carse Gray

Carse Castle *see* Kersie

Carse Castle

Stirlingshire & Clackmannan: About 3 miles north-east of Falkirk, near A904, just south of the River Carron, in Glenburgh area of Grangemouth.

Ruin or site NS 924823 [?] OS: 65 * Map: 6, no: 102

Possible site of castle of the Menteith of Kerse family, although it may have been at Kersie [NS 872912].

Other refs: Kerse Castle

Carse Gray

Angus & Dundee: About 2 miles north of Forfar, on minor roads south of A94 and east of B9128, just east of Carse Hill, at Carse Gray.

Private NO 464540 OS: 54 ** Map: 8, no: 199

Carse Gray incorporates a small altered 17th-century T-plan tower house of two storeys and a garret, to which has been added an 18th-century house.

Carse belonged to the Rynd family, but in 1641 the property was sold to the Ruthvens. The name was changed to Carse Gray when it was acquired in 1741 by Charles Gray of Balbunno, whose descendants still own the property.

Other refs: Carse

Carslogie House

Fife: About 1 mile west of Cupar, on minor road north of A91, at Carslogie.

Ruin or site NO 353144 OS: 59 ** Map: 7, no: 93

Carslogie House consists of a very ruined 16th-century tower house, much altered and remodelled in the 18th century with the insertion of large windows. It rose to four storeys.

The basement was vaulted, and the storey above had large windows.

The Clephane family held Carslogie from the late 14th century until after 1710. Alan Clephane of Carslogie fought on the side of Robert the Bruce at the Battle of Bannockburn in 1314, where he lost his right hand. He had one made in steel to replace it, fitted with springs so he could use his sword. The building was occupied until about 1870.

Carsluith Castle

Galloway: About 3.5 miles south of Creetown, just south of A75, short distance from the shore of Wigtown Bay, about 0.5 miles south-east of Carsluith village.

His Scot NX 495542 OS: 83 * Map: 1, no: 83**

Carsluith Castle consists of a rectangular 15th-century keep of three storeys, to which was added a taller stair-wing in the 16th century, making the castle L-plan. The stair-wing is crowned by a watch-chamber. The old part has a parapet crowning two walls and has open rounds. The walls are pierced by gunloops and shot-holes. The tower is dated 1586, and had a courtyard.

The entrance is in the re-entrant angle, and the basement is vaulted. A turnpike stair leads to the fine hall, on the first floor, which has a moulded fireplace. Private chambers occupied the floors above.

Carsluith was a Cairns property, but in 1460 passed to James Lindsay, Chamberlain of Galloway, who probably built the keep. His son was killed at the Battle of Flodden in 1513, and the property passed by marriage to Richard Brown, who built the 1568 addition.

Gilbert Brown of Carsluith was the last abbot of Sweetheart Abbey, and a noted supporter of the Catholic side at the Reformation. In 1596 the Privy Council complained to James VI that he was sheltering 'Jesuits and excommunicated papists', and in 1605 he was arrested and imprisoned in Blackness Castle. He was eventually allowed to retire to France, where he died in 1612. Richard's son, John Brown, was heavily fined for failing to answer the charge of murdering MacCulloch of Barholm. The Brown family emigrated to India in 1748, and abandoned the castle.

OPEN: Open all year – view from exterior?

Parking nearby.

Tel: 0131 668 8800 Fax: 0131 668 8888

Email: hs.explore@scotland.gov.uk Web: www.historic-scotland.gov.uk

Carstairs Castle

Lanarkshire & Glasgow area: In Carstairs, near the church, near A70, north of River Clyde and south of Mouse Water.

Ruin or site NS 939461 OS: 72 * Map: 3, no: 417

Site of 13th-century castle, of which nothing remains.

The property belonged to the Bishops of Glasgow from 1126, and there was a castle here, which was rebuilt or remodelled around 1290. The property was rented to James Hamilton of Finnart in 1535, but later passed to the Stewarts, then the Lockharts. Materials from the castle were used to build the parish church in 1794. The lands were acquired by Henry Monteith in 1819, and he built himself a Gothic mansion, which survives as St Charles Hospital, as well as replanning Carstairs.

Other refs: Casseltarras; Casteltarres

Carterton

Dumfriesshire: About 7 miles north-east of Lockerbie, on minor roads east of B723 or north of B7068, near Corrie Water, at or near Carterton.

Ruin or site   NY 203896   OS: 79   *   Map: 1, no: 264

Site of tower house, possibly within the earthworks of a fort.

Other refs: Garterton

Cartley Hole *see* Abbotsford

Cartsdyke

Renfrewshire: About 1 mile east of Greenock, on minor roads south of A8, 0.5 miles south of River Clyde, near Cartsburn, at Cartsdyke.

Ruin or site   NS 287756   OS: 63   *   Map: 3, no: 66

Site of 16th-century house of the Crawfords of Kilbirnie, who held the property from the 16th century.

 Sir Patrick Crawford of Cartsdyke fought for Mary, Queen of Scots, at the Battle of Langside in 1568. Sir Thomas Crawford of Cartsdyke invested heavily in the new port in the 17th century, and lost heavily in the Darien Scheme. Cartsdyke was once more important than Greenock itself.

Other refs: Crawfurdsdyke

Carvaldstan Castle *see* Careston Castle

Carvichen

Aberdeen & Gordon: About 0.5 miles south-east of Huntly, on minor road just south of A96 west of junction with A97, at or near Carvichen.

Ruin or site   NJ 540390   OS: 29   *   Map: 10, no: 128

Site of castle, some remains of which survived in the middle of the 19th century.

 There was apparently another tower, known as Torriesoul, in the same general area, although this may be another site.

Other refs: Corvichen; Torriesoul

Cary Castle *see* Castle Cary

Carzeid

Dumfriesshire: About 3 miles north of Dumfries, on minor roads west of A701, east of River Nith, at Carzeid.

Ruin or site   NX 969818   OS: 78   *   Map: 1, no: 187

Site of tower house and later farm, which stood within the now slight remains of a Roman fort.

Other refs: Carryill

Cash Tower

Fife: About 1.5 miles south-west of Auchtermuchty, on minor road south of A912, south of Strathmiglo, at Wester Cash.

Ruin or site   NO 222099   OS: 58   *   Map: 7, no: 40

Site of tower house, a property of the Scotts in 1548.

Caskieben Castle *see* Keith Hall

Casseltarras *see* Carstairs Castle

Cassencarie House

Galloway: About 3 miles east and north of Wigtown, on minor road east of A75, 0.5 miles south of Creetown, 0.25 miles east of River Cree, at Cassencarie.

Ruin or site   NX 476577   OS: 83   **   Map: 1, no: 79

Cassencarie House, a large and much-altered 17th-century ruined house, incorporates a 16th-century tower house. The house stood within a wooded park, and has also been recorded as Cassencarry.

 The lands were probably held by the church, but later passed to the Mures.

Cassillis House

Ayrshire: About 3 miles north-east of Maybole, on minor road north of B742, on the south bank of the River Doon, about 1.5 miles south-west of Dalrymple.

Private   NS 341128   OS: 70   **   Map: 3, no: 106

Cassillis House consists of a strong rectangular tower, built in the 14th century but much altered, to which a square tower was added in the 17th century, and large extensions in 1830.

The basement is vaulted, with a prison built into the walls, which are up to 16 feet thick. A 17th-century turnpike stair also survives – but few other old features remain.

 The property passed by marriage from the Montgomerys to the Kennedys in 1373 who had been Stewards of Carrick from 1367 or earlier. The 3rd Lord Kennedy was made first Earl of Cassillis in 1509, and killed at the Battle of Flodden in 1513. The second Earl was assassinated in 1527 by Sir Hugh Campbell of Loudoun, Sheriff of Ayr. Gilbert, the 3rd Earl, was captured at the Battle of Solway Moss in 1542. He was Treasurer from 1554 until his death, probably by poison, at Dieppe when a commissioner for the marriage of Mary, Queen of Scots, to the Dauphin of France. The 4th Earl, another Gilbert, fought for Mary at the Battle of Langside in 1568. He went on to boil the Commendator of Crossraguel Abbey, Allan Stewart, in sop to persuade him to sign over the lands of the abbey. In 1601 the 5th Earl, with 200 men, ambushed and murdered Kennedy of Bargany, during a dispute over land, but deviously escaped punishment. Bargany's son-in-law, Mure of Auchendrane, took his revenge by slaying Sir Thomas Kennedy of Culzean. Mure and his son were less lucky than the Earl, and were caught, tried and executed. This inspired Sir Walter Scott's play 'Auchendrane', or 'The Ayrshire Tragedy'. John, the 6th Earl, was Justice General 1649, and supported the Presbyterian side during the Restoration. The 12th Earl was created Marquis of Ailsa in 1831.

 Culzean Castle was the family seat from the 1770s until the 1940s, when the Marquis of Ailsa returned to Cassillis.

Casteltarres *see* Carstairs Castle

Castle Ascog *see* Asgog Castle

Castle Balliol *see* Loch Doon Castle

Castle Bloody

Orkney: About 2.5 miles north of Stromness, near A967, at Quholm.

Ruin or site   HY 251129   OS: 6   *   Map: 11, no: 35

Possible site of castle or stronghold, said to have been occupied in Norse times.

Castle Bradwude *see* Castle Brocket

Castle Brocket

Lanarkshire & Glasgow: About 3.5 miles south-east of Strathaven, just south of A726, south of Kype Water, at or near Castle Brocket.

Ruin or site   NS 735420   OS: 71   *   Map: 3, no: 346

Site of castle, on which was built a farm.

Other refs: Castlebrocket; Castle Bradwude

Castle Campbell – see below

Castle Caifen *see* Castle Coeffin

Castle Campbell

Stirlingshire & Clackmannan: About 0.5 miles north of Dollar, on minor road north of the A91, in Dollar Glen, just west of Gloom Hill, east of Burn of Sorrow.

NTS NS 962994 OS: 58 ** Map: 6, no: 108**

An impressive and picturesque ruin, Castle Campbell was built where the Burns of Care and Sorrow join, overlooked by Gloom Hill, and was originally known as Castle Gloom. A large strong 15th-century keep, altered in later centuries, stands at one corner of a substantial courtyard, enclosed by a curtain wall.

The courtyard is entered by an arched pend, originally through a gatehouse. The keep rises four storeys to a parapet with open rounds at each corner. The roof is flat, the upper floor being rib-vaulted to support it. The curtain wall has a corbelled-out parapet with machiolations.

One entrance to the keep was at ground level, and led to a vaulted basement and to a straight stair, in the thickness of the wall, which rose to the first floor. The other entrance, at first-floor level, was reached by an external stair. The hall, on the first floor, is vaulted, and has a prison in the thickness of one wall, reached through a hatch in the stone floor.

A later range also contains a hall. An arched loggia joins the lower storeys together.

It was a property of the Stewarts, but passed by marriage to Colin Campbell, 1st Earl of Argyll and Chancellor of Scotland, and he had the name changed to Castle Campbell by an Act of Parliament in 1489. The 2nd Earl, Archibald, was killed at the Battle of Flodden in 1513. The 4th Earl took a prominent part in the Battle of Pinkie in 1547, and in the siege of Haddington in 1548. John Knox stayed here in 1566.

The Marquis of Montrose defeated the 8th Earl and 1st Marquis of Argyll, another Archibald, at the battles of Inverlochy and Kilsyth in 1645, but failed to capture the castle, although he ravaged the lands. The 8th Earl was responsible for hanging, drawing and quartering Montrose in 1651 – Argyll himself was later executed in 1661 after the Restoration.

Cromwell's forces occupied the castle in 1653, and only part was restored after a burning by General Monck in 1654. The 9th Earl was condemned to death for treason, escaped to start a rebellion, but was captured and executed in 1685. George, the 6th Duke, sold the castle in the early 19th century to the Taits, who sold it to the Orr family in 1859. In 1948 the castle was taken over by The National Trust for Scotland, but is administered by Historic Scotland.

Other refs: Castle Gloom; Campbell Castle

OPEN: Open all year: Apr-Sep, daily 9.30-18.30; Oct-Mar, Mon-Wed and Sat 9.30-16.30, Thu 9.30-12.0, Sun 14.00-16.30, closed Fri; last ticket 30 mins before closing; closed 25/26 Dec and 1/2 Jan.

Gift shop. Tearoom. WC. Car parking. Group concessions. £. Owned by NTS but administered by Historic Scotland.

Tel: 01259 742408 Fax: 0131 668 8888

Email: hs.explore@scotland.gov.uk Web: www.historic-scotland.gov.uk

Castle Cary

Stirlingshire & Clackmannan: About 2 miles north and east of Cumbernauld, on minor roads south of A80, just east of the Walton Burn, near railway line, at Castlecary.

Private NS 786775 OS: 64 * Map: 6, no: 68**

Castle Cary consists of a rectangular late 15th-century keep with a crenellated parapet and open rounds. To this has been added a 17th-century L-plan wing of two storeys and an attic, the small wing of which houses another turnpike stair. A caphouse crowns the turnpike stair. The building incorporates reused Roman masonry.

The entrance leads to the barrel-vaulted basement, and to a turnpike stair which leads up to parapet level. The hall, on the first floor, has had a moulded fireplace. The interior has been altered, although an iron yett survives within the building. There is a walled garden.

The property was owned by the Livingstones until the first half of the 17th century, when it passed to the Baillies. The castle was burned by Jacobites during the 1715 Rising. In 1730 the property passed by marriage to the Dunbars of Fingask.

The castle is said to have two ghosts: General Baillie, the Covenanter general, who was defeated by the Marquis of Montrose at the Battle of Kilsyth in 1645; and Lizzie Baillie. Lizzie ran off with a poor Highland farmer, but reputedly haunts the castle searching for her father, as the news of her elopement is said to have killed him.

Other refs: Cary Castle

OPEN: Bed and breakfast – open all year to residents.

2 ensuite guest rooms. Vaulted dining room. Beamed lounge. Walled garden. Parking.

Tel: 01324 841330 Fax: 01324 841330

Email: bobhunter@easynet.co.uk

Castle Coeffin

Argyll & Dunbartonshire: About 8.5 miles north of Oban, on west coast of island of Lismore, on minor road and track west of B8045, 2 miles north of Achnacroish, at Castle Coeffin.

Ruin or site   NM 853437   OS: 49   **   Map: 5, no: 68

Standing on a rock, Castle Coeffin is a much ruined and overgrown 13th-century hall house and courtyard of the MacDougalls of Lorn. It passed in the 15th century to the Campbells, but was probably abandoned by the 17th century.

The castle is said to be named after Caifen, the son of a Norse king, who lived here. His sister, Beothail, died of a broken heart after her betrothed was killed. Her spirit was said to haunt the castle, and did not find peace until she was buried beside her love in Norway.

Other refs: Coeffin Castle; Castle Caifen

Castle Craig

Ross & Cromarty: About 6.5 miles north-east of Dingwall, on minor roads and foot north of B9163, on southern shore of Cromarty Firth, at Castle Craig.

Ruin or site   NH 632638   OS: 21   **   Map: 9, no: 86

Standing on a cliff-top site, Castle Craig consists of a ruined 16th-century tower house, one side of which has collapsed. The castle is surrounded by a large courtyard with round corner towers. The rectangular tower rises to four storeys and a garret within a parapet, which only extends along the gable. The parapet has open rounds, and the stone roof is supported by a vaulted garret storey.

There are two entrances, one in landward side, and one from the courtyard, both defended by gunloops. All the main storeys are vaulted. The kitchen was in the basement, and had a large fireplace; the hall was on the first floor; and there were private chambers above. A turnpike stair, in one corner, led to all floors.

The castle was built by the Urquharts, used as a residence by the Bishops of Ross, but abandoned about 1640.

Other refs: Craig Castle; Castlecraig

Castle Croft

Aberdeen & Gordon: About 3 miles south-west of Insch, on minor roads south of B9002 or west of B992, 2 miles west of Auchleven, at or near New Leslie.

Ruin or site   NJ 588253 [?]   OS: 37   *   Map: 10, no: 152

Nothing remains of Castle Croft, or New Leslie Castle, the last vestiges of which were removed before 1842.

New Leslie was a property of the Leslie family from about 1470, then held by the Leiths of Leith Hall from around 1600 until 1650. The castle was ruinous in 1724

Other refs: Croft; New Leslie Castle

Castle Dounie *see* Beaufort Castle

Castle Ewen

Argyll & Dunbartonshire: About 1.5 miles west and north of Kilfinan, on Rubha Beag, on minor roads and foot west of B8000, east side of Loch Fyne to north of Kilfinan Bay.

Ruin or site   NR 916796   OS: 62   **   Map: 5, no: 81

Little remains of a Iron Age fort, dun and medieval stronghold, marked by a cairn which was erected by members of Clan Ewen.

It was a stronghold of Clan Ewen of Otter, who claim descent from the kings of Ireland. The clan lost much power to the Campbells in the 15th century, and became a broken clan, although the site may have been used until the 16th century or later. The site was excavated in 1968-9, when finds included a 12th-century crucifix, pottery sherds from the 13th and 18th centuries, and a 15th-century coin.

Other refs: MacEwen's Castle; Caisteal Mhic Eogbainn

Castle Feather

Galloway: About 4 miles south of Whithorn, on minor roads south of A750 at Isle of Whithorn, south of Cutcloy, west of Burrow Head on shore of Solway Firth.

Ruin or site   NX 449342   OS: 83   **   Map: 1, no: 73

Little remains of Castle Feather, a 16th-century tower house, except foundations. It was built on a cliff-top promontory within the ramparts of an Iron Age fort.

Other refs: Feather

Castle Fergus *see* Lochfergus

Castle Forbes *see* Druminnor Castle

Castle Forbes

Aberdeen & Gordon: About 3.5 miles north-east of Alford, on minor roads east of B992, north of the River Don, 0.5 miles east of Keig, at Castle Forbes.

Private   NJ 622191   OS: 37   *   Map: 10, no: 168

Castle Forbes, a large castellated mansion of about 1815 designed by Archibald Simpson, stands on the site of a tower house of the Forbes family. The family's original seat was at Druminnor [NJ 513264], and the present mansion is still owned by the Forbeses.

Other refs: Putachie; Forbes Castle

Castle Fraser

Aberdeen & Gordon: About 6.5 miles south-west of Inverurie, on minor roads south of B993 or west of B977, 3 miles south of Kemnay, at Castle Fraser.

NTS   NJ 724126   OS: 38   ***   Map: 10, no: 224**

Impressive and well preserved, Castle Fraser is a tall and massive Z-plan tower house, mostly dating between 1575 and 1636. It consists of a large main block, a square tower at one corner, and a great round tower at the opposite corner. Two projecting wings form a courtyard, the final side being completed by other buildings, one with an arched gateway. It was built by John Bell.

The oldest part is a plain 15th-century keep of four storeys and an attic. The great round tower rises two storeys higher to finish in a flat roof. The corners of the main block and square tower are crowned by two-storey corbelled-out bartizans with shot-holes. The upper storeys of the main block and both towers project on corbelling, and have dormer windows. The walls are pierced with many gunloops, slits and shot-holes. Over the present entrance are panels dated 1576, 1683, and 1795.

The original entrance, in the re-entrant angle with the square tower, leads to the vaulted basement, containing a kitchen and cellars. It also leads to a wide turnpike stair, climbing to the first floor hall, above which there are smaller turret stairs to the private chambers on the floors above. The interior was remodelled in 1838.

The property was acquired by the Frasers in 1454, and in 1633 the family was created Lord Fraser. The Frasers were Covenanters, and their lands were ravaged in 1638, and in 1644 by Montrose. Later they were Jacobites, and the 4th Lord died a fugitive, falling from a cliff, after the 1715 Jacobite Rising. In 1976 the property was donated to The National Trust for Scotland. There is a walled garden.

One story associated with the castle is that a young woman was murdered in the Green Room of the castle's Round Tower – either in the 19th century or the distant past depending on the version of the tale – and that her body was dragged down stairs before being buried. It was said that blood from her corpse, which stained the stairs and the hearth of the chamber, could not be cleaned off, and the stairs were eventually boarded over to hide the stains. The stairs, on the other hand, may have been boarded over simply to provide greater comfort on the feet than cold stone.

Other unexplained events are said to include the sound of piano music and voices coming from the apparently empty hall; and the apparition of a woman in a long black gown, said to be Lady Blanche Drummond, who died in 1874.

Other refs: Fraser Castle; Muchalls-in-Mar

OPEN: Castle open 13 Apr-May and Sep, daily 13.30-17.30; Jun-Aug, daily 11.00-17.30; Oct, Sat-Sun 13.30-17.30; last admission 16.45; shop and tearoom open at 12.30 when castle opens at 13.30; garden open all year, daily 9.30-18.00; grounds open all year, daily 9.30-sunset.

Explanatory sheets. Many interesting rooms. Gift shop. Tea room. Picnic area. Garden and grounds. Adventure playground. Car and coach parking. Group concessions. £££.
Tel: 01330 833463
Email: information@nts.org.uk Web: nts.org.uk

Castle Gloom *see* Castle Campbell

Castle Gogar

Lothians: About 4 miles east of Edinburgh Castle, on minor road north of A8 near junction with A720, just west of the Gogar Burn.
Private NT 164730 OS: 65 * Map: 4, no: 49**
Castle Gogar is a large 17th-century L-plan tower house of three storeys and an attic. The main block and offset wing join only at the corners. A large stair-tower stands in one re-entrant angle, and is crowned with a square watch-chamber and a flat balustraded roof. There is a round tower, at a corner of the main block, and the

wing has bartizans. The walls are pierced by gunloops.

The basement is vaulted, and a small stairway rises to the first-floor hall, which has been altered. Private chambers occupy the floors above, and there are many mural chambers and hidden stairs.

The lands were given by Robert the Bruce to the Setons, passed to the Halyburtons around 1409, but it was the Coupers who built the house in 1625. The castle is still occupied.

Near the castle was a skirmish between an army under Cromwell and the Scots under General David Leslie. The English withdrew but defeated the Scots at Dunbar soon afterwards.

Other refs: Gogar House

Castle Grant

South Highland: About 1.5 miles north of Grantown-on-Spey, on minor roads east of A939 or north of B9102, about 1 mile south of Cottartown, at Castle Grant.
Private NJ 041302 OS: 36 * Map: 9, no: 158**
Castle Grant consists of a Z-plan tower house, incorporating work from the 15th century. It was massively enlarged in 1750 and later, with projecting lower wings enclosing a paved courtyard. The old part rises to four storeys and an attic, within

a corbelled-out parapet with machiolations. A stair-turret stands in the re-entrant angle and is crowned by a round caphouse. The windows of the old part are small.

The basement is vaulted. A wide stair rises in the wing to the altered first-floor hall, and the floors above were reached by a turnpike stair in a turret.

The property belonged to the Grants, and became their chief stronghold. There was an earlier castle at Freuchiehillock, about 0.25 miles to the south-east, which may have been held by the Comyns. The Grants were Hanoverians, and fought against the Jacobites in both the 1715 and 1745 Risings, although the castle was occupied by Jacobites. Robert Burns visited the castle in 1787. The family became Earls of Seafield in 1811. The castle became derelict, but is currently being restored.

The castle is said to be haunted by the ghost of Lady Barbara Grant, daughter of a 16th-century laird. She was imprisoned in a dark closet, off an upper bedroom in the old part of the castle, known as 'Barbie's Tower'. She had fallen in love with a man of low station, a suitor considered unsuitable by her father, who meanwhile chose another husband. Barbara died of a broken heart, choosing death rather than marriage to a man she did not love.

Her ghost is said to appear from behind tapestries concealing the closet, and cross the bedroom, stopping to wash her hands, then disappearing through the doorway leading to the turnpike stair.

Other refs: Grant Castle; Freuchie

Castle Grimness

Orkney: About 2 miles east of St Margaret's Hope, east of B904, west of Grutha, Castle, South Ronaldsay.
Ruin or site ND 473943 [?] OS: 7 * Map: 11, no: 52
Possible site of castle.

Castle Haven

Galloway: About 2 miles east of Borgue, on minor roads and foot east of B727 at Borgue, west of Kirkandrews, near shore.
Ruin or site NX 594483 OS: 82 ** Map: 1, no: 94
Castle Haven is a D-shaped galleried dun with the straight part of the wall along the cliff edge. The dun has two entrances, a main entrance at the north and a smaller one leading to the shore. Six entrances lead off the central courtyard into the gal-

leries. It is not certain if the surrounding walk was contemporary with the dun as it was occupied in medieval times. Earlier this century the site was cleared and restored by the landowner.
Other refs: Borgue Castle

Castle Heather

South Highland: About 2 miles south-east of Inverness, on minor roads east of B861 or south of B9006, at or near Castle Heather.
Ruin or site   NH 678426   OS: 26   *   Map: 9, no: 96
Site of castle, little of which remains except earthworks.
Other refs: Castle Leathers

Castle Hill of Findon *see* Findon Castle

Castle Hill of Manor *see* Castlehill Tower

Castle Hill, Auchleuchrie *see* Auchleuchrie

Castle Hill, Birnie

Moray: About 3.5 miles south of Elgin, on minor roads east of B9010 or west of A941, north-east of Thomshill, at or near Castlehill.
Ruin or site   NJ 217580   OS: 28   *   Map: 10, no: 40
Site of a castle or residence of the Bishops of Moray in the 12th century. The bishops moved from here to Kinneddar, then to Spynie. The last remains were cleared away at the beginning of the 19th century.
Other refs: Bishop's Palace, Birnie; Birnie

Castle Hill, Busby

Lanarkshire & Glasgow: About 2.5 miles west of East Kilbride, near A726, 0.5 miles south-east of Busby, east of Busbyside Farm, at Castle Hill.
Ruin or site   NS 589562   OS: 64   *   Map: 3, no: 269
There are scant remains of a castle on a hillock.
  It was apparently a property of the Semples, but passed to the Stewarts of Minto in 1490.

Castle Hill, Cargill

Perthshire: About 5 miles south of Blairgowrie, on minor road north of A93, just east of River Tay, 0.5 miles north-east of Cargill, west of Mains of Cargill.
Ruin or site   NO 157374   OS: 53   *   Map: 8, no: 103
Site of 12th-century castle on motte, which had a moat which could be filled by water from the river. It was a property of a Richard de Montifiquet.
Other refs: Cargill Castle

Castle Hill, Clunie *see* Clunie Castle

Castle Hill, Cullen *see* Cullen Castle

Castle Hill, Durris *see* Dores Castle

Castle Hill, Lanark *see* Lanark Castle

Castle Hill, North Berwick

Lothians: East of North Berwick, on minor roads north of A198, just south of shore of Firth of Forth, just west of Rugged Knowes, at Castle Hill.
Ruin or site   NT 563850   OS: 67   *   Map: 4, no: 202
Site of castle on motte, probably of the MacDuff Earls of Fife. The Earls had a ferry from North Berwick to Earlsferry in Fife.
OPEN: Access at all reasonable times.
Parking nearby.

Castle Hill, Pluscarden

Moray: About 5 miles south-west of Elgin, on minor roads north of B9010, 1 mile east of Pluscarden Abbey, near Inchallon.
Ruin or site   NJ 154571 [?]   OS: 28   *   Map: 10, no: 23
Site of castle, although the site is not certain. There is a motte nearer the abbey [NJ 142576].
  The lands were a property of Pluscarden Abbey, but passed to the Setons, later Lords Urquhart, after the Reformation. In 1595 the property was sold to the Mackenzies of Kintail, then to the Mackenzies of Tarbat, then through several families including the Sinclair Earl of Caithness in 1649, Brodie of Lethen, the Grants of Grant, and the Duffs.
  Originally founded by Alexander II in 1230, the abbey was one of only three Valliscaulian priories in Scotland, and dedicated to St Mary, St John the Baptist, and St Andrew. In 1390 it may have been torched by Alexander Stewart, the Wolf of Badenoch, along with Elgin Cathedral. In 1454 it became a Benedictine house, but the church and domestic buildings became ruinous after the Reformation. The abbey was refounded, and almost completely rebuilt, in 1948 as a Benedictine monastery, and there are now about 30 monks, priests and novices. The abbey is open to the public, and retreat facilities are available for men and women.
Other refs: Pluscarden

Castle Hill, Ranfurly *see* Ranfurly Castle

Castle Hill, Rattray *see* Rattray Castle

Castle Hill, Slamannan

Falkirk: About 5 miles south-west of Falkirk, east of B803 and north of B8022, Slamannan.
Ruin or site   NS 856732   OS: 65   *   Map: 6, no: 86
Site of castle on a small hill.
  The lands were held by the Livingstones from 1470 until 1716 when they were forfeited for their part in the Jacobite Rising.

Castle Hill, Tealing *see* Tealing House

Castle Hill, Whithorn

Galloway: To east of Whithorn, on minor roads east of A746.
Ruin or site   NX 448403   OS: 83   *   Map: 1, no: 72
Site of castle, a property of the Bishops of Galloway. The cathedral and priory of Whithorn lie about 400 yards to the west.
Other refs: Balnespick

Castle Hillock, Edzell *see* Edzell Castle

Castle Huntly

Perth & Kinross: About 1 mile west and south of Longforgan, on minor road south of A85, just north of the Huntly Burn, at Castle Huntly.
Private   NO 301292   OS: 53   *   Map: 8, no: 150**
Built on a steep rock surrounded by flat land, Castle Huntly consists of a huge 15th-century keep of four storeys and a garret. It was altered and enlarged with two-storey wings in the 17th and 18th centuries.
  The basement contains three vaulted chambers and a pit-prison. The hall, on the first floor, was barrel vaulted but this has been removed. The upper floors were reached by a turnpike stair in the thickness of the walls.
  The Grays held the property, and built the tower in 1452. They were a treacherous lot. Andrew, 2nd Lord Gray, Justice General of Scotland, betrayed James III to the Duke of Albany, then betrayed Albany to the young James IV. Patrick, the 4th Lord, surrendered Broughty Castle to the English. Patrick, 6th Lord, who was Master of Gray, supported Elizabeth I of England in the execution of Mary, Queen of Scots.
  The Grays held the property until 1614, when it was sold to the Lyon Lord Glamis, then to the Pattersons in 1777. It was owned by them until the 20th century, and is still occupied, although now a Young Offenders Institution.
Other refs: Huntly Castle; Castle Lyon

Castle Huntly – see previous page

Castle Karig Lion *see* Karig Lion Castle

Castle Kennedy

Galloway: About 3 miles west of Stranraer, on minor roads north of A75, between White Loch and Black Loch, about 0.5 miles north of Castle Kennedy village.

Ruin or site NX 111609 OS: 82 * Map: 1, no: 25**

Set among gardens and originally on an island in a loch, Castle Kennedy is a 17th-century E-plan tower house. It consists of a main block of four storeys and an attic; two projecting square wings of five storeys; and two square towers of seven storeys in the re-entrant angles, one containing the main turnpike stair. Three-storey wings were added later. The walls are pierced with large evenly spaced windows and shot-holes.

The main entrance leads to a vaulted passage, running through the entire basement. There is a large vaulted kitchen, and the basement rooms in the square wings and towers are also vaulted.

It was a property of the Kennedys from 1482. The existing castle was started in 1607 by John Kennedy, 5th Earl of Cassillis, and replaced an older stronghold, on Inch Crindil in White Loch [NX 104608]. The property passed about 1650 to the Hamiltons of Bargany, then around 1677 to the Dalrymples of Stair. A fire gutted the castle in 1716, and it was never restored. The modern Lochinch Castle stands about 0.5 miles to the north.

Other refs: Kennedy Castle; Lochinch Castle

OPEN: Lochinch Castle not open to the public. Gardens open daily Apr-Sep daily 10.00-17.00.

Gift shop. Tea room. Disabled access: admission free to disabled visitors. Disabled access. Car and coach parking. £

Tel: 01776 702024 Fax: 01776 706248

Castle Knowe *see* Leuchars Castle

Castle Lachlan

Argyll & Dunbartonshire: About 7 miles south-west of Strachur, on minor road and foot north of B8000, on north side of Lachlan Bay in Loch Fyne, south-west of Castle Lachlan.

Ruin or site NS 005953 OS: 55 * Map: 5, no: 93**

Castle Lachlan is a ruined 15th-century castle, consisting of ranges of later buildings, including a kitchen and hall, enclosing a small internal courtyard. The basements were vaulted, and a turnpike stair climbed to the upper floors.

The MacLachlans came from Ireland, where they had been kings of Ulster, but had settled around Loch Fyne by the 13th century, and had an earlier castle here, referred to in a charter of 1314. It may have been on an island in Loch Fyne. The family supported Bruce in the Wars of Independence, and sensibly were on good terms with the Campbells. The clan, however, were Jacobites and fought at Killiecrankie with Bonnie Dundee in 1689. They also took part in the 1715 and 1745 Jacobite Risings. The chief of MacLachlan was killed at the Battle of Culloden in 1746, and the castle was attacked by a Hanoverian warship, although it did little damage. Part was apparently habitable until 1790.

The MacLachlans managed to keep their lands, but the castle was not rebuilt and a new house, also called Castle Lachlan, was built nearby. It is still held by the same family.

The old castle was said to have a brownie.

Other refs: Lachlan Castle; Old Castle Lachlan

Castle Leathers *see* Castle Heather

Castle Leod

Ross & Cromarty: About 4 miles west of Dingwall, on minor road north of A834, about 1 mile north of Strathpeffer, south-west of Achterneed, at Castle Leod.

Private NH 485593 OS: 26 ** Map: 9, no: 54**

A fine and interesting building, Castle Leod consists of an altered 17th-century L-plan tower house of five storeys, with a later higher block filling in the re-entrant. This block is crowned by bartizans with conical roofs, while the older part has a corbelled-out parapet. The thick walls are pierced by many gunloops and slits; and many of the larger windows still have iron yetts.

The entrance, flanked by shot-holes, is in the newer block. The basement contains the old kitchen in the wing, and vaulted cellars in the main block. The hall, on the first floor, has a large fireplace, and private chambers occupy the floors above.

Castle Leod was built by Sir Roderick Mackenzie of Coigach about 1610. His grandson was created Viscount Tarbat, then Earl of Cromartie in 1703, but the 3rd Earl

was forfeited for his part in the Jacobite Rising of 1745. The property and titles were eventually recovered, and a wing was added in 1854. The castle is still occupied by the Mackenzie Earls of Cromartie.
Other refs: Leod Castle

Castle Levan

Renfrewshire: About 1.5 miles south-west of Gourock, on minor roads south of A770, in Levan, not far south of the Firth of Clyde.
Private NS 216764 OS: 63 * Map: 3, no: 39**
Standing on a strong site at the edge of a ravine, Castle Levan is a strong L-plan tower house of three storeys and a garret within a corbelled-out parapet with open rounds. It consists of a 14th-century keep or main block, and an adjoining offset larger 16th-century tower or wing, joining at one corner. The thick walls are pierced with small windows and slits.
There have been three entrances, two in the basement and one at first-floor level, which would have been reached by an external stair. The basement is vaulted, and contained a kitchen and cellars. Two narrow straight stairs, in the thickness of the walls, lead to the first-floor hall. There was a turnpike stair in the corner where the two blocks meet.
Castle Levan was built by the Mortons, but had been sold to the Semples by 1547. In 1649 it was acquired by the Stewarts of Inverkip. Although partly ruinous, it was restored and is occupied.
The castle is reputedly haunted by a 'White Lady', the ghost of a Lady Montgomery, who was starved to death by her husband for mistreating local peasants.
Other refs: Leven Castle

Castle Loch Castle

Galloway: About 6 miles east of Glenluce, on minor road, foot and boat south of B733 or north of B7005, in Castle Loch, about 0.75 miles west of Mochrum.
Ruin or site NX 294541 OS: 82 ** Map: 1, no: 40
Castle Loch Castle, built mostly in the 15th century, consists of a courtyard enclosing ranges of buildings, including a hall, chapel and kitchen, but is now very ruined. The island had a landing place. The island may have had an old chapel, dating from the 11th century, and occupation appears to go back to prehistoric times.
The property originally belonged to the Earls of March, and the castle was built by Patrick Dunbar of Kilconquhar. His son was killed at the Battle of Flodden in 1513.

In 1590 the island passed to Sir Patrick Vaux of Barnbarroch, and was occupied until the 17th century. The ruins were cleared and excavated in 1912, and again in 1950.

Castle Loch Heylipol

Argyll & Dunbartonshire: About 3 miles west of Scarinish on island of Tiree, north of B8068, north-east of Heylipol, on island in Loch Heylipol.
Ruin or site NL 986435 OS: 46 * Map: 5, no: 1
On a former island in the loch is the site of a strong castle of the MacDonalds, little or nothing of which remains, formerly square and turreted with a drawbridge. The castle dated from the 14th century or earlier, but was later held by the MacLeans, then the Campbell Earls and Dukes of Argyll, who had a causeway and factor's house built on the site in 1748, then altered and extended in the 19th century. The castle had been besieged by the Campbells in 1678-9, and was ruinous shortly afterwards.
The factor, called MacLaren, who had the house built is said to have died before he could enter it. His ghost reputedly haunts the house, as does a 'Green Lady', said to be responsible for unexplained noises in the 1970s. Lights are also said to be seen in the windows of the house when it is unoccupied.
Other refs: Loch Heylipol Castle; Island House

Castle Lyon *see* Castle Huntly

Castle Lyon *see* Karig Lion Castle

Castle Macnicol *see* Stornoway Castle

Castle Maud

Kincardine & Deeside: About 5.5 miles west and north of Banchory, on minor road and foot east of B993, on Moss Maud, 0.5 miles north of Craiglash, at Castle Maud.
Ruin or site NO 624995 OS: 45 ** Map: 10, no: 169
Little remains of a keep and a courtyard of the Durwards, which may date from the 14th century. It is also said to have been used for hunting by the Bishops of Aberdeen.
Other refs: Maud Castle

Castle Menzies – see next page

Castle Menzies

Perth & Kinross: About 1.5 miles north-west of Aberfeldy, on minor road just north of B846, about 0.5 miles north of River Tay, at Castle Menzies.
Private NN 837496 OS: 52 ** Map: 8, no: 20**
Castle Menzies is a fine altered and extended 16th-century tower house. It consists of a main block of three storeys and an attic, with two square towers of five storeys, projecting at opposite corners, making it Z-plan. Round bartizans crown most corners of the building, and the walls are pierced by gunloops. A huge wing was added in 1840.

The basement is vaulted, and the hall is on the first floor. A stair in one tower leads to all floors.

It was a property of the Menzies family. Their original castle was at Comrie, but this was burned in 1487, and Sir Robert Menzies built a new stronghold, called the Place of Weem, near the present castle. In 1502 this building in turn was destroyed by Neil Stewart of Garth, who imprisoned Robert Menzies in the dungeon at Garth, until he signed away some of his lands.

The castle was occupied by Cromwell's force, under General Monck in the 1650s, and captured and occupied by Jacobites in 1715. Bonnie Prince Charlie stayed here for two nights in 1746, but four days later the family were thrown out and the castle was taken by Hanoverian forces, led by the Duke of Cumberland, the butcher of Culloden.

The last of the Menzies line died in 1918, and the castle then passed through several families. Between 1939 and 1945 it was used as a Polish Army medical supplies depot. The castle became derelict, but is being restored by a trust established by the Clan Menzies Society, who acquired the building in 1957.
Other refs: Place of Weem; Menzies Castle
OPEN: Open Apr or Easter-mid Oct, Mon-Sat 10.30-17.00, Sun 14.00-17.00; last entry 16.30.
Access to all old part. Explanatory displays. Museum about Menzies Clan. Gift shop. Tea room. Disabled access to part of ground floor, tea room and gift shop. WC. Disabled access. Car and limited coach parking. Group concessions. £.
Tel: 01887 820982

Castle Mestag

Sutherland & Caithness: On island of Stroma, 2 miles north of mainland, about 10 miles north-east of Castletown, on minor roads and foot, on south-east tip of island.
Ruin or site ND 340764 OS: 12 * Map: 12, no: 61
Very little remains of a small castle on top of an inaccessible rock.

There may have been a stronghold at Flendie Clett [ND 359766], which was used by Norsemen, on the south-east of the island.
Other refs: Mestag Castle; Maesteg

Castle Newe

Aberdeen & Gordon: About 10 miles north of Ballater, on minor roads north of A944, north of River Don, about 1.5 miles east of Strathdon, at Newe.
Ruin or site NJ 380124 OS: 37 * Map: 10, no: 78
Not much remains of Castle Newe – pronounced 'Neyouw' – an altered Z-plan tower house of 1604 and mansion from 1831, which had a tall central tower and was designed by Archibald Simpson. The original castle consisted of a main block with rectangular towers at opposite corners. The building was demolished about 1927, and materials used to build an extension of the University of Aberdeen.

It was a property of the Forbes family, who made their fortune in India.
Other refs: Newe Castle

Castle of Avoch *see* Ormond Castle

Castle of Balloch *see* Taymouth Castle

Castle of Ballzordie *see* Kilgarie

Castle of Braigh *see* Brough Castle

Castle of Cullen of Buchan

Banff & Buchan: About 1.5 miles east and south of Macduff, on minor road south of B9031, at Mains of Cullen.
Ruin or site NJ 732636 [?] OS: 29 * Map: 10, no: 231
Site of castle, which was near the farm. The last remains were cleared away in the 19th century. It was a property of the Barclays.
Other refs: Cullen Castle

Castle of Dallas *see* Tor Castle

Castle of Eilean Rowan *see* Eilean Ran Castle

Castle of Esslemont

Aberdeen & Gordon: About 1.5 miles west and south of Ellon, just north of A920 east of Mains of Esslemont, about 0.5 miles south of River Ythan, at Esslemont Castle.
Ruin or site NJ 932298 OS: 38 ** Map: 10, no: 324
Castle of Esslemont is a very ruined L-plan tower house. It incorporates a round tower, surviving from a courtyard, which had at least two other towers.

It was a property of the Marshalls in the 14th century, but passed by marriage to the Cheynes. An earlier castle here was sacked and burned in 1493 during a feud between the Cheynes and the Hays of Ardendracht. The property passed to the Hay Earls of Errol in 1625, but in 1646 a force of Covenanters was besieged in the castle, 36 of them being killed, horses and arms being seized. It was sold to the Gordons in 1728, who abandoned the castle for a new mansion, Esslemont House, in 1769.
Other refs: Esslemont Castle

Castle of Faldonside

Borders: About 3 miles west and south of Melrose, on minor roads east of B6360, east of River Tweed, at or near Faldonside.
Ruin or site NT 502328 [?] OS: 73 * Map: 2, no: 167
Site of castle.
Other refs: Faldonside Castle

Castle of Fiddes

Kincardine & Deeside: About 4 miles south-west of Stonehaven, on minor roads south of A94, north side of Bruxie Hill, just south of Bendings, at Castle of Fiddes.
Private NO 825813 OS: 45 * Map: 10, no: 276**
Castle of Fiddes is a 16th-century L-plan tower house of three storeys, with a round stair-tower at one end of the main block. The round tower is corbelled out to square, and crowned by a corbiestepped watch-chamber. A round entrance stair-tower rises a storey lower in the re-entrant angle. Another stair-tower projects from the middle of the main block, and is capped by square corbelled-out watch-chamber. Bartizans, with conical roofs, crown two corners of the castle. The walls are pierced by shot-holes.

The basement is vaulted, and contains a kitchen with a large fireplace, and a wine-cellar with a small stair up to the hall above. The main stair rises only to the first floor, the upper floors reached by stairs in the round tower and the stair-turret. The hall was on the first floor, and there was a private room adjoining in the wing, with many private chambers on the floors above.

The property was held by the Arbuthnotts, but it was sold to the Thomsons of Arduthie in the late 17th century. The castle, now a farmhouse, was restored in the 1960s.
Other refs: Fiddes Castle

Castle of Fithie *see* Fithie

Castle of Flemington *see* Flemington Tower

Castle of Glenayes *see* Glenays Castle

Castle of Grange *see* Grange of Monifieth

Castle of Holydean

Borders: About 2.5 miles south of Melrose, on minor road west of B6359, near Holydean.

Private   NT 537303 [?]   OS: 73   **   Map: 2, no: 191

Little remains of a 16th-century castle, formerly with a large courtyard, most of which was demolished around 1760 to provide materials for a new farmhouse. It consisted of a courtyard with two strong towers, one of five storeys, as well as other ranges, with vaulted cellars, of which only the bakehouse remains. The arched gateway, with a gunloop, survives, as do some sections of walling.

The lands were a property of Kelso Abbey, but passed to the Kerrs after the Reformation. The castle was probably built by Sir Walter Kerr of Cessford around 1570.

Other refs: Holydean Castle

Castle of Inchgall *see* Lochore Castle

Castle of Innes *see* Innes House

Castle of Inverugie

Aberdeen & Gordon: About 1 mile north of Peterhead, by minor road and foot east of A952, on north side of Ugie River where it empties into the sea, 1.5 miles south-east of Inverugie.

Ruin or site   NK 124474 [?]   OS: 30   *   Map: 10, no: 367

Site of castle, a vestige of which survived in 1895.

Other refs: Old Castle of Inverugie

Castle of King Edward

Banff & Buchan: About 4 miles north of Turriff, just east of A947, 2 miles east of River Deveron, just south of Castleton Farm, at Castle of King Edward.

Ruin or site   NJ 722562   OS: 29   *   Map: 10, no: 222

Once a powerful stronghold, little remains of the Castle of King Edward, except some fragments of masonry and the ditch. The original castle was built in the 13th century, but most of what remains may date from the 16th century.

It was a property of the Comyn Earls of Buchan, who acquired the Earldom by marriage. The name is a corruption of Kinedar (Gaelic for 'head of the valley'). The old castle was destroyed by the forces of Robert the Bruce in 1308, after the Comyns were defeated at Inverurie and Aikey Brae, and thereafter Buchan was laid waste. The property later passed to the Ross family, then to Alexander Stewart, the Wolf of Badenoch, then the MacDonald Earl of Ross, until forfeited in 1455. It was acquired by the Forbes family in 1509.

Other refs: King Edward Castle; Kinedder

Castle of Ladyhill *see* Elgin Castle

Castle of Langholm *see* Langholm Tower

Castle of Mey

Sutherland & Caithness: About 7 miles north-east of Castletown, on minor roads north of A836, about 0.5 miles south of sea, west of Barrogill, at Castle of Mey.

Private   ND 290739   OS: 12   *   Map: 12, no: 57**

Castle of Mey is an altered 16th-century Z-plan tower house. It consists of a main block of three storeys and an attic, with four-storey square towers, one a stair-

tower, at opposite corners. Stair turrets rise in the re-entrant angles above first-floor level. Corbelled-out bartizans crown some corners. The walls are pierced by gunloops, but many of the windows have been enlarged. There was a walled courtyard. The building was extended and altered in the 18th century, in 1819 by William Burn, and again in 1957. There is a walled garden.

The original entrance led to a stair and into the vaulted basement. The basement contains the original kitchen, with a large fireplace, the wine-cellar, and another cellar. A second stair climbs to the floor above. The hall was on the first floor, with private chambers in the square tower and floors above.

The lands originally belonged to the Bishop of Caithness, but in 1566 were acquired by the Sinclair Earls of Caithness, who built the castle. The 6th Earl bankrupted the family, and the earldom was claimed by the Campbells, although this was disputed by Sinclair of Keiss. The Sinclairs eventually recovered the earldom and castle. MacLeod of Assynt, who betrayed the Marquis of Montrose, was imprisoned in the castle. In 1952 the castle was sold to the Queen Mother, who had it restored.

The castle is said to be haunted by the ghost of a daughter of the 5th Earl. She fell in love with a ploughman, and her father had her imprisoned in one of the attic rooms. She threw herself from one of the windows, and her sad spectre, a 'Green Lady', reportedly haunts the castle.

Other refs: Mey Castle; Barrogill Castle

OPEN: The gardens are occasionally open in the summer.

Castle of Old Wick

Sutherland & Caithness: About 1 mile south of Wick, on minor roads east of A9, just west of the sea, south of Old Wick.

His Scot   ND 369488   OS: 12   **   Map: 12, no: 65

One of the oldest keeps in Scotland, Castle of Old Wick consists of a simple square keep of at least three storeys. It stands on a promontory on cliffs above the sea, cut off by a ditch, and there are some remains of ruined ranges of buildings.

Built in the 12th century when this part of Scotland was ruled from Orkney by Norsemen, the castle was a property of the Cheynes in the mid 14th century, the Sutherland Lord Duffus the same century, then the Oliphants in the 15th century. In 1569, during a feud with the Sinclairs, the castle was besieged, starved into submission and captured by John Sinclair, Master of Caithness. It was sold to the Sinclairs in 1606 (or 1644), then the Campbells of Glenorchy in the 1670s, then to the Dunbars of Hemprigg who held it until 1910.

Other refs: Old Wick Castle; Castle Oliphant

OPEN: Access at all reasonable times - great care must be taken.

Parking nearby.

Tel: 0131 668 8800   Fax: 0131 668 8888

Email: hs.explore@scotland.gov.uk   Web: www.historic-scotland.gov.uk

Castle of Park *see* Park

Castle of Park

Galloway: About 0.5 miles west of Glenluce village, on minor roads north of A75, west of the Water of Luce, about 0.75 miles from the shore of Luce Bay.

His Scot   NX 189571   OS: 82   **   Map: 1, no: 33**

Castle of Park is a late 16th-century L-plan tower house of four storeys, with the stair-wing rising a storey higher to be crowned by a watch-chamber. The steeply pitched roof has corbiestepped gables: there does not appear to have been a parapet.

The entrance, at the foot of the stair-tower in the re-entrant angle, opens into a vaulted passage, leading to three vaulted chambers: a kitchen, with a huge arched fireplace; a wine-cellar, with a small stair to the hall above; and another cellar. It also leads to the main turnpike stair to the first-floor hall. The hall is a fine chamber with a moulded fireplace.

Two wings, added during the 18th century, have been demolished.

The lands were originally a property of Glenluce Abbey, but passed to the Hays, and Thomas Hay of Park built the castle in 1590 after the Reformation, his father having been the Commendator of the abbey. The property was acquired by the

Cunninghams in 1830, and they abandoned the castle for Dunragit, using Park to house farm labourers. It has been restored.

Other refs: Park Place

OPEN: The castle can be rented through the Landmark Trust.
Tel: 01628 825925 Fax: 01628 825417

Castle of Skeith *see* House of Skeith

Castle of Snusgar

Orkney: About 8 miles north of Stromness, east of B9056, 0.5 miles north of Skaill House, east of Bay of Skaill.

Ruin or site HY 236196 [?] OS: 6 * Map: 11, no: 32
Probable site of castle, remains of which are said to have survived in 1795.

Other refs: Snusgar

Castle of St John *see* Stranraer Castle

Castle of Stackel Brae

Orkney: To south of Eday, on minor roads and foot south of B9063, Stackel Brae.

Ruin or site HY 564288 [?] OS: 6 * Map: 11, no: 55
Site of castle, which may have been the predecessor of Carrick House. It is said that John Gow, the pirate, was held here before being taken away for trial and execution.

Other refs: Stackel Brae

Castle of Strom *see* Strom Castle

Castle of Tacis

Fife: About 3 miles north of Lower Largo, on minor roads east of A916, at or near Teasses.

Ruin or site NO 405085 [?] OS: 59 * Map: 7, no: 107
Site of castle, which was mentioned in 1525.

Castle of the Maidens *see* Edinburgh Castle

Castle of Thurso *see* Ormelie Castle

Castle of Troup

Banff & Buchan: About 6 miles west of Rosehearty, on minor roads and foot north of B9031, 0.5 miles north-west of Pennan, on promontory into sea, at Castle of Troup.

Ruin or site NJ 838663 OS: 30 * Map: 10, no: 282
Standing on a promontory above the sea is the site of 13th-century castle, within the earthworks of an Iron Age fort. The courtyard was elaborately patterned.

It was a property of a Hamelin de Troup, but may have been one of the Comyn strongholds destroyed by Robert the Bruce in 1307-8. Stone from here was used to build earthwork defences in the 1680s, then an artillery emplacement in the early 19th century. Troup House, a castellated pile of 1897, stands on the site of a mansion designed by John Adam in 1760.

Hell's Lum, which is nearby, is a fissure in the cliffs through which spray is forced by waves.

Other refs: Fort Fiddes; Troup

Castle of Wraiths *see* Wreaths Tower

Castle Oilen Greg *see* Eilean Dearg Castle

Castle Oliphant *see* Castle of Old Wick

Castle Qua *see* Craiglockhart Castle

Castle Rainy *see* Turriff Castle

Castle Robert

Dumfriesshire: About 3.5 miles north and east of Sanquhar, west of B740, west of the Crawick Water, just south of Nether Cog.

Ruin or site NS 804148 [?] OS: 78 * Map: 1, no: 136
Site of castle, which stood in a strong position. It was a property of the Williamsons in the 16th and 17th century. The castle may have been destroyed by fire as melted lead, presumably from the roof, was found here.

Other refs: Robert Castle

Castle Roy

South Highland: About 4 miles south of Grantown-on-Spey, just west of B970, 0.5 miles east of River Spey, 0.5 miles north of Nethy Bridge, at Castle Roy.

Ruin or site NJ 007219 OS: 36 ** Map: 9, no: 156
Castle Roy consists of a ruined rectangular castle of enclosure, with a square tower at one corner. It was built by the Comyns in the 13th century.

Other refs: Roy Castle

Castle Semple

Renfrewshire: About 2 miles east and north of Lochwinnoch, on minor roads north of A737 at Howwood, near Semple Collegiate Church, west of Low Semple.

Ruin or site NS 377602 [?] OS: 63 * Map: 3, no: 129
Site of castle, which was completely demolished around 1730. It was replaced by a large classical mansion, which in its turn was demolished in the 1960s – apart from one wing and the stables block.

It was a property of the Semple, or Sempill, family from the 14th century or earlier. John Semple, 1st Lord Semple, was killed at the Battle of Flodden in 1513, and William Semple was captured after the Battle of Pinkie in 1547. In 1560 the castle was seized by Protestants because the Semples opposed the Reformation. The family were Hanoverians, and fought against the Jacobites in 1715, and in 1746 at the Battle of Culloden. The castle had passed to the MacDowall family by 1727, and they built a classical mansion, demolishing the old castle in 1735. They sold the property to the Harveys around 1813, but the house and gardens deteriorated until Castle Semple was mostly demolished in the 1960s.

Nearby is Semple Collegiate Church, roofless but standing to the wallhead, which contains the elaborate tomb of its founder, John, 1st Lord Semple.

Castle Semple Country Park is based around Castle Semple Loch, and attractions include woodland walks, a visitor centre, and sailing, canoeing, windsurfing an rowing on the loch.

Other refs: Semple Castle; Eliotstoun

OPEN: Country park: open summer, 9.00-dusk; winter 9.00-16.30.
Country park: snack trailer in summer. Picnic areas. Information centre. Disabled access. Car parking. £ (use of loch).
Tel: 01505 842882

Castle Shuna

Argyll & Dunbartonshire: On south end of island of Shuna, about 8.5 miles north of Connel, on minor road and boat 0.5 miles west of A828 at The Knapp, at Castle Shuna.

Ruin or site NM 915482 OS: 49 ** Map: 5, no: 80
Castle Shuna is a ruined 16th-century tower house, with a later 17th-century round stair-tower projecting from one side.

A kitchen and cellar occupied the vaulted basement with the hall on the first floor and private chambers above.

It was built by the Stewarts of Appin, and is said never to have been completed. Near the castle are the remains of later buildings.

Other refs: Shuna Castle

Castle Sinclair *see* Girnigoe Castle

Castle Sinclair

Western Isles: On Barra about 2 miles north-west of Castlebay, by foot and boat west of A888 at Dun Mhic Leoid, on island in Loch Tangusdale or Loch St Clair.

Ruin or site NL 648997 OS: 31 ** Map: 11, no: 1
Castle Sinclair is a much-ruined tower house of three storeys of the MacNeils.

Other refs: Dun Mhic Leod; Iain Garbh's Castle

Castle Spioradain

Inverness & Nairn: About 6 miles south-west of Inverness, on minor roads north of B862, south side of Loch Dochfour at meeting with Loch Ness, at or near Bona Ferry.
Ruin or site NH 603375 OS: 26 * Map: 9, no: 77
Site of castle, held by the MacLeans of Dochgarroch around 1420. The castle may have been destroyed by Camerons around the turn of the 16th century. It was formerly on an island, and nothing remains except possibly a mound. It was partly removed at the beginning of the 19th century when the Caledonian Canal was constructed, coins and human bones being found at the site.
  The castle was said to be haunted, and its name 'Castle Spioradain' means fortress of ghosts. The story goes that a long-running feud between the MacLeans and the Camerons of Lochiel resulted in several Camerons being executed and hung from the battlements. Their ghosts were said to haunt the castle, and terrorise the neighbourhood.
Other refs: Bona Ferry; Castle Spiritual

Castle Spiritual *see* Castle Spioradain

Castle Spynie

Inverness & Nairn: About 3 miles south and east of Beauly, on minor roads east of A833, about 0.5 miles west of Easter Clunes, in The Aird, at Castle Spynie.
Ruin or site NH 541417 OS: 26 * Map: 9, no: 64
Not much remains of a broch, built on a rocky knoll.
Other refs: Spynie Castle

Castle Stalcaire *see* Castle Stalker

Castle Stalker

Argyll & Dunbartonshire: About 8 miles north of Connel, on minor road and boat west of A828 at Portnacroish, on a small island at mouth of Loch Laich, at Castle Stalker.
Private NM 921473 OS: 49 ** Map: 5, no: 83**
Standing dramatically on a small island, Castle Stalker is a tall, massive and simple keep, rectangular in plan, of four storeys and a garret. A flush parapet was remodelled in the 16th century, and a gabled caphouse crowns the stair. The thick walls are pierced by shot-holes.
  There are two entrances. The first, at ground level, is defended by a machiolation at parapet level and leads to the vaulted basement, which has a prison in one corner. A small mural stairway climbs to the first-floor hall. The main entrance, reached by an external stone stair, is at first-floor level and also protected by a machiolation. Private chambers occupied the storeys above the hall. A small courtyard has a landing place.
  Castle Stalker was built by Duncan Stewart of Appin, who was made Chamberlain of the Isles for his part in helping James IV destroy the MacDonald Lord of the Isles: it is believed to have been used by James IV as a hunting lodge. The assassination of Campbell of Cawdor in 1592 started a feud between the family and the Campbells. The Stewarts of Appin fought at the Battle of Inverlochy, under the Marquis of Montrose, in 1645 against the Campbells. In 1620 the castle was sold to the Campbells, but the Stewarts retrieved it after a long siege in 1685. A Stewart garrison surrendered to William and Mary's forces in 1690. In 1715 the clan fought for the Jacobites at Sheriffmuir during the Jacobite Rising. The 9th Chief did not support the 1745 Rising, but the clan were led by Stewart of Ardshiel. The 9th chief sold his estates in 1765. The castle was abandoned about 1780, was roofless in 1831, but restored from ruin in the 1960s.
Other refs: Stalker Castle; Castle Stalcaire
OPEN: Open by appt from Apr-Sep – tel for details (£6.00 admission charge). Times variable depending on tides and weather as reached by boat.
Parking nearby. Not suitable for coach parties. £££
Tel: 01883 622768 Fax: 01883 626238

Castle Stalker *see* Weaver's Castle

Castle Stewart *see* Castle Stuart

Castle Stewart *see* Ravenstone Castle

Castle Stewart

Galloway: About 3 miles north-west of Newton Stewart, on minor road west of A714, about 0.3 miles west of River Cree, just south of Penninghame.
Ruin or site NX 379691 OS: 83 ** Map: 1, no: 50
Castle Stewart consists of a 16th-century tower house of four storeys. It has was been much altered with the insertion of new windows and the removal of any vaulting. A courtyard contained a kitchen and other outbuildings, but these are now fragmentary. The castle was replaced by a modern house.
  The castle is named after Colonel William Stewart, who made his fortune fighting for Gustavus Adolphus of Sweden in the 30 Years War in the 17th century.
Other refs: Stewart Castle; Calcruchie

Castle Stripe

Moray: About 7 miles south-west of Charlestown of Aberlour, on minor road west of A95, north of River Avon, 0.3 miles south-east of Ballindalloch Castle, north of Bridge of Avon.
Ruin or site NJ 185361 [?] OS: 28 * Map: 10, no: 33
Not much remains of a tower house or keep and courtyard except low overgrown walls. The lands originally belonged to the Ballindalloch family, but passed to the Grants by 1499. They moved to Ballindalloch Castle [NJ 178365].
Other refs: Ballindalloch Old Castle; Old Ballindalloch

Castle Stuart

Inverness & Nairn: About 6 miles north-east of Inverness, on minor roads east of B9039 1 mile north of junction with A96, 0.5 miles south of Moray Firth, at Castle Stuart.
Private NH 742498 OS: 27 ** Map: 9, no: 113**
Overlooking the Moray Firth and the mountains beyond, Castle Stuart is an early 17th-century tower house, although it may incorporate work from the 14th century. It consists of a main block of four storeys and projecting square towers of six storeys at each end. One square tower has a flat roof and a modern parapet, while the other has corbiestepped gables and three bartizans with conical roofs. The main block is crowned by corbelled-out bartizans, capped by small gabled watch-chambers. There are stair-turrets in the re-entrant angles. The walls are pierced by evenly spaced windows, and gunloops and shot-holes.
  The original entrance was in the foot of one tower, which contains the main stair; but there is also a later entrance. The vaulted basement contains a passage to the original kitchen, with a wide arched fireplace and oven; the wine-cellar, with a small stair to hall on the first floor; and two cellars. The hall is on the first floor of the main block, with an adjoining private chamber and another room in the tower. The main block above first-floor level, and towers, are occupied by private chambers, reached by turnpike stairs in the turrets.
  The property was held by the Mackintoshes, but given by Mary, Queen of Scots, to James Stewart, Earl of Moray, who was her illegitimate half-brother. Moray was made Regent for James VI but was later assassinated, being shot and killed at Lin-

lithgow. The second Earl fared little better, and was also murdered, this time at Donibristle in Fife, the events recorded in the old ballad 'The Bonnie Earl o' Moray'. The castle was finished by James Stewart, 3rd Earl, about 1625, although it was seized by the Mackintoshes over a dispute about ownership and compensation. The Mackintoshes were bought off, and castle restored to the Stewarts. It was abandoned and unroofed about 1835, but has been privately restored and reoccupied by Charles and Elizabeth Stuart.

The Three Turret chamber was said to be haunted by some dreadful bogle. The story goes that the then Earl offered a reward of £20 (a princely sum in those days) to anyone who would spend a night in the haunted room. A local poacher, a tall and burly fellow called Big Angus, agreed and spent the night in the chamber. The next morning he was found dead in the courtyard, having apparently fallen from the turret, a terrible look of terror frozen on his face.

Other refs: Castle Stewart; Stuart Castle

OPEN: Overnight accommodation by reservation.
Accommodation available. 8 bedrooms with ensuite facilities and some with four poster beds.
Tel: 01463 790745 Fax: 01463 792604
Email: castlestuart@postservices.com
Web: www.castlestuart.com (also www.brigadoon.co.uk)

Castle Sween

Argyll & Dunbartonshire: About 11 miles north-west of Tarbert, on minor road 4 miles north-west of B8024 at Achahoish (much further by road), east coast of Loch Sween.

His Scot NR 712789 OS: 62 * Map: 5, no: 36**
Standing on a rocky ridge, Castle Sween is an impressive 12th-century castle of enclosure, consisting of a curtain wall, enclosing a rectangular courtyard, and a strong 15th- or 16th-century tower with other buildings.

The basement of the keep contained the kitchen and bakehouse, the hall was on the first floor, and above this were private chambers. A round tower at one corner contained a prison, although this may have actually been a cesspit.

One of the earliest castles in Scotland, it was built at a time when this part of Scotland was still under Norse rule, and is said to be named after Sueno, an 11th-

century Dane. The castle was held by the MacSweens until the middle of the 13th century, the Stewarts of Menteith from around 1262 until 1362, then the MacMillans and MacNeils of Gigha for the MacDonalds until 1481 when the Campbells became keepers of the castle for the Crown. The castle was captured and partly dismantled by Alaisdair Colkitto MacDonald in 1647. It was later used for industrial purposes, possibly metal working. One tower of the castle collapsed in the 19th century, but it has since been consolidated. Beware of caravans.

Other refs: Sween Castle

OPEN: Access at all reasonable times.
Parking nearby.
Tel: 0131 668 8800 Fax: 0131 668 8888
Email: hs.explore@scotland.gov.uk Web: www.historic-scotland.gov.uk

Castle Tioram

South Highland: About 3 miles north of Acharacle in Moidart, on minor roads north of A861, on a tidal island in the mouth of Loch Moidart, at Castle Tioram.
Private NM 663725 OS: 40 * Map: 9, no: 19**
A picturesque ruin in a wonderful setting, Castle Tioram stands on a tidal island. It consists of a massive 14th-century curtain wall, surrounding an irregularly shaped courtyard, in which a tower house and ranges of stone buildings were added in the 16th century and later. The walls were given open rounds, and a corbelled-out parapet.

The entrance is defended by a machiolation. The basements are vaulted, but the upper floors have gone.

Castle Tioram was modified by Amy MacRuari, wife of John, 7th Lord of the Isles, who was divorced by her husband so he could marry Margaret, daughter of Robert II. The Clan Ranald branch of the MacDonalds came through her, and this became the seat of the MacDonalds of Clan Ranald.

In 1554 it was attacked by a force under the Earls of Huntly and Argyll, and Cromwell's forces occupied the castle in 1651 after a siege. During the Jacobite Rising of 1715 the castle was torched so that Hanoverian forces could not use it, and the chief of Clan Ranald was killed at the Battle of Sheriffmuir. It was never reoccupied, but Lady Grange was imprisoned here for a few weeks in 1732 before being taken to the outer isles. The castle was sold in 1997.

Clan Ranald had a set of magic bagpipes which, when played, reputedly ensured victory in battle.

Other refs: Tioram Castle; Eilean Tioram Castle
OPEN: Care needs to be taken with tides.

Castle Truill

Sutherland & Caithness: About 6 miles south of Tongue, on minor road, track and miles by foot south of A838 in Tongue, 3 miles south-west of Cunside, east of Loch an Dherue.
Ruin or site NC 555480 OS: 10 * Map: 12, no: 9
Site of castle.
Other refs: Truill Castle

Castle Varrich *see* Caisteal Bharraich

Castle Wearie *see* Borve Castle

Castle Wemyss

Ayrshire: About 0.5 miles north-west of Wemyss Bay, on minor roads west of A78, on Wemyss Point, near old pier.
Ruin or site NS 188703 OS: 63 * Map: 3, no: 20
Castle Wemyss was a sprawling baronial mansion, which dated from the 19th century and was built by John Burns. It was visited by General Sherman, Trollope and Haile Selassie, but was demolished and only rubble remains.

Castle Wigg *see* Castlewigg

Castlebrocket *see* Castle Brocket

Castlecluggy *see* Cluggy Castle

Castlecraig *see* Castle Craig

Castledykes *see* Craiglockhart Castle

Castledykes *see* Kirkcudbright Castle

Castledykes, Dumfries *see* Dumfries Castle

Castlehaven *see* Ballone Castle

Castlehill *see* Dunimarle Castle

Castle Tioram – see previous page

Castlehill

South Highland: About 2 miles east and south of Inverness, on minor roads just east of B9006, at or near Castlehill.

Ruin or site NH 697442 OS: 26 * Map: 9, no: 104

Site of castle. Castlehill, which may stand on the site, dates from around the beginning of the 19th century.

Castlehill of Barcloy

Galloway: About 6.5 miles south of Dalbeattie, on minor roads west of A710, 1.5 miles south of Rockcliffe, at Castlehill Point.

Ruin or site NX 854524 OS: 84 * Map: 1, no: 157

Site of castle, which stands within the remains of an Iron Age fort on a promontory above the sea. The fort consisted of a large oval enclosure with a strong wall, and was defended on the landward side by a rock-cut ditch. The castle is listed by Timothy Pont, and may have been replaced by a tower near West Barcloy [NX 855532].

Other refs: West Barcloy; Barcloy Castle

Castlehill of Findon *see* Findon Castle

Castlehill of Strachan *see* Strachan

Castlehill Tower

Borders: About 4.5 miles south and west of Peebles, on minor road south of A72 from Kirkton Manor, west of the Manor Water, at Castlehill.

Ruin or site NT 214354 OS: 73 ** Map: 2, no: 47

Standing on an irregularly shaped rock, Castlehill Tower or Castlehill of Manor, is a ruined rectangular tower house, of which only two storeys remain. It incorporates work from the 15th century.

The basement is vaulted, and a stair leads to a passage, leading into the hall, which was once barrel-vaulted. A turnpike stair, in one corner of the tower, climbed to the upper floors.

Castlehill was built by the Lowis of Manor family, who held the property from early in the 15th century. It was sold to the Veitches in 1637, then passed to the Baillies of Jerviswood in 1672. It passed to William Douglas, Earl of March, in 1703, then was sold to Burnet of Barns in 1729, until acquired by the Tweedies of Quarter in 1838, who abandoned it around 1840.

Other refs: Castle Hill of Manor

Castlehill, Cambusnethan

Lanarkshire & Glasgow: About 1 mile south of Wishaw, south of B754, Gowkthrapple Road, north of River Clyde, at or near Castlehill Farm.

Ruin or site NS 788534 [?] OS: 64 * Map: 3, no: 372

Site of 17th-century tower house, a vault and gunloop from which survives. It was replaced after a fire in 1810 by Cambusnethan House [NS 781530], built in 1819 and designed by James Gillespie Graham.

The property was held by the Bairds, but passed to the Stewarts and Somervilles. This part passed to the Lockharts of Castlehill, who still held the property in the 20th century. The castle is said to be haunted by a headless horseman.

Other refs: Cambusnethan House; Gowkthrapple

Castlehill, Cardross *see* Cardross Manor House

Castlehill, Druminnor

Aberdeen & Gordon: About 1.5 miles north and east of Rhynie, on minor roads and foot east of A97, north of Castlehill.

Ruin or site NJ 516287 [?] OS: 37 * Map: 10, no: 117

Site of castle of the Forbes family from 1271 until 1440 when they moved to Druminnor Castle [NJ 513264].

Other refs: Druminnor Castle

Castlehill, Kippen

Stirling & Clackmannanshire: To north of Kippen, west of B822 and south of A811, Kier Know of Drum.

Ruin or site NS 651947 OS: 57 * Map: 6, no: 44

Only earthworks survive from a castle.

Other refs: Kier Know of Drum

Castlehill, Lanark

Lanarkshire & Glasgow: About 1.5 miles north of Lanark, on minor roads and foot south of A721 or east of A73 or west of A706, just north of Mouse Water, south of Castlehill Farm.

Ruin or site NS 882459 OS: 72 * Map: 3, no: 410

Site of castle, some remains of which survive including defensive ditches. The site was described as 'the picturesque remnant of the lofty tower of Castlehill' in about 1890.

Castlehill, Old Downie *see* Old Downie

Castleknowe of Lynturk *see* Lynturk Castle

Castlemains *see* Kirkcudbright Castle

Castlemilk

Lanarkshire & Glasgow area: About 1.5 miles south and east of Rutherglen, on minor roads south and west of the A749, just east of Machrie Drive, in Castlemilk housing scheme.

Ruin or site NS 608594 OS: 64 ** Map: 3, no: 281

Little remains of Castlemilk, a much-altered and extended tower house which incorporated work from the 15th century, except the basement. It formerly rose to three storeys with a modern parapet and garret, but had been much altered and extended, becoming the entrance block to a 19th-century castellated mansion.

Castlemilk, then known as Carmunnock, was a property of the Comyns, then the Douglases from the Wars of Independence, from 1455 the Hamiltons, then the Stewarts of Castlemilk in Dumfriesshire. Through marriage and inheritance the family name became Crawfurd Stirling Stuart.

Mary, Queen of Scots, may have lodged here rather than Craignethan the night before the Battle of Langside in 1568, when she lost and fled to England. Bought by Glasgow Corporation in 1938, the mansion was occupied as a children's home until the early 1960s. It was then mostly demolished, despite protests, in 1969.

The house and grounds are reputedly haunted. Ghosts include a 'White Lady' near a bridge over the burn; another is a 'Green Lady'; while a third is said to be an ancient Scottish soldier. This latter ghost allegedly fired a 'real' arrow into the back of the head of a local, who then needed stitches.

Yet another reported ghost was the 'Mad Major', believed to be an apparition that was said to gallop up to the house on moonlit nights. This was believed to be the return of Captain William Stirling Stuart from the Battle of Waterloo in 1815.

There may have been two other early castles of the Douglases on the lands of Carmunnock, which included Castlemilk and Busby.

Other refs: Carmunnock

Castlemilk

Dumfriesshire: About 7.5 miles north and west of Annan, on minor roads east of B723, just east of the Water of Milk, at Castlemilk.

Ruin or site NY 150775 OS: 85 * Map: 1, no: 249

Site of castle on motte, which dated from the 12th century. It had a small but strong tower.

It was built by the Bruces, but passed to the Stewarts of Castlemilk until exchanged

for lands in Carmunnock with the Maxwells (see Castlemilk [NS 608594]). The castle was occupied from at least 1547 until 1550 by the English, during the invasion by the Duke of Somerset, formerly the Earl of Hertford. The castle was destroyed by Cromwell's forces in the 1650s and nothing remains.

Castlemilk, a mansion dating from 1866, was built on the site of an earlier house, and was a property of the Jardines at the turn of the 19th century.

Castlerankine *see* Rankine Castle

Castleru *see* Rutherglen Castle

Castleton *see* Cowden Castle

Castleton

Perthshire: About 5 miles east of Crieff, north of A85, 0.5 miles east of Fowlis Wester, at or near Castleton.

Ruin or site NN 939240 OS: 58 * Map: 8, no: 38

Site of castle, a property of the Earls of Strathearn in the 12th century.

Castleton House *see* Muckhart Castle

Castleton of Eassie

Angus & Dundee: About 3.5 miles north-east of Meigle, on A94, Castleton of Eassie.

Ruin or site NO 333466 OS: 53 * Map: 8, no: 159

The rectangular earthworks survive from a castle.

Castletown

South Highland: About 3 miles south and east of Culloden, on minor roads east of B851, east of River Nairn, at or near Castletown.

Ruin or site NH 749427 OS: 27 * Map: 9, no: 114

Not much remains of a castle except an overgrown mound.

Castlewenrock *see* Saltcoats

Castlewigg

Galloway: About 2 miles north-west of Whithorn, on minor road west of A746, at Castlewigg.

Ruin or site NX 428432 OS: 83 ** Map: 1, no: 68

Castlewigg Castle consisted of a much-altered 16th-century L-plan tower house, to which had been added a more modern mansion. The tower was dated 1593, but the whole building was unroofed and derelict in the 1950s.

The moulded entrance led, through a lobby, to the vaulted basement.

It was a property of the Vaux family, but sold to the Stewarts of Bardye and Tonderghie in 1584. It was demolished in the 20th century.

Other refs: Castle Wigg; Wigg Castle

Catboll Castle *see* Cadboll Castle

Catcune Tower

Lothians: About 1 mile south of Gorebridge, on minor roads east of A7, north of the Gore Water, at Catcune.

Ruin or site NT 351605 OS: 66 * Map: 4, no: 144

No trace remains of Catcune, or Catclune, Tower, a 16th-century L-plan tower house, formerly with three vaulted cellars.

The lands were originally held by the Borthwick family, one of whom, William Borthwick, built Borthwick Castle in 1430. Catcune later passed of the Sinclairs, who probably built the tower.

Cathcart Castle

Lanarkshire & Glasgow area: About 0.5 miles south of Rutherglen, on minor roads south of the B767, east of the White Cart Water, in Cathcart.
Ruin or site NS 586599 OS: 64 ** Map: 3, no: 268
Not much survives of Cathcart Castle, an altered rectangular 15th-century keep, except the lower part of the formerly vaulted basement. It was surrounded by a rectangular courtyard, some ten feet from the keep, with round corner towers.

The Cathcarts held the property from the 12th century, were made Lords Cathcart in 1447, but built the castle about 1450. The property passed in 1546 to the

Semples, and although the family fought against her at Langside, Mary, Queen of Scots, is said to have stayed here the night before the battle. The castle was abandoned and unroofed around 1740 for nearby Cathcart House, although this house has long been demolished. The ruin was reduced to its base by the local council about 1980.

OPEN: Open all year, daily 7.00-dusk (as Linn Park).
Linn Park: Nature trail. Woodland walks. Children's zoo. Adventure playground. Limited disabled access. Parking nearby.
Tel: 0141 637 1147

Catslack Tower

Borders: About 8 miles west of Selkirk, on minor road just north of A708, north of Yarrow Water, near Catslackburn.
Ruin or site NT 340260 OS: 73 * Map: 2, no: 89
Site of tower house in a field. The property was held by the Crichtons of Cranston-Riddle about 1500.

Catter Castle

Stirlingshire & Clackmannan: About 0.5 miles south of Drymen, just south of A811 west of junction with A809, south of Drymen Bridge.
Ruin or site NS 473871 OS: 57 * Map: 6, no: 6
Site of castle of the Earls of Lennox, on an impressive motte, built to guard a ford over the Endrick Water. It was abandoned when Inchmurrin Castle was built in the 14th century. The property passed to the Buchanans.

A manor house was mentioned here in 1505. Part of may be incorporated into Catter House, a three-storey classical mansion, built in 1767 by the Graham Dukes of Montrose, which is just to the south [NS 471871].

Caverhill Tower

Borders: About 2.5 miles south-west of Peebles, on minor roads south of A72, just north of Manor Water, north-east of Kirkton Manor, at Caverhill.
Ruin or site NT 216383 OS: 73 * Map: 2, no: 50
Site of tower house, dating from the 16th century, some remains of which survived in 1838.

The property was held by the Caverhills, but passed to the Pattersons of Caverhill in the 16th century, and they probably built the tower.

Cavers Carre

Borders: About 4.5 miles south of Melrose, on minor road east of B6359, north of Ale Water, 1.5 miles east of Midlem, at Cavers Carre.
Private NT 551268 OS: 73 * Map: 2, no: 205
Possible site of tower house of the Kerrs, although the present house is no older than 1780.

Cavers House

Borders: About 2 miles east of Hawick, on minor roads east of A6088, at Cavers.
Ruin or site NT 540154 OS: 79 ** Map: 2, no: 194
Cavers House consists of a ruined 16th-century square tower house of five storeys and an attic, with extensive later alterations and extensions. The building may incorporate part of a 13th-century castle, but was altered in the 17th century, and remodelled in the classical style in the 1750s. It was extended in the 19th century, but partly demolished in 1953.

The Balliols had a stone castle on the site in the 12th and 13th centuries. It passed in the 1350s to the Douglases, who held the property until 1878. The old part was built by Sir Archibald Douglas, younger son of the Earl of Douglas, who died at the Battle of Otterburn in 1388. The castle was burned by Lord Dacre in 1523, by the English with the help of Scott of Branxholme in 1542, then again by the Earl of Hertford in 1545. It was rebuilt, and in 1887 extended and remodelled after it had passed by marriage to the Palmers, when the vault was taken out. It was unroofed and stripped in the 1960s.
Other refs: Warden's Tower, Cavers

Cawder Castle *see* Cadder Castle

Cawderstanes *see* Edrington Castle

Cawdor Castle

Inverness & Nairn: About 5 miles south-west of Nairn, on B9090 off A96, at Cawdor, just east of Allt Dearg, at Cawdor Castle.
Private NH 847499 OS: 27 *** Map: 9, no: 129**
One of the most magnificent and well-preserved strongholds in Scotland, Cawdor Castle incorporates a tall plain keep, dating from the 14th century, although the parapet and upper works were added in 1454. The castle has a deep ditch, and is reached by a drawbridge. Mainly three-storey ranges, gabled and crowned with bartizans and corbelled-out chambers, were built on all sides of the keep in the 16th and 17th centuries. There is a pit prison.

Across the drawbridge defending the entrance is a massive iron yett, which was brought here from Lochindorb Castle after 1455. The keep rises to four storeys and a garret within a flush parapet, and has very thick walls pierced by small windows. There are bartizans at each of the corners, as well as machiolated projections.

The entrance is now in the basement, but was originally at first floor level. Both the basement and the third floor are vaulted. A straight stair, in the thickness of one wall, leads up to the hall on the first floor – although this would formerly have been a stair down to the cellars. A turnpike stair climbs to the upper floors.

In the later ranges, there is an iron yett postern gate to the moat, some fine 17th-century fireplaces; and there are many portraits, furnishings and a collection of tapestries.

The title 'Thane of Cawdor' is associated with Macbeth, but Duncan was not murdered here, as the castle is not nearly old enough, and he was killed in battle near Spynie. The Calders had an earlier stronghold near here [NH 858512], but nothing remains.

The 1st Thane of Cawdor took the name of Calder when granted the lands by Alexander II in 1236, although one story is that the family were descended from a brother of Macbeth. The 3rd Thane was murdered by Sir Alexander Rait of nearby Rait Castle.

The 5th Thane built much of the present castle. The method of selecting the site for Cawdor Castle was unusual as it was chosen by a donkey allowed to roam at will until it came to a suitable spot. Cawdor is also built over a tree, the remains of which are in the vaulted basement. It was believed to be a hawthorn, but in fact it proved to be a holly tree and it died in about 1372, when the castle was built.

The Campbells obtained Cawdor by kidnapping the girl heiress, Muriel Calder, and marrying her at the age of 12 to the Earl of Argyll's son, Sir John Campbell, in

castle was slighted after it had been surrendered without a serious fight, although the English commander was not sure they could have taken the castle. It was restored, but burned in 1543, and damaged again by the Earl of Hertford in 1544, who also considered the castle difficult to capture. Sir Walter Kerr, also a Warden, was banished to France for his part in the murder of Walter Scott of Buccleuch in 1552, and was active against Mary, Queen of Scots. The Kerrs were made Earls, then Dukes of Roxburghe. The castle was abandoned about 1650, and materials were used for the building of Floors Castle in the 1720s.

Cessnock Castle

Ayrshire: About 1 mile south-east of Galston, on minor road east of B7037, in a ravine of the Burn Anne, 0.75 miles south of the River Irvine.

Private   NS 511355   OS: 70   *   Map: 3, no: 222**

Standing above a ravine, Cessnock Castle is a massive 15th-century rectangular keep of three storeys and an attic. To this has been added a large mansion, making the building U-plan. The keep has a corbiestepped gabled roof. The parapet has been removed, although the open rounds survive.

The basement is vaulted, the hall would have been on the first floor, with private

chambers on the floors above. The great hall, in the newer part, still has a late 16th-century painted ceiling.

Cessnock was a property of the Campbells. Mary, Queen of Scots, came to Cessnock after her defeat at Langside, when one of her ladies died here, and is said to haunt the castle. The reformers George Wishart and John Knox also visited, as did Robert Burns. The property then passed through the families of Dick, Wallace, and Scott, to the de Fresnes in 1946. The ground floor was sold off as a self-contained flat in 1981.

The spirit of John Knox is also said to haunt the castle.

1511. Campbell of Inverliver led the kidnapping, and all six of his sons were slain in the raid defending the party.

The Campbells of Cawdor, her descendants, remained at the castle. They gave refuge to Simon, Lord Lovat, during his flight from Hanoverian troops in 1746 during the Jacobite Rising, and hid him in a secret room in the roof. Fraser was eventually caught and executed. Bonnie Prince Charlie had visited the same year.

A ghost in a blue velvet dress has reputedly been seen here, as has an apparition of John Campbell 1st Lord Cawdor.

OPEN: Open May-mid-Oct, daily 10.00-17.30; last admission 17.00.

Fine collections of portraits, furnishings and tapestries. Explanatory displays. Three shops: gift shop, wool and book shop. Licensed restaurant and snack bar. Gardens, grounds and nature trails. Golf course and putting. Disabled access to grounds; some of castle. Car and coach parking. Group concessions. Conferences. £££.

Tel: 01667 404615   Fax: 01667 404674

Email: info@cawdorcastle.com   Web: www.cawdorcastle.com

Cessford Castle

Borders: About 5 miles south of Kelso, on minor roads south of B6401, about 0.25 miles north-east of Cessford village, east of Cessford Burn.

Ruin or site   NT 738238   OS: 74   *   Map: 2, no: 297**

Cessford Castle is an exceptionally massive ruined L-plan castle, rising to three storeys in the main block and four in the wing. It incorporates work from the 15th century and probably earlier, and there are some remains of a large courtyard wall, as well as apparently another wall and ditch beyond this. The walls are 12-feet thick in places.

The entrance is in the re-entrant angle. The basement and hall were both vaulted, and the hall was a fine apartment with a fireplace and window seats. The wing contained the kitchen. There is a 'dismal' dungeon.

The lands were held by the Sinclairs in the 14th century, but passed to the Kerrs in the following century. They apparently built the castle and soon rivalled the Ferniehirst branch of their family. Sir Andrew Kerr of Cessford fought and survived the Battle of Flodden in 1513, and became a Warden of the Marches, although Cessford was damaged by the English in 1519. When the Earl of Surrey besieged the castle in 1523, he reckoned Cessford the third strongest castle in Scotland. The

Champfleurie *see* Kingscavil

Chanonry

Ross & Cromarty: In Fortrose, on minor roads east of A832, on north coast of Moray Firth, Castle Street, at or near Cathedral site.
Ruin or site NH 727567 [?] OS: 27 * Map: 9, no: 110
Fortrose Cathedral was built in the 13th century by Bishop Robert, who moved his seat from Rosemarkie. Part of the cathedral complex included a fortified tower, which was built by Bishop John Fraser around 1500.

In 1571 the cathedral lands and property were fought over by the Leslies of Balquhain, who had been given the property by Bishop Leslie, and the Mackenzies of Kintail, granted it by Regent Moray. The Mackenzies retained the property, and were made Earls of Seaforth in 1623. They were forfeited in 1716 for their part in the Jacobite Rising, and although they later recovered their lands, the title of Earl of Seaforth was not recovered.

Most of the buildings and the church were demolished by Cromwell to build a fort at Inverness, and only part of the church and chapter house survives.
Other refs: Irvine's Tower; Seaforth Castle

Chapel

Dumfriesshire: About 1 mile west of Moffat, on minor roads west of A701, west of River Annan, at Chapel.
Ruin or site NT 074055 OS: 78 * Map: 1, no: 215
Little remains of a probable tower house and medieval chapel, believed to have been dedicated to St Cuthbert and founded by the Knights Templars.

Chapel

Borders: About 5 miles south-east of Selkirk, on minor road east of B6359 at junction with B6400 and B6453, south of Ale Water, at or near Chapel Farm.
Ruin or site NT 545255 [?] OS: 73 * Map: 2, no: 200
Site of tower house, which was demolished about 1839, and there was a chapel here in medieval times.

Chapel Hill *see* Carco Castle

Chapelhill

Borders: About 1 mile north and west of Peebles, on minor road west from A703, west of Eddleston Water, at Chapelhill.
Private NT 245422 OS: 73 * Map: 2, no: 57
Chapelhill, a harled two-storey farmhouse, is a much-altered 16th-century tower house.

The property was held by the chapel of Peebles Castle, but acquired by Kelso Abbey. In the middle of the 16th century it passed to the Pringles, who built the tower. The tower was used to store the vestments and valuables from the Cross Kirk in Peebles on its dissolution at the Reformation. The Pringles sold the property in 1657, and it later passed to the Williamsons, who held it in second half of the 18th century.

Chapelhouse

Ayrshire: About 4.5 miles west of Muirkirk, north of B743, north of Greenock Water, north of Greenock Mains, at Chapelhouse.
Ruin or site NS 634279 OS: 71 * Map: 3, no: 295
Not much survives of a small tower house along with the ruinous remains of a farm. There is said to have been a chapel here.

Chatelherault

Lanarkshire & Glasgow: About 2 miles south-east of Hamilton, on minor road west of A72, Chatelherault.
Private NS 737540 OS: 64 * Map: 3, no: 348**
Chatelherault is a magnificent hunting lodge and kennels, built in 1732-44 by the architect William Adam for James Hamilton, 5th Duke of Hamilton. The building has been restored, and houses an exhibition about the Clyde valley, geology and natural history of the park. The country park, which covers some 500 acres, has

18th-century gardens, terraces and parterre, as well as extensive country walks. There are also the ruins of Cadzow Castle.
OPEN: Open all year, Mon-Sat 10.00-17.00, Sun 12.00-17.00, Easter Sun-Sep open until 17.30; closed Christmas and New Year.
Guided tours. Explanatory displays. Tearoom. Picnic area. Garden. WC. Disabled access. Car and coach parking.
Tel: 01698 426213 Fax: 01698 421537

Chesterhill

Fife: In Anstruther Wester, on minor roads south of A917, north of shore.
Ruin or site NO 562034 OS: 59 * Map: 7, no: 145
Possible site of castle.

Chesterhouse Tower

Borders: About 3 miles south of Morebattle, on minor road and track south of B6436, on south-east side of Chesterhouse Hill.
Ruin or site NT 772203 OS: 74 * Map: 2, no: 310
Little remains of a tower house.

Chesters

Borders: About 2.5 miles south and east of Bonchester Bridge, on or near B6088, at or near Chesters.
Ruin or site NT 628106 OS: 80 * Map: 2, no: 245
Site of tower house, some remains of which survived in the 19th century.

Chingles Tower *see* Kirkton Tower

Chirnside

Borders: About 4.5 miles east of Duns, on minor roads north of A6105 or south of B6355, in village of Chirnside.
Ruin or site NT 870560 OS: 74 * Map: 2, no: 345
Site of tower house, near Chirnside burial ground. It was built by the Earl of Dunbar, and apparently demolished in the 18th century. The church dates from the 12th century, and has a Norman doorway, decorated with saw-tooth or chevron patterns. There is also a 16th-century doocot near the church.

Clachary

Galloway: About 3.5 miles south and east of Newton Stewart, on minor road east of A714, north of Bishop Burn, east of Causeway End, at or near Carse of Clary.
Ruin or site NX 424603 [?] OS: 83 * Map: 1, no: 64
Probable site of a palace of the Bishops of Galloway in the 15th and 16th centuries after they had moved from Penninghame Hall. The property passed to the Stewarts, later Earls of Galloway, and it is here that Mary, Queen of Scots, lodged with the Master of Garlies in 1563.
Other refs: Clary

Clackmannan Tower

Stirlingshire & Clackmannan: On western outskirts of Clackmannan, on minor roads south of B910, on footpath, east of the Black Devon river.
Private NS 905920 OS: 58 ** Map: 6, no: 99**
Standing on the summit of a ridge known as King's Seat Hill, Clackmannan Tower is a 14th-century keep of three storeys, which was heightened in the 15th century. Another taller tower was added in the late 15th century, with a machiolated corbelled-out parapet, making the house L-plan. The castle stands on the site of an older stronghold.

The original entrance to the old tower, at first-floor level, was reached by an external stair. When the new tower was added, a turnpike stair was inserted in the re-entrant angle, the entrance at ground level. Only the top of this stair survives, the lower part having been removed to allow the building of a wider scale-and-platt stair to the first-floor.

Both basements are vaulted, as are the first floors. The hall, in the main block, has a fine decorated 16th-century fireplace. There is an unusual long narrow gallery within the walls of the third floor, entered through one of the window recesses.

An adjoining mansion was added in the late 16th century, but was demolished

and nothing remains. Fragments of a courtyard wall, garden terrace and bowling green remain.

There was a royal castle or hunting lodge here, possibly from the 12th century, which was mentioned in the 13th century. Clackmannan was a property of the Bruces from 1359 until 1796, having been given to the family by David II. The family were bankrupted by 1708, and Henry Bruce of Clackmannan fought for the Jacobites in the 1745 Rising. On 26th August 1787, in the adjoining but now demolished mansion, Henry Bruce's widow, Catherine, 'knighted' Robert Burns, with the sword of Robert the Bruce. The tower and mansion were abandoned in 1791.

Clackriach Castle

Banff & Buchan: About 11 miles north of Ellon, on minor roads south of B9029, 1 mile south-east of Maud, south of South Ugie Water, just west of Mains of Clackriach.
Ruin or site   NJ 933471   OS: 30   *   Map: 10, no: 325
Little remains of Clackriach Castle, a 16th-century tower house of the Keiths.

Claddach Castle *see* Tarbet Castle

Claig Castle

Argyll & Dunbartonshire: To south of Am Fraoch Eilean, an island just off coast of Jura, about 5 miles south of Port Askaig, on minor road, boat and foot west of A846, at Claig.
Ruin or site   NR 472627   OS: 61   *   Map: 5, no: 19
Little remains of Claig Castle, a 13th-century castle of enclosure and later keep, except the basement. It was protected by a ditch.
It was a property of the MacDonalds, and is said to have been used as a prison as well as a stronghold.
Other refs: Am Fraoch Eilean Castle

Clan Cameron Museum, Achnacarry *see* Achnacarry

Clanyard Castle

Galloway: About 13 miles south of Stranraer, on minor road west of B7065, about 0.5 miles south-east of Clanyard Bay, at Low Clanyard.
Ruin or site   NX 109374   OS: 82   *   Map: 1, no: 22
Although once a great house, not much survives of Clanyard Castle, except one

gable and an adjoining wall. It was a 16th-century L-plan tower house of the Gordons of Kenmure, but ruinous by the end of the 17th century.
Other refs: Castle Clanyard; Claynurd

Clary *see* Clachary

Clatt *see* Knockespock House

Clatto Castle

Fife: About 5 miles south of Cupar, on minor roads west of A916, about 1 mile south of Clatto Reservoir, about 2.5 miles north of Kennoway.
Private   NO 358073   OS: 59   *   Map: 7, no: 96
Clatto, remodelled by David Bryce 1845-50, then again in 1964, stands on or near the site of a 16th-century castle.
The lands were held by the Ramsay family in the 13th century, but the castle was built after they had passed to the Learmonths. The property was held by the Law family in the 19th century.
The castle apparently had a tunnel communicating with a cavern at Clatto, and 'notable in olden times for the Seton's deeds of rapine and bloodshed'.

Claverhouse Castle

Angus & Dundee: About 7.5 miles north of Dundee, west of A928, 2 miles south of Glamis, near Hatton of Ogilvie.
Ruin or site   NO 380442 [?]   OS: 54   *   Map: 8, no: 168
Site of castle, which appears to have consisted of a large keep or tower house with a moat and drawbridge. Substantial remains survived until the end of the 19th century, although this appears to have been a 'modern monumental structure in the form of a ruin', but the site has been cleared and nothing now remains.
It was a property of the Ogilvies in the 14th century, but had passed to the Grahams by the 17th century. John Graham of Claverhouse, Bonnie Dundee or Bloody Clavers, took his title from this place and was brought up here. Graham was the victor at the Battle of Killiecrankie in 1689, against the forces of William and Mary, but was mortally wounded and died during the battle.
There was another Claverhouse Castle to the north of Dundee [NO 405339].
Other refs: Hatton of Ogilvie; Tower of Glen Ogilvie

Claverhouse Castle

Angus & Dundee: About 3.5 miles north of Dundee, on minor roads north or west of A90, at Claverhouse.
Ruin or site   NO 405339   OS: 54   *   Map: 8, no: 177
Site of castle, which was removed in 1792.
It was held by the Claverhouse family. There is another stronghold called Claverhouse [NO 380442] at Milton of Ogilvie.

Claynurd *see* Clanyard Castle

Claypotts Castle

Angus & Dundee: About 3.5 miles east and north of Dundee, just south of A92 at junction with B978, in West Ferry area of Dundee, at Claypotts.
His Scot   NO 452319   OS: 54   ***   Map: 8, no: 193**
An unusual and impressive building, Claypotts Castle is a Z-plan tower house. It consists of a rectangular main block of three storeys and a garret and two large round towers, crowned with square gabled chambers, at opposite corners. Two smaller stair towers rise in two of the re-entrant angles between the main block and round towers. The walls are pierced with gunloops and shot-holes.
The basement contains a kitchen and three cellars. The hall is on the first floor of the main block, with single chambers above; and the round towers contain eight private chambers. One tower carries the date 1569, and the other 1588.
The lands passed from the Abbey of Lindores to the Strachans about 1560, and the castle was started soon afterwards. It passed to the Grahams, one of whom was John Graham of Claverhouse, Viscount Dundee, also known as 'Bloody Clavers' for his cruel persecution of Covenanters in Galloway, and 'Bonnie Dundee' after his death at the Jacobite victory over the forces of William and Mary at the Battle of Killiecrankie in 1689. His lands were forfeited in 1694 and went to the Douglas Earl

of Angus, then later to the Homes. In the 19th century the castle was used to house farm labourers.

Claypotts is said to be haunted by a 'White Lady'. One tale is that she is the ghost of Marion Ogilvie, mistress of Cardinal David Beaton, who was murdered in 1546. She is said to be seen at one of the windows on the 29 May each year: the date of Beaton's death. It seems more likely, however, that she lived at Melgund Castle, as there was apparently no castle here in 1546. Claypotts is also said to have had a brownie.

OPEN: Open Jul-Sep, Sat-Sun 9.30-18.30; last ticket 18.00.
Parking Nearby. £.
Tel: 01786 450000 Fax: 0131 668 8888
Email: hs.explore@scotland.gov.uk Web: www.historic-scotland.gov.uk

Cleerie Castle *see* Adderston

Cleghorn House
Lanarkshire & Glasgow area: About 2 miles north-east of Lanark, on minor roads west of A706 or east of A73, north of the Mouse Water, at Cleghorn.
Ruin or site NS 898461 [?] OS: 72 * Map: 3, no: 412
Cleghorn House, a mansion which incorporated a castle, was demolished in the 20th century.

It was a property of the Lockhart family in 1649.

Cleish Castle
Perth & Kinross: About 3.5 miles south-west of Kinross, on minor roads south of B9097, about 0.5 miles west of the hamlet of Cleish, east of Cleish Mains.
Private NT 083978 OS: 58 *** Map: 8, no: 70
Cleish Castle is a strong 16th-century L-plan tower house. It consists of a main block of five storeys and an attic, and a narrower higher wing. There is a stair-turret above first-floor level. It may incorporate earlier work, and was remodelled in the 19th century.

The original entrance was in the re-entrant angle, but when the interior was altered a new entrance was inserted at first-floor level, reached by an external stair, and the old one was sealed.

The Colvilles owned the property from 1530. Mary, Queen of Scots, arrived here after escaping from Lochleven Castle in 1568. By 1840 the castle had passed from the Colvilles, and become ruinous to be restored in the 1920s. In the late 1960s the castle was drastically altered and reoccupied.

Cleland Castle
Lanarkshire & Glasgow: About 1 mile north-west of Wishaw, on minor roads north of B7029, north of South Calder Road, 0.5 miles west of Cleland, at or near Cleland House.
Private NS 784577 OS: 64 * Map: 3, no: 370
Site of castle, a property of the Cleland family.

A cave below the house is said to have been used as a place of concealment by William Wallace. Much of the cave has since fallen away.
Other refs: Kneelandtoun

Clerkington House *see* Rosebery House

Clessley Peel
Borders: About 6 miles south of Jedburgh, north of track between Southdean on A6088 and Lethem, about 1 mile north-east of Southdean.
Ruin or site NT 644099 OS: 80 * Map: 2, no: 257
Little remains of Clessley Peel, a small 16th-century tower house.

Clickhimin Broch
Shetland: Just south-west of Lerwick, on minor roads and foot north of A970, on promontory at the south Loch of Clickhimin, on mainland of Shetland.
His Scot HU 464408 OS: 4 *** Map: 11, no: 63
The settlement at Clickhimin was originally on an island, joined to the shore by a causeway. The first settlement dated from about 500 BC, and a small oval house of this period survives. The islet was later enclosed by a stone wall and the massive blockhouse built at the entrance. The blockhouse defended the broch, which is located at the centre of the islet, and survives to a height of 17 feet. When the broch went out of use a roundhouse was built inside it with some others round about it. At the end of the causeway, set into the path, is a stone with two footprints carved into it. Where similar stones have been found elsewhere they have been linked with the inauguration of kings, and the site was occupied by the Picts.
OPEN: Access at all reasonable times.
Parking nearby.
Tel: 0131 668 8800 Fax: 0131 668 8888
Email: hs.explore@scotland.gov.uk Web: www.historic-scotland.gov.uk

Clintwood Castle
Borders: About 4 miles north and east of Newcastleton, east of B6357, east of Dinlabyre, in Newcastleton Forest.
Ruin or site NY 538910 [?] OS: 79 * Map: 2, no: 192
Site of 16th-century tower house, probably of the Elliots. It may have stood on the site of or have incorporated an earlier castle, a property of the de Soulis family before they moved to Liddel Castle early in the 13th century.

There may have been another tower at Flight [NY 534904].
Other refs: Flight Tower

Cloak Castle
Renfrewshire: About 1.5 miles north of Lochwinnoch, on minor roads west of B786, near Meikle Cloak.
Ruin or site NS 344605 [?] OS: 63 * Map: 3, no: 110
Site of castle, long held by the Montgomerys. It was completely demolished for building materials.
Other refs: Shian Castle; Shine Castle

Cloberhill
Lanarkshire & Glasgow area: About 2 miles east of Clydebank, on minor roads near A82, off Towerhill Road, Knightswood.
Ruin or site NS 532703 OS: 64 * Map: 3, no: 237
Site of tower house, held by the Crawfords in 1567. In 1612 Hew Crawford of Cloberhill was involved with Crawford of Possil in attacking and capturing Corslie Castle.

Clonbeith Castle
Ayrshire: About 3 miles north-east of Kilwinning, on minor road south B778, north of the Lugton Water.
Ruin or site NS 338455 OS: 63 ** Map: 3, no: 104
Standing within a farm, little remains of Clonbeith Castle, a 16th-century tower house, except the vaulted basement. The upper floors have been demolished.

It was a property of the Cunninghams. Cunningham of Clonbeith murdered the Montgomery 4th Earl of Eglinton in 1596 during a feud. He was pursued by the Montgomerys and cut to pieces. The property was sold to the Montgomery Earl of Eglinton in 1717.

Cloncaird Castle

Ayrshire: About 4 miles east and south of Maybole, on minor road south of
B7045, north of the Water of Girvan, about 1.5 miles south-east of Kirkmichael.
Private NS 359075 OS: 70 ** Map: 3, no: 115
Cloncaird Castle is a square 16th-century tower house of four storeys and an attic,
the third storey projecting on corbelling. The castle was much extended and re-
modelled in the Gothic style in 1841.

The basement is vaulted, but the interior has been greatly altered.

In 1494 the Mures held the property. Patrick Mure of Cloncaird was killed at the
Battle of Flodden in 1513. The castle passed to other families, and was remodelled,
with the addition of the large mansion, in 1841. It is still occupied.

A ghost of a man is said to have been seen often on the stairs, even in recent times.

Closeburn Castle

Dumfriesshire: About 3 miles south-east of Thornhill, on minor road east of
A702, about 1 mile east of Closeburn village, south of Closeburn Mains.
Private NX 907921 OS: 78 *** Map: 1, no: 173
One of the oldest continuously inhabited houses in Scotland, Closeburn Castle is a
massive rectangular 14th-century keep, with a flush crenellated parapet, to which
has been added a 19th-century mansion. The tower still has an iron yett. A courtyard has had round towers at the corners.

The basement is vaulted, as is the hall and the top storey, and has a prison. The
hall has been subdivided. A turnpike stair leads to the upper floors in the thickness
of one wall. The interior has been altered.

The lands were granted to the Kirkpatricks in 1232, who built the castle. Roger
Kirkpatrick, along with Lindsay of Dunrod, joined Robert the Bruce in stabbing
John Comyn to death in a church in Dumfries in 1306. Sir Roger Kirkpatrick of
Closeburn captured the castles of Dalswinton and Caerlaverock from the English
in 1355. He was murdered by Sir James Lindsay in 1357 during a quarrel at Caerlav-
erock. The Empress Eugenie, wife of Napoleon III, was descended from the family.
The house was damaged by fire in 1748, and sold in 1783 to a Reverend James
Stewart-Menteith, then in 1852 to the Bairds. It is still occupied.

A red-breasted swan was said to appear here as a portent of a death in the Kirkpatrick family.

Clova Castle

Angus & Dundee: About 14 miles north of Kirriemuir, on minor road west of
B955 at Clova, just north of road, north of River South Esk, at Clova Castle.
Ruin or site NO 322734 OS: 44 * Map: 8, no: 157
Little remains of Clova Castle, a 16th-century tower house of the Ogilvies, except
some of a round stair-tower.

The Ogilvies also had another castle or old house at Clova [NO 327732], which
dated from the 17th century. The house had been demolished by 1842.

Cluggy Castle

Perth & Kinross: About 2 miles north-west of Crieff, on minor roads north of A85,
just north of Loch Monzievaird, just east of Ochtertyre, at Cluggy.
Ruin or site NN 840234 OS: 52 ** Map: 8, no: 21
Cluggy Castle consists of a ruined 15th-century keep, now only rising to two storeys, once surrounded by a ditch. The castle stood on a peninsula in the loch, and
was formerly of some strength, having a ditch and drawbridge.

The Comyns had a castle here in the 13th and 14th centuries. Malise Earl of Strathearn is said to have been besieged here by Robert the Bruce in 1306. By the middle of the 15th century the property had passed to the Murrays of Tullibardine. The
castle was still occupied in 1650, but probably abandoned in the 18th century for
the new house nearby.
Other refs: Castle Cluggy; Castlecluggy

Clunie Castle

Perth & Kinross: About 4.5 miles west of Blairgowrie, on minor roads south of
A923, just north of Clunie, on site to west of Loch of Clunie.
Ruin or site NO 111440 OS: 53 * Map: 8, no: 81
Not much remains of Clunie Castle, said to be a palace of Malcolm Canmore. It was
a royal castle, and Edward I of England stayed here in 1296. In 1377 Robert II ap-

pointed John Ross as keeper, but it had been completely demolished by the beginning of the 16th century and materials used to built the nearby tower house [NO
114440].
Other refs: Castle Hill, Clunie; Ward, The

Clunie Castle

Perth & Kinross: About 4.5 miles west of Blairgowrie, on minor roads and boat
south of A923, just east of Clunie, on island to south of Loch of Clunie.
Ruin or site NO 114440 OS: 53 ** Map: 8, no: 83
On a wooded island, Clunie Castle is a ruined L-plan tower house. It consists of a
15th-century keep of three storeys and a garret, to which has been added a higher
16th-century wing. A round stair-tower stands in the re-entrant angle. The castle
was altered in later centuries, roofed until the middle of the 20th century, and was
burned out. Materials for the castle came from the nearby royal castle, and the
island has a wall encircling it and is probably artificial.

The entrance, at the foot of the stair-tower, leads into the vaulted basement which
contained the kitchen. One chamber occupies each floor in the keep and in the
wing.

The island was used as a base by brigands and robbers in the 15th century. The
keep was probably built by Bishop Brown of Dunkeld, between 1485 and 1514
although it may be older. In 1562 his successor, Bishop Crichton, sold the lands to
his kinsmen the Crichtons of Elliok. James Crichton, who spent much of his youth
here, was known as the Admirable Crichton. He set out on his continental travels at
the age of 20, speaking 12 languages, as well as being skilled in swordsmanship,
riding and music. He was tutor to the son of the Duke of Mantua, but killed in a
duel about the age of 23 in 1583.

The lands passed to the Ogilvies, then to the Coxes of Lochlee in 1892.

There is believed to have been a chapel here, dedicated to St Catherine, and human bones are said to have been found on the island in the 18th century.

Cluny Castle

South Highland: About 5.5 miles south-west of Newtonmore, on minor road just
north of A86, north of River Spey, east of Balgowan, at Cluny Castle.
Private NN 645942 OS: 35 * Map: 9, no: 89
Cluny Castle, a large 19th-century mansion, with turrets, may incorporate or stand
on the site of a much-modified 14th-century castle of the Macphersons.

An 18th-century house here was sacked by the Duke of Cumberland in 1746.
Ewen Macpherson of Cluny was a Jacobite. After the Battle of Culloden he hid in a
refuge, 'Cluny's Cage', constructed from trees and brushwood, and here sheltered
Bonnie Prince Charlie. Macpherson escaped to France in 1755, and died there soon
afterwards.

The fate of the family is said to have rested with a black pipe chanter, believed, by
some, to have fallen from heaven.

Cluny Castle

Aberdeen & Gordon: About 8 miles south-west of Inverurie, on minor roads
south of B993 or north of A944, 2 miles south of Monymusk, south of Ton Burn,
at Cluny.
Private NJ 688128 OS: 38 ** Map: 10, no: 198
Cluny Castle, a large castellated mansion of 1836-40 which was designed by John
Smith, incorporates an altered 17th-century Z-plan tower house. The tower house
consisted of a main block, with two round towers at opposite corners. Most of the
original features have been lost, although part of the basement is vaulted.

The lands were held by the Gordons from the 15th century.

Cluny Crichton Castle

Kincardine & Deeside: About 2.5 miles north of Banchory, on minor roads north
of A980, west of the Raemoir Hotel, at Cluny Crichton
Ruin or site NO 686997 OS: 38 ** Map: 10, no: 194
Cluny Crichton Castle is a ruined 17th-century L-plan tower house of three storeys
and a garret, with shot-holes defending the entrance. There is a rectangular stair-
tower in the re-entrant angle.

The basement is not vaulted.

It was a property of the Crichtons of Cluny, but was later held by the Douglases of
Tilquhillie.

141

Clyne

Sutherland & Caithness: About 2 miles north of Brora, on minor roads west of A9, north-west of East Clyne.

Ruin or site   NC 895060 [?]   OS: 17   *   Map: 12, no: 33

Site of castle or old house, the location not certain. Balranald, the former manse, dates from 1775 but was much altered in 1830-40.

Other refs: Balranald

Clyth *see* Gunn's Castle

Cnoc Chaisteal

Sutherland & Caithness: About 2 miles west of Dornoch, on minor roads off A949, 0.25 miles south-west of Camore, 0.3 miles east of Evelix, at Cnoc Chaisteal.

Ruin or site   NH 777900   OS: 21   *   Map: 12, no: 23

Site of castle, standing on the highest part of a ridge. It is thought to have been built by the Sutherlands of Evelix about 1570.

Cnoc Mhic Eoghainn *see* Ballimore

Coaltown Tower

Lothians: About 4 miles south-west of Penicuik, on minor roads east of A702, north of River North Esk, at Coaltown.

Ruin or site   NT 181570 [?]   OS: 65   *   Map: 4, no: 57

Site of castle, all traces of which had been removed by 1915.

Cobairdy

Aberdeen & Gordon: About 4 miles north-east of Huntly, on minor roads west of A97, west of Burn of Connairdy, at Cobairdy.

Private   NJ 575438   OS: 29   *   Map: 10, no: 143

Cobairdy House, a mid 19th-century two-storey mansion, stands on the site of a 16th-century castle of the Murrays, which was then held the Burnets.

Cobbie Row's Castle *see* Cubbie Roo's

Cobbler Hotel *see* Arrochar House

Cochno Castle

Lanarkshire & Glasgow: About 2.5 miles north of Clydebank, on minor roads north of A810, 1 mile north of Duntocher, west of Cochno Burn, at or near Cochno House.

Ruin or site   NS 498745 [?]   OS: 64   *   Map: 3, no: 204

Site of 16th-century tower house.

The property was held by Paisley Abbey, but passed to the Hamiltons at the Reformation, who built the tower. Two of the family were keepers of Dumbarton Castle. The present three-storey Cochno House was built about 1757 for the Hamiltons of Barns. It has been owned by the University of Glasgow since 1956, and houses the animal husbandry and astronomical departments.

Cochrane Castle

Renfrewshire: About 1 mile west of Johnstone, on minor roads north of A737, near the Black Cart Water, on Auchengreoch Road at Red House.

Ruin or site   NS 418616 [?]   OS: 64   *   Map: 3, no: 159

Nothing remains of Cochrane Castle.

The lands were held by the Cochrane family from the 14th century, and the family became Barons Cochrane of Dundonald in 1647, then Earls of Dundonald in 1669. The property was sold by the family to the Johnstones of Cochrane about 1760. Although part of the castle survived at the end of the 18th century, nothing now remains. In 1896 the site was commemorated by a small corbiestepped tower, incorporating a stone with the Cochrane arms and the date 1592.

The family had another stronghold nearby at Johnstone, which was previously known as Easter Cochrane.

Cockairnie

Fife: About 2.5 miles east and north of Inverkeithing, on minor roads north of A921, just north of Couston Castle, at Cockairnie.

Private   NT 169853 [?]   OS: 65   **   Map: 7, no: 28

The mansion here, which rises to three storeys and an attic, apparently incorporates work from the 16th century.

There may have also been another castle nearby, known as Mount Laura Tower [NT 168856].

Other refs: Mount Laura Tower

Cockburn Castle *see* Cockburn Tower

Cockburn House

Lothians: About 1.5 miles west and south of Balerno, on minor road south of A70, near where the Water of Leith and the Cock Burn meet.

Private   NT 144657 [?]   OS: 65   **   Map: 4, no: 47

Site of 17th-century L-plan tower, probably incorporated into a later building.

Other refs: House of Cockburn

Cockburn Tower

Borders: About 1 mile north-west of Preston, on minor road north of B6355, west of Whiteadder Water, north of Cockburn.

Ruin or site   NT 770591 [?]   OS: 67   *   Map: 2, no: 309

Site of 16th-century tower house of the Cockburns, the last vestige of which was apparently removed in 1829.

Other refs: Cockburn Castle

Cockburnspath Castle

Borders: About 1.5 miles south of Cockburnspath, on minor road north of A1, just east of the Heriot Water.

Ruin or site   NT 785699   OS: 67   **   Map: 2, no: 318

Cockburnspath Castle consists of a very ruined 15th-century keep, with the remains of outbuildings, enclosed by a walled courtyard, which was entered by an arched gateway.

Cockburnspath was a property of the Cospatrick Earls of Dunbar, but on their forfeiture passed to the Homes, then to the Sinclairs, who in 1546 sold it to the Douglases. The tower was probably abandoned around the beginning of the 17th century, and replaced by Cockburnspath House (Sparrow Castle) in Cockburnspath village.

Other refs: Cockburnspath Tower

Cockburnspath House

Borders: In Cockburnspath, to the south of the village, near the A1.

Private   NT 775710 [?]   OS: 67   **   Map: 2, no: 313

Cockburnspath House, or Sparrow Castle, built in the 16th century, consists of two offset blocks joined only at the corner, with a round tower in the re-entrant angle. The roof level has been altered and the gables removed. The stair-tower has had the stair removed from the lower section. The first floor is now reached by an external stair.

The original entrance was in the foot of the stair-tower, and the basement of one of the blocks is vaulted.

It may have been a property of the Douglases. Although abandoned at one time, it has been restored and reoccupied.

Other refs: Sparrow Castle; Old Manor House

Cockburnspath Tower *see* Cockburnspath Castle

Cockburn's Tower

Borders: Just west of Cappercleuch, on minor road west of A708, near the mouth of Megget Water, west of St Mary's Loch, near Henderland.

Ruin or site   NT 230235 [?]   OS: 73   *   Map: 2, no: 52

Site of a 16th-century tower house, little of which remains except an overgrown mound.

William Cockburn of Henderland, a noted Border reiver, was reportedly hanged for treason from his own gates by James V in 1530, although the execution probably took place in Edinburgh and was by beheading. The event is recorded in the Border ballad 'The Border Widow's Lament'. After his execution, his wife tried to drown herself in a nearby burn, at a place known as the 'Lady's Seat'.
Other refs: Henderland

Cockcairnie House *see* Otterston Tower

Cockie's Field

Dumfriesshire: To the south-west of Lochmaben, to south of A709, near Kirk Loch, at Cockie's Field.
Ruin or site NY 075815 OS: 78 * Map: 1, no: 216
Possible site of tower. It is said to have been occupied by a notorious reiver, known as John Cock or John o' Cock. His strength was such that he was greatly feared, but some king's foresters, coming upon him while asleep, tried to slay him, only succeeding with the loss of seven of their number. An old ballad relates the story.
   The earthworks known as Woody or Dinwoody Castle [NY 073837] are part of an Iron Age fort, and do not appear to have been used into medieval times.
Other refs: Woody Castle; Dinwoody Castle

Cocklaw Castle

Borders: About 0.5 miles south-east of Hawick, on minor roads west of A6088 or east of B6399, at or near Ormiston.
Ruin or site NT 524421 OS: 79 * Map: 2, no: 181
Site of 15th-century castle. It was besieged by Henry 'Hotspur' Percy in 1403, after the Battle of Homildon Hill, the events recounted in the Scotichronicon by Walter Bower. The castle still existed in 1440, and was a property of the Gladstones before 1560.
Other refs: Ormiston

Cockpool Castle

Dumfriesshire: About 7.5 miles west of Annan, just north of B725 at Cockpool, just east of the Seaheugh Burn, short distance north of shore of Lochar Water.
Ruin or site NY 070677 OS: 85 * Map: 1, no: 213
Site of 14th- and 15th-century castle.
   Cockpool was the stronghold of the Murrays of Cockpool from 1320 until 1450 when they built nearby Comlongon Castle. Cockpool was occupied by the English during the invasion of 1547-50.

Coeffin Castle *see* Castle Coeffin

Coilsfield Castle

Ayrshire: About 3 miles west of Mauchline, on minor roads north of B743 or east of B730, 0.5 miles south-east of Tarbolton, west of Coilsfield Mains.
Ruin or site NS 444265 OS: 70 * Map: 3, no: 181
Site of castle which was occupied by Montgomerie House, itself demolished in the later 1960s.
   The lands were a property of Melrose Abbey from 1342, but passed to the Cunninghams of Caprington after the Reformation. The property was sold to the Montgomerys in 1661 and held by them into the 20th century. The castle was replaced by Montgomerie House in 1798, which was designed by John Paterson, but it was burned out in 1969 and completely demolished.
   Robert Burns's Highland Mary, Mary Campbell, was a byres woman at Coilsfield in 1786 and it was here that they parted. She may have been pregnant, but died soon afterwards.
Other refs: Montgomerie House

Coldcoat *see* Macbiehill

Coldoch

Stirlingshire & Clackmannan: About 3 miles south-west of Doune, on minor road south of B8031, about 1 mile north of River Forth, at Coldoch.
Private NS 699982 OS: 57 ** Map: 6, no: 55
Site of castle.

Robert Spittal of Stirling, tailor to James IV, probably built a stronghold here about 1513. The existing mansion of the Grahams would appear to be much later.

Coldstone

Aberdeen & Gordon: About 7 miles north and east of Ballater, on minor road and foot east of A97, 0.5 miles north of Logie Coldstone, at or near Parks of Coldstone.
Ruin or site NJ 434054 OS: 37 * Map: 10, no: 87
Site of castle, which consisted of a strong fortress, square in plan, enclosed by a wall and defended by a ditch at the end of the 16th century. It may have dated from the 12th century, but had been completely removed by 1865.
Other refs: Moat of Colstaine; Colstaine

Coldsyde

Borders: About 6 miles north-east of Newcastleton, by foot north of B6357, north of Liddel Water, south-east of Riccarton Farm.
Ruin or site NY 542945 [?] OS: 79 * Map: 2, no: 196
Probable site of tower house. This has been suggested as an alternative name for Riccarton Tower [NY 544958] although this does not seem likely as Riccarton is more than 0.5 miles to the north, and the two are marked separately on Blaeu's map of Liddesdale.
   There may have been another tower house at Nether Riccarton (now Riccarton Farm) [NY 549949].
Other refs: Nether Riccarton; Caldsyde

Cole Castle

Sutherland & Caithness: About 9 miles north-west of Brora, on minor roads 9 miles north-west of A9 at Brora, on east bank of Black Water, 2 miles north-west of Balnacoil.
Private NC 795133 OS: 17 ** Map: 12, no: 25
Standing on a rocky eminence, Cole Castle consists of a ruinous Iron-Age broch with remains of outlying earthworks. The walls stand to a height of about 12 feet, and features include double door checks in the entrance passageway.

Colgrain House *see* Camis Eskan

Colinton Castle

Lothians: About 3 miles south-west of Edinburgh Castle, on minor roads north of B701 at Colinton, just east of the Water of Leith, near Colinton House.
Ruin or site NT 216694 OS: 66 * Map: 4, no: 73**
Colinton Castle is a ruined 16th-century L-plan tower house, with a second stair-tower added early in the 17th century.
   The vaulted basement contains cellars and a kitchen, with a large fireplace and oven, in the wing. The hall was on the first floor of the main block.
   The property belonged to the Foulis family. The castle was burned in 1650, but restored. It was abandoned in 1800 when sold to Sir William Forbes of Pitsligo, a banker, who built nearby Colinton House. The painter, Alexander Nasmyth, advised Forbes to unroof and partly demolish the castle to make it a picturesque ruin. The house was later home to James Abercrombie, Lord Dunfermline, who was Speaker of the House of Commons and died here in 1858, the only Scot to have held the position until 2000.

Collairnie Castle

Fife: About 4 miles west and north of Cupar, south of minor road between A914 and A913, at Collairnie.
Private NO 307170 OS: 59 * Map: 7, no: 76**
Collairnie Castle is a 16th-century L-plan tower house, the wing of which rises to five storeys. The main block has been reduced in height, and the roof altered to oversail the turrets. The castle is dated 1581 and 1607.
   It has two fine panelled tempera ceilings in the second- and third-floor chambers, one decorated with the heraldic devices of 50 families, mostly of Fife origin.
   The property belonged to the Barclays from the 14th century, but passed by marriage to the Balfours in 1789. Mary, Queen of Scots, spent three days here on her way to St Andrews to meet Darnley in 1564. The building is part of a farm, and still occupied.

Colliechat Castle
Stirling & Clackmannanshire: About 4 miles east and south of Callander, on minor road north of A84, at or near Easter Colliechat.
Ruin or site NN 688038 OS: 57 * Map: 6, no: 52
Nothing remains of castle, which was probably a Z-plan tower house. There were remains at the end of the 19th century.

Collielaw
Borders: About 3 miles north-west of Lauder, on minor roads west of A68, 1.5 miles south of Oxton, just south-west of Collielaw.
Ruin or site NT 498517 OS: 73 * Map: 2, no: 163
Site of tower house, little or nothing of which remains.
Other refs: Colylaw

Colliston Castle
Angus & Dundee: About 4 miles north of Arbroath, on minor roads east of A933 at Colliston Mill, about 1 mile north-east of Colliston village, at Colliston Castle.
Private NO 612464 OS: 54 * Map: 8, no: 250**
Colliston Castle is a 16th-century Z-plan tower house of three storeys and an attic. It consists of a main block with round towers, one corbelled out to square, projecting at diagonally opposite corners. The walls are harled and pink-washed, and are

pierced by many gunloops and shot-holes. The parapet and open rounds are modern, being additions of 1894-5, when the entire upper storey was altered. Carved stones built into the front walling may have come from a Culdee chapel nearby. The windows were enlarged in the 18th century.
  The entrance is at the foot of the main tower, flanked by gunloops. The basement is vaulted, and contained the kitchen; a wine-cellar, with a stair to the hall above, now built-up; and other cellars. The original turnpike has been replaced by a scale-and-platt stair in a projecting tower. The hall, on the first floor, has been altered.
  The property belonged to Arbroath Abbey, but was granted to the Reids in 1539, who granted it to the Guthries, who built the castle. It was sold in 1691 to the Gordons, then in 1721 to the Chaplin family who held it until 1920. The property then passed through several families, and the building is still occupied.

Collochan Castle *see* Cullochan Castle

Colluthie House
Fife: About 4 miles north and west of Cupar, on minor road just south of A914, 0.5 miles south-east of Luthrie, north of Colluthie Hill, at Colluthie.
Private NO 340193 OS: 59 ** Map: 7, no: 87
Colluthie House, a house dating from the 18th century and remodelled in the 1840s and in 1883, is said to incorporate part of a castles of the Ramsays, built about 1356. The house has very thick walls in places. It was held by the Carnegies of Colluthie in 1583, who were later made Earls of Southesk. It was renovated in 1840 by the Inglis family.

Colmslie Tower
Borders: About 3 miles north-east of Galashiels, on minor roads north of A7, at Colmslie, near Hillslap Tower and Langshaw Tower, north of the Allan Water.
Ruin or site NT 513396 OS: 73 * Map: 2, no: 175
Colmslie Tower is a very ruined rectangular 16th-century tower house, little of which remains. The basement is vaulted, and part of a turnpike stair survives in one corner.
  Colmslie was a property of Melrose Abbey, and is believed to have been named after a chapel dedicated to St Columba. It was held by the Borthwicks, but passed to the Cairncross family, who apparently built the tower. It was acquired by the Pringles in the 17th century.

Colquhar Tower
Borders: About 3 miles north of Innerleithen, just east of the B709 at Colquhar, east of the Leithan Water.
Ruin or site NT 332416 OS: 73 * Map: 2, no: 87
Little remains of a 16th-century tower house of the Kerrs, which was later held by the Morrisons.

Colquhonnie Castle
Aberdeen & Gordon: About 10.5 miles north of Ballater, just north of A964, north of River Don, about 1 mile east of Strathdon, just east of Colquhonnie Hotel.
Ruin or site NJ 365126 OS: 37 ** Map: 10, no: 77
Not much survives of Colquhonnie or Colquhony Castle, a ruined 16th-century L-plan tower of Forbes of Towie, except the vaulted basement. It was apparently never completed as three of the lairds were killed while overseeing its building.
  The nearby Colquhonnie Hotel is said to be haunted by a phantom piper, one of the Forbeses, who fell in the 1600s from the top of the old tower.
OPEN: Hotel.
Hotel: eight bedrooms with ensuite facilities. Children (babysitting arranged if required), and dogs welcome.
Tel: 01975 651210 Fax: 01975 651210

Colstaine *see* Coldstone

Colstoun House
Lothians: About 2 miles south of Haddington, on minor roads east of B6368 and west of B6369, just east of the Colstoun Water, at Colstoun.
Private NT 514712 OS: 66 ** Map: 4, no: 187
Colstoun House, a later mansion, incorporated a 16th-century tower house, which may have included earlier work. There was a fire in 1907, although the building was restored. Much of the more modern house has recently been demolished, exposing the older work.
  It was a property of the Brown family from the 13th century or earlier. The Colstoun Pear was a magic pear given by Hugh of Yester or Gifford, a reputed wizard, to his daughter on her marriage to a Brown of Colstoun in the 13th century. So long as her family held and preserved the pear they would prosper. The pear, shrivelled to the size of a plum, is still kept at the house. It could be claimed, however, this was a very inexpensive dowry.
  Sir William Brown of Colstoun defeated the English in a battle at Swordwellrig, Annandale, in the 15th century, at which Sir Marmaduke Langdale and Lord Crosby were slain.
  The house is still occupied.
Other refs: Coulston

Coltness Castle
Lanarkshire & Glasgow: To north of Wishaw, on minor roads north of A722, south of South Calder Water, at Coltness.
Private NS 797564 OS: 64 ** Map: 3, no: 376
Site of castle, consisting of a tower house and later range of buildings. This was incorporated into a mansion of 1800, and had a picture gallery some 200 feet long.
  The lands were held by the Somervilles, but passed to the Logans of Restalrig in 1553, then in 1653 were sold to the Stewarts of Allanton. The property passed from the family, and at the end of the 19th century was held by the Houldsworths.

Colylaw *see* Collielaw

Colzium *see* Easter Colzium

Colzium Castle

Lanarkshire & Glasgow area: About 0.5 miles east of Kilsyth, on minor roads north of A803, near Colzium House.

Ruin or site   NS 729788   OS: 64   *   Map: 3, no: 342

Little remains of Colzium Castle, a 16th-century L-plan tower house with a hall block, except a fragment built into outbuildings. The basement was vaulted.

The lands were a property of the Callendar family, but passed by marriage to the Livingstones of Kilsyth. The castle was demolished in 1703 to build a new mansion nearby. The property passed to the Edmonstones of Duntreath who gifted the property to the local council.

The Battle of Kilsyth took place about 0.5 miles away, when the Marquis of Montrose defeated a Covenanter army led by General Baillie.

The gardens at Colzium include a fine collection of conifers and rare trees in a well-designed small walled garden. There is a fine display of crocuses and snowdrops in spring. Other attractions include a 17th-century ice house.

OPEN: Walled garden open Easter-Sep daily 12.00-19.00, Oct-Mar, Sat-Sun 12.00-16.00.

Tearoom. Picnic tables. WC. Glen walk. Ruins of the castle. Arboretum. Curling pond. Clock theatre. Pitch and putt course. Kilsyth Heritage Museum. Disabled access. Parking. £ (pitch and putt only).
Tel: 01236 624031   Fax: 01236 437513

Comiston House

Lothians: About 3 miles south of Edinburgh Castle, on minor roads north of B701 in Edinburgh, at Comiston House.

Private   NT 240687   OS: 66   **   Map: 4, no: 87

The existing house dates from no later than 1815, but nearby is a doocot or turret, apparently dating from the 16th century, which has gunloops and is built into the stable block.

The lands were held by Alexander de Meignes in 1355, but passed to Cunningham of Kilmaurs, then in 1531 to Foulis of Colinton, then to the Fairlies. In 1608 Comiston was held by the Creichs, then passed by marriage to the Cants, then by marriage to the Porterfield family. The present house was built for Lord Provost James Forrester, and is now a hotel.

Comlongon Castle

Dumfriesshire: About 8 miles south-east of Dumfries, on minor road west of B724, about 2 miles north of the Solway Firth, at Comlongon Castle Hotel.

Private   NY 079690   OS: 85   **   Map: 1, no: 217**

Standing in 120 acres of secluded woodland and gardens, Comlongon Castle is a massive 14th- or 15th-century keep of five storeys and a garret within a corbelled-out parapet. Parts of the parapet are roofed-in to form small gabled chambers, and there is a caphouse crowning the main stair. The castle formerly had a courtyard and moat, but this was removed when the adjoining castellated mansion was built in the 19th century. A fire damaged the new part late that century, and it was restored in 1901.

The entrance, still with its iron yett, is reached by an external stair. It leads to the vaulted basement, with a well, and to the turnpike stair, which climbs to the first-floor hall. The hall has a stone-flagged floor, two fireplaces – one in a deep arched recess – and two mural chambers, one reached by a stair in the thickness of the wall, which leads to a guardroom and dark prison. There were private chambers above, each with its own fireplace.

The castle was built by the Murrays of Cockpool, who held the property from 1331. The family became Earls of Annandale, and later Earls of Mansfield. It was sold by the 8th Earl in 1984, and restored. It is now a hotel.

The castle is believed to be haunted by a 'Green Lady', the ghost of Marion Carruthers of Mouswald, who died in the 16th century. She was the heir to her father's lands of Mouswald because he did not have a son – marrying her would mean that her husband would acquire her father's property. The poor girl was forced into a betrothal of marriage with Sir James Douglas of Drumlanrig – or to John MacMath his nephew, depending on the version of the story. Either way, she was to marry a

man she did not love, although the motive appears to have been to seize her lands rather than any desire for Marion herself.

Marion fled to Comlongon, the castle of her uncle. Even the Privy Council seemed to be against her and in 1563 ordered her into the wardenship of Borthwick Castle. Although she was sheltered in Comlongon by the then laird, Sir William Murray, she was so distressed from the long dispute that she committed suicide by jumping from the lookout tower. An alternative version is that she was murdered by the Douglases who gained access to her room and threw her from the roof. Because she was thought to have committed suicide, she was not given a Christian burial. It is said no grass will grow on the spot where the poor girl died. This happened on 25 September 1570.

Her apparition is said to have been witnessed, both in the grounds and castle, a forlorn sobbing girl. The sounds of her weeping have also been heard, and a ghostly presence, which has pushed past people, has also been recorded. Some say that she searches for a proper resting place as she was not given a Christian burial.

OPEN: Hotel – open all year round.

11 bedrooms, most with four-poster beds. Weddings and banquets. Parking.
Tel: 01387 870283   Fax: 01387 870266

Commendator's House *see* Dryburgh Abbey

Commendator's House *see* Inchcolm Abbey

Commendator's House *see* Melrose Abbey

Commendator's House *see* Pittenweem Priory

Compstone Castle *see* Cumstoun Castle

Comrie Castle

Perth & Kinross: About 4.5 miles west of Aberfeldy, on minor road just south of B846, just south of the River Lyon, in Appin of Dull, about 0.5 miles east of Comrie Farm.

Ruin or site   NN 787486   OS: 52   *   Map: 8, no: 15**

Comrie Castle consists of a ruined L-plan tower house, part of which dates from the 15th century. A corbelled-out stair-turret stood in the re-entrant angle, only the base of which remains. The walls are pierced by gunloops, and the basement is vaulted.

The castle was built by the Menzies family, but burned in 1487, after which they moved to Castle Menzies. The castle here was later repaired and occupied by junior branches of the family until about 1715.

Comyn's Castle

Lanarkshire & Glasgow area: About 1 mile north of East Kilbride, on minor roads north of B783, just south of Rogerton, 100 yards north of Mains Castle.

Ruin or site NS 628563 OS: 64 * Map: 3, no: 293

The motte, which was protected by ditches, had a tower or keep, and dated from the 12th century.

The property belonged to the Comyns, but had passed to the Lindsays of Dunrod by 1382, one of the family, along with Kirkpatrick of Closeburn, helping Robert the Bruce stab John Comyn in a church in Dumfries in 1306. The Lindsays moved to the nearby castle of Mains [NS 627560] in the 15th century.

Comyn's Castle *see* Dalswinton Castle

Comyn's Craig *see* Craig Castle

Condie

Perth & Kinross: About 3 miles west of Bridge of Earn, on minor road north of B935, 1 mile west of Forgandenny, at Condie.

Ruin or site NO 076182 OS: 58 * Map: 8, no: 67

Site of castle, which was replaced by a mansion, which was burned out in 1866 and apparently demolished. The castle consisted of a 16th-century rectangular tower house, altered with the addition of a stair-tower, which was extended in later centuries.

It was held by the Oliphants from 1601.

Other refs: Newtown of Condie

Congalton

Lothians: About 3 miles south and west of North Berwick, near B1347, at or near Congalton Mains.

Ruin or site NT 544805 [?] OS: 66 * Map: 4, no: 197

Site of castle or hall house, which was mentioned in 1224. Congalton was an ancient barony.

Contullich Castle

Ross & Cromarty: About 1 mile north-west of Alness, on minor road west of A836 2 miles north of junction with A9, at or near Contullich.

Private NH 637705 [?] OS: 21 * Map: 9, no: 88

Site of 11th-century castle and later keep, a property of the Munros.

Conzie Castle

Aberdeen & Gordon: About 5.5 miles north-east of Huntly, on foot just east of A97, 0.5 miles south of Bognie Brae, west of Burn of Forgue, west of Mains of Bognie.

Ruin or site NJ 595450 OS: 29 ** Map: 10, no: 156

Conzie Castle, built in the 17th century, is ruined, but once rose to four storeys. Two walls are more or less complete.

It was a property of the Morrison family, although the Dunbars of Conzie held it about 200 years.

Other refs: Bognie Castle

Coome *see* Cowholm

Copshaw Tower

Borders: West of Newcastleton, on minor road and foot west of B6357, on side of Park Hill.

Ruin or site NY 480876 OS: 79 * Map: 2, no: 145

Site of tower house, which was ruinous by 1793. It was a property of the Elliots.

Other refs: Park Tower

Copshaws Tower

Borders: About 10 miles north and east of Newcastleton, east of B6357, near Myredykes.

Ruin or site NY 583984 [?] OS: 80 * Map: 2, no: 221

Site of 16th-century tower house, held by John Elliot of Copshaw.

Other refs: Caddroun Burn Tower

Corb Castle

Perth & Kinross: About 7 miles north of Blairgowrie, on minor road east of A93, at Corb.

Ruin or site NO 164568 OS: 53 * Map: 8, no: 108

Site of castle or tower house, little of which survives except a mound.

It was held by the Lindsay Earls of Crawford, then the Rattray family in the 17th and 18th centuries, and was ruined by 1793.

Corbet

Ross & Cromarty: About 7.5 miles east of Tain, north of B9165, at or near Drumnacroy.

Private NH 900827 [?] OS: 21 * Map: 9, no: 142

Site of castle.

Corbet Tower

Borders: About 1 mile south of Morebattle, on minor roads south of B6401, just west of the Kale Water, east of Morebattle Hill.

Ruin or site NT 776239 OS: 74 ** Map: 2, no: 314

Corbet Tower is an unusual 16th-century tower house of four storeys and a garret, each floor containing a single small chamber. There are many gunloops. The parapet has been removed, and the roofline altered.

It was owned by the Kerrs, but burned by the English in 1522, and again by the Earl of Hertford in 1544. It was rebuilt in 1575. The tower was 'restored' in the 19th century, and is still occupied.

Other refs: Gateshaw

Corehead

Dumfriesshire: About 4.5 miles north of Moffat, on minor roads north of A701 in Moffat, south-east of Devil's Beef Tub, at or near Corehead.

Ruin or site NT 072124 [?] OS: 78 * Map: 1, no: 214

Site of tower house, a property of the Johnstones.

Corehouse Castle

Lanarkshire & Glasgow: About 1.5 miles south of Lanark, on minor roads off A73, Corehouse.

Private NS 882414 OS: 71 * Map: 3, no: 409**

Standing on a promontory above the Clyde, not much remains of Corra Castle, a 16th-century tower house and courtyard. It was defended on three sides by the steepness of the gorge, and on the landward side by a deep ditch.

It was a property of Kelso Abbey, but was granted to the Bannatyne family in 1400, then sold to the Somervilles of Cambusnethan in 1695. Mary, Queen of Scots, is said to have spent a night here after defeat at Langside in 1568. By the 19th century the property had passed to the Cranstouns, one of whom was raised to the bench as Lord Corehouse in 1826. The property is still owned by the same family.

The more modern Corehouse [NS 882416], a Tudor Revival mansion, was designed by Sir Edward Blore. It was built in the 1820s for the Cranstouns, one of whom was raised to the bench as Lord Corehouse in 1826. It was visited by William and Dorothy Wordsworth, who described the mansion as 'a neat, white lady-like house'.

The castle, mansion and nearby Cora Linn waterfall, are said to be named after 'Cora', a princess who leapt on horseback over the cliff into the water.

Other refs: Corra Castle

OPEN: Corehouse (more modern house) open by appt only.

Tel: 0131 667 1514

Corgarff Castle

Aberdeen & Gordon: About 10 miles north-west of Ballater, on minor roads west of A939, south of River Don, about 1 mile west of Corgarff village.

His Scot NJ 255086 OS: 37 * Map: 10, no: 46**

Corgarff Castle consists of a much-altered 16th-century tower house, rectangular in plan, of four storeys. The tower has later pavilions and star-shaped outworks.

It was used as a hunting lodge by the Earls of Mar, but passed to the Forbeses. The Forbeses feuded with the Gordons, and this came to a head when Adam Gordon of Auchindoun and a force of his family ravaged through Forbes lands and besieged

the castle. Corgarff was held by Margaret Campbell, wife of Forbes of Towie, and 27 others of her household, women, children and servants; the menfolk were away. Margaret, however, would not surrender the castle. Gordon of Auchindoun lost patience after she had shot one of Gordon's men in the knee with a pistol. He had wood and kindling set against the building, and torched the place. The building went up in flames, killing everyone inside. The story is recounted in the ballad 'Edom o' Gordon', although Towie Castle is given as another possible site of the massacre.

The Erskine Earls of Mar acquired the lands in 1626. The castle was used as a mustering point by the Marquis of Montrose for his campaign in 1645. It was torched by Jacobites in 1689 so that it could not be used by Government forces, and again in 1716 by Hanoverians to punish the Earl of Mar, who was forfeited for his part in the Rising. The castle returned to the Forbeses of Skellater.

The Jacobites occupied it during the Rising of 1745, this time the Forbeses being forfeited. In 1748 the government bought Corgarff and altered the buildings, with the addition of the pavilions and star-shaped outworks. It was later used as a base to help stop illicit whisky distilling.

The castle is said to be haunted, particularly the barrack room, and ghostly screams have reportedly been heard in the castle.

OPEN: Open Apr-Sep, daily 9.30-18.30; last ticket 18.00; open Oct-

Mar wknds only, Sat 9.30-16.30, Sun 14.00-16.30; last ticket 16.00.
Short walk to castle. Exhibition: one of the floors houses a restored barrack room. Explanatory displays. Gift shop. Car and coach parking. Group concessions. £.
Tel: 01975 651460 Fax: 0131 668 8888
Email: hs.explore@scotland.gov.uk Web: www.historic-scotland.gov.uk

Cormiston Towers

Lanarkshire & Glasgow: About 2 miles west of Biggar, on minor roads north of A72, north of River Clyde, at or near Cormiston Towers Farm.

Ruin or site NT 001372 OS: 72 * Map: 3, no: 440

Site of castle, which apparently stood at or near the farm.

Cornal Tower

Dumfriesshire: About 1.5 miles south-east of Moffat, on minor road south of A708, near the Cornal Burn about 0.5 miles north of Craigbeck.

Ruin or site NT 112044 OS: 78 * Map: 1, no: 235

Little remains of a small 16th-century tower house except foundations.

It was a property of Carruthers of Mouswald in the 15th century, but passed to the Johnstones of Corehead, then the Douglas Dukes of Queensberry after 1633.
Other refs: Polcornare; Procornal

Coroghon Castle

South Highland: On east end of island of Canna, on north side of Canna Harbour, on the north-east side of pier.

NTS NG 288055 [?] OS: 39 ** Map: 9, no: 3

Not much remains of Coroghon (which means 'fetters'), or Coroglon, Castle on the summit of a steep rock, except part of a gatehouse or forework, which is in a dangerous condition. It was a property of the Clan Ranald branch of the MacDonalds.

The surviving ruin may date from as late as the 17th century, but is probably considerably older.

The site is said to be haunted by the ghost of a woman imprisoned here by one of the MacDonald Lord of the Isles.
Other refs: Canna Castle

OPEN: Ruin may be in a dangerous condition – view from exterior.

Corra Castle *see* Corehouse Castle

Corra Castle

Galloway: About 4 miles north-east of Dalbeattie, on minor road just north of A711, just north of Kirkgunzeaon Lane, at Corra.

Ruin or site NX 867662 OS: 84 ** Map: 1, no: 162

Little remains of Corra Castle, a 16th-century tower house, except parts of a gable and wall.

Corranmore

Argyll & Dunbartonshire: About 2 miles south-west of Ardfern, just north of B8002, north side of Loch Craignish, 0.3 miles south-west of Corranmore, at or near Duine.

Ruin or site NM 790029 [?] OS: 55 * Map: 5, no: 52

Site of castle or house of the Campbells of Corranmore.

Corsbie Tower

Borders: About 2.5 miles west of Gordon, south of minor road west from A6089, just north of the Eden Water, near Corsbie.

Ruin or site NT 607438 OS: 74 ** Map: 2, no: 238

Standing on higher ground surrounded by a bog, Corsbie Tower is a ruined 16th-century tower house, formerly of five storeys and a vaulted basement. It was surrounded by ramparts, and a causeway led through the marshy land.

It was a property of the Cranstons of Oxenford, who held the property until the middle of the 17th century.

Corsby *see* Crosbie Castle

Corse Castle

Kincardine & Deeside: About 5.5 miles north of Aboyne, on minor road just
north of B9119 1 mile west of junction with A980, north of Corse Burn, at Corse
Castle.

Ruin or site   NJ 548074   OS: 37   ***   Map: 10, no: 134

Corse Castle is a ruined 16th-century Z-plan tower house. It consists of an L-plan
main block of four storeys and a garret; a square tower at one corner; and a round
tower, which has partly collapsed, at the opposite corner. A stair rises in a smaller
round tower, which was formerly crowned by a caphouse. Three open rounds
survive, and many gunloops and shot-holes pierce the walls. A lintel is dated 1581.

The main entrance is in the re-entrant angle at the foot of the square tower.

In 1476 Corse passed to Patrick Forbes, armour-bearer to James III, and became a
property of the Forbeses. One of the family was Patrick Forbes, Bishop of Aberdeen in the 17th century. Corse was raided by Highlanders in 1638, when the laird's
cousin was carried off for ransom. It was abandoned in the 19th century for the
nearby mansion.

Corsehill Castle

Ayrshire: To north of Stewarton, just east of A735 and west of railway line, about
0.25 miles south of Hillhouse.

Ruin or site   NS 416465   OS: 64   *   Map: 3, no: 158

Little remains of Corsehill Castle, a property of the Cunninghams of Kilmaurs.

Corsewall Castle

Galloway: About 6.5 miles north and west of Stranraer, on minor roads north of
A718 at junction with B738, about 1 mile south-east of Corsewall Point.

Ruin or site   NW 991715   OS: 76   **   Map: 1, no: 4

Not much survives of Corsewall Castle, a 15th-century keep and castle, except the
vaulted basement with the beginning of a stair. It formerly rose to three storeys,
and was surrounded by a ditch.

The property belonged to the Stewarts of Dreghorn, but passed in 1333 to the
Campbells of Loudoun. A seven-foot-long cannon was found here in the second
half of the 18th century, and a number of gold coins, a ring and some silver plate
were discovered in 1802.

Corsindae House

Aberdeen & Gordon: About 8 miles north of Banchory, on minor roads south of
A944 or north of B9119, 1 mile north of village of Midmar, at Corsindae.

Private   NJ 686088   OS: 38   **   Map: 10, no: 195

Corsindae House consists of a tall 16th-century L-plan tower house of three storeys
and an attic with a round stair-tower in the re-entrant angle. To this has been added
a large mansion, making the building U-plan. The whole house is harled and whitewashed.

The basement is vaulted.

Corsindae was a Forbes property. In 1605 John Forbes of Corsindae was arrested
and taken to Edinburgh for trial, accused of murder. The property had passed to
the Duffs of Braco by 1726. The house is still occupied.

Corslie Castle

Lanarkshire & Glasgow area: About 2.5 miles east of Barrhead, north-west of the
junction of A726 with B769, at Crosslees House.

Ruin or site   NS 545593 [?]   OS: 64   *   Map: 3, no: 246

Site of a tower house and walled courtyard, which may be occupied by Crosslees
House, although the location of the castle may be elsewhere.

It was a property of the Montgomery Earls of Eglinton. The castle was captured by
Robert Crawford of Possil in 1612 to recover a debt, but all he gained was imprisonment in Edinburgh Castle. The castle was abandoned around the end of the 17th
century.

Corsock Castle

Galloway: About 7 miles north of Castle Douglas, on minor roads south of A712,
0.5 miles south of village of Corsock, west of Urr Water, at Hallcroft.

Ruin or site   NX 758748   OS: 84   *   Map: 1, no: 123

Site of castle, the residence of Robert Nelson of Corsock, a noted Covenanter –
there is a memorial to him in the kirkyard of Kirkpatrick-Durham church. A panel

from the building is built into Corsock House.

Corsock House, a 19th-century castellated mansion built by David Bryce, was held
by the Mr Murray Dunlop about 1880, and is still occupied.

Corston Tower

Fife: About 2 miles south-west of Auchtermuchty, on minor road south of A91 at
Corston Mill, just north of the River Eden.

Ruin or site   NO 208098   OS: 58   **   Map: 7, no: 34

Corston Tower consists of a 16th-century tower house, one side wall of which survives to the wall head while the rest of the castle is very ruinous. The tower rose to
three storeys and an attic, and there was a watch chamber crowning the stair. There
was a courtyard, traces of which remain, and the basement was vaulted.

The property was passed to the Ramsays of Carnock in the 15th century. Sir John
Ramsay of Corston was made Lord Bothwell in 1483, although he did not hold the
lands for long as he refused to swear allegiance to James IV in 1488 and Bothwell
was given to the Hepburns. Corston stayed with the Ramsays until 1669 when it
passed to the Colquhouns.

Corstorphine Castle

Lothians: About 3 miles west of Edinburgh Castle, on minor roads north of A8, in
Corstorphine area of Edinburgh, Castle Avenue.

Ruin or site   NT 199723   OS: 66   *   Map: 4, no: 65

Nothing remains of a castle with a strong curtain wall, moat and corner towers,
which was built by Sir Adam Forrester between 1374 and 1405. It was occupied
until at least 1698, but was finally burned to the ground and most of it demolished
in 1797. Some remains survived at least until about 1870, and a 16th-century doocot
stands near the site – the doocot has supernatural protection: it is said that anyone
demolishing it will die within a short time.

The lands were held from 1374 by the Forrester family. Sir James Forrester was
killed at the Battle of Pinkie in 1547. The family were made Lords Forrester in 1633.
Also nearby is Corstorphine Old Parish Church, dating from around 1426, which
contains the tombs of Sir Adam Forrester, Lord Provost of Edinburgh (who died in
1405), and Sir John Forrester, Lord Chamberlain in the reign of James I.

The ground around the castles is still said to be haunted by a 'White Lady', the
ghost of a Christian Nimmo. She stabbed and killed her lover, one of the Forresters
of Corstorphine Castle, during an argument. She was tried and sentenced to death,
but although she managed to escape, was recaptured at Fala Moor and executed by
beheading in 1679.

There was probably an earlier stronghold at Broomhall [NT 194723], some remains of which may have been found.

Other refs: Broomhall

OPEN: Site accessible.

Parking Nearby.

Cortachy Castle

Angus & Dundee: About 3.5 miles north of Kirriemuir, on minor roads east of
B955, just west of River South Esk, just east of Cortachy village, at Cortachy
Castle.

Private   NO 398597   OS: 54   ***   Map: 8, no: 174

Cortachy Castle consists of a much-altered and extended 15th-century courtyard
castle. Three of the round corner towers survive, as well as parts of the curtain wall

built into later buildings. The main tower or keep has been engulfed in the extensions. There are many alterations, inside and out.

An older castle here belonged to the Stewart Earls of Strathearn in the 14th century. In 1473 it passed to the Ogilvie family, and then to the Earl of Airlie. He was a supporter of Charles I, and his castle of Airlie was destroyed by the Campbell Earl of Argyll – whereupon the family moved to Cortachy. Charles II spent a night at Cortachy in 1650 in the 'King's Room', and the following year the castle was sacked by Cromwell. The Ogilvies were forfeited for their part in the 1745 Jacobite Rising, but eventually recovered the titles in 1826. The house was extended by David Bryce in 1872, but fire gutted the Scottish baronial addition in 1883. The castle is still owned by the Ogilvies, although the Earl of Airlie now lives at the restored Airlie Castle.

The castle is said to be haunted by a ghostly drummer, who can be heard drumming whenever one of the Ogilvies nears death. The ghost is thought to be a spirit of a drummer, who angered the family – possibly by having an affair with the laird's wife – and was murdered, either by burning or by throwing him from the battlements. It is reputed that the drums were heard several times in the 19th century, and heralded deaths in the family.

Corvichen *see* Carvichen

Coshogle Castle
Dumfriesshire: About 5.5 miles south-east of Sanquhar, on minor road north of A76, just north of the Enterkin Burn, east of Coshogle.
Ruin or site NS 864052 OS: 78 * Map: 1, no: 161
Nothing remains of Coshogle Castle, although there were some remains in 1825. A heraldic panel, dated 1576, is built into a nearby cottage. It was a property of the Douglases of Drumlanrig.

Cossans Castle
Angus & Dundee: About 3 miles south of Kirriemuir, on minor roads east of A928 at Leys of Cossans, south of Roundy Burn, south of dismantled railway, at Cossans.
Ruin or site NO 393498 OS: 54 * Map: 8, no: 170
Site of a small 16th-century tower house, demolished in 1771 and the materials used to build the farmhouse, including a date stone of 1627. The castle had a ditch and drawbridge. Cossans was a property of the Lyon family from the 15th century.
Nearby [NO 401500] is St Orland's Stone, a Class 2 Pictish carved stone with a ringed cross, two fish-tailed serpents, horsemen and other Pictish devices.

Cot Castle
Lanarkshire & Glasgow area: About 2 miles east and north of Strathaven, just south of A71, south of the Avon Water, about 0.25 miles east of Bridgeholm Farm.
Ruin or site NS 739457 [?] OS: 64 * Map: 3, no: 349
Also known as Cat, Coat, Kemp and Kat, nothing remains of the castle, which was occupied by the Hamiltons about 1500. Limekilns were built on the site in the 19th century, and the site is at Cot Castle farm, itself now abandoned.
Other refs: Kat Castle; Kemp Castle

Coudcott *see* Macbiehill

Coudpil *see* Cow Peel

Coul House
Ross & Cromarty: About 1.5 miles south-west of Strathpeffer, on minor road east of A835 at Contin or west of A834, 0.5 miles east of Contin, at Coul House.
Private NH 463563 OS: 26 * Map: 9, no: 51
Site of castle, ruined by 1746.
It was a property of the Mackenzies of Coul, who held the property until the 19th century. The present building, dating from 1819, is a long low mansion, with an octagonal porch, and now used as a hotel.

Coull
Angus & Dundee: About 5.5 miles north of Forfar, on minor roads north of B957, 1 mile north of River South Esk, at or near Mains of Coull.
Ruin or site NO 444590 [?] OS: 54 * Map: 8, no: 189
Site of castle which survived until about 1750 but there are now no remains.
It was a property of the Ogilvies of Coull, who moved to Ruthven around 1744.

Coull Castle
Kincardine & Deeside: About 2.5 miles north of Aboyne, on minor roads east of B9094 at Bridgend, just east of Tarland Burn, south of Coull hamlet.
Ruin or site NJ 513023 OS: 37 ** Map: 10, no: 115
Coull Castle is a ruinous 13th-century castle of enclosure. It consisted of a pentagonal courtyard with a twin-towered gateway, a hall block opposite, a round keep, and at least one other tower. One account relates that it had five turrets and four hexagonal towers.
It belonged to the Durwards in the 13th century, hereditary 'door wards' to the kings of Scots. It was probably damaged in 1297, repaired about 1303 when garrisoned for the English, and destroyed during Robert the Bruce's campaign of 1307-8. It does not appear to have been rebuilt.
One story is that the bell of St Maddan of the nearby church of Coull would toll of its own accord when one of the Durward family was near death.
Other refs: Aboyne Castle

Coulston *see* Colstoun House

Coulter Motte
Lanarkshire & Glasgow: About 1.5 miles south-west of Biggar, on minor road just west of A72, east of River Clyde, at Coulter.
His Scot NT 018362 OS: 72 ** Map: 3, no: 443
The remains of a motte and bailey castle with a large mound.
Other refs: Wolfclyde
OPEN: Access at all reasonable times.
Parking nearby.
Tel: 0131 668 8800 Fax: 0131 668 8888
Email: hs.explore@scotland.gov.uk Web: www.historic-scotland.gov.uk

County Hotel, Peebles
Borders: In Peebles, off A72, High Street, at County Hotel.
Private NT 252405 OS: 73 * Map: 2, no: 61
The hotel buildings incorporate a vaulted cellar, which probably dates from the 16th century. This may be one of the six bastle houses which survived in the town as late as 1870.
The County Hotel is said to be haunted by the ghost of a young woman killed in a tunnel behind the dining room sometime in the early 1900s. Her indistinct apparition has reputedly been seen, and objects have mysteriously disappeared or been moved, ghostly whispers have been heard.
OPEN: Hotel. Open all year excluding Hogmanay and New Year's day.
Small family-run hotel.
Tel: 01721 720595

Courthill
Angus & Dundee: About 5.5 miles south and west of Montrose, on minor road north of A92, 2 miles north of Inverkeillor, north of Lunan Water, at or near Courthill.
Ruin or site NO 674514 OS: 54 * Map: 8, no: 261
Possible site of castle, which was associated with Red Castle [NO 687510]. It is said to take the name as it was where the lairds held their courts.

Cousland Tower
Lothians: About 2.5 miles east and north of Dalkeith, just south of Cousland, near minor road between Cousland and north of A6124.
Ruin or site NT 377683 OS: 66 * Map: 4, no: 151
Little remains of Cousland Tower, a 16th-century tower house, with a vaulted basement, and courtyard. The village, and probably the castle, was torched in 1547 by the English under the Duke of Somerset after the Battle of Pinkie.

The tower was a property the Sinclairs, but passed to the MacGills in the 17th century, then to Dalrymples of Stair. William Dalrymple of Cousland was accused of shooting a pistol at Henry Henderson of Fordell in 1756.

Couston Castle

Fife: About 2 miles west of Aberdour, on minor roads north of A921, on the south east side of Otterston Loch, north of railway line.
Private NT 168851 OS: 65 ** Map: 7, no: 26
Couston Castle is a 17th-century L-plan tower house, and has a round stair-tower in the re-entrant angle. It may incorporate an earlier castle. A lower wing was added in the 18th century.
  Couston was a property of the Logans of Couston, then the Murrays. Robert Blair, a Presbyterian minister and an outspoken opponent of Archbishop Sharp, died here in 1666, and is buried in Aberdour graveyard. The castle was restored in 1985.

Couston Castle

Lothians: About 2 miles north-west of Bathgate, on minor road north of A800 just east of junction with A801, south of the Couston Water, North Couston farm.
Ruin or site NS 955712 OS: 65 ** Map: 4, no: 5
Not much remains of a 15th-century L-plan castle, which was later altered. It was a property of the Hamiltons, then the Sandilands.
Other refs: North Couston

Couthalley Castle

Lanarkshire & Glasgow area: About 1.5 miles north-west of Carnwath, east of the B7016, just south of Woodend, west of the main Edinburgh-Carstairs railway line.
Ruin or site NS 972482 OS: 72 * Map: 3, no: 431
Little remains of Couthalley Castle, a 16th-century L-plan tower house with a courtyard and further towers and a gatehouse. It incorporates a 14th-century castle, and had a series of a shallow ditches so that access was only by a drawbridge. There were significant remains in 1815.
  It was the chief stronghold of the Somervilles from the mid 12th century, and burned by the English in 1320, although soon rebuilt. The family became Barons Somerville in 1430, before they removed to Drum in Midlothian in 1583. The castle had been besieged in 1557, but was rebuilt and then remodelled in 1586. James V visited, as did Mary, Queen of Scots, in 1563, and James VI. James, 13th Lord, was a Hanoverian and an aide-de-camp to Cope at Prestonpans and Hawley at Falkirk during the 1745-6 Jacobite Rising. This branch of the family died out in 1870.
Other refs: Cowthalley Castle

Covington Castle

Lanarkshire & Glasgow area: About 6 miles east and south of Lanark, on minor roads east of A73, on the west side of the River Clyde, north of Covington.
Ruin or site NS 975399 OS: 72 ** Map: 3, no: 432
Covington Castle or Tower is a ruined 15th-century keep of four storeys. The basement was vaulted, and the hall was on the first floor, with a turnpike stair in one corner. A pit-prison survives within the walls, and there are remains of the surrounding ditches and a 16th-century doocot.
  The earthworks may represent the castle of Colbin, a Flemish-Norman who held the property. It was granted to the Keith Earls Marischal by Robert the Bruce, but passed to the Lindsays in 1368, who built the castle in 1442. It was sold to the Lockharts in 1679, one of whom was Sir George Lockhart, President of the Lord of Session. The tower was excavated in the 1980s, prior to restoration work, and finds from here are in the Biggar Museum.

Cow Peel

Borders: About 3.5 miles south of Innerleithen, on B709, 0.75 miles south of Newhall.
Ruin or site NT 314310 OS: 73 * Map: 2, no: 79
Site of tower house, which stood by the bridge over the Paddock Burn.
Other refs: Coudpil

Cowden Castle

Stirlingshire & Clackmannan: About 2 miles north-east of Dollar, on minor roads just north of A91, about 0.25 miles north of Cowden Farm, at Cowden Castle.
Ruin or site NS 987997 OS: 58 * Map: 6, no: 111
Site of a 14th-century castle, which belonged to the Bishops of St Andrews. A 16th-century entrance arch survives. A later mansion here, remodelled in 1893 and held by the Christies, was demolished in 1952.
Other refs: Castleton

Cowden Hall

Renfrewshire: About 0.5 miles west of Neilston, on minor roads south of A736, south of Cowden Burn, east of Lochlibo Road, at Cowden Hall.
Private NS 466571 OS: 64 * Map: 3, no: 194
Cowden Hall, a mansion remodelled in the 19th century, is now very ruinous, but incorporates work from the 14th century.
  The lands were held by the Spreull family from 1306, but were sold in 1622 to the Blairs, who married into the Cochrane Earl of Dundonald family. The property passed to the Hamilton Marquis of Clydesdale in 1725, then to the Dukes of Hamilton, before being acquired by the Mures of Craigends in 1766.
Other refs: Cowdon Hall

Cowdenknowes

Borders: About 2.5 miles north-east of Melrose, on minor road just west of B6356, just east of the Leader Water, at Cowdenknowes.
Private NT 579371 OS: 73 *** Map: 2, no: 218
Once a powerful stronghold, Cowdenknowes consists of a 16th-century tower house of four storeys and a corbelled-out parapet, formerly with a courtyard and flanking towers. To this has been added a mansion, dating from the same century. The walls are pierced by gunloops.
  The property was owned by the Homes, and an older castle here, which was mentioned in 1493, was apparently destroyed at the beginning of the 16th century. Home of Cowdenknowes was a supporter of the Protestants at the time of the Reformation, and in 1582 was involved in the Raid of Ruthven, when James VI was imprisoned in Ruthven Castle for six months. The house is still occupied, but had passed from the family by the 19th century.
  The Homes were apparently a cruel lot:
  'Vengeance! Vengeance! When and where?
  Upon the house of Cowdenknowes, now and ever mair!'
  Perhaps justified considering the two pit prisons.
Other refs: Sorrowlessfield

Cowdon Hall *see* Cowden Hall

Cowhill Tower

Dumfriesshire: About 4.5 miles north of Dumfries, on minor roads east of A76, about just west of River Nith, south of modern Cowhill Tower.
Ruin or site NX 952824 OS: 78 ** Map: 1, no: 183
Cowhill Tower consists of a ruined 16th-century L-plan tower house, which was partly demolished in 1789. It is dated 1597.
  It was a property of the Maxwells. It was burned in 1560, then torched again in 1745 by Jacobites returning from England.

Cowholm

Dumfriesshire: About 3 miles north of Gretna, on minor roads and foot south of B6357, south of River Sark, at or near Cowholm.
Ruin or site NY 337721 [?] OS: 85 * Map: 1, no: 306
Probable site of castle a property of the Bells.
Other refs: Coome

Cowie Castle

Kincardine & Deeside: About 1.5 miles north-east of Stonehaven, on minor roads and foot east of A92, just west of the sea near St Mary's ruined church, at Cowie.
Ruin or site NO 887874 OS: 45 * Map: 10, no: 306
Cowie Castle, dating from as early as the 11th century, has traces of a stone wall

cutting off a coastal promontory, but the castle was probably dismantled early in the 14th century.

The castle was traditionally built by Malcolm Canmore, and Cowie was apparently made a burgh in the 11th century. The property was held by the Frasers, and Alexander Fraser of Cowie was Chamberlain to Robert the Bruce. He was slain at the Battle of Dupplin Moor in 1329. At the end of the 19th century Cowie was held by the Innes family, who had a mansion Cowie House.
Other refs: Castle of Cowie

Cowie House

Kincardine & Deeside: About 1 mile north-east of Stonehaven, on minor roads east of A92 or B979, just west of sea, north-east of village of Cowie, at Cowie House.
Private NO 880872 OS: 45 ** Map: 10, no: 300
Cowie House includes 17th-century work.

It was a property of the Frasers, but was held by the Innes family in the 19th century.

Cowthalley Castle *see* Couthalley Castle

Coxton Tower

Moray: About 3 miles east and south of Elgin, just south of B9103 about 0.5 miles south of junction with A96, at Coxtontower.
Ruin or site NJ 262607 OS: 28 ** Map: 10, no: 50**
Coxton Tower is a tower house, square in plan, of four storeys. It is roofed with stone slabs, and has corbiestepped gables, the pitch of the roof being steep. The

bartizans are stone roofed, and there is a corbelled-out open round at one corner. The thick walls are pierced by small windows, some still with iron yetts, and many shot-holes. The tower is dated 1644, although it appears to be considerably older, and it is marked on Blaeu's Atlas Novus map of Moray, which was compiled around 1590.

All the floors are vaulted, including the top storey to carry the heavy stone roof, making the tower effectively fire proof. Although there is now an entrance to the basement, this was probably inserted later: the original entrance was at first-floor level, and is now reached by an external stone stair of about 1846. This leads to the hall, and to the stair in one corner. The tower had a courtyard.

It was a property of the Inneses of Invermarkie until sold to the Duff Earl of Fife, who built a new house nearby. The tower is roofed, and in excellent condition.

Crag Tower

Borders: About 3 miles east and south of Jedburgh, on minor road east of A68, near hamlet of Oxnam.
Ruin or site NT 690190 [?] OS: 80 * Map: 2, no: 282
Site of tower house.

Craghouse *see* Urie House

Craig

Dumfriesshire: About 3 miles north-west of Langholm, on minor road west of B709, west of River Esk, at or near Craig.
Ruin or site NY 341884 [?] OS: 79 * Map: 1, no: 309
Site of tower house, listed as Craig. Both Over Craig and Nether Craig are located on Blaeu's Atlas Novus map of Eskdale.
Other refs: Over Craig; Nether Craig

Craig *see* Old Halls of Craig

Craig Castle

Aberdeen & Gordon: About 2.5 miles south-west of Rhynie, just south of B9002 1 mile west of junction with A97, south of Burn of Craig, at Craig Castle.
Private NJ 472248 OS: 37 ** Map: 10, no: 104**
Standing above a steep ravine, Craig Castle consists of a fine 16th-century L-plan tower house of four storeys with a more modern mansion attached. The once

open parapet has been built into the roof. The thick walls are pierced by gunloops, and are harled and pink-washed. The tower is dated 1548, but was altered or extended in 1832 and 1908. An older earthwork castle survives nearby.

The entrance, in the re-entrant angle, has a thick door and heavy iron yett. It opens into a vaulted vestibule, which leads to a passage to the wine-cellar, with a small stair to the hall above; a vaulted cellar; the kitchen, with a wide arched fireplace; and a small guardroom which has a pit prison beneath the floor.

The wide main turnpike stair, at the end of the passage, climbs to all floors. The hall has been a fine apartment but has later been partitioned. There is a private chamber in the wing. A gallery, in the thickness of one wall, opens into the hall. The second floor has contained an upper hall, now subdivided, a private room, and a long narrow mural chamber. Private chambers occupied the floors above.

There is a courtyard to the east, entered by a gateway dated 1726.

There was an earlier castle nearby [NJ 478245], said to have been held by the Comyns. The property belonged to the Gordons of Craig, one of whom, Patrick Gordon, died at the Battle of Flodden in 1513. His grandson, another Patrick, was killed at the Battle of Pinkie in 1547, and his son, William, was implicated with his chief, Huntly, in the murder of the Bonnie Earl of Moray at Donibristle in 1592. The Gordons held the property until 1892. The castle is still occupied, and in good condition.

There is reputedly a wishing well nearby [NJ 473245].
Other refs: Craig of Auchindoir Castle; Comyn's Craig

Craig Castle

Angus & Dundee: About 3.5 miles north of Alyth, on minor road and foot east of B954, south of River Isla, at or near Craig.
Ruin or site   NO 254527   OS: 53   *   Map: 8, no: 136
Site of castle, a property of the Ogilvies. It was apparently destroyed by the forces of James VI in 1595, then again in 1640 by the Earl of Argyll. The property passed to the Carnegies of Kinnaird in the 17th century.

Craig Castle *see* Craig House

Craig Castle *see* Castle Craig

Craig Douglas Castle

Borders: About 3.5 miles east of Cappercleuch, just north of the A708 at or near Craig Douglas, north of the Yarrow Water.
Ruin or site   NT 291249 [?]   OS: 73   *   Map: 2, no: 74
Nothing remains of Craig Douglas Castle, a stronghold of the Black Douglases. It was attacked without warning and destroyed by James II in 1450, when the Earl of Douglas was on pilgrimage to Rome. With the return of the Earl, his lands were restored, but after his treacherous murder by James II in 1452, the Black Douglases rebelled, but were eventually defeated at the Battle of Arkinholm and their lands forfeited.

This is one of the several castles associated with 'The Douglas Tragedy', an old and bloody ballad.

Craig House *see* Craighouse

Craig House

Angus & Dundee: About 1 mile south of Montrose, on minor road south of A92, just south of Montrose Basin, about 0.25 miles north of Kirkton of Craig, at Craig House.
Private   NO 704563   OS: 54   *   Map: 8, no: 269**
Craig House or Castle, has been a strong 17th-century courtyard castle, of which only two of the four sides remain. Two small square towers survive, probably from the 15th century, linked by a wall. These towers rise to three storeys and a garret, but one has a plain parapet with open rounds, while the other is crenellated. The towers have vaulted basements.

On two sides of the courtyard are three-storey blocks of the 17th century, although built on older foundations. One block is vaulted, containing four chambers, one of which was the kitchen. The hall would have occupied the floor above, and had a small stair down to the wine-cellar. The range is dated 1637.

A larger outer courtyard has two ruined round towers flanking the arched gateway.

The lands were held by the Woods, who built the original castle. Around 1617 it was acquired by the Carnegie Earls of Southesk. Lady Madelaine Carnegie married James Graham, Marquis of Montrose. The house is still occupied.
Other refs: Craig Castle

Craig of Auchindoir Castle *see* Craig Castle

Craig of Boyne Castle

Banff & Buchan: About 2.5 miles east of Portsoy, on minor roads north of B9139, just south of Boyne Bay, near Burn of Boyne, at Craig of Boyne.
Ruin or site   NJ 615660 [?]   OS: 29   *   Map: 10, no: 165
Craig of Boyne Castle is a very ruined 13th-century castle of enclosure of the Edmonstones (or the Comyns). When the Ogilvies of Dunlugas acquired the property around 1575, they built a new castle further up stream.

Craig of Inverugie *see* Ravenscraig Castle

Craigbarnet Castle

Lanarkshire & Glasgow area: About 2 miles west of Lennoxtown, on minor road just north of A891, at Craigbarnet.
Ruin or site   NS 594790   OS: 64   *   Map: 3, no: 273
Site of a large and important castle, replaced by a mansion in the 17th century, which itself was demolished in the 20th century except for a walled garden and barn.

The property was owned by the Stirlings, who were also granted the lands of Glorat in the 14th century. James IV visited in 1507. This branch of the family were keepers of Dumbarton Castle. Sir John Stirling of Craigbarnet, a friend of the Marquis of Montrose, abandoned the castle in 1660 and built a new mansion nearby. The mansion and the remains of the castle were removed in the 20th century when the site was cleared for tree-planting.

Craigcaffie Tower

Galloway: About 3 miles north-east of Stranraer, on minor road east of A77, about 0.25 miles from shore of Loch Ryan, at Craigcaffie.
Private   NX 089641   OS: 82   *   Map: 1, no: 16**
Craigcaffie Tower is a rectangular 16th-century tower house of three storeys and a garret. It has crenellated parapets on two sides, and open rounds at all four corners. A machiolation defends the entrance. There are corbiestepped gables and a steeply pitched roof; and it was defended by a ditch.

The entrance leads to a turnpike stair up to each floor. The basement is vaulted and the hall, on the first floor, has a moulded fireplace.

Robert the Bruce granted Craigcaffie to his illegitimate son, Neil, Earl of Carrick, from whom the Neilsons were descended. The Neilsons held the property until 1791, when it passed to the Dalrymple Earl of Stair. In the 19th century it was occupied by farm labourers. The tower has been restored and reoccupied.
Other refs: Kellechaffe

Craigcrook Castle

Lothians: About 2.5 miles west and north of Edinburgh Castle, on minor roads south of A90, north-east of Corstorphine Hill.
Private   NT 211742   OS: 66   **   Map: 4, no: 70
Craigcrook is a modified and extended 16th-century tower house, now Z-plan. It consists of a central block of three storeys, a projecting round tower at one corner, and a projecting square tower, although this been encased in later work. There are many other extensions and alterations.

The lands were held by the Grahams in the 14th century. The castle was probably built by the Adamson family, who were burgesses of Edinburgh. William Adamson of Craigcrook was killed at the Battle of Pinkie in 1547. Its owners have included Sir John Hall, Lord Provost of Edinburgh in 1689, as well as the Meins, Pringles, and Strachans, and Lord Jeffrey, the well-known judge and editor of the 'Edinburgh Review' who had William Playfair remodel the building. Walter Scott visited the castle. In the 19th century it was home to Archibald Constable, who started the

publishing firm. It was restored in 1989, but was recently put on the market.

Lord Jeffrey's ghost is said to haunt the building. Many disturbances have been reported in recent times, including unexplained footsteps and noises, things being moved around and thrown, and the doorbell ringing when nobody is apparently present. The library is also reputed to be unnaturally cold at times.

Craigdhu

Galloway: About 3 miles west of Whithorn, on minor road north of A747, at or near Craigdhu.

Ruin or site NX 401408 OS: 83 * Map: 1, no: 56

Little remains of a motte and bailey castle, said to have been used by the Bishops of Galloway.

Craigend Castle

Stirlingshire & Clackmannan: About 2.5 miles north of Milngavie, on minor roads between A81 and A809, about 0.25 miles north and west of Mugdock Castle, at Craigend.

Ruin or site NS 545778 OS: 64 * Map: 6, no: 20

Site of a castle, incorporated into a later mansion of 1812 designed by Alexander Ramsay for the Inglis family. The property was held by the Buchanan family in the 19th century. It was described as a splendid edifices, but only the stables survive as does Smith's folly. Craigend was used as a zoo before being abandoned and demolished.

OPEN: see Mugdock.

Craigends House

Renfrewshire: About 2.5 miles north-east of Kilbarchan, on minor roads south of B790 or east of B789, just south of River Gryffe, at Craigends.

Ruin or site NS 419662 OS: 64 * Map: 3, no: 161

Craigends House, a castellated mansion designed by David Bryce in 1857, was demolished in 1957. Only the stable blocks survive in a ruinous state, but the mansion had included old work, perhaps dating from 1477 or before.

The lands may have been a property of the Knoxes of Ranfurly, but had passed to the Cunninghams of Glencairn by the middle of the 15th century. Craigends was acquired by the Boyles of Kelburn in 1647, but later returned to the Cunninghams, who built the mansion. It was owned by the Glasgow publisher John Smith at one time.

Other refs: Old Craigends House

Craigentinny House

Lothians: About 3 miles east of Edinburgh Castle, in the Craigentinny area of Edinburgh, on minor roads west of the A199.

Private NT 290747 [?] OS: 66 ** Map: 4, no: 122

Craigentinny House is a much altered 16th-century L-plan tower house of three storeys and an attic, with a stair-turret in the re-entrant angle.

The original entrance, in the ground floor of the wing, leads to a wide stair to the first floor. The upper floors are reached by a turnpike stair, in the turret, in the re-entrant angle.

The castle was built by the Nisbets.

Craigenveoch Castle

Galloway: About 2.5 miles south-east of Glenluce, on minor roads east of A747, north side of Whitefield Loch, 1 mile south of Craigenveoch.

Ruin or site NX 237555 [?] OS: 82 * Map: 1, no: 36

Site of mansion, the site of which appears now to be forested. The house was built in 1876 for Admiral Sir John Dalrymple-Hay, but does not appear to have an older origin.

Craighall

Perth & Kinross: About 2 miles north of Blairgowrie [Rattray], on minor roads east of A93, just east of the River Erlicht, at Craighall.

Private NO 175480 OS: 53 * Map: 8, no: 113

Standing on a steep hill above a river, Craighall or Craighall-Rattray, a 19th-century mansion, incorporates part of a tower house. The castle was defended, on the landward side, by a ditch and towers.

It was a property of the Scotts of Balwearie, but passed to the Rattrays at the beginning of the 16th century – the Rattrays may have held the lands from the 11th century. Patrick Rattray of Craighall was driven from Rattray Castle in 1516 by the Earl of Atholl, who had him murdered in 1533. The family supported Charles I, and as a result the castle was besieged around 1650. Thomas Rattray of Craighall was Protestant Bishop of Dunkeld in 1627. Jacobites were sheltered at Craighall during the 1745 Rising. The family still occupy the castle.

Craighall

Fife: About 3 miles south-east of Cupar, on minor roads south of B939, about 0.5 miles south-east of Ceres, at Craighall.

Ruin or site NO 407107 OS: 59 * Map: 7, no: 108

Craighall incorporated a 16th-century tower house, but the whole classical mansion has been demolished. The basement of the old part was vaulted.

The castle was built by the Kinninmonds, but was sold in 1635 to the Hopes, one of whom was Sir Thomas Hope, King's Advocate to Charles II. Craighall was altered and extended at this time, then was remodelled by Sir William Bruce in 1697-90, but sold in 1729. Although an interesting ruin in the 20th century, it was demolished in 1955.

Craighlaw Castle

Galloway: About 7 miles east and north of Glenluce, on minor road west of B733, about 1.5 miles west of Kirkcowan, at Craighlaw.

Private NX 305611 OS: 82 ** Map: 1, no: 42

Craighlaw incorporates a square 16th-century tower house of three storeys and an attic, and has a stair-wing to the rear. The bartizans have been remodelled, and the tower much altered and extended.

The basement is vaulted, and contained the kitchen.

It was originally a property of the Mures, but was sold to the Gordons of Kenmure in 1513, and passed to the Hamiltons in 1741 and remains with them. It was enlarged and altered in 1870, and is still occupied.

Craighouse

Lothians: About 2 miles south and west of Edinburgh Castle, on minor roads west of A702, east of A70, on Craiglockhart Hill.

Private NT 234709 OS: 66 ** Map: 4, no: 82

Craighouse incorporates a much-altered 16th-century tower house. It consists of a narrow main block of four storeys with a square projecting stair-tower, and is dated 1565. To this has been added a lower extension, dated 1746.

The entrance is at the foot of the stair-tower. The basement is vaulted. The main turnpike stair rises to second-floor level, above which is a small turret stair.

The castle was built by the Symsons. In the 17th century Craighouse belonged to Lord Provost Sir William Dick, one of the wealthiest men of the day, who lost everything supporting Charles I, and the property passed to the Elphinstones. It was part of a psychiatric hospital, but is now a campus of Napier University.

In 1712 it was a property of Sir Thomas Elphinstone, who was married to the much younger Elizabeth Pittendale. Elizabeth is said to have fallen in love with Elphinstone's son John, and Sir Thomas caught them together. Thomas stabbed

Elizabeth to death in a terrible rage, although John escaped, and Sir Thomas committed suicide. John Elphinstone then inherited the property, and let the house, but a 'Green Lady', the spirit of Elizabeth, began to haunt the building. The hauntings only ceased when Elizabeth's remains were removed from the burial vault of her husband, and when John died he is said to have been buried beside her.
Other refs: Craig House

Craigie Castle

Ayrshire: About 4 miles south of Kilmarnock, on minor road north of B730, about 1 mile east of junction with A77, just east of Craigie Mains.
Ruin or site NS 408317 OS: 70 ** Map: 3, no: 150
Standing on a ridge, Craigie Castle consists of the ruins of a 13th-century groin-vaulted hall house and later castle. The hall house was vaulted in the 15th century, and remodelled into a tower house with ranges of outbuildings. The castle had two courtyards, and was defended by ditches.
  The groin-vaulted hall was once a fine chamber.
  The lands were held by a Walter Hose around 1150, but the original castle was probably built by the Lindsay family between 1230-40. It passed to the Wallaces of Riccarton in 1371, who had Blind Harry collect together stories and compile a poem about William Wallace, the famous freedom fighter. The castle was abandoned about 1600 when the Wallaces moved to Newton in Ayr.

Craigie Wood *see* Peelhill

Craigieburn

Dumfriesshire: About 2.5 miles east of Moffat, on minor road north of A708, north of Moffat Water, at Craigieburn.
Private NT 117053 OS: 78 * Map: 1, no: 237
Site of castle, nothing of which survives.
  Craigieburn House, a mansion, was the birthplace of Jean Lorimer, Robert Burns's 'Chloris', and Craigieburn Wood was frequented by Burns around 1789.
  The garden specialises in rare and unusual plants from south-east Asia. There is a fine gorge, sheltered woodland, formal borders, roses, a bog garden and alpines.
OPEN: Open Easter-Oct, Tue-Sun 12.30-18.00.
Plants for sale. Parking. £.
Tel: 01683 221250 Fax: 01683 221250

Craigievar Castle

Aberdeen & Gordon: About 4.5 miles south and west of Alford, on minor roads west of A980 1.5 miles north of junction with B9119, north of Rumblie Burn, at Craigievar.
NTS NJ 566095 OS: 37 *** Map: 10, no: 141**
A well-preserved and picturesque castle, Craigievar Castle is a massive L-plan tower house of seven storeys, and was completed in 1626. Turrets, gables, chimney-stacks and corbelling crown the upper storeys; in contrast to the lower storeys, which are completely plain. The walls are rounded at the corners, and are harled and pink-washed. The square tower, in the re-entrant angle, is crowned by a balustraded parapet enclosing a flat roof, with a caphouse topped by an ogee roof. The castle stood in a small courtyard, with round towers at the corners, one of which survives.
  The entrance, in the re-entrant angle, leads to a vestibule to three vaulted chambers, and to a straight stair in the centre of the house, which rises only to the first floor. The hall, with a private chamber, occupies the first floor, and is a magnificent vaulted apartment, with mixed groin- and barrel-vaulting, and a fine plaster ceiling. A narrow stair leads down to the wine-cellar, and there is a small minstrels gallery. The hall has a fine large fireplace with ornamental stone carving, and there is a laird's lug, reached from a narrow entrance in the adjoining passageway.
  The floors above are occupied by many private chambers, reached by five turret stairs. Many of these rooms are panelled.
  The property belonged to the Mortimer family from 1457 or earlier, and they held it until 1610. They began the castle, but ran out of money, and it was sold to the Forbeses of Menie, who finished the building in 1626. William Forbes, a zealous Covenanter, was responsible for the 'putting down' of Gilderoy the freebooter and his band, and having them hanged in Edinburgh. He commanded a troop of horse

in the Civil War, and was Sheriff of Aberdeen. Forbes of Brux and Paton of Grandhome, who were both Jacobites, hid in the laird's lug to avoid capture. The castle was taken over by The National Trust for Scotland in 1963.
  Craigievar is said to be haunted by a Gordon, who was murdered by being pushed from one of the windows of the Blue Room by Sir John Forbes – although it appears this window formerly had bars. Another ghost is said to be a fiddler, drowned in a well in the kitchen, who only appears to members of the Forbes family.
OPEN: Castle open, 13 Apr-Sep, daily 13.30-17.30; last admission 16.45; grounds open all year, daily 13.30-17.30.
Guided tours only. No coaches. No groups. £££.
Tel: 01339 883365

Craigievern Castle

Stirlingshire & Clackmannan: About 2 miles north-west of Drymen, on minor road north of A811, about 0.5 miles south of the Muir Park Reservoir, at Craigievern.
Private NS 495902 OS: 57 * Map: 6, no: 11
Little remains of Craigievern Castle, which was a property of the Buchanans.
  Craigievern is a T-plan 18th-century house.

Craiglockhart Castle

Lanarkshire & Glasgow area: About 0.5 miles north of Lanark, on minor roads and foot east of A73, north of Mouse Water, at Craiglockhart.
Ruin or site NS 875450 OS: 72 * Map: 3, no: 406
Site of castle of the Lockharts of The Lee. About 1900, it was a 'ruined, lofty, picturesque tower'.
  William Wallace is said to have held the castle before an attack on Lanark, and to have sheltered in nearby caves after murdering Hazelrigg, the English Sheriff of Lanark.
Other refs: Castle Qua; Castledykes

Craiglockhart Castle

Lothians: About 2.5 miles south-west of Edinburgh Castle, on minor road between A70 and A702, north of Craiglockhart Hill, north of Napier University.
Ruin or site NT 226703 OS: 66 ** Map: 4, no: 79
Craiglockhart Castle is a ruined square keep, dating from the 13th century, although it may be considerably older. The two lower storeys were vaulted.
  It was probably built by the Kincaids, but later passed to the Lockharts of The Lee.

Craigmaddie Castle

Lanarkshire & Glasgow area: About 2 miles north-east of Milngavie, on minor road east of A81, just east of Craigmaddie House.

Ruin or site NS 575765 OS: 64 ** Map: 3, no: 260

Not much remains of Craigmaddie Castle, a 16th-century tower house with a moat, except for the vaulted basement. It stands in the earthworks of a fort, and is overgrown.

The property belonged to the Galbraiths of Baldernock from 1238 or earlier, but passed by marriage to the Hamiltons of Cadzow in the 14th or early 15th century, who probably built the present castle. The family had moved to Bardowie by 1566.

Craigmill

Moray: About 4 miles south-east of Forres, near B9010, at or near Mains of Craigmill.

Ruin or site NJ 095542 OS: 27 * Map: 10, no: 14

Site of castle, a property of the Cummings or Comyns, of which there are no remains.

Craigmillar Castle

Lothians: About 3 miles south-east of Edinburgh Castle, on minor road south between A6095 and north of A68, just south of Craigmillar housing scheme.

His Scot NT 288709 OS: 66 ***** Map: 4, no: 121

A strong, imposing and well-preserved ruin, Craigmillar Castle consists of a 14th-century L-plan keep, surrounded by a 15th-century machiolated curtain wall with round corner towers. Early in the 16th century it was given an additional walled courtyard, protected by a ditch.

The keep is roofed with stone slabs, inside a parapet, and the stair is topped by a caphouse.

Domestic ranges were constructed around the courtyards.

The entrance to the keep is through a wide arched entrance, and leads to a vaulted lobby and to a turnpike stair. The basement is vaulted. The large hall, on the first floor, has a fine hooded moulded fireplace. The vaulted chamber in the wing was

once the kitchen. Another turnpike stair leads to the vaulted second floor.

The courtyard enclosed four-storey ranges, with vaulted basements, which contained a kitchen and a long gallery, as well as many other chambers.

The Prestons held the property from 1374, and built a new castle on the site of a much older stronghold. In 1477 James III imprisoned his brother John, Earl of Mar, in one of its cellars, where he died. The Earl of Hertford torched the castle in 1544, after valuables placed here by the citizens of Edinburgh had been seized. James V visited the castle to escape 'the pest' in Edinburgh. Mary, Queen of Scots, used Craigmillar often, and fled here in 1566 after the murder of Rizzio by, among others, her second husband Lord Darnley. It was also here that the Regent Moray, Borthwick and William Maitland of Lethington plotted Darnley's murder. Mary's son, James VI, also stayed here. In 1660 Sir John Gilmour bought Craigmillar, and had the castle altered into a comfortable residence.

A walled-up skeleton was found in one of the vaults in 1813.

OPEN: Open all year: Apr-Sep, daily 9.30-18.30; Oct-Mar, Mon-Wed and Sat 9.30-16.30, Thu 9.30-12.00, Sun 14.00-16.30, closed Fri; last ticket 30 mins before closing; closed 25/26 Dec and 1/2 Jan.
Exhibition and visitor centre. Gift shop. Car and coach parking. Group concessions. £.
Tel: 0131 661 4445 Fax: 0131 668 8888
Email: hs.explore@scotland.gov.uk Web: www.historic-scotland.gov.uk

Craigneach Castle

Moray: About 3 miles west of Charlestown of Aberlour, on minor roads south of B9102 or north of A95, 1 mile east of Carron, north of Spey River.

Ruin or site NJ 238425 [?] OS: 28 * Map: 10, no: 44

Not much remains of an L-plan tower house except for foundations. It may have been attacked and looted by Covenanters in 1645.

Other refs: Elchies Castle; Place of Elchies

Craigneil Castle

Ayrshire: About 5 miles north-east of Ballantrae, on minor roads south of A765 at Colmonell, just south of River Stinchar, near Craigneal.

Ruin or site NX 147853 OS: 76 ** Map: 3, no: 13

Standing on a rocky hill, Craigneil Castle is a ruined rectangular keep of four storeys, one corner of which fell into the adjacent quarry in 1886. It may date from as

early as the 13th century, although it appears to be substantially 15th century.

The hall, on the second floor, is vaulted. A turnpike stair rose in one corner.

Robert Bruce is said to have sheltered here during the Wars of Independence. It was a property of the Kennedys, and used as a half-way house for travellers between Cassillis and Castle Kennedy. The castle is said to have then been a prison and place of execution. By the end of the 19th century the property was held by the MacConnels of Knockdolian.

Craigneith Castle

Lanarkshire & Glasgow area: About 1.5 miles north-east of East Kilbride, on minor roads and foot south of A725, just east of the Rotten Calder, just west of Auchentibber.

Ruin or site NS 663553 OS: 64 * Map: 3, no: 311

Craigneith, a large mansion, incorporated a tower house, but little now remains.

Craignethan Castle

Craignethan Castle

Lanarkshire & Glasgow area: About 4.5 miles west and north of Lanark, on minor roads south of A72 at Crossford, on the north side of the River Neithan, just north of Tillietudlem.

His Scot NS 816464 OS: 72 ** Map: 3, no: 380**

Standing on a promontory above a deep ravine, Craignethan is an early castle built to withstand artillery. A strong tower was surrounded by a curtain wall on three sides, with a massively thick rampart protecting the landward side. There was also an outer courtyard.

The ruined main tower is squat and rectangular, with a corbelled-out parapet, open rounds at the corners, and a machiolation over the entrance.

The entrance leads, through a large lobby on the first floor, to the hall and to a turnpike stair by the guardroom. The kitchen is also on the first floor, and the basement is vaulted and contained cellars.

There were large flanking towers, only one of which survives, and a massively thick rampart before the tower, which has been completely demolished. The base of another flanking tower and of the gatehouse survive on one side. In the ditch, before the rampart, is a caponier, rediscovered in 1962 when the ditch was excavated. The crossing of the ditch was by a drawbridge, which led to the gatehouse. The outer courtyard consists of an enclosing wall with a gatehouse, a corner tower surmounted by a doocot, and another incorporated into a 17th-century house.

The property originally belonged to the Black Douglases, but passed to the Hamiltons with their forfeiture in 1455. Sir James Hamilton of Finnart, a talented architect and the King's Superintendent of Palaces, built most of the castle. Hamilton was beheaded for treason in 1540, although his son eventually inherited his lands. Mary, Queen of Scots, is said to have spent the night here before the Battle of Langside in 1568. The Hamiltons formed the main part of her army, but were defeated by the Regent Moray and Mary fled to England. The garrison of Craignethan surrendered after the battle, but the castle was retaken by the Hamiltons, then attacked in 1579 when given up without a siege. It was slighted, and much of the defences demolished. It was sold in 1665 to the Hays, who built the house in the outer courtyard. Sir Walter Scott featured Craignethan in 'Old Mortality', but called it 'Tillietudlem'. It passed into the care of the State in 1949.

The castle is said to be haunted by a headless ghost, perhaps the spirit of Mary, Queen of Scots, as well as other ghosts in the later house in the courtyard. The apparition of a woman wearing Stewart period dress has been witnessed in the courtyard, and other unexplained disturbances include pipe music and voices. Beware of the bogles in the toilets.

Other refs: Draffane

OPEN: Open Apr-Nov, daily 9.30-18.30; last ticket 30 mins before closing.

Exhibition and explanatory boards. Gift shop. Tearoom. Car parking. Group concessions. £.

Tel: 01555 860364 Fax: 0131 668 8888

Email: hs.explore@scotland.gov.uk Web: www.historic-scotland.gov.uk

Craignish Castle

Argyll & Dunbartonshire: About 4 miles west and north of Kilmartin, on minor road west of B8002, west of Loch Craignish, at Craignish Castle.

Private NM 773016 OS: 55 * Map: 5, no: 48**

Craignish Castle, a three-storey mansion of about 1832, incorporates the much-altered basement of a 16th-century tower house. The basement is vaulted, and there is a dungeon carved out of the rock.

It was a property of the Campbells, and withstood a six week siege by Alaisdair Colkitto MacDonald in the 1640s.

Craigoch

Galloway: About 8 miles south-east of Glenluce, just south of A747 on shore of Luce Bay, between Milton Point and Chippermore Point.

Ruin or site NX 305467 [?] OS: 82 * Map: 1, no: 41

Site of castle.

Craigoch Castle

Galloway: About 2 miles north of Leswalt, short distance east of B798 at Milton, just north of the Sole Burn.

Ruin or site NX 013668 OS: 82 * Map: 1, no: 7

Site of tower house.

There may have been another castle nearby [NX 014671], known as Auchengower or Auchingore, although this may be a confusion with Craigoch.

Other refs: Marslauch; Auchengower

Craigrownie Castle

Argyll & Dunbartonshire: To north-west of Kilcreggan, on minor roads west of B833, west of sea at Baron's Point, at south end of Loch Long, at Craigrownie.

Private NS 223813 OS: 63 * Map: 5, no: 124

Craigrownie Castle is a large castellated mansion, dating from about 1854. There does not appear to have been an older castle.

Craigs

Dumfriesshire: About 2 miles south-east of Dumfries, on minor roads south of A780 or east or north of B725, at or near Barnkin of Craigs.

Ruin or site NY 008726 OS: 84 * Map: 1, no: 196

Site of tower house, some remains of which survived in the 19th century.

Craigskean

Ayrshire: About 3.5 miles north of Maybole, on minor roads west of B7024, at Craigskean.

Ruin or site NS 299149 OS: 70 * Map: 3, no: 75

Site of castle, a vestige of which remained in the 19th century. Nothing now survives.

Craigston Castle

Banff & Buchan: About 4 miles north-east of Turriff, on minor road east of B9105, about 0.5 miles north-east of Fintry, at Craigston.

Private NJ 762550 OS: 29 ** Map: 10, no: 243**

An impressive fortress, Craigston Castle is a tall 17th-century tower house of five storeys and a garret. It consists of a main block with two projecting wings, these linked at fourth-floor level by an elaborate balcony supported on an archway. The roof is gabled, and there is a caphouse with a flat roof. The walls are harled; and the tower is dated 1607.

The basement is vaulted. The hall on the first floor has a series of carved wooden panels from the 17th century, although much of the interior decoration dates from the early 19th century.

The castle was a property of the Urquharts. One of the family was Captain John Urquhart, known as 'The Pirate' and born in 1696, was a Jacobite who had a narrow escape from death at the Battle of Sheriffmuir in 1715. Craigston is still occupied by the same family.

OPEN: By appt throughout the year: contact Mrs F. Morrison (01888 551640)

Guided tours. Explanatory displays. WC. Car and coach parking. ££.

Tel: 01888 551640 Fax: 01888 551717

Craigton

Stirling & Clackmannanshire: About 3 miles east of Callander, on minor road north of A84

Ruin or site NN 680054 OS: 57 * Map: 6, no: 49

Possible site of castle.

Crail Castle

Fife: In Crail, south of the A917, to the east of the harbour, near Castle Street and Castle Terrace, in Castle Garden.

Ruin or site NO 613074 OS: 59 * Map: 7, no: 162

Nothing remains of Crail Castle, except a fragment of masonry, which stood on the cliff top to the east of the harbour. It was used by David I, then Ada, mother of Malcolm IV and William I. By the 16th century it was ruinous, and given to the Spences of Wormiston, who may have rebuilt it. In 1706 it was demolished and the site reused, although part survived until the 19th century.

Other refs: Cunningham's

Crailloch

Galloway: About 2 miles east of Culshabbin, on minor road north of B7005, 1.5 miles east of Mochrum Loch, just east of Crailloch.

Ruin or site NX 326526 [?] OS: 82 * Map: 1, no: 46

Site of tower house, held by the Dunbars in 1539, on older motte.

Cramalt Tower

Borders: About 3 miles west of Cappercleuch, on minor road and submarine west of A708, in the Megget Reservoir.

Ruin or site NT 197227 OS: 72 * Map: 2, no: 43

Two ruined adjacent 16th-century tower houses were excavated, before the land was flooded by the Megget reservoir, but nothing remained except parts of the basement, with the start of a stair in one corner.

The lands were a property of the Hays, and the towers may have been used for hunting by James V and other kings of Scots.

Cramond Tower

Lothians: About 4 miles west and north of Edinburgh Castle, at Cramond, near shore of Firth of Forth, east of the mouth of the River Almond.

Private NT 191770 OS: 66 * Map: 4, no: 62**

Although part of a much larger castle at one time, Cramond Tower is a tall narrow

16th-century tower house, with a vaulted basement. It is located in the picturesque village of Cramond.

The property was owned by the Bishops of Dunkeld, but passed to the Douglases, and was then acquired in 1622 by an English merchant, John Inglis. His grandson abandoned the tower in 1680 for Cramond House, now the home of the Scottish Wildlife Trust. The tower became ruinous, but was consolidated by the local council, and finally restored and reoccupied in 1983.

Cramond is also the site of a Roman fort, remains having been found near Cramond Kirk, which itself has a 15th-century tower and interesting burial ground.

Other refs: Bishop's Tower, Cramond

Cranshaws Castle

Borders: About 0.5 miles west of Cranshaws, on minor road west of B6355, west of the Whiteadder Water, east of Cranshaws Hill.

Private NT 681619 OS: 67 * Map: 2, no: 277**

Cranshaws is an altered rectangular tower house, dating partly from the 15th century, of four storeys and a corbiestepped garret within a corbelled-out crenellated parapet. It has rounded corners, and was surrounded by a courtyard with ranges of buildings.

The entrance would have originally been beside the turnpike stair, which still rises in one corner. The basement was vaulted, but this has been removed, and the hall was on the first floor. The tower has been much altered inside.

Cranshaws was a property of the Swintons from 1400 until 1702, when it passed to the Douglases. The castle is supposed to have had a brownie, which undertook all

manner of chores. Having for a number of years gathered and threshed the corn, one of the servants complained that it was not neatly gathered. The next day the grain was found two miles away in the Whiteadder river, and the brownie abandoned the castle.

Cranston Castle *see* Oxenfoord Castle

Crathes Castle

Kincardine & Deeside: About 3 miles east of Banchory, on minor roads north of A93, about 0.5 miles north of River Dee, at Crathes.

NTS NO 734968 OS: 45 ** Map: 10, no: 233**

One of the finest surviving castles in Scotland, Crathes Castle is a massive 16th-century tower house of four storeys and an attic, square in plan, but with a small

projecting wing, to which later work has been added. The upper storeys are adorned with much corbelling, bartizans, stair-turrets and decoration, while the lower storeys are very plain, apart from a large modern window at first-floor level. There was an 18th-century wing, but this was burned out in 1966 and replaced by a two-storey range.

The basement is vaulted, and contained the old kitchen and cellars, the wine-cellar having a small stair to the hall above. The castle still has its iron yett. The hall is vaulted, and there is a 16th-century Italian fireplace. There are many fine tempera ceilings, and the top floor contains a long gallery.

The property was owned by the Burnets of Leys from the 14th century, their original castle being in the now drained Loch of Leys. The jewelled ivory 'Horn of Leys' is kept at Crathes, and was given to the Burnets in 1323 by Robert the Bruce. Around 1553 the family began to build the new castle, but it was not completed until 1596. It passed to The National Trust for Scotland in 1951.

One of the chambers, the Green Lady's room, is said to be haunted. The ghost reportedly first appeared in the 18th century, and is seen crossing the chamber, with a baby in her arms, to disappear at the fire-place. The young woman seems to have been a daughter of the then laird, and had been dallying with a servant. It appears that she was murdered to hide her pregnancy. A skeleton of a young woman and baby – or just the infant itself – were reportedly found by workmen under the hearthstone during renovations in the 19th century. The spectre is said to have been witnessed many times.

OPEN: Open Apr-Sep, daily 10.30-17.30; Oct, daily 10.30-17.30; last admission to castle 45 mins before closing; other times by appt only; grounds and garden open all year, 9.00-sunset. Timed ticket arrangement for castle; grounds may be closed at short notice on very busy days (limited parking).

Collections of portraits and furniture. Gift shop. Restaurant. Gardens, grounds and adventure playground. Plant sales. Disabled facilities, including access to ground floor and WC. Car and coach parking. £££

Tel: 01330 844525   Fax: 01330 881303

Email: information@nts.org.uk   Web: www.nts.org.uk

Craufurdland Castle

Ayrshire: About 2.5 miles north-east of Kilmarnock, on minor roads south of B7038 and west of A719, just north of the Craufurdland Water.

Private NS 456408 OS: 70 ** Map: 3, no: 188

Craufurdland Castle incorporates a much-altered 16th-century tower house, with a corbelled-out battlement, at one end, with extensions from the 17th century. It was remodelled as a castellated mansion, with further additions in the 18th and 19th centuries. A square gabled caphouse crowns the stair.

The basement is vaulted, but the tower has been much altered inside. The King's Room has a fine plaster ceiling with the date 1668.

The Crawfords held the property from the early 13th century. John Crawford of Craufurdland was killed at the Battle of Flodden in 1513. In 1793 the property passed to the Howiesons. The castle was restored in the 1980s, and is still occupied.

An underground passage is said to have connected the castle with Dean, some miles away.

Other refs: Crawfurdland Castle

Crawford Castle

Lanarkshire & Glasgow area: About 0.5 miles north of Crawford, on minor roads east of the A74, just north of the River Clyde, just south of Castle Crawford Farm.

Ruin or site NS 954213 OS: 72 ** Map: 3, no: 425

Little remains of Crawford Castle, located on an artificial mound and formerly surrounded by water. Parts of the walls survive to a height of three storeys. It was greatly altered in the 17th century, but abandoned at the end of the 18th century after being used as a farmhouse. It was partly demolished to provide materials for the present house.

The lands were a property of the Carmichaels, but passed to the Lindsays in the 12th century, who may have built a castle – although there may have been an even earlier stronghold here. The Carmichaels of Meadowflat were constables of the castle, and in 1297 William Wallace captured the stronghold from the English.

The property passed to the Douglas Earls of Angus in 1488, until they were forfeited in 1528. It was visited by James V, the king repaying the hospitality of the

keeper of the castle by making his daughter pregnant. After James's death the castle returned to the Earl of Angus, but in the 18th century the lands were sold to Sir George Colebrooke.
Other refs: Tower Lindsay; Lindsay Tower

Crawfordjohn *see* Boghouse Castle

Crawfordjohn Castle
Lanarkshire & Glasgow area: About 3.5 miles west of Abington, near B740 at Crawfordjohn, north of the Duneaton Water, at or near Crawfordjohn.
Ruin or site NS 879239 OS: 71 * Map: 3, no: 408
Site of castle, nothing of which survives, although there were some remains at the beginning of the 19th century. Materials from the castle were probably used to build nearby Boghouse [NS 878235].
   The lands were a property of John of Crawford in 1250, and there may have been a castle here, which had passed to the Crown by 1359. It was granted to the Douglases in 1366, but they were forfeited in 1455 and the property was apparently given to the Hamiltons, before passing to the Crawfords of Kilbirnie. It was exchanged with Sir James Hamilton of Finnart in 1533, and he probably built Boghouse using materials from here. The property was held by the Crown on Hamilton's execution in 1540, but returned to the Hamiltons in 1553, and they held the lands until 1693.
Other refs: Boghouse

Crawfordton Tower
Dumfriesshire: About 1 mile east of Moniaive, on minor road north of A702, just north of the Cairn Water, at or near Crawfordton.
Ruin or site NX 796905 [?] OS: 78 * Map: 1, no: 131
Site of tower. Crawfordton, a modern mansion, may stand on the site, and was held by the Walkers in the 19th century.

Crawfurdland Castle *see* Craufurdland Castle

Crawfurdsdyke *see* Cartsdyke

Creag an Fittick *see* Invergarry Castle

Creich Castle
Fife: About 5 miles north-west of Cupar, on minor roads north of A914, about 1 mile north of Luthrie, at Creich.
Ruin or site NO 329212 OS: 59 ** Map: 7, no: 83
Creich Castle is a ruined 16th-century L-plan tower house of three storeys and a collapsed garret, with a square stair-tower in the re-entrant angle. The tower formerly had corbelled-out bartizans, and a courtyard, being a place of some strength. The basement was vaulted, and there has been a turnpike stair.
   The Liddles originally owned the property, but were forfeited for treason and the property sold to the Beatons in 1502. One of the family, Elizabeth Beaton of Creich, was a mistress of James V and cousin to Cardinal David Beaton. Robert Beaton accompanied Mary, Queen of Scots to France in 1548, and later became Master of the Household. Mary Beaton was one of Mary, Queen of Scots 'Four Marys'.

Creich Castle *see* MacTire Castle

Crichton Castle
Lothians: About 2 miles east of Gorebridge, on minor road and footpath west of B6367, about 0.5 miles south-west of Crichton village.
His Scot NT 380612 OS: 66 ** Map: 4, no: 153**
A complex, large and interesting building, Crichton Castle consists of ranges of buildings from the 14th to 16th centuries, enclosing a small courtyard.
   The oldest part is a 14th-century keep, formerly of three storeys. The basement was vaulted, and had a pit-prison. A stair led up the hall and entrance on the first floor, and another turnpike stair led to the floors above. The castle had a small courtyard.
   In the 15th century a new gatehouse of three storeys was added, then further ranges enclosing the courtyard. Another block was added in the 16th century, Ital-

ian Renaissance in style, with an arcaded, diamond-faced facade.
   Outside the castle are the roofless stables, which are said to be haunted by the ghost of William Crichton.
   The castle was a property of the Crichtons, and probably first built about 1370. Sir William Crichton, Chancellor of Scotland, entertained the young Earl of Douglas and his brother before having them murdered at the 'Black Dinner' in Edinburgh Castle in 1440. John Forrester slighted the castle in retaliation. Crichton, however, founded the nearby Collegiate Church wherein priests were to pray for his salvation – he needed all the help he could get.
   The Crichtons were forfeited for treason in 1488, and the property later passed to Patrick Hepburn, Lord Hailes, who was made Earl of Bothwell. One of the family was James Hepburn, 4th Earl, third husband of Mary, Queen of Scots. In 1559 the castle was besieged and captured by the Earl of Arran and, after the Earl of Bothwell was forfeited, given to Francis Stewart, who added the Renaissance range. Mary, Queen of Scots, attended a wedding here in 1562. Francis Stewart was such a wild and unruly fellow that in 1595 he was also forfeited and he had to flee abroad. Crichton passed through many families, and became a romantic ruin: Turner painted the castle, and Walter Scott included it in 'Marmion'.
   The castle is said to be haunted by a horseman, who enters the castle by the original gate, which is now walled up.
OPEN: Open Apr-Sep, daily 9.30-18.30; last ticket 18.00.
Walk to property. Sales area. Car and coach parking. Group concessions. £
Tel: 01875 320017 Fax: 0131 668 8888
Email: hs.explore@scotland.gov.uk Web: www.historic-scotland.gov.uk

Cringletie House
Borders: About 2 miles north of Peebles, on minor roads west of A703, west of Eddleston Water, at or near Cringletie.
Private NT 234445 OS: 73 * Map: 2, no: 53
Site of tower house, on which was built Cringletie House, a castellated mansion, dating from 1861-3 and designed by David Bryce. The house is now used as a hotel.
   It was a property of the Murrays.
Other refs: Wester Wormiston
OPEN: Hotel.
Tel: 01721 730233 Fax: 01721 730244

Crockness *see* Martello Towers, Orkney

Croft *see* Castle Croft

Croft an Righ House
Lothians: About 1 mile east of Edinburgh castle, on minor roads south of A1, short distance east of Holyroodhouse, north side of Holyrood Park.
Private NT 271742 OS: 66 ** Map: 4, no: 113
Near to Holyrood Palace, Croft an Righ House is a much-altered early 17th-century L-plan tower house. It consists of a main block of two storeys and an attic and a

wing rising a storey higher. Two of the corners are crowned with bartizans, one of which has shot-holes.

The original entrance, now sealed, was in the re-entrant angle. The basement does not appear to have been vaulted, and the hall, on the first floor of the main block, has a fine plaster ceiling.

The house was probably built for James Stewart, Earl of Moray and Regent of Scotland. It is now used to house an area office of Historic Scotland.

Croftsike
Dumfriesshire: About 4 miles north of Gretna, on minor roads south of B6357, east of River Sark, at or near Croftsike.
Ruin or site NY 337744 [?] OS: 85 * Map: 1, no: 307
Probable site of tower house.

Cromarty Castle
Ross & Cromarty: About 0.5 miles south-east of Cromarty, on minor roads east of A832 on the Black Isle, at the mouth of the Cromarty Firth, at Cromarty House.
Ruin or site NH 794670 OS: 27 * Map: 9, no: 123
Nothing remains of Cromarty Castle, a strong L-plan tower house, which partly dated from the 12th or 13th century. It had bartizans and a parapet. A corbiestepped gabled block and other buildings were added in 1632. The castle was demolished in 1772, and Cromarty House, an imposing classical symmetrical mansion, built.

The property was owned by the Urquharts from the 1450s, although there had been a royal castle here from at least the 12th century. The Urquharts, however, lost everything as predicted by the Brahan Seer, and the property was sold to the Murray Lord Elibank in 1763, then in 1771 to the Ross family, who demolished the castle and built the mansion.

The old castle was said to be haunted by manifestations such as groans, cries and moans, and apparitions were also said to have been witnessed.

Crombie Castle
Banff & Buchan: About 2 miles west of Aberchirder, on minor roads north of B9117 or south of A9023, west of Crombie Burn, at Crombie.
Ruin or site NJ 591522 OS: 29 * Map: 10, no: 154**
Crombie Castle consists of an altered 16th-century L-plan tower house, with a later extension in the courtyard. Although the roof has been altered, one gable is crowned by open rounds and a machiolation defends the entrance. The walls are pierced by many gunloops and shot-holes.

The entrance, in the re-entrant angle, leads to the main stair and to a vaulted basement. The basement contains the kitchen, with a large arched fireplace and ovens; and the wine-cellar, with a small stair to the altered hall on the first floor.

Crombie was an Innes property, and James Innes of Crombie, who probably built the house, was killed at the Battle of Pinkie in 1547. A later owner, Alexander Innes, was brutally murdered in Aberdeen by his kinsman, Innes of Innermarkie. Crombie passed to the Urquhart family in 1631, then to the Meldrums, then the Duffs. The castle is roofed, but not occupied.

Cromwell's Citadel *see* Leith

Cromwell's Fort *see* Inverness Castle

Crooks Castle
Dumfriesshire: About 6.5 miles north-west of Langholm, on minor roads north of B709, east of Megget Water, at or near Crooks.
Ruin or site NY 296921 [?] OS: 79 * Map: 1, no: 293
Site of castle, some remains of which survived in the 18th century.
Other refs: Crucks

Crookston Castle
Lanarkshire & Glasgow area: About 3 miles east of Paisley, on minor roads east of the A736, on the south bank of the Levern Water, off Brockburn Road, in Crookston.
NTS NS 524628 OS: 64 * Map: 3, no: 233**
Surrounded by a large ditch, Crookston Castle is an unusual ruined irregularly-shaped 13th-century keep. It formerly rose to at least three storeys, and was strength-

ened by towers, only one of which is fairly intact, at the corners, making it X-plan. The entrance was defended by two doors and a portcullis. The basement is barrel-vaulted, with splayed ribs, and the hall, on the first floor, is also vaulted and has a large fireplace and windows with stone seats. A turnpike stair, in one corner of the hall, leads to the chambers above and to the towers. One tower has a small stair leading to a guardroom and a pit-prison.

The estate belonged to Robert de Croc in the 12th century, passing by marriage in the 13th century to the Stewarts. During the rebellion of the Earl of Lennox in the 15th century, James IV bombarded the castle with the large cannon, Mons Meg, leading to a quick surrender. The damage included the virtual destruction of two of the corner towers. The castle was seized in 1544 by the Regent Arran and Cardinal Beaton, while the Earl of Lennox was besieged in Glasgow Castle.

It was held by Henry Stewart, Lord Darnley, second husband of Mary, Queen of Scots. They may have been betrothed here, rather than at Wemyss Castle, or have stayed here after their marriage. Crookston passed through many families, including the Graham Dukes of Montrose, who in 1757 sold it to the Maxwells of Pollok. The castle became ruinous, but was partly restored in 1847 to commemorate Queen Victoria's first visit to Glasgow. Gifted to The National Trust in 1931, it was their first property.

Administered by Historic Scotland.

OPEN: Access at all reasonable times – collect key from keeper (Mrs McCourt) at bottom of path. Administered by Historic Scotland.
Parking nearby.
Tel: 0141 883 9606/0131 668 8800   Fax: 0131 668 8888
Email: hs.explore@scotland.gov.uk   Web: www.historic-scotland.gov.uk

Crookston Old House
Borders: About 6.5 miles west and north of Lauder, just south of B6368, about 0.5 miles east of junction with A7, east of Gala Water.
Ruin or site NT 425522 OS: 73 ** Map: 2, no: 108
Crookston Old House incorporates a 15th-century keep. It was extended in the 17th century, again in the 19th century, and is now a T-plan house of three storeys and a garret.

The basement has been vaulted, and there is a turnpike stair near the original entrance.

The castle was built by the Borthwicks around 1446.
Other refs: Old Crookston House

Crosbie Castle
Ayrshire: About 1.5 miles north-east of West Kilbride, on minor roads north of B781, just south of the Crosbie reservoir, at Crosbie.
Private NS 217500 OS: 63 ** Map: 3, no: 40
Crosbie incorporates a 17th-century L-plan tower house of two-storeys, with the off-centre stair-wing rising a storey higher. A large 19th-century mansion adjoins the castle. The house was used as a Youth Hostel at one time, and is now in the middle of a caravan park.

Crosbie was a property of the Crawfords of Auchenames. William Wallace sheltered here from the English in an earlier castle. The treacherous murder by the English of Wallace's uncle – who held the property – led to the torching of the Barns of Ayr in revenge, and the slaughter of many Southrons.
Other refs: Corsby

Crosbie House

Ayrshire: About 1.5 miles south-east of Troon, on minor roads east of B749 or
west of A78, west of Fullarton House, at Crosbie.
Ruin or site NS 344301 OS: 70 ** Map: 3, no: 109
Not much remains of a tower house, except part of the basement which was used
as an icehouse. The basement was vaulted. It was replaced by Fullarton House,
which was built in 1745, extended in later centuries, but demolished in 1966.
  Crosbie was a property of the Crawfords, but passed to the Fullertons in the 13th
century. They held the property until 1805, when it passed to the Bentinck Dukes
of Portland.
Other refs: Place of Fullarton; Fullarton House

Crossbasket Castle

Lanarkshire & Glasgow area: About 2 miles north-east of East Kilbride, on minor
roads north of B7012, on the east bank of the Calder Water.
Private NS 665563 OS: 64 ** Map: 3, no: 314
Crossbasket Castle consists of an altered 16th-century tower house of three storeys
and a garret within a corbelled-out parapet. To this a large 19th-century mansion
has been added. The walls are harled, and a caphouse crowns one corner. Most
windows have been enlarged.
  The interior has been much altered. The basement was vaulted, and the hall was
on the first floor.
  It was a property of the Lindsays of Dunrod, whose main seat was Mains, and used
as a dower house. It now houses a nursery and stores donations for the American-
based 'Missionaries of the Latter Day Rain'.

Crossdykes

Dumfriesshire: About 7 miles north-east of Lockerbie, on minor roads north of
B7068 or south of B709, east of Crossdykes Burn, at or near Crossdykes.
Ruin or site NY 242875 [?] OS: 79 * Map: 1, no: 272
Site of tower house.

Crossraguel Abbey

Ayrshire: About 2 miles south-west of Maybole, just south of the A77, at
Crossraguel.
His Scot NS 275084 OS: 70 ** Map: 3, no: 60
The Abbey, founded in the 13th century by Duncan, Earl of Carrick, has two forti-
fied buildings within its grounds.
  The 16th-century gatehouse, built by Abbot William Kennedy, is a square tower
house of three storeys and a garret within a parapet. A round tower is crowned by
a watch-chamber. The walls are pierced by gunloops.
  The Abbot's Tower, a 16th-century tower house, has a vaulted basement and hall,
and was remodelled by Abbot William Kennedy.
  Allan Stewart, Commendator of the abbey, was roasted 'in sop' in Dunure Castle
by the Kennedy Earl of Cassillis until he signed over the lands of the dissolved
abbey to the Kennedys. Substantial remains of the church, cloister, chapter house
and some of the domestic buildings survive.
Other refs: Abbot's Tower, Crossraguel
OPEN: Open Apr-Sep, daily 9.30-18.30; last ticket sold 18.00.
Exhibition. Sales area. WC. Parking. £.
Tel: 01655 883113 Fax: 0131 668 8888
Email: hs.explore@scotland.gov.uk Web: www.historic-scotland.gov.uk

Crucks *see* Crooks Castle

Cruggleton Castle

Galloway: About 2.5 miles south of Garlieston, on foot 0.5 miles east of B7063,
about 0.5 miles south-east of Cruggleton, on shore of Wigtown Bay.
Ruin or site NX 484428 OS: 83 ** Map: 1, no: 81
Standing on a cliff-girt promontory, little remains of Cruggleton Castle, except foundations of a 13th-century courtyard castle, with the basement of a 15th-century
keep, and 16th-century ranges enclosed within the walls. The site had been used as
an Iron Age fort, and the castle is said to have had eight towers at one time.
  The Lords of Galloway had a castle here, but it passed to the Comyns. The castle
is said to have been captured by Edward I of England, then recaptured by William

Wallace. The Comyns were forfeited by Robert the Bruce, and the original castle
was probably destroyed by Edward Bruce, Robert's brother. The property passed
to the Douglases, and the keep was built in the 1370s by Archibald the Grim, Lord
of Galloway. The castle was destroyed around 1455 after the Douglases had been
forfeited and defeated by James II.
  By the late 16th century the castle had been rebuilt. Robert Stewart, the Commendator of Whithorn Priory, was besieged here by John, 5th Lord Fleming, who
was trying to acquire the priory's lands. Later Stewart of Garlies captured Cruggleton in a surprise night attack. In 1591 the castle was occupied by James Kennedy,
who was denounced as an outlaw after he seized Alexander Myrtoun and imprisoned him in the castle dungeon.
  The property later passed to the Agnews of Lochnaw. The castle was abandoned,
ruinous by the 1680s, then plundered for materials. The site was excavated in 1978-
82.
  Cruggleton Church is the most complete Romanesque church in the area, and
although ruined before 1890, has been restored.
OPEN: Open all year – check at Cruggleton Farm

Cruivie Castle

Fife: About 1 mile north of Balmullo, on minor roads north of A92, just west of
South Straiton Farm.
Ruin or site NO 419229 OS: 59 ** Map: 7, no: 117
Cruivie Castle consists of a massive ruined 15th-century keep, formerly of four sto-
reys, and a later wing making it L-plan, probably dating from the 16th century. The
entrance is in the main block at first-floor level.
  The property passed by marriage from the Kinloch family to the Sandilands of
Calder around 1490. It was granted in 1540 to the Ramsays by James V, but around
1583 passed to the Carnegies of Colluthie, later Earls of Southesk.
Other refs: Cruvie Castle

Crumhaugh Tower

Borders: About 1.5 miles south-west of Hawick, near A7, south of the River
Teviot, about 0.3 miles north of Martinshouse.
Ruin or site NT 485138 [?] OS: 79 * Map: 2, no: 147
Crumhaugh is a very ruined 16th-century tower house.

Cruvie Castle *see* Cruivie Castle

Cubbie Roo's Castle

Orkney: On north side of the island on Wyre in Orkney, on minor roads 0.5 miles
south-east of pier, at Cubbie Roo's Castle.
His Scot HY 442264 OS: 6 ** Map: 11, no: 46
Standing on a small ridge, Cubbie Roo's Castle consists of a small 12th-century
keep surrounded by several rock-cut ditches. The keep is square in plan, and the
entrance would have been at first-floor level. The basement was not vaulted, and
would have been reached from the first-floor above. The keep was extended, and
there are foundations of later buildings.
  The name Cubbie Roo is a corruption of Kolbein Hruga, who built the tower
about 1150, as mentioned in the Orkneyinga Saga. The assassins of Earl John Har-
aldsson sought refuge here in 1231, and managed to fend off attacks by the Earl's
friends. Orkney was still held by the Norse, at this time, and did not become part of
Scotland until 1468.
  The nearby ruined Romanesque chapel of St Mary dates from the 12th century.
Other refs: Cobbie Row's Castle; Kolbein Hruga's Castle
OPEN: Access at all reasonable times.
Tel: 0131 668 8800 Fax: 0131 668 8888
Email: hs.explore@scotland.gov.uk Web: www.historic-scotland.gov.uk

Cuilean Castle *see* Culzean Castle

Culbin

Moray: About 3 miles north-west of Forres, on minor roads and foot north of
A96, north-west of Wellhill, in Culbin Forest.
Ruin or site NH 995615 [?] OS: 27 * Map: 10, no: 3
Site of castle or old house, which was buried in sand along with much of the estate.

The lands were a property of the de Moravia family or Murrays from the 13th century or earlier until they passed by marriage to the Kinnairds in the 15th, who held it until the end of the 17th century. By then sand had overrun most of the lands, some 9500 acres in total. The whole area is now covered in trees. Walter Kinnaird and his wife Elizabeth Innes have a fine tombstone, dated 1613, in Dyke kirkyard.

The forest is managed by Forest Enterprise and accessible to the public, and contains the highest sand dune system in Britain, and has over 550 different species of flowering plants and more than 130 species of lichen. The forest also features conifers and broad-leaved trees as well as open spaces, and is home to roe deer, badgers, red squirrels, wildcats, pine martins and otters. There are wildlife ponds.

Culcreuch Castle

Stirlingshire & Clackmannan: About 0.5 miles north of Fintry, on minor roads west of B822, west of the Fintry Hills, about 0.25 miles north of the Endrick Water, at Culcreuch.
Private NS 620876 OS: 57 * Map: 6, no: 40**
Set in 1600 acres of park land below the Fintry Hills, Culcreuch Castle consists of an

altered 15th-century keep of three storeys and a garret within a corbelled-out parapet. It has been altered, with the insertion of larger windows, and then extended in the 18th century. The original entrance, which has been built into later work, led to the barrel-vaulted basement, and to the main stair to the first-floor hall.

Culcreuch was a property of the Galbraiths of Culcreuch, but sold to the Setons in 1630, then to the Napiers two years later. In 1796 it was acquired by Alexander Speirs, who built a large and profitable cotton mill on his estate, but had passed from the family by 1875. The fine building is now a hotel, and has the largest colony of bats in Britain living in the roof area above the dining room. The Chinese Bird Room, within the old part of the building, has hand-painted Chinese wallpaper dating from 1723, believed to be the only surviving example of this period in Scotland.

The castle is reputed to have several ghosts. The Phantom Harper of Culcreuch relates to events believed to have taken place in 1582. One of the Buchanan family was mortally wounded by Robert Galbraith, son of the 16th chief. The dying man was taken to what is now the Chinese Bird Room, accompanied by his mistress. When he died, to comfort herself she began to play a wire-strung harp, known as a clarsach in Gaelic – and it is said that her soft music has often been heard since, particularly in the dead of night. The music has been reported from this and its adjoining room and also in the Laird's Hall.

Sightings of the apparition of a severed animal head have also been reported, which apparently flies around the battlements. Another manifestation is that of a cold grey mass, about the height and proportions of a human. This has been reported in all areas of the old castle.

OPEN: Hotel – open all year and to non-residents; country park –

open all year.
10 rooms with ensuite facilities. Restaurant and 2 bars. Meetings, functions, weddings and parties. Gift shop. Self-catering lodges. Country park. Disabled access to function suite, ground-floor bar and WC, as well as ground-floor bedroom. Large conference centre. Parking.
Tel: 01360 860228/555   Fax: 01360 860556
Email: david@culcreuch.com   Web: www.culcreuch.com

Cullen Castle *see* Castle of Cullen of Buchan

Cullen Castle *see* Cullen House

Cullen Castle

Moray: About 0.5 miles west of Cullen, just south of A98, on west side of Burn of Deskford, south of Seatown.
Ruin or site NJ 509670 [?] OS: 29 * Map: 10, no: 113
Site of a royal castle on motte, a vestige of which remained in the 19th century. There are traces of a ditch and rampart.

It was here that Elizabeth de Burgh, second wife of Robert the Bruce, died. Bruce founded a chapel nearby, at which prayers were to be said for her 'in perpetuity'.
Other refs: Seatown Castle; Castle Hill, Cullen

Cullen House

Banff & Buchan: About 0.5 miles south-west of Cullen, on minor roads west of A98, east of Burn of Deskford, south of Old Cullen, at Cullen House.
Private NJ 507663 OS: 29 * Map: 10, no: 111**
Situated on a strong site above a deep ravine, Cullen House incorporates an altered 16th-century L-plan tower house. It consists of a main block, of four storeys, and a stair-wing with a watch-chamber and bartizans which rise a storey higher. To this has been added very large wings in the 18th century. Additions were made by Robert Adam, then again in 1861 by David Bryce, until the house had 386 rooms.

The interior has been altered, but the basement would have been vaulted, and contained the kitchen and cellars.

The property passed by marriage from the Sinclairs to the Ogilvies of Auchleven, who built the castle. The family became Earls of Findlater. In 1645 the house was plundered by Royalists. James Ogilvie, 4th Earl of Findlater, was one of those responsible for union of the Scottish and English parliaments in 1707: he had been made Earl of Seafield in 1701. The castle was pillaged again in 1745 during the Jacobite Rising. The house was finally sold by the family in 1981, and was converted into flats in 1984-5. It was damaged by fire in 1987.

It is reputed that the ghost of the 3rd Earl haunts the castle. Although in good health most of the time, he suffered from bouts of uncontrollable insanity, and during one of these murdered his factor in 1770, and later killed himself. His ghost was said to have been seen in 1943, and ghostly footsteps have reportedly often been heard, including by journalists in 1964.
Other refs: Cullen Castle; Invercullen

Cullochan Castle

Dumfriesshire: About 3.5 miles west of Dumfries, on minor roads north of A75, just north of the Carogen Water, south of Cullochan hamlet.
Ruin or site NX 920755 OS: 84 * Map: 1, no: 178
Little remains of a 16th-century tower house on a motte.
Other refs: Collochan Castle

Culloden House

Inverness & Nairn: About 3.5 miles east of Inverness, on minor roads south of A96, in Culloden village, about 2 miles north-west of battlefield, at Culloden House Hotel.
Private NH 721465 OS: 27 ** Map: 9, no: 109
Culloden House, dating mostly from 1772-83, incorporates the cellars of a 17th-century tower house, and is set in 40 acres of park land.

Culloden was a property of the Mackintoshes, but sold in 1626 to the Forbes family. Duncan Forbes of Culloden, Provost of Inverness, was a Hanoverian, who fought with Butcher Cumberland at the Battle of Culloden. Many wounded Jacobites were brought here after the battle, and then shot: those who were not killed had their skulls bashed in with musket butts – Forbes, however, was against the slaughter. The house had many Jacobite mementoes, and is now used as a hotel.

The house is reputedly haunted by the ghost of Bonnie Prince Charlie, although this is disputed. The apparition of a man, dressed in tartan, is supposed to have been witnessed on several occasions in the passages, bedrooms and lounge.

OPEN: Hotel – open all year and to non-residents.

28 rooms with private facilities. Restaurant. Parking.

Tel: 01463 790461 Fax: 01463 792181

Email: USER@CULLODENHOUSE.CO.UK

Web: WWW.CULLODENHOUSE.CO.UK

Culnaha *see* Pitcalnie

Culnauld *see* Pitcalnie

Culrain Lodge *see* Carbisdale Castle

Culross Abbey House *see* Culross Palace

Culross Palace

Fife: In village of Culross, on minor roads north of B9037, on north side of Firth of Forth, at Culross Palace.

NTS NS 986862 OS: 65 * Map: 7, no: 5

Set in the picturesque village of Culross on the banks of the Forth, The Palace, although built between 1597 and 1611, does not apparently have any fortified fea-

tures, although one range is vaulted. The complex consists of ranges of gabled yellow-washed buildings, with decorative paint work and original interiors. There is an unusual steeply terraced garden.

The Palace was built for Sir George Bruce of Carnock, who made a fortune from coal mining, but about 1700 it passed to the Erskines. The building has been carefully restored by The National Trust for Scotland.

The NTS has a visitor centre and exhibition in the Town House of 1626, and the house of 1610, called The Study, is also open to visitors. Many other 16th- and 17th-century houses survive in the narrow streets of this ancient royal burgh.

Nearby is Culross Abbey House [NS 989862], which dates from 1608 and was built for Edward Bruce, Lord Kinloss. It was formerly an impressive building, but ruinous about 1800. It was altered in 1830, and again in 1955 when much reduced.

Other refs: Culross Abbey House

OPEN: Palace open Apr-Sep, 1-12 Apr, 17 Apr-May and Sep, daily 12.30-16.30, 13-16 Apr and Jun-Aug, daily 10.00-17.00; Oct, Sat-Sun 12.30-16.30; last admission 1 hr before closing; shop and tearoom open at 11.00 when palace opens at 12.30; Town House and Study same hours but last admission 15 mins before closing; groups at other times by appt.

Audio-visual show. Explanatory displays. Tea room. Town trail. Induction loop & Braille guide. ££. Combined ticket for Palace, Study and Town House available (£££).

Tel: 01383 880359 Fax: 01383 882675

Email: information@nts.org.uk Web: nts.org.uk

Culsalmond *see* Newton House

Culsalmond

Aberdeen & Gordon: About 9.5 miles south-east of Huntly, near A96 south of junction with A920, near River Urie, at or near Culsalmond.

Private NJ 650320 [?] OS: 29 * Map: 10, no: 176

Site of 16th-century castle, probably a property of the Gordons. The site may be at Newton House [NJ 661297], a late 17th-century house of four storeys and an attic.

Other refs: Newton House

Culzean Castle

Ayrshire: About 4.5 miles west of Maybole, on minor roads north of A77, in Culzean Country Park, on the shore of the Firth of Clyde.

NTS NS 233103 OS: 70 ** Map: 3, no: 48

Pronounced 'Cul-lane', Culzean Castle, a magnificent sprawling castellated mansion built between 1777-92, incorporates part of a 16th century L-plan tower house, which itself was built on the site of an older castle.

It was a property of the Kennedys from the 12th century, and they may have had stronghold here from then. Thomas Kennedy of Culzean was murdered by the Mure Lord Auchendrane in the course of a feud after the slaying of Kennedy of Bargany. The castle was completely rebuilt, although it incorporates much of the old castle, for the 9th and 10th Earls of Cassillis by Robert Adam. It passed to The National Trust for Scotland in 1945. A flat within the building was reserved for use by President Dwight Eisenhower for his services to Britain during World War II. The elegant interior includes the spectacular Oval Staircase and the Circular Saloon.

A ghostly piper is said to herald when one of the Kennedys is about to get married, and to play on stormy nights. His apparition has reportedly been seen in the grounds. There are reputedly two others ghosts who haunt the castle, one a young woman dressed in a ballgown. Sightings of a ghost were reported in 1972.

There is a country park and visitor centre: Culzean is one of the foremost attractions in Scotland.

Other refs: Cuilean Castle

OPEN: Castle, visitor centre, restaurants and shops open Apr-Oct 10.30-17.30, last admission 16.30; Mar, Nov and Dec, Sat-Sun: castle guided tours every 30 mins 12.00-14.30; other times by appt; walled garden closed at 17.00; shops and coffee shop also open Jan-Mar and Nov-Dec, Sat and Sun 12.00-16.00. Park open all year daily 9.30-sunset.

Fine interiors. Collections of paintings and furniture. Gift shops. Two restaurants. WC. Picnic areas. Gardens and adventure playground. Country park and visitor centre – one of the foremost attractions in Scotland. Car and coach parking. Group concessions. £££.

Tel: 01655 760274/269 Fax: 01655 760615

Email: information@nts.org.uk Web: nts.org.uk

Cumberland House *see* Provost Skene's House, Aberdeen

Cumbernauld Castle

Lanarkshire & Glasgow area: In Cumbernauld, on minor roads south of A80, near Cumbernauld House.

Ruin or site NS 773759 OS: 64 * Map: 3, no: 367

Little remains of Cumbernauld Castle, except for two vaulted chambers and some other buildings which are incorporated into Cumbernauld House. The house dates from the 18th century, and was designed by William Adam.

The lands passed from the Comyns to the Flemings in 1306, and the family moved here from Kirkintilloch in 1371. Sir Malcolm Fleming of Cumbernauld was murdered at the Black Dinner in Edinburgh Castle along with his friends, the Earl of Douglas and his brother, in 1440. One of the family was Mary Fleming, one of the 'Four Marys' of Mary, Queen of Scots, and Queen Mary visited the castle. The Flemings fought for Mary at Langside in 1568. The family were made Earls of Wigtown in 1606. The National Covenant was signed at Cumbernauld in 1646, and the building was burned out in 1746 by government dragoons after the Jacobite Rising. The property passed to the Elphinstones in 1747, then to Lord Inverclyde. The castle was superseded by Cumbernauld House, and by the end of 19th century the property had passed to Burns of Kilmahew. It is now used as offices.

Cumnock Castle *see* Black Bog Castle

Cumstoun Castle
Galloway: About 1.5 miles north of Kirkcudbright, on minor roads north of A755 and south of A75, just west of River Dee, at Cumstoun.
Ruin or site   NX 683533   OS: 84   **   Map: 1, no: 112
Little remains of Cumstoun Castle, a ruined 16th-century tower house, formerly of four storeys and an attic.

It was held by the Kennedys, MacLellans, and Dunbars, although it was a property of the Montgomerys in 1595, and had passed to the Maitlands by the 18th century. The castle was replaced by Compstone, a 19th-century mansion, which was still held by the Maitlands of Dundrennan in the 20th century.
Other refs: Compstone Castle

Cunningar
Aberdeen & Gordon: About 8 miles north of Banchory, just south of B9119, 0.5 miles north and west of Midmar Castle, at Cunningar.
Ruin or site   NJ 701060   OS: 38   *   Map: 10, no: 210
Site of castle on motte, which dates from the 12th century. It may have been replaced by Midmar Castle, and is said to have been abandoned by the end of the 16th century because of plague.

Midmar belonged to the Browns from the 13th century until 1422 when it passed to the Gordons, then to the Forbes, later to the Grants, then eventually to the Gordons of Cluny.
Other refs: Midmar

Cunninghamhead *see* Busbie Tower

Cunningham's *see* Crail Castle

Cupar Castle
Fife: In Cupar, north of A91, on Castlehill.
Ruin or site   NO 376146   OS: 59   *   Map: 7, no: 101
Site of 12th- or 13th-century royal castle, held by the MacDuff Earls of Fife, on School Hill. It was captured by Edward I of England in 1296, then visited by the future Edward II in 1303. The castle was still in use in 1339, and the court of the Stewartry of Fife was held here until 1425.

Castlehill was where 'Ane Pleasant Satyre of the Thrie Estaitis', by David Lindsay of The Mount, was first performed.

One tale sets the castle as the place where MacDuff's wife and children were murdered by Macbeth, but Dunimarle is a more likely location – if such an event ever took place.

There may have been another castle nearby, Well Tower [NO 374148], which appears on an old map of Cupar.
Other refs: Well Tower, Cupar

Curriehill Castle
Lothians: About 1 mile north of Balerno, north of the A70, near the outskirts of Currie.
Ruin or site   NT 165678 [?]   OS: 65   *   Map: 4, no: 50
Site of castle of the Skene family. It was held against Mary, Queen of Scots by the family. Sir John Skene of Curriehill was a prominent 16th-century lawyer, and appointed to the Supreme Court Bench in 1594. He was knighted and made a baronet of Nova Scotia. Other occupants included the Johnston Lord Warriston; James Anderson; General Thomas Scott of Malleny; and John Marshall, Lord Curriehill.
Other refs: Currie Hill

Cushnie Castle
Aberdeen & Gordon: About 6 miles west and south of Alford, on minor roads west of A980, in Glen of Cushnie, near the Cushnie Burn.
Private   NJ 525111   OS: 37   **   Map: 10, no: 122
Not much remains of Cushnie Castle, a 16th-century tower house, except a vault.

The existing House of Cushnie (or Cushnie Lodge) dates from the 17th or early 18th century.

The property passed by marriage from the Cushnie family – who had held the lands from the 12th century or earlier – to the Leslies in the early 14th century, but in 1628 passed to the Lumsdens. The house has been restored, and is occupied.
Other refs: Old Place of Cushnie; House of Cushnie

Cutreoch
Galloway: About 3 miles south and east of Whithorn, on minor road east of A750 at Isle of Whithorn, at Cutreoch.
Ruin or site   NX 467357   OS: 83   *   Map: 1, no: 77
Site of castle, the last remains of which were removed early in the 19th century.

Cuttlehill *see* Aberdour Castle

Cyderhall
Sutherland & Caithness: About 3 miles west of Dornoch, on minor roads south or east of A9, about 0.5 miles north of shore of Dornoch Firth, south of River Evelix, at Cyderhall.
Ruin or site   NH 758886   OS: 21   *   Map: 12, no: 21
Site of castle of the Gordons, built on lands earlier held by the Bishop of Caithness.

Cyderhall is reputed to be the burial place of Earl Sigurd, who died from blood poisoning when he was bitten by the bucktooth of the severed head of Maelbrigit, a mormaer of Moray. Maelbrigit had been slain by Sigurd, who had then tied his severed head to his saddle. The story is recounted in the Orkneyinga Saga.

D

Daer *see* **Kirkhope Tower**

Dairsie Castle

Fife: About 3 miles east and north of Cupar, on minor roads south of A91, just south of Dairsie Mains, west of the River Eden, west of railway.
Private NO 414160 OS: 59 ** Map: 7, no: 115
Dairsie Castle is a 16th-century Z-plan tower house. It consists of a main block and two small round towers. A third rectangular tower, containing the original entrance, was very ruined.

The basement was occupied by cellars, and a kitchen with a large fireplace, while the hall was on the first floor.

The original castle was a property of the Bishops and Archbishops of St Andrews. David II is said to have spent much of his boyhood here, and in 1335 the Scottish Estates met at the castle. The present building was mostly built by the Learmonth family, who held the property from the 16th century. It passed to the Spottiswoodes in 1616, and in 1621 the nearby church was built by John Spottiswoode, Archbishop of St Andrews. He is said to have written much of the 'History of the Church and State of Scotland' here. Sir Robert Spottiswoode, President of the Court of Session, was executed for being a Royalist in 1650. The castle then passed to his father-in-law, George Morrison, and later to the Scotts of Scotstarvit. The castle had become quite ruinous, but was completely rebuilt in the 1990s.

Dalblair Castle *see* Kyle Castle

Dalbog Castle

Angus & Dundee: About 4 miles south-west of Fettercairn, on minor road west of B966, 1.5 miles north of Edzell, west of River North Esk, just east of Wood of Dalbog farmhouse.
Ruin or site NO 596712 [?] OS: 44 * Map: 8, no: 245
Site of castle.

Dalcross Castle

Inverness & Nairn: About 7 miles east and north of Inverness, on minor road north of B9006 or south of A96, about 1.5 miles south-west of Croy, at Dalcross Castle.
Private NH 779483 OS: 27 ** Map: 9, no: 121**
Dalcross Castle is a restored 17th-century L-plan tower house. It consists of two offset wings, one rising to five storeys and an attic, the other three, joined only at one corner to form two re-entrant angles. A projecting square stair-tower, in one re-entrant angle, is crowned by a gabled watch-chamber and has a bartizan. Many of the windows still have their iron yetts, and the walls are pierced by many gun-loops and shot-holes. A lower extension was added in the early 18th century, and are also later additions.

The entrance, from the courtyard, is in the foot of the square stair-tower, and leads to the vaulted basement. The basement contains a wine-cellar, with a small stair to the hall above; a kitchen, with a very large arched fireplace; and other cellars. The main stair is wide, and leads up beyond the fine first-floor hall, which has a large fireplace.

Dalcross was originally a Fraser of Lovat property, and they built the castle in 1620. It passed to the Mackintoshes early in the 18th century. Hanoverian troops were marshalled here prior to the Battle of Culloden in 1746. The house was abandoned and became a ruin, but was restored and reoccupied in the 20th century.

Daldilling

Ayrshire: About 4 miles east of Mauchline, on minor road south of B743, 1.5 miles east of Sorn, north of River Ayr, at or near Daldilling.
Ruin or site NS 576263 [?] OS: 71 * Map: 3, no: 261
Site of castle. It was a property of the Reids of Daldilling, one of whom is said to have been a persecutor of Covenanters and to have hanged his victims here.

Dalduff Castle

Ayrshire: About 3 miles south-east of Maybole, on minor roads west of B7023, 0.5 miles north-west of Crosshill, west of Water of Girvan, at Dalduff.
Ruin or site NS 320070 OS: 70 * Map: 3, no: 89
Site of castle, not much of which survives. There are some remains built into the farm.

Dalgety

Fife: About 2 miles west of Aberdour, on minor roads south of A921, just east of Dalgety Bay, on shore of Firth of Forth, at Dalgety.
His Scot NT 169838 [?] OS: 65 * Map: 7, no: 27**
Nothing survives of Dalgety House, the favourite residence of Alexander Seton, Earl of Dunfermline and Chancellor of Scotland, who died in 1622. Seton is buried in the ruins of St Bridget's Kirk, which may date from the 12th century, but was altered in the 17th century with the addition of a burial vault and laird's loft.

There was a village of Dalgety, which stood about 0.5 miles south-east of the church, but there are no remains.
Other refs: St Bridget's Kirk, Dalgety
OPEN: Church: access at all reasonable times.
Parking nearby.
Tel: 0131 668 8800 Fax: 0131 668 8888
Email: hs.explore@scotland.gov.uk Web: www.historic-scotland.gov.uk

Dalgety Castle *see* Delgatie Castle

Dalginch *see* Barnslee

Dalhousie Castle

Lothians: About 14 miles south of Edinburgh, on minor road south of B704 between A6094 and A7, on west bank of South Esk, at Dalhousie.
Private NT 320636 OS: 66 ** Map: 4, no: 132
Dalhousie Castle incorporates an altered 16th-century L-plan tower house, within a 13th-century courtyard with corner towers and a moat, traces of which remain. The main entrance, through a tall archway, is crowned by two bartizans, and a large round tower survives, at one corner, from the courtyard. In the 17th century the castle was extended, and further substantial internal alterations were made by William Burn in 1820. The slots for the drawbridge survive, as does a bottle dungeon and the basement is vaulted.

The property belonged to the Ramsays from the 13th century, and Sir Alexander Ramsay was active for the Scots against the English during the Wars of Independence. However, he was starved to death in Hermitage Castle in 1342.

In 1400 the castle was held successfully against Henry IV of England, but Sir Alexander Ramsay of Dalhousie was killed at the Battle of Homildon Hill in 1402, as was another Alexander at the Battle of Flodden in 1513. The family supported Mary, Queen of Scots, and fought for her at Langside in 1568. In 1633 William Ramsay was created the 1st Earl of Dalhousie, and had the castle much extended and remodelled. Cromwell visited the castle in 1648.

The Ramsays lived at the castle until about 1900, then moved to Brechin Castle. The castle was used as a school from 1925-50, but since 1974 has been a hotel.

The building is said to be haunted by a 'Grey Lady', an apparition of a Lady Catherine. One version of the story is that she was the mistress of one of the Ramsay lairds, but his vengeful wife had her locked up in one of the castle turrets where the poor woman was starved to death. Another that she was his daughter and fell in love with the wrong man, was imprisoned in one of the chambers, and starved to death. Her apparition has been seen on the stairs, along the 'Black' corridor, and in the dungeons. Other manifestations include the rustling of her gown and unexplained noises such as the scratching or light tapping at doors. There was a sighting in 2000, during building work.

Another ghost is said to be that of one of the pupils from when the castle was a school. The story goes that a boy leapt from the top of the building and was killed.

A third spirit is alleged to be that of a dog, which died in the 1980s also after falling from the castle. Its apparition has allegedly been seen running on the stairs and along the passageways.

Other reported manifestations include a member of staff having her hair pulled when nobody else was present, and a guest being tapped on each shoulder several times by invisible hands.

OPEN: Hotel – open all year except closed 7-19 January 2001.
29 ensuite bedrooms in castle, 5 in lodge. Dungeon restaurant and library bar. Aqueous Spa and Orangery Restaurant. Conferences, banquets, meetings and weddings. Parking.
Tel: 01875 820153   Fax: 01875 821936
Email: res@dalhousiecastle.co.uk   Web: www.dalhousiecastle.co.uk

Daljarroch

Ayrshire: About 7 miles south of Girvan, on minor road just west of A714, west of River Stinchar, at Daljarrock.
Private   NX 196882   OS: 76   **   Map: 3, no: 25
The mansion, which dates from around 1750, incorporates a much-altered tower house. There was a fire in 1987, and many of the later additions were demolished.

Dalkeith Home Farm *see* Smeaton Castle

Dalkeith House

Lothians: About 0.5 miles north-west of Dalkeith, on minor road north of A6094, between the rivers North Esk and South Esk.
Private   NT 333679   OS: 66   **   Map: 4, no: 138
Dalkeith House or Palace, an 18th-century U-plan classical mansion, incorporates some of an old castle, possibly dating from as early as the 12th century. The house was remodelled in the 1570s or 1580s, and again in 1701-11 by James Smith.

The property originally belonged to the Grahams, but passed by marriage to the Douglases about 1350. Dalkeith was sacked in 1452 by the brother of the murdered 6th Earl of Douglas, but the castle held out, and in 1458 the family were made Earls of Morton. James IV first met Margaret Tudor, his wife-to-be, here in 1503. The castle was taken by the English after the Battle of Pinkie in 1547, and many Scots who had fled the battle were captured. The 4th Earl of Morton – Chancellor for Mary, Queen of Scots, and later Regent for the young James VI – remodelled the castle, and built a magnificent palace in 1575. James VI visited in 1581, after Morton had been executed. Charles I was entertained here in 1633.

In 1642 the property was sold to the Scott Earls – and later Dukes – of Buccleuch. Anna, Duchess of Buccleuch, stayed here and had the house remodelled. Her husband, the Earl of Monmouth, had been executed in 1685 for treason, after leading a rebellion against James VII. Bonnie Prince Charlie stayed here for two nights in 1745. The house was altered in the 1780s, and in 1831, but by 1885 had stopped being the main seat of the Dukes of Buccleuch and Queensberry. It is still occupied, although the house is said to be haunted by the apparition of a woman, which is said to have been seen in recent times.

The park was laid out in the 18th century, and includes working Clydesdale horses, adventure woodland play area, nature trails, 18th-century bridge, orangery and ice house.

OPEN: Country park open Mar-Oct, daily 10.00-18.00. House not open.
Country Park: Explanatory displays. Gift shop. Restaurant. Tearoom. WC. Picnic area. Woodland walks. Disabled access – cafe, shop and toilets. Car and coach parking. Group concessions. £.
Tel: 0131 665 3277   Fax: 0131 654 1666

Dalmahoy

Lothians: About 2 miles north-west of Currie, on minor roads south of A71, south of Gogar Burn, at or near Dalmahoy.
Private   NT 145690 [?]   OS: 65   *   Map: 4, no: 48
Set in fine grounds commanding extensive views, Dalmahoy is a three-storey symmetrical mansion, which was rebuilt by the architect William Adam about 1720. It probably stands on the site of a castle, and has been greatly extended in later centuries. It is now a hotel and country club.

The property was held from 1296 by the Dalmahoys of that Ilk, but was sold to the Dalrymples in 1725 or earlier, then to the Douglas Earls of Morton about 1750.

The building is reputedly haunted by the ghost of Lady Mary Douglas, a daughter of the first Earl of Morton to own the property. Her portrait hangs in the hotel, and her apparition is said to be a 'White Lady'. The ghost is said to be seen in both corridors and the bedrooms of the old part of the building, and to be a friendly ghost.

OPEN: Hotel – open all year.
215 bedrooms and suites with ensuite facilities. Award-winning Pentland Restaurant, cafe and bars. Swimming pool, gym, sauna and health and beauty salon. Two golf courses. Conferences and meetings. Parking.
Tel: 0131 333 1845   Fax: 0131 333 1433
Web: www.marriott.com/marriott/edigs

Dalmellington Castle

Ayrshire: Just east of Dalmellington, north of the B741 junction with A713, near the Muck Water.
Ruin or site   NS 482058   OS: 77   **   Map: 3, no: 198
Site of a strong 12th-century castle of the Cathcart family, probably occupied until the 16th century, and also known as Dame Helen's Castle. It had a motte and ditch. Another building, called Castle House, is said to have been constructed with stone from the castle.
Other refs: Dame Helen's Castle, Dalmellington

Dalmeny House

Lothians: About 2.5 miles east of South Queensferry, on minor roads east of B924 or A90, Dalmeny House.
Private   NT 167779   OS: 65   *   Map: 4, no: 52**
Site of castle or old house [NT 159776], also known as Dalmeny House, which was a residence of the Mowbrays of Dalmeny and Barnbougle (see Barnbougle). The property was sold to the Hamilton Earl of Haddington in 1615, who in turn sold it to the Primrose family in 1662, who were later made Earls of Rosebery. The present Dalmeny House was built in 1814-17, and is still home to the family.

The present house is Tudor Gothic in style, and there are vaulted corridors and a fine hammer-beam hall, although the main rooms are classical in style. The house has French furniture, tapestries and porcelain, as well as 18th-century portraits by Gainsborough, Raeburn, Reynolds and Lawrence, racing mementoes, and items associated with Napoleon. There are fine walks in the wooded grounds and along the shore.

OPEN: Open Jul-Aug, Sun-Tue 14.00-17.30; last admission 16.30; open other times by appt only.
Guided tours. Tea room. Disabled access and WC. Shore walk from Forth Bridge to Cramond. Car and coach parking. Group concessions. ££.
Tel: 0131 331 1888   Fax: 0131 331 1788   Web: www.edinburgh.org

Dalmoak Castle

Argyll & Dunbartonshire: About 1 mile north-west of Dumbarton, near A82 and A812, on west side of River Leven, south of Renton, at or near Dalmoak House.
Private   NS 385768 [?]   OS: 63   *   Map: 5, no: 152
The present building, dating from the late 19th century, is a castellated mansion, built for James Aitken. It does not appear to have any older origins.

Dalnaglar Castle

Perthshire: About 5 miles south of Spittal of Glenshee, on minor roads east of A93 or north of B951, east of Shee Water, at Dalnaglar Castle.
Private   NO 145647   OS: 43   *   Map: 8, no: 98
Dalnaglar Castle is a modern mansion, and does not apparently have any older origins.

Dalpeddar

Dumfriesshire: About 3 miles south-east of Sanquhar, just north of A76, north of River Nith, at or near Dalpeddar.

Private NS 820072 OS: 71 * Map: 1, no: 145

Site of tower house.

The area near Dalpeddar [NS 818073] is said to be haunted by the apparition of a tall woman and sometimes a young boy, dressed in white, and their figures have been recorded, appearing by the road. They are said to be the ghosts of 'Lady Hebron' and her son. The story goes that Lady Hebron was heiress to the small estate of Dalpeddar some time during the 16th century. She was married in due course and had a son, but her husband died and she was left a widow. Their uncle, however, wanted the property, and Lady Hebron and her son disappeared. Much later the bones of a woman and child were found, buried near the road: the lady had had her skull split. A Marion of Dalpeddar is said to have been murdered by one of the Crichton lairds and to haunt Sanquhar Castle [NS 786092], and the stories are obviously linked.

Dalpersie Castle *see* Terpersie Castle

Dalquharran Castle

Ayrshire: About 6 miles north-east of Girvan, north of the B741 at Dailly, on the north side of the Water of Girvan, 0.5 miles south-east of Dalquharran.

Ruin or site NS 273019 OS: 76 *** Map: 3, no: 59

Dalquharran Castle consists of a ruined 15th-century keep, with a round tower at one corner. It was extended to form an L-plan, and rises to three storeys and a garret within the corbelled-out crenellated parapet. The castle was extended and altered in the late 17th century.

The basement is vaulted.

Dalquharran Castle was a property of the Kennedy of Culzean family. About 1790 the old castle was abandoned for a new mansion, which was designed by Robert Adam, and enlarged about 1881. This house is also now ruinous.

Dalry House, Edinburgh

Lothians: About 1 mile west of Edinburgh Castle, on minor roads north of A70, Orwell Place, at Dalry House.

Private NT 235728 OS: 66 ** Map: 4, no: 84

Dalry House, standing in Orwell Place, dates from 1661 and was the country house of the Chiesly family. The building, with hexagonal stair-towers and fine plaster-work, is harled and whitewashed, and after renovation in 1965 is now an old people's day centre.

The house and area were said to be haunted by a ghost, 'Johnnie One Arm'. John Chiesly was executed for shooting Sir George Lockhart of Carnwath, after Lockhart, Lord President of the Court of Session, found against Chiesly in a divorce settlement. Chiesly had his arm chopped off before being hanged, but his dead body was taken from the gallows before he could be buried. His one-armed apparition is then said to have been seen often. In 1965 the remains of a one-armed man are said to have been found under a hearth, and his ghost has reputedly not been seen since his remains were buried. It is said his ghost was quite armless (groan).

OPEN: View from exterior.

Dalswinton Castle

Dumfriesshire: About 6 miles north of Dumfries, on minor road south of A76 at Auldgirth, about 1 mile south and east of Dalswinton village.

Ruin or site NX 945841 OS: 78 ** Map: 1, no: 182

Little remains of Dalswinton Castle, except the 16th-century vaulted basement, and a round tower containing a moulded entrance.

The lands belonged to the Comyns in the 13th century, and a castle here was occupied by the English in 1309 until captured and destroyed by the Scots in 1313. Robert the Bruce gave the lands to his son-in-law, Walter Stewart. The castle was rebuilt, but destroyed again along with the castle at Dumfries in 1357 as part of the terms of the release of David II from captivity in England. The lands later passed to the Maxwells. An elegant mansion, Dalswinton House, was built nearby, and is still occupied.

Other refs: Comyn's Castle, Dalswinton; Dalswinton Old House

Dalquharran Castle

Daltonhook

Dumfriesshire: About 3.5 miles south-west of Lockerbie, on minor roads west of
B723, east of River Annan, at or near Daltonhook.
Ruin or site   NY 113763 [?]   OS: 85   *   Map: 1, no: 236
Site of strong tower, some remains of which survived at the beginning of the 19th
century.

Dalveen Castle

Dumfriesshire: About 5 miles north of Carron Bridge, on minor road west of
A702, to west of Carron Water, at or near Dalveen.
Ruin or site   NS 884069 [?]   OS: 78   *   Map: 1, no: 167
Site of castle of the Douglases. One block, with a vaulted basement, survived in
1836, but it was then demolished to provide materials for Nether Dalveen. A panel,
dated 1622, is built into the farm.
Other refs: Nether Dalveen

Dalveich Castle *see* Ardveich Castle

Dalvey Castle

Moray: About 2 miles west of Forres, on minor roads north of A96, just west of
Muckle Burn, at Dalvey.
Private   NJ 003585   OS: 27   *   Map: 10, no: 4
Nothing remains of a castle of the Dunbars – originally called Grangehill – except
a walled garden. The name of the property was changed when it was acquired by
the Grants of Dalvey. They built a two-storey classical mansion on the site about
1770.
Other refs: Grangehill

Dalyell House *see* Dalzell House

Dalzell House

Lanarkshire & Glasgow area: About 1.5 miles south and east of Motherwell, on
minor roads south of A721, near north bank of the Clyde, south of Muirhouse.
Private   NS 756550   OS: 64   *   Map: 3, no: 357**
Standing on the edge of a rocky ravine, Dalzell House – other spellings can be
Dalyell or Dalziel – incorporates a 15th-century keep of three storeys and a garret,
within a corbelled-out parapet, in the large rambling mansion. The parapet has
three open rounds, and a later round caphouse crowns the stair. A new wing was
added in the 17th century with two towers: one round and one square. A strong
wall was built, at the same time, enclosing the courtyard. Further ranges of buildings were added within the courtyard in the 17th and 19th centuries.
   The original entrance was through a projection to hold a portcullis, the chain
grooves of which remain, but the present doorway leads to a large entrance hall
occupying the whole of the ground floor. A straight mural stair climbs to the first
floor, the upper floors being reached by a turnpike stair. The first-floor hall is vaulted,
and the original main entrance was reached by an external stair.

The 17th-century extension contains a vaulted kitchen on the ground floor, with
vaulted cellars beneath. The walls are pierced by shot-holes
   The property belonged to the Dalziel Earls of Carnforth from the 13th century,
who built the old castle, but was sold to the Hamiltons of Boggs in 1649. The family
became Lords Hamilton of Dalzell. Covenanters were sheltered in the grounds,
and held illegal conventicles under a huge oak tree, now known as the 'Covenanter's Oak'. The house was remodelled in the 1850s, the north wing used as a hospital during World War I, and the property held by the family until 1952. After a
period of decay, it was extensively repaired in the 1970s, and has been restored
again as private housing.
   The house is said to be haunted by three ghosts: 'Green', 'White' and 'Grey' Ladies. An apparition of the 'Green Lady' was reported in the Piper's Gallery, and
other manifestations include unexplained flashing lights, footsteps and other noises.
The smell of exotic perfume was also reported.
   The 'White Lady' is reportedly the ghost of a young female servant. Although
unmarried, she fell pregnant and in despair threw herself from the battlements and
was killed.
   The 'Grey Lady' haunted the north wing, and is said to date from when the house
was used as a hospital. Her apparition is said to be seen wearing a grey nurse's
uniform.
Other refs: Dalyell House; Dalziel House
OPEN: Dalzell Park open, daily dawn-dusk. Dalzell House not open.
Woodland walks. Arboretum. Parking.
Tel: 0141 304 1907   Fax: 0141 304 1839

Dalziel House *see* Dalzell House

Dame Helen's Castle, Dalmellington *see* Dalmellington Castle

Damsay

Orkney: About 3.5 miles west and north of Kirkwall, on Damsay, an island in the
Orkneys, by boat north of A965, in Bay of Firth, on Damsay.
Ruin or site   HY 390140 [?]   OS: 6   *   Map: 11, no: 43
There was probably a strong castle here, built by Norsemen in the 12th century, as
well as a church. It was visited by Svein Aliefson in 1136.

Dargavel House

Renfrewshire: About 1 mile south of Bishopton, on minor roads south of A8,
within the Royal Ordnance Factory, at Dargavel.
Private   NS 433693   OS: 64   **   Map: 3, no: 172
Dargavel House is a large L-plan tower house of three storeys and an attic, dating
from 1574. It was extended and remodelled in 1670, in 1849 by David Bryce, and
again in 1910. The main block has round towers projecting at two corners.
   The basement was vaulted, containing the kitchen and cellars, and the hall was on
the first floor. A main stair led to the first floor, while the upper floors were reached
by turnpike stairs.
   It was held by the Maxwells.

Darleith House

Argyll & Dunbartonshire: About 2 miles north of Cardross, on minor road north
of A814 at Cardross, near Darleith Farm.
Ruin or site   NS 345806   OS: 63   *   Map: 5, no: 142
Darleith House, a classical ruinous mansion, incorporates a much altered 16th-
century tower house with one round bartizan. It was extended and altered in later
centuries, including in 1903.
   It was a property of the Darleith family from 1510, but was sold in 1670 to the
Yuilles. It was being used as seminary in 1962, but is now ruinous.

Darnaway Castle

Banff & Buchan: About 4 miles south-west of Forres, on minor roads south of
A96, 1 mile west of River Findhorn, at Darnaway Castle.
Private   NH 994550   OS: 27   **   Map: 10, no: 2
Darnaway Castle, a large classical mansion of 1810 with battlements and turrets,
includes a 14th-century hall-block from an old castle. The oak roof of the hall is

particularly fine, rivalling that of Parliament Hall, an 'extraordinary early survival'. Little else of the old castle survives.

The original castle was built by Sir Thomas Randolph, Earl of Moray and Regent for the young David II. It passed to the Douglas Earls of Moray, then after 1455 to the Murray family. It was acquired by James Stewart, Earl of Moray, in the 16th century. He was murdered at Donibristle by the Gordon, Marquis of Huntly. Mary, Queen of Scots, held court here in 1564. The castle is still occupied by the Earls of Moray.

OPEN: Contact Darnaway Visitor Centre.
Tel: 01309 641469

Darngaber Castle

Lanarkshire & Glasgow: About 4 miles south of Hamilton, on minor roads west of B7078 or east of A723, south of Darngaber Burn, 0.3 miles south-east of Darngaber, at motte.
Ruin or site NS 729501 OS: 64 * Map: 3, no: 340
Nothing remains of a castle except a motte. The foundations could be traced in the middle of the 19th century. It was a property of the Hamiltons of Cadzow.

Darnhall Castle *see* Black Barony Castle

Darnick

Borders: About 0.5 miles west of Melrose, just south of A7, south of the River Tweed at Darnick.
Ruin or site NT 532343 OS: 73 ** Map: 2, no: 188
Fisher's Tower consists of the remains of a 16th-century tower house, which was altered in the following centuries into a two storey house. Two gunloops survive in one gable. It was a property of the Fisher family, and stands near to the better preserved tower. There was another [NT 532343] known as 'Little Peel', all traces of which have gone. There were at least two other fortified houses in Darnick.
Other refs: Fisher's Tower, Darnick; Little Peel, Darnick

Darnick Tower

Borders: About 0.5 miles west of Melrose, just south of A7, south of the River Tweed at Darnick.
Private NT 532343 OS: 73 * Map: 2, no: 187**
Darnick Tower is a tower house of three storeys and a garret within a corbelled-out parapet, which incorporates a 15th-century castle. A projecting square tower of four storeys is crowned by a caphouse and watch-chamber. There is a later two-storey wing, and the building was altered again in the 19th century.

The entrance is at the foot of the stair-tower. The basement was formerly vaulted and the hall, on the first floor, has a large fireplace.

Darnick was a property of the Heiton family, but was torched and 'cast down' by the Earl of Hertford in 1545, although it was rebuilt by 1569. It is still occupied.

A ruinous much-altered second tower stands nearby within the garden, and is known as 'Fisher's Tower'. There was another [NT 532343] known as 'Little Peel', all traces of which have gone. There were at least two other fortified houses in Darnick.

Darnley Castle

Lanarkshire & Glasgow area: About 1.5 miles east of Barrhead, on minor roads south of A726 at Darnley Toll, just east of Brock Burn, at Darnley.
Ruin or site NS 527586 OS: 64 * Map: 3, no: 235
Site of castle, some remains of which survive, including a round stair-tower.

It was a property of the Stewarts, who became Earls of Lennox in 1488. One of the family was Henry Stewart, Lord Darnley, second husband of Mary, Queen of Scots. The property was sold to the Graham Duke of Montrose in 1689. It passed to the Maxwells of Nether Pollok, who removed the upper storeys in 1820 and demolished other parts. The building was used as a mill, but has been renovated.
OPEN: 'The Mill' restaurant.
Restaurant. Parking.
Tel: 0141 876 0458

Daugh

Aberdeen & Gordon: About 5 miles north of Huntly, on minor roads west of B9022 or north of A96, near Burn of Cairnie, at or near Daugh.
Ruin or site NJ 507473 [?] OS: 29 * Map: 10, no: 110
Site of a much-modified castle.
Other refs: Doagh

Davidston House

Aberdeen & Gordon: About 4 miles south of Keith, on minor roads south of B9115 east of Bomakelloch, just east of Burn of Davidston, at Davidston House.
Private NJ 419451 OS: 28 ** Map: 10, no: 82
Davidston House is a much-altered and extended 16th- or 17th-century L-plan tower house of three storeys. Round bartizans crown two of the corners of the tower, and the gables are corbiestepped. A number of windows have been built up and others enlarged, while a modern doorway has been opened in the wing.

The building has been almost completely altered inside. The basement is not vaulted.

It was a property of the Gordons, and the tower and courtyard are said to have been restored in the 1970s.

Daviot Castle

Inverness & Nairn: About 6 miles south-east of Inverness, just west of A9 at Daviot, west of River Nairn, at or near Daviot.
Ruin or site NH 730405 [?] OS: 27 * Map: 9, no: 111
Not much remains of a 15th-century keep and courtyard of the Lindsay Earls of Crawford. The property later passed to the Mackintoshes, who built the nearby house.

Davoch of Grange

Moray: About 3.5 miles east of Keith, on minor roads just north of A95, north of River Isla, at or near Davoch of Grange
Ruin or site NJ 480515 [?] OS: 28 * Map: 10, no: 106
Site of castle, described as a stately edifice defended by a ditch. There were remains in the 19th century, but nothing now survives.

It was a property of Kinloss Abbey from the 12th or 13th century.
Other refs: Grange Castle; Tower of Strathisla

Davochcarte *see* Docharty

Davochmaluach *see* Dochmaluag Castle

Davochpollo *see* Docharty

Dawick *see* Easter Dawyck

Dawyck House

Borders: About 8 miles south-west of Peebles, on minor roads east of B712, east of River Tweed, at Dawyck.
Private NT 168352 OS: 72 ** Map: 2, no: 32
Dawyck House was built in 1832-7 by the architect William Burn after a previous

house on the site burned down in 1830. The house was extended in 1898, and again in 1909 by Sir Robert Lorimer.

The property was held by the Veitch family from the 13th century, but passed to the Naesmiths at the close of the 17th century. James Naesmith, who died in 1706, was known as the 'Deil o Dawick'. The property passed to the Balfours in the 20th century.

Dawyck Botanical garden is nearby.

Dean Castle

Ayrshire: About 1 mile north-east of Kilmarnock, on minor roads east of B7038, between Fenwick and Craufurdland Water, in Dean Castle County Park.
Private NS 437394 OS: 70 **** Map: 3, no: 174
Interesting and well preserved, Dean Castle consists of a 14th-century keep of three storeys and a garret within a flush crenellated parapet. A 15th-century palace block, with a square projecting tower, is crowned by a gabled caphouse. This block has a corbelled-out parapet and corbiestepped gables. The keep and palace block are within a courtyard enclosed by a curtain wall. Adjoining is a three-storey house of the late 17th century.

The basement of the keep has two vaulted chambers, one a kitchen, the other a wine-cellar. The main entrance was originally at first-floor level by an external stair. The thick walls, beside the original entrance, contain a small guardroom, with a trapdoor leading to a prison, and a small stair descending to the wine-cellar. The

hall is a fine large chamber, with two stone benches running along the walls. The second floor is occupied by an upper hall and chapel. A turnpike stair leads up to the parapet, and is crowned by a corbiestepped caphouse.

The hall block has a kitchen and cellars in the basement, and a hall on the first floor, with private chambers on the floors above.

The lands were originally held by the Lockharts, then the Soulis family, who had a castle nearby. By the beginning of the 14th century it was held by the Balliols, but the lands were given to the Boyds by Robert the Bruce after the Balliols were forfeited. The castle is said to have been besieged by the English during the Wars of Independence.

The keep was built by the Boyds about 1460, although it may incorporate earlier work. Robert Boyd became Guardian of James III during his minority, and practically ruled Scotland from 1466-9. He later had to flee to Denmark, and his brother was executed for treason. William, 10th Lord Boyd, was created Earl of Kilmarnock in 1661.

The 4th Earl was Privy Councillor to Bonnie Prince Charlie during the Jacobite Rising of 1745. He was a Colonel in the Prince's guard, but captured after the Battle of Culloden in 1746 and executed by beheading. The lands were forfeited, but the 5th Earl recovered the estates in 1751, and in 1758 became the 15th Earl of Errol and took the name Hay. Dean was sold, first to the Cunningham Earl of Glencairn, then to the Scotts of Balcomie. In 1735 a fire gutted the hall block, and most of the

castle was abandoned.

The castle passed to Lord Howard de Walden in 1828. It was restored from 1905 using material from Balcomie Castle, and the entire building was donated by Lord Howard to Kilmarnock in 1975. The castle now houses a museum, and is surrounded by a public park. The castle also has a copy of the 'Kilmarnock Edition' of Robert Burns's work.

Before William Boyd, 4th Earl of Kilmarnock, was executed, servants were terrified by an apparition of his severed head rolling about the floor. When Boyd joined the Jacobite Rising, he told the Earl of Galloway about the haunting, who predicted Boyd would lose his head. Boyd was executed, by beheading, in 1746.
Other refs: Kilmarnock Castle
OPEN: Open daily Apr-Oct 12.00-17.00; open end Oct to end Mar wknds only; closed Christmas and New Year; park open daily dawn-dusk.
Guided tours. Explanatory displays. Museum of armour and musical instruments. Gift shop. Restaurant. WC. Picnic area. Park. Disabled access – but not into castle. Car and coach parking. Country park and castle free.
Tel: 01563 522702 Fax: 01563 572552

Dean House

Lothians: About 1 mile north-west of Edinburgh Castle, on minor roads south of A90, west of Dean village, at Dean Cemetery.
Ruin or site NT 235740 [?] OS: 66 * Map: 4, no: 85
Site of 16th-century tower house of the Nisbets of Dean, which was demolished in 1845 when the cemetery was laid out. The house had many turrets, corbels and corbiestepped gables. The great hall was decorated with painted wooden panels of the early 17th century, six of which are on display in the Royal Museum of Scotland.

William Nisbet of Dean was Provost of Edinburgh when James VI visited Edinburgh in 1617, and was knighted.

Dechmont House

Lothians: About 2.5 miles west and south of Broxburn, on minor roads north or west of A89, east of Bangour Hospital, at or near Dechmont.
Ruin or site NT 040707 [?] OS: 65 * Map: 4, no: 19
Dechmont House, a much-modified and extended tower house, was completely demolished in the 20th century. It was here that Dr David Livingstone could not be persuaded to stay in Scotland, and returned to Africa where he later died.

Dee Castle

Aberdeen & Gordon: About 5 miles east of Ballater, on minor road just south of B976, just south of the Dee, at or near Deecastle.
Ruin or site NO 438968 [?] OS: 37 * Map: 10, no: 91
Site of 15th-century castle, a property of the Gordons. The castle was apparently burned in 1641, and its part is thought to be built into a chapel on the site, which now a dwelling.
Other refs: Kinacoul Castle; Candecaill

Deinbee *see* Denbie

Delgatie Castle

Banff & Buchan: About 2 miles east of Delgatie, on minor roads east of A947 or west of B9170, west of Wood of Delgaty, at Delgatie Castle.
Private NJ 755506 OS: 29 **** Map: 10, no: 239
An imposing and well-preserved building, Delgatie Castle consists of a 15th-century keep of five storeys and a garret, although it may incorporate older work. The walls are very thick, and are harled and whitewashed. The original windows are small, and there are many gunloops. There is an adjoining 16th-century gabled house, and lower ranges of buildings.

The original entrance is now engulfed by the 16th-century addition. A later entrance leads, through a fine vaulted vestibule, to a turnpike stair in one corner of the keep. The basement is vaulted, and contains the old kitchen with a wide fireplace. The hall, on the first floor, is ribbed- and groin-vaulted, the apex boss being adorned with the Hay arms. The fireplace lintel is dated 1570, and there are many mural chambers. Tempera-painted ceilings survive on the second floor, dating from

1590s. The wings were added in 1769, and the castle was extended again in the 19th century.

Delgatie was originally a property of the Comyn Earls of Buchan, but passed to the Hays on the Comyns' forfeiture in the 14th century. The Hays were made Earls of Errol in 1452. Sir Gilbert Hay of Delgatie, with many others of the family, was killed at the Battle of Flodden in 1513. Mary, Queen of Scots, spent three days here after the Battle of Corrichie, when the Gordon family were defeated by her forces. The 9th Earl was summoned for treason in 1594 for supporting the Gordon Earl of Huntly, and part of the west wall was battered down by James VI's forces. However, the 9th Earl went on to fight at Glenlivet in 1594, when the royal forces, under the Earl of Argyll, were defeated, but the rebellion failed and he was forfeited. Sir William Hay of Delgatie was standard bearer to the Marquis of Montrose, during his campaign of 1645. Although defeated at Philiphaugh, Hay managed to return the standard to Buchanan Castle, but he was executed with Montrose at Edinburgh in 1650, and buried beside him in St Giles Cathedral.

The Hays supported the Jacobites during the 1715 and 1745 Risings and suffered for it, Delgatie passing to the Gardens of Troup in 1762, the Duffs in 1798, then the Ainslies about 1868, but then returning to the Hays. It was made the Clan Hay centre in 1948, and is still occupied.

It is said to be haunted by a the ghost of a spirited young woman, known as Rohaise. She is thought to have defended the castle from an attack, and haunts the bedroom off the main stair, which now bears her name. It is said she likes to visit men who stay in the chamber.

It appears the ghost could be quite frightening, at least in the imagination. Troops stationed here during World War II twice fled outdoors following unexplained disturbances, although a search of the building found nothing.

Other refs: Dalgety Castle

OPEN: Open Apr-Oct, daily 10.00-17.00.

Many rooms, two with original painted ceilings of 1592 and 1597. Guided tours available by arrangement. Explanatory boards. Gift shop. Tearoom. WC. Picnic area. Disabled access to tearoom and front hall only. Accommodation available including in castle (£169-535 per week). Short breaks available. £

Tel: 01888 563479   Fax: 01888 563479

Email: jjohnson@delgatie-castle.freeserve.co.uk   Web: www.delgatiecastle.com

Delnabo

Moray: About 1 mile south-west of Tomintoul, on minor roads west of A939, just west of Water of Ailnack, at Delnabo.
Private   NJ 160170   OS: 36   *   Map: 10, no: 25
Delnabo, a two-storey building with turrets, dates from the 19th century, but stands on the site of a 17th-century house.

It was a property of the Grants of Carron in the 17th century, and Margaret Sinclair, widow of one of the Grants, married Gregor MacGregor, chief of the Glen-

strae family, who were proscribed at the time. The Gordon 2nd Marquis of Huntly, who had supported Montrose in his campaign of 1644 for Charles I, was captured here in 1647 to be executed two years later.

Delny Castle

Ross & Cromarty: About 3 miles east and north of Invergordon, on minor roads south of A9 in Delny, 1 mile north of shore of Cromarty Firth.
Ruin or site   NH 735724   OS: 21   *   Map: 9, no: 112
Site of 14th-century castle of the Earls of Ross, who were MacDonalds in the 15th century. William, 3rd Earl, died here in 1322, and the property later passed to the Munros. It was held by Black Andrew Munro in 1512, an unpleasant character, who was hanged at Balnagown by the Rosses. Munro made his female servants thresh corn naked, and another version is that he was murdered by his own household in 1522. The site is occupied by a farm.

Denbie

Dumfriesshire: About 6.5 miles south and east of Lochmaben, on minor road east of B725, south of River Annan, at or near Denbie.
Ruin or site   NY 109729   OS: 85   *   Map: 1, no: 232
Probable site of castle, which stood in park land.
Other refs: Deinbee

Denfind *see* Pitairlie Castle

Denholm

Borders: About 5 miles east and north of Hawick, near junction of A698 and B6405, south of River Teviot, at or near village of Denholm.
Ruin or site   NT 568183   OS: 80   *   Map: 2, no: 213
Site of tower house of the Douglases. The village, and probably the tower, were torched by the Earl of Hertford in 1545.

Denmiln *see* Denmylne Castle

Denmuir *see* Ayton

Denmylne Castle

Fife: About 1 mile south and east of Newburgh, just east of the A913, just north of Den of Lindores, 1 mile north-west of Lindores Loch.
Ruin or site   NO 249175   OS: 59   *   Map: 7, no: 49**
Denmylne Castle is a ruined 16th-century tower house of three floors and a garret, which has a corbelled-out parapet at only one gable. The building is cross-shaped, consisting of a main block with a centrally projecting stair-tower, matched by a smaller rectangular tower on the opposite side of the main block. The windows are large, and there are a number of gunloops. The castle had a courtyard.

The moulded entrance, at the foot of the stair-tower, leads to a wide turnpike stair. The basement contains two vaulted chambers.

The property was held by the Balfours from 1452 until 1710. James Balfour of Denmylne died at the siege of Roxburgh in 1460, while his son, John, died at the Battle of Flodden in 1513. Sir James Balfour of Denmylne and Kinnard, appointed Lord Lyon King of Arms in 1639, compiled a collection of manuscripts, which form the basis of much of authenticated Scottish history. He officiated at the coronations of Charles I and Charles II, and died in 1657. His brother, Sir Andrew, founded the first botanical garden in Edinburgh. The Balfours are buried in the ruinous parish church at Abdie.
Other refs: Denmiln

Dennistoun Castle

Renfrewshire: About 2 miles south of Kilmacolm, on minor roads south of A761, north of River Gryffe, at or near Craigends Dennistoun.
Ruin or site   NS 364673   OS: 63   *   Map: 3, no: 123
Site of castle. It was a property of the Dennistoun or Danzieltoun family. They moved to Colgrain, but continued to use the castle here until at least the 16th century.

Denoon Castle

Angus & Dundee: About 7 miles south-west of Kirriemuir, on minor roads south of A94, east of Castleward, at or near Easter Denoon.
Ruin or site   NO 348438 [?]   OS: 54   *   Map: 8, no: 161
Site of castle, nothing of which remains.

Deskford Castle

Banff & Buchan: About 3.5 miles south of Cullen, on minor roads east of B9018 at Kirkton of Deskford, west of Burn of Deskford, at Deskford.
Ruin or site   NJ 509617   OS: 29   *   Map: 10, no: 112
Little remains of Deskford Castle or Tower. It was a 16th-century tower house of four storeys with a courtyard, which was mostly demolished in the 1830s.
   It was a property of the Sinclairs, before passing to the Ogilvies, who abandoned it for Cullen House.

Deskie Castle

Moray: About 3 miles north of Tomnavoulin, on minor road east of B9008, east of River Livet, in Glenlivet, at or near Deskie.
Ruin or site   NJ 198302   OS: 36   *   Map: 10, no: 36
There are slight remains of a castle, a property of the Stewarts.

Deuchar Tower

Borders: At Yarrow, just north of A708, north of Yarrow Water, south of Deuchar Hill.
Ruin or site   NT 360280   OS: 73   *   Map: 2, no: 95
Not much survives of Deuchar Tower, a 16th-century tower house, except several mounds and part of a wall built into the garden.
   The property was held by the Homes in 1502, but had passed to the Murrays of Deuchar by 1643, and then to the Dewars.

Devon *see* Dowane

Devon Tower *see* Sauchie Tower

Dheirrig *see* Eilean Dearg Castle

Dilspro *see* Grandhome House

Dingwall Castle

Ross & Cromarty: To east of Dingwall, on minor roads east of A862, west of the shore of the Cromarty Firth, in garden of The Castle.
Ruin or site   NH 553589   OS: 26   *   Map: 9, no: 68
Little remains of Dingwall Castle, except a round tower and an underground vault.
   It is said that Macbeth's father had a stronghold at Dingwall, and that Macbeth was brought up there. Thorfinn the Mighty, the Norse Earl of Orkney, who was probably related to Macbeth, also had a centre here, and Dingwall ('field of the thing') is called after the 'Thing' or court of justice.
   William the Lyon built a castle here in the late 12th century, and the Earls of Ross rebuilt it in stone in the 14th or 15th century. James IV had a hall added after his visit in 1503, and in 1507 Andro, Bishop of Caithness, carried out some improvements after assaults by the MacDonalds and Mackenzies. It was derelict by 1625, and ruinous by the mid 18th century.
   The Castle, a two-storey house with crenellations, was built in 1821 and stands nearby.

Dingwall Castle, Edinburgh

Lothians: Centre of Edinburgh, Waverley Station.
Ruin or site   NT 259739   OS: 66   *   Map: 4, no: 99
Nothing remains of a castle, consisting of a tower and courtyard with a round tower at each corner, the site now occupied by Waverley Station. It was probably built for John Dingwall, who was provost of Trinity College Church from 1525-32. The building was later used as a prison, but a ruin by 1647. Trinity College was founded in 1462 by Mary of Gueldres, but demolished and the site cleared for the coming of the railway in 1848.

Dinlabyre

Borders: About 4 miles north and east of Newcastleton, just south of B6357, south of Liddel Water, at Dinlabyre.
Private   NY 528920   OS: 79   **   Map: 2, no: 184
The house, which appears to date from the 19th century, incorporates a tower house. There are dated stones with 1668 and 1682.
   It was a property of the Elliots, but by the middle of the 18th century had passed to the Olivers.

Dinning

Dumfriesshire: About 3.5 miles south of Thornhill, on minor roads west of A76, east of River Nith, north of Dinning.
Ruin or site   NX 892901   OS: 78   **   Map: 1, no: 170
Dinning consists of the well-preserved remains of a motte and bailey castle.

Dinvin Motte

Ayrshire: About 3 miles south of Girvan, just east of A714 at Dinvin.
Ruin or site   NX 200932   OS: 76   **   Map: 3, no: 29
Site of 12th-century castle on an impressive motte with a double rampart and ditches. The motte may have had a wall, and a ramp leads up to the entrance.

Dinwoodie

Dumfriesshire: About 5.5 miles north of Lochmaben, on minor roads east of M74, at or near Dinwoodie Mains.
Ruin or site   NY 108907 [?]   OS: 78   *   Map: 1, no: 231
Built into the porch of a farmhouse is an armorial panel, which is dated 1631 and has the initials RM. There is said to have been a chapel nearby, a property of the Knights Templars.

Dinwoody Castle *see* Cockie's Field

Dirleton Castle

Lothians: About 2 miles west of North Berwick, on minor roads north of A198, in Dirleton village.
NTS   NT 518840   OS: 66   ***   Map: 4, no: 191**
Standing on a rock in a picturesque flower garden, Dirleton Castle consists of towers and ranges of buildings around a courtyard, which was once surrounded by a wide ditch. The old part of the castle, dating from the 13th century, is grouped around a small triangular court, and consists of a large drum tower, a smaller round tower and a rectangular tower. The chambers in the drum tower are polygonal, one on top of the other. The basement is vaulted, like a dome, and has a fireplace decorated with dog-tooth mouldings. The upper chamber would probably have been the lord's room, and is a particularly fine apartment.
   The entrance to the castle is by a wooden bridge across the wide ditch, and is through a gatehouse, formerly with a drawbridge and portcullis.
   On one side of the castle is a range of buildings with a very thick outer wall. The basement, partly dug out of solid rock, contained the bakery, with ovens and a well, and several large vaulted cellars. Adjacent to the bakery is the vaulted kitchen with two huge fireplaces and a service room leading to the hall. The hall, on the first floor, was very large, and one end is raised and was probably screened. A stair linked the hall and cellars at one end, and at the other a stair led down to the dungeon, beneath which is a pit-prison. A wing also ran along the other side of the courtyard.
   The castle was built in the 13th century by the Vaux family. It was captured after a hard siege in 1298, when the English employed large engines, but retaken by the Scots in 1311 and partly demolished. In the 15th century the castle passed to the Halyburton family, who extended it; and in the 16th century to the Ruthvens, who again remodelled much of the castle. After the forfeiture of the Ruthvens in 1600, following the 'Gowrie Conspiracy', the lands were acquired by Thomas Erskine of Gogar. In 1649 several women and men, who had confessed to witchcraft after the witch-finder, John Kincaid, had found 'devil's marks' on them, were imprisoned in the castle, later to be strangled and burned at the stake. In 1650 the castle was besieged by General Monck, during Cromwell's invasion of Scotland. A party of mosstroopers had been attacking Cromwell's lines of communication, with some success, but they were quickly forced to surrender. Three of the leaders were sub-

Dirleton Castle

sequently shot. The castle had been damaged in the attack, and was probably slighted. In 1663 the property was bought by Sir John Nisbet, who built the house of Archerfield to replace the castle.

OPEN: Open all year: Apr-Sep, daily 9.30-18.30; Oct-Mar, Mon-Sat 9.30-16.30, Sun 14.00-16.30; last ticket sold 30 mins before closing; closed 25/26 Dec and 1/2 Jan. Administered by Historic Scotland.
Explanatory displays. Gift shop. WC nearby. Limited disabled access. Parking nearby. £.
Tel: 01620 850330   Fax: 0131 668 8888
Email: hs.explore@scotland.gov.uk   Web: www.historic-scotland.gov.uk

Dirlot Castle

Sutherland & Caithness: About 8 miles west and south of Watten, on minor roads and foot south of B870 at Westerdale, just north of River Thurso, south of Dirlot.
Ruin or site   ND 126486   OS: 12   *   Map: 12, no: 46
Nothing survives of a keep and courtyard on a rock in a very remote location. It is said to have been only accessible by a drawbridge.

It was a property of the Cheynes, but passed to the Gunns in the 15th century. It was later held by the Sutherlands, one of them said to have been a daring pirate, then to the Mackays in 1499.

Disblair House

Aberdeen & Gordon: About 2 miles west of New Machar, on minor roads west of A947, at or near Disblair House.
Ruin or site   NJ 862197 [?]   OS: 38   *   Map: 10, no: 294
Site of castle or old house. The present house dates from the 19th century, and there is a heraldic panel and doocot.

Doagh *see* Daugh

Docharty

Ross & Cromarty: About 1 mile north-west of Dingwall, on minor roads north of A834, north of River Peffery, at or near Lower Docharty.
Ruin or site   NH 534603 [?]   OS: 20   *   Map: 9, no: 62
Site of 16th-century tower house of the Munros. It was held by Black Andrew Munro

at the beginning of the 16th century, but was sold to the Bains of Tulloch in 1553.

Along with the three other Davoch Marys, the daughter of the house entertained James IV at Dingwall Castle in 1503 by a feat of harp playing. The other Marys were of Dochmaluag [Davochmaluach], a Mackenzie; Davochcairn, a Munro; and Davochpollo, which was a Munro property which passed to the Dingwall family in 1552. Docharty, itself, is from Davochcarte.
Other refs: Davochpollo; Davochcarte

Dochmaluag Castle

Ross & Cromarty: About 1.5 miles west of Dingwall, on minor roads north of A834, in Strath Peffer, north of River Peffer, at Dochmaluag.
Ruin or site   NH 521601   OS: 20   *   Map: 9, no: 60
Dochmaluag Castle is a ruinous 17th-century tower house, formerly of three storeys, which may incorporate earlier work.

It was a property of the Mackenzies from the 15th century. One story is that the daughter of the then laird entertained James IV during a visit to Dingwall Castle in 1503. The castle was garrisoned by Cromwell in the 1650s.
Other refs: Davochmaluach

Dochroyle

Ayrshire: About 2 miles south of Barrhill, on minor roads south of A714, at or near Dochroyle.
Ruin or site   NX 230793   OS: 76   *   Map: 3, no: 46
Site of castle.

Dod

Angus & Dundee: About 2.5 miles east of Forfar, on minor roads south of A932 or north of B9128, at or near Mid Dod.
Ruin or site   NO 492499 [?]   OS: 54   *   Map: 8, no: 207
Site of a small castle, nothing of which remains.
Other refs: Old House of Dod

Dolphingstone Castle

Lothians: About 1.5 miles west of Tranent, north of junction of A199 with A1, at Dolphingstone.

Ruin or site   NT 384729 [?]   OS: 66   *   Map: 4, no: 154

Site of castle, probably of the Ainslie family, remains of which survived at the beginning of the 20th century. The Ainslie family came to Scotland early in the 13th century and, although forfeited by Robert the Bruce, recovered their lands in 1377, and retained them until recent times. An alternative owner is recorded as being a MacLeod, and it is said that Cromwell stayed here.

Other refs: Dolphinstone Castle

Dolphinston Tower

Borders: About 4 miles south-east of Jedburgh, on minor roads east of A68, east of Jed Water, at Dolphinston.

Ruin or site   NT 683150 [?]   OS: 80   *   Map: 2, no: 278

Site of a strong tower house and castle, which has been completely demolished – the site is occupied by Dolphinston Farm.

The lands were a property of one Dolphin, a son of one Cospatrick in the 11th century, hence the name. The property was held by the Ainslie family from the 13th century or earlier, but passed by marriage to the Kerrs in the 16th century. There was a castle here in the 14th century, as it was destroyed by the English around 1360, but was quickly rebuilt, possibly at a nearby site [NT 682148].

The stronghold is said to have had a brownie, which – however – left after being given a present which it disliked, reputedly saying:

'Since ye've gien me a harden ramp,
Nae mair o' your corn I will tramp.'

Other refs: Dolphiston

Dolphinstone Castle *see* Dolphingstone Castle

Dolphinton

Lanarkshire & Glasgow: About 4 miles south-west of West Linton, on or near A702, at or near Dolphinton.

Ruin or site   NT 105465 [?]   OS: 72   *   Map: 3, no: 459

Site of castle, a property of the Hepburns in the 15th century.

Dolphiston *see* Dolphinston Tower

Donibristle Castle

Fife: About 1.5 miles east of Inverkeithing, on minor roads south of A921, west of Dalgety Bay, east of the shore at Donibristle Bay, at Donibristle.

Ruin or site   NT 157827 [?]   OS: 65   *   Map: 7, no: 23

Site of castle.

The lands were a property of the Abbey of Inchcolm, but passed to the Stewart Earls of Moray. It was at the shore here in 1592 that the 'Bonnie' Earl of Moray was murdered by the Gordon Earl of Huntly, as recounted in the old ballad, and the castle torched. Moray reportedly said, as he was dying after Gordon of Gight had slashed him across the face with his sword: 'You have spoilt a better face than your own.' Moray's mother had a painting made of his hewn body, which is now kept at Darnaway Castle. Donibristle was rebuilt about 1700, then accidentally burned down again in 1858, and valuable portraits were lost. Only two service wings survive.

The lands were sold in the 1960s, and developers built the new town of Dalgety Bay for our sins.

Doon of Tynron *see* Tynron Doon

Doonside Castle *see* Brigend Castle

Dores Castle

Angus & Dundee: About 3 miles south-east of Coupar Angus, south of A923, about 1 mile south-east of Pitcur, near Lochindores

Ruin or site   NO 253358 [?]   OS: 53   *   Map: 8, no: 135

Site of castle, which is said to have been used by Macbeth in the 11th century.

Dores Castle

Kincardine & Deeside: About 4 miles east of Banchory, on minor roads just north of B9077, just south of River Dee, between Kirkton of Durris and Balfour, at Castle Hill.

Ruin or site   NO 779968   OS: 45   *   Map: 10, no: 256

Site of 13th-century castle of the Comyns, later held by the Frasers until they moved to nearby Durris House.

Other refs: Castle Hill, Durris; Durris Castle

Dorlaithers Castle

Banff & Buchan: About 2.5 miles south-west of Turriff, on minor roads south of B9024, south of Burn of Gask, at or near Dorlaithers.

Ruin or site   NJ 703474 [?]   OS: 29   *   Map: 10, no: 212

Site of castle, nothing of which survives.

Dormont

Dumfriesshire: About 4.5 miles south and east of Lockerbie, on minor roads east of B7020, south-west of River Annan, 0.5 miles north of Dalton, at or near Dormont.

Ruin or site   NY 112749 [?]   OS: 85   *   Map: 1, no: 234

Site of tower house, also recorded as Dormond. Dormont House was built in 1823, and is a property of the Carruthers family.

Dornal Castle

Ayrshire: About 5 miles south-east of Barrhill, on minor road east of B7027, north of Loch Dornal, at or near Dornal.

Ruin or site   NX 295769 [?]   OS: 76   *   Map: 3, no: 70

Site of castle.

Other refs: Over Castle Dornal

Dornoch Palace

Sutherland & Caithness: In Dornoch, near Cathedral, on minor roads west of A949.

Private   NH 797897   OS: 21   *   Map: 12, no: 26**

Dornoch Palace or Castle consists of an altered 13th- or 14th-century keep of five storeys with a round 16th-century stair-tower. The keep has two open rounds, and a gabled roof. Many of the windows have been enlarged, but the walls are still pierced by shot-holes. Adjoining this is a four-storey 16th-century wing with its own stair-tower. The castle has a courtyard and garden, and was extended and altered in the 19th century.

The entrance was at the foot of the stair-tower. The basement is vaulted, the hall would have been on the first floor, with private chambers on the floors above. The building has been very altered inside.

Dornoch Palace was built by the Bishops of Caithness, and the cathedral is close by. It passed to the Gordon Earls of Sutherland after the Reformation. In 1567 George Sinclair, 4th Earl of Caithness, had the town and cathedral burned and the castle besieged to secure possession of the young Earl of Sutherland, although he is also said to have been abducted from Skibo. The castle held out for a month, but eventually surrendered on fair terms, although hostages given by the garrison were subsequently murdered. The castle was then burned, and left a ruin until restored in the 19th century as a courthouse and jail. It is now a hotel.

Other refs: Bishop's Palace, Dornoch

OPEN: Hotel.

Tel: 01862 810216   Fax: 01862 810091

Dornock

Dumfriesshire: About 2 miles east of Annan, on minor roads south of B721, north shore of Solway Firth, at Dornock.

Ruin or site   NY 231659   OS: 85   *   Map: 1, no: 268

Site of tower house, possibly a property of the Carruthers or the Carlyles of Torthorwald.

The medieval church stood nearby [NY 230660], which was dedicated to St Marjorie. There are three carved gravestones, dating from the 12th or 13th century, in the old burial ground.

Other refs: Dundronok

Douglas Castle

Lanarkshire & Glasgow area: About 0.75 miles north of Douglas, on minor roads north of the A70, on the south side of the Douglas Water.

Ruin or site   NS 843318   OS: 72   *   Map: 3, no: 390

Little remains of Douglas Castle, a 13th-century stronghold, except for the remains of a corner tower and vaulted cellars.

The castle was built by the Douglases, who took their name from the 'Douglas'

('black water') Water. It was held by the English in 1307, during the Wars of Independence, when Sir James Douglas trapped the English garrison while they were at worship in the chapel, and recaptured the castle for the Scots. He had the garrison slaughtered and dumped in the cellar, before torching the castle, in what became known as 'Douglas's Larder'.

The castle was rebuilt, but was sacked in 1455 by James II after the Battle of Arkinholm, when the Black Douglases were defeated and their lands forfeited. It was recovered by the Douglases, who were made Dukes of Douglas in 1707, and replaced by a tower house, but this was destroyed in 1755 by a fire. The castle was used by Sir Walter Scott as 'Castle Dangerous'. The house was rebuilt by the Adam brothers from 1757, and was a large castellated mansion with round towers and turrets. The property passed to the Home Earls of Home, but the castle was demolished between 1938 and 1948, because of subsidence due to coal mining.

The castle was believed to be haunted by a phantom black dog.

Douglaston House

Lanarkshire & Glasgow: About 0.5 miles east of Milngavie, on minor roads east of A81 or north of A807, north of Douglaston Loch, on golf course, at Douglastown.

Private   NS 565742 [?]   OS: 64   *   Map: 3, no: 256

Site of castle, which was replaced by Douglaston House, which is now used as the clubhouse of the golf course.

The lands were a property of the Grahams, and in 1591 Walter Graham of Douglaston quarrelled with Hamilton of Bardowie. The property had passed to the Crawfords by 1796, then to the Kerrs by the end of the 19th century.

Douloch Castle *see* Dubh Loch Castle

Dounarwyse *see* Aros Castle

Doune Castle

Stirlingshire & Clackmannan: About 0.25 miles south-east of Doune, on minor road south of the A820, just north of where the River Teith and the Ardoch Burn meet.

His Scot   NN 728011   OS: 57   ***   Map: 6, no: 59**

Standing on a strong site in a lovely location, Doune Castle, built in the 14th century, consists of two strong towers linked by a lower range. These buildings form two sides of a courtyard, the other sides enclosed by a high curtain wall. Other ranges were planned to surround the whole courtyard, but were apparently never built. The curtain wall has open rounds at the corners, and corbelled-out semi-circular bartizans midway between the rounds.

The larger gatehouse, or lord's tower, with the arched entrance or pend to the castle through the basement, is rectangular in plan, with a semi-circular tower pro-

jecting at one corner. It rises to five storeys and a gabled garret within a flush parapet.

The smaller, or kitchen, tower rises to four storeys and a gabled garret, also within a flush parapet.

The lord's tower has vaulted cellars, in the basement, and a fine vaulted hall on the first floor, reached by an external stone stair from the courtyard. The hall has a magnificent double fireplace and a gallery. A stair, in the thickness of the walls, climbs to the storeys above, which contain many chambers.

The joining range contains a lesser hall, and was also originally reached by a separate outside stair.

The kitchen tower has an enormous arched fireplace, an oven and drains; and above this were more private chambers, a suite of which was used by Mary, Queen of Scots.

The castle was built by Robert Stewart, Duke of Albany, who virtually ruled Scotland during the reign of Robert III and the imprisonment in England of the young James I. When Albany died in 1420, his son, Murdoch, succeeded him as Regent and as Duke, but when James I was freed in 1424 he had Murdoch executed.

Doune was kept as a royal hunting lodge, prison, and dower house for the widows of James III, James IV and James V. It was occasionally used by Mary, Queen of Scots, and held by forces loyal to her until 1570.

Doune was occupied by the Marquis of Montrose in 1645, and by Government troops during the Jacobite Risings of 1689 and 1715. It was taken by Jacobites in 1745, and used as a prison, although many of the prisoners escaped. It was restored in the late 19th century, although the mortar used has all had to be removed.

The ballad 'The Bonnie Earl o' Murray' tells the tale of the murder of the Earl of Moray at Donibristle by the Gordon Earl of Huntly during a feud, and has the last verse:

'O lang will his Lady,
Look owre the Castle Doune,
Ere she see the Earl o' Moray,
Come sounding through the toun.'

OPEN: Open all year: Apr-Sep, daily 9.30-18.30; Oct-Mar Mon-Wed and Sat 9.30-16.30, Thu 9.30-12.00, Sun 14.00-16.30, closed Fri; last admission 30 mins before closing; closed 25/26 Dec and 1/2 Jan.

Explanatory displays. Gift shop. Picnic area. Car parking. Group concessions. £

Tel: 01786 841742   Fax: 0131 668 8888

Email: hs.explore@scotland.gov.uk   Web: www.historic-scotland.gov.uk

Doune of Invernochty

Aberdeen & Gordon: In Strathdon, just west of A944, just west of River Don south of meeting with River Nochty.

Ruin or site   NJ 352129   OS: 37   **   Map: 10, no: 72

Doune of Invernochty consists of a large motte, second in size only to the Motte of Urr, with a surrounding wide and deep ditch. It has traces of a wall around the top, and had a wet moat fed from a river by a system of dams and sluices. There was a chapel on the motte, which was used until about the 17th century.

It was built for the Earl of Mar in the 12th century, but may have been abandoned as early as the 14th century.

Other refs: Invernochty

Doune of Rothiemurchus *see* Rothiemurchus

Dounie Castle *see* Beaufort Castle

Dounreay Castle

Sutherland & Caithness: About 8 miles west of Thurso, on minor roads north of A836, south of sea, north and within the grounds of Dounreay Nuclear Plant at Lower Dounreay.

Ruin or site   NC 983669   OS: 11   **   Map: 12, no: 36

Dounreay Castle is a ruined 16th-century castle, consisting of a main block and stair-wing, which contained a scale-and-platt stair. The hall was on the first floor of the main block. There is an adjoining single-storey block and some remains of a barmkin. The castle is derelict and roofless.

The lands were a property of the Bishop of Orkney, but passed to the Sinclairs of Dunbeath in 1564. This was disputed by the Sinclair Earl of Caithness, and the castle was besieged in 1614. It was still being used by the Earls in 1726, but later passed to the Forbeses, then the Mackays of Reay, and later of Tongue. It was occupied until 1863, unroofed and ruinous in 1910, and probably does not glow in the dark.

Dovecotwood Castle

Lanarkshire & Glasgow area: To north of Kilsyth, on minor roads north of A803, near the Garrel Burn, at or near Allanfauld.

Ruin or site   NS 717789 [?]   OS: 64   *   Map: 3, no: 333

Site of a strong castle, of which there were still some remains in the 19th century. This is probably the same site as Kilsyth Castle [NS 717786].

Dowalton Castle *see* Longcastle

Dowane

Lanarkshire & Glasgow: About 1.5 miles south-west of Lanark, on minor roads south of A72 or B7018, at or near Greenrig.

Ruin or site   NS 857422 [?]   OS: 71   *   Map: 3, no: 399

Probable site of castle.

The lands were a property of Lesmahagow Priory, but were granted to the Dowane family. They later passed to the Weirs.

Other refs: Greenrig; Devon

Dower House *see* Hamilton House

Dowhill Castle

Perth & Kinross: About 3.5 miles south of Kinross, on minor road and footpath south of B9097, south of Dowhill.

Ruin or site   NT 118973   OS: 58   **   Map: 8, no: 85

Little remains of Dowhill Castle, a 16th-century tower house, which was extended by a range of buildings, with a round tower at one corner, in the 17th century. It had a courtyard with round towers. It was a property of the Lindsays.

Dowies

Galloway: About 4.5 miles west and north of Whithorn, on minor road south of B7021, south of the Monrieth Burn, north of the Fell of Barhullion, at Dowies.

Private   NX 381430   OS: 83   **   Map: 1, no: 51

Dowies is an altered early 17th-century tower house of two storeys and an attic, and is cross-shaped. It consists of a main block with a centrally placed square wing on one side and a matching round stair-tower on the other. The walls are pierced by small windows with roll mouldings and slits and shot-holes.

The entrance was originally in the stair-tower, but the building has been greatly altered, and little of the original building survives except a turnpike stair.

Dowies was a property of the Maxwell family from 1481 and occupied by them

until 1683 when they moved to Myrton Castle. It became a farmhouse, was derelict, but has been restored in the 1980s and is occupied.

Other refs: Moure

Downfield

Fife: About 3 miles south-east of Ladybank, on minor roads west of A916, 1 mile east of Coaltown of Burnturk, at or near Downfield.

Ruin or site   NO 342075   OS: 59   *   Map: 7, no: 88

Not much remains of a castle except the vaulted basement. The lands are mentioned in the 16th century.

Other refs: The Vault, Downfield; Dunfield

Downie Castle *see* Old Downie

Downieken Castle

Angus & Dundee: About 2 miles north and east of Monifieth, on minor roads east of B962, 0.5 miles south-east of Newbigging, at or near Downieken.

Ruin or site   NO 505357   OS: 54   *   Map: 8, no: 216

Site of castle.

Draffan Castle

Fife: About 3.5 miles north-west of Crail, on minor roads west of A917 at Kingsbarns, south-west of North Quarter.

Ruin or site   NO 572110   OS: 59   *   Map: 7, no: 150

Supposed site of castle, which was said to have been built by Norsemen.

Other refs: Castle of Draffan

Draffane *see* Craignethan Castle

Dreel Castle

Fife: In Anstruther Easter, south of B9131, in Wightman's Wynd (Castle Street) near shore.

Ruin or site   NO 565035   OS: 59   *   Map: 7, no: 146

Very little remains of Dreel Castle, formerly a tall and narrow keep of the Anstruther family, except some masonry in the wall of Wightman's Wynd. The family were descended from William de Candela, who held the lands here in the 12th century. Charles II was entertained here in 1651, and Cromwell captured the castle the same year and sacked the town. It was the meeting place of the 'Beggars' Benison of Anstruther' secret society, founded in 1739, 'a Scottish society of an erotic and convivial nature composed of the Nobility and Gentry of Anstruther'. The castle had been demolished by the beginning of the 19th century.

Other refs: Anstruther Castle; Castle of Dreel

Dreghorn Castle

Lothians: About 3 miles south of Edinburgh Castle, on minor roads south of B701, east of Howden Burn, at Dreghorn Barracks.

Private   NT 225684   OS: 66   *   Map: 4, no: 77

Nothing remains of a castle, dating from 17th-century or earlier. The site is in the present barracks.

In 1671 it was a property of the Murrays, one of whom was Sir William Murray, Master of Works to Charles II. It passed to the Pitcairns, then in 1720 to the Homes of Kello, then through several families to John MacLaurin, Lord Dreghorn, after his elevation to the bench. He died in 1796, and it then became a property of the Trotters, who in 1820 built a castellated mansion nearby. This house was destroyed by the army in 1955.

Dreva Tower

Borders: About 1 mile north of Drumelzier, on minor roads west of B712 or east of A701, north of River Tweed, at or near Dreva.

Private   NT 140359   OS: 72   *   Map: 2, no: 21

Site of tower house, a property of the Tweedie family from the beginning of the 15th century.

Drochil Castle – see below

Drimnin Castle

South Highland: About 12.5 miles north-west of Lochaline, on minor roads north-west of B849, near sea on east side of Sound of Mull, east of Drimnin House.

Ruin or site NM 547550 OS: 47 * Map: 9, no: 12

Site of castle of the MacLeans of Coll in the 16th century, which was demolished to build a chapel in 1838, itself now a ruin. The castle was probably abandoned in the middle of the 18th century for nearby Drimnin House [NM 554550], which was a property of the Gordons. It dates from the 1850s, and replaced a house burned out in a fire in 1849.

Drochil Castle

Borders: About 6 miles north-west of Peebles, on minor road west of B7059 about 0.25 miles north of junction with A72, west of the Lyne Water.

Ruin or site NT 162434 OS: 72 * Map: 2, no: 26**

Drochil Castle is a large ruined 16th-century Z-plan tower house of four storeys and a garret. It consists of an almost square central block with two projecting towers, corbelled out to square above first floor level, at opposite corners.

The basement is barrel-vaulted, and contained the kitchen and cellars. Passages ran the length of the building from which individual chambers were reached – rather than each chamber opening into the next. A turnpike stair rose at one end of the passage. The hall was on the first floor with an adjoining private chamber, while many rooms occupied the floors above.

Drochil Castle was built in the 1570s by James Douglas, Earl of Morton. Morton was made Chancellor of Scotland in 1563, but was dismissed for his part in the murder of Rizzio, Mary's secretary. He was Regent from 1572-8, but in 1581 was tried and executed by the Maiden – the Scottish equivalent of the guillotine – for his part in the murder of Lord Darnley, Mary's husband. Drochil was abandoned about 1630, but is an impressive ruin, although screened by trees.

Drongan Castle

Ayrshire: In Drongan, west of B730, north of the Water of Coyle.

Ruin or site NS 450179 OS: 70 * Map: 3, no: 185

Little survives of a 15th-century castle of the Crawford family, of which substantial remains survived in the 19th century. The property had passed to the Crawfords in 1390.

Druchtag Motte

Galloway: About 2 miles north of Port William, on minor roads north of A747, north of Mochrum, at Druchtag.

His Scot NX 349467 OS: 82 ** Map: 1, no: 47

The well-preserved motte of an early castle, which dates from the 12th or 13th century. There may have been a later castle near here, and the lands of Druchtag are mentioned in 1577 and later. They were part of the Monreith estate, which was held by the MacCullochs, then the Maxwells.

Other refs: Motte of Boghouse; Boghouse

OPEN: Access at all reasonable times.

Tel: 0131 668 8800 Fax: 0131 668 8888

Email: hs.explore@scotland.gov.uk Web: www.historic-scotland.gov.uk

Druid's Temple Hill

Renfrewshire: About 2 miles east and south of Barrhead, on minor roads south of A77, Cathcart Castle Golf Course, Williamwood.

Ruin or site NS 559575 [?] OS: 64 * Map: 3, no: 253

Possible site of castle.

Other refs: Eastwood Castle; Giffnock Castle

Drum Castle

Kincardine & Deeside: About 3 miles west of Peterculter, on minor roads north of A93, 1.5 miles north of the Dee, at Drum.

NTS NJ 796005 OS: 38 ** Map: 10, no: 265**

One of the oldest occupied houses in Scotland and surrounded by extensive gardens, Drum Castle consists of a plain late 13th-century keep of four storeys. To this has been added a large L-shaped range of 1619, and the castle was extended again in the 19th century.

The keep has rounded thick walls, which are pierced by small windows, gunloops and slits. Surrounding a flat roof, which may once have had a garret, the corbelled-out parapet has open rounds. An external stone stair leads to the entrance at first-floor level.

The vaulted basement is lit only by slits, and is reached down a straight stair, in the thickness of the walls, from the barrel-vaulted lesser hall on the first floor, now the library and reached from the newer house. An external stair climbs to the entrance.

The main hall, which is also vaulted, is on the second floor. A turnpike stair rises in the thickness of one corner.

The 17th-century extension consists of an L-shaped range of three storeys and a garret, with square gabled projecting towers and a round stair-tower. There are other additions, which together with the older parts, form a courtyard completed by a curtain wall with a gateway.

The basement of the extension is vaulted, and contained the kitchen with a large fireplace and cellars. A large hall occupies the first floor, and a turnpike stair led up to the private chambers above.

Drum was a property of the Irvines from 1323, when the lands were given to them by Robert the Bruce after Sir William de Irwyn, or Irvine, whose seat was at Bonshaw, had been his standard bearer. The Irvines were much involved in the feuding between the Keiths and the Forbeses.

Sir Alexander Irvine was killed at the Battle of Harlaw in 1411, slain by and slaying MacLean of Duart 'Hector of the Battles'. The Irvines supported Charles I, and Drum was besieged and plundered by Argyll in 1644, and sacked again in 1645 when the womenfolk were turned out of the castle. The family were Jacobites, and fought in the 1715 and 1745 Jacobite Risings.

The courtyard was remodelled by David Bryce in 1876. In 1975 the castle was given to The National Trust for Scotland.

OPEN: Castle open 13 Apr-May and Sep, daily 13.30-17.30; Jun-Aug, daily 11.00-17.30; Oct, Sat-Sun 13.30-17.30; last admission 16.45. Garden as house, 10.00-18.00. Grounds open all year, daily 9.30-sunset.
Collections of furniture and pictures. Garden of historic roses. Woodland walks. Gift shop. Tearoom. WC. Disabled facilities. Parking. £££.
Tel: 01330 811204
Email: information@nts.org.uk Web: nts.org.uk

Drum House

Lothians: About 4.5 miles south-east of Edinburgh Castle, on minor roads west of A68 or east of A7, east of Gilmerton, at Drum.
Private NT 301688 OS: 66 * Map: 4, no: 125
Little remains of a 16th-century tower house of the Somervilles, replaced by an Adam mansion of 1726-34, which has some fine plasterwork. James Somerville of Drum was killed after a duel with Thomas Learmonth in 1628. Drum later passed to the Nisbets of Cairnhill.
Other refs: The Drum; Somerville House

Drumbreck Castle *see* Dumbreck Castle

Drumcoltran Tower

Galloway: About 5 miles north and east of Dalbeattie, on minor roads north of A711, about 0.25 miles north of Kirkgunzeaon Lane, among farm buildings, at Drumcoltran.
His Scot NX 869683 OS: 84 * Map: 1, no: 163**
Drumcoltran Castle is a 16th-century L-plan tower house. It consists of a main block of three storeys and a garret, within a corbelled-out parapet; and a stair-tower with

no parapet, rising a storey higher to be crowned by a watch-chamber. The tower is roofed but does not have internal flooring.

It was a property of the Herries of Terregles family, but passed by marriage to the Maxwells in 1550. It was sold to the Irvings in 1669, then to the Hynds in 1799, then the Herons, and then back to the Maxwells in 1875. The tower was occupied until the 1890s.

OPEN: Access at all reasonable times – apply to key holder.
Parking nearby.
Tel: 0131 668 8800 Fax: 0131 668 8888
Email: hs.explore@scotland.gov.uk Web: www.historic-scotland.gov.uk

Drumdollo Castle

Aberdeen & Gordon: About 4.5 miles east of Huntly, on minor roads north of A96 or south of A97, 0.3 miles south-east of Drumdollo.
Ruin or site NJ 606387 [?] OS: 29 * Map: 10, no: 159
Site of castle, which was demolished around 1840. It was a property of the Leslies, and had a date stone of 1508.

Drumelzier Castle

Borders: About 3 miles south and east of Broughton, on minor road and footpath east of A701, on the west side of the Tweed, west of Drumelzier.
Ruin or site NT 124334 OS: 72 * Map: 2, no: 18**
Drumelzier Castle consists of a ruined 16th-century L-plan tower house of three storeys and an attic, but incorporates older work. It was extended by a square tower at one corner, also of three storeys and an attic.

Drumelzier was a property of the Tweedies from the 14th century until 1632 when it passed to the Hays of Yester. John Tweedie of Drumelzier – and others – assassinated John Fleming, Chancellor of Scotland, while he was out hawking. A James Tweedie of Drumelzier was pardoned for the murder of William Geddes in 1558 during a feud. The castle was abandoned for the nearby 18th-century house, now incorporated into farm buildings, and was ruinous by 1790. The Hays held the property until about the middle of the 19th century.
Other refs: Drummelzier Castle

Drumgin Castle

Galloway: About 3.5 miles north-west of Whithorn, on minor roads and foot north of B7021 or east of A746, north of White Loch, 0.3 miles west of Drumgin.
Ruin or site NX 402444 OS: 83 * Map: 1, no: 57
Site of tower house or castle, formerly surrounded by a marsh, itself built on the site of a moated manor house. It is mentioned in 1455, and this castle appears to have been superseded by Ravenstone Castle [NX 409441].
Other refs: Old Castle of Ravenstone; Ravenstone

Drumhead Tower *see* Blairhenechan Tower

Drumin Castle

Moray: About 7.5 miles north of Tomintoul, on minor road just north of B9136 at Drumin, south-east of River Avon at meeting with River Avon, at Drumin.
Private NJ 184303 OS: 36 ** Map: 10, no: 31
Drumin Castle, a massive ruined 14th-century keep, formerly of four storeys, was probably built by Alexander Stewart, the Wolf of Badenoch or his son, another Alexander (or Andrew). It was later sold to the Gordons, but may have returned to the Stewarts. The family were Jacobites, forfeited after the Rising of 1745, and the property passed to the Gordons. Some consolidation work was carried out in 1997. There is a modern house nearby.
Other refs: Castle Drumin

Druminnor Castle

Aberdeen & Gordon: About 1 mile south-east of Rhynie, on minor roads east of A97, 1 mile east of Water of Bogie, north of Correen Hills, at Druminnor.
Private NJ 513264 OS: 37 ** Map: 10, no: 116**
Druminnor Castle consists of a much-altered 15th-century keep of three storeys and a garret. It was extended in the 16th century, to L-plan, and a slender stair-turret, in the re-entrant angle, was also added. A round stair-tower, corbelled out to square and crowned by a watch chamber, projects at one end. The walls are

pierced by gunloops. There were further alterations in 1660, and 1825 when a new wing was added, but this has since been demolished.

The entrance is in the foot of the stair-tower. The basement is vaulted, and contained the kitchen with a wide arched fireplace. The hall, on the first floor, is a fine chamber.

The lands were a property of the Forbes family from the 13th century or earlier, and they held a castle at Castlehill [NJ 516287]. They built the present castle in 1440. This was the original Castle Forbes, and the family feuded with the powerful Gordons – 20 Gordons were slaughtered at a banquet held at the castle in 1571. The Battle of Tillyangus was fought soon afterwards, and the Forbeses were routed by the Gordons, and the castle sacked. Druminnor was sold in 1770, the family having moved to Castle Forbes [NJ 622191], but purchased in the 1960s by a descendant of the original Forbes family. It was restored and is occupied.

Other refs: Castle Forbes

Druminnor Castle *see* Castlehill, Druminnor

Drumlanrig Castle

Dumfriesshire: About 3 miles north and west of Thornhill, on minor roads west of A76, just west of River Nith, at Drumlanrig.

Private NX 851992 OS: 78 * Map: 1, no: 156

The remains of a 14th-century castle, including cellars, were built into the large 18th-century courtyard mansion. The castle consists of four ranges around the court, with higher rectangular towers at the corners, and stair-towers within the courtyard. The towers have pepper-pot turrets.

The original castle was built by the Douglases soon after 1357, but sacked by the English in 1549. It was destroyed in 1575 because the family supported Mary, Queen of Scots, who had stayed here in 1563. However, it was restored or rebuilt as James VI stayed here in 1617, by when it had assumed a courtyard design. Drumlanrig was occupied by a Cromwellian force in 1650.

A huge new mansion, set around the courtyard, was built between 1675 and 1689 by the architect William Wallace for William Douglas, 3rd Earl of Queensberry, who was made Duke in 1684, and seems to have nearly bankrupted himself. However, the Duke spent only one night in his splendid new mansion, decided he did not like it, and moved back to Sanquhar Castle, where he died in 1695. His son, the 2nd Duke, transferred his seat to Drumlanrig and Sanquhar was left to decay. Bonnie Prince Charlie stayed at the castle in 1746 after his retreat from Derby, and his men sacked and damaged the building and stabbed a painting of William of Orange.

Drumlanrig became derelict, but passed to the Scott Dukes of Buccleuch in 1810. The castle was restored in 1827, and service wings were added by William Burn. The house is in good condition, and there is a fine collection of pictures, including paintings by Rembrandt, Holbein and Leonardo, as well as many other works of art.

Three ghosts are said to haunt the castle. One is reputed to be the spirit of Lady

Anne Douglas; another a young woman in a flowing dress; a third a monkey or other creature. Another story is that someone was murdered in the 'Bloody Passage', and that the blood could not be washed from the floor.

There is also a prophecy by Thomas the Rhymer about the castle – House of Hassock is another name for the castle.

'When the Marr Burn runs where never man saw
The House of the Hassock is near to a fall'

This is said to have been fulfilled when Charles 3rd Duke diverted the Marr Burn to make a fountain south of the castle. His two sons died young. The burn has since been returned to its original course.

Other refs: House of the Hassock; Hassock

OPEN: Open May-mid Aug: Mon-Sat 11.00-16.00, Sun 12.00-16.00; country park, gardens & adventure woodland end Apr-Sep 11.00-17.00; other times by appt only.

Fine collection of pictures, including paintings by Rembrandt, Holbein and Leonardo, as well as many other works of art. Guided tours. Gift shop. Tea room. Visitor centre. Park land, woodland walks and gardens. WC. Picnic area. Adventure woodland play area. Working craft centre. Demonstrations of birds of prey (except Thu). Disabled access. Car and coach parking. Group concessions. ££.

Tel: 01848 330248 Fax: 01848 600244
Email: bre@drumlanrigcastle.org.uk

Drumlanrig's Tower, Hawick

Borders: In Hawick, south of A7.

Private NT 502144 OS: 79 ** Map: 2, no: 166

Drumlanrig's Tower, formerly the Tower Hotel, consists of an altered and extended 16th-century L-plan tower house, once surrounded by a moat.

It was a property of the Douglases of Drumlanrig, and the only building left unburned after the torching of Hawick by the Earl of Surrey and the English in 1570. It was later occupied by Anna, Duchess of Buccleuch, wife of the executed Duke of Monmouth. From the 17th century part of the basement was used as a prison, this becoming the wine-cellar on its conversion to a coaching inn. It has been restored to house an exhibition of local history, during which a parapet was uncovered, as well as fireplaces, windows and a gunloop.

There were several strongly fortified bastle houses in the town, and remains of a bastle house at 51 High Street survive, with a vaulted basement, built into what is now a shop.

Other refs: Hawick Tower; Black Tower of Drumlanrig

OPEN: Open late Mar-Oct, Sun 12.00-17.00; late Mar-May and Oct, Mon-Sat 10.00-17.00; Jun-Sep, Mon-Sat 10.00-17.30; Jul-Aug 10.00-18.00.

Visitor centre. Period rooms and costumed figures. Explanatory displays. Gift shop. Disabled access. Parking nearby at Common Haugh. £.

Tel: 01450 373457 Fax: 01450 373993

Drumlochy Castle

Perth & Kinross: About 1.5 miles north-west of Blairgowrie, on minor roads west of A93 in Blairgowrie, north of Lornty Burn, 0.25 miles west of Milton of Drumlochy.

Ruin or site NO 158469 OS: 53 * Map: 8, no: 105

Little remains of Drumlochy Castle, a 16th-century stronghold, except part of one wall and a round tower.

It was a property of the Herons of Drumlochy. It was destroyed during a feud with the Blair family, whose castle of Glasclune is nearby.

Drummellan Castle

Ayrshire: About 3.5 miles south of Maybole, east of B741, east of Water of Girvan, at Drummellan.

Ruin or site NS 298032 [?] OS: 76 * Map: 3, no: 74

Site of castle, the last remains of which were removed in the 19th century. A mansion was built nearby.

The property passed to the Kennedys in the 14th century.

Drummelzier Castle *see* Drumelzier Castle

Drummochreen

Ayrshire: About 4.5 miles south of Maybole, on minor roads and foot north of B741, just north of Water of Girvan, 1 mile north-east of Dailly, Drummochreen.
Ruin or site   NS 280026   OS: 76   **   Map: 3, no: 62
Little remains of a castle or old house but one upstand of masonry and some traces of a courtyard with a ditch.

Drummond Castle

Perth & Kinross: About 2.5 miles south and west of Crieff, on minor road west of A822, in Drummond Park, at Drummond Castle.
Private   NN 844181   OS: 58   ****   Map: 8, no: 23
Built on a rocky outcrop, Drummond Castle consists of a 15th-century keep of five storeys and a garret. To this has been added a lower 17th-century extension, and a late 18th-century mansion, which was later remodelled from the buildings surrounding the keep. The keep has a corbelled-out parapet, with open rounds, and a square stair-tower projects from one side.

The entrance, at first floor level, is reached from the courtyard by an external stone stair. A lesser hall occupied the first floor, and the vaulted basement is reached by a narrow stair in the thickness of the wall. A turnpike stair, in the tower projecting from the keep, leads up to the main hall. The upper floors have been remodelled.

The extension comprises a rectangular gatehouse range of three storeys, through which a vaulted pend, with massive iron gates, enters the courtyard. Another range of buildings was demolished to foundations.

Sir Malcolm Drummond distinguished himself at the Battle of Bannockburn in 1314, and was given the lands here – although the existing castle was not begun until the 15th century. Margaret, daughter of the Drummond laird who built the castle, was a lover of James IV, and they were reputedly married and had a daughter. However, some of the nobles wanted James to marry Margaret Tudor, sister of Henry VIII, and form an alliance with England. To this end, and to 'free' James, Margaret, and two of her sisters, were murdered with poisoned sugared fruit, and are buried side by side in Dunblane Cathedral.

The Drummonds were made Earls of Perth. Mary, Queen of Scots, visited the castle in 1566-7 with Bothwell. The castle was badly damaged by Cromwell in the 1650s, and slighted after having been occupied by Hanoverian troops during the Jacobite Rising of 1715. The 5th Earl had commanded the Jacobite cavalry at the Battle of Sheriffmuir that year, and the 6th commanded the left wing of the Jacobite army at the Battle of Culloden in 1746. The family was forfeited as a result, although the Earldom of Perth was recovered by them in 1853, as was Stobhall where they now live.

The castle passed to the Willoughbys, then the Earl of Ancaster. It was restored in 1822, when a turreted extension was added to the mansion. The castle and magnificent formal garden featured in the film version of 'Rob Roy'.
OPEN: Castle not open. Gardens open Easter & May-Oct 14.00-18.00; last admission 17.00.
Gift shop. Disabled partial access. WC. Car and coach parking.
Tel: 01764 681257/433   Fax: 01764 681550
Email: thegardens@drummondcastle.sol.co.uk

Drummond House *see* Hawthornden Castle

Drummore Castle

Galloway: About 16 miles south of Stranraer, near B7041 just south-west of Drummore, about 0.3 miles south of shore of Drummore Bay.
Ruin or site   NX 136364   OS: 82   *   Map: 1, no: 28
Little or nothing remains of a 16th-century tower house of the Adairs of Kilhilt. It was rectangular in plan, and the basement was vaulted and divided into three with a turnpike stair. The castle was still habitable in 1684, and there were significant remains until it was demolished in 1963.
Other refs: Drumore Castle

Drummuir

Moray: About 4 miles south-west of Keith, on minor road north of B9115, about 2.5 miles east of modern Drummuir Castle, at Mains of Drummuir.
Private   NJ 407448   OS: 28   **   Map: 10, no: 80
Drummuir consist of a very altered 17th-century L-plan tower house of three storeys. The walls are pierced by small windows and shot-holes.

It was a property of the Leslies, but sold to the Duffs in 1670, and abandoned around 1700 for Kirkton House, then Drummuir Castle, a large 19th-century castellated mansion, which has been recently restored.

Alexander Duff of Drummuir seized Inverness for the Jacobites in 1715. The castle is now occupied by the Gordon-Duff family, has fine plasterwork, and collections of paintings and other artefacts. There is a walled garden.

The house and gardens are regularly open in the summer, and there is also the Loch Park Adventure Centre on the estate which offers activities such as canoeing, kayaking, gorge walking, rowing, and fly fishing.
Other refs: Mains of Drummuir
OPEN: Modern castle open 28/29 Aug and 8-29 Sep: tours at 14.00 and 15.00.
Modern castle: Guided tours. WC. Disabled access and WC. Parking. £.
Tel: 01542 810332   Fax: 01542 810302

Drumore Castle *see* Drummore Castle

Drumquhassle Castle

Stirlingshire & Clackmannan: About 1.5 miles south and east of Drymen, on minor road south of A811, just east of Endrick Water, at or near Park of Drumquhassle.
Ruin or site   NS 483869   OS: 57   *   Map: 6, no: 9
Site of a castle or old house, dating from the 16th century.

It was a property of the Cunninghams. Sir John Cunningham of Drumquhassle was keeper of Dumbarton Castle, and in 1577 was Master of the King's Household.

Drumry Castle

Lanarkshire & Glasgow: About 2 miles east and south of Duntocher, on minor roads north of A82, between Drumchapel and Kilbowie, off Drumry Place, at Drumry.
Ruin or site   NS 515710   OS: 64   *   Map: 3, no: 225
Site of three-storey tower house, with a corbelled-out turret in one corner, and later extensions, which were cleared away by the council in 1959. The castle had gardens and an orchard.

The lands were a property of the Callendar family, but passed in 1346 to the Livingstones. Sir Robert Livingstone of Drumry was Lord Treasurer of Scotland, but executed in 1447. The last Livingstone holder died at the Battle of Flodden in 1513, and the property passed by marriage to James Hamilton of Finnart. In 1528 Drumry was exchanged with Laurence Crawford of Kilbirnie for Crawfordjohn and Kilbirnie, and Crawford probably built the castle. He was later accused of treason, and the property passed to the Semples in 1545. The castle became ruinous, but was apparently restored in 1836. It was used to house farm labourers, but became ruinous again, and no trace now remains as it was demolished in the 1960s. It was, however, described as being in good condition in 1951.
Other refs: Peel of Drumry; East Kilpatrick

Drumsargad Castle

Lanarkshire & Glasgow area: About 3.5 miles north-west of Hamilton, on minor roads north of A724, 1 mile east of Flemington, just south of Hallside, at or near Calder Glen.
Ruin or site   NS 667597   OS: 64   *   Map: 3, no: 315
Little remains of a castle – spelt variously Drumsargad, Drumsagard or Drumsharg – which crowned a rounded flat-topped mound. It was ruinous by the end of the 18th century.

The lands were a property of the Oliphants (or Olifards) from the 13th century, but passed by marriage to the Murrays. John Murray of Drumsargad married Mary, daughter of Malise, Earl of Strathearn in 1299, and was forfeited by Edward I of England in 1306 for supporting Robert the Bruce.

In 1370 the lands, along with Bothwell in 1360, passed to the Douglases, then in

1455 on their forfeiture to the Hamiltons, who held them until the 1920s. The name was changed in the 17th century to Cambuslang, and the site cleared by the 1880s. The main residence had become Westburn House, which dated from 1685, but this was demolished in the 20th century.
Other refs: Drumsharg; Westburn House

Drumsharg *see* Drumsargad Castle

Drumsoy Castle

Ayrshire: About 0.5 miles south of Drongan, on minor road west of B730, south of Water of Coyle, at Drumsuie.
Ruin or site NS 439175 [?] OS: 70 * Map: 3, no: 175
Site of tower house, which was demolished early in the 19th century. A cottage is said to occupy the site. It was a property of the Crawfords in 1567.
Other refs: Drumsuie Castle

Drumsuie Castle *see* Drumsoy Castle

Drumtochty Castle

Kincardine & Deeside: About 2 miles north-west of Auchenblae, on minor roads north of B966, east of Drumtochty Forest, at Drumtochty Castle.
Private NO 699801 OS: 45 ** Map: 10, no: 208
Standing in acres of wooded grounds, the present 19th-century mansion, designed by James Gillespie Graham, may incorporate part of an old castle. The mansion was built for the Reverend J. S. Gammell of Countesswells, but was later used as a hotel, then a school.

Drumwalt Castle *see* Old Place of Mochrum

Dryburgh Abbey

Borders: About 3 miles north-east of Melrose, on minor road south of B6356 at Dryburgh, just east of the River Tweed, part of Dryburgh Abbey.
His Scot NT 591317 OS: 73 * Map: 2, no: 228**
A picturesque and substantial ruin, the Abbey was founded by David I as a Premonstratensian establishment, dedicated to St Mary. Most of the buildings date from the 12th and 13th centuries, and part of the church survives as do substantial portions of the cloister, including the fine chapter house, parlour and vestry. The Abbey was torched by the English in 1322 and 1385. The lands passed to the Erskine family after the Reformation, and the family were Commendators. The abbey had been burned in 1544, again by the English, and was never rebuilt, although it was occupied by monks until at least 1584.

The Commendator's House, for the Abbey's secular owners, was created in the 16th century by altering the dormitory of the abbey, immediately over the chapter house, into a comfortable but fortified house. New windows were inserted, and an entrance was made from the east side. The walls were pierced by shot-holes.

David Erskine, Lord Cardross, stayed in the abbey until his death in 1671. It was later sold to the Scotts of Ancrum. Sir Walter Scott and Earl Haig are both buried here.

The abbey ruins are said to be haunted by ghostly monks.
Other refs: Commendator's House, Dryburgh Abbey
OPEN: Open all year: Apr-Sep, daily 9.30-18.30; Oct-Mar, Mon-Sat 9.30-16.30, Sun 14.00-16.30, last ticket 30 mins before closing; closed 25/26 Dec and 1/2 Jan.
Gift shop. WC. Picnic area. Disabled access. Car and coach parking. Group concessions. £.
Tel: 01835 822381 Fax: 0131 668 8888
Email: hs.explore@scotland.gov.uk Web: www.historic-scotland.gov.uk

Dryburgh Abbey Hotel *see* Mantle House

Dryhope Tower

Borders: About 2 miles east and north of Cappercleuch, on minor road north of A708 at Dryhope, about 0.3 miles north of St Mary's Loch, west of Dryhope Burn.
Ruin or site NT 267247 OS: 73 * Map: 2, no: 68**
Dryhope Tower is a ruined 16th-century tower house, formerly of three or four storeys. The basement is vaulted, and a turnpike stair in one corner led up to the

hall, on the first floor, which was also vaulted. A courtyard, with a curtain wall, enclosed ranges of buildings.

Dryhope was a property of the Scotts, and the home of Mary (or Marion) Scott, the Flower of Yarrow. The ballad the 'Dowie Holms of Yarrow' records, in several versions, the bloody events associated with her. In 1576 she married Walter Scott of Harden, 'Auld Wat', a famous Border reiver. The tower was slighted in 1592 after the Scotts had been involved in some dastardly events against James VI at Falkland Palace, but rebuilt by 1613.
OPEN: Access at all reasonable times.

Duart Castle

Argyll & Dunbartonshire: On east side of island of Mull (ferry from Oban), about 3 miles south of Craignure, on minor road east of A849, on Duart Point, at Duart.
Private NM 749354 OS: 49 *** Map: 5, no: 41**
An extremely impressive and daunting fortress, Duart Castle consists of a large 13th-century curtain wall, enclosing a courtyard on a rocky knoll. In 1390 Lachlan Lubanach, 5th Chief, built the keep on the outside of the curtain wall, enclosing the existing well. There are later ranges of buildings within the walls. The entrance was through a gatehouse with a portcullis.

The keep has very thick walls, and the ground floor was vaulted with the main hall, on the first floor, which has a great fireplace, and round headed windows with

stone seats, although a new window has been cut in one wall. The upper floors are reached by a narrow turnpike stair in the thickness of the wall.

A 16th-century range of three storeys and a garret has four vaulted cellars, and another three-storey block was added in the 17th century.

The MacLeans of Duart claim descent from Gillean of the Battle Axe. Lachlan Lubanach married Lady Elizabeth, daughter of the Lord of the Isles, granddaughter of Robert II King of Scots, and was granted the first known charter for Duart dated 1390 as her dowry. While fighting with the MacDonalds, the 6th chief Red Hector was killed at the Battle of Harlaw in 1411, slaying and being slain by Sir Alexander Irvine of Drum.

During a feud in the clan, Ewen MacLaine of Lochbuie was slain and beheaded in battle – and his ghost, the headless horseman, rides in Glen Mor.

Lachlan Cattanach, 11th Chief, became so unhappy with his Campbell wife that he had the poor woman chained to a rock in the Firth of Lorn to be drowned at high tide. However, she was rescued and taken to her father, the Campbell Earl of Argyll. As a result, MacLean was murdered in his bed in Edinburgh by Sir John Campbell of Cawdor.

In 1604 MacLean of Duart, along with many other chieftains, was kidnapped and imprisoned while being entertained aboard ship off Aros Castle. In 1674 the castle was acquired by the Campbell Earl of Argyll. The MacLeans remained staunch supporters of the Stewarts throughout the Jacobite Risings. Although garrisoned, the castle was not used as a residence, and was abandoned after the Jacobite Rising of 1745 to become derelict and roofless. It was acquired in 1911 by Fitzroy MacLean, who restored the castle. It houses a exhibition of clan displays, and featured in the recent film 'Entrapment' with Sean Connery.

OPEN: Open May-mid Oct, daily 10.30-18.00.

13th-century keep, exhibitions, dungeons and state rooms. Tea room and gift shop. WC. Picnic areas. Disabled access to tea room and gift shop. Car and coach parking. Group concessions. ££.

Tel: 01680 812309/01577 830311   Fax: 01577 830311
Web: www.duartcastle.com

Dub Castle

Aberdeen & Gordon: In Aberdeen, Gilcomston.
Ruin or site   NJ 935065 [?]   OS: 38   *   Map: 10, no: 327
Site of castle.

Dubh Loch Castle

Argyll & Dunbartonshire: About 2 miles north-east of Inveraray, on minor roads north of A83 at the northern end of Loch Shira (Loch Fyne), on southern shore of Dubh Loch.
Ruin or site   NN 114107 [?]   OS: 56   *   Map: 5, no: 112
Site of castle, little or nothing of which survives except a mound, on southern shore of Loch Dubh. It was a stronghold of the MacNaughtons, before moving to Dunderave. It is said to have been abandoned in the late 15th or mid 16th century because of plague.

Other refs: Loch Dubh Castle; Douloch Castle

Dubs

Renfrewshire: About 0.5 miles east of Barrhead, on minor roads south of B773, south of Dovecothall, off Dubs Road, at Dubs.
Private   NS 516591   OS: 64   **   Map: 3, no: 228
Standing on a knoll above a burn, Dubs consists of a very altered two-storey house or tower standing in a small courtyard.

It was a property of the Maxwells from 1271 until the 1830s. Maxwell of Dubs fought for the Hanoverians during the Jacobite Rising of 1745. It is said that he hid his money, not trusting family or bankers, in Darnley Glen, but never returned to collect it. Occasional finds of silver and gold coins are reportedly made.

Duchal Castle

Renfrewshire: About 1.5 miles west and south of Kilmacolm, on minor road and foot south of B788, where the Blackkelty Water and the Burnbank Water meet.
Ruin or site   NS 334685   OS: 63   *   Map: 3, no: 99
Little remains of Duchal Castle, a 13th-century keep and courtyard of the Lyles, later made Lords Lyle in 1440 and Lord High Justiciars of Scotland. The castle was abandoned for nearby Duchal House, which was built about 1768, although part may date from 1710.

The family took part in the Lennox rebellion of 1489, and James IV besieged Duchal, apparently bringing with him the cannon Mons Meg. Later he visited the castle to see one of his mistresses, Marion Boyd. They had a son, who was made Archbishop of St Andrews, but died at the Battle of Flodden in 1513 with his father. In 1544 the property passed to the Montgomerys of Lainshaw, and was sold to the Porterfields, who held it until the middle of the 19th century. The castle became ruinous soon after. At the end of the 19th century the property was held by the Shaw-Stewarts of Ardgowan.

The castle was said to have been haunted by the spirit of an excommunicated monk in the 13th century, apparently a very 'corporeal' ghost. The monk would stand on the walls of Duchal and shout and swear at the occupants. The ghost could not be got rid of – arrows melted when they hit the ghost – until a son of the laird, a particularly goodly youth, cornered it in the great hall. In the ensuing battle the son was killed and the hall wrecked, but the ghost departed and was not witnessed again.

Duchray Castle

Stirlingshire & Clackmannan: About 3 miles west of Aberfoyle, on minor roads south of B829 at Milton, about 1 mile south of Loch Ard, at Duchray Castle.
Private   NS 480998   OS: 57   **   Map: 6, no: 8
Duchray Castle is an altered rectangular 16th-century tower house of three storeys with a round tower at one corner and a turret crowning the opposite corner. The building has corbiestepped gables, and the basement is vaulted.

Duchray was sold to the Grahams of Downie in 1569, who built the castle. It was the mustering point for an army led by the Earl of Glencairn, who defeated a Cromwellian force at Aberfoyle in 1653. In the 1690s two Graham sisters entertained officers of William and Mary, while Rob Roy MacGregor was smuggled out the back. The castle was torched after the Jacobite Rising of 1745, but restored and remodelled in 1825. It is still occupied.

Dudhope Castle

Angus & Dundee: About 0.5 miles south of Dundee Law, on minor road just north of A923, about 0.5 miles north-west of Dundee railway station, at Dudhope.
Private   NO 394307   OS: 54   *   Map: 8, no: 171**
Dudhope Castle is a 17th-century courtyard castle, consisting of two long blocks, with round corner towers, and a twin-towered gateway. The towers have conical roofs. A 16th-century tower house, which was originally part of the castle, has been demolished, and no traces remain.

The basement of one block is vaulted, and contained the kitchen, with a wide arched fireplace. The castle has been very altered inside.

The lands were a property of the Scrimgeours from 1298 until 1668. James VI visited the castle in 1617. Sir John Scrimgeour was created Viscount Dudhope in 1641, but the 2nd Viscount was killed fighting for Charles I at the Battle of Marston Moor in 1644. The 3rd Viscount was made Earl of Dundee.

Dudhope was sold to John Graham of Claverhouse in 1668, and became his chief residence. Known both as 'Bonnie Dundee' and 'Bloody Clavers', he led the Jacobites to victory at the Battle of Killiecrankie in 1689, although he himself was slain. The castle was later adapted for use as a woollen mill, then a barracks from 1796 until 1879, and finally a storeroom. Although derelict, it was restored from 1989 as an office. The grounds are a public park.

Dudwick Castle

Aberdeen & Gordon: About 4 miles north-east of Ellon, on minor roads east of A948, west of A92, at or near Mains of Dudwick.
Private   NJ 975370 [?]   OS: 30   *   Map: 10, no: 344
Site of castle, which was later extended into a mansion, but completely demolished about 1860.

It was held by the Mitchell family, but passed to the Kings in the first quarter of the 17th century. One of the family was General James King, who fought in the Swedish army of Gustavus Adolphus, and was made Lord Ythan in 1642. King returned to Sweden, where he died in 1652. The castle was later used as a farmhouse.

Duff House, Banff

Aberdeenshire: South of Banff, on minor roads east of A97, west of River Deveron, at Duff House.
His Scot   NJ 692633   OS: 29   *   Map: 10, no: 202**
Duff House is a fine classical mansion with colonnades and corner towers, dating from 1735, and designed by William Adam for William Duff of Braco, later Earl of Fife. Adam and Duff fell out over the cost of building the house, and work stopped in 1741 – the subsequent legal action was eventually won by Adam. The house is now used to display works of art from the National Galleries of Scotland.

OPEN: Open all year: Apr-Oct, daily 11.00-17.00; Oct-Mar, Thu-Sun 11.00-16.00.

Sales area. Refreshments. WC. Disabled facilities including lift and toilets. Parking. £ (free admission to shop, tearoom, grounds and woodland walks).

Tel: 01261 818181   Fax: 01261 818900

Duff House – see previous page

Duffus Castle

Moray: About 3 miles north-west of Elgin, on minor roads west of B9012 or east of B9135, 1.5 miles east of Duffus, south of Lossiemouth Airfield, at Old Duffus.
His Scot NJ 189672 OS: 28 * Map: 10, no: 34**
One of the best examples of a 12th-century motte and bailey castle in Scotland, Duffus Castle consists of an extensive outer bailey with a wet moat, a walled and ditched inner bailey, and a large motte. On the motte was built a square 14th-century stone shell-keep of two storeys. There were ranges of buildings in the outer bailey. The motte was not strong enough to support the keep and part has collapsed down the slope. The castle was surrounded by the now drained Loch of Spynie.
  The original castle was built by Freskin, Lord of Strathbrock, a Fleming who also held property in West Lothian. David I stayed here while supervising the construction of nearby Kinloss Abbey. It was destroyed by the Scots in 1297, but rebuilt in stone by the Cheynes in the late 13th or early 14th century. It passed by marriage to the Sutherland Lord Duffus in 1350, and the family held the property until 1843. The castle was sacked in 1452 by the Douglas Earl of Moray, and again in 1645 by Royalists. John Graham of Claverhouse, 'Bonnie' Dundee' stayed here in 1689. The castle was abandoned for nearby Duffus House at the end of the 17th century.
OPEN: Access at all reasonable times.
Car parking.
Tel: 0131 668 8800 Fax: 0131 668 8888
Email: hs.explore@scotland.gov.uk Web: www.historic-scotland.gov.uk

Duffus Castle *see* Invershin Castle

Duke Murdoch's Castle

Stirlingshire & Clackmannan: About 3.5 miles west of Aberfoyle, on minor roads west of B829 at Milton, on a small island, Dundochil, near the south shore of Loch Ard.
Ruin or site NN 473014 OS: 57 ** Map: 6, no: 7
Not much remains of a 14th-century castle on an island in the loch. It was a hunting lodge of Murdoch, Duke of Albany, who was executed by James I in 1425.
Other refs: Dundochil

Dumbarton Castle

Argyll & Dunbartonshire: In Dumbarton, on minor roads south of the A814, on a promontory on the north side of the River Clyde.
His Scot NS 400745 OS: 64 ** Map: 5, no: 156
Little remains of Dumbarton Castle, which now mostly consists of 18th and 19th century fortifications, except the 14th-century entrance.

Meaning 'fortress of the Britons', Dumbarton is first mentioned around 450 as the stronghold of Alcluith of the kings of Strathclyde. In 756 it was captured by Picts and Northumbrians, and in 870 was besieged by Irish raiders, who captured the rock only after four months of fighting, starving the garrison into surrender. Owen the Bald, the last King of Strathclyde, died at the Battle of Carham in 1018, and Strathclyde was absorbed into the kingdom of Scots.
  Dumbarton became a royal castle, and was a formidable fortress. William Wallace was held here before being taken to London for execution in 1305. In 1333 the young King David II and his queen Joan sheltered in the castle during fighting with the English. In 1489 James IV besieged Dumbarton twice to oust the Earl of Lennox, the second time successfully, and then used it as a base to destroy the Lord of the Isles.
  The castle changed hands many times in the 16th century, between various factions, but after the disastrous Battle of Pinkie in 1547, the young Mary, Queen of Scots, was kept at Dumbarton for some months before being taken to France. The castle changed hands again, but was retaken in 1562 and held for Mary until 1571. The Earl of Morton and Patrick Stewart, Earl of Orkney, were imprisoned here in 1581 and 1614 respectively. The castle was captured and recaptured several times in the 1640s, but in 1654 a Royalist force made a successful surprise attack on Cromwell's garrison.
  The old castle was badly damaged during this period, and improvements were begun in 1675 and carried on until the middle of the 18th century. Further renovations were made to develop the castle for coastal defence during the 1790s, and nothing remains of the medieval castle except the 14th-century portcullis arch.
  In Dumbarton itself is a 17th-century town house of the Cunningham Earls of Glencairn [NS 395752], known as the 'Earl of Glencairn's Greit House' or 'Glencairn Tenement'. It was built in 1623, and in 1923 acquired by the town council.
OPEN: Open all year: Apr-Sep, daily 9.30-18.30; Oct-Mar, Mon-Wed and Sat 9.30-16.30, Thu 9.30-12.00, Sun 14.00-16.30, closed Fri; last ticket 30 mins before closing; closed 25/26 Dec and 1/2 Jan.
Exhibition in Governor's House. Gift shop. WC. Car parking. Group concessions. £.
Tel: 01389 732167 Fax: 0131 668 8888
Email: hs.explore@scotland.gov.uk Web: www.historic-scotland.gov.uk

Dumbraxhill *see* Duntervy Castle

Dumbreck Castle

Aberdeen & Gordon: About 3.5 miles west of Ellon, on minor roads north of A920, at or near Mains of Dumbreck.
Ruin or site NJ 898289 [?] OS: 38 * Map: 10, no: 312
Site of 16th-century castle. A gunloop is built into one of the walls of Mains of Dumbreck. The lands were a property of the Dumbreck family, but passed to the Meldrums, who built the castle.
Other refs: Drumbreck Castle

Dumcrieff

Dumfriesshire: About 1.5 miles south of Moffat, on minor roads south of A708, west of Moffat Water, at or near Dumcrieff.

Ruin or site   NT 102036   OS: 78   *   Map: 1, no: 227

Site of tower house. Dumcrieff House, a later mansion, may stand on the site.

Dumcrieff was a property of the Murrays, but passed to the Clerks of Penicuik, and then in 1785 was the home of John Loudoun Macadam, of road-making fame. It was then held by Dr James Currie, who wrote a biography of Robert Burns, and later Dr John Rogerson, who was court doctor at St Petersburg for about 50 years. He died in 1823, and at the end of the 19th century it belonged to the Rollo Lord Rollo, after whom the chocolates were named – well maybe not.

Other refs: Duncreith

Dumfries Castle

Dumfriesshire: In Dumfries, west of B725 south of junction with A756, just east of the River Nith.

Ruin or site   NX 975754   OS: 84   *   Map: 1, no: 189

Only earthworks remain of Dumfries Castle, a royal castle built by William the Lyon before 1214.

The castle was taken by Robert Bruce the Elder in 1286 after the death of Alexander II. It was held by the English from 1298, but briefly taken by his son Robert the Bruce, later Robert I, after the stabbing of the Red Comyn in a church in Dumfries in 1306. It was recaptured and held by the English, during which time they strengthened it with the addition of a keep, until 1314 when it was seized by the Scots.

The castle was destroyed in 1357 as part of the conditions of release of David II from captivity in England. Dumfries was torched by the English about 1448 and repeatedly thereafter, including in 1536.

Lord Maxwell, after sacking the English town of Penrith in revenge, built a tower house [NX 971762] in 1545 as a fortress and refuge (in Castle Street). This building is said to have had four storeys with a vaulted basement, a turnpike stair and bartizans. However, the tower was taken and the town sacked by the English in 1547, and again in 1570. It was garrisoned in 1675 when in need of repair, but by 1724 had been demolished and the site is occupied by a church.

In 1583 the townsfolk built a tower house of two storeys, called the 'New Wark', to defend Dumfries. Part of this building survived until 1719, although this is probably the same site as above.

Other refs: Castledykes, Dumfries; New Wark, Dumfries

Dumfries House *see* Ward of Lochnorris

Dun *see* House of Dun

Dun Airnistean

Western Isles: About 3 miles west of Port of Ness, on minor road and foot north of A857, Airnistean, on coast, Lewis.

Ruin or site   NB 489627   OS: 8   **   Map: 11, no: 29

A castle is said to have stood on a small island here, but there are only slight traces. Iron Age pottery, now in the Museum of Scotland, has been found here, and this was probably a dun, although it may have been used in medieval times.

Other refs: Airnistean

Dun an Garbh-Sroine

Argyll & Dunbartonshire: About 4.5 miles south-west of Kilmelford, just east of A816, west of Garraron, Dun an Garbh-Sroine.

Ruin or site   NM 803089   OS: 55   *   Map: 5, no: 56

The remains of a fort or castle, roughly rectangular in plan, stand near the shore. It was a property of the MacIver Campbells, and was used from the 13th until the 17th century.

Other refs: Lergychonzie

Dun an Sticar

Western Isles: About 6 miles north of Lochmaddy on North Uist, on foot east of B893, 0.5 miles south of Newtonferry, on island in Loch an Sticar, at Dun an Sticar.

Ruin or site   NF 898778   OS: 18   ***   Map: 11, no: 16

Although originally an Iron Age dun, Dun an Sticar was inhabited by Hugh MacDonald, one of the MacDonalds of Sleat and son of Hugh the Clerk, until 1602. He sheltered here after plotting to slaughter his kin, but was eventually captured to be starved to death in Duntulm Castle on Trotternish in Skye.

The massive walls of the dun had a gallery, part of which can be seen, and survive to a height of over ten feet. The entrance can be traced, and there are two splendid causeways out to a neighbouring islet, Eilean na Mi-Chomhairle ('island of the bad council'?), then another causeway out to the dun.

OPEN: View from exterior – care should be taken.

Parking nearby.

Dun Aonais

Western Isles: About 4 miles north-west of Lochmaddy on island of North Uist, on foot and boat just east of A865, in Loch Aonais, at Dun Aonais.

Ruin or site   NF 889737 [?]   OS: 18   **   Map: 11, no: 15

The remains of a dun, Dun Aonais or Aonghais ('dun of Angus'), which stands on a small round island in Loch Aonais. The wall encloses the island near to the water edge, and there was a causeway joining it to the mainland.

The dun was occupied until 1516 or later, and takes its name from a MacDonald Aonghais Fionn, 'Angus the Fair', its last occupier.

Dun Ara

Argyll & Dunbartonshire: To north of island of Mull, about 5 miles west of Tobermory, on minor roads and foot 4.5 miles east of B882, 0.5 miles north-west of Glengorm Castle.

Ruin or site   NM 427577   OS: 47   **   Map: 5, no: 16

Standing on a large outcrop of rock, Dun Ara consists of the ruinous remains of a wall enclosing the summit of the rock with an outwork at a lower level defending the entrance. Within the wall are the foundations of a probable hall and other buildings.

Beneath the summit are the traces of other buildings, and it is likely that the castle was built on the site of a dun or fort. There are also the remains of a harbour and boat-landing.

Dun Ara was a stronghold of the MacKinnons, who held lands here from 1354 or earlier. The castle appears to have still been in use in the 17th century.

Dun Athad

Argyll & Dunbartonshire: About 6 miles south-west of Port Ellen on Islay, on minor road and foot 5.5 miles west of A846, on southern tip of The Oa, south of Upper Killeyan.

Ruin or site   NR 284406   OS: 60   **   Map: 5, no: 4

Dun Athad, originally an Iron Age dun, was reused by Sir James MacDonald in 1615, while trying to reclaim the island for his family.

Other refs: Dunaidh Castle

Dun a' Ghallian

Western Isles: About 4 miles west of Sollas, by minor road and boat north of A865, Grimnish, Loch an Eilean, North Uist.

Private   NF 748760   OS: 18   **   Map: 11, no: 5

The island in Loch an Eilean has the remains of a probably defensive – and probably medieval – wall, which enclosed a paved area. The entrance, also paved, consists of a 20 foot passage, which changes direction at one point. The island may have been occupied by Norsemen, and finds from here include a dagger, carved knife, pottery and animal bones.

Dun Ban, Loch Caravat

Western Isles: About 8 miles south and east of Bayhead on North Uist, on foot and boat north of A865, islet in Loch Caravat, south of Beinn na Coille, at Dun Ban.

Ruin or site NF 843608 OS: 22 ** Map: 11, no: 13

On an island in Loch Caravat, Dun Ban – originally an Iron Age dun – was given mortared walls in medieval times, and had a hall block opposite the entrance. It probably dates from the 14th or 15th century, and it is said that the building was still roofed, with flat stones, in 1850. There may have been a causeway.

Dun Ban, Ulva

Argyll & Dunbartonshire: On west side of island of Ulva, on minor roads, ferry and track west of B8073, 4 miles west and north of Ulva House, in inlet between Ulva and Gometra, at Dun Ban.

Private NM 384416 OS: 47 ** Map: 5, no: 10

Situated in the narrow channel between Ulva and its neighbouring island of Gometra, Dun Ban consists of the remains of a rectangular building standing on the summit of a small islet. The islet has steep cliffs, and the only relatively easy approach, from the foreshore, is defended by a wall. There was a causeway across to Gometra, and a small harbour.

  The island was a property of the MacQuarries from 1473 or earlier until the 18th century, although they had a old mansion or castle [NM 442389] near the present Ulva House, the site now occupied by a farm.

Other refs: Glackingdaline Castle; Ulva House

Dun Beag

South Highland: About 8 miles south of Dunvegan on island of Skye, on foot north of A863, north west of Struanmor, at Dun Beag.

His Scot NG 339386 OS: 32 ** Map: 9, no: 4

Dun Beag ('small dun') is a well-preserved ruined broch on a small knoll. The entrance passage, an adjoining cell and mural stair rising about 20 steps all survive.

The broch was occupied in the 18th century, and finds from here included pottery, an armlet of glass, a gold ring, bronze objects, and glass beads as well as coins from the reigns of Henry II, Edward I, James VI, George II and George III.

OPEN: Access at all reasonable times.

Parking.

Tel: 0131 668 8800 Fax: 0131 668 8888
Email: hs.explore@scotland.gov.uk Web: www.historic-scotland.gov.uk

Dun Bhoraraic

Argyll & Dunbartonshire: About 2.5 miles south and east of Port Askaig, island of Islay, on minor roads and foot south of A846, west and north of Lossit Farm.

Ruin or site NR 417658 OS: 60 ** Map: 5, no: 15

Standing on a small hill, Dun Bhoraraic consists of the remains of a broch, the walls of which are over twelve-feet thick. The remains of a guard cell defending the entrance and a mural chamber can be traced. It was used by the MacDonalds in medieval times.

Other refs: Dunborerraig

OPEN: Permission must be sought from Dunlossit Estate.

Dun Bragar

Western Isles: About 5 miles north-east of Carloway, by foot just south of A858, just west of Bragar, Loch an Duna, Lewis.

Private NB 285474 OS: 8 * Map: 11, no: 25**

Standing on an island in a small lochan, Dun Bragar is a ruinous broch, the walls of which survive to a height of 14 feet on the south side. The broch may still have been in use as late as the 16th and 17th century, as John Roy MacPhail was caught in his bed here.

Other refs: Loch an Duna, Bragar

Dun Buidhe

Western Isles: About 1.5 miles east of Balivanach, on minor road and foot east of B892, Loch Dun Mhurchaidh, Benbecula.

Ruin or site NF 794546 OS: 22 ** Map: 11, no: 11

Standing on a small island in Loch Dun Mhurchaidh is Dun Buidhe 'yellow dun', which was connected by a causeway to a second island to the mainland. The causeway is defended by a wall at the mainland end.

  The main part of the oval dun is very ruinous, and survives to a height of about three feet. A secondary wall, enclosing the island, is better preserved and is over seven feet high at one point. There are the remains of several buildings and structures within the walls, and the island is said to have been reused by the Norsemen.

Dun Canna *see* Dun Channa

Dun Carloway

Western Isles: About 15 miles west of Stornoway on island of Lewis, on minor road west of A858, 1.5 miles south-west of Carloway, at Dun Carloway.

His Scot NB 190412 OS: 8 * Map: 11, no: 22**

Dun Carloway is the best preserved broch in the Western Isles, and stands to a height of 30 feet. There is a guard cell off the entrance passage. Inside the courtyard are three doorways leading to the staircase opposite the main entrance, and to side cells. The natural rock protrudes jaggedly into the interior of the courtyard

and given this it would seem likely that there was a timber floor erected higher up which provided the main living space. A ledge of stones, or scarcement, protruding from the wall, could have supported such a floor.

In the 17th century the Morrisons of Ness used the broch as their stronghold against the MacAulays of Uig. However, one of the MacAulays climbed up the outer wall, using a dagger to find holds in the masonry – although the stone is so well laid it is hard to see how, and he may have used a grappling hook. The sleeping Morrisons were then suffocated by throwing smouldering heather over them.

OPEN: Access at all reasonable times.
Car and coach parking. The Doune Broch Centre is nearby.
Tel: 0131 668 8800 Fax: 0131 668 8888
Email: hs.explore@scotland.gov.uk Web: www.historic-scotland.gov.uk

Dun Channa

South Highland: On west tip of Canna.
Ruin or site NG 206048 OS: 39 ** Map: 9, no: 1
Built on a relatively inaccessible rocky stack, the landward side has been further strengthened by a wall, now much ruinous. There are foundations within the wall, which may be medieval in origin.
Other refs: Dun Canna

Dun Chonnuill

Argyll & Dunbartonshire: On south-east side of Dun Chonnuill island, the most easterly of the Garvellachs, a chain of islands south of Mull in the Firth of Lorn.
Ruin or site NM 680125 OS: 55 ** Map: 5, no: 27
Dun Chonnuill is a ruined 13th-century castle, although the site was fortified from prehistoric times. The remains consist of a ruinous wall surrounding the summit of a knoll with the foundations of several buildings within the walls. On another crag to the north are the remains of a triangular dun, and at its foot are the foundations of more buildings. A wall has been built between the two knolls.

It was probably a property of the MacDougalls, although one story is that a MacLauchlan from Ireland took and fortified the island in the 14th century. It was later held by the MacDonalds, then the MacLeans.
Other refs: Dunchonnel Castle

Dun Creich *see* MacTire Castle

Dun da Lamh

South Highland: About 2.5 miles west and south of Laggan, on minor roads and foot north of A86, south of River Spey, at Dun da Lamh.
Ruin or site NN 582929 OS: 35 ** Map: 9, no: 73
Set on a rock commanding the lands around, Dun da Lamh consists of the remains of an impressive fort. It is defended by a strong wall which survives to a height of about nine feet.
Other refs: Black Craig

Dun Dornaigil

Sutherland & Caithness: About 3.5 miles south of end of Loch Hope, on minor road 10 miles south of A838 at Hope, just east of Strathmore River, at Dun Dornaigil.
His Scot NC 457450 OS: 9 ** Map: 12, no: 7
Dun Dornaigil or Dun Dornadilla survives to almost 22 feet in one section (now supported by a modern buttress) which places it among the best preserved examples in Scotland. The entrance is crowned with a huge triangular lintel. The broch has not been excavated and the interior is full of rubble.
OPEN: Access at all reasonable times.
Parking.
Tel: 0131 668 8800 Fax: 0131 668 8888

Dun Eibhinn

Argyll & Dunbartonshire: North-west of Scalasaig, on foot north of A870, Dun Eibhinn, Colonsay.
Private NR 382944 OS: 61 ** Map: 5, no: 9
A well-preserved dun, the 'fort of Eyvind', from a Norse name. The enclosing wall and entrance can be traced, and there have been buildings within the fort. The dun was apparently used by the MacDuffies in medieval times.

Dun Eiphinn, Gometra

Argyll & Dunbartonshire: About 5 miles west of Ulva House, 0.5 miles south of Gometra House, off track, Dun Eiphinn, Gometra.
Private NM 358402 OS: 47 ** Map: 5, no: 7
Set on a rocky hillock, Dun Eiphinn is an Iron Age fort or dun. A wall enclosed the top of the crag, the entrance can be traced, and there were also outworks. The dun may have still been in use in medieval times as pottery and coins were found here which date from the turn of the 14th century.

Dun Gallanach *see* Gallanach Castle

Dun Grugaig

South Highland: About 3.5 miles south-east of Glenelg, on minor road west of A87 at Shiel Bridge, north of river, in Gleann Beag.
Ruin or site NG 852159 OS: 33 * Map: 9, no: 31
The remains of a D-plan dun stand above a steep gorge. The walls stand to a maximum height of about 16 feet, and mural chambers and a blocked entrance passage can be traced.
Other refs: Caisteal Chonil

Dun Grugaig

South Highland: About 1.5 miles south-east of Elgol, off A881, Glasnakille, Skye.
Private NG 535124 OS: 32 * Map: 9, no: 10**
Standing on a small rocky outcrop above the sea, Dun Grugaig consists of a strong wall cutting off the promontory on the landward side. The wall, which survives to a height of 13 feet above the inside level, has mural galleries and there are the treads of a stair. A massive lintel survives above the entrance, and the passageway is still roofed over.

Dun Horavaig *see* Caisteal Camus

Dun Lagaidh

South Highland: About 2.5 miles south of Ullapool, on minor roads and foot west of A835, on west side of Loch Broom, at Dun Lagaidh.
Ruin or site NH 142913 OS: 20 ** Map: 9, no: 42
Dun Lagaidh is a dun, standing within an earlier fort, which was later used as a castle. The dun has very thick walls, and there are the remains of a guard chamber and an intramural stair, later utilised as an entrance. The site was reused in the 12th century as a castle.

Dun Mhic Laitheann

Western Isles: About 5.5 miles north-east of Lochmaddy, on minor road, foot and boat east of A865, Groatay, North Uist.
Ruin or site NF 978731 OS: 18 ** Map: 11, no: 18
The ruins of a dun situated on a steep tidal rock to the south-west of the islet of Groatay. The walls survive to a height of over three feet, and the entrance can be traced. There are also the remains of a rectangular building, and the site may have been reused in the mid 17th century.

Dun Mhic Leod *see* Castle Sinclair

Dun na Muirgheidh

Argyll & Dunbartonshire: About 2 miles north-east of Bunessan, on minor road and foot north of A849, east of Knockan, on promontory on south shore of Loch Scridain, Dun na Muirgheidh, Mull.
Ruin or site NM 413236 OS: 48 ** Map: 5, no: 14
The ruins of a fort, standing on a rock promontory, cut off by four walls on the landward side. The massive walls survive to a height of five feet, and the entrance to the fort can be traced. There are the foundations of two rectangular medieval buildings within the fort, and it appears to still have been in use during this period.

Dun Naoimh Castle *see* Dunyvaig Castle

Dun Raouill

Western Isles: About 12 miles north of Lochboisdale, by foot 1 mile east of A865, south shore of Loch Druidibeg, Dun Raouill, South Uist.
Private NF 778371 OS: 22 * Map: 11, no: 9
The remains of a rectangular fortification and possible small harbour on a small island in the loch. The 'dun' is probably medieval, and there are traces of other buildings and a garden.

Dun Ringill

South Highland: About 11 miles south and west of Broadford on Skye, on minor road and foot east of A881 at Kilmarie (footpath by bridge or stepping stones) along shore.
Ruin or site NG 562171 OS: 32 *** Map: 9, no: 13
An Iron Age stronghold, Dun Ringill consists of a dun, with mural passageways, and an altered entrance within which are the foundations of two small medieval rectangular buildings. The dun was defended by a ditch.
   It was used by Clan MacKinnon before they moved to Dunakin or Castle Maol in the late 16th century.
Other refs: Fingon

Dun Sgathaich

South Highland: About 8 miles north and west of Armadale on island of Skye, on minor road west of A851, in Sleat, about 1 mile west of Tokavaig, just east of sea.
Ruin or site NG 595121 OS: 32 ** Map: 9, no: 16
Standing on a rock with an enclosing wall following the irregular contours, Dun Sgathaich is a ruined 14th-century courtyard castle, probably incorporating an older castle or dun. The entrance is reached by a flight of steps, protected by a draw-bridge, door and flanking tower. Ranges of buildings surrounded at least three sides of the courtyard, dating or rebuilt in the 16th and 17th centuries, but are now very fragmentary. The castle appears to have been a place of some strength.
   Meaning 'Dun of the Shadow', Dun Sgathaich is associated with Diarmid, a companion of Finn MacCool. The warrior queen Sgathaich trained men in the art of fighting, and Diarmid came here to be instructed by her. Another tradition is that the castle was built in a single night by a witch.
   Although the castle was originally held by the MacAskills, in the 14th century the lands of Sleat and Dun Sgathaich belonged to the MacLeods. They managed to fight off attacks by the MacDonald Lord of the Isles in 1395 and 1401, but early in the 15th century the property passed to the MacDonalds.
   James I captured the castle in 1431 because of a rebellion by the MacDonalds. It was forfeited to the Crown around the 1490s with the destruction of the Lord of the Isles by James IV, but was besieged by the MacLeods in support of the MacDonalds in 1515, although unsuccessfully. It was probably abandoned around 1618 when the MacDonalds of Sleat moved to Duntulm, although they later returned to Armadale on Sleat.
Other refs: Dunscaith; Dunscaich

Dun Telve

South Highland: About 2 miles south-east of Glenelg, on minor road west of A87 at Shiel Bridge, north of river, in Gleann Beag.
His Scot NG 829172 OS: 33 *** Map: 9, no: 29
The Glenelg brochs, Dun Telve and Dun Troddan [NG 833172] are two of the best preserved brochs in Scotland. A large part of the wall of Dun Telve is missing but within the remaining sector of wall are scarcements to support upper floors, and voids above the interior doors. The entrance has a bar-hole and door-checks. There are various outbuildings around the broch although they may be later in date. Artefacts recovered when the site was excavated included pottery fragments, stone cups (possibly used as lamps) and a few quern stones.
Other refs: Glenelg
OPEN: Access at all reasonable times.
Parking nearby.
Tel: 0131 668 8800 Fax: 0131 668 8888
Email: hs.explore@scotland.gov.uk Web: www.historic-scotland.gov.uk

Dun Torcuill

Western Isles: About 4.5 miles north-west of Lochmaddy, by foot east of A865, Loch an Duin, Dun Torcuill, North Uist.
Private NF 888737 OS: 18 *** Map: 11, no: 14
On a small island in the loch, connected to the mainland by a short causeway, is a well-preserved dun or possible broch. The entrance, cells and gallery can be traced, and the walls survive to a height of about ten feet, although the inside of the building is choked with rubble and undergrowth. There are the remains of a later building, and the dun may have been occupied in the 16th or 17th centuries.

Dun Totaig *see* Caisteal Grugaig

Dun Troddan

South Highland: About 2.5 miles south-east of Glenelg, north of minor road west of A87 at Shiel Bridge, north of river, near Corrary, in Gleann Beag.
His Scot NG 833172 OS: 33 *** Map: 9, no: 30
Dun Troddan is a fine broch, and neighbour to Dun Telve [NG 829172], which is located 0.3 miles further along the glen. As with Dun Telve a section of the wall survives and the structure of the building – two skins held together with horizontal slabs – can be seen. It is possible to go up a section of the staircase within the gallery. Off the entrance is a corbelled guard cell. When the site was excavated in 1920 a circle of posts was located in the central area, presumably to hold the posts which supported an upper timber floor.
Other refs: Glenelg
OPEN: Access at all reasonable times.
Parking nearby.
Tel: 0131 668 8800 Fax: 0131 668 8888
Email: hs.explore@scotland.gov.uk Web: www.historic-scotland.gov.uk

Dun Trudernish

Argyll & Dunbartonshire: About 7.5 miles north-east of Port Ellen, on minor road and foot east of A846, 0.25 miles north-east of Trudernish, Trudernish Point, Islay.
Ruin or site NR 468526 OS: 60 ** Map: 5, no: 18
The ruins of a fort, standing on a rocky promontory, defended on the landward side by three walls. One wall survives to a height of about eight feet, and is vitrified in places. The entrance can be identified. A second wall stands to a height of around six feet, and appears to date from the medieval period. The entrance through this wall can also be traced, and there are the probable remains of a causeway. The outermost wall is more ruinous.

Dun Vulan

Western Isles: About 9.5 miles north-west of Lochboisdale, on minor road and foot west of A865, Rubha Ardvule, South Uist (marked as Danger Area on OS map).
Private NF 713297 OS: 22 *** Map: 11, no: 3
A broch or dun with walls surviving to a height of about 14 feet. There is a wall chamber and a stairway to a first-floor gallery, and the entrance can be identified. The site was occupied from the Bronze Age until at least 300 AD, and there is apparently a medieval building outside the broch wall. Finds from the broch and surrounding area include tools, wooden artefacts, animal bones, shells and pottery.
   The headland the broch stands on, Rubha Ardvule, is said to be named after a Norse Princess called Vule.

Dunachton Castle

South Highland: About 5 miles east and north of Kingussie, on minor roads north of A9, north of Loch Insh, at or near Dunachton Lodge.
Ruin or site NH 820047 [?] OS: 35 * Map: 9, no: 128
Little or nothing remains of Dunachton Castle, except a small cellar built into the present house.
   The lands were a property of the MacNivens, but passed to the Mackintoshes of Torcastle about 1500. The castle was burned down in 1689 by the MacDonalds of Keppoch, and not rebuilt.
   A Class 1 Pictish symbol stone was found here, and is carved with a deer's head.

Dunadd

Argyll & Dunbartonshire: About 3.5 miles south of Kilmartin, on minor road and foot west of A816, south of the River Add, on hill at Dunadd.

His Scot   NR 836936   OS: 55   *   Map: 5, no: 62**

Dating from the 1st century AD, Dunadd is built on an imposing rock and consists of lines of fortifications, some well preserved. It was a stronghold of the Scots after they first arrived from Ireland in the 3rd to 6th century. It was the place of inaugurations of their kings, with a basin, footprint and other carvings in the rock. St Columba ordained Aidan, son of Gabhrain, the 6th King of the Dalriadan Scots. The Stone of Destiny was kept here. In the Annals of Ulster it is recorded that Dunadd was besieged by the Picts in 683 and 736, and a the carving of a boar, which looks Pictish in execution, was found here. Kenneth MacAlpin united the Scots and Picts. The fort was abandoned in the 10th century.

OPEN: Access at all reasonable times.

Parking nearby.

Tel: 0131 668 8800   Fax: 0131 668 8888

Email: hs.explore@scotland.gov.uk   Web: www.historic-scotland.gov.uk

Dunagoil

Argyll & Dunbartonshire: About 10 miles south of Rothesay, on minor road and foot south of A844, south side of Dunagoil Bay, Port Dornoch, Bute.

Private   NS 085531   OS: 63   *   Map: 5, no: 104

Standing on a site defended by crags except on the landward side, the fort is encircled by the remains of a wall. Parts of the wall are vitrified. Finds from the fort, now in Rothesay Museum, include glass and lignite bracelets, a brooch, ring-headed pins, pottery and axe-heads, dating from both the Bronze and Iron Age.

Nearby at Little Dunagoil [NS 087532] is another small fort, occupied from the Bronze Age until the 13th century. The remains of Norse longhouses were found here, and finds including pottery, an axe and fragments of a comb and bracelet are also kept in the Rothesay Museum.

Dunaidh Castle *see* Dun Athad

Dunain

South Highland: About 4 miles south-west of Inverness, on minor roads west of A82, at or near Dunain House.

Ruin or site   NH 626423   OS: 26   *   Map: 9, no: 85

Site of castle. Dunain House, a 19th-century baronial mansion, may be built on the site.

Other refs: Dunean

Dunakin *see* Caisteal Maol

Dunalastair

Perth & Kinross: About 4 miles east of Kinloch Rannoch, on minor roads south of B846, north of River Tummel, at eastern end of Dunalastair Water, at Dunalastair.

Ruin or site   NN 710589 [?]   OS: 52   *   Map: 8, no: 8

Site of castle, probably of the Robertsons.

Dunaskin *see* Laight Castle

Dunaverty Castle

Argyll & Dunbartonshire: About 8 miles south of Campbeltown, on minor roads south of B842 at Southend, on point at south tip of Kintyre, at Dunaverty.

Ruin or site   NR 688074   OS: 68   **   Map: 5, no: 28

Once an important stronghold on a steep promontory above the sea, virtually nothing remains of Dunaverty Castle, a 13th-century castle of enclosure. The landward side was protected by a series of ditches. The promontory is now known as 'Blood Rock'.

This was one of the strongholds of the Scottish kingdom of Dalriada, and was captured and burned. It was recaptured from rebels by Alexander II in 1240, and garrisoned against Norsemen in 1263 when it was a property of the MacQuillans. It was later held by the MacDonald Lord of the Isles, and is said to have sheltered Robert the Bruce. In 1493 James IV seized the castle from the MacDonalds, but it was almost immediately retaken and the king's governor was hanged from the walls, within sight of the king's departing ship. The castle was damaged by the English, led by Sussex, during their raid on Kintyre in 1558.

Archibald MacDonald's 300 strong garrison was massacred to a man after surrendering to the Covenanter forces of General David Leslie in 1647. The castle was finally dismantled during Argyll's rebellion of 1685, and little remains.

OPEN: Access at all reasonable times – care should be taken.

Dunbar Castle

Lothians: In Dunbar, on minor road north of A1087, on north shore just west of harbour.

Ruin or site   NT 678794   OS: 67   **   Map: 4, no: 222

Although once one of the most important castles in Scotland, little remains of Dunbar Castle, except foundations of a very ruined keep and courtyard. The ruins date

in part from the 12th century, although there was a stronghold here from at least the 9th century.

The Cospatrick Earls of Dunbar held the castle in the 13th century, but it was captured by the English in 1297. Black Agnes, Countess of Douglas, held the castle successfully for six weeks in 1338 against English armies, using a giant catapult against the besiegers' stone-hurling mangonels. She reputedly said after the battle, as the English fled: 'behold of the litter of English pigs'. The 11th Earl of Dunbar was forfeited for treason; and the castle was slighted in 1488, but later rebuilt by James IV. In 1489 the ships of Sir Andrew Wood defeated an English navy just off Dunbar.

The castle passed to the Duke of Albany, who remodelled the castle for artillery about 1515, but it was burned by the English in 1548. Further fortifications were added by the French in 1550, but destroyed under the terms of the Treaty of Leith. However, in 1566, two days after Rizzio's murder, Mary, Queen of Scots, and Darnley arrived here – although he had been involved in the murder. In 1567 ten weeks after Darnley was himself murdered, Mary was brought here after being abducted by James Hepburn, 4th Earl of Bothwell, who was the keeper of the castle. She later married him.

The castle surrendered and was destroyed after Mary had fled to England. Much of the ruin was demolished in the 19th century to build the harbour. The remains of the castle are very ruinous, and continue to deteriorate.

OPEN: Access at all reasonable times – care should be taken.

Parking nearby.

Dunbeath Castle

Sutherland & Caithness: About 1 mile south of Dunbeath, on minor roads east of A9, north-east of Dunbeath Mains, just west of the sea, at Dunbeath Castle.

Private   ND 158282   OS: 17   **   Map: 12, no: 49**

Standing on top of cliffs above the sea, Dunbeath Castle is a 17th-century E-plan tower house of four storeys, to which has been added modern wings, although it may incorporate work from the 15th century. Two-storey bartizans crown three corners and two stair-turrets are corbelled-out above first-floor level to be topped by square watch-chambers. The walls are harled and whitewashed, and are pierced by many gunloops and shot-holes.

The castle has been much altered inside, but the basement is vaulted. It contained the kitchen, with a large fireplace, and a wine-cellar, with a small stair to the hall above, as well as other cellars. There is a very narrow secret stair. A turnpike stair, in one of the turrets, leads to the upper floors.

The property was held in 1452 by the Crichtons, but by 1507 had passed to the Innes family. They held it until 1529 when Dunbeath was acquired by the Sinclairs of Geanies, who built much of the existing building about 1620. The castle was besieged and taken by a force for the Marquis of Montrose in 1650, but quickly recaptured after his defeat at the Battle of Carbisdale. The house was altered in the 1850s and 1881, and is still occupied.

Dunblane, Bishop's Palace *see* Bishop's Palace, Dunblane

Dunbog Castle
Fife: About 3 miles east and south of Newburgh, on minor road south of A913 at Glenduckie, at or near Dunbog.
Ruin or site   NO 285181 [?]   OS: 59   *   Map: 7, no: 66
Site of L-plan castle of the Bannermans.

Not much remains of Dunbog House, a mansion of the Dundas Marquis of Zetland. It has been mostly demolished, but is said to occupy the site of a house of Balmerino Abbey, known as the Preceptory of Gadvan. Dunbog is said to have been built by Cardinal David Beaton, and the mansion incorporated some of a 16th-century building. This may also be the site of the castle mentioned above. The property, however, had passed to the Beatons of Creich by 1578.
Other refs: Preceptory of Gadvan; Gadvan

Dunborerraig *see* Dun Bhoraraic

Dunchonnel Castle *see* Dun Chonnuill

Duncreith *see* Dumcrieff

Duncrub
Perth & Kinross: About 4.5 miles north-east of Auchterarder, on minor road west of B9141, about 1 mile north-west of Dunning, at or near Mains of Duncrub.
Ruin or site   NO 007157 [?]   OS: 58   *   Map: 8, no: 51
Site of castle of the Rollo family, who held the lands from 1380. Lord Rollo of Duncrub was executed by beheading in 1645 after being captured at the Battle of Philiphaugh fighting for Montrose. The 4th Lord Rollo fought for the Jacobites in the 1715 Rising, but was later pardoned and died at Duncrub in 1758.

Dundaff Castle *see* Graham's Castle

Dundarg Castle
Banff & Buchan: About 6 miles west of Fraserburgh, on minor roads and foot north of B9031, 1 mile north-west of New Aberdour, south of sea, at Dundarg.
Ruin or site   NJ 895649   OS: 30   *   Map: 10, no: 309
Not much remains of Dundarg or Dundargue Castle. It dates from the 13th century, was much rebuilt in the 16th century, and stands within the earthworks of an Iron Age fort.

Dundarg is associated with St Drostan, and the site is said to have been given to him by Bede the Pict as related by the Book of Deer. The Comyn Earls of Buchan had a castle here, which was destroyed by Robert the Bruce in 1308. It was rebuilt in 1333, and held by the English, but besieged, captured and destroyed again by the Regent Andrew Moray the next year. Moray used cannon, the first known use of such in Scotland.

Dundarg was occupied again, and is mentioned between 1450-55 when it was a castle of the Black Douglases, probably being slighted again after they were forfeited. It passed to the Borthwicks, who had the site refortified in 1550 by French engineers. It was sold to the Cheynes of Esslemont, and probably abandoned soon after. A new house was built within the outer courtyard in the 1930s.

Dundas Castle
Lothians: About 1.5 miles south of South Queensferry, on minor road west of A8000, just north of Dundas Loch, at Dundas Castle.
Ruin or site   NT 116767   OS: 65   *   Map: 4, no: 42**
Dundas Castle or Tower is a massive 15th-century keep of four storeys and a flat roof, now L-plan with the addition of a later wing. A round caphouse with a rib-vaulted ceiling crowns the main turnpike stair. The corbelled-out parapet has open

rounds at the corner.

The entrance, in the re-entrant angle, still has an iron yett. The basement is vaulted and has a stair, in one corner, which leads to the hall on the first floor. The castle has been greatly altered inside with brick partition walls. The main stair climbs only to the first floor. There were fine private chambers above the hall, some of them vaulted.

The Dundas family held the lands from about 1124 until 1875, and built the castle in 1424. It was besieged in 1449, and visited by both Charles II and Cromwell in 1651. The castle was abandoned when the nearby Gothic mansion, designed by William Burn, was built in 1818, and later converted for use as a distillery. It is empty, but in fairly good condition. The house was sold to the Stewarts in 1875.
Other refs: Old Dundas

Dundavid *see* Duntulm Castle

Dundee Castle
Angus & Dundee: To the south of Dundee, near the shore of the Firth of Tay, west of the Tay Road Bridge, on Black Rock.
Ruin or site   NO 404302 [?]   OS: 54   *   Map: 8, no: 176
Nothing remains of Dundee Castle, once a strong fortress.

Dundee was besieged and sacked more often than any other town in Scotland apart from Edinburgh. The castle was damaged by William Wallace, repaired by Edward I of England, then comprehensively destroyed by Robert the Bruce after having been recaptured from the English in 1312. It was not rebuilt, and until the 16th century Dundee did not have a town wall. The town suffered much in Cromwell's invasion of 1651. One sixth of the town's population was massacred, and the plunder was enormous, probably because other Scottish towns had sent their valuables to Dundee for safekeeping. Why, if it was sacked so much?

There was a tower within the city, known as Mauchline Tower [NO 403304], but this was demolished in 1812; while in Panmure Street [NO 403305] there was a fortified position on the town walls.
Other refs: Mauchline Tower, Dundee; Lion's Round, Dundee

Dunderave Castle

Argyll & Dunbartonshire: About 3 miles east of Inveraray, on minor road just south of A83, at Dunderave Point, on the north bank of Loch Fyne, at Dunderave.

Private NN 143096 OS: 56 ** Map: 5, no: 116**

Dunderave Castle is a 16th-century L-plan tower house of four storeys and an attic with a square tower, in the re-entrant angle, and a round tower at one corner. Bartizans crown the corners and the walls are pierced by gunloops. A panel above

the entrance is dated 1596.

The entrance, at the foot of the stair-tower, leads into a passage to the vaulted basement. The basement contains the kitchen with a wide arched fireplace, the wine-cellar with a small stair to the hall above, and another cellar. The hall, on the first floor, has a turnpike stair in one corner which climbs to the chambers above. There was a private room next to the hall.

The property belonged to the MacNaughtons, who had moved here from Dubh Castle near Inveraray. The last MacNaughton holder intended to wed the younger daughter of Sir James Campbell of Ardkinglas, but found himself married to the wrong daughter. After fleeing to Ireland with his love the younger daughter, Dunderave passed to the Campbells probably around 1689 – with a good deal less slaughter than common for them. By the early 19th century the castle had been abandoned and roofless, but it was restored and extended by Sir Robert Lorimer in 1911-12 for the Noble family. It is still occupied.

Dundeugh Castle

Galloway: About 4.5 miles north of St John's Town of Dalry, on minor road east of A713 at Dundeugh, east of Water of Ken, 0.25 miles NW of Power Station.

Ruin or site NX 602880 OS: 77 * Map: 1, no: 96

Very little remains of a 16th-century L-plan tower house, consisting of a very ruinous main block and stair-tower. It was a property of the Gordons of Kenmure, and there may have been a stronghold here from the 11th century.

Dundochil *see* Duke Murdoch's Castle

Dundonald Castle

Ayrshire: About 3.5 miles north-east of Troon, on minor road west of B730 about 0.5 miles south of junction with A759, just south-west of Dundonald.

His Scot NS 364345 OS: 70 * Map: 3, no: 122**

Dundonald Castle consists of a remodelled 13th-century keep, formerly the gatehouse of an earlier castle. The entrance was blocked and the basement and hall on the first floor were given vaults, the hall vault being particularly fine. Most of the wall of the adjoining courtyard survives. The castle appears to have had a moat.

Dundonald was built by the Stewarts in the 13th century, and is said to have been slighted in the Wars of Independence. It was extended and remodelled around 1350 by Robert II, who died at Dundonald in 1390. Robert III also used the castle, and he died here in 1406. The property was bought by Sir William Cochrane in 1636, and in 1644 he used the old castle as a quarry from which to build the man-

sion of Auchans – itself now a ruin. Dr Johnson and Boswell visited in 1773.

Administered by Friends of Dundonald Castle.

OPEN: Open Apr-Sep, daily 10.00-17.00. Managed by the Friends of Dundonald Castle.

Visitor centre. Gift shop. Tearoom. WC. Disabled access only to visitor centre. Car and coach parking. £.

Tel: 01563 850201

Dundonald Castle

Argyll & Dunbartonshire: Near Killean, near A83, on the Mull of Kintyre.

Ruin or site NR 700445 [?] OS: 62 * Map: 5, no: 32

Site of castle, some remains of which may survive.

It was a stronghold of the MacDonald Lord of the Isles, but passed to the Campbells.

Dundronok *see* Dornock

Dunduff Castle

Ayrshire: About 4.5 miles north and west of Maybole, on minor road east of A719, about 0.25 miles north-east of Dunduff Farm.

Private NS 272164 OS: 70 ** Map: 3, no: 58

Dunduff Castle consists of an L-plan tower house, part of which may date from the 15th century, with a rectangular stair-tower in the re-entrant angle. It was rebuilt or remodelled around the turn of the 16th century.

The basement is vaulted, and contained the kitchen and wine-cellar, with a small stair up to the hall on the first floor. The entrance leads to the stair, while a passageway on the first floor gave access to a private chamber in the wing. The hall, also on the first floor, is a fine room.

It was a property of the Kennedys. It has recently been restored, and is occupied.

Dundurcus Castle

Moray: About 3 miles north-east of Rothes, on minor roads and foot south of B9015, north of River Spey, 0.5 miles north-east of Dundurcus Farm.

Ruin or site NJ 307513 [?] OS: 28 * Map: 10, no: 58

Probable site of castle.

Dundurn

Perth & Kinross: About 4 miles west of Comrie, on minor road and foot south of A85 at Tynreoch, just south of River Earn, west of Dundurn, at Dundurn fort.

Ruin or site NN 708233 [?] OS: 51 * Map: 8, no: 7

Site of Iron Age fort or early castle. It was a major stronghold of the Picts, but besieged in 683. Giric, one of the early Kings of Scots, was slain here in 889.

Dunean *see* Dunain

Dunfallandy

Perth & Kinross: About 1.5 miles south of Pitlochry, on minor road south of A9 or A924, just west of River Tummel, at Dunfallandy.

Ruin or site NN 949560 OS: 52 * Map: 8, no: 41

Site of castle of the Ferguson family. The Fergusons of Dunfallandy were Jacobites, and the laird narrowly escaped execution after the Jacobite Rising of 1745. The house was rebuilt in 1812, and occupied by the Fergusons until recently.

A fine Pictish sculpted stone stands nearby [NN 946564], and is said to have been 'long regarded with much superstitious awe'.

Dunfermline Palace

Fife: In Dunfermline, on minor roads south of A994 or north of B9156, north of Pittencrieff Park, just south of the Abbey church, at Dunfermline Abbey.

His Scot NT 089872 OS: 65 *** Map: 7, no: 13

Part of the buildings to the south of the Abbey Church were remodelled as a Royal Palace in 1587. The ruins are particularly impressive from Pittencrieff Glen, and consist of a range of buildings modelled into the palace from the guest range of the Abbey. The building had wide mullioned windows and elaborate vaulting.

There appears to have been a Royal Palace here from the 14th century, when Edward I stayed here in 1303-4, although he described Dunfermline as 'not a church but a den of thieves' and had the place sacked and torched. David II was born at the palace in 1323, but it may have been burned by Richard II of England in 1385. It was

restored, and James I was born here in 1394. James IV, James V, and Mary, Queen of Scots, all visited. The Palace was remodelled in 1587 by Queen Anne, wife of James VI, and Charles I was born at the Palace in 1600, as was his sister Elizabeth, Queen of Bohemia, the 'Winter Queen'. Charles I used the palace in 1650, but it was abandoned soon afterwards, and unroofed by 1708.

The Abbey was founded about 1070 by Queen Margaret, wife of Malcolm Canmore, and it was at Dunfermline that they had been married. Margaret was made a saint, and she and Malcolm were buried in the church, which became a place of pilgrimage. Abbot George Durie, the last abbot, was responsible for removing their remains, and taking them to the continent, where the Jesuits of Douai secured her head, although it may have been lost during the French Revolution. The rest of their remains are said to have been taken to the church of St Lawrence at Escurial by Philip II of Spain. Robert the Bruce's body – although not his heart – is buried here. The Abbey was sacked in 1560, and fell into disrepair, although part of the church continued to be used.

The church, domestic buildings of the abbey, and the remains of the Royal Palace are open to the public.

In 1624 nine-tenths of Dunfermline was destroyed by fire.

Other refs: Palace of Dunfermline

OPEN: Open Apr-Sep, daily 9.30-18.30; Oct-Mar, Mon-Wed and Sat 9.30-16.30, Thu 9.30-12.00, Sun 14.00-16.30, closed Fri; last ticket 30 mins before closing; choir of abbey church closed winter; closed 25/ 25 Dec and 1/2 Jan.

Explanatory displays. Gift shop. Parking nearby. Group concessions. Group concessions. £.

Tel: 01383 739026 Fax: 0131 668 8888

Email: hs.explore@scotland.gov.uk Web: www.historic-scotland.gov.uk

Dunfermline Tower *see* Malcolm's Tower

Dunfield *see* Downfield

Dunglass Castle

Argyll & Dunbartonshire: About 2 miles east of Dumbarton, south of the A82 at the Esso Oil Terminal, just north of the shore of the River Clyde.

Private NS 436735 OS: 64 ** Map: 5, no: 162

Not much of the 14th-century castle of Dunglass remains, except a wall with a seagate and a ruined range with turrets. In the 16th century, a turreted house was built within the walls of the old castle, and this was extended and remodelled in the 19th century.

The property passed by marriage to the Colquhouns, one of whom was Chamberlain of Scotland in the 15th century. Sir Humphrey Colquhoun of Luss built the 16th century house. Having been defeated in a skirmish and being pursued, Colquhoun fled to Bannachra Castle. A treacherous servant, however, pointed him out at a window, and a skilled bowman shot and killed Colquhoun.

The castle passed to the Edmonstones in 1738, but became ruinous soon afterwards, and in 1783 was partly demolished to build a new quay. In 1812 Buchanan of Auchentorlie bought the castle, and extended and remodelled it. Now surrounded by an Esso Oil Terminal, visitors need to be accompanied by a security guard: the house is apparently in too dangerous a condition to be approached closely.

Dunglass Castle

Borders: About 1 mile north of Cockburnspath, at Dunglass, on minor road east of the A1, south of the Dunglass Burn.

Ruin or site NT 766718 OS: 67 * Map: 2, no: 306

Site of a strong 14th-century castle.

Dunglass was a Home property from the beginning of the 15th century or earlier, but on their forfeiture in 1516 passed to the Douglases. The castle was burned by the English in 1532 and in 1547. James VI stayed here in 1603, but the castle was blown up in 1640. Apparently an English servant was so angered by insults directed against his countrymen that he ignited the castle's store of gunpowder, killing himself, the Earl of Haddington, and many of the Covenanting garrison. Dunglass House, its successor, was demolished in 1947.

Dunglass Collegiate Church, near the site of the castle, was founded by Alexander Home in 1423, and held against the English in 1547. The building is almost complete, open to the public, and in the care of Historic Scotland.

A fort, to the south-west, was occupied by the English during the invasion of 1547-50.

OPEN: Collegiate church: access at all reasonable times.

Parking nearby.

Tel: 0131 668 8800 Fax: 0131 668 8888

Email: hs.explore@scotland.gov.uk Web: www.historic-scotland.gov.uk

Dunikrannil *see* Loch nan Clachan Dun

Dunimarle Castle

Fife: About 1 mile west of Culross, just north of the B9037, just north of the sea.

Private NS 977859 OS: 65 * Map: 7, no: 4

The remains of a vaulted tower and part of a wall survive of a 16th-century, or earlier, castle. The present Dunimarle Castle, an 18th-century two-storey house with a large round tower of four storeys, was remodelled and enlarged around 1840, and stands near the site.

The castle is built on the traditional site of the murder of Lady MacDuff and her children, as related in Shakespeare's Macbeth. The lands were long held by the Blairs, but passed to the Erskines in the 19th century. When the last owner died, the property was left to trustees, and part of the mansion opened as an art gallery – although this had to close. A collection of furniture and other items from here, however, are currently on display at Duff House, near Banff, which is under the guardianship of Historic Scotland.

Other refs: Old Dunimarle Castle; Castlehill

Dunino Den

Fife: About 3 miles south and east of St Andrews, on minor roads and foot east of B9131, south of Kenly Water, at Dunino Law.

Ruin or site   NO 542113   OS: 59   *   Map: 7, no: 142

Site of castle or fortified house, the last remains of which were removed in 1815. This site has also been identified as a nunnery.

The lands were a property of the Thomsons in the 17th century.

OPEN: Open at all reasonable times – access is by worn steps and care should be taken.

Dunivaig Castle *see* Dunyvaig Castle

Dunkeld Castle *see* Bishop's Palace, Dunkeld

Dunkeld House

Perthshire: To west of Dunkeld, on minor roads west of A923, north of River Tay, north of cathedral.

Ruin or site   NO 024427   OS: 52   *   Map: 8, no: 55

Site of castle and mansion, a property of the Murrays, later Dukes of Atholl. It was stormed by forces of Oliver Cromwell in 1653, then blown up with gunpowder. It was rebuilt in 1679 by the architect William Bruce, but completely demolished at the beginning of the 19th century. A new house, Dunkeld New Palace, was started but never completed, then a new mansion was built for the Duke of Atholl in 1900, which is now the Dunkeld House Hotel.

Dunlappie

Angus & Dundee: About 5 miles north of Brechin, on minor roads west of B966, 1 mile west of Edzell, west of West Water, at or near Dunlappie.

Ruin or site   NO 587679   OS: 44   *   Map: 8, no: 244

Possible site of castle, known as Poolbrigs. Dunlappie was a property of the Abernethy family from the 12th century until 1390.

Other refs: Poolbrigs

Dunlop House

Ayrshire: About 2.5 miles north of Stewarton, on minor roads east of A735, 1 mile east of Dunlop, at Dunlop House.

Private   NS 428493   OS: 64   *   Map: 3, no: 168

Dunlop House, a large Jacobean mansion built in 1833, stands on the site of a 16th-century castle of the Dunlops, who had held the property from the 13th century. It is from here that the well-known 'Dunlop cheese' originates, created in the 17th century.

Other refs: Hunthall

Dunmore Tower *see* Airth Tower

Dunnideer Castle

Aberdeen & Gordon: About 1 mile west of Insch, on minor roads and foot north of B9002, 0.5 miles south of Dunnideer, in ramparts of fort and settlement, at Dunnideer.

Ruin or site   NJ 613282   OS: 37   **   Map: 10, no: 163

Standing within the earthworks of an Iron Age fort, Dunnideer Castle is a very ruined 13th-century castle. Parts of the fort are vitrified.

The stronghold is said to have been built by Gregory the Great around 890, but it was probably built about 1260 by John Balliol, father of John I, Toom Tabard, who was forced to abdicate by Edward I of England in 1297. The Tyrie family occupied the castle until 1724.

King Arthur is said to have held court here with Giric, King of Scots, in the 9th century.

Other refs: Castle of Dunnideer

Dunninald *see* Black Jack's Castle

Dunninald Castle

Angus & Dundee: About 2.5 miles south of Montrose, on minor roads east of A92, at Dunninald Castle.

Private   NO 704543   OS: 54   *   Map: 8, no: 268

Dunninald Castle was built to replace Black Jack Castle [NO 708535] in the 17th century, itself replaced by a mansion dating from 1824 and designed by James Gillespie Graham. The 17th-century Dunninald Castle survives as a ruin in the grounds of the newer building.

The property was held by the Grays, but the new castle built for the Arklay family.

Dunnottar Castle

Kincardine & Deeside: About 2 miles south of Stonehaven, on minor roads east of A92 or A957, on promontory jutting into sea, 0.5 miles east of Dunnottar Mains.

Private   NO 882839   OS: 45   ***   Map: 10, no: 301**

Set on a virtually impregnable cliff-top promontory some 160 feet above the sea, Dunnottar Castle is a spectacular ruined courtyard castle, parts of which date from the 12th century, although there was probably a stronghold here from the earliest times. The entrance is through a doorway, defended by a portcullis, and several rows of gunloops, and then up a flight of steps and through a tunnel.

The large site has many buildings. An early 15th-century L-plan keep of four storeys and formerly a garret stands at one corner. The walls are pierced by gunloops, and all corners are crowned by open rounds. The basement is vaulted, and contained a kitchen and cellars. There was a lesser hall, on the first floor, and the main hall on the second floor had private chambers adjoining and above.

In the 16th and early 17th centuries, ranges were built around a large courtyard, enclosing a bowling green. One range contained a hall and private chamber, another a long gallery floor, and a third much accommodation. Other buildings included a large chapel, a stable block, a forge, barracks, and a priest's house.

St Ninian established a church here at the beginning of the 5th century. There was a stronghold from early times, and it was besieged by the Picts, then in 900 by Norsemen when Donald, King of Scots, was slain.

An early castle here was captured by William Wallace from the English in 1296, one story relating that he burned 4000 Englishmen here. Edward III of England took the castle in the 1330s and strengthened it, but it was quickly recaptured by Sir Andrew Moray, the Regent.

The Keiths acquired the property in 1382, exchanging Struthers in Fife for Dunnottar with Lindsay of The Byres. The 5th Earl Marischal was a noted scholar, and founded Marischal College in Aberdeen. By the beginning of the 16th century, Dunnottar was one of the strongest fortresses in Scotland. Mary, Queen of Scots, stayed here in 1562.

Despite its strength, it was captured by Catholic nobles in their rebellion of 1594. The Marquis of Montrose unsuccessfully besieged it in 1645. The 9th Earl entertained King Charles II here in 1650, and in 1651 the Scottish crown jewels were brought here for safety during Cromwell's invasion of Scotland. General Lambert besieged the castle in 1652, but this proved extremely difficult, and the castle was only reduced after eight months by starvation and mutiny. The regalia and state papers were smuggled out to be hidden in nearby Kinneff Church until recovered

at the Restoration.

In 1685 Covenanters, numbering some 167 women and men, were packed into one of the cellars during a hot summer and 9 died while 25 escaped. The others, when freed, were found to have been tortured.

The castle was held for William and Mary in 1689 and many Jacobites were imprisoned here. The Earl Marischal threw in his lot with the Stewarts during the Jacobite rising of 1715, and was subsequently forfeited. The Duke of Argyll partly destroyed Dunnottar in 1716, and it was more fully slighted in 1718.

Between the wars, the castle was consolidated and partly reroofed. External shots of the castle were used, along with Dover and Blackness, in the making of the film Hamlet with Mel Gibson.

Sightings of several ghosts have been reported here. The apparition of a girl, around 13 years old and dressed in a dull plaid-type dress, is said to have been witnessed in the brewery. She leaves by the doorway next to the building, but then vanishes.

Other ghosts are said to include a young deer hound, which faded away near the tunnel; a tall Scandinavian-looking man going into the guardroom at the main entrance, who then also vanished; and noises of a meeting coming from Benholm's Lodging when nobody was apparently present.

OPEN: Open Easter-Oct, Mon-Sat 9.00-18.00, Sun 14.00-17.00; winter Mon-Fri only, 9.00 to sunset; last admission 30 mins before closing.
Getting to the castle involves a walk, steep climb, and a steeper one back. Exhibition. Sales area. WC. Car and coach parking. Group concessions. Parking.
Tel: 01569 762173   Fax: 01330 860325
Email: info@dunechtestates.com   Web: www.dunechtestates.com

Dunollie Castle

Argyll & Dunbartonshire: About 1 mile north of Oban, on minor road and foot north of A85 in Oban, on headland just east of sea, just south-west of Dunollie.
Ruin or site   NM 852314   OS: 49   ***   Map: 5, no: 67
Standing on a rocky ridge overlooking the sea, Dunollie Castle consists of a 13th-century castle of enclosure and a 15th-century keep of four storeys. Ranges of buildings once stood in the courtyard, but these are mostly ruined and overgrown.

The keep had a vaulted basement. There was a lesser hall on the first floor, and a main hall on the second floor, reached by two straight stairs. A turnpike stair led to the upper chambers.

In 698 Dunollie, then a fortress of the kings of Dalriada, was captured and destroyed. The present castle was built by the MacDougalls of Lorn in the 13th century, direct descendants of Somerled, and one of the most powerful families in Scotland at that time. They were bitter enemies of Robert the Bruce. A MacDougall force defeated Bruce at Dalry, nearly killing him and wrenching a brooch from his cloak. This brooch become known as the Brooch of Lorn and was kept at the castle, then at Gylen Castle on Kerrera [NM 805265]. Bruce returned and ravaged MacDougall lands in 1309 after defeating them at the Pass of Brander.

In 1644 the castle was attacked by Argyll, and in 1647 besieged by General David Leslie and an army of Covenanters. It was attacked again in 1715 when the MacDougalls were fighting for the Stewarts during the Jacobite Rising. The lands were forfeited, but restored in 1745.

The MacDougalls built nearby Dunollie House in 1746, and the castle was abandoned. The castle is still owned by the MacDougalls, but in a dangerous condition.
OPEN: Can be reached from a lay-by on the Ganavan road, but not from the drive to Dunollie House, which is NOT open to the public. Care should be taken.

Dunoon Castle

Argyll & Dunbartonshire: In Dunoon, just south of harbour, just west of A815, in park, just west of sea.
Ruin or site   NS 175764   OS: 63   *   Map: 5, no: 120
Little remains of Dunoon Castle, once an important stronghold, except grass-covered foundations.

There is said to have been an earlier stronghold here, but there was a castle here from the 11th century. It was later a Stewart property.

It was captured by Edward Balliol and the English in 1334, but was recovered by the Scots soon afterwards. The town was torched by the Earl of Lennox for the English in 1544, but the castle remained in Scottish hands. Mary, Queen of Scots, visited here in 1563. In 1646 the Campbells massacred the Lamonts at Dunoon after a raid on Lamont lands. They torched Toward and Asgog Castles, and took

several hundred prisoners, murdering most of them, and taking the rest back to Dunoon, where 36 were hanged from one tree alone.

The castle was abandoned in the 1650s, and little remained by the 19th century, the ruins being plundered for materials to built Castle House in 1820. The site is now a public park.

There was a bishop's palace in Dunoon [NS 173765] in 1479, the site now occupied by a school playground.
Other refs: Bishop's Palace, Dunoon

Dunphail Castle

Moray: About 6.5 miles south of Forres, on minor roads west of A940 1.5 miles south of junction with B9007, east of River Divie, west of Dunphail House.
Ruin or site   NJ 007481   OS: 27   **   Map: 10, no: 6
Not much remains of Dunphail Castle, a ruinous 14th-century stronghold of the Comyns, except the vaulted basement.

The Comyns were besieged here in 1330 by the Regent Andrew Moray, after they had fled from Darnaway Castle in an attempt to waylay and slat Moray. Moray managed to capture five of the garrison, including Alasdair Comyn of Dunphail, who had been out foraging for food. Moray had the men executed and their heads flung over the walls of the castle, reputedly with the words 'Here's beef for your bannocks'. The last of the Comyn garrison tried to flee, but were slaughtered by the Regent's men. In the 18th century five skull-less skeletons were found buried near the castle. Headless ghosts are said to haunt the castle, and tales of the sound of fighting and groans have been reported.

The castle may have been reused by the Dunbar family, but nearby Dunphail House, built in 1828 and designed by William Playfair, was built for the Cummings.

Dunragit House

Galloway: About 3.5 miles west of Glenluce, on minor road north of A75, about 0.5 miles north of Dunragit village.
Private   NX 150582   OS: 82   **   Map: 1, no: 29
Dunragit House incorporates part of a massive 16th-century tower house. It may have replaced Old Hall of Dunragit [NX 143592], of which there are no remains.

It was held by the Cunninghams.
Other refs: Old Hall of Dunragit

Dunrobin Castle

Sutherland & Caithness: About 1 mile north-east of Golspie, on minor roads south of A9 (signposted), at Dunrobin Castle.
Private   NC 852008   OS: 17   **   Map: 12, no: 29
Dunrobin Castle consists of an altered 15th-century keep – parts of which may date from the 1300s – and 17th-century courtyard mansion, with round corner turrets, which was greatly enlarged in the 18th and 19th centuries. The keep is vaulted on all floors, and still has its original iron yett. With the keep, the 17th-century L-plan block of three storeys and a garret formed a courtyard. A large round tower joins up this block and the keep. The castle was remodelled and enlarged between 1845 and 1851, and again in 1915-21 by Sir Robert Lorimer.

The Sutherland family were created Earls of Sutherland in 1235, and had a castle here in the 13th century: Dunrobin may be called after Robert or Robin, the 6th Earl. The property passed by marriage to the Gordons. The family were forfeited for their part in Huntly's rebellion of 1562.

At Helmsdale Castle, Isobel Sinclair poisoned John, the 11th Earl, and his wife hoping to secure the succession of her son, but the future 12th Earl escaped, and she managed to poison her own son. The young Earl of Sutherland escaped to Dornoch Palace or Skibo Castle, where he was eventually captured by the Earl of Caithness and forced to marry Lady Barbara Sinclair, who was twice his age. When he came of age he divorced her. The family supported the government in the Jacobite Risings, although in 1746 the castle was held briefly by troops of Bonnie Prince Charlie.

The lands passed by marriage to the Trentham Marquis of Stafford in the 18th century. They were involved in the Clearances, burning cottages and throwing people out of their homes to so that the land could be cleared for sheep. During the World War I the castle was used as a naval hospital, and as a boy's public school between 1963 and 1972. It is still held by the same family.

The upper floors of the castle are reputedly haunted by the spectre of a daughter

of the 14th Earl. She decided to elope with her lover but her father, who considered the man unsuitable for his daughter, found out, and had her imprisoned in one of the attic rooms. She tried to escape by climbing down a rope, from one of the upstairs windows, but her father surprised her, and she fell to her death. It is said that the one of the rooms she haunted has since been disused.

OPEN: Open Apr-mid Oct: Apr, May and Oct, Mon-Sat 10.30-16.30, Sun 12.00-16.30; Jun and Sep, Mon-Sat 10.30-17.30, Sun 12.00-17.30; Jul and Aug, daily 10.30-17.30; last entry 30 mins before close.
Collections of furniture, paintings and memorabilia. Museum, which features a collection of Pictish stones. Formal gardens. Guided tours. Explanatory displays. Gift shop. Tea room. WC. Disabled access: phone to arrange. Car and coach parking. Group concessions. £££.
Tel: 01408 633177 Fax: 01408 634081
Email: dunrobin.est@btinternet.com Web: www.greathousesofscotland.co.uk

Dunrod Castle

Renfrewshire: About 3.5 miles south and west of Greenock, on minor roads east of A78, just west of railway line, at or near Dunrod.
Ruin or site NS 224732 [?] OS: 63 * Map: 3, no: 42
Site of castle, a vestige of which survived in 1856.
 Dunrod was a property of the Comyns but passed to the Lindsays after John Lindsay of Dunrod 'made sure' that the Red John Comyn was dead. Comyn had been stabbed by Robert the Bruce – later Robert I, King of Scots – in a church in Dumfries in 1306. In 1619 the property was sold to Archibald Stewart of Blackhall by Alexander Lindsay of Dunrod. Lindsay became penniless, selling charms to sea captains, and died in a barn. An old verse relates:
 'In Innerkip the witches ride thick,
 And in Dunrod they dwell;
 But the greatest loon among them a'
 Is auld Dunrod himsel'.

Duns Castle

Borders: About 1 mile north-west of Duns on minor road north of A6112 near junction with A6105, in Duns Castle Country Park.
Private NT 777544 OS: 67 ** Map: 2, no: 315
Duns Castle incorporates parts of a modified 14th-century keep, later altered to an L-plan, and much altered and extended in the 18th and 19th centuries.
 The castle may have been built by Thomas Randolph, Earl of Moray, in 1320, but

had passed to Home of Ayton by 1489. It was damaged by the Earl of Hertford in 1547, and in 1639 used by the Covenanter General David Leslie, who later went on to defeat the Marquis of Montrose at the Battle of Philiphaugh in 1645. It passed to the Cockburns, then the Hays of Drumelzier, who had James Gillespie Graham remodel and extend the house.
 The ghost of Alexander Hay, who was killed at the Battle of Waterloo in 1815, is said to haunt the castle.
OPEN: Accommodation available.
Wooded and landscaped grounds. Nature reserve and lake. Golf and fishing.
Tel: 01361 883211 Fax: 01361 882015
Email: aline-hay@lineone.net Web: www.dunscastle.co.uk

Dunscaich *see* Dun Sgathaich

Dunscaith *see* Dun Sgathaich

Dunskeath Castle

Ross & Cromarty: About 1.5 miles north-east of Cromarty, on minor road and foot east of B9175, on north side of Cromarty Firth, at North Sutor, at Dunskeath.
Ruin or site NH 807689 [?] OS: 21 * Map: 9, no: 124
Little remains of a 12th-century castle of enclosure, except earthworks.

Dunskey Castle

Galloway: About 0.5 miles south-east of Portpatrick, on minor road and foot south of A77, on cliffs near the sea.
Ruin or site NX 004534 OS: 82 * Map: 1, no: 6**
Protected by a ditch on the landward side, Dunskey Castle consists of a large ruined 16th-century L-plan tower house of four storeys. To this has been added a low adjoining block of two storeys, containing the courtyard entrance. A rectangular stair-tower stands in the re-entrant angle, and the tower was crowned by bartizans, now very ruined. Little remains of outbuildings within the courtyard.
 The basement of the tower is vaulted, and contains three cellars, one the wine-cellar with a small stair up to the hall above. The main entrance leads through the tower in the re-entrant to the wide scale-and-platt stair in the wing, which ascends

only to the hall on the first floor of the main block. The hall has several large windows and a fireplace. The upper chambers in the main block and wing were reached by a stair-tower in the re-entrant angle.

The adjoining block has a long gallery at first floor level, entered from the hall, over vaulted cellars.

The present stronghold was started about 1510 by the Adairs of Kilhilt, although in 1489 an older castle here was torched by MacCulloch of Myrton in retaliation for the murder of Dionysius of Hamilton by William Adair of Dunskey. The abbot of Soulseat Abbey was imprisoned and tortured in the castle to force him to sign away the abbey lands. The castle was altered and remodelled in the 16th century, but was sold in 1620 to Hew Montgomery, then in the 1660s to John Blair, Minister of Portpatrick. It was a ruin by 1684, but recently put up for sale.

The castle was said to have had a brownie, and is reputed to be haunted by the ghost of a nurse maid, who dropped a baby from one of the windows onto the rocks far below.

OPEN: View from exterior – climb and walk from Portpatrick.
Parking Nearby.

Dunstaffnage Castle

Argyll & Dunbartonshire: About 3.5 miles north-east of Oban, on minor road north of A85 at Dunbeg, on headland north of Dunstaffnage Bay, near the sea, at Dunstaffnage.

His Scot   NM 882344   OS: 49   ***   Map: 5, no: 75

On a promontory in the Firth of Lorn, Dunstaffnage Castle consists of a massive 13th-century curtain wall, with round towers, and an altered 16th-century gatehouse. The wall is 60 feet high in places, crowned by a parapet, and is pierced by arrow slits. Ranges of buildings within the walls contained a hall and kitchen. In 1725 a two-storey house was added, which was altered in the 19th century.

A stronghold here was held by the kings of Dalriada in the 7th century, and one of

the places where the Stone of Destiny was kept. The present castle was built by the MacDougalls. The castle was besieged and captured by Robert the Bruce in 1309 after the MacDougalls had been defeated at the Pass of Brander. Bruce made the castle a royal property with the Campbells as keepers.

In 1455 the 9th Earl of Douglas fled here to seek help from the Lord of the Isles after James II had destroyed the power of the Black Douglases. James IV visited twice. The 9th Earl of Argyll burned the castle in 1685 during his rebellion of the same year. In 1715 and 1746 government troops occupied the castle during the Jacobite Risings, and Flora MacDonald was briefly imprisoned here after helping Bonnie Prince Charlie. The castle was put into the care of the State in 1958.

There is a fine ruined chapel nearby.

The castle is said to be haunted by a ghost in a green dress, the 'Ell-maid of Dunstaffnage' and her appearance heralds events, both bad and good, in the lives of the Campbells (or the owners of the castle, anyway). When she was seen to be smiling then there were happy events to come, but if she was sad or weeping it augured trouble. She is said to be a gruagach, a spirit woman closely associated

with the fortunes of a castle or house. Ghostly footsteps, as heavy as a booted man, have also been reported, as well as bangs and thumps, although the spirit was also said to be able to hand on handicraft skills.

OPEN: Open Apr-Sep, daily 9.30-18.30; Oct-Mar, daily 9.30-16.30; last ticket 30 mins before closing; closed 25/26 Dec and 1/2 Jan.
Explanatory panels. Gift shop. WC. Car and coach parking. Group concessions. £. Joint entry ticket available with Bonawe Iron Furnace.
Tel: 01631 562465   Fax: 0131 668 8888
Email: hs.explore@scotland.gov.uk   Web: www.historic-scotland.gov.uk

Dunsyre Castle

Lanarkshire & Glasgow area: About 6 miles east of Carnwath on minor roads north of A721 at Newbigging, east of A702 just north of Dolphinton, at or near Dunsyre.

Ruin or site   NT 073482 [?]   OS: 72   *   Map: 3, no: 458

Site of castle, near the parish church. The basement was vaulted, and there were at least two further storeys with a turnpike stair.

It was originally a property of the Newbigging family, but granted to the Douglases in 1368. In 1492 it was exchanged for Hermitage Castle by the Hepburn Earls of Bothwell, among a cluster of their properties of Dunsyre, Elsrickle, Walston and Dolphinton. The property later passed to the Lockharts of The Lee. Until about 1740 the ruins of the castle were still used to hold courts, and 'possessed its instruments of torture', although little or nothing now remains. The location is approximate.

Duntarvet Castle *see* Duntervy Castle

Duntarvie Castle

Lothians: About 3 miles south and west of South Queensferry, just west of B8020 between B9080 and A904, short distance north of M9.

Private   NT 091765   OS: 65   ***   Map: 4, no: 38

Duntarvie Castle was a large ruined 16th-century tower house. It consists of a rectangular main block of four storeys, with square towers, rising a storey higher, projecting at each end. Tall corbelled-out stair-turrets, in the re-entrant angles, are crowned by stone-roofed caphouses.

The basement is vaulted, and contained the kitchen with a wide fireplace and cellars, one with a small stair to the hall above. A straight stair led to the first floor, the upper floors being reached by the turret stairs. The hall was on the first floor, with adjoining chambers, and a small stair in one corner led up to a room above. The upper floors were occupied by many chambers in the main block and towers.

Duntarvie was a possession of the Durham family. It is currently being restored, although, during preliminary work, part of one tower collapsed in a gale.

Duntervy Castle

Lanarkshire & Glasgow area: About 4.5 miles south-west of Lanark, west of the M74, near Brocketsbrae.

Ruin or site   NS 828401   OS: 72   *   Map: 3, no: 384

Site of a 15th-century castle, which was held by the Durham family in the 16th century. The Durham Aisle was built by the family, and is part of the first post-Reformation church in Lesmahagow.
Other refs: Dumbraxhill; Duntarvet Castle

Duntreath Castle

Stirlingshire & Clackmannan: About 4 miles north of Milngavie, on minor road south of the A81, just east of the Blane Water, at Duntreath.

Private   NS 536811   OS: 64   ***   Map: 6, no: 17

Duntreath Castle, which is pronounced 'Duntreth', consists of a large altered 15th-century courtyard castle, with a massive rectangular keep of three main storeys and a garret, in one corner of the courtyard. The corbelled-out crenellated parapet and the corbiestepped gabled roof are later modifications. Extensions, from the 17th century and later, have been demolished, including a large and complex gatehouse, but a Victorian wing and replacement gatehouse remain.

Duntreath was a property of the Earls of Lennox, but passed on their forfeiture in 1425 to the Edmonstones of Culloden, and is still owned by the same family. The castle was abandoned around 1740 for lands at Redhall in Ireland, and became ruinous, but in 1857 it was restored, remodelled and extended. By 1958 all but the original keep, and a Victorian range and gatehouse, had been demolished. The house is still occupied by the Edmonstones.

Duntrune Castle

Argyll & Dunbartonshire: About 6.5 miles north-west of Lochgilphead, on minor roads west of B8025, on the north side of Loch Crinan, on Rubha an Moine, at Duntrune Castle.

Ruin or site   NR 794956   OS: 55   *   Map: 5, no: 54**

Duntrune, or Duntroon, Castle was originally a 13th century castle of enclosure. It consisted of a wall, crowned by a broad parapet and rounded at the corners, enclosing an irregularly shaped courtyard. In one corner an L-plan tower house was added in the 16th or 17th century. The corners of the tower are also rounded below roof level.

The entrance, in the re-entrant angle, leads to the barrel-vaulted basement, con-

taining the kitchen and cellars, with a small stair to the hall on the first floor. There were private chambers above.

It was a property of the Campbells of Duntrune. The castle was besieged by a force led by Alasdair Colkitto MacDonald in 1644, after the Battle of Inverlochy, when the lands of the Campbells were ravaged by the Marquis of Montrose's army. It was burned by the Earl of Argyll in 1685. In 1792 the lands were sold to the Malcolms of Poltalloch, who still own the castle.

The castle is said to be haunted by a ghostly piper. A MacDonald had been sent as a spy to try to capture the castle in 1615, but was discovered, and the only way he could warn his companions was to play the pipes. Both his hands or all of his fingers were chopped off in revenge, and he died to be buried under the kitchen flagstones.

The ghost was thought to have been exorcised in modern times, when part of the basement was used as a church. A handless or fingerless skeleton was reputedly found sealed beneath the floor, and the remains were buried. However, the ghost became active in the 1970s, and unexplained knockings on doors were reported, as well as furniture and other objects being thrown about the rooms. Or so it is said.

Duntulm Castle

South Highland: About 6.5 miles north of Uig on west side of island of Skye, on a promontory above the shore, west and north of the hotel, at Duntulm.

Ruin or site   NG 410743   OS: 23   **   Map: 9, no: 6

On a strong site once cut off on the landward side by a ditch and protected on the other sides by cliffs and steep slopes, Duntulm Castle consists of a very ruined 15th-century keep, with the remains of 17th century ranges, around a courtyard. The vaulted basement of the keep remains. It was once a strong and comfortable fortress and residence.

Duntulm was originally an Iron Age broch or dun, later used by the Norsemen because of its strong position. Little of an early castle of the MacLeods remains, most of the existing ruin dating from when Trotternish was held by the MacDonalds of Sleat in the 17th century after they had removed from Dun Sciath. James V had visited the castle in 1540.

Hugh MacDonald was imprisoned and starved to death in a dungeon here after

he had tried to seize the lands of Trotternish by murdering his kin. He was given only salted beef and no water, and died raving: his ghostly groans are said to have been heard. The castle was abandoned around 1730 when the MacDonalds moved to Monkstadt House, then Armadale Castle in Sleat. The last tall upstand of masonry fell in a storm in the 1980s.

The castle has many other ghost stories.

The ghost of the 8th chief, Donald Gorm, brawling and drinking with spectral companions, has also been recorded in many tales. Another alleged apparition was that of Margaret, a sister of MacLeod of Dunvegan, who was married to one of the MacDonalds. She had lost an eye in an accident, but her husband threw her out, sending her back to Dunvegan on a one-eyed horse with a one-eyed servant and one-eyed dog. Her weeping ghost is said to haunt the castle.

A nursemaid also reputedly dropped a baby out of one of the windows, onto the rocks below. Her terrified screams are said to be heard sometimes as the poor woman was murdered in reprisal.

The MacDonalds moved to Monkstadt [NG 380675], itself now ruined, because of the ghosts – reputedly – although it looks a lot more sheltered and comfortable than Duntulm.

Other refs: Dundavid; Monkstadt

OPEN: View from exterior – care must be taken as dangerously ruined.

Parking Nearby.

Dunure Castle

Ayrshire: About 5 miles north-west of Maybole, on minor roads west of A719, on shore of Firth of Clyde at village of Dunure, south of harbour.

Ruin or site   NS 253158   OS: 70   *   Map: 3, no: 54**

Once a strong fortress on the summit of a rocky promontory, Dunure Castle consists of a ruined 13th-century keep, which was later altered and extended, surrounded by a curtain wall, and a 15th-century block, at lower level, containing kitchens, a hall and private chambers. There is a well preserved doocot.

Dunure was a property of the Kennedys of Dunure, Earls of Cassillis. One of the family married Mary, daughter of Robert III, and another was Bishop of St Andrews and founded St Salvator's College. In 1570 Allan Stewart, Commendator of Crossraguel Abbey, was roasted in sop here by the Kennedy Earl of Cassillis until he signed away the lands of the abbey. Kennedy of Bargany, an enemy of Cassillis, hearing of the treatment of Stewart, stormed the castle and rescued the Commendator, apparently doing some damage to the buildings. Cassillis was instructed to pay Stewart a pension, although he kept the lands, and led to a feud with the Kennedys of Bargany. Dunure may have been torched and blown up sometime around the middle of the 17th century. By 1696 the castle was abandoned and ruined, and it appears to have been systematically dismantled.

The castle was recently excavated and consolidated so the ruins could be opened to the public.

Ghostly cries have reputedly been heard emanating from the chamber in which Stewart was roasted.

OPEN: View from exterior?

Parking Nearby.

Dunvegan Castle

South Highland: About 1 mile north of the village of Dunvegan on island of Skye, on minor road north of A850, east shore of Loch Dunvegan, at Dunvegan Castle.
Private NG 247491 OS: 23 *** Map: 9, no: 2
Dunvegan Castle consists of a massive 14th-century keep, a 16th-century tower known as the Fairy Tower, and a joining hall block from the 17th century, as well as a later wing. The Fairy Tower was built by Alasdair Crotach MacLeod, whose fine tomb is at St Clement's Church [NG 047833] at Rodel on Harris. The castle was completely restored in 1840-50, and given ornamental turrets and modern battlements in the 19th century. It was repaired after a fire in 1938-40.

The castle has been continuously occupied by the chiefs of MacLeod since 1270, who trace their ancestry back to Leod, a son of Olaf the Black, Norse King of the Isle of Man. It is still owned by the 29th Chief of MacLeod.

Dunvegan is the home to the famous Fairy Flag, 'Am Bratach Sith' in Gaelic. There are many legends surrounding this piece of silk, which is now reduced in size (from

pieces being removed and kept for luck) and somewhat threadbare. One is that it was given to one of the chiefs by his fairy wife at their parting. This is said to have taken place at the Fairy Bridge, three miles to the north east, at a meeting of rivers and roads. The chief had married his wife thinking she was a mortal woman, but she was only permitted to stay with him for 20 years before returning to Fairyland.

The flag, however, originates from the Middle East, and it has been dated between 400 and 700 AD, predating the castle by hundreds of years. The flag is believed to give victory to the clan whenever unfurled, and reputedly did so at the battles of Glendale in 1490 and Trumpan in 1580.

The Fairy Flag was also believed to make the marriage of the MacLeods fruitful, when draped on the wedding bed, and to charm the herrings out of Dunvegan Loch when unfurled. Belief in its power was such that during World War II pilots from the clan carried a picture of the flag as a talisman.

Other interesting items at Dunvegan include a drinking horn, 'Rory Mor's Horn', holding several pints of claret, which the heir of the MacLeods had to empty in one go; and the Dunvegan Cup, gifted to the clan by the O'Neils of Ulster in 1596. There are also mementoes of Bonnie Prince Charlie and Flora MacDonald, and information about St Kilda, which was formerly a property of the family.

At Borreraig was a college of piping of the MacCrimmons, renowned pipers to the MacLeod chiefs.
OPEN: Open all year: Mar-Oct, daily 10.00-17.30; Nov-Mar, daily 11.00-16.00; closed 25/26 Dec and 1/2 Jan; last entry 30 mins before closing.
Guides in each of the public rooms. Explanatory panels and displays. Audio-visual theatre. Gift shops. Restaurant. WC. Gardens. Boat trips (£££) to seal colony. Pedigree Highland cattle fold. Car and coach parking. Group/student/OAP concessions. Holiday cottages available. £££.
Tel: 01470 521206 Fax: 01470 521205
Email: info@dunvegancastle.com Web: www.dunvegancastle.com

Dunyvaig Castle

Argyll & Dunbartonshire: On south coast of island of Islay, 3 miles east of Port Ellen, on minor road and foot south of A846 just east of Lagavulin, east of Lagavulin Bay, at Dunyvaig.
Ruin or site NR 406455 OS: 60 ** Map: 5, no: 13
Little remains of Dunyvaig Castle, except the remains of a small 15th-century keep on top of a rock with a small inner and larger outer courtyard of the 13th century. An arched entrance and part of a groined arch survive in the inner courtyard.

There was a stronghold here from early times. The castle first belonged to the MacDonald Lord of the Isles, who had their main stronghold at Finlaggan, also on Islay. The Lord of the Isles was forfeited by James IV in 1493, and the castle passed to the MacIans of Ardnamurchan after the MacDonald keeper rebelled against the Crown. The property was leased back to the MacDonalds in 1519, but then given to the Campbells in 1543, who leased it back after much dispute to a branch of the MacDonalds. In 1598 the last MacDonald of Dunyvaig defeated the MacLeans of Duart at the Battle at Gruinart. However, he was ordered to surrender the castle, then forfeited in 1608, and Dunyvaig was put into the stewardship of the Bishops of the Isles for the King. In 1612 the castle was taken by Alasdair 'Old' Colkitto MacDonald, but it was retaken by the Campbells of Cawdor in 1615, and although Colkitto escaped, the rest of his men were slain or later hanged. Fighting continued and the castle changed hands again. It was besieged and taken by 'Old' Colkitto in 1647. After a siege by a Covenanter army under David Leslie it was forced to surrender when the water supply failed, and Colkitto was finally hanged from the walls. The Campbells of Cawdor occupied the castle until about 1677, but demolished it soon afterwards, and moved to Islay House. The ruin has been consolidated.
Other refs: Dun Naoimh Castle; Dunivaig Castle
OPEN: Access at all reasonable times – care should be taken.
Parking nearby.

Dupplin Castle

Perth & Kinross: About 4 miles south-west of Perth, on minor road north of B9112 or south of A9, about 1.5 miles south-west of Milton of Aberdalgie, at Dupplin.
Private NO 056195 OS: 58 * Map: 8, no: 63
Dupplin Castle, a 19th-century Tudor mansion, stands on the site of a 13th-century castle.

It was a property of the Oliphants. Sir William Oliphant, the defender of Stirling Castle against Edward I of England in 1304, had a castle built or extended here. Nearby, in 1322, Edward Balliol, son of John, defeated an army, led by the Regent Mar, and declared himself king, although his success was short lived. In 1461 the burgesses of Perth destroyed the castle during a dispute with Lord Oliphant.

The castle was rebuilt, and in 1623 sold to the Douglas Earl of Morton, but then passed to the Hay Earl of Kinnoull. In 1688 the castle was remodelled and extended, but was destroyed by fire in 1827. A new mansion of 1828-32 was built on the site, but this was also mostly demolished. Dupplin was later a property of the Dewars.

Dura House

Fife: About 2.5 miles east of Cupar, on minor roads north of B940, west of Ceres Burn, 0.5 miles north of Pitscottie, at Dura House.
Private NO 413141 OS: 59 * Map: 7, no: 113
The mansion, which was remodelled with a castellated extension in 1861 by John Milne, incorporates a building of the mid 17th century, itself probably incorporating a house or possibly castle of 1603 or earlier. It was held by the Wemyss family in 1624.

Durie House

Fife: About 1 mile north-west of Leven, on minor roads north of A915 or south of A916, at Durie House.
Private NO 372025 OS: 59 ** Map: 7, no: 99
Site of castle. The present Durie House dates from 1762, and is a three-storey classical mansion.

The property belonged to the Durie family from the 13th until the beginning of the 16th century, when it passed to Sir Alexander Kemp, a favourite of James V – although it later returned to the Duries. Mary, Queen of Scots, stayed here in 1565.

George Durie, the last abbot of Dunfermline Abbey, was responsible for removing the remains of Saint Margaret and Malcolm Canmore from the Abbey, and taking them to the continent. The Duries were forfeited, and the property sold to the Gibsons in 1614, who took the title Lord Durie. Sir Alexander Gibson, a noted judge, was kidnapped and held prisoner by one of the Armstrongs, so that the case he was presiding over would be found in favour of the Earl of Traquair. Durie's sons were also well-known lawyers. It was sold in the 18th century to the Christies. The house is still occupied.

Durisdeer Castle

Dumfriesshire: About 3.5 miles north and east of Carronbridge, on minor road east of A702, about 0.5 miles west of village of Durisdeer, near Carronglen.
Ruin or site   NS 886037 [?]   OS: 78   *   Map: 1, no: 168
Site of 13th-century castle of the Menzies family. It was held by the English during the Wars of Independence.
Other refs: Carronglen

Durris Castle *see* Dores Castle

Durris House

Kincardine & Deeside: About 6.5 miles east of Banchory, on minor road south of B9077, about 1 mile south of the Dee, 1.5 miles east of Kirkton of Durris, at Durris House.
Private   NO 799968   OS: 45   *   Map: 10, no: 266**
Durris House is an altered and extended 16th-century L-plan tower house of three storeys and a garret. It consists of a main block and stair-wing, which is crowned by a corbelled-out watch-chamber. The re-entrant angle of the L has been filled in with later work. All that remains of an earlier courtyard castle is the vaulted basement of one tower.
   The original entrance was in the stair-wing. The basement is vaulted, and probably part of the older castle. The floor levels have been altered, but the hall would have been on the first floor, with private chambers above.
   The property was held by the Frasers in the 13th century. The castle was burned by the Marquis of Montrose in 1645 at the same time as Castle Fraser. It was sold at the end of the 17th century, and later greatly remodelled and extended, passing to the Innes family, then to the MacTires. The house, divided into three, is still occupied.
   A 'Green Lady' is said to haunt the castle, reputedly the wife of the Fraser lord when Montrose torched the house on 17 March 1645. The poor woman is said to have been distraught, feeling that she was responsible after having cursed Montrose, and she drowned herself in a nearby burn. Her curse may have had some effect, however, as Montrose was finally defeated in 1650, captured, and taken to Edinburgh where he was executed.

Dykeraw Tower

Borders: About 7 miles south of Jedburgh, south on minor road from A6088 at Southdean, near or at Dykeraw.
Ruin or site   NT 629085 [?]   OS: 80   **   Map: 2, no: 247
Site of 15th-century castle, which was torched by the English in 1513.

Dysart

Angus & Dundee: About 2.5 miles south-west of Montrose, near A92, at or near East Mains of Dysart.
Ruin or site   NO 695550 [?]   OS: 54   *   Map: 8, no: 266
Possible site of castle, nothing of which remains. The lands were held by the Melvilles, but then passed to the Guthries, then the Lyles.

E

Eagerness *see* Eggerness Castle

Eaglescairnie

Lothians: About 2.5 miles south of Haddington, on minor roads east of B6368 or west of B6369, about 1.5 miles north-west of Gifford, at Eaglescairnie.
Private   NT 518696   OS: 66   *   Map: 4, no: 190
Eaglescairnie, an 18th-century mansion, stands on the site of a castle. The property was held by the Halyburtons in the 17th century.

Eaglesham Castle

Renfrewshire: In or near Eaglesham, about 4 miles west and south of East Kilbride, near junction of B764 and B767, west of the White Cart Water.
Ruin or site   NS 571520 [?]   OS: 64   *   Map: 3, no: 258
Site of castle of the Montgomery family, who held the property from the 12th century. Sir John, 9th of Eaglesham, captured Percy 'Hotspur' at the Battle of Otterburn in 1388, and built a new castle at Polnoon. The family became Earls of Eglinton in 1508. Castlehill Farm lies to the north-west of the present village. The present Eaglesham Castle or House is a grand modern mansion, and the motte site was used for meetings and festivals.

Earlshall

Fife: East of Leuchars, on minor roads east from A919 at Leuchars, near RAF Leuchars.
Private   NO 465211   OS: 59   **   Map: 7, no: 124**
Earlshall is a 16th-century courtyard castle. It consists of a main house, occupying two sides, a smaller detached tower of three storeys, the lower two being vaulted, and a range of 17th-century outbuildings. The entrance to the courtyard is by an archway, dated 1546.
   The main house consists of a main block of three storeys and a garret, and a wing. A round stair-tower is corbelled out to square and crowned by a watch-chamber. On the other corner of the main block is a large tower, with a small stair-turret in the angle between it and the principal block.
   The entrance, in the stair-tower, leads to the vaulted basement. The hall, on the first floor, has a large carved fireplace and panelled walls. On the second floor is a gallery, which has a tempera-painted ceiling from the 1620s.
   Sir William Bruce built the castle in 1546. He had fought at, and unusually, survived the Battle of Flodden in 1513. Mary, Queen of Scots, visited in 1561. One of the family was killed at the Battle of Worcester in 1651, fighting for Charles II; and another Sir Andrew is known as 'Bloody Bruce'. He and his men killed Richard Cameron, a noted Covenanter, at Airds Moss. Bruce then hacked off Cameron's head and hands, and took them back to Edinburgh.
   The castle was abandoned and ruinous before being restored for R. W. R. Mackenzie by Sir Robert Lorimer in 1892. The gardens were relaid, and formal garden replanted. The castle has been sold several times in the 20th century, the last time in 1994, and is still occupied.
   The castle is said to be haunted by the ghost of Sir Andrew Bruce, the 'Bloody Bruce', and his footsteps are reportedly heard on the stairs.

Earlston Castle *see* Earlstoun Castle

Earlston Tower *see* Rhymer's Tower

Earlstoun Castle

Galloway: About 2 miles north of St John's Town of Dalry, on minor road west of B7000, short distance east of north Earlstoun Loch, at Earlstoun.
Private   NX 613840   OS: 77   *   Map: 1, no: 100**
Earlstoun Castle is an altered 16th-century L-plan tower house which probably incorporates earlier work. It consists of a main block of three storeys and a garret,

and a stair-wing which rises a storey higher. A round stair-turret is corbelled out in the re-entrant angle. The tower has later been extended, with two wings; and there was an adjoining courtyard, little of which remains.

The entrance, in the re-entrant angle, leads to the foot of a wide turnpike stair and into the vaulted basement, which contained the kitchen. The first-floor hall has a fine fireplace, but has been subdivided. The upper floors were occupied by private chamber, and reached by the turret stair. There is a later kitchen in one of the additions.

The property belonged to the Hepburn Earls of Bothwell, but passed to the Sinclairs in the mid 16th century. In 1615 it passed by marriage to the Gordons of Airds. One of the family, William Gordon, was killed at the Battle of Bothwell Brig in 1679, and the castle was occupied by troops engaged in suppressing Covenanters. The castle is still occupied.

Other refs: Earlston Castle

Earl's Palace, Birsay

Orkney: About 12 miles north of Stromness on Orkney, on minor road just north of A966, just east of Birsay Bay, north-west of Loch of Boardhouse, at Birsay.

His Scot HY 248279 OS: 6 *** Map: 11, no: 34

Once a fine and stately building, the Earl's Palace at Birsay is a ruined 16th-century courtyard castle. It consists of two-storey ranges of buildings, enclosing a courtyard, with taller towers at three of the corners. The walls are pierced by many shot-holes and gunloops. The entrance to the courtyard was through the basement of one of the ranges

The basements were vaulted. A long gallery occupied the first floor, above the entrance, and another range contained a kitchen with a large fireplace.

The palace was started by Robert Stewart, Earl of Orkney, about 1574 and completed by his son, Patrick Stewart, before 1614. Father and son oppressed the islanders, and taxed them to pay for the palace at Birsay and at Kirkwall. Earl Patrick was charged with treason and executed in 1615 after his son, Robert Stewart, had risen against the Crown and seized the palace here. The rising was put down by the Earl of Caithness, and Robert was also executed. The building was badly damaged in a gale of 1868.

Nearby [HY 239285] on an island is the Brough of Birsay, an early Christian settlement, which was later used by Norsemen.

Other refs: Birsay Palace

OPEN: Access at all reasonable times.
Parking nearby
Tel: 0131 668 8800 Fax: 0131 668 8888
Email: hs.explore@scotland.gov.uk Web: www.historic-scotland.gov.uk

Earl's Palace, Kirkwall

Orkney: To west of Kirkwall on Orkney, on minor road just south of A960, across road from cathedral, off Palace Road, next to Bishop's Palace.

His Scot HY 449107 OS: 6 *** Map: 11, no: 49

The Earl's Palace is a 17th-century U-plan tower house or palace of two storeys and an attic. It consists of a main block, one long projecting wing, and another small offset square wing. The square wing has turrets, at first-floor level, at two of the corners. Large oriel windows, also at first-floor level, have moulded transoms and mullions. The walls are pierced by shot-holes. The gables are corbiestepped. The palace is dated 1607. A courtyard wall linked the adjacent Bishop's Palace with the Earl's Palace.

The main moulded entrance, in the re-entrant angle with the long wing, opens into a vaulted lobby and a fine scale-and-platt stair climbs to the first floor. A passageway, from the main entrance, leads to vaulted cellars in the basement and to the kitchen with a massive fireplace.

Another entrance, through a porch, also led into the basement.

The hall, on the first floor, has been a fine chamber with a large fireplace and oriel windows in both walls. An adjoining withdrawing chamber also has oriel windows. There were private chambers on the floor above.

The palace was built by Patrick Stewart, Earl of Orkney, the illegitimate half-brother of Mary, Queen of Scots. He oppressed the Orcadians, and was imprisoned in 1609. His son led a rebellion in the islands in 1614, capturing the Palace and castle, as well as Earl's Palace at Birsay. The rising was put down by the Earl of Caithness, and

Patrick and Robert Stewart were both executed in Edinburgh in 1615. The Bishops of Orkney occupied the palace until 1688.

OPEN: Open Apr-Sep, daily 9.30-18.30.
Explanatory displays. Parking nearby. £
Tel: 01856 875461 Fax: 0131 668 8888
Email: hs.explore@scotland.gov.uk Web: www.historic-scotland.gov.uk

Earnside Castle

Moray: About 4.5 miles north-west of Forres, on minor road north of A96, north of Alves Wood, at or near Earnside.

Ruin or site NJ 109624 OS: 28 * Map: 10, no: 18

Site of 15th-century castle, which was a property of the Cummings (or Comyns) of Altyre in 1450. Nothing remains, and it was replaced by Earnside House [NJ 107623].

East Arthurlie *see* Arthurlie House

East Bangour *see* Strathbrock Castle

East Buccleuch *see* Buccleuch Castle

East Cairns Castle *see* Cairns Tower

East Clyth *see* Gunn's Castle

East Coates House

Lothians: About 0.5 miles west of Edinburgh Castle, on minor roads north of A8, near St Mary's Episcopal Cathedral.

Private NT 241734 OS: 66 *** Map: 4, no: 88

Near St Mary's Episcopal Cathedral, East Coates House is an early 17th-century L-plan tower house of two storeys and a garret. It was considerably added to in the 18th and 19th centuries. A stair-turret, in the re-entrant angle, is corbelled out to a square at the top. Two large bartizans crown one gable, and the walls are pierced by gunloops.

The entrance is in the foot of the stair-wing. The building has been much altered inside.

The house was built by Lord Provost Sir John Byres in 1615. The house is in good condition, was part of a music school attached to the nearby cathedral, but is now the Episcopal Church's Theological Institute.

Other refs: Easter Coates House

East Kersland *see* Kersland

East Kilbride *see* Calderwood Castle

East Kilpatrick *see* Drumry Castle

East Nisbet Castle *see* Nisbet House

East Preston *see* Preston

East Raffles *see* Raffles Tower

East Reston Tower

Borders: About 2 miles south of Coldingham, on minor roads south of A1 or east of B6438 or west of B6355, west of Eye Water, at or near East Reston.

Ruin or site NT 903612 OS: 67 * Map: 2, no: 354

Probable site of tower house.

Other refs: Langton Tower

East Wemyss Castle *see* MacDuff's Castle

Eastend

Lanarkshire & Glasgow area: About 7 miles south-east of Lanark, on minor road south of A73, about 1.5 miles west of Thankerton, just south of Glade Burn, at Eastend.

Private NS 949374 OS: 72 ** Map: 3, no: 423

Eastend incorporates a 16th-century tower house of three storeys, with a corbelled-out crenellated parapet and open rounds. To this has been added tall corbiestepped gabled wings of 1673, an 18th-century bow-fronted range encasing the tower on one side, and in the late 19th century large castellated extensions.

The tower has been completely altered inside, including the removal of the basement vault.

The Carmichaels of Eastend held the property from early times. The house is still occupied.

Easter Braikie Castle

Angus & Dundee: About 6 miles south of Brechin, on minor roads south and east of A934 or north of B965, 1.5 miles east of Friockheim, 0.5 miles north-east of Braikie Castle, Easter Braikie.

Ruin or site NO 637515 OS: 54 * Map: 8, no: 257

Site of tower house, which was demolished about 1823 and replaced with a mansion.

There is a also tower at Braikie [NO 628509].

Easter Carriber *see* Carriber Castle

Easter Clune Castle

Kincardine & Deeside: About 6 miles south-west of Banchory, on minor roads south of B976, south of the Water of Feugh, at Easter Clune.

Ruin or site NO 612914 OS: 45 * Map: 10, no: 161

Very little remains of a 16th-century tower house.

It was probably built by Archbishop James Stewart, who died in 1503, or by Archbishop Ross. It was replaced by Easter Clune House, which is dated 1719.

Easter Coates House *see* East Coates House

Easter Cochrane Castle *see* Johnstone Castle

Easter Colzium

Lothians: About 4.5 miles south-east of West Calder, on minor road south of A70 at Harperrig Reservoir, at Colzium.

Ruin or site NT 083586 OS: 65 * Map: 4, no: 34

Site of castle or tower house, on which stands a modern house.

Other refs: Colzium

Easter Dawyck

Borders: About 5 miles west and south of Peebles, on minor road east of B712 at Stobo, east of the River Tweed, at or near Easter Dawyck.

Ruin or site NT 191376 OS: 72 * Map: 2, no: 39

Site of tower house of the Veitch family. The tower was demolished by Sir Walter Scott's father in the 18th century to build a farm.

Other refs: Dawick

Easter Deans

Borders: About 4 miles south of Penicuik, on minor road between A701 and A703 at Easter Deans.

Private NT 226532 OS: 73 * Map: 2, no: 51

The later farmhouse incorporates a 16th-century tower house. It was a property of the Ramsays.

Easter Elchies

Moray: About 0.5 miles north of Charlestown of Aberlour, on minor roads south of B9102, just north of River Spey, at Easter Elchies.

Private NJ 279444 OS: 28 * Map: 10, no: 55**

Easter Elchies is a small 17th-century L-plan tower house which has been much altered and added to, and was partly rebuilt in 1857. The stair-wing, in the centre of the main block, is crowned by a watch-chamber. The gables are corbiestepped and the pitch of the roof is steep.

The original entrance was in the re-entrant angle but the present entrance is now in the stair-wing.

Easter Elchies was a Grant property, one of the family, Patrick Grant being a well-known judge. During recent restoration, many of the Victorian extensions were removed. The house is now used as offices for the Macallan Distillery.

OPEN: Distillery tours available by appt.

Tel: 01340 871471 Fax: 01340 871212

Easter Fordel

Perth & Kinross: About 7 miles south of Perth, on minor roads north of B996, about 0.5 miles east of Fordel, at Easter Fordel.

Ruin or site NO 143124 OS: 58 ** Map: 8, no: 95

Not much remains of castle, the ruins consisting of a long range with a tower, rising to three storeys and an attic, at one end. A round stair-tower, with a gunloop, also survives.

Other refs: Fordel

Easter Gladstones *see* Gladstone Castle

Easter Greenock Castle

Renfrewshire: About 1.5 miles east of Greenock, south of the A8, near railway line between Glasgow and Greenock, about 0.25 miles south of the Firth of Clyde.

Ruin or site NS 300755 [?] OS: 63 * Map: 3, no: 77

Site of 16th-century castle, which was completely demolished for the building of the Caledonian railway in 1886. It was a large building, with corbiestepped gables,

but nothing remains except the gate piers and a well.

It was originally a property of the Stewarts of Castlemilk, but passed to Sir James Hamilton of Finnart, until his execution, then to the Shaws of Sauchie in 1540, then later to the Cathcarts, then back to the Stewarts. The buildings were dated 1635, 1637 and 1674. In the 1730s a new house was built, but in 1745 the family moved to Ardgowan, and the house at Greenock was sub-let to tenants. The cellars were used as a prison.

Other refs: Greenock Castle; Wellpark

Easter Happrew

Borders: About 4.5 miles south-west of Peebles, on minor road west of B712, west of River Tweed, about 1 mile north-east of Stobo, at Easter Happrew.

Ruin or site NT 191395 OS: 72 * Map: 2, no: 40

Site of tower, which stood to the south of the farm.

Easter Kinnear Castle

Fife: About 1.5 miles north and west of Balmullo, on minor roads south of the
A914, at Easter Kinnear.

Ruin or site   NO 404232   OS: 59   *   Map: 7, no: 106

Not much survives of a 17th-century tower house of the Kinnear family. Easter
Kinnear was a property of the family from the 13th century.

Easter Lilliesleaf *see* Lilliesleaf Tower

Easter Powrie *see* Wedderburn Castle

Easter Stanhope *see* Stanhope Tower

Easthills *see* Hills Tower

Eastshield Tower

Lanarkshire & Glasgow area: About 2.5 miles north-west of Carnwath, at junction
of B7016 with minor road, at Eastshield.

Ruin or site   NS 960500   OS: 72   **   Map: 3, no: 428

Little remains of a 16th-century tower house except one end wall and stair tower.
It was a property of the Inglis family.

Eastwood Castle *see* Druid's Temple Hill

Ecclefechan Hall *see* Kirkconnel Tower

Ecclesiamagirdle House

Perth & Kinross: About 4.5 miles south of Perth, on minor roads south of B935,
about 1.5 miles south-west of Bridge of Earn, at Ecclesiamagirdle.

Private   NO 107164   OS: 58   *   Map: 8, no: 79**

Ecclesiamagirdle House is a 17th-century T-plan house of two storeys and an attic.
The stair-wing rises a storey higher and contains a watch-chamber, reached by a
corbelled-out stair-turret. The courtyard gateway is dated 1648, and there is a later
wing.

The entrance is in the stair-wing. The basement is vaulted and the hall would have
been on the first floor.

Ecclesiamagirdle means the church of St Grill or Grillan, Grillan being one of St
Columba's 12 followers: there is a small church nearby. After the Reformation, the
lands of Ecclesiamagirdle were sold to the Halyburtons of Pitcur, but by 1629 had
passed to the Carmichaels of Balmedie.

'The lasses o' Exmagirdle may weel be dun,

For frae Michaelmas to Whitsunday they never see the sun.'

Ecclesiamagirdle lies beneath the northern slopes of the Ochil hills, and sees little
sun in the winter.

Other refs: Exmagriddle; Eglismagirdle

Echizingles Tower *see* Kirkton Tower

Eckford Tower

Borders: About 4 miles south and west of Kelso, on minor roads east of A698,
near or at Eckford, east of the River Teviot.

Ruin or site   NT 709261   OS: 74   *   Map: 2, no: 289

Site of 16th-century tower house, which was burned by the English in 1554 by Sir
Ralph Eure, then again in 1570 by the Earl of Sussex.

Eddercalda House *see* Calda House

Edderstoun *see* Adderston

Edderton Castle

South Highland: About 3.5 miles west and north of Tain, on minor roads south of
A9, 1 mile south of Edderton, east of Edderton Burn, at or near Edderton Mains.

Ruin or site   NH 716838 [?]   OS: 21   *   Map: 9, no: 108

Site of castle, said to have been built by William the Lyon in 1179. The site may have
been at Edderton Mains although it is also suggested to be at Blackpark [NH 675832].
A third possibility is at Meikle Daan [NH 688847].

Standing in the graveyard of the 18th-century church is a carved cross-slab [NH
719842] . On one side is a cross, below which is a rider within a curved frame, while
on the other side is a large ringed cross on a tall stem. There are the ruins of an
earlier church to the east of the modern building.

Eddlewood Castle

Lanarkshire & Glasgow: About 1.5 miles south of Hamilton, off A723, 1 mile
north-west of Quarter Iron Works, on banks of Meikle Burn.

Ruin or site   NS 722518 [?]   OS: 64   *   Map: 3, no: 335

Site of castle of the Hamiltons of Eddlewood and Neilsland, who held the property
until 1750. It may have been destroyed by the Regent Moray after the Battle of
Langside in 1568. A mound of rubbish marked the site, but nothing apparently now
remains.

Eden Castle

Banff & Buchan: About 3.5 miles south of Banff, on minor roads west of A947,
east of River Deveron, at Mains of Eden.

Ruin or site   NJ 698588   OS: 29   **   Map: 10, no: 207

Not much survives of a 16th-century Z-plan tower house of the Meldrums, which
was extended by the Leslies in 1613. Alexander Leslie of Eden wrote the ballad 'The
Banks o' Deveron Water' for Helen Christie. In 1712 the castle was sold the Duff
Earl of Fife.

Edgerston *see* Eggerston Castle

Edinample Castle

Stirlingshire & Clackmannan: About 1 mile south-east of Lochearnhead, on
minor roads east of A84, just south of Loch Earn, north of the Falls of Edinample,
at Edinample.

Private   NN 601226   OS: 51   **   Map: 6, no: 33**

Edinample Castle is an altered 16th-century Z-plan tower house, although it may
incorporate an earlier tower. It consists of a main block with round towers at opposite corners, and was remodelled in the late 18th century, then extended by a four-
storey range.

The basement is vaulted, and contained the kitchen and wine-cellar with stairs to
the hall above. The main stair, to the first floor, is in one of the round towers, where
there is a dungeon in the thickness of the walls, reached from a guardroom above.

The property originally belonged to the MacGregors, but was acquired by the
Campbells, while the MacGregors were a proscribed clan. The castle is said to have

been built by Sir Duncan Campbell of Glenorchy – Black Duncan of the Castles – around 1584. By the early 1970s the castle had been abandoned and was derelict, but has since been restored.

St Blane, a 6th-century saint, reputedly cursed the place: that the owners would be neither rich nor lasting. Another legend is that one of the lairds took tombstones away from a local graveyard to build the castle, and was told by a witch 'You'll put the Estate through your backside yet with the gill stoup!' – and the laird, of course, drank his way through his money and estate.

The building is said to be haunted. Black Duncan of the Castles ordered that the castle should have a parapet walk around it. The builder forgot to add this feature, but tried to show that it was possible to walk around the roof as it stood. Black Duncan pushed him from the roof, so saving the fee. So – 'tis said – at certain times the ghost of the builder can be seen clambering around the roof.

Edinbeg Tower *see* Wester Kames Castle

Edinbellie Castle

Stirlingshire & Clackmannan: About 2 miles east of Balfron, on minor road north of B818, north of Endrick Water, south of Ballindalloch Muir, at Edinbellie Farm.
Ruin or site   NS 577890   OS: 57   *   Map: 6, no: 26
Site of tower, some remains of which survived in 1840.

It was a property of the Napiers of Merchiston from 1509, and may be the birthplace of John Napier in 1550, who invented logarithms, although this is more likely to have been Merchiston.

In 1750 the sons of Rob Roy MacGregor forcibly abducted Jean Kay from here. She was a young widow and heiress to Edinbellie, and was (probably) forced to marry Robin Oig MacGregor. When she died her family protested to the authorities, and Robin Oig was hanged three years later.

Edinburgh Castle

Lothians: In the centre of Edinburgh, on minor road south of A1 (Princes Street), just west of Waverley Station.
His Scot   NT 252735   OS: 66   ***   Map: 4, no: 94**
Standing on a high rock, Edinburgh Castle was one of the strongest and most important castles in Scotland and, although the present complex of buildings dates from no earlier than the 15th century, it has a long and bloody history.

There was a fortress on the castle rock from the earliest times, but the oldest building is a small Norman chapel of the early 12th century, dedicated to St Margaret, wife of Malcolm Canmore. After Malcolm's death at Alnwick in 1093, the castle was besieged by his brother, Donald Bane, in support of his claim to the throne. In 1173, after the capture of William I the Lyon at Alnwick, it was surrendered to the English, but later recovered by the Scots.

The castle had an English garrison from 1296 until 1313 during the Wars of Independence, when the Scots, led by Thomas Randolph, climbed the rock, surprised the garrison, and retook it. The castle was slighted, but there was an English garrison here again until 1341, when it was retaken by a Scottish force disguised as merchants bringing provisions to the garrison. In 1367-71 David II rebuilt the castle

with strong curtain walls and towers, and a large L-plan keep, David's Tower, which was named after him.

After the murder of the young Earl of Douglas and his brother at the 'Black Dinner' at the castle in 1440, it was attacked and captured by the Douglases after a nine month siege, and required substantial repairs. James III's brother, Alexander, Duke of Albany, escaped after being imprisoned in David's Tower in 1479. James, himself, was confined in the tower by his nobles in 1482, but Alexander returned from exile, took his side, and had him released.

A new great hall was built in 1483, and other repairs were executed, but increasingly the royal palaces were favoured as comfortable residences over the castle – although the castle remained of vital importance as the state armoury, prison, record repository, and major fortress of Edinburgh.

In 1566 Mary, Queen of Scots, gave birth to the future James VI in the castle. After her abdication, it was held on her behalf, until English help forced it to surrender in 1573. Having been badly damaged by artillery, the castle was rebuilt to such an extent afterwards, and in subsequent periods, that all that survives of David's Tower is embedded in the Half Moon Battery.

The castle was captured in 1640 after a three-month siege by the Covenanters, and Cromwell besieged it throughout the autumn of 1650. Much new work on the fortifications was done by Charles II, and many of the present buildings date from the 17th and 18th centuries. The Jacobites failed to take it in both the 1715 and 1745 Jacobite Risings, although some of them were incarcerated in it later, as were Napoleonic prisoners of war in the early 19th century.

The castle is the home of the Scottish crown jewels, and the Stone of Destiny – on which the Kings of Scots were inaugurated – and is an interesting complex of buildings with spectacular views over the capital.

The castle is reputedly haunted by many ghosts, including a headless drummer seen in 1960, a ghostly piper sent to explore an underground tunnel thought to lead down to Holyroodpalace, and the spectre of a dog whose remains are buried in the pet's cemetery.

Other refs: Castle of the Maidens
OPEN: Open all year: Apr-Sep, daily 9.30-17.15 (last ticket sold); Oct-Mar, daily 9.30-16.15 (last ticket sold), castle closes 45 mins after last ticket is sold; times may be altered during Tattoo and state occasions; closed 25/26 Dec and 1/2 Jan.
Explanatory displays. Guided tours. Gift shop. Restaurant. WC. Disabled access. Visitors with a disability can be taken to the top of the castle by a courtesy vehicle; ramps and lift access to Crown Jewels and Stone of Destiny. Car and coach parking (except during Tattoo). £££.
Tel: 0131 225 9846   Fax: 0131 668 8888
Email: hs.explore@scotland.gov.uk   Web: www.historic-scotland.gov.uk

Edingham Castle

Galloway: About 1 mile north of Dalbeattie, on minor road east of A711, just east of Edingham Farm, just west of Kingunzeon Lane.
Ruin or site   NX 839626   OS: 84   **   Map: 1, no: 152
Little remains of a small 16th-century tower house above the vaulted basement. There was a turnpike stair in one corner.

Edingight House

Moray: About 7.5 miles south of Cullen, on minor roads east of B9018 or west of A95, just west of Burn of Braco, at Edingight.
Private   NJ 517557   OS: 29   **   Map: 10, no: 118
Edingight House is an altered two-storey house, part of which may date from 1559, which was built for the Innes family. It was extended in 1615 and restored in 1955. It does not appear to have any surviving defensive features, but is still occupied.

Edinglassie Castle

Aberdeen & Gordon: About 7 miles west of Huntly, on minor roads south of A920, just west of River Deveron, near Burn of Edinglassie, at Mains of Edinglassie.
Ruin or site   NJ 423388   OS: 28   *   Map: 10, no: 83
Site of castle of the Gordons. It was burned in 1688 (or 1690) by General Mackay for William and Mary during the Jacobite Rising.

Edington Bastle

Borders: About 1.5 miles south-east of Chirnside, on minor roads east of B6437 or north of B6460, just to south of Whiteadder Water, just north of Hutton Castle.
Ruin or site   NT 890552   OS: 74   *   Map: 2, no: 352
Site of castle or bastle, formerly in a strong position by a loop of the Whiteadder Water, which was apparently destroyed by the English in the 16th century.

Edington Castle

Borders: About 1.5 miles east of Chirnside, just south of A6105, west of minor road to Edington.
Ruin or site   NT 896562   OS: 67   **   Map: 2, no: 353
Site of castle, formerly with a moat. It probably dated from the 16th or 17th century and was abandoned about 1708. All that remains is a wall built from the remains of the castle. There was also a bastle near here [NT 889552], which was destroyed by the English in the 16th century.
Other refs: Ithington Castle; Mains Castle

Edmonston Castle

Lanarkshire & Glasgow area: About 4 miles north-east of Biggar, on minor road between A702 and A721, at Edmonston, west of the Candy Burn.
Private   NT 070422   OS: 72   **   Map: 3, no: 457
Edmonston Castle is a ruined 15th-century keep of three storeys and had a small adjoining courtyard. A stair-turret survives at one corner, as does a gunloop in the basement. The basement was vaulted. The tower was roofless but intact until 1872, when it was partially demolished by blowing it up. A house built in the courtyard had been demolished in 1815 and a new dwelling built.
It was a property of the Edmonstones, but passed to the Douglases in 1322 until it was sold in 1650 to Baillie of Walston, who held it until the early 18th century. It was then a property of the Browns, before being sold to Wodropps of Elsrickle and Dalmarnock.
Other refs: High House of Edmonston

Edmonstone Castle

Lothians: About 4 miles south-east of Edinburgh Castle, on minor roads between A6106 and A68, west of Danderhall, at Edmonstone.
Private   NT 304704 [?]   OS: 66   *   Map: 4, no: 126
Site of castle, on which a more modern mansion was built.
It was a property of the Edmonstones from 1248, who were said to have come to Scotland with Queen Margaret, wife of Malcolm Canmore. It passed to the Rait family at the beginning of the 17th century, then by marriage to the Wauchopes of Niddrie in 1671. One of the family John Wauchope, Lord Edmonstone, was a Lord of Session.

Edradour Castle *see* Red Castle

Edrington Castle

Borders: About 5 miles east and south of Chirnside, on minor road north of B6461, east of Paxton, east of Whiteadder Water, north of Cawderstanes.
Ruin or site   NT 941534   OS: 67   *   Map: 2, no: 361
Site of tower house, formerly of four storeys, and once a place of some strength.
It featured often in the wars between England and Scotland, and is said to have been destroyed by the Duke of Gloucester in 1482. It was rebuilt and seized by the Homes of Wedderburn. Having been held for some time by the English, Edrington was returned to the Scots in 1534. There were substantial remains in the 18th century, but only a fragment now survives, incorporated into farm buildings.
There was apparently another tower near here [NT 944540], known as Edrington Bastle, and used as a prison by the garrison of Edrington Castle.
Other refs: Cawderstanes

Edzell Castle

Angus & Dundee: About 6 miles north of Brechin, on minor roads west of B966 at Edzell village, about 0.3 miles north of West Water, at Edzell Castle.
His Scot   NO 585693   OS: 44   **   Map: 8, no: 242**
Edzell Castle consists of an early 16th-century tower house, later enlarged and ex-

tended with ranges of buildings around a courtyard. A large pleasance, or garden, was created in 1604, and was surrounded by an ornamental wall, to which a summerhouse and a bath-house were added. The fine carved decoration of the garden walls is unique.
The L-plan tower, at one corner of the main courtyard, replaced an older castle. It rises to four storeys and a garret, and has open rounds at all corners and small projecting half-rounds at the centre of each wall.
The entrance, reached through an arched doorway from the courtyard, is in the re-entrant angle. It leads to the vaulted basement, one cellar having a small stair to the hall on the first floor above. The hall has two fireplaces and the upper floors were reached by a wide stair.
An L-shaped gabled range of three storeys was added in the late 16th century. This is very ruinous, but once contained many comfortable chambers.
The pleasance is large and surrounded by a wall. The summerhouse is a rectangular two-storey building with its own stair tower, gunloop and bartizan. The basement is vaulted.
The lands passed by marriage from the Stirlings of Glenesk to the Lindsay Earls of Crawford in 1357. The castle replaced the nearby motte [NO 584688]. Mary, Queen of Scots, held a Privy Council at Edzell in 1562, and stayed in the castle. Cromwell garrisoned it in 1651. During the Royalist uprising of 1653, John Lindsay was kidnapped from Edzell, but he was rescued by Cromwell's forces.
The Lindsays had to sell the property in 1715, because of huge debts, and it was bought by the Maule Earl of Panmure. The Maules were forfeited for their part in the 1745 Jacobite Rising, and the castle was garrisoned by Hanoverian troops, who did much damage. The Maules recovered Edzell in 1764, but the castle was abandoned soon afterwards.
One story associated with the castle is that the one of the Lindsays lairds was cursed by a gypsy woman, after he had hanged her sons for poaching. The tales goes that his pregnant wife died that day, while he himself was devoured by wolves – as foretold.
The castle is said to be haunted by a 'White Lady', reputedly the spirit of Catherine Campbell, second wife of David Lindsay, 9th Earl of Crawford. She died in 1578, but is said to have been interred alive in her family vault. She eventually regained consciousness, but died of exposure at the castle gates. The ghost has reportedly been witnessed in recent times, including in 1986.
Other refs: Stirling Tower; Castle Hillock, Edzell
OPEN: Open all year: Apr-Sep, daily 9.30-18.30; Oct-Mar, Mon-Wed and Sat 9.30-16.30, Thu 9.30-12.00, Sun 14.00-16.30, closed Fri; last ticket 30 mins before closing; closed 25/26 Dec and 1/2 Jan.
Visitor centre. Exhibition and explanatory panels. WC. Garden. Picnic area. Reasonable disabled access and WC. Car and coach parking. Group concessions. £
Tel: 01356 648631   Fax: 0131 668 8888
Email: hs.explore@scotland.gov.uk   Web: www.historic-scotland.gov.uk

Eggerness Castle

Galloway: About 1 mile north-east of Garlieston, on minor roads east of B7004 at Garlieston, just west of sea at Wigtown Bay, east of Eggerness.

Private   NX 495478   OS: 83   **   Map: 1, no: 82

Standing on a rocky promontory are the remains of an Iron Age fort with two ramparts and ditches. The site was reused as a medieval castle, and is from 'Edgar's ness'.

Other refs: Eagerness

Eggerston Castle

Borders: About 6 miles south and east of Jedburgh, on minor roads east of A68, about 1 mile east of the Jed Water, at or near Eggerston.

Ruin or site   NT 691115 [?]   OS: 80   *   Map: 2, no: 283

Site of castle, which was seized by 'assured' Scots for the English in 1544.

Other refs: Edgerston

Eglinton Castle

Ayrshire: About 1.5 miles north of Irvine, on minor roads north of B7080, near Eglinton Park visitor centre.

Ruin or site   NS 323423   OS: 70   *   Map: 3, no: 92

Eglinton Castle, a huge very ruined 18th-century castellated mansion, was built on the site of a 16th-century stronghold of the Montgomery Earls of Eglinton.

The property passed by marriage, along with Ardrossan, from the Eglintons to the Montgomery family in the 14th century, who were made Earls of Eglinton in 1508. The family long feuded with the Cunningham Earls of Glencairn. The castle here was burned in 1528 by the Cunninghams in retaliation for the sacking of Kerelaw Castle. Hugh Montgomery, 4th Earl, was murdered near the bridge of Annick by the Cunninghams of Clonbeith and of Robertland, and others of that family. The Montgomerys killed every Cunningham they could find, and cut Cunningham of Clonbeith to pieces.

The castle was replaced by a large mansion in 1802, and it was at the new castle that the Eglinton Tournament was held in 1839, a medieval tournament, attracting thousands of visitors. However, the house was abandoned when the family ran out of money building the harbour at Ardrossan. It was unroofed in 1925 to be used for target practice, blown up in the 1950s, and the shell of the house was partly demolished in 1973. All that survives is a single corner tower and some low walls.

The ruins stand in a public park.

Eglismagirdle *see* Ecclesiamagirdle House

Eilean Amalaig Castle

Argyll & Dunbartonshire: About 4.5 miles south of Craignure on Mull, by foot and boat 1 mile south of A849 at Ardachoil, on small island, Eilean Amalaig, west side of Loch Spelve.

Ruin or site   NM 708298   OS: 49   **   Map: 5, no: 34

Site of castle of the MacLeans of nearby Duart. It was at Loch Spelve that the MacLeans marshalled their birlinns or galleys.

At the end of the 16th century, Sir Lachlan MacLean was advised not to sail his galleys anticlockwise around the island or trouble would befall. He ignored this warning, and soon afterwards was killed on Islay at the Battle of Gruinart in 1598 by the MacDonalds.

Eilean Assynt *see* Assynt Castle

Eilean Darroch

South Highland: About 4.5 miles north and west of Spean Bridge, by boat east of B8005, 1 mile east of Achnacarry, on island in bay on west side of Loch Lochy.

Ruin or site   NN 187876   OS: 41   *   Map: 9, no: 45

Site of fortified island on a crannog. One tale about the island is that the laird asked his family to come to see him one at a time, but as each one arrived they were thrown into the water by a tilting log and drowned. One way to deal with troublesome relations.

Eilean Dearg Castle

Argyll & Dunbartonshire: About 9 miles north and west of Rothesay, on foot and boat west of B866 at Port an Eilean, on island in Loch Riddon or Ruel, on Cowal, on Eilean Dearg.

Ruin or site   NS 008771   OS: 63   *   Map: 5, no: 95

Eilean Dearg Castle is a much-ruined castle, dating from the 14th or 15th century, consisting of a keep and courtyard. It is said to have been similar to Castle Stalker. Musket flints and balls were found during excavation, when the remains of the keep, a range of buildings, and a chapel were found.

It was a property of the Stewarts at the end of the 13th century, but held by the Campbells from the 1440s or before, and used by the Campbell Earl of Argyll during his rebellion of 1685. The castle was blown up with gunpowder the same year following naval action, and not reused.

Other refs: Castle Oilen Greg; Dheirrig

Eilean Donan Castle

South Highland: About 8 miles east of Kyle of Lochalsh, south of Dornie, on an island, on A87, on the north side of Loch Duich at mouth of Loch Long, at Eilean Donan.

Private   NG 881259   OS: 33   **   Map: 9, no: 34**

One of the most beautifully situated of all Scottish castles, Eilean Donan Castle consists of a 13th-century wall surrounding a courtyard. In one corner of the courtyard stands a strong 14th-century keep of three storeys and a gabled garret. Adjoining ranges of outbuildings and fortifications were added in later centuries. The keep has a flush parapet, with open rounds and corbelled machiolations.

The main entrance is up a flight of stairs from the courtyard. The basement is barrel-vaulted, and the hall is on the first floor. Access to private rooms above the hall.

Alexander III gave the lands to Colin Fitzgerald, son of the Irish Earl of Desmond and Kildare, for his help in defeating King Haakon and his Norsemen at the Battle of Largs in 1263. The family changed their name to Mackenzie, and Eilean Donan became their main stronghold. Robert the Bruce was sheltered here in 1306.

In 1331 Randolph, Earl of Moray, executed 50 men at Eilean Donan and adorned the castle walls with severed heads. The castle was captured by the Earl of Huntly in 1504, and in 1509 the MacRaes became constables of the castle. In 1539 Eilean Donan was besieged by Donald Gorm MacDonald, a claimant to the Lordship of the Isles, but he was killed by an arrow shot from the castle.

William Mackenzie, 5th Earl of Seaforth, had it garrisoned with Spanish troops during the Jacobite rising of 1719, but three frigates battered it into submission with cannon, and it was blown up from within. Although very ruinous, it was completely rebuilt in the 20th century.

The ghost of one of the Spanish troops, killed either at the castle or the nearby

Eilean Donan Castle around 1900 – it was completely restored in the 20th century

battle, is said to haunt the castle. Another apparition, Lady Mary, is said to have been seen in one of the bedrooms.

OPEN: Open Apr-Oct, daily 10.00-17.30.

Guided tours available. Visitor centre. New exhibitions. Gift shop. Tearoom. WC and disabled WC. Car and coach parking. Group concessions. ££.

Tel: 01599 555202   Fax: 01599 555262

Eilean Dunic Raonuill *see* Loch nan Clachan Dun

Eilean Ghruididh

South Highland: About 7.5 miles north-west of Kinlochewe, by boat north of A832, on island Eilean Ghruididh, on the south side of Loch Maree.

Ruin or site   NG 951693   OS: 19   *   Map: 9, no: 36

Eilean Ghruididh was fortified and there are the remains of a wall around the island.

This is thought to have been a stronghold of the MacBeaths in the 13th century, and was then held by the MacLeods from about 1430 until 1513.

Other refs: Loch Maree; Eilean Gruididh

Eilean Gruididh *see* Eilean Ghruididh

Eilean Molach

Stirling & Clackmannanshire: About 6 miles north of Aberfoyle, by boat off A821 at Trossachs Pier Complex, in Loch Katrine, Eilean Molach

Ruin or site   NN 488083   OS: 57   *   Map: 6, no: 10

The island in the loch was used as a stronghold by the MacGregors in the middle of the 16th century. There was a lodge here in the 19th century, which was destroyed by fire.

Other refs: Island Varnach; Ellen's Isle

Eilean na Circe

Argyll & Dunbartonshire: About 6 miles west of Lochgilphead, by boat east of B8025, in Caol Scotnish, on Eilean na Circe.

Ruin or site   NR 767892   OS: 55   *   Map: 5, no: 46

There are remains of a fortified residence on the island.

Eilean nam Faoileag

Perthshire: About 9 miles west of Kinloch Rannoch, on island in Loch Rannoch south of B846, Eilean nam Faoileag.

Ruin or site   NN 530577   OS: 51   *   Map: 8, no: 2

Possible site of castle. The island was used as a prison and refuge by the Robertsons of Struan. The present tower was rebuilt in the 19th century.

Eilean nan Bannoabh Castle *see* Kenmore Castle

Eilean nan Craobh

South Highland: About 0.25 miles south-west of Corpach, by boat or pier south of A830, on Eilean nan Craobh, an island in Loch Eil.

Ruin or site   NN 090763   OS: 41   *   Map: 9, no: 37

Site of castle or residence of the Camerons of Lochiel in the 15th and 16th centuries.

Other refs: Loch Eil

Eilean Ran Castle

Stirlingshire & Clackmannan: In or near Killin, near the A827, about 0.5 miles west of Loch Tay, probably between River Lochay and River Dochart.

Ruin or site   NN 577334 [?]   OS: 51   *   Map: 6, no: 27

Site of castle, which was originally on an island.

It was a property of the MacNabs in 1525, and was burned out in the 1650s or 1660s. The lands around Killin later passed to the Campbells.

Other refs: Castle or Eilean Rowan; Eilean Rowan Castle

Eilean Rossdhu Castle *see* Rossdhu Castle

Eilean Rowan Castle *see* Eilean Ran Castle

Eilean Tighe Bhainn *see* Loch Tromlee

Eilean Tioram Castle *see* Castle Tioram

Eilean Vhow Castle

Argyll & Dunbartonshire: About 5 miles north of Tarbet, on island to north of Loch Lomond, east of the A82, about 2 miles south and east of Ardlui.

Ruin or site   NN 332128   OS: 56   **   Map: 5, no: 138

Eilean Vhow Castle is a ruined 16th-century tower house. The basement was vaulted, but little remains above this level.

It was a property of the MacFarlanes, and became one of their main seats after the destruction of Inveruglas in the 1650s. James VI visited the castle, and the clan moved to Arrochar in 1697. It was still inhabited in 1743, but had been abandoned by the early 19th century, although a hermit apparently still lived in the vault, which was known as the 'Hermit's Cave', at this time.

Other refs: Vow

Elchies Castle *see* Craigneach Castle

Elcho Castle

Perth & Kinross: About 4 miles east and south of Perth, on minor roads east of A912 at Scoonieburn or Bridge of Earn, just south of River Tay, at Elcho.

His Scot   NO 165211   OS: 58   **   Map: 8, no: 109**

Impressive and well preserved, both stronghold and comfortable residence, Elcho Castle is a 16th-century tower house, built in the plan of a Z with an extra tower at one corner. It consists of a long rectangular main block, with a square stair-tower projecting from one corner, and three other towers projecting on the opposite

side. One of these is a round stair-tower, corbelled out to square at the top, while the other square towers contain apartments. Some windows still have iron yetts, and the walls are pierced by many gunloops. Two turnpike stairs are corbelled out above first floor level and give access to the upper floors and the towers along with the round stair-tower.

One round tower and some walling remain from a courtyard, which formerly enclosed many buildings.

The entrance to the tower, in the re-entrant angle, leads to a wide turnpike stair and into the vaulted basement, which contains a large kitchen with an enormous fireplace, and cellars. The hall, on the first floor, has some remains of plasterwork and has a large fireplace. The lord's apartments were also on this floor. The upper floors and towers contained many more comfortable chambers.

William Wallace is supposed to have sheltered here, but nothing of this early castle remains. The Wemyss family held the property from 1468, and built the existing castle towards the end of the 16th century. The family were made Lords Elcho in 1633, as well as Earls of Wemyss the same year. David, Lord Elcho, fought and survived the Battle of Culloden on the Jacobite side in 1746, but had to flee to France. By the 1780s Elcho Castle was abandoned by the family, although it may have been used to house farm workers, and fell into decay. It was reroofed in 1830, and has been in the care of the State since 1929.

A small spring [NO 165210] is said to have been used by William Wallace.
OPEN: Open Apr-Sep, daily 9.30-18.30; last ticket sold 18.00.
Gift shop. Picnic area. WC. Parking. £.
Tel: 01738 639998 Fax: 0131 668 8888
Email: hs.explore@scotland.gov.uk Web: www.historic-scotland.gov.uk

Elderslie *see* Wallace's Buildings

Eldinhope Tower
Borders: About 4 miles east of Capperclauch, about 0.5 miles south east of B709, by the Eldinhope Burn.
Ruin or site NT 305238 OS: 73 * Map: 2, no: 78
Very little remains of a tower house except overgrown foundations.

It was a property of the Scotts of Howpaslie in 1492, but passed to the Scotts of Branxholme, then to the Scott Earl of Buccleuch by 1628.
Other refs: Aldinhope

Elgin *see* Thunderton House, Elgin

Elgin *see* Bishop's House, Elgin

Elgin Castle
Moray: In Elgin, just north of A96, about 0.5 miles west of Elgin Cathedral, just south of River Lossie on Ladyhill.
Ruin or site NJ 212628 OS: 28 * Map: 10, no: 38
Very little survives of a 12th-century royal castle, built on Ladyhill.

King Duncan is said to have died here in the 11th century from wounds inflicted by Macbeth at a battle near Spynie. Edward I of England stayed here for four days in 1296, during the Wars of Independence, and again in 1303, but it was recaptured by the Scots in May 1308 and never rebuilt. There are excellent views from the top.

The chapel of the castle was dedicated to the Virgin Mary, hence Ladyhill.
Other refs: Castle of Ladyhill
OPEN: Access at all reasonable times.
Parking nearby

Elibank Castle
Borders: About 4 miles east of Innerleithen, on minor roads south of A72, south of the River Tweed.
Ruin or site NT 397363 OS: 73 ** Map: 2, no: 102
Elibank Castle consists of a ruined 16th-century L-plan tower house of four storeys and probably a garret. The basement and second floors were vaulted, and there was a terraced garden and a courtyard with a gatehouse. It was apparently once a place of some strength and comfort.

The lands were a property of the Liddles, but passed to the Murrays of Glenpoit in about 1594, who probably built or rebuilt an existing castle. Sir Gideon Murray was

chamberlain to Walter Scott of Buccleuch, and received the lands in 1594. In 1611 he captured Walter Scott of Harden, a Border reiver, but offered him his life if Scott would marry Murray's daughter Agnes, 'Muckle Mou'd Meg', rather than be hanged. Harden sensibly married the girl. Murray's son became Lord Elibank in 1643, but the castle was a ruin by 1722. Alexander Murray, son of the 4th Lord Elibank, was a Jacobite.
Other refs: Eliburn

Eliburn *see* Elibank Castle

Elie Castle
Fife: In Elie, on minor road west of A917, south of minor road, overlooking beach and harbour area.
Ruin or site NO 488001 OS: 59 ** Map: 7, no: 127
Elie Castle is a 17th-century L-plan tower house of three storeys and a garret, although it incorporates work from the 15th century. It consists of a long main block

and a projecting rectangular stair-tower, rising a storey higher, and crowned by a corbelled-out square caphouse. The gables are corbiestepped, and the basement is vaulted.

Some original painting and panelling survives.

It was held by the Gourlays of Kincraig.

Elie House
Fife: About 0.75 miles north of Elie, on minor roads north or east of A917, at Elie House.
Ruin or site NO 496008 OS: 59 * Map: 7, no: 129
Elie House is apparently mostly modern, but incorporates an L-plan house dating from about 1697, itself built on the foundations of an earlier castle.

The original castle was built by Sir Andrew Anstruther in 1366, although by the 17th century the property had passed to the Scots. This house was altered and extended again about 1740, and in the 19th century, by when it had passed to the Bairds. It was altered again in the 20th century, while being used as a convent.

Eliock House
Dumfriesshire: About 2 miles south-east of Sanquhar, on minor roads south of A76 at Eliock Bridge, south of the River Nith, west of the Eliock Burn, at Eliock.
Private NS 796074 OS: 78 ** Map: 1, no: 133
Eliock House, a 17th-century and later H-plan mansion, incorporates the vaulted basement, with shot-holes, of a 16th-century tower house in one wing.

It was a property of the Dalziels in 1388, but then passed to the Crichtons, then in

1462 to the Charteris family. It was held by Robert Crichton, Lord Advocate of Scotland to Mary, Queen of Scots, and James VI. He was the father of 'Admirable Crichton', who may have been born here, or at Clunie Castle, on its island. The property was sold to Stewart of Balquhane in 1593, then in the 17th century returned to the Dalziels, but later sold to the Veitch family, who held it in the 19th century.
Other refs: Elliok Castle

Eliotstoun *see* Castle Semple

Elistone *see* Illieston House

Ellanrayne Castle *see* Loch Earn Castle

Ellen's Isle *see* Eilean Molach

Ellibister
Orkney: About 6 miles north of Finstown, on minor road west of A966, at or near Ellibister.
Ruin or site HY 386212 [?] OS: 6 * Map: 11, no: 42
This is said to be the site of a castle.

Elliok Castle *see* Eliock House

Elliotston Tower *see* Elliston Castle

Elliston *see* Illieston House

Elliston Castle
Renfrewshire: About 3 miles west and south of Johnstone, on minor road north between B776 and A737, about 0.5 miles south-east of Howwood.
Ruin or site NS 392598 OS: 63 * Map: 3, no: 140
Elliston Castle is a large very ruined 15th-century castle and courtyard. The basement was vaulted.
It was a property of the Semple family, but was abandoned about 1550 for Castle Semple, and partly demolished in 1735.
Other refs: Elliotston Tower

Ellon Castle
Aberdeen & Gordon: To the north-east of Ellon, on minor roads and foot north of A920 or east of A948, north of River Ythan.
Ruin or site NJ 960307 OS: 30 ** Map: 10, no: 341
Ellon Castle consists of a very ruined 16th-century tower house, with gunloops, and the remains of other ranges, incorporating parts of a 13th-century castle.
The Comyns built the first castle which was probably destroyed around 1308, but later rebuilt. It was held by the Kennedys of Kermuck, who had an earlier stronghold at Kinmuck (Kermuck or Kenmuck) [NJ 989351]. They were outlawed for the murder of John Forbes of Waterton in 1652; and the property sold to the Gordons. James Gordon created a terraced garden about 1706, but his sons were murdered by their tutor, and the property passed to the Gordon Earl of Aberdeen in 1752. In 1782 the 4th Earl remodelled and extended the building, destroying much of the old castle. This house was replaced by a mansion of 1851, which was itself demolished in 1929.
Other refs: Ardgith Castle; Old Ellon Castle

Ellridgehill *see* Elsrickle

Elphinstone Tower *see* Airth Tower

Elphinstone Tower *see* Baronial Hall, Gorbals

Elphinstone Tower
Lothians: About 2 miles south-east of Tranent, south of Elphinstone, on minor road south of B6414.
Ruin or site NT 391698 OS: 66 ** Map: 4, no: 160
Elphinstone Tower consists of a simple ruined 14th-century keep, formerly of three storeys with a stone-flagged parapet.
The basement was vaulted. The hall and original kitchen, screened by a partition, were on the first floor. The upper floors contained private chambers. Many small rooms and stairs were contained in the thickness of the walls, including a peephole, where the hall could be watched in secret.

The Elphinstones held the lands from the 13th century. Sir Alexander Elphinstone was killed in 1435, and the property apparently passed by marriage to the Johnstones soon afterwards. In 1545 the Protestant martyr, George Wishart, was brought from nearby Ormiston, and at Elphinstone was handed over to Cardinal Beaton, who took Wishart back to St Andrews for trial and execution by burning in 1546. An adjoining mansion of 1600 was demolished in 1865, as was much of the tower in 1955 due to subsidence from coal workings, and more has since been lost.

Elrick House

Aberdeen & Gordon: About 1 mile south of New Machar, on minor roads north of B979 or west of A947, east of Elrick Burn, at or near Elrick House.

Private   NJ 883183 [?]   OS: 38   *   Map: 10, no: 303

Site of castle or old house. The present mansion dates from the second half of the 18th century, but there is a 16th-century doocot.

Elshieshields Tower

Dumfriesshire: About 2 miles north-west of Lochmaben, on minor road north of B7020 at Lochmaben, just east of the Water of Ae, at Elshieshields.

Private   NY 069850   OS: 78   **   Map: 1, no: 212**

A good example of a fortified but comfortable residence, Elshieshields Tower is a late 16th-century L-plan tower house of three storeys and an attic. Three large bartizans and a square tower, of two storeys, crown the corners. The walls are harled. The house was extended in the 18th century, and was remodelled and enlarged in the 19th and 20th centuries.

The original doorway is in the re-entrant angle, but the basement is not vaulted. The hall is on the first floor, with private chambers above.

The tower was a property of the Johnstones, but burned by Maxwell of Kirkhouse in 1602. It was repaired, and the house is still occupied and in good condition.

Elsrickle

Lanarkshire & Glasgow: About 5 miles east of Carnwath, on or near A721, at or near Elsrickle.

Ruin or site   NT 062435   OS: 72   *   Map: 3, no: 456

Site of castle, a property of the Hepburns in the 15th century. The lands had passed to the Wodropps of Dalmarnock by the 18th century.

Other refs: Ellridgehill

Embo *see* Old House of Embo

Endovie *see* Balfluig Castle

Enoch Castle

Dumfriesshire: About 3.5 miles north of Thornhill, short distance east of A702 at Enoch, west of the Carron Water.

Ruin or site   NS 879009   OS: 78   *   Map: 1, no: 165

Site of a 13th- or 14th-century castle, which stood on a peninsula between the Carron river and a deep ravine. A gateway apparently once held the date 1281 or 1581.

Enoch is said to have been captured by William Wallace in 1296. It was a property of the Menzies family from at least 1376, and occupied by them until sold in 1703 to the Douglas Duke of Queensberry. In 1810 it passed by marriage to the Scott Duke of Buccleuch.

Enrick

Galloway: About 1.5 miles south and east of Gatehouse of Fleet, on minor roads and foot north of A75 and west of B727, south of Enrick, at Palace Yard.

Ruin or site   NX 614544   OS: 83   *   Map: 1, no: 101

Site of castle, known as 'Palace Yard', of which only earthworks remain. The castle consisted of a 13th-century hall house of the Abbots of Tongland, which passed to the Bishops of Galloway. Edward I stayed here in 1300.

Other refs: Ainrick; Palace Yard

Enzieholm *see* Bogle Walls, Enzieholm

Erchless Castle

Inverness & Nairn: About 8 miles west and south of Beauly, on minor roads south of A831, north of River Beauly at meeting with Erchless Burn, at Erchless.

Private   NH 410408   OS: 26   **   Map: 9, no: 50**

Erchless Castle is an altered 16th-century L-plan tower house. It consists of a main block of four storeys and a projecting stair-wing, rising a storey higher. There are two stair-turrets, and a bartizan crowns one corner. The gables are corbiestepped, and the pitch of the roof is steep. The walls are harled and whitewashed, and pierced

by gunloops and shot-holes. There is a 19th-century extension.

The original entrance would have been in the re-entrant angle, but this has been moved. The basement is vaulted. The wide turnpike stair, in the wing, climbs only to the first floor, the upper floors being reached by the turret stairs. The hall is on the first floor, and private chambers on the floors above.

The lands originally belonged to the Frasers, but passed by marriage to the Chisholms in the 15th century, and Erchless became the main castle of the family. In 1689 the castle was attacked by 500 Jacobites, led by Bonnie Dundee. The Chisholms, however, fought for the Jacobites at the Battle of Sheriffmuir in 1715; and in 1746 the chief's son and 30 of his men were killed at the Battle of Culloden.

Mary, sister of the last Chisholm lord, tried to counter evictions in Strathglass during the Clearances. The property passed from the Chisholms, but the castle is still occupied and in good condition.

Errol Park

Perth & Kinross: About 7.5 miles east of Perth, on minor roads north of B958, just west of village of Errol, about 1 mile north of the River Tay, at or near Errol Park.

Private   NO 245228   OS: 53   *   Map: 8, no: 130

Errol Park, a mansion which dates from after a fire of 1874, stands on the site of a castle.

William the Lyon gave the property to his butler, William de Haya. Sir Gilbert Hay of Errol was a loyal supporter of Robert the Bruce, and made hereditary High Constable. The 9th Chief was made Earl of Errol in 1452.

Francis Hay, the 9th Earl, was summoned for treason in 1594, and went on to fight at the Battle of Glenlivet, where James VI's forces, led by the Earl of Argyll, were defeated by an army led by the Gordon Earl of Huntly and Hay. Hay was forfeited, but returned in 1597 to be excommunicated in 1608.

The Hays left Errol in 1634 to move to Slains, itself now a ruin.

Errolly *see* Airlie Castle

Erskine Castle

Renfrewshire: About 0.5 miles north of Erskine, on minor road north of A726, south-east of Erskine Bridge, on south shore of River Clyde.

Ruin or site   NS 462720 [?]   OS: 64   *   Map: 3, no: 190

Site of castle, which was extended in 1778. The castle was abandoned around 1829 for the large mansion of Erskine House [NS 454724], and no remains survived by 1856. Erskine House, designed by Sir Robert Smirke, was begun in 1828.

The lands were held by the Erskines from 1226 or earlier, and they acquired property around Alloa and became Earls of Mar. The property was sold to Sir John Hamilton of Orbiston in 1638, then in 1703 to the Stewart Lords Blantyre, who built the new mansion. Since 1916 it has been used as a hospital for limbless sailors and soldiers.

Erth *see* Airth Castle

Eslie

Kincardine & Deeside: About 2 miles south of Fettercairn, by minor roads and foot west of B974, south-east of Bogmuir,

Ruin or site   NO 654709   OS: 45   *   Map: 10, no: 177

Site of castle.

Esslemont Castle *see* Castle of Esslemont

Ethie Castle

Angus & Dundee: About 5 miles north-east of Arbroath, on minor roads 2 miles east of A92, about 0.75 miles west of the sea, at Ethie Castle.

Private   NO 688468   OS: 54   **   Map: 8, no: 265**

Once a fortress of some strength, Ethie Castle consists of a large altered 15th-century keep, which may incorporate older work. It was enlarged in the mid 16th century to an L-plan tower of four storeys, and extended again in the late 16th and 17th centuries, to form a large complex, with both inner and outer courtyards. The original castle was surrounded by a courtyard and moat with flanking towers, of which a round tower, with built-up gunloops, is incorporated into the later work.

Ethie Castle

The present main entrance, which was formerly a gateway into the courtyard, now leads into the house. The basement of the old tower is vaulted, and contained the kitchen and cellars. One of the cellars, probably the wine-cellar, has a small stair, in the thickness of the walls, leading up to the hall on the first floor. A new kitchen was added in one of the later ranges, and has a wide arched fireplace and a well.

Ethie was a property of the Beatons, and was used by Cardinal David Beaton when he was Abbot of Arbroath in the 1530s, and Archbishop of St Andrews until his murder in 1546. It passed to the Carnegies in 1549, who were made Earls of Ethie in 1647, but exchanged this title for Earls of Northesk in 1662. The 7th Earl was a distinguished admiral, and third in command at the Battle of Trafalgar in 1805. The castle passed from the family in the 20th century, and is now owned by the Forsyths. It is in good condition, and still occupied.

The ghost of Cardinal Beaton, who was murdered at St Andrews in 1546, is said to haunt the house, and the sound of his ghostly footsteps climbing a stair have reportedly been heard. Another ghost was apparently that of a child, who mostly haunted one of the rooms where a skeleton of a child was said to have been found. When the bones were buried, this haunting stopped. Another apparition is reputedly a 'Green Lady'

Ethiebeaton

Angus & Dundee: About 1.5 miles north-west of Monifeith, on minor road north of A92 or south of B961, at or near Ethiebeaton.
Ruin or site   NO 479342   OS: 54   *   Map: 8, no: 204
Site of castle, a property of the Beatons and said to have been associated with Cardinal David Beaton.

Ettrick House

Borders: About 22 miles south-west of Selkirk, on minor roads west of B709, north of Ettrick Water, near Ettrick Kirk.
Private   NT 259144 [?]   OS: 79   *   Map: 2, no: 66
Site of castle of the Scotts. The stronghold and a village of 50 houses stood near the existing church, but these were demolished about 1700. A new mansion, Ettrick Hall, was built nearby, but this has also gone.

Near the church is the birthplace of James Hogg, the 'Ettrick Shepherd', the well-known poet.
Other refs: Old Ettrick

Evelaw Tower

Borders: About 2.5 miles east and north of Westruther, on minor roads north of B6456, about 1.5 miles east of Wedderlie, south of Eve Law.
Ruin or site   NT 661526   OS: 74   **   Map: 2, no: 271
Evelaw Tower is a ruined 16th-century L-plan tower house of three storeys and a garret. It consists of a main block and a small stair-wing, the top floor of which is

vaulted. The walls are pierced by small windows with iron yetts and gunloops.

The basement of the main block was vaulted, and contained the kitchen. A wide turnpike stair climbed to the first-floor hall, and a turnpike stair in the turret led to the private chambers on the floors above.

Evelaw was a property of the Abbey of Drylaw, but sold to the Douglases in 1576. It passed by marriage to the Sinclairs of Longformacus, then was sold in 1731 to the Smiths.

Evelick Castle

Perth & Kinross: About 6 miles east and north of Perth, on minor roads 2 miles north of A85, on east side of Pole Hill, at Evelick.
Ruin or site   NO 205260   OS: 58   *   Map: 8, no: 118**
Evelick Castle is a substantial ruined 16th-century L-plan tower house of three storeys, consisting of two offset blocks, joining only at one corner. A round stair-tower stands in one re-entrant angle. Most of the attic storey has gone, and some of the windows have been enlarged. The walls are pierced by many gunloops.

There were two entrances, the main one being at the foot of the stair-tower. The basement has been vaulted, but this has fallen in – as have the other floors.

The Lindsays of Evelick were descended from 'Earl Beardie', 4th Earl of Crawford, and held the property from 1497 or earlier. One of the family, Thomas Lindsay, was brutally murdered here by his step-brother, James Douglas. Douglas stabbed Lindsay five times, held him under the water in a burn, and finally dashed his brains out with a rock. The last Lindsays of Evelick was drowned in 1799. The building is ruinous, and not in a good condition.
Other refs: Castle of Evelick

Ewes Castle

Borders: About 1.5 miles west of Stow, on minor road then footpath west of A7, on north bank of the Lugate Water.
Ruin or site   NT 434448   OS: 73   *   Map: 2, no: 114
Site of tower house and courtyard, little of which remains except a mound of rubble.

Exmagriddle *see* Ecclesiamagirdle House

Eyemouth

Borders: Just north of Eyemouth, on minor roads north of A1107, just south of coast.
Ruin or site   NT 945645 [?]   OS: 67   *   Map: 2, no: 362
An artillery fort was built here by the English during the invasion by the Duke of Somerset in 1547, and occupied for several years. Most of it was destroyed in 1550.

F

Faichfield House

Banff & Buchan: About 3.5 miles west of Peterhead, on minor road north of A950, 1.5 miles east of Longside, at Faichfield House.
Ruin or site NK 065467 OS: 30 * Map: 10, no: 361
A castle or old house, dating from the early 17th century, was demolished in the 1960s.

Fairburn Tower

Ross & Cromarty: About 4 miles west of Muir of Ord, on minor roads west of A832, about 0.25 miles north of River Orrin, 1 mile south of Coul of Fairburn, at Fairburn.
Private NH 469523 OS: 26 * Map: 9, no: 52**
An impressive castle, Fairburn Tower is a 16th-century tower house of four storeys and a garret within corbiestepped gables. To this has been added a stair-wing early in the 17th century. Two round bartizans crown the gables and the stair was topped by a caphouse. The thick walls are pierced by small windows, gunloops and shot-holes. There has been a courtyard.

The present entrance, at the foot of the stair-tower, is not in the re-entrant angle, although there was an earlier entrance at first-floor level, reached by an external stair. The hall, on the first floor, has a straight stair down to the vaulted basement, to which there was originally no other entrance. There are many moulded fire-places.

Fairburn was a stronghold of the Mackenzies. It featured in one of the Brahan Seer's prophecies, when a cow managed to climb all way to the watch-chamber at the top of the tower. It could not be brought down again until it had calved – an event, according to the Seer, heralding the end of the Mackenzies of Kintail and Seaforth.

The tower was abandoned when Fairburn House was built in 1874-8, although Fairburn House is now a nursing home. The tower is currently being restored.

One ghost story involves one of the lairds. His apparition is said to have crossed the Conon Ferry some hours after his death, accompanied by the unfortunate fer-ryman.

Fairlie Castle

Ayrshire: About 3 miles south of Largs, on minor road west of A78 at Fairlie, in Fairlie Glen.
Ruin or site NS 213549 OS: 63 * Map: 3, no: 36**
Ruined but well-preserved, Fairlie Tower is a plain 15th-century keep of four storeys, with a later corbelled-out parapet and bartizans. The walls are pierced by gunloops. The basement is vaulted, and a small stair leads up to the hall and kitchen on the first floor. The castle was built by the Fairlies, but sold to the Boyles in 1650.

Fairnilee

Borders: About 2.5 miles south and west of Galashiels, just north of meeting of A707 and B7060, just north of River Tweed, at Fairnilee.
Private NT 458327 OS: 73 * Map: 2, no: 125**
Fairnilee consists of a 16th-century tower house of three storeys with corbiestepped gables. It was part of a larger rectangular mansion, most of which has been demol-ished. Shot-holes survive beneath many of the windows.

The basement is not vaulted. A turnpike stair climbed to the upper floors, but only its well remains. The inside has been greatly altered.

Fairnilee was held by the Kerrs of Linton at the end of the 16th century, but passed to the Rutherfords. Alison Rutherford, later married to Patrick Cockburn, wrote 'The Flowers of the Forest' here, which commemorates the disastrous Battle of Flodden in 1513. A large mansion was built close by in the 19th century. This was complete in the 1880s, but by the early part of the 20th century most of it, apart from the old tower, had fallen or been demolished.
Other refs: Fernilee Tower; Old Fairnilee House

Fairnington House

Borders: About 3.5 miles north of Jedburgh, on minor road between A68 and A699, at Fairnington.
Private NT 646280 OS: 74 ** Map: 2, no: 261
Fairnington House incorporates an altered 16th-century tower house of three sto-reys and a garret as one wing of the large house. The walls are harled and yellow-washed, and many of the windows have been enlarged. A modern external stone stair leads to an entrance at first-floor level.

The house has been altered inside.

Fairnington was a property of the Burnets in the 12th century, but had passed to the Hepburn Earls of Bothwell by the late 15th century, who probably built the original castle. It was sacked by the English in 1544. In 1581 the lands were given to Francis Stewart, Earl of Bothwell; but they passed to the Rutherfords in 1647, who built the extension. The house is in good condition and still occupied.

Nearby is the site of the Battle of Ancrum Moor, fought in 1545, when an English army was defeated by a Scottish force under the Douglas Earl of Angus.

Fala Luggie Tower

Lothians: About 5 miles east and south of Gorebridge, on minor road and foot south of A68 at Fala, north of Fala Flow Loch.
Ruin or site NT 425590 OS: 66 ** Map: 4, no: 166
Little remains of a tower house, except one wall. The basement was vaulted.

Faldonside Castle *see* Castle of Faldonside

Falkland Palace

Fife: About 4 miles north of Glenrothes, in Falkland, just north of A912.
NTS NO 254075 OS: 59 ** Map: 7, no: 51**
A fortified but comfortable residence remodelled in Renaissance style, Falkland Palace is a courtyard castle, consisting of ranges of buildings around an open court. The late 15th-century gatehouse range survives complete, and has some good inte-riors. An adjoining range is ruined, and only traces remain of a range opposite the gatehouse. The last side of the courtyard was completed by a wall. Parts of the palace may date from the 13th century, but little remains of an older castle here, except the base of two round towers.

The courtyard is entered through a twin-towered gatehouse range, which has guardrooms on both sides of the entrance, one with a pit-prison. The basement is vaulted, and the first floor has a large chapel, the Chapel Royal, with fine mullioned windows and a 16th-century oak screen at one end. The painted ceiling dates from 1633. There is also a fine tapestry gallery, and access to the keeper's apartments.

The ruined adjoining range once contained the king's guard hall, royal audience chamber, and privy dining room, over vaulted cellars. The restored cross house contains a refurbished room, reputedly the King's Room, where James V died in 1542, as well as the Queen's Room on the first floor.

Little remains of the range opposite the gatehouse, but this may have contained a hall, and also had a Renaissance front.

Falkland was used as a hunting seat by the kings of Scots from the 12th century.

The property was owned by the MacDuff Earls of Fife in the 14th century, and the castle destroyed by the English in 1337. It was rebuilt, and in 1371 passed to Robert Stewart, Duke of Albany. He had David, Duke of Rothesay, his nephew and the heir of Robert III, imprisoned here and starved to death, or murdered, in 1402. After 1425 and the forfeiture of the Dukes of Albany, Falkland was acquired by the Crown, and used by Mary of Guiderland, wife of James II. The Palace is first mentioned in 1455. It became a favourite residence of the Stewart kings, and was used and re-modelled by James III, James IV, and James V, who was virtually held prisoner here by the Douglas Earl of Angus in his childhood, and died at the palace in 1542. The castle was still in use in the 16th century, but little remained by 1610.

Mary, Queen of Scots, visited the palace in 1563, James VI stayed at Falkland, as did Charles I in 1633, and Charles II in the 1650s. Despite a visit by George IV in 1822, the palace deteriorated until 1887 when restored by the 3rd Marquis of Bute. In 1952 The National Trust for Scotland assumed responsibility for the palace.

The tapestry gallery is said to be haunted by a 'White Lady'.

OPEN: Open Apr-Oct, Mon-Sat 11.00-17.30, Sun 13.30-17.30; Jun-Aug, Mon-Sat 10.00-17.30, Sun 13.30-17.30; last admission to Palace 16.30, garden 17.00; groups at other times by appt only.

Explanatory displays. Visitor centre. Gift shop. Visitor centre. Picnic area. Extensive gardens. Real tennis court. WC. Disabled access. Tape tour for visually impaired. Car parking nearby. ££.

Tel: 01337 857397   Fax: 01337 857980

Email: information@nts.org.uk   Web: nts.org.uk

Falside Castle

Lothians: About 2.5 miles south-west of Tranent, on minor road between east of A6094 at Crookston and A199 at Tranent, just south-west of Falside Hill.

Private   NT 378710   OS: 66   *   Map: 4, no: 152**

Standing dramatically on a high ridge, Falside Castle consists of an L-plan tower

house, and incorporates a plain 15th-century keep of four storeys. It was later extended by a block with turrets, dormer windows and decorated mouldings.

The entrance to the older part leads into the vaulted basement and to a straight stair, in the thickness of the wall, leading to the first floor. A turnpike stair, in another corner, climbs to the upper floors.

The property was held by an Alexander de Such, but he was forfeited by Robert the Bruce and it passed to the Setons of Falside. The tower was torched by the English before the Battle of Pinkie in 1547, suffocating and killing all those inside. In 1631 it was sold to an Edinburgh merchant burgess, named Hamilton. Falside was restored from ruin in the 1970s.

Other refs: Fawside Castle; Fa'side Castle

Farme Castle

Lanarkshire & Glasgow area: In Rutherglen, on minor roads east of A730, not far south of the River Clyde.

Ruin or site   NS 620624   OS: 64   *   Map: 3, no: 291

Site of 15th-century castle, which had been incorporated into a large castellated mansion around a courtyard. The old part consisted of a three-storey keep with a crenellated parapet and corbiestepped gables. One of the rooms had a fine painted ceiling which was removed in 1917. The castle was demolished, along with the later additions, in the 1960s during the building of an aluminium works.

It was property of the Stewarts from the 14th century, but passed to the Douglases, then the Crawfords between 1482 and 1599, the Stewarts of Minto (who owned it in 1645), then the Flemings, then the Duke of Hamilton, then the Faries who held it in the 20th century.

Farnell Castle

Angus & Dundee: About 3.5 miles south and east of Brechin, on minor road north of A934, just north of the Pow Burn, just west of Farnell village.

Private   NO 624555   OS: 54   *   Map: 8, no: 253**

Farnell Castle consists of a 16th-century tower house, to which has been added a stair-tower and extension. The tower has large corbiestepped gables. The walls are pierced by shot-holes, and are pink-washed. The building is decorated with tiny

carved shields and the initials I. M. for Jesu Maria, surmounted by a heavenly crown.

The entrance is in the foot of the stair-tower. The house has been greatly altered inside.

Farnell was originally a property of the Bishops of Brechin, but passed to the Campbells in 1566 – the Bishop of the time was a member of the family – then to the Lindsays in 1568, then by marriage in the 17th century to the Carnegies of Kinnaird, later Earls of Southesk. The family were forfeited for their part in the Jacobite Rising of 1715, but recovered the property in 1764. The castle was used to house farm workers, then abandoned, but has been restored and is still occupied.

Farr Castle *see* Borve Castle

Faseyside Tower

Borders: About 8 miles north and east of Newcastleton, on west of B6357, at or near Saughtree.

Ruin or site   NY 563966 [?]   OS: 80   *   Map: 2, no: 209

Site of 16th-century tower house.

Faslane Castle

Argyll & Dunbartonshire: About 0.5 miles east and south of Faslane, on minor road and foot east of A814, on eastern side of Gare Loch.

Ruin or site   NS 258879 [?]   OS: 56   *   Map: 5, no: 125

Set in woodland, only a motte remains of a 12th-century castle of the Earls of Lennox. The stronghold is said to have been abandoned by the end of the 14th century. The Earls had moved their main seat to Balloch in the 13th century, and the property passed to the MacAulays of Ardincaple, then later to the Colquhouns of

Luss. There are some remains of a medieval chapel [NS 249899] dedicated to St Michael, believed to be where Henry Stewart, Lord Darnley, was christened.

The Earls of Lennox had another castle at Shandon [NS 257878], some miles to the south, which consists of a motte and ditches.

Other refs: Shandon

Fasque

Kincardine & Deeside: About 5 miles north-west of Laurencekirk, on minor roads north of B974, just east of the Crichie Burn, at Fasque.

Private   NO 648755   OS: 45   *   Map: 10, no: 175

Site of castle of the Ramsays of Balmain. The present castellated mansion was built in 1809, probably by the architect John Paterson for Sir Alexander Ramsay. The property passed to the Gladstones in 1829, one of whom, William Ewart Gladstone, was Prime Minister four times between 1830 and 1851. It is still held by the Gladstone family.

The house is said to be haunted by the ghost of Helen Gladstone, youngest sister of the Prime Minister, as well as the spirit of a butler called MacBean.

Other refs: Balmain

OPEN: Open May-Sep, daily 11.00-17.30; last admission 17.00.

William Gladstone library, state rooms, kitchen, extensive domestic quarters and family church. Explanatory displays. Sales area. WC. Picnic area. Collections of farm machinery. Deer park with Soay sheep and walks. Car and coach parking. ££.

Tel: 01561 340569   Fax: 01561 340569

Fast Castle

Borders: About 4 miles north and west of Coldingham, on minor road and footpath north of A1107, on cliffs above North Sea, about 0.5 miles north of Dowlaw.

Ruin or site   NT 862710   OS: 67   **   Map: 2, no: 343

Standing on a cliff-top promontory, little remains of Fast Castle, formerly a 15th-century keep and courtyard, which was once approached by a drawbridge over the steep chasm.

It was occupied by the English after the Battle of Neville's Cross in 1346, but in 1410 a surprise attack by Patrick Cospatrick, son of the Earl of Dunbar, recaptured it for the Scots. Margaret Tudor stayed here in 1502. After destruction by the Duke of Albany in 1515, the castle was rebuilt by the Homes in 1521. It was taken by the English around 1547, recovered by the Scots before 1566 when Mary, Queen of Scots stayed here, but recaptured by the English in 1570. After passing by marriage in 1580 to the Logans of Restalrig, it was soon abandoned and became ruinous after their forfeiture in 1600 – a result of involvement in the Gowrie Conspiracy and increasing bankruptcy. It was sold to the Douglases in 1602, then passed to the Home Earls of Dunbar, to the Arnots, to the Homes, and finally to the Halls.

It was reputedly used by smugglers, having a 'secret' cave below the castle. There are tales of treasure buried here, possibly hidden by Sir Robert Logan of Restalrig, who died in 1606.

Walter Scott used the castle is his novel 'Bride of Lammermoor', calling it Wolf's Crag.

Other refs: Wolf's Crag

OPEN: Access at all reasonable times – visit involves walk and care must be taken.

Car parking nearby.

Fast Castle

Borders: About 1.5 miles east and north of Denholm, south of A698, west of the Rule Water.

Ruin or site   NT 590190 [?]   OS: 80   *   Map: 2, no: 227

Site of 12th-century castle, a property of the Turnbulls of Bedrule.

Fatlips Castle

Borders: About 5 miles west of Jedburgh, on minor road north of B6405, on north side of Teviot River, about 1 mile east of Minto.

Ruin or site   NT 582209   OS: 74   *   Map: 2, no: 220**

Fatlips Castle is a rectangular 16th-century tower house of three storeys and a garret. The parapet is rounded at each of the four corners. The stair is crowned with a conical caphouse.

The entrance leads to the vaulted basement and to a turnpike stair in one corner.

Fatlips was a property of the Turnbulls, who according to tradition had very full lips, hence the name. The family are said to have been so unruly that James IV forced 200 of them to come before him with halters around their necks – he then hanged several for good measure. Fatlips passed to the Stewarts, who in 1705 sold it to Sir Gilbert Elliot of Minto. The tower was restored in 1897 but, although still roofed, is becoming derelict.

Other refs: Minto Tower

Fatlips Tower

Lanarkshire & Glasgow area: About 5 miles west and south of Biggar, on minor road and foot west of A73, just north-west of Tintoside, north of the Lanimer Burn.

Ruin or site   NS 969340   OS: 72   *   Map: 3, no: 430

Fatlips Tower is a very ruined 16th-century bastle or tower house, which stood in a strong location.

Fawside Castle *see* Falside Castle

Fa'side Castle *see* Falside Castle

Fearn *see* Vayne Castle

Fearnan

Perthshire: About 3.5 miles west of Kenmore, on minor roads north of A827, north side of Loch Tay, at Fearnan.

Ruin or site   NN 725446   OS: 52   *   Map: 8, no: 10

Site of castle or old house.

Feather *see* Castle Feather

Feddal

Perth & Kinross: About 1 mile south-west of Braco, on minor road just west of B8033, west of River Knaik, between Easter and Wester Feddal.

Ruin or site   NN 824089   OS: 57   **   Map: 8, no: 17

The ruined house, dated 1683 but remodelled in the 19th century, may incorporate older work. It was a property of the Stewarts.

Fedderate Castle

Banff & Buchan: About 2 miles north-east of New Deer, on minor road and foot west of A981, just south-east of Mains of Fedderate, at Fedderate Castle.

Ruin or site   NJ 897498   OS: 30   *   Map: 10, no: 310

Little remains of Fedderate Castle, a large L-plan tower house of four storeys, once surrounded by a moat, approached by a causeway and drawbridge.

The castle was built by the Crawford family, and incorporates work from the 13th century. It was extended in 1519, and later passed to the Gordons. It was one of the last places to hold out for James VII after the Battle of Cromdale in 1690, but was besieged and captured by William of Orange's forces. Its very ruined condition is due to an attempt to blow it up to clear the field for agriculture.

The castle is said to be haunted.

Other refs: Old Castle of Fedderate; Castle of Fedderate

Fenton Tower

Lothians: About 2 miles south of North Berwick, on B1347 south from North Berwick, south of Kingston.

Ruin or site   NT 543822   OS: 66   *   Map: 4, no: 195**

Fenton Tower is a ruined 16th-century L-plan tower of three storeys and a garret. It is dated 1587.

The entrance leads to the vaulted basement and to a wide turnpike stair, to the first floor, while the upper floors are reached by a turret stair. A small separate turnpike stair links the one basement chamber, probably the wine cellar, with the first floor.

The property was originally owned by the Fentons, then the Whitelaw family, who were forfeited in 1587, then passed to the Carmichaels. Sir John Carmichael, the Scottish Warden of the Marches, argued with the English Warden, Sir John Foster,

at a meeting at Carter's Bar in 1575. A battle resulted which the Scots eventually won, slaying many and taking captive several of the English leaders, embarrassing the Scottish leadership of the time. In 1600 Carmichael was ambushed and murdered by the Armstrongs after he had tried to bring some of them to justice for reiving.

Fergus Loch

Ayrshire: About 4 miles east of Ayr, north of B742, Fergus Loch.
Ruin or site NS 395183 [?] OS: 70 * Map: 3, no: 142
Site of castle, a property of the Kennedy Earls of Cassillis. There may have been some remains in the 19th century.

Ferguslie Castle

Renfrewshire: About 1 mile west of Paisley Abbey, on minor roads north of A737, at Ferguslie.
Ruin or site NS 467637 OS: 64 * Map: 3, no: 196
Site of castle, a vestige of which survived in the 19th century, which was replaced by a mansion, itself now apparently demolished.
Ferguslie was a property of Paisley Abbey, but in 1544 was given to the Hamiltons. The castle was replaced by Ferguslie House which was owned by the Wilsons in 1837.

Fern *see* Brandy Den

Ferney Castle

Borders: About 2.5 miles north of Chirnside, on minor roads east of B6437 or south of B6438, 1 mile south of Reston, at or near Ferneycastle.
Ruin or site NT 880602 [?] OS: 67 * Map: 2, no: 349
Site of castle.

Fernie Castle

Fife: About 4 miles west of Cupar, just west of A914, about 1 mile north-east of Monimail, south of village of Fernie.
Private NO 316147 OS: 59 ** Map: 7, no: 78
Situated in 17 acres of woodland, Fernie Castle consists of an altered 16th-century

L-plan tower house, to which has been added a three-storey block with a round tower at one corner. There may have been a castle here from the 13th century. The stair-wing is crowned by a corbiestepped gabled watch-chamber. There are other extensions, and the walls are harled and yellow washed.
Fernie was a property of the MacDuff Earls of Fife, but passed to the Balfour family, then by the 15th century to the Fernies. The castle went by marriage to the Lovells, who in 1586 sold it to the Arnots, but it then passed by marriage back to the Balfours. The Balfours were forfeited for their part in the Jacobite Rising of 1715, although they recovered the property in 1720. In recent years the castle has become a hotel.
The west tower of the building is said to be haunted by a 'Green Lady', a girl who ran off with her lover. They sought refuge in the castle, but were discovered by her father's men – her father disapproved of her lover. The poor woman fell three floors from the west tower to her death, and her apparition is said to have been seen in some of the bedrooms. Other manifestations include electrical equipment and lights switching themselves on and off.
OPEN: Hotel – open all year round.
15 bedrooms with ensuite facilities. Restaurant, Keep Bar and lounge. Dinners, meetings and corporate entertaining. Parking.
Tel: 01337 810381 Fax: 01337 810422
Email: mail@ferniecastle.demon.co.uk Web: www.ferniecastle.demon.co.uk

Ferniehirst Castle

Borders: About 1.5 miles south of Jedburgh, on minor road east of A68, east of the Jed Water.
Private NT 653179 OS: 80 ** Map: 2, no: 266**
Ferniehirst Castle consists of an extended and altered tower house, which incorporates the cellars from the 16th-century castle, with later wings. A large conical-roofed stair-turret is corbelled out above first-floor level, and bartizans, with shot-holes, crown the top of the tower.
The original entrance leads to a stair known as the 'Left-Handed Staircase', the story being that when Sir Andrew Kerr, who was himself left-handed, returned from Flodden in 1513 he had his followers trained to use their weapons with their left hands. This is said to be the origin of 'Corrie-fisted' or 'Kerr-handed'. The basement is vaulted, and the hall has a 16th-century fireplace.
Ferniehirst was a property of the Kerrs, and first built around 1470, but taken and sacked by the English in 1523. It was recaptured with French help in 1549, and the leader of the English garrison beheaded. Sir Thomas Kerr, protector of Mary, Queen of Scots, invaded England in 1570, hoping to have her released, but all that resulted was a raid on Scotland, during which Ferniehirst was damaged. James VI attacked the castle in 1593, because of help given by the family to the Earl of Bothwell. The castle was rebuilt about 1598. Between 1934 and 1984 it was leased by the Scottish Youth Hostel Association, except for during World War II when it served as an army billet.

A 'Green Lady' is said to haunt the castle in some tales, and unusual occurrences were reported during its time as a youth hostel, although the story is refuted.
OPEN: Open Jul, Tue-Sun 11.00-16.00.
Collection of portraits. Turret library. Guided tours. Explanatory displays. Gift shop. WC. Riverside walk. Sheep of Norse origin. Car and coach parking. £.
Tel: 01835 862201 Fax: 01835 863992

Fernilee Tower *see* Fairnilee

Ferryport-on-Craig Castle *see* Tayport Castle

Fettercairn House
Kincardine & Deeside: About 0.5 miles north-east of Fettercairn, on minor roads west of B966 or east of B974, at or near Fettercairn House.
Ruin or site NO 656740 OS: 45 * Map: 10, no: 178
Site of castle. The present house was started in 1666, and then extended and altered in 1839 and 1877.

It was a property of the Middletons from the 13th century until sold in 1777. One of the family was John Middleton, a general, who saw action at Philiphaugh in 1645, Preston in 1648 and Worcester in 1651. He was captured, but escaped and went abroad. He led a Royalist rising in Scotland in 1653, and at the Restoration was made Earl of Middleton. The family were forfeited following the Jacobite Rising of 1715. The property passed to the Belshes, then by marriage to the Forbeses of Pitsligo in 1797, then to Lord Clinton in 1866 whose family still held it in the 20th century.
Other refs: Middleton

Fetteresso Castle
Kincardine & Deeside: About 1.5 miles west of Stonehaven, on minor roads west of A92, north of Carron Water, west of Kirkton of Fetteresso, south of Home Farm.
Ruin or site NO 843855 OS: 45 * Map: 10, no: 283
Fetteresso Castle, a mansion dating from the 17th century which was altered and extended in later centuries, stands on the site and incorporates part of a 15th-century castle. Part of the basement is groin vaulted. Fine illustrated panels, including a pig playing the bagpipes, were rescued from here in 1954 and taken to Muchalls Castle.

The lands were a property of the Strachans, but passed by marriage in the 14th century to the Keith Earls Marischal, who built the castle. It was torched by the Marquis of Montrose in 1645. James VIII, the old Pretender, stayed here over Christmas 1715 during the Jacobite Rising. It was completely rebuilt in 1671, and additions were made by the Duffs in 1782 and 1808. Although remodelled in 1947 and used as a hotel, it became ruinous and was stripped and unroofed. It has since been rebuilt, and divided into seven apartments.

The castle is said to be haunted. One ghost is reputedly a 'Green Lady', whose apparition is said to have been witnessed, as well as the sounds of her feet and skirt on the stairs. On one occasion the ghost is said to have had a baby in its arms, and to have disappeared into a wall, later shown to be a sealed-up doorway. On another occasion the sounds of feet, followed by the dragging of something metallic along the floor of a passage, were also heard. The ghost is also reputed to haunt a house on the High Street of Stonehaven, and there is an unlikely tale of a tunnel linking Fetteresso, this house and Dunnottar Castle.

Fetternear House
Aberdeen & Gordon: About 4 miles south-west of Inverurie, on minor roads west of B993, west of River Don, 0.5 miles north-west of Kemnay, south of Fetternear House.
Ruin or site NJ 723171 OS: 38 ** Map: 10, no: 223
Only foundations remain of a 13th-century castle and palace of the Bishops of Aberdeen. Nearby is the large ruin of Fetternear House, which incorporates a 16th-century tower house of three storeys, and a round tower. Part of the basement of the old part is vaulted. The house was extended and altered in the 17th century, with the addition of a hall block, again in 1690, and the 19th century.

The property originally belonged to the Bishops of Aberdeen, who had built a castle here by the mid 13th century, which was extended by Bishop Kinnimond in the 1330s. William Wallace is said to have been sheltered here in 1297. After the Reformation, the property passed to the Leslies, who built the tower house in the 1560s, partly from the demolished palace. Fetternear passed to the Abercrombies in 1627, but returned to the Leslies in 1690. It was burned out in 1919, and is a substantial ruin. It has recently been consolidated.

The Fetternear Banner, a pre-Reformation banner of the fraternity of the Holy Blood, was kept here by the Leslies. Patrick Leslie of Fetternear was a count of the Holy Roman Empire.
Other refs: Bishop's Palace, Fetternear; Old House of Fetternear

Fettykil *see* Leslie House

Fichlie *see* Peel of Fichlie

Fiddes Castle

Aberdeen & Gordon: About 4 miles south of Ellon, on minor roads south of B9000 or west of A92, at or near Fiddes.
Ruin or site NJ 939244 [?] OS: 38 * Map: 10, no: 332
Site of castle.

Fiddes Castle *see* Castle of Fiddes

Fiddleton Bankend *see* Glenvorann

Fidra

Lothians: About 2 miles north of Dirleton, by minor roads and boat north of A198, on island of Fidra, in Firth of Forth.
Ruin or site NT 513868 [?] OS: 66 * Map: 4, no: 186
Site of castle, traces of which are said to survive. There are also the ruined remains of a medieval church, dedicated to St Nicholas, and part of a monastic complex, dating from about 1220.

Finavon Castle

Angus & Dundee: About 4.5 miles north-east of Forfar, on minor roads east of A94 at Finavon Castle, south of Lemno Burn, east of modern Finavon Castle.
Ruin or site NO 497566 OS: 54 ** Map: 8, no: 211
Once a strong and important castle, Finavon Castle consists of a ruined altered L-plan tower house of five storeys and a garret, which incorporates a 14th-century castle. A substantial bartizan crowns one corner, and the walls are pierced by gun-loops. Large windows have been inserted in one side. Little remains of the wing of the tower house, and there has been a courtyard.
   The basement is vaulted, and has a massive iron-studded oak door. A large doocot stands nearby, and could house 2000 birds.
   Finavon was held by the Lindsay Earls of Crawford from 1375. David, 3rd Earl, and his brother-in-law Ogilvie of Inverquharity – badly wounded at Battle of Arbroath in 1446 – were brought back to the castle. The Earl soon died, and his wife suffocated Ogilvie, her brother, with a pillow to ensure the succession of her own son. Alexander Crawford, her son, was 4th Earl, and called 'The Tiger' or 'Earl Beardie', a cruel and ruthless character. He hanged a minstrel from hooks who (correctly) foretold of the Lindsays defeat at the Battle of Brechin in 1452. Crawford fled after the battle, but James II pardoned him – so that he could more easily deal with Crawford's former allies, the Black Douglases. On the Covin Tree, grown from a chestnut dropped by a Roman soldier, Crawford hanged Jock Barefoot for cutting a walking stick from the tree. Jock's ghost is said to haunt the castle.
   In 1530, David, 8th Earl, was murdered by a Dundee cobbler in brawl, and David, 10th Earl, married Margaret, daughter of Cardinal Beaton, at Finavon in 1546.
   The property was sold in 1629 to Lord Spynie, after Edzell became their preferred residence, and it was then owned by the Carnegies until it was sold in 1775 to the Gordon Earl of Aboyne, then in 1815 to the Gardynes.
   'When Finavon Castle runs to sand
   The end of the world is near at hand.'
OPEN: Finavon Doocot open Apr-Oct, daily: keys from the Finavon Hotel
Doocot: NTS. Explanatory board. Car and coach parking. Tel: 01738 631296.

Fincastle *see* Amhuinnsuidhe Castle

Fincastle House

Perth & Kinross: About 3 miles west of Killiecrankie, on minor road west of B8019, in Glen Fincastle, at Fincastle House.
Private NN 870622 OS: 43 * Map: 8, no: 25
Fincastle House, an 18th-century mansion, has a wing of 1640.
   It was a property of the Stewarts, but by the 19th century had passed to the Colquhouns. The name is derived from the many castles in the area, said at one time to number some 15 strongholds.

Fincharn Castle

Argyll & Dunbartonshire: About 5.5 miles north-east of Kilmartin, on foot north of B840, on promontory to south of Loch Awe, 2 miles east of Ford, at Fincharn.
Ruin or site NM 898044 OS: 55 ** Map: 5, no: 77
Fincharn Castle is a strong but ruined 16th-century tower house and courtyard.
   An earlier castle here was held by the MacDougalls for the English in 1308. It was a property of the Scrimgeours from about 1370 until 1688. One of the family, John Scrimgeour of Glassery, was killed at Flodden in 1513. The castle later returned to the MacDougalls.
   One tale is that one of the chiefs, Mac Mhic Iain, wronged the wife of one of his men, who took his revenge by burning the castle and slaying the chief.
Other refs: Glassery Castle; Fionnchairn Castle

Findlater Castle

Banff & Buchan: About 2 miles east of Cullen, on minor roads and foot north of A98, on shore south of the sea, at Findlater Castle.
Ruin or site NJ 542673 OS: 29 ** Map: 10, no: 130
Built on a dizzying cliff-top promontory, not much remains of a 14th-century keep and castle, the large fortress of the Ogilvies of Findlater, who held it from 1445 or

earlier. It was defended by two ditches on the landward side.
   It was a property of the Sinclairs in the 12th century, but passed to the Ogilvies. About 1560 the Ogilvie laird of the time argued with his son, disinherited him, and signed the property over to Sir John Gordon, 3rd son of the Earl of Huntly.
   In 1562, the Gordons rebelled against Mary, Queen of Scots – refusing her entrance to the castle – but were defeated at the Battle of Corrichie, and Sir James Gordon was beheaded. The castle returned to the Ogilvies, but was abandoned after 1600 when the family moved to Cullen. They were made Earls of Findlater in 1633.
   The ruins are in a dangerous condition.

Findlay Castle *see* Fintry Castle

Findlaystone *see* Finlaystone House

Findochty Castle

Moray: About 2.5 miles east and north of Buckie, on minor road just south of A942, just west of Findochty village, about 0.25 miles south of sea.
Ruin or site NJ 455673 OS: 28 ** Map: 10, no: 100
On a rock at the end of a drained loch, Findochty Castle is a ruined 16th-century L-plan tower house. The basement was vaulted, and the hall was on the first floor.
   The castle was built by the Gordons, but later passed to the Ogilvies. The Ord family acquired the property in 1568, and were responsible for developing the village as a fishing port. The castle was consolidated towards the end of the 19th century.
Other refs: House of Findochty

Findon Castle

Banff & Buchan: About 5.5 miles east of Macduff, on minor roads and foot west of B9123, just south-west of Gardenstown, south of sea at Gamrie Bay, at Findon.
Ruin or site NJ 795644 OS: 29 * Map: 10, no: 263
Only earthworks remain of Findon Castle, a 14th-century castle of the Troup family, which later passed to the Gardens. It stood a knoll, and was used from early times: it is said that it was used by the Scots in the 10th or 11th century to guard against Norse attack.
Other refs: Castlehill of Findon; Castle Hill of Findon

Findrassie Castle

Moray: About 2 miles north-west of Elgin, on minor roads north of B9012, about 1.5 miles south of Duffus Castle, at Findrassie.
Private NJ 195651 OS: 28 * Map: 10, no: 35
Site of castle of the Leslies of Findrassie, who held the property from the first half of the 16th century until it was sold in 1825. The present house dates from around 1780, but has vaulted outbuildings.

Findrowie Castle

Angus & Dundee: About 3 miles west and north of Brechin, on minor roads north and west of A94, 0.5 miles south of the Cruick Water, north of dismantled railway, at Findrowie.
Ruin or site NO 554607 [?] OS: 44 * Map: 8, no: 235
Site of 16th-century L-plan tower house, with bartizans, of the Arbuthnott family, which was completely demolished in the 19th century. A date stone of 1584 survives at Balmoon, while others of 1638 and 1642 remain at the farm.

Finella's Castle

Kincardine & Deeside: About 1 mile south-west of Fettercairn, on foot east of B966 near Cairnton of Balbegno, at Finella's Castle (Green Castle).
Ruin or site NO 633723 OS: 45 ** Map: 10, no: 171
Situated on the top of a rise, Finella's Castle is an Iron Age fort, and consists of an inner and outer enclosing wall, the ground sloping steeply away on three sides.
  This was the stronghold where – reputedly – Finella, wife of the Mormaer of the Mearns, murdered Kenneth III, King of Scots, in 994. Kenneth slew her son, and she built an elaborate statue, trapped with bolts, which was activated when the King removed an apple from the contraption, and so he was slain. She also died, for her pains, reputedly in the Den of Finella, at St Cyrus. An alternative story is that she simply persuaded Kenneth's men to murder him, which – given the record of the Kings of Scots in the 9th and 10th centuries – was probably not too difficult.
Other refs: Green Castle

Fingalton

Renfrewshire: About 2.5 miles south of Barrhead, on minor roads west of B769, near Walton Burn, at or near Craigton.
Ruin or site NS 499550 [?] OS: 64 * Map: 3, no: 205
Possible site of castle. The lands were a property of the Hamiltons from the 14th to the 16th centuries.

Fingask Castle

Perth & Kinross: About 7.5 miles east and north of Perth, on minor roads north of A85, just north of village of Rait, at Fingask.
Private NO 228275 OS: 53 * Map: 8, no: 126**
Fingask Castle consists of an altered 16th-century L-plan tower house, dating from 1594, of three storeys and a garret, to which extensions were made in 1675, and a long wing was added in modern times. The walls are pierced by gunloops and shot-holes, and some of the windows still have iron yetts.
  The present entrance is defended by a vaulted guardroom, and the vaulted basement contains a kitchen, with a wide arched fireplace. The hall, on the first floor, is a fine chamber, and has a smaller adjoining room. Private chambers occupied the floor above.
  The property belonged to the Bruces of Clackmannan from 1399 or earlier, but was sold to the Threipland family in 1672. The castle was besieged in 1642. Patrick

Threipland, Provost of Perth, was knighted in 1674 for suppressing Covenanters, but died a prisoner in Stirling Castle two years later.
  His son was one of the first to join the Jacobite Rising of 1715. James VIII, the Old Pretender, stayed at Fingask twice in 1716, but the family were forfeited after the Rising. During the Jacobite Rising of 1745, the elder son was killed at the Battle of Prestonpans; but the family were forfeited again after its failure, and the castle sacked and partially demolished in 1746.
  Sir Stewart Threipland, a younger son, escaped to France after helping Bonnie Prince Charlie, and securing for himself some of the Loch Arkaig Treasure. He returned to Edinburgh in 1747, and was later able to buy back Fingask in 1783. The house was restored early in the 20th century, and again in 1967.

Fingon *see* Dun Ringill

Finlaggan

Argyll & Dunbartonshire: On island of Islay about 3 miles west of Port Askaig, on minor road and boat north of A846, on island near north end of Loch Finlaggan, at Finlaggan.
Ruin or site NR 388681 OS: 60 * Map: 5, no: 12**
Little remains of Finlaggan except foundations on two islands. Remains have recently been found of a 15th-century keep on the smaller or 'council' island. The ruins of a chapel, dedicated to St Finlaggan a contemporary of St Columba, and many other buildings stand on the larger island, Eilean Mor.
  There was a kingdom of the Isles, subject to Norway, from about 900. In the 12th century, Somerled, of mixed Norse and Celtic blood, pushed the Norsemen out of much of Scotland and took control of their territories. He was assassinated at Renfrew in 1164 when at war with Malcolm IV, King of Scots. He was succeeded by his sons Reginald in Kintyre and Islay, Dugald in Lorn, Mull and Jura, and Angus in Bute, Arran and North Argyll.
  The whole area became part of the kingdom of Scots in 1266 after the Battle of Largs in 1263. Angus Og MacDonald – grandson of Donald, a son of Reginald: hence MacDonald – a friend and supporter of Robert the Bruce, died at Finlaggan in 1328, and his son, John of Islay, was the first to use the title 'Lord of the Isles'. The independence of the Lords, however, and their power and influence, caused constant trouble for the kings of Scots. A campaign by the 2nd Lord led to the bloody Battle of Harlaw in 1411, and the 3rd Lord was twice imprisoned by James I. James IV eventually destroyed the power of the Lords in a campaign in 1493, and had John, the then Lord of the Isles, imprisoned until his death in 1503. Attempts were made to restore the Lordship, but these were ultimately unsuccessful.
  Visitor centre near the island, with archaeological finds and display of the crowning ceremony of the Lord of the Isles.
OPEN: Open Apr, Tue, Thu and Sun 14.30-17.00; May-Sep, Mon-Tue 10/00-13.00 and 14.30-17.00, Wed-Fri 14.30-17.00, Sun 14.30-17.00, closed Sat; Oct, Tue, Thu and Sun 14.00-16.00.
Visitor centre. Parking nearby.
Tel: 01496 810629 Fax: 01496 810856
Email: lynmags@aol.com Web: www.islay.com

Finlarig Castle

Stirlingshire & Clackmannan: About 0.5 miles north-east of Killin, on minor road east of the A827, at the west end of Loch Tay, east of the River Lochay, at Finlarig.
Ruin or site NN 575338 OS: 51 ** Map: 6, no: 25
Little remains of Finlarig Castle, a 17th-century Z-plan tower house. Two ruined square towers with shot-holes survive, although another has been demolished, and a passage leads past two cellars to the kitchen.
  The lands were held by the Menzies family, but the castle was built in 1621-9 by the Campbell 'Black Duncan of the Cowl' or 'Black Duncan of the Castles'. Parliament was summoned to appear here in 1651, but only three members turned up. Rob Roy MacGregor visited about 1713.
  Close by is said to be a beheading pit, containing a block and a sunken cavity for the head. Noble folk were executed in the pit, while the common people were hanged on a neighbouring oak tree. The pit may in fact be a water collection tank – but this does not make such a good story. This branch of the family became Earls of Breadalbane.

Finlaystone House

Renfrewshire: About 3 miles east of Port Glasgow, on A8, west of Glasgow Airport, on south side of River Clyde, at Finlaystone.

Private NS 365737 OS: 63 ** Map: 3, no: 124

Finlaystone House, a grand symmetrical mansion, mostly dating from 1760 and later, was remodelled between 1898 and 1903. The building incorporates a 15th-century castle.

Finlaystone was a property of the Dennistouns in the 12th century, but passed by marriage to the Cunninghams of Kilmaurs in 1404. They were made Earls of Glencairn in 1488, although the 1st Earl was slain at the Battle of Sauchieburn the same year. Alexander Cunningham, 5th Earl, supported the Reformation and had John Knox preach here in 1556. He opposed Mary, Queen of Scots, at the Battle of Carberry Hill in 1567.

The 9th Earl led a rising for Charles II in 1654, but the rebellion was a failure, and he was imprisoned, narrowly escaping execution. After the Restoration he was made Chancellor of Scotland.

Robert Burns – whose patron was James, 14th Earl – also visited the house, and scratched his name on a window pane with his diamond ring. He also wrote a lament for the earl, and called his son James Glencairn Burns.

The earldom became dormant in 1796, and the property passed by marriage to the Cunningham Grahams of Gartmore. It was sold in 1863 because of debt, and later passed to the McMillans.

Other refs: Findlaystone

OPEN: Gardens and grounds open all year, daily 10.30-17.00; visitor centre and refreshments open May-Aug, daily 11.00-16.30.

Visitor centre with Clan MacMillan exhibits, doll museum, and Celtic art display. Gift shop. Tearoom. WC. Gardens. Disabled access to grounds & WC. Parking. £.

Tel: 01475 540505 Fax: 01475 540285

Web: www.finlaystone.co.uk

Fintry Castle *see* Mains Castle

Fintry Castle

Stirlingshire & Clackmannan: About 1 mile east of Fintry, just north of the B818 0.25 miles east of junction with B822, just north of Endrick Water, 0.25 mile west of Spittalhill.

Ruin or site NS 641863 OS: 57 * Map: 6, no: 42

Little survives of a 15th- and 16th-century castle of the Grahams of Fintry, which was ruined by 1724.

Other refs: Findlay Castle; Tower of Fintrie

Fintry House *see* Linlathen House

Finzean House

Kincardine & Deeside: About 5 miles south-east of Aboyne, on minor road west of B976, at or near Finzean House.

Private NO 591934 [?] OS: 37 * Map: 10, no: 153

Site of castle, which was replaced by Finzean House, 'a fine old building forming three sides of a quadrangle.' It was apparently burned down, although later rebuilt. It was a property of the Fotheringhams at the end of the 19th century.

Fionnchairn Castle *see* Fincharn Castle

Fisherie

Banff & Buchan: About 5 miles north-east of Turriff, on minor roads west or south of A98, north of the burn of Fisherie, at or near Mains of Fisherie.

Ruin or site NJ 765580 [?] OS: 29 * Map: 10, no: 247

Site of castle. The property was held by the Duffs.

Fisher's Tower, Darnick *see* Darnick

Fithie

Angus & Dundee: About 3.5 miles south-east of Brechin, on minor roads south of A934, at or near Fithie.

Ruin or site NO 635545 OS: 54 * Map: 8, no: 256

Site of castle, the remains of which were incorporated into a cottage.

The lands were held the Fithie family from the 13th century, before passing to the Carnegies in 1549 or the early 17th century.

Other refs: Castle of Fithie

Flask Tower

Dumfriesshire: About 2.5 miles north of Langholm, on minor roads and foot east of A7, east of Ewes Water, near Flask Wood.

Ruin or site NY 373884 [?] OS: 79 * Map: 1, no: 318

Site of tower house, which is referred to in 16th-century charters.

Other refs: Flaskholm; Flaskhoome

Flaskholm *see* Flask Tower

Flaskhoome *see* Flask Tower

Flemington Tower

Angus & Dundee: About 5.5 miles north-east of Forfar, on minor roads east of B9134 at Crosston, near Aberlemno Cross, at Flemington.

Private NO 527556 OS: 54 *** Map: 8, no: 222

Flemington Tower is a ruined 17th-century L-plan tower house of three storeys. It consists of two offset blocks, forming two re-entrant angles. Stair-turrets rise in both angles, one reaching all floors above the first, the other only connecting the first and second floors. The walls are pierced by gunloops and shot-holes.

The entrance is in the re-entrant angle. The basement contains two vaulted chambers, one being the old kitchen, with a wide arched fireplace. The main turnpike stair in the wing rises only to the first-floor hall, which has been subdivided. Private chambers, on the floors above, were reached by the two turret stairs.

It was a property of the Dishington family from the beginning of the 15th century, but later passed to the Ochterlony family. The Ochterlony family supported the Jacobites in the Rising of 1745, and fugitives hiding in the castle only narrowly escaped discovery. The castle was abandoned in 1830, then used to house farm servants

Other refs: Castle of Flemington

Flemington Tower

Borders: About 5 miles south of West Linton, on minor road east of B7059, just east of meeting of Flemington Burn and Lyne Water.

Ruin or site   NT 166451   OS: 72   **   Map: 2, no: 30

Flemington Tower is a small ruinous 16th-century tower house, reduced to two storeys and given a modern roof and new entrance. A fireplace and well for a turnpike stair are all that survive inside, and the basement is vaulted. The tower was occupied until the end of the 19th century.

It was a property of the Hays, but later passed to the Veitch family.

Fletcherfield Castle

Angus & Dundee: About 1.5 miles south-east of Kirriemuir, on minor road west of A926, about 0.5 miles east of Logie, at Fletcherfield.

Ruin or site   NO 403522   OS: 54   *   Map: 8, no: 175

Site of tower of the Lyon family.

Flight Tower *see* Clintwood Castle

Floors Castle

Borders: About 1 mile north-west of Kelso, on minor roads west of A6089 or south of B6397, north of River Tweed, at Floors Castle.

Private   NT 711346   OS: 74   *   Map: 2, no: 290

Probable site of castle. 'Fleurs' is marked on Blaeu's Atlas Novus map of The Merse, which was compiled about 1590.

The largest inhabited mansion in Scotland, the present house consists of a large towered and turreted central block with other wings and ranges. The building dates from 1721, and was designed by William Adam for the Kerr 1st Duke of Roxburghe. Building materials were brought from Cessford Castle. In the 19th century, the house was remodelled by William Playfair with a profusion of spires and domes. Floors is still the home of the Duke and Duchess of Roxburghe, and was used in the film 'Greystoke'. There is a walled garden with fine herbaceous borders.

One story is that the house is haunted by the ghost of a gardener, who is said to be experienced – rather than seen – outside the main entrance. In the grounds is a holly tree, reputedly where James II was killed by an exploding cannon while besieging Roxburgh Castle. The apparition of a horseman has allegedly been seen riding towards the site of the old stronghold.

OPEN: Open Easter-Sep, daily 10.00-16.30; last admission 16.00.

Collections of furniture, tapestries, works of art and porcelain.. Gift shop. Licensed restaurant. WC. Playground. Walled garden and park. Disabled access to house; lift for wheelchairs; WC. Car and coach parking. Group concessions. ££.

Tel: 01573 223333   Fax: 01573 226056

Flowerdale

Ross & Cromarty: About 1.5 miles south-east of Gairloch, on minor road east of A832, on east side of Loch Gairloch, north-east of Charlestown, near Flowerdale House.

Ruin or site   NG 814754   OS: 19   *   Map: 9, no: 25

Site of stronghold, which could only be reached by a drawbridge across the moat.

It was a property of the Mackenzies after Red Hector, son of the Mackenzie of Kintail, was granted Gairloch in 1494. Flowerdale House, a long two-storey mansion, was built in 1738, and replaced the earlier residence. The property is still held by the Mackenzies of Gairloch and Conon.

Other refs: Tigh Dige; Moat House

Fodderance *see* Lintrose House

Folkerton Castle

Lanarkshire & Glasgow: About 4.5 miles south of Lanark, on minor roads east of B7078 or north of A70, north of Douglas Water, at or near Tower Farm.

Ruin or site   NS 866364 [?]   OS: 71   *   Map: 3, no: 403

Site of tower house.

The lands were a property of Theobold the Fleming in 1147. They were held by the Folkerton family from the 13th century until about 1495.

Forbes Castle *see* Castle Forbes

Ford House

Lothians: Just north-west of Pathhead, on minor roads west of A68, west of Tyne Water, at Ford.

Private   NT 389644   OS: 66   **   Map: 4, no: 156

Ford House, which dates from 1680, is a fine L-plan house of two storeys with an octagonal stair-tower in the re-entrant angle. It stands in a walled garden, was restored in 1956, and is in good condition. It was built by the Frasers of Lovat. Ford was the point of crossing the Tyne until the building of Lothian Bridge.

Fordel *see* Easter Fordel

Fordell Castle

Fife: About 1.5 miles north of Inverkeithing, on minor road east of B981, just north of junction with B916.

Private   NT 147854   OS: 65   *   Map: 7, no: 21**

Standing on the edge of a ravine, Fordell Castle is a 16th-century Z-plan tower house. It consists of a rectangular main block and two square towers at opposite corners, both of which house a turnpike stair. One tower has a corbiestepped gabled roof, while the other has a flat roof and parapet with a conical-roofed turret crowning a corbelled-out stair-tower in the re-entrant angle. Corbelled-out bartizans crown the other corners of the main block.

The castle had a courtyard with a drawbridge, but these were demolished in the 19th century.

There are two entrances, at the foot of each of the stair-towers. The basement contains a vaulted passage and three vaulted chambers. One chamber was the kitchen, while a small mural stair leads from the wine cellar to the hall. The hall is on the first floor of the main block, along with a private chamber. There are more apartments on the upper floors of the main block and towers, reached by a stair in the corbelled-out tower. A vaulted and panelled chamber, known as Queen Mary's room, has a vaulted roof to support the flat roof of the tower.

Fordell was a property of the Airths of Plean, but had passed by marriage to the Hendersons by 1511. Mary, Queen of Scots, stayed here when one of her ladies, Marion Scott, was married to George Henderson of Fordell, and the castle may have been torched in 1568. The castle was sacked by Roundheads after the Battle of Inverkeithing in 1651. A new mansion was built nearby, although the property passed by marriage to Hon. Hew Adam Dalrymple Hamilton Haldane Duncan, second son of the Earl of Camperdown, in 1866, who then added Mercer-Henderson to his name – correspondence must have been a nightmare. The castle is still occupied.

There was also a chapel, dedicated to St Theriot, along with a holy and wishing well. Coal was mined on the estate from 1600, and there was a light railway from Fordel to St Davids.

Fordyce Castle

Banff & Buchan: About 2.5 miles south-west of Portsoy, on minor roads south of A98, east of Burn of Fordyce, west of Durn Hill, in square of village of Fordyce.

Private   NJ 556638   OS: 29   *   Map: 10, no: 139**

Fordyce Castle consists of a 16th-century L-plan tower house of three storeys. A harled wing of two storeys and an attic, built around 1700, extended it into a T-plan building. The old part has a corbelled-out stair-turret, in the re-entrant angle, above first-floor level. The top storey has bartizans, with conical roofs, and there are many gunloops and shot-holes. The castle is dated 1592

The entrance is in the re-entrant angle, at the foot of the stair-wing. The basement is vaulted, and the main stair, in the wing, only climbs to the first floor, while the upper floors are reached by a stair in the corbelled-out turret. The house has been much altered inside, although the hall would have been on the first floor, with private chambers on the floors above, and in the wing.

The castle was built by Thomas Menzies of Durn, Provost of Aberdeen. It was used as the village school, and has been recently restored.

Forfar Castle

Angus & Dundee: To west of Forfar, near A926 north of junction with A929, east of Loch of Forfar.

Ruin or site   NO 456507 [?]   OS: 54   *   Map: 8, no: 195

Site of 13th-century royal castle, apparently surrounded by water. There were some remains in the 17th century but nothing survives.

The castle was associated with Malcolm Canmore and Queen Margaret, and used by William the Lyon and Alexander II. It was garrisoned by the English during the Wars of Independence, visited by Edward I in 1296, but recaptured by the Scots, who slaughtered the garrison, on Christmas Day 1308, then demolished the defences. It was apparently rebuilt, then captured and slighted again in 1313. It had been abandoned by the 1330s.

Forglen House

Banff & Buchan: About 2 miles north-west of Turriff, on minor roads east of B9025, west of River Deveron, south of Todlaw Wood, at Forglen House.
Private   NJ 696517   OS: 29   **   Map: 10, no: 205
Forglen House, a castellated mansion built in 1840, incorporates part of a 16th century-castle.

The lands were held by the Ogilvies of Dunlugas, but passed by marriage to the Abercrombies, who built the present house. The house is still occupied.

Formartine Castle *see* Gight Castle

Forres Castle

Moray: In Forres, just south-east of B9011 junction with A940, east of Mosset Burn at Castle Bridge.
Ruin or site   NJ 035588   OS: 27   *   Map: 10, no: 9
Site of royal castle from the 12th or 13th century, which was strengthened by a keep, strong curtain wall and corner towers. Nothing remains.

An earlier stronghold here is said to have been destroyed by Norsemen about 850, and this is the probable site of the murder of Dubh, King of Scots, in 966. The King is said to have been slain by the governor of the castle, who concealed his body in a deep pool, but the sun would not shine on the spot until his corpse was found.

In the late 15th-century it was a property of the Murrays, although it is also said to have been held by the Dunbars of Westfield from the 14th until the 17th century. David II had stayed here in 1367. The lands had passed to the Grants at the beginning of the 18th century, and the castle site was given to the town.

Little remained of the castle by the mid 18th century, and the site is now a public park.
OPEN: Access at all reasonable times.
Parking nearby.

Forse Castle

Sutherland & Caithness: About 4.5 miles north-east of Dunbeath, on minor roads and foot south of Forse, just north of sea, at Forse Castle.
Ruin or site   ND 224338   OS: 11   **   Map: 12, no: 52
Standing on a promontory cut off by a ditch, Forse Castle, probably dating from the 12th or 13th century, consists of a ruined keep and courtyard, with the remains of outbuildings. The promontory was cut off on the landward side by a ditch, now crossed by a narrow causeway.

It was a property of the Cheynes, but later passed to the Keiths, then the Sutherlands, and was probably abandoned in the 18th century. About two miles to the north is its successor, Forse House – the estate previously being known as Nottingham until the mid 19th century. The house is a three-storey symmetrical mansion, built in 1753, and still occupied.
Other refs: Nottingham; Achastle

Fort Augustus

Inverness & Nairn: At or near Fort Augustus, on minor roads west of A82, at southern tip of Loch Ness, at or near Bunoich.
Ruin or site   NH 382091   OS: 34   *   Map: 9, no: 49
Site of castle [NH 382090]. Part of the barracks from an early 18th-century fort, which was known as Kilwhimin, remains behind the Lovat Arms Hotel [NH 377090], while a larger fort [NH 382091] was built by General Wade in 1729-42 nearer the loch, and called Fort Augustus after Butcher Cumberland. One of the bastions remains to full height.

The fort was captured after a bombardment by the Jacobites in 1746, but restored and occupied until the Crimean War. It was sold to Lord Lovat in 1857, and pre-

sented by him to the Benedictine Order in 1876.

Part of the complex is open to the public as a heritage centre. There are displays about Loch Ness and the Great Glen, the Jacobite Risings, the capturing of the fort and the history of the Scottish Highlander. There is also the Clansmen Centre which features a turf house, weapon demonstrations and 17th-century life in the Highlands, and cruises on Loch Ness. Parts of the abbey are also accessible, including the church, chapels, cloister and grounds.
Other refs: Kilwhimin; Kilchumin
OPEN: Open all year, daily 9.00-17.00 (closes 18.00); reduced hours in winter; closed Christmas Day.
Explanatory displays. Gift shop. Restaurant and tearoom. Picnic area. WC. Disabled access. Car and coach parking. Group concessions. ££.
Tel: 01320 366233   Fax: 01320 366228
Email: abbey@monk.co.uk

Fort Charlotte

Shetland: In Lerwick on island of Shetland, on minor roads north (or south) of A970.
His Scot   HU 475415   OS: 4   **   Map: 11, no: 64
Fort Charlotte is a 17th-century pentagonal artillery fort, which had accommodation for 100 men. It was built to defend the harbour from the Dutch, who – nevertheless – burned the barrack block and much of the town of Lerwick in 1673. The fort was rebuilt in 1781, and called Fort Charlotte after the wife of George III. The fort never saw action, but is well preserved, although modern buildings encroach.
Tel: 0131 668 8800   Fax: 0131 668 8888
Email: hs.explore@scotland.gov.uk   Web: www.historic-scotland.gov.uk

Fort Fiddes *see* Castle of Troup

Fort George

Inverness & Nairn: About 9 miles north-east of Inverness, on minor roads west of B9006, on promontory on south side of the Moray Firth, at Fort George.
His Scot   NH 763566   OS: 27   **   Map: 9, no: 116
Fort George is a magnificent example of a massive Georgian artillery fort. It was built after the Jacobite rising of 1745-6 to designs by William Skinner, but was not completed until 1769, by which time it was redundant. Many of the buildings were designed by William and John Adam. It extends over 16 acres and could accommodate nearly 2000 men; and is still used as a barracks. Reconstruction of barrack rooms in different periods, and a display of muskets and pikes. The Regimental

Museum of the Queen's Own Highlanders features uniforms, medals and pictures.
The fort is said to be haunted by a ghostly piper.
OPEN: Open all year: Apr-Sep, daily 9.30-18.30; Oct-Mar 9.30-16.30, Sun 14.00-16.30; last ticket 45 mins before closing; closed 25/26 Dec and 1/2 Jan.
Reconstruction of barrack rooms in different periods, and display of muskets and pikes. Visitor centre with explanatory panels. Gift shop. Tea room. WC. Picnic area. Disabled access and WC. Car and coach parking. Group concessions. ££.
Tel: 01667 462777   Fax: 01667 462698
Email: hs.explore@scotland.gov.uk   Web: www.historic-scotland.gov.uk

Fort William

South Highland: Just north of Fort William, just north of A82, south of River Lochy, by railway station, at Fort William.
Ruin or site   NN 104742   OS: 41   **   Map: 9, no: 38
Fort William is named after the now ruinous fort [NN 104742], which was built by General Monck for Cromwell during the 1650s, then reconstructed and renamed in 1690, during the reign of William of Orange. It was bombarded in the spring of 1746 by Jacobites, but could not be taken. It was garrisoned until 1866, after which most of it was demolished, although remains of the ramparts and bastions as well as the sallyport survive. The West Highland Museum in the town contains information about the fort.

Fortar Castle *see* Forter Castle

Forter Castle

Angus & Dundee: About 12 miles north of Alyth, on minor road north of B951 at Meikle Forter, in Glen Isla, west of River Isla, at Meikle Forter.
Private   NO 183646   OS: 43   **   Map: 8, no: 114
Situated in the narrow glen, Forter Castle is a 16th-century L-plan tower house of four storeys and a garret. It consists of a main block and an offset square wing. A stair-turret projects above the first floor in the main re-entrant angle, and round bartizans crown two corners of the main block. There are a number of shot-holes.
   The entrance, at the foot of the wing in the re-entrant angle, leads to a wide stair to the first floor only, while the floors above are reached by the stair in the turret. The basement was vaulted, and contained the kitchen with a wide fireplace and two cellars. The hall, on the first floor, has a large fireplace.
   The lands belonged to the Abbey of Coupar, but passed to the Ogilvies after the Reformation. The castle was plundered and burned by the Earl of Argyll in 1640, when he turned out the Countess of Airlie, as recounted in the old ballad 'The Bonnie House o' Airlie'. The castle was later restored.
   The property was sold to the MacThomas family, who built a new house at Crandart. They feuded with the Ogilvies, and were eventually ruined and had to sell the property in 1676. Forter Castle became very ruined, but was restored around 1990 and is occupied.
Other refs: Fortar Castle

Forteviot

Perthshire: About 4.5 miles south-west of Perth, on B935, Forteviot.
Private   NO 049176   OS: 58   **   Map: 8, no: 59
Site of palace of the Pictish and Scottish kings, traditionally at Halyhill to the west of the village. It is here that Kenneth MacAlpin is said to have slaughtered his rivals at a drunken feast to secure his position as joint ruler of the Scots and Picts. Kenneth died here in 858, and the palace may still have been in use in the 13th century and visited by William the Lyon.
   A church existed here from the 8th century, on the site of which the present Forteviot Parish Church is believed to have been built. A bronze bell, dated 900, is preserved here, and there are medieval carved stones.
OPEN: Church open by arrangement: tel 01738 625854.

Forthar Tower

Fife: About 3 miles north-east of Glenrothes, on minor roads south of A92, 0.5 miles south-west of Kettlebridge, at or near Forthar.
Ruin or site   NO 301064   OS: 59   *   Map: 7, no: 72
Site of castle, which is mentioned in 1551, although there are no remains.

Fotheringham Castle

Angus & Dundee: About 4 miles south of Forfar, on minor roads south of B9127, south of Fotheringham Hill, at or near Fotheringham Home Farm.
Ruin or site   NO 459441   OS: 54   *   Map: 8, no: 196
Site of castle, the site of which was occupied by a large castellated mansion of 1859 designed by David Bryce, itself demolished.
   The lands were held by the Fotheringhams from the 14th century until the present day, the family having come to Scotland with Queen Margaret, wife of Malcolm Canmore, in the 11th century.

Foulage Tower *see* Foulitch Tower

Foulden Bastle

Borders: About 3 miles east of Chirnside, on minor roads south of A6105, north of Whiteadder Water, west of Foulden hamlet, at Foulden Bastle.
Ruin or site   NT 920555 [?]   OS: 74   *   Map: 2, no: 355
Site of bastle or tower house of the Ramsays, the last vestige of which was removed around 1835. A doocot survived the bastle, only to be demolished in the 1960s. In the graveyard of Foulden Church is a stone for Ramsay of Dalhousie with the inscription: 'Hier lyeth ane honorabil man Georg Ramsay in Fulden Bastle who departit 4 Jan 1592 and of his age 74'. Ramsay was apparently a notorious Border reiver.
   Nearby [NT 931558] is a two-storey tithe barn, which was used to store grain as payment of 'tithes' or tenth of produce to the church.
OPEN: Barn: HS. View exterior only. Tel: 0131 668 8800; fax: 0131 668 8888.

Foulfourde *see* Fulford Tower

Foulis Castle

Ross & Cromarty: About 5 miles south-west of Alness, on minor roads north of A9, north of the Cromarty Firth, at Foulis Castle.
Private   NH 589642   OS: 21   *   Map: 9, no: 75
Foulis Castle, a white harled two-storey mansion, incorporates part of an earlier tower house, from which some walling and gunloops survive.
   It was a property of the Munros. The Munros built a castle here in the 12th century. They had acquired the lands on agreement that they should find a snowball in midsummer if requested to do so. One of the chiefs was killed at the Battle of Pinkie in 1547, while another, Robert Munro, known as the 'Black Baron' joined the army of Gustavus Adolphus in the 30 Years War and was killed at Ulm in 1633. The castle was sacked and torched in 1746 by Jacobites, as the family fought against Bonnie Prince Charlie in the Jacobite Rising. The house was rebuilt as a large classical mansion in 1754-92.
   The Munros held the property in the 20th century. The castle was restored, and the house is still occupied.
Other refs: Fowlis Castle

Foulitch Tower

Borders: About 2 miles north of Peebles, on minor roads and foot east of A703, east of Eddleston Water, about 0.5 miles north-east of Winkston.
Ruin or site   NT 256436   OS: 73   *   Map: 2, no: 65
Site of castle, some remains of which survived in 1856 by a later farm, but this has also gone.
   In the 16th century it was a property of the Caverhills, but then passed through several families. In the 17th century it was held by the Williamsons, but later passed to the Littles of Winkston.
Other refs: Foulage Tower

Foulshiels Tower

Borders: About 2 miles north of Newcastleton, on foot west of B6399, on west side of Hermitage Water, north of Foulshiels, west of Leahaugh Cottage.
Ruin or site   NY 492916 [?]   OS: 79   *   Map: 2, no: 153
Site of tower house of the Elliots.

Foumerkland Tower

Dumfriesshire: About 5 miles north-west of Dumfries, on minor road west of B729, about 0.5 miles north of Cairn Water, north of Foumerkland.
Private   NX 909807   OS: 78   **   Map: 1, no: 174**
An excellent example of a simple fortified house, Foumerkland Tower is a rectangular 16th-century tower house of three storeys and an attic. Bartizans, with conical roofs, crown two corners of the tower. The tower had a courtyard.
   Each floor only has a single room. The basement is vaulted and contained the kitchen. A turnpike stair, in one corner, climbs the full height of the building. The hall is on the first floor.
   Foumerkland belonged to the Abbey of Holywood, but passed to the Maxwells

after the Reformation, and they built the tower in 1590, although it may incorporate an old stronghold. In 1720 the property was sold to Robert Ferguson, who also acquired the nearby tower of Isle. Foumerkland was occupied until about 1935, but after a period of neglect was repaired.

Fountainhall *see* Penkaet Castle

Foveran Castle

Aberdeen & Gordon: About 4.5 miles south-east of Ellon, on minor roads south of A975 south of Newburgh, 1 mile west of mouth of Ythan River and sea, at or near Foveran.
Ruin or site NJ 990244 [?] OS: 38 * Map: 10, no: 349
Site of 12th- or 13th-century castle of the Turing family, which collapsed about 1720. The property passed to Forbes of Tolquhon about 1750, and there are no remains.
Foveran House [NJ 991242], built about 1770, stands near the site.
One of Thomas the Rhymer's prophecies is:
'When Turing's Tower falls to the land,
Gladsmuir shall be near at hand;
When Turing's Tower falls to the sea,
Gladsmuir the next year shall be.'
This is said to perhaps refer to the Battle of Prestonpans in 1745, which is near Gladsmuir.
Other refs: Turing's Tower

Fowlis Castle

Angus & Dundee: About 5 miles north-west of Dundee, on minor roads south of A923 or 2 miles north of A85 at Star Inn Farm, just south of Fowlis village.
Private NO 321334 OS: 53 * Map: 8, no: 156**
Once a strong fortress, Fowlis Castle consists of a 17th-century rectangular tower house of three storeys and an attic, with a later wing , known as 'The Lady's Tower'. The stair-tower is crowned by a modern conical roof, and rises above the main block. The tower once had a courtyard.
Fowlis was a property of the Maules from 1330. It passed to the Mortimers, then by marriage in 1377 to Sir Alexander Gray of Broxmouth, who became Lord Gray of Fowlis. The Grays were a treacherous lot during the time of Mary, Queen of Scots, and much of the scheming to have her executed probably took place at the castle. In 1669 the 9th Lord Gray sold Fowlis to the Murrays of Ochtertyre. The building, once a village tavern, fell into disrepair, but is once again occupied as a farmhouse.
Other refs: Fowlis Easter

Fowlis Castle *see* Foulis Castle

Fowlis Easter *see* Fowlis Castle

Francie of Canonbie *see* Hallgreen

Fraoch Eilean Castle

Argyll & Dunbartonshire: About 3.5 miles south-west of Dalmally, on minor road and boat south-west of A85, on island in Loch Awe, on Fraoch Eilean.
Ruin or site NN 108251 OS: 50 ** Map: 5, no: 111
Little remains of a strong 12th- or 13th- century castle, consisting of a ruined courtyard and hall house. It was still occupied or reoccupied in the mid 17th century, and abandoned around the middle of the 18th century.
It was a property of the MacNaughtons from 1267, and was used by their chiefs. It later passed to the Campbells.
A tale about the island is that Fraoch, a hero, came here to fetch apples for Mego, a fair maiden, and was slain by a serpent guarding the fruit. Fraoch, however, means heather.

Fraser Castle *see* Castle Fraser

Freefield House

Aberdeen & Gordon: About 11.5 miles north of Inverurie, on minor roads east of B992 1 mile south of A920, 1 mile west of North Rayne, at Freefield House.
Ruin or site NJ 676314 OS: 29 * Map: 10, no: 192
Site of castle of the Leith family. George Leith of Freefield was killed by Leslie of Pitcaple, starting a feud between the families. The present Freefield House, which stands near the site of the castle, is a plain mid 18th-century mansion, which was altered in 1885.

Frenchland Tower

Dumfriesshire: About 0.5 miles east of Moffat, on minor road and foot north of A708, just west of Frenchland Burn, at Frenchland.
Ruin or site NT 102054 OS: 78 ** Map: 1, no: 228
Frenchland Tower is an altered 16th-century tower house of three storeys, the gables standing to their full height, but the side walls have collapsed. The main block dates to the 16th century, while a stair wing, with a scale and platt stair, was added in the 17th century when the building was altered and extended.
It was a property of the French family from the 13th century.

Frendraught Castle

Aberdeen & Gordon: About 6 miles east of Huntly, on minor roads west of B9001, 1 mile west of Largue, at Frendraught House.
Private NJ 620418 OS: 29 ** Map: 10, no: 166
Site of 13th-century castle, which was torched in 1630. The present house dates from 1656, was remodelled in 1753, extended in 1790, and incorporates a small part of the old castle.
It was a property of the Crichtons, and James V visited in 1535. The castle was torched in 1630 during a feud over land with the Gordons. Six Gordons, including John Gordon, Lord Rothiemay, and John Gordon, Viscount Aboyne, were burned and killed in the castle, although the Crichton laird escaped with his folk. Crichton of Frendraught was tried and acquitted of their murders, although one of his servants was executed. Lady Rothiemay certainly believed in Crichton's involvement: she employed Highlanders to attack and plunder his lands and family. Lady Rothiemay was eventually imprisoned in 1635, although she was later released.
Crichton's son, James, was made Viscount Frendraught in 1642, and although a Covenanter, fought for the Marquis of Montrose in 1650. He was captured after being wounded, and died soon afterwards.
The property passed to the Morrisons about 1690. The house was restored in 1974 and is still occupied.
The castle is said to be haunted by the ghost of Crichton's wife, Lady Elizabeth Gordon, daughter of the Earl of Sutherland, who may have been involved in the torching of the castle. Her ghost has reportedly been seen, most often on the stairs, in the 18th and 20th centuries, and her apparition has been described as a dark woman wearing a white dress edged with gold. Other activity includes arguing, footsteps coming down the stairs and crashing sounds, as well as doors being locked and unlocked, opened or shut.

Freswick Castle *see* Bucholly Castle

Freswick House

Sutherland & Caithness: About 11 miles north of Wick, on minor road east of A9, just south of Gill Burn, on south side of Freswick Bay, at Freswick House.
Private ND 378671 OS: 12 ** Map: 12, no: 66
Freswick House is a tall 17th-century house of five storeys. It consists of a main block and wing with a stair-tower projecting from the middle of one side. The roof is steeply pitched and there are corbiestepped gables. It was extended in the 18th century, but the basement is vaulted. There is a courtyard surrounded by ranges of buildings.
The property was owned by the Mowats, and they built a castle nearby at Bucholly. In 1427 Mowat of Freswick, and his followers, were burned to death in the chapel of St Duthac at Tain by MacNeil of Creich. The present house replaced the castle, but was sold to the Sinclairs of Rattar in 1661. It was badly damaged in a thunder storm in the 1770s, but by 1791 had been remodelled. It is still occupied.
Other refs: House of Freswick

Freuchie *see* **Castle Grant**

Freugh Tower
Galloway: About 4 miles south-east of Stranraer, by foot north of A757, north of West Freugh Airfield, 0.25 miles north-east of East Galdenoch.
Ruin or site NX 111562 OS: 82 * Map: 1, no: 24
Site of tower house, which had been demolished by 1847.
  It was a property of the MacDowalls from the 15th century or earlier, and in 1654 the tower was burned and the family moved to Balgreggan. The MacDowalls of Freugh were made Earls of Dumfries in 1768.

Fruid Castle
Borders: About 4 miles south of Tweedsmuir, on minor roads south of A701, at southern end of Fruid Reservoir, Fruid.
Ruin or site NT 106180 OS: 78 * Map: 2, no: 8
Site of castle, which dated from the 12th century, a property of the Frasers. There was a later tower house, and part of the site is now in the reservoir.

Fuirdstone Castle
Angus & Dundee: About 4.5 miles west of Brechin, on minor roads south of A90, north of River South Esk, 200 yards west of Balnabreich.
Ruin or site NO 542589 OS: 54 * Map: 8, no: 227
Site of castle, mentioned in 1612, the last remains of which were removed at the beginning of the 19th century.
Other refs: Balnabreich Castle; Furdstone Castle

Fulford Tower
Lothians: About 2.5 miles north of Penicuik, on minor road west of A702, east of Woodhouselee Hill, near Fulford, at or near Woodhouselee.
Ruin or site NT 238645 [?] OS: 66 * Map: 4, no: 86
Site of 14th-century castle. It was incorporated into the mansion of Woodhouselee in the 17th century, when the property was held by the Purvis family, and stones from Old Woodhouselee were used to repair the building in 1665. It was rebuilt in 1796, and passed to the Tytler family, one of whom, Patrick Tytler was an eminent Scottish historian. Sir Walter Scott visited the house. Remains from Wrychtishousis, including a fireplace and sundial, were brought here. The mansion was completely demolished about 1965, except for the U-plan stables, and the site grassed over.
  It is said that the mansion was haunted by a ghost of Lady Hamilton, apparently transferred from Old Woodhouselee: this could either be a confusion of site or – more interestingly but less likely – that her ghost came here with the stone used for the rebuilding in 1665.
Other refs: Woodhouselee; Foulfourde

Fullarton Castle
Ayrshire: To south of Irvine, on minor roads off A737, west side of River Irvine, Fullarton.
Ruin or site NS 319383 [?] OS: 70 * Map: 3, no: 88
Site of castle, which was held in the 13th century by the Fullertons (also see Crosbie House [NS 344301]).
Other refs: Castle of Fullarton; Fullerton Castle

Fullarton House *see* **Crosbie House**

Fullerton Castle *see* **Fullarton Castle**

Fulton Tower
Borders: About 4.5 miles south-west of Jedburgh, on minor road north of B6357, on the east side of Rule Water, about 2 miles south of Bedrule.
Ruin or site NT 605158 OS: 80 ** Map: 2, no: 237
Fulton Tower is a ruined 16th-century L-plan tower house, rectangular in plan with a round stair-tower at one corner. The basement was not vaulted.
  It was a property of the Homes of Cowdenknowes, before passing by marriage to the Turnbulls of Bedrule in 1570.

Furdstone Castle *see* **Fuirdstone Castle**

Fyrish House
Ross & Cromarty: About 2.5 miles west of Alness, on minor roads north of A9, north of Mains of Novar, at Fyrish.
Private NH 614690 OS: 21 * Map: 9, no: 82
Fyrish House, an early 18th-century mansion, stands on the site of castle of the Munros. The mansion was the home of Sir Hector Munro, a general who served mostly in India, and suppressed a 'mutiny' at Patna.

Fyvie Castle
Banff & Buchan: About 1 mile north of Fyvie village, on minor roads west of A947, just south of Ythan River, just north of Loch of Fyvie, at Fyvie Castle.
NTS NJ 764393 OS: 29 *** Map: 10, no: 246**
Set in the rolling countryside of Aberdeenshire, Fyvie Castle is one of the most magnificent castles in Scotland. The building consists of a massive tower house with very long wings, and is adorned with turrets, dormer windows and carved finials, and corbiestepped gables. It was defended by the River Ythan, and down the centuries was developed from a strong castle into a comfortable and striking residence. The castle was formerly built around a courtyard, but the north and east side were lost in the 18th century. There are also many original interiors.
  The vaulted basement has both barrel- and groined-vaults. The fine wide main turnpike stair is decorated with 22 coats of arms. Many of the chambers are panelled in wood, and have plaster ceilings and tempera painting.
  Fyvie was originally a property of the Lindsays. William the Lyon held court here in 1214, as did Alexander II in 1222. Edward I of England stayed in 1296, during the Wars of Independence, then Robert the Bruce in 1308. Margaret Keith, wife to the Earl of Crawford, was besieged here by her nephew.
  The property passed to the Prestons in 1402, then about 1433 to the Meldrums, then the Seton Earls of Dunfermline in 1596. The Marquis of Montrose occupied the castle in 1644, and in the 1650s it was held by a Cromwellian force. The property passed to the Gordon Earls of Aberdeen in 1733 and finally to the Leith family in 1889, each of whom added to the castle. It was put onto the open market in 1982, and is now owned by The National Trust for Scotland.
  Thomas the Rhymer is recorded as having made a prophecy concerning Fyvie and the 'weeping stones' – this would be around the turn of the 14th century, before the Lindsays were in possession.
  When the castle was first being built, stones were removed from church lands by demolishing a nearby chapel, but fell into a nearby river. The then laird refused Thomas shelter in the castle, and the Rhymer is said to have prophesied that unless the three stones were recovered the castle and estate would never descend in direct line for more than two generations. Only two of the stones were found, and

the prophecy is said to have come true. One of the stones is in the charter room, while another is reported to be built into the foundations – and were said to 'weep', oozing with water, when tragedy is going to strike the owners.

The castle is reputedly haunted by several ghosts. One, the 'Grey Lady' is said to be the spectre of a lady starved to death here. The ghost is said to have been at her most active in the 1920s and 1930s. When workmen were renovating one room, they found a secret room behind a wall which contained a skeleton. When the skeleton was removed disturbances increased until the remains were returned to the chamber.

Another ghost is said to be the 'Green Lady', the spectre of Lilias Drummond, wife of Alexander Seton, who died in 1601. Her appearance bodes ill for the family. She may have been starved to death by her husband, Alexander Seton, who remarried quickly after her death. The ghost is said to have scratched her name on the window sill of the newlyweds' bedroom, soon after they were married – and the writing can still be seen.

The castle also reputedly has a ghostly drummer.

OPEN: Open 13 Apr May-Sep, daily 13.30-17.30; Jul-Aug, daily 11.00-17.30; Oct, Sat-Sun 3.10-17.30, last admission 16.45. Tearoom and shop as castle but open 12.30 when castle open 13.30. Grounds open all year, daily 9.30-sunset.

Collections of portraits, arms and armour and tapestries. Gift shop. Tearoom. WC. Picnic area. Garden and grounds. Plant sales. Disabled access to tearoom and WC. Car parking. £££.

Tel: 01651 891266 Fax: 01651 891107
Email: information@nts.org.uk Web: www.nts.org.uk

G

Gadgirth House

Ayrshire: About 4.5 miles east of Ayr, just east of B742, just east of River of Ayr, at or near Gadgirth.

Ruin or site NS 409223 [?] OS: 70 * Map: 3, no: 151

Site of 14th-century castle, some of which may have been incorporated in Gadgirth House. The house dated from 1801, but was completely demolished in 1968 and the site cleared.

It was a property of the Chalmers family, but by the end of the 19th century held by the Burnets. Mary, Queen of Scots, is said to have visited, and John Knox to have preached at Gadgirth.

An older castle [NS 405219], known as Old Ha', was defended by the River Ayr on two sides as well as by a ditch. It is believed to have preceded Gadgirth, and was probably a property of one Reginaldus de Camera around the turn of the 13th century.

Other refs: Old Ha', Gadgirth

Gadvan *see* Dunbog Castle

Gagie House

Angus & Dundee: About 5.5 miles north-east of Dundee, on minor roads east of A929 at Inveraldie or west B978, south of Sweet Burn, at Gagie House.

Private NO 448376 OS: 54 * Map: 8, no: 192**

Gagie House consists of a small rectangular 17th-century tower house of two storeys, which was later altered and extended into a T-plan mansion. The walls are harled and whitewashed, and two bartizans crown one gable. The pitch of the roof has been changed, and windows have been sealed or enlarged.

The house has been greatly altered inside to join up with the more modern additions.

The lands originally belonged to the Oliver family, but were sold to the Guthries in 1610, who probably built the original house. The house and extensions have been restored, and the house is still occupied.

Galdenoch Castle

Galloway: About 6 miles west and north of Stranraer, on minor road south of B738 0.5 miles from junction with B7043, at Meikle Galdenoch.

Ruin or site NW 974633 OS: 82 ** Map: 1, no: 1

Galdenoch Castle is a ruined 16th-century L-plan tower house. It consists of a main block of three storeys and an attic, and a wing which rises a storey higher. A round bartizan crowns one corner, and the gables have been corbiestepped. The house is dated 1547, and stands next to the farm.

The entrance, in the re-entrant angle, leads to the main stair and into the vaulted basement. The hall, on the first floor, has a large fireplace. A very narrow turnpike stair climbs to the floors above.

Galdenoch Castle was built by Gilbert Agnew of Lochnaw, who was killed at the Battle of Pinkie in 1547. The family were ruined supporting the Covenanters, for which they had been heavily fined.

The castle was reputed to have been haunted at one time, the spirit seeming to enjoy grabbing old women. The ghost is said to have been exorcised by the mighty singing of a priest.

Other refs: Caldenoch Castle

Gallanach Castle

Argyll & Dunbartonshire: About 3.5 miles south-west of Oban, on minor roads west of A816 in Oban, just east of the Sound of Kerrera, at or near Gallanach.

Private NM 827260 [?] OS: 49 ** Map: 5, no: 60

Site of castle, probably of the MacDougalls.

Other refs: Dun Gallanach

Galdenoch Castle

Galloway House

Galloway: About 15 miles south of Newton Stewart, on minor road south of B7004, Garlieston.

Private NX 478453 OS: 83 * Map: 1, no: 80**

Commanding fine views over Wigtown Bay and the Solway Firth, Galloway House dates from 1740 and is a large plain mansion with projecting wings. The property was owned by the Stewart Earls of Galloway, descended from Stewart of Bonkyl. The family were made Lord Garlies in 1607, then Earls of Galloway in 1623.

The gardens, created in 1740 by Lord Garlies, are currently under restoration but are open to the public.

OPEN: Gardens open Mar-Oct, daily 9.00-17.00; house not open.

Parking. £.

Tel: 01988 600680

Gallowhill

Renfrewshire: About 1 mile south of Renfrew, on minor roads just east of A741, east of White Cart Water, near Arkleston Road, at Gallowhill.

Private NS 499650 [?] OS: 64 * Map: 3, no: 207

Gallowhill, a 16th-century dwelling or fortified house of the Hamiltons, was replaced by a mansion of 1867. It had passed to the Cochrane Earls of Dundonald by the middle of the 17th century. There are no remains.

Gamelshiel Castle

Lothians: About 3.5 miles north and west of Cranshaws, on footpath north of B6355 at Milknowe, about 0.5 miles north of Whiteadder Reservoir.

Ruin or site NT 649648 OS: 67 ** Map: 4, no: 221

Little remains of a keep of the 14th or 15th century.

Gamescleuch Tower

Borders: About 0.5 miles east of Ettrick, on minor road south of B709, just south of the Ettrick Water.

Ruin or site NT 284147 OS: 79 ** Map: 2, no: 72

Not much survives of Gamescleuch Tower, except part of the vaulted basement and the hall on the first floor. There was a stair in a small tower projecting from one side.

It was a property of the Scotts of Tushielaw until 1530, but passed to the Scotts of Thirlestane. The tower was built for Simon Scott at the end of the 16th century, but is said to have never been occupied as his step-mother poisoned him on the eve of his marriage.

Garden Tower *see* Tower of Garden

Gardyne Castle

Angus & Dundee: About 7 miles north-west of Arbroath, on minor road south of A932 at Pitmuies or north-west of B961, 1 mile south-west of Friockheim, at Gardyne.

Private NO 574488 OS: 54 ** Map: 8, no: 240**

Gardyne Castle is an extended 16th-century tower house, part of which dates from the 14th century, but the tower itself was built in 1468. A round stair-tower, corbelled out to square and crowned by a watch-chamber, now stands in the middle of one front. Two corbelled-out and crenellated bartizans, with conical roofs, top two corners. The walls are pierced by shot-holes.

The old part of the house has been very little altered. The basement is vaulted, and the hall is on the first floor.

The property belonged to the Gardynes of Leys, who feuded for years with the neighbouring Guthries. A marriage between the families in 1558 produced a son, but he was stabbed to death by a Gardyne cousin. Patrick Gardyne was slain in 1578 by William Guthrie, and in 1588 the Gardynes slew a Guthrie chief. Two years later the Guthries fell upon the Gardyne family and murdered their chief and others. Both families were forfeited by James VI, losing their lands, but while the Guthries recovered theirs, the Gardyne family never did.

By 1682 Gardyne had been acquired by James Lyle of Dysart, and the family remained in possession until the 20th century. The building has been renovated, is in good condition, and still occupied.

Gardyne Castle

Gargunnock House

Stirlingshire & Clackmannan: About 5 miles west of Stirling, on minor roads south of A811, about 0.5 miles east of village of Gargunnock.

Private NS 715944 OS: 57 * Map: 6, no: 57**

Gargunnock House incorporates a 16th-century L-plan tower house of three storeys and an attic. To this has been added wings and extensions, to both ends, in the 17th century and later. The old part is crowned by one bartizan. Nothing remains of a courtyard and moat. The tower may include older work.

The original entrance was in the re-entrant angle, but this has been sealed and harled over. The basement is vaulted.

William Wallace drove the English from a castle here, Gargunnock Peel, but there is no trace of this stronghold. Gargunnock was a property of the Setons in 1460, but passed to the Erskine Earls of Mar, who added to the castle after 1624. By 1740, Colonel Campbell of Ardkinglas (Glentirran?), Governor of Stirling Castle, had acquired the property. It was sold to the Stirlings at the end of the 18th century, who still held it in the 20th century. It is still occupied.

Garleton Castle

Lothians: About 1.5 miles north of Haddington, to south of B1343, 1.5 miles west of Athelstaneford, just north of the Garleton Hills.

Private NT 509767 OS: 66 ** Map: 4, no: 184

Garleton Castle is a 16th-century courtyard castle, once consisting of three blocks enclosed by a curtain wall. The main L-plan block is mostly gone, and had two

projecting wings. One of the other blocks was made into farm cottages, while the last is still almost entire. This rectangular block of two storeys and a garret has corbiestepped gables, and a projecting round stair-tower. The walls are pierced by gunloops.

The vaulted basement contained a kitchen, with a wide arched fireplace, and another chamber. The building has been very altered inside.

Parts of the curtain wall and a round tower survive.

Garleton was the property of the Lindsays. Sir David Lindsay of the Mount, the famous 16th-century playwright who wrote 'The Satire of the Three Estates', is thought to have been born here. Garleton passed to the Towers of Inverleith, who sold it to the Setons.

The building was said to be haunted by the apparition of a man at one time, and the sounds of heavy footsteps have reputedly also been heard.

Garlies Castle

Galloway: About 2.5 miles north-east of Newton Stewart, on minor road and rough track north of A714, short distance north of Peat Rig Strand.
Ruin or site   NX 422692   OS: 83   **   Map: 1, no: 63
Garlies Castle consists of a 14th-century courtyard castle, with a ruined 15th-century keep, and the overgrown remains of ranges of buildings. Little remains of the keep, except the vaulted basement with a lobby leading to a small guardroom, a turnpike stair, and two cellars. There was also a pit-prison. The hall fireplace has been reset in the wine-cellar.

Garlies was held by the Stewarts from 1263 until the 20th century. They were descended from Alexander, High Steward of Scotland in 1263, and made Earls of Galloway in the 1670s.

Garmore *see* Maiden Castle

Garnieston Castle

Banff & Buchan: About 3 miles north of Turriff, near A947, about 1 mile south of Castle of King Edward, at or near Plaidy.
Ruin or site   NJ 734551 [?]   OS: 29   *   Map: 10, no: 234
Site of castle of the Delgarno family.

Garoch Castle *see* Tulloch Castle

Garrion Tower

Lanarkshire & Glasgow area: About 2.5 miles south of Wishaw, on minor roads south of the A71, on the north bank of the River Clyde, at Garrion.
Ruin or site   NS 797511   OS: 64   **   Map: 3, no: 375
Garrion Tower is a small 16th-century L-plan tower house of three storeys and a garret, to which a large modern mansion has been added. The main block is taller than the stair-wing. The walls are pierced by small windows, where original, and shot-holes.

The original entrance was in the re-entrant angle, and led to the vaulted basement. The hall was on the first floor, while the floors above were occupied by private chambers.

The property was held by the Bishops of Glasgow, then the Forest family. In the 16th century it passed by marriage to Sir James Hamilton of Finnart, who may have built the tower, then to the Hamiltons of Garrion. The building is in good condition, and still occupied.

Garrison of Inversnaid *see* Inversnaid

Garryhorn

Ayrshire: About 3 miles north of Maybole, on minor roads west of B7024, at Garryhorn.
Ruin or site   NS 296138   OS: 70   *   Map: 3, no: 73
Site of castle, a vestige of which survived in the 19th century, although nothing apparently remains. It was used by Sir Robert Grierson of Lagg towards the end of the 17th century when persecuting Covenanters.

Garscadden Castle

Lanarkshire & Glasgow area: About 1.5 miles south-west of Bearsden, on minor road north of A82, in Drumchapel, 0.5 miles north of Garscadden Road, at Garscadden House.
Ruin or site   NS 522710   OS: 64   **   Map: 3, no: 232
Garscadden Castle or Peel consisted of a 15th-century castle, which was incorporated into the large 17th- and 18th-century castellated mansion. The mansion was destroyed by fire in 1959 and has been demolished.

Garscadden was a property of the Flemings until 1369, then the Erskines until 1444, then the Galbraiths of Gartconnel until 1571. It passed to the Colquhouns of Camstraddan around 1664, then in the 18th century was held by the Colquhouns of Killermont, who extended the mansion.

Around the end of the 18th century, the laird of Garscadden was attending a drinking party at Law when another reveller mentioned how pale Garscadden appeared. Their host told him that Garscadden had been dead for two hours, but he had not mentioned it for spoiling the party. This event is reportedly the origin of the phrase 'as gash as Garscadden', meaning deathly pale.

Gartartan Castle

Stirlingshire & Clackmannan: About 2 miles south of Aberfoyle, on minor road west of A81, just north of Gartmore House, at Gartartan Castle.
Ruin or site   NS 530978   OS: 57   **   Map: 6, no: 15
Gartartan Castle is a ruined 16th-century Z-plan tower house, consisting of a rectangular main block and two round towers at opposite corners. Both had corbelled-out stair-turrets, one containing a wide turnpike stair from the entrance to the hall on the first floor. Not much remains of the chambers above the hall.

The property belonged to the Lyles, but passed to the MacFarlanes in 1531, who built the castle. It was allowed to decay after it passed to the Grahams of Gartmore, who had moved to Gartmore House by 1780, although Gartartan may have been partly habitable until the 19th century. The Grahams sold Gartmore in the 20th century.
Other refs: Gartmore

Gartconnel Castle

Lanarkshire & Glasgow area: In Bearsden, near junction of A810 with A809, probably in Bearsden Academy grounds, at Gartconnel.
Ruin or site   NS 537732   OS: 64   *   Map: 3, no: 242
Site of a 14th-century castle of the Galbraiths of Culcreuch, of which only a ditch survives.

Garterton *see* Carterton

Garth Castle

Perth & Kinross: About 6 miles west of Aberfeldy, on minor roads west of B846 at Keltneyburn, just north of burn from Coire Pheiginn, at Garth.
Private   NN 764504   OS: 52   *   Map: 8, no: 12**
Standing on a steep crag, Garth Castle is a plain 14th-century keep, square in plan, with a flush parapet crowning two walls.

The entrance, at ground level, has a strong iron yett. The stair climbs, within the thickness of the walls, up to parapet level. The basement is vaulted and lit by slits. The hall, on the first floor, was also vaulted at one time, as was the storey above.

The castle was built by Alexander Stewart, the Wolf of Badenoch, Lord of Badenoch and Earl of Buchan, 4th son of Robert II. He torched Elgin Cathedral and town, as well as Forres, after being excommunicated by the Bishop of Elgin for forcing marriage upon his wife, the Countess of Buchan, then deserting her. He died here in 1396, and is buried in Dunkeld Cathedral.

In 1502 Nigel Stewart of Garth attacked nearby Weem Castle, burned it, and took Sir Robert Menzies prisoner. Stewart put Menzies in the vaulted dungeon at Garth, threatening to have him killed unless he signed away some of his lands. Stewart was nearly executed for the crime, only the intervention of the Earl of Atholl saving him. Stewart was later suspected of murdering his wife, Mariota, and imprisoned in Garth until his death in 1554. The castle is said to be haunted by the ghost of Mariota.

The property then passed to the Stewarts of Drumcharry. The castle was aban-

doned about the middle of the 18th century, and became ruinous. It was partly restored in 1880, and again in the 1960s. It is occupied.
Other refs: Caisteal a Cuilean Curta

Garthland Castle

Galloway: About 3.5 miles south of Stranraer, on minor roads west of A716, just west of the Garthland Burn, at or near Garthland Mains.
Ruin or site   NX 077554   OS: 82   *   Map: 1, no: 12
Site of 13th-century castle of the MacDowalls of Garthland, demolished about 1803 or 1840 to build a farm. It consisted of square tower, which rose to about 45 feet, and other buildings.

Gartincaber House

Stirlingshire & Clackmannan: About 2 miles south-west of Doune, on minor road just south of B826, about 0.75 miles west of Loch Watston, at Gartincaber.
Private   NN 698001   OS: 57   *   Map: 6, no: 54
Gartincaber House, a late 17th-century mansion altered in the late 18th century and extended in 1820 and 1843, incorporates part of a tower house or castle.

Gartlea

Lanarkshire & Glasgow: About 1 mile south of Airdrie, on minor roads west of A73 or east of B802, at Gartlea.
Ruin or site   NS 765648 [?]   OS: 64   *   Map: 3, no: 364
Possible site of a 16th-century castle of the Crawfords of Rochsolloch.

Gartly Castle

Aberdeen & Gordon: About 4 miles south of Huntly, on minor roads east of A97, 1 mile north-east of village of Gartly, east of Water of Bogie, at or near Mains of Gartly.
Ruin or site   NJ 534335 [?]   OS: 29   *   Map: 10, no: 125
Nothing remains of Gartly Castle, a 15th-century castle with a keep, which was defended by a deep ditch.
   The Barclays held the lands from the 12th until the 16th century. Mary, Queen of Scots, stayed here in October 1562 before her forces went on to defeat the Gordons at the Battle of Corrichie. The remains were finally removed around 1975.
Other refs: Mains of Gartly

Gartmore *see* Gartartan Castle

Gartness Castle

Stirlingshire & Clackmannan: About 2 miles south-east of Drymen, on minor road west of A81, south of the Endrick Water, at or near Gartness.
Ruin or site   NS 502865   OS: 57   *   Map: 6, no: 12
Standing above a river, nothing remains of Gartness Castle except a mound. A date stone with 1574 survived at Gartness Mill. The lands were held by the Napiers from 1495.
   Nearby is a waterfall on the Endrick Water known as 'Pots of Gartness.'

Gartsherrie House

Lanarkshire & Glasgow: To north of Coatbridge, on minor roads west of B804 or north of A89, east of Drumpellier Country Park, at Gartsherrie.
Ruin or site   NS 726659   OS: 64   *   Map: 3, no: 337
Site of castle, which was probably replaced by Gartsherrie House, itself demolished.
   Gartsherrie was a property of the Colt family from the 14th century, but in the 19th century passed to Whitelaws. The mineral rights, however, were sold to the Bairds who developed many furnaces for producing iron here, the last of which closed in 1967. The family had apparently been quite sharp in their practices. The site of the castle is now occupied by a container base.

Gartshore House

Lanarkshire & Glasgow: About 1.5 miles east of Kirkintilloch, on minor roads south of B8048, 1.5 miles west of Drumgrew Bridge, at Gartshore.
Ruin or site   NS 692737   OS: 64   *   Map: 3, no: 324
Site of castle. Gartshore House was a 17th-century mansion, which consisted of a

double-tenement block of two storeys and an attic with other additions. It was set in fine surrounding woodland, but completely demolished in the 20th century.
   The lands were a property of the Hamiltons, but by 1579 had passed to the Gartshore family, then in the 18th century to the Starks of Auchinvole, and by the end of the 19th to the Whitelaws of Gartsherrie.

Garvie Castle

Argyll & Dunbartonshire: About 10 miles south-west of Strachur on Cowal, on minor road east of A886, east of River Ruel, at or near Garvie.
Ruin or site   NS 035903 [?]   OS: 55   *   Map: 5, no: 99
Site of 16th-century castle of the Campbell Earls of Argyll.

Garvock Hill

Fife: About 1 mile east of Dunfermline Abbey, south of A907, Garvock Hill.
Ruin or site   NT 105875   OS: 65   *   Map: 7, no: 16
Site of castle and large mansion. In 1785 a strong wall survived as well as a round tower with loops. It may have already been abandoned in the middle of the 17th century, and nothing remains.
   The lands apparently belonged to the Wellwood family, but they moved to a house in Maygate, Dunfermline.

Gascon Hall

Perth & Kinross: About 4 miles north-east of Auchterarder, on minor roads east of B8062 at Kinkell Bridge, just north of River Earn, at or near Orchard, at Gascon Hall.
Ruin or site   NN 986175   OS: 58   *   Map: 8, no: 49
Site of 13th-century castle, little of which remains.
   It was a property of the Oliphants. William Wallace hid here during the Wars of Independence. Sir William Oliphant held Stirling Castle against Edward I and the English in 1304. One of the family was killed at the Battle of Flodden in 1513, while another was captured after the Battle of Solway Moss in 1542.
   The Oliphants of Gask were Jacobites, and fought in the Risings of 1689, 1715 and 1745. Bonnie Prince Charlie is said to have visited, and the house was torched by Hanoverian troops in 1746. Carolina Oliphant, Lady Nairne, the well-known song-writer was born here.
   The nearby house of Gask [NN 995189] was built in 1801. The Oliphants sold Gask in the 20th century, and moved to Ardblair.
Other refs: Gask House; Old House of Gask

Gask House

Aberdeen & Gordon: About 2 miles south of Turriff, on minor roads west of A947 or south of B9024 just west of junction with A947, north of Burn of Gask, at or near Gask.
Ruin or site   NJ 730472 [?]   OS: 29   *   Map: 10, no: 228
Site of castle or old house, which was said to have dated from the 14th century. It was demolished around 1950.
   It was a property of the Forbes family, but passed to the Duff Earls of Fife in the 19th century.

Gask House *see* Gascon Hall

Gateshaw *see* Corbet Tower

Gauldwell Castle

Moray: About 3.5 miles north and west of Dufftown, on foot south of A95, north of River Fiddich, south of Easter Gauldwell, east of Wester Gauldwell.

Ruin or site NJ 311452 OS: 28 * Map: 10, no: 59

Little remains of Gauldwell Castle, a large 13th-century castle of enclosure. It consisted of a curtain wall enclosing a courtyard, with a hall block, and was altered and extended in later centuries.

It was held by Freskin, who was Flemish. His descendants were the Murrays of Abercairny. The castle was a property of the Earls of Moray. Mary, Queen of Scots, stayed here in 1562.

Other refs: Boharm Castle; Bucharin Castle

Geanies Castle

Ross & Cromarty: About 8 miles east and south of Tain, on minor roads south of B9165, just west of the sea, 2.5 miles north-east of Hilton of Cadboll, 0.25 miles east of Mains of Geanies.

Ruin or site NH 894798 [?] OS: 21 * Map: 9, no: 139

Site of castle, nothing of which remains.

It was a property of the MacLeods of Geanies, but by 1624 had passed to the Sinclairs. It was sold in 1838 to Kenneth Murray, a merchant from Tain. Geanies House appears to date from no later than the 18th century, and replaced the castle.

Gedeleth *see* Broomhall

Geilston House

Argyll & Dunbartonshire: About 3.5 miles west and north of Dumbarton, near A814 to west of Cardross, north side of River Clyde, at Geilston.

NTS NS 339783 [?] OS: 63 ** Map: 5, no: 140

Geilston is a two-storey L-plan house, which may incorporate work from the 15th century, although it appears to mostly date from the 17th century and later. The walls are harled, and the house has corbiestepped gables. It is said to have been thatched until the beginning of the 19th century. There is a fine walled garden as well as a wooded glen.

It was a property of the Woods family in the 16th century, who had a tower here, but passed to the Henrys by the 19th century. The gardens have been cared for by The National Trust for Scotland since 1983.

OPEN: Garden open Apr-Oct, daily 9.30-17.00; house not open.

£.

Tel: 01389 841867

Email: information@nts.org.uk Web: nts.org.uk

Gelston Castle

Galloway: About 2.5 miles south and east of Castle Douglas, on minor roads south of B727 at village of Gelston or west of B736, at Gelston Castle.

Private NX 773577 OS: 84 * Map: 1, no: 125

Gelston Castle, a mansion built in the 19th century for the Douglases, apparently has no older origins.

There is a motte nearby at Ingleston [NX 775579]. During excavation the former buildings on it were found to have been torched, probably in the second half of the 12th century when there was unrest in Galloway.

Other refs: Ingleston

Giffen Castle

Ayrshire: About 4 miles south-east of Beith, just north of B706, about 0.5 miles north-east of Burnhouse.

Ruin or site NS 377507 OS: 63 ** Map: 3, no: 128

Little survives of Giffen Castle, a square 15th-century keep, which was altered in later centuries.

It was a property of the Montgomerys of Eglinton. The castle was abandoned in 1722, most of it collapsed in 1838, and it was demolished in 1920.

Giffnock Castle *see* Druid's Temple Hill

Gight Castle

Aberdeen & Gordon: About 4 miles east of Fyvie, on minor road south of B9005, just north of River Ythan, 1 mile south of Cottown, south of Mains of Gight, at Gight.

Ruin or site NJ 827392 OS: 29 * Map: 10, no: 277**

Pronounced 'Gecht', Gight Castle is a ruined 16th-century L-plan tower house with ranges of outbuildings of a later date. The basement of the tower is vaulted, a long passage running through the building to a turnpike stair. The hall was on the first floor.

The Gordons built the castle in the 1570s, and were an unruly bunch. The 1st Laird, William Gordon, was killed at the Battle of Flodden in 1513. The 6th laird broke his sword across the head of Laird of Leask, harassed his second wife's mother to change her will in his favour (at pain of death), and tried to extort money out of his first wife's brother. The 7th laird was a tax collector, but after virtually plundering the town of Banff kept all the money.

Catherine Gordon married John Byron, but in 1787 had to sell Gight to pay off his gambling debts. Their son was the poet Lord Byron. The Gordon Earl of Aberdeen acquired the castle.

Ghostly pipes can reputedly be heard from a piper sent to explore an passage under the castle, but who never returned, and was never seen again.

Other refs: Formartine Castle

Gilbertfield Castle

Lanarkshire & Glasgow area: About 2.5 miles north of East Kilbride, on minor roads south of A724, south east of Cambuslang, north of Dechmont Hill, at Gilbertfield.

Ruin or site NS 653588 OS: 64 ** Map: 3, no: 306

Gilbertfield Castle is a ruined 16th-century L-plan tower house of three storeys and an attic. Although there is no parapet, two bartizans crown the corner, and the walls are pierced by shot-holes.

The entrance, in the re-entrant angle, led to a broad turnpike stair and to the vaulted basement. The basement contains a kitchen, with a large fireplace, and a wine-cellar with a small stair to the hall above in the main block. The hall was on the first floor with private chambers on the floors above.

Gilbertfield was a property of the Hamiltons, one of whom was the poet William Hamilton of Gilbertfield around the turn of the 18th century. Hamilton was responsible for the translation of Blind Harry's epic poem 'Sir William Wallace'. The castle is not in a good state of repair: one gable fell down about 1950 and is reduced to the ground.

Gilberton *see* Brunstane House

Gilkerscleugh House

Lanarkshire & Glasgow area: About 2 miles west of Abington, on minor road south of M74 at Duneaton Bridge to B740 at Crawfordjohn, at or near Gilkerscleugh Mains.

Ruin or site NS 900236 [?] OS: 72 * Map: 3, no: 414

Site of 17th-century L-plan tower house of three storeys, altered and modernised, but demolished in the 20th century. A round stair-tower projected from one corner, and the house had corbelled gables and small turrets.

The lands were held by the Hamiltons from 1598 until the 19th century. The house was demolished in the 1950s after a fire.

Gillbank House

Lanarkshire & Glasgow: About 2 miles south of Strathaven, on minor roads west of A726 or east of A723, south of Avon Water, at or near Gillbank.

Ruin or site NS 706426 OS: 71 * Map: 3, no: 327

Site of tower house, the last remains of which were removed in 1852.

The lands were held by the Auchinlecks. One of the family is said to have been active with William Wallace: they reputedly raided Lanark from here.

Gillesbie Tower

Dumfriesshire: About 7 miles north-east of Lockerbie, on minor road north of
B723, just west of the Dryfe Water, about 0.3 miles north-west of Gillesbie.
Ruin or site NY 171919 OS: 79 ** Map: 1, no: 255
Not much remains of Gillesbie Tower, a 16th-century tower house of the Grahams,
except the basement and earthworks.

Gilmilnscroft

Ayrshire: About 4 miles east and south of Mauchline, on minor roads south of
B713 or B743, south of River Ayr, 0.5 miles south of Sorn, at Gilmilnscroft.
Private NS 556255 OS: 71 ** Map: 3, no: 251
Gilmilnscroft is a T-plan house, which dates from the 17th century and may incor-
porate a tower house. It was a property of the Farquhars at the end of the 19th
century, restored in 1968, and still occupied.

Gilmour Castle

Dumfriesshire: About 2 miles east of Sanquhar, on foot west of B797 1 mile
north-east of junction with A76, west side of Menneck Water, just south of
Auchengruith.
Ruin or site NS 822093 OS: 78 * Map: 1, no: 147
Site of castle.
Other refs: Castle Gilmour

Gilnockie Tower *see* Hollows Tower

Gilnockie Tower

Dumfriesshire: About 2 miles north of Canonbie, on minor road east of A7 at
Hollows, just south of the River Esk, near Hollows Tower.
Ruin or site NY 386782 OS: 85 * Map: 1, no: 324
Little survives of Gilnockie Tower, a 16th-century tower house.
  It was a stronghold of the unruly Armstrong clan, who were said to be able to
muster 3000 men. The tower was built in 1518, but burned by Lord Dacre, the
English Warden of the West March, in 1523. In 1530 Johnnie Armstrong and 50
followers were summarily hanged on the spot, without trial, by James V after being
tricked into joining the king on a hunting party, the event recorded in the old
ballad.

Gilston Peel

Borders: About 7 miles east and south of Gorebridge, on B6368 between A7 and
A68 at Soutra, north of the Armet Water, at Gilston.
Ruin or site NT 443562 OS: 66 ** Map: 2, no: 117
Not much remains of a 16th-century tower house, which has been incorporated
into a later building.

Girnigoe Castle

Sutherland & Caithness: About 3 miles north of Wick, on minor roads and
footpath east of A9 in Wick, 0.5 miles west of Noss Head, at Castle Sinclair/Castle
Girnigoe.
Ruin or site ND 379549 OS: 12 * Map: 12, no: 67**
Standing on a rocky promontory in the sea, Girnigoe Castle and Castle Sinclair
were two separate fortresses, although they stood very close together. Not much
remains of Castle Sinclair.
  Girnigoe Castle is a 15th-century altered keep, and consists of a main block and
two projecting wings, creating a U-plan building. It had a walled courtyard, within
which Castle Sinclair was built, which had a gatehouse with a drawbridge to span a
deep ditch cutting off the promontory.
  The main block of Girnigoe is of five storeys but, due to the uneven level of the
ground, the main block basement is a storey lower than the wings. The entrance
was in the stair-wing. The vaulted basement contained the kitchen, with a small
stair up to the hall above. The hall, on the first floor, has been a fine chamber, and
has a decorated oriel window.
  In 1472 the Sinclair Earls of Orkney were forced to resign the earldom and were
given Caithness as compensation. The 2nd Earl, William Sinclair, built a castle here
but died at the Battle of Flodden in 1513. In 1571 the 4th Earl had John, Master of

Caithness, his son and heir, imprisoned in the dungeons for seven years. The Master was fed on salted beef, and denied water so that he died mad with thirst.
  The 5th Earl built Castle Sinclair, but feuded with the Earl of Sutherland, and put
down a rebellion in Orkney in 1615. Cromwell had the castle garrisoned in the
1650s. The 6th Earl had huge debts to Campbell of Glenorchy, and the earldom
was claimed by the Campbells. In 1679 the castle was besieged and captured by
Sinclair of Keiss, who also seized the earldom. The Sinclairs were brought to battle
at Altimarlech, where they were slaughtered in such numbers that the Campbells
reportedly could cross the river without getting their feet wet. However, the Sinclairs recovered the earldom in 1681. The castle was damaged during the attack,
and not reused. The property passed to the Dunbars of Hempriggs, but was sold
back to the Sinclairs about 1950, and the castle is now held in trust.
  There is a car park and faint path, but the ruins and cliffs are dangerous and great
care should be taken if visiting.
Other refs: Castle Girnigoe; Castle Sinclair

Glackingdaline Castle *see* Dun Ban, Ulva

Gladstone Castle

Lanarkshire & Glasgow: About 3.5 miles south-east of Carnwath, on minor roads
south of A721 or north of B7016, at Gladstone.
Ruin or site NT 030428 OS: 72 * Map: 3, no: 446
Site of castle, remains of which survived in the 19th century, although the site was
occupied by a farm building in 1911. The castle had a square tower, and two stones
with the dates of 1619 and 1778 survive and are incorporated into a barn.
  Gladstone or Easter Gladstones was a property of the Gladstone family from the
13th until the end of the 17th century. The family then removed to Biggar, and
were ancestors of William Ewart Gladstone, who was Prime Minister four times
between 1830 and 1851, and had his seat at Fasque in Kincardine.
Other refs: Easter Gladstones

Gladstone's Land, Edinburgh

Edinburgh: 477b Lawnmarket, High Street, Edinburgh.
NTS NT 255736 OS: 66 * Map: 4, no: 96**
Gladstone's Land, built in 1620 and retaining an arcaded front, is a typical six-storey
tenement and was the home of prosperous Edinburgh merchant, Thomas Glad-
stone. There are unusual tempera paintings, and the rooms and ground-floor shop
are furnished and equipped as they would have been in the 17th century.
**OPEN: Open Apr-Oct, Mon-Sat 10.00-17.00, Sun 14.00-17.00; last
admission 16.30.**
*Explanatory displays. Gift shop. Tours for the blind by appt. Disabled access to ground
floor. Parking nearby. £.*
Tel: 0131 226 5856 Fax: 0131 226 4851
Email: information@nts.org.uk Web: nts.org.uk

Glamis Castle

Angus & Dundee: About 5.5 miles south-west of Forfar, just off A94, 1 mile north
of Glamis village, south of the Dean Water, at Glamis Castle.
Private NO 387481 OS: 54 *** Map: 8, no: 169**
One of the most famous, and reputedly haunted, castles in Scotland, Glamis Castle
consists of a greatly extended 14th-century keep. It was altered to an L-plan in the

Glamis Castle

16th century, and has a large round stair-tower in the re-entrant angle. The keep was heightened, and the battlements were replaced with bartizans and dormers. It was extended again, with lower wings and round towers, in the 17th, 18th and 19th centuries.

The keep has three vaulted storeys with thick walls.

The original kitchen was in the vaulted basement, with a huge fireplace and well. A lesser hall, also vaulted, was on the first floor, while the great hall, a fine chamber with a large fireplace and magnificent plaster ceiling, is on the second. There are many private chambers on the floors above. There is a wide turnpike stair rising 143 steps from the basement to the battlements.

Malcolm II is said to have been slain here in 1034, although if he was it was in an earlier building. Glamis is traditionally associated with Macbeth, and in the old keep is 'Duncan's Hall', but any connection is probably only based on Shakespeare's play.

In the 15th century the lands were held by Sir John Lyon, Chancellor of Scotland, who married a daughter of Robert II. The family were made Lords Glamis in 1445.

Janet Douglas was the beautiful widow of John Lyon 6th Lord Glamis and, unfortunately for her, sister of the Earl of Angus. This meant that she was hated by James V. James was ill treated and imprisoned in his youth by the Earl of Angus, who had married his mother, Margaret Tudor, after the death of James IV at Flodden in 1513. James's spite was extended to members of the Earl of Angus's family, and Janet was accused of both trying to poison the king as well as of a false charge of witchcraft. The poor woman had no way of escaping James's wrath, and was burned to death on Castle Hill in Edinburgh on 3 December 1537.

Her apparition, the 'Grey Lady of Glamis' is said to haunt the building, and has been seen in the chapel and clock tower.

Mary, Queen of Scots, stayed here in 1562. In 1578 the 8th Lord was killed in a brawl with the Lindsays in Stirling, and his brother was one of those involved in the kidnapping of the young James VI in the 'Raid of Ruthven'. The castle is still held by the Lyons, now Earls of Strathmore and Kinghorne, and the present Queen Mother comes from this family.

The ghost of Alexander Lindsay, 4th Earl of Crawford, 'Earl Beardie', is said to haunt a walled-up room where he played cards with the devil. Here he is compelled to play until the 'day of doom', and he was certainly a cruel and ruthless character. Indeed, one story is that his mother smothered her own brother so that he would succeed to the Earldom of Crawford. It is said that Crawford's ghost can also be seen at the castle of Lordscairnie, in Fife, on Hogmanay.

Other stories of ghosts and beasts abound and are widely reported, including that of the spirit of a little African boy, which along with many other tales appear to have no foundation.

OPEN: Open Apr-Oct, daily 10.30-17.30; Jul-Aug, from 10.00; last admission 16.45; at other time groups by appt.

Collections of historic pictures, porcelain and furniture. Guided tours. Three additional exhibition rooms. Four shops. Licensed restaurant. WC. Picnic area. Play park. Extensive park, pinetum, nature trail and garden. Disabled access to gardens and ground floor; WC. Car and coach parking. Group concessions. £££.

Tel: 01307 840393   Fax: 01307 840733
Email: glamis@great-houses-scotland.co.uk
Web: www.great-houses-scotland.co.uk/glamis

Glamis Tower *see* Kinghorn Castle

Glammis Castle *see* Kinghorn Castle

Glanderston Castle
Renfrewshire: About 2 miles south of Barrhead, on minor roads south of A736, north of Glanderston Dam, at or near Glanderston Mains.
Ruin or site   NS 499563 [?]   OS: 64   *   Map: 3, no: 206
Site of castle, replaced by a T-plan mansion of 1697, which was then used as a farmhouse. The mansion incorporated the foundations of the castle.

It was a property of the Stewart Earls of Lennox in 1507, but passed by marriage to the Mures of Caldwell. A long feud was fought regarding the property between the Mures and the Maxwells of Nether Pollok.

Glasclune Castle
Perth & Kinross: About 2 miles north-west of Blairgowrie, on minor road north of A923 at Kinloch, north of the Lornty Burn, at Glasclune.
Ruin or site   NO 154470   OS: 53   **   Map: 8, no: 102
Once a place of some strength, Glasclune Castle is a ruined 16th-century Z-plan castle, comprising a main block, now very ruined, with a tower, containing a kitchen, and a round tower at opposite corners. Shot-holes pierce the walls below the windows and corbelling, for a bartizan, survives at one corner.

Glasclune was a property of the Blairs, who feuded for years with the Herons of Drumlochy – the family that is, not the birds. In the 19th century most of the castle remained, but it is now very ruined.

229

Glasgoego *see* Kinellar House

Glasgow Castle

Lanarkshire & Glasgow area: In Glasgow, just north-west of Glasgow Cathedral, on minor roads south or east of A8.
Ruin or site NS 602655 OS: 64 * Map: 3, no: 276
Almost nothing remains of a 12th-century castle.

It was a royal castle in 1258, but it had become the Bishop's residence by the 14th century. It was recaptured from the English by William Wallace in 1296, but garrisoned by Edward I of England in 1301. Bishop Cameron built a large keep of five storeys in the 15th century, and the castle was further extended by the addition of a courtyard and a gatehouse with round towers. The castle changed hands six times in various conflicts between 1513 and the final defeat in 1568 of the Hamiltons and other families fighting on behalf of Mary, Queen of Scots. The castle was abandoned as a residence in the 17th century, but then used as a prison. It was cleared for the building of the Royal Infirmary in 1789. A stone, marking the site, is in the grounds of the infirmary.

The nearby cathedral is the only Scottish medieval cathedral to have survived the Reformation – St Magnus Cathedral in Kirkwall was built when Orkney was not a part of Scotland. Some stones from the castle are on display in the crypt.
Other refs: Bishop's Castle, Glasgow; Castle of Glasgow

Glassaugh House

Banff & Buchan: About 2.5 miles south-west of Portsoy, on minor roads south of A98, near Burn of Fordyce, at or near Glassaugh.
Ruin or site NJ 558645 [?] OS: 29 * Map: 10, no: 140
Site of castle or old house. It was replaced by Glassaugh House, a now ruinous L-plan mansion of three storeys, around 1770.

Glassaugh was a property of the Abercrombies, one of whom was General Abercrombie who commanded the British forces at the Battle of Ticonderoga in 1758 against the French in Canada – and had served on the staff of the Duke of Cumberland. The property later passed to the Duffs of Glassaugh and Fetteresso, who occupied it until the 20th century. The building was used to house farm animals, and is now a shell.

Glasserton House

Galloway: About 2.5 miles south-west of Whithorn, on minor road south of junction of A747 with A746, south of Home Farm, at Glasserton.
Ruin or site NX 419377 OS: 83 * Map: 1, no: 62
Glasserton House, a mansion dating from 1780, occupies the site of a 15th-century castle, later of the Stewart Earls of Galloway, which was burned down in 1730.

Glassery Castle *see* Fincharn Castle

Glassford

Lanarkshire & Glasgow area: About 2 miles west of Stonehouse, on minor roads north of A71, just north of Glassford.
Ruin or site NS 728473 [?] OS: 64 * Map: 3, no: 339
Site of castle, the site of which appears to be occupied by housing.
Other refs: Quarter; Westquarter

Glassingall

Stirling & Clackmannanshire: About 2 miles north and east of Dunblane, on minor road east of B8033 and west of A9, at Glassingall.
Private NN 798045 [?] OS: 57 * Map: 6, no: 74
Probable site of castle. Glassingall House is a plain mid 18th-century house of two storeys, and may stand on the site. Glassingall House was a grand Gothic mansion of 1864, but it has been demolished.

The lands were a property of the Chisholms of Glassingall, but by the 19th century had passed to the Smiths, then the Wallaces. William Chisholm of Glassingall was prominent during the Reformation.

Glen Caladh Castle

Argyll & Dunbartonshire: About 3 miles north-east of Tighnabruaich on Cowal, on minor roads and foot east of A8003, on west side of Loch Ruel, on mainland above Eilean Dubh.
Ruin or site NS 000767 OS: 62 * Map: 5, no: 92
Site of castle, little or nothing of which remains, which was demolished in the 20th century. 'Calow' is marked on Blaeu's Atlas Novus map of Bute, compiled about 1590.
Other refs: Caladh Castle

Glenae Tower

Dumfriesshire: About 7 miles south-east of Thornhill, 0.5 miles north of Ae on minor roads and foot east of A701, on hillside east of Water of Ae in forest of Ae.
Ruin or site NX 984905 OS: 78 ** Map: 1, no: 191
There are some remains of a 16th-century tower house of the Dalziels. The family appear to have moved to Kirkmichael Tower, and this tower was then abandoned.

Glenane

Lanarkshire & Glasgow: About 1 mile north of Lesmahagow, on minor road east of B7078, west of River Nethan, at or near Kerse.
Ruin or site NS 812421 [?] OS: 71 * Map: 3, no: 377
Site of a tower house, which was replaced by Kerse, a mansion.

It was a property of the Weirs in 1612.

Glenapp Castle

Ayrshire: About 1.5 miles south-east of Ballantrae, on minor roads south or west of A77, 0.5 miles north-west of Smyrton, at Glenapp Castle.
Private NX 093808 OS: 76 * Map: 3, no: 8
Glenapp Castle, a very large castellated mansion, was built in 1870 by the architect David Bryce for the Hunters. It has no older origins.

Glenays Castle

Ayrshire: About 4.5 miles south-west of Ayr, near A719, near Low Glenayes.
Ruin or site NS 285180 [?] OS: 70 * Map: 3, no: 65
Site of castle, little or nothing of which remains. A farm was built on the site, but this is also gone.

The property was held by the Montgomerys of Brigend, and the Kennedys.
Other refs: Castle of Glenayes

Glenbarr Abbey

Argyll & Dunbartonshire: About 12 miles north of Campbeltown, on A83, Glenbarr.
Private NR 669365 OS: 68 * Map: 5, no: 26
Glenbarr Abbey is an 18th-century house, built in the Gothic revival style and designed by James Gillespie Graham. It has been the home of the lairds of Glenbarr since 1796. There are tours, which are conducted by the 5th laird, Angus MacAlister, who also owns the property. Items on display include china, a display of patchwork, a thimble collection, antique toys, jewellery, and gloves worn by Mary, Queen of Scots. The fine grounds feature river-side and woodland walks.
OPEN: Open Easter-Oct, daily 10.00-17.30; closed Tue.
Guided tours. Museum. Explanatory displays. Gift shop. Tearoom. Woodland and riverside walk. Picnic facilities. WC. Car and coach parking. Group concessions. £.
Tel: 01583 421247 Fax: 01583 421255
Web: www.kintyre-scotland.org.uk/glenbarr

Glenbervie House

Kincardine & Deeside: About 7 miles south-west of Stonehaven, on minor roads north of A94 to the south of Glenbervie village, north of the Bervie Water.
Private NO 769805 OS: 45 ** Map: 10, no: 251
Glenbervie House, a mansion of the 18th and 19th centuries, incorporates two large round towers, probably from a 14th-century courtyard castle, and the gable of a 17th-century tower. Both round towers have splayed gunloops.

The basement is vaulted.

Glenbervie was held by the Melville family from the 12th century. Edward I of England stayed here in 1296, and John Melville did homage like any sensible fellow would. John Melville, Sheriff of Kincardine, was murdered and boiled in a cauldron on Hill of Garvock by four local lairds, who drank some of the broth, and were afterwards outlawed. In 1468 the castle passed by marriage first to the Auchinlecks, then to the Douglases. In 1572 it was besieged by Sir Adam Gordon. Glenbervie. It was sold to the Burnets of Leys in 1675, who in turn sold it to the Nicholsons in 1721. The house is still occupied.

Glenborrodale Castle
South Highland: About 7 miles west and south of Salen, on Ardnamurchan, on minor road north of B8007, on north side of Loch Sunart, at Glenborrodale Castle.
Private   NM 620601   OS: 40   *   Map: 9, no: 17
Glenborrodale Castle is a 19th-century mansion, and has no older origins. It is now used as a hotel.
OPEN: Hotel.

Glenbuchat Castle *see* Badenyon Castle

Glenbuchat Castle
Aberdeen & Gordon: About 4.5 miles west of Kildrummy, on minor road west of A97, at meeting of River Don and Water of Buchat, at head of Glen Buchat.
His Scot   NJ 397149   OS: 37   ***   Map: 10, no: 79
Glenbuchat Castle is a roofless, but otherwise complete, late 16th-century Z-plan tower house of three storeys and a garret. It consists of a main block, with large square towers at diagonally opposite corners. In the two re-entrant angles, cor-belled out above first-floor level, are large stair-turrets. Round and square bartizans crown the corners of the tower. The hall, on the first floor, has large windows, and the walls are pierced by shot-holes. The castle is dated 1590, and had a courtyard.

The entrance is in one of the square towers from the courtyard. The basement is vaulted, and contained a kitchen, with a large fireplace, and a wine-cellar, with a small stair to the hall above. A wide stair leads to the hall, which has been subdi-vided at some time. The private chambers of the upper floors were reached by the two turret stairs.

The castle was built by the Gordons, whose earlier stronghold was at Badenyon [NJ 340190]. It was occupied by James VI's forces during the Catholic rebellion of the Gordon Earl of Huntly of 1592. Brigadier-General John Gordon of Glenbuchat fought for the Jacobites in both the 1715 and 1745 Risings, and led the Gordons and Farquharsons at the Battle of Culloden in 1746 – when aged 70. He was hunted after the battle, but managed to escape to Norway, disguised as a beggar, and died in France. The castle was a ruin by 1738, sold to the Duff Earl of Fife the same year, and replaced by Glenbuchat House [NJ 397148].
Other refs: Glenbucket Castle
OPEN: Access at all reasonable times.
Parking nearby.
Tel: 0131 668 8800   Fax: 0131 668 8888
Email: hs.explore@scotland.gov.uk   Web: www.historic-scotland.gov.uk

Glenbucket Castle *see* Glenbuchat Castle

Glencairn Castle *see* Abergairn Castle

Glencairn Castle *see* Maxwelton House

Glencassley Castle
Sutherland & Caithness: About 11 miles north-west of Invershin, on minor roads north of A837, 4 miles north and west of Invercassley, north of River Cassley, in Glencassley.
Private   NC 442078   OS: 16   *   Map: 12, no: 6
Glencassley Castle, dating from about 1860 and 1875, is a shooting lodge, and has no older origins.

Glendarroch
Argyll & Dunbartonshire: About 2 miles south and west of Lochgilphead, on minor road and foot west of A83, just north of Ardrishaig, west of Glendarroch.
Ruin or site   NR 849866   OS: 55   *   Map: 5, no: 66
Site of a castle or stronghold built within the remains of a fort, defended by gorges on two sides. There is a rock-cut ditch and the ruins of two rectangular building.
It is said to have been the refuge of a robber, and to have been used by the MacIv-ers in the 17th century.
Other refs: Robber's Den, Glendarroch; Kilduskland

Glendearg *see* Hillslap Tower

Glendevon Castle
Perth & Kinross: About 5 miles north of Dollar, on minor road north of A823, just north of the River Devon, 1 mile north-west of Glendevon, at Glendevon Castle.
Private   NN 976055   OS: 58   ***   Map: 8, no: 45
Situated on high ground, Glendevon Castle is an altered Z-plan tower house incor-porating a keep from the 15th century. It consists of a main block with square towers at diagonally opposite corners. Much of the building has been reduced in height, but one tower still rises to four storeys. A round stair-tower is capped by a conical roof.

The main entrance, at the foot at one of towers, leads to a scale-and-platt stair. The basement of the tower is vaulted, and unlit and the two chambers of the main block could not be reached from above. The hall is on the first floor.

Glendevon belonged to William, Earl of Douglas, who was treacherously mur-dered by James II at Stirling Castle in 1452, and his body tossed out of a window. The castle was rebuilt in the 16th century by the Crawford family. It passed to the Rutherfords in the 18th century, and was used as a farmhouse in the 20th century.

Glendinning Castle
Dumfriesshire: About 8 miles north and west of Langholm, on minor roads 4 miles north of B709 at Bentpath, on Megget Water, at Glendinning.
Ruin or site   NY 299965   OS: 79   *   Map: 1, no: 295
Site of castle, a vestige of which remained in 1845 although there are apparently now no remains.
It may have been a property of the Johnstones, and was held by Johnstone of Westerhall in the 19th century.

Glendivan
Dumfriesshire: About 3.5 miles north of Langholm, on minor roads and foot east of A7, east of Ewes Water, south-east of Briery Shaw, at or near Glendivan.
Ruin or site   NY 374907 [?]   OS: 79   *   Map: 1, no: 319
Site of tower house, possibly of the Armstrongs.
Other refs: Glendouin; Jingles

Glendoick House
Perth & Kinross: About 6 miles east of Perth, on minor roads north of A90, about 0.5 miles north of hamlet of Glendoick, at Glendoick House.
Private   NO 208237   OS: 58   *   Map: 8, no: 120
Glendoick House, a mansion built about 1746, incorporates part of a late 16th-

century tower. It was built by the Murrays, one of whom Sir Thomas Murray was made a Lord of Session (Glendoick) in 1674 . The property passed to the Craigies in 1726, one of whom, Robert Craigie, was lord president of the Court of Session in 1754. It is now held by the Cox family.

Glendorch Castle
Lanarkshire & Glasgow area: About 3.5 miles south of Crawfordjohn, on road and track south of B740, west of the Glendorch Burn, at Glendorch.
Ruin or site   NS 871189   OS: 71   *   Map: 3, no: 404
Not much remains of a 16th-century tower house, with a barrel-vaulted basement, and courtyard, some of which was built into a barn.
   It was a property of the Fowlis family, who were involved in mining gold and lead in the area.

Glendouin *see* Glendivan

Gleneagles Castle
Perth & Kinross: About 2.5 miles south and west of Auchterarder, on minor roads west of A823, about 0.25 miles north of Gleneagles House.
Ruin or site   NN 929093   OS: 58   **   Map: 8, no: 36
Gleneagles Castle consists of the very ruined remains of a 14th- or 15th-century keep and courtyard, with traces of other buildings. Part of the keep survives to the height of three storeys.
   The basement does not appear to have been vaulted, but contained the kitchen and three cellars. A hall, on the first floor, was vaulted, and there were probably at least two further storeys above this. There are remains of a stair in one corner.
   The property belonged to the Haldanes from the 12th century. The castle was abandoned around 1624 with the building of Gleneagles House. The family supported the Hanoverians during the Jacobite Risings, and the property passed to the Duncans in 1799.
   The 12th-century chapel was restored by General Sir Aylmer Haldane as a family war memorial in 1925.

Glenelg *see* Dun Telve

Glenelg *see* Dun Troddan

Glenelg *see* Bernera Barracks

Glenfarquhar Castle
Kincardine & Deeside: About 2 miles north of Auchenblae, on minor roads north of B966 or west of A90, just west of Mains of Glenfarquhar.
Ruin or site   NO 718804   OS: 45   *   Map: 10, no: 219
Not much remains of a castle except the ditch and some foundations. Materials from the castle were used to build Mains of Glenfarquhar around 1857, and a stone survives in the stable with the date 1674.
   The lands were a property of the Falconers.

Glengarnock Castle
Ayrshire: About 2 miles north of Kilbirnie, on minor roads north of A760, about 0.5 miles north of Blackbarn, in Glen Garnock, just east of the River Garnock.
Ruin or site   NS 311574   OS: 63   **   Map: 3, no: 86
On a strong site on a promontory by a river, Glengarnock Castle is a very ruined 15th-century keep. It has later alterations and extensions, one a vaulted kitchen, in a courtyard. The landward side was defended by a deep ditch.
   The lands were held by the de Morville family, Constables of Scotland, in the 12th and 13th centuries, then the Riddels, but passed to the Cunninghams, who held the property until the early 17th century. Mary, Queen of Scots, visited here in 1563. The castle was abandoned in the 18th century, and stripped for materials. Part of it collapsed in a storm of 1839, although the castle was consolidated in 1841.

Glengarrisdale Castle *see* Aros Castle

Glengeith
Lanarkshire & Glasgow: 0.25 miles south-west of Elvanfoot, on minor road and foot west of A702 or south of B7040, at Glengeith.
Ruin or site   NS 947166   OS: 78   **   Map: 3, no: 421
Not much remains of a small tower or bastle house, probably dating from the 16th century, which had a vaulted basement.

Glengonnar Castle
Lanarkshire & Glasgow: About 4 miles north of Leadhills, just east of B797, 0.5 miles south of Lettershaws, at Glengonnar.
Ruin or site   NS 899201   OS: 71   *   Map: 3, no: 413
Site of tower or bastle house, a property of the Bulmers who were involved in mining lead and gold.

Glengorm Castle
Argyll & Dunbartonshire: About 4 miles west and north of Tobermory, on north side of Mull, on minor road west of B882 in Tobermory, at Glengorm Castle.
Private   NM 439572   OS: 47   *   Map: 5, no: 17
Glengorm Castle, a castellated mansion of 1860, has no older origins.

Glengyle Castle
Stirling & Clackmannanshire: About 13 miles north-west of Aberfoyle, on minor roads north of B829, north end of Loch Katrine, 2.5 miles north-west of Stronachlachar, at Glengyle.
Ruin or site   NN 385135   OS: 56   *   Map: 6, no: 2
There was apparently a castle here, some remains of which survived in the 19th century. It was a property of the MacGregors. Rob Roy's father was styled 'of Glengyle'.

Glenhoul
Galloway: About 4 miles north of St John's Town of Dalry, on minor roads between A713 and B7000, east of Water of Ken, at Glenhoul.
Ruin or site   NX 608879   OS: 77   *   Map: 1, no: 98
The mansion may stand on the site of a castle.

Glenkindie House
Aberdeen & Gordon: About 3 miles south-west of Kildrummy, on minor road north of A97 at Glenkindie, north of River Don 0.5 miles east of meeting with Kindie Burn.
Private   NJ 437140   OS: 37   **   Map: 10, no: 90
The present Glenkindie House is a U-plan house. One of the wings probably dates from the 16th century, although the house was remodelled in 1741. A matching wing is 17th century, but the main block of the house dates from the 19th century, and was built on the site of the castle. The building was altered several times.
   The lands were held by the Strachans. The castle, which was built in 1595, was pillaged by Donald Farquharson of Monaltrie in 1639, then torched in 1644 by Argyll. The property later passed to the Leiths. The house was remodelled in 1785, and again in 1900.

Glenmuick *see* Knock Castle

Glenochar Castle
Lanarkshire & Glasgow area: About 2 miles south of Elvanfoot, by foot west of A702 at Glenochar, west of Daer Water, near Glenochar Burn.
Ruin or site   NS 946139 [?]   OS: 78   *   Map: 3, no: 419
Little survives of a small 16th-century tower or bastle house and courtyard, which was occupied until the middle of the 18th century. It had a vaulted basement, and there are some remains of a stair. The tower had several ancillary buildings.
   It was a property of the Bulmer family. The whole site has been excavated. A hoard of 16th-century coins was found near the tower.

Glenquiech *see* Quiech Castle

Glenrae Castle
Lanarkshire & Glasgow area: About 5 miles north and east of Sanquhar, on foot east of B740, east of burn, 0.5 miles south and west of Nether Whitecleugh, 0.5 miles NE of Glenrae Brae.
Ruin or site   NS 833185   OS: 71   *   Map: 3, no: 386
Site of castle, a vestige of which remained in the 19th century.

Glensanda Castle
South Highland: About 10 miles east of Lochaline, on rough tracks 8.5 miles east of A884 or 5 miles south of B8043, on west side Loch Linnhe, at mouth of Glensanda.
Ruin or site   NM 824469   OS: 49   **   Map: 9, no: 28
One of the most remotely situated castles in Scotland, Glensanda Castle is a small square 15th-century keep of four storeys which stands on a rock at the mouth of the loch. The few windows are small.
   The stair climbs in the thickness of the walling. The basement is not vaulted, and the hall was on the first floor. The roof and the garret storey have gone. It probably had a courtyard, the ruins of one outbuilding remaining.
   The property originally belonged to the MacMasters, but passed to the MacLeans in the 15th century. The castle was built by Ewen MacLean of Kingairloch in about 1450. Restoration is proposed.
Other refs: Caisteal Mernaig; Caisteal na Gruagaich

Glenstrae Castle
Argyll & Dunbartonshire: About 2.5 miles north-west of Dalmally, on minor roads north of B8077, north of River Strae, north of Castles Farm.
Ruin or site   NN 138296   OS: 50   *   Map: 5, no: 115
Site of castle.
   It was a property of the MacGregors of Glenstrae and Stronmilchan from the beginning of the 15th century until 1604, when the property passed to the Campbells with the proscription of the MacGregors. The castle was burned in 1611 by Sir Duncan Campbell.

Glensykeburn *see* Rusko Castle

Glentirran
Stirling & Clackmannanshire: About 1 mile east of Kippen, on minor roads south of A811, west of the bridge of Boquhan Burn, at or near Glentirran.
Ruin or site   NS 668944 [?]   OS: 57   *   Map: 6, no: 47
Site of castle or old mansion, nothing of which survives.
   Glentirran was a property of the Livingstones from the 16th century or earlier, and Sir Alexander Livingstone of Glentirran was made a baronet of Nova Scotia in 1685. The property passed to the Campbells in the 18th century, who also held Gargunnock.

Glentress Tower
Borders: About 4 miles north of Innerleithen, east from B709, just north of the Glentress Burn, about 0.5 miles east of Glentress.
Ruin or site   NT 348433   OS: 73   *   Map: 2, no: 90
Little remains of Glentress Tower, a 16th-century tower house, except the basement and traces of other buildings.

Glenvorann
Dumfriesshire: About 6.5 miles north of Langholm, on A7, west of Eweslees Burn, at or near Fiddleton Bankend.
Ruin or site   NY 387965 [?]   OS: 79   *   Map: 1, no: 325
Site of tower house, a fragment of which may have been found in 1912. It was a property of Hobbie (Armstrong?) of Glenvore in 1590.
Other refs: Glenvore; Fiddleton Bankend

Glenvore *see* Glenvorann

Glorat House
Lanarkshire & Glasgow area: About 1 mile north-west of Milton of Campsie, on minor road north of A891 between Milton of Campsie and Lennoxtown, at Glorat.
Private   NS 641779   OS: 64   *   Map: 3, no: 301
Glorat House, a mansion dating from about 1625 which was rebuilt in 1869 and extended ten years later, incorporates part of a tower house or castle.
   The Stirlings held the property from 1430, one of whom Sir John Stirling was armour bearer to James I. George Stirling of Glorat died of wounds received at Pinkie in 1547. Another Stirling of Glorat killed Malcolm Kincaid in 1581. The house is still occupied by the Stirlings.

Goblin Ha' (Hall), Yester *see* Yester Castle

Godsbrigge *see* Scotsbrig

Gogar House *see* Castle Gogar

Goldielands Tower
Borders: About 2 miles west and south of Hawick , on minor roads just south of A7, south of the River Teviot.
Ruin or site   NT 478128   OS: 79   **   Map: 2, no: 142
Goldielands Tower is a ruined 16th-century tower house, rectangular in plan, formerly of five storeys. It had a courtyard with two outbuildings and corner towers. The tower had a vaulted basement, with an entresol floor, and turnpike stair, which now ends at the second floor. The chamber above housed both the hall and kitchen. The parapet and attic storey have gone.
   The property passed to the Scotts in 1446, and Scott of Goldielands was ordered to demolish Dryhope Tower in 1592. Walter Scott of Goldielands was one of the leaders of the party that helped to rescue Kinmont Willie from Carlisle Castle in 1596, as recounted in the old ballad, and his burial marker is now in the Hawick Museum. The last laird of Goldielands was hanged from his own gates for treason.

Golspie Tower
Sutherland & Caithness: About 0.25 miles north of Golspie, on minor road north of A9, west of Allt nan Sgeith, at or near Golspie Tower Farm.
Ruin or site   NC 836009   OS: 17   *   Map: 12, no: 28
Site of large tower house, a property of the Gordons in 1636 and the Earls of Sutherland.

Gordon Castle
Borders: North of Gordon, west of A6089 north of junction of A6105, south-east of Greenknowe, near cutting of dismantled railway.
Ruin or site   NT 646438 [?]   OS: 74   *   Map: 2, no: 262
Possible site of castle, although the location is not certain. The lands were a property of the Gordons from the middle of the 12th century until 1580 when they passed to the Setons. The Gordon family acquired lands in Strathbogie in Aberdeenshire, with their main seat at Huntly Castle, and became Earls, Marquises of Huntly and Dukes of Gordon.

Gordon Castle
Moray: About 8.5 miles east of Elgin, on minor roads north of A98 or west of B9104, 0.5 miles north of Fochabers, 0.5 miles east of Spey, at Gordon Castle.
Private   NJ 350596   OS: 28   *   Map: 10, no: 70
Little remains of Gordon Castle, a 15th-century stronghold of the Gordons.
   The original keep was greatly extended, possibly into a Z-plan tower, and incorporated a huge block of six storeys, part of which still survives. The castle was remodelled in 1769, and a huge mansion was built around the old part. It was sold to the government in 1936 in lieu of death duties, and deteriorated during World War II. Most of it was demolished when bought back by the Gordon-Lennox family, except for the six-storey block, and two separate wings. The building now looks a bit odd.
   Robert Burns visited in 1787.
Other refs: Castle Gordon; Bog o' Gight Castle

Gordon Castle – see previous page

Gordonstoun

Moray: About 3.5 miles south-west of Lossiemouth, on minor roads east of B9012 or west of B9135, about 1 mile east of Duffus, at Gordonstoun.
Private NJ 184690 OS: 28 ** Map: 10, no: 32
Gordonstoun incorporates a 16th-century tower house, rectangular in plan, with single-storey wings. In 1616 wings of two storeys, crowned with bartizans, were added.
    Although much altered inside, part of the basement is still vaulted.
    It was originally a property of the Ogstons, but was sold to the Innes family in 1473, who in turn sold it to the Gordons in 1616, and it was renamed Gordonstoun. In 1730 the house was remodelled, and in 1775 was given the present classical front. The lands passed to the Cummings of Altyre in 1795. In 1934 the property was bought by Kurt Hahn, and turned into Gordonstoun School, the famous public school for royalty such as the Duke of Edinburgh and Prince Charles and other rich folk.
Other refs: Plewlands

Gorm Castle

Argyll & Dunbartonshire: On west side of island of Islay about 6 miles north-west of Bowmore, on minor roads and boat west of B8018, on island in Loch Gorm, at Gorm.
Ruin or site NR 235655 OS: 60 ** Map: 5, no: 3
Site of 15th-century castle of the MacDonalds, once a place of some strength, on a small island in the loch. It passed to the MacLeans, and is said to have been besieged in 1578 by the MacDonalds. It was used by the MacLeans before they were defeated at the Battle of Traigh Gruinart. The castle was refortified, or still in use, in 1615 when Sir James MacDonald fought against the Campbells on Islay and Kintyre. He was unsuccessful, and his forces had to surrender. The castle was garrisoned by the Campbells until the 1640s.
Other refs: Loch Gorm Castle; Guirm Castle

Gorrenberry Tower

Borders: About 6 miles north of Newcastleton, on minor road west of B6399, north of the Hermitage Water, 2 miles west of Hermitage Castle, at Gorrenberry.
Ruin or site NY 464973 [?] OS: 79 * Map: 2, no: 128
Site of tower house of the Elliots, some remains of which survived until the 1830s. The castle is said to have had a brownie.

Gourock Castle

Renfrewshire: To east of Gourock, on minor roads south of A770, about 0.5 miles south of Kempock Point on the south coast of the Firth of Clyde.
Ruin or site NS 244771 [?] OS: 63 * Map: 3, no: 53
Site of castle, a vestige of which survived about 1875, said to be small and unimportant. It was a property of the Earls of Douglases until 1455, then passed to the Stewarts of Castlemilk. The castle appears to have been demolished by 1747, and the lands were sold to the Darroch family in 1784.
    Gourock Castle, a plain mansion of 1747, was built nearby.

Gowkthrapple *see* Castlehill, Cambusnethan

Gowrie House, Perth

Perthshire: In centre of Perth, County Buildings.
Ruin or site NO 120235 [?] OS: 58 * Map: 8, no: 87
Gowrie House was a fortified town house with a large garden, and built by the Countess of Huntly in 1520. It was sold to the Ruthven Earl of Gowrie, and it was here that in 1600 the Gowrie Conspiracy took place. This may have been a plot to kidnap or murder James VI, but the result was the death of the Earl of Gowrie and his brother, the Master of Ruthven. The family were forfeited and their name proscribed (see Huntingtower). The property was held by the Hay Earl of Kinnoul, who entertained Charles II here in 1663. It was acquired by the city of Perth, who gave it to the Duke of Cumberland, butcher of Culloden, in 1746, who in turn sold it to the government. It was used as a cavalry barracks until demolished in 1805. The site is occupied by the County Buildings.
Other refs: Whitehall of Perth

Graden Tower

Borders: About 4.5 miles south-east of Kelso, on minor roads north of B6352, 2 miles north-west of Town Yetholm, at or near Old Graden.
Ruin or site NT 799300 [?] OS: 74 * Map: 2, no: 324
Site of tower house, also recorded as Graden Place, which was completely demolished by the English in the 1540s. It was a property of the Kerrs of Graden.

Grahams Walls

Borders: About 1 mile south of Romanno Bridge, on foot east of B7059, east side of Lyne Water, just south of Newlands Church.
Ruin or site NT 162465 OS: 72 * Map: 2, no: 27
Site of castle, a property of the Graham family. Remains of it were apparently used to build both Newlands Church and Whiteside Tower.
    The patronage of the nearby church was given to Dunfermline Abbey in 1317 by a John Graham.

Graham's Castle

Stirlingshire & Clackmannan: About 4 miles east of Fintry, on foot just north of the B818, just north of the Carron River Reservoir.
Ruin or site NS 682858 OS: 57 * Map: 6, no: 50
Little remains of a 13th-century castle, except the impressive moat, although it once had very thick walls.
    It was a stronghold of Sir John Graham, who fought at Stirling Bridge in 1297, and died fighting alongside William Wallace at the Battle of Falkirk in 1298. Graham is buried in Falkirk Kirkyard. Wallace is said to have found refuge here. The Grahams were made Viscounts Dundaff and Earls, Marquis and Dukes of Montrose.
Other refs: Dundaff Castle

Grandhome House

Aberdeen & Gordon: About 0.5 miles south-east of Dyce, on minor roads north of A92 or west of B997, just east of River Don, at Grandhome House.
Private NJ 899117 [?] OS: 38 * Map: 10, no: 314
Site of castle or old house. The present mansion incorporates work from the 17th century or earlier.
    The lands were a property of the Keiths, then the Ogilvies, Buchanans, Gordons and the Jaffrays. Towards the end of the 17th century it passed to the Patons of Farrochie, who changed the name from Dilspro (which does sound like a medicine) to Grandhome. Paton of Grandhome was a Jacobite, and hid in the laird's lug at Craigievar to escape capture.
Other refs: Dilspro

Grandtully Castle

Perth & Kinross: About 2.5 miles north-east of Aberfeldy, on minor road just south of A827, about 0.25 miles south of River Tay, at Grandtully.
Private NN 891513 OS: 52 ** Map: 8, no: 29**
An impressive and well preserved fortress, Grandtully Castle consists of a 16th-century Z-plan tower house of three storeys and a garret with 17th-century altera-

tions and extensions. To this was added a large mansion in the same style in 1893. The tower may incorporate older work as the walls are very thick.

There was an earlier castle, about 1 mile to the east, dating from about 1414.

The tower consists of a rectangular main block and square towers, projecting at opposite corners, with a tall round stair-tower rising in one re-entrant angle. Conical-roofed bartizans crown several of the corners

The entrance, at the foot of the stair-tower, is flanked by a guardroom with a pit-prison. The basement is vaulted, and the old kitchen in one of the square towers. The hall, on the first floor of the main block, was panelled.

Grandtully was a property of the Stewarts from the 14th century. The castle is in a strategic position and was used by the Marquis of Montrose, General Mackay, Argyll, the Earl of Mar in the Jacobite Rising of 1715, and Bonnie Prince Charlie in the 1745 Rising. Grandtully was abandoned for Murthly Castle in the late 19th century, but restored and reoccupied by the Stewarts in the 1920s.

After defeat at the Battle of Killiecrankie, a soldier killed an officer in one of the bartizans, the blood staining the floor and said to be permanently visible.
Other refs: Grantully Castle

Grange *see* Grange House

Grange
Fife: About 1 mile north of Kinghorn, on minor roads west of A921, about 0.5 miles west of Seafield Tower, at Grange.
Private NT 270886 OS: 66 ** Map: 7, no: 58
Grange, a mansion, incorporates part of an altered 16th-century tower house with a round tower. The basement is not vaulted, and the round tower probably housed a turnpike stair.

It was a property of the Kirkcaldy family from 1540 or earlier. James Kirkcaldy was Lord High Treasurer to James V and to Mary, Queen of Scots. Kirkcaldy was forfeited, and the property passed to the Hamiltons, but was then recovered by Sir William Kirkcaldy, his son, in 1564. He had been involved in the murder of Cardinal David Beaton, and was captured and sent to France, where he distinguished himself as a soldier. He returned and joined the rebellion against Mary and Bothwell in 1567, pursuing Bothwell all the way to Shetland. However, after her flight to England, Kirkcaldy held Edinburgh Castle for Mary from 1571-3. Although he surrendered on the condition he would not be harmed, he was hanged after the fall of the castle. Kirkcaldy was forfeited, and the property passed to the Douglases, then the Stewarts, but returned to the Kirkcaldy family. The last of the line died in 1739, and the property passed to the Melvilles.
Other refs: Kirkcaldy of Grange

Grange Castle *see* Davoch of Grange

Grange House
Lothians: About 1.5 miles south of Edinburgh Castle, on minor roads west of A7, north of Braid Hills, between Grange Loan, Lauder Place and Dick Place.
Ruin or site NT 258718 OS: 66 * Map: 4, no: 98
Grange House was a 16th-century L-plan tower house of three storeys and an attic, with battlements and corbelled-out bartizans. The house was greatly extended and

remodelled to designs by William Playfair around 1830, but was completely demolished in 1936.

The lands were originally a property of St Giles Cathedral, but passed to the Wardlaw family in the 14th century, then to the Cants, the Dicks in 1679, and later the Lauders. Bonnie Prince Charlie stayed here in 1745.

The house reputedly had many ghosts, one of whom a miser, who – from time to time – is said to have rolled a barrel of gold through the house.

Grange House
Stirlingshire & Clackmannan: In Bo'ness, near the southern shore of the Forth of Forth, near the A904 at Grangepans.
Private NT 015815 [?] OS: 65 ** Map: 6, no: 113
Site of an altered 16th-century tower house of the Hamiltons. It was held by the Cadells in the 19th century.
Other refs: Grange; Grangepans

Grange House, Kerelaw *see* Kerelaw Castle

Grange of Monifieth
Angus & Dundee: To the north-east of Monifieth, on minor roads north of A930 or south of A92, near Grange House.
Ruin or site NO 490330 [?] OS: 54 * Map: 8, no: 206
Site of castle of the Durhams, nothing of which remains. The castle was demolished in 1829.

The lands were held by Arbroath Abbey, but in 1322 passed to the Durhams. The Marquis of Montrose was held here on his way to Edinburgh to be executed. He nearly escaped by getting his guards drunk, but was spotted and recaptured.
Other refs: Monifieth; Castle of Grange

Grangehill *see* Dalvey Castle

Grangepans *see* Grange House

Grant Castle *see* Castle Grant

Grantfield *see* Midmar Castle

Granton Castle
Lothians: About 3 miles north and west of Edinburgh Castle, west of A901, at Granton, just south of the shore of the Firth of Forth.
Ruin or site NT 225772 OS: 66 * Map: 4, no: 78
Nothing remains of Granton Castle, a 16th-century L-plan tower house, except the gates and a 17th-century doocot. The castle was extended by a wing in the 17th century, and there was also a courtyard and walled garden.

The lands were owned by the Melvilles from the 12th century until bought by Sir George Mackenzie of Tarbat. In 1739 the property passed to the Campbell Duke of Argyll, who renamed the castle Royston House when the adjacent property of Royston was itself renamed 'Caroline Park' after his daughter – or alternatively after George II's queen. The castle became ruinous, and was demolished in the 1920s.
Other refs: Royston Castle; Old Granton House

Grantully Castle *see* Grandtully Castle

Green Castle *see* Tronach Castle

Green Castle *see* Finella's Castle

Greena Tower
Borders: About 4.5 miles south and west of Newcastleton, on minor roads east of B6357, west of Liddel Water, south side of Greena Hill, north of Longrow.
Ruin or site NY 461807 [?] OS: 79 * Map: 2, no: 127
Site of tower house of the Armstrongs.

Greenan Castle
Ayrshire: About 2.5 miles south-west of Ayr railway station, on minor roads north of A719 on the shore of the Firth of Clyde, near Greenan.
Ruin or site NS 312193 OS: 70 * Map: 3, no: 87**
Standing on a headland above the sea, Greenan Castle is a ruined rectangular 16th-

century tower house, once of four storeys. It had open rounds and a caphouse, and the walls were pierced by shot-holes. There was a courtyard, but little remains, and ditches defended the castle on the landward side.

The basement was vaulted, the hall was on the first floor, and the floors above were occupied by private chambers.

There was a castle here in the 12th century, which was held by a Roger de Scale-broc. The property passed to the Davidsons, but was sold to the Kennedys in 1588. In 1602 Sir Thomas of Kennedy of Culzean, younger son of Gilbert, 3rd Earl of Cassillis, spent his last night at Greenan before being murdered by Mure of Auchendrane.

The castle has been suggested as the site of Arthur's Camelot.

Greenhead Tower
Borders: About 1 mile east of Selkirk, on minor roads east of A7 at Selkirk, north of Bell Hill, at or near Greenhead.
Ruin or site NT 492295 [?] OS: 73 * Map: 2, no: 154
Site of a square 16th-century tower house. The lands were a property of the Browns in the 14th century.

Greenknowe Tower
Borders: About 0.5 miles west of Gordon, just north of lay-by on A6105.
His Scot NT 639428 OS: 74 * Map: 2, no: 254**
Built for comfort as well as defence, Greenknowe Tower is a 16th-century L-plan tower house. It consists of a main block of four storeys and a higher wing. Three of the corners had bartizans, and the walls are pierced by gunloops. The castle is dated 1581.

The entrance, in the re-entrant angle, still has an iron yett. It leads to the main turnpike stair to the hall above, and into the vaulted basement which contains the kitchen with an arched fireplace. The hall has a wide decorated fireplace. The private chambers on the floors above of both the wing and main block were reached by a turnpike stair in the re-entrant angle.

Greenknowe passed by marriage from the Gordons to the Setons of Touch, who built the castle. In the 17th century it was acquired by the Pringles of Stichel, one of whom Walter Pringle was a noted writer and Covenanter. It later passed to the Dalrymples, and was occupied until the middle of the 19th century. It was put into the care of the State in 1937.

OPEN: Access at all reasonable times.
Parking nearby.
Tel: 0131 668 8800 Fax: 0131 668 8888
Email: hs.explore@scotland.gov.uk Web: www.historic-scotland.gov.uk

Greenlaw Castle

Borders: To west of Greenlaw, on minor roads west of A697, north side of
Marchmont Road, north of Blackadder Water.
Ruin or site   NT 719463 [?]   OS: 74   *   Map: 2, no: 294
Site of castle of the Homes, which was abandoned as a residence in 1729, although
it was used to house farm labourers until the 1820s. The last vestige was removed
in 1863 and nothing remains.
Other refs: Grey Peel; Tenandry House

Greenlaw House

Lothians: North of Penicuik, east of A701, west of River North Esk, Glencorse.
Private   NT 248620   OS: 66   *   Map: 4, no: 91
Greenlaw House, which incorporated a 17th-century laird's house, was remodelled from 1804 into a large barracks and prison which could hold up to 6000 prisoners from the Napoleonic wars. The building served as the military prison for
Scotland from 1845 to 1888. In 1875 it was extended to become the army depot for
south-east Scotland, but was completely demolished and the site is occupied by
later buildings.
   The ghost of a young woman is reported to have been seen at a spot called 'Lover's Leap' at a gorge above the River Esk. The story goes that she had been cavort-
ing with one of the French prisoners imprisoned at Greenlaw. Her father had her
imprisoned, and while incarcerated her French lover was murdered, died or moved
elsewhere. When the girl was released, she found her lover gone, and then threw
herself into the river at 'Lover's Leap'.

Greenlaw Tower

Galloway: About 1.5 miles north-west of Castle Douglas, on minor roads west of
A713, just east of the River Dee, just south of Mains of Greenlaw.
Ruin or site   NX 741636   OS: 84   **   Map: 1, no: 120
Site of tower house, defended by earthworks, which was occupied in the 16th
century. It was apparently still occupied in the middle of the 18th century but little
survives.

Greenock Castle *see* Easter Greenock Castle

Greenock Castle

Renfrewshire: In Greenock, near the A8, just south of the Firth of Clyde.
Ruin or site   NS 280765 [?]   OS: 63   *   Map: 3, no: 63
Site of castle. Greenock was a property of the Cathcarts, then the Hamiltons – the
castle may have been built or modified by James Hamilton of Finnart – then the
Shaws. The castle was replaced by a mansion of the Shaws of Greenock.
Other refs: Wester Greenock Castle

Greenrig *see* Dowane

Greenvale *see* Perceton House

Greenwich *see* Greenwrae

Greenwrae

Dumfriesshire: About 3.5 miles north of Gretna, on minor roads south of B6357,
east of River Sark, at or near Greenwrae.
Ruin or site   NY 326729   OS: 85   *   Map: 1, no: 302
Probable site of tower house.
Other refs: Greenwich

Grey Coat Peel

Borders: Around 6.5 miles south of Hawick, near minor road about 4 miles south
of B6399, near Peelbraehope.
Ruin or site   NT 475045 [?]   OS: 79   *   Map: 2, no: 141
Site of 16th-century tower house.
Other refs: Peelbraehope

Grey Peel *see* Greenlaw Castle

Grey Peel

Borders: About 2 miles south and west of Jedburgh, on minor roads or foot
north of B6357 or west of A68, 0.5 miles north-west of Langlee.
Ruin or site   NT 639179   OS: 80   *   Map: 2, no: 253
Site of tower house, apparently a property of the Douglases. There is now no trace.

Grieston Tower

Borders: About 1.5 miles south-west of Innerleithen, on minor road south of
B7062, south of the River Tweed, south of Howford, at Grieston.
Ruin or site   NT 314358   OS: 73   *   Map: 2, no: 80
Site of tower house, a property of the Middlemast family in the 16th and 17th
centuries. There were some remains in 1857, but nothing survives.

Gryffe Castle

Renfrewshire: About 0.5 miles north of Bridge of Weir, on minor road north of
A761 just west of junction with B790, at Gryffe.
Private   NS 385663   OS: 63   *   Map: 3, no: 135
Site of castle, which is mentioned in the 15th century.
   Gryffe Castle, a small asymmetrical mansion dating from 1841, may incorporate or
be built on the site of an earlier castle. In the 19th century it was a property of the
Barbours, although the house was built by Robert Freeland of Broomward.

Grymm's Castle

Renfrewshire: About 2 miles south-east of Kilmacolm, on minor road east of
A761, at or near Barlogan.
Ruin or site   NS 377676 [?]   OS: 63   *   Map: 3, no: 130
Site of castle.

Guirm Castle *see* Gorm Castle

Gunnery of MacLeod

Western Isles: About 2 miles east of Borve, south of unlisted road, on Ludag
Point, Isle of Berneray.
Private   NF 933815   OS: 18   **   Map: 11, no: 17
The Gunnery of MacLeod is said to have been the stronghold of the MacLeods of
Berneray. Norman MacLeod of Berneray was born here in 1614.

Gunn's Castle

Sutherland & Caithness: About 8 miles south and west of Wick, on foot south of
A9, just north of shore, south of East Clyth, near Hanni Geo.
Ruin or site   ND 307386   OS: 11   *   Map: 12, no: 59
Not much remains of a once strong and splendid castle on a rock, except part of
the basement of a keep or tower.
   It was owned by the Gunn family, who feuded with the Keiths of Ackergill. Dugald
Keith attacked the Gunns of Braemore and carried off Helen Gunn to Ackergill.
She threw herself from a castle tower rather than submit to Keith, and her ghost is
said to haunt Ackergill. The Gunns ravaged the Keiths' lands, but were defeated at
battles at Tannach Moor in 1438, and again at Dirlot in 1464. The chief of the Gunns
and four of his sons were killed. Another Gunn chief, Justiciar of Caithness, was
'basely' murdered by the Keiths in 1478. James Gunn slew Keith of Ackergill and
his son at Drummoy in revenge.
Other refs: East Clyth; Clyth

Gurness Broch

Orkney: About 1 mile north-east of Evie on Orkney, on minor roads and foot
north of A966, south shore of Eynhallow Sound, on Aikerness, at Gurness
His Scot   HY 381268   OS: 6   **   Map: 11, no: 41
Excavated in the 1930s, Gurness is a fine broch and settlement. The settlement is a
spread of buildings between the broch and the surrounding ramparts and ditches.
The broch has a solid wall base with a guard cell on each side of the entrance
passage, and survives to a height of ten feet. In the courtyard is a well with stone
steps.
   The settlement was occupied by the Picts, and a stone carved with Pictish devices

was found here, as were the remains of one of their houses. There is a museum, with prehistoric and some Pictish artefacts, at the site. Walk to broch.

Other refs: Broch of Gurness

OPEN: Open Apr-Sep, daily 9.30-18.30; last ticket 30 mins before closing – combined ticket available for Orkney monuments.

Explanatory displays. Disabled access. Car and limited coach parking. Group concession. £

Tel: 01831 579478   Fax: 0131 668 8888

Email: hs.explore@scotland.gov.uk   Web: www.historic-scotland.gov.uk

Guthrie Castle

Angus & Dundee: About 6.5 miles east of Forfar, on minor roads north of A932, just west of hamlet of Guthrie, south-east of Guthrie Hill, at Guthrie Castle.

Private   NO 563505   OS: 54   *   Map: 8, no: 236**

Guthrie Castle consists of an altered 15th-century keep of three storeys and a garret, square in plan, to which has been added a modern mansion. The keep has a small projecting stair-wing crowned by a caphouse, and a restored crenellated parapet with open rounds.

The original entrance is in the middle of one side and opens into a lobby which leads to the vaulted basement and to a straight stair, in the thickness of the walling, to the first-floor hall. The upper floors were reached by the turnpike stair in the wing. There are some fine wall paintings and a walled garden.

The original tower was built by the Guthries around 1470. One of the family, Sir Alexander, was killed at the Battle of Flodden in 1513.

A Guthrie married a Gardyne in 1558 and their son, quarrelling with his relatives, was stabbed to death by his Gardyne cousin, so starting a long feud. Patrick Gardyne was slain in 1578 by William Guthrie, but 10 years later the Gardynes succeeded in murdering a Guthrie laird. Two years after this the Guthries fell upon the Gardyne family, and murdered their laird and others. Both families were forfeited by James VI and lost their lands, but while the Guthries recovered theirs, the Gardynes never did.

The castle was remodelled by David Bryce in 1848, and still held by the family in the 20th century.

Gylen Castle

Argyll & Dunbartonshire: About 4 miles south-west of Oban, on south coast of island of Kerrera, on minor roads and foot south of Cnoc Biorach on promontory, at Gylen.

Ruin or site   NM 805265   OS: 49   *   Map: 5, no: 58**

On a rocky promontory jutting into the sea, Gylen or Gylem Castle – the 'castle of fountains' – is a 16th-century L-plan tower house, which consists of a square main block and a stair-tower. The main block rises to four storeys, while the wing is a storey higher and crowned by a corbelled-out caphouse. There was an adjoining courtyard.

A vaulted passageway runs through the main block to the courtyard, and a vaulted cellar is entered from the pend. The main entrance, in the re-entrant angle from the courtyard, leads to the foot of the main turnpike stair, which climbs to all floors. The hall and kitchen are on the first floor. An oriel window projects at third-floor level.

Gylen was a property of the MacDougalls. An earlier castle here was where Alexander II died during an expedition to recover the Western Isles in the mid 13th century, although Dalrigh near Horse Shoe Bay is given as an alternative site. The existing castle, built by Duncan MacDougall, was completed in 1582, but captured and burned by a Covenanter army, led by General David Leslie, in 1647. The Brooch of Lorn, a brooch torn from Robert the Bruce's cloak, was also stolen, and not returned by the Campbells of Inverawe until the 19th century.

The castle was never restored, although it has been consolidated.

OPEN: Access at all reasonable times – care should be taken.

H

Hackness *see* Martello Towers, Orkney

Haddington Castle

Lothians: In Haddington, south of the A1.

Ruin or site   NT 513738 [?]   OS: 66   *   Map: 4, no: 185

Site of 12th-century castle or palace, nothing of which remains, the site probably occupied by the County Buildings. The remains of vaults were found in the 19th century. The castle was visited by William the Lyon and the birthplace of Alexander II in 1168. The 6th Earl of Atholl was apparently murdered here in 1242.

A fort was built at Haddington during the invasion of 1547 by the Duke of Somerset. It successfully resisted French sieges and attacks, from July 1548 until September 1549, and it was only a lack of supplies and disease which eventually forced the English to withdraw.

There were a least three old, possibly fortified, town houses in Haddington, one called Bothwell's Castle, a property named after the Hepburn Earls of Bothwell which was held by the Cockburns of Sanybed; another Busbie Castle; while a third was Blair's Castle, which was demolished about 1850. There was also a building believed to have been the Preceptory of the Knights Templar in Haddington, which has also been demolished.

Haddo House

Aberdeen & Gordon: About 10 miles north-west of Ellon, on minor roads south of B9005 or east of B9170, 1 mile south of River Ythan, at Haddo House.

NTS   NJ 868347   OS: 30   *   Map: 10, no: 297

Nothing survives of a castle of the Gordons, who had held the lands from 1429. The present Haddo House, an Adam mansion of 1731-6, was built for William Gordon, 2nd Earl of Aberdeen.

Patrick Gordon of Haddo was killed at the Battle of Arbroath in 1446. In 1644 Sir John Gordon of Haddo, who had been active with the Marquis of Montrose, was captured after being besieged in the castle for three days. He was imprisoned in 'Haddo's Hole' in St Giles Cathedral before being executed by beheading. The castle was destroyed. His son, however, became Lord Chancellor of Scotland and Earl of Aberdeen, while the 4th Earl was Prime Minister but resigned in 1854. The family were made Marquises of Aberdeen in 1915, and the house is now in the care of The National Trust for Scotland.

The apparition of Lord Archibald Gordon is said to have been seen in the Premier's Bedroom. He was the youngest son of the 1st Marquis of Aberdeen, and killed in a car accident, one of the first people in Britain to die in such a way.

Other refs: Place of Kellie; House of Haddo

OPEN: Open 13 Apr-Sep, daily 13.30-17.30; Oct, Sat-Sun 13.30-17.30; last admission 16.45. Garden open Mar-Oct, daily 9.30-18.00; Nov-Feb, daily 9.30-16.00; closed 24-25 Dec. Shop and tearoom, 11.00-17.30. Country park open all year daily 9.30-sunset; occasionally some rooms may be closed to the public.

Generally guided tours, Mon-Sat. Exhibition of paintings. Explanatory displays. Gift shop. Restaurant. WC. Adjoining country park. Disabled access. Car and coach parking. Group concessions. £££

Tel: 01651 851440   Fax: 01651 851888

Email: information@nts.org.uk   Web: nts.org.uk

Haggishaugh

Borders: About 6 miles north-east of Newcastleton, on minor roads south of B6357, south of Liddel Water, at or near Larriston House.

Ruin or site   NY 545944 [?]   OS: 79   *   Map: 2, no: 199

Site of tower house. Larriston House, which dates from the 18th century, may stand on or near the site. It was a property of the Elliots, and it is said that a cannon ball was found here. By the end of the 19th century it was held by the Jardines of Dryfeholm.

Other refs: Larriston House

Haggs Castle

Lanarkshire & Glasgow area: In Glasgow, just south of the B768, north end of Pollok Country Park, in the Pollokshaws suburb of Glasgow.
Private NS 560626 OS: 64 * Map: 3, no: 255**
On the edge of extensive park land, Haggs Castle is an altered 16th-century L-plan tower house of three storeys and an attic. Stair-turrets project above first-floor level in the middle of two walls. The walls are pierced by many squared gunloops and shot-holes, and there is much moulded decoration around the windows, door and wallhead. The castle is dated 1585.

The basement was vaulted and contained the original kitchen, with a large fire-place; and a wine-cellar, with a small stair to the hall above. The fine hall, on the first floor, has an impressive stone fireplace.

The castle was built by John Maxwell of Pollok in 1585, and the family were involved in a long feud with the Johnstones. It was used by Covenanters in the 17th century, and the Maxwells were heavily fined in 1684, although they were saved from paying by the Revolution of 1689. The castle was abandoned around 1753 for Pollok House, derelict by the 1850s, but restored and extended around 1890. It was Glasgow's Museum of Childhood, but sold and converted into flats as private housing.

Hailes Castle

Lothians: About 1.5 miles west and south of East Linton, north of minor road south 1.5 miles from East Linton off A1, on south bank of Tyne.
His Scot NT 575758 OS: 67 * Map: 4, no: 205**
In a lovely location above a river, Hailes Castle consists of a 14th-century keep, extended by ranges and towers in the 15th and 16th centuries, within a thick 13th-

century curtain wall. The castle had a large courtyard, fragments of which remain.

The keep, of at least three storeys, stood at one corner of the original castle and contains a vaulted pit-prison. The upper part of the tower was later made into a doocot. A 14th-century tower had a vaulted basement with another pit-prison. The 15th-century work consists of a hall (or chapel), and a basement bakehouse, between the keep and tower. There were other buildings, one upstand having a postern gate, and the remains of a well, but these are very fragmentary.

Hailes was a Hepburn property, having passed from the Cospatrick Earl of Dunbar and March and the de Gourlay family. It was probably Sir Patrick Hepburn – who played a valiant part in the Battle of Otterburn in 1388 by saving the Douglas banner from falling into the hands of the English – who extended the castle. In 1400 the Earl of March and Harry 'Hotspur' Percy failed to take the castle, and were themselves surprised and routed. Archibald Dunbar captured the castle in 1443, and slew all he found within in the walls. Patrick Hepburn became Earl of Bothwell, but was killed at the Battle of Flodden in 1513. The castle was torched in 1532, and in 1547 occupied by Lord Gray of Wilton for the English. James Hepburn, 4th Earl of Bothwell, brought Mary, Queen of Scots, here after abducting her in 1567. In 1650 the castle was partly dismantled by Cromwell. It passed to the Stewarts, then the Setons, who in 1700 sold the castle to the Dalrymples of Hailes, but was then abandoned for the mansion of New Hailes. In 1835 Hailes was being used as a

granary. The castle was transferred into State care in 1926.

There are stories of an underground passage, which appears to have led under the river, or even to Traprain Law.
OPEN: Access at all reasonable times.
Parking nearby.
Tel: 0131 668 8800   Fax: 0131 668 8888
Email: hs.explore@scotland.gov.uk   Web: www.historic-scotland.gov.uk

Haimer Castle

Sutherland & Caithness: About 2 miles east of Thurso, on minor roads south of A836, at or near Haimer.
Ruin or site ND 143673 OS: 12 * Map: 12, no: 48
Site of castle of the Sinclairs, little or nothing of which survives.
Other refs: Castle of Haimer

Haining Castle *see* Almond Castle

Halberry Castle

Sutherland & Caithness: About 9 miles south of Wick, on minor roads and foot east of A9, just west of sea, at Halberry Head.
Ruin or site ND 302377 OS: 11 * Map: 12, no: 58
Standing on a promontory above the sea, Halberry Castle is a very ruined 15th-century keep and castle of the Gunn family. It was defended on the landward side by a ditch.

Halcro

Orkney: About 5.5 miles south and east of St Margaret's Hope, on minor roads east of A961, on south-east side of South Ronaldsay, at or near Halcro.
Ruin or site ND 462855 [?] OS: 7 * Map: 11, no: 51
Possible site of castle.

It may have been held by Sir Hugh Halcro, who was knighted at the Battle of Bannockburn in 1314.

Halhill Castle

Inverness & Nairn: About 7 miles north-east of Inverness, on minor roads south of B9039, south of shore of Moray Firth, at or near Fisherton.
Ruin or site NH 759519 [?] OS: 27 * Map: 9, no: 115
Site of castle, originally of the Mackintoshes.

It was sacked by the Dunbars of Cumnock and of Durris in 1502. After it had been occupied by Sir James Ogilvie of Strathnairn – whose wife was the daughter of Dunbar of Cumnock – it was plundered in 1513 by a party of Mackintoshes and Roses, possibly in retaliation.

Halhill Tower

Fife: About 5 miles west of Cupar, on minor roads north of A91, north of Collessie, at or near Halhill.
Ruin or site NO 292132 [?] OS: 59 * Map: 7, no: 68
Site of 16th-century tower house of the Melvilles. One of the family was Sir James Melville, courtier and diplomat, who died in 1607. The castle was demolished by Lord Melville when he added the lands to Melville Park.

Halkerton *see* Haulkerton Castle

Hall of Rule *see* Hallrule

Hall of Tolophin

Aberdeen & Gordon: About 4 miles west and south of Rhynie, on foot north of B9002, 0.3 miles north-east of Silverford, Moss of Tolophin.
Ruin or site NJ 438256 OS: 37 * Map: 10, no: 92
Site of castle or hall house, possibly dating from the 15th century, said to have been a summer residence of the Gordons of Craig. Their castle of Craig [NJ 472248] is about 2.5 miles to the east.

Hall Yard

Perth & Kinross: About 2 miles west of Kinross, south of A977, near Wood of Coldrain.

Ruin or site   NO 084013 [?]   OS: 58   *   Map: 8, no: 72

Site of castle.

Hallbar Tower

Lanarkshire & Glasgow area: About 2 miles south-west of Carluke, on minor road north of B7056, about 0.5 miles south-west of Braidwood.

Private   NS 839471   OS: 72   *   Map: 3, no: 388**

Standing on a commanding hilly site, Hallbar Tower is a 16th-century tower house, square in plan, of four storeys and a garret. It is claimed it may incorporate a castle from as early as the 11th century. The corbelled-out parapet only crowns two wall-heads, and was restored in the 19th century. A square caphouse, with a pyramidal roof, tops the stair in one corner. The main roof of the castle is stone-flagged, and the garret roof is vaulted to carry the weight. There are traces of a courtyard.

The entrance leads to the basement, and to a mural stair which rises steeply around each side of the tower as it climbs. The first-floor hall has a fireplace.

Hallbar was a Douglas Earls of Douglas stronghold, but acquired in 1581 by the Stewarts of Gogar. It passed to Maitland of Thirlestane the same century, then the Douglases, then to Sir George Lockhart of The Lee around 1662. It was semi-derelict, but has been restored.

Braidwood House is a modern mansion, and replaced the tower.

Other refs: Braidwood Castle; Tower of Hallbar

OPEN: Holiday accommodation is available.

Tel: 0171 930 8030   Fax: 0171 930 2295

Email: aniela@vivat.demon.co.uk

Hallcraig House

Lanarkshire & Glasgow area: About 1.5 miles west of Carluke, on minor roads west of A73, on north side of Jock's Burn, 0.5 miles south of Scoularhall, at Hallcraig.

Ruin or site   NS 829500 [?]   OS: 72   *   Map: 3, no: 385

Site of mansion, which may have incorporated a castle, but was completely demolished in the 20th century.

Hallforest Castle

Aberdeen & Gordon: About 4 miles south of Inverurie, on minor road and foot north of B994 at Hallforest, 1 mile west of Kintore, at Hallforest.

Ruin or site   NJ 777154   OS: 38   **   Map: 10, no: 255

Hallforest Castle is a ruined 14th-century keep, rectangular in plan, of five or six storeys.

The basement and first floor are vaulted. The basement contained a cellar, below a kitchen, beneath the first vault; and a hall, below a private chamber, beneath the second. The entrance would have been at the level of the hall.

It was built as a hunting lodge for Robert the Bruce, and given to Sir Robert Keith,

Marischal of Scotland, in 1309. The castle was visited by Mary, Queen of Scots, in 1562. Hallforest was used until about 1639, and is said to have often been attacked in the fighting before and during the Civil War.

Hallgreen

Dumfriesshire: About 0.25 miles south-east of Canonbie, south of B6357, east of River Esk, at or near Hallgreen.

Ruin or site   NY 400758   OS: 85   *   Map: 1, no: 329

Site of tower house.

Other refs: Francie of Canonbie

Hallgreen Castle

Kincardine & Deeside: To east of Inverbervie, on minor roads east of A92, in the village, to south of Bervie Bay just west of the sea, at Hallgreen.

Private   NO 832721   OS: 45   **   Map: 10, no: 279

Hallgreen Castle is a much-altered 16th-century L-plan tower house of three storeys and an attic. It incorporated earlier work from the 14th century, and has been extended by a modern mansion. The old part has steep roofs and corbiestepped gables. Bartizans, with splayed gunloops, crown the corners. Many windows have been enlarged and others sealed.

The basement of the house is vaulted and the hall would have been on the first floor with private chambers above.

Hallgreen was a property of the Dunnet family, who built the castle about 1376, but it passed to the Raits in the 15th century, one of whom was a captain of the guard to James IV. Although still roofed, the house became empty and derelict, but has since been restored and is occupied.

Several ghosts are said to haunt the castle, including that of a cloaked man, a woman who reputedly killed herself after the death of her child, and two servant girls.

There is said to have been a castle at Inverbervie in the 13th century, and there was walled mansion which was demolished around 1825. This was known as Marischal's Lodging or Arbuthnott's Lodging.

David II and Queen Johanna landed at Inverbervie from France in 1341.

Other refs: Inverbervie; Bervie

OPEN: Hotel.

Tel: 01561 362861   Fax: 01561 362444   Email: scotiagrendel@onet.co.uk

Hallguards Castle

Dumfriesshire: About 2 miles south-west of Ecclefechan, on minor roads north of B725, south of River Annan, 0.3 miles south-east of Hoddom Castle, at or near Hallguards.

Ruin or site   NY 162728 [?]   OS: 85   *   Map: 1, no: 253

Site of 14th-century castle.

It is said to have been built by of the Bruces, but the property passed to the Herries family, then later to the Carruthers. The castle was demolished under the terms of a Border treaty, and Hoddom became the main stronghold.

Other refs: Hoddomtown Castle

Hallhead

Aberdeen & Gordon: About 5 miles north-east of Tarland, on minor roads north of B9119 or west of A980, south of Rumblie Burn, at Mains of Hallhead.

Private   NJ 525092   OS: 37   **   Map: 10, no: 121

Hallhead is an altered 17th-century T-plan tower house. It consists of a main block of two storeys and an attic, and a centrally projecting stair-tower, which rises a storey higher. A small stair-turret is corbelled out in one re-entrant angle. The walls are harled, and gables corbiestepped. The tower has had a courtyard.

The entrance is in the re-entrant angle, but the basement is not vaulted, and the building has been altered inside.

It was a property of the Gordons of Esslemont. It has been used as a farmhouse from the 19th century, but is not occupied.

Other refs: Mains of Hallhead

Hallrule

Borders: About 1 mile north of Bonchester Bridge, on minor road north of B6357, west of Rule Water, at or near Hallrule

Ruin or site NT 593140 OS: 80 * Map: 2, no: 230

Site of tower house, a property of the Turnbulls, burned and demolished by the English in 1545. There was also a 'town' or village, probably a little way to the south, which was torched by the Marquis of Dorset in 1523, then by the Armstrongs of Liddlesdale in 1544. On Blaeu's Atlas Novus map of Teviotdale is marked both 'Hall of Roull [Rule]' and further north 'Tou[r? or w?] of Roull [Rule]. 'Town o' Rule' is just west of B6357.

Other refs: Hall of Rule; Tower of Rule

Halltown of Nemphlar *see* Nemphlar

Hallyards

Lothians: About 0.5 miles south of Kirkliston, on minor road north of A8 just east of junction with M9 & M8, on south bank of River Almond, at Hallyards.

Ruin or site NT 129738 OS: 65 * Map: 4, no: 44

Hallyards is a very ruined, overgrown 17th-century tower house, formerly with a round stair-turret, although there may have been an earlier stronghold here as it is mentioned in 1579. It was ruinous by 1892, and subsidence caused by mining hastened its destruction.

It was acquired by the Skenes around 1615, but passed to the Erskine Earl of Mar in 1619, then sold to the Marjoribanks family in 1696.

Hallyards

Borders: About 3 miles south-west of Peebles, on minor roads south of A72, just west of Manor Water, at Hallyards.

Private NT 216375 OS: 73 ** Map: 2, no: 49

Hallyards, a 19th-century mansion altered by the architect Sir Robert Lorimer in 1897, incorporates part of a 16th-century tower house. Most of the old part was demolished.

It was a property of the Scotts of Hundleshope in 1647. The house was occupied by the historian Professor Adam Ferguson, and visited by Sir Walter Scott in 1797.

Hallyards Castle

Fife: About 3.5 miles east of Cowdenbeath, on minor road between A92 and B925, 1 mile south-west of Loch Gelly, 0.5 miles north of Auchtertool.

Ruin or site NT 212914 OS: 58 * Map: 7, no: 36

Very little survives of a 16th-century courtyard castle, except some upstands of masonry and grassy mounds.

It was held by the Skene family, but passed to Sir James Kirkcaldy of Grange, Lord High Treasurer to James V, but then appears to have returned to the Skenes. James V stayed here on his way to Falkland Palace, after the rout at Solway Moss in 1542, and died soon afterwards at the Palace. The castle is said to have been the mustering point for Fife Jacobites in the 1715 Rising. In 1788 the name was changed to Camilla after the property passed by marriage to Moncrieffe of Reidie.

Other refs: Camilla

Halmyre House

Borders: About 2 miles south-east of West Linton, on minor roads west of A701 north of junction with B7059, south of Dead Burn, at Halmyre House.

Private NT 174496 OS: 72 ** Map: 2, no: 36

Halmyre House, substantially extended and remodelled in 1858, incorporates two vaulted basement chambers from a 16th-century tower house, as well as other work.

It was a property of the Tweedies of Drumelzier in the 16th and early 17th centuries, but sold to the Gordons in 1808.

Halton *see* Hatton House

Halton House *see* Peel Ring of Lumphanan

Hamilton Castle *see* Hamilton Palace

Hamilton House

Lothians: South-east of Prestonpans, on roads north of B1361, in the Preston area, between Preston Tower and Northfield House.

NTS NT 389739 OS: 66 * Map: 4, no: 157

One of four old houses around the village of Preston, Hamilton House consists of a main block of two storeys with projecting wings at both ends. A hexagonal stair tower stands in one re-entrant angle. The roof is steep and stone-tiled. The walls are whitewashed, and the house is dated 1626.

The building has been completely altered inside.

The house was a property of the Hamiltons. Although ruinous at one time, the building has been restored by The National Trust for Scotland.

Other refs: Magdalens House; Dower House

OPEN: House is let and open only by prior arrangement, phone 01721 722502.

Hamilton Palace

Lanarkshire & Glasgow: North of Hamilton, on minor roads off B7071, in Hamilton Low Parks, 200 yards south of Mausoleum.

Ruin or site NS 726504 OS: 64 * Map: 3, no: 336

Site of castle, which was almost entirely rebuilt at the beginning of the 18th century, and then again in 1822 to form a magnificent mansion. The whole building

was demolished in 1927 because of mining subsidence. Many of the furniture, paintings and porcelain from here are now on display at Lennoxlove.

The castle, first mentioned in 1455, was a property of the Hamiltons, and known as 'The Orchard'. The castle was burned down, probably by the forces of the Regent Morton in 1579, although by 1591 it had been repaired or rebuilt. The building was then developed down the centuries until little survived of the castle except foundations.

Other refs: Hamilton Castle; The Orchard, Hamilton

Hangingshaw

Borders: About 4.5 miles west of Selkirk, on minor roads north of A708, north of the Yarrow Water, at Hangingshaw.

Ruin or site NT 397303 OS: 73 * Map: 2, no: 101

Site of 15th-century castle of the Murrays of Philiphaugh, which was accidentally burned at the end of the 18th century. The present house is a two-storey Jacobean mansion, built in 1846.

One laird was the 'outlaw' Murray who – according to the ballad – came before James IV on charges of treasonably occupying the Ettrick Forest, although he claimed that he had recovered the territory from the English. An sensible agreement was reached whereby Murray acknowledged James as his king, and the king made Murray Sheriff of Ettrick Forest.

Hangingside *see* Hawthornside

Harburn Castle

Lothians: About 2.5 miles south-east of West Calder, on minor roads east of B7008, at or near Harburn.

Ruin or site   NT 044608 [?]   OS: 65   *   Map: 4, no: 20

Site of castle, already ruined when Cromwell refortified it in the 1650s against mosstroopers, who were active in the area. Harburn House, a nearby mansion of three storeys with a courtyard, was built in 1804, and is now a conference centre and hotel. The house is situated in a large estate.

OPEN: Harburn House: hotel – open all year by appointment.
Accommodation available.
Tel: 01506 461818   Fax: 01506 416591
Email: Harburn@compuserve.com   Web: www.harburnhouse.com

Harden

Borders: About 3.5 miles west of Hawick, on minor road north of B711, just north of the Harden Burn.

Private   NT 449149   OS: 79   **   Map: 2, no: 120

Harden incorporates a rectangular 16th-century tower house of three storeys, which is said to have replaced an earlier tower demolished in 1590. The building was extended and altered between 1680-90, and again in the 19th century.

The basement is not vaulted.

Harden was a property of the Homes, but sold to the Scotts in 1501. One of the family was Auld Wat of Harden, a Border reiver, who married Marion or Mary Scott, the Flower of Yarrow, the bloody events surrounding her recorded in the ballad 'The Dowie Holms (or Dens) o' Yarrow'. The family moved to Mertoun in the 18th century, and the house was used as a farmhouse. In the mid 19th century it was restored and reoccupied, and is now the seat of the Home Lord Polwarth.

Harehead Castle

Borders: About 7 miles north-west of Duns, on minor road east of B6355, east of Whiteadder Water, north-east of Cranshaws, at or near Harehead.

Ruin or site   NT 692630 [?]   OS: 67   *   Map: 2, no: 284

Site of castle, which is believed to have burned down in the 18th century. It was a property of the Carmichael Earls of Hyndford.

Harelaw Tower

Dumfriesshire: About 3.5 miles north-east of Canonbie, just south of B6357, about 0.3 miles north of the Liddel Water (Border with England), near Harelaw Mill.

Ruin or site   NY 436790 [?]   OS: 85   *   Map: 1, no: 332

Site of 16th-century tower of the border reiver Hector Armstrong, who in 1569 betrayed the Earl of Northumberland into the hands of the Regent Moray.

Harlawhill

Lothians: To the north-east of Prestonpans, on minor roads south of B1348.

Private   NT 390745 [?]   OS: 66   *   Map: 4, no: 159

Standing in a walled garden, Harlawhill is a 17th-century L-plan house of two storeys. The interior has been much altered to connect with later extensions. There is no vaulting.

It was a property of the Hamiltons, and the house is still occupied.

Harrow Hope

Borders: About 6 miles west of Peebles, on minor roads and track north of B712 or south of A72, at or near Harrow Hope.

Ruin or site   NT 163393 [?]   OS: 72   *   Map: 2, no: 28

Site of residence of the Bishops of Glasgow, which was mentioned in 1299.

Harskeith *see* Hartsgarth Tower

Harthill Castle

Aberdeen & Gordon: About 5.5 miles north-west of Inverurie, on minor road south of B9002 0.5 miles west of A96, south of Kirkton of Oyne, just north of Torries, at Harthill.

Private   NJ 687252   OS: 38   **   Map: 10, no: 196**

Harthill Castle is a large 17th-century Z-plan tower house. It consists of a main block of four storeys and a garret with towers at opposite corners, one round and one square. Bartizans crown the corners, and the walls are pierced by gunloops. The tower had a courtyard, and remains of a gatehouse and part of a courtyard wall survive.

The entrance is in the main re-entrant angle. The basement is vaulted and contained a guardroom, and the main turnpike stair is in the square tower. The kitchen, with a large arched fireplace, occupied one end of the basement of the main block. Both the kitchen and wine-cellar had small stairs to the hall on the first floor. There is a dome-vaulted cellar in the basement of the round tower.

The hall, on the first floor, was a fine chamber with a large fireplace and stone seats. Private chambers, in the two towers and on the floors above the hall, were reached by turnpike stairs in the thickness of the walls.

Harthill was probably built by the Leith family, who had held the property from 1531. One of the family, Patrick Leith, was noted for his boldness and leadership in the army of the Marquis of Montrose. He was captured by General Middleton in 1647, and beheaded at the age of 25. The last Leith of Harthill apparently deliberately torched the castle, and the property passed to the Erskines of Pittodrie. The house was restored in the 1970s, and is occupied.

Hartree Tower

Borders: About 1 mile south of Biggar, on minor road east of A702, east of the Hartree Hills.

Ruin or site   NT 046360   OS: 72   *   Map: 2, no: 1

Nothing remains of a 16th-century tower house, the site of which is occupied by a later mansion, itself incorporated into a later building.

It was a property of the Browns from 1434 or earlier until sold in 1634 to the Dicksons of Hartree. The tower was inhabited until the 1780s, but demolished about 1790 to build a new house. The Dicksons held the property at the end of the 19th century. The mansion was altered and extended down the centuries, and looks a bit of a mess.

Hartsgarth Tower

Borders: About 3.5 miles north of Newcastleton, on minor road west of B6399, west of Hermitage Water, just north of the Hartsgarth Burn, at Hartsgarth.

Ruin or site   NY 494926   OS: 79   *   Map: 2, no: 156

Site of tower house of the Elliots.

Other refs: Harskeith; Herskerth

Hartshaw Tower

Stirlingshire & Clackmannan: About 2.5 miles east of Clackmannan, on minor roads north of A907 or south of A977, near Brucefield, at Hartshaw Farm.

Ruin or site   NS 958915   OS: 58   *   Map: 6, no: 107

Site of castle, dating from the 15th century, which was a property of the Stewarts of Rosyth. Hartshaw Mill and Farm were built from the remains, and there is a stone with the date 1574.

Brucefield House is an 18th-century symmetrical mansion with two small wings, built by Alexander Bruce of Kennet.

Hartside Castle

Borders: About 4.5 miles north-west of Lauder, on minor roads west of A68, 1.5 miles west of Oxton, at Hartside.

Ruin or site   NT 469537   OS: 73   *   Map: 2, no: 136

Site of castle.

Harviestoun Castle

Stirlingshire & Clackmannan: About 1 mile east of Tillicoultry, on minor roads north of A91, north of River Devon, at Harviestoun.

Ruin or site   NS 937978 [?]   OS: 58   *   Map: 6, no: 104

Site of a castellated mansion, dating from 1804 and enlarged and altered around 1860, but blown up and demolished in 1970. Nothing remains except gate lodges and stables. There was, however, an earlier house on the site, possibly dating from 1610. Robert Burns visited in 1787, and it was here he had the inspiration for 'The Banks of Devon'. The later mansion was built by the Taits around 1780, but later passed to the Orr family. Kerr of Harviestoun presented Castle Campbell to The National Trust for Scotland in 1948.

Hassendean Castle

Borders: About 4.5 miles north-east of Hawick, on minor roads just east of B6359 near junction with B6405, at or near Hassendean.

Ruin or site   NT 547203 [?]   OS: 73   *   Map: 2, no: 202

Little or nothing remains of a strong tower of the Scott family. Sir Alexander Scott of Hassendean was killed at the Battle of Flodden in 1513.

The nearby kirk and graveyard were washed away in a flood in 1796.

Other refs: Hazeldean

Hassock *see* Drumlanrig Castle

Hatton Castle

Banff & Buchan: About 3 miles south-east of Turriff, on minor roads east of A947 or south of B9170, 1 mile south of Idoch Water, at Hatton House.

Private   NJ 758469   OS: 29   **   Map: 10, no: 240

Hatton Castle, mostly built in 1814, incorporates a substantial part of the 15th-century castle of Balquhollie.

It was a property of the Mowat family from the 13th century until 1723, when they sold it to the Duffs, who built the castellated mansion. The house is in good condition, and still occupied.

Other refs: Balquhollie Castle

Hatton Castle

Angus & Dundee: About 5.5 miles east of Coupar Angus, on minor road just east of B954 just south of village of Newtyle, north-west of Hatton Hill, at Hatton.

Ruin or site   NO 302411   OS: 53   *   Map: 8, no: 151**

Hatton Castle is a 16th-century Z-plan tower house. It consists of a main block of three storeys and an attic, with square towers projecting at opposite corners. Round stair-towers rise in the outer re-entrant angles. The walls are pierced by many gun-loops and shot-holes.

The moulded entrance leads to a wide turnpike stair, which climbs only to the first floor, in one of the square towers. The vaulted basement contains cellars and a kitchen with an enormous arched fireplace. The hall was on the first floor with adjoining private chambers. The many rooms on the floors above, both of the main block and towers, were reached by turret stairs.

The lands were granted by Robert the Bruce to Isabella Douglas, who married William Oliphant, Justiciar of Scotland. The castle was built in 1575. The property passed to Halyburton of Pitcur in 1627, then to the son of Mackenzie of Rosehaugh. The castle was garrisoned by the Covenanter Earl of Crawford in 1645, but was captured by the Marquis of Montrose. In 1983 it was purchased by a member of the Oliphant family as a centre for the Clan Oliphant, and has been restored.

Other refs: Newtyle Castle

Hatton House

Lothians: About 3 miles north west of Balerno, on minor road north of A71 east of junction with B7030, just north of Burnwynd.

Private   NT 128687   OS: 65   *   Map: 4, no: 43

Site of L-plan tower house, incorporating 15th-century work. It was surrounded by a large old mansion, dating from the 17th century, but was gutted by fire in 1952 to be demolished three years later. Much remains of the garden terraces, grotto, gazebo and gates of 1692 (which have been moved from their original position).

The property belonged to the Hattons in the 13th century, but passed to the Lauders in 1377, who built a castle here. One of the family was killed fighting for the Black Douglases in the 1450s, and the property forfeited, although the castle had to be besieged in 1453 to wrest it from the family. It was later recovered by the Lauders, and refortified by them in 1515.

James Hepburn, 4th Earl of Bothwell, stayed here the night before he abducted Mary, Queen of Scots, in 1567. In the 1580s Sir William Lauder argued with his son and wife, and had them imprisoned in the castle. The property passed to the Maitlands in 1652, and they built much of the house that stood in 1952. It was sold in 1792 to the Davidsons of Muirhouse, then again in 1870 when it was bought by the Douglas Earl of Morton.

Beware of farmers.

Other refs: Halton

Hatton Manor

Banff & Buchan: About 5 miles south of Turriff, on minor roads west of B992, 0.3 miles north-west of Kirkton of Auchterless.

Private   NJ 709420   OS: 29   **   Map: 10, no: 215

Site of castle, part of which may be built into the late 18th-century house. There is a round tower with a gunloop, and 17th- or 18th-century panelling in two rooms, as well as a walled garden.

Hatton of Ogilvie *see* Claverhouse Castle

Haughton House

Aberdeen & Gordon: About 0.5 miles north-east of Alford, on minor roads north of A944, south of River Don, at or near Haughton.

Private   NJ 583169 [?]   OS: 37   *   Map: 10, no: 148

Site of castle or old house. Haughton House, which dates from about 1800, is a mansion of three storeys and an attic with a later extension.

The lands were a property of the Farquharsons from the second half of the 17th century.

Haulkerton Castle

Kincardine & Deeside: About 1 mile north of Laurencekirk, on minor roads north of A937 in Laurencekirk, north of the Luther Water, at or near Mains of Haulkerton.

Ruin or site   NO 713731 [?]   OS: 45   *   Map: 10, no: 218

Site of 16th-century castle of the Falconers, who were descended from the royal falconers of Kincardine Castle. The castle was ruinous by 1790, there were some remains in the 19th century, but only two date stones survive with 1556? and 1648.

The family acquired the lands in 1150 and moved to nearby Inglismaldie in 1693. They were made Lords Falconer in 1647, then Earls of Kintore in 1778.

Other refs: Hawkerton; Halkerton

Haven

Ross & Cromarty: About 10 miles east and north of Tain, on minor roads and foot north of B9165 at Portmahomack, 1.5 miles of Tarbat Ness, near Blar a' Chath.

Ruin or site   NH 925870 [?]   OS: 21   *   Map: 9, no: 145

Site of castle.

Hawick *see* Lovells' Castle, Hawick

Hawick Tower *see* Drumlanrig's Tower, Hawick

Hawkerton *see* Haulkerton Castle

Hawkhead Castle

Renfrewshire: About 1 mile east of Paisley, on minor roads north of A726 or south of A737, on south side of White Cart Water, at or near Ross House.
Ruin or site NS 501626 [?] OS: 64 * Map: 3, no: 210
Site of castle, which consisted of a large square tower or keep, extended in 1634 by ranges to form a courtyard. It was remodelled in 1782 and later, surrounded by wooded parks and garden, but nothing now remains.
  It was a property of the Ross family from the end of the 14th century until 1866, when the lands were divided. Hawkhead Hospital occupies the site.

Hawkhill *see* Tulliallan Castle

Hawkshaw Castle

Borders: About 9 miles south of Broughton, on minor road east of A701, on east side of Tweed, near the Hawkshaw Burn.
Ruin or site NT 079225 [?] OS: 72 * Map: 2, no: 3
Site of 14th-century castle of the Porteous family, little of which remains above ground. The family held the property until about 1725.

Hawthornden Castle

Lothians: About 1 mile south of Loanhead, on minor roads north of A6094, just south of the River North Esk, about 0.5 miles east of Roslin village.
Private NT 287637 OS: 66 ** Map: 4, no: 120
Standing on a cliff overlooking a deep gorge, Hawthornden consists of ruined 15th-century keep, to which has been added a 17th-century L-plan house of three storeys and a garret. Defended by three gunloops, the entrance leads through a pend to a courtyard, where the main part of the 17th-century house stands.

The castle has been modernised inside, and is being restored again.
  The property originally belonged to the Abernethy family from the 13th century, but passed by marriage to the Douglases, who sold it to the Drummonds about 1540. The caves and passageways carved out of the rock beneath the castle were reputedly used by Robert the Bruce and Sir Alexander Ramsay of Dalhousie, who was later starved to death in Hermitage Castle. The castle was sacked by the Earl of Hertford, later Duke of Somerset, in 1544 and again in 1547. Mary, Queen of Scots, is said to have spent three nights here.
  Hawthornden was the home of the poet William Drummond. His fiancee, Mary Cunningham of Barns, was burned to death on the eve of their wedding, and Drummond became a learned recluse. He was a staunch Jacobite. Dr Johnson visited Hawthornden. The house is still occupied.
Other refs: Drummond House

Hawthornside

Borders: About 1 mile west of Bonchester Bridge, on minor road and foot just west of A6088, just west of Hawthornside.
Ruin or site NT 565121 OS: 80 * Map: 2, no: 211
Site of tower house. The present farmhouse is said to have been built from the remains of the tower.
Other refs: Hangingside; Peel Knowe

Haystoun

Borders: About 1.5 miles south and east of Peebles, on minor roads south of B7062, 1 mile south-east of Kings Muir, east of the Glensax Burn, at Haystoun.
Private NT 259383 OS: 73 * Map: 2, no: 67
Standing on a knoll overlooking a burn, Haystoun is a much-altered 16th-century L-plan tower house, now forming three sides of a courtyard. There is a walled garden. It was built by the Elphinstones, who held the property from 1500 until 1622. In 1635 the Hays of Smithfield acquired the castle, and greatly extended and altered the old tower. The house is still occupied, and in good condition.
Other refs: Hendestoun

Hazeldean *see* Hassendean Castle

Hazelside Castle

Lanarkshire & Glasgow: About 1.5 miles south-west of Douglas, on minor road north of A70, west of Douglas Water, at or near Hazelside.
Ruin or site NS 815289 [?] OS: 72 * Map: 3, no: 379
Site of castle.

Ha' Hill *see* Pitgair Castle

Ha' Tower

Perth & Kinross: About 1.5 miles west of Dunning, on minor roads and foot east of B934 in Dunning, just south-west of Clevage, north of Woodhead.
Ruin or site NO 043145 OS: 58 * Map: 8, no: 58
Very little remains of a tower house of the Grahams.

Heatherlands Tower

Borders: About 2 miles south of Morebattle, on minor road south of B6401, 0.25 miles south of Whitton, north of Chesterhouse Hill, at Heatherlands.
Ruin or site NT 759215 OS: 74 * Map: 2, no: 303
Site of tower house, a vestige of which survived in the middle of the 19th century.

Helmsdale Castle

Sutherland & Caithness: In Helmsdale, on minor road just west of A9, just north of River Helmsdale, beneath tourist information office.
Ruin or site ND 027152 OS: 17 * Map: 12, no: 38
Site of castle of the Sutherland Earls of Sutherland, built about 1488 and altered in 1616 by the Gordons of Navidale. It was an L-plan building with a stair in the re-entrant angle.
  It was here that in 1567 Isobel Sinclair, the Earl's aunt, poisoned John, the 11th Earl of Sutherland, and his wife in order make her own son Earl. She also tried to poison the Earl's heir, but the cup of poison was drunk by her own son, who died two days later. She killed herself before being executed in Edinburgh. The whole affair was apparently a plot hatched by George Sinclair, 4th Earl of Caithness.
  The property later passed to the Gordons. The castle was ruined by 1858, and was removed in the 1970s when the A9 was realigned.

Hempisfield Tower *see* Amisfield Tower

Hempriggs Castle

Moray: About 5 miles north-east of Forres, on minor road just south of B9089, about 3.5 miles south of Burghead, at or near Hempriggs.
Ruin or site NJ 103641 [?] OS: 28 * Map: 10, no: 16
Site of 15th-century castle of the Dunbars, who also held property in Caithness. It was demolished in the first half of the 19th century to build the farm.

Hempriggs House

Sutherland & Caithness: About 2.5 miles south of Wick, on minor road east of A9, 0.5 miles east of Loch Hempriggs, at Hempriggs House.
Private ND 359473 OS: 12 * Map: 12, no: 64
Hempriggs, a plain altered and extended two-storey mansion, incorporates part or is built on the site of a castle. The existing house mostly dates from 1692 and 1875, and is now a rambling building.
   Hempriggs was a property of the Sinclairs, but passed to the Dunbars of Hempriggs and Ackergill, from Moray, who held it until the 20th century. The house is now a residential home.

Henderland *see* Cockburn's Tower

Henderstoun *see* Haystoun

Herbertshiel Castle *see* Whistleberry Castle

Herbertshire Castle

Stirlingshire & Clackmannan: About 5 miles west of Falkirk, west of the A872, in Dunipace, just south of the River Carron.
Ruin or site NS 804830 OS: 65 * Map: 6, no: 75
Site of large, altered and extended 16th-century L-plan tower house. The castle was demolished in the 20th century, and nothing remains.
   The property passed from the Sinclairs of Rosslyn, Earls of Orkney, to Alexander Elphinstone, 1st Earl of Linlithgow, in 1608. It was later held by the Stirlings, who sold it to William Morehead in 1768. It was acquired by Forbes of Callendar in 1835.

Herdmanston

Lothians: About 4.5 miles west and south of Haddington, on minor roads north of B6355, on south bank of the River Tyne, near or at Herdmanston.
Ruin or site NT 474700 [?] OS: 66 * Map: 4, no: 177
Site of 16th-century L-plan tower of the Sinclair family. It was captured and held by Lord Gray of Wilton acting for the English in 1548, when it was a place of some strength.

Hermitage Castle

Borders: About 5 miles north of Newcastleton, on minor road west of B6357 at Hermitage, just north of Hermitage Water.
His Scot NY 497960 OS: 79 ** Map: 2, no: 160**
One of the most impressive and oppressive of Scottish fortresses, Hermitage Castle consists of a 13th-century courtyard and large 14th-century keep of four storeys, around which has been constructed a massive castle. The keep had small square towers added at three of the corners, and the entrance was at first-floor level and defended by two portcullises. In the 15th century a new rectangular wing was extended from the main keep.
   The walls are pierced by small windows and splayed gunloops. A timber gallery projected around the whole building, the holes to support the joists still visible.
   The entrance leads into the central courtyard, but the buildings within are very ruined.

The property belonged to the Dacres, who had a castle here in the 13th century, but passed to the de Soulis family, who strengthened the castle. One of the family was a man of ill repute and said to dabble in witchcraft. Many local children were apparently seized by Soulis and never seen again. The local people, according to one story, eventually rebelled and Soulis was wrapped in lead and boiled in a cauldron at Ninestane Rig (a stone circle about 1.5 miles north-east of Hermitage), although he may actually have been imprisoned in Dumbarton Castle for supporting the English. The family were forfeited in 1320.
   The castle passed to the Grahams, then by marriage to the Douglas family. William Douglas, 'The Knight of Liddlesdale', was prominent in resisting Edward Balliol in 1330s. He seized Sir Alexander Ramsay of Dalhousie, however, while at his devotions in St Mary's Church in Hawick, and imprisoned him in a dungeon at the castle and starved him to death. In 1353 Douglas was murdered by his godson, another William Douglas, after he had tried to block his claim to the lordship of Douglas.
   In 1492 Archibald, 5th Earl of Angus, exchanged Hermitage for Bothwell with Patrick Hepburn, Earl of Bothwell. In 1566 James Hepburn, 4th Earl of Bothwell was badly wounded, in a skirmish with the Border reiver 'Little Jock' Elliot of Park – the latter was shot and eventually died – and was paid a visit on his sick bed by Mary, Queen of Scots. Mary and Bothwell were later married, but after she fled Scotland in 1568, he escaped to Norway. Bothwell was eventually imprisoned in the Danish castle of Dragsholm until his death – his mummified body is said to be preserved there. The castle and title passed from the Hepburns to Francis Stewart, Earl of Bothwell, then after he was forfeited to the Scotts of Buccleuch. The castle was partly restored in the 19th century.
   Ghostly screams and cries can sometimes reputedly be heard from the victims of Lord Soulis, and his own ghost has been reported here. The ghost of Alexander Ramsay is said to have been seen within the walls, as has that of Mary, Queen of Scots, clad in a white dress.
OPEN: Open Apr-Sep, daily 9.30-18.30, last ticket sold 18.00.
Sales area. Car and coach parking. Group concessions. £.
Tel: 01387 376222   Fax: 0131 668 8888
Email: hs.explore@scotland.gov.uk   Web: www.historic-scotland.gov.uk

Heron's Hole *see* Longformacus

Herskerth *see* Hartsgarth Tower

Hessilhead Castle

Ayrshire: About 2.5 miles east of Beith, on minor roads south of B777, just north of Hessilhead, north of the Dusk Water.
Ruin or site NS 379533 OS: 63 * Map: 3, no: 132
Nothing remains of an altered and extended 15th-century keep and castle, remodelled and extended further in 1685, but mostly demolished in 1776. It was apparently built on a loch and was defended by large ditches
   It was a property of the Montgomerys of Eglinton. One of the family was the 16th-century poet, Alexander Montgomery.

Heston Island

Galloway: About 7 miles south of Dalbeattie, on minor roads and boat south of A711, on Heston Island east of Balcary Point, south of Almorness Point.
Ruin or site NX 839503 [?] OS: 84 * Map: 1, no: 151
Site of castle or manor, a vestige of which remains.
   It was a property of the MacDowalls, but burned by Edward Bruce, brother of Robert the Bruce, in 1308 during the Wars of Independence. It was used in the 1330s and 40s by Edward Balliol. The property was long held by Dundrennan Abbey.
Other refs: Isle of Heston

Heugh Head

Borders: About 2 miles south and west of Coldingham, on minor roads just north of A1, 0.25 miles north-east of Reston, at Heugh Head
Ruin or site NT 877625 OS: 67 * Map: 2, no: 348
Site of tower house of the Craw family who held property here in 1562.

Hewke

Dumfriesshire: About 4 miles north of Lockerbie, on minor roads east of B723, just east of Dryfe Water, at Hewke.
Ruin or site   NY 144887   OS: 78   *   Map: 1, no: 247
Site of tower house.

High House of Edmonston *see* Edmonston Castle

Hill House

Fife: About 1 mile south of Dunfermline Abbey, on minor road just east of B9156, at Hill House.
Private   NT 092860   OS: 65   **   Map: 7, no: 15
Hill House consists of a 17th-century L-plan house of three storeys and a five-storey tower, in the re-entrant angle, which is crowned by a parapet. The walls are adorned with inscriptions of a religious nature.

The house has been much altered inside, but contains several fine fireplaces removed from 17th-century buildings in Culross.

William Menteith of Randieford acquired the lands of Hill in 1621, and 'twas he who built the house and wrote the goodly sayings.

Hill of Ardmore *see* Ardmore

Hill of Beith

Ayrshire: To east of Beith, on minor road north of B777, at Hill of Beith.
Ruin or site   NS 360541 [?]   OS: 63   *   Map: 3, no: 118
Site of castle, marked on Blaeu's Atlas Novus Map of Cunningham.

The lands were held by Kilwinning Abbey from the end of the 12th century, but passed to the Cunninghams at the Reformation. The Court Hill [NS 361539] stands nearby.

Hill of Tarvit Mansion House

Fife: About 2.5 miles south of Cupar, on minor roads east of A916 or north of B939, 1.5 miles west of Ceres, Hill of Tarvit.
NTS   NO 380119   OS: 59   *   Map: 7, no: 104**
The original house dating from 1696, with 19th-century wings, was virtually rebuilt in 1906 by Sir Robert Lorimer for Mr F. B. Sharp, a Dundee industrialist. Sharp wanted to house his fine collections of paintings and pictures including works by Raeburn and Ramsay, furniture including Chippendale, Flemish tapestries and Chinese porcelain and bronzes. There are formal gardens, also designed by Lorimer, and Scotstarvit Tower is nearby and open to the public.
Other refs: Wemyss Hall; Upper Wemyss
OPEN: Open Easter wknd, then May to Sep, daily 13.30-17.30; Jul-Aug, daily 11.00-17.30; Oct, Sat-Sun 13.30-17.30; last admission 16.45. Tearoom as house except open at 12.20 when house opens 13.30. Grounds and garden open all year, 9.30-sunset.
Explanatory displays. Gift shop. Tearoom. Picnic area. Restored Edwardian laundry. Woodland walk. Scotstarvit Tower is nearby. Disabled access to ground floor and grounds suitable and WC. Gardens: scented border for the visually impaired, with Braille captions. ££.
Tel: 01334 653127
Email: information@nts.org.uk   Web: nts.org.uk

Hill Tower *see* Calfield Tower

Hillhouse *see* Stobo Castle

Hillhouse Tower *see* Whithaugh Tower

Hillhouse Tower

Borders: About 1.5 miles east of Newcastleton, on minor roads and foot east of B6357, in Newcastleton Forest, north-east of Hillhouse.
Ruin or site   NY 505871   OS: 79   *   Map: 2, no: 170
Site of tower house, described as a strong square tower, some remains of which survived in 1795.

Hills Tower

Lanarkshire & Glasgow: About 4 miles east of Carnwath, on minor roads north of A721, 1.5 miles west of Dunsyre, at Easthills.
Ruin or site   NT 049481   OS: 72   *   Map: 3, no: 454
Site of tower house, with a vaulted basement, of which nothing remains. In 1299 the property was held by the Denholms, but it passed to the Baillies of Lamington, then the Hamiltons, and finally the Lockharts.
Other refs: Easthills

Hills Tower

Galloway: About 5 miles south-west of Dumfries, on minor roads north of A711, about 0.5 miles east of Lochrutton Loch, at Mains of Hills.
Private   NX 912726   OS: 84   *   Map: 1, no: 175**
Hills Tower consists of a 15th-century rectangular keep of four storeys and a garret within a crenellated parapet. To this has been added a two-storey house, in the 18th century, within an adjoining courtyard. The courtyard has a small gatehouse, which still has an iron yett. The gatehouse was converted into a doocot. The stair of the keep is crowned by a caphouse with a conical roof.

The entrance to the keep, from the courtyard, leads to a vaulted basement and to the foot of a turnpike stair. The hall, on the first floor, has a fireplace flanked by aumbries.

Hills was a property of the Maxwells, the family eventually succeeding to the Earldom of Nithsdale. William Maxwell, the 5th Earl and a Jacobite, made a famous escape from the Tower of London on the eve of his execution after being captured at Preston in 1715. His wife was allowed to visit him before his execution, and he escaped wearing her clothes, reputedly disguised as her servant. She eventually joined him in Rome. Hills passed by marriage to the MacCullochs of Ardwall. The building was restored in the 1970s.
Other refs: Hill's Castle

Hillside

Fife: About 3 miles west of Burntisland, on minor road north of A921, to north of Aberdour, Hillside.
Ruin or site   NT 191856   OS: 65   *   Map: 7, no: 32
Site of castle, some remains of which were built into the later mansion. The last remains were demolished, along with a 16th-century doocot, in 1960. The mansion was held by the Stewarts of Dunearn in the 19th century, and Hillside was visited by James Hogg among other notables.

Hillslap Tower

Borders: About 3.5 miles north and east of Galashiels, on minor roads north of A7, near Langshaw Tower and Colmslie Tower, south of Allan Water.
Private   NT 513394   OS: 73   *   Map: 2, no: 174**
Hillslap Tower is a 16th-century L-plan tower house of four storeys. It consists of a main block and a stair-wing, which rises a storey higher. A stair-turret projects from above first-floor level in the re-entrant angle. The walls are pierced by gunloops, and the tower is dated 1585. The tower has a courtyard with a range of buildings.

The entrance leads to the main stair, which climbs to the large hall on the first floor of the main block, the other floors reached by the stair-turret. The basement is vaulted.

Hillslap was a property of the Cairncross family. Walter Scott used it in his novel 'The Monastery', calling it Glendearg. It was reroofed and restored in the 1980s.
Other refs: Glendearg; Calfhill Tower

Hill's Castle *see* Hills Tower

Hindhaughhead

Borders: About 7 miles south and west of Jedburgh, north of A6088, about 1.5 miles east of Chesters, north of Jed Water, east of Falside.
Ruin or site   NT 643103   OS: 80   *   Map: 2, no: 256
Site of 15th-century castle, some foundations of which survive along with the remains of later buildings. The castle and village were destroyed by Sir John Ratcliffe for the English in 1513, but a building here was occupied by a Lady Shaw in the 17th century.

Hillslap Tower – see previous page

Hirendean Castle

Lothians: About 6.5 miles south-east of Penicuik, on minor road 4 miles south of B6372, about 1 mile south of Gladhouse Reservoir, in the Moorfoot Hills.
Ruin or site NT 298512 OS: 66 * Map: 4, no: 124
Little survives, except two ruined walls, of a 16th-century tower house of at least three storeys. The lands were a property of Newbattle Abbey, but passed to the Kerrs after the Reformation and they built the castle.

Hirsel, The *see* The Hirsel

Hoddom Castle

Dumfriesshire: About 5 miles north-west of Annan, on minor roads north of B725, south of the River Annan, at Hoddom.
Private NY 157730 OS: 85 ** Map: 1, no: 252**
Hoddom (also recorded as Hoddam) Castle is massive 16th-century L-plan tower house of four storeys and an attic within a parapet. To this had been added a 19th-century mansion, which has since been demolished. The remaining castle consists of a main block and higher stair-tower. A corbelled-out parapet and bartizans crown the tower. The entrance surround is moulded, and there are remains of a court-yard wall and dry ditch.

The property was held by the Herries family in the 14th and 15th centuries, but passed to the Carruthers. Hoddom was built by the Maxwell Lord Herries, who acquired the lands in the middle of the 16th century. He demolished a chapel to build the castle, but later constructed a watch-tower on Repentance Hill as recompense. This may have been to appease his conscience, but more likely to appease the powerful Archbishop of Glasgow, whose chapel he had demolished. The castle was taken in 1588 and held by Douglas of Drumlanrig, but in 1569 Hoddom was recaptured by forces loyal to Mary, Queen of Scots. In 1570 the English captured and blew up the tower. It was rebuilt and acquired by the Murrays of Cockpool about 1627, then the Carnegie Earls of Southesk in 1653. It was sold to the Sharp family in 1690, who extended the castle with a wing by William Burn, but sold again, this time to the Brooks in 1878. It stands in a caravan park.

Hoddomtown Castle *see* Hallguards Castle

Holehouse *see* Hollows Tower

Holenly *see* Holylee

Hollows Tower

Dumfriesshire: About 2 miles north of Canonbie, on minor road east of A7, west of the River Esk, just north of Hollows.
Private NY 383787 OS: 85 * Map: 1, no: 323**
Situated on a strong site, Hollows or Gilnockie's Tower is a rectangular 16th-century tower house of four storeys and a garret within a corbelled-out parapet. There was probably a courtyard.

The entrance leads to a turnpike stair, which climbs to the upper floors. The basement is vaulted, and the hall, on the first floor, has a wide moulded fireplace.

Hollows was a stronghold of the unruly Armstrong clan after nearby Gilnockhall or Gilnockie Castle had been destroyed by the English in 1523. Johnnie Armstrong of Gilnockie was hanged without trial by James V in 1530, with 50 of his family, as recorded in the old ballad. A stone memorial marks the mass grave at Carlanrig [NT 403048].

The tower has been reroofed and restored, and now houses the Clan Armstrong Centre, although the Armstrongs were never a clan.

There may have been another tower to the south, known as 'Priore Johns'.
Other refs: Gilnockie Tower; Holehouse

OPEN: Guided tours – check opening; summer months 11.00-14.30.
Guided tours. Explanatory displays. Gift shop. WC. Car parking. Group concessions. £.
Tel: 01387 371876

Holm Castle

Lanarkshire & Glasgow area: About 0.5 miles north-west of Stonehouse, on minor roads north of A71, north of Avon Water, at or near Holm.
Ruin or site NS 746474 OS: 64 * Map: 3, no: 352
Site of castle, which was ruinous by the 19th century.
Other refs: Holmhead

Holmains Castle

Dumfriesshire: About 4 miles south of Lochmaben, on minor roads north of minor road between A75 at Byeloch and B7020 at Newton, at or near Holmains.
Ruin or site NY 083767 OS: 85 * Map: 1, no: 221
Site of a castle, said never to have been a place of great strength. It was ruinous by 1795.

It was a property of the Carruthers, and in 1563 John Carruthers, and others, were accused of assaulting Kirkpatrick of Closeburn and slaying several people.
Other refs: Howmains Castle

Holmhead *see* Holm Castle

Holy Island

Ayrshire: About 2 miles east of Lamlash on Arran, by boat and foot east of A841, on north-west side of Holy Island.

Ruin or site   NS 052308   OS: 69   *   Map: 3, no: 6

A small tower was built on the north-west of the island to defend Lamlash Bay, a fragment of which stood until about 1879. It is said to have been built by Somerled.

Holy Island is associated with St Molaise, and there is said to have been a house of friars here, although there is little evidence to support this. There was an old chapel, but nothing remains. The island is now home to a Buddhist retreat and centre.

Other refs: Smugglers' Cave, Holy Island

Holydean Castle *see* Castle of Holydean

Holylee

Borders: About 4 miles east of Innerleithen, on minor roads just north of A72, north of River Tweed, at or near Holylee.

Private   NT 392376 [?]   OS: 73   *   Map: 2, no: 100

Site of tower house. Old Holylee, a rectangular two-storey house which has been harled, stands on the site of a tower house.

It was a property of the Bannatyne family from 1734 to 1827, and replaced by the nearby 18th-century three-storey mansion.

Other refs: Old Holylee; Holenly

Holyroodhouse

Lothians: About 1 mile east of Edinburgh Castle, on minor roads south of A1, on the north-east edge of Holyrood Park.

Private   NT 269739   OS: 66   *   Map: 4, no: 110**

Holyroodhouse consists of ranges surrounding a rectangular courtyard, one of which dates from the 16th century. The present building was designed by Sir William Bruce for Charles II in 1671-8.

Holyrood Abbey was founded by David I around 1128 although sacked in 1322 and 1385 by the English. James III found the guest range of the abbey a comfortable alternative to Edinburgh castle, and James IV and James V extended the house. The English burned the abbey in 1544 and 1547, and all that survived their destruction was a block, with round corner turrets, built in 1529 to contain private chambers for James V.

David Rizzio, Mary, Queen of Scots's secretary was murdered here in her presence by men including by her husband, Lord Darnley. The palace was rebuilt in the late 17th century, a new block being built to balance the original tower with a connecting wall. The original 16th-century interiors survive in the old block, and the ruins of the abbey church adjoin.

Bonnie Prince Charlie stayed here for six weeks in 1745, and held court after the Battle of Prestonpans; while the Duke of Cumberland made it his residence after the Rising. The palace is the official residence of the monarch in Scotland. The State apartments house tapestries and paintings, and the Picture Gallery has portraits of over 80 Kings of Scots, painted by De Wet in 1684-6, and nearly all entirely made up.

A 'Grey Lady', thought to be the spirit of one of Mary's companions, has reputedly been seen in the Queen's Audience Chamber. Ghostly footsteps are said to have been heard in the long gallery.

Administered by the Lord Chamberlain.

Other refs: Palace of Holyroodhouse

OPEN: Open all year (except when monarch is in residence, Good Friday, 7-16 May, 24 Jun-12 Jul & 25/26 Dec): Apr-Oct daily 9.30-17.15; Nov-Mar daily 9.30-15.45.

Guided tours Nov-Mar. Gift shop. WC. Garden. Disabled access. Car and coach parking. Group concessions (10% groups of 15 or more). £££

Tel: 0131 556 1096/7371   Fax: 0131 557 5256

Email: information@royalcollection.org.uk   Web: www.royal.gov.uk

Home *see* Smeaton Castle

Home *see* Hume Castle

Hoolet House *see* Howlet's House

Hopeton Tower

Borders: About 3.5 miles north of Peebles, on minor road east of A703 at Eddleston, 0.3 miles east of Eddleston, near Longcote Burn.

Ruin or site   NT 249467 [?]   OS: 73   *   Map: 2, no: 60

Site of tower house, a property of the Murrays of Black Barony in the 17th century.

Other refs: Wormiston

Hopetoun House

Lothians: About 2.5 miles west of South Queensferry, on minor roads north of A904, south shore of Firth of Forth, at Hopetoun House.

Private   NT 089790   OS: 65   *   Map: 4, no: 36**

Situated on the shores of the Firth of Forth, Hopetoun House is a large and stately palatial mansion, with a central block and flanking wings. It dates between 1699 and 1707, and was built by William Bruce for the Hope family. Sir Charles Hope was made Earl of Hopetoun in 1703, then later Marquis of Linlithgow, and had the house remodelled by William Adam from 1721, the work being continued by John and Robert Adam. The house was transferred to a charitable trust in 1974. There are fine interiors including paintings by famous artists, 17th-century tapestries, rococo ceilings and Meissen ceramics. The house is set in 100 acres of rolling park land, including woodland walks, a red deer park, and a spring garden.

The ghost of a dark-cloaked man is said to have been seen on one of the paths in the grounds, and to be a harbinger of death or misadventure in the Hope family.

OPEN: Open daily 2 Apr-26 Sep 10.00-17.30; wknds only in Oct; last admission 16.30; other times closed except for group visits by prior appt.

Fine interiors. Collections of furniture and pictures. Gift shop. Restaurant. WC. Picnic area. Exhibitions. Park land. Croquet. Car and coach parking. Group concessions. ££.

Tel: 0131 331 2451   Fax: 0131 319 1885

Hopetoun Tower *see* Midhope Castle

Hoppringle Castle

Borders: About 4 miles north of Stow, on minor road east of A7, east of Gala Water, 1 mile north of Fountainhall, north of Toddle Burn, at or near Hoppringle.

Ruin or site   NT 434511   OS: 73   *   Map: 2, no: 115

Site of castle, once a place of some strength and importance, the site believed to be occupied by the later farm.

It was the original stronghold of the Hoppringle, or Pringle, family.

Hopsrig *see* Bombie

Horsburgh Tower

Borders: About 2 miles east and south of Peebles, on minor road south of Glentress from A72, on north bank of Tweed.

Ruin or site   NT 285392   OS: 73   **   Map: 2, no: 73

Horsburgh Tower is a very ruined 16th-century L-plan tower house, with the remains of a stair-turret.

The lands were held by the Horsburghs from the 13th century until the beginning of the 20th century.

Horsleyhill

Borders: About 2.5 miles north-east of Hawick, on B6359, south of Hassendean Burn, at or near Horsleyhill.

Ruin or site   NT 532193 [?]   OS: 79   *   Map: 2, no: 186

Site of tower house, probably of the Scotts.

Hoselaw Tower

Borders: About 2 miles north and west of Town Yetholm, on minor road from B6352, south-west of Hoselaw, near chapel.

Ruin or site   NT 802318 [?]   OS: 74   *   Map: 2, no: 325

Site of 17th-century tower house, remains of which survived in the 19th century.

Houndwood House

Borders: About 3 miles south-east of Granthouse, on minor road north of A1 at junction with B6437, at Houndwood House.

Private   NT 855630   OS: 67   **   Map: 2, no: 341

The present mansion of Houndwood House incorporates a 16th-century tower house, with a vaulted basement, which has a turnpike stair in one corner. The house is dated 1656, but was remodelled and castellated in the 19th and 20th centuries. Parts are said to date from the 12th century.

The lands were originally held by Coldingham Priory, and the monks are said to have had a hunting lodge here. They were acquired by the Homes after the Reformation, but later passed to Logan of Restalrig. Mary, Queen of Scots, is said to have visited in 1565. In the 18th century the property passed to the Turnbulls, then to the Coulsons, then the Cooksons, until 1919 when it was acquired by the Browns.

The house was said to be haunted by a ghost called 'Chappie', and manifestations were reported in the 19th century, including unexplained heavy footsteps, knocking and rapping, and deep breathing and moans. The apparition of a the lower part of a man, dressed in riding breeches, is said to have been witnessed in the grounds outside the house. The story goes that a man was killed by a party of soldiers in the 16th century, and cut in half.

The sounds of ghostly horses have also been reported here.

There may have been another tower at Houndwood village [NT 842638], although this may be a confusion with the building here.

House of Auchiries

Banff & Buchan: About 4 miles south of Fraserburgh

Private   NJ 977606   OS: 30   **   Map: 10, no: 345

House of Auchiries consists of three blocks, forming a rough Z-plan. The building dates from the first half of the 18th century, although it may incorporate earlier work as the kitchen is vaulted and there are shot-holes. Two of the blocks are roofless, while the third is used as a farm.

It was a property of the Keith Earls Marischal in the 17th century, but was sold to the Ogilvies in 1703 who held it for 100 years. Alexander Forbes, Lord Pitsligo, who was a Jacobite, only just managed to escape from here when surprised by Hanoverian forces in 1756.

House of Boyndlie *see* Boyndlie House

House of Byth *see* Byth House

House of Cockburn *see* Cockburn House

House of Cushnie *see* Cushnie Castle

House of Dun

Angus & Dundee: About 3 miles north-west of Montrose, on minor road north of A935 at Mains of Dun, at or near House of Dun.

NTS   NO 667599 [?]   OS: 54   *   Map: 8, no: 260

Site of castle, little of which survives except one vault about 400 yards west the present mansion. House of Dun, a fine classical mansion, was built in 1730 by William Adam for David Erskine Lord Dun.

The Erskine family held the lands from 1375, and had a castle here. One of the family was John Erskine, a scholar and reformer in the time of Mary, Queen of Scots.

Other refs: Dun

OPEN: Open Easter wknd, then May-Sep, daily 13.30-17.30; Jul-Aug, daily 11.00-17.30; Oct, Sat-Sun 13.30-17.30; last admission 17.00. Tea room opens at 11.00. Garden and grounds open all year 9.30-sunset.

Explanatory displays. Gift shop. Restaurant. Adventure playground. Fine plasterwork and a collection of portraits, furniture and porcelain. Walled garden and handloom weaving workshop. On Sundays during summer there is a special steam train service from Brechin Station, run by Caledonian Co Ltd. Disabled access to ground floor and basement and WC. Info in Braille. £££

Tel: 01674 810264   Fax: 01674 810722

Email: information@nts.org.uk   Web: nts.org.uk

House of Kairs *see* Kair House

House of Lethan *see* Lethen House

House of Mergie

Kincardine & Deeside: About 4 miles west and north of Stonehaven, on minor road south of A957 (Slug Road), just north of the Cowie Water, at Mergie.

Private   NO 796887   OS: 45   **   Map: 10, no: 264

House of Mergie is a tall 17th-century tower house of three storeys, now T-plan. It consists of a rectangular main block and a small projecting stair-wing. The building has been altered, the roof level lowered and shot-holes sealed.

The basement is not vaulted. The old kitchen has a wide arched fireplace.

Mergie was a property of the Douglases, but passed to Paul Symmer, an officer in Cromwell's army. It was sold in 1772 to Alexander Garrioch, a staunch Jacobite, who had fought in the 1715 Rising. A later owner, Colonel Duff of Fetteresso, caught Robert Burns poaching on his estate. The building is still occupied and used as a farmhouse.

Other refs: Mergie House

House of Monymusk *see* Monymusk Castle

House of Penick *see* Penick Castle

House of Royston *see* Caroline Park House

House of Ruthven *see* Huntingtower Castle

House of Schivas

Aberdeen & Gordon: About 5.5 miles north-west of Ellon, on minor roads north of B9005, north of River Ythan, south of South Quilquox, at House of Schivas.

Private   NJ 898368   OS: 30   *   Map: 10, no: 313**

House of Schivas is a fine altered 16th-century L-plan tower house. It consists of a main block and offset wing with a large round stair-tower projecting from the main block. A stair-turret rises in the main re-entrant angle. The walls are pierced by shot-holes. The tower has been extended by lower wings.

The entrance, from the modern courtyard, is in the re-entrant angle. The basement is vaulted and contains the kitchen and two cellars, reached by a vaulted passageway. The foot of the wing is occupied by a square timber stair, which rises only to the first floor, the upper floors being reached by the narrow turnpike stair in the turret. The wider turnpike, in the round tower, climbs to all floors. The hall, on the first floor, is panelled and has a large fireplace. The second floor has contained a now divided upper hall and two private chambers.

The property belonged to the Schivas family, but passed to the Lipps, the Maitlands, then to the Gordons in 1467. In 1509 it was acquired by the Grays, who probably built the house. By 1721 the property had passed to the Forbeses, but it was then acquired by the Gordon Earl of Aberdeen. It was used as a farmhouse in the 19th century, restored after a fire in 1900, and is still occupied.
Other refs: Schivas; Shivas

House of Skeith

Banff & Buchan: About 4 miles south of Cullen, on minor roads east of B9018, 1 mile south of Kirktown of Deskford, east of Burn of Deskford, at or near Mains of Skeith.
Ruin or site   NJ 504603 [?]   OS: 29   *   Map: 10, no: 109
Site of castle or old house, nothing of which survives although there was a vestige in 1866. The lands were held by the Ogilvies.
Other refs: Skeith; Castle of Skeith

House of The Binns *see* The Binns

House of the Hassock *see* Drumlanrig Castle

House of Tongue

Sutherland & Caithness: About 1.5 miles north of Tongue, on minor roads just north of A838, on south coast of Kyle of Tongue, at Tongue House.
Ruin or site   NC 592588   OS: 10   **   Map: 12, no: 13
Site of tower house of the Mackays, which was demolished by 1830. The present House of Tongue dates from 1678, and was the main seat of the Mackay Lord Reay, although the property later passed to the Dukes of Sutherland, and is still held by them. There is a walled garden.
Other refs: Tongue; Old House of Tongue

House of Tyrie

Banff & Buchan: About 4 miles south-west of Fraserburgh, on minor road south of A98, near the Water of Tyrie, near Tyrie Mains.
Ruin or site   NJ 936632 [?]   OS: 30   *   Map: 10, no: 330
Site of 17th-century house, with round towers, of the Frasers, nothing of which remains. It had terraces, orchards, and a canal, but was ruinous by 1732. There was also a motte nearby, a property of the Comyns, but this has also gone.
Other refs: Tyrie House

Houston House

Lothians: In Uphall, on minor road south of A899, just west of junction with B8046, near the Brox Burn.
Private   NT 058716   OS: 65   *   Map: 4, no: 28**
Standing on a woody ridge, Houston House consists of an early 17th-century L-plan tower house of four storeys and an attic. The tower was greatly altered and extended in later centuries, with the addition of new wings around a rectangular courtyard. A small stair-tower projects from the original house, and the walls are harled.
   The basement is vaulted, but the inside of the tower has been much altered. A scale-and-platt stair has replaced the original turnpike stair in the re-entrant angle. The vaulted kitchen has a large arched fireplace. The hall, now the dining room, occupied the first floor of the main block.
   The lands were originally held by the Houstons, one of whom, Sir Peter Houston, was killed at the Battle of Flodden in 1513. The property passed to the Sharp, or Shairp, family about 1569. Sir John Shairp received a pair of hawking gloves from Mary, Queen of Scots, which were long kept at the house. One of the family was Archbishop Sharp, who was murdered at Magus Muir in 1679. Shairp of Houston voted against the Act of Union of 1707 during the last Scottish Parliament. Houston was sold by the family in 1945, the building extended in the 1960s, and it is now a hotel.
OPEN: Hotel.
Tel: 01506 853831   Fax: 01506 854220

Houston House

Renfrewshire: About 1 mile east and north of Bridge of Weir, on minor roads north of B790, east of B789, just north of village of Houston.
Private   NS 412672   OS: 64   **   Map: 3, no: 156
Not much remains of a 16th-century courtyard castle of the Stewart Earls of Lennox, except an altered range, dated 1625, but incorporating earlier work. The name is derived from 'Hugh's town' from Hugh of Padvinan, whose descendants took the name Houston.
   The castle was mostly demolished in 1780, except for one range, when a new mansion was built on the same site. In 1782 it was acquired by the Speirs of Elderslie, and additions were made in 1872 and 1893.
Other refs: Kilpeter

Howlet's House

Lothians: About 3 miles north-west of Penicuik, on minor road and foot west of A702 at Floterston, just north of Loganlea reservoir in Pentland hills, at Howlet's.
Ruin or site   NT 194625   OS: 66   *   Map: 4, no: 63
Site of castle, with thick walls and a vaulted basement.
Other refs: Hoolet House

Howliston Tower

Borders: About 4 miles north-west of Stow, on minor road west from A7, south of the Comely Burn, at or near Howliston.
Ruin or site   NT 412489   OS: 73   *   Map: 2, no: 104
Little remains of a tower house, built into the farm, which was a property of the Home family in 1626, but had passed to the Mitchells by 1690.

Howmains Castle *see* Holmains Castle

Howpaslie *see* Old Howpasley

Hudshouse Tower

Borders: About 9 miles north-east of Newcastleton, on minor roads east of B6357, on north bank of Liddel Water, south of Hudshouse Rig.
Ruin or site   NY 576980   OS: 80   *   Map: 2, no: 217
Site of tower house of the Croziers, marked by a mound of rubble, by the ruinous farm. There may have been another tower nearby [NY 580988], which was held by Martin Crozier of Rakestonleis in 1590, although this may be the same site.
Other refs: Caddroun Burn Tower

Huildie's Tower *see* Ayton Castle

Humbie Old Place

Lothians: About 5 miles east of Pathhead, on minor roads and foot south of B6368, north-west of Humbie Mains.
Ruin or site   NT 467627 [?]   OS: 66   *   Map: 4, no: 176
Site of castle or old house, the last remains of which had been removed by 1853. It was replaced by Humbie House.
   The lands were held by the Hepburns, but passed by marriage to the Scotts, who were Lords Polwarth from 1835.
Other refs: Old Humbie House

Hume Castle

Borders: About 3 miles south of Greenlaw, on minor road west of B6364 at Hume.
Ruin or site   NT 704414   OS: 74   *   Map: 2, no: 287
Standing on a commanding position with fine views over the Tweed valley, Hume Castle was first built in the 12th or 13th centuries, and was an important stronghold of the Home family. It was considered impregnable before the advent of gunpowder.
   The lands were held by the Home family from the 13th century, having come to them by marriage, and they were made Barons Home in 1478. The castle was captured by the English in 1547, although only after a stout resistance from the garrison led by Lady Home – her husband had been killed the day before in a skirmish

before the Battle of Pinkie. In 1549 it was retaken by Lord Home, her son, and the English garrison slaughtered. It was visited by Mary, Queen of Scots, in 1566, but in 1569 was again besieged by the English, with artillery, and within 12 hours had surrendered. The Homes were made Earls of Home in 1605. In 1650 the castle was surrendered to Colonel Fenwick, one of Cromwell's commanders, and demolished. The family moved to The Hirsel, and the castle was not rebuilt.

The property passed to the Home Earls of Marchmont in the 18th century, and the castle, which by now was almost 'level with the ground', was rebuilt as a crude folly in 1794, incorporating the foundations of the old castle.

The verse:
'I, Willie Wastle,
Stand firm in my castle;
And a' the dog o' your toon
Will no pull Willie Wastle doon.'
is believed to be from the siege of Hume in 1650, and was apparently sent in defiance by the keeper of the castle to Colonel Fenwick. Fenwick must have laughed.
Other refs: Home
OPEN: Open all year, daily 9.00-21.00.
Explanatory displays. Car and coach parking.

Hundalee Tower

Borders: About 1 mile south and west of Jedburgh, on minor roads west of A68, on west side of Jed Water, at Hundalee.
Ruin or site   NT 646187   OS: 80   *   Map: 2, no: 260
Site of tower house, some foundations of which survive.

Hunterston Castle

Ayrshire: About 2.5 miles north of West Kilbride, on minor roads west of A78, near Hunterston House, about 0.75 miles east of Nuclear Power Station.
Private   NS 193515   OS: 63   *   Map: 3, no: 22**
Once defended by a moat and rampart in a marshy area, Hunterston Tower is a rectangular 15th-century keep of three storeys and a garret within a crenellated parapet. It was much altered and extended in later centuries to form three sides of a courtyard. A square stair-tower projects from the keep.

The basement is vaulted and has a modern entrance. The main entrance is on the first floor, and leads to the hall with a fireplace. The upper floors were reached by a turnpike stair in one corner.

It was a property of the Hunters, hereditary foresters of the island of Little Cumbrae from the 12th century until recent times. John Hunter of Hunterston was killed at the Battle of Flodden in 1513, and his great-grandson, Mungo Hunter, was killed at Pinkie in 1547. The tower was abandoned by the family in the late 18th century for the nearby mansion. The old castle was remodelled as a chauffeur's quarters and a garage, the latter in the basement. The mansion is still occupied by the Hunters.

Hunter's Hall, Galashiels

Borders: To south of Galashiels, on minor roads south of A7, south of Gala Water.
Ruin or site   NT 494357   OS: 73   *   Map: 2, no: 157
Site of castle, a hunting lodge used by the kings of Scots. It was demolished in 1814 for an extension to the parish school, itself now demolished and the site occupied by a housing development.
Other refs: The Peel, Galashiels; Peel, Galashiels

Hunthall *see* Dunlop House

Hunthill

Borders: About 1 mile south-east of Jedburgh, on minor roads east of A68, about 1 mile east of the Jed Water, at Hunthill.
Private   NT 665191   OS: 80   *   Map: 2, no: 272
Hunthill, a 19th-century three-storey house, stands on the site of a strong 16th-century tower house of the Rutherfords. The castle was sacked by the English in 1571, and apparently demolished in the 18th century.

Huntingtower Castle

Perth & Kinross: About 2 miles north-west of Perth railway station, outskirts of Perth, on minor road just north of A85 west of junction with A9, at Huntingtower.
His Scot   NO 083252   OS: 58   ***   Map: 8, no: 71**
A well-preserved and interesting castle, Huntingtower consists of three different phases of building. The oldest part is a 15th-century keep of three storeys and a garret, rectangular in plan, with open rounds at the angles. Nearby, but not touching, a 16th-century L-plan tower house was built, consisting of a main block of four storeys and a wing rising a storey higher. The only communication between these was a wooden bridge. Towards the end of the 16th century, a connecting range of three storeys was built, containing a stair for both the keep and L-plan tower. A one-storey hall block, projecting from the tower, and ending in a two-storey building, has been demolished. There was also a courtyard with other outbuildings but these have gone.

The basement of the keep is vaulted. The entrance was at first-floor level and was reached by an external stair.

Some rooms have fine painted ceilings, mural paintings and plasterwork, as well as decorative beams in the hall.

The property was held by the Ruthvens from the 12th century, and originally called Ruthven Castle. The Ruthvens fought against the English during the Wars of Independence, and were made Sheriffs of Perth in 1313. William, Master of Ruthven, was killed at the Battle of Flodden in 1513. Mary, Queen of Scots, visited the castle in 1565 while on honeymoon with Darnley, although the 3rd Lord Ruthven, Patrick, took part in the murder of Rizzio, Mary, Queen of Scot's secretary. In 1582 the 4th Lord Ruthven, who had been made Earl of Gowrie in 1581, kidnapped the young James VI – known as the 'Raid of Ruthven' – and held him in Huntingtower for a year until the King escaped during a hunting trip. The Earl was beheaded in 1585.

In 1600 John Ruthven, 3rd Earl of Gowrie and his brother, Alexander, Master of Ruthven, were murdered in Gowrie House in Perth by James VI and his followers, following the 'Gowrie Conspiracy', a possible plot to murder the king. The Ruthvens were forfeited, their lands seized, and their name proscribed. The castle, renamed Huntingtower, remained royal property until Charles I gave it to William Murray, the 1st Earl of Dysart. The property passed to the Murray Earls of Tullibardine in 1663, then to the Marquises and Dukes of Atholl in 1676. Lord George Murray, Bonnie Prince Charlie's general in the 1745-6 Jacobite Rising, was born here. The property was sold in 1805, and Huntingtower was used to house labourers. It passed into the care of the State in 1912.

The space between the battlements of the two towers is known as 'The Maiden's Leap'. Dorothy, daughter of the 1st Earl of Gowrie is supposed to have jumped from one tower to the next. While visiting her lover, John Wemyss of Pittencrieff, in his chamber, and about to be discovered by her mother, she leapt to the other tower and returned to her own bed before being discovered. She eloped with her lover the following night.

The castle and grounds are said to be haunted by a 'Green Lady', also known as 'My Lady Greensleeves'. Her footsteps have reputedly been heard, along with the

rustle of her gown, and she has reportedly appeared on several occasions, sometimes as a warning of death, sometimes to help passers-by – including an ill child and a man being robbed.

Other refs: Ruthven Castle; House of Ruthven

OPEN: Open all year: Apr-Sep, daily 9.30-18.30; Oct-Mar, Mon-Wed and Sat 9.30-16.30, Thu 9.30-12.00, Sun 14.00-16.30, closed Fri; last ticket sold 30 mins before closing; closed 25/26 Dec and 1/2 Jan.

Gift shop. Picnic area. Car parking. Group concessions. £.

Tel: 01738 627231 Fax: 0131 668 8800

Email: hs.explore@scotland.gov.uk Web: www.historic-scotland.gov.uk

Huntly

Borders: About 1.5 miles west of Gordon, on minor road north of A6105, at or near Huntlywood.

Ruin or site NT 618429 OS: 74 * Map: 2, no: 242

Site of castle, some vestige of which is said to have survived in the 19th century. The lands were a property of the Gordons from the 12th century, and family became Earls of Huntly after acquiring lands in Strathbogie in Aberdeenshire, where their main castle was Huntly.

Other refs: Huntlywood

Huntly Castle

Aberdeen & Gordon: To the north of Huntly, on minor road north of A920 in Huntly, just south of River Deveron, south of Huntly Lodge.

His Scot NJ 532407 OS: 29 ** Map: 10, no: 124**

A fine building with a long and violent history, Huntly Castle consists of a strong 15th-century keep, rectangular in plan, with a large round tower at one end and a smaller circular tower at the opposite corner. The upper storey of the keep was remodelled in the late 16th century with decorative stonework and new windows, including three oriels. An adjoining large courtyard had ranges of buildings on two sides, and nothing remains of an older tower except foundations.

From the entrance to the castle, a straight stair leads down to the vaulted base-

ment, which contains three cellars and a prison in the large round tower. The floor above, at ground level, is also vaulted and contains two cellars and a kitchen, with a private chamber in the round tower. Two turnpike stairs lead up from this chamber, one to the first floor, one up to the roof. The hall, on the main first floor, was a fine chamber, but was later subdivided, and there are fine decorative fireplaces.

An older castle here, then called Strathbogie, was built by the MacDuff Earls of Fife on a nearby mound, and passed to the Gordons early in the 14th century. The motte, just to the west, can still be seen. Robert the Bruce stayed here before defeating the Comyn Earl of Buchan at a battle nearby in 1307. This old castle was burned down in 1452 by the Douglas Earl of Moray, and a new castle was built close by. In 1496 Perkin Warbeck, a pretender to the English throne, married Catherine Gordon here in the presence of James IV.

In 1506 the name was changed from Strathbogie to Huntly. The 4th Earl was defeated (and died, reportedly from apoplexy) by the forces of Mary, Queen of Scots, at the Battle of Corrichie in 1562, and his son executed. The castle was slighted and pillaged at this time, the treasure from St Machar's Cathedral in Aberdeen being seized.

The castle was restored, but in 1594 attacked by James VI and damaged again, to be restored once again in 1602. The 2nd Marquis of Huntly was hanged for his support of Charles I, and in 1640 the castle was occupied by a Covenanting army, who destroyed much of the interior. In 1644 it was taken by forces of the Marquis of Montrose, then captured by General David Leslie in 1647 after starving out and slaughtering the garrison. It was garrisoned by Hanoverian soldiers during the Jacobite rising of 1745-6, but by then had been abandoned as a residence. It was then used as a quarry and dump until cleared in 1923.

'Ne'er misca a Gordon in the raws of Strathbogie.'

Other refs: Strathbogie Castle; Peel of Strathbogie

OPEN: Open all year: Apr-Sep, daily 9.30-18.30; Oct-Mar, Mon-Wed and Sat 9.30-16.00, Thu 9.30-12.00, Sun 14.00-16.30, closed Fri; last ticket sold 30 mins before closing; closed 25/26 Dec and 1/2 Jan.

Exhibition. Gift shop. WC. Disabled WC. Parking. £.

Tel: 01466 793191 Fax: 0131 668 8888

Email: hs.explore@scotland.gov.uk Web: www.historic-scotland.gov.uk

Huntly Castle *see* Castle Huntly

Huntly House, Edinburgh

Lothians: 142 Canongate, Royal Mile, Edinburgh.

Private NT 265739 OS: 66 * Map: 4, no: 105**

Huntly House, one of the best old buildings in the Old Town, was built in 1570 for the Gordon Earls and Marquises of Huntly, and later became the headquarters of the Incorporation of Hammermen. It is now the main museum of local history for Edinburgh, and there are fine collections of silver, glassware, pottery, and other items such as street signs and Greyfriars Bobby collar and feeding bowl. Painted beams here were taken from Pinkie House, Musselburgh.

OPEN: Open all year: Mon-Sat, 10.00-17.00; also during Festival, Sun 14.00-17.00; closed Christmas and New Year.

Gift shop. Disabled access. Parking nearby.

Tel: 0131 529 4143 Fax: 0131 557 3346

Huntlywood *see* Huntly

Hutchinfield Tower

Borders: About 1 mile north of Peebles, east of minor road from A703 (south from Mailingsland), about 0.3 miles east and south of Langside Farm.

Ruin or site NT 255422 OS: 73 * Map: 2, no: 63

Very little remains of a 16th-century tower house, except part of the vaulted cellar. It was a property of the Horsburgh family, but passed to the Williamsons in 1659.

Hutton Castle

Borders: About 2 miles south and east of Chirnside, on minor road between north of B6460 and south of A6105, south of the Whiteadder River.

Private NT 888549 OS: 67 ** Map: 2, no: 351

In a strong position, Hutton Castle (which is also recorded as Hutton Hall) incorporates a 16th-century tower house, which has been much extended and altered in later centuries. The old part consists of a small square tower of three storeys, and possibly includes 15th-century work. It has a flat roof within a parapet, but may have had a garret storey. A very altered 16th-century stair-tower projects from the tower. There was a courtyard.

The basement is vaulted.

It was a property of the Homes, destroyed or slighted by an English army in the 16th century, and is still occupied.

Hynd Castle

Angus & Dundee: About 6.5 miles south-east of Forfar, on minor roads and foot east of B978, south of Lawsonhall, west of dismantled railway, at Hynd.
Ruin or site NO 504415 OS: 54 * Map: 8, no: 214
Not much survives of Hynd or Hyne Castle, a 15th-century stronghold, except the walls of the lower storey. The castle stands on a small hillock, and was apparently once surrounded by water.

Illieston House – see above

I

Iain Garbh's Castle *see* Castle Sinclair

Idoch Castle

Aberdeen & Gordon: About 3 miles east of Turriff, near B9170, near Idoch Water, at or near Mains of Idoch.
Ruin or site NJ 770490 [?] OS: 29 * Map: 10, no: 252
Site of 14th-century castle, the last remains of which were removed in 1850. It is said that a large quantity of human bones were found here. There is a fine doocot.

Illieston House

Lothians: About 2 miles south east of Broxburn, on minor roads between B7015 in south and B7030 in east, just west of the River Almond, at Illieston.
Private NT 010700 OS: 65 * Map: 4, no: 15**
Illieston House is an altered 17th-century T-plan tower house of two storeys and an attic. It consists of a main block with a projecting square wing. A small stair-turret is corbelled out at second-floor level. The stair-wing rises a storey higher than the main block, and is crowned by a watch-chamber. A vaulted wing, which contained the kitchen, has been demolished, but there are later additions.

The present entrance is by a modern doorway, although it would have been at the foot of the stair-wing. The house has been altered inside.

The kings of Scots are said to have had a hunting lodge here, which was used often by James II and James IV. The property was held by the Ellis family (the name being from 'Elliston'), but later passed to the Hope Earls of Hopetoun. It is still occupied and in good condition, although it was roofless in 1856.
Other refs: Elliston; Elistone

Inaltrie Castle

Moray: About 3 miles south of Cullen, on minor roads east of B9018, just east of Burn of Deskford, 1 mile north of Kirkton of Deskford, at Inaltry.
Ruin or site NJ 518631 OS: 29 * Map: 10, no: 119
Only one wall remains of a 13th-century castle, probably a property of the Lawties of Inaltrie or Inaltry. The lands were sold to the Ogilvie Earl of Findlater around 1721.
Other refs: Old Castle of Inaltrie

Inch *see* Inch Crindil

Inch Castle

Renfrewshire: About 0.5 miles east of Renfrew, on minor roads north of A877, on south bank of River Clyde, at King's Inch.
Ruin or site NS 515675 [?] OS: 64 * Map: 3, no: 224
Site of castle, built by David I, nothing of which remains, located on an island in the river known as King's Inch. The property passed to the Stewarts, then to the Ross family towards the end of the 15th century. The castle was rebuilt in the 15th century with a four-storey keep or tower. The keep had corbiestepped gables, and a central stair-tower was corbelled out above first-floor level. Inch was a ruin by the 18th century, the last Ross owner died in 1732, and the property sold to the Speirs of Elderslie in 1760.

Elderslie House was built close by – named after Elderslie, near Paisley – a mansion dating from the 1770s. It was enlarged and remodelled in later centuries, and a property of the Speirs family. The house was demolished in 1924 and no trace survives. The site is no longer an island and occupied by Braehead Power Station.

Inch Crindil

Galloway: About 3 miles east of Stranraer, on minor roads, foot and boat north of A75, on island in White Loch, Inch Crindil.
Ruin or site NX 104608 OS: 82 * Map: 1, no: 20
Site of castle, mentioned in the 15th and 16th centuries. It was a property of the Kennedys from 1482, and replaced by Castle Kennedy [NX 111609] in 1607.

253

Inch House

Lothians: About 2.5 miles south-east of Edinburgh Castle, on minor roads west of A68, east of A7, just south of Cameron Toll.

Private NT 278709 OS: 66 ** Map: 4, no: 118

Inch House, or The Inch, consists of a 17th-century L-plan tower house of four storeys and a garret, and incorporates earlier work. A lower extension was added in 1634, another was added in the 18th century, and the house was remodelled in 1891.

The original entrance was in the square stair-tower in the re-entrant angle. The inside of the tower has been altered, but two vaulted basement chambers survive.

The lands were originally a property of the Abbey of Holyrood, but had passed to the Gilmours by 1600. Lochend House was burned by William Gilmour of the Inch about 1601, although the Winram family are also said to have held the property. The house is now a community centre, and surrounded by a public park.

Other refs: The Inch; King's Inch

Inchbervie Castle

Perth & Kinross: About 6 miles north of Perth, on minor roads and foot east of B9099, about 0.75 miles east of Stanley, west bank of River Tay, at Inchbervie.

Ruin or site NO 123329 OS: 53 ** Map: 8, no: 89

Little remains of Inchbervie Castle, which was built in the 14th or 15th century, except a ruined D-plan tower with a vaulted roof. The walls are pierced by gun-loops, and some foundations of a courtyard and outbuildings survive. The building was greatly altered in the 19th century, burned in 1887, but afterwards rebuilt.

The basement was vaulted.

The lands may have been held by Dunfermline Abbey, and William Wallace is said to have sheltered here. It was a property of the Nairn family. The name was changed at the beginning of the 18th century after Lady Amelia Stanley: her fourth son, William Murray, succeeded to the title Lord Nairne in 1683. The 3rd Lord Nairne, a Jacobite, had to flee from the dining room of the castle to avoid capture after the Rising of 1745.

Other refs: Stanley House; Inchbervis Castle

Inchbervis Castle *see* Inchbervie Castle

Inchbrackie Castle

Perth & Kinross: About 2.5 miles east of Crieff, on minor roads east of A822, south of A85, 0.75 miles south-east of Milton of Cultoquhey, south-east of Inchbrackie Farm.

Ruin or site NN 903218 OS: 52 * Map: 8, no: 31

Virtually nothing remains of Inchbrackie Castle, once surrounded by a moat.

It belonged to the Mercers, then the Grahams from 1513, and was destroyed by Cromwell's forces in 1651. Inchbrackie's Ring, a sapphire set in gold, was given to the laird of Inchbrackie in the 1720s by Kate McNiven, a reputed witch, who was burned at Crieff. She spat it into his hand as she was being burned. He had tried to save her, and she promised that if his family kept the ring they would prosper. The castle didn't, and the lands were sold in 1882.

Inchbrayock House

Angus & Dundee: About 1 mile south of Montrose, on minor roads east of A92, at or near Inchbrayock.

Ruin or site NO 718562 OS: 54 * Map: 8, no: 272

Site of castle or old house. The 19th-century house has a lintel dated 1638.

Inchcolm Abbey

Fife: On island of Inchcolm in Firth of Forth, 2 miles south of Aberdour on north coast of Fife, by boat from South or North Queensferry.

His Scot NT 191827 OS: 66 ** Map: 7, no: 31

Inchcolm Abbey, although ruined, is the best preserved monastic complex in Scotland, the cloister and chapter house being complete. A new range of buildings, including a square fortified tower, were added on the south side about 1609. The tower rises to four storeys, and has a parapet.

The abbey was founded in 1123 by Alexander I, King of Scots, after he had been rescued here from the sea, his boat having capsized crossing the Forth at Queens-

ferry. The abbey was sacked by the English in 1542 and 1547, and garrisoned by the French in 1548. The property passed to the Crown at the Reformation in 1560, and was given to Henry Stewart of Beith in 1609. His son married the heiress of the Regent Moray, and became the Earl of Moray. He was murdered by the Gordon Earl of Huntly on the sands at nearby Donibristle, the deed recorded in the ballad 'The Bonnie Earl o' Moray'. The island was later used as a naval quarantine station, fort, and Russian naval hospital. In 1924 it passed into the care of the State.

Other refs: Commendator's House, Inchcolm

OPEN: Open Apr-Sep, daily 9.30-18.30; ferry (£) (30 mins) from South or North Queensferry (phone 0131 331 4857)

Exhibition. Explanatory boards. Gift shop. Disabled access and WC. £.

Tel: 01383 823332 Fax: 0131 668 8888

Email: hs.explore@scotland.gov.uk Web: www.historic-scotland.gov.uk

Inchdrewer Castle

Banff & Buchan: About 3 miles south-west of Banff, on minor roads west of B9121 just north of junction with A97, at Inchdrewer.

Private NJ 656607 OS: 29 * Map: 10, no: 180**

Inchdrewer Castle is an altered 16th-century L-plan tower house of five storeys. A wing was added in the 17th century, which extended the building to a T-plan. The tower had a stair-turret, in the re-entrant angle, but a round stair-tower was later added at one corner. A courtyard enclosed ranges of outbuildings, which are very ruined.

The entrance was in the re-entrant angle. The basement was vaulted and the hall was on the first floor.

The lands belonged to the Curror family, but were sold to the Ogilvies of Dunlugas in the 16th century, who built the castle. The family was made Lords Banff in 1692.

In 1713 a later Lord Banff was murdered in the castle after unexpectedly returning home from Edinburgh. He was probably killed by his own servants, who had been robbing him, and set the building alight to destroy the evidence. In the early 19th century Inchdrewer passed to the Abercrombies of Birkenbog.

The castle became ruined, but has been partly restored, although it does not appear to be occupied.

The castle is said to be haunted.

Inches *see* Inshes House

Inchewan *see* Inshewan

Inchgalbraith Castle

Argyll & Dunbartonshire: About 1.5 miles south and east of Luss, on island, Inchgalbraith, to the west of Loch Lomond, about 0.5 miles east of A82 at Bandry.

Ruin or site NS 369904 OS: 56 ** Map: 5, no: 147

Inchgalbraith Castle is a ruined 16th-century tower house, square in plan. The tower occupies most of the island, and was ruinous and overgrown by the early part of the 18th century.

It was a property of the Galbraiths, but passed to the Colquhouns of Luss in the 16th century. It was probably abandoned soon afterwards.

Inchgall Castle *see* Lochore Castle

Inchgarvie

Lothians: An island in the Firth of Forth, between North and South Queensferry, on which one pier of the Forth Railway Bridge stands.

Ruin or site NT 137795 OS: 65 ** Map: 4, no: 45

Not much remains of a 15th-century castle, to which James IV added a strong tower in 1513. It was altered in later centuries, and used as a prison for a time.

It was a property of the Dundas family from 1491, and used by Royalists in the 1650s. It was refortified against John Paul Jones, a Scotsman who entered the American navy in 1775 and harried shipping in British waters during the American War of Independence; then again in the 20th century against German bombers trying to destroy the Forth Railway Bridge.

Inchinnan Castle

Renfrewshire: About 1 mile east and south of Erskine, south of shore of Clyde at Newshot Island, about 0.5 miles north of Inchinnan town, at or near Garnieland.
Ruin or site NS 482697 OS: 64 * Map: 3, no: 199
Site of castle, known as Inchinnan Castle or Palace, which was rebuilt and enlarged about 1506 by Matthew Stewart, 2nd Earl of Lennox. There were considerable remains in 1710, but nothing now remains.

Inchinnan was held by the High Steward in 1151, but acquired by the Stewart Earls of Lennox. The property passed to the Crown in 1571, then to several members of the Stewart family, eventually coming to the Earls of Lennox and Richmond. They sold the lands to the Campbells of Blythswood.

Inchinnan was an important early Christian site, as was Govan, and many old coffins and burials have been unearthed here.

Inchkeith

Fife: On Inchkeith, an island in the Forth of Forth, near the lighthouse.
Ruin or site NT 293828 OS: 66 * Map: 7, no: 69
Little survives of a 16th-century fort.

The English built a fort here in 1549 during their invasions of 1547-50. It was quickly captured by the Scots, and in 1550 had a French garrison installed. The Scottish parliament ordered the fort demolished in 1567, but it survived until 1773, and was not removed until a lighthouse was built in 1803. The island was refortified in 1878 with gun batteries to control access into the Forth. All that survives is a length of wall, with gunloops, and a panel on the lighthouse with the year 1584 and the initials of Mary, Queen of Scots.

Inchmurrin Castle

Argyll & Dunbartonshire: About 3 miles north of Balloch, on south-east of island, Inchmurrin, to south of Loch Lomond, about 1 mile east of A82 at Auchentullich.
Ruin or site NS 373863 OS: 57 ** Map: 5, no: 148
Inchmurrin Castle is a ruined 14th-century keep and castle, or hall house, of the Earls of Lennox.

There may have been an earlier castle here, which was used as a hunting lodge by Robert the Bruce. Sir John Colquhoun and his followers were murdered here in 1439 by Highlanders. It was the home of the widow of Murdoch Stewart, Duke of Albany, who had been executed along with his sons by James I. She was imprisoned in Tantallon Castle for two years, and died here in 1460. This part of the Earldom, along with the title, went to the Stewarts of Darnley. In 1506 James IV stayed at the castle, as did James VI in 1585 and 1617. The island passed to the Graham Dukes of Montrose around the beginning of the 18th century, and the castle was ruinous by 1724.

Inchmurtach

Fife: About 3 miles south-east of St Andrews, on minor roads and foot east of B9131, 0.5 miles east of Prior's Muir.
Ruin or site NO 565132 [?] OS: 59 * Map: 7, no: 147
Site of bishop's palace, a residence built by William Lamberton, Bishop of St Andrews, about 1314. A parliament is believed to have been held here in the reign of David II, and some remains survived at the end of the 18th century.
Other refs: Bishop's Palace, Lower Kenly; Lower Kenly

Inchneuk *see* Inchnock Castle

Inchnock Castle

Lanarkshire & Glasgow area: About 2.5 miles north of Coatbridge, on minor roads north of B804, about 0.5 miles north east of Marnock.
Ruin or site NS 718694 [?] OS: 64 * Map: 3, no: 334
There are slight remains of a tower house of the Forsyths of Dykes, which was ruinous by the mid 17th century. The property later passed to Hamilton of Dalyell, and then to a John Hay, although it may also have been a possession of the Steel family as there was a tomb [NS 719692] for the family nearby.
Other refs: Inchnoch; Inchneuk

Inchoch Castle *see* Inshoch Castle

Inchtalla Castle

Stirlingshire & Clackmannan: About 3 miles east of Aberfoyle, west of the B8034 junction with the A81, in the Lake of Menteith, west of Inchmahome Priory.
Ruin or site NN 572004 OS: 57 ** Map: 6, no: 24
On an island in the Lake of Menteith, Inchtalla – the Earl's Isle – Castle is a ruined 15th-century castle, although there was probably a stronghold here from the 13th century or earlier. The ruins consist of a hall or tower, with private chambers above, and other buildings including a kitchen, enclosed within a courtyard. Much of it is said to have been built with materials from the nearby priory in the 17th century.

The lands were part of the Earldom of Menteith, and held by the Comyns, but passed to the Grahams. In 1361 Robert Stewart, 1st Duke of Albany, acquired the property by marriage; but in 1425, with the execution of Murdoch the 2nd Duke, it passed back to the Grahams. Inchtalla was then the main stronghold of the earldom until Doune Castle was built, and was occupied until about 1700.

On another island in the Lake of Menteith is Inchmahome Priory, which is open to the public; while a third, the smallest island, is called the 'Dog Isle' and is where the earls are said to have had their dog kennels.
Other refs: Menteith Castle; Talla Castle
OPEN: Inchmahome Priory: includes ferry; closed in winter.
Tel: 01877 385294

Ingleston *see* Gelston Castle

Inglismaldie Castle

Kincardine & Deeside: About 5 miles north-east of Brechin, on minor roads north of A94 at North Water Bridge, north of River North Esk, at Inglismaldie.
Private NO 644669 OS: 45 ** Map: 10, no: 173
Inglismaldie Castle consists of an altered late 16th-century L-plan tower house of

three storeys and a garret. It was extended by a long 17th-century wing, and was remodelled as a mansion in 1884.

The basement is vaulted. The main stair leads only to first-floor level, which would have been occupied by the hall. Some fine original carved woodwork survives. The house has been very altered inside and out.

It was a property of the Livingstones from 1588, but in 1635 passed to the Carnegies. In 1693 it was sold to the Falconers of Halkerton. One of the family married Joseph Home of Ninewells, and was the mother of David Hume the philosopher. It was sold to the Ogilvies in 1960, and the house is still occupied.

Inneravon Castle *see* Inveravon Castle

Innergellie House

Fife: About 0.5 miles north of Kilrenny, on minor road north of A917, at Innergellie House.
Private NO 575052 OS: 59 * Map: 7, no: 151
Probable site of castle. The present house is a Baroque three-storey mansion dating from 1740, but has a date stone of 1630.

The property was part of the dowry of Anabella Drummond, wife of Robert III. It passed to the Beatons, then the Barclays of Kippo, until sold to the Lumsdens of Airdrie by 1642, one of whom Sir James Lumsden fought for Gustavus Adolphus of Sweden, and was present at the Battle of Dunbar in 1650. It remained with the Sandys-Lumisdaines until the 1960s.

Innerkip Castle *see* Inverkip Castle

Innermessan Castle

Galloway: About 2 miles north-east of Stranraer, on minor road west of A77 at Innermessan, short distance east from shore of Loch Ryan.

Ruin or site   NX 084634   OS: 82   *   Map: 1, no: 14

Site of 15th-century castle, the site now occupied by a farmhouse.

It was a property of the Agnews of Lochnaw from 1429 until the end of the 17th century. The tower was abandoned as a residence around 1687, and sold to the Dalrymple Earl of Stair in 1723. It was used as a cavalry barracks, but then decayed, and was demolished to build the farm.

There is a motte nearby [NX 084633].

Innerpeffray Castle

Perth & Kinross: About 3.5 miles south-east of Crieff, on minor roads and foot south of B8062, just north of River Earn, just south of hamlet of Innerpeffray.

Ruin or site   NN 904179   OS: 58   *   Map: 8, no: 32**

Innerpeffray Castle is a ruined early 17th-century L-plan tower house, complete to the wallhead, with a square stair-tower in the re-entrant angle. The gables are corbiestepped, and the walls are pierced by gunloops.

The entrance, at the foot of the stair-tower, leads to the vaulted basement and to the main turnpike stair, which climbs to all floors. The basement contains the kitchen, with a large arched fireplace and bread oven, and a wine-cellar with a small stair to the hall above. The hall and an adjoining chamber in the wing occupied the first floor, and there were private chambers on the floors above.

The lands were held by Inchaffray Abbey, but were acquired after the Reformation by the Drummond Lords Madderty, who built the castle in 1610.

Innerwick Castle

Lothians: About 5 miles south-east of Dunbar, on minor roads south of the A1, about 0.75 miles east of Innerwick, just north of the Thornton Burn.

Ruin or site   NT 735737   OS: 67   **   Map: 4, no: 225

Little remains of Innerwick Castle, a 15th-century keep and courtyard, except vaults, ruined walls and a rock-cut ditch.

The castle was built by the Stewarts, but passed to the Hamiltons in 1398. In 1547 the English smoked out the garrison and dismantled the castle, while in 1548 the castle seems again to have been in the hands of the Scots, as the Master of Hamilton and eight other men held Innerwick against the English. Eight of the garrison were picked off with muskets, while the last threw himself to his death from one of the walls. The defences were slighted. The castle was sufficiently complete to be used as a base to attack Cromwell's lines of communication in the 1650s. The property was sold to the Nisbets in 1663.

Innes House

Moray: About 4 miles east and north of Elgin, on minor roads north of A96 or east of B9013, 1.5 miles north of Urquhart, at Innes House.

Private   NJ 278649   OS: 28   *   Map: 10, no: 54**

Innes House consists of an altered but fine 17th-century L-plan tower house. A square stair-tower, in the re-entrant angle, rises a storey higher than the main block and is crowned by a flat-roofed caphouse. The walls are harled, and the pitch of the roof is steep.

The basement was vaulted, and the wine-cellar had a small stair up to the hall above. The hall was on the first floor, and private chambers occupied the floors above. There have been many alterations and additions.

The house was built by the Innes family and designed by William Aytoun, master mason. James III visited here. Alexander, the 16th Lord Innes, was beheaded by the Regent Morton, while the 17th Lord resigned the property in favour of Alexander Innes of Crombie, which led to a feud. The 18th Lord was murdered by Innes of Innermarkie in 1580, and the 19th outlawed in 1624. The 20th Lord was a prominent Covenanter, and it was he who built the present house between 1640 and 1653. Innes was sold to James Duff, 2nd Earl of Fife, in 1767, and later passed to the Tennant family.

Other refs: Castle of Innes; Palace of Innes

Innerwick Castle – see opposite column

Innis Chonnel Castle

Argyll & Dunbartonshire: About 14 miles north-east of Kilmartin, by boat west of B840, on island just west of shore of Loch Awe, 0.5 miles east of Dalaveich, at Innis Chonnel.

Ruin or site NM 976119 OS: 55 * Map: 5, no: 90**

Innis Chonnel Castle is a 13th-century castle of enclosure, rectangular in plan, with thick curtain walls, although it may incorporate earlier work. It was extensively remodelled in the 15th century. The inner courtyard had towers at two corners, and enclosed ranges of buildings, including a hall and a kitchen with a large fireplace. The castle was divided into inner, middle and outer courtyards.

The entrance from the courtyard is at first-floor level.

The castle was the original stronghold of the Campbells from the 11th century, and the seat of Mac Cailean Mor, who was killed at the Red Ford of Lorn in 1294. John MacDougall held it against Robert the Bruce in 1308. The Campbells were made Earls of Argyll in 1457.

Innis Chonnel was abandoned as the Campbells' main a residence for Inveraray in the 15th century, although it was still used as a prison. The young heir to the Lordship of the Isles, Donald, son of Angus, was imprisoned here after the Battle of Bloody Bay, off Mull, in 1484. He eventually escaped, but after invading Badenoch in 1503, was again captured and imprisoned, this time in Edinburgh Castle, for 40 years. The castle was ruinous by the 19th century.

Other refs: Ardchonnel Castle

Inshes House

Inverness & Nairn: About 2 miles south-east of Inverness, on minor roads south of B9006 just west of junction with A9, 1.5 miles south of Moray Firth, at Inshes.

Ruin or site NH 695437 OS: 26 * Map: 9, no: 100

Site of castle, one tower of which survives from the courtyard. Inshes House, a mansion built in 1767, stands just south of the site of a castle, and is being restored.

Other refs: Inches

Inshewan

Angus & Dundee: About 4 miles north of Forfar, on minor roads north of B957, just north of River South Esk, at Inshewan.

Private NO 447569 OS: 54 * Map: 8, no: 191

Inshewan, a modern house, stands on the site of a castle of the Ogilvies, who held the property in the 20th century.

Other refs: Inchewan

Inshoch Castle

Inverness & Nairn: About 3.5 miles east of Nairn, on minor roads north of A96, about 1.5 miles north-east of Auldearn, north of Penick, at Inshoch.

Ruin or site NH 936567 OS: 27 ** Map: 9, no: 149

Inshoch Castle is a ruined 16th-century Z-plan tower house. It consisted of a rectangular main block with two round towers, one a stair-tower, at opposite corners, and an extension.

It was a property of the Hays of Lochloy.

Other refs: Inchoch Castle

Inverallan

South Highland: About 0.5 miles south-west of Grantown on Spey, on minor roads east of A95, north of River Spey, Inverallan burial ground.

Private NJ 027269 OS: 36   Map: 9, no: 157

Several heraldic panels survive, apparently from the castle or seat of the lairdship of Shillochan.

Inverallan was an early Christian site, and there was a church here, nothing of which survives, dedicated to St Futach or Fiacre, a 7th-century Irish saint. In the burial ground is a Class 1 Pictish carved stone, and the weathered Figgat's or Futach's Cross, an early Christian monument is also here. There was also a holy well here [NJ 028266], dedicated to St Futach.

Other refs: Shillochan

OPEN: Access at all reasonable times.

Inverallochy Castle

Banff & Buchan: About 4 miles south-east of Fraserburgh, on foot south of B9033, 1 mile west of St Combs, 1.5 miles south of Inverallochy village, south of Mains Croft.

Ruin or site NK 041630 OS: 30 ** Map: 10, no: 358

Little remains of Inverallochy Castle, a 16th-century tower house of the Cumming or Comyn family, although there was a castle here from the 13th century. A courtyard enclosed later ranges of fine buildings. The property later passed to the Frasers of Lovat.

Inveramsay

Aberdeen & Gordon: About 2 miles north-west of Inverurie, on minor road just east of A96, just west of River Urie, at or near Inveramsay.

Ruin or site NJ 742240 OS: 38 * Map: 10, no: 236

Site of castle of the Erskines.

Other refs: Peelwalls

Inveraray Castle

Argyll & Dunbartonshire: North of Inveraray, off A83, west of Loch Fyne near mouth of River Aray.

Private NN 096093 OS: 56 * Map: 5, no: 106

Site of 15th-century castle of the Campbell Earls of Argyll. It consisted of a keep of four storeys and a garret, and had bartizans with conical roofs. James V visited in

1533, as did Mary, Queen of Scots, in 1562. It was torched in 1644 by the Marquis of Montrose, and the castle demolished as part of the 3rd Duke of Argyll's rebuilding of a new castle and town.

The present castle was begun in 1743, and is a symmetrical classical mansion with towers and turrets, which was remodelled by William and John Adam. The castle houses many interesting rooms, with collections of tapestries and paintings, and superb displays of weapons. Rob Roy MacGregor's sporran and dirk handle are on display. The Clan Room features information of special interest to members of Clan Campbell.

Several ghost stories are recorded in various places about Inveraray, although these are refuted. The old castle was said to be haunted by a ghostly harper, one of Montrose's victims from the attack in 1644.

The library is also reputedly haunted, and strange noises and crashes have reportedly been heard there.

Other ghosts include a spectral birlinn, which is reputedly seen when one of the Campbells is near death, seen in 1913 on the death of Archibald Campbell, as well as gatherings of ravens. The ghost of a young servant, who was murdered by Jacobites, is said to haunt the MacArthur room.

The apparitions of Redcoats, some of Cumberland's men, are said to have been seen marching on the road through Glen Aray, not far from the castle.

**OPEN: Open Apr-Oct, Mon- Thu and Sat 10.00-13.00 and 14.00-17.45,
Sun 13.00-17.45, closed Fri; Jul and Aug, Mon-Sat 10.00-17.45, Sun
13.00-17.45; last admissions 12.30 and 17.00.**

*Guided tours. Collections of tapestries and paintings. Displays of weapons. Rob Roy
MacGregor's sporran and dirk handle. Clan Room. Gift shop. Tea room. WC. Picnic
area. Woodland walks. Disabled access to ground floor only. Car and coach parking.
Group concessions. ££*

Tel: 01499 302203   Fax: 01499 302421
Email: enquiries@inveraray-castle.com   Web: www.inveraray-castle.com

Inveravon Castle

Stirlingshire & Clackmannan: About 3 miles west and north of Linlithgow, on
minor roads south of the B904, near or at Inveravon.

Ruin or site   NS 953798   OS: 65   *   Map: 6, no: 105

Very little remains of a 15th-century castle and courtyard of the Douglas family,
except the vaulted basement of a round tower. It was besieged then demolished by
James II in 1455, during the destruction of the Black Douglas family.

Other refs: Inneravon Castle

Inverawe House

Argyll & Dunbartonshire: About 1 mile north-east of Taynuilt, on minor roads
north of A85, on north bank of River Awe, at Inverawe House.

Private   NN 023316   OS: 50   **   Map: 5, no: 97

The later mansion may incorporate a castle of the 14th century. It was a property of
the Campbells, and Mary, Queen of Scots, is said to have visited.

  The house is thought to be haunted by a 'Green Lady', believed to be the ghost of
Mary Cameron of Callart, who married the then laird, Diarmid Campbell. Campbell
died in 1645 of wounds received at the Battle of Inverlochy, while fighting against
the Marquis of Montrose, and is buried at Ardchattan Priory. Mary died after him,
and her ghost is said to haunt the house. It has supposedly been seen in the Ticonderoga Room, and there are reports of the ghost in the 20th century.

  Another ghost is said to be that of Duncan Campbell, who died at Ticonderoga in
Canada in 1758.

  At the house are four fishing lochs, with tuition available, as well as a smokery
exhibition and nature trail.

**OPEN: Fisheries and smokery exhibition: open May-Nov, daily 8.00-
18.00. House private - not open to public.**

*Fisheries and smokery exhibition: explanatory displays. Mail order available for
smokery. Gift shop. Tearoom. Picnic area. Nature trail. Wildfowl reserve. WC. Disabled
access. Car and coach parking. £ (fishing). Holiday cottages available.*

Tel: 01866 822446 (office 01866 822777)   Fax: 01866 822274
Email: info@inverawe.co.uk   Web: www.inverawe.co.uk

Inverbervie *see* Hallgreen Castle

Inverbreakie

Ross & Cromarty: About 0.5 miles north-east of Invergordon, on minor roads
north of B817, north of shore of Cromarty Firth, at or near Inverbreakie.

Ruin or site   NH 715700 [?]   OS: 21   *   Map: 9, no: 107

Site of 13th-century castle of enclosure.

Inverbreakie Castle *see* Invergordon Castle

Inverbroom House *see* Balloan Castle

Invercauld House

Kincardine & Deeside: About 2 miles east and north of Braemar, on minor roads
north of A93, north of River Dee, at Invercauld House.

Private   NO 174924   OS: 43   **   Map: 10, no: 26

Invercauld House, a castellated mansion with battlements and turrets, incorporates a vaulted cellar from a 16th-century tower house. There is a walled garden.

  Invercauld was a property of the Farquharsons from the 14th century. Farquharson of Invercauld fought for the Jacobites in the Rising of 1715, and it was from
here that the Earl of Mar, leader of the Rising, called out the Highlanders for the
Old Pretender, James Francis Edward, James VIII to some.

Invercullen *see* **Cullen House**

Inveresk Lodge

Lothians: About 1 mile south of Musselburgh, on minor road south of A6124, at
Inveresk, just east of the River Esk.

NTS   NT 348716   OS: 66   **   Map: 4, no: 143

One wing of Inveresk Lodge, a 17th-century mansion, is a 16th-century tower house.
The lands of Little Inveresk were held by Dunfermline Abbey, but passed to the
Maitlands of Thirlestane after the Reformation, until sold to the Scotts of Buccleuch
in 1709.

  The gardens of the house are open to the public, and feature a large range of
plants. Visitor centre.

**OPEN: House not open; gardens open all year: Apr-Oct, Mon-Fri
10.00-18.00, Sat-Sun 14.00-18.00; Nov-Mar, Mon-Fri 10.00-16.30, Sun
14.00-17.00.**

*Visitor centre. Explanatory displays. No dogs. Disabled access. Limited parking by
garden wall. £.*

Tel: 01721 722502   Fax: 01721 724700
Email: information@nts.org.uk   Web: nts.org.uk

Inverey Castle

Kincardine & Deeside: About 4.5 miles west of Braemar, on minor roads 4.5
miles west of A93 in Braemar, near meeting of The Dee and Ey rivers, at Inverey.

Ruin or site   NO 086893   OS: 43   *   Map: 10, no: 11

Site of 17th-century tower house of the Farquharsons. The castle was demolished
in 1689 after the Battle of Killiecrankie.

  John Farquharson of Inverey, the 'Black Colonel' murdered John Gordon of Brackley in 1666, as recorded in the old ballad. He fought for the Jacobites in 1689, and
defeated a force attacking Braemar Castle, which he then burned. Farquharson
summoned servants by firing a pistol, and his exploits evading government dragoons were legendary. He is said to haunt Braemar Castle, leaving behind a burning candle.

  There is a strange tale concerning his own death. The Black Colonel wished to be
buried at Inverey, side by side with his mistress, but when he died he was interred
at Braemar at the request of his widow and family. His spirit did not apparently rest
easy, and three times his coffin mysteriously appeared above ground – and his
apparition also terrified his relatives – until they relented and his remains were
taken back to Inverey.

Invergarry Castle

South Highland: About 7 miles south-west of Fort Augustus, on minor roads east
of A82, on west bank of Loch Oich, south of Glengarry Castle Hotel, at
Invergarry.

Ruin or site   NH 315006   OS: 34   *   Map: 9, no: 47**

A very impressive ruin, Invergarry Castle is a large 17th-century L-plan tower house
consisting of a main block of five storeys with a six-storey round stair-tower. The
walls are pierced by shot-holes. The fortress stands on the 'Rock of the Raven', the
slogan of the family.

  The basement does not appear to have been vaulted. A wide scale-and-platt stair
climbed to the first floor in the wing, while the upper floors were reached by a stair-
tower in the re-entrant angle as well as the round stair-tower.

  The castle was built by the MacDonalds, or Clan Ranald, of Glengarry after raids by
the Mackenzies in 1602. It was torched in 1654 by forces of General Monck during
Cromwell's occupation of Scotland. In 1688 Alastair MacDonald of Glengarry fortified it for James VII, but eventually submitted to the government of William and
Mary in 1692. It was retaken by Alasdair Dubh of Glengarry in 1715, but recaptured
by Hanoverian forces in 1716. The castle was back in the hands of the MacDonalds
by 1731, and during the Jacobite Rising of 1745-6 was twice visited by Bonnie
Prince Charlie. Afterwards it was burned by the 'Butcher' Duke of Cumberland. A
new mansion was built nearby, on the site of which is the Glengarry Castle Hotel.

  The old castle was said to have had a brownie.

Other refs: Sleismenane; Creag an Fittick

**OPEN: Glengarry Hotel – open 26 Mar-8 Nov. Ruin can be seen from
grounds of hotel – the interior of castle is in dangerous condition.**

Tel: 01809 501254   Fax: 01809 501207

Invergarry Castle – see previous page

Invergordon Castle

Ross & Cromarty: About 0.5 mile north of Invergordon, on minor roads south of A9 or north of B817, near Invergordon Mains Steading.

Ruin or site   NH 705700   OS: 21   *   Map: 9, no: 105

Site of castle, called Inverbreakie [NH 715700?], which is mentioned in the 13th century. A house here was burned down in 1801, but rebuilt in 1873 as an Eliza-

bethan mansion, then itself completely demolished in 1928. It was a property of the Gordon family from the beginning of the 18th century. They changed the name and established the town and port of Invergordon in the 18th century. The property was held by the MacLeods of Cadboll in the 1870s. No more.

Other refs: Inverbreakie Castle

Invergowrie Castle

Angus & Dundee: About 2.5 miles west of Dundee, on minor roads north of A85, near Ninewells Hospital, Invergowrie.

Ruin or site   NO 363309   OS: 54   *   Map: 8, no: 163

Not much survives of a castle, which is said to have been visited by Alexander I in the 13th century. Invergowrie House [NO 363304] may have replaced this castle.

Invergowrie House

Angus & Dundee: About 2 miles west of Dundee, on minor roads east or north of A85, 0.5 miles north of Firth of Tay, just south-east of Ninewells Hospital, in Invergowrie

Private   NO 363304   OS: 54   **   Map: 8, no: 162

Invergowrie House incorporates a 16th-century tower house of three storeys, itself possibly incorporating work from the 13th century, although this earlier stronghold was more probably nearby [NO 363309]. To the tower house was added large mansion in 1836. A bartizan crowns one corner of the old part, and there is a corbelled-out stair-tower. Nearly all the windows have been enlarged and the original entrance, defended by a shot-hole, has been sealed.

The tower has been greatly altered inside, but the basement is still vaulted and contained the original kitchen.

The lands belonged to the Abbey of Scone, but passed to the Carnegies, then the Grays, who built or rebuilt the tower in 1568. The lands were forfeited after the Gowrie Conspiracy, and given to David Murray, one of James VI's henchmen. In 1615 the lands were sold to Robert Clayhills of Baldovie. The house was remodelled by William Burn in 1837 and, although divided into flats, is in good condition.

Inveriach House *see* Arrochar House

Inverie

South Highland: About 7 miles east and north of Mallaig, by boat east of A830, at Inverie in Knoydart.

Ruin or site   NM 776995 [?]   OS: 33   *   Map: 9, no: 24

Site of castle, a property of the MacDonalds of Glengarry. It is believed to have been destroyed in 1745 because the clan supported the Jacobites. The mansion here was described as 'within and without is a curious structure, in the old Celtic style' whatever that means.

Inverkeithing

Fife: In Inverkeithing, on B981.

Private   NT 129827   OS: 65   *   Map: 7, no: 20**

Inverkeithing Friary was a Franciscan establishment founded around 1268 by Philip Mowbray. The site is now a public garden, although the former guest house survives. It probably dates from the 14th century but was remodelled in the 17th century. The ground floor is vaulted, and vaults also survive in the garden. A museum is located on the upper floor of the building via an external stair, and there are displays and information on Inverkeithing and Rosyth, as well as on Admiral Greig who founded the Russian Navy.

Inverkeithing was made a royal burgh in 1165, and had a town wall and four gates, although these were removed in the 16th century. Other buildings of note are St Peter's Parish Church, which has a 14th-century tower, Fordell's Lodging, a 17th-century town house, and the 18th-century tolbooth. There is also Rosebery House [NT 131829], in King Street, a much-altered 16th-century house, named after the Primrose Earl of Rosebery who bought it in 1711.

Other refs: Rosebery House, Inverkeithing; Fordell's Lodging, Inverkeithing

OPEN: Open all year, Wed-Sun 11.00-17.00; closed pub hols.

Explanatory displays. Gift shop. Parking nearby.

Tel: 01383 313595/838

Inverkip Castle

Renfrewshire: About 5 miles south-west of Greenock, on minor roads west of the A78, about 0.5 miles north of Inverkip, near Ardgowan House.

Ruin or site   NS 205728   OS: 63   *   Map: 3, no: 30**

Inverkip Castle is a ruined 15th-century keep, square in plan, of three storeys and a garret. The corbelled-out crenellated parapet has open rounds at three corners. The original main entrance was at first-floor level, and reached by an external stone stair. A later wing has been demolished.

The basement was vaulted.

A 13th-century castle here was captured and held by the English during the Wars of Independence, although it was besieged by Robert Boyd for Robert the Bruce in 1306. The Stewarts acquired the lands in 1390, and they built the present castle, possibly incorporating some of the older building. It was abandoned early in the 19th century when the large classical mansion of Ardgowan, which is nearby, was built by the same family. The castle was repaired in 1936.

Other refs: Ardgowan Castle; Innerkip Castle

Inverlaidnan

South Highland: About 3 miles west and south of Carrbridge, on minor roads and tracks west of A9, west of River Dulnain, at Inverlaidnan.

Ruin or site   NH 862214   OS: 36   **   Map: 9, no: 132

The ruinous remains of a substantial 17th-century house, a property of the Grants. Bonnie Prince Charlie stayed here in 1746. The house was apparently burned but rebuilt.

Other refs: Old House of Inverlaidnan; House of Inverlaidnan

Inverlochy Castle

South Highland: About 1.5 miles north-east of Fort William, on minor roads north of A82, just south of River Lochy, north of Claggan, at Inverlochy Castle.

His Scot   NN 120754   OS: 41   *   Map: 9, no: 39**

Inverlochy Castle is a ruined 13th-century castle of enclosure of the Comyns of

Badenoch. It has a rectangular courtyard with a round tower at each corner, one larger than the others, probably the keep and known as 'Comyn's Tower'. There are two entrances, opposite each other, which had portcullises.

The Comyns were destroyed by Robert the Bruce around 1308, and the castle was granted to the Gordons of Huntly in 1505. Major consolidation work is underway.

Two battles were fought nearby. In 1431 Donald Balloch and Alasdair Carrich led the MacDonalds to victory over an army of Stewarts, the Earl of Caithness being among those who were slain. In the second, the Marquis Montrose led a force of Highlanders to victory over the Covenanters, led by his arch foe, the Campbell Earl of Argyll.

The modern castle stands nearby [NN 138767], and is now a hotel.

OPEN: Open all year – view from exterior for present.

Parking nearby.

Tel: 0131 668 8800   Fax: 0131 668 8888

Email: hs.explore@scotland.gov.uk   Web: www.historic-scotland.gov.uk

Invermark Castle

Angus & Dundee: About 14 miles north-west of Edzell, on minor roads about 10 miles west of B966, north of River North Esk, east of Loch Lee, at Invermark.

Ruin or site   NO 443804   OS: 44   *   Map: 8, no: 188**

Standing in a strategic position, Invermark Castle is a ruined plain 14th-century keep of four storeys and garret. The parapet and a two-storey bartizan were added in the late 16th century. The walls are pierced by gunloops. The keep had a courtyard.

The entrance, at first-floor level by an arched doorway, was reached by an external

stair, and still has an iron yett. The hall was on the first floor, and a stair led down to the vaulted basement.

Invermark was a property of the Lindsays of Crawford, and the castle rebuilt in 1526. David, 9th Earl of Crawford, died here in 1558, and in 1607 Invermark became the hiding place of Lord Edzell's son, another David, who was involved in the murder of Lord Spynie in Edinburgh. It was still habitable in 1729, but by 1803 was ruined, materials having been removed to build the church and manse.

Invermarkie Castle

Aberdeen & Gordon: About 6.5 miles south of Keith, on minor roads south of A920, north of River Deveron, at or near Invermarkie.

Ruin or site   NJ 429396 [?]   OS: 28   *   Map: 10, no: 85

Site of castle.

It was built by John Gordon, who was given the lands for his part in the Battle of Brechin in 1452 when forces loyal to James II defeated the Earl of Crawford. The property passed to the Innes family, but the castle was demolished in the 17th century, and replaced by a shooting lodge of the Duffs.

Invermay Tower

Perth & Kinross: About 5.5 miles south-west of Perth, on minor roads south of B935, about 1 mile south of Fortviot, just south of Water of May, at Invermay.

Ruin or site   NO 061163   OS: 58   *   Map: 8, no: 64**

Invermay Tower is a late 16th-century L-plan tower house. It consists of a main block of three storeys and a stair-tower which projects from one end. Another wing, with a new stair-tower, was added in 1633. The stair-tower is corbelled out, above second floor level, to form a watch-chamber. A later two-storey range was also added.

The property was owned by the Bonnar family, but passed to the Belshes of Invermay, who built the castle. By 1560 it had passed to the Stewarts of Innermeath. A large plain 18th-century mansion was built nearby. The tower is not occupied.

Other refs: Old House of Invermay

Inverness Castle

Inverness & Nairn: In Inverness, on minor roads south of A82, near the east bank of River Ness, about 0.25 miles south of railway station, at Inverness Castle.

Ruin or site   NH 667451   OS: 26   *   Map: 9, no: 92

Nothing except a well, some walling and a stair survives of the royal castle of Inverness, and a mock castle of 1835, housing the Sheriff Court and Police Department, stands on the site.

Inverness was strategically important, and the Picts had a major stronghold here, which may have been the seat of their kings. Malcolm Canmore destroyed a castle of Macbeth here in 1057. David I and William the Lyon built a keep and courtyard, which was seized by Edward I of England during the Wars of Independence, but recaptured for Robert the Bruce in 1310.

James I summoned 50 Highland chiefs, including Alexander, Lord of the Isles, to meet him at Inverness Castle in 1427. They were all imprisoned until they gave hostages and pledges of good behaviour. The Lord of the Isles returned in 1429 to burn the town, although the castle held out. His son, John, became Earl of Ross in 1437, and in 1455 he captured the castle during the Douglas's fight against James II. For many years he acted as a semi-independent prince, but in 1476 was forced to submit to James III, losing both the Ross earldom and the Lordship of the Isles. He became a pensioner at court, although the MacDonalds were not subdued for many years. James I, III and IV all stayed here.

In 1508 the Gordon, Earl of Huntly, was made keeper of the castle, previously having been held by the Mackintoshes, and in 1555 Mary of Guise was imprisoned here. In 1562 Mary, Queen of Scots's, forces captured the castle from the Gordons and hanged the keeper. The Marquis of Montrose failed to take the castle in 1644, but a party of Royalists seized it in 1649.

The castle was then in a bad state of repair, and Cromwell built a Citadel nearby [NH 664463], which Charles II had destroyed at the request of Highland chiefs in the 1660s. A clock tower marks this latter site, and parts of the ramparts and bastions survive.

The old castle was patched up by the government. It was captured by the Jacobites in 1715, but retaken by Hanoverian forces the same year. It was repaired again in 1718, but finally captured and blown up by the Jacobites in 1746 after the Battle

of Culloden. A mock castle of 1835 was built on the site, and part houses a small exhibition.
Other refs: Cromwell's Fort, Inverness
OPEN: Exhibition open in summer.

Invernochty *see* Doune of Invernochty

Inverquharity Castle

Angus & Dundee: About 3.5 miles north-east of Kirriemuir, on minor roads east of B955, south of River South Esk, at Inverquharity.
Private NO 411579 OS: 54 **** Map: 8, no: 179
Inverquharity Castle consists of an altered 15th-century keep, rectangular in plan, of four storeys and a garret. To this was added a wing in the 16th century, making the castle L-plan. This wing had been demolished, but has since been replaced and the castle restored. A corbelled-out parapet has a large gabled caphouse, open rounds, and a machiolation defending the entrance.

  The arched entrance leads to the stair, and into the vaulted basement. The fine hall, on the first floor, is also vaulted and has an arched moulded fireplace. It is reached by a dog-legged stair in the thickness of the walling. The floors above were occupied by private chambers with fireplaces.

  It was a property of the Ogilvies from 1420. One of the family, Alexander, was smothered at Finavon Castle by his sister in 1446, and John Ogilvie of Inverquharity was slain by the Lindsays in 1581. Another Alexander Ogilvie was captured after the Battle of Philiphaugh in 1645, while fighting for the Marquis of Montrose, and beheaded in Glasgow. Another fought for James VII at the Battle of the Boyne in 1690. The Ogilvies were involved in a long feud with the Lindsays. The property was sold in the late 18th century, the castle restored in the 1960s, and it is occupied.

  Inverquharity is said to have been haunted by a Sir John Ogilvie. Desiring the beautiful daughter of the local miller John White, Ogilvie had her father hanged when she refused him, then raped her and her mother. The local priest prayed for vengeance, and Ogilvie was struck down dead, although his ghost is said to have so plagued the castle that it had to be abandoned at one time.

Inverquiech Castle

Perth & Kinross: About 2 miles east of Alyth, on minor road north of A926, just north of meeting of River Isla and Alyth Burn, at or near Inverquiech.
Ruin or site NO 273964 OS: 53 * Map: 8, no: 142
Little remains of Inverquiech Castle, a 13th-century courtyard castle. It may have been built by Alexander II or an earlier king as a hunting lodge. It was visited by Edward I of England in 1296. The Lindsays were made keepers of the castle in 1394, but it was later a property of the Rollo family, and probably used until the 17th century.
Other refs: Balloch Castle

Invershin Castle

Sutherland & Caithness: About 3.5 miles north-west of Bonar Bridge, on foot west of A836, east bank of Kyle of Sutherland, west of Invershin.
Ruin or site NH 573964 OS: 21 * Map: 12, no: 10
Very little remains of Invershin Castle, except a mound or motte, perhaps dating from the 12th century. Invershin was a property of the de Moravia family, from whom the Sutherlands were descended.
Other refs: Duffus Castle

Inversnaid

Stirlingshire & Clackmannan: About 16 miles north-west of Aberfoyle, on minor road west of B829, 3 miles west of Stronachlachar, west end of Glen Arklet, at Garrison.
Private NN 348097 OS: 56 * Map: 6, no: 1
Not much remains of a barracks, dating from 1719. It consisted of two barrack blocks in a large courtyard, but all that survives are walls with gunloops, built into a steading.

  The barracks were built after the Jacobite Rising of 1715 to protect against the MacGregors, and Rob Roy's men attacked the workmen during construction. The barracks were commanded by General Wolfe, before he was a general, but were abandoned by 1800. In 1820 part of the building was used as an inn, but it had been demolished by 1828.

  Rob Roy held property in the area, and probably inherited the lands from his father, Donald MacGregor of Glengyle. Rob Roy was forfeited for his part in the 1715 Rising, but pardoned in 1725. He had been responsible for much blackmail – the term being credited as an invention of the clan – and thievery, including the taking of £1000 from rents of the Marquis of Montrose. MacGregor died at Balquhidder in 1734. His son and cousin took the barracks in 1745.

  Rob Roy's Cave, about 1 mile north of the Inversnaid Hotel, is said to have sheltered Robert the Bruce, and to have been used by Rob Roy to plan his night-time raids.
Other refs: Garrison of Inversnaid

Inverugie Castle

Banff & Buchan: About 2.5 miles north-west of Peterhead, on minor roads south of A952, just north of River Ugie, in village of Inverugie.
Ruin or site NK 102484 OS: 30 ** Map: 10, no: 366
Once an imposing castle, Inverugie Castle is a ruined 16th-century tower house, which incorporates work from the 13th century. Only the basement remains of the main block, formerly of four storeys and a garret, which had two round towers facing a courtyard, and a round stair-tower. There were ranges of buildings around the courtyard.

  The property belonged to the Cheynes, and in 1267 Sir Reginald le Cheyne was Lord Chamberlain of Scotland. The family were allied with the Comyns, and consequently enemies of Robert the Bruce, who destroyed their power. The property passed by marriage to the Keiths, High Marischals of Scotland, one of whom founded Marischal College in Aberdeen in 1598. The Keiths were Jacobites, and forfeited and forced into exile after the Jacobite Rising of 1715. James Keith, born at Inverugie in 1696, rose to the rank of Major-General in the Russian army, and Field Marshall in the service of Frederick of Prussia in 1747. His elder brother, the Earl Marischal, became the Prussian ambassador to the Court of France and Governor of Neufchatel.

  Inverugie passed to Ferguson of Pitfour in 1764, and the courtyard buildings were

still occupied in the late 17th century. The castle was still floored in the late 18th century, when it was surmounted by an observatory. The tower was blown up in 1899 to clear the land – unsuccessfully – for agriculture.

One of True Thomas's predictions was:

'Inverugie by the sea,

Lordless shall thy landis be.'

which refers to an earlier castle by the sea.

Inverugie Castle

Moray: About 5.5 miles north-west of Elgin, on minor roads west or south of B9012, about 1 mile south of Hopeman, at or near Inverugie.

Ruin or site   NJ 152687 [?]   OS: 28   *   Map: 10, no: 22

Site of castle on a rocky promontory of the Young family, nothing of which remains. The present house dates from 1864, and was built after the property had passed to the Mortimers.

Inveruglas Castle

Argyll & Dunbartonshire: About 3.5 miles north of Tarbet, east of Inveruglas on A82, on island, Inveruglas Isle, to north of Loch Lomond.

Ruin or site   NN 323096   OS: 56   *   Map: 5, no: 135

On an island in Loch Lomond, Inveruglas Castle is a ruined Z-plan tower house. It consists of a rectangular main block with two round towers at opposite corners, one much larger than the other. The walls are pierced by shot-holes, and the island has a jetty and landing stage.

It was a property of the MacFarlanes. The 11th chief of MacFarlane was killed at the Battle of Flodden in 1513, and Duncan, the 13th chief, was killed at the Battle of Pinkie in 1547. The clan fought against Mary, Queen of Scots, at the Battle of Langside, and were part of the Marquis of Montrose's army that defeated the Campbell Marquis of Argyll at the Battle of Inverlochy in 1645. The castle was torched by Cromwell's men in the 1650s, and the building shows evidence of having been burned. The clan moved to Tarbet.

Inverurie *see* Bass of Inverurie

Irvine Castle *see* Seagate Castle

Irvine Tower

Dumfriesshire: About 2.5 miles south of Langholm, on minor road west of A7, west of River Esk, at or near Old Irvine.

Ruin or site   NY 367810 [?]   OS: 79   *   Map: 1, no: 314

Site of tower house.

Irvine's Tower *see* Chanonry

Island House *see* Castle Loch Heylipol

Island Muller Castle

Argyll & Dunbartonshire: About 3 miles north-east of Campbeltown, on foot east of B842 near turn off for Ballymenach, on east coast of Kintyre, on promontory, at Island Muller.

Ruin or site   NR 756224   OS: 68   **   Map: 5, no: 44

Island Muller Castle is a ruined 15th-century keep and castle of the MacDonalds of Dunyvaig.

Other refs: Smerby

Island Varnach *see* Eilean Molach

Isle Castle *see* Loch Dochart Castle

Isle Maree

South Highland: About 8.5 miles north-west of Kinlochewe, by boat north of A832, on Isle Maree on the north side of Loch Maree.

Ruin or site   NG 931724   OS: 19   *   Map: 9, no: 35

Possible site of tower, said to have been built by a Norse prince.

On the island in is the site of a chapel and remains of a burial ground, which are believed to have been founded by St Maelrubha. This is believed by some to have been an earlier place of pagan worship, associated with bull sacrifice, and later associated with St Maelrubha's day.

Also on the island is a healing well which was used for curing lunacy as late as the 19th century. The sufferer was towed several times around the island, then left by themselves tethered overnight. On oak tree stood beside the well, and coins and nails were hammered into the trunk with pieces of rag.

Other refs: St Maelrubha's Chapel, Loch Maree; Loch Maree

Isle of Heston *see* Heston Island

Isle of May

Fife: Boat leaves from The Harbour, Anstruther, Fife.

Private   NT 655995   OS: 59   *   Map: 7, no: 165**

Not much remains of a 16th-century castle. Patrick Learmonth added a round tower, with gunloops to fortify part of the former Cluniac priory.

The island is believed to have been where St Adrian was murdered by Norsemen around 875, and became a place of pilgrimage: St Adrian's shrine was visited by barren women. David I founded the priory in the 12th century, but little of it survives. A spring here was visited by the pilgrims.

After the Reformation, the island passed to the Learmonths, then the Balfours of Montquhanie, later to Cunningham of Barnes. In 1636 a lighthouse was built on the island, the first in Scotland, by Alexander Cunningham of Barnes. The property later passed to the Scotts of Scotstarvit, then the Scotts of Balcomie, then to the Commissioners of Northern Lights. The lighthouse was rebuilt in 1815-6, then again in 1886 when it reached a height of 240 feet.

The island is home to large numbers of sea birds, including puffins, as well as a colony of grey seals. There are boat trips to the island from Anstruther, lasting about five hours with three hours ashore.

OPEN: Can be visited May-Sep: telephone for sailing times.

Explanatory displays. Snack bar on board. Visitor centre and picnic area on Isle of May. WC. Car and coach parking at harbour. £££.

Tel: 01333 310103

Isle of Whithorn Castle

Galloway: About 3.5 miles south-east of Whithorn, just north of A750 at junction with B7063, at Isle of Whithorn, short distance from the sea.

Private   NX 476367   OS: 83   ***   Map: 1, no: 78

Isle of Whithorn Castle is a 17th century L-plan tower house of three storeys and a garret, crowned by two corbelled-out bartizans. A stair-tower rises in the re-entrant angle and the walls are harled and whitewashed. The tower has been altered, externally and internally.

The original entrance was in the foot of the stair-tower, and the basement is vaulted.

It was a property of the Houstons of Drummaston. The tower was altered about 1830 when it was occupied by John Reid, Superintendent of Customs. It is still occupied.

Isle Tower

Dumfriesshire: About 6 miles north and west of Dumfries, on minor road east of A76, just south of the River Nith, at Isle.

Private   NX 935823   OS: 78   ***   Map: 1, no: 180

Isle Tower is a rectangular 16th-century tower house of three storeys and an attic, with corbelled-out bartizans crowning two corners. The castle is dated 1587, and a modern house and outbuildings adjoin, although there was probably a stronghold here from 1414 or earlier.

The entrance, now reached from the modern house, has a fine iron yett, and leads to the vaulted basement and to a turnpike stair in one corner. The hall, on the first floor, has a fireplace.

The property was owned by the Fergusons from the 14th century. Robert Burns farmed Ellisland, an adjoining property, and may have used the tower. It is occupied, and in good condition.

Isle Tower

Dumfriesshire: About 5.5 miles south-east of Dumfries, north of minor road and foot north of B725, just west of the Lochar Water, about 0.25 miles north of Bankend.

Ruin or site   NY 028689   OS: 84   **   Map: 1, no: 199

Once standing on an island, little remains of Isle Tower. It consisted of a small 17th-century tower house of three storeys and a centrally projecting stair-wing. The walls were pierced by gunloops.

It was a property of the Maxwells.

Other refs: Lochar Tower; Bankend Castle

Ithington Castle *see* Edington Castle

Jarlshof

Shetland: About 20 miles south of Lerwick, on minor roads and foot south of A970, Sumburgh.

His Scot   HU 398095   OS: 4   ***   Map: 11, no: 60

Not much remains of a 16th-century house.

This is one of the most remarkable archaeological sites in Europe. There are remains from the Bronze Age, Iron Age, Pictish and Norse settlements, as well as a medieval farm. There is also a 16th-century Laird's House, once home of the Earls Robert and Patrick Stewart, and the basis of Jarlshof in Walter Scott's novel 'The Pirate' – apparently not one of his better works.

There is a small visitor centre with artefacts from the excavations.

OPEN: Open Apr-Sep, daily 9.30-18.30; last ticket 18.00.

Visitor centre with exhibition. Gift shop. Car and coach parking. Group concessions. £.

Tel: 01950 460112

Email: hs.explore@scotland.gov.uk   Web: www.historic-scotland.gov.uk

Jedburgh *see* Queen Mary's House, Jedburgh

Jedburgh *see* Stone Hill, Jedburgh

Jedburgh Castle

Borders: In Jedburgh, on minor road south of B6358 from A68, just south of Jedburgh Abbey.

Ruin or site   NT 647202   OS: 74   *   Map: 2, no: 263

Site of 12th-century castle.

It was one of the strongholds handed over to the English after the Treaty of Falaise to release William the Lyon from captivity. Malcolm the Maiden died here in 1165. Alexander III was married at the castle in 1285, but a ghostly apparition warned of his impending death – which came true when Alexander fell, with his horse, from a cliff at Kinghorn. The castle was occupied by the English after the Battle of Neville's Cross in 1346 until 1409, when it was retaken by the Scots and demolished, the work paid for by the Crown. The town itself was burned in 1410, 1416, 1464 and 1523, as well as being seized by the English in 1513. Six bastle houses were then built to protect the population, but the town was again torched by the English under the Earl of Hertford in 1544 and the bastles were slighted. These were apparently rebuilt and one in Kirkwynd was occupied by the Kerrs in the 1620s. Another tower, known as David's or Davie's Tower stood near the meeting of Abbot's Close and Castlegate, and was a property of Jedburgh Abbey. The site is occupied by a mansion. All traces of old houses have disappeared except for Queen Mary's House [see separate entry].

A jail was erected on the site of the old castle in 1823, a Howard reform prison, and the only type of its kind now remaining in Scotland. The prison is now a museum, with a display of exhibits relating to 19th-century prison life.

The ghostly apparition who warned of Alexander's death has apparently appeared many times, and is always the harbinger of death.

OPEN: Castle Jail open Apr-Oct, daily Mon-Sat 10.00-16.45, Sun 13.00-16.00; open on Bank Holidays.

Explanatory displays. Gift shop. WC. Picnic area. Disabled access. Car and coach parking. Group concessions. £.

Tel: 01835 863254

Jerviston

Lanarkshire & Glasgow area: About 1 mile north-east of Motherwell, on minor road north of A723, on north bank of Calder Water, near Colville Park.

Private   NS 757583   OS: 64   ***   Map: 3, no: 360

Jerviston is an altered 16th-century L-plan tower house of three storeys and an attic. A round stair-turret is corbelled out, in the re-entrant angle, above first-floor

John Knox House, Edinburgh

Lothians: The Netherbow, 43-45 High Street, Edinburgh.
Private   NT 262738   OS: 66   ***   Map: 4, no: 102
John Knox House, which may be the oldest house in Edinburgh, dates from the 15th century and John Knox is said to have died here. The house was home to James Mossman, keeper of the Royal Mint to Mary, Queen of Scots. The original floor in the Oak Room survives, and there is a magnificent painted ceiling. An exhibition covers the life and times of John Knox and the Reformation, and information about Mossman.
OPEN: Open all year: Mon-Sat 10.00-17.00; closed Christmas; last admission 30 mins before closing.
Explanatory displays. Gift shop. Cafe. WC. Parking nearby. £
Tel: 0131 556 9579

John the Bangster's House

Perthshire: About 3.5 miles south of Crieff, on minor roads east of A822, to north-east of Muthill.
Ruin or site   NN 872174   OS: 58   *   Map: 8, no: 26
Site of castle, which was defended by a ditch, the last remains of which were removed around 1840.
It was said to be held by John the Bangster, a noted brigand.

Johnscleugh

Lothians: About 5 miles west and north of Cranshaws, on minor road north from B6355, north of the Whiteadder Water, at Johnscleugh.
Private   NT 631665   OS: 67   **   Map: 4, no: 217
Standing in an exposed position, Johnscleugh is a plain sturdy 16th-century tower house, rectangular in plan, with a short semi-circular stair-tower. There are no windows at basement level, and the building has been lowered.
The interior has been greatly altered, but part of the basement is vaulted.
It was a property of the Lauder family, and is still occupied as a farmhouse.

Johnstone Castle

Renfrewshire: In Johnstone, on minor road south of A737, just south of Quarrelton in Tower Place.
Private   NS 425623   OS: 64   ***   Map: 3, no: 165
Originally called Easter Cochrane, Johnstone Castle is an altered 16th-century L-plan tower house. It consists of a main block of three storeys and a garret, and a wing, remodelled as a massive Gothic tower, which rises a storey higher. A two-storey bartizan crowns the gable of the main block, and there is a massive chimney-stack from the original kitchen. The walls are pierced by slits.
The entrance, in the re-entrant angle, has a porter's lodge. The entrance leads to a vaulted passage, from which the basement chambers are reached. The basement contains the kitchen, with a wide arched fireplace; and the wine-cellar with a small stair, in the thickness of the wall, climbing to the hall above. The hall, on the first floor, has been altered.
The property was owned by the Cochranes, who became Earls of Dundonald in 1669, and called their property Easter Cochrane. It passed to the Houstons in 1733, who changed the name back to Johnstone. They extended the castle in 1771, and in 1812 it was remodelled in the Gothic style. Frederick Chopin visited the castle in 1848. The castle was taken over by the local council, and most of the mansion was demolished in 1950: only the old part survives. It stands in a housing estate, and is apparently used as a store.
Other refs: Easter Cochrane Castle

Jordanhill

Lanarkshire & Glasgow area: About 3 miles west and north of Glasgow city centre, on minor roads south of A82, in the grounds of Jordanhill College.
Ruin or site   NS 538683   OS: 64   *   Map: 3, no: 243
Site of 16th-century tower house of the Crawford family, which they held until the 19th century. Sir Thomas Crawford of Jordanhill fought at and survived the Battle of Pinkie in 1547, although he was captured by the English and ransomed. He did not support Mary Queen of Scots, and after she had fled Scotland he captured Dumbarton Castle from her forces in 1570. In 1577 Crawford was made Provost of Glasgow, and he had Partick Bridge built.

---

level. The tower has been crowned with bartizans, but only part of the corbelling remains.
The entrance, in the stair-wing in the re-entrant angle, leads to the vaulted basement, which contains the kitchen and a cellar. The main turnpike stair rises only to the first floor in the wing, while the upper floors were reached by the turret stair. The hall is on the first floor.
It was a property of the Baillies. There is a modern mansion nearby, and the building was derelict at one time.

Jerviswood House

Lanarkshire & Glasgow area: About 1 mile north of Lanark, on minor road north of the A706, on the south bank of the Mouse Water, at Jerviswood.
Private   NS 884455   OS: 72   ***   Map: 3, no: 411
Jerviswood is an altered 16th-century L-plan tower house of three storeys and a garret, beneath a steeply-pitched roof.
The basement is not vaulted and contained a kitchen with a fireplace and oven. The interior was greatly altered to provide lodgings for farm workers, although several original fireplaces survive.
The property belonged to the Livingstones, who built the original tower, but was sold to the Baillies of Lamington in 1636. One of the Baillies, Robert Baillie, the Covenanter, was hanged, drawn and quartered in 1684, and parts of his body were displayed in Ayr, Edinburgh, Glasgow, Jedburgh and Lanark. Robert wrote to his son, George: 'if ye have a strong heart ye may go and see me nagled; but if ye have not the heart for it, ye may stay away'. The folk of Lanark gave their part of his body a decent burial.
George married the daughter of the Earl of Marchmont, and the family eventually moved to Mellerstain, and were later made Earls of Haddington. The house was restored and is occupied, receiving a Civic Trust commendation in 1984.

Jingles *see* Glendivan

Jocksthorn *see* Kilmaurs Place

K

Kaim of Mathers Castle

Kincardine & Deeside: About 6 miles north and east of Montrose, on minor roads and track east of A92, 0.5 miles east of St Cyrus, just north of sea, south of West Mathers.

Ruin or site   NO 763649   OS: 45   *   Map: 10, no: 244

Not much remains of a 15th-century castle, on cliff-tops, which consists of one wall of a keep or tower. The site is being eroded by the sea, which also destroyed the nearby village.

It was a property of the Barclays of Mathers. One of the family, David Barclay, was involved in the murder of Sir John Melville, and used the castle as refuge. Melville was murdered around 1420 by being boiled in a cauldron by several local lairds.

Other refs: Mathers Castle; West Mathers Castle

Kair House

Kincardine & Deeside: About 2.5 miles north-west of Arbuthnott, on minor roads north of B967 or east of A90, east of Bervie Water, at Kair House.

Ruin or site   NO 769765   OS: 45   *   Map: 10, no: 250

Site of castle. The present house is a two-storey classic mansion with wings and dates from the beginning of the 19th century.

Other refs: House of Kairs

Kally *see* Cally Castle

Kames Castle

Argyll & Dunbartonshire: On island of Bute, about 2.5 miles north-west of Rothesay, at junction of A844 with A886 on Kames Bay, Port Bannatyne, at Kames.

Private   NS 064676   OS: 63   *   Map: 5, no: 103**

Kames Castle is a massive 14th-century keep, formerly surrounded by a moat, to which later and lower buildings were added in the 18th century. The keep rises to four storeys, with a corbelled-out crenellated parapet and a caphouse topping the stair. A 16th-century stair-wing contained a scale-and-platt stair, but this was removed at the beginning of the century and the stone used to build cottages in the courtyard. The original windows are small, but new larger windows have been inserted.

The entrance leads to a vaulted basement, which contains a well, and to a straight narrow stair, which climbs to the parapet within the thickness of the walling. The hall is on the first floor, and there would have been private chambers on the floors above.

Kames was a property of Bannatyne family from the beginning of the 14th century or earlier. The house was extended in the 18th century, but later passed to the Stewarts.

OPEN: Cottages in the courtyard of the castle can be rented.

Tel: 01700 504500   Fax: 01700 504554

Email: kames-castle@easynet.co.uk   Web: www.kames-castle.co.uk

Kand *see* Cander

Karig Lion Castle

Stirlingshire & Clackmannan: Just north of Bo'ness off the coast, north of A904, on the south shore of Firth of Forth.

Ruin or site   NS 987812   OS: 65   *   Map: 6, no: 110

Nothing remains of a castle, marked on Blaeu's Atlas Novus map of Lothian as 'Remains of Cast Karig Lion', located somewhere off the coast north of Bo'ness at Kinneil. It was a dower house, and was used by Margaret Lyon, daughter of Lord Glamis and widow of John Hamilton, 1st Marquis of Hamilton, who himself died in 1604. The castle stood on what is now reclaimed land, and the site was occupied by the Kinneil Iron Works.

Other refs: Castle Karig Lion; Castle Lyon

Karlinghoups *see* Carlops

Karlock *see* Carlock

Kat Castle *see* Cot Castle

Keillor Castle

Angus & Dundee: About 2 miles south-west of Newtyle, on minor roads west of B954, at or near Keillor.

Ruin or site   NO 268403   OS: 53   *   Map: 8, no: 139

Site of castle, nothing of which survives except a panel built into a wall of the house.

Other refs: Wester Keillor

Keillour Castle

Perth & Kinross: About 3 miles west of Methven, on minor roads north of A85, at Keillour Castle.

Private   NN 979256   OS: 58   *   Map: 8, no: 47

Keillour Castle, a mansion dating from the 19th century, is said to have been built on the site of an earlier castle or house.

Keir House

Stirlingshire & Clackmannan: About 3.5 miles north and west of Stirling, on minor roads south of B824, about 1 mile north of River Teith, about 0.5 miles east of Arnhall Castle.

Private   NS 770989   OS: 57   *   Map: 6, no: 64

Keir House incorporates part of a 15th-century castle in the mostly mid 18th-century mansion, which was enlarged in 1810, 1841-51 and 1899.

The property originally belonged to the Leslies, but passed to the Stirlings in 1448. The Stirlings of Keir fought for the Jacobites in both the 1715 and 1745 Risings, and the family were forfeited, although they later recovered their lands. The house is still occupied, and there are extensive gardens.

Keirs Castle

Ayrshire: About 3.5 miles north-west of Dalmellington, on minor road south of A713 south of Waterside, west of River Doon, at Keirs.

Ruin or site   NS 430081   OS: 77   *   Map: 3, no: 169

Very little remains of a 13th-century castle of enclosure except overgrown mounds. One story is that William Wallace besieged Keirs Castle, but was driven from the walls.

Other refs: Kiers Castle

Keiss Castle

Sutherland & Caithness: About 7 miles north of Wick, on minor roads east of A9, just east of Keiss Castle, west of sea.

Ruin or site   ND 357616   OS: 12   *   Map: 12, no: 63**

Standing on a cliff-top promontory above the sea, Keiss Castle is a ruined 16th-century Z-plan tower house of three storeys and an attic. It consists of a main block and two round towers at opposite corners, one a stair-tower crowned by a square caphouse. There is a bartizan at one corner and the walls, which are not very thick, are pierced by shot-holes. The windows are small.

The basement was vaulted, the hall was on the first floor, and the upper floors were occupied by private chambers.

It was a property of the Sinclairs. Sinclair of Keiss recovered the Earldom of Caithness from the Campbells in 1681 after the 6th Earl had left huge debts. The castle was abandoned for the nearby new Keiss Castle [ND 355617]. The new mansion was built in 1755, remodelled and extended in 1860 to David Bryce's designs, and is a castellated pile.

Part of the old castle collapsed when the cliff below it fell, and the ruin is in a very dangerous condition.

Other refs: Old Keiss Castle

Keiss Castle – see previous page

Keith Hall

Aberdeen & Gordon: About 1 mile south-east of Inverurie, on minor road north of B993 or south of B9170, east of River Urie, at Keith Hall.

Private NJ 787212 OS: 38 ** Map: 10, no: 258

Once called Caskieben, Keith Hall consists of a 16th-century Z-plan tower house to which has been added a large mansion in 1662. The old part consists of a main block of four storeys and a garret with square towers, projecting from opposite corners, and round stair-towers. There are ranges of domestic buildings.

Caskieben was a property of the Leslies in 1224, and there was an earlier moated castle nearby [NJ 788213]. The property passed to the Johnstones of Caskieben, who sold it to the Keiths, later Earls of Kintore, in 1662. They changed the name to Keith Hall and held the property until the 1980s. The house was remodelled as 14 houses and flats in 1984.

Other refs: Caskieben Castle

Keith Inch Tower

Banff & Buchan: About 1 mile east of Peterhead, on minor roads east of A952, on Keith Inch just east of the sea on north side of Peterhead Bay.

Ruin or site NK 138458 [?] OS: 30 * Map: 10, no: 369

Site of 16th-century L-plan tower house and courtyard of the Keith Earls Marischal, which was later extended with artillery fortifications. The tower rose to four storeys and a garret, and had a later wing. The family were forfeited in the 1715 Jacobite Rising and the property was sold to the Arbuthnotts, who built a new house. The old tower was demolished in 1813 and nothing remains.

Other refs: Tower of Keith Inch; Peterhead

Keith Marischal

Lothians: About 3 miles south of Pencaitland, about 1 mile north-west of Humbie, on minor road north of B6371, north of the Keith Water.

Private NT 449643 OS: 66 ** Map: 4, no: 172

Keith Marischal incorporates a very altered late 16th-century L-plan tower house.

To this has been added a long 17th-century L-plan extension to form three sides of a courtyard. The courtyard was filled in by a castellated block in the 19th century.

The basement of the tower is vaulted, as is the extension. The hall, on the first floor, is also vaulted, and has a moulded stone fireplace.

The house was built by the Keith Earls Marischal. George Keith negotiated James VI's marriage to Anne of Denmark, and in gratitude to the King of Denmark sent him a ship-load of timber to be used in the building of the house. Agnes Simpson lived here. She was accused of witchcraft by James VI, who charged her with raising a storm to drown him and his new bride on their way home from Norway. After torture the unfortunate woman confessed, and she was strangled, then burned.

Kelburn Castle

Ayrshire: About 2 miles south of Largs, on minor road east of A78, in Kelburn Country Centre.

Private NS 217567 OS: 63 * Map: 3, no: 41**

With fine views over the Clyde and set in park land, Kelburn Castle is a tall 16th-century Z-plan tower house, to which has been added a large symmetrical mansion, although part of the building may date from the 12th or 13th century. The tower, of four storeys and rectangular in plan, has round towers projecting at two corners, making it Z-plan. One round tower contains the main stair, and rises a storey higher than the main building to be capped by a conical-roofed watch-chamber. The castle is dated 1581. The castle was extended in 1700, 1722, and again in 1879 and 1890.

The original entrance is now a window. The basement was vaulted and contained the old kitchen. The house has been much altered inside, and contains fine 18th-century interior work.

The Boyles held the lands of Kelburn from the 12th or 13th century, and fought in the Battles of Largs in 1266 and Bannockburn in 1314. John Boyle of Kelburn, a supporter of James III, was killed at the Battle of Sauchieburn in 1488, and another of the family was slain at Pinkie in 1547. The Boyles were made Lord Boyle in 1699, and Earls of Glasgow and Viscounts Kelburn in 1703, as a reward for helping persuade reluctant Jacobites sign the Act of Union. They still occupy the castle, making Kelburn one of the oldest houses continuously occupied by the same family.

The grounds are open to the public as a Country Centre, established in 1977. There are walled gardens, containing rare shrubs and trees, as well as many unique historical and natural features.

OPEN: Castle open: Jul-1st week in Sep; daily tours 13.45, 15.00 and 16.15; other times by appt only. Country centre and gardens open: Easter-Oct, daily 10.00-18.00. Also grounds only open: Nov-Easter, daily 11.00-17.00.

Guided tours of house. Explanatory displays. Gift shop. Licensed tea room. Cafe. WC. Picnic area. Riding centre open all year. Assault and adventure courses. Secret Forest. Disabled limited access and WC. Car and coach parking. Group concessions. ££ (+£ entrance to castle).

**Tel: 01475 586685/204 (castle) Fax: 01475 568121/328 (castle)
Email: info@kelburncastle.com Web: www.kelburncastle.com**

Kellechaffe *see* Craigcaffie Tower

Kellie Castle

Fife: About 4 miles north and east of Elie, on minor road north of B9171, east of Newton of Balcormo.

NTS NO 520052 OS: 59 ** Map: 7, no: 135**

One of the finest castles in Scotland, Kellie Castle is a 16th-century E-plan tower house. It consists of a three-storey main block with three large square towers which form the E. The towers rise to five storeys, and two have bartizans. Two smaller stair-towers project from one side. The oldest part of the castle, one of the towers, dates from the early 16th century; another tower was added in 1573. The main block and a large tower were added to connect the older parts of the building in 1603-6.

The basement is vaulted throughout the building. A square stair rises, from the main entrance, to the large hall on the first floor. Four turnpike stairs also climb to

hall level. The Vine Room, on one of the upper floors, has a ceiling painted by De Witt, and there are fine plaster ceilings.

There is a magnificent walled garden.

An earlier castle here belonged to the Siwards, but the present castle was built by the Oliphants, who held the lands from 1360 until 1613, when the 5th Lord Oliphant had to sell the property. It was bought by Sir Thomas Erskine of Gogar, made Earl of Kellie in 1619, a favourite of James VI. Erskine was involved in the 'Gowrie Conspiracy', and may have been one of those who murdered the Master of Ruthven and his brother, the Earl of Gowrie, at Gowrie House in Perth.

Kellie was abandoned in 1829, but in 1878 James Lorimer, Professor of Public Law at Edinburgh University, leased Kellie as an almost roofless ruin and proceeded to restore it. Robert Lorimer, his son, spent most of his childhood at Kellie, and was later a famous architect. In 1970 Kellie passed into the care of The National Trust for Scotland.

A spiral stair in the castle is reputedly haunted by the spirit of Anne Erskine, who died by falling from one of the upstairs windows. The ghost of James Lorimer is also said to have been seen seated in one of the passageways.

OPEN: Open 13 Apr-Sep, daily 13.30-17.30; Oct, Sat-Sun 13.30-17.30; last admission 16.45. Grounds and garden open all year, daily 9.30-sunset.

Victorian nursery, old kitchen, and audio-visual show. Explanatory displays. Giftshop. Tearoom. Magnificent walled garden. WC. Disabled access to ground floor and grounds. Car park. ££.

Tel: 01333 720271 Fax: 01333 720326

Email: information@nts.org.uk Web: nts.org.uk

Kellie Castle

Angus & Dundee: About 2.5 miles west of Arbroath, on minor roads north of A92 or south of B9127, east of Arbirlot, south of Elliot Water, at Kellie (Kelly) Castle.

Private NO 608402 OS: 54 ** Map: 8, no: 249**

A fine example of a fortified house, Kellie Castle consists of a 15th-century keep of

five storeys, which was extended by a wing to L-plan. It forms one corner of a courtyard, with lower ranges making up the other sides. The entrance, by a pend through a gatehouse, is flanked by a round tower with gunloops.

The keep has steep roofs and corbiestepped gables, and is crowned by two bartizans, one round with a conical roof, the other rectangular. The rectangular tower rises to three storeys, and is crowned by a watch-chamber.

The entrance is in the re-entrant angle from the courtyard. The basement is vaulted, and the hall, on the first floor of the main block, is panelled in pine.

The property originally belonged to the Mowbray family, but was held by the Stewarts until 1402 when it was acquired by the Ochterlony family. It is also, however, said to have been a property of the Elliots from the 14th to 17th centuries. It was sold in 1614 to the Irvines, who extended the house to the present form. It was acquired in 1679 by the Maule Earl of Panmure.

Harry Maule, the Earl's son, was one of the most successful leaders of the Jacobite Rising of 1715. His elder brother, James was severely wounded and taken prisoner at the Battle of Sheriffmuir, but was rescued by Harry. Both brothers were outlawed, and forfeited, when the Rising failed, but escaped to the Continent, never to return.

The castle became ruinous, but was restored in the 19th century and acquired by the Maule family. Kellie is still occupied.

Other refs: Kelly Castle; Auchterlony

Kelloe Bastle

Borders: About 2.5 miles east of Duns, on minor roads south of A6105, 0.5 miles north-west of Kelloe Mains.

Ruin or site NT 828543 OS: 74 * Map: 2, no: 337

Site of bastle house or tower in a field. Kelloe, a mansion, was held by the Fordyce-Buchans in the 19th century.

Kelly *see* Cally Castle

Kelly Castle *see* Kellie Castle

Kelly House

Renfrewshire: About 2 miles south of Inverkip, on minor road east of A78, north of the Kelly Burn, near Wemyss Bay, at or near Kelly Mains.

Ruin or site NS 198685 [?] OS: 63 * Map: 3, no: 28

Site of a mansion and earlier house.

It was held by the Bannatynes from the 15th century until 1792 when it was purchased by John Wallace and a new house was built. Sir James Young, pioneer of oil technology, later lived at Kelly. Another new house, designed by William Leiper, was built in 1890 by the Stephen family, but burned down in 1913, probably by suffragettes.

Kellyly

Borders: About 5.5 miles north-east of Newcastleton, south of B6357, south of Liddel Water, at or near Kelly Cleuch Burn.
Ruin or site NY 537928 OS: 79 * Map: 2, no: 189
Possible site of tower house.

Kelsoland *see* Brisbane House

Kelspoke Castle

Argyll & Dunbartonshire: About 6 miles south of Rothesay, off B881, north of Kilchattan Bay, Bute.
Ruin or site NS 106541 OS: 63 * Map: 5, no: 110
There are scanty remains of an L-plan tower house.

Keltie Castle

Perth & Kinross: About 1 mile south-west of Dunning, on minor road south of B8062, north of the Ochil Hills, at Keltie.
Private NO 008133 OS: 58 * Map: 8, no: 52**
Keltie Castle is a plain 17th-century L-plan tower house of three storeys and a garret beneath a steep roof. A bartizan is corbelled out at second-floor level. The walls are pierced by shot-holes.
The basement is not vaulted, but contained the kitchen with traces of an arched fireplace. A turnpike stair leads to the hall on the first floor.
The lands belonged to the Bonnar family from 1452, but were sold to the Drummonds in 1692, who held the property until 1812. It then passed to the Ogilvie Earl of Airlie, then to Lord Rollo in 1833, and was held in turn by several families. It is still occupied.
During renovations the skeleton of a woman was found walled-up in one of the rooms.

Kemnay House

Aberdeen & Gordon: About 5.5 miles south and west of Inverurie, on minor roads south of B993, 0.5 miles south of Kemnay, east of River Don, at Kemnay House.
Private NJ 733154 OS: 38 ** Map: 10, no: 232
Kemnay House incorporates a tall 17th-century L-plan tower house, the wings of which have been extended. A stair-turret rises above second-floor level in the re-entrant angle. The walls are cream-washed, and the windows of the tower are small. The tower had a courtyard, of which traces remain. The house was altered and extended in 1833.
The original entrance was in the re-entrant angle, but a new doorway has been inserted. The basement is vaulted, and contained the kitchen in the wing.
Kemnay belonged to the Douglases of Glenbervie in the 16th century, but passed to the Crombies, who built the present house in the 17th century. It was sold to Thomas Burnet of Leys in 1688. He was a staunch Hanoverian, but while travelling through Paris his Jacobite enemies had him imprisoned in the Bastille. The house is still occupied.

Kemp Castle *see* Cot Castle

Kemps Castle

Dumfriesshire: About 1 mile south-west of Sanquhar, on minor roads and foot west of A76, on west bank of Euchan Water at meeting with Barr Water, Kemps.
Ruin or site NS 773089 OS: 78 * Map: 1, no: 126
Only earthworks survive of a castle.
Other refs: Castle Kemps

Kemp's Walk Fort

Galloway: About 4.5 miles west of Stranraer, on minor road west of B738, above Broadsea Bay, Larbrax.
Ruin or site NW 975598 OS: 82 * Map: 1, no: 2**
Kemp's Walk is a promontory fort overlooking Broadsea Bay. It has three large ramparts and ditches crossing the easiest approach. The other sides of the promontory have steeper slopes and would have been easier to defend. There are no traces of hut circles within the fort. This is the largest of Galloway's promontory forts, and was probably used into medieval times.

Kenmore Castle

Perth & Kinross: About 6 miles south-west of Aberfeldy, south of A827, on Eilean nan Bannoabh, an island at north-east end of Loch Tay, just west of Kenmore.
Ruin or site NN 766454 OS: 52 ** Map: 8, no: 13
On Eilean nan Bannoabh, 'island of female saints', Kenmore Castle was built by the Campbells in the 1560s. The island was besieged by the Marquis of Montrose in 1645, and occupied by General Monck's forces during Cromwell's invasion of the 1650s.
Other refs: Eilean nan Bannoabh Castle

Kenmuir

Lanarkshire & Glasgow: About 4 miles east and north of Rutherglen, on minor roads south of A74, north of River Clyde, north of Mount Vernon, at or near Kenmuir.
Ruin or site NS 660622 [?] OS: 64 * Map: 3, no: 309
Site of castle.

Kenmure Castle

Galloway: About 1 mile south of New Galloway, just east of A762, on hillock west of Water of Ken, at Kenmure.
Ruin or site NX 635764 OS: 77 ** Map: 1, no: 103
Kenmure Castle consists of a 16th-century tower house of three storeys and an attic, a later wing, and further work added in the 18th and 19th centuries. A square stair-tower rises at one corner of the tower, the top storey of which is corbelled out. A later semi-hexagonal stair-tower stands in the re-entrant angle, and contains the entrance. There is much fine decorative stonework. The walls are pierced by shot-holes.
There may have been a stronghold here of the Lords of Galloway, and John Balliol may have been born at Kenmure, rather than Buittle Castle, and he used an early castle at Kenmure. On his forced abdication as King of Scots, the property may have been held by the Maxwells, but passed to the Gordons of Lochinvar about 1297, who were made Viscounts Kenmure in 1633. The castle was torched after the Gordons had entertained Mary, Queen of Scots, here in 1568, and burned again by Cromwell in 1650 after the family supported Charles I. The 6th Viscount was beheaded in the Tower of London for supporting the Jacobite Rising of 1715 after being captured at the Battle of Preston, and the family were forfeited. The property was recovered, and the castle restored from ruin in the 18th century. It was visited by Robert Burns. After a fire in the early 20th century it was stripped of materials in the 1950s, and is now a ruined shell.
Other refs: Castle Kenmure

Kennedy Castle *see* Castle Kennedy

Kennedy's Castle *see* Stranraer Castle

Kennoway Castle *see* MacDuff's Castle

Keppoch Castle

South Highland: About 3.5 miles east of Spean Bridge, on minor road south of A86 at Roy Bridge, between River Spean and River Roy, at Keppoch.
Ruin or site NN 270807 OS: 41 * Map: 9, no: 46
Site of castle near motte, which was altered and strengthened in the 16th century. It was a property of the MacDonnels or MacDonalds of Keppoch, but passed to the Mackintoshes in 1690. The lands were disputed with the Mackintoshes, and the last clan battle was fought here. The castle was demolished in 1663 after the Keppoch Murder.

Keppoch House

Argyll & Dunbartonshire: About 3 miles south-east of Helensburgh, on minor roads east of A814, at or near Keppoch House.
Private NS 330798 [?] OS: 63 * Map: 5, no: 136
Site of castle. Keppoch House, a three-storey mansion with a classical front, dates

from 1820 and may be built on the site.

The lands were a property of the Stirlings of Glorat in 1545, but passed to the Ewings in the 17th century. The house is still occupied.

Other refs: Lyleston

Kerelaw Castle

Ayrshire: About 2.5 miles west of Kilwinning, on minor roads north of A78, just outside Stevenston to the north-west.

Ruin or site NS 269428 OS: 63 ** Map: 3, no: 57

Kerelaw Castle is an altered massive ruined 13th- or 14th-century keep and courtyard, which is much overgrown. The basement was vaulted, and the building was remodelled in the 16th or 17th century.

Kerelaw was a property of the Lockharts in 1191. The castle was built by the Cunningham Earls of Glencairn, but apparently destroyed in a feud in 1488, then sacked by the Montgomerys of Eglinton in 1528. Eglinton Castle was burned in retaliation. The 9th Earl was active as a Covenanter, and led an unsuccessful rebellion against Cromwell's occupation in 1653. He was made Chancellor of Scotland after the Restoration from 1661 to 1664.

The ruined castle was remodelled around 1830 as a garden folly for Kerelaw or Grange House, an 18th-century mansion which has itself been demolished, and large Gothic windows were inserted.

Other refs: Grange House, Kerelaw

Kermuck Castle *see* Kinmuck Castle

Kerse Castle

Ayrshire: About 4 miles east of Dalrymple, on minor road and foot east of A713, north of B730, just east of Kerse Loch, north of Knockshinnoch.

Ruin or site NS 432144 [?] OS: 70 * Map: 3, no: 170

Site of castle.

Kerse Castle *see* Kersie

Kerse Castle *see* Carse Castle

Kersie

Stirlingshire & Clackmannan: About 5 miles east and south of Stirling, on minor roads north of the A905, on the south bank of the River Forth, at or near Kersie Mains.

Private NS 872912 OS: 58 ** Map: 6, no: 90

Kersie is a 17th-century L-plan tower house of three storeys and a garret, with a wide stair-tower in the re-entrant angle. The walls are harled, and the gables plain. At one corner are the remains of an earlier tower. There was an earlier castle on the site or nearby.

The original entrance is at the foot of the stair-tower. The house has been much altered inside, but two moulded fireplaces survive. In the basement are the remains of a wide-arched fireplace and a sealed gunloop.

Kersie was probably built by the Menteiths of West Kerse, but the property later passed to the Livingstones, then the Hopes. It was sold to the Dundas family in 1794, who were made Earls of Zetland in 1838, then in 1892 Earl of Ronaldsay. The house is in good condition, and used as a farmhouse.

Other refs: Kerse Castle; Carse Castle

Kersland

Ayrshire: About 1.5 miles north-east of Dalry, on minor roads north of A737, east of Garnock Water, at or near Kersland.

Ruin or site NS 306508 OS: 63 * Map: 3, no: 84

Site of castle, little of which remains except for part of the vaulted basement built into the present building.

The property was held by the Kerrs in 1604.

Other refs: East Kersland

Kidlaw

Lothians: About 3 miles south-west of Gifford, on minor roads south of B6368 or B6355, at or near Kidlaw.

Ruin or site NT 509642 OS: 66 * Map: 4, no: 183

Site of tower house, used as a stronghold and prison, the last remains of which were removed in 1827. It is said that James V had vagrants imprisoned in the tower.

Kier Know of Drum *see* Castlehill, Kippen

Kiers Castle *see* Keirs Castle

Kiessimul Castle *see* Kisimul Castle

Kilallan House

Renfrewshire: About 1.5 miles east of Kilmacolm, on minor roads east of A761 at Kilmacolm, about 0.5 miles south-east of Lawfield Dam, at Killallan.

Private NS 383689 OS: 63 ** Map: 3, no: 133

Kilallan House is a small strongly built house of the early 17th century, which rises to two storeys and a garret within corbiestepped gables. There is a projecting tower with a turnpike stair. The basement has not been vaulted. The house has been extended and was renovated in 1783, in 1927 and again in 1963.

Adjoining the house is the ruined church of St Fillan, a place of worship since the 8th century. Nearby is a large hollowed stone and a spring of water, called Fillan's Seat and Fillan's Well. The house was used for a time as the manse, and is in good condition and now a farmhouse.

In 1659 Reverend Alexander Jamieson was ordered to remain in the house by the Privy Council. It was believed that he had suffered from the malice of the Witches of Pollok.

Other refs: Killallan

Kilberry Castle

Argyll & Dunbartonshire: About 10 miles west of Tarbert, on minor road west of B8024 at Kilberry, east of the sea, in Knapdale, at Kilberry Castle.

Private NR 709642 OS: 62 * Map: 5, no: 35

Kilberry Castle, a mansion of 1844 which was enlarged in 1871, incorporates parts of a late 15th-century L-plan castle.

It was a property of the Campbells, who built the castle about 1497, and burned by an English pirate, Captain Proby, in 1513.

An important collection of early stone crosses and sculpted stones, which date from medieval times, is located here. The stones were collected from the estate.

OPEN: Sculpted stones: access at all reasonable times.

Tel: 0131 668 8800   Fax: 0131 668 8888

Email: hs.explore@scotland.gov.uk   Web: www.historic-scotland.gov.uk

Kilbirnie House

Ayrshire: About 0.75 miles west of Kilbirnie, on minor road south of A760, just south of Farm of Place.

Ruin or site NS 304541 OS: 63 ** Map: 3, no: 80

Kilbirnie House consists of a ruined 13th-, 14th- or 15th-century rectangular keep, which rose to four storeys, altered and extended with a plain three-storey wing and round stair-tower of 1627. The keep had two vaulted floors, and there were gardens, an avenue, and orchards. Not much remains of the wing.

The lands were originally held by the Barclays, but passed by marriage to the Crawfords in 1470, who may have built the castle. The property was sold to the Lindsay Earls of Crawford in 1661, then to the Boyle 4th Earl of Glasgow in 1833. The house was accidentally burned in 1757, not restored, and is very overgrown and ruined.

The name Kilbirnie is said to be taken from a cell or mission of St Brendan, Abbot of Clonfert, Columba's uncle, who was in Scotland about 563.

Other refs: Place of Kilbirnie; Old Place of Kilbirnie

Kilbride *see* Law Castle

Kilbryde Castle

Stirlingshire & Clackmannan: About 3 miles north-west of Dunblane, on minor roads north of the A820, on the west side of the Ardoch Burn, at Kilbryde.
Private NN 756036 OS: 57 * Map: 6, no: 62**
Kilbryde Castle consists of a 16th-century L-plan tower house of three storeys and an attic, which incorporates a 15th-century castle. The tower has square bartizans

crowning the corners of the main block. The stair-wing rises two storeys higher than the main block. The castle was remodelled and extended around 1877.

The entrance, in the foot stair-wing, leads to a turnpike stair and to a passageway to four basement chambers, including the kitchen.

Kilbryde was originally a property of the Graham Earls of Menteith. A castle was built here about 1460, and is incorporated into the existing building. The property was sold to the Campbells of Aberuchill in 1669, one of whom, Sir Colin, Lord Aberuchill of Session, was prominent in his activities against Rob Roy MacGregor, but still had to pay blackmail to be left alone by the MacGregors.

The house is still occupied by the Campbells, and the gardens, which have been restored and developed, are open to the public.

OPEN: Garden open to the public all year by appt only; castle not open.
Parking.
Tel: 01786 824505 Fax: 01786 825405

Kilbuaick Castle *see* Kilbulack Castle

Kilbucho Place

Borders: About 4 miles east and south of Biggar, on minor road west of A701 at Broughton, south of the Kilbucho Burn, at Kilbucho Place.
Private NT 095352 OS: 72 * Map: 2, no: 4
Kilbucho Place is a 17th-century L-plan house, which incorporates work from the 16th century. It has been much altered inside, and formerly rose to three storeys and a garret.

The lands belonged to the Grahams, but passed to Sir William Douglas, the Knight of Liddesdale, in the 14th century. The property was sold to the Stewart Earl of Traquair in 1631, but acquired by John Dickson, Lord Hartree, around 1650. After 1815 it passed to the William family. The house is still occupied, and in good condition.

Kilbulack Castle

Moray: About 4 miles east of Forres, just south of A96, about 1 mile north of Burgie Castle, near the distillery.
Ruin or site NJ 095605 OS: 27 * Map: 10, no: 15
Site of 15th-century castle, a property of the Dunbars. It was demolished at the beginning of the 19th century, and the materials used to build a farm.
Other refs: Kilbuaick Castle; Killbuyack Castle

Kilchrist Castle

Argyll & Dunbartonshire: About 2 miles south-west of Campbeltown on the Mull of Kintyre, on minor road east of B842, just south of Killeonan Burn, at Kilchrist Burn.
Private NR 692180 OS: 68 * Map: 5, no: 29
Kilchrist Castle is a modern mansion.

Kilchumin *see* Fort Augustus

Kilchurn Castle

Argyll & Dunbartonshire: About 2 miles west of Dalmally, on minor road and foot west of A85 west of junction with A819, on peninsula at northern tip of Loch Awe, at Kilchurn.
His Scot NN 133276 OS: 50 ** Map: 5, no: 114**
A picturesque and much photographed ruin, Kilchurn Castle is a courtyard castle of the 15th century. It consists of a rectangular keep of four storeys and a garret, which was extended with ranges of buildings in the 16th and 17th centuries.

The basement of the keep is vaulted, and contained the kitchen. The hall, on the

first floor, only had a small fireplace. The floors above are gone.

The courtyard has round towers at the corners, which are pierced by shot-holes. The other ranges are late 17th-century barrack-blocks, and there are two large kitchen fireplaces.

The lands originally belonged to the MacGregors, but were acquired by the Campbells of Glenorchy, who built the castle. The castle was strengthened and improved by Black Duncan of the Seven Castles, Sir Duncan Campbell, at the end of the 16th century after damage inflicted by the MacGregors. The Campbells withstood a two-day siege in 1654 by General Middleton before he retreated from Monck's Cromwellian forces.

Sir John Campbell of Glenorchy acquired the extensive lands of the 6th Earl of Caithness by foreclosing on his vast debts, and even claimed the title of Earl. He led a bloody campaign in the north in 1680, and reportedly slew so many Sinclairs that the Campbells crossed the Wick River without getting their feet wet. This was when the song 'The Campbells are Coming' was composed. Although he failed to hold the Earldom of Caithness, he was made Earl of Breadalbane instead.

The castle was inhabited by the Campbells until 1740 when they moved to Balloch, which is now called Taymouth. Kilchurn was garrisoned by Hanoverian troops in 1745 but unroofed by 1775. The castle was recently consolidated and repaired.

There are regular sailings from Loch Awe pier to Kilchurn by steamer – phone ferry company 01838 200400/200449.

OPEN: Open Apr-Sep, daily 9.30-18.30 – tel to check.
Parking nearby.
Tel: 0131 668 8800 Fax: 0131 668 8888
Email: hs.explore@scotland.gov.uk Web: www.historic-scotland.gov.uk

Kilconquhar Castle

Fife: About 2 miles north of Elie, on minor roads east of B941, north of village of Kilconquhar.

Private   NO 494027   OS: 59   **   Map: 7, no: 128

The large mansion of Kilconquhar Castle incorporates a much-altered 16th-century tower house of five storeys, with bartizans at the corners. All windows, except those of the turrets, have been enlarged as part of the encircling mansion, which was designed by William Burn in 1831, and remodelled by David Bryce around 1839.

The property belonged to the Earls of Dunbar and March, but was sold to the Bellenden family in 1528. The house was probably built by Sir John Bellenden, Lord Justice Clerk, who worked with the notorious Master of Gray in destroying the Chancellor, the Earl of Arran. It was sold to Sir John Carstairs in 1640. After fire damage and much alteration, it is now part of a holiday time-share development.

Kilcoy Castle

Ross & Cromarty: About 3 miles east of Muir of Ord on the Black Isle, on minor roads north of A832 or south of A835, 2 miles east and south of Tore, at Kilcoy Castle.

Private   NH 576512   OS: 26   **   Map: 9, no: 72**

Kilcoy Castle is a 17th-century Z-plan tower house. It consists of a main block of four storeys and two round towers, at opposite corners, which rise a storey higher. One tower is corbelled out to square and topped by a gabled watch-chamber. Round bartizans crown two corners of the main block, and there are two stair-turrets, corbelled-out above first floor level, in the re-entrant angles. The walls are pierced by gunloops and shot-holes, and there is much heraldic decoration. The main roofs are slated, but those over the stair-turrets are stone-slabbed.

The original entrance was in the re-entrant angle, with one of the towers, although the present doorway is in the centre of the main block. The basement is vaulted, and contains four chambers, including the kitchen and a wine-cellar, with a small stair to the hall above. The hall, on the first floor, has an adjoining private room. The lintel of the hall fireplace is carved with three Mackenzie shields, dated 1679, and is decorated with mermaids playing harps and other motifs. The floors above, reached by the turret stairs, contained many private chambers in the main block and towers.

Kilcoy was acquired in 1618 by Alexander Mackenzie, son of the 11th baron of Kintail, chief of the clan, who built the castle. The castle was abandoned and became ruinous. It was restored around 1891, with the addition of a substantial rear wing, and then again in 1968. It is still occupied.

Kildonan *see* Kildonnan

Kildonan

Ayrshire: About 0.5 miles north-west of Barrhill, on minor roads north of A714, on east side of Duisk River, at or near Kildonan.

Ruin or site   NX 227831   OS: 76   *   Map: 3, no: 44

Site of castle.

Kildonan, a large mansion built between 1914-23 and for the Wallaces by James Miller, stands on the site of an earlier house.

Kildonan Castle

Ayrshire: About 10 miles south of Brodick on south-east of Isle of Arran, on minor roads south of A841, north of Sound of Pladda, at Kildonan.

Ruin or site   NS 037210   OS: 69   **   Map: 3, no: 5

Not much remains of an overgrown rectangular 13th-century keep. It had a vaulted basement and hall, and may have been built in the site of an older stronghold.

It was a property of the MacDonald Lord of the Isles, but in 1406 the castle was granted to John Stewart of Ardgowan, then in 1544 passed to the Hamiltons. The ruin may be in a dangerous condition (and beware of naturists!).

Kildonan Dun

Argyll & Dunbartonshire: About 5 miles north-east of Campbeltown, just east of B842, Kildonan, Kintyre.

Ruin or site   NR 780277   OS: 68   *   Map: 5, no: 49**

Excavations at this drystane-walled D-plan dun indicate that it was built in the 1st or 2nd century AD, then reoccupied in the 9th to 12th centuries. The wall is seven feet thick, and the door check and bar holes can still be seen. Also visible are the double stairway to the wallhead and a mural cell.

Kildonnan

Galloway: About 5 miles south of Stranraer, on minor roads west of B7042, Rhinns of Galloway, at or near Kildonan.

Ruin or site   NX 059518   OS: 82   *   Map: 1, no: 9

Site of castle.

Other refs: Kildonan

Kildrummy Castle

Aberdeen & Gordon: About 1 mile south-west of hamlet of Kildrummy, on minor roads west of A97, just south of Mains of Kildrummy, at Kildrummy Castle.

His Scot   NJ 454164   OS: 37   *   Map: 10, no: 98**

Although now ruinous, Kildrummy Castle, built in the 13th century, was one of the largest and most powerful early castles in Scotland, and remains a fine ruin in a picturesque setting. The high curtain walls enclosed a courtyard with six round towers at the corners and gate. One of these, the largest, called 'The Snow Tower', may have been the main keep, and is similar to that at Coucy.

The gatehouse is much reduced, but was formerly defended by two towers, and resembles Edward I's Welsh castle of Harlech. Nearby was the two-storey hall block, the walls of which are the best preserved part of the castle. There was also a chapel, three tall lancet windows of which remain. The towers at either end of this wall survive in part.

The original castle was built by Gilbert de Moray, Bishop of Caithness, in the 13th century, although there was an earlier stronghold on a motte in Kildrummy burial ground [NJ 473177].

Kildrummy Castle was captured by Edward I of England in 1296, then again in 1306 from a garrison led by Nigel Bruce, younger brother of Robert the Bruce, after the castle was set alight by a traitor. Nigel Bruce, and the rest of the garrison, were executed by hanging. The traitor was rewarded with much gold – poured molten down his throat.

The castle was restored before 1333, and besieged by the Earl of Atholl acting for the English in 1335. It was successfully defended by Bruce's sister, Christian. Her husband, Sir Andrew Moray, the Regent, relieved the castle and killed the Earl of Atholl at or after the Battle of Culbean. David II besieged it in 1363, and seized it from the Earl of Mar.

It was in royal hands from 1361-8 until Alexander Stewart, son of the Wolf of Badenoch, acquired it after he had forced Isabella Douglas, Countess of Mar, to marry him in 1404. He may have had the poor women's husband, Sir Malcolm Drummond, kidnapped from Kindrochit Castle. Stewart led the king's forces at the Battle of Harlaw in 1411. After 1435 it was held by the Crown, but it was stormed by the Erskines to no avail in 1442. It later passed to the Cochranes, then the Elphinstones from 1507-1626, until they were compelled to give it the Erskine Earls of Mar. It was also sacked and torched in 1530 by the freebooter John Strachan of Lynturk; and captured in 1654 by Cromwell's forces.

The castle was badly damaged in 1690, when it was burned by Jacobites, but complete enough for the Earl of Mar to use it as his base when he led the Jacobite Rising in 1715. In 1731 it passed to the Gordons of Wardhouse.

After the collapse of the Jacobite cause Kildrummy was deliberately dismantled and used as a quarry. This was halted at the beginning of the 19th century, but the ruins were not consolidated until 1898. In 1951 it was put into the care of the State.

A secret passage was found at the castle last century.

OPEN: Open Apr-Sep, daily 9.30-18.30; last admission 18.00.
Gift shop. WC. Disabled WC. Parking. £
Tel: 01975 571331 Fax: 0131 668 8888
Email: hs.explore@scotland.gov.uk Web: www.historic-scotland.gov.uk

Kilduff House

Lothians: About 2 miles north of Haddington, on minor road north of B1343, south of Kilduff Hill, at or near Kilduff House.
Ruin or site NT 516774 [?] OS: 66 * Map: 4, no: 189
Possible site of castle or old house.

Kilduskland *see* Glendarroch

Kilgarie

Angus & Dundee: About 4.5 miles north of Brechin, on minor roads 4.5 miles north of A94, at Kilgarie.
Ruin or site NO 565660 [?] OS: 44 * Map: 8, no: 237
Site of castle of the Spaldings.
Other refs: Castle of Ballzordie; Lundie Castle

Kilhenzie Castle

Ayrshire: About 1 mile south and east of Maybole, on minor roads south of the A77, just east of the main railway line to Girvan and the south.
Private NS 308082 OS: 70 ** Map: 3, no: 85
Kilhenzie Castle is a much-altered and extended 16th-century tower house of two storeys and a garret. Corbelled-out bartizans, with conical roofs, crown each corner. A 17th-century wing of three storeys made the castle into an L-plan. A round stair-tower, in the re-entrant angle, contains a wide turnpike stair. The house was a ruin until the 19th century, but restored and incorporated into a castellated mansion.

The tower has been much altered inside.

Kilhenzie was held by the Baird family, but passed to the Kennedys in the 17th century.

Kilhilt

Galloway: About 2.5 miles south of Stranraer, near A77, just south of Lochans, at Kilhilt.
Ruin or site NX 062564 OS: 82 * Map: 1, no: 11
Site of a house or castle of the Adairs of Kilhilt, who built Dunskey Castle about 1510. The last remains were apparently removed about 1933.

Kilkerran *see* Barclanachan

Kilkerran Castle

Ayrshire: About 7 miles east and north of Girvan, on minor roads south of B741, about 1.5 miles east and south of Dailly, just north of Dobbingstone Burn.
Ruin or site NS 293005 OS: 76 * Map: 3, no: 69
Very little remains of a strong 15th-century keep of four storeys and a garret, a property of the Fergusons. The basement was vaulted.

Two miles to the north and east is 'Kilkerran' [NS 305030], to where the Ferguson Lord Kilkerran removed about 1730, and which incorporates the old tower of Barclanachan.
Other refs: Barclanachan; Kinlockkerran

Kilkerran Castle

Argyll & Dunbartonshire: South-east of Campbeltown on Kintyre, on minor roads east of A83 in Campbeltown, on the south shore of Campbeltown Loch, at Kilkerran.
Ruin or site NR 729194 OS: 68 * Map: 5, no: 39
Not much remains of a 15th-century keep and castle of the MacDonald Lord of the Isles, although this may have been called Moil Castle [NR 725209]. It may have been rebuilt by James IV towards the end of the 15th century as a base against the Lord of the Isles. It was also used during James V's campaign in 1536, although he found it difficult to subdue the locals. James granted the property to the Campbell Earls of Argyll, who brought the area under their sway after much bloodshed and it was settled by Lowlanders. The castle may have been abandoned around the middle of the 17th century, although another castle is recorded at Lochhead [NR 718202], built by the Campbells in 1609.

Kilkerran – the church of Ciaran, a 6th-century Celtic saint – was the old name of Campbeltown, before the Campbells changed it.
Other refs: Campbeltown; Kinlochkerran

Killallan *see* Kilallan House

Killaser Castle

Galloway: About 9 miles south of Stranraer, on minor roads west of A716 at Ardwell, just south of the Killaser Burn, between Cairnhandy and Barnhill Farm.
Ruin or site NX 096451 OS: 82 * Map: 1, no: 17
Very little remains of a 15th-century rectangular keep or tower except some remains of the vaulted basement. The castle was defended by a ditch.

It was a property of the MacCullochs of Ardwell.
Other refs: Killessar Castle

Killbuyack Castle *see* Kilbulack Castle

Killernie Castle

Fife: About 7 miles west of Cowdenbeath, on minor road north of B914, about 0.5 miles east and north of Saline, south-west of Saline Hill.
Ruin or site NT 032924 OS: 58 * Map: 7, no: 8
Not much survives of a 16th-century Z-plan tower house. There are remains of the two round corner towers, one of which housed a stair.

The property was held by James Colville of East Wemyss in 1542, but he was forfeited, and Killernie passed to the Duries. It was also a property of the Scotts of Balwearie.

Killessar Castle *see* Killaser Castle

Killiesmont

Moray: About 1.5 miles north-west of Keith, on minor roads north of B9017, at Killiesmont.
Ruin or site NJ 415525 [?] OS: 28 * Map: 10, no: 81
Site of castle, although the location is very approximate.

Killiewarren

Dumfriesshire: About 5 miles west of Thornhill, on minor roads west of A702, 1 mile north-west of Tynron, north of Shinnel Water, at Killiewarren.
Private NX 796935 OS: 78 * Map: 1, no: 132**
Killiewarren is a 17th-century tower house, rectangular in plan and rising to three storeys. It dates from 1617, but has been much altered, inside and out. There is no vaulting or turnpike stair, and the windows have been enlarged. The walls are whitewashed.

It was a property of the Douglases, and is now used as a farmhouse.
Other refs: Killywarren

Killincraig *see* Brisbane House

Killochan Castle

Ayrshire: About 3 miles north-east of Girvan, on minor roads south of B741 near Burnhead, just north of the Water of Girvan, just south of Burnhead.
Private NS 227004 OS: 76 **** Map: 3, no: 45
One of the best preserved and impressive castles in Ayrshire, Killochan Castle is a tall 16th-century L-plan tower house, which replaced an earlier castle on the site. The tower consists of a main block of five storeys and a higher wing. A square stair-tower stands in the re-entrant angle. A conical-roofed round tower, at one corner,

has a corbelled-out parapet. Two bartizans crown the top of the tower. The entrance is defended by a machiolated projection at parapet level. The walls are pierced by shot-holes. The tower is dated 1586.

The entrance leads to a wide scale-and-platt stair, which climbs to the first floor, while the floors above were reached by a turnpike stair in the re-entrant angle. The basement is vaulted, and contained the original kitchen and two cellars. The hall is on the first floor, and has an adjoining private chamber.

There is an 18th-century wing of two storeys.

The property belonged to the Cathcarts from the 14th century. One of the family, Robert Cathcart of Killochan, was killed at the Battle of Flodden in 1513. In the feud between the Cassillis and Bargany Kennedys, the Cathcarts supported their neighbours of Bargany, and John Cathcart, builder of the castle, commanded the rearguard at a battle at Pennyglen, during which Bargany was mortally wounded. The Cathcarts occupied Killochan, although not continuously, until 1954.

Killumpha Tower

Galloway: About 13 miles south of Stranraer, on minor road west of B7065 and east of A716, at Killumpha.
Private NX 113407 OS: 82 ** Map: 1, no: 26
Killumpha is a tower house of two storeys with bartizans, which has been altered and extended. It is still occupied.

Killundine Castle *see* Caisteal nan Con

Killywarren *see* Killiewarren

Kilmacolm Castle

Renfrewshire: South side of Kilmacolm, near A761, to the south of the old part of the town, east of the River Gryffe.
Ruin or site NS 361693 [?] OS: 63 * Map: 3, no: 119
Site of castle, which may have been held by the Porterfields. There is a family tomb, dated 1560, in the burial ground of the Old Kirk.

Kilmahew Castle

Argyll & Dunbartonshire: About 1 mile north of Cardross, on minor roads north of the A814, 0.5 miles east of Kirkton, north-west of Kilmahew House.
Private NS 352787 OS: 63 ** Map: 5, no: 143
Kilmahew Castle consists of a ruined 15th-century keep of five storeys and formerly a garret. It had a corbelled-out parapet, and there has been a machiolated projection above the entrance. The castle was remodelled as a Gothic mansion, but was never completed.

The basement does not appear to have been vaulted, but it contained the kitchen. The hall was on the first floor.

Kilmahew was a property of the Napier family from the late 13th century until 1820. The property was sold to James Burns in 1859, who built a new mansion nearby.

Kilmaluag Castle *see* Raasay House

Kilmarnock Castle *see* Dean Castle

Kilmaron Castle

Fife: About 1 mile north-west of Cupar, on minor roads east of A913, at Kilmaron Castle.
Ruin or site NO 357162 OS: 59 * Map: 7, no: 95
Kilmaron Castle, a mansion built to the designs of James Gillespie Graham about 1820, was demolished in the 20th century, and only a stable block remains. It had no older origins.

It was built for the Baxters of Kilmaron.

Kilmaronock Castle

Argyll & Dunbartonshire: About 1 mile south west of Drymen, on minor road north of A811, just south of the Endrick Water, at Kilmaronock.
Ruin or site NS 456877 OS: 57 ** Map: 5, no: 163
Kilmaronock Castle consists of a ruined 15th-century keep, formerly of four storeys, with thick walls.

Part of the vaulted basement and the vaulted second-floor hall survive. A stair in one corner led down from the hall to the basement, while that in another corner rose to the private chambers on the upper floors.

The lands were a property of the Earls of Lennox, but given to the Flemings in 1329, then passed by marriage to the Dennistouns later that century. The property was held by the Cunningham Earl of Glencairn from the end of the 14th century, then by the Cochrane Earls of Dundonald, then passed to a John McGoune in the 18th century.

Kilmaronock House, built in 1901, stands nearby.
Other refs: Mains of Kilmaronock Castle

Kilmartin Castle

Argyll & Dunbartonshire: At Kilmartin, just east of A816 to the north of the village, just east of the Kilmartin Burn, about 1 mile south of Carnasserie Castle.
Private NR 836991 OS: 55 *** Map: 5, no: 63
Kilmartin Castle is a small formerly ruined 16th-century Z-plan tower house. It consists of a main block of three storeys, with projecting round towers at opposite corners. A small stair-tower stands against one side of the main block. The walls are pierced by shot-holes, and the windows still have iron yetts.

The entrance leads to the vaulted basement, which contains three chambers, one the kitchen, linked by a passage. A turnpike stair climbs to all floors in one of the round towers. The hall, with a large fireplace, was on the first floor of the main

block, and had an adjoining private chamber. There were more private rooms above the hall.

The castle was the residence of John Carswell, who moved to Carnasserie Castle when made Protestant Bishop of the Isles. It later became a property of the Campbells, and has recently been restored.

Kilmaurs Place

Ayrshire: About 2.5 miles north of Kilmarnock, on minor road east of the A735, south of the B751, just south of the Irvine Water, just east of Kilmaurs.
Private NS 412411 OS: 70 ** Map: 3, no: 155
Kilmaurs Place is a T-plan house, dating from 1620, which has been much altered with the insertion of larger windows. The gables are corbiestepped, and the walls harled and whitewashed. A ruined adjacent building has a vaulted basement, and was fortified.

Kilmaurs was a property of the Cunninghams from the 13th century, after they had helped Alexander III win the Battle of Largs in 1263. In 1413 William Cunningham, Lord Kilmaurs, endowed a collegiate church at Kilmaurs. The family were made Earls of Glencairn in 1488.

There appears to have been an earlier castle of the Cunninghams at Jocksthorn [NS 420408], although little now remains, and it was ruinous by 1608.
Other refs: Jocksthorn

Kilmory Castle

Argyll & Dunbartonshire: On island of Bute, about 4 miles south-west of Rothesay, on minor road just east of A844 at Meikle Kilmory, 0.5 miles east of St Ninian's Bay, at Kilmory.
Ruin or site NS 051611 OS: 63 ** Map: 5, no: 101
Not much remains of a tower house or castle, except one small turret, with two shot-holes, and the wall of a rectangular building.

It was a property of the Jamiesons of Kilmory, hereditary coroners of Bute, from the 15th century, but the property passed to the Stewarts in 1780.
Other refs: Meikle Kilmory

Kilmory Castle

Argyll & Dunbartonshire: About 1 mile south of Lochgilphead, on minor road east of A83, at Kilmory Castle.
Private NR 870868 OS: 55 * Map: 5, no: 73**
Kilmory Castle is said to date from the 14th century, but has been much enlarged and modified down the centuries. It was a property of the Campbells from 1828, but is now local council buildings.

The garden, which was first planted in the 1770s, has over 100 species of rhododendron and has been fully restored. There are woodland walks, nature trails, herbaceous borders, as well as a sensory trail.
OPEN: Garden: open all year, daylight hours; closed Christmas and New Year; castle not open.
Disabled access. Car parking.
Tel: 01546 604360 Fax: 01546 604208

Kilmun Church

Argyll & Dunbartonshire: About 6 miles north of Dunoon, just east of A880, north-east shore of Holy Loch, Kilmun.
Private NS 166821 OS: 56 * Map: 5, no: 119**
The church, which stands on the site of a 7th-century Celtic monastery, mostly dates from 1841 and 1899, but the 15th-century tower of the collegiate church survives. The collegiate church was founded in 1441 by Sir Duncan Campbell, and the building is still used as the parish church. The site is dedicated to St Munn, who was a follower of St Columba.

The tower of the church may have been used as a residence by the Campbells, and this is also the location of the mausoleum of the Campbell Dukes of Argyll. There are 18th-century markers in the burial ground.
OPEN: Open May, Jun and Sep, Tue-Thu 13.30-16.30; Jul-Aug, Mon-Fri 13.30-16.30; other times by arrangement.
Guided tours. Gift shop. Tearoom. WC. Disabled access. Car and coach parking. Donations welcome.
Tel: 01369 840342

Kilnmaichlie House

Moray: About 8 miles north of Tomintoul, on minor road 4 miles south of A95 at Lagmore 0.5 miles west of B9008, west of River Avon, at Kilnmaichlie.
Private NJ 181321 OS: 36 ** Map: 10, no: 29
Kilnmaichlie House is a 16th-century T-plan house. It consists of a main block of three storeys and a centrally projecting square stair-tower which rises a storey higher to be crowned by a watch-chamber. The walls are yellow-washed and were pierced by shot-holes.

The entrance would have originally been in the foot of the stair-tower but has been moved. There is a pit prison.

The lands were held by Alexander Stewart, the Wolf of Badenoch, then later were a property of the Stewarts of Kilnmaichlie and Drumin. The family were Jacobites, and after the failure of the Jacobite Rising of 1745-6, the Grants acquired the property. The house is still occupied as a farmhouse.

Kilnsike Peel

Borders: About 4.5 miles south of Jedburgh, on minor road between A7 and Chesters on A6088, about 0.5 miles east and north of Westerhouses.
Ruin or site NT 634130 OS: 80 ** Map: 2, no: 250
Not much survives of a 16th-century tower or bastle house, except the basement.

Kilpeter *see* Houston House

Kilpurnie Castle *see* Kinpurnie Castle

Kilravock Castle

Inverness & Nairn: About 6 miles south-west of Nairn, on minor roads south of B9091, just north of River Nairn, 1 mile east of Croy, at Kilravock.
Private NH 814493 OS: 27 ** Map: 9, no: 126**
Pronounced, 'Kilrock', Kilravock Castle is a plain massive 15th-century keep of five storeys and a garret to which has been added a long tall 17th-century block, making the building L-plan. The keep has rounds at the corners, and a square caphouse. The windows throughout are small. In the 17th century the keep was extended by a square stair-wing, against one corner, a five-storey block with a steep gabled roof and stair-turret, and a square tower. The walls are pierced by gunloops and shot-holes. Later and lower work has also been added.

The original entrance to the keep was at the foot of the stair, but is now enclosed in a square wing. The basement is vaulted, as is the basement of the later block, and contains three cellars.

The castle passed by marriage from the Bissets to the Roses of Kilravock in the 13th century, and they built the castle. Mary, Queen of Scots, visited the castle in 1562, and Hugh, the 17th laird, entertained Bonnie Prince Charlie the day before the Battle of Culloden in 1746. The next day the Duke of Cumberland called on his

way to the battlefield. Robert Burns visited in 1787.

The castle is now a guest house and sports centre, and there is also a youth hostel.
OPEN: Open days May-Oct, Wed; guided tours at 11.00, 14.00, 15.00 and 16.00; groups other days by appt only; dinner, bed and breakfast available Apr-Sep; open for conferences all year.
Guided tours. Gift shop. Tearoom. WC. Car and coach parking. £
Tel: 01667 493258 Fax: 01667 493258
Email: castles@kilravock-rose.freeserve.com Web: www.kilravock.com

Kilspindie Castle
Borders: About 4 miles south of Cockburnspath, on minor roads west of A6112, 1 mile south-west of Granthouse, north of Eye Water, at Butterdean.
Ruin or site NT 797648 [?] OS: 67 * Map: 2, no: 323
Site of castle, little of which remains, that formerly had a moat and is said to have been associated with a monastic order.

Kilspindie Castle
Lothians: Just north-west of Aberlady, on minor road west from A198 north of junction with A6137, near shore of Aberlady Bay, south of Kilspindie.
Ruin or site NT 462801 OS: 66 * Map: 4, no: 174
Virtually nothing remains of a 16th-century tower house of the Douglases, which passed to the Hays in 1621.

Kilspindie Castle
Perth & Kinross: About 7 miles east of Perth, on minor roads north of A90, at or near Kilspindie.
Ruin or site NO 219258 OS: 58 * Map: 8, no: 123
Site of Kilspindie Castle, an altered 14th-century keep, which was demolished in 1840. The basement was vaulted, and contained three cellars and the kitchen. The hall and two other chambers were on the first floor.

William Wallace and his mother are supposed to have taken refuge here according to a poem by Blind Harry. Much later the castle was a property of the Lindsays.

Kilsyth Castle
Lanarkshire & Glasgow area: In Kilsyth, south of A803, near B8084, north of River Kelvin.
Ruin or site NS 717786 [?] OS: 64 * Map: 3, no: 332
Site of a 15th-century castle which consisted of a tower house and a courtyard with later ranges of buildings.

It was a property of the Livingstone family, who were Royalists. The castle was garrisoned and strengthened against Cromwell in 1650, but quickly captured and the tower was blown up while the rest of the buildings were burned. The Livingstones were made Viscounts Kilsyth in 1661 following the Restoration, but were forfeited after the Jacobite Rising of 1715.
Other refs: Allanfauld Castle

Kilwhimin *see* Fort Augustus

Kinacoul Castle *see* Dee Castle

Kinaldy Castle
Fife: About 3.5 miles south of St Andrews, on minor roads east of A915 or west of B9131, just north of Kinaldy Burn, at Kinaldy.
Ruin or site NO 513104 OS: 59 * Map: 7, no: 131
Site of castle.

The Ayton family held the property from 1539 to the 18th century. Thomas the Rhymer prophesied that none of woman born would succeed to the lands of Kinaldy, save of Ayton blood. The property later passed to the Monypennys, although presumably they were born of woman.

Kinbeachie Castle
Ross & Cromarty: About 5.5 miles north-east of Dingwall, on minor roads and foot south of B9163, south of Kinbeachie.
Ruin or site NH 634622 OS: 21 * Map: 9, no: 87
Nothing remains of a 16th-century castle, a property of the Urquharts. The building was dated 1546 and 1612, and the last remains were removed in 1959.

A modern mansion was built nearby.

Kinblethmont
Angus & Dundee: About 4 miles north of Arbroath, on minor roads south of B965, about 2.5 miles south-west of Inverkeillor, at Kinblethmont.
Ruin or site NO 638470 OS: 54 * Map: 8, no: 258
Not much remains of a 17th-century castle, near the more modern mansion, which was burned out in 1887.

In the late 15th century the lands were a property of the Lindsay Earls of Crawford, but passed to the Carnegies, who built the castle.

Kinbrace
Sutherland & Caithness: About 2.5 miles south of Kinbrace, on minor road just east of A897, east of River Helmsdale, at or near Kinbrace Farm.
Ruin or site NC 874285 [?] OS: 17 * Map: 12, no: 32
Site of castle or stronghold, the location of which is not certain. It was here that around 1140 Lady Frakark was burned to death by Svein Aliefson as told in the sagas. Svein is said to have had a stronghold at Bucholly.
Other refs: Cairn Shuin

Kincaid House
Lanarkshire & Glasgow: To south of Milton of Campsie, on minor roads west of B757, at Kincaid House Hotel.
Private NS 650760 OS: 64 * Map: 3, no: 304
Site of castle, which may have been at NS 632753.

The lands of Kincaid passed to the Galbraiths, but they sold them to the Kincaid family in 1280. They built a castle, possibly at the site above, but by 1690 had moved to this new site, where they had a house. This house was extended in 1712, then in 1812, and is now used as a hotel.
OPEN: Hotel.
Tel: 0141 776 2226 Fax: 0141 775 0031
Web: btinternet.com/kincaidhouse

Kincardine Castle
Stirling & Clackmannanshire: About 2 miles south of Doune, near junction of A84 with A873, 1 mile south of Blair Drummond, at Kincardine.
Ruin or site NS 721986 OS: 57 * Map: 6, no: 58
Site of castle which was defended by a ditch.

It was a property of the Muschetts of Kincardine, but passed to the Drummonds at the beginning of the 14th century. It was in ruins by 1714, and little now remains.

Kincardine Castle

Perth & Kinross: About 0.75 miles south-east of Auchterarder, on minor roads south of A824 or A9, just north of the Ruthven Water, at Kincardine Castle.
Ruin or site   NN 948115   OS: 58   *   Map: 8, no: 40
Little remains of a 14th-century castle, which consisted of a keep and rectangular courtyard.
  It was a property of the Grahams of Montrose from about 1250, who were made Earls of Kincardine in 1644. The castle was demolished by the Campbell Earl of Argyll in 1646 after the Graham Marquis of Montrose had led a brilliant campaign against the Covenanters, although he was finally defeated at Philiphaugh. The castle was abandoned, and a new mansion built nearby in the 19th century.

Kincardine Castle

Kincardine & Deeside: About 1.5 miles north-east of Fettercairn, on minor roads north of B966, west of the Devilly Burn, in the Howe of the Mearns, at Kincardine.
Ruin or site   NO 671751   OS: 45   *   Map: 10, no: 190
Not much remains of a square 12th-century castle of enclosure with a twin-towered gateway, a hall and other buildings on three sides of the courtyard. The castle stood within a marsh, and the entrance was defended by a ditch and drawbridge.
  Kincardine was a royal castle, and William the Lyon and Alexander II both stayed here. John Balliol may have been forced to abdicate here by Edward I of England, during the Wars of Independence, and the English king visited in 1296. Robert II also stayed here in 1383. The Woods were hereditary keepers of the castle in the 15th and 16th centuries. Mary, Queen of Scots, stayed here in 1562 during her campaign against the Gordons. The castle was finally demolished in 1646.
  There was a royal burgh of Kincardine, near the castle, but by the 17th century it was in decline and little now remains, except the ruin of the castle and a burial ground. The lands were incorporated into the Fasque estate in 1845.
Other refs: Phesdo

Kincardine Castle

Sutherland & Caithness: About 2 miles south of Bonar Bridge, near A9, on south side Dornoch Firth, at or near Kincardine.
Ruin or site   NH 607895   OS: 21   *   Map: 12, no: 14
Site of castle.
  A spring, below the high water level, is known as Lady's Well, and a Pictish carved stone was located nearby [NH 605894].

Kincausie *see* Kingcausie

Kinclaven Castle

Perth & Kinross: About 5 miles south of Blairgowrie, on minor roads and foot south of A93 at Bridge of Isla, just west of River Tay, 0.5 miles east of Kinclaven Farm.
Ruin or site   NO 158377   OS: 53   *   Map: 8, no: 104
Kinclaven Castle is a very ruined rectangular castle of enclosure, possibly dating from the 11th century, with the remains of a keep. Ditches protected the castle on the landward side, and it was a place of great strength.
  A castle here was built by Alexander II around 1230-40 on the site of an older stronghold, said to have been visited by Malcolm Canmore in the 11th century. Edward I stayed here in 1296, and it was held by the English until 1297, when it was captured and slighted by William Wallace in 1299. It was again taken by forces under Edward III in 1335, but destroyed again in 1336. The castle remained a royal castle, and would appear to still have been in use as late as 1455.

Kincraig Castle

Fife: About 1 mile west and north of Earlsferry, on minor roads west or south of A917, on hill above Shell Bay, at Kincraig.
Ruin or site   NO 466003   OS: 59   *   Map: 7, no: 125
Site of castle of the Gourlays of Kincraig, who had held the property from the 13th century.

Kindrochit Castle

Kincardine & Deeside: To south of Braemar, on minor road just west of A93 in Braemar, by a ravine of the Clunie, at Kindrochit.
Ruin or site   NO 152913   OS: 43   **   Map: 10, no: 21
Not much remains of a strong royal castle, with square corner towers, and a later 14th-century keep, built about 1390. It was used by Robert II.
  In 1390 it was granted to Sir Malcolm Drummond. While supervising work on it, he was kidnapped and died in captivity about 1402, possibly at the hands of Alexander Stewart, son of the Wolf of Badenoch. Isabella, Countess of Mar and Drummond's widow, was forced to marry Stewart at Kildrummy Castle in 1404. Stewart then acquired both the Earldom of Mar and the Lordship of Garioch from her.
  The castle was ruined by 1618, and excavated in the 1920s.
  It was reputedly destroyed when plague broke out among those in the castle, and the folk of Braemar blockaded them inside. Cannons were used to destroy the castle, and trap anyone remaining alive inside. In 1746 a Hanoverian soldier was lowered into one of the vaults in search of treasure, but fled when he found a ghostly company seated around a table, piled with skulls. During excavations nothing of this was found, but the Kindrochit Brooch was unearthed, and the walls were traced.
OPEN: Access at all reasonable times.
Parking.

Kinedder *see* Castle of King Edward

Kinellan *see* Loch Kinellan

Kinellar House

Aberdeen & Gordon: About 3 miles south-east of Kintore, on minor roads north of A96, 1 mile west of Blackburn, at or near Kinellar House.
Private   NJ 815129 [?]   OS: 38   *   Map: 10, no: 272
Site of castle or old house. The present mansion is a U-plan building and dates from the 18th century with later additions and alterations.
Other refs: Glasgoego

Kinfauns Castle

Perth & Kinross: About 2.5 miles east of Perth, on minor road north of A85, about 0.25 miles north of River Tay, at Kinfauns Castle.
Ruin or site   NO 151226   OS: 58   *   Map: 8, no: 100
Site of castle, nothing of which remains, on which a Gothic mansion of 1825, which was designed by Sir Robert Smirke, was built with a tall central tower. The building is set in landscaped gardens.
  The castle was a property of the Charteris family, who were descended from Thomas de Longueville, 'The Red Rover'. He was a French knight, who turned to piracy after murdering a nobleman in the presence of Philip IV of France, and known as the Red Rover from the colour of his sails. Around 1301 William Wallace captured him and managed to get Philip of France to pardon him. De Longueville then joined

Wallace and after Wallace's death followed Robert the Bruce. In reward for his services at the capture of Perth from the English in 1313, he received a grant of lands and married the heiress of Charteris of Kinfauns, whose name he assumed. His two-handed sword was preserved at Kinfauns Castle.

The family feuded with the Ruthvens of Perth and in 1552 John Charteris was murdered by the Ruthvens in Edinburgh's High Street. The property later passed to the Carnegies, the Blairs, then to the 12th Lord Gray in 1741, and the Stewart Earls of Moray in 1895. The house is now a hotel.

OPEN: Hotel – open all year.
16 rooms with ensuite facilities. Restaurant. Conferences and functions. Parking.
Tel: 01738 620777   Fax: 01738 620778

King Edward Castle *see* Castle of King Edward

King Fergus's Hunting Lodge *see* Loch Laggan Castle

Kingancleugh Tower *see* Kingencleugh Castle

Kingask
Fife: About 2.5 miles south-east of St Andrews, on minor road just north of A917, at or near Kingask.
Ruin or site   NO 541145 [?]   OS: 59   *   Map: 7, no: 141
Site of castle.

It was a property of a David Grundistoun in 1552, but had passed to the Lindsay Earl of Crawford by 1669.

Kingcausie
Kincardine & Deeside: About 1.5 miles south-east of Peterculter, on minor road south of B9077 just east of junction with B979, south of the Dee, at Kingcausie.
Private   NJ 863001   OS: 38   **   Map: 10, no: 295
Site of castle, dating from the 16th century. Pronounced 'Kincowsie', the present Kingcausie, a baronial castellated mansion, incorporates a 17th-century house near the site of a castle. This was burned in 1680, and the walls were built into a new mansion, itself remodelled by David Bryce in 1852.

The property was held by the Irvines of Kingcausie, and is still owned by the same family.

The house is said to be haunted by the ghost of a two-year-old child. James Turner Christie, the infant, fell down the stairs after slipping through his nanny's arms and was killed. The pattering of child's footsteps have reputedly been heard several times when there is nobody about. The Chinese Room is also reputedly haunted. The bedclothes are said to have been flung off one of the occupants.
Other refs: Kincausie

Kingencleugh Castle
Ayrshire: About 1 mile south of Mauchline, on minor road south of A76, just north of the River of Ayr, at Kingencleugh.
Ruin or site   NS 503256   OS: 70   **   Map: 3, no: 213
Little remains of a 16th-century L-plan tower house of the Campbells of Loudoun. Adjacent to the tower is a later house, dating from 1765. John Knox is said to have preached at the tower, and the Campbells of Kingencleugh held the property until at least end of the 18th century.
Other refs: Kingancleugh Tower

Kingennie
Angus & Dundee: About 3 miles north and east of Broughty Ferry, on minor road just north of B961, 1 mile east of Murroes, at or near Kingennie House.
Ruin or site   NO 477354 [?]   OS: 54   *   Map: 8, no: 202
Site of castle. A date stone with 1639 is built into a farm building.

It was a property of the Wedderburns in the 17th century.

Kinghorn Castle
Fife: In Kinghorn, near A921, just north of the Firth of Forth, 3-5 Burt Avenue, in the town.
Ruin or site   NT 269871 [?]   OS: 66   *   Map: 7, no: 57
Site of castle, nothing of which remains.

The stronghold, dating from the 12th century, was a royal castle. Kinghorn was made a royal burgh between 1165 and 1172. Alexander III fell from cliffs nearby in 1286 on his way to the castle and his young wife. The property passed to Sir John Lyon of Glamis, Chancellor of Scotland, towards the end of the 14th century, a descendant of whom was made Earl of Kinghorn in 1606. Kinghorn was burned by the English in 1547 after the Battle of Pinkie. There was nothing left of the castle by 1790.
Other refs: Glamis Tower; Glammis Castle

Kingledores
Borders: About 2.5 miles north and east of Tweedsmuir, on minor road west of A701, west of the Tweed, at or near Kingledores.
Ruin or site   NT 107283 [?]   OS: 72   *   Map: 2, no: 9
Site of tower house.

Kingsbarns Castle
Fife: About 4 miles north of Crail, on minor roads and foot east of A917, north of Kingsbarns, near footpath on sea shore.
Ruin or site   NO 599126   OS: 59   *   Map: 7, no: 158
Site of royal castle, some remains of which survived in the 19th century. The castle contained barns to store grain for Falkland Palace, hence the name, but seems to have been of no great size. Little remains of the harbour.
Other refs: Castle of Kingsbarns

Kingscavil
Lothians: About 2.5 miles east of Linlithgow, on minor roads north of B9080, 0.5 miles north-west of Bridgend, at or near Kingscavil.
Ruin or site   NT 038766 [?]   OS: 65   *   Map: 4, no: 17
Site of castle, parts of which may be built into Champfleurie, a 19th-century L-plan mansion, designed by David Rhind.

In the early 16th century the captain of Blackness Castle was Sir Patrick Hamilton of Kingscavil. He took part in chivalric jousts at Stirling Castle in 1507, but was slain in 1520 in a fight with the Douglases on Edinburgh's High Street, known as 'Cleanse the Causeway'. Hamilton of Kingscavil's son, Patrick, Abbot of Fearn, became Scotland's first Protestant martyr, and was burned at St Andrews in 1528.
Other refs: Champfleurie

Kingseat
Perth & Kinross: About 5.5 miles north of Blairgowrie, on minor roads east of A93 at Strone Bridge, on east side of Black Water, at Kingseat.
Private   NO 147545   OS: 53   *   Map: 8, no: 99
Kingseat, a mansion dating mostly from the 19th century, incorporates part of a tower or fortified house, rising to two storeys and an attic. A gunloop and four iron yetts are built into garden walls.

Kingsnow House *see* Manor Castle

King's Castle, Kirkwall *see* Kirkwall Castle

King's Haugh
Moray: About 8 miles south of Dufftown, on minor road and foot west of A941, near Black Water, at King's Haugh.
Ruin or site   NJ 363303   OS: 37   *   Map: 10, no: 75
Possible site of castle or residence of Malcolm Canmore.

King's Inch *see* Inch House

Kininmonth House

Banff & Buchan: About 4.5 miles north and east of Mintlaw, on minor roads east of A92 and west of A952, at or near Kininmonth.
Private NK 033530 [?] OS: 30 * Map: 10, no: 356
Site of castle. The present T-plan house dates from around 1740 although it has an earlier wing.
 The lands were a property of the Hays of Delgatie, but were sold to the Cummings around 1682.
Other refs: Kinninmonth

Kininvie House

Moray: About 2.5 miles north of Dufftown, on minor road north of B9014 or south of A95, just east of Fiddich, at Kininvie House.
Private NJ 319441 OS: 28 *** Map: 10, no: 62
Kininvie House is a 16th-century L-plan tower house, which was extended in the early 18th century and later, but may include earlier work. The tower consists of a main block of four storeys and a garret, with a round stair-tower projecting from one corner. The stair-tower rises a storey higher to be crowned in a gabled corbelled-out watch-chamber. The whitewashed walls are rounded at the corners, and pierced by slits, at basement level, and small windows.
 The entrance leads to the vaulted basement, and to a turnpike stair climbing to all floors. The tower has been much altered to join up with the modern mansion, but the hall would have been on the first floor, with private chambers on the floors above.
 Kininvie was a Leslie property from 1521. The stone effigy and tomb of Alexander Leslie of Kininvie, who died about 1549, are located in Mortlach Parish Church [NJ 323392]. James V is reputed to have hidden in the kitchen while travelling as the Gudeman of Ballengeich. The house was extended in 1840, and the Leslies still own the property. It is occupied.

Kinkell

Fife: About 2.5 miles east of St Andrews, on minor road north of A917, at or near Kinkell Ness, just south of the sea.
Ruin or site NO 539158 [?] OS: 59 * Map: 7, no: 140
Site of castle.
 The lands were a property of the Collegiate Church of St Mary on the Rock, but passed to the Monypennys of Pitmillie, then the Hamiltons of Kinkell. They may have also been held by the Kinninmonds of Craighall.

Kinkell Castle

Ross & Cromarty: About 3 miles south of Dingwall, on minor roads just west of A835, about 1 mile south-east of Conon Bridge, at Kinkell Castle.
Private NH 554543 OS: 26 **** Map: 9, no: 70
Kinkell Castle is a 17th-century tower house. It comprises a main block of three storeys and a garret, a large round stair-tower at one corner, and a slender stair-turret, corbelled out above first-floor level, in the opposite corner. The round tower rises another storey, and is crowned by a watch-chamber. The roof is steeply pitched, with corbiestepped gables, and the walls are harled and pierced by shot-holes and gunloops. There was an extension, but this has been removed.
 The entrance is in the re-entrant angle at the foot of the round stair-tower. The vaulted basement contained a kitchen, with a wide arched fireplace; and a cellar in the main block, reached from a vaulted passage. A small stair climbs to the hall above. The hall, on the first floor, has a fireplace dated 1594.
 Kinkell was a property of the Mackenzies of Gairloch. The building was used as a farmhouse before being abandoned, then became ruinous. It was restored in 1969, the extension was removed, and it is now occupied.

Kinloch

Angus & Dundee: About 3 miles south-east of Alyth, on minor road north of A94, south of River Isla, at or near Kinloch.
Ruin or site NO 268444 [?] OS: 53 * Map: 8, no: 140
Site of castle or old house, which dated from the 17th century or earlier. It was replaced by Kinloch House, which is now a hotel.
 It was a property of the Kinlochs of Kinloch, and the property still held by the family in the 20th century.

Kinlochaline Castle

South Highland: About 2.5 miles north of Lochaline, on minor roads east of A884, at northern end of Loch Aline, on west side of River Aline, at Kinlochaline.
Private NM 697476 OS: 49 *** Map: 9, no: 22
Standing in a striking location, Kinlochaline Castle is an altered 15th-century keep, rectangular in plan, of four storeys and a parapet walk. The corbelled-out parapet has open rounds, and was remodelled in the 16th century.
 An external stone stair leads to the hall, on the first floor, with a guardroom beside the entrance. The hall has an arched fireplace over which is a stone panel featuring a naked woman. A stair leads down to the vaulted cellars, which are lit only by slits, while another turnpike stair, in one corner, climbs to the parapet. There are stairs and passageways in the thickness of the walls. The garret storey has gone.
 The castle was the seat of the MacInnes clan, hereditary bowmen to the MacKinnons. Following the murder of the laird and his sons by the MacKinnons at nearby Ardtornish in 1319, the lands were given to the MacLeans of Duart. The castle was damaged by the Marquis of Montrose's lieutenant Alasdair Colkitto MacDonald in 1644, and later by Cromwell's forces in the 1650s. The castle was attacked by the Campbell Earl of Argyll in 1679 during a feud. It was abandoned about 1690, restored about 1890, but then deserted. It is about to be or has been restored as a house.
Other refs: Caisteal an Ime

Kinlochkerran *see* **Kilkerran Castle**

Kinlockkerran *see* **Kilkerran Castle**

Kinmont Tower *see* **Woodslee Tower**

Kinmont Tower *see* **Sark Tower**

Kinmuck Castle

Aberdeen & Gordon: About 4 miles north-east of Ellon, on minor roads west of A92, at or near Mains of Kinmuck.
Ruin or site NJ 988353 OS: 30 * Map: 10, no: 348
Site of 14th-century castle, a property of the Kennedys in 1413. Materials from it were used to build Ellon Castle [NJ 960307].
Other refs: Castle of Kinmuck; Kermuck Castle

Kinnaird Castle

Angus & Dundee: About 5.5 miles west of Montrose, on minor roads north of A934, about 0.5 miles south of River South Esk, in Kinnaird Park deer park, at Kinnaird.
Private NO 634571 OS: 54 ** Map: 8, no: 255
Kinnaird, a 19th-century mansion which was further enlarged in 1854-60 by the architect David Bryce, incorporates parts of a 15th-century castle.
 There was a stronghold here in the 14th century. It was a property of Carnegies from the beginning of the 15th century, and Duthac Carnegie died at the Battle of Harlaw in 1411. Walter Carnegie of Kinnaird fought at the Battle of Brechin in 1452,

against the Earl of Crawford, although the castle was later burned, in revenge, by the Lindsays. John Carnegie of Kinnaird was killed the Battle of Flodden in 1513.

Sir Robert Carnegie was ambassador to France in 1550. The castle was visited by James VI. The Carnegies were made Earls of Southesk in 1633, and Charles I and Charles II stayed here.

The family were Jacobites, and forfeited after the 1715 Jacobite Rising, but had recovered their estates and titles by 1858. The house is still occupied by the Earl of Southesk.

One story connected with the castle is that the corpse of James Carnegie, the 2nd Earl of Southesk, who died in 1669, was reportedly taken by a ghostly black coach driven by black horses. Carnegie is said to have studied in Padua, where he supposedly learnt black magic.

Kinnaird Castle

Perth & Kinross: About 9 miles east and north of Perth, on minor road north of A85, at Kinnaird.
Private   NO 242291   OS: 53   ****   Map: 8, no: 129
A tall and impressive fortress, Kinnaird Castle is a rectangular 15th-century keep of four storeys and a gabled garret within the parapet. The parapet has machiolated projections, and there is an octagonal round at one corner.

There are two entrances: one at first-floor level, reached by an external stone stair,

entering through a buttress; the other at basement level, still with an iron yett.

The basement is partly vaulted, the central part of the floor supported by corbels. There is a pit-prison, carved from the rock, and another dungeon excavated from the masonry of the buttress.

The straight stair climbs, within the thickness of the wall, to the hall, on the first floor, which has a large mural chamber reached from the stair. The upper floors are reached by a turnpike stair.

A small two-storey range, containing a kitchen with an enormous arched fireplace, stands close by, and was built in the 17th century.

Kinnaird was a property of the Kinnaird family, descended from Randolph Rufus who settled here in the 1170s. They built a castle in the 13th century, although little or nothing of this building has survived. Kinnaird passed to the Colvilles. In 1449 Sir Robert Colville killed John Auchinleck, and the Douglas Earl of Angus besieged and sacked the castle, and wasted the lands. James VI visited Kinnaird in 1617, to hunt, during his only return trip to Scotland after the Union of the Crowns in 1603. The property was sold to the Threipland family, later of Fingask, in 1674. It was abandoned and became ruined, but renovated in 1855 and recovered by the Threiplands to be reoccupied.

Kinnaird Head Castle

Banff & Buchan: To north of Fraserburgh, on minor roads north of A98, north of harbour just south of the sea, at Kinnaird Head.
His Scot   NJ 999675   OS: 30   ***   Map: 10, no: 352
Kinnaird Head Castle consists of an altered massive 15th-century keep, rectangular in plan, of four storeys and formerly with a garret. The parapet, with open rounds at the corners, has a machiolated projection in the centre of each parapet. The walls are harled and whitewashed.

The entrance was at first-floor level, and a turnpike stair has been removed. The basement is vaulted, and the hall was on the first floor.

The Wine Tower, standing about 50 yards away, is a lower tower, now of three storeys, all of them vaulted. It is said to have been so called as it was used as a wine

cellar for the main castle, and probably its predecessor. The unlit first floor is only entered by a trapdoor from the second floor, which is itself only reached from an outside ladder. The basement has no stair to the floors above. The upper vault has three finely carved heraldic pendants, with the Fraser arms and those of James V. The upper chamber may have been used as a chapel.

It was a property of the Frasers of Philorth. Sir Alexander Fraser built the harbour at Fraserburgh – the town was originally called Faithlie – came near to bankrupting himself, and had to sell much of his property in 1611. A lighthouse was built into the top of the castle in 1787, and the outbuildings were built around it in 1820 by Robert Stevenson, grandfather of Robert Louis Stevenson. It now forms part of a lighthouse museum.

Sir Alexander Fraser is said to have had his daughter's lover, of whom he disapproved, chained in the sea cave below the Wine Tower, where the poor man drowned. His daughter, Isobel, threw herself to her death on finding that her lover had been killed. An apparition is said to been seen by the Wine Tower whenever there is a storm.
Other refs: Kinnaird's Head; Wine Tower, Fraserburgh
OPEN: Open daily all year as Lighthouse Museum, Apr-Oct , Mon-Sat 10.00-18.00, Sun 12.30-18.00; Nov-Mar, Mon-Sat 10.00-16.00, Sun 12.00-16.00; closed 25/26 Dec & 1/2 Jan – joint entry ticket.
Visitor centre with explanatory displays and audio-visual display. Gift shop. Tearoom. W.C. Disabled access to museum/toilet. Car and coach parking. Group concessions. £.
Tel: 01346 511022   Fax: 01346 511033

Kinnaird House

Fife: About 3 miles east and south of Newburgh, on minor road west of A913, 0.5 miles east and north of Lindores, at Kinnaird.
Ruin or site   NO 273174 [?]   OS: 59   *   Map: 7, no: 62
Site of old house or castle.

The lands were a property of Lindores Abbey from the end of the 12th century, but by 1630 had passed to Sir James Balfour of Denmylne and Kinnaird, Lord Lyon King of Arms and author of 'Annales of Scotland'.

Kinnairdy Castle

Banff & Buchan: About 2 miles south-west of Aberchirder, on minor road east of A97 just south of junction with B9117, east of River Deveron, at Kinnairdy.
Private NJ 609498 OS: 29 * Map: 10, no: 160**
Kinnairdy Castle, said to date from as early as the 14th century, is an altered keep of five storeys and a garret. To this a narrow stair-wing was added, making the castle L-

plan. The castle was later extended by a long lower two-storey wing. The roofline has been altered, and there are corbiestepped gables.

The original entrance, at first-floor level, was reached from the courtyard parapet by a bridge. A straight stair led down to the vaulted basement. The hall, on the first floor, contains an oak-panelled aumbry with carving among the finest in Scotland, decorated with the carved heads of Sir Alexander Innes and Christine Dunbar, his wife, along with the date 1493.

The castle was a property of the Innes family. Sir Alexander Innes got into trouble with his creditors, and was imprisoned. The property was sold in 1629 to the Crichtons of Frendraught, but passed to the Reverend John Gregory in 1647, and it was here that his brother fathered 29 children and built Scotland's first barometer – he must have needed something to do in the evenings. The Innes family eventually bought Kinnairdy back, and the castle has been restored.

Kinnaird's Head *see* **Kinnaird Head Castle**

Kinneddar Castle

Moray: About 1 mile south of Lossiemouth, on minor roads and foot east of B9135 or west of A941, just north of the Kirkyard at Kinneddar.
Ruin or site NJ 224696 OS: 28 * Map: 10, no: 42
Site of a 12th century castle of the Bishops of Moray, the ruins of which were still visible in the 19th century. It consisted of a concentric hexagonal stone castle, with a ditch and keep.

Bishop Richard of Moray stayed at Kinneddar at the end of the 12th century, and he may have built the castle. About 1280 Bishop Archibald had the castle enlarged or rebuilt, and it was still used in the 14th century. It was ruined by the 17th century, and apparently demolished in the 19th.

The site of the former parish church, used for a while as the cathedral in the 12th century, is nearby.

Kinneddar was also an important Pictish site, and fragments of carved stones have been found here.
Other refs: Bishop's Palace, Kinneddar

Kinneff Castle

Kincardine & Deeside: About 2 miles north-east of Inverbervie, on minor roads east of A92, at or near Kinneff just west of the sea, north of Castle Hill.
Ruin or site NO 856747 OS: 45 * Map: 10, no: 288
Site of 14th-century keep and castle, little of which remains. The castle was held by the English in 1336 for Edward Balliol. It may not have been used afterwards, and little survived by the beginning of the 18th century.

The Scottish regalia was kept in Kinneff Church in the 1650s, where it was buried for 9 years after being smuggled out of Dunnottar. The castle was besieged by Cromwell's forces in 1651-2, and the regalia was recovered at the Restoration.

Kinneil House

Stirlingshire & Clackmannan: About 1 mile south and west (outskirts) of Bo'ness, on minor road south of A993, south of the Bo'ness and Kinneil Railway.
His Scot NS 983806 OS: 65 ** Map: 6, no: 109
Kinneil House or Palace incorporates a much-altered 16th-century tower house, to which was added a three-storey wing of 1553, originally a separate range. The house was further extended and altered in 1600, and in 1677 when a block linking the two parts of the house was built. There was a large courtyard, with two flanking ranges.

The basement of the old part is vaulted, but the house has been much altered inside. There are tempera paintings in two rooms, some of the best preserved in Scotland.

The lands were held by the Hamiltons from the 14th century, having been given to them by Robert the Bruce. The Hamilton Earl of Arran was Governor for Mary, Queen of Scots, until 1554, and then led her party until 1573 – he built a large tower here in 1553. As a result the house was sacked by the Earl of Morton in 1568-70, and part blown up with gunpowder, but it was later rebuilt, and in the 17th century was greatly remodelled by the Dukes of Hamilton. The building was occupied by Cromwell's forces in the 1650s.

Kinneil was abandoned about 1828, and became ruinous, and in 1936 was to be demolished. It has been restored, however, and is surrounded by a public park. A museum occupies the renovated stable block. James Watt had a workshop here, where he carried out experiments on the development of the steam engine.

The area is said to be haunted by the ghost of Ailie or Alice, Lady Lilburne, the young wife of a Cromwellian officer billeted here in the 1650s or the mistress of the Duke of Hamilton, depending on the version of the story. After having tried to escape several times because she was homesick, she was imprisoned in one of the upper chambers. However, she threw herself from the window into the Gil Burn, 200 feet below. Her screams and wails are said still to be heard on dark winter nights, and her spectre is said to haunt the glen.
Other refs: Palace of Kinneil
OPEN: Access at all reasonable times – view from exterior.
Car parking.
Tel: 0131 668 8800 Fax: 0131 668 8888
Email: hs.explore@scotland.gov.uk Web: www.historic-scotland.gov.uk

Kinnelhead Tower

Dumfriesshire: About 4 miles west and south of Moffat, on minor road west of A74 at Beattock, just west of the Kinnel Water, west of Kinnelhead.
Ruin or site NT 028017 OS: 78 * Map: 1, no: 200
Little remains of Kinnelhead Tower, a 16th-century tower house, except the remains of a vaulted basement and some walls.

The lands were a property of the Johnstones, and held by them until 1965.

Kinnell Castle

Angus & Dundee: About 0.5 miles north-east of Friockheim, north of B965, south-west of Kinnell, near Lunan Water.
Ruin or site   NO 599500 [?]   OS: 54   *   Map: 8, no: 248
Site of castle, nothing of which remains, possibly a property of the Ogilvies. It was ruinous in the 17th century, and demolished in 1811.
Other refs: White Walls, Kinnell; Whitehills Castle

Kinnell House

Stirlingshire & Clackmannan: About 0.5 miles east of Killin, on minor roads east of A827, just south of River Dochart at the west end of Loch Tay, at Kinnell.
Private   NN 578329   OS: 51   **   Map: 6, no: 28
Although much altered in later centuries, Kinnell House incorporates a 16th-century castle. The existing house consists of a long harled building, and has good 18th-century interiors. There is a walled garden.
  It was a property of the MacNabs from 1580, but later acquired by the Campbells.

Kinninmonth *see* Kininmonth House

Kinnordy

Angus & Dundee: About 1 mile west of Kirriemuir, on minor roads and foot north of B951, east of Loch of Kinnordy, at crannog.
Ruin or site   NO 367547   OS: 54   *   Map: 8, no: 165
Site of castle, on crannog, although the Loch of Kinnordy was partly drained in 1730.
  It was held by the Earls of Angus.

Kinnordy

Angus & Dundee: About 1 mile west and north of Kirriemuir, on minor roads west of B955, 0.5 miles north of Loch of Kinnordy, at Kinnordy.
Private   NO 366553   OS: 54   *   Map: 8, no: 164
Kinnordy, a mansion, may incorporate part or be built on the site of a castle of the Ogilvies of Inverquharity. It was sold to the Lyles of Gardyne in 1770, who held it in the 20th century.

Kinnoull Castle

Perth & Kinross: About 1 mile east of Perth railway station, on minor roads east of A93, at Bridgend of Tay, just east of the River Tay.
Ruin or site   NO 123228   OS: 58   *   Map: 8, no: 88
Site of castle, a vestige of which only remained until the end of the 18th century.
  It was a property of the Hays from 1360. George Hay of Kinnoull was a gentleman of the bedchamber to James VI, knighted in 1609, and made Chancellor in 1622. After being created Viscount Hay in 1627, he was made Earl of Kinnoull in 1633. He is buried in the old church of Kinnoull.
Other refs: Bridgend of Tay

Kinord Castle *see* Loch Kinord Castle

Kinpurnie Castle

Angus & Dundee: About 1 mile south-west of Newtyle, on minor roads west of B954, 0.5 miles south of Auchtertyre, at Kinpurnie Castle.
Private   NO 285405   OS: 53   *   Map: 8, no: 144
Kinpurnie Castle, a 20th-century mansion, has no older origins.
Other refs: Kilpurnie Castle

Kinross House

Perthshire: To east of Kinross, on minor road east of B996, west side of Loch Leven, Kinross House.
Private   NO 126020   OS: 58   *   Map: 8, no: 90**
Site of castle or old house, near Kinross House, which was held by the Douglases in the 16th century.
  Kinross House, which is one of the finest examples of 17th-century architecture in Scotland, was built by Sir William Bruce, who was Royal Architect to Charles II.

There are formal walled gardens with yew hedges, roses and herbaceous borders, which are open to the public.
OPEN: House not open; gardens open May-Sep, daily 10.00-19.00.
Gift shop. Disabled access. Car parking. £.
Tel: 01577 862900

Kintore Castle

Aberdeen & Gordon: About 3.5 miles south of Inverurie, near A96 at junction with B977, on west side of River Don, in Kintore.
Ruin or site   NJ 794163 [?]   OS: 38   *   Map: 10, no: 261
Site of 12th-century castle, which was used as a royal hunting lodge. Edward I of England stayed here in 1296. The property was granted to the Keiths by Robert the Bruce in 1309. The family were made Earls of Kintore in 1677.

Kinvaid Castle

Perth & Kinross: About 5 miles north and west of Perth, on minor roads north of B8063, near Shochie Burn, 1 mile north-west of Kinvaid, east of Millhole.
Ruin or site   NO 063300 [?]   OS: 53   *   Map: 8, no: 65
Site of 15th-century castle, built by Bishop Brown of Dunkeld. The castle may have been some distance away at Kinvaid [NO 063300].

Kippilaw House

Borders: About 3.5 miles south of Melrose, on minor road east of B6359 south of junction with A699.
Private   NT 548286   OS: 73   *   Map: 2, no: 203
Kippilaw House, a later mansion, incorporates part of 16th-century tower house. The house was extended at the end of the 18th century, and again in 1886 when the whole interior was altered.

Kippo

Fife: About 1.5 miles south-west of Kingsbarns, on minor roads west of A917, north of B940 or east of B9131, at Kippo.
Ruin or site   NO 579105   OS: 59   *   Map: 7, no: 152
Site of tower house, which is mentioned in 1590.

Kipps Castle

Lothians: About 2 miles south of Linlithgow, on minor roads east of B792 or south of A803, 0.5 miles east of Lochcote Reservoir, at Kipps.
Ruin or site   NS 989739   OS: 65   **   Map: 4, no: 10
Kipps is a ruinous 17th-century tower house, formerly of three storeys, although it was later extended. It consists of a main block, with a vaulted basement, a round stair-turret and a rectangular stair-tower.
  The house was built by the Boyds, but later passed to the Sibbalds. One of the family was Sir Robert Sibbald, 17th-century naturalist and antiquary, a founder member of the Royal College of Physicians of Edinburgh in 1681, and first professor of medicine at Edinburgh in 1685. He was the king's physician and geographer in Scotland. Kipps was inhabited until the 1880s, but is now ruinous.

Kirk o' Field

Lothians: Old College, University of Edinburgh, Edinburgh.
Ruin or site   NT 260735   OS: 66   *   Map: 4, no: 100
Site of the house where in 1567 Lord Darnley, second husband of Mary Queen of Scots, and his servant were strangled before the building was blown up using gunpowder. There may have been more than one plot that night.
OPEN: Site only.

Kirkbank Castle *see* Ormiston Tower

Kirkbuddo

Angus & Dundee: About 5.5 miles south of Forfar, on minor road just east of B9127 short distant west of junction with B978, at or near Kirkbuddo House
Ruin or site   NO 502435   OS: 54   *   Map: 8, no: 213
Site of castle.
  It was a property of the Lindsays in the late 15th century, but later held by the Guthries.

Kirkcaldy of Grange *see* Grange

Kirkconnel House

Dumfriesshire: About 5 miles south of Dumfries, on minor roads east of A710, about 0.75 miles west of the River Nith, at Kirkconnel.

Ruin or site   NX 979679   OS: 84   **   Map: 1, no: 190

Kirkconnel House incorporates a much-altered 16th-century tower house of four storeys at one end. It was extended with a stair wing into an L-plan. The tower house has a corbelled-out parapet, and the walls are pierced by gunloops. There are many extensions and alterations, including larger windows inserted in 1780.

The basement is vaulted, and has unusual cross-shaped shot-holes.

Kirkconnel was held by the Kirkconnel family by 1320 or earlier, but passed by marriage to the Maxwells in 1410, and they built the tower. It was later held by the Bells, but returned to the Maxwells, and is still occupied.

Kirkconnel Tower

Dumfriesshire: About 4.5 miles east of Ecclefechan, on minor roads south of B722 at Fulton, south of the Kirtle Water, south of Kirkconnel Church.

Ruin or site   NY 253752 [?]   OS: 85   *   Map: 1, no: 279

Site of 16th-century tower house, apparently a property of the Bells at one time. This was probably the home of Helen Irvine of Kirkconnel, the heroine of one of the Border Ballads, who was slain by a rejected suitor, one of the Bells of Blacket House. Helen got in the way of a bullet meant for her lover, Adam Fleming:

'I wish I were where Helen lies,
Night and day on me she cries,
O that I were where Helen lies,
On fair Kirkconnel lea!

'Curst be the heart that thought the thought,
And curst be the hand that fired the shot,
When in my arms burd Helen dropt,
And died to succour me!'

The lovers are said to be buried in Kirkconnel Church. The Irvines moved to another Kirkconnel Tower [NY 191752] in 1609.

Other refs: Bell's Tower

Kirkconnel Tower

Dumfriesshire: To north-west of Ecclefechan, on minor roads west of B725, at Kirkconnel.

Ruin or site   NY 192752   OS: 85   *   Map: 1, no: 261

Very little remains of a 16th-century tower house except one fragment of the formerly vaulted basement with a gunloop.

It was a property of the Irvines, who moved here from Kirkconnel, near Sprinkell, in 1609. Kirkconnel Hall is a modern mansion, and now used as a hotel.

Other refs: Ecclefechan Hall

Kirkcudbright Castle

Galloway: To west of Kirkcudbright, on minor road west of A711, just east of the River Dee, at Castledykes.

Ruin or site   NX 677508   OS: 83   *   Map: 1, no: 110

Site of 13th-century castle, only the surrounding ditch remaining. It had a thick wall with corner towers, one of which may have been a keep, around a large courtyard with a twin-towered gatehouse.

There may have been an earlier stronghold here built by the Lords of Galloway or by Malcolm IV after a rebellion in Galloway, but the earliest mention of a castle is in 1288. The Lordship of Galloway had passed to the Balliols. Edward I of England stayed here for 10 days in July 1300 when the castle was held by the English during the Wars of Independence. The property passed to the Douglases after the Balliol's forfeiture, but reverted to the Crown on their own forfeiture in 1455, and was visited by James II. Henry VI of England sheltered here in 1461, but the site was given to the town by James IV in 1509. Stone from the castle may have been used to build MacLellan's Tower in the town in 1577. The old castle was excavated in 1911-13.

Other refs: Castledykes; Castlemains

Kirkcudbright Castle *see* MacLellan's Castle

Kirkdale Tower

Galloway: About 6 miles west and south of Gatehouse of Fleet, on minor roads north of A75, 1 mile north-west of Barholm, west of Kirkdale Burn, at Kirkdale.

Ruin or site   NX 513535   OS: 83   *   Map: 1, no: 84

Some remains of a tower house survive, located between Kirkdale House, an 18th-century mansion designed by Robert Adam for the Hannay family, and the stable block. The mansion was destroyed by fire in 1893, and rebuilt.

Kirkhill Castle

Ayrshire: About 4.5 miles east and north of Ballantrae, on minor road south of A765 at Colmonell, just south of the River Stinchar.

Ruin or site   NX 146859   OS: 76   ***   Map: 3, no: 12

Kirkhill Castle is a ruinous 16th-century L-plan tower house of three storeys and a garret, and stands beside a 19th-century mansion. The tower has corbelled-out round bartizans at the corners of the main block. Many of the windows still have iron yetts, and the walls are pierced by small shot-holes. The castle is dated 1589.

The basement is vaulted. A scale-and-platt stair rose to the first floor.

Kirkhill was built by the Kennedys of Bargany, who acquired the lands after the Reformation. A descendant was Sir Thomas Kennedy of Kirkhill, Lord Provost of Edinburgh in 1680. In 1843 Kirkhill was sold to Colonel Barton of Ballaird, a hero of the Battle of Waterloo in 1815, who built the new mansion.

Kirkhill House

Lothians: To north-west of Broxburn, on minor roads north of A899, at Kirkhill.

Private   NT 074723   OS: 65   ***   Map: 4, no: 32

Kirkhill House is a much-altered 16th-century tower house, which consists of a main block of three storeys with a semi-circular stair-tower projecting from one side. The building has been reduced in height and the roof altered.

It was a property of the Stewart Earl of Buchan in 1770. The house and adjoining steading were converted into flats and houses in the 1970s.

Kirkhill of Meigle *see* Belmont Castle

Kirkhope Tower

Borders: About 1 mile north west of Ettrickbridge, on minor roads north of B7009, just west of Tower Burn.

Private   NT 379250   OS: 73   ***   Map: 2, no: 98

Kirkhope Tower is a 16th-century tower house, rectangular in plan, of four storeys and a garret within a parapet. A rectangular bartizan crowns one corner, and a

caphouse crowns another. A parapet walk crowned three sides of the tower. Kirkhope had a courtyard with ranges of buildings, some remains of which survive.

The entrance leads to the vaulted basement. The hall is on the first floor, and a turnpike stair climbs to the upper floors

Kirkhope was a property of the Scotts, but burned by the Armstrongs in 1543. This was the home – in his youth – of the famous Border reiver, 'Auld Wat', Walter Scott of Harden. With Walter Scott of Buccleuch, Auld Wat rescued Kinmont Willie – William Armstrong of Kinmont – from Carlisle Castle after he had been imprisoned by the English in 1596, as recorded in the ballad 'Kinmont Willie'. In 1576 Auld Wat had married Mary (or Marion) Scott of Dryhope, the 'Flower of Yarrow' who is associated with the Border ballad 'The Dowie Dens of Yarrow'. The tower was occupied until the middle of the 19th century, and has been restored.

Kirkhope Tower
Borders: About 9 miles south and west of Peebles, on minor road south from A72 to Kirkton Manor, near Manor Water, on branch to Old Kirkhope.
Ruin or site NT 194307 OS: 72 * Map: 2, no: 41
Not much remains of a 16th-century tower house.
Other refs: St Gordians

Kirkhope Tower
Lanarkshire & Glasgow: About 6 miles south of Elvanfoot, on minor road south of A702, on west side of Daer Reservoir, at Kirkhope.
Ruin or site NS 968065 OS: 78 ** Map: 3, no: 429
Site of tower or bastle house, probably dating from the 16th century. The basement was vaulted and there was a projecting stair tower. The Barony of Daer was created in 1646 for the Douglas Earl of Selkirk, but passed to the Duke of Hamilton in 1885.
Other refs: Daer

Kirkintilloch Peel
Lanarkshire & Glasgow area: In Kirkintilloch, south of the A803, near the meeting of the Luggie and Glazert Water.
Ruin or site NS 651740 [?] OS: 64 * Map: 3, no: 305
Site of 12th- and 13th-century castle, which may not have been used after the 14th century.

Kirkintilloch was granted to the Comyns around 1211, but passed to the Flemings, later Earls of Wigtown, after the Wars of Independence. They preferred a site at Cumbernauld, and this part of the property was sold to the Kennedys by 1747. The castle may not have been used after the Wars of Independence early in the 14th century, and there are no remains except earthworks and ditches.

There may have been another castle, near Lenzie railway station, but all traces of this have also disappeared.
Other refs: Lenzie Castle; Peel of Kirkintilloch

Kirklands Tower *see* Belmont Castle

Kirklands Tower
Fife: In Saline, near meeting of B913 and B914, near the church.
Ruin or site NT 025925 OS: 58 * Map: 7, no: 7
Site of castle, nothing of which remains. The property was held by the Bishops of Dunkeld.

Kirkmichael House
Ayrshire: About 3 miles east and south of Maybole, on minor road west of B7045, just south of Kirkmichael village, south of the Dyrock Burn.
Private NS 342085 OS: 70 ** Map: 3, no: 107
The present house, a large fine mansion dating from the 19th century, incorporates a four-storey block with a round stair-turret, which dates from around the end of the 16th century.

It may have been a property of the Kilpatricks, was owned by the Shaw-Kennedys at the end of the 19th century, and is now used as a school.

Kirkpatrick Tower
Dumfriesshire: About 3.5 miles north-west of Gretna, on minor roads south of A74 at Kirkpatrick Fleming, north of Kirtle Water, at or near the village.
Ruin or site NY 275701 [?] OS: 85 * Map: 1, no: 285
Site of 16th-century tower house. There are two stones, one dated 1543 or 1548, the other 1674.

Kirkside Castle
Kincardine & Deeside: About 3 miles north and east of Montrose, on minor roads east of A92, 1 mile south-east of St Cyrus, just west of the sea, at Kirkside.
Private NO 738637 OS: 45 ** Map: 10, no: 235
Kirkside, an 18th-century mansion, incorporates part of a 17th-century castle of the Stratton family. The house is still occupied.

Kirkton
Fife: About 3.5 miles north of Leuchars, on minor road east of B945, south and east of Kirkton Barns.
Ruin or site NO 447260 [?] OS: 59 * Map: 7, no: 119
Kirkton, a ruined mansion of three storeys, has one round corner tower and incorporates a 16th-century castle. It formerly had a courtyard

The property originally belonged to the Lockharts, but passed to the Balfours, who held the property in the 16th century, and later to the Youngs. In 1700 it was acquired by John Gillespie of Newton Rires. The house has been partly restored.
Other refs: Balledmond

Kirkton Hall *see* Ballanreoch Castle

Kirkton of Carluke
Lanarkshire & Glasgow area: To the west of Carluke, short distance east of the railway station, on minor roads west of A73.
Ruin or site NS 844502 [?] OS: 72 * Map: 3, no: 391
Kirkton of Carluke, a mansion which was demolished in the mid 20th century, incorporated an altered tower house of three storeys. The old part had a projecting stair-tower, containing a narrow turnpike stair, but had been altered with a new roof and larger windows. The basement was vaulted, and the first floor contained the hall.

The property belonged to the Weirs of Stonebyres, but passed to Lockhart of The Lee in 1662.
Other refs: Carluke

Kirkton Tower
Dumfriesshire: About 1.5 miles north of Lockerbie, on foot west of B723, east of Dryfe Water, near Kirk Burn.
Ruin or site NY 132838 OS: 78 * Map: 1, no: 242
Site of a strong tower, a property of the Johnstones of Kirkton. There were some remains in 1836, but nothing now apparently survives.

Kirkton Tower
Dumfriesshire: About 3.5 miles north of Langholm, on minor road west of A7, west of Ewes Water, at or near Kirkstile.
Ruin or site NY 368907 [?] OS: 79 * Map: 1, no: 315
Site of tower house, a property of the Armstrongs.
Other refs: Echizingles Tower; Chingles Tower

Kirkurd
Borders: About 3 miles south-west of Romannobridge, on minor road west of A72, at or near Kirkurd.
Ruin or site NT 139446 [?] OS: 72 * Map: 2, no: 20
Site of tower house.

Kirkwall Castle

Orkney: In Kirkwall on Orkney, near A960, south and east of the cathedral.

Ruin or site   HY 448109 [?]   OS: 6   *   Map: 11, no: 48

Site of 14th-century castle of the Sinclair Earls of Orkney. Henry Sinclair, the 1st Earl, captured both Shetland and the Faroes, and travelled as far as Greenland and Canada. The 2nd Earl, another Henry, was captured by the English at the Battle of Homildon Hill in 1402, and was Admiral of Scotland. William was made Earl of Caithness in 1455, but forced to resign the Earldom of Orkney to the Crown in 1470.

The Earldom was granted to Robert Stewart, an illegitimate son of James V, in 1568. Patrick Stewart, Earl of Orkney and son of Robert, left Orkney and was imprisoned at Dumbarton. His son rebelled and seized the palace at Birsay, as well as the Earl's Palace in Kirkwall and the castle here. The rising was put down by the Sinclair Earl of Caithness and Robert was hanged and Earl Patrick beheaded in 1615. The castle appears to have been destroyed at this time.

The last remains were used to build a tolbooth and town hall, and nothing remains.

Other refs: King's Castle, Kirkwall

Kirkwood

Dumfriesshire: About 5.5 miles south of Lochmaben, on minor roads north of B725, west of River Annan, at or near Kirkwood Mains.

Ruin or site   NY 121744   OS: 85   *   Map: 1, no: 238

Site of tower house, which had a park.

Kirnie Tower

Borders: About 1 mile north-east of Innerleithen, 0.5 miles north of the A72, on the south east slope of Kirnie Law.

Ruin or site   NT 349373 [?]   OS: 73   *   Map: 2, no: 92

Site of tower house, square in plan. The last remains were removed about 1840 for building materials.

Kirtlehead

Dumfriesshire: About 5.5 miles west of Langholm, on minor road north of B7068, west of Winterhope Reservoir, at or near Kirtlehead.

Ruin or site   NY 269823   OS: 79   *   Map: 1, no: 283

Site of tower house.

Kisimul Castle

Western Isles: Just south of Castlebay on Barra, by boat south of A888 in Castlebay, in Castle Bay, at Kisimul Castle.

His Scot   NL 665979   OS: 31   **   Map: 11, no: 2**

Kisimul Castle consists of curtain wall shaped to fit the island on which it stands, said to date from at least the 13th century, perhaps as early as the 11th, or it may be much later. One of the first stone buildings within the walls is said to be St Cieran's Chapel, although again the date, or indeed that it is a chapel at all, is a matter of dispute. A hall was added, followed by other stone ranges, then a keep of five storeys which had a high parapet and few windows.

The keep has a hall on the top floor, and private chambers occupied the floors below. The upper floors were reached by an external stair.

Although Clan MacNeil claim descent from Neil of the Nine Hostages, High King

of Ireland at the end of the 4th century, the first to settle in Scotland seems to have been Hugh, King of Aileachh and Prince of Argyll. His son, 21st in descent, was called Neil of the Castle, and built a stronghold here in 1030, or so it is claimed. The castle was besieged several times during the clan wars. The clan nominally supported Bonnie Prince Charlie in the Jacobite Risings, and even in 1750 an agent reported to the exiled Bonnie Prince Charlie that MacNeil of Barra would bring 150 men to a new rising in Scotland. The 40th Chief, Roderick, went bankrupt and was forced to sell Barra and all his lands in 1840 to the Gordons of Cluny, then it passed by marriage to the Cathcarts. The castle was bought back by the MacNeils of Barra in 1937, and was restored in the 1950s and 60s.

The castle has been put into the care of Historic Scotland.

Other refs: Kiessimul Castle

OPEN: Open Apr-Sep, daily 9.30-18.30; last ticket 30 mins before closing.

Parking nearby. £. Boat trip.

Tel: 01871 810336/449   Fax: 0131 668 8888

Email: hs.explore@scotland.gov.uk   Web: www.historic-scotland.gov.uk

Kittlehall

Borders: About 5 miles south-east of Biggar, on minor roads and foot west of A701, west of River Tweed, east of Holms Water, south of Rachan Mill.

Ruin or site   NT 113337   OS: 72   *   Map: 2, no: 11

Site of tower house of the Geddes of Rachan family, nothing of which remains. The tower was ruinous by 1775. The Geddes family held the property from 1406 until 1752 when it was sold to the Tweedies of Quarter. By 1897 it had passed to the Marshall family.

Other refs: Rachan

Kneelandtoun *see* Cleland Castle

Knightswood Castle

Lanarkshire & Glasgow area: About 2 miles east of Clydebank, on minor roads south of A82, at or near Knightswood Cross.

Ruin or site   NS 530695 [?]   OS: 64   *   Map: 3, no: 236

Site of 15th-century castle.

The property was earlier held by the Knights Templar, who had their temple at Anniesland.

Knight's Law Tower *see* Penicuik Tower

Knock

Dumfriesshire: About 4 miles north-west of Langholm, near B709, west of Bentpath, south of River Esk, at or near Mid Knock.

Ruin or site   NY 299908 [?]   OS: 79   *   Map: 1, no: 294

Site of tower house.

Other refs: Knockholme

Knock Castle

Kincardine & Deeside: About 1.5 miles west of Ballater, on minor road north of B976, 1 mile west of meeting of Dee and Muick, north of Ardmeanach, just east of Knock.

His Scot   NO 352952   OS: 44   *   Map: 10, no: 71**

Knock Castle is a small ruined 16th- or 17th-century tower house, rectangular in plan, of four storeys. Corbelled-out bartizans crown two corners, and a third corner is crowned by a watch-tower. The walls are pierced by shot-holes, and the tower formerly had a courtyard. The castle may have also been known as Glenmuick, although this may refer to another stronghold.

The vaulted basement has fallen in, as have all other floors, but contained the kitchen, with a small stair up to the hall on the first floor above. A turnpike stair, in one corner of the hall, climbed to the upper floors.

There was a castle here in the 12th century, a property of the Earl of Mar, then the Bissets in the 13th century. It may have been this stronghold which was attacked and destroyed in 1590 by Clan Chattan. The property had passed to the Gordon Earls of Huntly. The feud between the Gordons and the Forbeses resulted in Henry Gordon, 2nd of Knock, being slain in a raid. Later, while the seven sons of the next laird were out cutting peat, apparently on Forbes's land, Forbes of Strathgirnock surprised and beheaded all seven sons, and tied their heads to their peat-spades. When the laird of Knock heard of their deaths, he fell down the stair of his own tower, and was also killed. Forbes of Strathgirnock was summarily executed for the deed in his own house by Gordon of Abergeldie.

Other refs: Glenmuick; Old Castle of Knock

OPEN: Not currently accessible to the public.

Knock Castle

Ayrshire: About 2.5 miles north of Largs, on minor road east of A78, not far from shore of Firth of Clyde, at Knock.

Ruin or site NS 194631 OS: 63 * Map: 3, no: 23**

Knock Castle is a ruined 16th-century Z-plan tower house. It consists of a main block of four storeys and a garret, which had round towers at opposite corners. One end has fallen in, while the other end is roofed and had been restored. The walls are pierced by shot-holes and one gunloop. There has been a courtyard, not much of which remains except a moulded doorway.

One entrance leads to the main turnpike stair, while one nearby opens into the dark unvaulted basement. The interior has been completely altered.

The property passed by marriage to the Frasers of Lovat about 1380, who held it until 1645. The family supported the Marquis of Montrose, and had to sell the property to Montgomery of Skelmorlie. It was later sold again, and passed through several families. In 1853 the castle was turned into a garden folly for the nearby Knock Castle, a castellated pile designed by J. T. Rochead and completed in 1852, which was held by the Elder family. One end of the old castle was restored.

Knock Castle *see* Caisteal Camus

Knock Innon Castle *see* Knockinnan Castle

Knockamillie Castle

Argyll & Dunbartonshire: About 4 miles south of Dunoon, on minor roads west of A815 at Innellan, on the east side of Cowal, west of coast of Firth of Clyde, at Knockamillie.

Ruin or site NS 152711 OS: 63 * Map: 5, no: 117

Not much remains of a 16th-century courtyard castle of the Lamonts. It was destroyed by the Campbells about 1646, who may have built a later house here, itself now mostly gone.

Knockbuie *see* Minard Castle

Knockdavie Castle

Fife: About 2 miles north-west of Burntisland, just south of B9157, about 0.25 miles north of Stenhouse Reservoir, north of Stenhouse Farm.

Ruin or site NT 213883 OS: 66 * Map: 7, no: 37

Little remains of an early 17th-century tower house except the foundations of a main block with a round stair-turret and a projecting rectangular tower.

It was a property of the Douglases in the 17th century, one of whom is said to have been a persecutor of Covenanters.

Knockdaw Castle

Ayrshire: About 6 miles north and east of Ballantrae, on minor road east of A77, at or near Knockdon.

Ruin or site NX 151896 OS: 76 * Map: 3, no: 14

Site of tower house, little of which remains except part built into a shed. It was a property of the Kennedys.

Other refs: Knockdon

Knockderry Castle

Argyll & Dunbartonshire: About 1 mile north of Cove, on minor road just off B833, on eastern shore of Loch Long, at Knockderry Castle.

Private NS 216834 OS: 56 ** Map: 5, no: 123

Perched at the edge of a rocky outcrop, Knockderry Castle, a mansion of 1855

which was enlarged in 1896 by the architect William Leiper, is said to have been built on the basement of a small castle or watch-tower dating from the Norse occupation of the area in the 13th century.

The house is said to be haunted.

Knockdolian Castle

Ayrshire: About 3 miles north-east of Ballantrae, just east of the B7044 at junction with A765, just west of the River Stinchar.

Ruin or site NX 123854 OS: 76 * Map: 3, no: 10**

Knockdolian Castle is a well-preserved 16th-century tower house, rectangular in

plan, of four storeys and a garret within a parapet. The corbelled-out parapet, only crowning two of the walls, has open rounds, and there is a roofless caphouse. The walls are pierced by small windows, gunloops and shot-holes. There has been an adjoining courtyard.

The entrance leads into the vaulted basement, containing two vaulted cellars, and to the turnpike stair which climbs to all floors and the parapet. The hall, on the first floor, has a large fireplace.

There may have been an earlier castle nearby [NX 120862]. Knockdolian was a property of the Graham family, but later passed to the MacCubbins, who made extensive repairs to the castle in the mid 17th century. Nearby is Knockdolian House, a large mansion built about 1842 for the MacConnels.

A verse associated with the castle is:

'Ye may think on your cradle
I'll think on my stane
And there'll ne'er be an heir
To Knockdolian again.'

A mermaid used to sing all night from a stone near the castle which so irritated the lady of the house that she had the rock broken up. The mermaid returned only once to sing the above verse. The heir to the lands died in his cradle and the line died out. Or so the harpers sadly sang.

Knockdon *see* Knockdaw Castle

Knockdon Castle

Ayrshire: About 2.5 miles north of Maybole, on minor roads west of B7024, near or at Knockdon.

Ruin or site   NS 305132 [?]   OS: 70   *   Map: 3, no: 82
Site of castle.

Knockespock House

Aberdeen & Gordon: About 3.5 miles south-east of Rhynie, on minor roads east of A97, south of B9002, north of A944, just north of Correen Hills, at Knockespock.

Private   NJ 544241   OS: 37   **   Map: 10, no: 132
Knockespock House, a complex mansion of two storeys and an attic, incorporates a 16th-century tower house of the Gordons. This is said to have been a seat of the Bishops of Aberdeen.

Near the house is a Class 1 Pictish stone, carved with a crescent and v-rod above a double disc and fragment of a mirror.
Other refs: Clatt

OPEN: Pictish stone on private property – permission should be sought in advance.

Knockhall Castle

Aberdeen & Gordon: About 1 mile north-west of Newburgh, on minor roads west of A975, west of River Ythan, south of Tarty Burn, near Mains of Knockhall.

Ruin or site   NJ 992265   OS: 38   ***   Map: 10, no: 350
Knockhall Castle is a ruined 16th-century L-plan tower house of four storeys and a garret, which has been extended and altered in the 17th century. The walls are pierced by gunloops. The castle had a courtyard, and some remains of a round flanking tower survived in 1970. The castle is dated 1565.

The basement is vaulted and contained a kitchen, with a wide fireplace, in the wing and a cellar in the main block. The hall was on the first floor, and private chambers occupied the floors above. The lower windows and entrance have been blocked up.

Knockhall was built by the Sinclairs of Newburgh in 1565, but sold in 1633 to the Udnys. It was attacked and captured in 1639 by Covenanters led by the Hay Earl of Errol and the Keith Earl Marischal. In 1734 it was accidentally burned, the family being saved by their fool, Jamie Fleeman, and never restored.

Knockhill

Dumfriesshire: About 4 miles south of Lockerbie, on minor roads east of B723, 1.5 miles west of Ecclefechan, at or near Knockhill.

Ruin or site   NY 166740 [?]   OS: 85   *   Map: 1, no: 254
Site of tower house, called 'Duke of Hoddoms' or 'Knockhill ye dukes howse', which stood within park land. The tower is mentioned in 1691.

It was replaced by a later mansion, dating from 1777, possibly on the site of the tower. It was a property of Andrew Johnstone of Knockhill in 1745, who was transported to the West Indies for his part in the Jacobite Rising. He returned in 1777.

Knockholme *see* Knock

Knockinnan Castle

Sutherland & Caithness: About 1.5 miles north of Dunbeath, west of A9.

Ruin or site   ND 181312   OS: 11   *   Map: 12, no: 50
Not much remains of an L-plan tower house and courtyard, a property of the Sinclair family. It may never have been completed.
Other refs: Knock Innon Castle

Knockshinnoch

Ayrshire: About 1 mile south-west of New Cumnock, on minor roads south of B741, east of Connel Burn, south of Connel Park, at Knockshinnoch.

Ruin or site   NS 609126   OS: 71   *   Map: 3, no: 282
Site of castle, formerly with very thick walls. It was demolished by 1850.

Knownoble

Lanarkshire & Glasgow: About 3 miles north of Wishaw, on minor roads and track south of A723 or north of B7029, just north of Cleland, at or near Knownoble

Ruin or site   NS 794589 [?]   OS: 64   *   Map: 3, no: 373
Site of castle of the Cleland family, some remains of which could still be traced in 1880.
Other refs: Knownoblehill

Knownoblehill *see* Knownoble

Kolbein Hruga's *see* Cubbie Roo's Castle

Kyle Castle

Ayrshire: About 5 miles east of Cumnock, on minor roads 4 miles east of A70, east of Dalblair, near the meeting of Guelt Water and Glenmuir Water

Ruin or site   NS 647192   OS: 71   *   Map: 3, no: 303
Little remains of a 15th-century keep, castle and courtyard of the Cunninghams, which later passed to the Stewarts of Bute.
Other refs: Dalblair Castle

L

Lachlan Castle *see* Castle Lachlan

Lachop House *see* Lauchope House

Ladhope Tower
Borders: Just north of Galashiels, on minor roads north of A7, near the clubhouse of the golf club.
Ruin or site NT 494366 OS: 73 ** Map: 2, no: 158
Ladhope Tower is a ruined 16th-century tower house of the Darling family, the basement of which was used as a store for Appletreeleaves Farm. The basement was probably vaulted.
Other refs: Appletreeleaves Tower

Ladiestane *see* Larriston Tower

Ladyland Castle
Ayrshire: About 2.5 miles north of Kilbirnie, on minor road north from A760, about 1 mile east of Glengarnock Castle, at Ladyland.
Private NS 324579 [?] OS: 63 * Map: 3, no: 94
Site of 16th-century tower house, most of which was demolished in 1815 except a fragment.
 It was a property of the Barclay family until 1718, and the occupants were accused of 'adhering' to 'papastrie' during the Reformation. Hugh Barclay seized Ailsa Craig Castle in 1597 and held it for the Spanish. In 1609 the castle was described as a 'strong tower', although the little that remains today is built into a garden wall. The present picturesque house of Ladyland [NS 322578] dates from 1817-21.

Lagg Tower
Dumfriesshire: About 7 miles south-east of Moniaive, on minor road east of B729 north of Dunscore, close to Lagg Farm.
Ruin or site NX 880862 OS: 78 ** Map: 1, no: 166
Lagg Tower is a ruined 16th-century tower house of four storeys, which formerly had a courtyard with outbuildings. There was a turnpike stair on one side of the entrance.
 It was a property of the Griersons from 1408 or earlier, and they built the tower. Roger Grierson of Lagg was killed at the Battle of Sauchieburn in 1488, and others of the family were killed at Flodden in 1513. Robert Grierson of Lagg was prominent in persecuting Covenanters. In 1685 he surprised an illegal Coventicle and, after killing some of the worshippers, including James Clement, denied them a Christian burial. A granite monument marks the spot. Grierson, himself, is buried in the burial ground of the old parish church [NX 927832].

Lagwine Castle *see* Banck Castle

Lagwyne Castle *see* Banck Castle

Laigh Castle *see* Pollok House

Laigh Place *see* Netherplace

Laight Castle
Ayrshire: About 3 miles north-west of Dalmellington, on foot north from A713 south of Waterside, south of a loop of the Dunaskin Burn.
Ruin or site NS 450089 OS: 77 * Map: 3, no: 184
Laight Castle is a very ruined tower house of the Crawfords. It was defended by a ditch, and appears to have been a rectangular tower house with an adjoining stair-tower.
Other refs: Dunaskin; Castle of Laight

Laighwood *see* Bishop Sinclair's Tower

Lainshaw Castle
Ayrshire: About 1 mile south-west of Stewarton, on minor roads west of B769, just north of the Annick Water, at Lainshaw House.
Ruin or site NS 410453 OS: 64 * Map: 3, no: 154
Nothing remains of a 15th-century castle of the Stewarts, which passed to the Montgomerys in 1570. The property was sold to the Cunninghams in 1779, one of Glasgow's 'tobacco lords'.
 The present Lainshaw House, a classical mansion, was built around 1800, and given a Tudor-Gothic style extension in 1824.

Lamberton
Borders: About 4 miles north-east of Berwick upon Tweed, on minor roads south of A1, at Lamberton.
Ruin or site NT 965573 [?] OS: 74 * Map: 2, no: 364
Site of tower house, located just inside the Scottish border. It was probably held by the Rentons, and burned and destroyed along with the village by the Earl of Hertford in 1545. The only trace of the village is the scant remains of the church, where James IV and Margaret Tudor are said to have been married. Lamberton Toll was formerly the site of runaway marriages, and for a time rivalled Gretna Green, although the Toll House has been demolished.

Lamb's House, Leith
Lothians: About 2 miles north-east of Edinburgh Castle, Leith.
Private NT 269764 OS: 66 * Map: 4, no: 111
The house of Lamb, a Leith merchant. Mary Queen of Scots rested here after arriv-

ing from France in 1561. The house has been restored and is now an old people's day centre.
OPEN: View from exterior.

Lamington Tower
Lanarkshire & Glasgow area: About 5 miles south-west of Biggar, on minor roads north of A702 at Lamington, just west of Mains, just east of the River Clyde.
Ruin or site NS 980320 OS: 72 ** Map: 3, no: 435
Not much remains of a 15th-century keep, the basement of which was vaulted.
 The lands were named from Lambin, a Fleming, who held them under Malcolm IV. They were granted in 1368 to William Baillie. Mary, Queen of Scots, visited in 1565, and another William Baillie of Lamington was her Master of the Wardrobe. The family fought for Mary at the Battle of Langside in 1568, and were subsequently forfeited. The tower was occupied until around 1750, but blown up in 1780 so that the stones might be used to build dykes.
 The Baillie family became Lords Lamington in 1880, and built Lamington House, a small mansion.

One tale is that Marion Braidfute, heiress of the 13th-century owner of Lamington, was taken off to Lanark by Hazelrigg, Edward I's sheriff and governor of the town and castle there. She was the wife of William Wallace, and cruelly slain by the English, probably after helping her husband escape – as he was already an outlaw. Wallace avenged her death by killing Hazelrigg and massacring the English garrison of Lanark.

Lanark Castle

Lanarkshire & Glasgow area: In Lanark, on minor roads south of A73, near Castlebank.
Ruin or site NS 875435 OS: 72 * Map: 3, no: 405
Site of 12th-century castle, which stood on Castle Hill, a prominent knoll.
  It was visited by 12th-century kings of Scots, but occupied by the English during the Wars of Independence, until recovered by Robert the Bruce in 1310. William Wallace had massacred the garrison here, and murdered Hazelrigg, the English governor, after his wife, Marion Braidfute, had been killed by Hazelrigg.
Other refs: Castle Hill, Lanark

Lang *see* Langton

Langhaugh Tower

Borders: About 7 miles south and west of Peebles, on minor road south of A72 from Kirkton Manor, just east of the Manor Water, at Langhaugh.
Ruin or site NT 202310 OS: 73 * Map: 2, no: 45
Little remains of a 16th-century tower house except stony mounds.
  It was a property of the Bairds of Posso, but occupied by the Cockburns as tenants. In 1561 this led to a dispute between Janet Scott, widow of Baird of Posso, and a William Cockburn.

Langholm Tower

Dumfriesshire: In Langholm, just north of the A7, on the north-east side of the main street of the town, in the Buccleuch Arms Hotel.
Ruin or site NY 365855 OS: 79 * Map: 1, no: 313
Not much survives of a 16th-century tower house, except the cellar surviving in a wing of the former Buccleuch Arms Hotel. It may have been held by the Armstrongs, but Langholm was sold by the Maxwells to Douglas of Drumlanrig.
  There was another tower just north of the meeting of the Ewes Water with the River Esk.

Langholm Tower

Dumfriesshire: Just north of Langholm, on minor road west of A7, just north of meeting of Ewes Water and River Esk.
Ruin or site NY 361849 OS: 79 * Map: 1, no: 312
Not much remains of a 16th-century tower house apart from the remains of one gable.
  It may have been built by the Armstrongs, but passed to the Maxwells. The tower was betrayed to the English in 1544, but recaptured in 1547 by the Scots. It was later sold to Douglas of Drumlanrig, and abandoned by 1725. There was another tower in the town of Langholm, the vaulted basement of which is built into one wing of the former Buccleuch Arms Hotel.
  The Battle of Arkinholm was fought nearby, where the Black Douglases were defeated by the forces of James II in 1455.
Other refs: Castle of Langholm

Langrig

Renfrewshire: About 3 miles south-east of Barrhead, off minor roads south of A77, in woodland west of the site of the former Mearnskirk Hospital.
Ruin or site NS 536550 OS: 64 * Map: 3, no: 241
The foundations of buildings survive, believed to be from a grange or tower house.
  The property was held by the Knights Templars, but passed to the Knights Hospitallers. This appears to be the site of the Maxwell's original castle, before they moved to Mearns in 1449.
Other refs: Lanrig

Langshaw Tower

Borders: About 3.5 miles north-east of Galashiels, on minor road north of A7, near Colmslie Tower and Hillslap Tower, north of Allan Water.
Ruin or site NT 516397 OS: 73 ** Map: 2, no: 180
Little remains of a late 16th-century L-plan tower house, formerly of three storeys, and a later extension, dating from the 17th century. The tower was occupied until the 18th century and part of it was used as the local school.
  It was held by the Borthwicks, then the Murrays.

Langskaill House

Orkney: On the south-west side of the island of Gairsay in Orkney, just north of the shore, 1 mile east of the mainland at Queenamuckle.
Private HY 435219 OS: 6 ** Map: 11, no: 45
Langskaill House is a 16th- and 17th-century courtyard castle. It consists of ranges of buildings around three sides of the courtyard, with the last side completed by a wall with a gateway. Only one range of one storey and an attic survives. There are two gunloops defending the entrance. The house is dated 1674.
  The house stands on the site of the drinking hall of Svein Aliefson, who spent his life farming and raiding the Western Isles and Ireland, as recorded in the Orkneyinga Saga. He was killed in Ireland. In the 17th century Langskaill was a property of the Craigies of Gairsay.

Langton

Renfrewshire: About 3.5 miles south of Barrhead, on minor road west of B769, south-west of Langton.
Ruin or site NS 501541 [?] OS: 64 * Map: 3, no: 209
Probable site of castle.
Other refs: Lang

Langton Castle

Borders: About 2.5 miles west of Duns, south of minor road north of A6105, north of Langton Burn.
Ruin or site NT 756534 OS: 67 * Map: 2, no: 302
Site of 15th-century castle.
  The property was held by the Viponts, who had held the property from the middle of the 12th century, one of whom was killed at the Battle of Bannockburn in 1314. It passed by marriage to the Cockburns in the 14th century. James IV had artillery brought here in September 1496 during the Raid of Ellem. Mary, Queen of Scots, visited in 1566, and the castle was still occupied at the end of the 17th century. The property was sold in 1758 to the Gavin family, then to the Campbell Marquis of Breadalbane who in 1862 built a new mansion, designed by David Bryce, and later passed to the Baillie-Hamiltons. The mansion was completely demolished in the 1950s, except for a 'noble entrance gateway' of 1877.

Langton Tower *see* East Reston Tower

Langwell Castle

Sutherland & Caithness: About 5 miles south-west of Dunbeath, on minor road and foot west of A9 at Berriedale, between Langwell and Berriedale Water, east of Langwell House.
Ruin or site ND 116227 OS: 17 * Map: 12, no: 43
Not much remains of a 15th-century keep and courtyard.
  It was a property of the Sutherland family. Langwell House, which stands nearby, is a rambling mansion, part dating from the 18th century, with corbiestepped gables. The property was sold to the Sinclairs in 1788, then to the Hornes in 1813, then to the Bentinck Dukes of Portland in 1860, who still occupy it. There is a fine walled garden.
Other refs: Achastle

Lanrick Castle

Stirlingshire & Clackmannan: About 2.5 miles west and north of Doune, on minor road south of A84, near the south bank of the River Teith, at Lanrick.
Private NN 685031 OS: 57 * Map: 6, no: 51
Lanrick Castle, a large castellated and turreted mansion, incorporates part of a tower house.

It was a property of the Haldanes of Gleneagles, but later passed to the MacGregors. In 1840 William Jardine, the tea tycoon, built the new mansion.

Lanrig *see* Langrig

Lanton Tower

Borders: About 2 miles north-west of Jedburgh, on minor road south of A698, at Lanton.

Private NT 618215 OS: 74 ** Map: 2, no: 240

Lanton Tower is an altered 16th-century tower house, rectangular in plan, of three storeys and garret, to which has been added a modern mansion. Many windows have been enlarged, and the upper part has been altered.

The basement has been vaulted, and two gunloops pierce the walls.

The tower was sacked in 1513. It was a property of the Cranstons in 1627, but had passed to Douglas of Cavers by 1687. It was restored in 1989.

There were possibly two other towers in the village, [NT 620218 and NT 621219], although it is possible this is the same site. The last remains of both were recorded as being removed about 1800.

Larabank Castle

Renfrewshire: About 3 miles north of Kilbirnie, on minor roads west of A760, 1.5 miles west of Lochwinnoch, south of Glenlora.

Ruin or site NS 328586 [?] OS: 63 * Map: 3, no: 96

Site of castle, the last remains of which were removed in the 19th century.

Other refs: Lorabank Castle

Larg Castle

Galloway: About 4 miles north and west of Glenluce, on minor road 4 miles north of A75 at Glenluce, west of the Main Water of Luce, at or near Mains of Larg.

Ruin or site NX 167644 OS: 82 * Map: 1, no: 30

Site of castle with a courtyard. The lands were a property of Soulseat Abbey, but passed at the Reformation to John Vaux of Longcastle and Barnbarroch, then in the 17th century to the Lynns.

Larg Tower

Galloway: About 1.5 miles east and north of Newton Stewart, east of A712 just north of Larg, west side of Larg Hill, west of The Lane.

Ruin or site NX 432663 OS: 83 * Map: 1, no: 69

Little remains of a tower house except some masonry. It was a property of the Mackies, who held the property from around 1320, and ruinous in 1684.

Other refs: Larg Castle

Largie Castle

Kincardine & Deeside: About 2.5 miles north of Inverbervie, on minor road west of A92, about 0.5 miles south-west of Roadside of Kinneff, at or near Largie.

Ruin or site NO 835760 OS: 45 * Map: 10, no: 280

Site of 16th-century castle, a property of the Grahams of Largie. A dated stone with 1611 is built into a farm building.

Largie Castle

Argyll & Dunbartonshire: About 17 miles south and west of Tarbert, on A83, near Rhunahaorine, east of Sound of Gigha, at Old Largie Castle.

Ruin or site NR 708483 OS: 62 * Map: 5, no: 33

Site of castle, fragments of which remain including a cellar and part of the barmkin wall. A farm, High Rhunahaorine, was built on the site, itself now very ruinous.

The property was held by the MacDonalds of Largie, descendants of the Lord of the Isles, from the middle of the 15th century until the 20th century, and is said to have had a brownie. The family moved to 'new' Largie Castle, 0.5 miles north-east of Tayinloan.

Other refs: Old Largie Castle

Largo Castle

Fife: About 0.5 miles north of Lower Largo, east of minor road north from A917, near ruin of Largo House, south of Largo Law.

Ruin or site NO 418034 OS: 59 * Map: 7, no: 116

Nothing remains of a 15th-century keep and castle, except one round conical-roofed tower, which was built in the 16th century.

The lands of Largo were given by James III to Sir Andrew Wood in 1482-3, and he built a castle here. Wood had many exploits in his ship 'The Yellow Carvel', particularly in 1489 when he routed an English fleet in the Forth, and in 1504 when he defeated another English fleet at Dundee, taking three of the ships as prizes. He served James IV, and was employed in expeditions to Western Isles to destroy the Lord of the Isles, as well as commanding the 'Great Michael', the largest ship in the world at the time. Wood died in 1540.

The lands passed to the Blacks in 1618, the Gibsons in 1633, then the Durhams in 1663, who held them until 1868. Around 1750 the old castle was mostly demolished to build Largo House, designed by John Adam, itself now a ruined shell.

Larriston House *see* Haggishaugh

Larriston Tower

Borders: About 6.5 miles north-east of Newcastleton, on minor roads south of B6357, just south of the Larriston Burn, south-east of Larriston Rigg.

Ruin or site NY 557937 [?] OS: 80 * Map: 2, no: 207

Site of 16th-century tower house of the Elliots. William Elliot of Larriston, with others, was charged with making a raid into Tynedale in 1593.

Other refs: Ladiestane

Lasonn *see* Abbot's Tower

Lathallan Castle

Fife: About 5 miles north and east of Elie, on minor roads south of A915, at or near Lathallan.

Ruin or site NO 460063 [?] OS: 59 * Map: 7, no: 122

Site of castle of the Spence family.

John Spence of Lathallan sat in parliament in 1434, and another of the family features in the old ballad 'Sir Patrick Spens' when the ship he was captaining was lost with all hands. The property later passed to the Lumsdens.

Lathallen *see* Brotherton Castle

Latheron Castle

Sutherland & Caithness: About 3.5 miles north-east of Dunbeath, near junction of A9 with A895, 0.5 miles north of the sea, at or near Latheron village.

Ruin or site ND 199334 OS: 11 * Map: 12, no: 51

Not much remains of a castle of the Gunn family, except one overgrown wall. The castle was ruinous but in good condition in 1726.

Latheron House, dating from the 18th century, was much enlarged in the 19th century.

Clan Gunn Heritage Centre and Museum is located in the village of Latheron.

OPEN: Museum open in summer except Sun.

Lathrie *see* Lathrisk House

Lathrisk House

Fife: About 4 miles north of Glenrothes, on minor roads north of B936, about 1.5 miles north-west of Freuchie, at Lathrisk House.

Private NO 273085 OS: 59 ** Map: 7, no: 61

The mansion, which mostly dates from about 1740 although it was extended in 1786, incorporates three barrel-vaulted cellars, probably from the 16th century.

It was a property of the Johnstones from 1783 until the 20th century.

Other refs: Lathrie

Lauchope House

Lanarkshire & Glasgow area: About 3.5 miles north-east of Motherwell, on minor roads north of A8 or south of B799, south of Chapelhall, at or near Lauchope Mains.

Ruin or site NS 781617 OS: 64 * Map: 3, no: 368

Site of strong tower house, which had very thick walls, a property of the Muirheads. It gave refuge to Hamilton of Bothwellhaugh, as the then laird was Hamilton's brother-in-law, after he had shot the Regent Moray at Linlithgow in 1570. The tower was burned in revenge the same year, but restored and incorporated into a later mansion. It would appear to have been demolished.

Other refs: Lachop House

Lauder Tower

Borders: In Lauder, near A68, near Lauder Church.

Ruin or site NT 530475 OS: 73 * Map: 2, no: 185

Site of tower house of the Lauder family, formerly with gardens and orchards. A stronghold, called Lauder Fort, was built here by Edward I of England, during the Wars of Independence, and rebuilt by Edward II in 1324. It was strengthened by the Duke of Somerset and the English in 1548, although it was retaken by the Scots, with French help, by 1550. It was demolished at the end of the 17th century, and nothing now remains.

Laur *see* Lour Tower

Lauriston Castle

Kincardine & Deeside: About 4 miles south-east of Laurencekirk, on minor roads west of B9120 at Mains of Lauriston, 1 mile north of the sea, at Lauriston.

Private NO 759667 OS: 45 ** Map: 10, no: 241

Lauriston Castle consists of part of a keep and courtyard castle, dating from the 13th century, to which has been added a late 18th-century mansion. Two parts of the old castle survived, linked by a section of curtain wall, which enclosed the courtyard, but one part has since been demolished.

Lauriston belonged to the Stirlings, then to the Straitons from the 13th century until 1695. The castle was captured by the English under Edward III in 1336. One of the family, Alexander Straiton, was slain at the Battle of Harlaw in 1411, and another, David Straiton, an early Protestant martyr, was killed for his faith in 1534 at Greenside in Edinburgh. In 1695 the property was acquired by the Falconers of Phesdo. The house became ruinous, part was demolished, while part rebuilt and reoccupied. The whole building is now apparently derelict.

Lauriston Castle

Lothians: About 3 miles west and north of Edinburgh Castle, between Davidson's Mains and Cramond, on minor road north of the B9085.

Private NT 204762 OS: 66 * Map: 4, no: 68**

Lauriston Castle is a much-altered 16th-century tower house of three storeys and an attic, to which was added a two-storey Jacobean extension, designed by William Burn, in 1824-7. The tower has a round stair-tower, and two large pepperpot bartizans crown one side.

The basement of the old part is vaulted. The first-floor hall has a hidden stair leading to a spy hole.

The castle was built by the Napiers of Merchiston. One of the family, John Napier, was the inventor of logarithms. In 1656 the property was sold to Charles II's solicitor, Robert Dalgleish, and in 1683 to the Laws. In 1827 it passed to the Allans, and then later to the Rutherfords, the Crawfords of Cartsburn, then the Reids, who were the last owners, and gave it to the city of Edinburgh. The castle has a fine Edwardian-period interior, housing good collections of Italian furniture, Blue John, Grossley wool mosaics, Sheffield plate, mezzotint prints, Caucasian carpets, and items of decorative art.

The ghostly sound of feet have reportedly been heard in the castle.

OPEN: Open Apr-Oct, daily except Fri 11.00-13.00 and 14.00-17.00; Nov-Mar, Sat and Sun only 14.00-16.00, closed Mon-Fri; grounds open all year.

Good collections of Italian furniture, Blue John, Grossley wool mosaics, Sheffield plate,

mezzotint prints, Caucasian carpets, and items of decorative art. Guided tours of house only. WC. Disabled access to grounds & WC. Car and coach parking. Group concessions. ££ (castle).

Tel: 0131 336 2060   Fax: 0131 557 3346

Law Castle

Ayrshire: About 0.5 miles north-east of West Kilbride, on minor road east of B7047 near junction with B781, beneath Law Hill.

Private NS 211484 OS: 63 * Map: 3, no: 34**

Commanding a wide view over the Clyde, Law Castle is a 15th-century keep, rectangular in plan, of four storeys and a garret. A corbelled-out parapet has open

rounds and the walls are pierced by gunloops.

The basement is vaulted and contains two cellars, one with a stair to the hall above. The hall, on the first floor, has a screened-off kitchen with a wide fireplace. There is a turnpike stair in one corner.

The castle was a property of Boyds, one of whom married Mary, daughter of James II, and became Earl of Arran, but later had to flee the country. It was sold to the Bontine family in 1670, and has been restored and occupied as flats.

Other refs: Kilbride; Tower of Kilbride

Law Tower

Lanarkshire & Glasgow area: About 1 mile west of Bearsden, on minor roads north of A810, east of Duntocher, at or near Law.
Ruin or site NS 515738 [?] OS: 64 * Map: 3, no: 226
Site of 16th-century tower house, nothing of which remains. The castle was destroyed around 1890 and materials used in Edinbarnet House.

Law was a property of the Livingstone family, but passed by marriage to Sir James Hamilton of Finnart after 1513. It was sold to the Stirlings of Glorat about the same time as he exchanged Drumry with the Crawfords of Kilbirnie for Crawfordjohn and Kilbirnie, probably around 1528. The property was then held by the Stirlings of Glorat.
Other refs: Tower of Law

Leask House

Aberdeen & Gordon: About 4.5 miles north-east of Ellon, on minor roads east of A92 or west of A975, west of Mains of Leask.
Ruin or site NK 026331 [?] OS: 30 * Map: 10, no: 355
Site of castle or old house. The present ruinous mansion of two storeys was built in 1826-7 by Archibald Simpson. It was burned out in 1927.

It was a property of the Cummings or Comyns at the beginning of the 18th century, but passed to the Gordons of Hilton and Straloch, who were descended from the Gordons of Pitlurg, and they changed the name to Pitlurg. The Gordon 6th laird of Gight broke his sword across the head of Laird of Leask. The property later passed to the Skenes, and they used the old name House of Leask.
Other refs: Pitlurg House; House of Leask

Leccamore Dun

Argyll: Off unlisted road, 1.5 miles N of Toberonochy, Luing.
Private NM 750107 OS: 55 * Map: 5, no: 42**
Built on the top of a ridge, this is a well-preserved Iron Age dun, which consists of an enclosing wall with outlying ditches. There are two entrances, one with cells on both sides of the passage, and the remains of a flight of steps which may have once given access to the upper part of the dun. The walls stand to a height of ten feet. There are many cup marks on one of the slabs in the entrance. There have been other structures within the dun, and during excavations finds included some worked antler, stone implements, bronze and a fragment of an iron blade.
OPEN: Seek permission from farmer at Leccamore.

Leckie House *see* Old Leckie House

Lee Castle

Renfrewshire: About 4 miles north-west of East Kilbride, on minor roads east of A726, in Beechgrove Park behind Clarkston Road.
Ruin or site NS 580590 [?] OS: 64 * Map: 3, no: 262
Site of 14th-century castle, which was extended in the 18th century. Nothing remains.

It was a property of Cochrane of Lee in the 15th century, but passed to the Pollocks of Balgray during the following century, then apparently to the Maxwells.

The foundations were removed in the 1840s when human bones were discovered in 'subterranean houses', the bones said to be of 'almost superhuman magnitude'.
Other refs: Williamwood; Netherlee

Lee Castle *see* The Lee

Lee Tower

Borders: About 1.5 miles north of Innerleithen, on minor road west of B709, west of the Leithen Water.
Ruin or site NT 328396 OS: 73 ** Map: 2, no: 85
Lee Tower is a ruinous 16th-century tower house, and stands within a farm. The basement was vaulted. It was a property of the Homes, then the Kerrs.
Other refs: Ley Tower

Lee, The *see* The Lee

Leith

Lothians: About 2 miles north-east of Edinburgh Castle, near A199, Johnston Street, Leith.
Ruin or site NT 268766 OS: 66 * Map: 4, no: 108
Not much remains of the Citadel built at Leith by Cromwell in the 1650s. It was pentagonal in plan, but most of it has been demolished except for a vaulted pend. Also in Leith is Lamb's House [NT 269764].
Other refs: Cromwell's Citadel, Leith

Leith *see* Martello Tower, Leith

Leith Hall

Aberdeen & Gordon: About 3.5 miles north-east of Rhynie, on minor roads north of B9002, 1 mile north of Kennethmont, south of Knockandy Hill, at Leith Hall.
NTS NJ 541298 OS: 37 ** Map: 10, no: 129
Leith Hall incorporates a 17th-century tower house, rectangular in plan, of three storeys and an attic, with bartizans crowning the corners. To this have been added 18th- and 19th-century blocks to form four sides of a courtyard. The walls are yel-

low-washed, and the original windows are small. Small drum towers date from the 19th century.

The basement of the tower is vaulted, and contained the original kitchen. The hall was on the first floor, with private chambers on the floors above, but the old part has been much altered inside.

The Leith family held the property from 1650 or earlier until 1945, when it was given to The National Trust for Scotland.

Guests in 1968 reported manifestations in their bedroom, including the sounds of a woman's laugh and a party going on when nobody else was apparently there. Sightings of the apparition of a man, bearded and bandaged about the head, were also reported. The ghost is thought to be John Leith, who was killed in a brawl and shot in the head in 1763, or Colonel Alexander Leith who died in 1900 and had fought at the Battle of Balaclava. A woman in Victorian dress has also reputedly been seen, as well as a young child and governess.
Other refs: Peill Castle
OPEN: Open Easter wknd, then May-Sep, daily 13.30-17.30; Oct, Sat-Sun 13.30-17.30, last admission 16.45. Garden and grounds open all year 9.30-sunset.
Jacobite mementoes. Exhibition on family's military history. Exhibition. Tearoom. WC. Picnic area. Garden and 286 acres of extensive grounds with trails, ponds and a bird hide. Disabled facilities and WC. Car and coach parking. Group concessions. £££.
Tel: 01464 831216 Fax: 01464 831594
Email: information@nts.org.uk Web: nts.org.uk

Leithenhall *see* Wamphray Tower

Leitholm Peel

Borders: About 4 miles east and south of Greenlaw, on minor road north of B6461, about 0.5 miles west of Leitholm, near Stainrig House.
Ruin or site NT 784438 OS: 74 ** Map: 2, no: 316
Little remains of a 16th-century tower house.

Lennox Castle

Lothians: About 0.5 miles north-east of Balerno, from the A70 on the south bank of the Water of Leith, just south of Currie.
Ruin or site NT 174671 OS: 65 * Map: 4, no: 55
Lennox Castle was a massive 15th-century keep, rectangular in plan, of which only the basement remains. The basement was divided into three vaulted cellars, and the hall above was also vaulted. The base of a turnpike stair survives close to the entrance. The castle reputedly had a tunnel to another building on the opposite bank of the river.

It was a property of the Stewart Earls of Lennox, and visited for hunting by Mary, Queen of Scots, the Regent Morton, and James VI. The property later passed to George Heriot, known as 'Jinglin Geordie', who was a goldsmith in the time of Queen Anne, and bequeathed his large fortune to found George Heriot's School.

Lennox-Plunton Castle *see* Plunton Castle

Lennoxlove

Lothians: About 1 mile south of Haddington, on minor road between B6369 and B6368, north of the Coulston Water, at Lennoxlove.
Private NT 515721 OS: 66 * Map: 4, no: 188**
Originally known as Lethington, Lennoxlove incorporates an altered L-plan tower house of three storeys and an attic. The parapet has open rounds. The tower incorporates work from the 14th century, and probably earlier. Many of the windows have been enlarged, and the wallheads of the tower have been heightened and a two-storey caphouse added. A two-storey range projects from the tower, and there is another extension from the 17th century.

The main entrance, in the re-entrant angle, leads to a stair which climbs to the first floor; another entrance opens into the vaulted basement. The first floor of the main block is vaulted, and contained the hall, and the original kitchen was in the wing at the same level. A turnpike stair climbs to the upper floors. There are fine interiors with good panelling, fireplaces and plasterwork.

It was originally a property of the Giffords, but sold to the Maitlands about 1350, who built or extended a castle here. It was burned by the English in 1549. William Maitland of Lethington, secretary to Mary, Queen of Scots, lived here. He was involved in the plot to murder Lord Darnley, but supported Mary after she abdicated. He was taken prisoner after Edinburgh Castle was captured in 1573 and died, possibly from poison, soon afterwards.

The property passed to the Maitland Duke of Lauderdale in 1645, but was sold to the Stewart Lord Blantyre. Instrumental in having the name changed to Lennoxlove was Frances Stewart, Duchess of Richmond and Lennox, a great beauty, who is said to have been the model for Britannia. Lennoxlove passed to the Bairds, then in

1947 to the Duke of Hamilton, since when it has been the family seat.

Among the treasures it contains are the death mask of Mary, Queen of Scots, and the casket which may have contained the 'Casket Letters'. There is also porcelain, paintings and furniture from the Hamilton Palace collection.
Other refs: Lethington Castle
OPEN: Open Easter-Oct, Wed, Thu, Sat and Sun, 14.00-16.30; check if house is open on Sat before setting out.
Fully guided tours. Explanatory displays. Garden cafe. WC. Disabled access to house and gardens. Parking. ££.
Tel: 01620 823720 Fax: 01620 825112
Email: info@lennoxlove.org Web: www.lennoxlove.org

Leny House

Stirlingshire & Clackmannan: About 1.5 miles west and north of Callander, on minor road north of A84, north of Kilmahog, at Leny.
Private NN 613089 OS: 57 ** Map: 6, no: 37
Leny House consists of a 16th-century L-plan tower house with corbiestepped gables. To this has been added a large 19th-century mansion, surrounding the tower on three sides, with bartizans.

The basement is vaulted, but the inside of the tower has been greatly altered.

The property originally belonged to the Leny family, but passed by marriage to the Buchanans, whose descendants held it until the 20th century. In 1746 Francis Buchanan was hanged after Stewart of Glenbuckie, leader of Stewarts on their way to join the Jacobite army, was shot in the head at Leny. The building is now used as a hotel.
OPEN: Hotel
Tel: 01877 331078 Fax: 01877 331335
Email: res@lenyestate.com Web: www.lenyestate.com

Lenzie Castle *see* Kirkintilloch Peel

Leod Castle *see* Castle Leod

Lergychonzie *see* Dun an Garbh-Sroine

Leslie Castle

Aberdeen & Gordon: About 3 miles south-west of Insch, on minor roads west of B992 at Auchleven or south of B9002, at Leslie.
Private NJ 599248 OS: 37 * Map: 10, no: 158**
Built on the site of an earlier castle, Leslie Castle is a 17th-century L-plan tower house of three storeys with a square stair-tower, rising a storey higher, in the re-entrant angle. Bartizans crown the corners. The walls are pierced by numerous windows, shot-holes and gunloops. An adjoining courtyard had a ditch, drawbridge, gatehouse and other buildings, which were demolished in 1661, although traces of the moat remain. The walls of Leith Hall are now harled and whitewashed.

The entrance, at the foot of the stair-tower, leads to the wide scale-and-platt stair and into the basement. The basement is vaulted. The main block contains the kitchen, which has a large fireplace, and the wing is occupied by two cellars, one the wine-cellar with a small stair to the hall above. The hall, on the first floor of the main block, has an adjoining withdrawing room. A private chamber in the wing has a vaulted strong-room. The upper floors were occupied by private chambers.

It was a property of the Leslies from the end of 12th century, descended from a Fleming called Bertolf, and Norman de Lesselyn swore fealty to Edward I at Aberdeen in 1294. The property passed by marriage to the Forbeses of Monymusk in the 17th century, and they built or rebuilt the tower in 1661. In 1671 it was sold to the Leiths of Leith Hall. The tower became roofless and ruinous about 1820, but in the 1980s was restored to be reoccupied by a Leslie. The castle was used as a hotel, but has recently been put up for sale – offers over £750,000.
Other refs: Old House of Leslie; Castle of Leslie

Leslie House

Fife: To north of Glenrothes, on minor road south of A911, just north of River Leven, about 0.5 miles east of Leslie, at Leslie House.
Private NO 259019 OS: 59 ** Map: 7, no: 54
Site of castle, nothing of which remains except a vaulted kitchen and cellars. These were incorporated into a 17th-century courtyard mansion, designed by William

Bruce, while the gardens were designed by William Adam in 1731. This mansion was burned down in 1763, and only the west wing was rebuilt in 1765-7 as a three-storey classical mansion. It was remodelled in the 19th century, and again in 1906-7 by Sir Robert Lorimer.

It was a property of the Leslies from the 12th century until the 20th century. The family were made Lord Leslie of Leven in 1445, Earls of Rothes in 1457, then Dukes of Rothes in 1680. Leslie is now a Church of Scotland eventide home.

Other refs: Fettykil; Palace of Leslie

Lesmoir Castle

Aberdeen & Gordon: About 2 miles west of Rhynie, beside A941, south-west of Tap o' Noth, at Mains of Lesmoir.

Ruin or site   NJ 470280   OS: 37   *   Map: 10, no: 103

Very little remains of Lesmoir or Lesmore Castle, a 16th-century stronghold of the Gordons set on a knoll in 13th-century earthworks. The castle was used by Jock o' Scurdargue early in the 15th century. In 1647 the Covenanter General David Leslie captured the castle by draining the wet moat, hanged the garrison in his usual compassionate way, and sacked the castle. It was sold in 1759 to the Grants of Rothiemaise, who dismantled it.

Other refs: Castle of Lesmoir

Lesnoreis *see* Ward of Lochnorris

Lessendrum House

Aberdeen & Gordon: About 3.5 miles east and north of Huntly, on minor roads south of A97, about 1 mile north of Drumblade, at Lessendrum.

Ruin or site   NJ 578415   OS: 29   **   Map: 10, no: 146

Lessendrum, a mansion repaired and enlarged in 1816 and 1837 by Archibald Simpson, incorporates an L-plan 17th-century house. The building may have some work from 1470.

It was a property of the Bissets of Lessendrum, who are one of the oldest families in this part of the country. The present house is ruined and overgrown after a fire in 1928.

Lessudden House

Borders: About 4 miles north-west of Melrose, near A699 junction with A68, on south of St Boswells, at Lessudden.

Private   NT 595306 [?]   OS: 74   **   Map: 2, no: 231

Lessudden House consists of a very altered 16th-century tower house of three storeys and a garret, to which has been added a small 17th-century wing and later work.

The interior of the house has been greatly altered, and the vault removed from the basement kitchen. A 17th-century scale-and-platt staircase climbs to the upper floors in the wing.

The property was owned by the Scotts of Lessudden. The family were persecuted for becoming Quakers, and fined and their children taken from them. Sir Walter Scott was descended from the family. The house is still occupied.

The village of Lessudden, near to St Boswells, formerly had 16 bastle houses, but was burned by the English in 1544 and 1545.

Lethen House

Inverness & Nairn: About 4 miles south-east of Nairn, on minor roads east of A939 or south of A96, north of Muckle Burn, at Lethen House.

Private   NH 937518   OS: 27   *   Map: 9, no: 150

Lethen House, a three-storey mansion with lower wings, is dated 1785, although it was altered in 1790 and 1875. It replaced a house of 1634 or earlier.

Lethen was a property of the Brodies, and the newer house is still occupied by the family. It was torched in 1645 by Royalists as the Brodies were Covenanters, then again in 1680.

Other refs: House of Lethan

Lethendry Castle

South Highland: About 3.5 miles east of Grantown-on-Spey, on minor roads south and east of A95, 1 mile south of Cromdale, in Haughs of Cromdale, at Lethendry.

Ruin or site   NJ 084274   OS: 36   **   Map: 9, no: 159

Lethendry Castle is a ruinous L-plan tower house, which now consists of the vaulted basement and traces of a stair in the wing.

It was a property of the Grants, and seized by Jacobites in 1690.

Lethendy Tower *see* Tower of Lethendy

Lethenty Castle

Aberdeen & Gordon: About 2 miles north of Inverurie, on minor roads east of B9001 or west of B9170, 1 mile north of River Urie, at or near Hillend of Lethenty.

Ruin or site   NJ 764254 [?]   OS: 38   *   Map: 10, no: 245

Site of 17th-century castle, not much of which remains except the basement of a tower.

It was a property of the Skenes, and sacked in 1640 by Covenanters, then again in 1645.

Lethington Castle *see* Lennoxlove

Lethnot Castle *see* Lichnet Castle

Letterfourie

Moray: About 2.5 miles south-east of Buckie, on minor roads south of A98, east of Burn of Buckie, 0.5 miles east of Drybridge, at Letterfourie.

Private   NJ 447625   OS: 28   **   Map: 10, no: 97

Letterfourie, an Adam mansion of 1776, replaced a 16th-century tower house of the Leslies. The later house was a property of the Gordons.

Lettrick Tower

Galloway: About 4.5 miles south of Moniaive, on minor roads west of B729, at or near Lettrick.

Ruin or site   NX 788828   OS: 78   *   Map: 1, no: 128

The mansion may be built on the site of a tower house.

Leuchars Castle

Fife: About 0.5 miles north of Leuchars, east of A92, south of Leuchars Castle (modern), at Castle Knowe.

Ruin or site   NO 454219   OS: 59   *   Map: 7, no: 120

Site of 13th-century castle of enclosure on Castle Knowe.

It was built by the de Quincy family after having passed by marriage from one Ness, son of William, a local laird. It was demolished by Robert the Bruce, but rebuilt in support of Edward Balliol in 1336. It was retaken by the Scots, then appears to have been destroyed. A tower house, built in the 16th century, was demolished in the mid 18th century, and the remains used as a quarry.

The parish church of St Athernase, a fine old building, stands in Leuchars and dates from 1183.

Other refs: Castle Knowe

Leuchars House

Moray: About 3.5 miles north-east of Elgin, on minor road east of B9013, 0.5 miles east of River Leslie, at Leuchars House.

Private   NJ 260649   OS: 28   *   Map: 10, no: 49

Site of 16th-century tower house, although the present house appears to date from no later than the 19th century. The property belonged to Innes of Leuchars.

The house is still occupied.

Leven Castle *see* Castle Levan

Lews Castle

Western Isles: Off A866, W of Stornoway, Lews Castle, Lewis.
Private   NB 419335   OS: 8   *   Map: 11, no: 26**
Lews Castle was built by the Mathesons in the 19th century, on the west side of
Stornoway Harbour. Cnoc na Croich [NB 417323] – 'Gallows Hill' – is traditionally
the site where criminals were executed, and nearby are the remains of a cham-
bered cairn. The pleasant wooded park and gardens have shore, woodland, and
river walks as well as moorland.
OPEN: Castle not open; park open all year.

Leys *see* Loch of Leys

Leys Castle

South Highland: About 3 miles south of Inverness, on minor roads east of B861,
at Leys Castle.
Private   NH 680410   OS: 26   *   Map: 9, no: 97
Leys Castle is a grand castellated mansion, but has no defensive origins.

Ley Tower *see* Lee Tower

Lhanbryde

Moray: About 4 miles east of Elgin, near A96, at or near Lhanbryde.
Ruin or site   NJ 275613 [?]   OS: 28   *   Map: 10, no: 51
Site of castle or old house.

Liberton *see* MacBeth's Castle, Liberton

Liberton House

Lothians: About 3 miles south-east of Edinburgh Castle, just south of Liberton
Drive west of A701, on east side of Braid Hills, just south-east of Liberton Tower.
Private   NT 267694   OS: 66   **   Map: 4, no: 107
Liberton House is a 17th-century L-plan tower house. It consists of a main block of
three storeys and a four-storey wing, with a round stair-tower corbelled-out to square,
at the top, in the re-entrant angle. The walls are pierced by small windows and
gunloops, and are now harled and orange-washed. The house has been much altered over the centuries.
   The basement is not vaulted, and contained a kitchen and bakehouse, as well as
the hall.
   The name Liberton comes from 'leper's town': the leper colony which was once
reputedly located near here. Liberton House was built by William Little, Provost of
Edinburgh, around 1605 to replace nearby Liberton Tower. The house is said to be
haunted, and a photograph taken at the beginning of the century purports to show
the image of an apparition of a man not seen when the photograph was taken.
However, there were countless fakes.
   Public access is restricted to the hall and old kitchen. The garden has also been
restored, and there is a 17th-century doocot by the entrance.
OPEN: Open Mar-Oct, 10.00-16.30 by prior appt only.
Limited parking.
Tel: 0131 467 7777   Fax: 0131 467 7774
Email: mail@nicholas-groves-raines-architects.co.uk

Liberton Tower

Lothians: About 3 miles south-east of Edinburgh Castle, just north of Liberton
Drive west of A701, on east side of Braid Hills, just north-west of Liberton House.
Ruin or site   NT 265697   OS: 66   **   Map: 4, no: 103**
Liberton Tower is a plain 15th-century keep, square in plan, of four storeys with a
stone-flagged pitched roof and a flush parapet.
   The entrance was at first-floor level and was reached by an external stair. The
basement is vaulted, as is the top-most storey. Three straight stairs, with windows
where they turn at the corners, are contained within the thick walls, one leading
down to the basement from the hall, the other two climbing to the private chambers on the floors above.
   The property originally belonged to the Dalmahoy family, but was sold to William
Little, Provost of Edinburgh, in 1587. He built nearby Liberton House, and aban-

doned the castle. The tower is in a good state of preservation, and has recently
been restored.
OPEN: Available for let through Country Cottages in Scotland.
Tel: 0990 851133

Lichnet Castle

Banff & Buchan: About 7 miles east of Macduff, on minor roads north of B9031,
0.5 miles north-east of Gardenstown, north of Lichnet.
Ruin or site   NJ 809653 [?]   OS: 29   *   Map: 10, no: 269
Site of castle.
Other refs: Lethnot Castle; Lighnot Castle

Lickleyhead Castle

Aberdeen & Gordon: About 3 miles south of Insch, on minor road east of B992
just south of Auchleven, south of Gadie Burn, at Lickleyhead.
Private   NJ 627237   OS: 37   **   Map: 10, no: 170**
Lickleyhead Castle is a fine altered 17th-century L-plan tower house of three storeys and a garret, to which has been added newer work. It consists of a main block,
with two round turrets, and an offset projecting wing. A narrow stair-turret, corbelled out to square and crowned by a watch-chamber, rises in one re-entrant angle. The gables are corbiestepped. A wing was added in the 1730s, and the castle
was altered again in 1820.
   The entrance, in the main re-entrant angle, leads to the vaulted basement, containing a kitchen and cellar lit by small slit windows. A wide turnpike stair climbs to
the first floor, the floor above reached by a turnpike stair in the stair-turret.
   Lickleyhead was originally a property of the Leslies, but passed to the Leiths. It
was sold in 1625 to the Forbeses, who built most of the existing castle, although it
probably incorporates earlier work.
   One of the family was William Forbes, who shot off his own hand while firing a
gun. He accepted 5000 merks from the Covenanters to murder Alexander Irvine, a
supporter of Montrose, for which Forbes was eventually tried and executed.
   The property passed to the Hays at the end of the 17th century, then to the Duffs,
Gordons and others, until returning to the Leslies at the beginning of the 19th
century. The house is in good condition and occupied.

Lickprivick Castle

Lanarkshire & Glasgow area: About 1.5 miles south-west of East Kilbride, on
minor roads south of A726, east of B764, near Mossneuk.
Private   NS 616527   OS: 64   *   Map: 3, no: 288
Site of castle, mostly dating from the 17th century, but incorporating a 14th-cen-
tury keep. The castle had towers and battlements, but was ruinous by 1773 and the
remains had been cleared away by 1840. The site is occupied by a housing estate.
   The property was held by the Lickprivick family in the 14th century, and may have
passed to the Maxwells of Calderwood.

Liddel Castle

Borders: About 2.5 miles north and east of Newcastleton, just north of B6357, just south of the Liddel Water.
Ruin or site   NY 510900   OS: 79   *   Map: 2, no: 172
Site of 12th-century castle of enclosure, of which earthworks, dividing off inner and outer courtyards, survive.
  It was a property of the de Soulis family. Edward I visited in 1296 and 1298 during the Wars of Independence. The castle was probably destroyed early in the 14th century and never reused.

Lighnot Castle *see* Lichnet Castle

Lilliesleaf Tower

Borders: About 4.5 miles south-east of Selkirk, near B6359 in the village of Lilliesleaf, south of the Ale Water.
Ruin or site   NT 537253 [?]   OS: 73   *   Map: 2, no: 190
Site of tower house or castle, said to have been two storeys high, one thick wall of which survived at the beginning of the 19th century. There are no remains.
  Lilliesleaf was a property of the Riddel family from the middle of the 12th century until 1823.
Other refs: Easter Lilliesleaf

Lin *see* Lunelly Tower

Lincluden Collegiate Church

Dumfriesshire: About 1 mile north of Dumfries, on minor roads east of A76, just west of the River Nith, at Lincluden.
His Scot   NX 967779   OS: 84   *   Map: 1, no: 186
A nunnery here was founded by Uchtred, son of Fergus, Lord of Galloway, but was converted to a collegiate establishment in 1389 by Archibald the Grim, 3rd Earl of Douglas, as he considered it had fallen into a state of disrepute, disgrace and disrepair. There is a fine stone effigy in a recessed tomb of Margaret, daughter of Robert III and wife of Archibald, 4th Earl of Douglas. The college was dissolved during the Reformation, and part of the domestic buildings of the collegiate church was later fortified. Along with other alterations, a semi-octagonal turret with gunloops was added. Much of the chancel and south transept survive, as does the north range.
  The lands were acquired by Provost Stewart after the Reformation, and he altered the buildings. The property later passed to the Douglases of Drumlanrig, then the Gordons of Lochinvar.
OPEN: Access at all reasonable times.
Disabled access. Parking nearby.
Tel: 0131 668 8800   Fax: 0131 668 8888
Email: hs.explore@scotland.gov.uk   Web: www.historic-scotland.gov.uk

Lindores Castle

Fife: About 2 miles south east of Newburgh, just north of B937, south of Lindores, east of Lindores Loch.
Ruin or site   NO 265168   OS: 59   *   Map: 7, no: 56
Site of 13th-century stone castle, said to be a stronghold of the MacDuff Earls of Fife. It is believed to have been destroyed by Edward I of England in 1300, although there were still some slight remains around 1800.
  Nearby William Wallace defeated an English force, led by the Earl of Pembroke, in 1298.
Other refs: MacDuff's Castle, Lindores

Lindores Castle *see* Old Lindores Castle

Lindsay Tower *see* Crawford Castle

Linlathen House

Angus & Dundee: About 1 mile north of Broughty Ferry, on minor roads north of A92, north of Dighty Water, at or near Linlathen.
Ruin or site   NO 463329 [?]   OS: 54   *   Map: 8, no: 198
Site of castle or old house.
  The property passed to the Grahams of Fintry in the first half of the 17th century,

and they changed the name. It was changed back when it was sold in 1803, and it was a property of the Erskines at the end of the 19th century. The house has apparently been demolished.
Other refs: Fintry House

Linlithgow Palace

Lothians: In Linlithgow, on minor road north of A803, on the south shore of Linlithgow Loch.
His Scot   NT 003774   OS: 65   ***   Map: 4, no: 12**
Once a splendid palace and still a spectacular ruin, Linlithgow Palace consists of ranges of buildings set around a rectangular courtyard, and may include 12th-century work.
  The oldest part of the castle is the hall-block. The original entrance, once defended by a portcullis, leads under the hall and into the courtyard. On one side of the entrance is a guardroom, with a dungeon beneath. This block also contains a well-room and vaulted kitchen, with a fireplace and oven, and a wine-cellar.
  The first floor was occupied by the fine hall, with a minstrels gallery and a fine Renaissance fireplace, as well as private chambers.
  The present entrance, through a later block, has a small turreted gatehouse. The basement of this block is vaulted. A chapel, on the first floor, has canopied niches, which once contained statues.
  On the side of the courtyard opposite the hall-block are the King's private chambers, one of which has a fine fireplace.
  The range, opposite the present entrance, was rebuilt in the 17th century. The basement contains six chambers, and the first floor was occupied by a hall with two large fireplaces.
  Stair-towers, within the courtyard, lead to all floors and to the battlements, which run all round. There is a fine carved fountain in the courtyard.
  There was a 12th-century castle here, which was captured and strengthened by Edward I of England in 1301 during the Wars of Independence, then known as the Peel of Linlithgow. It was slighted, after being retaken by the Scots by driving a cart under the portcullis, and remained a ruin until about 1350. It was repaired by David II, then mostly rebuilt by James I at the beginning of the 15th century. It became a favourite residence of the kings of Scots, and the work continued under James III and James IV. Mary, Queen of Scots, was born here in 1542.
  After the Union of the Crowns in 1603 the palace was left in charge of a keeper. It was last used by Charles I in 1633 although his son, James, Duke of York, stayed here before succeeding to the throne as James VII in 1685. In the 1650s Cromwell had garrisoned the palace. It was also visited by Queen Anne with her father in the 1680s, Bonnie Prince Charlie in 1745 and the Duke of Cumberland. In 1746 General Hawley retreated here after being defeated by the Jacobites at the nearby Battle of Falkirk. The soldiers started fires to dry themselves, and the palace was accidentally set blaze. It was never restored.
  The palace is said to be haunted by a 'Blue Lady', who walks from the entrance of the palace to the door of the nearby parish church of St Michael.
  Queen Margaret's bower, at the top of one of the stair-towers, is reputed to be

haunted by the ghost of either Margaret Tudor, wife of James IV, or Mary of Guise, wife of James V.

It was in the parish church that a blue-robed apparition is said to have warned James IV not to march into England – but the King ignored the warning, invaded England, and was killed at the disastrous Battle of Flodden in 1513.

Other refs: Peel of Linlithgow

OPEN: Open all year: Apr-Sep, daily 9.30-18.30; Oct-Mar, Mon-Sat 9.30-16.40, Sun 14.00-16.30; last ticket sold 30 mins before closing; closed 25/26 Dec and 1/2 Jan.

Explanatory panels and exhibition. Gift shop. WC. Picnic area. Disabled access. Car parking. Group concessions. £.

Tel: 01506 842896

Email: hs.explore@scotland.gov.uk Web: www.historic-scotland.gov.uk

Linnbridgeford

Dumfriesshire: About 5 miles north-east of Ecclefechan, on minor roads east of B722, at or near West Linnbridgeford

Ruin or site NY 266793 OS: 85 * Map: 1, no: 281

Site of tower house.

Other refs: West Linnbridgeford

Linnhouse

Lothians: About 2.5 miles east of West Calder, on minor road between B7008 and A71, west of the Morton Reservoir, just west of the Linnhouse Water.

Private NT 062630 OS: 65 *** Map: 4, no: 29

Linnhouse consists of a 16th-century L-plan tower house of three storeys, the wing rising a storey higher. To this was added a second L-plan building in the 17th century, making the house E-plan. A stair-turret is crowned by a corbelled-out watch-chamber. The building is dated 1589, although there may have been an older castle on the site.

The original entrance was in the re-entrant angle, although it is now a window, and led to the vaulted basement of the wing and to a turnpike stair. The basement of the main block contains the kitchen, but is not vaulted. The hall was on the first floor, and there were many private chambers on the floors above.

The tower was probably built by Francis Tennant, Provost of Edinburgh, in 1571. He was taken prisoner fighting for Mary, Queen of Scots. It passed to the Muirheads about 1631, who sold it in 1767. It is still occupied.

Linthill House

Borders: About 1.5 miles south-west of Eyemouth, north of B6355, near confluence of Eye and Ale Waters, at Old Linthill.

Private NT 937628 OS: 67 *** Map: 2, no: 360

Linthill is an altered 17th-century L-plan tower house of three storeys and a garret. A square tower, in the re-entrant angle, rises a storey higher to be crowned by a watch-chamber. The roof is very steep and has corbiestepped gables.

The old entrance, now sealed, was in the foot of the stair-tower, but the current entrance is at the first-floor level, reached by an external stone stair. The basement is not vaulted, but contained the original kitchen. A scale-and-platt stair climbs to the upper floors. The hall, on the first floor of the main block, has been subdivided, and much of the interior has been altered.

Linthill was a property of the Homes. In 1752 the widow of Patrick Home of Linthill was brutally murdered by her servant, Norman Ross. He was executed and is the last man in Scotland to be mutilated and hung in a gibbet afterwards. The house is still occupied.

Linton Tower

Borders: About 6.5 miles south-east of Kelso, near parish church from B6436, at Linton.

Ruin or site NT 774262 [?] OS: 74 * Map: 2, no: 311

Site of tower house.

The property belonged to the Somervilles from the 12th century. The tower was torched by the English in 1523, and destroyed by the Duke of Somerset's forces about 1547. The Linton worm or dragon is said to have been defeated by Sir John Somerville, who was knighted because of this feat of beast slaying.

Lintrose House

Angus & Dundee: About 2 miles south of Coupar Angus, on minor road south of A923, about 0.5 miles east of Campmuir, at Lintrose.

Private NO 225379 OS: 53 ** Map: 8, no: 125

Lintrose House, a large modern mansion, incorporates part of a 16th-century castle, called Fodderance, of the Halyburtons. The property later passed to the Murrays.

Other refs: Fodderance

Lion's Round, Dundee *see* Dundee Castle

Little Brighouse *see* Bridge Castle

Little Clyde

Lanarkshire & Glasgow: About 2.5 miles east of Elvanfoot, on minor roads east of M74, north west of remains of Roman camp, at Little Clyde.

Ruin or site NS 993160 OS: 78 * Map: 3, no: 436

Site of a strong rectangular tower house, which had been demolished by the middle of the 19th century. It is believed to have stood where the midden of the farm is located.

Little Cumbrae Castle

Ayrshire: On an islet just east of Little Cumbrae Island in the Firth of Clyde, about 4 miles north-west of West Kilbride, about 2 miles from the mainland.

Ruin or site NS 153514 OS: 63 *** Map: 3, no: 16

Little Cumbrae Castle is a ruined 15th-century keep, rectangular in plan, of three storeys and a garret within a corbelled-out parapet with open rounds. The walls are pierced by many shot-holes.

The original entrance is at first-floor level, and is reached by an external stone stair. A later entrance was added at ground level leading into the basement, which contained two cellars. The vaulted hall and kitchen, on the first floor, were divided by a screen. A turnpike stair leads from the ground-floor door and climbs to the second floor, where the chambers were reached by a passage in the thickness of the wall.

It was a property of the Crown, but held by the Hunters of Hunterston until 1515, when Hew Montgomery, Earl of Eglinton, acquired the property following a dispute between the Crown and the Hunters over the ownership of falcons. In the 1650s the 6th Earl imprisoned Archibald Hamilton, a friend of Cromwell, in the castle before sending him to Stirling to be hanged. Cromwell had the castle sacked, and it was never reoccupied.

Little Dean *see* Littledean Tower

Little Endovie *see* Balfluig Castle

Little Hope *see* Broughton Place

Little Peel, Darnick *see* Darnick

Little Rigend Castle *see* Waterhead Castle

Little Sauchie *see* Old Sauchie

Little Swinton

Borders: About 3 miles north of Coldstream, on minor roads south of B6461 or west of A6112, 1 mile south-west of village of Swinton, at or near Little Swinton.

Ruin or site NT 825459 [?] OS: 74 * Map: 2, no: 336

Apparently a castle or bastle here was destroyed in 1482 by an English army under the Duke of Gloucester, as was another at Meikle Swinton (probably Swinton village, although this may refer to Swinton House). The lands were long a property of the Swinton family.

Other refs: Meikle Swinton

Little Tarrel

Ross & Cromarty: About 8 miles east of Tain, on minor road south of B9165, about 2 miles south of Portmahomack, south of Rockfield House, at Little Tarrel.

Private NH 911819 OS: 21 ** Map: 9, no: 143

Little Tarrel is an altered 16th-century L-plan tower house of two storeys and a garret. The walls are pierced by gunloops and shot-holes. The entrance, at first-floor level, is reached by an external stone stair.

The basement has been vaulted, and contained the kitchen with a sealed arched fireplace.

It may have been a property of the Gordon Earl of Huntly or the Munros. The house had become ruinous, but was restored in the 1980s and is occupied.

Other refs: Rockfield Castle

Littledean Tower

Borders: About 6.5 miles west of Kelso, on minor roads north of A699, about 0.5 miles east of Littledean, just south of River Tweed.

Ruin or site NT 633314 OS: 74 ** Map: 2, no: 249

Littledean Tower consists of a 16th-century block, rectangular in plan, of four storeys and an attic, to which was added a large D-plan tower later the same century. The walls are pierced by gunloops. The rectangular block is very ruined, and the D-plan tower is now a shell.

The entrance to the D-plan tower, over which is a small guardroom, leads to a narrow vaulted passage to the vaulted basement. A turnpike stair climbed to the hall, on the first floor, which has a large fireplace. The castle had a courtyard with a curtain wall.

It was a property of the Kerrs, but burned in 1544 by the English, the D-plan tower probably dating from after this. Littledean was the birth place of Dun Scotus, John of Duns, who won renown as an eminent scholar from some – and the name 'dunce' from others.

A ghostly horsemen, the spirit of one of the Kerr lords, is said sometimes to be seen near the castle. A cruel man who scorned his wife and his servants, he is said to have become involved with a witch, whose severed arm is said to have strangled him in his bed.

Other refs: Little Dean

Livingston Peel

Lothians: In Livingston village, near B7015, north of River Almond.

Ruin or site NT 040676 OS: 65 * Map: 4, no: 18

Site of 12th-century castle, little or nothing of which remains. It was surrounded by a wet moat and defended by high ramparts.

It was held by the English in 1302, and against Robert the Bruce in 1313, although by 1314 all castles in Lothian were captured by the Scots. The lands belonged to the Livingstones (or Livingstons), the name coming from one 'Leving' who was mentioned in the 12th century. The family became Earls of Callendar and Linlithgow. A keep or tower house was still complete when it was drawn by Timothy Pont about 1590. It was held by the Murrays, and one of the owners, Sir Patrick Murray of Livingstone, collected plants and formed the basis of the Old Physic Garden, the first botanic garden in Edinburgh. The tower was built by the Cunninghams, but demolished when the property passed to the Primrose Earl of Rosebery in 1812.

Other refs: Peel of Livingston; Livingston House

Loch Alterwall

Sutherland & Caithness: About 6.5 miles south-east of Castleton, by minor roads and foot north of B876, 0.5 miles south-west of Alterwall.

Ruin or site ND 279645 OS: 12 * Map: 12, no: 56

Not much remains of a castle on a former island in loch except a mound. The castle was ruinous by 1726, and the loch drained in the middle of the 19th century.

Other refs: Alterwall

Loch an Duna, Bragar *see* Dun Bragar

Loch an Eilean Castle

South Highland: About 3.5 miles south of Aviemore, on minor roads and boat east of B970, about 1 mile east of Spey River, Rothiemurchus estate, in Loch an Eilean.

Ruin or site NH 899079 OS: 36 ** Map: 9, no: 140

Loch an Eilean Castle consists of a ruined 14th-century keep, hall block, and other buildings enclosed by a small courtyard. It was modified in later centuries.

The castle was probably built by Alexander Stewart, the Wolf of Badenoch, who

obtained the Earldom of Ross by forcing the widowed heiress, Euphemia, to marry him. They lived apart, and when the Bishop of Moray criticised Alexander and then excommunicated him, he retaliated in 1390 by burning Forres, and the town and cathedral of Elgin.

The castle was later held by the Mackintoshes, then the Gordons, then apparently a property of the Grants in 1567. It was attacked by the Jacobites after their defeat in Cromdale in 1690, but successfully held out. It was last used in 1715 when Mackintosh of Balnespick was confined here to prevent him opposing the Jacobites.

Other refs: Lochaneilean Castle; An Eilean Castle

Loch an Sgoltaire Castle

Argyll & Dunbartonshire: On island of Colonsay about 2 miles north of Scalasaig, on minor road and boat north of A870, north-west of Kiloran, on island in Loch an Sgoltaire.

Ruin or site NR 386972 OS: 61 * Map: 5, no: 11

Considerable remains survive of a castle.

The island was held by the MacDuffies, but passed to the MacDonalds in the 17th century, then to the Campbell Dukes of Argyll. It was acquired by the MacNeils about 1700.

The well-preserved priory on the adjoining island of Oronsay contains several stone effigies and a sculpted cross.

Other refs: Loch Sgoltaire

Loch Avich *see* Caisteal na Nighinn Ruaidhe

Loch a' Phearsain

Argyll & Dunbartonshire: About 0.5 miles north-east of Kilmelford, on minor road, foot and boat east of A816, on an island to the south of Loch a' Phearsain.

Ruin or site NM 855135 OS: 55 * Map: 5, no: 69

The island was fortified and encircled by a wall, which enclosed several buildings. It was occupied at the end of the 17th century. It may have been used by a bandit called MacPherson, hence the name.

Loch Beanie

Perth & Kinross: About 3.5 miles east of Spittal of Glenshee, on minor road and track east of A93 at Dalhenzean, on island in Loch Beanie.

Ruin or site NO 160686 OS: 43 * Map: 8, no: 106

A residence of the laird of Gleenshee and Strathardle stood on a crannog.

Loch Bradan Castle *see* Bradan Castle

Loch Brora

Sutherland & Caithness: About 3.5 miles north-west of Brora, on minor roads and boat north of A9, on island, Eilean nan Faoileag, south end of Loch Brora.
Ruin or site   NC 856060 OS: 17   *   Map: 12, no: 30
Site of castle, a hunting seat of the Earls of Sutherland.

Loch Dochart Castle

Stirlingshire & Clackmannan: About 11 miles west and south of Killin, just (by boat) north of A85, west of Portnellan, on island in Loch Dochart.
Ruin or site   NN 407257 OS: 51   **   Map: 6, no: 4
Loch Dochart Castle is a ruined 16th-century tower house of three stories. It consisted of a main block of two storeys and an attic, with a round tower at one corner. A square tower projects from the middle of the main block, and there are two stairturrets.

The main block housed a hall and private chamber, with private chambers above.

It was built by Sir Duncan Campbell of Glenorchy, Black Duncan of the Castles, between 1585 and 1631, but burned out in 1646. The ruins have been cleared and consolidated.

The castle is traditionally associated with Rob Roy MacGregor.
Other refs: Lochdochart; Isle Castle

Loch Doon Castle

Ayrshire: About 7 miles south of Dalmellington, on minor road 6 miles south of A713 at Dalmellington, on west side of Loch Doon, at Craigmalloch.
His Scot NX 483950 OS: 77   **   Map: 3, no: 200
Loch Doon Castle is a ruined 13th-century courtyard castle, polygonal in plan, which formerly enclosed ranges of buildings, including a 16th-century tower house. The tower house was not rebuilt when the castle was moved, which seems a bit odd.

The castle was built by the Bruce Earls of Carrick, but captured by the English in 1306, Sir Christopher Seton, Robert the Bruce's brother-in-law, being seized after the siege and later hanged at Dumfries. The castle was retaken by the Scots by 1314.

In 1333 it was one of the six strongholds which held out for David II against Edward Balliol. In 1510 Loch Doon was captured from the Kennedys by William Craw-

ford of Lochmores, being gutted by fire, but was restored and reoccupied until abandoned in 17th century. It originally stood on an island in the middle of the loch but, when in 1935 the water level was raised by a hydroelectric scheme, the castle was moved to the present site.
Other refs: Castle Balliol; Balliol's Castle
OPEN: Access at all reasonable times.
Parking.
Tel: 0131 668 8800   Fax: 0131 668 8888
Email: hs.explore@scotland.gov.uk   Web: www.historic-scotland.gov.uk

Loch Dubh Castle *see* Dubh Loch Castle

Loch Earn Castle

Perth & Kinross: Just off shore from St Fillans, by boat west of A85 at St Fillans, on island at extreme end of Loch Earn.
Ruin or site NN 690243 OS: 51   **   Map: 8, no: 6
Loch Earn Castle, a ruined but once strong fortress, was a property of the MacNeishes from about 1250 to 1420, then occasionally afterwards.

After the clan had been defeated at the Battle of Glenboltachan, the remnant of the MacNeishes survived by plundering the surrounding area from the island. The MacNabs, however, slew the chief of the MacNeishes and most of his folk, having crossed the mountains with a boat to get them out to the island. The MacNabs then used MacNeish's head (a depiction of it, anyway) as their heraldic crest.

The island was later used by the Ardvorlich family as a residence.
Other refs: Ellanrayne Castle; Neish Island

Loch Eil *see* Eilean nan Craobh

Loch Gorm Castle *see* Gorm Castle

Loch Goul, Bishop's Palace *see* Bishop's Palace, Loch Goul

Loch Heylipol Castle *see* Castle Loch Heylipol

Loch Doon Castle – see above

Loch Kinellan

Inverness & Nairn: About 1 mile west of Strathpeffer, on minor roads and boat north of A834 at Kinellan Farm, on (manmade) island in Loch Kinellan.

Ruin or site   NH 472576   OS: 26   **   Map: 9, no: 53

Site of stronghold of the Mackenzies of Seaforth on a crannog in the loch.

  Robert the Bruce is said to have visited William 4th Earl of Ross here, although his wife and womenfolk had been delivered up to the English by the Earl. The Earldom of Ross passed into the control of the MacDonald Lord of the Isles, but the Mackenzies of Seaforth supported the Stewart kings in defeating the MacDonalds, and gained much of their lands. The island was held by the Mackenzies, and in 1494 the widow of Kenneth Mackenzie was kidnapped from the island by a band of Munros. They were pursued and slaughtered near Castle Leod.

  One story associated Kinellan is that the then Earl of Ross sent his wife, Margaret, back to John MacDonald, Lord of the Isles, her brother. Margaret happened to have one eye, and the Earl had her accompanied by a one-eyed horse, a one-eyed servant, and one-eyed dog. Angering the Lord of the Isles in this way would not seem very sensible, although there is a very similar tale from Duntulm on Skye, where the lady was a MacLeod and her husband a MacDonald.

Other refs: Kinellan

Loch Kinord Castle

Kincardine & Deeside: About 4.5 miles west of Aboyne, on minor road and boat, east of A97 or west of B9119, on island in Loch Kinord.

Ruin or site   NO 440996   OS: 44   *   Map: 10, no: 93

Site of castle, on the western-most island, a property of the Gordons of Huntly in the 16th century.

  In 1335 it was occupied by the supporters of Edward Balliol, including the Earl of Atholl, after they had been defeated at the Battle of Culbean by the Regent, Andrew Moray, but they soon surrendered. The castle was visited by James IV in 1505, but besieged and captured by the Covenanter General David Leslie in 1647. It was restored but was razed by an order of parliament soon afterwards, probably in 1648.

Other refs: Castle of Kinord; Kinord Castle

Loch Laggan Castle

South Highland: About 11 miles east and north of Tulloch Station, by boat south of A86, on island in Loch Laggan, 1.5 miles east of Aberarder.

Ruin or site   NN 498875   OS: 34   *   Map: 9, no: 55

Site of castle of the Macphersons, some remains of which survive. The building is said to have been a hunting lodge for the early Kings of Scots, and the nearby island is called Eilean nan Con ('island of dogs'). The building was burned at some time.

  The mansion house of Ardverikie [NN 508876], which was built in 1840 by the Hamilton Marquis of Abercorn, stands on the south side of Loch Laggan. It was visited by Queen Victoria in 1847, passed to the Ramsdens, and mostly destroyed by fire in 1873. The house was used in the BBC series 'Monarch of the Glen'. A mound in the grounds is said to mark the site of the burial places of Fergus and four other kings.

Other refs: King Fergus's Hunting Lodge; Ardverikie

Loch Leven Castle *see* Lochleven Castle

Loch Maberry Castle

Galloway: About 5.5 miles south-east of Barrhill, in loch south of B7027, on island nearer west side of Loch Maberry.

Ruin or site   NX 286752   OS: 76   *   Map: 1, no: 39

Site of 12th- or 13th-century castle of enclosure, which consisted of an oval courtyard enclosing ranges of buildings. The walls survives to a height of six feet or so in places, and enclosed the island near the water's edge. A causeway apparently linked the island with another to the south, then to the shore.

  It is said that lepers were brought here by monks from Glenluce Abbey.

Loch Maree *see* Isle Maree

Loch Maree *see* Eilean Ghruididh

Loch na Sreinge

Argyll & Dunbartonshire: About 5 miles north-west of Dalavich, on minor roads west of B840, on an island in Loch na Sreinge.

Ruin or site   NM 926170   OS: 55   *   Map: 5, no: 85

Site of castle, which was used by bandits.

Loch nan Clachan Dun

Western Isles: About 2.5 miles west of Sollas, by foot and boat just south of A865, Loch nan Clachan, North Uist.

Ruin or site   NF 768738   OS: 18   **   Map: 11, no: 7

The remains of a choked and overgrown dun, on an island in the loch, which was connected to the mainland by a causeway. The island is marked on Blaeu's Atlas Novus map as 'Ylen Dunikrannil', and therefore would appear to have been occupied at the end of the 16th century.

Other refs: Dunikrannil; Eilean Dunic Raonuill

Loch of Leys

Kincardine & Deeside: About 1 mile north of Banchory, east of A980, at or near Lochead of Leys.

Ruin or site   NO 700980 [?]   OS: 45   *   Map: 10, no: 209

Site of castle of the Burnets from the early 14th century on an island in a now drained loch. Alexander Burnet of Leys married Janet Hamilton in 1543, and acquired a sizeable dowry of church lands. With this new wealth, they built Crathes Castle and abandoned Leys.

  The castle was reputedly haunted. Alexander Burnet fell in love with Bertha, a relative who was staying at the castle. His mother, Agnes, wanted a more advantageous match for her son and poisoned Bertha. Agnes was apparently frightened to death by a spectre of Bertha, and a ghost is said to still appear on the anniversary of Bertha's death.

Other refs: Leys

Loch Ranza Castle *see* Lochranza Castle

Loch Ronald

Galloway: About 5 miles north-east of Glenluce, on minor roads and foot north of A75, Loch Ronald.

Ruin or site   NX 267643 [?]   OS: 82   *   Map: 1, no: 38

Possible site of a castle, near to the east side of Loch Ronald. There are some remains of a building at Woodhill.

Other refs: Woodhill

Loch Rusky *see* Rusky Castle

Loch Rutton

Dumfriesshire: About 4.5 miles south-west of Dumfries, on minor road and boat south of A75 at Drummore, south of Lochfoot, on island in Lochrutton Loch.

Ruin or site   NX 898730   OS: 84   *   Map: 1, no: 172

Site of hall house, which was used from the 13th to the 17th centuries, built on a crannog.

Loch Sgolitaire *see* Loch an Sgoltaire Castle

Loch Sguabain Castle

Argyll & Dunbartonshire: About 9.5 miles south-west of Craignure, by foot and boat south of A849, on crannog in Loch Sguabain, Mull.

Ruin or site   NM 631307   OS: 49   *   Map: 5, no: 22

On a small island at the north end of Loch Sguabain is a fortified island, possibly a crannog, occupied into the 16th century or later. A wall encloses the island, and survives to a height of four feet. This island is traditionally the home of Ewen of the Little Head whose headless ghost is said to ride a horse down Glen Mor when one of the MacLaines of Lochbuie is near death. The island residence was the reason for the conflict with his father: the house was too humble for his wife – always blame a woman! Also see Moy Castle.

Other refs: Caisteal Eoghainn a' Chinn Bhig

Loch Slin Castle

Ross & Cromarty: About 4.5 miles east of Tain, on minor roads north of B9165, east of Loch Eye, about 0.5 miles east of Lochslin village.
Ruin or site   NH 849806   OS: 21   *   Map: 9, no: 130
Loch Slin Castle consists of the ruinous remains of an L-plan castle, made up of two towers which adjoined at one corner with a stair, and outbuildings. It incorporates work from the 14th century. There were considerable remains at the end of the 19th century, and the castle stood some 60-feet high.
  It was held by the Munros in the 17th century, then the Mackenzies.
Other refs: Lochslin Castle

Loch Stack Castle

Sutherland & Caithness: About 7 miles east of Scourie, by boat north of A838, on island in Loch Stack.
Ruin or site   NC 275434 [?]   OS: 9   *   Map: 12, no: 4
Site of castle, a residence of the Mackays of Reay.

Loch Strom Castle *see* Strom Castle

Loch Tromlee

Argyll & Dunbartonshire: About 1.5 miles north of Kilchrenan, by boat and minor road east of B845, on island in Loch Tromlee.
Ruin or site   NN 044249   OS: 50   *   Map: 5, no: 100
Not much remains of a square tower, said to date from the 16th century, on an island in the loch. It was a property of the MacCorquodales of Phantilands, who were said to be descended from one Thorkil in the time of Kenneth MacAlpin. Thorkil is said to have retrieved the severed head of Alpin, Kenneth's father and king of the Dalriadan Scots, from the Picts. The MacCorquodales were described in 1612 as 'notorious thieves and supporters of Clan Gregour [the MacGregors]'. The castle was sacked by Alasdair Colkitto MacDonald in 1646.
Other refs: Eilean Tighe Bhainn

Lochaneilean Castle *see* Loch an Eilean Castle

Lochar Tower *see* Isle Tower

Lochbuie *see* Moy Castle

Lochcote Tower

Lothians: About 2.5 miles south-west of Linlithgow, on minor road east of A706, just over 1 mile north and east of Torphichen, just north of Lochcote Reservoir.
Ruin or site   NS 976737   OS: 65   **   Map: 4, no: 8
Little remains of a 16th-century tower house, formerly of four storeys with bartizans, and a courtyard with ranges of buildings, except one angle tower. The tower is vaulted, and was used as a doocot.
  It was a property of the Crawfords.

Lochdochart *see* Loch Dochart Castle

Lochend House

Lothians: About 1.5 miles east of Edinburgh Castle, between Calton Hill and Holyrood Park, on minor road south of A1.
Private   NT 273743   OS: 66   **   Map: 4, no: 115
Lochend House incorporates a much-altered 16th-century castle, considerably reduced in size, to which a more modern house has been added. The old part consists of an L-plan block of three storeys, with a steeply pitched roof.
  Although the interior has been completely altered, the thick walls still contain a number of aumbries, and there are the remains of a huge fireplace, in which a whole ox could have been roasted.
  The lands of Restalrig belonged to the Lestalric family in the 13th century, but passed by marriage to the Logans early in the 14th century. They remained with them until their forfeiture around 1601 for their part in the Gowrie Conspiracy against James VI, and the castle was burned by William Gilmour of the Inch. Sir

Robert Logan, the last of the family to hold the property, is said to have buried treasure at Fast Castle in Berwickshire [NT 862710].
  The lands were acquired by Arthur Elphinstone, 6th Lord Balmerino, in 1704, but he was executed in London for his part in the Jacobite Rising after being captured at the Battle of Culloden in 1746. The house is still occupied.
Other refs: Restalrig Castle

Lochfergus

Galloway: About 1 mile east of Kirkcudbright, on minor road just north of B727, at Lochfergus.
Ruin or site   NX 699511 [?]   OS: 84   *   Map: 1, no: 114
Very little remains of a 12th-century castle of Fergus, Lord of Galloway, which stood on an island in the now drained loch. A later castle of the MacLellans of Bombie was burned in 1499.
Other refs: Castle Fergus

Lochhead Castle

Argyll & Dunbartonshire: South of Campbeltown, on minor roads south of A83, to west of Campbeltown Loch, at Castlehill Church.
Ruin or site   NR 718202   OS: 68   *   Map: 5, no: 37
Site of castle, which is occupied by Castlehill Church. It was a property of Archibald Campbell, 7th Earl of Argyll, and built in 1609. This presumably replaced Kilkerran Castle [NR 729194] and Moil Castle [NR 725210].
Other refs: Campbeltown

Lochhouse Tower

Dumfriesshire: About 1 mile south of Moffat, on minor road just south of A701, just west of Roman Road, about 0.5 miles north of Evan Water.
Private   NT 082034   OS: 78   ***   Map: 1, no: 220
Lochhouse Tower is a strong 16th-century tower house of three storeys and an attic, formerly within a corbelled-out parapet. The tower is rectangular in plan, and has rounded corners. There are several gunloops.
  The original entrance led to a turnpike stair, in one corner, and into the vaulted basement. The interior has been greatly altered.
  It was a property of the Johnstones of Corehead in the 16th and 17th centuries. It was restored about 1980, and is still occupied.

Lochinch Castle *see* Castle Kennedy

Lochindorb Castle

South Highland: About 6.5 miles north-west of Grantown-on-Spey, on minor road and boat west of A939, north-east of Lochindorb Lodge, on island in Lochindorb.
Ruin or site   NH 974364   OS: 27   **   Map: 9, no: 154
Meaning the 'loch of trouble' in Gaelic, Lochindorb Castle is a ruined 13th-century stronghold of enclosure with round corner towers, occupying all the island. There are traces of a hall block, chapel and other buildings within the courtyard.
  It was a property of the Comyns. The castle was occupied by the English during the Wars of Independence, and Edward I of England visited in 1303. It was held again for the English in 1335 when Andrew Moray the Regent besieged it unsuccessfully, and had to withdraw before a large army led by Edward III.
  The castle was then used as a prison. At the end of the 14th century it was a property of Alexander Stewart, the Wolf of Badenoch. Lochindorb passed to the

Douglas Earls of Moray, who strengthened it, but was dismantled after their fall in 1455, and not reused. The iron yett was taken to Cawdor Castle. Substantial remains survived at the end of the 18th century.

The property passed to the Stewart Earls of Moray, then was sold to the Campbells of Cawdor in 1606, who sold it to the Ogilvie Earl of Seafield in 1750.

During investigation of the castle and island, five granite balls were found, which had probably been cast here by a trebuchet during a siege.

OPEN: View from exterior (from shore of loch).

Lochinvar Castle

Galloway: About 3.5 miles north-east of St John's Town of Dalry, on minor road 2 miles north of A702, on islet in Lochinvar.

Ruin or site   NX 656853   OS: 77   *   Map: 1, no: 107

Lochinvar Castle consists of the ruins of a rectangular keep or tower, and traces of other buildings. The island appears now to be submerged after the water level was raised.

The lands of Lochinvar were originally held by the Balliol Lords of Galloway, but passed to the Gordons in 1297, who had a castle here until at least 1640. In the 16th century the Gordons of Lochinvar removed to their larger castle of Kenmure. A Gordon of Lochinvar murdered MacLellan of Bombie in Edinburgh's High Street in 1527. The Lochinvar branch of the family became Viscounts Kenmure in 1633.

Lochleven Castle

Perth & Kinross: About 1 mile east of Kinross, on minor roads and ferry east of B996, on Castle Island in Loch Leven.

His Scot   NO 138018   OS: 58   *   Map: 8, no: 93**

Lochleven Castle consists of a small 15th-century keep, rectangular in plan, of five storeys, standing at one corner of a 14th-century courtyard. A corbelled-out para-

pet, with three open rounds, crowns the keep. The courtyard has a small round tower, with gunloops, at one corner, and the entrance is through an arched gateway. The courtyard enclosed ranges of buildings, including a hall and kitchen, but these are very ruinous. The castle used to occupy most of the island, but the level of the loch has been lowered.

The original entrance to the keep was at second-floor level, from an external stair, and leads to the hall through a hooded arch. A turnpike stair leads down to the vaulted kitchen on the first floor. The basement is also vaulted, but has a modern entrance. The chamber above the hall has an oratory, with altar-shelf and piscina.

Lochleven was a royal castle from 1257, and stormed by William Wallace after being captured by the English. The English besieged the castle in 1301, but it was relieved by Sir John Comyn before it could be captured. It was visited by Robert the Bruce. The castle was held again against Edward Balliol and the English in 1335. By the end of the 14th century it had passed to the Douglases of Lochleven. Mary, Queen of Scots, was held here from 1567 until she escaped in 1568, during which time she signed her abdication – her ghost is said to haunt the castle. The property

passed to the Bruces, then the Grahams, and the Montgomerys, and was taken into State care in 1939.

Other refs: Loch Leven Castle

OPEN: Open Apr-Sep, daily 9.30-18.30; last ticket 18.00 – includes boat trip from Kinross.

Gift shop. WC. Picnic area. Car parking at Kinross. £.

Tel: 01786 450000

Email: hs.explore@scotland.gov.uk   Web: www.historic-scotland.gov.uk

Lochloy Castle

Inverness & Nairn: About 3 miles east of Nairn, on minor roads north of A96, about 1 mile south of the sea, south of Loch Loy, at or near Lochloy.

Ruin or site   NH 926578 [?]   OS: 27   *   Map: 9, no: 146

Site of castle of the Hays. William Hay of Lochloy, who died in 1470, is buried in Elgin Cathedral.

Lochmaben Castle

Dumfriesshire: About 0.5 miles south of Lochmaben, on minor road east of B7020, just south of Castle Loch (Nature Reserve).

His Scot   NY 088812   OS: 78   **   Map: 1, no: 224

Once an important and powerful castle, Lochmaben Castle consists of a complex of very ruined buildings, dating in part from the 13th century, with a 15th-century keep and later additions. It had a strong curtain wall, and was surrounded by a moat.

An older castle, of which only a motte survives, may be where Robert Bruce, later Robert I, King of Scots, was born (see following entry). In 1298 Edward I of England

chose this stronger site to build a castle. The castle was strengthened after being besieged by Robert the Bruce in 1299, and it was attacked again by the Scots in 1301. It was seized by Bruce in 1306, recovered by the English, but finally surrendered to the Scots after the Battle of Bannockburn in 1314.

It was held by the English from 1333 until 1384 when it was taken by Archibald the Grim, the Douglas Lord of Galloway. In 1410 the Maxwells were made hereditary keepers. It was acquired by James II after he destroyed the Black Douglases in

1455, and in 1542 it was where the Scottish army was mustered by James V before going on to defeat at Solway Moss.

Mary, Queen of Scots, and Darnley attended a banquet here in 1565. In 1588 James VI besieged and captured the castle from the Maxwells. The castle was abandoned around 1603, and became ruinous to be robbed of much stone in the 18th century.

OPEN: Access at all reasonable times – view from exterior.
Car parking
Tel: 0131 668 8800 Fax: 0131 668 8888
Email: hs.explore@scotland.gov.uk Web: www.historic-scotland.gov.uk

Lochmaben Castle

Dumfriesshire: Just south of Lochmaben, west of A709 at junction with B7020, between Kirk Loch and Castle Loch, on north of golf course.
Ruin or site NY 082822 OS: 78 * Map: 1, no: 219
Site of 13th-century castle of enclosure, of which only a motte remains.

It was the chief stronghold of the Bruce Lords of Annandale and may be where Robert the Bruce, later Robert I, King of Scots, was born. In 1298, during the Wars of Independence, Edward I of England built a new castle of Lochmaben nearby, and the old castle was abandoned.

Lochmodie Castle

Ayrshire: About 4 miles south and west of Maybole, near B741, 0.5 miles north of Dailly, north of Water of Girvan, at Lochmodie.
Ruin or site NS 263024 OS: 76 * Map: 3, no: 56
Little remains of a castle except one upstand of masonry, materials from which are believed to have been used to build Dalquharran Castle.
Other refs: Old Dalruharran

Lochnaw Castle

Galloway: About 4.5 miles north-west of Stranraer, on minor road south of B7043, at the south end of Loch Naw, at Lochmodie.
Private NW 991628 OS: 82 * Map: 1, no: 3**
Lochnaw Castle consists of a small 16th-century tower house, square in plan, of four storeys and a garret. It was extended by a three-storey wing in the 17th century, making it L-plan. In the 18th century it was enlarged again, making it a U-plan, although this part has been demolished, as has an adjoining mansion of 1822. The

tower has a corbiestepped gabled roof, and a high machiolated parapet, with open rounds at three corners, and a caphouse and watch-chamber above the stair.

The basement of the tower is vaulted, and has a turnpike stair in one corner. The tower has been altered inside, but still has the original moulded fireplaces and painted beams.

An older castle on an island in Lochnaw was destroyed by Archibald the Grim, Earl of Douglas and Lord of Galloway, in 1390. The Agnews of Lochnaw had been made keepers of the castle in 1360, and built the existing stronghold. Andrew Agnew of Lochnaw was killed at the Battle of Pinkie in 1547. The castle was sold by the Agnews, but bought back in 1957, and is still occupied. The Agnews are buried in the kirkyard of the old church at Leswalt [NX 015637].

Lochnaw Castle

Galloway: About 4 miles west and north of Stranraer, south of B7043, on island in Lochnaw, about 0.25 miles north of 16th-century Lochnaw Castle.
Ruin or site NW 994633 OS: 82 * Map: 1, no: 5
Little survives of a 14th-century keep and castle except the basement. The castle was probably dismantled in 1426 when a new castle was built nearby.

The castle existed by 1363 when David II made the Agnews keepers. In 1390 Archibald the Grim, Earl of Douglas and Lord of Galloway, captured and destroyed the castle. The Agnews later recovered the property in 1426, and built another castle nearby. However, the site appears to have been reused, and was occupied in the 16th and early 17th centuries, including by an Andrew McKracken at one time.

Lochnell House

Argyll & Dunbartonshire: About 6 miles north of Oban, on minor roads west of A828, on north side of Ardmucknish Bay, at Lochnell.
Private NM 887390 OS: 49 ** Map: 5, no: 76
Lochnell House, a later mansion incorporates part of a castle in one wing. It was built by the Campbell family, suffered a serious fire about 1859, and only part restored. It is now held by the Cochrane Earl of Dundonald.

The house is said to have had a brownie, and ghostly music has reportedly been heard here.

Lochore Castle

Fife: About 3 miles north of Cowdenbeath, near minor road west of B920, south of the village of Lochore, east of Loch Ore, in Lochore County Park.
Ruin or site NT 175959 OS: 58 ** Map: 7, no: 29
Lochore Castle consists of the ruins of a 14th-century keep, formerly of four storeys, and castle on a motte, originally on an island in a loch. The castle had a courtyard, enclosing ranges of buildings, with round corner towers.

The island was known as Inchgall – 'isle of strangers' – and the motte constructed by Duncan of Lochore. The property passed to the Valances before 1296, who extended the castle, then built the keep in the 14th century. In 1547 the castle was described by the English as one of 'the four strongest castles in Fife'. The property passed to the Wardlaws of Torrie, then in 1656 it was acquired the Malcolms of Balbedie. The area was devastated by mining, but landscaped as part of one of the largest operations of its kind in the UK and is now a park. The loch was drained towards the end of the 18th century.
Other refs: Inchgall Castle; Castle of Inchgall
OPEN: Park: open Apr-Sep, daily 9.00-19.30; Oct-Mar, daily 9.00-17.00.
Park: Visitor centre. Explanatory displays. Cafe. Picnic areas. WC. Play area. Walks. Activities. Disabled access. Car and coach parking.
Tel: 01592 414300

Lochorwart _see_ Borthwick Castle

Lochraig _see_ Asknish House

Lochranza Castle

Ayrshire: About 10 miles north and east of Brodick on northern end of isle of Arran, on minor roads just north of A841, on south shore of Loch Ranza, at Lochranza.
His Scot NR 933507 OS: 69 * Map: 3, no: 1**
Lochranza Castle is a ruined L-plan tower house, remodelled in the 16th century, although it incorporates much of a 13th or 14th century hall house. The main block is of three storeys and an attic, while the wing rose two storeys higher and was capped by a watch-tower. A bartizan crowned one corner, and there is a machiolated projection, over the entrance, at parapet level.

The entrance led to a turnpike stair, which climbed to all floors, as did a smaller stair in the thickness of the walls. The basement of the main block is vaulted, and contained the kitchen and a cellar, but other parts are not vaulted. A small stair, in the thickness of the wall, climbed to the hall, but has been sealed up. The hall has a raised dais.

Lochranza was used as a hunting lodge by the kings of Scots, and is said to have been used by Robert the Bruce. The castle may have been built by the Stewarts of

Lochranza Castle – see previous page and below

Menteith, the MacDonald Lord of the Isles or the Campbells, who appear to have held the property in 1315. It passed to the Montgomerys, later Earls of Eglinton, in 1452. James IV used it as a base to attack the MacDonald Lords of the Isles in the 1490s, and it was occupied by the forces of James VI in 1614 and Cromwell in the 1650s. In 1705 it was sold to Anne, Duchess of Hamilton, but it had been abandoned by the end of the 18th century. The property was sold again recently.

Other refs: Loch Ranza Castle

OPEN: Key available from Post Office/local shop.

Car parking.

Tel: 0131 668 8800   Fax: 0131 668 8888

Email: hs.explore@scotland.gov.uk   Web: www.historic-scotland.gov.uk

Lochslin Castle *see* Loch Slin Castle

Lochtower

Borders: About 5.5 miles south-east of Kelso, on minor road south of B6352, 1 mile west of Town Yetholm, Lochtower, on an island in Yetholm Loch.

Ruin or site   NT 805282   OS: 74   *   Map: 2, no: 328

Site of tower house, on an island reached by a causeway in Yetholm Loch, remains of which survived until the latter part of the 19th century.

It was a property of the Kerrs, and was torched – along with many other towers in the area – by the English under the Earl of Surrey in 1523. Walter Scott used the then ruin and surrounding area as 'Avenel Castle' in the 'Monastery'.

Other refs: Yetholm Loch

Lochwood *see* Bishop's House, Lochwood

Lochwood Tower

Dumfriesshire: About 6 miles south of Moffat, on minor road west of B7020 and east of A701, at Lochwood.

Ruin or site   NY 085968   OS: 78   **   Map: 1, no: 222

Lochwood Tower, once a strong castle, is a ruined 16th-century L-plan tower house, and incorporates work from the 15th century. A courtyard contained ranges of buildings, including the kitchen, enclosed by a wall.

The entrance to the tower was in the wing, and led to a wide turnpike stair. The basement was vaulted, but not much remains above this level, although the hall would have been on the first floor of the main block, with private chambers above.

Lochwood was the main stronghold of the Johnstones, who had held the property from the 14th century. The castle was captured by the English in 1547, and held by them until 1550. In 1585 the tower was burned by the Maxwells and Armstrongs during a feud. The castle was rebuilt, but abandoned around 1724. The family became Earls of Hartfell in 1643, Earls of Annandale in the 1660s, then Marquises of Annandale in 1701. James VI is reputed to have said of its builder: 'however honest he might have been in outward appearance, he must have been a rogue at heart'. The ruins of the castle have been consolidated.

Lockerbie Tower

Dumfriesshire: In Lockerbie, on minor roads west of B723, by the main street.

Ruin or site   NY 136815   OS: 78   *   Map: 1, no: 243

Site of 16th-century tower house(s), little or nothing of which remains.

Lockerbie was a property of the Johnstones. In 1585 two towers here were besieged and captured by the Earl of Morton. One tower withstood another attack in 1593 when Lord Maxwell attempted to capture and destroy it. The Johnstones surprised Lord Maxwell at the siege, and he was defeated and slain, the wounds given by the Johnstones being known as a 'Lockerbie Lick'. The tower was later used as the town jail, and survived into the 20th century. The new police station is built on the site.

Logan House

Lothians: About 2.5 miles north-west of Penicuik, on minor road and foot north of A702, west of Glencorse Reservoir, just north of Logan Burn, at Logan.

Private   NT 204630 [?]   OS: 66   *   Map: 4, no: 67

Not much remains of a castle of the Sinclairs of Rosslyn, dating from the 14th and 15th centuries although it may have included earlier work from as early as 1230, in the grounds of Logan House. The castle consisted of two towers, but was mostly demolished by the turn of the century, and little now remains.

The kings of Scots are said to have had a hunting seat here, and a keep was built in 1230. One story is that Sir William Sinclair, 3rd Earl of Orkney, wagered his life that he could help the king kill a famous white stag before it escaped across the Glen-

corse Burn. This he did, and was granted the lands in reward, although he was slain fighting the Moors, along with Sir James Douglas and other Scottish knights, after taking Bruce's heart to Granada on a crusade. The castle appears to have been abandoned by the middle of the 16th century, although the property was held by the Cowan family in the 19th century.
Other refs: Logan Tower

Logan House
Galloway: About 10 miles south of Stranraer, on minor road north of B7065, about 2 miles north of Port Logan, at Logan Botanic Garden.
Ruin or site   NX 097426   OS: 82   *   Map: 1, no: 18
Little remains of a 15th-century castle, which is said to have been burned down in 1500, except part built into a garden wall. The basement was vaulted.
  It was a property of the MacDowalls, who held the property until the 20th century. Andrew MacDowall of Logan was a Lord of Session in 1755, and wrote 'Institutional Laws of Scotland'. Logan House is a castellated mansion, and stands near Logan Botanic Garden, a specialist garden of the Royal Botanic Garden in Edinburgh. The garden has a wide range of unusual and exotic plants, supported by the relatively mild climate, including tree ferns, cabbage palms, unusual shrubs, climbers and tender perennials, set in the walled, water, terrace and woodland gardens.
Other refs: Balzieland Tower
OPEN: House not open; gardens open Mar-Oct, daily 10.00-18.00
Botanic garden: Gift shop. Licensed salad bar. WC. Guided tours by arrangement. Plant centre. Discovery Centre. Soundalive self-guided tours. Disabled access. Parking. Group concessions. £.
Tel: 01776 860231   Fax: 01776 860333

Logan Tower *see* Logan House

Logie Almond Tower *see* Logie-Almond House

Logie House
Angus & Dundee: About 1.5 miles south of Kirriemuir, on minor roads east of A928 or west of A926, at Logie.
Private   NO 394521   OS: 54   **   Map: 8, no: 172
Logie House consists of a plain 16th-century tower house, rectangular in plan, with a round stair-tower projecting from one corner. It was extended and altered in the late 17th century, when the roofline was lowered, and it was added to again in the 18th century. The walls are harled, and have been pierced by shot-holes.
  The basement is vaulted, and contains a passageway which leads to cellars and the kitchen. There is a wide turnpike stair. The hall, on the first floor, has been subdivided, and the interior has been greatly altered.
  Logie was a property of the Wisharts. One of the family, George Wishart, was chaplain to the Marquis of Montrose from 1644, and followed him into exile. He returned after the Restoration, and was made Bishop of Edinburgh in 1662. The property later passed to the Kinlochs of Kilrie, who held it in the 20th century. The house is in good condition.
Other refs: Logie-Wishart; Logie Wishart

Logie House
Aberdeen & Gordon: About 4.5 miles north-west of Inverurie, on minor roads north of A96 1 mile east of junction with B9002, north of River Urie, at Logie House.
Private   NJ 706258   OS: 38   **   Map: 10, no: 214
Logie House incorporates a much-modified 17th-century tower house of three storeys and a garret, which has round bartizans. A round stair-tower rises at one corner. To this was added a two-storey block, in the 18th century, and another two-storey wing about 1760 around a courtyard. It was extended in later years. The house was burned out in 1974, although one wing is habitable.
  It was a property of the Elphinstone family from 1670 until 1903. It was latterly used as a hotel until the fire.
Other refs: Logie-Elphinstone

Logie House
Moray: About 5.5 miles south of Forres, on minor roads west of A940, east of River Findhorn, north-west of hamlet of Logie, at Logie House.
Private   NJ 006508   OS: 27   *   Map: 10, no: 5
Site of castle. The present Logie House, a tall late 18th-century whitewashed mansion with corbiestepped gables and a bartizan, incorporates work from 1655, if not earlier. It was a property of the Cummings, or Comyns, of Altyre, then later the Cunninghams.

Logie House
Fife: About 3 miles west of Leuchars, on minor roads south of A914 or west of A92, about 1 mile west of Balmullo, at Logie House.
Private   NO 408206   OS: 59   *   Map: 7, no: 110
Logie House, which is an early 18th century house extended in later centuries, incorporates part of an L-plan tower house, dating from the 16th century. There are sealed-up gunloops.
  The lands were a property of the Wemyss family from the 15th century or earlier, and held by them until at least the reign of James VI. One of the lairds is the subject of the old ballad 'The Laird of Logie'. The story is that the laird was imprisoned in the tolbooth of Edinburgh, and about to be executed by the king. Using a cunning plan, he was freed by his lover and together they escaped abroad.
Other refs: Logie-Murdoch

Logie-Almond House
Perth & Kinross: About 7.5 miles north-west of Perth, on minor roads south of B8063 at Chapelhill, just north of the River Almond, at Logie-Almond.
Ruin or site   NO 014297   OS: 53   *   Map: 8, no: 54
Logie-Almond House, a formerly ruined mansion which incorporated parts of a 16th-century castle, was demolished in the 1960s, except for one round tower with gunloops.
  It was probably originally a property of the Hays, but had passed to the Drummonds by the 16th century. It was later acquired by the Murray Earls of Mansfield.
Other refs: Logie Almond Tower

Logie-Elphinstone *see* Logie House

Logie-Murdoch *see* Logie House

Logie-Wishart *see* Logie House

Logierait Castle
Perth & Kinross: About 6 miles north of Dunkeld, on minor road and foot south of A825 at Logierait, on promontory at meeting of River Tay and Tummel.
Ruin or site   NN 975513   OS: 52   *   Map: 8, no: 44
Only a ditch and foundations remain of a 14th-century castle of enclosure of Robert III. Rob Roy MacGregor escaped from here in 1717, and in 1745 the Jacobites used the castle to confine 1600 prisoners captured after the Battle of Prestonpans. There is a Celtic cross memorial to the Murray 6th Duke of Atholl on the site.
Other refs: Rath of Logierait

Long Castle *see* Longcastle

Longcastle
Galloway: About 6 miles north-west of Whithorn, on minor road south of A714, on island in what was Dowalton Loch, east of Boreland of Longcastle.
Ruin or site   NX 394469   OS: 83   *   Map: 1, no: 53
There are scant remains of a keep and castle of the MacDowalls, who held the property from 1330 or earlier. The property had apparently passed to the Vaux family by the Reformation. It stood in a loch, which was drained towards the end of the 19th century. Two of the islands in the loch proved to be crannogs, and finds from here are now in the Museum of Scotland.
Other refs: Dowalton Castle; Long Castle

Longformacus

Borders: About 5.5 miles west and north of Duns, on minor roads west of A6105 or B6355, south of Dye Water, at or near Longformacus.
Ruin or site   NT 685573   OS: 74   *   Map: 2, no: 281
Site of 16th-century tower house, just west of the manse, some remains of which are built into a garden wall.
   The property was owned by the Earls of Moray, then the Cospatrick Earls of Dunbar, then the Sinclairs of Rosslyn. Longformacus House dates from the early 18th century, and is an extended classical mansion.
Other refs: Peelhill; Heron's Hole

Longniddry House

Lothians: East of Longniddry, on minor roads south of A198.
Ruin or site   NT 444762   OS: 66   *   Map: 4, no: 171
Little or nothing remains of Longniddry House, although vaulted chambers survived in the 19th century. It was a property of the Douglases of Longniddry, who were active in the Reformation.

Longslack Sike

Borders: About 3 miles east and south of Bonchester Bridge, on minor roads and foot north of A6088, 1 mile east of Chesters, south of Jed Water, at or near Longslack Sike.
Ruin or site   NT 645104 [?]   OS: 80   *   Map: 2, no: 259
Site of tower house, some remains of which survive along with later buildings.

Lonmay Castle

Banff & Buchan: About 6 miles south-east of Fraserburgh, on minor roads east of B9033, west of the sea, 1.5 miles south of St Combs, near Netherton of Lonmay.
Ruin or site   NK 062608 [?]   OS: 30   *   Map: 10, no: 360
Nothing remains of a 13th-century castle of the Frasers.
Other refs: Castle of Lonmay

Lorabank Castle *see* Larabank Castle

Lordscairnie Castle

Fife: About 3 miles north and west of Cupar, west of minor road between A913 and A914, at Lordscairnie.
Ruin or site   NO 348178   OS: 59   *   Map: 7, no: 91**
Once standing on an islet in a loch, Lordscairnie Castle is a 15th-century keep of four storeys and an attic, to which a stair-wing was added in the 16th century, making the castle L-plan. Above the entrance, in the stair-tower, is a machiolation, and the keep once had bartizans. A single round tower of a 16th-century gatehouse is all that remains of a courtyard.
   The basement is vaulted, which has fallen in; the hall was on the first floor; and the floors above, which were divided, contained private chambers.
   It was a property of the Lindsay Earls of Crawford from around 1350, and probably

the 4th Earl, 'Earl Beardie' or the 'Tiger Earl', who built the castle. It was abandoned in the 18th century, and the loch drained about 1803. The castle was recently put up for sale.
   There is reputedly treasure buried nearby.
   The castle is said to be haunted by the ghost of the 4th Earl of Crawford, which can be seen playing cards with the devil on the stroke of midnight of New Years' Eve. Or not.

Lossit House

Argyll & Dunbartonshire: About 7 miles west of Campbeltown, on minor road south of B843, 0.3 miles south-west of Machrihanish, at or near Lossit.
Private   NR 633202   OS: 68   *   Map: 5, no: 23
Site of castle or old house, which was a property of the MacNeils of Tirfergus and Lossit in 1683.

Loudoun

Ayrshire: About 1 mile north-east of Galston, on minor roads north of A71, 0.5 miles east of Loudoun Castle, north of River Irvine, west of Woodhead.
Ruin or site   NS 516377   OS: 70   *   Map: 3, no: 227
Site of castle on motte of the Campbells of Loudoun. It was destroyed by the Kennedy Earl of Cassillis towards the end of the 15th century, and the Campbells then moved to the present Loudoun Castle.

Loudoun Castle

Ayrshire: About 1 mile north of Galston, on minor road east of A719, about 0.5 miles north of the River Irvine.
Ruin or site   NS 506378   OS: 70   **   Map: 3, no: 216
Loudoun Castle, a large ruined castellated mansion, incorporates a tower house. Part of the castle dates from the 15th century, but it was extended in the 17th century, then engulfed by a castellated mansion of 1804-11.

Loudoun was a property of the Crawfords in the 14th century, but passed by marriage to the Campbells. John Campbell, Chancellor of Scotland, was made Earl of Loudoun in 1641. The castle was surrendered to General Monck for Cromwell in 1650 after a siege, during which part of the building was destroyed, but the Earl took part in an uprising in support of Charles II in 1653. It passed to Francis, Lord Hastings, who built much of the mansion, although he later ran out of money. The castle was used by Belgian troops during World War II, and in 1941 was accidentally torched and gutted. It remains a large impressive ruin, and is now the centre piece of a theme park.
   The castle was reputedly haunted by a 'Grey Lady', who was apparently seen often before its destruction in 1941, and is said to have been witnessed since. The ghost of a hunting dog, with glowing eyes, is also said to roam the area.
OPEN: Loudoun Castle Park open Easter-Oct from 10.00.
Guided tours for school parties. Woodland and country walks. Theme park with rollercoasters, go karts, log flume, carousel and much else (!). Gift shop. Restaurant. Tearoom. WC. Picnic area. Disabled limited access and WC. Car and coach parking. Group concessions. £££.
Tel: 01563 822296   Fax: 01563 822408
Email: loudouncastle@btinternet.com   Web: www.loudouncastle.co.uk

Lour Tower

Borders: About 4.5 miles east and south of Broughton, on minor road and foot south from B712, about 1 mile south of Stobo, just west of Lour.
Ruin or site   NT 179356   OS: 72   *   Map: 2, no: 37
Not much remains of a very ruinous 16th-century tower house and outbuildings, although it may be older. It stands within an Iron Age fort.
   It was held by the Veitch family from the 13th century, but passed to the Nae-smiths towards the end of the 18th century. It was inhabited until 1715, but ruin-ous by 1775.
Other refs: Laur; The Lour

Lovat Castle

Inverness & Nairn: About 1 mile east of Beauly, on minor roads north of B9164, just south of River Beauly, at Wester Lovat.
Ruin or site   NH 539461   OS: 26   *   Map: 9, no: 63
Site of castle, which was first built in the 12th century.
   It was a property of the Bissets of Lovat, but passed by marriage to the Frasers in the 13th century. The castle may have been destroyed by Cromwell in the 1650s or used to build a new house in 1671. The Frasers were Jacobites, however, and it is said that it was destroyed by the Duke of Cumberland after the Battle of Culloden in 1746. Simon Fraser, Lord Lovat, was executed by beheading. The family were forfeited, but had recovered their lands and titles by 1857.

Lovells' Castle, Hawick

Borders: About 0.5 miles south-west of Hawick, on minor road south of A7, west of Slitrig Water.
Ruin or site   NT 499140   OS: 79   *   Map: 2, no: 164
Nothing remains of a castle of the Lovells, except a motte.
Other refs: Hawick

Low Ardwell

Galloway: About 9 miles south of Stranraer, on minor roads west of A716, on the Rhinns of Galloway, at or near Low Ardwell.
Ruin or site   NX 082465 [?]   OS: 82   *   Map: 1, no: 13
Site of castle.

Low Auldgirth *see* Auldgirth

Lower Kenly *see* Inchmurtach

Luce

Dumfriesshire: About 3 miles north of Annan, on minor roads north of B722, just east of River Annan, at or near Luce.
Ruin or site   NY 189713 [?]   OS: 85   *   Map: 1, no: 259
Site of tower house.

Ludquharn

Banff & Buchan: About 5 miles west of Peterhead, on minor roads south of A950 or east of A92, near Burn of Ludquharn.
Ruin or site   NK 035455 [?]   OS: 30   *   Map: 10, no: 357
Site of castle of the Keiths.

Luffness House

Lothians: About 0.75 miles east of Aberlady, just south of A198, just south of the shore of Aberlady Bay.
Private   NT 476804   OS: 66   ***   Map: 4, no: 178
Luffness House incorporates a much-altered 16th-century tower house, although parts date from the 13th century. It is now a T-plan building, with a stair-tower and turret, and the house was altered and extended in the 17th century, then again in the 18th and 19th centuries. The castle was formerly surrounded by a moat.
   The lands were a property of the Cospatrick Earls of Dunbar and March, but passed by marriage to the Lindsays in the 12th century. They built a castle in the 13th century, once a large and strong fortress. The property (or at least part of it) was given to the Church in memory of the 8th Earl, Sir David Lindsay, a crusader. He

died in the 1160s while on crusade, and on his deathbed promised land for a reli-gious house provided his body was returned to Scotland. A Carmelite friary was built nearby in 1293, some of which survives, including the stone burial slab of a crusader.
   A fort was built around the castle by the French in 1549 to stop the English supply-ing the fort at Haddington, but destroyed on the orders of Mary of Guise in 1552. The property passed to the Hepburn Earls of Bothwell after the Reformation, and Mary, Queen of Scots, visited Luffness. In 1739 it was sold to the Hope Earl of Hopetoun. It was altered and extended by William Burn in 1822, and David Bryce in 1846 and 1874. It is in good condition, and still occupied by the Hope family.
Other refs: Aberlady Castle

Lugate Castle

Borders: About 1 mile south-west of Stow, on minor road west of A7, south of the Lugate Water, near Lugate farm.
Ruin or site   NT 444436   OS: 73   *   Map: 2, no: 118
Site of castle, which stood near the farm.

Lugbanck *see* Banklug Castle

Lugton

Lothians: To north-west of Dalkeith, on minor roads north of A68, on north side of River North Esk, at or near Lugton.
Ruin or site   NT 327677 [?]   OS: 66   *   Map: 4, no: 135
Site of castle of the Douglases. The property passed to the Scott Dukes of Buc-cleuch in 1693.

Lumphanan *see* Peel Ring of Lumphanan

Lumsdaine

Borders: About 2.5 miles north-west of Coldingham, on minor roads north of A1107, at or near Lumsdaine.
Ruin or site   NT 873690 [?]   OS: 67   *   Map: 2, no: 347
Site of tower house, a property of the Lumsden family. There was a village here in medieval times, which was torched in 1532 by Sir George Douglas.

Lumsden Castle *see* Blanerne Castle

Lundie Castle *see* Kilgarie

Lundie Castle

Angus & Dundee: About 7 miles east and south of Coupar Angus, on minor roads north of A923, 1.5 miles south-west of Auchterhouse, at or near Lundie Castle.

Ruin or site   NO 309361   OS: 53   *   Map: 8, no: 153

Site of 16th century castle, which consisted of the ruins of a large square tower in 1823, although there are now no remains. Materials from the castle were used to build the later house. It has a date stone with 1683.

Lundie was a property of the Duncan family, who were made Earls and Viscounts of Camperdown. One of the family, Adam Duncan, was a famous admiral, and defeated a Dutch fleet at Camperdown in 1797.

The family built Camperdown House [NO 365327], a 19th-century mansion, set in nearly 400 acres of fine park land. The grounds are now a country park.

Lundin Tower

Fife: About 1 mile west of Lower Largo, on minor roads north and west of A915, just east of Lundin Wood.

Ruin or site   NO 399029   OS: 59   **   Map: 7, no: 105

Site of a much-altered 16th-century tower house, which had been incorporated into Lundin House. All of the house, except an altered stair-turret from the 16th or 17th century, was demolished in 1876.

There was a castle here in the 14th century, belonging to the Lundin family, who held the property from the 12th century. It passed by marriage to the Drummonds in 1670, who were forfeited after the 1745 Jacobite Rising. Mary, Queen of Scots, is said to have stayed at the tower in 1565.

Lunelly Tower

Dumfriesshire: About 4 miles east of Lockerbie, on minor roads north of B7068, north of Bankshill, north of the Water of Hill.

Ruin or site   NY 197824   OS: 79   *   Map: 1, no: 263

Not much remains of a 16th-century tower house. There was an earlier stronghold on the site. The lands were a property of the Corrie family, but passed to the Johnstones in 1516 and they built the tower.

Other refs: Lin

Lunga

Argyll & Dunbartonshire: About 2.5 miles south of Arduaine, on minor roads south of A816 or west of B8002, 1 mile south of Craobh Haven, at Lunga.

Private   NM 795064   OS: 55   **   Map: 5, no: 55

Lunga, a mansion dating partly from the 17th century, still has a gunloop.

It was a property of the Campbells of Craignish, but passed to the MacDougalls of Lunga in the 1780s.

Lurdenlaw Tower

Borders: About 2.5 miles south and east of Kelso, on minor road between B6396 and B6352, at or near Lurdenlaw.

Ruin or site   NT 769321 [?]   OS: 74   *   Map: 2, no: 307

Site of tower house.

Luskie *see* Nunton Castle

Lustruther *see* Slacks Peel

Luthrie

Fife: About 4 miles north and west of Cupar, on minor roads north of A914, in village of Luthrie.

Ruin or site   NO 332196 [?]   OS: 59   *   Map: 7, no: 85

Site of castle or old house.

Luthrie was a property of the Crown until the 16th century, when it passed to John Murray, barber-surgeon to James V.

Lyleston *see* Keppoch House

Lynturk Castle

Aberdeen & Gordon: About 3 miles south-east of Alford, on minor roads west of A944 or east of A980, 1 mile south-west of Kirkton of Tough, at Lynturk.

Ruin or site   NJ 598122   OS: 37   *   Map: 10, no: 157

Site of 16th-century castle of the Strachans, little of which survives except earthworks. A 19th-century house has been built in the earthworks.

John Strachan of Lynturk was involved in the murder of Alexander Seton of Meldrum in 1526, along with the Master of Forbes. Strachan besieged Kildrummy Castle in 1531, and managed to get the Master of Forbes executed by implicating him in a plot to assassinate James V. Strachan went into exile in 1550. The property passed to the Irvines, then to the Gordons, until 1816 when it was sold to the MacCombies. The castle was ruinous by 1782.

Other refs: Castleknowe of Lynturk; Castle of Lynturk

M

Macbeth's Castle

South Highland: To east of Inverness, on minor roads south of A82, The Crown.
Ruin or site   NH 674456   OS: 26   *   Map: 9, no: 94
Site of castle, the site occupied by housing.
   It is said to have been held by Macbeth in the 11th century, and destroyed by Malcolm Canmore.

MacBeth's Castle, Liberton

Lothians: About 3 miles east and south of Edinburgh Castle, west of A7, Liberton School.
Ruin or site   NT 275694   OS: 66   *   Map: 4, no: 117
Site of a tall tower house, the stronghold of MacBeth or Malbet, a baron in the reign of David I. On the site was an old house which dated from the 17th century or earlier. The house was demolished after 1840, and the site is occupied by the present school.
Other refs: Malbet; Liberton

Macbiehill

Borders: About 2 miles east of West Linton, on minor roads north of A701 at Whitmuir, just north of Dead Burn, at or near Macbiehill.
Ruin or site   NT 185514 [?]   OS: 72   *   Map: 2, no: 38
Site of mansion, built in 1835 to the designs of William Burn, which incorporated a tower house, but was demolished in the 1950s. The tower may also have been known as Coldcoat or Coudcott, although this may refer to another castle nearby. The property was held by the Montgomerys in the middle of the 17th century, but had passed to the Beresfords before the end of the century.
Other refs: Coudcott; Coldcoat

MacDuff's Castle

Fife: On the northern outskirts of East Wemyss, south of A955, on footpath near the shore.
Ruin or site   NT 344972   OS: 59   **   Map: 7, no: 89
MacDuff's Castle consists of a ruined 14th-century keep and courtyard. The oldest part is a gate-tower standing at one end of the main block. The keep was enclosed by a curtain wall with ranges of buildings, little of which remain, around a courtyard. An outer courtyard with corner towers was later added.
   There may have been a castle here of the MacDuff Thanes or Earls of Fife in the 11th century, although nothing survives from that date – the castle was torched by Edward I of England. The existing castle was built by the Wemyss family in the 14th century, but passed by marriage to the Livingstones, who exchanged it for other lands with the Colvilles of Ochiltree in 1530. In 1630 it returned to the Wemyss family, later Earls of Wemyss, but was little used afterwards, the family having several other castles. In 1666 the Countess of Sutherland, who was a daughter of the 2nd Earl of Wemyss, lodged her children here during an outbreak of plague in

Edinburgh. The upper parts of the keep were dismantled in 1967.
   The ghost of a woman, the 'Grey Lady' reputedly haunts the castle. She is said to be Mary Sibbald, who was found guilty of thievery, and died from the resultant punishment.
Other refs: East Wemyss Castle; Kennoway Castle
OPEN: View from exterior.

MacDuff's Castle, Lindores *see* **Lindores Castle**

MacEwen's Castle *see* **Castle Ewen**

Machan *see* **Broomhill Castle**

Machermore Castle

Galloway: About 1 mile south-east of Newton-Stewart, on minor road south of A75, just east of the River Cree, at Machermore.
Private   NX 416644 [?]   OS: 83   **   Map: 1, no: 61
Machermore Castle, a modern mansion, may incorporate a square tower house.
   The old castle was probably held by the MacDowalls, although by 1866 the property had passed to the Dunbars.

MacLellan's Castle

Galloway: In Kirkcudbright, just south-west of the junction of A755 with A711, just south of the River Dee, in the centre of the town.
His Scot   NX 683511   OS: 83   *   Map: 1, no: 111**
MacLellan's Castle is a large 16th-century L-plan tower house. It consists of a main block and a wing, a projecting rectangular tower, and two towers in the re-entrant angle. Part of the main block rises to five storeys, but the rest of the building is four storeys high. There are bartizans, which formerly had conical roofs, at two corners

of the main block and at the two corners of the wing. The castle is roofless, but had corbiestepped gables. The walls are pierced by gunloops, and the building is dated 1582.
   The entrance, at the foot of the smaller of two towers in the re-entrant angle, opens onto a straight stair to the hall and to a passage to three vaulted basement cellars. Another passage leads to the vaulted kitchen, which has its own door to the courtyard.
   The hall has a fine fireplace, and a small turnpike stair leads to three private chambers. Another turnpike stair, in a turret, climbs to the floors above from the main stair.
   In 1569 Sir Thomas MacLellan of Bombie, Provost of Kirkcudbright, acquired the

Franciscan Greyfriars Monastery, demolishing all but part of the chapel, now the Episcopalian Church, and built the castle nearby around 1582. The MacLellans were made Lords Kirkcudbright in 1633, and one of the family fought at the Battle of Philiphaugh in 1645. They abandoned the castle around 1752, because of financial troubles, and it was sold to Sir Robert Maxwell of Orchardton, only to be sold again to the Douglas Earl of Selkirk in 1782. It was put into State guardianship in 1912.
Other refs: Kirkcudbright Castle
OPEN: Open Apr-Sep, daily 9.30-18.30; last ticket 18.00.
Sales area. Exhibition. WC. Parking. £.
Tel: 01557 331856   Fax: 0131 668 8888
Email: hs.explore@scotland.gov.uk   Web: www.historic-scotland.gov.uk

MacLeod's Castle

Western Isles: About 2 miles south-west of Stornoway, on minor road south of A866 at Sandwick, on east side of Stornoway Bay, at or near Holm.
Ruin or site   NB 442305   OS: 8   *   Map: 11, no: 28
Site of castle.
   Standing on the north side of Stornoway Bay, an old stronghold of the MacLeods – known helpfully as MacLeod's Castle – was demolished by Cromwell's troops in 1653, although a fragment survived at least until the 19th century. It is marked on John Speed's map as 'Stoy Castle'.
Other refs: Stoy Castle

MacTire Castle

Sutherland & Caithness: About 3.5 miles east and south of Bonar Bridge, on minor roads and foot south of A9, south of Creich Mains, at Dun Creich.
Ruin or site   NH 652883   OS: 21   *   Map: 12, no: 15
Site of castle, traces of which remain, within the ramparts of the Iron Age fort. It was built by the MacTires, and ruined by 1590 or before.
Other refs: Dun Creich; Creich Castle

Maesteg *see* Castle Mestag

Magdalens House *see* Hamilton House

Maiden Castle

Fife: About 2 miles north-west of Methil, just east of A916, about 0.5 miles south of Kennoway, about 1 mile north of Windygates.
Ruin or site   NO 349015   OS: 59   **   Map: 7, no: 92
Site of 12th-century motte and bailey castle, with at least three outer ditches and ramparts.
   It is associated with the MacDuff Thanes of Fife. One story is that a passage from here goes to Barnslee, about three miles away.

Maiden Castle

Lanarkshire & Glasgow area: About 3.5 miles north and west of Kirkintilloch, on minor roads north of A891, about 0.5 miles east of Lennoxtown, near Glorat House.
Ruin or site   NS 643785   OS: 64   *   Map: 3, no: 302
The remains of a 12th-century motte and bailey castle, which was held by the Earls of Lennox.
Other refs: Garmore

Mailer

Perth & Kinross: About 2 miles south of Perth, on minor road west of A912 at Craigend and east of B9112 at Aberdalgie, just north of River Earn, at or near Mailer.
Ruin or site   NO 099202 [?]   OS: 58   *   Map: 8, no: 77
Site of castle.

Main Castle

Lanarkshire & Glasgow area: About 3.5 miles south-east of Darvel, on minor road and track about 2.5 miles south of A71, just west of the Avon Water.
Private   NS 602345   OS: 71   **   Map: 3, no: 275
Site of 15th-century keep and castle with earthworks.

Mains Castle *see* Edington Castle

Mains Castle

Lanarkshire & Glasgow area: About 1 mile west and north of Milngavie, on minor road east of A809 just north of Crossburn, at Mains.
Ruin or site   NS 535752   OS: 64   *   Map: 3, no: 239
Site of castle, which was replaced by a mansion, itself demolished to build a school.
   It was a property of the Galbraiths of Culcreuch, but passed by marriage to the Douglases of Dalkeith in 1373, and they held the property until the 20th century.

Mains Castle

Lanarkshire & Glasgow area: About 1 mile north of East Kilbride, on minor roads north of B783, just south of Rogerton, at High Mains.
Private   NS 627560   OS: 64   *   Map: 3, no: 292**
Mains Castle is a plain late 15th-century keep, rectangular in plan, of three storeys and an attic. The parapet has a square corbelled-out caphouse at one corner. The castle formerly had a courtyard, enclosing extensive ranges of buildings little of which remain.
   The entrance, through an arched doorway, opened into the vaulted basement and onto a turnpike stair, which climbs to the upper floors in the thickness of the

walls. A passage, reached from the stair, leads to a trapdoor to a vaulted pit-prison. The hall, on the first floor, has a plain fireplace, while the floors above have been subdivided.
   The property was originally held to the Comyns, but passed to the Lindsays of Dunrod by 1382. One of the family, along with Kirkpatrick of Closeburn, had helped Robert the Bruce murder John Comyn in a church in Dumfries in 1306. There was an earlier castle on the nearby motte [NS 628562]. A later Lindsay, while curling on the ice of a nearby loch, was angered by one of his servants, and had a hole cut in the ice and the man drowned by forcing him under the ice. The property was sold because of debt about 1695, and unroofed in 1723 to become ruinous. It has been restored, and was recently been put up for sale.
   The castle is reputedly haunted by the ghost of a woman strangled by her jealous husband.

Mains Castle

Stirlingshire & Clackmannan: About 6 miles east and north of Killin, on minor road and foot 6 miles east of junction with A827 at Killin, just south of Loch Tay, just north of Ardeonaig.

Ruin or site   NN 668360   OS: 52   *   Map: 6, no: 48

Little remains of a 16th-century tower house, which was rectangular in plan. It was not vaulted. It was a property of the Campbells.

Mains Castle

Angus & Dundee: On northern outskirts of Dundee, on minor roads west of A929 near junction with A972, east of Caird Park, at Mains of Fintry.

Private   NO 410330   OS: 54   **   Map: 8, no: 178**

Mains Castle is a courtyard castle, mostly of the 16th century, but partly from the 15th century. Ranges of buildings form three sides of a courtyard, the last side

being completed by a high wall with a parapet. The gateway is defended by a massive corbelled-out machiolation. The castle is dated 1562.

The main range, dating from the end of the 15th century, has a six-storey square stair-tower and corbiestepped gables. The entrance, at the foot of the stair-tower, led to the hall and to a private chamber on the first floor. The basement is not vaulted, and contained stables and cellars. The kitchen and bakehouse were in an adjoining range, which was rebuilt in the late 17th century.

The property originally belonged to the Stewarts, then the Douglas Earls of Angus from the 14th century, but passed in 1530 to the Grahams, who built the castle. One of the family, Sir David Graham, nephew of Cardinal Beaton, was executed for plotting to restore Catholicism to Scotland around 1592. The property was sold to the Erskines in the 19th century, then the Cairds, before being given to the City of Dundee. Although ruined and derelict for many years, it has been restored. The grounds are a public park.

Other refs: Mains of Fintry Castle; Fintry Castle

Mains of Balfour

Aberdeen & Gordon: About 2.5 miles south-east of Aboyne, on minor road west of B976, south of Burn of Birse, at or near Mains of Balfour.

Ruin or site   NO 551964   OS: 37   *   Map: 10, no: 136

Not much remains of a castle or old house except foundations.

Other refs: Balfour

Mains of Drummuir *see* Drummuir

Mains of Dyce

Aberdeen & Gordon: About 0.5 miles north of Dyce, just east of A947, just south of River Don, at or near Mains of Dyce.

Private   NJ 889138 [?]   OS: 38   *   Map: 10, no: 307

Possible site of castle. The present house dates from 1835.

The lands were a property of the Skenes.

Mains of Fintry Castle *see* Mains Castle

Mains of Gartly *see* Gartly Castle

Mains of Hallhead *see* Hallhead

Mains of Kilmaronock Castle *see* Kilmaronock Castle

Mains of Mayen

Moray: About 6 miles north and east of Huntly, on minor road just south of B9117, on slope above River Deveron, at Mains of Mayen.

Private   NJ 576477   OS: 29   *   Map: 10, no: 145**

Mains of Mayen is a 17th-century L-plan tower house of two storeys, with a large round stair-tower in the re-entrant angle. The house may incorporate earlier work. The gables are corbiestepped, and a steep roof has stone slates.

The original entrance was in the foot of the stair-tower, but this has been moved. The basement is not vaulted, and the interior has been very altered in the late 17th century.

The property originally belonged to the Abernethys from the 14th century until 1612, when it passed to the Gordons. In 1649 it was sold to the Halkett or Hacket family, and then passed by marriage back to the Abernethys. One of the family, James Abernethy, shot and murdered John Leith of Leith Hall in 1752, and had to flee abroad after being outlawed. The property later passed to the Duffs, who built nearby Mayen House in 1788. Mains of Mayen was restored in the 1960s.

Other refs: Mayen

Mains of Moyness *see* Moyness Castle

Mains of Mulben

Moray: About 5 miles east of Keith, on minor roads north of A95 at junction with B9013 or north of B9013, just north of Burn of Mulben, at Mains of Mulben.

Private   NJ 353512   OS: 28   *   Map: 10, no: 73

Mains of Mulben incorporates a 16th-century tower house in what is now a T-plan house, and mostly dates from the late 17th century.

It was built by the Grants. John Grant of Mulben fought against the Gordons at the Battle of Glenlivet in 1594. The property later passed to the Macphersons. The house is still occupied, and used as a farm.

Other refs: Mulben

Makerstoun House

Borders: About 3.5 miles west and south of Kelso, on minor roads south of B6397 and B6404, about 0.75 miles south of Makerstoun, just north of River Tweed.

Private   NT 672315   OS: 74   *   Map: 2, no: 275

Makerstoun House, a square three-storey building, incorporates a 16th-century castle.

It was a property of the MacDougalls from 1373 until 1890, when it passed to the Scotts of Gala. It was sacked by the Earl of Hertford in 1545.

Malbet *see* MacBeth's Castle, Liberton

Malcolm Canmore's Tower *see* Malcolm's Tower

Malcolm's Tower

Fife: In Dunfermline, not far west of the Abbey church, in Dunfermline [Pittencrieff] Park, on minor road south of A994.

Ruin or site   NT 087873   OS: 65   *   Map: 7, no: 12

Malcolm's Tower is a large 14th-century keep, of which only the base remains, although there may have been a stronghold here from the 11th century. The castle gets its name from Malcolm Canmore, king of Scots.

One tale is that the tower was where Malcolm Canmore and Margaret were married in 1068. Margaret founded the great abbey of Dunfermline, and was later made a saint. Nearby is St Margaret's Cave, which is open to the public. It was at the tower that Maud, later wife of Henry I of England, was born.

Other refs: Dunfermline Tower; Malcolm Canmore's Tower

OPEN: Park open all year.

Malleny House

Lothians: Just east of Balerno, on minor road south of A70, just south of the Water of Leith.

NTS   NT 166667   OS: 65   *   Map: 4, no: 51

Malleny House, an extended 17th-century mansion with a round stair-tower, incorporates earlier work from at least 1589. It was extended again in 1823.

The property belonged to the Hamiltons, but passed to the Kerrs, then the Murrays of Kilbaberton, who built much of the present house. It passed in the 17th century to the Scotts of Murdieston, but was sold to the Primrose Lord Rosebery in 1882. It is now owned by The National Trust for Scotland, and the grounds – although NOT the house – are open to the public.

There may have been another stronghold nearby [NT 171654], known as Malleny Castle, which was in ruins in 1773.

Other refs: Malleny Castle

OPEN: House not open; garden open all year: Apr-Oct, daily 9.30-19.00; Nov-Mar, 9.30-16.00.

Disabled access to garden. Car and coach parking. £.

Tel: 0131 449 2283

Email: information@nts.org.uk   Web: nts.org.uk

Mallscastle

Dumfriesshire: About 2 miles south-east of Lockerbie, on minor road north of A74, west of the Water of Milk, at Mallscastle.

Private   NY 153795   OS: 85   *   Map: 1, no: 250

Site of castle.

Maltan Walls

Borders: To east of Ancrum village, near B6400 west of junction with A68, just west of Ale Water.

Ruin or site   NT 632246   OS: 74   *   Map: 2, no: 248

Site of castle or old building, a vestige of which still survived at the end of the 19th century. There were the remains of vaults and one gable in the 18th century, but all are now gone.

It has been suggested as a preceptory of the Knights of Malta. The lands were held by the Bishops of Glasgow, and they may have had a residence or palace.

Other refs: Mantle Walls; Nether Ancrum

Manderston

Borders: About 1.5 miles east of Duns, on minor roads north of A6105, at Manderston.

Private   NT 810545   OS: 74   *   Map: 2, no: 332**

Site of castle.

Featuring the only silver staircase in the world, Manderston is a fine Edwardian mansion, part of which dates from the original house of 1790, when it was a property of the Homes. The house was virtually rebuilt between 1903-5 by John Kinross for Sir James Miller, a millionaire racehorse owner, whose family had acquired the property in 1890. The house stands in 56 acres of gardens.

OPEN: Open mid May-end Sep, Thu and Sun 14.00-17.00; Bank Holiday open Mon May and Aug, 14.00-17.00; other times group visits by appt.

Fine interiors, above and below stairs. Museum. Restaurant and tea room. WC. Gardens. Woodland and lake-side walks. Car and coach parking. Accommodation. £££.

Tel: 01361 883450/882636   Fax: 01361 882010

Email: palmer@manderston.co.uk   Web: www.manderston.co.uk

Mangerton Tower

Borders: About 1 mile south of Newcastleton, on east of Hermitage water, between B6357 and minor road.

Ruin or site   NY 479853   OS: 79   *   Map: 2, no: 143

Little remains of a 16th-century tower house, except part of the basement, a prop-

erty of the Armstrongs and residence of the head of their family.

The Armstrongs were very powerful on the Border, and the English Warden of the Marches attacked and sacked the tower in 1523. One of the family John 'Black Jock' Armstrong was executed for reiving in 1530. The tower was also torched in 1543, 1569 and 1601. The Armstrongs of Mangerton were accused of raiding Tynedale in 1593, and the last Armstrong lairds were hanged in 1610 for raiding England – many of the family went to Ulster. Most of their towers, of which there were many, were then demolished. The property, including the tower, passed to the Scotts in 1629.

By the side of the B6357 is the Milnholm Cross, which was put here around 1320, to commemorate Alexander Armstrong who was murdered in Hermitage Castle.

OPEN: Cross: Access at all reasonable times.

Cross: Car parking.

Manner *see* Manorhead Tower

Mannerston

Lothians: About 3 miles east and north of Linlithgow, just east of B9109, about 0.5 miles south of Blackness, at Mannerston.

Private   NT 048790 [?]   OS: 65   **   Map: 4, no: 25

Mannerston, a later mansion, incorporates part of an early 16th-century castle, which belonged to Sir James Hamilton of Finnart.

Manor Castle

Galloway: About 4 miles south and west of Kirkcudbright, on minor roads south of B727, west of Kirkcudbright Bay, 1 mile south of Balmangan, on Manor Point.

Ruin or site   NX 654443   OS: 83   *   Map: 1, no: 106

Site of castle, traces of which remained in the 19th century.

Manor Castle

Stirlingshire & Clackmannan: About 2 miles east of Stirling, south of the A907, just north of the River Forth, south of Manor Powis.

Ruin or site   NS 827948   OS: 57   *   Map: 6, no: 79

Not much survives of a 16th-century tower house, latterly T-plan.

It was a property of the Callendars from 1479, but had passed to the Dundas family by 1729. It was then abandoned for Airthrey Castle, and the property was sold to the Haldanes about 1750, then in 1796 to the Abercrombies.

Other refs: Kingsnow House

Manorhead Tower

Borders: About 10 miles so south and west of Peebles, from A72 on minor road from Kirkton Manor near Manor Water.

Ruin or site   NT 195276   OS: 72   *   Map: 2, no: 42

Not much remains of a 16th-century tower house except the formerly vaulted basement, which has been incorporated into farm buildings.

It was a property of the Inglis family. The first Inglis of Manor was given the lands for killing Sir Thomas Struthers, an English champion, in single combat in 1395. The property was sold to the Horsburghs around the beginning of the 18th century.

Other refs: Manner

Mantle House

Borders: About 3 miles south-east of Melrose, on minor road west of B6356, east of River Tweed, at Dryburgh.

Private   NT 589322   OS: 73   **   Map: 2, no: 226

Mantle House, a castellated mansion now known as Dryburgh Abbey Hotel, was remodelled in 1892, but stands on the site of a much older building. It was home to Lady Grizel Baillie, and has recently undergone a major renovation.

A ghost story, however, dates from the 16th century or earlier. Before the nearby abbey was dissolved, a young lady of the house fell in love with a monk, and they became close. The abbot, on hearing of the monk's earthly love, had the poor man killed. When the young lady found out she was devastated, and threw herself into the Tweed and was drowned. Her apparition, a 'Grey Lady', has been seen on the chain bridge and in outbuildings of the hotel. Disturbances apparently increased during building work.

Other refs: Dryburgh Abbey Hotel

OPEN: Hotel – open all year.

37 luxury bedrooms. Restaurant and bar. Swimming pool. Conferences, meetings, weddings and dinners. Parking.

Tel: 01835 822261 Fax: 01835 823945 Email: enquiries@dryburgh.co.uk

Mantle Walls *see* Maltan Walls

Marchmont House *see* Redbraes Castle

Marcus *see* Markshouse

Markfield Tower *see* Otterston Tower

Markle

Lothians: About 0.5 miles north-west of East Linton, near Edinburgh-London railway line, on minor road north of A1.

Ruin or site NT 579775 OS: 67 * Map: 4, no: 206

Markle is a ruined 14th-century castle, which consists of two ranges and a small square courtyard with ditches and ramparts. There was a college of priests near or at the site. Markle was torched in 1401 and 1544 by the English.

Markshouse

Angus & Dundee: About 5 miles west of Brechin, near A90, south of Noran Water and north of River South Esk, at or near Easter Marcus.

Ruin or site NO 517582 [?] OS: 54 * Map: 8, no: 219

Site of castle.

Other refs: Marcus

Marlfield House

Borders: About 5.5 miles south of Kelso, on minor roads south of B6401, 2 miles west of Morebattle, south of Kale Water, at Marlfield.

Private NT 735255 OS: 74 ** Map: 2, no: 296

Marlfield House, a three storey house with a main block and corner towers, incorporates part of a castle, dating from the 16th century or earlier. The building was remodelled in the mid 18th century, possibly by William Adam, and again in 1891.

The house is reputed to be haunted by a ghost, that pushes past people in one of the passageways, and is said to have been active in recent years.

Other refs: Marlfield House

Marlfield House *see* Marlfield House

Marslauch *see* Craigoch Castle

Martello Tower, Leith

Lothians: About 3 miles north-east of Edinburgh Castle, on minor roads north of A199, in Leith Docks.

Private NT 269777 OS: 66 ** Map: 4, no: 112

The Martello Tower, a round tower and gun emplacement, was built in 1805 to defend the entrance to Leith harbour from attack by the French during the Napoleonic Wars. The name is from Mortella in Corsica, where one such tower had kept the British at bay. There are two other Martello Towers, both in Orkney, at Hackness [ND 338912] and Crockness [ND 324934], which were built to defend the anchorage at Scapa Flow.

Other refs: Leith

Martello Towers, Orkney

Orkney: South-east side of Hoy, on minor roads and foot east of B9047, south side of Longhope, Hackness.

His Scot ND 338912 OS: 7 ** Map: 11, no: 38

The tower here is one of a pair which was built in 1813-15 to protect Longhope and Scapa Flow, and the British ships which were moored there, against French and American pirates, including John Paul Jones. The squat round tower housed a 25

pounder gun and its crew, and was refortified in 1866. The name is from Mortella in Corsica.

There is also a Martello Tower at Crockness on the north side of Longhope [ND 324934], and another at Leith [NT 269778], near Edinburgh. There were around 100 such towers built in Britain, but only these three in Scotland.

Other refs: Hackness, Martello Tower; Crockness, Martello Tower

OPEN: For access contact key holder.

A visit involves a walk.

Tel: 0131 668 8800 Fax: 0131 668 8888

Email: hs.explore@scotland.gov.uk Web: www.historic-scotland.gov.uk

Martnaham Castle

Ayrshire: About 4.5 miles south-east of Ayr, on minor roads and foot between east of A713 and south of B742, on a peninsula to south of Martnaham Loch.

Ruin or site NS 395173 OS: 70 * Map: 3, no: 141

Martnaham Castle, now standing on a peninsula which was formerly an island, is a very ruined 16th-century tower house and courtyard.

Mary Queen of Scots House *see* Queen Mary's House, Jedburgh

Maryculter House

Kincardine & Deeside: About 7 miles south and west of Aberdeen, on minor roads north of B9077, just south of River Dee, near Templars, at Maryculter.

Private NO 845999 OS: 38 ** Map: 10, no: 285

Picturesquely situated on the banks of the Dee in woodland and landscaped gardens, Maryculter House is a 17th-century mansion. It was later altered and extended, but vaulted cellars from the perceptor's house are built into the hotel, including the cocktail bar. The house suffered a fire in 1720, but was repaired or rebuilt.

There was a preceptory of the Knights Templars here, founded by Walter Bisset between 1225 and 1236, which passed to the Knights of St John of Jerusalem about 1309 when the Templars were suppressed. It later passed to the Menzies family, who built the 17th-century house.

The foundations of the nearby Templar's church, which was used by the parish until 1782, can also be traced.

One of the Knights was Godfrey Wedderburn of Wedderhill. Godfrey went on crusade to the Holy Land, where he distinguished himself, but he was badly wounded and was nursed back to health by a beautiful Saracen woman. Godfrey was pious man, and the couple appear to never have been anything more than friends. When he had recovered, he returned to Maryculter and the preceptory.

Years later the Saracen woman travelled to Scotland and looked for Godfrey. She found him at Maryculter and greeted him warmly. The preceptor (the head of the Order) did not believe that they were not lovers, or that he could be friendly with an enemy of the Church: he was not one of the pure to whom all things are pure. Because the preceptor believed that Godfrey was lying, that he had broken his vows, Godfrey was forced to kill himself using his own dagger. The Saracen also plunged a knife into her own chest, but called down a curse on the preceptor. As she died a lightning bolt struck the Templar, and killed him, leaving a smoking hollow where he had been. This hollow, the 'Thunder Hole', which was formerly much deeper, can still be seen.

It is said that Godfrey and the Saracen were buried side by side, but that his apparition returns to ride over the hill of Kingcausie while the ghost of the beautiful Saracen woman has been seen in the woods.

OPEN: Hotel – open all year.

23 bedrooms with ensuite facilities. Dining room and bars. Banquets, weddings and conferences. Parking.

Tel: 01224 732124 Fax: 01224 733510

Email: info@maryculterhousehotel.co.uk

Web: www.maryculterhousehotel.co.uk

Maryton

Angus & Dundee: About 3 miles west and south of Montrose, on minor road north of A934, south of Montrose Basin, at or near Maryton.

Ruin or site NO 686563 OS: 54 * Map: 8, no: 263

Site of castle, a property of the Grahams of Montrose.

Mar's Castle, Aberdeen

Aberdeen & Gordon: In Aberdeen, to the south of the old town, on minor roads east of A956, 0.5 miles west of the sea.

Ruin or site   NJ 945078   OS: 38   *   Map: 10, no: 338

Site of 15th-century castle and town house of the Stewart Earls of Mar. The Earldom passed to the Erskines in 1565. The building was dated 1494.

Mar's Work, Stirling

Stirling & Clackmannanshire: Castle Wynd, Stirling.

His Scot   NS 794937   OS: 57   **   Map: 6, no: 72

Mar's Work is a ruinous Renaissance-style mansion, which was built in 1570 by the 1st Earl of Mar, Regent of Scotland during the minority of James VI and hereditary keeper of Stirling Castle. The fine facade survives with a gatehouse adorned with sculptures.

The Earls of Mar used the mansion until 'Bobbing' John Erskine, 6th Earl of Mar, fled Scotland after leading the 1715 Jacobite Rising. The building was converted into a barracks, but damaged by cannon during the 1745-6 Jacobite Rising.

OPEN: Access at all reasonable times.

Parking nearby.

Tel: 0131 668 8800   Fax: 0131 668 8888

Email: hs.explore@scotland.gov.uk   Web: www.historic-scotland.gov.uk

Masterton House

Lothians: About 0.75 miles south-east of Newtongrange, on minor roads east of B6482, at Masterton.

Ruin or site   NT 345636 [?]   OS: 66   *   Map: 4, no: 141

Masterton House was a small late 16th-century L-plan tower house of three storeys. It had a round stair-tower, corbelled out to square, in the re-entrant angle. The basement was vaulted, and a turnpike stair climbed to all floors. There was at least one gunloop.

It may have been a property of the Kerrs. The house appears to have been demolished.

Mathers Castle *see* Kaim of Mathers Castle

Mauchline Castle

Ayrshire: In Mauchline, on minor roads between B743 and A76 in Castle Street in the town.

Private   NS 496273   OS: 70   **   Map: 3, no: 203

Mauchline Castle is an altered 15th-century keep, to which has been added a 17th-century L-plan wing, as well as other extensions and alterations of 1690, 1800 and

1820. The arms of Abbot (of Melrose) Hunter (died 1471) adorn the building.

The basement and hall, on the first floor, are both vaulted, but the inside of the castle has been much altered.

The castle was a built by Melrose Abbey to manage its Ayrshire estates. It passed to the Campbells of Loudoun after the Reformation, and was used as the factor's house. Robert Burns paid his rent here, and was married in one of the extensions to the keep. The castle is in good condition.

Other refs: Abbot Hunter's Tower

Mauchline Tower *see* Dundee Castle

Maud *see* Old Maud

Maud Castle *see* Castle Maud

Maxwelton House

Dumfriesshire: About 2.5 miles east of Moniaive, on minor road south of A702 and north of B729, about 0.5 miles north of the Cairn Water, at Maxwelton.

Private   NX 822898   OS: 78   **   Map: 1, no: 146

Maxwelton is a 17th-century tower house of two storeys and an attic, although an older castle, dating from the 14th and 15th centuries, may be incorporated. To this has been added a large mansion around three sides of a courtyard. The tower stands at one end of a more modern wing, and has a round tower, formerly containing a stair, in the re-entrant angle.

The house has been much altered inside, but part of the basement is vaulted.

The property originally belonged to the Dennistouns, but passed by marriage to the Cunninghams in the 15th century. The family were made Earls of Glencairn in 1488, but the property was sold to the Laurie family in 1611. It was the home of the heroine of the song 'Annie Laurie'. The Lauries sold the property in 1966, and the house is still occupied.

Other refs: Glencairn Castle

Maybole Castle

Ayrshire: In Maybole, near junction of A77 with B7023, in Castle Street of the town.

Private   NS 301100   OS: 70   *   Map: 3, no: 78**

Maybole Castle is an altered 16th-century L-plan tower house of four storeys and a garret, to which has been added a lower wing. Large round bartizans are corbelled out at two corners. There is much fine decorative stonework.

The original entrance, at the foot of the stair-tower, opened into the vaulted basement. The hall was on the first floor, and the chambers on the upper floors were subdivided. Much of the interior is panelled.

The tower was probably built by Gilbert Kennedy, 5th Earl of Cassillis, and High Lord Treasurer of Scotland – the Kennedys were known as the 'Kings of Carrick'

because they held so much land in the area and could 'lord' it over most of Carrick.

It was here that traditionally Lady Jean Hamilton, wife of the 6th Earl of Cassillis, was imprisoned after she had run off with Sir Johnnie Faa, King of the Gypsies. Cassillis pursued and caught them, and hanged Faa and his followers from the gallows tree at Maybole – making his wife watch. The story is recounted in an old ballad, and Cassillis House has also been given as the location, although there is little other evidence.

The house is in good condition, and used as the factor house for the estates of the Kennedy Marquis of Ailsa.

Maybole formerly had several fine town houses, including those held by the Kennedys of Knockdaw, Culzean, and Ballimore.

Mayen *see* Mains of Mayen

Mayshiel

Lothians: About 4.5 miles north-west of Cranshaws, on minor road south of B6355, south of Kell Burn, 1.5 miles west of Whiteadder Reservoir, at Mayshiel.
Private NT 622641 OS: 67 ** Map: 4, no: 216
Mayshiel is a plain altered 17th-century tower house of two storeys and a garret, now L-plan. It consists of a main block and a stair-wing. The walls are pierced by at least one gunloop. The tower had a courtyard, a fragment of which remains.

The entrance, through an arched doorway in the re-entrant angle, leads to a wide turnpike stair in the wing. The basement is not vaulted, and the interior has been very altered.

Mayshiel was a property of the Priory of the Isle of May until the Reformation, when it was acquired by the Stewarts in 1586. It later passed to the Cockburns.

McCulloch's Castle

Dumfriesshire: About 6 miles south of New Abbey, on minor road east of A710, on coast, 0.25 miles of Arbigland House, at McCulloch's Castle.
Private NX 997577 OS: 84 ** Map: 1, no: 194
Site of castle, shown by excavation to have been used from the Iron Age until about 1500. It was presumably a property of the MacCulloch family, but passed to the Murrays.

The castle was moved to a new site [NX 992572] called Arbigland Hall, now a sunken rose garden, itself abandoned for Arbigland House. The property passed from the Murrays, then to the Carnegie Earl of Southesk, the Craiks in 1679, then the Blacketts in 1852, who still own the property.
Other refs: Arbigland

McWhurter's Tower *see* Blairquhan

Mearns Castle

Renfrewshire: About 3 miles south-west of Barrhead, on minor roads south of A77, just east of Newton Mearns, about 0.3 miles north of the Earn Water.
Private NS 553553 OS: 64 *** Map: 3, no: 249
Mearns castle is an altered 15th-century keep, square in plan, of four storeys, which stood on a rocky outcrop. It was enclosed by a wall, and is said to once have had a drawbridge.

The entrance leads to the vaulted basement and to a straight mural stair to the first-floor hall, which is also vaulted. The original main entrance was through an arched doorway at first-floor level, now sealed, which would have been reached by an external stair.

The property originally belonged to the Pollocks, but passed by marriage to the Maxwells of Caerlaverock in 1300, and they built an earlier castle. The licence to build the existing castle was given in 1449. One of the family was killed at the Battle of Flodden in 1513, while another, an ambassador to France, was imprisoned in the Tower of London in 1542 until ransomed. The property later passed to the Maxwells of Nether Pollok in 1648, then the Stewarts of Blackhall. The castle was abandoned and became ruinous, but restored in 1971 to link two Church of Scotland buildings. It is apparently deteriorating.

Meggernie Castle

Perth & Kinross: About 8 miles north of Killin, on minor road 14 miles west of junction with B846 at Keltneyburn, just south of River Lyon, at Meggernie.
Private NN 554460 OS: 51 **** Map: 8, no: 3
Meggernie Castle consists of a 16th-century tower house, square in plan, of five storeys to which has been added a modern mansion, although it may incorporate older work. The roof is steep and the tower is crowned with square corbelled-out

bartizans at the corners. The walls are harled and whitewashed, and are pierced by shot-holes below some of the windows.

The entrance opens into the vaulted basement. The hall would formerly have been on the first floor, with private chambers on the floors above.

The castle was built by 'Mad' Colin Campbell of Glenlyon around 1585, and he was responsible for the kidnapping of the Countess of Errol. The property passed to Menzies of Culdares. James Menzies of Culdares, 'Old Culdares' was a Jacobite who took part in the Rising of 1715, and sheltered Jacobite fugitives while entertaining government troops during the 1745 Rising. The property passed to the Stewarts of Cardney, who held it until 1885. The castle is in excellent condition and is occupied.

The castle is reputedly haunted by the top half and lower half of a woman, which has apparently been seen many times, both in the castle and in the grounds. She is said to have kissed visitors to Meggernie, waking them from sleep.

She is said to be the ghost of the beautiful wife of one of the Menzies lords. He was a very jealous man, and in a fit murdered her and cut her in half, hoping to dispose of her body later. Her husband excused his wife's disappearance by saying that she had drowned on holiday. He managed to dispose of her lower half, but was then apparently murdered himself.

An apparition of her top half is said to haunt the upper floors, where this part of her body was hidden; while her lower half is reputedly seen on the ground floor and near the family burial ground, where this part of her was buried. During renovation, the upper bones of skeleton were reportedly discovered, but the haunting continued even after the skeleton was buried. Or so it is said.

Megginch Castle

Perth & Kinross: About 8 miles east of Perth, south of A85.
Private NO 242246 OS: 53 *** Map: 8, no: 128
Surrounded by woodlands, Megginch Castle is an altered Z-plan tower house of three storeys and a garret, consisting of a 15th-century main block and a 16th-century wing. A semi-circular stair-tower stands in the re-entrant angle, capped by a square corbelled-out watch-chamber. Bartizans, with conical roofs, crown two corners, and the walls are pierced by gunloops. The 16th-century wing is dated 1575, while the stair-tower and second block are pre-1460. The house was considerably altered in 1707, Robert Adam added a wing in 1790, and other additions were made in 1820 and 1928. After a fire in 1969, the 18th- and 19th-century wing

was totally restored.

It was a property of the Hays of Leys at the end of the 15th century, and sold to the Drummonds of Lennoch in 1664. The 3rd Drummond of Megginch was the first member of Parliament for Perthshire for the Union parliament of 1707. Rob Roy MacGregor was imprisoned in Perth Tolbooth by Drummond, and part of the film 'Rob Roy' with Liam Neeson was made here. The Drummond family still live in the house.

There are extensive gardens, dating from 16th and 18th centuries. The 16th-century garden is an astrological garden, and unusual topiary features a golden yew crown and peacock. The 1830s parterre is surrounded by 1000-year-old yews.

OPEN: Castle not open; gardens open Jun- Sep, daily 14.30-17.00; other times by prior arrangement.

Guided tours by arrangement and extra charge. Disabled partial access. Car and coach parking. £.

Tel: 01821 642222 Fax: 01821 642708

Meikle Daan

Ross & Cromarty: About 1.5 miles west of Edderton, on minor roads south of A9, north and west of Allt Muigh Bhlaraidh, at Meikle Daan.

Private NH 688847 OS: 21 * Map: 9, no: 99

Meikle Daan is a plain two-storey house, dating from 1680, but incorporates earlier work. It was a property of the Munros.

Meikle Kilmory *see* Kilmory Castle

Meikle Swinton *see* Little Swinton

Meikle Tarrel

Ross & Cromarty: About 8 miles east of Tain, on minor road south of B9165, about 3 miles south-west of Portmahomack, south of Tarrel, at Meikle Tarrel.

Ruin or site NH 900810 OS: 21 * Map: 9, no: 141

Site of castle or fortified house, a property of the Munros.

Meikleour House

Perth & Kinross: About 4 miles south and west of Blairgowrie, on minor roads south of A93, on east bank of Tay, 0.5 miles south of Meikleour village, at Meikleour House.

Private NO 153387 OS: 53 * Map: 8, no: 101

Site of castle. Meikleour House, a substantial mansion extended in 1869 and re-modelled by David Bryce, stands on the site of several earlier houses.

The property was acquired by the Mercer family in 1162, then passed to the Murray Lords Nairne, and later to the Marquises of Landsdowne. The house is still occupied by the same family. The Meikleour Hedge, a famous beech hedge which lines the A93 along the edge of the estate, is 100-feet high.

Meldrum House

Aberdeen & Gordon: About 1 mile north of Oldmeldrum, on minor roads east of A947 or west of B9170, at Meldrum House.

Private NJ 812291 OS: 38 ** Map: 10, no: 271

Meldrum House, a large sprawling mansion, incorporates a 17th-century castle with a vaulted basement. The house was extended in the 17th and 18th centuries, and altered again in 1934.

It was a property of the Meldrums from 1236 until the middle of the 15th century, when it passed to the Setons. Alexander Seton of Meldrum was murdered in 1526 by the Master of Forbes and John Strachan of Lynturk. In 1670 Meldrum was acquired by the Urquharts, who were Jacobites. It is now a hotel.

The house is traditionally believed to be haunted by a 'Green Lady', who has reputedly been seen many times. Recent reports, however, have her clad in white, or this may be another ghost. Sightings of this apparition have been reported several times, as recently as 1985 when she reputedly gave a male guest a cold kiss during a thunder storm. It was believed by some that this spectre only appeared to children on their own, who reported a lady in white had been taking care of them.

OPEN: Hotel – open all year.

9 bedrooms with ensuite facilities. Restaurant and private bar. Functions, small conferences and weddings. Own 18 hole golf course available to residents. Parking.

Tel: 01651 872294 Fax: 01651 872464 Web: www.meldrumhouse.co.uk

Melgund Castle

Angus & Dundee: About 4.5 miles south-west of Brechin, on minor roads and foot south of B9134, 1.5 miles east of Crosston, south of Mains of Melgund.

Ruin or site NO 546564 OS: 54 * Map: 8, no: 232**

An impressive and interesting building, Melgund Castle is a 16th-century L-plan tower house and hall-block. It consists of a main block of four storeys, formerly with a garret, and a higher stair-wing, which was once capped by a large watch-chamber. A corbelled-out parapet has open rounds. The walls are pierced by small windows and many gunloops.

The entrance, in the stair wing, leads to a wide turnpike stair and to two cellars in the vaulted basement. The first floor and upper floors contained private chambers.

The hall-block of two storeys and an attic has a corbelled-out parapet and a round tower, with shot-holes, at one corner. It contained the kitchen, with a large fire-

place; the wine-cellar, with a private stair to the hall above; and other cellars in the vaulted basement. The hall, on the first floor, was a magnificent chamber. A turnpike stair climbs to the upper floors beside the round tower.

Another range of buildings is completely ruinous.

Melgund was built by Cardinal Beaton, Archbishop of St Andrews and Chancellor of Scotland, and Margaret Ogilvie, his mistress (or wife). It passed to the Gordon Marquis of Huntly in the 17th century, then to the Maules, then to the Murrays, later Murray Kynmonds, then to the Elliot Earls of Minto and Viscounts Melgund. It is currently being restored.

The ghost of Cardinal Beaton reputedly haunts the castle, one of several places his spirit is said to frequent.

Mellerstain

Borders: About 5 miles east of Earlston, on minor roads west of A6089 or east of B6397, at Mellerstain.

Private NT 648392 OS: 74 ** Map: 2, no: 264**

Mellerstain House is a magnificent castellated mansion, which was designed by William and Robert Adam. It replaced an earlier house, which the Baillies had held from 1642 or earlier. The wings date from 1725, while the central block was not completed until 1778, and replaced an earlier building. Mellerstain was built for George Baillie of Jerviswood, and is now owned by the Baillie-Hamiltons, Earls of Haddington.

OPEN: Open Easter weekend (Fri-Mon), then May-Sep, daily except Sat 12.30-17.00; groups at other times by appt; restaurant, 11.30-17.30.

Collections of paintings and furniture. Fine interiors. Gift shop. Tearoom. Gardens and grounds. Disabled access to ground floor and grounds. Car and coach parking. ££.

Tel: 01573 410225 Fax: 01573 410636

Email: mellerstain.house@virgin.net

Web: http://muses.calligrafix.co.uk/mellerstain

Mellingshaw Tower

Dumfriesshire: About 4 miles north-west of Moffat, on minor roads west of A74, west of Evan Water, in Greskine Forest, just south of Mellingshaw Water.

Ruin or site   NT 037088   OS: 78   *   Map: 1, no: 203

Not much survives of a 16th-century tower house of the Johnstones except one corner, which contained a turnpike stair. It may have been T-plan, and rose to at least three storeys. It formerly had a courtyard.

Melrose Abbey

Borders: To the east of Melrose, on minor road north of A6091 in Melrose, east of B6361, about 0.25 miles south of the River Tweed, behind the Abbey.

His Scot   NT 550344   OS: 73   **   Map: 2, no: 204

An elegant and picturesque ruin, Melrose Abbey was founded as a Cistercian house by David I about 1136, and dedicated to the Blessed Virgin Mary. The church is particularly well preserved, while the domestic buildings and the cloister are very ruinous. The Abbey suffered in the wars with the English, and was sacked in 1322, 1385 and 1545, after which it never recovered. It was dissolved at the Reformation, although the nave of the church was crudely vaulted and used as a parish church from 1618 until 1810, when it was finally abandoned. The lands were given to the Douglases, who had been Commendators of the abbey. The heart of Robert the Bruce is buried in the nave, and many of the powerful Douglas family are also interred here.

The Commendator's House is a 16th-century tower house, developed out of the abbot's house by heightening it and providing gunloops and shot-holes. It was later altered and given a new roof and windows. There is an inscribed lintel over the door, dated 1590.

The entrance opened into a vaulted lobby, and leads to a passage which connects with four basement chambers, two of which are vaulted. On the first floor there are now three chambers. The building now houses an exhibition of carvings and other artefacts.

Other refs: Commendator's House, Melrose Abbey

OPEN: Open all year, daily 9.30-18.30; last ticket sold 30 mins before closing; closed 25/26 Dec and 1/2 Jan.

Audio guide and explanatory displays. Gift shop. WC. Picnic area. Museum in former Commendator's House. Car and coach parking (£). Group concessions. £.

Tel: 01896 822562   Fax: 0131 668 8888

Email: hs.explore@scotland.gov.uk   Web: www.historic-scotland.gov.uk

Melville Castle

Lothians: About 1.5 miles west of Dalkeith, on minor roads east of A7, just west of the North Esk, at Melville.

Private   NT 310669   OS: 66   **   Map: 4, no: 129

Site of castle, which was visited by Mary, Queen of Scots. The old castle was demolished when the present derelict house, a symmetrical castellated mansion of three storeys, designed by James Playfair, was built at the end of the 18th century.

The property took its name from Norman de Malavilla in the 12th century. It passed to Sir John Ross of Hawkhead in the late 14th century, but was sold to David Rennie in 1705, then passed by marriage to Henry Dundas, 1st Viscount Melville, later Duke of Lauderdale. Dundas was a very powerful man in Scotland, and there is a memorial to him in the gardens of St Andrew Square in Edinburgh. The house was used as a hotel, but although only abandoned in the 1980s, is now derelict. It may be about to be restored.

Melville House

Fife: About 4.5 miles west of Cupar, on minor roads east of A914 and west of A91 at junction with B937, at Melville House.

Private   NO 298138   OS: 59   **   Map: 7, no: 70

Melville House, a tall classical mansion, was built in 1692 to replace the old bishop's palace at Monimail [NO 299141], and includes cellars from a 16th-century building. There were apparently also shot-holes in each of the wings, although these can no longer been seen.

After the Reformation the property passed to the Balfours of Pittendreich, but was sold to the Melvilles in 1592. The family were made Lords Melville of Monimail in 1616, then Earls of Melville in 1690 after playing an active part in the Revolution of 1689. The family lived here until 1950.

Menie House

Aberdeen & Gordon: About 2 miles north of Balmedie, on minor roads east of A92, about 0.5 miles west of sea, at Menie House.

Private   NJ 978206   OS: 38   **   Map: 10, no: 346

Menie House, a two-storey Jacobean house of about 1840, incorporates an 18th-century house at one corner, and stands on the site of a 15th-century castle. It was a property of the Forbes family.

The castle is said to be haunted by a 'Green Lady', who is reported to have been seen in the basement of the old part of the house.

Menmuir

Angus & Dundee: About 4.5 miles north-west of Brechin, on minor roads north of A90, east of Kirkton of Menmuir, near Tigerton.

Ruin or site   NO 534643 [?]   OS: 44   *   Map: 8, no: 224

Site of royal palace or castle, dating from the 13th century. The Crown held the lands until the middle of the 14th century.

Menstrie Castle

Stirlingshire & Clackmannan: About 3 miles north-west of Alloa, on minor road south of A91, north of River Devon, in Menstrie.

Private   NS 852968   OS: 58   *   Map: 6, no: 85**

Menstrie Castle consists of a small 16th-century L-plan tower house of two storeys and an attic, the wing of which was later greatly extended into a long block. The gables are corbiestepped, and a bartizan, with gunloops, crowns one corner. Another range was added, forming three sides of a courtyard, the last side being completed by a wall. The curtain wall, and ranges of outbuildings, have been demolished.

The entrance to the tower leads through a pend or passage, with stone benches, to the vaulted basement. The tower has been altered inside.

Menstrie was a property of the Alexander family from around 1481, and they were made Earls of Stirling about 1567. One of the family, Sir William Alexander, was born in 1575 and the 1st Earl of Stirling. He was the founder of Nova Scotia, although he was later ruined and died bankrupt. The castle was burned by the Marquis of Montrose in 1645 because the family supported the Campbell Earl of Argyll. The Holbournes acquired Menstrie in 1649, one of whom was General James Holbourne, who fought against Cromwell at the Battle of Dunbar in 1650. The property was sold to the Abercrombies in 1719. Alexander Abercrombie was a committed Hanoverian.

The house was saved from demolition in the 1950s, and stands in a housing estate. There is a museum about Sir William, and the Nova Scotia Baronetcies.

OPEN: Open Easter wknd, then May-Sep, Wed and Sun 14.00-16.00. Administered by NTS and staffed by Clackmannanshire Council.

Parking nearby.

Tel: 01259 213131

Menteith Castle *see* Inchtalla Castle

Menzies Castle *see* Castle Menzies

Merchiston Castle

Lothians: About 1 mile south and west of Edinburgh Castle, on minor road west of the A702, in the Merchiston area of Edinburgh, part of Napier University.

Private   NT 243717   OS: 66   *   Map: 4, no: 89**

Merchiston Castle consists of an altered strong 15th-century keep, now L-plan, of four storeys and a gabled attic. A corbelled-out parapet has rounds at each corner.

The basement is vaulted and contains a cellar, reached by a narrow stair, while the ground floor houses the kitchen with a wide fireplace. A turnpike stair, in one corner, climbs to the upper floors. The castle has been altered inside, and later extensions have been demolished.

Merchiston was a property of the Napiers of Merchiston. Mary, Queen of Scots, visited the castle. In 1572 it was besieged by the Regent Morton, who bombarded it from Edinburgh Castle. Sir Archibald Napier refused to surrender the castle to the Regent Mar, and it resisted another siege. John Napier, the inventor of logarithms, was born at the castle in 1550.

In 1833 the castle was let to Charles Chalmers and a school was founded at Mer-

chiston. In 1914 the property was let to Merchiston Castle School Ltd, but in 1924 the school moved to a new site at Colinton. In 1935 the castle passed to the City of Edinburgh, and was used by the National Fire Service during World War II, although the surrounding 19th-century buildings were then demolished.

The building became derelict and was threatened with demolition. In 1958 the castle was 'restored' and incorporated into Napier College of Commerce and Technology, now Napier University, by slapping a corridor through the wing, the kind of restoration that could only happen in the 1960s. The gate survives to the east of the main university building. A ceiling from Prestongrange was brought here.

OPEN: View from exterior.

Mergie House *see* House of Mergie

Mersington Tower

Borders: About 3.5 miles east and south of Greenlaw, on minor roads east of A697, near Mersington.
Ruin or site   NT 775443   OS: 74   *   Map: 2, no: 312
Site of 15th century castle, nothing of which remains.

The lands were a property of the Kerrs, then the Swintons, but the tower was torched by the Earl of Hertford in 1545 during the Rough Wooing. Alexander Swinton, Lord Mersington, was one of those who led an attack on the Chapel Royal at Holyrood during a riot in 1688.

Mertoun House

Borders: About 7 miles west of Kelso, on minor road south of B6404, just north of the River Tweed, at or near Merton House.
Ruin or site   NT 618318   OS: 74   *   Map: 2, no: 241
Site of castle of the Halyburtons. The property passed to the Scotts of Harden, later Lords Polwarth, from around 1680 until 1912. The property is now held by the Duke of Sutherland.

Merton House, built in 1702 and designed by Sir William Bruce, was altered and extended in 1843 by William Burn and again in 1912, although these extensions were demolished in the 1950s. It replaced a two-storey harled building of 1677, which may have stood on the site of the tower.

Mertoun Gardens consist of 26 acres of beautiful grounds with fine walks and river views, featuring grand trees, herbaceous borders, and flowering shrubs. There is a walled garden and well-preserved round doocot, dated 1576.
Other refs: Old Mertoun House
OPEN: House not open; gardens open Apr-Sep wknds and Mon Bank Holidays 14.00-18.00; last admission 17.30.
Guided tours. Disabled access. WC. Parking. £.
Tel: 01835 823236   Fax: 01835 822474

Mervinslaw Pele

Borders: About 5.5 miles south of Jedburgh, on minor road south of A68, about 0.5 miles from road, on south slopes of Mervins Law, west of Black Burn (Jed).
Ruin or site   NT 672117   OS: 80   *   Map: 2, no: 274**
Mervinslaw Pele is a ruined but well-preserved 16th-century tower house, or peel tower, of three storeys.

The basement does not appear to have been vaulted, and the small hall or living room was on the first floor. There were no stairs, and the upper floors would have been reached by ladders. Not much remains of a courtyard, with ranges of buildings.

It was a property of the Olivers.

Mestag Castle *see* Castle Mestag

Methven Castle

Perth & Kinross: About 5 miles west and north of Perth, on minor road north of A85, about 0.75 miles east of village of Methven, at Methven Castle.
Private   NO 042260   OS: 53   **   Map: 8, no: 57
Methven Castle is a 17th-century tower house, square in plan, of five storeys, with round towers with ogee roofs at each corner. The windows are large and evenly spaced, and there are lower and later extensions.

The property belonged to the Mowbrays from the 11th century, but passed to the

Stewart Earls of Atholl, who were forfeited for treason in 1427, the lands being retained by the Crown. The castle was used as a dower house for Margaret Tudor, wife of James IV, who died at the castle in 1540. In 1584 the property was given to Esme Stewart by James VI, then was held by the Dukes of Lennox until sold to the Smythes of Braco in 1664, who held it until 1923 when it was sold again. The castle was restored in the 1950s and 1980s, and is occupied as company offices.

Robert the Bruce was defeated at a battle nearby in 1306 by the Earl of Pembroke.

Mey Castle *see* Castle of Mey

Middleton

Renfrewshire: About 2.5 miles north east of Johnstone, on minor roads north of A740, 1 mile west of Linwood, at or near Middleton.
Ruin or site   NS 451651   OS: 64   *   Map: 3, no: 186
Site of castle.

Middleton *see* Fettercairn House

Middleton House

Angus & Dundee: About 6 miles north-west of Arbroath, on minor roads north of B961 west of junction with A933, 1 mile south-west of Friockheim, at Middleton.
Private NO 583487 OS: 54 ** Map: 8, no: 241
Middleton House, an 18th-century mansion of the Gardyne family, incorporates, or is built on the site of, a 16th-century tower house. The family held the property in the 20th century.

Middleton of Colquhoun *see* Tresmass

Midhope Castle

Lothians: About 5 miles east and north of Linlithgow, on minor road north of A904, about 1 mile west of Hopetoun House, west of the Midhope Burn.
Private NT 073787 OS: 65 * Map: 4, no: 31**
Midhope Castle is a 16th-century tower house of five storeys and a garret, to which has been added a later and lower wing. Two-storey bartizans crown three of the

corners, a caphouse for the stair crowning the fourth. The roof is steeply pitched. It forms one side of a courtyard, and there is a fine walled garden.
  The entrance, at first floor level, is reached by a short external stair. The basement is vaulted, and the wing contained the kitchen. The original stair was turnpike, but a scale-and-platt stair was later added. The hall, on the first floor, has been subdivided, and the inside of the tower has been much altered.
  Midhope originally belonged to the Drummonds, but later passed to the Livingstone Earls of Linlithgow, then to the Hopes. It was used to house farm workers after the building of nearby Hopetoun House, but was abandoned and became semi-derelict. It is being restored.
Other refs: Hopetoun Tower

Midhowe Broch

Orkney: On south-west side of island of Rousay in Orkney, 1 mile north and west of end of B9064, about 4 miles north-west of Trumland, at Midhowe.
His Scot HY 371306 OS: 6 ** Map: 11, no: 39
Midhowe broch occupies a neck of land overlooking Eynhallow Sound. Two ditches with a wall between them cuts it off from the adjoining land. There are a number of houses around the broch – several more have been destroyed by coastal erosion. The broch is different from the majority of northern brochs, having a gallery at ground level rather than the usual solid-base construction. The gallery was apparently faulty in its design and its outside wall had to be buttressed with vertical slabs. The partitions in the interior were probably constructed during a late phase of use.

Other features in the interior include a hearth and a watertank filled by an underground spring.
  The chambered tomb of Midhowe is close by.
Other refs: Broch of Midhowe
OPEN: Access at all reasonable times.
Parking nearby.
Tel: 0131 668 8800 Fax: 0131 668 8888
Email: hs.explore@scotland.gov.uk Fax: www.historic-scotland.gov.uk

Midmar *see* Cunningar

Midmar Castle

Aberdeen & Gordon: About 5.5 miles north of Banchory, on minor roads south of B9119, north of Midmar Forest, at Midmar Castle.
Private NJ 704053 OS: 38 ** Map: 10, no: 213**
A fine and well-preserved stronghold, Midmar Castle is a late 16th century Z-plan tower house, which was probably built by the architect George Bell. It consists of a main block of four storeys and a garret, and two towers at opposite corners, one a

six-storey round tower with a flat crenellated roof, the other being square. Two stair-turrets have conical roofs and another projects on corbelling from second-floor level and is topped by an ogee-roofed caphouse. Bartizans crown some of the corners. The roofs are steep and the walls are harled. Lower 17th-century ranges have been added.
  Midmar belonged to the Browns from the 13th century until 1422 when it passed to the Gordons, then to the Forbeses, later to the Grants, then through several families until finally returning to the Gordons of Cluny. It was then abandoned about 1850, but reoccupied in the 1970s.
  There was an earlier castle, known as Cunningar [NJ 701060], about 0.5 miles to the north.
Other refs: Ballogie Castle; Grantfield

Migvie Castle

Kincardine & Deeside: About 8 miles north-east of Ballater, on minor road east of A97 or west of B9119 at Tarland, in Migvie.
Ruin or site NJ 437066 OS: 37 * Map: 10, no: 89
Very little remains of a 13th-century castle of enclosure of the Earls of Mar, probably destroyed by the Bruces in 1307-8 and never rebuilt. The property passed to the Rutherfords of Tarland, then later to the Gordon Earl of Huntly.

Milliken

Renfrewshire: About 1.5 miles north-west of Johnstone, on minor roads south of A761, 1 mile north-east of Kilbarchan, Milliken.
Ruin or site NS 418634 OS: 64 * Map: 3, no: 160
Probable site of tower house.
  The lands were a property of the Wallaces of Elderslie, but passed to the Hou-

stons, then in 1733 to a James Milliken, a wealthy sugar merchant. He demolished the old house or castle, and built a new mansion, itself replaced after a fire by a Grecian-style house in 1829. The property passed to the Mackenzies, then the architect George Boswell. He demolished Milliken House, and remodelled other buildings into the White House of Milliken in the 1920s.

Milnton *see* Tarbat House

Milton

Ayrshire: About 6 miles west of Dalmellington, on minor road just west of B7045 north of junction with B741, 0.25 miles N of Straiton, west of Water of Girvan, at Milton.
Ruin or site   NS 377054   OS: 77   *   Map: 3, no: 127
Possible site of castle, on which was built the farm.
  Milton was a property of the Blairs in the 16th century.

Milton Brodie House

Moray: About 4 miles north-east of Forres, on minor roads south of B9089 or north of A96, north of Kinloss Burn, at Milton Brodie.
Private   NJ 094627   OS: 27   *   Map: 10, no: 13
Milton Brodie House, a mansion remodelled in 1835, may incorporate or be built on the site of a castle of the Brodies.
Other refs: Windy Hills

Milton Keith Tower

Moray: In Keith, on minor roads north of A95 or south of B9116, above (east of) River Isla, at Milton Keith.
Ruin or site   NJ 429512   OS: 28   **   Map: 10, no: 86
Not much remains of a or a 15th or 16th-century tower house, formerly of three storeys and with a vaulted basement.
  The property was acquired by the Ogilvies from the Abbey of Kinross after the Reformation, passed to the Oliphants in the late 17th century, and abandoned and 'destroyed' in 1829.
Other refs: Milton Tower

Milton of Colquhoun *see* Tresmass

Milton Tower *see* Milton Keith Tower

Minard Castle

Argyll & Dunbartonshire: About 8 miles north-east of Lochgilphead, on minor road east of A83, south of Minard Bay on west shore of Loch Fyne, at Minard Castle.
Private   NR 973943   OS: 55   *   Map: 5, no: 89
Set in fine countryside on the west side of Loch Fyne, Minard Castle is a modern mansion and has no fortified origins. The oldest part of the house dates from the 18th century, when the house was known as Knockbuie and held by the Campbells. It was extended and remodelled with a new castellated front in the mid 19th century, when it was a property of the Lloyds, who were related to the former Campbell owners, until the 1940s. It became a hotel, but was sold to the Gayre family in 1974, and is now a private residence. Accommodation available.
Other refs: Knockbuie
OPEN: B&B (Apr-Oct) and self-catering accommodation available.
Three bedrooms with ensuite facilities for B&B. Lodge and courtyard flats. Parking.
Tel: 01546 886272   Fax: 01546 886272
Email: reinoldgayre@bizonline.co.uk
Web: www.oas.co.uk/ukcottages/minardcastle/

Mindork Castle

Galloway: About 1.5 miles south and west of Kirkcowan, on minor roads south of B733, 1 mile east of High Mindork, north of Mindork Fell, just north of road.
Ruin or site   NX 322588   OS: 82   *   Map: 1, no: 45
On raised ground now within a conifer plantation, little remains of Mindork Castle, although part of it still stood at the end of the 18th century.
  It was a property of the Dunbars.

Mingary Castle

South Highland: About 1 mile east of Kilchoan, on minor roads and foot south of B8007 (the castle can be reached along the shore from Kilchoan pier), on south coast of Ardnamurchan, at Mingary.
Ruin or site   NM 502631   OS: 47   ***   Map: 9, no: 9
Mingary Castle is a strong 13th-century castle of enclosure, with a high wall encircling the rock on which it stands. The main entrance was on the sea side, but there

Mingary Castle – see above

was another entrance across a drawbridge, over a walled ditch. Ranges of two-storey buildings stand inside the curtain wall, dating from the 17th and 18th centuries, as well as a three-storey rectangular block. Alterations of various kinds were made between the 16th and 18th centuries.

Mingary was probably built by the MacIans of Ardnamurchan. It was occupied by James IV in 1493 and 1495 during his campaigns against the MacDonalds; and demolished or slighted in 1517. The MacIans supported the MacDonalds in the 1550s, and MacLean of Duart captured the chief of MacIan, then unsuccessfully attempted to besiege the castle with Spanish soldiers from an Armada galleon in Tobermory Bay. The Campbells, however, took Mingary from the MacIans. It was captured by Alaisdair Colkitto MacDonald in 1644 for the Marquis of Montrose, but was recaptured by the Covenanter General David Leslie in 1646, then returned to the Argyll Campbells in 1651. The castle was garrisoned for the Government during the Jacobite Rising of 1745, and probably still habitable around 1848. Although the building is fairly complete to the wallhead, it may be in a dangerous condition. The castle can be reached from along the shore from Kilchoan pier.

Minnigaff Motte

Galloway: To north of Newton Stewart, on minor roads north of B 7079, on promontory between River Cree and Penkiln Burn, at Minnigaff.
Ruin or site NX 410665 OS: 83 * Map: 1, no: 60
The motte stands between the confluence of two rivers, the landward side being defended by a wide ditch. The motte was probably raised at the beginning of the 13th century. It was held for the English and stormed by William Wallace in 1298. It was slighted and may not have been reused.

Minto House

Borders: About 5.5 miles north-east of Hawick, on minor road north of B6405, on north side of Teviot river, near Minto House.
Ruin or site NT 573203 OS: 73 * Map: 2, no: 216
Site of 16th-century tower house incorporated into Minto House, a large four-storey Adam mansion of the 1740s, which was rebuilt and altered in the 19th century.

The property belonged to the Turnbulls, but in the 14th century passed to the Scotts, and later was sold to the Elliots, who were made Earls of Minto in 1813. Gilbert John Murray Kynmond, 4th Earl, who succeeded in 1891, was Governor General of Canada 1898-1904, and Viceroy of India 1905-10. The house has been mostly demolished, having been neglected for years, and set on fire in 1992.

Minto Tower *see* Fatlips Castle

Moat

Lanarkshire & Glasgow: About 2.5 miles north of Abington, just east of A73, just west of Clyde, 1 mile south of Roberton, at Moat.
Ruin or site NS 941272 OS: 72 * Map: 3, no: 418
The earthwork here is believed to date from the 14th century. It may have been constructed by Mary of Stirling, needing a secure base as she did not support Robert the Bruce. She resigned her lands at Roberton in 1346, hoping for a pardon from David II.

Moat House *see* Flowerdale

Moat House, Elderslie *see* Wallace's Buildings

Moat of Colstaine *see* Coldstone

Moat, Lesmahagow

Lanarkshire & Glasgow: About 2 miles east of Lesmahagow, off minor roads 3 miles east of M74, at Moat.
Ruin or site NS 846396 OS: 71 * Map: 3, no: 393
Site of castle, which had a vaulted basement and was 'loopholed in its lower part'. It is said to have been built to resist the Annandale thieves.

Mochrum *see* Old Place of Mochrum

Moil Castle

Argyll & Dunbartonshire: To north-east of Campbeltown, near B842, north side of Campbeltown Loch, at Moil.
Ruin or site NR 725210 [?] OS: 68 * Map: 5, no: 38
Site of castle, a property of the MacDonald Lord of the Isles. Two other castles are recorded around Campbeltown: Kilkerran Castle [NR 729194] and Lochhead Castle [NR 718202].
Other refs: Campbeltown

Monboddo House

Kincardine & Deeside: About 4 miles north of Laurencekirk, on minor roads north of B966, 1 mile east of Auchenblae, at Monboddo.
Private NO 744783 OS: 45 * Map: 10, no: 237**
Monboddo House incorporates a simple 17th-century tower house, rectangular in plan, of two storeys and an attic, to which a large mansion has been added. The walls are harled and pierced by gunloops, the windows quite large, and conical-roofed bartizans crown two of the corners. The roofline has been altered. The old part is dated 1635.

The basement is not vaulted, and contains the kitchen with a large fireplace. The hall, on the first floor, was panelled.

Monboddo was a Barclay property from the 13th century, but by 1593 had passed to the Strachans, then later to the Irvines, then to the Burnets. The house was reoccupied in the 1970s with the demolishing of the modern mansion, and stands in a modern housing estate.

Monckton Castle *see* Monkton House

Moncur Castle

Perth & Kinross: About 9 miles east and north of Perth, on minor road and foot east of B953 or north of A85 at Moncur hamlet, just west of the Huntly Burn.
Ruin or site NO 284295 OS: 53 * Map: 8, no: 143**
Moncur Castle is a ruined 16th-century Z-plan tower house. It consists of a three-storey main block, with a square tower and a round tower at opposite corners.

The vaulted basement of the main block contained the kitchen, with a fireplace, and two cellars. The hall, on the first floor, had an adjoining private chamber.

It was a property of the Moncurs from the 15th century. The castle was gutted by fire in the 18th century, and not reoccupied.

Mondynes Castle

Kincardine & Deeside: About 7 miles south-west of Stonehaven, on minor roads west of B966 at junction with A94, east of Monbuddo, at or near Mains of Mondynes.
Ruin or site NO 772795 [?] OS: 45 * Map: 10, no: 253
Site of 13th-century castle, probably of the Barclays. The site may be at Castleton [NO 759788] rather than Mains of Mondynes.

Moniack Castle

Inverness & Nairn: About 2.5 miles south-east of Beauly, on minor roads south of A862, west of the Moniack Burn, 1 mile east of Balchraggan, at Moniack Castle.
Private NH 552436 OS: 26 * Map: 9, no: 66**
Moniack Castle incorporates a 17th-century L-plan tower house, consisting of a main block of three storeys and a two-storey wing, which has been much altered and extended over the centuries. A large round stair-tower stands in the re-entrant angle, and is corbelled out to square, above second-floor level, to form a watch-chamber. The walls are harled, and the windows small, but the roofline has been altered, and the parapet is modern.

The entrance, at the foot of the stair-tower, leads to a wide turnpike stair, but the inside of the tower has been very altered, and there is no vaulting.

It was a property of the Frasers of Lovat. Simon Fraser, Lord Lovat, lived here. He was an active Jacobite, although he was imprisoned in France and supported the government in the 1715. He took part in the 1745 Rising, but was captured, tried and executed in 1747.

In the grounds of the castle is a carved Pictish stone, bearing a bird-headed man carrying a club as well as prehistoric cup and ring marks.

Highland Wineries is based at the castle, and Moniack Castle now gives its name to a range of wines and foods, including elderflower and silver birch; and also mead and sloe gin, and there are also meat and game preserves. There is also a wine bar and bistro.

Other refs: Highland Wineries; Wester Moniack

OPEN: Open Mar-Oct, daily 10.00-17.00, closed Sun; Nov-Feb, 11.00-16.00.

Guided tours. Gift shop. Restaurant. Tearoom. Picnic area. WC. Car and coach parking.
Tel: 01463 831283   Fax: 01463 831419

Monifieth *see* Grange of Monifieth

Monikie Castle

Angus & Dundee: About 4 miles north of Monifieth, just off B962 at Kirkton of Monikie, about 0.5 miles north of Monikie Reservoir Country Park.
Ruin or site   NO 517390 [?]   OS: 54   *   Map: 8, no: 218
Site of 16th-century castle, nothing of which survives except two armorial panels built into a cottage, one with the date 1587.

   Monikie was a property of the Lindsays.

Monimail Tower

Fife: About 6 miles west of Cupar, on minor road between Collessie and Letham, west of A914 and east of A91 at junction with B937, at Monimail.
Private   NO 299141   OS: 59   *   Map: 7, no: 71**
Monimail Tower is a 16th-century tower house, square in plan, of four storeys and a flat roof within a parapet, although parts may date from the 14th century. The parapet has open rounds and a caphouse crowns the stairhead. A ruined round tower and fragments of a curtain wall and range of buildings also survive.

   It is said to have first been built by Bishop William Lamberton before 1328, and was a property of the Bishops of St Andrews. It was altered by Cardinal David Beaton, who was murdered at St Andrew's Castle and his naked body hung from one of the windows of the castle. Archbishop Hamilton, who succeeded Beaton, also used the palace. He was cured of asthma at Monimail by the celebrated Italian physician, Jerome Cardan, and was one of those who tried to persuade Mary, Queen of Scots, not to go into exile in England. He was, himself, hanged at Stirling Castle in 1571.

   After the Reformation, the property passed to the Balfours of Pittendreich, but was sold to the Melvilles in 1592. The family were made Lords Melville of Monimail in 1616, and Earls of Melville in 1690, after they had been prominent in helping William and Mary come to the throne. Nearby Melville House was built in 1692 to replace the old palace, and includes cellars from a 16th-century building. The family lived here until 1950.

   The tower is being restored, and houses an exhibition on the history and parish.

Other refs: Beaton's Tower

OPEN: Visitors should phone to ensure entry.
Tel: 01337 810420

Monk Castle

Ayrshire: About 3 miles north of Kilwinning, on minor road west of A737, about 1.5 miles south of Dalry, west of the River Garnock.
Ruin or site   NS 292474   OS: 63   **   Map: 3, no: 68
Monk Castle is a small ruined 16th-century T-plan tower house, consisting of a main block of two storeys and an attic and a centrally projecting stair-tower, which rises a storey higher.

   The basement was vaulted.

   It was originally a property of the Abbey of Kilwinning, but passed to the Hamiltons after the Reformation. Although a shell the walls appear to have been consolidated.

Monkbie *see* Mumbiehirst Tower

Monkbiehirst *see* Mumbiehirst Tower

Monkland House

Lanarkshire & Glasgow area: About 1 mile south of Coatbridge, on minor roads west of the A725, at Shawhead.
Private   NS 730633   OS: 64   *   Map: 3, no: 343
Monkland House was a 16th-century L-plan tower house, and built on sloping ground, so that one side has extra storeys. The old tower had been extended by later ranges. The main block had round towers at two corners, and a round stair-

tower stood in the re-entrant angle. The walls were pierced by shot-holes, but most of the windows had been enlarged.

   The vaulted basement contained three cellars, in the main block, and the kitchen in the wing. The hall, on the first floor, had been subdivided, and the house had been very altered inside, apart from a turnpike stair.

   The lands were originally owned by Newbattle Abbey, but passed to the Kerrs of Ferniehirst, then later to the Hamiltons who held them in 1554. The property was acquired by Sir James Cleland of Monkland, who built the house. The building was demolished following a series of fires since 1950, and the site is occupied by a housing development.

Other refs: Pedderslourn; Peddersburn

Monkredding House

Ayrshire: About 2 miles north-east of Kilwinning, on minor road north of B778, about 0.75 miles west of Clonbeith Castle, at Monkredding.
Private   NS 325454   OS: 63   *   Map: 3, no: 95**
Monkredding House is a small much-altered 16th-century tower house, to which has been added a more modern mansion to form three sides of a square courtyard. The tower is harled and whitewashed. The windows are small, the walls have been pierced by shot-holes, but the roofline and gables have been altered.

   The entrance is at the foot of the stair-tower, and the basement is vaulted. Apart from this, the inside of the tower has been much altered.

   The property belonged to the Abbey of Kilwinning, but passed to the Nevans. It was acquired by Cunninghams of Clonbeith in 1698, and is still occupied.

Monkstadt *see* Duntulm Castle

Monkton House

Lothians: About 1 mile south of Musselburgh, on minor road north of A6124, at Inveresk, east of the River Esk.
Private   NT 334703   OS: 66   **   Map: 4, no: 139
Monkton House incorporates an altered 16th-century L-plan tower house, extended in the 16th and 17th centuries, and added to again and remodelled in the late 17th century. The old tower has thick walls, which are pierced by gunloops and small moulded windows.

The original entrance opened into a turnpike stair, which has been removed. The basement is vaulted. One of the extensions contains the vaulted kitchen.

Monkton was a property of Newbattle Abbey, but was acquired by the Hays of Yester after the Reformation. They were forfeited for their part in the Jacobite Rising of 1715, and it passed to the Falconers, then to the Hopes of Pinkie. It is still occupied.

General Monck, Cromwell's commander, is said to have made Monkton his favourite residence in Scotland.

Monkton House
Ayrshire: About 1 mile north of Prestwick, east of A79 or west of A77, south of Monkton, beneath runway of Prestwick Airport.
Ruin or site   NS 359271   OS: 70   *   Map: 3, no: 116
Site of castle, nothing of which remains.
It was a property of the Hamiltons, who were made Earls of Abercorn in 1606, but passed to the Baillies of Monkton.
Other refs: House of Monkton; Monckton Castle

Monk's Tower
Borders: About 3 miles north-east of Hawick, on minor roads south of B6359 or north of A698, just south of village of Hassendean, near unlisted road.
Ruin or site   NT 547199   OS: 79   *   Map: 2, no: 201
Site of tower house, owned by the church.

Monk's Tower, Perth *see* Perth Castle

Montfode Castle
Ayrshire: About 1 mile north of Ardrossan, on minor road east of A78, at Montfode, not far east of the shore of the Firth of Clyde.
Ruin or site   NS 226441   OS: 63   **   Map: 3, no: 43
Not much remains of a 16th-century Z-plan tower house of the Montgomerys, except one round turret and some walling. It was ruinous by the middle of the 19th century, and mostly demolished to build a mill.

Montgomerie House *see* Coilsfield Castle

Montgreenan Castle
Ayrshire: About 3.5 miles north-east of Kilwinning, on minor roads west of A736, just south of the Lugton Water.
Ruin or site   NS 342452 [?]   OS: 63   *   Map: 3, no: 108
Site of a strong old castle with a courtyard, little of which remains except some walling.
It was apparently a bishop's palace, but later passed to the Cunninghams of Montgreenan. The family was forfeited around 1680, the castle became ruinous, and was mostly demolished in 1765.
Other refs: Mountgreenan

Montrose Castle
Angus & Dundee: To the south of Montrose, near A92 where crosses entrance to Montrose Basin, on Rossie Island or Inchbraoch.
Ruin or site   NO 710568 [?]   OS: 54   *   Map: 8, no: 271
Site of 12th-century royal castle of enclosure, which stood on Forthill.
It was used by William the Lyon, but captured by Edward I of England in 1296, who stayed at the castle, during the Wars of Independence. It may have been where John Balliol abdicated in 1296, was captured by William Wallace, and probably destroyed by Robert the Bruce around 1308. It was rebuilt, held by the English, recaptured by the Scots, then abandoned by the 1330s.
Sir James Douglas may have set out for Granada from here, to take the heart of Robert the Bruce on crusade.

Monymusk Castle
Aberdeen & Gordon: About 6.5 miles south-west of Inverurie, on minor roads north of B993 at Monymusk, just south of River Don, east of Monymusk village.
Private   NJ 688155   OS: 38   *   Map: 10, no: 199**
Monymusk Castle consists of a tall much-altered 16th-century tower house, to which

lower ranges of buildings, with a round tower, have been added. The main L-plan part of the house is now of five storeys, although the two upper storeys are an 18th-century alteration: the corbelling for the parapet and bartizans remaining above second-floor level. The walls are yellow-washed, but many of the windows have been enlarged. There is a walled garden.

The lands were originally owned by the priory of Monymusk, until seized by Forbes of Corsindae during the Reformation. The property was sold in 1712 to the Grants of Cullen, who still occupy the house.

The Monymusk Reliquary was a casket containing the relics of Saint Columba and was carried before the Scottish army at the Bannockburn in 1314 when the army of Edward II of England was given a sound thrashing by Robert the Bruce. The Reliquary is preserved in the National Museum of Scotland. In the nearby parish church [NJ 685152] is a fine Class 2 Pictish cross-slab, elaborately decorated and embellished, which was originally at the castle.

The castle is said to have had several ghosts: a man reading in the library who would disappear when approached; a 'Grey Lady', who appeared from a cupboard in the nursery, checked the children and left; a pale lady, who crossed one of the upper rooms and bathroom; and the 'Party Ghost', a red-haired man, dressed in kilt, sporran, laced shirt and silver-buttoned jacket, who would barge through party guests, and could later be heard laughing, joking and running on the stairs by guests in the upper chambers.
Other refs: House of Monymusk
OPEN: Walled garden, open Nov-Mar, Mon, Wed, Fri and Sat, 10.00-15.00, Sun 12.00-15.00; Apr-Oct, Mon-Sat 10.00-17.00, Sun 12.00-17.00. Church open all year.
Parking. Donations welcome.
Tel: 01467 651543

Monzie Castle
Perth & Kinross: About 2 miles north and east of Crieff, on minor roads west of A822 or north of A85, north of the Shaggie Burn, about 0.5 miles south-west of Monzie.
Private   NN 873245   OS: 52   **   Map: 8, no: 27
Monzie Castle is a small early 17th-century L-plan tower house of two storeys and an attic, to which has been added a large castellated mansion in the 19th century. The roof is steeply pitched, and the walls are pierced by shot-holes. The tower is

dated 1634, although it may incorporate work from the 16th century or earlier.
The entrance, in the wing, leads to a scale-and-platt stair, which climbs to the first floor then on to the upper floors. The basement is not vaulted, and the hall, on the first floor, has been subdivided.
The property belonged to the Campbells from early times until 1869, when it was sold to the Johnstones of Lathrisk. The house was restored around 1908 by Sir Robert Lorimer, after being burned out. It is still occupied, and now a property of the Crichtons.
OPEN: Open mid May-mid Jun, daily 14.00-17.00; by appt other times.
Parking. £.
Tel: 01764 653110

Morac *see* Caisteal Morar na Shein

Mordington House

Borders: About 3.5 miles west and north of Berwick upon Tweed, on minor roads north of A6105, 1 mile east of Foulden, at or near Mordington House.
Ruin or site   NT 951558 [?]   OS: 74   *   Map: 2, no: 363
Site of castle. The lands were held by the Mordington family, but given to Thomas Randolph by Robert the Bruce in the 14th century. The property passed by marriage to the Douglases of Dalkeith, later Earls of Morton, who held the property until 1581.
   The village of Mordington and bastle were burned by an English army under the Duke of Gloucester in 1482, but it is not clear whether this refers to the castle here or another building – there is little trace now of the village. Mordington passed to a son of the Douglas Earl of Angus in 1634, and the family were made Lords Mordington in 1641, although the last Lord died in 1741. Mordington later passed to the Rentons of Lamberton. Cromwell used a castle or house here as his headquarters in July 1650, but in the 18th century this was apparently replaced by a large Georgian mansion, which itself was demolished in 1973.
Other refs: Mornington

Moredun Hall

Perth & Kinross: About 3.5 miles south-east of Perth, on minor roads east of A912, about 0.5 miles north of River Earn, just north of Easter Moncrieffe.
Ruin or site   NO 145193   OS: 58   *   Map: 8, no: 97
Little remains of Moredun Hall, a 16th-century castle of the Moncrieffes of Kinmonth, who had held the lands from 1248.
   The present Moncrieffe House was built after the previous house, dating from 1679, was burned down in 1957, killing the 23rd laird.

Moredun House

Borders: About 4 miles north of Peebles, on minor road east of A703 at Eddleston, north of the Longcote Burn.
Private   NT 243472   OS: 73   *   Map: 2, no: 56
Moredun House incorporates a much-altered 16th-century tower house.

Morham Castle

Lothians: About 3 miles south east of Haddington, on minor roads between B6369 and B6370, in Morham.
Ruin or site   NT 557723   OS: 66   *   Map: 4, no: 201
Site of castle, a property of the Hepburn Earls of Bothwell.
   There was a village near the castle, but by the beginning of the 19th century this had disappeared and there are no remains, except for the small parish church.

Moriston Tower *see* Morriston Tower

Mormond *see* Strichen

Mornington *see* Mordington House

Morphie Castle

Kincardine & Deeside: About 4.5 miles north of Montrose, on minor roads west of A94 or east of A937, north of River North Esk, south-west of Hill of Morphie, at Morphie.
Ruin or site   NO 713642   OS: 45   *   Map: 10, no: 217
Site of castle of the Grahams, the last remains of which had gone by 1863. It was located on a promontory, and defended by a wall, ditch and drawbridge.
Other refs: Castle of Morphie

Morrison's Haven Fort

Lothians: About 1 mile west and south of Prestonpans, south of B1348, near Prestongrange Industrial Museum.
Ruin or site   NT 372737   OS: 66   *   Map: 4, no: 149
Site of a fort, which was built in 1547 by a John Acheson, an officer in the Scots Guard in Paris. It was destroyed by Cromwell in 1650, although remains survived into the 19th century, including an underground passage. The site is beneath a road.
Other refs: Acheson's Haven Fort

Morriston Tower

Borders: About 3 miles north-east of Earlston, on minor roads north of A6105, at or near Morriston Cottage.
Ruin or site   NT 595423 [?]   OS: 74   *   Map: 2, no: 232
Site of tower house of the Kerrs of Morriston, which was completely demolished at the end of the 18th century. Members of the family are buried at Ledgerwood Church.
Other refs: Moriston Tower

Mortlach

Moray: To south-east of Dufftown, on minor road west of A941, at Mortlach Distillery.
Private   NJ 327397   OS: 28   **   Map: 10, no: 64
The large distillery incorporated a 15th-century keep or tower house. The distillery was founded in 1823 by George Gordon and James Findlater, and has passed through several hands until owned by United Distillers.

Mortlach *see* Balvenie Castle

Morton Castle

Dumfriesshire: About 2.5 miles north and east of Thornhill, on minor roads east of A76, just south of Morton Loch, south of Morton Mains.
His Scot   NX 891992   OS: 78   ***   Map: 1, no: 169
Built on a strong site, Morton Castle consists of a ruined 15th-century keep or altered hall house, and a triangular courtyard, although little remains of two sides. The two-storey hall house, which contained a hall over a basement, stands on the third side, and has a round corner tower at one end. Part of the gateway also survives, one of the D-shaped flanking tower still standing to four storeys. The passage was defended by a portcullis and drawbridge over a pit.
   Dunegal, Lord of Nithsdale, is said to have had a stronghold here in the 12th century. The property belonged to the Adairs, but passed to Thomas Randolph early in the 14th century. An older castle here was destroyed in 1357. The property passed to the Earls of March, who built the existing castle. In 1459 it was acquired by the Douglases, later made Earls of Morton. The castle was occupied until about 1715.
OPEN: Access at all reasonable – view from exterior.
Parking nearby
Tel: 0131 668 8800   Fax: 0131 668 8888
Email: hs.explore@scotland.gov.uk   Web: www.historic-scotland.gov.uk

Morton Hall *see* Mortonhall

Morton House

Lothians: About 4 miles south of Edinburgh Castle, on minor road south of B701, north of Swanston Burn, east of Fairmilehead, Winton Loan, at Morton House.
Private   NT 254679   OS: 66   **   Map: 4, no: 95
Morton House is a plain tall house, once harled, with later additions, which dates from 1702, but contains older work. It was part of the same estate as Mortonhall, and a property of the Sinclairs of Rosslyn, given to them by Robert the Bruce in 1317.

Morton Tower *see* Sark Tower

Mortonhall

Lothians: About 3 miles south of Edinburgh Castle, on minor road north of B701 (Frogston Road East), Mortonhall
Private   NT 262683   OS: 66   *   Map: 4, no: 101
Site of keep, which had a moat and drawbridge, a property of the Sinclairs in the 14th century, and granted to Sir Oliver Sinclair of Rosslyn by James III in 1486. It passed to the Ellis family, then to John Trotter, 1st Baron, in 1635. The 9th Baron had the castle demolished, and built a classical mansion nearby in 1769, which was altered in 1835. Original interiors remain, and the house has been divided into apartments.
Other refs: Morton Hall

Mosfennan *see* Mossfennan

Moss Castle

Dumfriesshire: About 5 miles north-west of Annan, on minor roads and foot east of B7020, south-west of Murraythwaite, at Moss Castle.

Ruin or site   NY 126723   OS: 85   *   Map: 1, no: 239

The remains of an Iron Age settlement consist of a round ditch and bank. The site may have been reused for a medieval castle, a property of the Cockpool family in the 15th century.

Murraythwaite is a modern mansion, but was long a property of the Murrays.

Other refs: Murraythwaite

Moss Castle

Lanarkshire & Glasgow area: About 2.5 miles west and south of Crawfordjohn, on minor roads north of B740, 1 mile west and north of Eastertown Farm, at Mosscastle.

Ruin or site   NS 845227   OS: 71   *   Map: 3, no: 392

Site of castle, a vestige of which remained in the 19th century.

Other refs: Mosscastle; Tower of Mausonly

Moss Tower

Borders: About 4 miles south of Kelso, on minor roads between A698 and B6401, at Mosstower.

Ruin or site   NT 714265 [?]   OS: 74   *   Map: 2, no: 292

Site of a strong 15th-century castle, little of which remains, a property either of the Earls of Bothwell or the Scotts of Buccleuch. It was situated in a marsh, and a causeway provided the only access. Torched by the English in 1523, and besieged, captured and slighted by the forces of the Earl of Hertford in 1544, the stronghold was twice restored. However, after being sacked once again, this time in 1570, the tower was left ruined, and was demolished in the second half of the 18th century.

Mossburnford Castle

Borders: About 4 miles south and east of Jedburgh, on minor roads east of A68, just east of Jed Water, at or near Mossburnford.

Ruin or site   NT 675168 [?]   OS: 80   *   Map: 2, no: 276

Site of castle, which was still inhabited in the middle of the 18th century. The present Mossburnford House was built in the 19th century.

Mosscastle *see* Moss Castle

Mossfennan

Borders: About 2 miles south-west of Drumelzier, on minor road west of A701, west of the Tweed, at or near Mossfennan.

Ruin or site   NT 117317 [?]   OS: 72   *   Map: 2, no: 14

Site of tower house.

The present Mossfennan House, dating from the 18th century, was later altered and extended. It was sold to the Welsh family in 1753.

Other refs: Mosfennan

Mote of Lochorwart *see* Borthwick Castle

Motte of Boghouse *see* Druchtag Motte

Motte of Urr

Galloway: About 2.5 miles north-west of Dalbeattie, on minor road west of B794, just west of the Water of Urr.

Ruin or site   NX 815647   OS: 84   **   Map: 1, no: 139

Motte of Urr is probably the best example of a motte and bailey earthwork castle in Scotland, and dates from the 12th century, although the bailey may be even older and incorporate a hill fort.

It was a stronghold of the Lords of Galloway before they moved to Buittle in the 1240s. Devorgilla of Galloway, heiress of Allan, Lord of Galloway, married John Balliol whose son became John I, King of Scots. They were a devoted couple, and they founded Balliol College, Oxford. Devorgilla built Sweetheart Abbey [NX 964663], where they are buried, and wore an amulet containing Balliol's heart around her neck.

OPEN: Access at all reasonable times.

Parking nearby.

Moulin Castle *see* Black Castle of Moulin

Mounie Castle

Aberdeen & Gordon: About 3 miles west and north of Oldmeldrum, on minor road just south of A920, north of Netherton of Mounie, at Mounie.

Private   NJ 766287   OS: 38   *   Map: 10, no: 248**

Mounie Castle is a 17th-century T-plan tower house. It consists of a long main block of three storeys and a centrally projecting round stair-tower. The round stair-tower is corbelled out to square, and crowned by a watch-chamber. The gables are corbiestepped. A more modern detached wing has been added.

The entrance is in the foot of the stair-tower, but there are two other modern doorways. The vaulted basement contains a kitchen, with a wide arched fireplace, and a cellar. The hall, on the first floor, has been subdivided by later partitions, and there are other alterations.

Mounie was a property of the Setons, but sold to the Farquhars in 1634, and passed to the Hays of Arnbath in 1701. It was later recovered by the Setons, who sold it in 1970, and the castle is still occupied.

A Class 1 stone, found at Daviot, was brought here and has a crescent and v-rod above a mirror and comb, and a second crescent, this time without a rod.

OPEN: Pictish stone: on private property – permission should be sought in advance.

Mount Laura Tower *see* Cockairnie

Mount Stuart House

Argyll & Dunbarton: About 3.5 miles south of Rothesay, on minor roads off A844, Mount Stuart, Bute.

Private   NS 105595   OS: 63   **   Map: 5, no: 108**

A fine Victorian Gothic stately home with splendid interior decoration, Mount Stuart was designed by the Scottish architect Robert Rowand Anderson for the 3rd Marquis of Bute, and is still the seat of the Stewarts of Bute. It was built on the site of an earlier house of 1719, designed by Alexander MacGill and later William Adam, which was burned down in a disastrous fire in 1877.

The house is surrounded by 300 acres of fine landscaped grounds, gardens and woodlands with an adventure play area. There is an octagonal glass pavilion with tropical plants.

A Special Day Return Ticket is available, which includes travel from Glasgow and admission to house – tel for details.

OPEN: House and garden open Easter, then May-mid Oct, daily except closed Thu and Thu: house 11.00-16.30, last tour 15.30, gardens 10.00-17.00.

Fine collection of family portraits. Visitor reception area. Guided tours. Gift shop. Tearoom. Picnic areas. Audio-visual presentation. Adventure play area. WC. Disabled facilities: access to house and most of gardens. Car and coach parking. Group concessions available. £££

Tel: 01700 503877   Fax: 01700 505313

Email: contactus@mountstuart.com   Web: www.mountstuart.com

Mountblairy *see* Balravie Castle

Mountgreenan *see* Montgreenan Castle

Mountquhanie Castle

Fife: About 4.5 miles north and west of Cupar, on minor roads north from A914, near Mountquhanie House.

Ruin or site   NO 347212   OS: 59   **   Map: 7, no: 90

Mountquhanie consists of a ruined early 16th-century tower house, rectangular in plan, of four storeys. To this has been added 16th-century, and later, additions. The tower has a parapet with corbelled-out open rounds at three corners, and the original windows are small. The main entrance is at first-floor level, and reached by an external stone stair, from the courtyard. Within the courtyard is a small round tower, with a conical roof and gunloops, and a long two-storey range, with corbiestepped gables.

The basement of the main tower is vaulted, and had no stair to the first-floor hall.

It was a property of the Balfours from before 1459. One of the family, Sir Michael Balfour, a favourite of James IV, was killed at the Battle of Flodden in 1513, while others were involved in the murders of Cardinal David Beaton and Lord Darnley, second husband of Mary, Queen of Scots, and had to flee to Noltland in Orkney. The property was sold to the Lumsdens of Innergellie about 1600. Major-General Robert Lumsden, a veteran of the Gustavus Adolphus wars, fought against Cromwell at the Battle of Dunbar in 1650, and was Governor of Dundee in 1651. He surrendered to an army, led by General Monk, but was murdered by English troops and the town sacked and about one sixth of the inhabitants slaughtered. In 1676 the property was sold to the Crawfords. The tower was still inhabited until about 1800, but is now ruinous, although one of the later ranges is still occupied.

Moure *see* Dowies

Moure Castle

Galloway: About 4 miles north-west of Whithorn, on minor road south of B7021, north of Dowies, near Monreith Burn.

Ruin or site NX 382433 [?] OS: 83 * Map: 1, no: 52

Site of castle, little of which remains. It may have been a moated manor.

It was a property of the Mundeville family, but passed by marriage to the Maxwells in 1451. The Maxwells moved to nearby Dowies [NX 381430] about 1600.

Other refs: Ballingray

Mousa Broch

Shetland: About 10 miles south of Lerwick in Shetland, on minor road, boat and foot east of A970, on west side of island of Mousa (boat from Sand Lodge pier, Sandwick).

His Scot HU 457236 OS: 4 ***** Map: 11, no: 62

The best preserved of all brochs in Scotland, and one of the foremost Iron Age monuments in Britain or even Europe, the broch at Mousa consists of a dry-stone tower rising to about 35 feet in height. The solid base of the tower has three small cells, but above this the walls are hollow and contain galleries. A narrow stair climbs through the galleries to the wallhead. There may have been a wooden roof, and floors within the tower.

An eloping couple took shelter in the broch when their ship was wrecked about 900, as recounted in Egil's Saga. The Orkneyinga Saga tells the story of the abduction of Margaret by Erlend in 1153. He and his followers sheltered within the broch, and although they were besieged within, they managed to withstand the attack. Erlend and Margaret, mother of Earl Harald Maddadson, were eventually married.

Other refs: Broch of Mousa

OPEN: Open all year – accessible by boat from Sandwick: weather permitting.

Tel: 0131 668 8800 Fax: 0131 668 8888

Email: hs.explore@scotland.gov.uk Web: www.historic-scotland.gov.uk

Mouswald Tower

Dumfriesshire: About 9 miles west and north of Annan, on minor roads south of A75 and 1 mile north of B724, about 0.75 miles north of village of Mouswald.

Ruin or site NY 061739 OS: 85 ** Map: 1, no: 208

Little remains of Mouswald Tower or Place, a 16th-century tower house, except one wall.

It was a property of the Carruthers, but passed by marriage to the Douglases of Drumlanrig. Simon Carruthers of Mouswald was killed in a raid in 1548. Marion Carruthers of Mouswald is said to haunt Comlongon Castle. She was forced into a betrothal of marriage with a Douglas of Drumlanrig, a man she did not love, and although sheltered in Comlongon by Sir William Murray, committed suicide by jumping from one of the upstairs windows – or may have been murdered. Her apparition is said to have been seen at Comlongon, as have the sounds of her weeping, as well as a ghostly presence which has pushed people.

Mow Tower *see* Mowhaugh Tower

Mowhaugh Tower

Borders: About 3.5 miles south-east of Morebattle, on minor road 4.5 miles south from B6401, just east of the Bowmont Water

Ruin or site NT 816204 OS: 74 * Map: 2, no: 333

Site of a substantial 16th-century tower house, which was destroyed, killing the occupants, after it was undermined by the English under Sir William Eure in 1546.

Other refs: Mow Tower

Moy Castle

Inverness & Nairn: About 10.5 miles south-east of Inverness, on minor roads and boat east of B9154, 0.5 miles south-east of Moy, on island in Loch Moy.

Ruin or site NH 775343 OS: 27 * Map: 9, no: 120

Virtually nothing remains of a 14th-century castle of the Mackintosh family, used from 1337 until 1665, and said to have had a garrison of 400 men in 1422. The island had several other buildings and a paved road, as well as two huge ovens.

It was nearby, at Moy Hall, that in 1746 forces under the Montgomery Earl of Loudoun tried to capture Bonnie Prince Charlie during the Jacobite rising, and were surprised and routed. This house was burned down in about 1800, and its successor was demolished because of dry rot. A new house was built on the site in the 1950s, and is occupied by the Mackintoshes. A bed the Prince slept in is preserved at the hall.

Other refs: Moy Hall

Moy Castle

Argyll & Dunbartonshire: On island of Mull, about 10 miles south-west of Craignure, on minor road and foot 6 miles south of A849 at Strathcoil, along beach, east of Lochbuie House.

Ruin or site NM 616247 OS: 49 *** Map: 5, no: 21

In a beautiful situation on a rocky crag by the seashore, Moy Castle is a ruinous plain 15th-century keep of three storeys and a gabled garret, remaining entire to the wallhead. It has a flush crenellated parapet. Open rounds, which were once roofed over, crown two of the corners, while a caphouse for the stair and a gabled

watch-chamber crown the others. The few windows are small.

The entrance leads to the vaulted basement. The hall would have been on the first floor, with private chambers above. The tower was harled, and a landing place survives, just beside the castle. Part of the beach appears to have been cleared.

The MacLaines owned the property, an unruly branch of the MacLeans. MacLean of Duart, desiring Lochbuie, captured one of the MacLaines, and confined him on the Treshnish Isle of Cairnburgh to prevent him producing an heir. His only female companion was an old and ugly woman who, however, he contrived to make pregnant. MacLaine, himself, was murdered, but the woman managed to escape, and produced a son, who eventually regained the property.

Iain the Toothless, the chief, and his son and heir, Ewen of the Little Head, fought in 1538 over the latter's marriage settlement: apparently Ewen's wife was not satisfied with their house on a fortified island in Loch Squabain [NM 631307], and desired something more luxurious. Ewen was slain in the subsequent battle, his head being hewn off and his horse riding away for two miles with the decapitated body. A cairn [NM 649326?] was said to mark the spot where Ewen finally fell from his horse, but has been destroyed. His ghost, the headless horseman, is said to been seen riding in Glen Mor when one of the MacLaines is about to die.

MacLaine of Lochbuie, having supported the Marquis of Montrose in the 1640s with his kinsmen from Duart, rode with 300 men to join Bonnie Dundee in 1689.

The castle was abandoned in 1752, and when Boswell and Johnson visited Lochbuie in 1773 they stayed in a small house nearby, which was in turn replaced by a large Georgian mansion. The MacLaines sold the property in the 20th century, and there is a burial vault, dating from 1864, at the old chapel [NM 626236], as well as a number of 18th-century memorials.

Other refs: Castle of Moy; Lochbuie

OPEN: View from exterior.

Walk to castle.

Moy Hall *see* Moy Castle

Moy House

Moray: About 1.5 miles north-west of Forres, on minor roads north of A96, east of Muckle Burn, west of River Findhorn, at Moy House.

Private NJ 016599 OS: 27 * Map: 10, no: 7

Moy House, a three-storey mansion designed by John Adam in 1762, was built for the Grants, then altered by Colin Williamson of Dyke, who went on to built the White House in Washington. It was built on the site of a 17th-century castle.

Moyness Castle

Inverness & Nairn: About 4.5 miles east and south of Nairn, on minor roads south of A96, 0.5 miles north of Muckle Burn, at or near Mains of Moyness.

Ruin or site NH 951538 [?] OS: 27 * Map: 9, no: 152

Site of castle, a property of the Hays, nothing of which survives except a mound.

Other refs: Mains of Moyness

Muchalls Castle

Kincardine & Deeside: About 4 miles north and east of Stonehaven, on minor roads west of A92 at Muchalls, 0.5 miles west of sea, at Muchalls Castle.

Private NO 892908 OS: 45 **** Map: 10, no: 308

Little altered and well preserved, Muchalls Castle is an early 17th-century courtyard castle, incorporating older work from as early as the 13th century. An L-plan block and curtain wall enclose the square stone-flagged courtyard. A semi-circular stair-tower stands in the main re-entrant angle, and bartizans crown many of the corners. The wing, housing the main stair to the first floor, is corbelled out to form a watch-chamber. The roof levels have been altered. The curtain wall has open rounds at the corners, and formerly had a parapet. Gunloops defend the entrance.

The entrance, at the foot of the wing, leads to the stair and to a vaulted passage opening into a groin-vaulted kitchen and cellars. The hall, on the first floor, is a fine chamber, and has a plaster ceiling, as well as a large fireplace and overmantel, dated 1624. Other chambers also have plaster ceilings. There is said to be a secret stair.

Muchalls Castle – see above

Muchalls originally belonged to the Frasers, but was sold to the Hays in 1415. It had passed by 1619 to the Burnets, who built the castle here (and Crathes Castle as well). James VIII, the Old Pretender, stayed here in 1716 during the Jacobite Rising. It later passed from the family, and was used as a hotel. The castle was put up for sale in 1997 for an asking price of offers over £650,000.

The castle is reputedly haunted by the ghost of young woman, a 'Green Lady', who is said to have been drowned in a cave, which formerly could be reached by a subterranean stair from the wine-cellar. She had been awaiting her lover, but somehow slipped into the water and was killed. Her ghost, clad in a green gown, has reportedly been seen in one of the rooms, sitting in front of a mirror. Another report has the apparition disappearing into a cupboard, which was later shown to conceal a secret passageway.

Muchalls-in-Mar *see* Castle Fraser

Muckerach Castle *see* Muckrach Castle

Muckhart Castle

Stirlingshire & Clackmannan: About 2.5 miles east and north of Dollar, near junction of A823 and A91, at or near Yetts o' Muckhart.
Ruin or site   NO 003007 [?]   OS: 58   *   Map: 6, no: 112
Site of 13th-century castle, a property of the Bishop of St Andrews. Muckhart was garrisoned by the English during the Wars of Independence, but recovered after 1311 by the Scots. William Lamberton, Bishop of St Andrews, is said to have stayed here around 1320.
Other refs: Castleton House

Muckrach Castle

South Highland: About 3.5 miles south-west of Grantown-on-Spey, just north of A95 0.5 miles west of Dulnain Bridge, north of River Dulnain, at Muckrach.
Private   NH 986251   OS: 36   *   Map: 9, no: 155**
Muckrach Castle is a late 16th-century L-plan tower house. It consists of a main block, of three storeys and a garret, and a projecting stair-wing. The wing has rounded corners, but is corbelled out to square above second-floor level to be crowned by a gabled two-storey watch-chamber. The walls are not very thick, but are pierced by gunloops.

There has been a large courtyard, with ranges of buildings, which has had round corner towers.

The entrance, in the re-entrant angle, leads to a wide turnpike stair which climbs as far as the second floor. The basement is vaulted and the hall is on the first floor.

Muckrach was a property of the Grants of Rothiemurchus, and the castle built about 1598. Although ruinous and roofless at one time, the castle was restored in the 1980s, and can be rented as a holiday home.
Other refs: Muckerach Castle

Mugdock Castle

Stirlingshire & Clackmannan: About 1.5 miles north of Milngavie, on minor roads west of the A81, on the west side of Mugdock Loch, about 0.5 miles west of Mugdock village.
Ruin or site   NS 549772   OS: 64   *   Map: 6, no: 21**
Formerly a large fortress of great strength, Mugdock Castle is a courtyard castle, dating from the 14th century, but altered and extended as late as the end of the 19th century.

Of the first castle, two towers and part of the gatehouse, connected by a high curtain wall, remain. The castle was enlarged in the 15th century, with a wall enclosing an outer courtyard.

One tower is fairly complete and rises to four storeys. The main entrance is at first-floor level, reached by an external stone stair, and leads to a vaulted chamber on the first floor. A turnpike stair, in one corner, climbs to the upper floors.

Of the other tower, only the vaulted basement remains. Later buildings, outside the courtyard, date from 1655.

It was a property of the Grahams from the middle of the 13th century. One of the family was James Graham, 5th Earl and 1st Marquis of Montrose, who succeeded his father in 1626 and may have been born here. He joined the Covenanters in 1638, but was opposed to Scottish intervention in the English Civil War. Lord Sin-

clair sacked the castle while Montrose was in prison in 1641. However, Montrose went on to conduct a brilliant campaign against the Covenanters in 1644-5 winning battles at Tippermuir, Aberdeen, Inverlochy, Auldearn, Alford, and Kilsyth, but was finally defeated by David Leslie at Philiphaugh. Montrose escaped to the continent, but returned in 1650 to be defeated at Carbisdale, and was captured and hanged in Edinburgh. The family was forfeited, and Mugdock was acquired by Montrose's enemy, the Campbell Marquis of Argyll. It was recovered by the Grahams in 1661 when Argyll, himself, was executed.

In the 18th century it was replaced by Buchanan Castle. In 1875 a large castellated mansion was built in the ruins of the old castle, destroying much of it, for J. Guthrie Smith. This house itself became derelict after being used by the government during World War II, and was demolished. The ruins of the castle were presented to the local council, have been consolidated, and are in a public park.
OPEN: Park open all year: summer 9.00-21.00; winter 9.00-17.30.
Explanatory displays. Giftshop. Restaurant. Tearoom. Picnic and barbecue areas. WC. Play areas and walks. Craigend stables and bridle routes. Disabled access and WC. Tactile map. Car and coach parking.
Tel: 0141 956 6100   Fax: 0141 956 5624

Muir of Clunes

South Highland: About 3.5 miles south-east of Beauly, on minor roads south of A862 or east of A833, at or near Easter Clunes.
Ruin or site   NH 554414   OS: 26   *   Map: 9, no: 69
Possible site of castle.

Muirburnhead

Dumfriesshire: About 3.5 miles south-west of Newcastleton, on minor roads and tracks north of B6357, in Tinnisburn Forest, at or near Muirburnhead.
Ruin or site   NY 444826   OS: 79   *   Map: 1, no: 334
Site of tower house of the Armstrongs.

Muirfad Castle

Galloway: About 4 miles south-east of Newton Stewart, on minor roads east of A75, east of River Cree, at Muirfad.
Ruin or site   NX 457631   OS: 83   *   Map: 1, no: 76
Site of castle, of which there were substantial remains in 1800 but nothing now survives.

It was a property of the Gordons of Muirfad, and the last of the family was killed at the Battle of Flodden in 1513.

Muirhead

Dumfriesshire: About 0.25 miles west of Lockerbie, on minor roads north of A709, at or near Muirhead.
Ruin or site   NY 129818 [?]   OS: 78   *   Map: 1, no: 241
Site of strong tower, a vestige of which remained about 1845. It was probably a property of the Johnstones.
Other refs: Myrehead

Muirhouse Tower

Borders: About 0.5 miles east of Stow, on minor road east of A7, south of B6362, at or near Muirhouse.
Ruin or site   NT 473452   OS: 73   *   Map: 2, no: 140
Site of tower house, square in plan, all traces of which were removed in 1832.

Mulben *see* Mains of Mulben

Mumbiehirst Tower

Dumfriesshire: About 2.5 miles north of Canonbie, on minor road west of B6318, east of River Esk, at or near Nether Mumbie.
Ruin or site   NY 379797 [?]   OS: 85   *   Map: 1, no: 321
Site of castle.
Other refs: Monkbie; Monkbiehirst

Muness Castle

Shetland: On south-east end of island of Unst in Shetland, on minor roads east of A968, west of Mu Ness, at Muness Castle.

His Scot HP 629012 OS: 1 * Map: 11, no: 65**

Muness Castle is a ruined 16th-century Z-plan tower house. It consists of a main block of three storeys and formerly a garret, with round towers at diagonally opposite corners. Stair-turrets are corbelled-out above first-floor level. The walls are pierced by gunloops below many of the windows. The castle is dated 1598.

The entrance opens into a scale-and-platt stair to the upper floors and into a passageway to the vaulted basement. This passage leads to three cellars, one of which is the wine-cellar, with a small stair to the hall above; and another the kitchen, with a fireplace and oven. The hall is on the first floor of the main block, along with two other private chambers. Stairs in the turrets, as well as the scale-and-platt stair, led to the upper floor.

The castle was built by Laurence Bruce of Cultmalindie, a Scottish incomer to Shetland, who moved here after being involved in a murder. In 1573 he was appointed Chamberlain of the Lordship of Shetland, but his was a corrupt and repressive regime. Ill feeling developed between Bruce and Patrick Stewart, Earl of Orkney, and the Earl landed a force to besiege the castle in 1608, but then withdrew. The castle was burned in 1627, possibly by French pirates, although it was later restored. It was abandoned about 1750, and unroofed by 1774. The upper storey was partly dismantled for materials in the 19th century.

OPEN: Access at all reasonable times – apply to key holder.
Tel: 0131 668 8800 Fax: 0131 668 8888
Email: hs.explore@scotland.gov.uk Web: www.historic-scotland.gov.uk

Murdostoun Castle

Lanarkshire & Glasgow area: About 1 mile north of Newmains, on minor roads north of A71, north of South Calder Water, at Murdostoun Castle.

Private NS 825573 OS: 65 ** Map: 3, no: 382

Murdostoun Castle, a modern mansion, incorporates a 15th-century keep. The building is now used as a hospital.

It was a property of the Scotts, but passed in 1446 to the Inglis family and they built the keep. In 1719 it passed to the Hamiltons, and in 1856 was sold to Robert Stewart, Provost of Glasgow, who was responsible for securing Glasgow's water supply from Loch Katrine.

Murieston Castle

Lothians: About 2 miles east of West Calder, on minor road south of A71, west of main south railway line, west of the Murieston Water, at Murieston Castle Farm.

Private NT 050636 OS: 65 ** Map: 4, no: 26

Murieston Castle, a ruined 16th-century tower house, was partially rebuilt and made into a folly in 1824. The present building is two storeys high, and there is a roofless bartizan.

Murraythwaite *see* Moss Castle

Murroes Castle

Angus & Dundee: About 2.5 miles north of Broughty Ferry, on minor road east of B978 south of Kellas and west of B961, just west of the Sweet Burn, at Murroes.

Private NO 461350 OS: 54 * Map: 8, no: 197**

Built on sloping ground, Murroes Castle is a 16th-century tower house, with a long main block of two storeys and a centrally projecting round stair-tower. The walls are pierced by gunloops and shot-holes, and the original windows have moulded surrounds.

Two entrances, on different sides of the building, are at different levels, one at ground level, the other reached by an external stone stair, because of the slope of the ground.

The entrance now leads to the kitchen, formerly the hall, subdivided in modern times. There is no vaulting.

It was a property of the Fotheringhams from the 14th century. By the end of the 19th century the house had been converted to house farm labourers, but it was restored in 1942 and is occupied.

Murthly Castle

Perth & Kinross: About 3.5 miles south-east of Dunkeld, on minor roads west of B9099 or east of A9, south of River Tay, at Murthly.

Private NO 070399 OS: 52 * Map: 8, no: 66**

Murthly Castle incorporates an altered 15th-century square keep, to which has been added ranges of buildings in later centuries, forming three sides of a courtyard. The keep rises to four storeys and a garret, and has a small tower at one corner containing a turnpike stair. Bartizans were added, in the late 16th century, and have gunloops.

The first extension seems to have been a plain gabled tower, and is now linked by later buildings.

An early castle may have been a hunting seat of the kings of Scots. It originally belonged to the Abercrombies, but passed to the Stewarts of Grandtully in 1615. In 1829 a new mansion was built nearby, designed by James Gillespie Graham, although never apparently finished, but this was demolished in 1949. The property passed to the Fotheringhams in the 19th century. The castle is in good condition, and still occupied.

Other refs: Old Murthly Castle

Muthill

Perth & Kinross: About 3 miles south of Crieff, near A822 in Muthill.

Private NN 877164 OS: 58 ** Map: 8, no: 28

A mansion of the 19th-century here is said to incorporate a 14th-century castle.

Myrehead *see* Muirhead

Myres Castle

Fife: About 0.5 miles east of Auchtermuchty, just west of B936, about 0.3 miles north of Dunshalt.

Private NO 242110 OS: 59 * Map: 7, no: 47**

Originally surrounded by a marsh, Myres Castle is a 16th-century Z-plan tower house, consisting of a main block and two round towers, projecting from opposite corners. To this 17th-century work has been added, making the building E-plan. One round tower was heightened, with a corbelled-out square chamber. The walls are pierced by gunloops. There is a walled garden, laid out in the same style as one at the Vatican.

There was an earlier castle here, owned by Robert Coxwell, a favourite of James I and page to him when he was imprisoned in England. It passed by marriage to the Scrimgeours, constables of Dundee and mace-bearers (Clavigers) to the king. The castle was built in 1530 by John Scrimgeour, Master of Works to James V. Mary, Queen of Scots, visited during hunting trips. In 1611 the castle passed to the Pattersons, then the Moncrieffes of Reidie about 1750, was extended and modified in 1828 by the Bruces, and acquired by the Fairlies in 1887. It was used by the army during World War II, when it housed Polish troops. The castle was put up for sale in 1997 with an asking price of over £550,000.

Myrton Castle

Galloway: About 6 miles west and north of Whithorn, on minor road south of B7021, just east of White Loch of Myrton, near Monreith Mains.

Ruin or site NX 360432 OS: 83 * Map: 1, no: 48**

Built on a 12th-century motte, Myrton Castle is a ruined 16th-century L-plan tower house. It rose to four storeys and a garret, within a parapet, and had open rounds at the corners. There was another building at the base of the motte.

It was originally a property of the MacCullochs. Sir Alexander MacCulloch of Myrton torched Dunskey Castle in 1503, and was the King's Master Falconer. James IV visited in 1504 (and 1511) during a pilgrimage to the shrine of St Ninian at Whithorn. The tower was ruined by the late 17th century, and a new house built nearby. The property was sold to the Maxwells of Monreith in 1685, who removed to Myrton from nearby Dowies. They altered the building, and a wing was still occupied in the 19th century. The Maxwells built Monreith House close by, which is still occupied.

N

Nairn Castle

Inverness & Nairn: In Nairn, on minor roads south of A96 near junction with A939, near River Nairn, to the south of the town, east of railway station, Constabulary Gardens.

Ruin or site NH 885566 [?] OS: 27 * Map: 9, no: 136

Site of 12th-century castle, which was built by William the Lyon. The castle had a central keep.

The castle was garrisoned for the English during the Wars of Independence, but retaken by the Scots in 1308. The keepers of the castle were the Calders as Thanes of Cawdor, although the lands were held by Thomas Randolph, Earl of Moray. The property passed to the MacDonald Earls of Ross, but reverted to the Crown in 1475. The castle was probably finally destroyed around 1581.

There may have been a stronghold here in the 11th century, and Nairn is traditionally one of the places where Macbeth is said to have murdered Duncan. The Calders are said to have been descended from Macbeth's brother. Duncan, however, was slain after a battle with Macbeth near Spynie in Moray.

Naughton Castle

Fife: About 2 miles west and south of Wormit, on minor roads between B946 and A914, just north of Bottomcraig, near Naughton House.

Ruin or site NO 373246 OS: 59 * Map: 7, no: 100

Built on a strong defensive site, Naughton Castle is a very ruined 16th-century tower house and courtyard, which enclosed later ranges of buildings. It was once a large building, and there may have been a castle here from the 13th century, built by a natural son of William the Lyon, Robertus de Lundon.

It was a property of the Hays in the 12th century, but passed by marriage in 1494 to the Crichtons, one of whom, Sir Peter Crichton, was Master of the Wardrobe to James III. The property passed back to the Hays about 1625, then in 1737 to the Morrisons, then to the Beatons in the 19th century.

Nease Tower *see* Calfield Tower

Neidpath Castle

Borders: About 1 mile west of Peebles, on A72, just north of the River Tweed.

Private NT 236405 OS: 73 ** Map: 2, no: 54**

Nestling on the side of steep gorge overlooking a bend of the River Tweed, Neidpath Castle is an altered L-plan keep with rounded corners. The keep dates from the 14th century, but was substantially remodelled in the 16th century, with the alteration of the upper storeys. It was altered again in the late 17th century, when a wide stair was inserted and an additional storey created beneath the vault of the hall. A small courtyard, with ranges of buildings, was added in the 16th and 17th centuries.

The original entrance was in the south side. The basement of the main block and wing are both vaulted. Turnpike stairs climb within the walls. The much-altered first floor has a wide stair leading to the vaulted hall on the second floor. The third floor is also vaulted. Turnpike stairs lead to the upper floors, and there is a dark pit prison which is only reached from a hatch in the floor above.

An earlier castle here belonged to Sir Simon Fraser. He defeated the English at Roslin Moor in 1302, but was later captured and executed by the English. The property passed by marriage to the Hays in 1312, who built the existing castle. Mary, Queen of Scots, stayed at Neidpath in 1563, as did her son James VI in 1587.

The Hays were Royalists, and in 1650 Neidpath held out against Cromwell's army longer than any other stronghold south of the Forth. Cannon damaged the castle, and the defenders were eventually forced to surrender.

The castle was later partly repaired, and in 1686 was sold to the Douglas Duke of Queensberry, but passed in 1810 to the Earl of Wemyss and March. Walter Scott and William Wordsworth both visited the castle in 1803. Neidpath has featured in many films.

Neidpath is reputedly haunted by the ghost of a young lass, the 'Maid of Neid-path', who was written about by Sir Walter Scott, although there have been manifestations in recent times. The ghost is believed to be that of Jean Douglas, the youngest of the three daughters of Sir William Douglas, Earl of March. She was born in 1705, and fell in love with the son of the laird of Tushielaw, which was owned by the Scott family. Her father did not think her lover, although a man of property, was of high enough birth for an Earl's daughter and forbad them to marry. The lad was sent away from the area, and the Earl hoped that Jean would forget him. Jean was devastated and her health deteriorated. Her lover eventually returned, but by then she had become so ill that he no longer recognised her. Wounded to the core by this final hurt, she died of a broken heart. Her ghost then began to haunt Neidpath, waiting for her lover to return for her in death as he had not in life.

Sightings of Jean's ghost report that she is clad in a full-length brown frock with a large white collar. Doors are said to open and close by themselves, unexplained noises have been reported, and objects move by themselves, including on one occasion a wooden plank.

OPEN: Open Easter week, then May Bank Holiday wknds, then Jul-2nd Sun in Sep, Mon-Sat 11.00-18.00, Sun 13.00-17.00; outwith these times tel to confirm.

Gift shop. Museum. Unique batiks depicting Mary Queen of Scots. Tartan collection. WC. Disabled access only to museum and ground floor of castle (up 5 steps). Picnic area. Group concessions. Car and coach parking. £.

Tel: 01721 720333 Fax: 01721 720333

Neish Island *see* Loch Earn Castle

Nemphlar

Lanarkshire & Glasgow area: About 2 miles west and north of Lanark, on minor roads south or west of A73, north of River Clyde, Nemphlar.

Private NS 854447 OS: 72 * Map: 3, no: 397**

Nemphlar is a small 16th-century tower or bastle house, the upper floor of which is still occupied. The basement is vaulted, and there is a blocked-up stair. The building is dated 1607 and has the initials D. F. and D. L., possibly for the Forrest and Lockhart families.

Other refs: Halltown of Nemphlar

Ness Castle

Inverness & Nairn: About 2.5 miles south-west of Inverness, on minor roads south of B862, south of River Ness, at Ness Castle.
Private   NH 652414   OS: 26   *   Map: 9, no: 90
Ness Castle is a modern mansion.

Ness of Burgi Fort

Shetland: About 20 miles south of Lerwick, on minor road and foot south of A970, 1 mile south-west of Sumburgh, at Ness of Burgi.
His Scot   HU 386085   OS: 4   *   Map: 11, no: 58**
Positioned across the neck of the promontory is a blockhouse similar to that found in association with the broch at Clickhimin. The blockhouse is a rectangular block of walling with an entrance passage running through it, which has door checks and bar holes part of the way along it. The blockhouse is protected by a rampart with a ditch on either side (the pile of stones is excavation debris).
OPEN: Access at all reasonable times – access is difficult.
Tel: 0131 668 8800   Fax: 0131 668 8888
Email: hs.explore@scotland.gov.uk   Web: www.historic-scotland.gov.uk

Nether Abington

Lanarkshire & Glasgow: About 1 mile north of Abington, on minor roads just east of A73, just west of River Clyde, at Nether Abington.
Ruin or site   NS 932250   OS: 71   *   Map: 3, no: 415
Nether Abington consists of a relatively well preserved motte and bailey castle.

Nether Ancrum *see* Maltan Walls

Nether Arthurlie *see* Arthurlie House

Nether Auchendrane

Ayrshire: About 3.5 miles south of Ayr, on minor roads west of A77, east of B7024, just west of the River Doon, at Nether Auchendrane.
Private   NS 338167   OS: 70   **   Map: 3, no: 102
Nether Auchendrane, extended and altered in the 19th century, incorporates a 17th-century house which may contain earlier work. The property was known as Blairston(e).
  It was a property of the Mures, although it later passed from the family, and is still occupied, now being an old peoples home.
Other refs: Blairstone; Auchendrane House

Nether Craig *see* Craig

Nether Dalveen *see* Dalveen Castle

Nether Glens *see* Parkglen Wood

Nether Horsburgh Castle

Borders: About 4 miles east of Peebles, on minor road north of A72 at Nether Horsburgh.
Ruin or site   NT 304396   OS: 73   **   Map: 2, no: 77
Not much remains of Nether Horsburgh Castle, a 16th-century tower house, formerly of three storeys, and a courtyard. Part of the tower survives to third-floor level.
  The basement was vaulted and had a stair to the first-floor hall. A turnpike stair, in one corner, climbed to the upper floors.
  It was originally a property of the Horsburghs, but sold to the Shaws of Shillingshaw in the 17th century because of debt.

Nether Oliver Castle *see* Oliver Castle

Nether Pollok *see* Pollok House

Nether Pollok *see* Netherplace

Nether Riccarton *see* Coldsyde

Nether Tofts *see* Purves Hall

Nether Whitehaugh Castle *see* Whitehaugh Castle

Netherlee *see* Lee Castle

Netherplace

Renfrewshire: About 2 miles south-east of Barrhead, on minor roads west of A77, 0.5 miles west of Newton Mearns, at Netherplace.
Ruin or site   NS 520556 [?]   OS: 64   *   Map: 3, no: 229
Possible site of castle. The present house of Netherplace, which dates from the 18th century, may stand on the site.
Other refs: Laigh Place; Nether Pollok

Netherplace

Dumfriesshire: To south of Lockerbie, on minor roads south of A709, at or near Netherplace.
Ruin or site   NY 137811 [?]   OS: 78   *   Map: 1, no: 244
Site of strong tower, some remains of which survived at the turn of the 19th century. It was probably held by the Johnstones.

New Cumnock *see* Black Bog Castle

New Leslie Castle *see* Castle Croft

New Wark, Dumfries *see* Dumfries Castle

Newark Castle

Borders: About 3 miles west of Selkirk, on minor roads south of A708, south of the Yarrow Water, in the grounds of Bowhill.
Ruin or site   NT 421294   OS: 73   *   Map: 2, no: 106**
Standing in the grounds of the mansion of Bowhill, Newark Castle is a ruined 15th-century keep of five storeys, rectangular in plan, which formerly had a corbelled-out parapet. Two-storey 16th-century caphouses crown two corners of the keep. The tower had a large courtyard, parts of which remain.
  The entrance, now at ground level, leads to a vaulted basement. A straight stair, in one corner, which becomes a turnpike above first-floor level, climbs to all floors. The hall, on the first floor, has an area screened off to provide a kitchen. The main entrance was at first-floor level, and was reached by an external stair. The castle had a courtyard with a gatehouse and wall, sections of which survive.
  The castle replaced an 'auld wark' [NT 425286?], east of the present castle and

nothing of which remains, and was acquired by Archibald, Earl of Douglas, around 1423. It was kept by the Crown after the downfall of the Black Douglases, and given to Margaret of Denmark, wife of James III, in 1473. The castle was besieged by the English in 1547 by Lord Gray of Wilton, although apparently not captured, and burned in 1548. In 1645 one hundred followers of the Marquis of Montrose, mostly Irish women, many of them pregnant, were then shot, stabbed, slashed or bludgeoned to death. The castle and area are said to be haunted by the folk butchered here, and their cries and moans have reputedly been heard.

Other prisoners, again mostly women and children, were taken to the market place in Selkirk, and there later also shot. The castle was altered for Anna, Duchess of Monmouth and Buccleuch, about 1690-1700. Her husband, James, Duke of Monmouth, was executed in 1685 for rebelling against James VII. Wordsworth visited the castle in 1831 with Sir Walter Scott. The ruin has been consolidated.

Bowhill, dating mainly from 1812 and the home of the Duke and Duchess of Buccleuch, houses many work of art and historical mementoes.

Other refs: Old Wark, Newark

OPEN: Park open 24 Apr-30 Aug, except closed Fri apart from Jul; Bowhill open Jul 13.00-16.30; other times by appt for educational groups.

See Bowhill.

Tel: 01750 22204 Fax: 01750 22204

Newark Castle

Fife: About 2 miles east and north of Elie, on footpath south of A917, about 0.5 mile west of St Monans, on the sea.

Ruin or site NO 518012 OS: 59 ** Map: 7, no: 133

Newark Castle or Newark of St Monans is a very ruined 15th-century castle, which was altered and extended in the 16th and 17th centuries. Not much remains except

vaulted cellars, part of a block with thick outer walls and a large round tower, as well as fragments of a walled courtyard and other buildings.

It was originally a property of the Kinloch family, but passed to the Sandilands of Cruivie. The Sandilands became bankrupt and sold the castle in 1649 to the Covenanter General Sir David Leslie. Leslie served under Gustavus Adolphus, and joined the army of Covenanters in 1643. He fought at Marston Moor in 1644 and defeated the Marquis of Montrose at Philiphaugh in 1645. However, he was defeated by Cromwell at Dunbar 1650, and was captured at the Battle of Worcester in 1651, after which he spent nine years in the Tower of London. He died in 1682. The castle passed to the Anstruthers, then to the Bairds of Elie.

Other refs: Newark of St Monans

Newark Castle

Renfrewshire: In Port Glasgow, just north of the A8, on the south shore of the River Clyde, at Newark.

His Scot NS 331745 OS: 63 ** Map: 3, no: 97**

Standing on a spit of land into the sea, Newark Castle consists of a much-extended simple square 15th-century keep. To this was added a 16th-century gatehouse block and a large late 16th-century range, to form three sides of a courtyard. The remaining side was formerly completed by a wall.

The old keep rises to four storeys, the top storey being built from the original parapet. The windows of the keep have been enlarged.

The entrance leads to a vaulted basement and to a turnpike stair, in one corner, which climbs to all floors.

The tall gatehouse block is three storeys high with a gabled roof. An arched gateway leads to a vaulted pend, which opens into the courtyard. A turnpike stair climbs to all floors from a guardroom.

The later large range has bartizans at the corners, and the walls are pierced by gunloops. A semi-circular stair-tower, with a conical roof, is corbelled out above first-floor level. This building is dated 1597.

The basement is vaulted and contains a kitchen, with a wide fireplace, a cellar, and a wine-cellar with a small stair to the hall above. The hall, on the first floor and reached by the main stair, has a richly decorated fireplace. The second storey contains a gallery.

Newark was originally a property of the Dennistouns or Danielstouns, but passed by marriage to the Maxwells of Calderwood in 1402, who built the castle. James IV was a frequent visitor. One of the family, Patrick Maxwell, was involved in the murders of Patrick Maxwell of Stanely and the Montgomery Earl of Eglinton, in 1584 and 1596 respectively, during a series of feuds. The castle was abandoned as a residence early in the 18th century, and was handed over into State care in 1909.

OPEN: Open Apr-Sep, daily 9.30-18.30; last ticket 18.00.

Sales area. WC. Car and coach parking. Group concessions. £.

Tel: 01475 741858 Fax: 0131 668 8888

Email: hs.explore@scotland.gov.uk Web: www.historic-scotland.gov.uk

Newark Castle

Ayrshire: About 3 miles south of Ayr, on minor road west of B7024, at Newark.

Private NS 324173 OS: 70 ** Map: 3, no: 93**

Newark Castle is a tower house of four storeys and a garret within a corbelled-out parapet, to which has been added a 17th-century extension. The tower house incorporates work from the 15th century. The parapet has open rounds and a square gabled caphouse.

The 17th-century range contains the present entrance. The building was remodelled and extended in 1848, and again in 1907-8. The east wing, dating from the 19th century, was demolished in 1977.

The original entrance, from the courtyard, led to a turnpike stair built into the thickness of one corner of the original tower. The basement is vaulted and the hall is on the first floor.

The castle was built by the Kennedys of Bargany. Mary, Queen of Scots, is supposed to have stayed here after defeat at the Battle of Langside before fleeing to England. By 1601 Newark had passed to the Crawfords of Camlarg, but was sold to the Kennedy Earl of Cassillis in 1763. It is in good condition, and still occupied.

Other refs: Newark of Bargany

Newark of Bargany *see* Newark Castle

Newark of St Monans *see* Newark Castle

Newbattle Abbey

Lothians: About 1 mile south-west of Dalkeith, on minor roads just east of B703, just west of River South Esk, east of Eskbank, at Newbattle Abbey.

Private   NT 333660   OS: 66   **   Map: 4, no: 137

One range of Newbattle Abbey was remodelled into a fortified house, and incorporates a fine 14th-century vaulted undercroft. The house was altered and extended in 1650, again in the late 18th century, and the 19th century.

Newbattle Abbey was founded in 1140 by David I as a Cistercian house dedicated to the Blessed Virgin Mary, and became a very rich establishment. It was visited by Alexander II – Marie de Coucy, his wife, was buried here. It was burned by the English in 1385, 1544 and 1548. The Kerrs acquired the abbey after the Reformation, having been Commendators, and were made Lords Newbattle in 1591, and Earls of Lothian in 1606. They demolished most of the abbey, and greatly altered the little that was left – the vaulted undercroft of the dormitory and rereredorter survives, as well as the warming house. Additions were made by William Burn in 1836, and David Bryce in 1858. The house was altered again in 1936 and 1968, given to the nation by the 11th Marquis of Lothian, and is now an adult education college. Fine plasterwork and wood carving survives.

Newbattle has a reputation for being haunted, and it is said that few folk like to stay in the building after dark.

Newbie Castle

Dumfriesshire: About 1.5 miles south-west of Annan, on minor roads south of B724, west of Newbie village, just east of Newbie Mains, north shore of Solway Firth.

Ruin or site   NY 174647   OS: 85   *   Map: 1, no: 256

Site of castle, which was completely demolished about 1816, and only some masonry survives. The castle is said to have had a moat and drawbridge.

It was a property of the Johnstones.

Newbyres Tower

Lothians: In Gorebridge to the west of main street, on minor roads east of the A7 and west of B704, at Newbyres.

Ruin or site   NT 344614   OS: 66   *   Map: 4, no: 140

Little remains of a 16th-century L-plan tower house and courtyard, which was demolished in 1963. It was a property of the Borthwick family, but later sold to the Dundases of Arniston.

Newe Castle *see* Castle Newe

Newhall

Perthshire: About 7 miles north-east of Perth, on minor roads east of A94, 0.25 miles south-west of Kinrossie, at Newhall.

Ruin or site   NO 186319   OS: 53   *   Map: 8, no: 115

Nothing survives of a castle, which is mentioned in the 16th century. There were some remains in 1810.

Newhall Castle

Lothians: About 4.5 miles south-west of Penicuik, on minor roads south of A702, just north of River North Esk, 1 mile north-east of Carlops, at Newhall.

Ruin or site   NT 175566   OS: 66   *   Map: 4, no: 56

Site of castle, part of which may be incorporated into the later house of 1703, which was altered and enlarged in 1785, and remodelled by David Bryce in 1852. Two panelled rooms, dating from about 1704, survive. The castle stood above two ravines.

It was a property of the Crichton family from 1529 or earlier, and its inhabitants were accused of 'adhering' to 'papastrie' around 1570. It was sold to the Penicuik family in 1646, then in 1703 to Sir David Forbes, when Newhall was called an 'old decayed castle'. Newhall was the inspiration of 'The Gentle Shepherd' by Allan Ramsay, when the house was owned by the Browns. A walled garden survives, and there were some remains of the castle at the end of the 19th century.

Newhall Tower

Fife: About 1.5 miles north of Crail, on minor road west of A917, at or near West Newhall.

Ruin or site   NO 598100 [?]   OS: 59   *   Map: 7, no: 157

Site of castle. The property was held by the Meldrums in 1578, but later absorbed into the Cambo estate, which was itself held by the Erskines from the 1680s.

Newlands

Dumfriesshire: About 3.5 miles north-west of Locharbriggs, on minor roads east of A76 or west of A701, about 0.5 miles north of Quarrelwood, at Newlands.

Ruin or site   NX 962851   OS: 78   *   Map: 1, no: 185

Site of castle, said to have been of great strength. It was replaced by a later house.

Newmilns Tower

Ayrshire: In Newmilns behind the Loudoun Arms in Main Street, near A71, north of the River Irvine.

Ruin or site   NS 536374   OS: 70   *   Map: 3, no: 240**

Newmilns Tower is a small altered 16th-century tower house, rectangular in plan, of three storeys and an attic within a parapet. Corbelled-out open rounds crown the corners, but the roof has been lowered.

The basement is vaulted, and there is one chamber on each floor.

Newmilns was a property of the Campbells of Loudoun. In the 17th century it was used as a prison for Covenanters. The castle was captured by a Covenanter force, led by John Low, and the prisoners were rescued, although Low was killed in the fight. His gravestone is in the wall surrounding the castle.

Newmore Castle

Ross & Cromarty: About 2.5 miles north-east of Alness, on minor roads north of A9, south of Newmore Wood, west of Newmore House, east of Rosebank.

Ruin or site   NH 680720   OS: 21   **   Map: 9, no: 98

Not much remains of Newmore Castle, a 17th-century castle, except the vaulted basement with a round stair-turret. There are many gunloops.

It was a property of the Munros, then later the Mackenzies. It was superseded by Newmore House, built in 1875, a property of the Inglis family.

Other refs: Rosskeen

Newton

Lothians: About 2 miles south of Musselburgh, west of A720, on minor road east from B6415, at Newton.

Private   NT 332699   OS: 66   *   Map: 4, no: 136

Newton, a three-storey mansion of 1820 and 1855, incorporates part of a 16th-century castle, including vaulted cellars. A nearby round tower, with gunloops, has a doocot in its top storey.

The lands were held by the Newton family in the 13th century, but by about 1710 had passed to Lord Edmonstone.

Newton

Angus & Dundee: About 7.5 miles north and east of Alyth, on minor roads north of B951, near Inzion Burn, at or near Newton.

Ruin or site   NO 287577   OS: 53   *   Map: 8, no: 146

Site of castle.

Newton Castle

Angus & Dundee: About 12 miles north-west of Kirriemuir, on minor road north of B951, just east of Newton Burn north of meeting with River Isla, at or near Newton.

Ruin or site   NO 230602   OS: 44   *   Map: 8, no: 127

Site of castle, a property of the Ogilvies. It was destroyed by the Earl of Argyll in 1640, and there were some remains in the middle of the 19th century.

Newton Castle

Perth & Kinross: Just north-west of Blairgowrie, on minor roads west of A923 in Blairgowrie, at Newton.

Private   NO 172453   OS: 53   *   Map: 8, no: 111**

On a strong position on high ground, Newton Castle is a 16th-century Z-plan tower house, although it may incorporate, or be built on the site of, an older castle. It consists of a main block of three storeys and a garret, with a square stair-tower at one corner and a round tower diagonally opposite. This round tower is corbelled out to square at the top to form a watch-chamber. The walls of the tower are pierced

by gunloops and whitewashed.

The original entrance, at the foot of the square stair-tower, led to the vaulted basement and to a stair to the upper floors. The hall would have been on the first floor with private chambers above. The tower has been altered inside, but some 17th-century panelling survives.

Newton was a property of the Drummonds, who feuded with the Blairs of nearby Ardblair. The tower was sacked by the Marquis of Montrose in 1644, and torched by Cromwell in the 1650s, although the defenders of the tower are supposed to have survived in the vaults while the building burned around them. Newton later passed to the Macphersons, is in good condition and still occupied.

The castle is said to be haunted by a 'Green Lady', dressed in green silk, who searches through the grounds of the castle. She is reputed to be the ghost of Lady Jean Drummond of Newton, who fell in love with one of the Blairs of Ardblair. The families feuded, and Lady Jean seems to have died of a broken heart when she was betrothed to another, drowning herself in a local marsh.

Other refs: Place of Newton of Blair; Newton of Blair

Newton Castle

Ayrshire: In Newton on Ayr, near A719, east of Garden Street, close to the shore of the Firth of Clyde.

Ruin or site   NS 339223   OS: 70   *   Map: 3, no: 105

Site of 15th-century keep and strong castle, which was later altered and extended, and stood within gardens and groves.

There was a castle here from about 1200, which was captured by Norsemen in 1263 before the Battle of Largs. It was a property of the Wallaces in 1468, but in the 16th century passed to the Hamiltons, then to the Wallaces of Craigie in 1588, who later moved to Craigie Castle. The castle was demolished or blown down in 1701, and by 1837 only one wall survived. The site is now occupied by a car park.

Other refs: Newton upon Ayr; Sanquhar-Hamilton Castle

Newton Castle

Stirlingshire & Clackmannan: About 0.25 miles south-east of Doune, on minor road south of the A820, just across from Doune Castle, on the east side of Ardoch Burn.

Private   NN 731013   OS: 57   *   Map: 6, no: 60**

Newton Castle is a 16th-century L-plan tower house of four storeys and a garret. A stair-turret, in the re-entrant angle, is corbelled-out above first-floor level. The wing of the L is rounded with semi-circular corbiestepped gables. The walls are pink-washed. The tower has been extended with lower additions and had a courtyard.

The original entrance, in the re-entrant, led to a wide turnpike stair which rises only to the first floor, the upper floors being reached by the turret-stair. A straight stair leads down into the vaulted basement. The hall was on the first floor.

Newton was built by the Edmonstone family, hereditary keepers of nearby Doune Castle. The family were Jacobites, and in 1708 the Laird of Newton was arrested for trying to put James VIII on the throne. The property was sold to John Campbell, a Glasgow merchant, in 1858. The house is still occupied.

Other refs: Old Newton, Doune

Newton House *see* Culsalmond

Newton House

Aberdeen & Gordon: About 9 miles north-west of Inverurie, on minor roads off B992, Newton.

Private   NJ 662297   OS: 38   **   Map: 10, no: 184

Site of 16th-century castle, which was said to be unroofed in 1591. Newton House is a late 17th-century house of four storeys and an attic, the walls of which are harled. Newton was a property of the Leslies at one time.

In the grounds is a carved Pictish stone, some seven feet high and brought here in the 19th century. It has a double disc above a snake and z-rod. The left-hand disc has a small semicircular notch very deliberately carved into the outline. It stands next to another stone which carries no symbols but does have the Ogham inscription with the word EDDARRNONN (as at Brodie Castle). There is also a second inscription which has not been translated.

Other refs: Culsalmond

OPEN: On private property – permission should be sought in advance.

Newton House

Lanarkshire & Glasgow: About 1.5 miles north-east of Cambuslang, on minor roads east of A724 or west of B758, south of River Clyde, at Newton.

Ruin or site   NS 663613   OS: 64   *   Map: 3, no: 312

Newton House, built in 1602, was probably fortified. It burned down in 1684, and was replaced by a mansion, itself now demolished.

The lands were a property of the Hamiltons of Silvertonhill.

Newton House

South Highland: About 2.5 miles east of Beauly, on minor road north of B9164, 0.5 miles east of Kirkhill, west of Moniack Burn, at or near Newton House.

Ruin or site   NH 562456   OS: 26   *   Map: 9, no: 71

The ruins of a 17th-century mansion stand by Newton House, a modern mansion.

Newton Mearns

Renfrewshire: About 3 miles south-east of Barrhead, on minor roads east of A77, Rob's Hill, Newton Mearns.

Ruin or site   NS 535560   OS: 64   *   Map: 3, no: 238

Site of castle of the Maxwells, dating from the 13th century. There are no remains and the site is occupied by housing.

Newton of Blair *see* Newton Castle

Newton Tower

Borders: About 6 miles east of Jedburgh, on minor road south of A698, south of
River Teviot, just south-west of Newton.
Ruin or site   NT 597205 [?]   OS: 73   *   Map: 2, no: 233
Site of tower house, probably of the Turnbulls.

Newton upon Ayr *see* Newton Castle

Newtown of Condie *see* Condie

Newtyle Castle *see* Hatton Castle

Newyearfield

Lothians: In Livingston, on minor roads north of A705 or west of A899, at or near
Newyearfield.
Ruin or site   NT 047686 [?]   OS: 65   Map: 4, no: 24
Site of tower house, nothing of which remains, but a vestige of which survived at
the end of the 18th century. It is said to have been a royal hunting seat of the kings
of Scots. Nearby was a reputed healing well. Water from the Rose Well was believed
to be a cure for scrofula, 'the King's Evil', when sprinkled on the sufferer by the
monarch before sunrise on the first day on the new year.
Other refs: Rose Well, Newyearfield

Niddrie Marischal

Lothians: About 3 miles east and south of Edinburgh Castle, near A6095, in the
Niddrie housing scheme of Edinburgh.
Ruin or site   NT 295715 [?]   OS: 66   *   Map: 4, no: 123
Site of 16th-century tower house of four storeys, to which had been added a 17th-
century wing, and later large extensions. The tower had a parapet, and the walls
were pierced by gunloops.
 The basement was vaulted, but the tower had been remodelled inside.
 In the 14th century the property belonged to the Niddries, but around 1390 passed
to the Wauchopes. A castle here was burned by an Edinburgh mob in the 16th
century. Mary, Queen of Scots, visited the castle several times. The Wauchopes
were forfeited, and the property was acquired by the Sandilands family, before
returning by marriage to the Wauchopes in 1608. The house was occupied until
the 1930s, but then completely demolished, and a housing estate built on the site.

Niddry Castle

Lothians: About 2 miles north-east of Broxburn, on minor road north between
A89 and B8020, just east of main railway line between Edinburgh and Glasgow.
Private   NT 097743   OS: 65   *   Map: 4, no: 40**
Niddry Castle is an altered 15th-century keep, now L-plan, consisting of a main

block and wing. It rises to four storeys and an attic, formerly within a parapet, only
the corbelling for which remained. The parapet had open rounds at all corners, but
was obliterated when two storeys were added to the building in the 17th century. A
small stair-turret, in the re-entrant angle, led to the garret storey.
 The entrance, in the re-entrant angle, leads through a lobby to the vaulted basement, which contained a dungeon in the wing, and to a turnpike stair which climbs,
in the thickness of the walls, to all floors. The hall, on the first floor, has a very large
fireplace.
 The castle, known as Niddry-Seton to distinguish it from Niddrie Marischal, was a
property of the Setons. One of the family, George Seton, was killed at the Battle of
Flodden in 1513. The Setons supported Mary, Queen of Scots, and she came here
after she had escaped from Lochleven Castle in 1568. The following day she rode to
Hamilton, but her army was defeated at the Battle of Langside, and she fled to
England to be imprisoned for the rest of her life until executed at Fotheringhay in
1587. Niddry was acquired by the Hopes in the 17th century, but abandoned soon
afterwards. The castle has been restored, and is occupied.
 There are the remains of a formerly fine massive walled garden.
OPEN: View from exterior.

Nisbet House

Borders: About 2 miles south of Duns, on minor road east of A6112, north of the
Hoew Burn, west of the Blackadder Water.
Private   NT 795512   OS: 74   *   Map: 2, no: 321**
Nisbet House is an altered 17th-century tower house of four storeys, although it
probably contains earlier work. It consists of a main block with two projecting round
towers at one end and two square stair-towers at the opposite end. Small corbiestepped stair-turrets are corbelled out in two re-entrant angles, and a bartizan
crowns the main block. The walls are pierced by many gunloops. A square tower
was added in the 18th century.
 The entrance leads to the vaulted basement, which contains a kitchen and several
cellars. The first-floor hall has an adjoining private chamber, and there are small
linked rooms in the round towers.
 The castle was built by the Nisbets, but the family had to flee after two of the
family had been executed during the Civil War in the 1650s. The Kerrs acquired the
property, but in the 19th century it was held by the Sinclairs.
Other refs: East Nisbet Castle

Noltland Castle

Orkney: On north-east side of island of Westray in Orkney, on minor roads west
of B9066, about 0.5 miles west of Pierowall, at Noltland.
His Scot   HY 430487   OS: 5   *   Map: 11, no: 44**
A strong and grim stronghold, Noltland Castle is a large ruined 16th-century Z-plan
tower house. It consists of a main block of four storeys and an attic with square
towers, one of five storeys and a garret high, at opposite corners. The thick walls
are pierced by many gunloops. Remains of a corbelled-out parapet, with open
rounds, survive around the taller tower and part of the main block. A later courtyard survives with the remains of an L-plan range of buildings.
 The entrance is in the re-entrant angle with one of the square towers. It leads to a
wide turnpike stair and into the vaulted basement of the main block, which contains a kitchen with a large fireplace and oven; and cellars, one with a small stair to
the hall above. The hall, on the first-floor of the main block, had a fireplace and very

small windows, and had a stone roof. There was an adjoining private chamber, another in the square tower, as well as more rooms on the floors above. The castle may never have been completed.

An earlier castle here was built by a Thomas de Tulloch in 1420, and towards the end of the 15th century besieged by the Sinclairs of Warsetter. The present castle was built by Gilbert Balfour, who was Master of the Household to Mary, Queen of Scots. He acquired the property by marrying Margaret Bothwell, whose brother was Bishop of Orkney and granted the lands to Balfour. Balfour had been involved in the murders of Cardinal Beaton in 1546, for which he was imprisoned, and Lord Darnley in 1567. He supported Mary after she fled to England, but when her cause became hopeless he fled Scotland, and served in the Swedish army until his death, being executed for treason against the Swedish king, in 1576.

The castle was besieged and captured in 1592 by Patrick Stewart, Earl of Orkney, in order to get payment of a debt. Some of the Marquis of Montrose's men took refuge here after their defeat in 1650, and the castle was later held by Cromwell's men. Noltland was damaged by fire in 1746, and abandoned about 1760. It passed into the care of the State in 1911.

A death in the Balfour family was reputedly heralded by a ghostly howling dog, the 'Boky Hound', while births and marriages were announced by an eerie spectral light. The castle is also said to have had a brownie, an old man who helped folk at need, beaching boats or clearing roads, and is said to have been well liked by the Balfour family. The brownie left when the castle was abandoned.

OPEN: Open Jul-Sep, daily 9.30-18.30; last ticket 18.00.
Tel: 0131 668 8800   Fax: 0131 668 8888
Email: hs.explore@scotland.gov.uk   Web: www.historic-scotland.gov.uk

North Barr *see* Northbar

North Berwick Priory

Lothians: In North Berwick, on minor road south of A198, just south of railway station, in Old Abbey Road.
Private   NT 546850   OS: 66   *   Map: 4, no: 198**
Although most of the buildings were demolished, part of North Berwick Priory, probably the refectory range, was fortified and a four-storey tower, with a stair-tower, added to one end. The range is now ruined, but is fairly complete to the wall head; and the older part has four vaulted cellars. The walls are pierced by gun-loops.

The Cistercian nunnery was founded about 1150 by Duncan, Earl of Fife, but in 1588, after the Reformation, passed to the Homes. The building stands in the grounds of an old people's home.

North Couston *see* Couston Castle

North Synton

Borders: About 2.5 miles south of Selkirk, on minor road just north of B6400, 1 mile north-east of Ashkirk, north of Ale Water, at North Synton.
Private   NT 485237   OS: 73   **   Map: 2, no: 148
North Synton consists of a much-altered 16th-century tower house of three storeys with a centrally projecting wing. The basement is vaulted.

The property was acquired by the Veitch family in 1407, who built the tower, but had passed to the Cunninghams by the end of the 17th century. It is still occupied as a farmhouse.

Northbank Peel

Borders: About 6 miles south of Jedburgh, near footpath between Lethem and Southdean from minor road north of A6088, south of Shaw Burn.
Ruin or site   NT 661095   OS: 80   *   Map: 2, no: 270
Very little remains of a 16th-century peel or tower house of the Oliver family.

Northbar

Renfrewshire: About 2 miles north-west of Renfrew, on minor roads north of A8, on south side of River Clyde, north of Inchinnan village, at or near Northbar House.
Private   NS 481693   OS: 64   *   Map: 3, no: 197
Site of castle, nothing of which remains. Northbar House, built around 1742, is a three-storey corbiestepped mansion.

The lands were sold to the MacGilchrists in 1672, then in 1741 were acquired by the Semples. The property was sold to the Buchanans in 1798, then to the Stewart Lords Blantyre in 1812. Another suggested site for Northbar is NS 465714.
Other refs: North Barr; Semple House

Northfield House

Lothians: Just south of Prestonpans, on minor road north of B1361, near Prestonpans railway station, near Hamilton House and Preston Tower.
NTS   NT 389739   OS: 66   *   Map: 4, no: 158**
Standing within a walled garden, Northfield House is an altered late 16th-century L-plan house of three storeys and a garret. Large bartizans crown all corners, and the pitch of the roof is steep.

The hall was on the first floor, but the building has been altered inside. In 1956 16th-century tempera wall and ceiling paintings were discovered behind plaster-work.

The property probably belonged to the Hamiltons, but by 1611 had passed to Joseph Marjoribanks, an Edinburgh merchant. It was sold in 1746 to the Nisbets, and later to the Symes, then in 1890 to the MacNeils. The house is in good condition, and still occupied.

Norwood Hall *see* Pitfodels Castle

Nottingham *see* Forse Castle

Novar House

South Highland: About 2.5 miles west and south of Alness, on minor roads north of A9 or west of A836, 1.5 miles north and east of Evanton, at Novar House.
Private   NH 612680   OS: 21   *   Map: 9, no: 80
Possible site of castle or old house. Novar House is a symmetrical mansion, which dates from 1720 and later, although a date stone with 1634 survives (possibly from Fyrish? [NH 614690]). It was a property of the Munros. One of the family was General Sir Hector Munro, who served in India in the second half of the 18th century.

Nucke

Dumfriesshire: About 0.5 miles east of Ecclefechan, on minor roads east of M74, north of Mein Water, near Burnfoot.
Ruin or site   NY 204747 [?]   OS: 85   *   Map: 1, no: 265
Site of a tower house, a property of the Bells.

Nunraw Castle

Lothians: About 3 miles south of East Linton, on minor road west from B6370, 0.5 miles south-east of Garvald, east of the Whittinghame Water.
Private   NT 597706   OS: 67   *   Map: 4, no: 210**
Nunraw consists of a strong 15th-century keep of four storeys and an attic within a corbelled-out parapet. The parapet has open rounds at the corners. A mansion was added to the keep in 1860.

The basement and the first-floor hall of the keep are vaulted. During a 19th-century renovation, a painted refectory ceiling was discovered, dated 1461, part of which is now in the Museum of Scotland in Edinburgh.

The castle was built by the Nunnery of Haddington, but passed to the Hepburn Earls of Bothwell after the Reformation, then to the Dalrymples. It was captured by the English in 1547. The new mansion was added in the 1860s, and the property later passed to the Hay family. In 1946 a new monastery was founded here, the Abbey of Sancta Maria, and the castle is incorporated into the buildings.

There was a village here, dating from medieval times, but nothing now remains.
Other refs: Whitecastle

Nunton Castle

Galloway: About 3 miles south-west of Kirkcudbright, on foot and track west of B727, 0.5 miles north-west of Lower Nunton, at Nunton Castle.
Ruin or site   NX 648491 [?]   OS: 83   *   Map: 1, no: 104
Site of castle, some remains of which survived in the 19th century.
Other refs: Luskie

O

Oakwood Tower *see* Aikwood Tower

Ochiltree Castle

Lothians: About 3.5 miles east and south of Linlithgow, on minor road south of B9080, west of B8046, at Wester Ochiltree.

Private NT 032748 OS: 65 ** Map: 4, no: 16

Standing on a high ridge, Ochiltree Castle is an altered 16th-century L-plan tower house of three storeys and an attic, to which has been added a 17th-century wing. A stair-tower stands in the re-entrant angle. Bartizans crown two of the corners.

The entrance has been moved, but was probably in the foot of the stair-tower. The inside of the tower has been much altered, but the vaulted basement contained a kitchen, and the hall was on the first floor.

It was a property of James Hamilton of Finnart from 1526 until 1540, but then acquired by the Stewarts of Ochiltree. It was used as a farmhouse, then modernised in the 1930s, fell into disrepair in the 1970s, but was restored and reoccupied in the 1980s. It was put up for sale in 1997.

Other refs: Ochiltree Place; Wester Ochiltree

Ochiltree Castle

Ayrshire: To east of Ochiltree, north of minor road north of A70 near junction with B7036, south of Lugar Water, at Ochiltree.

Ruin or site NS 510212 [?] OS: 70 * Map: 3, no: 221

Site of keep, castle and later mansion. There is a motte to the north west [NS 502218]

The property belonged to the Colvilles from the 14th century, but was exchanged for East Wemyss with Sir James Hamilton of Finnart in 1530. The lands were acquired by the Stewarts of Avondale in 1534. One of the family, James Stewart of Ochiltree, was made Earl of Arran in 1581, and Chancellor of Scotland from 1584-5. He was overthrown in 1585, and murdered in 1596. In 1609 Lord Stewart of Ochiltree was involved in the murder of James, Lord Torthorwald. The property passed to the Cochrane Earls of Dundonald about 1675, and John Claverhouse, Viscount Dundee, was married here in 1684. Ochiltree was sold to the MacRaes about 1737, then passed to other families, and it was in a bad state of repair in 1856 when it was owned by the Boswells. It was, however, in good order when it was completely demolished around the middle of the 20th century, and the site is occupied by a modern house.

Ochiltree Place *see* Ochiltree Castle

Oggs Castle *see* Ogs Castle

Ogilface *see* Bridge Castle

Ogilface Castle

Lothians: About 4 miles west of Bathgate, on minor roads north of A89, near Barbauchlaw Farm, west of Woodend Farm.

Ruin or site NS 927690 OS: 65 * Map: 4, no: 3

Site of castle, strongly built but of no great size, of which foundations survived in the 19th century.

It was a property of the de Bosco family, but passed to the Livingstone Earls of Linlithgow. It is said to have been used by Covenanters as a place of refuge.

Ogilvie Castle

Perth & Kinross: About 4 miles south-west of Auchterarder, on minor roads south of A9 at Blackford, 1 mile south of Blackford, south of Braes of Ogilvie.

Private NN 896072 OS: 58 * Map: 8, no: 30

Not much remains of a 14th-century keep of the Grahams, once a place of some strength.

Ogs Castle

Lanarkshire & Glasgow area: About 4 miles east and south of Carnwath, on minor road north of A721, just south of the South Medwin Water, at Ogscastle.

Private NT 030446 OS: 72 * Map: 3, no: 447

Site of castle, some vestiges of which remained in the 19th century. It was demolished in 1808, and nothing above ground remains, although the site has been excavated.

Other refs: Oggs Castle; Ogscastle

Ogscastle *see* Ogs Castle

Old Aberdeen, Bishop's Palace *see* Bishop's Palace, Old Aberdeen

Old Arniston House *see* Arniston House

Old Balbithan *see* Balbithan House

Old Ballikinrain

Stirlingshire & Clackmannan: About I mile south-east of Balfron, on minor roads north of B818, south of Endrick Water, at Old Ballikinrain.

Private NS 561880 OS: 57 ** Map: 6, no: 22

Although altered and given an 18th-century facade, Old Ballikinrain incorporates a 17th-century building, which still retains a drawbar to defend the entrance.

The property was owned by the Napiers from the 17th century until 1862.

Ballikinrain Castle was a 19th-century baronial mansion, built around a steel frame and designed by David Bryce, which was burned out in 1913, probably by Suffragettes. It was restored and is still occupied as a Church of Scotland Residential School.

Other refs: Ballikinrain

Old Ballindalloch *see* Castle Stripe

Old Bar Castle *see* Bar Castle

Old Bishopton *see* Bishopton House

Old Caberston *see* Caberston Tower

Old Cambus

Borders: About 2 miles south-east of Cockburnspath, near A1107, at or near Old Cambus.

Ruin or site NT 805695 OS: 67 * Map: 2, no: 330

Site of castle or residence of Coldingham Priory. It was given to the priory by Edgar, King of Scots, in 1098, and there was an old church here, dedicated to St Helen, but it has been demolished. The manor was laid waste by the Douglas Earl of Angus about 1530.

It was from here that Robert the Bruce planned to besiege Berwick in 1317, and was building siege engines, when he received a papal bull addressed to 'Robert, Governor of Scotland'. He refused the bull, saying it was wrongly addressed as he was King of Scots. Several other messengers from the Pope were waylaid and robbed of other wrongly addressed bulls.

Other refs: Aldcambus

Old Castle Lachlan *see* Castle Lachlan

Old Castle of Barnwyil *see* Barnweill Castle

Old Castle of Fedderate *see* Fedderate Castle

Old Castle of Inaltrie *see* Inaltrie Castle

Old Castle of Inverugie *see* Castle of Inverugie

Old Castle of Knock *see* Knock Castle

Old Castle of Ravenstone *see* Drumgin Castle

Old Craigends House *see* Craigends House

Old Crawfordton

Dumfriesshire: About 2.5 miles east and south of Moniaive, on minor road south of A702 at junction with B729, south of Cairn Water, at Old Crawfordton.
Ruin or site   NX 815889   OS: 78   *   Map: 1, no: 140
Little survives of a 17th-century tower house, probably of the Crichtons, except the basement. It is being restored.

Old Crookston House *see* Crookston Old House

Old Dalruharran *see* Lochmodie Castle

Old Downie

Angus & Dundee: About 3 miles south-east of Monifieth, on minor roads east of B962, 1 mile east of Newbigging, at or near Old Downie.
Ruin or site   NO 519364   OS: 54   *   Map: 8, no: 221
Site of castle on a small hill, some remains of which are said to have survived in the 19th century. It was a property of a Duncan de Dunny in 1264, and may later have passed to the Grahams.
Other refs: Castlehill, Old Downie; Downie Castle

Old Dundas *see* Dundas Castle

Old Dunimarle Castle *see* Dunimarle Castle

Old Ellon Castle *see* Ellon Castle

Old Ettrick *see* Ettrick House

Old Fairnilee House *see* Fairnilee

Old Gala House

Borders: In Galashiels, on minor road from A7, on south side of Buckholm Hill, near Ladhope Tower, in Scot Crescent, at Old Gala House.
Private   NT 492357   OS: 73   **   Map: 2, no: 155
Old Gala, a rambling mansion, incorporates an altered 16th-century tower house at one end, and an extended T-plan building of 1611 in the middle. There is a painted ceiling, dating from 1635.
  It may stand on the site of a 15th-century castle of the Douglases, which was destroyed in 1544. The property passed by marriage from the Pringles of Gala to the Scotts in 1632. The building is now used as a community and art centre, and there is a museum with displays about the occupants of the house and Galashiels.
OPEN: Open late Mar-early Nov, Tue-Sat 10.00-16.00; Jul-Aug, Mon-Sat 10.00-16.00, Sun 14.00-16.00; Oct, Tue-Sat 13.00-16.00.
Explanatory displays. Gift shop. Tearoom. Garden. Disabled limited access. Gallery with visual art exhibitions. Parking nearby.
Tel: 01896 752611

Old Graitney

Dumfriesshire: About 0.5 miles south-west of Gretna, on minor roads south of B721, east of Kirtle Water, about 200 yards south of Old Graitney.
Ruin or site   NY 312663   OS: 85   *   Map: 1, no: 298
Site of castle, a property of the Johnstones which was burned by the Maxwells in 1585.
Other refs: Auld Hoose, Old Graitney; Old Gretna

Old Granton House *see* Granton Castle

Old Greenlaw Castle

Borders: On minor roads west of A697 or south of A6105, 1 mile south of Greenlaw, at or near Old Greenlaw.
Ruin or site   NT 726448 [?]   OS: 74   *   Map: 2, no: 295
Site of castle, a property of the Cospatrick Earls of Dunbar from the 12th century, then the Homes.

Old Gretna *see* Old Graitney

Old Hall of Auchincross

Ayrshire: About 3 miles west of New Cumnock, on minor roads west of A76, north of River Nith, at Hall of Auchincross.
Ruin or site   NS 582141   OS: 71   *   Map: 3, no: 264
Site of castle or old house to the north-west of Hall of Auchincross.
Other refs: Auchincross

Old Hall of Dunragit *see* Dunragit House

Old Halls of Craig

Galloway: About 2 miles north-west of Glenluce, on minor roads and foot north of A75, west of Water of Luce, north-west of Airyhemming.
Ruin or site   NX 172598 [?]   OS: 82   *   Map: 1, no: 31
Site of castle, nothing of which remains.
Other refs: Craig

Old Ha', Gadgirth *see* Gadgirth House

Old Holylee *see* Holylee

Old House of Barras *see* Barras Castle

Old House of Carnousie *see* Carnousie Castle

Old House of Dod *see* Dod

Old House of Embo

Sutherland & Caithness: About 2.5 miles north and east of Dornoch, on minor roads east of A9, west of the sea, at or near Embo.
Ruin or site   NH 809922 [?]   OS: 21   *   Map: 12, no: 27
Site of tower house. The present Embo House was built in 1790, and does not appear to have any defensive features.
  It was a property of the Gordons of Embo.
Other refs: Embo

Old House of Fetternear *see* Fetternear House

Old House of Gask *see* Gascon Hall

Old House of Inverlaidnan *see* Inverlaidnan

Old House of Invermay *see* Invermay Tower

Old House of Leslie *see* Leslie Castle

Old House of Straloch *see* Straloch House

Old House of Tongue *see* House of Tongue

Old Howpasley

Borders: About 11 miles south-west of Hawick, on minor roads south of B711, 1 mile south of Craik, east of Howpasley Burn, at Old Howpasley.
Private   NT 349067   OS: 79   *   Map: 2, no: 91
Site of tower house, which was torched by the English in 1547 (or 1543). It was a property of the Scotts of Howpasley.
Other refs: Howpaslie

Old Humbie House *see* Humbie Old Place

Old Jeddart

Borders: About 4 miles south and east of Jedburgh, on minor road just north of A68, on west bank of Jed Water, at or near Old Jeddart.
Ruin or site   NT 670144 [?]   OS: 80   *   Map: 2, no: 273
Site of tower house, recorded as Old Jeddart or Jedward, the last remains of which were removed about 1800.
Other refs: Old Jedward

Old Jedward *see* Old Jeddart

Old Keiss Castle *see* Keiss Castle

Old Kendal

Aberdeen & Gordon: About 4 miles east of Inverurie, on minor roads south of B993 1 mile west of junction with A947, at or near Old Kendal.
Ruin or site   NJ 838225   OS: 38   *   Map: 10, no: 281
Site of castle of the Burnets.
Other refs: Ardiherald

Old Kippencross

Stirlingshire & Clackmannan: About 1 mile south of Dunblane, on minor roads south or east of B8033, east of the Allan Water, at Old Kippencross.
Private   NS 785999 [?]   OS: 57   **   Map: 6, no: 67
Old Kippencross, a mansion dating from 1767, incorporates the vaulted basement of greatly altered L-plan tower house of 1617. The walls are harled.
  Kippencross was a property of the Pearsons in 1624, but passed to the Stirlings of Kippendavie after 1768. Kippencross is a three-storey classical mansion of about 1770, altered and extended in the 19th century. A walled garden dates from 1703.

Old Largie Castle *see* Largie Castle

Old Leckie House

Stirlingshire & Clackmannan: About 6.5 miles west of Stirling, on minor road south of A811, one mile west of Gargunnock, at Old Leckie.
Private   NS 690946   OS: 57   ***   Map: 6, no: 53
Old Leckie is a late 16th-century T-plan tower house. It consists of a main block of three storeys, and a centrally projecting stair-wing. A stair-turret is corbelled out from first-floor level, and another is above second-floor. A lower wing was added in the mid 18th century.
  The entrance still has an iron yett, but the house has been altered inside, including the removal of the stair from the stair-tower.
  The property belonged to the Leckie family, who built the present castle, but was sold to the Moirs in 1659, who held it until the beginning of the 20th century. Bonnie Prince Charlie was entertained at the house in 1745 by the wife of the laird, while her husband was imprisoned in Stirling Castle.
Other refs: Leckie House

Old Lindores Castle

Fife: About 2 miles south-east of Newburgh, on minor roads south of A913, north of Lindores Loch, just north-east of Lindores House.
Ruin or site   NO 264168   OS: 59   *   Map: 7, no: 55
Site of castle, which was mentioned in 1480 and a property of the MacGills. It is, however, very close to Lindores Castle [NO 266168].
Other refs: Lindores Castle

Old Manor House *see* Cockburnspath House

Old Manse

Fife: In Anstruther Easter, on minor roads south of the A917, just north of the harbour.
Private   NO 567036   OS: 59   **   Map: 7, no: 148
Old Manse consists of an altered 16th-century L-plan tower house of three storeys with a corbelled-out stair turret in the re-entrant angle. A wing was added in 1753 making the house T-plan.
  It was held by the Reverend James Melville around 1571. The house was restored in the 1970s.

Old Mansion House *see* Auchterhouse

Old Mar *see* Braemar Castle

Old Maud

Banff & Buchan: About 0.5 miles south-west of Maud, on minor road just east of B9106, 0.5 miles north and east of Drymuir, at or near Mains of Old Maud.
Ruin or site   NJ 917469 [?]   OS: 30   *   Map: 10, no: 320
Site of castle, a property of the Keith Earls Marischal. The remains were apparently destroyed with the building of the railway, itself now dismantled.
Other refs: Maud; Castle of Old Maud

Old Mertoun House *see* Mertoun House

Old Montrose Castle

Angus & Dundee: About 3 miles west of Montrose, on minor roads north of A934, on west side of Montrose Basin, south of The (Dreaded?) Lurgies, at or near Old Montrose.
Ruin or site   NO 675570 [?]   OS: 54   *   Map: 8, no: 262
Site of castle of the Grahams, a fragment of which remained at the end of the 19th century.
  The lands were exchanged by Robert the Bruce for Cardross with Sir David Graham, a follower of Bruce. The 1st Earl of Montrose was killed at the Battle of Flodden in 1513. The 5th Earl, later Marquis of Montrose, was born here.

Old Murthly Castle *see* Murthly Castle

Old Newton, Doune *see* Newton Castle

Old Ormiston *see* Ormiston Castle

Old Ormiston Castle *see* Ormiston Tower

Old Place

Lanarkshire & Glasgow area: About 1.5 miles west of Kilsyth, on minor roads north of A803 at Queenzieburn, at or near Old Place.
Ruin or site   NS 690780 [?]   OS: 64   *   Map: 3, no: 321
Site of castle of the Livingstones of Kilsyth, which was ruinous by 1740.

Old Place of Ardoch *see* Ardoch

Old Place of Auchinleck *see* Auchinleck Castle

Old Place of Balgair *see* Balgair Castle

Old Place of Balneil *see* Balneil

Old Place of Broughton

Galloway: About 1.5 miles south-west of Garlieston, on minor roads and foot west of B7004, 0.3 miles north-east of Broughton Mains farm.

Ruin or site   NX 456452   OS: 83   *   Map: 1, no: 75

Site of castle, nothing of which remains except an oval enclosure and a date stone of 1628 built into the farmhouse wall. It was a property of the Murrays.

Other refs: Broughton

Old Place of Cushnie *see* Cushnie Castle

Old Place of Kilbirnie *see* Kilbirnie House

Old Place of Mochrum

Galloway: About 7 miles east of Glenluce, on minor road north of B7005 and south of B733, just north of Mochrum Loch, at Old Place of Mochrum.

Private   NX 308541   OS: 82   **   Map: 1, no: 44**

Standing in open moorland, Old Place of Mochrum is a courtyard castle. The courtyard encloses a 15th-century keep and a 16th-century tower house, formerly only

joined by the courtyard wall. Ranges of buildings, including a gatehouse and a block connecting the keep and tower, were later built around the other sides of the courtyard. An underground passage runs beneath the courtyard from the tower house to one of the wings.

The rectangular keep has four storeys and a garret, and has very thick walls. Two sides are crowned by corbelled-out parapets with open rounds at the corners. The gables are corbiestepped. The entrance opens into the vaulted basement, which contained a kitchen with a wide fireplace. The floors above have been very altered. A turnpike stair is crowned by a gabled caphouse.

The tower house is also rectangular and has a projecting square stair-tower topped by a watch-chamber. The windows are larger than the keep, and it has been much altered inside.

It was a property of the Dunbars, a branch of the Cospatrick Earls of Dunbar and March. One of the family was Gavin Dunbar, Archbishop of Glasgow and Chancellor of Scotland to James V. The property passed to the MacDowalls about 1694, who were made Earls of Dumfries in 1768, then in 1876 to the Stewart Marquises of Bute, who still own the property. The castle became ruinous, but has been restored and is still occupied.

Other refs: Mochrum; Drumwalt Castle

Old Place of Sorbie *see* Sorbie Castle

Old Place, Blantyre

Lanarkshire & Glasgow: About 2 miles east of East Kilbride, on minor roads off B7012, near Blantyre Old Parish Church, High Blantyre.

Ruin or site   NS 680568   OS: 64   *   Map: 3, no: 318

Site of castle or fortified house, apparently with a moat. It was demolished about 1800 and replaced by a farm.

The lands were a property of Blantyre Priory, which was founded by Patrick Earl of Dunbar in 1239 and dedicated to the Holy Rood. At the Reformation the property

passed to the Stewarts of Minto, Lords Blantyre, although they appear to have used the priory as their seat, then later Cardonald Place.

Other refs: Blantyre Castle

Old Polmaise House *see* Polmaise Castle

Old Risk

Galloway: About 3 miles north-east of Newton Stewart, on minor road and foot north of A712, east of the Penkiln Burn, about 0.5 miles north of Risk.

Ruin or site   NX 443695 [?]   OS: 83   *   Map: 1, no: 71

Little remains of a castle except foundations, which was defended by marshy ground.

Other refs: Castle of Old Risk

Old Sauchie

Stirlingshire & Clackmannan: About 3 miles south-west of Stirling, on minor roads west of A872, west of Howieton Fishery, at Old Sauchie.

Private   NS 779883   OS: 57   **   Map: 6, no: 65

Old Sauchie is a ruined 16th-century L-plan tower house of four storeys. To this has been added a 17th-century wing and other additions, now used as an estate office. The old tower has two bartizans, and a stair-turret. The tower has corbiestepped gables, and the walls are pierced by gunloops and shot-holes.

The entrance, in the re-entrant angle, leads to the vaulted basement, which contained the kitchen and cellars, and to a wide stair to the first-floor hall. A turnpike stair, in the turret, climbs to the upper floors.

It was a property of the Erskines, but passed to the Ramsay family in the 18th century, then in 1865 to Sir Alexander Gibson-Maitland.

The Battle of Sauchieburn was fought nearby in 1488, where the forces of James III were defeated by his rebellious nobles. The king was murdered after the battle, and is buried in Cambuskenneth Abbey.

Other refs: Sauchieburn Castle; Little Sauchie

Old Scarlaw *see* Scarlaw Peel

Old Skelbo House *see* Skelbo Castle

Old Slains Castle

Aberdeen & Gordon: About 4.5 miles south-west of Cruden Bay, on minor roads east of A975, south-east of Mains of Slains, on a promontory into the sea, at Old Slains.

Ruin or site   NK 053300   OS: 38   **   Map: 10, no: 359

Not much survives of a 13th-century castle, which was once a major stronghold and occupied a large area. It consisted of a strong 15th-century keep, a fragment of which survives, and a courtyard defended by ditches.

It was originally a property of the Comyns, but passed to the Hay Earls of Errol early in the 14th century. James VI had it destroyed and blown up with gunpowder after the Earl had taken part in the rebellion led by the Earl of Huntly in 1594. The Hays built a new castle and mansion at Slains [NK 102362], near Cruden Bay, of which a substantial ruin remains.

Other refs: Slains Castle

Old Tarbat House *see* Tarbat House

Old Thirlestane Castle

Borders: About 2 miles east of Lauder, 0.3 miles south-west of A697 at Thirlestane village, east of the Boonsdreigh Water.

Ruin or site   NT 564474   OS: 73   **   Map: 2, no: 210

Little remains of a tower and courtyard, except the vaulted basement. The tower consisted of a rectangular block and a wing containing a stair.

The Maitlands held the property from the middle of the 13th century or earlier, but moved to Thirlestane Castle, near Lauder, in about 1595.

Other refs: Thirlestane

Old Walls

Dumfriesshire: About 1.5 miles north of Lockerbie, near B723, east of Dryfe
Water, at or near St Michael's Walls.
Ruin or site   NY 140849   OS: 78   *   Map: 1, no: 245
Site of a strong tower, some remains of which survived about 1845. There may
have been another tower or stronghold nearby, known as Walls, and there is also
Peelhouses [NY 142840].
Other refs: Walls; Peelhouses

Old Wark, Newark *see* Newark Castle

Old Wick Castle *see* Castle of Old Wick

Old Woodhouselee Castle

Lothians: About 1.5 miles north-east of Penicuik, on minor road east of B7026,
south of the River North Esk, near track of dismantled railway (cycle route).
Ruin or site   NT 258617   OS: 66   *   Map: 4, no: 97
Located on a high crag over the River North Esk, not much survives of a 16th-
century L-plan tower house, except three vaulted cellars and a ruined wing.

It may have been built by Oliver Sinclair in the first half of the 16th century, but
was a property of the Hamiltons of Bothwellheugh. Lady Hamilton and her young
child were stripped naked and turned out of their home here by the Regent Moray.
The baby died and Lady Hamilton went mad, to die soon afterwards. Her husband,
James Hamilton of Bothwellheugh, shot and killed Regent Moray at Linlithgow in
1570. The castle was demolished in the late 17th century, and materials used to
build Woodhouselee, itself now gone.

The ruins are said to be haunted by a 'White Lady', the ghost of Lady Hamilton,
dressed in white, searching for her baby. The ghost has also been described as a
'Green Lady'.
Other refs: Woodhouselee

Oliver Castle

Borders: About 6 miles south of Broughton, on minor road north of A701, on the
west side of the Tweed, at Oliver.
Ruin or site   NT 098248 [?]   OS: 72   *   Map: 2, no: 5
Site of 12th-century castle of enclosure of the Frasers, and later the Tweedies. The
castle was razed to the ground. The old house of Oliver is an altered 18th-century
house.

Thomas Tweedie of Oliver Castle was involved in the murder of Lord Fleming in
1524, which started a feud between the families.

Over Oliver was a 16th-century tower house of the Tweedies of Oliver, while Nether
Oliver passed from the Flemings to the Hays.
Other refs: Over Oliver Castle; Nether Oliver Castle

Orbiston House

Lanarkshire & Glasgow: At northern edge of Strathclyde Park, on minor road
west of A721, Motherwell, at Orbiston.
Ruin or site   NS 732580   OS: 64   **   Map: 3, no: 344
Not much remains of a keep or tower, which was extended by a mansion in the
19th century. The basement and second storey of the keep were both vaulted, and
the building probably dated from the 15th century or earlier.

It was a property of the Oliphants in the 12th century, but passed to the Hamiltons who held it until 1827.

Orchard *see* Carco Castle

Orchardton Tower

Galloway: About 4 miles south of Dalbeattie, on minor roads south of A711,
about 1 mile south of Palnackie, west of Orchardton Burn.
His Scot   NX 817551   OS: 84   **   Map: 1, no: 141**
The only free-standing circular tower house in Scotland, Orchardton Tower is a
round tower house of four storeys. It was built in the 15th and 16th centuries. The
tower has a corbelled-out parapet, and a gabled caphouse crowning the turnpike
stair. Remains of courtyard buildings survive.

The entrance, at first-floor level, is reached by an external stone stair, while the
basement is entered through a separate arched doorway. The hall, on the first
floor, like the chambers above, was circular. The upper storeys have no floors.

The lands of Orchardton passed to the Cairns early in the 15th century, and they
built the tower. One of the family was present at the murder of MacLellan of Bombie, along with Gordon of Lochinvar, in the High Street of Edinburgh in 1527.

The tower passed to the Maxwells. During the Jacobite Rising of 1745, one of the
family, Sir Robert Maxwell, was wounded and captured at Culloden in 1746 and
taken to Carlisle for trial and probable execution. He tried to destroy his personal
papers, but was prevented, and his commission as an officer in the French army
found. He was thereafter treated as a prisoner of war, and was sent to France rather
than being executed. He later returned to Orchardton. Walter Scott made use of
this story in his novel 'Guy Mannering'.
OPEN: Access at all reasonable times.
Car parking.
Tel: 0131 668 8800   Fax: 0131 668 8888
Email: hs.explore@scotland.gov.uk   Web: www.historic-scotland.gov.uk

Ord House

South Highland: About 1 mile west of Muir of Ord, on minor roads west of A832,
at or near Ord House.
Private   NH 514505   OS: 26   *   Map: 9, no: 58
Ord House, a property of the Mackenzies, dates from about 1810 with later additions, but has a date stone of 1637.

Ormacleit Castle

Western Isles: About 9.5 miles north of Lochboisdale on island of South Uist, on
minor roads west of A865, about 0.5 miles east of the sea, at Ormacleit Castle.
Private   NF 740319   OS: 22   *   Map: 11, no: 4
One of the last castles built in Scotland, Ormacleit consists of a T-plan house of two
storeys. It had a courtyard, and was started in 1701 and completed in 1708. A massive kitchen fireplace survives.

The castle was built as the residence of Ailean, Chief of Clan Ranald, a MacDonald. It was accidentally destroyed by fire in 1715, on the eve of the Battle of Sheriffmuir during the Jacobite Rising, when the Clan Ranald chief was killed. It was never rebuilt, although part has recently been reoccupied.
Other refs: Ormiclate Castle

Ormelie Castle

Sutherland & Caithness: To south of Thurso, on minor roads west of B874, west of River Thurso, in Ormlie part of Thurso.
Ruin or site ND 110680 [?] OS: 12 * Map: 12, no: 42
Site of castle, a property of the Earls of Orkney. It was destroyed by fire at the beginning of the 16th century, and a manse was built on the site in 1818.
Other refs: Ormlie Castle; Castle of Thurso

Ormiclate Castle *see* Ormacleit Castle

Ormiston *see* Cocklaw Castle

Ormiston Castle

Lothians: About 4 miles east of Dalkeith, south of A6093 on minor road to B6371, north of Ormiston Mains.
Ruin or site NT 413677 OS: 66 * Map: 4, no: 164
Parts of a castle, also known as Ormiston Hill House, were built into the later house, which is itself now ruined.
The property originally belonged to the Lindsays, but passed to the Cockburns in the 14th century. In 1545 George Wishart, the Protestant martyr, was taken from Ormiston to Cardinal Beaton, who had him burned to death at St Andrews.
The castle was occupied by the English in 1547 as Cockburn of Ormiston sided with them. The Earl of Arran retook Ormiston, burned it and even cut down the trees around it as revenge for Cockburn's treachery. In 1748 it was sold to the Hope Earl of Hopetoun.
Other refs: Old Ormiston

Ormiston Tower

Borders: About 3.5 miles south and west of Kelso, on west side of River Teviot, on minor roads between Roxburgh and Nisbet, south-east of Old Ormiston.
Ruin or site NT 700279 [?] OS: 74 * Map: 2, no: 285
Site of 15th-century castle, held by the Dicksons in the 16th and 17th centuries, and demolished in the 19th century. It was sacked and torched by the English in 1523, and the courtyard was burned by the English in 1544. There were some remains in the 19th century, and the site is marked by a mound.
Other refs: Old Ormiston Castle; Kirkbank Castle

Ormiston Tower

Borders: About 1.5 miles west of Innerleithen, on minor road and foot (?) south of A72, on north bank of the Tweed, south of Glenormiston Farm.
Ruin or site NT 315378 OS: 73 * Map: 2, no: 81
Site of tower house. It was completely demolished about 1805 when Glenormiston House was built, itself extended in 1824 and 1846, but demolished in the 1950s.
It was a property of the Stewarts of Traquair from 1533, although it is also recorded as being a property of the Dicksons of Ormiston – this may be a confusion with Ormiston Tower [NT 700279]. The property was sold in 1789, and purchased by William Chambers, the well-known author and publisher, in 1849. At the turn of the 19th century it was held by the Thorburns.

Ormlie Castle *see* Ormelie Castle

Ormond Castle

Ross & Cromarty: About 3 miles south-west of Fortrose on Black Isle, on minor roads south of A832, about 1 mile south of Avoch, west of Moray Firth, at Ormond.
Ruin or site NH 696536 OS: 26 * Map: 9, no: 102
Standing on Castle or Lady Hill, little remains of a rectangular 12th-century castle of enclosure with square corner towers, except foundations. It was probably built by William the Lyon about 1200-14, and was the seat of the Ormond family.

It was a property of the Murrays. One of the family was Sir Andrew Moray who, along with William Wallace, defeated an English army at the Battle of Stirling Bridge in 1297. He died soon afterwards. His son, another Andrew, was made Guardian of Scotland in 1332, and did much to free Scotland from Edward Balliol and the English. He was responsible for the capture of Kildrummy Castle in 1335, and Bothwell Castle in 1336. He died here in 1338.
The property passed to the Douglases, who took from it the title of the Earl of Ormond. The title was created around 1445 for Hugh Douglas, but he was executed and forfeited in 1455 with the fall of the rest of his Black Douglas family. The property was kept by the Crown, and the castle may have been destroyed about 1650.
The sacrament house, a mural cupboard in which the consecrated elements of bread and wine were retained for the use of the sick and the dying, at Avoch may have come from the Chapel of Our Lady at the castle.
There may have been a castle at Avoch (which is pronounced as 'Auch' or 'Och') [NH 705550], but this appears just to be an alternative name for Ormond.
Other refs: Castle of Avoch; Avoch Castle

Orrock House

Aberdeen & Gordon: About 1.5 miles north of Balmedie, on minor roads west of A92, at or near Orrock House.
Private NJ 964196 [?] OS: 38 * Map: 10, no: 342
Site of castle or old house. The present tall and plain mansion dates from the end of the 18th century.
It was a property of the Mitchells from 1708, but passed to the Fordyce family in 1770. Alexander Fordyce, a London banker, became bankrupt and had to sell the property to the Orrock family about 1780. John Orrock, a merchant, changed the name to Orrock after lands lost in Fife and built the house. It is still occupied.
Other refs: Over Blairton

Ospisdale House

Sutherland & Caithness: About 5.5 miles west of Dornoch, on minor roads north of A9, about 1 mile north of shore of Dornoch Firth, at or near Ospisdale.
Ruin or site NH 713897 [?] OS: 21 * Map: 12, no: 17
Ospisdale House, an 18th-century mansion, is built on or near the site of a 16th-century tower house. In the 19th century the property was held by the Gilchrist family.

Otterston Tower

Fife: About 2 miles west of Aberdour, on minor roads north of A921, south side of Otterston Loch, just north of railway line.
Private NT 165852 OS: 65 ** Map: 7, no: 25
Otterston, a mansion of three storeys and an attic, was much altered in 1851 and partly demolished. It incorporates an L-plan tower house, dating from 1589. Two round towers from the barmkin survive.
The property was owned by the Hendersons at the beginning of the 16th century, but had passed to the Mowbrays of Barnbougle by 1589, who built the tower, and held it until the 19th century. The house is occupied.
There may have been another castle, Markfield Tower, nearby [NT 164850].
Other refs: Cockcairnie House; Markfield Tower

Oulch Castle *see* Tulloch Castle

Outer Woodhead

Dumfriesshire: About 2.5 miles north and east of Canonbie, on minor roads north of B6318, at or near Outer Woodhead.
Ruin or site NY 403797 [?] OS: 85 * Map: 1, no: 330
Possible site of tower house.

Over Blairton *see* Orrock House

Over Castle Dornal *see* Dornal Castle

Over Craig *see* Craig

Otterston Tower – see previous page

Over Oliver Castle *see* Oliver Castle

Over Riccarton *see* Riccarton Tower

Overglinns *see* Balgair Castle

Overhowden
Borders: About 3.5 miles north-west of Lauder, on minor roads west of A68, 1 mile west of Oxton, at Overhowden.
Ruin or site   NT 488522   OS: 73   *   Map: 2, no: 151
Site of tower house, now occupied by a farmhouse.

Overton *see* Wallans

Overton Tower
Borders: About 5 miles south of Jedburgh, on minor road west of A68, mile north of Edgerston.
Ruin or site   NT 685128   OS: 80   **   Map: 2, no: 280
Overton Tower is a ruined 16th-century tower house, formerly rising to two storeys and a garret. There are some remains of other buildings, probably within a courtyard. It was a property of the Frasers.

Overtoun Castle
Argyll & Dunbartonshire: About 1.5 miles north-east of Dumbarton, on minor road north of A82 at Milton, east of Overtoun Burn, at Overtoun.
Private   NS 424761   OS: 64   *   Map: 5, no: 159**
Site of castle. Overtoun Castle or House, a large baronial mansion of the mid 19th century, was designed by James Smith and may be built on the site. The castle was built for James White, a successful chemical manufacturer.
   The estate is open to the public.
OPEN: Park open all year, daily.
Guided walks during summer season. Picnic area. Parking.

Oxenfoord Castle
Lothians: About 3.5 miles east and south of Dalkeith, on minor road east of the A68 at junction with B6372, west of the Tyne Water.
Private   NT 388656   OS: 66   *   Map: 4, no: 155
Oxenfoord Castle, also recorded as Oxfurd, an Adam mansion built in 1780-85 and then enlarged by William Burn in 1842, incorporates a 16th-century L-plan tower house. There was a stair-tower in the re-entrant angle, and there were bartizans crowning the corners.
   It was a property of the Riddels, but passed to the MacGills in the 12th century, one of whom was David MacGill of Oxenfoord, King's Advocate in 1582. It passed by marriage to the Dalrymples of Stair in 1760, and was the seat of the Earls of Stair. James Boswell stayed here in 1786. It was used as a girls private boarding school from 1931, although it closed in 1984.
   There may have also been a castle nearby at Cranston, whose inhabitants were accused of 'adhering to papistrie' at the end of the 16th century, although this may refer to Oxenfoord.
Other refs: Cranston Castle; Oxfurd

Oxfurd *see* Oxenfoord Castle

P

Palace an Righ

Perthshire: About 3.5 miles west of Tummel Bridge, near B846, north of River Tummel, Palace an Righ.
Ruin or site   NN 717593   OS: 52   *   Map: 8, no: 9
Possible site of royal palace.

Palace of Dunfermline *see* Dunfermline Palace

Palace of Holyroodhouse *see* Holyroodhouse

Palace of Innes *see* Innes House

Palace of Kinneil *see* Kinneil House

Palace of Leslie *see* Leslie House

Palace of Spynie *see* Spynie Palace

Palace Walls *see* Woll

Palace Yard *see* Enrick

Palacerigg

Lanarkshire & Glasgow: About 2 miles east of Cumbernauld, on minor roads south of B8054 or east B8039, North Palacerigg Country Park.
Private   NS 783733 [?]   OS: 64   *   Map: 3, no: 369**
Site of castle, a property of the Flemings of Cumbernauld.
  The country park, which covers some 700 acres, has a visitor centre and a Scottish and North European animal collection with roe deer, bison, lynx, wildcat and owls.
OPEN: Park open all year: Apr-Sep, daily 9.00-18.00; Oct-Mar 9.30-16.30.
Guided tours. Explanatory displays. Gift shop. Tearoom. Picnic areas. Nature trails. Bridle paths. Pony trekking. Golf course. Disabled access to visitor centre.
Tel: 01236 720047   Fax: 01236 458271

Panmure Castle

Angus & Dundee: About 2.5 miles north of Carnoustie, on minor roads and foot west of B9128 and north of A92, east of the Monikie Burn, at Panmure.
Ruin or site   NO 546376   OS: 54   *   Map: 8, no: 230
Little remains of a 12th-century castle of enclosure, rhomboid in plan, which had corner towers and a hall and chapel.
  The lands passed to the Maules by marriage about 1224. The castle was held by the English in the Wars of Independence, but recaptured by the Scots in 1306, when Andrew Moray had the defences slighted, then again in 1312. It may have been abandoned for many years, but had been rebuilt before 1487. Sir Thomas Maule of Panmure was killed at the Battle of Harlaw in 1411, while his grandson, another Sir Thomas, was slain at the Battle of Flodden in 1513. The family were made Earls of Panmure in 1633, but were forfeited in 1716 after fighting for the Jacobites at the Battle of Sheriffmuir during the Jacobite Rising. They later recovered their titles.
  The castle was used until the middle of the 17th century, and replaced by Panmure House [NO 537386], a mansion dating from the end of the 17th century but almost completely rebuilt in 1852-5. The house has been demolished and only a stable block remains.

Parbroath Castle

Fife: About 4 miles north west of Cupar, on minor roads north of A914, north of junction with A913.
Ruin or site   NO 322176   OS: 59   *   Map: 7, no: 80
Very little remains of Parbroath Castle, formerly protected by a ditch, except part of the vaulted basement.
  It was a property of the Setons, one of whom captured and held Broughty Castle against the Lords of the Congregation in 1571.

Parck

Borders: About 2.5 miles north of Newcastleton, east of B6399, east of Hermitage Water, north-east of Redheugh.
Ruin or site   NY 500910 [?]   OS: 79   *   Map: 2, no: 165
Site of tower house of the Elliots.
  John o' the Park, otherwise known as Wee Jock Elliot, stabbed and seriously wounded James Hepburn, 4th Earl of Bothwell, after having been shot himself. Bothwell had been rounding up local members of the Elliot family for reiving. Elliot soon died from his wound, but although Bothwell was injured, he recovered after a visit from Mary, Queen of Scots, and later became her third husband.
  The lands of the Elliots were devastated in 1569.
Other refs: Park

Pardovan Castle

Lothians: About 3 miles east of Linlithgow, on minor roads south of A904 or north of B9080, north of Union Canal, north-west of Philipstoun, at Pardovan.
Ruin or site   NT 044773   OS: 65   *   Map: 4, no: 23
Site of 16th-century castle of the Hamiltons, little or nothing of which remains. It had a three-storey main block, with a tower rising another two storeys.

Parisholm

Lanarkshire & Glasgow: About 3 miles east of Muirkirk, just south of A70, at eastern end of Glenbuck Loch, at or near Parish Holm.
Ruin or site   NS 762280 [?]   OS: 71   *   Map: 3, no: 361
Site of small tower house, some remains of which survived in 1864.

Park

Renfrewshire: About 1.5 miles west of Bishopton, east of B789, south of Formakin, by Formakin Burn.
Ruin or site   NS 409706 [?]   OS: 64   *   Map: 3, no: 152
Site of castle, dating from the 13th century.
  It was a property of the Park family, but passed to the Houstons around the turn of the 16th century.
  Formakin House was designed by Sir Robert Lorimer at the beginning of the 20th century, and built by J. A. Holms, although he ran out of money before World War I.

Park

Banff & Buchan: About 4 miles north-west of Aberchirder, on minor road south of B9023 0.5 miles south of junction with A95 at Cornhill, at Park.
Private   NJ 587571   OS: 29   **   Map: 10, no: 151
Set in extensive grounds with ornamental walks, park and woodlands, Park is a large mansion. It dates from 1292, and was rebuilt into a Z-plan tower house in 1563, extended again in 1723, and later centuries.
  Park was a property of the Gordons, and Sir William Gordon of Park was active for the Jacobites during the 1745 Rising. Although he escaped to France, he lost his lands and property, and died in 1751, the estate eventually passing to the Gordon-Duffs. Butcher Cumberland and his army camped here on their way south after slaughtering the Jacobites at Culloden. The house is now owned again by the Gordons.
  Park is said to be haunted by a 'Green Lady'. The story goes that a young servant girl became pregnant and was dismissed from service. She committed suicide by hanging herself, and her ghost is said to have been seen in the grounds, as well as in the house and looking from the window of a second-floor chamber. The appari-

tion of a cloaked and hooded woman was also witnessed by a guest.

Other apparitions and occurrences include a monk, who was walled up in one of the castle chambers on the ground floor; and the sounds of a child's voice and music box, only heard in the upper quarters. Quick changes in temperature have also been experienced, as well as vague shapes moving across rooms. Objects are also reputedly frequently moved or disappear only to reappear later.

Other refs: Castle of Park

OPEN: Open all year to residents by arrangement.

Castle offers dinner, bed and breakfast and self-catering accommodation. Murder mystery evenings. Weddings and functions on request. Parking.

Tel: 01466 751667 Fax: 01466 751667

Email: booking@castleofpark.net Web: www.castleofpark.net

Park *see* Parck

Park Place *see* Castle of Park

Park Tower *see* Copshaw Tower

Parkglen Wood

Renfrewshire: About 2.5 miles east of Kilmacolm, on minor roads south of B789, near Haddockston, Parkglen Wood.

Ruin or site NS 400707 OS: 63 * Map: 3, no: 146

There are some foundations of buildings, which may be the scant remains of a tower house.

Other refs: Nether Glens

Parkhall

Lanarkshire & Glasgow area: About 2.5 miles north-east of Douglas, on minor road south of A70, about 0.75 miles east of junction with M74, south of the Douglas Water, at Parkhall.

Private NS 863330 OS: 72 * Map: 3, no: 401

Site of a castle. The site may be at Parkhall, a modern mansion, or at NS 864325, where the remains of an L-plan building were recorded.

Parkhill House

Aberdeen & Gordon: About 1 mile north of Dyce, on minor roads south of B997, north of River Don, at or near Parkhill House.

Ruin or site NJ 898140 [?] OS: 38 * Map: 10, no: 311

Site of castle or old house. Parkhill House, which dated from the 18th century, was demolished around 1960, and a new house built.

Parkhill was a property of the Skenes of Dyce.

Partick Castle

Lanarkshire & Glasgow area: About 2.5 miles west of Glasgow Cathedral, on minor roads north of A814, west of River Kelvin on north of River Clyde, off Castlebank Street, near Partick railway station.

Ruin or site NS 559663 OS: 64 * Map: 3, no: 254

Site of castle, which had gardens and orchards.

The lands were a property of the Bishops of Glasgow from 1136, who built a residence here. A new L-plan tower house was built in 1611 by George Hutcheson, probably on the site of Bishop's residence. The house was inhabited by labourers in 1770, but subsequently became ruinous. It was demolished about 1836, and nothing remains, the site occupied by a scrap dealers.

Other refs: Bishop's Castle, Partick

Parton Place

Galloway: About 6.5 miles north-west of Castle Douglas, near A713, east side of Loch Ken, 1 mile south-east of Parton, at or near Parton House.

Private NX 710695 [?] OS: 84 * Map: 1, no: 116

Site of castle or old house, although the site is not certain.

Parton was a property of the Glendonwyn family from the 15th century until 1850 when it passed to the Murrays.

Patrickholm

Lanarkshire & Glasgow area: About 0.5 miles south-west of Larkhall, on track from minor roads west of the B7078, west and above the Avon Water.

Private NS 756500 OS: 64 ** Map: 3, no: 356

Site of castle. The present 19th-century ruined house contains vaulted cellars from an earlier building.

It was a property of the Hamiltons of Raploch, and is said to have been a rendezvous for government forces during Covenanting times.

Pavilion *see* Westhouses

Paxton House

Borders: About 4 miles west of Berwick-upon-Tweed, off A1, Paxton.

Private NT 935530 OS: 74 * Map: 2, no: 359**

In a picturesque setting overlooking the Tweed, Paxton House, a fine classical mansion with a central block with columns and two flanking wings, was built in 1756 for Patrick Home of Billie. The house was built for his intended bride, Sophie de Brandt, from the court of King Frederick the Great of Prussia.

The house was designed by Robert, John and James Adam, and in 1811 a gallery and library were added to designs by Robert Reid. There is access to 12 period rooms, and a fine collection of furniture. Paxton is now an outstation of the National Galleries of Scotland, and houses 70 paintings.

There are 80 acres of garden, woodland and park land.

OPEN: Open Good Fri-Oct, daily 11.00-17.00; last admission 16.15; shop and tearoom, 10.00-17.30; grounds 10.00-sunset; open to groups/schools all year by appt.

Exhibitions of pictures and furniture. Gift shop. Licensed tearoom. Gardens, woodlands and park land. Picnic area. Plant centre. Adventure playground. Partial disabled access to house. Car and coach parking. ££ Function suite for hire.

Tel: 01289 386291 Fax: 01289 386660

Email: info@paxtonhouse.com Web: www.paxtonhouse.com

Peddersburn *see* Monkland House

Pedderslourn *see* Monkland House

Peebles Castle

Borders: In Peebles, just south of the A702 west of junction with B7062, north of the River Tweed.

Ruin or site NT 249403 OS: 73 * Map: 2, no: 59

Site of 12th-century castle of enclosure on motte.

It is probably where Henry, Earl of Huntingdon, son of David I and father of kings Malcolm IV and William I the Lyon, died in 1152. William, Alexander II and Alexander III all stayed here. The castle was garrisoned for Edward I of England between 1301-2, and the English king also visited. The castle may have been abandoned early in the 14th century, although another reference asserts that it (or part of it) remained in use until 1685. It was then used as a quarry, and a parish church built on the site.

There were apparently six bastle houses in Peebles in 1870 – part of one may be built into the County Hotel. Part of the burgh wall, built in 1570, also survives, bordering a car park.

The Steeple was a fortified watch-tower, and stood at the end of the High Street [NT 250404]. It dated from the end of the 15th century, was also used as a jail and store for town records, and was demolished in 1776.

Other refs: The Steeple, Peebles

Peel Hill, Selkirk *see* Selkirk Castle

Peel Knowe *see* Hawthornside

Peel of Buchanan *see* Buchanan Castle

Peel of Claggans

Stirling & Clackmannanshire: About 3 miles south of Aberfoyle, on minor roads west of A81, 0.5 miles south of Gartmore, north of Kelty Water, north-east of Borland House.

Ruin or site NS 521966 OS: 57 * Map: 6, no: 13

There are slight remains of a D-shaped enclosure with a ditch. Foundations of a building were removed from here in the 19th century.

Peel of Drumry *see* Drumry Castle

Peel of Fichlie

Aberdeen & Gordon: About 3 miles south of Kildrummy village, on minor road east of A97, north of River Don, just east of minor road at Fichlie.

Ruin or site NJ 460139 OS: 37 ** Map: 10, no: 101

Peel of Fichlie consists of a fine rectangular motte with traces of walling on the summit.

The lands were held by the Earls of Mar in 1228, but passed to the Durwards and they may have built the castle.

Other refs: Fichlie

Peel of Gartfarran

Stirling & Clackmannanshire: About 3 miles south of Aberfoyle, just east of A81, south of Kelty Water, Flanders Moss, Gartfarran.

Ruin or site NS 536954 OS: 57 ** Map: 6, no: 18

The fine earthworks of Peel of Gartfarran consist of a ditch and bank which enclose a trapezoidal area. The Peel was still being used in the 13th or 14th centuries.

Peel of Kirkintilloch *see* Kirkintilloch Peel

Peel of Linlithgow *see* Linlithgow Palace

Peel of Lintrathen

Angus & Dundee: About 4.5 miles north of Alyth, on minor road east of B954, 1.5 miles west of Bridgend of Lintrathen, south-west of Loch of Lintrathen, at Peel.

Ruin or site NO 263540 OS: 53 * Map: 8, no: 138

Site of castle, a property of the Durwards from the 12th until the 14th century. Lintrathen passed to the Ogilvies.

This is one of the places where they may have kept the Bell of St Maddan.

Peel of Livingston *see* Livingston Peel

Peel of Strathbogie *see* Huntly Castle

Peel Ring of Lumphanan

Kincardine & Deeside: About 5 miles north-east of Aboyne, on minor roads south of A980 or north of A93, 0.5 miles south-west of Lumphanan, at Peel of Lumphanan.

His Scot NJ 576037 OS: 37 * Map: 10, no: 144

Site of 12th-century castle of enclosure, now consisting of a large but low motte

with a wide ditch. It was enclosed by a strong stone wall, held by the Durwards in the 13th century, and visited by Edward I of England in 1296. Halton House, a 15th-century block, was built on the motte and occupied until 1782. Nothing remains of this building except foundations.

It was at Lumphanan that Macbeth is believed to have been waylaid and slain by MacDuff or Malcolm Canmore in 1057. Macbeth's Cairn [NO 578053] is where he is believed to have been buried before his body was reputedly taken to Iona, and there is also a large boulder, Macbeth's Stone [NJ 575034] near which he is said to have been killed, and Macbeth's Well [NJ 580039], a spring from which he is believed to have drunk before the battle.

Other refs: Lumphanan; Halton House

OPEN: Access at all reasonable times.

Parking.

Tel: 0131 668 8800   Fax: 0131 668 8888

Email: hs.explore@scotland.gov.uk   Web: www.historic-scotland.gov.uk

Peel Tower

Borders: About 11 miles north-east of Newcastleton, on minor roads and foot east of B6357, east of Wormscleuch, north-east of Bagraw Ford, at Peel.

Ruin or site NY 605995 [?] OS: 80 * Map: 2, no: 236

Site of tower house.

Peel, Galashiels *see* Hunter's Hall, Galashiels

Peel, The *see* The Peel, Busby

Peelbraehope *see* Grey Coat Peel

Peelhill

Borders: About 0.5 miles west of Longformacus, on minor roads south of B6355, just south of Dye Water, east of Whinrig.

Ruin or site NT 683572 OS: 74 * Map: 2, no: 279

Site of tower house, little of which remains except the vestige of a ditch.

The property was owned by the Earls of Moray, then the Cospatrick Earls of Dunbar, then the Sinclairs of Rosslyn, who probably built the castle.

Other refs: Craigie Wood

Peelhill *see* Longformacus

Peelhouses *see* Old Walls

Peelwalls

Borders: About 2.5 miles south and west of Eyemouth, on minor roads just west of B6355, south of Eye Water, at or near Peelwalls House.

Ruin or site NT 922599 OS: 67 * Map: 2, no: 356

Site of castle, a property of the Homes. The present Peelwalls House, dating from the early 19th century, is a two-storey classical mansion.

Peelwalls *see* Inveramsay

Peelwalls *see* Bastleridge

Peffermill House

Lothians: About 2.5 miles south-east of Edinburgh Castle, on minor road north of A6095, south of Duddingston Loch, near the Braid Burn.

Private NT 284717 OS: 66 ** Map: 4, no: 119

Peffermill House is an altered 17th-century tower house of three storeys and a garret, with a semi-circular stair-tower in the re-entrant angle.

The entrance is at the foot of the stair-tower, and leads to the wide turnpike stair and the partly vaulted basement. The basement contains a kitchen with a large arched fireplace. The hall, on the first floor, has been subdivided, and the house has been much altered inside.

The property originally belonged to the Prestons of Craigmillar, but was sold to the Edgars, who built the house. It later passed to the Osbornes, then the Alexanders. The house is in good condition, and still occupied.

Peill Castle *see* Leith Hall

Penick Castle

Inverness & Nairn: About 3.5 miles east of Nairn, by foot south of A96, about 1 mile east of Auldearn, east of Meadowfield.
Ruin or site NH 934563 [?] OS: 27 * Map: 9, no: 148
Nothing remains of a 16th-century tower house of three storeys. It was removed towards the end of the 19th century.
 It was a property of the Deans of Moray.
Other refs: House of Penick

Penicuik Tower

Lothians: About 0.5 miles south-west of Penicuik, south of A766, north of River North Esk.
Ruin or site NT 220596 OS: 66 * Map: 4, no: 75
Probable site of an old tower house, which was demolished by the Clerks of Penicuik in the second half of the 17th or early 18th century. It was apparently known as Terregles, and a folly was built here in 1750 by Sir John Clerk.
Other refs: Terregles; Knight's Law Tower

Penkaet Castle

Lothians: About 1 mile south-west of Pencaitland, on minor roads south of A6093, east of B6371, at Fountainhall.
Private NT 427677 OS: 66 * Map: 4, no: 167**
Standing in a walled garden, Penkaet Castle consists of an altered 16th-century tower house, which was extended in the 17th century. It consists of a very long main block of two storeys and a garret, with small projecting wings at both ends. A round stair-tower stands in the centre of one side.
 The basement is not vaulted, and the hall was on the first floor, with private chambers above. Original wood panelling remains.
 It was originally a property of the Maxwells, but passed to the Cockburns, then the Pringles. The name was changed to Fountainhall, after it was sold in 1685 to the Lauders. They held it until 1922, when it was sold to the Holbourne family. In recent years the name has been changed to Penkaet Castle.
 The castle is reputedly haunted by several ghosts.
 One is said to be the spectre of Alexander Hamilton. He was a beggar, who was accused of witchcraft after cursing the lady of the house and her eldest daughter. They both died from a mysterious illness, after they had thrown Hamilton off their property. He was executed in Edinburgh, and his ghost is said to have been witnessed near the castle.
 Another is reported to manifest itself by banging doors and moving furniture. It may be the spirit of John Cockburn, who had apparently committed – or been the victim of – a murder. The sounds of footsteps and the dragging of a heavy object have also apparently been heard.
 A four-poster bed, once slept in by Charles I, is reportedly haunted as it often appears to have been used – some say by a manifestation of the king himself – although it has not actually been slept in.
 Manifestations were reported in the 20th century – the house was investigated in the 1920s, when many unexplained noises and events were recorded, although the investigation was not as thorough as it would be today.
Other refs: Fountainhall; Woodhead

Penkill Castle

Ayrshire: About 3 miles east of Girvan, on minor road south of B734, just north of Penwhappie Burn, about 1 mile south of Old Dailly.
Private NX 232985 OS: 76 * Map: 3, no: 47**
Penkill Castle is a 16th-century tower house of three storeys and a garret, to which was added a 17th-century wing, making it L-plan. A round stair-tower stood in the re-entrant angle, but this was replaced by a Victorian tower. Two conically roofed corbelled-out bartizans crown the tower.
 The basement is vaulted. The hall, on the first floor, has a large fireplace.
 Penkill was a property of the Boyds, who built the tower. The tower became ruinous, but was restored in 1857 by William Bell Scott, the Pre-Raphaelite artist and

poet. The castle had many pre-Raphaelite artefacts, but these were dispersed in the 1960s and 1970s, and again when the castle was sold in the late 1980s. The building is still occupied.

Penneld *see* Penwold

Penningham Hall *see* Bishop's Palace, Penninghame

Penshiel Grange

Lothians: About 3 miles west of Cranshaws, on minor road south from B6355, south-east of the Whiteadder Reservoir, east of the Faseny Water.
Ruin or site NT 642632 OS: 67 ** Map: 4, no: 219
Penshiel Grange is a ruined 16th-century tower house, consisting of a ruined rectangular block and a vaulted basement. The walls are pierced by gunloops.
 Penshiel was originally a monastic grange, but by 1621 had passed to the Hamilton Earl of Melrose.

Penston

Lothians: About 2.5 miles east of Tranent, on B6363 or minor road south of A199, east of Macmerry, at or near Penston.
Ruin or site NT 444722 [?] OS: 66 * Map: 4, no: 170
Site of strong old mansion, which had been demolished by the 19th century.
 Penston was a property of the Balliols from the 13th century, but passed to the Baillies of Lamington. There were good seams of coal found here, and the village grew in size, although the miners were treated little better than slaves. The population dwindled, however, as mining was abandoned, and the village now consists of a farm and a few cottages.

Penwold

Renfrewshire: About 3 miles north-west of Johnstone, on minor road west of A761, 0.5 miles north of Kilbarchan, near Pannell Farm.
Ruin or site NS 400642 OS: 64 * Map: 3, no: 145
Little remains of a castle except foundations.
 The property was held by a Henry St Martin in the 12th century.
Other refs: Penneld

Perceton House

Ayrshire: About 2.5 miles east and north of Irvine, on minor roads north of B769, south of Annick Water, at Perceton.
Private NS 354406 OS: 70 * Map: 3, no: 113
Site of castle or old house. It was a property of the Mures of Perceton, but held by the Barclays in the 20th century. There was a village here from early times, and there are the remains of an old church [NS 351406], used as a burial ground for the Macreddies and Mures of Perceton.
 The present Perceton, a late 18th-century mansion, is the headquarters of the Irvine Development Corporation.
Other refs: Greenvale

Perth Castle

Perth & Kinross: In Perth, just west of the River Tay, near the bridge across the Tay, near the A93 at end of Skinnergate, west side of Curfew Row.
Ruin or site NO 119238 OS: 58 * Map: 8, no: 86
Site of 13th-century castle, some remains of which survived in 1860.
 It was washed away in 1210 along with the bridge, but then rebuilt and captured by Edward I of England in 1298. It was recovered by the Scots in 1311, led by Robert the Bruce, who had the walls razed and the moat filled in. The castle was seized by Edward III and rebuilt, but besieged and captured by Robert the Steward in 1339 for the Scots, and does not appear to have been used afterwards.
 The town had strong walls, which survived into the 18th century, but little or nothing remains. The Spey Tower, which stood near the county buildings, was part of the fortifications, and Cardinal Beaton had several Protestants imprisoned here who were then burned as heretics. This tower was demolished in 1766, while an-

other, Monk's Tower, was demolished in 1806.

   Gowrie House, scene of the Gowrie Conspiracy, also stood in the town until demolished in 1805.

   A fragment of walling in George Street is from Cromwell's Citadel of 1652.

Other refs: Spey Tower, Perth; Monk's Tower, Perth

Peterhead *see* Keith Inch Tower

Phesdo *see* Kincardine Castle

Philorth Castle

Banff & Buchan: About 2 miles south of Fraserburgh, on minor roads east of A92, west of Water of Philorth, at or near Philorth.

Ruin or site   NK 003641 [?]   OS: 30   *   Map: 10, no: 353

Site of 17th-century castle, later extended and altered, little of which survived a fire in 1915. It consisted of an L-plan house, with pepperpot round towers, but was extended and altered in 1874 and before.

   It was the main castle of the Frasers, who held the property from the 14th century, and in 1669 became Lords Saltoun. The 7th laird, Alexander Fraser, built a harbour at Fraserburgh and bankrupted himself in the process, moving here from Cairnbulg which had to be sold. The family moved back to Cairnbulg after the fire.

   A prophecy states:

   'As lang as there's a Cock o' the North,

   There'll be a Fraser in Philorth.'

Other refs: Castle of Philorth

Physgill *see* Port Castle

Physgill House

Galloway: About 2.5 miles south and west of Whithorn, on minor roads south of A747, at Physgill House.

Private   NX 428366   OS: 83   *   Map: 1, no: 67

Site of tower house and courtyard, which is mentioned in 1684 and 1725. The present mansion dates from 1780, was later modified and extended, and stands on the site of the earlier building.

Pickeringshaw Tower *see* Breaken Tower

Pilmuir House

Lothians: About 3.5 miles south-west of Haddington, on minor roads east between B6356 and west of B6355.

Private   NT 486695   OS: 66   **   Map: 4, no: 179

Pilmuir House is a fine 17th-century T-plan house of three storeys and a garret. A stair-tower, in the re-entrant angle, is corbelled out, and there is a watch-chamber crowning the stair-wing. The walls are harled and whitewashed.

   Pilmuir belonged to the Cairns family, but passed by marriage to the Borthwicks. It is still occupied.

Pilrig House

Lothians: About 1.5 miles north-east of Edinburgh Castle, on minor roads west of Leith Walk, in Pilrig area of Edinburgh.

Private   NT 265757   OS: 66   **   Map: 4, no: 106

Pilrig House is a much-altered 17th-century L-plan tower house of three storeys and a garret, with a stair-tower in the re-entrant angle.

   The interior has been much altered, but the basement contained the kitchen with a large fireplace. The hall, on the first floor, has been subdivided.

   It was owned by the Monypennys from the 16th century, but passed in 1623 to Gilbert Kirkwood, a goldsmith. It was acquired by the Balfours in 1718. It was bequeathed to the local council in 1941, but was left unused and then vandalised. After a fire, which gutted the building, it was restored, divided and reoccupied in 1985, and stands in a public park.

Pilrig House – see below

Pinkie House

Lothians: In Musselburgh, on minor road south of the A199, south of Musselburgh race course.

Private   NT 353727   OS: 66   *   Map: 4, no: 145**

Pinkie House is an altered 16th-century L-plan tower house, of three storeys, to which has been added 17th-, 18th- and 19th-century extensions. The old part consists of a strong main block and square tower, and has steeply pitched roofs. The square tower rises to five storeys, and is topped by a flat roof with a crenellated parapet and bartizans.

   The interior has been largely modernised, but the basement is vaulted, and a wide

turnpike stair climbs as far as the second floor. A long gallery has a fine painted wood ceiling, and there are also many good plaster ceilings.

   Pinkie was a property of the Abbey of Dunfermline, but passed, after the Reformation, to the Setons, one of whom was 1st Earl of Dunfermline and Chancellor to James VI. He altered the house in 1613, and died here in 1622. Charles I stayed here, as did Bonnie Prince Charlie following victory over Sir John Cope and his army at Prestonpans in 1745 during the Jacobite Rising. The property was sold to the Hay Marquis of Tweeddale in 1694, then in 1778 to the Hopes of Craighall. The house is part of Loretto, a private boarding school.

   The house is said to be haunted by a 'Green Lady', Lilias Drummond, who died in

1601 and was the wife of Alexander Seton. Her appearance bodes ill for the family. Her ghost, or another, is said to be sometimes accompanied by a child, and she is also believed to haunt Fyvie Castle.

Pinmore

Ayrshire: About 4 miles south and east of Girvan, on minor road north of B734 east of junction with A714, just south of the River Stinchar at Pinmore.
Private   NX 206904   OS: 76   *   Map: 3, no: 31
Site of castle of the Hamiltons, on which a 19th-century house stood. The castle dated from the 16th and 17th centuries, but was destroyed by fire in 1876. It was rebuilt in the same style, but was burned and gutted, then demolished in 1981.

Pinwherry Castle

Ayrshire: About 8 miles east of Ballantrae, just north of A714 at Pinwherry, just south of the Duisk River where it meets the River Stinchar.
Ruin or site   NX 198867   OS: 76   **   Map: 3, no: 27
Standing on high ground, Pinwherry Castle is a ruined and overgrown 16th-century L-plan tower house, formerly rising to five storeys. A square stair-tower is corbelled out above first-floor level in the re-entrant angle. The gables were corbiestepped, and round bartizans crowned two of the corners. The castle has had a courtyard.
   The entrance is at the foot of the wing in the re-entrant angle, and the basement was vaulted.
   Pinwherry was held by the Kennedys until 1644 when sold to the Pollocks. It was abandoned before the end of the 18th century.

Pirn

Borders: On eastern outskirts of Innerleithen, just south of A72, north of the Tweed, at or near Pirn (school).
Ruin or site   NT 337370 [?]   OS: 73   *   Map: 2, no: 88
Site of tower house. Pirn House, dating from about 1700 and altered in 1746, may have stood on the site. The house was demolished in 1950, and the site is now occupied by a school.

Pitairlie Castle

Angus & Dundee: About 2.5 miles north of Monifieth, on minor road just east of B962, 1 mile south of Monikie, 0.5 miles north of Newbigging, at or near Pitairlie
Ruin or site   NO 502367 [?]   OS: 54   *   Map: 7, no: 212
Site of 17th-century castle, a panel from which is built into a farm and dated 1631.
   Pitairlie was a property of the Lindsays from the 15th to 17th centuries, then passed to the Maules.
   There may have been another castle at Denfind [NO 505372?], although this may be the same site.
Other refs: Denfind

Pitcairlie House

Fife: About 2 miles north of Auchtermuchty, on minor road north of B936, at Pitcairlie.
Private   NO 236148   OS: 58   **   Map: 7, no: 46
Pitcairlie, a mansion of about 1730 which was remodelled about 1740 and again in 1815, incorporates a very altered 16th-century Z-plan tower house. The old part is a four-storey tower house. A corbelled-out parapet has open rounds at the corners, and a caphouse crowns the stairhead. Many of the windows have been sealed, while others have been enlarged.
   The basement is vaulted.
   Pitcairlie was a property of the Abernethy family, but passed by marriage to the Leslies in 1312. One of the family was David Leslie, the Covenanter general, who fought with Gustavus Adolphus of Sweden, helped win the Battle of Marston Moor in 1644, and defeated the Marquis of Montrose at Philiphaugh in 1645. He was defeated by Cromwell at Dunbar in 1650, and captured at the Battle of Worcester a year later, although he was released and made Lord Newark. The family became bankrupt, and it was eventually sold in the mid 18th century to the Cathcarts of

Carbiston, with whose descendants it remained until the 20th century. The house is still occupied.
OPEN: Accommodation available
Tel: 01337 827418   Fax: 01337 828464
Web: hmclay@pitcairlie.prestel.co.uk

Pitcalnie

Ross & Cromarty: About 4 miles north of Cromarty, on minor roads east of B9175, north of Pitcalnie, on east side of Nigg Bay, near Bayfield House.
Ruin or site   NH 810730 [?]   OS: 21   *   Map: 9, no: 125
Site of castle, probably of the Ross family, part of which may be incorporated in a farm near Bayfield House. It was a property of the Munros at the beginning of the 16th century.
Other refs: Culnaha; Culnauld

Pitcaple Castle

Aberdeen & Gordon: About 4 miles north-west of Inverurie, on minor roads just north of A96, south of River Urie, at Pitcaple Castle.
Private   NJ 726261   OS: 38   *   Map: 10, no: 226**
Pitcaple Castle is a Z-plan tower house of three storeys and an attic. It consists of a main block and projecting round towers at opposite corners, and dates partly from the 15th century. A bartizan crowns one corner, and the harled walls are pierced by gunloops and shot-holes. The towers and bartizan have concave conical roofs. The castle was formerly surrounded by a walled courtyard with a gatehouse, drawbridge and moat. The building became ruinous by the end of the 18th century, but was restored in 1830 by William Burn, and extended in 1873.
   The basement of the main block is vaulted, as are four storeys of one of the round towers. The hall is on the first floor and there are many chambers on the floors above and in the towers.
   The lands were a property of the Leslies from 1457. The 4th Laird killed George Leith of Freefield, starting a feud between the families. James IV visited Pitcaple, as did Mary, Queen of Scots, in 1562. In 1650 the Marquis of Montrose was imprisoned here on his way to Edinburgh to be executed, and Charles II visited the same year. The laird was killed at the Battle of Worcester in 1651 fighting for Charles.
   In 1757 the castle passed by marriage to the Lumsdens. The house is in good condition, and still occupied.
   When a robin is found in the castle it is reputedly the harbinger of bad news and the herald of death. A robin was discovered when the laird was killed at the Battle of Worcester in 1651.

Pitcarry

Kincardine & Deeside: About 1 mile north of Inverbervie, on minor roads north of B967 or west of A92, north of Bervie Water, at or near Pitcarry.
Ruin or site   NO 830740 [?]   OS: 45   *   Map: 10, no: 278
Site of castle.

Pitcastle

Perth & Kinross: About 3.5 miles south-east of Pitlochry, on minor roads east of A9, east of River Tummel, at Pitcastle.
Ruin or site   NN 973554   OS: 52   **   Map: 8, no: 43
Pitcastle consists of a very ruined two-storey house or tower of the Robertsons. The studded door and other remnants are kept at Blair Castle.

Pitcon

Ayrshire: About 1 mile north and east of Dalry, on minor roads east of B780, west of River Garnock, at or near Pitcon.
Ruin or site   NS 299506 [?]   OS: 63   *   Map: 3, no: 76
Site of castle or old house, a property of the Boyds in the 16th century. The present Pitcon is a late 18th-century mansion.

Pitcruvie Castle

Fife: About 1.5 miles north of Lower Largo, west of minor road north of A917, just west of Pitcruvie Farm, west of Largo Law, just east of Boghall Burn.
Ruin or site   NO 413046   OS: 59   **   Map: 7, no: 112
In a romantic position, Pitcruvie is a ruined rectangular keep of the late 15th cen-

tury. It had a small later stair-wing, of which little survives.

The entrance was originally at first-floor level, but this has been sealed. The basement and hall were vaulted.

It was built by the Lindsays, ancestors of the Earls of Crawford. The lands were sold to the Watsons in the 17th century.

Other refs: Balcruvie Castle

Pitcullo Castle

Fife: About 3 miles east and south of Leuchars, on minor roads west of A92, about 1.5 miles south-west of Balmullo, at Pitcullo.
Private   NO 413196   OS: 59   *   Map: 7, no: 114**

Pitcullo Castle is a late 16th-century L-plan tower house, consisting of a main block of three storeys and a stair-wing. To this has been added 17th-century alterations, including a square tower. A corbelled-out stair-turret, in the re-entrant angle, was crowned by a square caphouse, while a semi-circular stair-tower projects from the rear of the building. A wall, near the entrance, is pierced by a gunloop, and the walls are harled and whitewashed.

The main entrance is at the foot of the stair-wing. The basement is vaulted and contained a kitchen with a fireplace and oven. The main stair in the wing only climbs to first-floor level, the upper floors reached by the turnpike stair in the turret as well as another stair. The hall was on the first floor with private chambers in the wing and on the floors above.

Pitcullo was originally the property of the Sibbalds, but passed to the Balfours in the 16th century, and was later held by the Trents. It was restored, with much demolition and alteration, in the 1960s and 1971, and is still occupied.

Pitcur Castle

Angus & Dundee: About 3 miles south-east of Coupar Angus, on minor road just south of A923, in the Sidlaw Hills, at Pitcur.
Ruin or site   NO 252370   OS: 53   *   Map: 8, no: 133**

Pitcur Castle is a massive ruined 16th-century L-plan tower house, of four storeys and formerly a garret, to which has been added a later wing making the building T-plan. A round stair-tower stands in one re-entrant angle. The windows are mainly small.

The arched and moulded entrance still has an iron yett. The basement was vaulted, and contained the kitchen in the main block. The hall, on the first floor of the main block, has been a fine chamber. Private chambers occupied the floors above.

Pitcur was owned by the Chisholms from 1315 or earlier, but in 1432 passed by marriage to the Halyburtons of Dirleton. James Halyburton of Pitcur, who was Provost of Dundee from 1550 until 1583, fought against Mary, Queen of Scots, at the Battle of Langside in 1568. The property was sold to the Menzies family in 1880.

Piteadie Castle *see* Pitteadie Castle

Pitfichie Castle

Aberdeen & Gordon: About 3.5 miles west of Kemnay, on minor roads north of A993, just west of River Don, 1 mile north of Monymusk, at Pitfichie.
Private   NJ 677168   OS: 38   *   Map: 10, no: 193**

Pitfichie Castle is a 16th-century tower house, consisting of a rectangular block of four storeys and a large round tower projecting at one corner. A semi-circular stair-tower is corbelled out to square and crowned by a gabled caphouse. The castle had a courtyard.

The arched entrance, at the foot of the round tower, led to the vaulted basement, which contained the kitchen, and to the main stair. The hall was on the first floor and there were private chambers above.

Pitfichie was a property of the Urie family, one of whom, Sir John Urie, or Hurry, led Covenanter armies which were defeated by the Marquis of Montrose at the battles of Auldearn and Alford in 1645. In 1650 William Urie of Pitfichie, and others, raided the lands of Forbes of Forneidlie, mistreating the locals and driving off their cattle to Pitfichie, for which he was outlawed.

The property passed to Forbes of Monymusk in 1657, and the castle was abandoned and roofless by 1796. It became ruinous, a large section collapsing in 1936, but in the 1980s was restored and is now occupied.

Pitfirrane Castle

Fife: About 2.5 miles west of Dunfermline, on minor road south of A994, just west of Crossford.
Private   NT 060863   OS: 65   *   Map: 7, no: 9**

Pitfirrane Castle is an altered and extended 16th-century L-plan tower house. It consists of a 15th-century keep, or main block, of three storeys and an attic, to which has been added a square stair-tower, which rises a storey higher. The cor-

ners are crowned by bartizans. The tower is dated 1583.

Another large L-plan wing was added in the 17th century, and there have been alterations and extensions in later centuries, including by David Bryce in 1854 .

The interior has been much altered.

It was a property of the Halkett family from 1399, one of whom George Halkett was Provost of Dunfermline, and died by falling from one of the windows of Pitfirrane. It passed by marriage to the Wedderburns of Gosford, but they assumed the name of Halkett. Sir Peter Halkett of Pitfirrane fought for the Hanoverians against the Jacobites in the Rising of 1745-6, but was taken prisoner. He died in 1755. The family held the property until 1877 when the castle was sold to Lawrence Dalgleish. It is now the clubhouse for a golf course.

Pitfodels Castle

Aberdeen & Gordon: About 2 miles south-west of Aberdeen, on minor roads south of A93, on north side of River Dee, Garthdee Road, Cults, at Norwood Hall.
Private   NJ 918032   OS: 38   *   Map: 10, no: 321

Site of castle, nothing of which survives except a motte or mound. Pitfodels was held by the Reids, but passed by marriage in the 16th century to the Menzies family. The castle was apparently abandoned about 1622.

Set in seven acres of wooded grounds, Norwood Hall is a fine mansion with an imposing staircase. The house was rebuilt in 1881 for the Ogston family, and stands near the site of the old castle, which was on high ground slightly to the south-east of the present building. Norwood Hall is now a family-owned hotel.

The building is reputedly haunted by two ghosts.

One is said to be the apparition of the mistress of Colonel James Ogston, and her ghost has been seen on the main stair. The poor woman despaired after Ogston would not leave his wife, and she supposedly waits for his return.

The other is believed to be Ogston himself, and is described as an elegant gentleman. The apparition has been seen in the dining room in recent times. It moves from the wine cupboard across the chamber, stopping for a brief moment in front

of the log fire before moving through to the kitchen.
Other refs: Norwood Hall
OPEN: Hotel – open all year.
Norwood Hall: 21 bedrooms with ensuite facilities. Dining room, restaurant and bar. Seminars, conferences, meetings, weddings, murder mystery dinners, BBQs and haggis hunts. 2 night short breaks available. Children free B&B when sharing parents room. Disabled access to restaurant only. Parking.
Tel: 01224 868951 Fax: 01224 869868
Email: info@Norwood-hall.co.uk Web: www.norwood-hall.co.uk

Pitfodel's Lodging

Aberdeen & Gordon: In Aberdeen, in the corner of Castlegate and Marischal Street, just north of the harbour and sea.
Ruin or site NJ 945063 [?] OS: 38 * Map: 10, no: 337
Site of 16th-century house, of three storeys with bartizans, of the Menzies of Pitfodels family. It was one of the first stone houses in Aberdeen, but has been demolished. The family had their castle at Pitfodels [NJ 918032] at Cults, the site near Norwood Hall, which was built for the Ogston family in 1881.

Pitfour Castle

Perth & Kinross: About 5.5 miles east of Perth, on minor road south of B958 junction with A90, south of St Madoes, 1 mile north of River Tay, at Pitfour Castle.
Private NO 199209 OS: 58 * Map: 8, no: 117
Pitfour Castle, a mansion of 1784 and 1829, may incorporate part of a castle, although the site of the older building is said to have been nearer the Tay.
  It was a property of the Lindsay Earls of Crawford in the late 15th century, but later passed to the Hays, then the Richardsons, who held it in the 20th century.

Pitgair Castle

Banff & Buchan: About 5.5 miles east and south of Macduff, on minor roads north of A98, east of Pitgair, near Minnonie.
Ruin or site NJ 774606 [?] OS: 29 * Map: 10, no: 254
Site of 13th-century castle, a vestige of which survives.
Other refs: Wallace's Castle; Ha' Hill

Pitillock *see* Pittillock House

Pitkerro House

Angus & Dundee: About 2 miles north of Broughty Ferry, on minor road north of B961 just east of B978, just west of the Sweet Burn, at Pitkerro.
Private NO 453337 OS: 54 * Map: 8, no: 194
Pitkerro House is a small altered 16th-century tower house of two storeys, to which a large 19th-century mansion has been added. A projecting round stair-tower is corbelled out to square, and topped by a watch-chamber. The tower is dated 1593.
  The original entrance is in the foot of the stair-tower. The basement is not vaulted, and contains the old kitchen and three cellars. The hall was on the first floor.
  Pitkerro was a property of the Durhams from 1534 and they built the tower. It was later sold to the Dick family. In 1902 Sir Robert Lorimer restored the building, and it is still in good condition and occupied.

Pitkindie House

Perthshire: About 3 miles north and west of Inchture, on minor roads west of B953, 0.5 miles north-west of Abernyte, at or near Pitkindie.
Ruin or site NO 248317 OS: 53 * Map: 8, no: 132
Site of castle, some fragments of which are built into the farm.
Other refs: Pittkindie House

Pitlair *see* Pitlochie Castle

Pitlessie Castle

Fife: About 2 miles east of Ladybank, near A92, at Pitlessie.
Ruin or site NO 336096 [?] OS: 59 * Map: 7, no: 86
Site of a castle, which was a property of the Hamiltons of Bynnie at the beginning of the 17th century. Pitlessie House, an early 19th-century house with later additions, may be built on the site.

Pitlochie Castle

Fife: About 3.5 miles west and south of Auchtermuchty, near junction of A91 with A912, north of River Eden, at Pitlochie.
Ruin or site NO 175095 OS: 58 * Map: 7, no: 30
Site of castle.
  Pitlochie was a property of the Kinloch family, but had passed to the Lundies of Balgonie by 1452, and apparently held by them in 1557 when the 'tower and fortalice' are mentioned. The lands were, however, acquired by the Sandilands family in 1509 and were part of the barony of Pitlair.
Other refs: Pitlair

Pitlour

Fife: About 1.5 miles west of Auchtermuchty, on minor roads north of A91, 1 mile north of Strathmiglo, at Pitlour.
Private NO 209113 OS: 58 * Map: 7, no: 35
Probable site of castle. The present Pitlour, a fine classical mansion, was built in 1783-4.
  The lands were a property of the Scotts in the 15th and 16th centuries.

Pitlurg Castle

Banff & Buchan: About 3.5 miles south of Keith, on minor road south of B9115 0.5 miles west of junction with A96, north of Burn of Davidston, at Mains of Pitlurg.
Ruin or site NJ 436455 OS: 28 ** Map: 10, no: 88
Not much remains of a 16th-century Z-plan tower house and courtyard of the Gordons, except one round tower with two vaulted storeys. The family were descended from Jock o' Scurdargue, and held the property until 1724. The castle was ruinous by the 19th century. An effigy of Sir John Gordon of Pitlurg is in the Boray Aisle, the remains of St Martin's Church at Cairnie.
  The ruins of St Fidamnan's Chapel, dating from the 15th century or earlier and dedicated to St Adamnan, stands to the south-east [NK 030325].

Pitlurg House *see* Leask House

Pitmedden House

Aberdeen & Gordon: About 4 miles west and south of Ellon, on minor roads east of A920 or west of B999, to west of Pitmedden village, at Pitmedden House.
NTS NJ 885281 OS: 38 * Map: 10, no: 304
Site of castle. The present Pitmedden House is a 17th-century house, remodelled in 1853 and in 1954, and may incorporate part of an older building. It had been burned in 1818.
  The castle was a property of the Pantons about 1430, then the Setons, the Bannermans in the 17th century, then the Keiths. The house has a five-acre walled garden, which is open to the public, and features sundials, pavilions and fountains dotted among formal flower beds.
OPEN: House not open; garden, museum and visitor centre open May-Sep, daily 10.00-17.30; last admission 17.00; grounds open all year, daily.
Museum of Farming Life. Gift shop. Tea room. WC. Disabled facilities and access. Woodland walk and wildlife garden. Car and coach parking. ££.
Tel: 01651 872352 Fax: 01651 841188

Pitmilly House

Fife: About 0.5 miles east of Boarhills, on minor roads just south of A917, south of Kenly Water, at Pitmilly House.
Private NO 579134 OS: 59 * Map: 7, no: 153
Site of castle. Pitmilly House is a modern mansion.
  The Monypenny family held the property from the 12th century until 1974.

Pitreavie Castle

Fife: About 2 miles south of Dunfermline, on minor roads east of A823, just north of A823(M), at Pitreavie.
Private NT 117847 OS: 65 ** Map: 7, no: 18
Pitreavie Castle is an altered early 17th-century U-plan tower house, which was remodelled in later centuries. The walls are pierced by gunloops, and the original

entrance still has an iron yett. There is much fine plasterwork and panelling, and the basement was vaulted.

The tower was built by the Wardlaws of Balmule, who acquired the lands in 1608. One of the family was Sir Cuthbert Wardlaw, Chamberlain to Queen Anne, wife of James VI. The property was sold to the Primrose Lord Rosebery in 1703, then in 1711 to the Blackwood family, who altered the building, but by the mid 19th century Pitreavie was empty and abandoned. Restored, remodelled and enlarged in 1885 by the Beveridge family, it was owned by the Royal Navy and the Royal Air Force, but was then put up for sale when the base was closed.

The Battle of Inverkeithing or Pitreavie was fought nearby in 1651. A Cromwellian force routed a Royalist army, mostly made up of Highlanders, with the loss of 1600 killed and 1200 taken prisoner. A party of MacLeans, many of them wounded, sought refuge in the castle, but were dispersed by missiles from the battlements. The MacLeans are said to have cursed the Wardlaws for their poor treatment – the laird of Pitreavie died within 18 months, and the family had lost the property within 50 years.

Pitroddie

Perthshire: About 4 miles north-east of St Madoes, on minor roads north of A90, at or near Pitroddie Farm.
Ruin or site   NO 214252   OS: 53   *   Map: 8, no: 122
Site of castle, some stones of which are built into the farm.
The lands were a property of the Lindsays of Evelick in 1665.

Pitsligo Castle

Banff & Buchan: About 3.5 miles west of Fraserburgh, on minor roads south of B9031 just south-east of Rosehearty, 0.5 miles south of sea, at Pitsligo.
Ruin or site   NJ 938669   OS: 30   *   Map: 10, no: 331**
A large and impressive castle, Pitsligo is a 15th-century courtyard castle, consisting of a massive square keep with a stair-tower, a tall drum tower at one corner, and ranges of buildings enclosing the central courtyard. The whole complex is surrounded by a walled pleasance with an arched gateway.

The original keep, now a shell, has two main vaulted storeys, but the parapet and

floor above the upper vault were demolished in the early 18th century.

The subsidiary buildings and courtyard are ruined and roofless, with vaulted basements, one containing a kitchen.

Pitsligo was a Fraser property, but passed to the Forbeses of Druminnor. In 1633 the family were created Lord Pitsligo. Alexander Forbes, 4th Lord Pitsligo, was forfeited for his part in the Jacobite Rising of 1745, and the castle looted by mercenaries. Forbes lived the rest of his life in caves, one of which is still called 'Lord Pitsligo's Cave' until he died in 1792, aged 84. The lands were recovered by the family, but the castle was unroofed when it passed to the Gardens of Troup. It has recently been consolidated, when it was sold to a member of the Forbes family.

Pittarrow Castle

Kincardine & Deeside: About 3 miles north and east of Laurencekirk, on minor roads west of A94, in the Howe of the Mearns, at or near Pittarrow.
Ruin or site   NO 727751   OS: 45   *   Map: 10, no: 227
Site of 15th-century castle of the Wisharts, which was demolished in 1802. It was the birthplace of the Protestant martyr George Wishart, who was charged with heresy and fled to Germany and Switzerland, then to Cambridge. He returned to Scotland in 1543, and preached widely, only to be arrested on the orders of Cardinal David Beaton, and burned alive at St Andrews. Pittarrow later passed to the Carnegies.

Pittarthie Castle

Fife: About 6 miles north and east of Elie, on foot about 0.5 miles north of the B940 at Lochty, south and west of Chesters Farm.
Private   NO 522091   OS: 59   *   Map: 7, no: 136**
Pittarthie Castle is a large L-plan tower house of three storeys and an attic. A stair-tower stands in the re-entrant angle. The walls are pierced by many gunloops and shot-holes.

The vaulted basement contains a kitchen, with a large arched fireplace. A turnpike stair climbs to the hall on the first floor.

The property passed from the Monypennys of Pitmilly in 1590 to the Murrays, then in 1598 to the Logans. By the early 17th century the property had been acquired by the Borthwicks, who in 1644 sold it to the Bruces of Kinross. It was remodelled in 1653. In the 18th century the Bruces were forfeited, probably because of the Jacobite Rising, and the lands sold to the Cunninghams of Glencairn. The castle is being restored.

Pitteadie Castle

Fife: About 3 miles north and east of Burntisland, on minor road south of B9157, south of Pitteadie House.
Ruin or site   NT 257891   OS: 66   **   Map: 7, no: 53
Pitteadie Castle is a ruined strong 15th-century keep, altered and extended in the 17th century with the addition of a stair-tower topped by a watch-chamber. Bartizans have crowned the other three corners of the keep. The castle had a walled courtyard with two fine Renaissance gateways.

The entrance was at first-floor level and was reached by an external stair. The basement is vaulted.

The Valance family probably built the original keep, and held the property in 1519. The lands later passed to the Sinclairs, then the Sandilands, then the Boswells of Balmuto. In 1671 the property was sold to the Calderwoods, and was inhabited into the 18th century.
Other refs: Piteadie Castle

Pittencrieff House

Fife: In Dunfermline, a short distance from the abbey church, south of A994, in Pittencrieff Park.
Private   NT 087873   OS: 65   **   Map: 7, no: 11
Built with stone from the nearby royal palace at Dunfermline, Pittencrieff House is a 17th-century T-plan house of three storeys and a garret. It consists of a main block and stair-tower, which rises a storey higher to be crowned by a watch-chamber. The walls are harled and yellow-washed. It was extended in 1740.

The entrance is in the foot of the stair-tower.

Pittencrieff was a property of Dunfermline Abbey, and passed to the Setons and Wemyss family after the Reformation, then the Clerks in the 17th century, but was sold in 1762. John Wemyss of Pittencrieff was the suitor of Dorothy Ruthven towards the end of the 16th century. Dorothy made the 'Maiden's Leap' at Huntingtower Castle, and two later eloped. In 1612 John Wemyss of Pittencrieff had been excommunicated for slaying his brother. By 1763 the property was held by a Colonel Forbes, who in that year sold it to the Grants, then the Phins. It was held by the Hunts from 1800, and the house was remodelled, to form three galleries, by Sir Robert Lorimer in 1908 when it was bought by Andrew Carnegie. It houses a collection of costumes and displays on the history of the house and park, as well as an art gallery.

The house and park were given to the town by Andrew Carnegie, and is administered by the local council.

OPEN: Open all year: May-Oct 11.00-17.00; Nov-Apr 11.00-16.00; closed Christmas and New Year; Pittencrieff will be closed from 2/10/00 until 14/1/01.

Audio-visual presentation. Explanatory displays. Gift shop. Picnic area in park. Gardens. WC in park. Disabled access to ground floor. Parking in park.
Tel: 01383 722935/313838   Fax: 01383 313837

Pittenweem Priory

Fife: In Pittenweem, on minor roads south of A917, off Cove Wynd between High Street and East Shore.
Private   NO 549027   OS: 59   **   Map: 7, no: 143
Parts of the Pittenweem Priory complex were remodelled in the 16th century into a three-storey house. A fortified gatehouse, dating from the 15th century but altered, survives with heavy machiolations. Other parts of the priory buildings may be built into the 'Great House', which mostly dates from 1588, and the Prior's Lodging survives with a vaulted basement.

The priory was founded here in the 13th century by Augustinians from the Isle of May around the cave of St Fillan, who was said to have preached here in the 7th century. After the Reformation, the priory lands were granted to the Stewarts of Darnley in 1606, while the buildings were given to the burgh.
Other refs: Commendator's House, Pittenweem
OPEN: View from exterior.

Pittheavlis Castle

Perth & Kinross: About 1 mile south-west of Perth railway station, on minor roads south of A93 junction with B9112, in south-west outskirts of Perth, at Pittheavlis.
Private   NO 097222   OS: 58   *   Map: 8, no: 76**
Alongside more modern houses, Pittheavlis Castle is a late 16th-century L-plan tower

house. It consists of a main block of three storeys and a garret, and a stair-wing. Two bartizans crown the corners, and the walls are pierced by gunloops.

The lands belonged to the Rosses of Craigie, but in 1586 were sold to the Stewarts, who probably built the tower. By 1636 it had passed to the Oliphants of Bachiltron, but was later used as a farmhouse. It is still occupied, and in good condition.

Pittillock House

Fife: About 2.5 miles north of Glenrothes, on minor roads south of A912 or west of A92, west of Muirhead, at Pittillock House.
Private   NO 278052   OS: 59   **   Map: 7, no: 64
Pittillock House incorporates a 16th-century L-plan tower house, but the whole building was remodelled as a symmetrical mansion in about 1850.

The lands were originally held by the MacDuff Earls of Fife, but passed to the Bruces, then to the Lumsdens who held the property until 1651. It was acquired by Baillie of Falkland, but later passed to the Balfours of Balbirnie.

There may have been another castle nearby, known as Conland, although this may be the same site.
Other refs: Pittlochy; Pitillock

Pittkindie House *see* Pitkindie House

Pittlochy *see* Pittillock House

Pittodrie House

Aberdeen & Gordon: About 5 miles north-west of Inverurie, on minor roads south of A96, 1 mile west of Chapel of Garioch, at Pittodrie House.
Private   NJ 697241   OS: 38   **   Map: 10, no: 206
Set in 200 acres in the foothills of the impressive and foreboding hill of Bennachie, Pittodrie House incorporates a greatly altered and extended 15th- or 16th-century L-plan tower house, although it includes earlier work. A turnpike stair survives, as does a detached wing, which has a vaulted cellar and gunloops. The castle was extended in 1675, 1841 by Archibald Simpson, 1900 and 1926.

It was an Erskine property from around 1558. It is now used as a hotel, and was greatly extended in 1990.

The chamber which was formerly the nursery is said to be haunted.
Other refs: Balhaggardie
OPEN: Hotel – open all year.
27 bedrooms with private facilities. Dining room and bar. Hill walking and sports. Functions, conferences, corporate events and meetings. Parking.
Tel: 01467 681444   Fax: 01467 681648
Email: info@pittodrie.macdonald-hotels.co.uk
Web: www.macdonald-hotels.co.uk

Pittulie Castle

Banff & Buchan: About 3.5 miles west of Fraserburgh, on minor road and foot south of B9031, 1 mile south-east of Rosehearty, 0.5 miles south of sea, at Pittulie Castle.
Ruin or site   NJ 945671   OS: 30   *   Map: 10, no: 339**
Pittulie Castle is a ruined 16th-century tower house. It consists of a long main block of two storeys and an attic and a four-storey square tower at one corner. A later wing made the building U-plan, enclosing a small courtyard. The last side was completed by a wall with a gateway. A stair-turret is corbelled out in one re-entrant angle. Bartizans crown two corners. There are some remains of a courtyard wall and doocot.

The basement of the tower is not vaulted, and contained a kitchen; a wine-cellar, with a small stair to the hall above; and another cellar. The main stair climbs to the first floor, in the square tower, while the upper floors were reached by a turnpike stair in a corbelled-out stair-turret. The hall, on the first floor, is very large and had a fireplace at each end.

The lands were held by the Frasers from the 14th century until around 1630, when they passed by marriage to the Ogilvies. Part of the castle was inhabited until about 1850.

Place of Barras *see* Barras Castle

Place of Belton *see* Belton House

Place of Bonhill

Bonhill Place: South of Alexandria, on minor road east of A82, west of River Leven, in Bonhill.

Ruin or site NS 390793 OS: 63 * Map: 5, no: 155

Place of Bonhill, a later mansion, incorporated an old house or castle, but was demolished in 1950. The site appears to be occupied by a school.

The property was originally held by the Lennox family, but Bonhill passed to the Lindsays in the 15th century, then to the Smolletts in the 17th century.

It is said that a tunnel led down from a hidden entrance behind the drawing room fireplace to the banks of the River Leven. A piper was sent to explore the passage, but vanished without trace. Afterwards it was said that faint pipe music could often be heard within the walls.

Other refs: Bonhill

Place of Elchies *see* Craigneach Castle

Place of Fullarton *see* Crosbie House

Place of Kellie *see* Haddo House

Place of Kilbirnie *see* Kilbirnie House

Place of Newton of Blair *see* Newton Castle

Place of Snade

Dumfriesshire: About 5 miles south-east of Moniaive, on minor roads west of B729, just west of Cairn Water, at or near Snade.

Ruin or site NX 847857 [?] OS: 78 * Map: 1, no: 155

Site of 14th-century castle, probably a property of the Hays of Yester. Little or nothing survives, although there were some remains in 1856.

Other refs: Snade; Snaid

Place of Tillyfour

Aberdeen & Gordon: About 7 miles west of Inverurie, on minor roads north of B993 or east of B992, just east of River Don, 3 miles north of Monymusk, at Tillyfour.

Private NJ 659195 OS: 38 * Map: 10, no: 182**

Place of Tillyfour is a 16th-century L-plan tower house of two storeys and a garret, which was restored from ruin and extended in 1884. The old part consisted of two offset blocks, creating two re-entrant angles, in one of which is a corbelled-out stair-turret. The walls are pierced by slit windows. The building is dated 1626. A courtyard is entered by an arched gateway.

The inside of the house has been gutted, and the basement is not vaulted.

This may have been a hunting lodge of the Earls of Mar, but the property was acquired by the Leslies of Wardhouse in 1508, who built a castle here. It passed to the Gordons after 1640, and was restored about 1884. It is in good condition, and still occupied.

Other refs: Tillyfour Castle; Tilliefour

Place of Weem *see* Castle Menzies

Plane Tower *see* Plean Castle

Plean Castle

Stirlingshire & Clackmannan: About 6 miles south-east of Stirling, on minor road south of the B9124 to A9, just east of the main railway line to Stirling.

Private NS 850870 OS: 65 * Map: 6, no: 84**

Plean Castle, or Plane, is an altered 15th-century keep, originally of three storeys to the parapet, above which there would have been an attic within the gables. Out-sized windows were added to a new storey above the parapet, which destroyed the upper part during a 'restoration' of about 1900. A courtyard housed ranges of buildings, including a kitchen.

The basement is not vaulted. A straight stair climbs to the first-floor hall, while the upper floors are reached by a turnpike stair.

The lands passed by marriage to the Somervilles in 1449. The property was sold in 1643 to the Nicholsons, and later held by the Elphinstones. The castle was abandoned and became ruinous, was remodelled about 1900, then became derelict again. It has been restored, and is occupied.

Other refs: Plane Tower

Plewlands *see* Gordonstoun

Plora Tower

Borders: About 2 miles east of Innerleithen, on minor roads south of A72, about 0.5 miles south of Walkerburn.

Ruin or site NT 359360 OS: 73 * Map: 2, no: 94

Not much remains of a 16th-century tower house of the Lowis family. It had a courtyard with outbuildings and a terraced garden, and was fairly complete at the beginning of the 19th century. The tower may still have been roofed in 1838.

Plotcock Castle

Lanarkshire & Glasgow area: About 4 miles south of Hamilton, on minor roads between east of A723 and west of B7078, south of the Darngaber Burn, just south of Thinacres.

Ruin or site NS 740501 OS: 64 * Map: 3, no: 351

Little survives of a 16th-century tower house in a bend of Plotcock Glen, parts of which were destroyed in 1828. It was protected by a ditch.

Other refs: Thinacres Castle

Plunton Castle

Galloway: About 4 miles south of Gatehouse of Fleet, on minor road south of B727, just south of Lennox Plunton, just east of the Plunton Burn.

Ruin or site NX 605507 OS: 83 ** Map: 1, no: 97

Plunton Castle is a 16th-century L-plan tower house of three storeys and an attic. Two round bartizans crown the corners of tower, and the castle was surrounded by a moat.

The entrance, at the foot of the stair-tower, leads to the vaulted basement. The hall was on the first floor, and there were private chambers on the floors above.

It was a property of the MacGies in the early 16th century, put passed to the Lennox family, who built the tower. Sir Walter Scott used the castle as the scene for his unsuccessful melodrama 'The Doom of Devorgoil'.

Other refs: Lennox-Plunton Castle

Pluscarden *see* Castle Hill, Pluscarden

Pokelly

Ayrshire: About 1.5 miles east of Stewarton, on minor roads east of B778, west of A77, at or near Pokelly.

Private NS 442458 OS: 64 * Map: 3, no: 178

Site of castle.

Polcornare *see* Cornal Tower

Poldean

Dumfriesshire: About 3 miles south of Moffat, on minor roads east of M74 or south of A708, east of River Annan, at or near Poldean.

Ruin or site NT 104001 [?] OS: 78 * Map: 1, no: 229

Site of tower house, a property of the Bells.

Polkemmet House

Lothians: About 1.5 miles west of Whitburn, on minor roads north of B7066, south of M8 motorway, in Polkemmet Country Park.

Ruin or site NS 925650 [?] OS: 65 * Map: 4, no: 2

Polkemmet, a two-storey mansion incorporating a house of 1620 or earlier, was extended and castellated in the 19th and 20th century.

The property was held by the Shaws, but was sold to the Baillies in 1820. The house was completely demolished, and the grounds are now Polkemmet Country Park.

Other refs: Polkemmet Country Park

OPEN: Park: open all year, daily 9.00-18.00.

Park: Restaurant. Picnic and BBQ sites. WC. Play areas. Disabled access. Car and coach parking.

Tel: 01501 743905

Polkmyl Tower *see* Bonhard House

Pollok Castle

Renfrewshire: About 1 mile north-west of Newton Mearns, on minor roads west of B769, south-east of Ryat Linn Reservoir, at Pollok.

Private   NS 522570   OS: 64   *   Map: 3, no: 231

Pollok House, dated 1686 and 1687, incorporated part of a 15th-century keep, and

was restored after a fire in 1882. It was demolished in 1947, and nothing now remains except foundations.

It was a property of the Pollocks from the 12th century. John Pollock of Pollok supported Mary, Queen of Scots, and fought for her at the Battle of Langside in 1568. John Pollock, his son, was killed in 1593 at Lockerbie, while supporting the Maxwells in a feud against the Johnstones. The Pollocks were a turbulent lot and involved in feuding with local families, and held the property until the 20th century.

In the grounds is a motte, probably the original 12th-century stronghold of Fulbert de Pollok.

Pollok House

Lanarkshire & Glasgow area: In the Pollokshaws area of Glasgow, on minor roads west of B768 or B769, in Pollok Country Park, north of the White Cart Water, at Pollok House.

NTS   NS 549619   OS: 64   **   Map: 3, no: 248

Site of castle, with a ditch and drawbridge, a vestige of which remains with a garden wall, close to the stable yard. The present house, first built about 1750 and remodelled and extended by the architect Sir Robert Rowand Anderson in 1890, replaced the stronghold.

It was a property of the Maxwells from the mid 13th century. Pollok was gifted to the City of Glasgow in 1966, and the Burrell Collection is situated within the grounds. The house is open to the public, and houses the Stirling Maxwell collection of Spanish and European paintings, furniture, ceramics and silver.

Another earlier castle lay on the southern bank of the White Cart Water, but was destroyed when the gardens of the house were laid out. It was a property of the Pollock family, but passed to the Maxwells.

The house stands in a country park with rhododendrons, magnolias, prunus, azaleas, Japanese maples and fine woodland and shrubbery.

Other refs: Laigh Castle; Nether Pollok

OPEN: Open Apr-Oct, daily 10.00-17.00; Nov-Mar, daily 11.00-16.00; closed 25/26 Dec and 1/2 Jan.

Guided tours. Giftshop. Tearoom. WC. Partial disabled access. Parking. ££.

Tel: 0141 632 0274   Fax: 0141 649 0823

Email: information@nts.org.uk   Web: nts.org.uk

Polmaise Castle

Stirlingshire & Clackmannan: About 3 miles east and south of Stirling, on minor roads north of A905, just north of Fallin, on southern shore of River Forth, at Polmaise.

Ruin or site   NS 835924   OS: 57   *   Map: 6, no: 82

Site of castle, which was replaced by a three-storey mansion of 1691, altered and extended in later centuries, itself completely demolished.

Polmaise was a property of the Cunninghams, but passed by marriage to the Murrays of Touchadam in 1568 who held it until the 20th century. The site of the castle and mansion is apparently now a sewerage works.

Other refs: Old Polmaise House

Polmont House

Falkirk: About 3 miles east of Falkirk, near B810, north of Polmont railway station, Polmont.

Ruin or site   NS 933782   OS: 65   *   Map: 6, no: 103

Probable site of castle. Polmont House, which dated from about 1785, may have stood on the site, and is believed to have been built by Gilbert Laurie, who had been Lord Provost of Edinburgh. The house was altered in later centuries, but demolished in the 20th century and the site is occupied by a housing scheme.

Polmont was a property of the Hamiltons in the 17th century, and they were made Barons Polmont in 1643.

Polmood

Borders: About 2 miles north-east of Tweedsmuir, on minor road east of A701, on east side of the Tweed, at Polmood.

Private   NT 114270 [?]   OS: 72   *   Map: 2, no: 12

Site of tower house.

Polmood was a property of the Hunters. The present house, dating from 1638 or earlier, has corbiestepped gables and harled walls, and forms three sides of a small courtyard. It was greatly altered around 1887.

Polnoon Castle

Renfrewshire: About 3 miles south-west of East Kilbride, on minor road south and west of B764, about 1 mile south-east of Eaglesham, west of the White Cart Water.

Ruin or site   NS 586513   OS: 64   *   Map: 3, no: 267

Not much remains of a 14th-century keep, on a motte, of the Montgomerys, except mounds. It was built by using the ransom gained from Sir Henry 'Hotspur' Percy, who Sir John Montgomery of Eaglesham had captured at the Battle of Otterburn in 1388; and for a long time was the chief castle of the family. The Montgomerys moved to Eglinton, and the castle was ruinous by the end of the 17th century.

Polrossie

Sutherland & Caithness: About 6.5 miles west of Dornoch, on minor roads south of A9, north side of Dornoch Firth, south-east of Loch Ospisdale, at or near Polrossie.

Ruin or site   NH 724884   OS: 21   *   Map: 12, no: 18

Site of castle or old house, which is mentioned around 1630.

Other refs: Balrossie

Polwarth Castle

Borders: About 2.5 miles south-west of Duns, on minor roads south of A6105, south-east of village of Polwarth.
Ruin or site   NT 749500 [?]   OS: 74   *   Map: 2, no: 300
Site of castle.

The property originally belonged to the Polwarth family in the 13th century or earlier, but passed to the Cospatrick Earl of March, then to Sinclair of Herdmanston, then to the Homes, who probably built the castle. Sir Patrick Home hid in his own family's burial vault at Polwarth Kirk [NT 750495] after getting into trouble with James VII. Grizel (later the well-known Grizel Baillie of Mellerstain), his 12-year-old daughter, supplied him with food and drink from Redbraes Castle. Sir Patrick escaped to Holland, and later returned with William of Orange to become Lord Polwarth in 1690 and Earl of Marchmont in 1697. The property was later acquired by the Scotts.

Poneil

Lanarkshire & Glasgow: About 2.5 miles north of Douglas, on minor road west of B7078, south of Poneil Water, at or near Poneil.
Ruin or site   NS 840343 [?]   OS: 72   *   Map: 3, no: 389
Site of tower house.

The lands were held by Theobold the Fleming in 1147, then by the Folkerton family until about 1495.

Poolbrigs *see* Dunlappie

Port Castle

Galloway: About 3 miles south-west of Whithorn, on minor roads south of A747, on cliffs above Port Castle Bay, south of Physgill House, just east of St Ninian's Cave.
Ruin or site   NX 426358   OS: 83   *   Map: 1, no: 65
Site of castle, consisting of a courtyard enclosed by thick walls, which stands on a rocky promontory.
Other refs: Physgill

Portencross Castle

Ayrshire: About 2 miles west of West Kilbride, on minor road west of B7048 at Portencross, on the shore of the Firth of Clyde.
Ruin or site   NS 176488 [?]   OS: 63   *   Map: 3, no: 19**
Standing on a rock, Portencross Castle is an altered 14th- or 15th-century keep of three storeys and a garret. It was originally rectangular in plan, but a tall four-storey wing was added at one end. The parapet is corbelled out.

There are two entrances at right angles to each other in the re-entrant angle: one in the wing, one in the main block. The basement is vaulted, and contained the kitchen, with a straight stair to the hall above. In the wall, between the main block and wing, is a turnpike stair. The hall, on the first floor of the main block, is vaulted, and has an entresol floor at the base of the vaulting. The upper part of the building is ruinous.

The property, known as Ardneil, belonged to the Ross family, but they supported

the Comyn (losing) side in the Wars of Independence, and Robert the Bruce gave the lands to the Boyds of Kilmarnock. There was an earlier stronghold at Auld Hill [NS 178491], which consisted of a walled enclosure and hall house within an earlier fort. This was still occupied in the 14th century, and possibly later, but replaced by Portencross Castle.

Robert II and Robert III visited the castle on their way to Rothesay on Bute. The Boyds held the property until 1785, when it passed to the Fullertons of Overton. A gale stripped off the roof in 1739 although the ruins are in good condition.

A ship from the Spanish Armada sank near the castle in 1588.
Other refs: Ardneil; Auld Hill, Portencross

Portlethen Castle

Kincardine & Deeside: East of Portlethen, on minor roads east of A90, about 0.5 miles west of the sea and Portlethen Village, at or near Portlethen.
Ruin or site   NO 929967 [?]   OS: 45   *   Map: 10, no: 323
Site of 17th-century courtyard castle, nothing of which remains, except three dated stones.

Portrack Castle

Dumfriesshire: About 6 miles north and west of Dumfries, on minor road east of A76, just south of the River Nith, near Portrack House.
Ruin or site   NX 935832   OS: 78   *   Map: 1, no: 181
Little survives of a 16th-century castle of the Maxwells except some masonry.

Portsoy Castle

Banff & Buchan: To west of Portsoy, on minor roads north of A98, at or near Castlebrae.
Ruin or site   NJ 585660 [?]   OS: 29   *   Map: 10, no: 149
Site of castle, no remains of which survive.

It was a property of Sir Walter Ogilvie of Boyne in 1550, when the village was made a burgh of barony.

Possil

Lanarkshire & Glasgow: About 3 miles north of Glasgow Cathedral, west of A879, 1 mile west of Bishopbriggs, at north-east side of Possil Loch.
Ruin or site   NS 592705 [?]   OS: 64   *   Map: 3, no: 271
Site of castle, a property of the Crawfords. In 1612 Crawford of Possil seized Corslie Castle in an attempt to recover a debt, but all he managed to get was a term of imprisonment in Edinburgh Castle. The property was divided into Easter and Wester Possil.

Possil House, a plain mansion with wooded grounds, was further south. It was a property of the Alison family, and the Possilpark area of Glasgow was laid out in the grounds.

Posso Tower

Borders: About 6 miles south and west of Peebles, on minor road south of A72 from Kirkton Manor, west of the Manor Water, at Posso.
Ruin or site   NT 200332   OS: 73   *   Map: 2, no: 44
Not much remains of Posso Tower, a 16th-century tower house, except the choked basement, and foundations and one upstand of masonry of outbuildings. There may also be traces of an orchard and gardens.

It was a property of the Bairds of Posso, which later passed to the Naesmiths. It was ruined by 1775 after being replaced by a new house nearby.

Powrie Castle

Angus & Dundee: About 3 miles north-east of Dundee, on minor road east of A929 at Fintry, just west of South Powrie.
Private   NO 421346   OS: 54   *   Map: 8, no: 183**
Once a large, strong and comfortable stronghold, Powrie Castle now consists of a ruined 15th-century keep and a restored 17th-century wing. These were once linked together by an enclosing curtain wall or range, within a courtyard.

The keep has two round towers at opposite corners, making it into a Z-plan. It had a vaulted basement, fine hall and other chambers.

The two-storey 17th-century range consists of a main block, with a round tower at one corner. The basement is vaulted and contains a kitchen, with a wide arched fireplace, and bakery, and there have been two comfortable chambers on the first floor.

The lands were acquired about 1170 by the Ogilvies, but passed to the Fotheringhams in 1412, who built the keep. The castle was sacked by the Scrimgeours of Dudhope in 1492. Nicholas Fotheringham of Powrie died at the Battle of Flodden in 1513. The castle was attacked again in 1547 by the English, the same year that one of the family, Thomas Fotheringham, was killed at Pinkie. Alexander Fotheringham of Powrie fought for the Jacobites at Sheriffmuir during the Rising of 1715 and, although captured, later managed to escape.

The wing is in good condition.

Other refs: Wester Powrie Castle

Poyntzfield

South Highland: About 5.5 miles west and south of Cromarty, on minor roads south of B9163 or east of B9160, at or near Poyntzfield.

Ruin or site   NH 711642   OS: 21   *   Map: 9, no: 106

Possible site of castle. Poyntzfield, which was built in 1720 but altered in 1757, is a symmetrical mansion with wings at right-angles to the main block. It stands on the site of an older house.

The property was known as Ardoch and was held by the Gordons, but passed to the Munros around 1757 who renamed it Poyntzfield after the laird's wife whose surname was Poyntz. It is still occupied.

Other refs: Ardoch

Preceptory of Gadvan *see* Dunbog Castle

Press Castle

Borders: About 2 miles west of Coldingham, on minor roads south of A1107 or west of B6438, north of Mid Grange Burn, at Press Castle.

Private   NT 871653   OS: 67   *   Map: 2, no: 346

Press Castle, a 19th-century castellated two-storey house, may stand on the site of a castle. A nearby doocot bears the date 1607.

Preston

Borders: About 2 miles north of Duns, on or near A6112 or B6355, north of Whiteadder Water, at Preston.

Ruin or site   NT 795573   OS: 67   *   Map: 2, no: 322

Site of tower houses, one at West Preston, one at East Preston. They were both properties of Logan of Restalrig, and completely demolished in the 18th century.

Other refs: East Preston; West Preston

Preston Tower

Lothians: South-east of Prestonpans, on minor road north of B1361 west of junction with A198, near Northfield House and Hamilton House.

NTS   NT 393742   OS: 66   *   Map: 4, no: 161**

Preston Tower consists of a strong 15th-century L-plan keep of four storeys, although it may possibly incorporate work from the 14th century. Two further storeys were added in the 17th century, when an extension was also built. The corbelled-out parapet has open rounds at each of the corners. Outbuildings and the courtyard have disappeared.

The basement is vaulted, and near the entrance, which still has an iron yett, is a pit-prison. The entrance to the vaulted hall, on the first floor, could only be reached by an external stair. The hall has a large fireplace, and a mural chamber. A turnpike stair climbs to the upper floors, within the thickness of the walls, while another turnpike stair, in the re-entrant angle at parapet level, gave access to the ruinous 17th-century addition.

Preston is said to have been a property of the Homes, but is recorded as being held by the Setons in the 13th century before passing to the Liddles. It passed by marriage, at the end of the 14th century, to the Hamiltons of Rossavon, Fingalton and Preston, who probably built the tower. Preston was torched in 1544 by the Earl of Hertford, and again in 1650 by Cromwell. After being restored, it was accidentally burned again in 1663, then abandoned for nearby Preston House. One of the family was Robert Hamilton, who was a noted Covenanter and prominent in the

battles of Drumclog and Bothwell Brig. The family were forfeited in 1684, but recovered the property in the 19th century. The tower was consolidated in 1936, purchased by The National Trust for Scotland in 1969, and is under the guardianship of the local council.

OPEN: Gardens open all year, daily dawn to dusk – tower: view from exterior?

Garden. Parking nearby.

Tel: 01875 810232

Prestongrange House

Lothians: About 2 miles east of Musselburgh, on minor roads south of B1348, 0.25 miles south of the Firth of Forth, south of mining museum, at Prestongrange.

Private   NT 373737   OS: 66   **   Map: 4, no: 150

Prestongrange House, a large mansion, incorporates work from the 16th century, but was extensively altered and extended in 19th century.

The estate passed from Newbattle Abbey, who had started coal mining here by the 13th century, to the Kerr Earls of Lothian, and then to the Morrisons in 1609. In 1746 it was sold to William Grant, Lord Advocate, then passed by marriage to the Grant-Sutties, after a Grant daughter had married Sir George Suttie of Balgone. A painted ceiling, dating from 1581, was discovered during alterations and removed to Merchiston Castle, which is now part of Napier University.

Prickinghaugh Tower *see* Breaken Tower

Printonan *see* Bite-About Pele

Procornal *see* Cornal Tower

Proncy Castle

Sutherland & Caithness: About 2.5 miles north-west of Dornoch, on minor road and foot west of A9, south of Harriet Plantation, just north of Proncy.
Ruin or site NH 772926 OS: 21 * Map: 12, no: 22
Not much remains of a keep, except a mound covering the basement.
It was owned by the Sutherlands, then the Gordons of Proncy.

Provan Hall

Lanarkshire & Glasgow area: About 3.5 miles west and north of Coatbridge, on minor roads north of M8, south of B806, just east of Garthamlock, at Provan.
NTS NS 667663 OS: 64 * Map: 3, no: 316**
Provan Hall is a late 16th-century tower house, forming one side of a walled court-yard, which encloses later buildings. The courtyard has a moulded arched gateway.
The rectangular tower rises to two storeys and a garret. It has a conically roofed stair-tower, and a steeply pitched roof.
The basement is vaulted, and contains the kitchen with a wide arched fireplace, and two cellars. The first floor has two rooms, each with a hooded fireplace. This floor was originally reached only by an external stair.
The lands were owned by Glasgow Cathedral, but by the 16th century had been acquired by the Baillie family, who built the hall. The property later passed by marriage to the Hamiltons; and Mary, Queen of Scots, is said to have stayed here, as did James IV, her grandfather. Provan Hall was attacked in the 17th century as the family were Royalists. The property passed through several owners until held by Reston Mathers.
The property was sold to The City of Glasgow in 1667. In 1935 it was given to The National Trust for Scotland.
Reston Mathers is said to haunt the hall. Another story is that one of the owners murdered his wife in a first-floor bedroom, and a White Lady is said to have been seen and heard calling for her son from the garden gate.
Other refs: Blochairn House
OPEN: Managed by the City of Glasgow Council. Open all year except Dec 25/26 and Jan 1/2, and when special events in progress: tel to confirm.
Parking.
Tel: 0141 771 4399

Provand's Lordship, Glasgow

Lanarkshire & Glasgow: Opposite Glasgow Cathedral, 3 Castle Street, Glasgow.
Private NS 605655 OS: 64 * Map: 3, no: 277**
Provand's Lordship, the oldest house in Glasgow, dates from 1471 and was built as part of St Nicholas's Hospital. There are period displays and furniture, as well as a recreated medieval herb garden.
OPEN: Open all year, Mon-Sat 10.00-17.00, Fri and Sun 11.00-17.00.
Explanatory displays. Disabled access. Car and coach parking.
Tel: 0141 553 2557 Fax: 0141 552 4744

Provost Ross's House, Aberdeen

Aberdeen & Gordon: In Shiprow, Aberdeen.
Private NJ 935060 OS: 38 * Map: 10, no: 326**
Built in 1593, Provost Ross's House is the third oldest in Aberdeen, and is named after Provost Ross who acquired it in 1702. Ross was involved in trading with Holland, and died in Amsterdam in 1714.
It now houses part of the Aberdeen Maritime Museum, which gives an insight into the maritime history of the city, including the oil industry. There is a unique collection of ship models, paintings, artefacts, computer interaction and set-piece exhibitions, as well as a National Trust for Scotland visitor centre.
Other refs: Maritime Museum, Aberdeen
OPEN: Open all year, Mon-Sat 10.00-17.00, Sun 11.00-17.00; closed 25/26 Dec and 1/2 Jan.
Guided tours. Explanatory displays. Gift shop. Restaurant. WC. Disabled access and induction loop. Public car parking nearby.
Tel: 01224 377700 Fax: 01224 213066

Provost Skene's House, Aberdeen

Aberdeen & Gordon: In Aberdeen, on roads east of A92, at 45 Guest Row off Broad Street, at Provost Skene's House.
Private NJ 943064 OS: 38 * Map: 10, no: 334**
Provost Skene's House is a fine 16th-century fortified town house, and dates from about 1545. Magnificent 17th-century plaster ceiling and wood panelling survives, and the painted gallery features a unique cycle of tempera wall and ceiling painting depicting Christ's life.
The house was a property of George Skene of Rubislaw, a wealthy merchant and provost of the city, from 1669. The Duke of Cumberland stayed here for six weeks in 1746 on his way to Culloden and the defeat of the Jacobites. Other rooms include a suite of Georgian chambers, and an Edwardian nursery.
Other refs: Cumberland House
OPEN: Open all year, Mon-Sat 10.00-17.00, Sun 13.00-16.00; closed 25/26/31 Dec and 1/2 Jan.
Period room settings. 17th-century ceiling and wall paintings, costume gallery, and local history exhibitions. Sales area. Coffee shop. WC. Public parking nearby.
Tel: 01224 632133 Fax: 01224 632133
Web: www.aberdeen.net.uk

Pubil Tower *see* Caisteal an Duibhe

Puddingburn Tower

Borders: About 2 miles south-west of Newcastleton, on minor roads and foot west of B6357, between Black Grain and Dowsike by Stanygill Burn.
Ruin or site NY 455858 OS: 79 * Map: 2, no: 122
Site of 16th-century tower house. This may have been the stronghold of Jock Armstrong o' the Side, although there was another tower at Syde.
Other refs: Puddingburn Hall

Pulcree

Galloway: About 1 mile north of Gatehouse of Fleet, on minor road and foot east of B796, west of Water of Fleet, east of Pulcree.
Ruin or site NX 593584 OS: 83 * Map: 1, no: 93
Only the earthworks remain of a castle.

Pumpherston

Lothians: About 2 miles east of Livingston, on minor roads east of B8046, on north side of River Almond, at Pumpherston farm.
Ruin or site NT 075686 OS: 65 * Map: 4, no: 33
Site of a castle, apparently once a place of considerable strength. Nothing now remains, and the site is occupied by Pumpherston Farm.

Purves Hall

Borders: About 3.5 miles south-east of Greenlaw, on minor roads east of A697 at Ploughlands, at Purves Hall.
Private NT 761447 OS: 74 ** Map: 2, no: 305
Purves Hall incorporates a much-altered tower house, to which additions and alterations were made in 1673, the 18th century, and in 1908-10.
The property was known as Tofts or Nether Tofts, and an Adam of Tofts signed the Ragman Roll in 1296. It was later held by the Furde family, then the Rutherfords, then the Homes. The castle was attacked by the English during the Rough Wooing about 1544. It had passed to the Belshes by 1610. One of the family was Sir Alexander Belshes of Tofts, who was Senator in the College of Justice. The lands were acquired by the Purves family about 1670, and they changed the name to Purves Hall. It was used as a hotel, but is now a residence again.
A rhyming couplet relates: 'befa' what e'er befa', there'll aye be a gowk in Purves-ha".
Other refs: Tofts; Nether Tofts

Purvishaugh *see* Purvishill Tower

Purvishill Tower
Borders: About 1.5 miles east of Innerleithen, north of A72, about 0.5 miles
north-west of Walkerburn.
Ruin or site NT 355375 OS: 73 * Map: 2, no: 93
Very little remains of a 16th-century tower house except a stony mound. The re-
mains of the building were removed around the middle of the 19th century.
   It was held by the Purves family, possibly from the 11th century, but later passed
to the Horsburghs. Blaeu's Atlas Novus map, however, locates Purvis Hill on the
south bank of the Tweed.
Other refs: Purvishaugh

Putachie *see* Castle Forbes

Quarrelwood Castle
Moray: About 2.5 miles west and north of Elgin, on minor roads north of A96 or
south of B9012, at or near Quarrywood.
Ruin or site NJ 181642 [?] OS: 28 * Map: 10, no: 30
Nothing remains of a 14th-century keep and castle, also known as Quarrywood.
   It was built by the Lauders around the middle of the 14th century, but passed to
the Sutherlands who held it until about 1750. The castle then became ruinous, and
the last remains were removed in the 19th century.
Other refs: Quarrywood House

Quarrywood House *see* Quarrelwood Castle

Quarter *see* Glassford

Quarter House
Borders: About 2.5 miles south of Broughton, on minor roads west of A701,
north of Holms Water, at or near Quarter House.
Private NT 100334 [?] OS: 72 * Map: 2, no: 7
Site of tower house, either at Quarter or nearby at Cardon [NT 099332].
   The present Quarter House, dating from the 18th century or earlier, is a two-
storey harled mansion. It was sold to the Tweedies in 1741.
Other refs: Cardon

Queen Mary's House – see next page

Queen Mary's House, Jedburgh

Borders: In Jedburgh, on Queen Street, on minor roads west of the A68, near Jedburgh Abbey.

Private NT 651206 OS: 74 *** Map: 2, no: 265

Surrounded by a garden, which is now a public park, Queen Mary's House is an altered 16th-century T-plan tower house. It consists of a main block of three storeys and a centrally projecting wing, which rises a storey higher. A stair-turret is corbelled out in one re-entrant angle, and a vaulted pend led to a courtyard, little of which remains.

The entrance to the house, in the re-entrant angle, leads to a turnpike stair. The basement is vaulted, and the hall is on the first floor.

The house belonged to the of Scotts of Ancrum. Mary, Queen of Scots, stayed in a chamber on the second floor. She was very ill and lay for many days near to death after her visit to James Hepburn, Earl of Bothwell, at Hermitage Castle in 1566. Above Mary's chamber is another similar room where the Queen's Four Marys are supposed to have stayed.

The building is open to the public, and houses a museum displaying exhibits relating to the visit by Mary to Jedburgh.

There were six other bastle houses in Jedburgh, which have all gone, including one in Kirk Wynd, a property of the Kerrs.

Other refs: Mary Queen of Scots House; Jedburgh

OPEN: Open Mar-Nov, Mon-Sat 10.00-16.45, Sun 12.00-16.30; Mar and Nov, Mon-Sat 10.30-15.45, Sun 13.00-16.00

Award-winning visitor centre. Explanatory displays. Gift shop. Formal garden. WC. Disabled access to ground floor only. Parking nearby. £.

Tel: 01835 863331 Fax: 01450 378506

Quiech Castle

Angus & Dundee: About 4 miles north-east of Kirriemuir, on minor roads east of B955 and west of B957, just north of River South Esk, near Shielhill Bridge.

Ruin or site NO 426580 [?] OS: 54 * Map: 8, no: 184

Site of castle, on a steep rock in a bend of a river, of the Comyn Earls of Buchan. The castle was still occupied at the end of the 17th century, ruins survived in 1744, but there were no remains by 1853.

Other refs: Shielhill; Glenquiech

Quothquan

Lanarkshire & Glasgow: About 2.5 miles west and north of Biggar, on minor roads north of A72 or south of B7016, east of River Clyde, at or near Quothquan.

Ruin or site NS 995395 OS: 72 * Map: 3, no: 437

Site of castle or old house of the Chancellor family of Quothquan and Shieldhill. The family supported Mary, Queen of Scots, at the Battle of Langside in 1568, and Quothquan was burned down by the forces of the Regent Moray. The family moved to Shieldhill.

R

Raasay House

South Highland: On island of Raasay, about 2 miles north of East Suinish pier, on minor road at Clachan, in the grounds of Raasay House.

Ruin or site NG 546366 OS: 32 * Map: 9, no: 11

Near Raasay House is the site of a 16th-century tower house of three storeys, called Kilmaluag Castle because of the proximity to St Moluag's church. The main residence of the MacLeods of Raasay was at Brochel Castle, but they moved here in the 17th century. This tower or a later residence was torched in 1745 after the Jacobite Rising, and replaced in 1747 by Raasay House, built by the 10th chief – Bonnie Prince Charlie was briefly sheltered on Raasay in 1746. The last traces of the castle were removed in 1846, and it was this year that the 12th and last chief of MacLeod had to sell the property.

Raasay was purchased by a George Rainy of Edinburgh, who was responsible for clearing much of the island in the excesses that seemed common for the time: he built a large wall separating the north of the island from the south and cleared 94 families, forbad marriage and burned houses in an attempt to encourage emigration.

Between 1961 and 1979 the property was owned by an Edinburgh based property developer who was nicknamed Dr No because of his negative attitude toward any requests for improvement by the islanders.

In the garden is a Pictish stone [NG 547368], carrying a cross set inside a square above a tuning fork, crescent and v-rod. The stone was found during the building of a road.

Raasay House – the Raasay Outdoor Centre (which is approved by the Adventure Activities Licensing Authority) – offers multi-activity holidays and day activities. A heritage museum (tel: 01478 660207) is located in the west wing, and has displays of artefacts from Raasay.

Other refs: Kilmaluag Castle; Torr Iain Ghairbh

OPEN: Open Mar-Nov, Mon-Sat 9.00-19.00.

Outdoor sports tuition. Guided tours. Explanatory displays. Gift shop. Restaurant and cafe. Garden. WC. Disabled access. Car and coach parking. Accommodation.

Tel: 01478 660266 Fax: 01478 660200
Email: raasay.house@virgin.net Web: www.freespace.virgin.net/raasay.house/

Rachan *see* Kittlehall

Raeberry Castle

Galloway: About 4 miles south-east of Kirkcudbright, on minor roads and foot 2.5 miles south of A711, south of Howwell, on cliffs above shore, in Danger Area.

Ruin or site NX 699437 [?] OS: 83 * Map: 1, no: 113

Standing on cliffs overlooking the sea, little remains of Raeberry Castle. It was defended on the landward side by a strong wall and deep ditch, spanned by a huge drawbridge.

It was a property of the MacLellans, and it was from here that in 1452 Patrick MacLellan of Bombie was seized and taken to Threave Castle, where he was murdered by the Earl of Douglas. The castle buildings were demolished in the mid 16th century, and the outer wall and defences in the 18th century.

Raeburnfoot

Dumfriesshire: About 1 mile north of Eskdalemuir, on minor roads north of B709 at Eskdalemuir, east of River Esk, at or near Raeburnfoot.

Ruin or site NY 252991 [?] OS: 79 * Map: 1, no: 278

Site of tower house of the Beatties, possibly within the earthworks of the Roman fort.

Raecleugh Tower

Dumfriesshire: About 5 miles north-west of Moffat, on minor road north of B719 just east of junction with A74, just east of Evan Water, at Raecleugh Farm.
Ruin or site NT 038118 OS: 78 * Map: 1, no: 204
Very little remains of a 17th-century tower house with a formerly vaulted basement. This tower is recorded as a bastle house by Biggar Museum Trust, although it is difficult to see how it differs from sites listed as tower houses.
  It was a property of the Johnstones of Raecleugh.

Raemoir

Kincardine & Deeside: About 2 miles north of Banchory, on minor roads north of B977, at or near Raemoir.
Private NO 695995 [?] OS: 38 * Map: 10, no: 204
Site of castle or hall house. It may be incorporated into Raemoir Hotel, a mansion which was held by the Innes family at the end of the 19th century.

Raesknowe *see* Allannmouth Tower

Raffles Tower

Dumfriesshire: About 7 miles west and north of Annan, near A75 at Raffles, just east of the Raffles Burn.
Ruin or site NY 086721 OS: 85 * Map: 1, no: 223
Site of 16th-century tower house, which was ruinous but well preserved at the end of the 18th century, but little remained 50 years later. It was square in plan, and rose to three storeys.
  It was a property of the Carruthers family.
Other refs: East Raffles

Rais Tower *see* Tower Rais

Rait Castle

Inverness & Nairn: About 2.5 miles south of Nairn, on minor road south of B9101 0.5 miles west of junction with A939, north of Laiken Forest, south-east of Raitcastle.
Ruin or site NH 894525 OS: 27 * Map: 9, no: 138**
Rait Castle consists of a ruined 13th-century hall house, altered in the 16th and 17th centuries, and with a round tower at one corner and a garderobe tower. The building is complete to the wallhead, and consists of a long hall over an unvaulted basement with large arched windows. The castle had a courtyard further defended by round towers, and there are the remains of what was probably a chapel.
  It was a property of the Raits. Sir Alexander Rait killed the 3rd Thane of Cawdor around 1395. Rait passed to the Comyns or Cummings, then the Mackintoshes, then the Campbells of Cawdor. The Duke of Cumberland is said to have stayed here before victory at the Battle of Culloden against the Jacobites in 1746.
  The tale (although there is more one version) goes that in 1524, when the castle was held by the Cummings, they invited the Mackintoshes here for a feast, possibly a wedding banquet, but planned to murder their guests. The Mackintoshes appar-

ently learned of the plan and came heavily armed, and managed to flee from Rait after killing many of their treacherous hosts. The Cumming laird was furious – he suspected his daughter had betrayed his plan as she was in love with one of the Mackintoshes – pursued the terrified girl through the building. She tried to escape out of an upstairs window, but her father hacked off her hands with his sword as she hung from a window ledge, and she fell to her death. Her ghost, a handless phantom in a blood-stained dress, then began to haunt Rait.
  The Cumming laird and his followers were, themselves, apparently slain at Balblair in retribution.
Other refs: Raitcastle

Raith Tower

Fife: About 1.5 miles west of Kirkcaldy railway station, on minor roads west from A921, near Raith House.
Ruin or site NT 256917 OS: 59 ** Map: 7, no: 52
Little remains of a tower house of the Melvilles, who held the property from the 13th century or earlier. Descendants of the family became Earls of Melville. The property was sold to the Fergusons in the 17th century. The family built Raith House, dating from 1694, which was altered and extended in later centuries.
  The current Raith Tower, west of Raith House, is a derelict 19th-century Gothic folly.

Ralston

Renfrewshire: About 2 miles north-east of Paisley, on minor roads north of A737 or west of A736, south of Paisley Road, at Ralston Golf Club.
Ruin or site NS 507642 OS: 64 * Map: 3, no: 217
Site of castle or old house, which was replaced by Ralston House, a mansion built in 1810, but demolished in 1934.
  It was held by the Ralston family (or Ralphston – the 'town of Ralph') from the 13th century until 1704, when the property was sold to the Cochrane Earls of Dundonald. It later passed to the Hamiltons, but by 1800 had been acquired by the Orr family, who built the mansion.

Rammerscales House

Dumfriesshire: About 3 miles south of Lockerbie, on minor roads west of B9020, at Rammerscales.
Private NY 081786 OS: 85 ** Map: 1, no: 218
Standing on a high slope of the Torthorwald Hills, Rammerscales is a fine 18th-century mansion of four storeys, with fine views over Annandale. In Adam style and mostly unaltered, the mansion was home to the Mounsey family in the 18th century, but is now a property of the Bell Macdonald family. It houses rare contemporary art and a library with 600 volumes. Extensive and attractive grounds with walled gardens.
OPEN: Last week in Jul; 1st three weeks in Aug: daily except Sat 14.00-17.00.
Guided tours for parties. Picnic area. Extensive and attractive grounds with walled gardens. Car and coach parking. Group concessions. ££.
Tel: 01387 810229/811988 Fax: 01387 810940

Randerston *see* Randolphstoun Castle

Randerston

Fife: About 3 miles north of Crail, on minor road east of A917 about 1 mile south of Kingsbarns, at Randerston.
Private NO 608108 OS: 59 ** Map: 7, no: 160
Randerston is an altered 16th-century L-plan tower house of three storeys. A round stair-tower, in the re-entrant angle, is corbelled out to square and topped by a gabled watch-chamber. The walls are pierced by gunloops. Two bartizans crown the tower, but these have been lowered in height.
  The entrance is not in the foot of the stair-tower, but in the opposite side of the house. It opens into a corridor, leading to two vaulted chambers in the main-block, while the vaulted chamber in the wing was probably the kitchen. The upper floors have been very altered.
  The lands had passed to the Balcomie family by the 15th century, but the family joined the English against James I and were forfeited. The lands were given to the

Myrtoun, or Morton, family, who probably built the house. In 1629 Randerston was sold to the Moncrieffes of Balcaskie, who sold it to the Balfours of Denmylne in 1663. It is now a farmhouse and still occupied.

Randolphstoun Castle

Fife: About 2.5 miles north of Crail, on minor roads and footpath north of A917, about 0.5 miles east of Randerston, on shore.
Ruin or site   NO 618109   OS: 59   *   Map: 7, no: 163
Site of the castle, which survived until at least 1528, of John FitzRandolph, which was probably built in the remains of an Iron Age fort.
Other refs: Randerston

Ranfurly Castle

Renfrewshire: About 0.5 miles south-west of Bridge of Weir, on minor roads south of A761, in Ranfurly Golf Course.
Ruin or site   NS 384652   OS: 63   *   Map: 3, no: 134
Ranfurly or Ranforlie is a small ruined early 15th-century keep and courtyard. Only two storeys remain of the keep, and three cellars of the ranges of buildings within the courtyard. The castle probably replaced the nearby motte [NS 384650].

It was a property of the Knox family, one of whom was John Knox, while another was a Protestant Bishop of the Isles. It passed in 1665 to the Cochrane Earls of Dundonald, then was sold to the Hamiltons of Holmhead, then to the Aitkenheads.
Other refs: Castle Hill, Ranfurly

Rankeilour Castle

Fife: About 3 miles west and south of Cupar, on minor roads south of A91, at or near Rankeilour House.
Ruin or site   NO 330119   OS: 59   *   Map: 7, no: 84
Site of a castle, which is mentioned in 1540.

The lands were a property of the Rankeilour family, but passed to the Sibbalds of Balgonie, then in the second half of the 17th century to the Hopes, later Earls of Hopetoun. Rankeilour House, a mansion dating from the beginning of the 19th century, was built by the 4th Earl of Hopetoun.

Rankine Castle

Stirlingshire & Clackmannan: About 2 miles west of Denny, on minor roads north of A803 and south of B818, south of the Castlerankine Burn, at Castlerankine.
Ruin or site   NS 787819   OS: 64   *   Map: 6, no: 69
Site of 12th- or 13th- century castle of enclosure, although it was still in use between the 14th and 16th centuries.

It may have been a property of the Morham family around 1300.
Other refs: Castle Rankine; Castlerankine

Rannas Castle

Moray: About 2 miles east of Buckie, on minor roads south of A98, at Rannas.
Private   NJ 460649   OS: 28   **   Map: 10, no: 102
Site of castle of the Hays of Rannas, of which only a wing and walled garden survive. Andrew Hay of Rannas was reputedly 7'2" tall and fought for the Jacobites in the 1745 Rising. His size made it difficult for him to conceal his identity, and after six years as a fugitive in Scotland, he spent a further 11 years on the continent. He returned in 1763, and in 1789 sold Rannas to clear the debts of his great nephew, who held Leith Hall – his sister had married John Leith.

Raploch Castle

Lanarkshire & Glasgow area: To north of Larkhall, near B7078, east of Avon Water at Fairholm, at Raploch.
Ruin or site   NS 763515   OS: 64   *   Map: 3, no: 362
Site of castle, which may be occupied by a housing development.

The lands were a property of the Comyns, but were given by Robert the Bruce to the Hamiltons in 1312, who built the castle. It was destroyed after the Battle of Langside in 1568, because of the family's support for Mary, Queen of Scots. Hamilton of Raploch captured Colonel Rumbold in 1685 at Lesmahagow as Rumbold was involved in the Ryehouse Plot.
Other refs: Roplock Castle

Rarey

Argyll & Dunbartonshire: About 7 miles south of Oban, on minor road south of B844, west of River Euchar, at or near Raera.
Ruin or site   NM 832206   OS: 49   *   Map: 5, no: 61
Site of castle, which was defended by a ditch and the steepness of the slopes down to the river. The buildings had been burned at one time.

It was a property of MacDougalls, but granted to the Campbells of Lochaw in 1311. It was recovered by the MacDougalls, and the site occupied until the 16th or 17th century. It was replaced by the nearby house at Rarey, which dates from the 18th century.

Rath of Logierait *see* Logierait Castle

Rathillet House

Fife: About 4 miles north of Cupar, on minor roads north of A914, 0.3 miles west of Rathillet, at or near Rathillet House.
Private   NO 359208   OS: 59   *   Map: 7, no: 97
Site of castle. The hall of the manor was repaired in the 13th century. The present house is a symmetrical house and dates from 1790.

The lands were held by the Halkerstone or Hackston family until about 1772. David Hackston of Rathillet was a noted Covenanter, and one of those present when Archbishop Sharp was brutally murdered on Magus Muir in 1679. He fought at the Battle of Bothwell Brig the same year. He was eventually captured and his hands hacked off before being hanged.

Rathven

Moray: About 0.5 miles east of Buckie, on minor roads north of A98 or south of A942, at or near Rathven.
Ruin or site   NJ 444655 [?]   OS: 28   *   Map: 10, no: 95
Site of castle.

Rattray Castle

Banff & Buchan: About 8 miles south-east of Fraserburgh, on minor roads north of A952, 1 mile west of Rattray Head, and east end of Loch of Strathbeg, at Rattray.
Ruin or site   NK 089580   OS: 30   *   Map: 10, no: 363
Only earthworks remain of Rattray Castle, a 13th-century stronghold of the Comyn Earls of Buchan, which was destroyed by Robert the Bruce in 1308.

There was a burgh of Rattray, first recorded in 1220, which was made a royal burgh in 1564. Its harbour was badly silted up by 1654, and a great storm in 1720 completed the process of sealing the river from the sea, thus creating the Loch of Strathbeg. The burgh declined from then on, and little is left today, except the castle site and the ruins of a 13th-century chapel. The site of the castle has been excavated.
Other refs: Castle Hill, Rattray

Rattray Castle

Perth & Kinross: About 1.25 miles east of Rattray, on minor roads south of A926 at Easter Rattray, about 0.5 miles north of River Ericht, at motte.
Ruin or site   NO 210454   OS: 53   *   Map: 8, no: 121
Site of large castle on motte of the Rattray family, who held the property from the 11th century. It was their main seat until 1516, when the Earl of Atholl had them driven from the castle. They moved to Craighall.
Other refs: Bendochty; Castle of Rattray

Ravelston House

Lothians: About 2 miles west of Edinburgh Castle, on minor roads north of A8 or south of A90, east of Corstorphine Hill, at Ravelston.
Private   NT 217741   OS: 66   *   Map: 4, no: 74
Little remains of a 17th-century castle. An old house here had a square tower at one end and a round tower at the opposite corner, but was almost completely destroyed by fire in the early 19th century. A courtyard gateway with gunloops survives, as does a stair-tower, stable wing and some carvings.

The house was built by the Foulis family.

Ravenscraig Castle

Fife: About 1 mile north and east of Kirkcaldy railway station, on the coast south of the A955, about 1 miles west of Dysart.

His Scot NT 291925 OS: 59 * Map: 7, no: 67**

Ravenscraig Castle is an altered 15th-century castle and courtyard, and one of the first castles in Britain built to withstand and return artillery. It consists of two D-plan towers, with very thick walls, and a courtyard cut off from the mainland by a deep ditch. The towers were linked by a two-storey block with a broad parapet. The walls are pierced by gunloops. The castle was never completed as first planned. The single rooms on each floor of the towers are small because of the thickness of the walls. The basements are vaulted.

James II, who died when a cannon exploded during the siege of Roxburgh Castle, started to build Ravenscraig, before 1460, for Mary of Gueldres. She died at the castle in 1463. It was forced upon William Sinclair, then Earl of Orkney, by James III

in return for Kirkwall Castle, on Orkney, which the King wanted for himself. Ravenscraig was then held by the Sinclairs, who completed the castle as it is today, and inhabited until about 1650. It passed by marriage to the Sinclair-Erskines, but was sold by the family in 1898, and put into the care of the State in 1955.

Only part of the building is now accessible.

Other refs: Ravenshaugh Castle

OPEN: Access at all reasonable times – some of the building cannot be entered.

Parking.

Tel: 0131 668 8800 Fax: 0131 668 8888

Email: hs.explore@scotland.gov.uk Web: www.historic-scotland.gov.uk

Ravenscraig Castle

Banff & Buchan: About 2.5 miles north-west of Peterhead, on minor roads and foot west of A952, 0.5 miles north of Inverugie, south of River Ugie, at Ravenscraig.

Ruin or site NK 095488 OS: 30 ** Map: 10, no: 364

Ravenscraig Castle is a massive ruined L-plan tower house of four storeys, which incorporates a 15th-century keep. The basement is vaulted, and a round stair-turret, in the re-entrant angle, was crowned by a caphouse. It was defended by a rock-cut ditch.

The lands originally belonged to the Cheynes, but passed by marriage to the Keiths of Inverugie in the 14th century, and they built the castle about 1491. James VI visited the castle in 1589.

Other refs: Craig of Inverugie Castle

Ravenshaugh Castle *see* Ravenscraig Castle

Ravensneuk Castle

Lothians: About 1.5 miles south of Penicuik, on footpath west of A701, east of Ravensneuk farm, south of the River North Esk, in South Bank Wood.

Ruin or site NT 224590 OS: 66 * Map: 4, no: 76

Little remains of a 16th-century castle, except the basement, part of which appears to have been vaulted. It was a property of Oliver Sinclair of Pitcairn, favourite of James V and leader of the Scottish forces at the disastrous Battle of Solway Moss in 1542. Much of the castle was demolished by the Clerks of Penicuik around the beginning of the 18th century to build a park wall.

Ravenstone *see* Drumgin Castle

Ravenstone Castle

Galloway: About 3.5 miles north-west of Whithorn, on minor roads north of B7021 and south A746, about 0.5 miles east of White Loch, at Ravenstone.

Ruin or site NX 409441 OS: 83 ** Map: 1, no: 58

Ravenstone Castle was an altered 16th-century tower house, which incorporated work from the 15th century. There were later wings, although these had been demolished by the 20th century.

The lands belonged to the MacDowalls, but had passed to the MacLellans by 1560, who modified an earlier castle. In the mid 17th century it was acquired by the Stewarts, and then known as Castle Stewart. It was held by Lord Borthwick in the 19th century, when described as 'a fine old mansion'.

There appears to have been an older castle nearby [NX 402444], known as the Old Castle of Ravenstone.

Other refs: Castle Stewart; Remeston

Red Castle

Ross & Cromarty: About 7 miles east of Tain, north of B9165, east of Mains of Arboll, west and south of Drumancroy.

Ruin or site NH 892825 [?] OS: 21 * Map: 9, no: 137

Site of castle, the last vestige was removed around 1870.

Other refs: Arboll

Red Castle

Ross & Cromarty: About 3.5 miles east of Muir of Ord, on minor roads south of A832, on north shore of Beauly Firth, 1 mile south of Kilcoy Castle, at Redcastle.

Ruin or site NH 584495 OS: 26 * Map: 9, no: 74**

Standing on a strong position above a steep ravine, Red Castle is an altered 16th-century L-plan tower house, which incorporates some of a 12th-century castle. It consists of a main block and wing, with a square stair-tower, in the re-entrant angle, and 17th-century extensions, including a round and a square tower. The gables are crowned with corbelled-out bartizans, and the walls are pierced by shot-holes.

The entrance is in the re-entrant at the foot of the stair-tower. The hall, on the first floor, has an adjoining private chamber. The inside of the castle has been very altered.

The original castle was probably built at the end of the 12th century by David, Earl of Huntingdon, brother of William the Lyon. It had passed to the Bissets by 1230, but in 1278 was held by Sir Andrew de Besco, then the Frasers. It was acquired by the Douglases, but the Douglas Earl of Ormond, who owned the property, was executed in 1455 with the fall of Black Douglases. The property was kept by the Crown. Mary, Queen of Scots, visited in 1562. The castle passed to the Mackenzies in 1570, who held it until 1790, although the house was burned in 1659 when the family joined Montrose. It was a property of the Baillies of Dochfour in the 19th century, who had it remodelled in 1840. It was used to house troops in World War II, but the building became derelict after it was neglected and its roof stripped. It is in a dangerously ruined condition.

Other refs: Edradour Castle; Redcastle

Red Castle

Angus & Dundee: About 5 miles south of Montrose, on minor roads east of A92 , just south of the mouth of Lunan Water at sea, south of Lunan, at Red Castle.
Ruin or site   NO 687510   OS: 54   **   Map: 8, no: 264
Red Castle consists of the crumbling ruins of a 12th-century castle, to which a keep was added in the 14th or 15th century. There is an impressive-looking section of the curtain wall and one half of the keep.

The original castle was built by the Berkleys, and was used by William the Lyon for hunting. Robert the Bruce gave the castle to Hugh, 6th Earl of Ross, in 1328, and it later passed to the Stewart Lord Innermeath. It was attacked by Protestants led by James Gray in 1579, 1580 and 1581. It was last occupied by an Episcopal minister, James Rait, and the property later passed to the Guthries.

Other refs: Redcastle

OPEN: Access at all reasonable times – the castle may be in a dangerous condition.
Parking nearby.

Redbraes Castle

Borders: About 3 miles north-east of Greenlaw, near minor road between B6460 and A6105 at Polwarth, near Howe Burn.
Ruin or site   NT 746485 [?]   OS: 74   *   Map: 2, no: 299
Site of castle of the Homes of Polwarth, which once had a moat, only a fragment of which remains.

Sir Patrick Home hid in his own family's burial vault at Polwarth Kirk [NT 750495] after getting into trouble with James VII. Grizel (later the well-known Grizel Baillie of Mellerstain), his 12-year-old daughter, supplied him with food and drink from Redbraes. Sir Patrick escaped to Holland, and later returned with William of Orange to become Lord Polwarth in 1690 and Earl of Marchmont in 1697. The building was remodelled between 1726-35, but replaced by Marchmont House, a mansion which was built between 1750-4 and may have been designed by William Adam. Marchmont House was remodelled in 1830 by William Burn, and in 1913-20 by Sir Robert Lorimer. Redbraes was demolished and little now remains.

Other refs: Marchmont House

Redcastle *see* Red Castle

Redcastle *see* Red Castle

Redhall Castle

Dumfriesshire: About 2.5 miles north-west of Gretna, on minor roads east from B6357, just north of the Kirtle Water, just south of M74, at Redhall.
Private   NY 290694   OS: 85   *   Map: 1, no: 289
Site of castle.

Redhall Castle

Lothians: About 4 miles west of Edinburgh Castle, south of the A8, east of the A720, near or in South Gyle.
Ruin or site   NT 190718 [?]   OS: 66   *   Map: 4, no: 61
Site of 16th-century castle, the site of which is overgrown. It was a property of Sir Adam Otterburn, Lord Provost and Scottish ambassador to pacify Border skirmishes with the English. The castle was taken by Cromwell's forces after a two day siege in 1650. Around 1758 the castle was demolished for materials to build Redhall House, which was designed by James Robertson, and there is a doocot nearby with a 16th-century panel bearing the Otterburn arms.

Redheugh Castle

Borders: About 2 miles north of Newcastleton, on minor road west of B6399, west of Hermitage Water, at Redheugh.
Ruin or site   NY 498902 [?]   OS: 79   *   Map: 2, no: 161
Site of castle, the main stronghold of the Elliots. Robert Elliot, the 13th Chief, was killed at the Battle of Flodden in 1513. In 1565 the Elliots feuded with the Scotts, after some of the family had been executed for stealing cattle, but the feud ended in an indecisive battle. James Hepburn, the Earl of Bothwell, was wounded in a skirmish with the Elliots, but their lands were devastated in 1569 in retaliation. The castle here was probably abandoned by the beginning of the 17th century. Pottery dating from the 14th to the 19th century have been found here.

There may have been another tower [NY 494906] about 0.5 miles to the north.

Redhouse Castle

Lothians: About 1.5 miles south of Aberlady, just south of B1377 between Longniddry and Ballencrieff, west of Spittal, north of railway line, at Redhouse.
Ruin or site   NT 463770   OS: 66   *   Map: 4, no: 175**
An extensive ruin, Redhouse Castle is an altered 16th-century courtyard castle. It consists of a rectangular courtyard enclosing a four-storey tower house, and ranges of buildings with vaulted cellars. The tower house was later extended by an adjoining tower, and a Renaissance entrance was added. At one corner of the courtyard is a doocot.

It was a Douglas property, but acquired by the Laings, then passed by marriage to the Hamilton family. George Hamilton, the last of the family, was executed for his part in the 1745 Jacobite Rising. The property was forfeited, and the castle allowed to fall into ruin.

Redkirk

Dumfriesshire: About 1 mile west and south of Gretna, on minor roads south of B721, north side of Solway, at or near Redkirk.
Ruin or site NY 300659 OS: 85 * Map: 1, no: 296
Site of tower house.

Rednock Castle

Stirlingshire & Clackmannan: About 4 miles south west of Callander, on minor road north of A873 just west of junction with A81, at Castle of Rednock.
Ruin or site NN 600022 OS: 57 * Map: 6, no: 32
Not much remains of a 16th-century tower house of the Grahams, except a ruined turret. There may have been a castle here from the 13th century, a property of the Menteiths of Ruskie
Other refs: Castle of Rednock

Redpath

Borders: About 2 miles south of Earlston, on minor roads west of B6356, east of Leader Water, at or near Redpath.
Ruin or site NT 585358 OS: 73 * Map: 2, no: 223
Site of tower house or castle, known as Cairncross Tower.
Other refs: Cairncross Tower

Reedie

Fife: About 0.5 miles south of Auchtermuchty, on minor roads east of A912 or west of B936, north of Reedieleys Farm.
Ruin or site NO 234107 [?] OS: 58 * Map: 7, no: 45
Site of old mansion or castle, a property of the Moncrieffes of Reidie, who later moved to Myres Castle.
Other refs: Reidie

Reidie *see* Reedie

Remeston *see* Ravenstone Castle

Renatton *see* Rineten

Renfield

Renfrewshire: To north of Renfrew, on minor roads north of A8, between the Clyde and Cart Water, at Blythswood
Ruin or site NS 501684 OS: 64 * Map: 3, no: 211
Site of castle or old mansion.
  The property was held by the Stewart Earl of Moray but passed to the Hays in 1568, then later to the Campbells of Blythswood, who changed the name, and then apparently to the Elphinstones. The house at Renfield was abandoned around 1810, and a new house built further from the river. This was called Blythwood House, a large Greek-Revival mansion, and was demolished in 1935. The sites are occupied by a golf course.
Other refs: Blythswood; Ronnise

Renfrew Castle

Renfrewshire: In Renfrew, on minor roads west of the A741, south of the River Clyde.
Ruin or site NS 509680 [?] OS: 64 * Map: 3, no: 220
Site of 12th-century castle, built by Walter Fitzalan, the High Steward of Scotland. It was attacked by Somerled, King of the Isles, in 1164 – but he was assassinated before the castle could be taken. The castle is mentioned in the 15th century, but nothing remains, although the ditch was still visible in 1775. Materials from the castle were used to build a soap works, itself replaced by Castlehill House. This later house has also been demolished.

Renn Tower *see* Roan Tower

Renton Peel

Borders: About 4 miles west of Coldingham, on minor roads east of A1, 0.5 miles east of Grantshouse, east of Eye Water, at Renton.
Ruin or site NT 824654 OS: 67 * Map: 2, no: 335
Site of tower house, marked by a mound near the farmhouse. It was a property of the Logans of Restalrig, and one of the strongholds torched by the Earl of Hertford in 1545. The remains of the tower were demolished in the 18th century.

Repentance Tower

Dumfriesshire: About 5 miles north-west of Annan, south of B725 at Hoddom Mains, on top of Repentance Hill, about 0.5 miles south of River Annan.
Private NY 155723 OS: 85 * Map: 1, no: 251**
Commanding a good view over the west part of the Border, Repentance Tower is a 16th-century tower house, square in plan, of three storeys. It has a parapet and a stone-slabbed roof. The walls are pierced by small windows, gunloops and shot-holes. Over the lintel of the entrance is inscribed the word 'REPENTANCE'.
  The entrance, at first-floor level, is now reached by an external stone stair. The only access to the vaulted basement is from the first floor, and a timber stair climbed to the floor above. The second floor roof is vaulted, to support the heavy roof, and has a small fireplace.
  The tower was built by John Maxwell, Lord Herries, of nearby Hoddom Castle, in the mid 16th century. He demolished a chapel to build Hoddom Castle, and either because of his conscience or the protestations of the Archbishop of Glasgow, whose chapel it was, he built this watch-tower to give warning of English raiders. It withstood an English siege in 1570. A graveyard surrounds the tower.

Reres Castle *see* Rires Castle

Rescobie Castle

Angus & Dundee: About 3 miles east of Forfar, on minor road just north of B9113, on northern side of Roscobie Loch, at or near Roscobie.
Ruin or site NO 510517 OS: 54 * Map: 8, no: 217
Site of castle, nothing of which remains, which stood on an island.
  It was at an earlier stronghold here that King Edgar had his uncle, Donald Bane, imprisoned. Donald Bane had been blinded for trying to usurp the throne.
Other refs: Barnsdale Castle; Roscobie

Restalrig Castle *see* Lochend House

Reston

Borders: About 2 miles south-west of Coldingham, on or near B6438, south of Eye Water, at east end of village of Reston.
Ruin or site NT 883621 OS: 67 * Map: 2, no: 350
Site of tower house, a property of the Logans of Restalrig. There were some remains at the beginning of the 19th century, but it was completely demolished to provide building materials.
Other refs: West Reston

Rhymer's Tower

Borders: About 3 miles north-east of Melrose, west of A68 in Earlston, south of the Leader Water, behind garage.
Ruin or site NT 572383 OS: 73 * Map: 2, no: 215
Not much remains of a small 15th-century keep, formerly with a vaulted basement. It is associated with Thomas Learmonth – True Thomas or Thomas the Rhymer – a 13th-century poet and seer who, in his youth, reportedly spent seven years in fairyland, after falling asleep under the Eildon Tree, where he met and kissed the Queen of the Fairies. Returning older and wiser, he was famed for his predictions over the remaining seven years before he disappeared altogether. In the 14th century Earlston was a property of the Purves family.
Other refs: Earlston Tower

Riccarton

Lothians: About 5 miles south west of Edinburgh castle, near minor road north of the A70, not far from Heriot Watt University campus.
Ruin or site NT 183695 [?] OS: 66 * Map: 4, no: 58
Site of 16th century tower house. It consisted of a long L-plan block of 1621 added to an older tower house, perhaps dating from as early as the 14th century, to make a variation on a Z-plan. A large extension was added in 1827, designed by William Burn, but the building was completely demolished in 1956.

It was originally a property of the Stewarts, having been given to Walter the High Steward by Bruce on his marriage to Marjorie, daughter of Robert the Bruce; but passed to the Craig family, one of whom was the distinguished 16th-century lawyer, Sir Thomas Craig of Riccarton. The property passed by marriage to the Gibsons in 1823.
Other refs: Riccarton House

Riccarton Castle

Ayrshire: About 1 mile south of Kilmarnock railway station, near A71, south of River Irvine, Fleming Street in Riccarton.
Ruin or site NS 427364 [?] OS: 70 * Map: 3, no: 166
Site of castle.

The name Riccarton is said to be derived from 'Richard's town' from one Richard Wallace. The lands were held by the Wallaces in the 13th and 14th centuries, who built a castle here. Malcolm Wallace, William's father, is said to have been born here. A plaque marks the site.

Riccarton House *see* Riccarton

Riccarton Tower

Borders: About 6.5 miles north and east of Newcastleton, on foot north of B357, 0.5 miles north of Riccarton Farm, on east bank of Riccarton Burn.
Ruin or site NY 544958 [?] OS: 79 * Map: 2, no: 198
Site of 16th-century tower house, a property of the Croziers or Elliots. There are some remains into which has been built a sheepfold.
Other refs: Over Riccarton

Riddell Tower

Borders: About 4 miles south-east of Selkirk, on minor roads just north of B6400, north of the Ale Water, near Riddell.
Ruin or site NT 516245 OS: 73 * Map: 2, no: 179
The remains of a 16th-century tower house, probably L-plan, is incorporated in the now ruined Riddell House. The house was much modified and extended down the centuries, and part of the tower was demolished during alterations.

The Riddels held the property until 1823, although by the end of the 19th century Riddell House was held by the Sprots. The house was burned out in 1943 and remains a shell.

Nearby [NT 520249] are the remains of a motte and bailey castle, which was built by the Riddels around 1150, and on the site of which is the General's Tower, a folly of 1885.
Other refs: West Lilsly; West Lilliesleaf

Ridford

Renfrewshire: About 2.5 miles north west of Paisley, near junction of A761 with A737, 0.75 miles west of Ferguslie Park, near Barskiven Hill.
Ruin or site NS 455635 [?] OS: 64 * Map: 3, no: 187
Site of castle, possibly a property of the Hamiltons.

Rineten

Aberdeen & Gordon: About 7 miles north-west of Ballater, on minor road north of B976, 0.5 miles west of River Gairn, at or near Rineten.
Ruin or site NJ 276003 [?] OS: 37 * Map: 10, no: 52
Site of castle.
Other refs: Renatton

Ringsdale Castle

Lanarkshire & Glasgow area: About 2 miles south of Larkhall, on minor roads north of A71, west of the Avon Water.
Ruin or site NS 764493 [?] OS: 64 * Map: 3, no: 363
Site of castle, on a bank of the Avon, nothing of which remains except some fallen stones and the traces of a ditch.

Ringwodhay *see* Broadhaugh

Rires Castle

Fife: About 3 miles north and west of Elie, on minor roads east of B941, about 0.5 miles west of Balcarres House, at Rires.
Private NO 464046 OS: 59 * Map: 7, no: 123
Site of 14th-century castle, which replaced an earlier stronghold. It consisted of a rectangular tower with thick walls, but was completely demolished about 1840 and nothing remains except traces of the ditch.

The castle was built about 1392 by Sir John Wemyss. In 1402 the Duke of Rothesay besieged and captured the castle using a wooden engine constructed at St Andrews.
Other refs: Reres Castle

Roan Tower

Borders: About 1.5 miles north of Newcastleton, on minor road west of B6357, between Ryedale and Ralton Burn, at Roan.
Ruin or site NY 488895 OS: 79 * Map: 2, no: 150
Site of tower house, near the modern house, of which there were significant remains at the beginning of the 18th century. It was probably held by the Armstrongs.
Other refs: Renn Tower

Robber's Den, Glendarroch *see* Glendarroch

Robert Castle *see* Castle Robert

Robertland Castle

Ayrshire: About 1.5 miles north-east of Stewarton, on minor road south of B769, just north of Swinzie Burn, at Robertland.
Ruin or site NS 441470 OS: 64 ** Map: 3, no: 176
Site of 16th-century tower house, on which the existing Robertland was built around 1804. The property belonged to the Cunninghams. David Cunningham of Robertland, with others of his family, was responsible for the shooting of Hew Montgomery, 4th Earl of Eglinton in 1586. Cunningham and his companions were quickly hunted down and slain, but the feud between the families lasted at least another 20 years. Sir William Cunningham of Robertland was a friend of Robert Burns.

Robgill Tower

Dumfriesshire: About 5 miles north-east of Annan, on minor road south of A74, south of the Kirtle Water, at Robgill Tower.
Private NY 248716 OS: 85 ** Map: 1, no: 276
Robgill Tower is a very altered 16th-century tower house, formerly rising to three storeys. It was complete in the middle of the 19th century, but then demolished to the basement, and the remains were incorporated into a new mansion.

The basement was vaulted and housed the kitchen with a fine arched fireplace.

It was a property of the Irvines, and torched by the English in 1544. It was sold by the Irvines in the 19th century, and held by the Pattersons about 1890.

Robroyston House

Lanarkshire & Glasgow: About 2.5 miles south-west of Kirkintilloch, on minor roads south of B812 or east of B765, north of Robroyston, at or near Robroyston Mains.
Ruin or site NS 634692 [?] OS: 64 * Map: 3, no: 296
Site of castle or old house, dating from the 17th century or earlier. The house was extended around 1849, but has been demolished and little survives.

It was at Robroyston that William Wallace was betrayed, captured then eventually executed in London.

Rochsoles House

Lanarkshire & Glasgow: About 1.5 miles north of Airdrie, on minor roads south of B803 or east of B802, to east of Glenmavis, at Rochsoles.
Ruin or site   NS 756678   OS: 64   *   Map: 3, no: 359
Site of castle, which was replaced by a mansion of which only the stable block of 1839 survives.
   The lands were a property of the Crawfords, then the Cochranes, then the Gerard family who held them in the 20th century.

Rochsolloch

Lanarkshire & Glasgow: To south of Airdrie, on minor roads south of A89, near Rochsolloch Road, Victoria Place, at or near Rochsolloch Farm.
Ruin or site   NS 754649 [?]   OS: 64   *   Map: 3, no: 355
Site of castle, replaced by a mansion, itself demolished and replaced by a farm in the 19th century.
   Rochsolloch was a property of the Crawfords, but in 1685 sold to the Aitchisons, and later passed to the Alexanders. There was much industry on the estate, and by 1840 there were 15 mines.
Other refs: Ruchsallach

Rockfield Castle *see* Little Tarrel

Rockhall

Dumfriesshire: About 6 miles east of Dumfries, on minor roads north of A75, west of Rockhall Moor, at Rockhall Hotel.
Private   NY 054754   OS: 85   **   Map: 1, no: 207
Rockhall is a plain much-altered 16th-century tower house with a stair-tower, which was extended in the 17th century. Slit-windows light the basement.
   The house has been much altered inside, but the vaulted basement contains the old kitchen and a cellar.
   The lands were held by the Kirkpatricks, but in the 15th century passed by marriage to the Griersons of Lagg. Sir Robert Grierson, persecutor of Covenanters, lived here. His pet monkey, killed by his servants after his death, is said to haunt the house, blowing a whistle. The property was held by the Griersons until the 20th century. Rockhall is in a good condition, was a hotel, but is now a private house again.

Rohallion Castle

Perth & Kinross: About 1.5 miles south of Dunkeld station, on minor roads and foot west of B867, 0.5 miles north-west of Rohallion Lodge, just east of Birnam Hill.
Private   NO 039401   OS: 53   **   Map: 8, no: 56
Rohallion Castle is a small 16th-century Z-plan tower house, which was partly re-built in 1974. It consists of a rectangular main block with round towers at opposite corners. The walls are pierced by shot-holes and there were a series of outer defences.
   It was a property of the Ruthvens. William, 4th Lord Ruthven, sheltered here after involvement in the Raid of Ruthven in 1582.

Romanno Tower

Borders: About 2.5 miles south of West Linton, on minor road south of A701, just east of Romanno Bridge, near Romanno House.
Ruin or site   NT 167483   OS: 72   *   Map: 2, no: 31
Site of 16th-century tower house. Romanno House is a two-storey mansion, which dates from the 18th century.
   It was a property of the Murrays of Romanno from 1513 until 1676, and apparently held against James VI in 1591. The lands passed by marriage to the Penicuiks of Newhall, then in 1720 was sold to the Kennedys, who still held it at the end of the 19th century.
   Romanno Bridge was apparently the scene of a battle between two Romany families, the Faws and Shaws, in 1683.
Other refs: Tower of Romanno

Ronnise *see* Renfield

Roplock Castle *see* Raploch Castle

Roscobie *see* Rescobie Castle

Rosebery House

Lothians: About 4 miles south-west of Gorebridge, on minor road just east of B6372, west of River South Esk, at Rosebery House.
Private   NT 305574   OS: 66   **   Map: 4, no: 127
Site of castle or old house, known as Clerkington House, which was replaced by Rosebery House, a much-altered mansion which may incorporate work from the 17th century. Clerkington, a large and ancient mansion house, was demolished in 1805-12.
   This was part of the ancient barony of Nicholson, and sold to the Primroses in 1695. Archibald Primrose was made Viscount Rosebery in 1700, then Earl of Rosebery in 1703. It was sold in 1712, but bought back by the 4th Earl in 1821.
Other refs: Clerkington House

Rosebery House *see* Inverkeithing

Roseburn House

Lothians: About 1.5 miles west of Edinburgh Castle, on minor road south of A8, just north of Murrayfield Rugby Stadium.
Private   NT 226731   OS: 66   **   Map: 4, no: 80
Roseburn House consists of an altered and extended 16th-century L-plan tower house, with a round stair-tower at one corner. The walls are thick and whitewashed, and there is a courtyard.
   The basement is vaulted, but the inside of the house has been altered. The house is occupied.
   Cromwell is said to have spent a night here in 1650.

Roslin Castle *see* Rosslyn Castle

Rosneath Castle

Argyll & Dunbartonshire: About 1 mile south and east of Rosneath, on minor roads east of the B822, at the south-east end of the bay, at Castle Point.
Ruin or site   NS 272823   OS: 56   *   Map: 5, no: 127
Rosneath Castle, originally a 16th-century castle, was remodelled in 1633 as a more comfortable residence, but was burned down in 1802, then replaced by a large elegant mansion of 1806 close to the old castle.
   There is said to have been a royal castle here in the 12th century, which was destroyed by William Wallace. The lands were held by the Earls of Lennox, but in 1489 the property passed to the Campbells, Earls, Marquis and Dukes of Argyll. The house was sold on the death of Princess Louise, Dowager Duchess of Argyll, in 1939. After use as the administrative centre for the American Naval Base at Rosneath during World War II, the building was abandoned to be blown up in 1961. The site is now used as a caravan park.

Ross Castle

Dumfriesshire: About 4 miles north of Lochmaben, on minor roads west of B7020 or east of A701, west of Kinnel Water, at Mains of Ross.
Ruin or site   NY 067887   OS: 78   *   Map: 1, no: 211
Site of castle. Some remains may be incorporated into the 18th century farm house.

Ross House

Lanarkshire & Glasgow: About 1.5 miles east of Hamilton, on minor road east of A72, between Avon Water and River Clyde, at Ross House.
Private   NS 739558   OS: 64   *   Map: 3, no: 350
Site of castle. Ross House, a Georgian mansion, was built here in 1788, then replaced by a baronial mansion in 1830.
   The lands were a property of the Crown and a hunting forest, but passed to Kelso Abbey in 1222, then to the Hamiltons of Rossavon in 1339. This branch of the family also acquired Carmunnock on the forfeiture of the Douglases in 1455. The family were active during the Reformation, and one of the family was at the Battle

of Drumclog. The property passed to the Aikman family in 1856. The house is still occupied.
Other refs: Rossavon Castle

Ross Priory

Argyll & Dunbartonshire: About 3.5 miles north-east of Balloch, on minor roads north of A811, on southern shore of Loch Lomond, 1 mile north of Gartocharn, at Ross Priory.
Private   NS 415877   OS: 56   *   Map: 5, no: 158
Ross Priory, a mansion of 1693 which in 1810-16 was remodelled by James Gillespie Graham, may incorporate some of a 14th-century castle of the Buchanans of Ross, itself rebuilt in 1695. The house was much frequented by Sir Walter Scott while he was writing 'Rob Roy'. The mansion was held by the Buchanans until 1925, but is now owned by the University of Strathclyde.

Rossavon Castle *see* Ross House

Rossdhu Castle

Argyll & Dunbartonshire: About 2 miles south of Luss, on minor road east of the A82, near Loch Lomond at Rossdhu, near Rossdhu House, Loch Lomond Golf Course, near shore of Loch Lomond.
Private   NS 361896   OS: 56   **   Map: 5, no: 145
Rossdhu Castle is a very ruined 15th- or 16th-century tower house, and not much remains except one gable.
   The lands were a property of the Colquhouns of Luss from the 13th century. The castle was visited by Mary, Queen of Scots, and abandoned in 1770. James Colquhoun led his clan to defeat in a battle with the MacGregors in Glen Fruin in 1603. The tower was mostly demolished to provide materials for the nearby Rossdhu House, which was completed in 1774. Dr Johnson and James Boswell visited Rossdhu during their 'Tour of the Hebrides', although Lady Helen Colquhoun found the Doctor boorish and his manner insufferable.
   There was a castle on Eilean Rossdhu [NS 360894], little of which remains except fallen masonry. This was probably the predecessor to Rossdhu Castle, and built on a crannog. It is believed to have been abandoned when Rossdhu was built.
Other refs: Eilean Rossdhu Castle

Rossend Castle

Fife: In Burntisland, south of the A921, overlooking the harbour.
Private   NT 225859   OS: 66   **   Map: 7, no: 41
Standing on a rocky hill above the harbour, Rossend Castle is an altered and extended 16th-century tower house, now E-plan, although it may incorporate work from the 13th and 14th centuries. The original tower rose to three storeys with a parapet, and is dated 1544.
   The entrance was in a stair-wing. The main stair climbs to the hall, on the first floor, then to the second floor. The upper part of the castle is reached by a turnpike stair.
   The lands originally belonged to the Abbey of Dunfermline, who had a castle or residence here, but passed to the Duries. In 1563, while Mary, Queen of Scots, was staying in the castle, the French poet Chatelard secreted himself in the Queen's bedchamber. He had done the same at Holyrood, and been pardoned, but this second attempt led to his execution by beheading at the Mercat Cross in St Andrews. The property passed to the Melvilles of Murdocairnie, although it may have been held by the Duries again, before once again returning to the Melvilles. The castle was held against Cromwell, but easily captured by his forces in 1651, and he stayed at Rossend. It was later acquired by Wemyss of Caskieburn, who was created Lord Burntisland in 1672. The Jacobites held it briefly in 1715.
   It was used as a boarding house until 1952, after which it deteriorated and became roofless. It was saved from demolition in 1971, restored, and is now an office for a firm of architects.
Other refs: Abbots Hall, Burntisland
OPEN: View from exterior.

Rossie *see* Rossie Ochil

Rossie Castle

Angus & Dundee: About 1.5 miles south-west of Montrose, on minor roads south or east of A92, north-west of Kirkton of Craig, west of Craig House, at Rossie Castle.
Ruin or site   NO 702561   OS: 54   *   Map: 8, no: 267
Site of castle, of which there were remains in the 19th century.
   It was a property of the Rossie family, but the lands had passed to the Scotts of Logie by 1650. A modern Rossie Castle, built in 1800 and held by the Millars in 1880, has apparently been demolished.

Rossie Ochil

Perth & Kinross: About 6 miles south of Perth, on minor roads 3 miles south of B935 at Forgandenny, east of the Water of May, at Rossie Ochil.
Private   NO 087130   OS: 58   *   Map: 8, no: 73
The later mansion may incorporate an earlier house or castle.
   It was a property of the Blairs, but passed to the Oliphants of Newton in 1583.
Other refs: Rossie

Rosskeen *see* Newmore Castle

Rossland

Renfrewshire: About 1 mile west of Erskine, on minor roads east of A8, 1 mile east of Bishopton, on north side of Craigton Burn, at or near Rossland.
Ruin or site   NS 442707 [?]   OS: 64   *   Map: 3, no: 180
Site of castle.
Other refs: Rostad

Rosslyn Castle

Lothians: About 2 miles south of Loanhead, 0.5 miles south east of Roslin village, on minor road south of B7006.
Private   NT 274628   OS: 66   *   Map: 4, no: 116**
Once a formidable and splendid fortress, Rosslyn Castle consists of a ruined 14th-century round keep, altered and extended with ranges of buildings and towers in the 15th and 16th centuries, some of these complete. It stands on a high bank, above a river, and is defended by a wide ditch on the only weak side. The keep and ranges of buildings were arranged around a courtyard.
   A 16th-century block of five storeys, still mainly entire, is rectangular in plan, with a projecting square tower at one end. The walls are pierced by gunloops.
   The three lower floors each have four vaulted chambers, with another in the tower. The main block rooms are reached by a long corridor, and there is a wide scale-and-platt stair from the basement to the top floor. The block contains a kitchen, with a huge fireplace. The hall, on the third floor, has a finely carved fireplace, dated 1597. The third and fourth floors were altered in the 17th century, but have ornamental plaster ceilings.
   Rosslyn was the main stronghold of the Sinclair Earls of Orkney and Caithness, who lived like princes. During the Wars of Independence, an English army was heavily defeated by the Scots in 1303 near the castle. Sir William Sinclair, who probably built the keep, was one of the knights who set out on crusade with Robert the Bruce's heart, and was killed fighting the Moors in Granada in 1330. The castle was accidentally burned in 1452. It was sacked and torched by the Earl of Hertford in

1544, and attacked again in 1650 by Monck during Cromwell's invasion of Scotland. A mob damaged it in 1688. The property passed by marriage to the Sinclair-Erskines, who were made Earls of Rosslyn in 1802, still own the castle, and part of it is habitable, and can be rented through the Landmark Trust.

Rosslyn Chapel, intended as a Collegiate Church, was founded by William Sinclair, Earl of Caithness and Orkney, in 1446, and is open all year to the public (tel: 0131 440 2159). The chapel is richly carved with Biblical stories, and has the largest number of 'Green Men' found in any medieval building. The crypt is pretty creepy, and in the burial vault below ten of the Sinclair lairds and their kin lie, said to be laid out in their armour without coffins. Ghostly flames were said to be seen here when one of the Sinclairs was about to die. The chapel is also reputedly haunted by the ghost of the apprentice, who carved the famous Apprentice Pillar, and is said to have been murdered by his teacher.

A spectre of a dog, killed with its English master after a battle in the Glen in 1302, reputedly haunts the castle, and its howling has been reported.
Other refs: Roslin Castle

Rostad *see* Rossland

Rosyth Castle

Fife: About 2 miles west and south of Inverkeithing, in Rosyth Dockyard, west of minor road from B981, south of Rosyth.
His Scot   NT 115820   OS: 65   *   Map: 7, no: 17**
Once standing on a small island connected to the mainland by a causeway, Rosyth Castle is an altered 15th-century keep, now L-plan. It consists of a main block of three storeys and a projecting stair tower, and stands in a ruined 16th-century courtyard. The courtyard was formerly enclosed by a high barmkin wall and ranges of buildings, but these have mostly gone on two sides. The castle is dated 1561.

The entrance is in the re-entrant angle and leads, through a lobby, to the vaulted basement and to a stair to the first-floor hall. The hall is barrel-vaulted, and has a large 17th-century window. The second floor was occupied by a single chamber, and there was a garret.

It was a property of the Stewarts of Rosyth from 1428 until the beginning of the 18th century. It was for the family that Walter Bower, Abbot of Inchcolm, compiled a history of Scotland, known as the 'Scotichronicon', in the 1440s. One of the family, Robert Stewart, was a supporter of Mary, Queen of Scots, and a later lord, James Stewart, was imprisoned in 1647 for being a Royalist. Rosyth was sacked by Cromwell's forces in 1650. In the 18th century it passed to the Primrose Earl of Rosebery, then to the Hope Earl of Hopetoun. It stands in the dockyard at Rosyth, now surrounded by reclaimed land.
OPEN: Access by appt.
Tel: 0131 668 8800   Fax: 0131 668 8888
Email: hs.explore@scotland.gov.uk   Web: www.historic-scotland.gov.uk

Rothes Castle

Moray: About 3.5 miles north of Charlestown of Aberlour, on minor road just west of A941 to south of Rothes, west of River Spey, just south of The Linn.
Ruin or site   NJ 277490   OS: 28   *   Map: 10, no: 53
Little remains of a 13th-century keep and courtyard, except some of the curtain wall and other masonry.

Edward I visited here in July 1296. In the 12th century the lands were held by the Pollocks, but passed by marriage to the Watsons, then to the Leslies, who in 1457 were made Earls of Rothes. The castle was torched by the Innes family, may have been damaged by Montrose, and largely demolished around 1660 to prevent it being used by thieves, who were harrying the area. The Leslies had moved to a house in Fife, but were created Dukes of Rothes in 1680. The property was sold to Grant of Elchies in 1700, then in 1708 to the Ogilvie Earl of Findlater, then back to the Grants Earls of Seafield.

Rothesay Castle

Argyll & Dunbartonshire: In Rothesay on island of Bute, on minor roads south A886, south of Rothesay Bay.
His Scot   NS 086646   OS: 63   *   Map: 5, no: 105**
Surrounded by a wet moat and built on a mound or motte, Rothesay Castle consists of an enormous 12th-century shell keep, with four massive round towers. In the late 15th century a large rectangular keep and gatehouse were added, built for comfort as well as defence, and then completed by James V after 1541. Parts of the castle were restored in the late 19th century.

The entrance leads through a long vaulted passage, in the floor of which is a trapdoor to a pit-prison. The first-floor hall can be reached by a narrow mural stair or by external steps within the castle walls. There were private chambers on the floors above the hall.

The castle was attacked by Norsemen in the 1230s, who cut a hole in the wall with their axes. It was captured in 1263 by King Haakon of Norway, before he was defeated at the Battle of Largs. The Stewarts were keepers of the castle.

The castle was held by the English during the Wars of Independence, but taken by

Robert the Bruce, only to be captured again by the English in 1334, to be recaptured once again by the Scots.

It was a favourite residence of Robert II and Robert III, who died here in 1406. In 1401 Robert III made his son Duke of Rothesay, a title since taken by the eldest son of the kings of Scots and currently held by Prince Charles. The castle was besieged by the Earl of Ross in 1462, the Master of Ruthven in 1527, and in 1544 captured by the Earl of Lennox on behalf of the English. It had been visited by James V, who completed the gatehouse block. In the 1650s it was held for Charles I, but later taken by Cromwell, whose men damaged the castle. Argyll's forces torched the castle in 1685, and it was very ruined until 1816 when repaired and partly rebuilt – somewhat crudely – by the 2nd Marquis of Bute between 1872 and 1879. It was placed in the care of the State in 1951.

According to a 19th-century ballad, the castle is haunted by a Lady Isobel, her apparition seen on the 'Bloody Stair', behind the chapel. Her family was killed by Norsemen, and rather than submit to marriage with a Norseman, she stabbed herself to death.

OPEN: Open all year: Apr-Sep, daily 9.30-18.30; Oct-Mar, Mon-Wed and Sat 9.30-16.30, Thu 9.30-12.00, Sun 14.00-16.30, closed Fri; last ticket sold 30 mins before closing; closed 25/26 Dec and 1/2 Jan.
Explanatory panels. Car parking nearby. Group concessions. £.
Tel: 01700 502691　Fax: 0131 668 8888
Email: hs.explore@scotland.gov.uk　Web: www.historic-scotland.gov.uk

Rothiemay Castle

Moray: About 5.5 miles north of Huntly, on minor roads east of B9118 or south of B9117, just north of River Deveron, just east of Milltown of Rothiemay.
Ruin or site　NJ 554484　OS: 29　*　Map: 10, no: 137
Site of 15th-century castle, formerly comprising a mostly 16th-century Z-plan tower house, which was extended in the late 17th century, then remodelled in the 19th century. Little or nothing remains.

The original castle was built by the Abernethys, but later passed to the Gordons.

Mary, Queen of Scots, may have spent a night here in 1562. It was attacked by George Gordon of Gight in 1618. In 1630 William Gordon of Rothiemay, and others, were burned to death at the castle of Frendraught in suspicious circumstances, although the Crichton laird was cleared of involvement. In revenge, Lady Rothiemay employed Highlanders to attack and harry Crichton's lands and family. Lady Rothiemay was eventually imprisoned in 1635, but later released.

The castle was captured and looted by the Marquis of Montrose in 1644, and held by Cromwell's forces in the 1650s. Rothiemay passed to the Duffs in 1741, then to the Forbeses in 1890. It was completely demolished in 1956.

Rothiemurchus

South Highland: About 2 miles south of Aviemore, on minor roads west of B970, east of Spey River, at Doune.
Private　NH 885098　OS: 36　**　Map: 9, no: 135
Doune of Rothiemurchus, a mansion dating from the late 18th century, is a property of the Grants of Rothiemurchus. It was home to Elizabeth Grant, author of 'Memoirs of a Highland Lady'.

The house was said to be haunted by the son of a laird, who suffered from bouts

of madness. During one of these he reputedly strangled a servant girl on the stairs, then died himself after falling over the balustrade. His ghost reportedly haunts the house, and is said to mostly manifest itself in one of the bedrooms. The house also had a brownie.
Other refs: Doune of Rothiemurchus
OPEN: Open Apr-Oct.
Guided tours only. Rothiemurchus visitor centre. Gift shop and refreshments (Apr-Oct). Limited parking. £.
Tel: 01479 812345　Fax: 01479 811778
Email: rothie@enterprise.net　Web: www.rothiemurchus.net

Rotmell

Perth & Kinross: About 4 miles north of Dunkeld, on minor roads east of A9, east of River Tay, 1 mile south of Dowally, at or near Rotmell Farm.
Ruin or site　NO 004470 [?]　OS: 53　*　Map: 8, no: 50
Site of royal castle, demolished in 1810.

Rough Castle

Falkirk: About 1.5 miles east of Bonnybridge, on minor roads east of B816, Rough Castle.
His Scot　NS 835798　OS: 65　**　Map: 6, no: 81
Rough Castle consists of the earthworks of a large Roman fort which stood on the Antonine Wall. The buildings have gone, but mounds and terraces mark are the sites of barracks, granary and bath buildings. The military road, which linked all the forts on the wall, is still well defined, and there is also a fine length of rampart and ditch.
OPEN: Access at all reasonable times.
Parking.
Tel: 0131 668 8800　Fax: 0131 668 8888
Web: www.historic-scotland.gov.uk

Rough Hill

Lanarkshire & Glasgow: About 1 mile north-west of East Kilbride, on minor roads north of A726, north-west of College Milton, at Rough Hill.
Ruin or site　NS 607553　OS: 64　*　Map: 3, no: 280
Site of castle on motte, which appears to have had a large rectangular tower. A vault was found here in 1807.

Rough Island

Dumfriesshire: About 4 miles south of Moniaive, on minor roads west of B729 or south of A702, just south of Lochurr, on an island, Rough Island, in Loch Urr.
Ruin or site　NX 763845　OS: 78　**　Map: 1, no: 124
Site of 13th-century hall house, built on a crannog in the loch. A peninsula on the south shore of the loch is cut off by an earthwork, and may have been used as a bailey.

Roughlee

Borders: About 4.5 miles south of Jedburgh, on minor roads and foot west of A68 or east of A6088 at Chesters, just north of Jed Water, 0.3 miles south of Roughlee.
Ruin or site　NT 656104　OS: 80　*　Map: 2, no: 268
Foundations survive of a tower or bastle house.
Other refs: Rucchly

Roundstonefoot *see* Runstonfoote

Rowallan Castle

Ayrshire: About 3 miles north of Kilmarnock, on minor road north of B751, north of the Carmel Water, at Rowallan.
His Scot　NS 435424　OS: 70　**　Map: 3, no: 173**
Once surrounded by marshland, Rowallan Castle is an altered 16th-century courtyard castle. It consists of two ranges of buildings and a drum-towered gatehouse around a courtyard, of which the last side is completed by a wall.

The oldest part is a range of buildings, with a vaulted basement, from the 16th century. The gatehouse of three storeys and an attic dates from 1562. A 17th-century range is ruinous.

Rowallan originally belonged to the Comyns, but passed by marriage to the Mures. Robert II's wife was Elizabeth Mure, daughter of Adam Mure of Rowallan, and their son became Robert III. Mungo Mure was killed at the Battle of Pinkie in 1547.

The property passed by marriage to the Boyle 1st Earl of Glasgow at the beginning of the 18th century, then to the Campbell Earls of Loudoun. It was acquired by the Corbetts early in the 20th century, but is apparently now in the care of Historic Scotland, although not currently open.

OPEN: Not currently accessible to the public.

Roxburgh Castle

Borders: About 1 mile west of Kelso, just south of A699, on a spit of land between the Tweed and Teviot Rivers.
Ruin or site   NT 713337   OS: 74   *   Map: 2, no: 291
Not much remains of a 14th-century courtyard castle.

Roxburgh Castle was one of the main strongholds of Scotland in 1174 when, along with Berwick, Edinburgh and Stirling, it was surrendered to the English after the capture of King William the Lyon at Alnwick. It was occupied by the English, and in

1306 Mary, sister of Robert the Bruce, was hung from a cage suspended from the walls. It was retaken by the Scots under James Douglas in 1314, but later held by the English for many years. Henry V made repairs after a siege by the Scots in 1417. In 1460 James II was killed when one of the cannons, with which he was bombarding the castle, blew up beside him, but Roxburgh was then stormed and demolished. A holly tree between Floors and the River Tweed is said to mark where James was killed.

In 1545 the English built a rectangular fort on the site, but it was dismantled in 1550 under the terms of the Treaty of Boulogne.

A ghostly horsemen is reputedly sometimes seen riding towards the castle.
OPEN: Access at all reasonable times.
Parking nearby

Roxburghe House *see* Sunlaws House

Roy Castle *see* Castle Roy

Royston Castle *see* Caroline Park House

Royston Castle *see* Granton Castle

Rucchly *see* Roughlee

Ruchsallach *see* Rochsolloch

Rue Castle
Borders: About 2.5 miles west of Jedburgh, on minor road south from A698, at Ruecastle.
Ruin or site   NT 613202 [?]   OS: 74   *   Map: 2, no: 239
Site of 13th-century castle, which was torched in 1513 by Lord Dacre, and in 1545 by the Earl of Hertford.

Ruglen Castle *see* Rutherglen Castle

Rumgally House
Fife: About 2 miles east of Cupar, on minor roads north of B940, south of River Eden, at Rumgally House.
Private   NO 407149   OS: 59   **   Map: 7, no: 109
The house, which has been altered and extended, incorporates probably a 16th-century L-plan tower house, with a round tower in the re-entrant angle. There is a small corbelled-out turret, and the walls are harled.

Rumgally was a property of a James Butellare in 1446, but had passed to the Scotts of Balwearie by 1528. It may have also been held by the Wemyss family, although by 1658 had been acquired by James MacGill, minister of Largo. The house is still occupied.

Runstonfoote
Dumfriesshire: About 3 miles north-east of Moffat, just west of A708 at Roundstonefoot, just west of the Moffat Water.
Ruin or site   NT 140085 [?]   OS: 78   *   Map: 1, no: 246
Site of 16th-century castle, one wall of which with a gunloop survived in 1857, but nothing now remains.
Other refs: Roundstonefoot

Ruskie Castle *see* Rusky Castle

Rusko Castle
Galloway: About 3 miles north of Gatehouse of Fleet, on minor road just east of B796, just west of Water of Fleet, at Rusko.
Private   NX 584605   OS: 83   *   Map: 1, no: 90**
Standing on a tree-clad hillside, Rusko Castle is an altered 15th-century keep, to which had been added a long and lower 17th-century wing, which was ruinous and has been demolished. The rectangular keep rises to three main storeys and a garret within a corbelled-out parapet. There is a gabled caphouse at one corner.

The entrance, through a lobby, leads to the turnpike stair and to the vaulted basement. The hall, on the first floor, is a large chamber with a fine moulded fireplace.

The property was held by the Cairns, but passed by marriage to the Gordons of Lochinvar early in the 16th century, and they held it until the 20th century. The castle was inhabited until around 1930, but then became roofless. It was restored in the 1970s, and is occupied.
Other refs: Glensykeburn

Rusky Castle
Stirlingshire & Clackmannan: About 3 miles south and west of Callander, on foot east of A81, on island to west of Loch Rusky.
Ruin or site   NN 616034   OS: 57   *   Map: 6, no: 39
Site of castle on a small island in the loch, traditionally held by Sir John Menteith, who imprisoned William Wallace in Dumbarton Castle before having him taken to London for execution. There were no remains by the end of the 19th century, and the water level of the loch has been raised drowning the island.
Other refs: Loch Rusky; Ruskie Castle

Rutherglen Castle

Lanarkshire & Glasgow area: In Rutherglen, near A730, south of the River Clyde, at King Street where joins Castle Street.
Ruin or site   NS 614618   OS: 64   *   Map: 3, no: 285
Rutherglen Castle was a large 13th-century courtyard castle, which was defended by a series of towers.

It was used by the kings of Scots, and occupied by the English during the Wars of Independence. The castle was retaken for the Scots in 1309, then again in 1313 by Robert the Bruce's brother, Edward.

It passed to the Hamiltons of Ellistoun. The family supported Mary, Queen of Scots, and the castle was burned by Regent Moray about 1569. It was repaired, but abandoned early in the 18th century. There are no remains, and the site is occupied by modern buildings.
Other refs: Castleru; Ruglen Castle

Ruthven

Aberdeen & Gordon: About 4.5 miles north of Huntly, on minor roads west of A96 or east of B9022, south-east of Ruthven.
Ruin or site   NJ 510468 [?]   OS: 29   *   Map: 10, no: 114
Site of castle on motte, a property of the Gordons. It was held by the Comyns, but given to the Gordons by Robert the Bruce in the first quarter of the 14th century. The Gordons main stronghold was at Huntly. There is the tomb and stone effigy of Sir Thomas Gordon of Ruthven, Tam o' Ruthven, in the ruins of St Carol's Church at Ruthven.

It was probably replaced by nearby Auchanachie Castle [NJ 498469].

Ruthven Barracks

South Highland: About 1 mile south of Kingussie, just north of B970 east of A9, south of River Spey, west of Burn of Ruthven, at Ruthven Barracks.
His Scot   NN 764997   OS: 35   **   Map: 9, no: 118
Nothing remains, except the substantial earthworks, of a 13th- or 14th-century castle of the Comyns, later held by Alexander Stewart, the Wolf of Badenoch, as the chief stronghold of his lordship. In 1451 it passed to the Gordon, Earl of Huntly, but in that year was sacked by John MacDonald, Earl of Ross. It was rebuilt by 1459

when James II visited. Mary, Queen of Scots stayed at the castle. It was twice damaged by fire, and in 1689 attacked by Jacobites.

In 1718 the castle was demolished and replaced by a barracks, for Hanoverian troops, on the earthworks of the old castle. It was held by government forces in 1746, but was eventually taken and burned by Jacobite forces after Culloden.

Alexander Stewart, the Wolf of Badenoch, was responsible for the burning of Elgin Cathedral and town, and the town of Forres. He reputedly dabbled in witchcraft. One story is that in 1394 a visitor to the castle, dressed all in black, challenged Stewart to a game of chess. In the morning there was nobody left alive in the castle, for Stewart had reputedly played with the devil. The shades of Stewart and his followers, still playing chess with the devil, reputedly haunt the place. So the story goes. Stewart, however, was buried in Dunkeld Cathedral.
OPEN: Access at all reasonable times.
Car parking.
Tel: 0131 668 8800   Fax: 0131 668 8888
Email: hs.explore@scotland.gov.uk   Web: www.historic-scotland.gov.uk

Ruthven Castle

Angus & Dundee: About 3.5 miles east of Alyth, on minor roads south of A926, just east of River Isla, 1 mile south-east of village of Ruthven village, at Ruthven House.
Ruin or site   NO 302479   OS: 53   **   Map: 8, no: 152
Virtually nothing remains of a 15th-century castle, except one D-shaped tower with gunloops and a vaulted basement. The castle was mostly demolished in 1790 when the nearby mansion was built.

It was a property of the Lindsay Earls of Crawford, but had passed to the Crichtons by 1510. In 1744 the property was sold to the Ogilvies of Coul, who built Ruthven Mansion nearby, and was still held by the family in the 20th century.
Other refs: Castle of Ruthven

Ruthven Castle *see* Huntingtower Castle

Ryehill Castle

Dumfriesshire: About 1 mile south-east of Sanquhar, just south of A76 at Ryehill, just east of the River Nith.
Ruin or site   NS 794086   OS: 78   *   Map: 1, no: 130
Site of a 12th-century castle, although there was apparently a later tower house on the site. It was a property of the Crichtons in the 16th century.

S

Saddell Castle

Argyll & Dunbartonshire: About 8 miles north of Campbeltown, on minor road east of B842 south of Saddell in Kintyre, at Saddell Bay, west of Kilbrannon Sound, at Saddell.

Ruin or site NR 789316 OS: 68 * Map: 5, no: 51**

Saddell Castle consists of an altered 15th-century keep of four storeys and a garret, and a range of 18th-century outbuildings, which replaced the original courtyard. It may incorporate work from an earlier stronghold. The keep has a corbelled-out

parapet, with open rounds at the corners and a semi-circular round above the entrance. The keep is dated 1508.

The entrance opens into a lobby, which leads to the main turnpike stair to all floors. Just inside the entrance is a pit-prison. The basement, below ground level and reached down a flight of stairs, contains two cellars. The hall, on the first floor, had one end screened off as a kitchen with a fireplace and oven. The upper floors were occupied by private chambers.

The castle stands on what were the lands of Saddell Abbey, founded by Reginald, son of Somerled. Angus Og MacDonald is said to have sheltered Robert the Bruce here in 1306. The lands passed to the Bishop of Argyll, David Hamilton, in 1507, who built the present castle. It was held for the Bishops by the MacDonalds, but later passed to the Campbell Earl of Argyll. In 1559 the Earl of Sussex sacked the castle. The castle housed servants after the building of nearby Saddell House at the end of the 17th century. The building was restored in the 19th century, and had to be reroofed just before World War II. It is in the care of the Landmark Trust.

The castle is said to be haunted. A 'White Lady' is reputed to walk the battlements, and the castle also has a ghostly monk.

Salenside Castle

Borders: About 5 miles south of Selkirk, on minor roads west of A7, south of the Ale Water, at Salenside.

Ruin or site NT 464207 OS: 73 * Map: 2, no: 130

Site of 16th-century tower house, once a strong fortress. A cottage may stand on the site, and has a modern tower of three storeys with a stair-tower.

Saltcoats

Ayrshire: In Saltcoats, by B714, Windmill Street, Castlewenrock, Saltcoats.

Ruin or site NS 243411 OS: 70 * Map: 3, no: 51

There may have been a castle here, known as Castlewenrock.

Saltcoats was made a burgh of barony for the Montgomery Earl of Eglinton in 1529.

Other refs: Castlewenrock

Saltcoats Castle

Lothians: About 0.5 miles south of Gullane, on minor road south of A198, at Saltcoats, on Luffness Links, north of Mill Burn.

Ruin or site NT 486819 OS: 66 ** Map: 4, no: 180

Saltcoats Castle is an unusual ruined 16th-century courtyard castle. Ranges of buildings, rising to two storeys and an attic, were arranged around a central courtyard, except at one end where a block of four storeys stood. This block is made up of two towers, rounded at the bases but corbelled out to square above basement level, which are joined by an arch, which carried a parapet. The walls are pierced by gunloops.

The basement of the main block has been vaulted.

Saltcoats was a property of the Livingstones, but in the 18th century passed to the Hamiltons of Pencaitland. It was inhabited until the early 19th century, but partly demolished about 1820.

Saltoun Hall

Lothians: About 5 miles south-west of Haddington, about 2 miles east of Pencaitland, on minor road south of B6355, just east of the Birns Water.

Private NT 461685 OS: 66 * Map: 4, no: 173

Saltoun Hall, a later mansion in the Elizabethan style, incorporates part of a strong castle, which may date from as early as the 12th century.

It was a property of the de Morvilles in the 12th century, but passed to the Abernethy family before 1300, who were later made Lords Saltoun. Saltoun was occupied by the English in 1547, led by Cockburn of Ormiston, but retaken by the Earl of Arran for the Scots in a surprise attack. It was sold in 1643 to Sir Andrew Fletcher of Saltoun, 'The Patriot', who was prominent in resisting the Union of Parliaments of Scotland and England in 1707. The hall was occupied by the Fletchers until the 20th century, but has been subdivided and is still occupied.

It is reputedly haunted by a 'Grey Lady'.

Salvage *see* Selvage

Sandside House

Sutherland & Caithness: About 0.5 miles north-west of Reay, on minor roads north of A836, south-west of Sandside Bay, at Sandside House.

Ruin or site NC 952652 OS: 11 * Map: 12, no: 34

Site of castle or old house.

It was a property of the Mackays, and the 1st Lord Reay built a house in 1628, although there was already a building on the site. The lands passed to the Bentinck Duke of Portland, and the present large rambling mansion dates from the middle of the 18th century and was extended in 1889.

Sanquhar Castle

Dumfriesshire: About 0.25 miles south of Sanquhar, on minor roads south of A76, just east of River Nith at meeting with Euchan Water.

Ruin or site NS 786092 OS: 78 ** Map: 1, no: 127

Sanquhar Castle is a ruined 13th-century castle, consisting of an altered keep and ranges of buildings around a courtyard. A four-storey tower stands at one corner. A ruined hall block and later wing, with a gateway passage and a semi-circular tower, also survive. The rest of the castle is very ruined.

The lands originally belonged to the Ross family, but passed by marriage to the Crichtons in the 14th century. James VI visited the castle in 1617. The family were made Earls of Dumfries in 1633, but in 1639 sold the property to Sir William Douglas of Drumlanrig, who was later made Duke of Queensberry. The 1st Duke had Drumlanrig Castle built, but only spent one night in his new mansion, decided he did not like it, and moved back to Sanquhar. However, the family moved to Drumlanrig after his death, and Sanquhar was abandoned to become ruined. The 3rd

Marquis of Bute began rebuilding it in 1896, but this was abandoned on his death in 1900.

Two ghosts reputedly haunt the castle. One is the 'White Lady', which is said to be the spirit of a young golden-haired woman, Marion of Dalpeddar, who is said to have disappeared in 1590. She may have been murdered by one of the Crichton lords, and a skeleton of a girl was reportedly found during excavations in 1875-6. This is obviously linked to the ghost story at Dalpeddar [NS 820072]. Another ghost is said to be that of John Wilson, who was hanged by another of the Crichtons, and manifests itself with groans and the rattling of chains.

Sanquhar-Hamilton Castle *see* Newton Castle

Saok Castle *see* Savoch Castle

Saphock Castle *see* Savoch Castle

Sark Tower
Dumfriesshire: About 3 miles west and south of Canonbie, on minor roads south of B6357, east of River Sark, at or near Tower-of-Sark.
Ruin or site NY 333750 [?] OS: 85 * Map: 1, no: 305
Site of castle, a property of the Armstrongs. It was held by William Armstrong of Kinmont in the 1590s, and it was from here that Scott of Buccleuch planned his escape from Carlisle Castle, as related in the old ballad 'Kinmont Willie'.
Other refs: Kinmont Tower; Morton Tower

Sarkbridge
Dumfriesshire: To east of Gretna, near B721, at or near Sarkbridge.
Ruin or site NY 326669 [?] OS: 85 * Map: 1, no: 301
Site of castle, possibly a property of the Johnstones.

Sauchie Tower
Stirlingshire & Clackmannan: About 2 miles north of Alloa, on minor roads west of A908 north of junction with B9140, south of the River Devon.
Private NS 896957 OS: 58 * Map: 6, no: 95**
Sauchie Tower is a 15th-century keep, square in plan, of four storeys. It has a cor-belled-out parapet, with open rounds at all four corners, and a hexagonal cap-house with a conical roof. The tower had a courtyard enclosing later buildings, but these were demolished in the 1930s.

The arched entrance, at basement level, leads through a lobby, defended by a guardroom, to a turnpike stair in one corner. The basement is vaulted, and there is a pit-prison in the thickness of one wall. The hall, on the first floor, has a wide fireplace, and three of the windows have stone seats.

Sauchie was granted to the de Annan family by Robert the Bruce in 1321. In 1420 it passed by marriage to the Shaws, who built the keep. The family plotted against James III, and Sir James Shaw, Governor of Stirling Castle, refused the king access to his son, later James IV. James III was murdered soon afterwards in 1488 after the Battle of Sauchieburn. The family were Masters of the King's Wine Cellar in 1529. The tower was abandoned for a mansion within the courtyard in 1631, then the

family moved to Schawpark, near Fishcross. Both these houses have been demolished.

The property passed to the Cathcarts in 1752, one of whom William, created Earl of Cathcart in 1814, was ambassador to Russia in the Napoleonic Wars. The tower became ruinous, but is being restored.
Other refs: Devon Tower

Sauchieburn Castle *see* Old Sauchie

Sauchrie Castle
Ayrshire: About 3 miles north of Maybole, on minor roads west from B7024, at or near Sauchrie.
Private NS 303147 OS: 70 * Map: 3, no: 79
Site of 16th-century castle. The present Sauchrie, a small mansion, appears to date from no earlier than the late 18th century.

Saughton House
Lothians: About 3 miles east of Edinburgh Castle, in Saughton Park.
Ruin or site NT 205713 [?] OS: 66 * Map: 4, no: 69
Site of 17th-century L-plan tower house, which was burned down in the 1950s and afterwards demolished. It consisted of a three-storey main block and garret, and two projecting wings.

The entrance opened into a turnpike stair, and the basement was vaulted, with the hall on the first floor.

It originally belonged to the Watsons, but passed to the Ellis family, who built the house. It was used as a private lunatic asylum, before being bought by the local council, after which the grounds were turned into a park. The 1908 the Scottish National Exhibition took place in the grounds. Only a footbridge survives.

Saughton Mills *see* Stenhouse

Savoch Castle
Aberdeen & Gordon: About 6 miles north and west of Ellon, on minor roads west of A948, near Greens of Savoch.
Ruin or site NJ 918389 [?] OS: 30 * Map: 10, no: 322
Probable site of castle, although the location may be very approximate.
Other refs: Saok Castle; Saphock Castle

Scalloway Castle
Shetland: In Scalloway on the mainland of Shetland, on minor roads south of A970, on peninsula into East Voe of Scalloway.
His Scot HU 404392 OS: 4 * Map: 11, no: 61**
Scalloway Castle is a 17th-century L-plan tower house of four storeys and a garret. It consists of a main block and a smaller square offset wing, with a large stair-turret, corbelled out above first-floor level, at one corner. Bartizans crowned the corners of the tower, and the walls are pierced by shot-holes. The castle was dated 1600.

The arched entrance is in the main re-entrant angle, at the foot of the square wing. It leads to a scale-and-platt stair, which climbed only to the first floor, and into the vaulted basement. A passage led to a cellar, and to the kitchen, with a fireplace and well. The hall occupied the first floor of the main block. A stair in the corbelled-out turret, and another in the re-entrant angle, led to the upper floors, which were occupied by private chambers.

The castle was built by Patrick Stewart, Earl of Orkney, in 1600. He was unpopular with both the Orcadians and the folk of Shetland, forcing local people to work on the castle and taxing them to pay for materials. Earl Patrick was executed in 1615. The castle was occupied by Cromwell's forces in the 1650s, and abandoned by the end of the 17th century. In 1908 the castle was given over to the State, and the vaults were repaired or rebuilt.

OPEN: Access at all reasonable times.
Explanatory displays. Car parking.
Tel: 0131 668 8800 Fax: 0131 668 8888
Email: hs.explore@scotland.gov.uk Web: www.historic-scotland.gov.uk

Scarlaw Peel
Borders: About 3 miles west of Longformacus, on minor roads from B6355 and A6105, just north of Watch Water Reservoir, south-east of Scar Law.
Ruin or site NT 658567 OS: 74 * Map: 2, no: 269
Not much remains of a 16th-century tower house, the remains of which were built into a cottage, itself now ruinous.
Other refs: Old Scarlaw

Schivas *see* House of Schivas

Scone Palace
Perth & Kinross: About 2.5 miles north of Perth railway station, on A93, east of River Tay, 0.5 miles west of Old Scone, at Scone Palace.
Private NO 114267 OS: 58 ** Map: 8, no: 82
Scone Palace, a large castellated mansion dating from 1802 and designed by William Atkinson, incorporates part of the palace built by the Ruthvens in the 1580s, itself probably created out of the Abbot's Lodging.

Scone was a centre of the Picts, and in the 6th century a Culdee cell of the early Celtic church was founded here. The Kings of Scots were inaugurated at the Moot Hill, near the present palace, from the reign of Kenneth MacAlpin. An abbey was founded here in the 12th century, and the Stone of Destiny, also called the Stone of Scone, was kept here, until taken to Westminster Abbey by Edward I in 1296 – although this was returned to Edinburgh Castle in 1996. The last king to be inaugurated here was Charles I in 1651, who stayed at the Palace.

The abbey was sacked by a Protestant mob in 1559, and there are no remains. The property passed to the Ruthvens in 1580. However, after the Gowrie Conspiracy in 1600, when the Ruthven Earl of Gowrie and his brother, the Master of Ruthven, were murdered by James VI and others, Scone passed to the Murrays, as David Murray of Gospertie had been one of those to save the King's life. The family moved from Balvaird Castle [NO 169118], and were made Viscounts Stormont in 1602, and Earls of Mansfield in 1776.

James VIII held 'court' here in 1716 during the Jacobite Risings, and Bonnie Prince Charlie visited in 1745.

The old village of Scone was moved to New Scone in 1804-5, as it was too close to the Palace for the then owners.

The palace is said to be haunted by ghostly footsteps heard in the south passage.
OPEN: Open Easter-4th Mon Oct daily 9.30-17.15; last admission 16.45; grounds close at 17.45; other times by appt.
Fine collections of furniture, clocks, needlework and porcelain. Gift shops. Restaurant. Tearoom. WC. Picnic area. 100 acres of wild gardens. Maze. Adventure playground. Meetings and conferences. Disabled access to state rooms & restaurant. Car and coach parking. Group concessions. £££.
Tel: 01738 552300 Fax: 01738 552588
Email: sconepalace@cqm.co.uk Web: www.scone-palace.co.uk

Scotsbrig
Dumfriesshire: About 1.5 miles north-east of Ecclefechan, on minor roads north of B725 at Middlebie, near Middlebie Burn, at or near Scotsbrig.
Ruin or site NY 214769 [?] OS: 85 * Map: 1, no: 266
Site of tower house, apparently a property of the Bells. Scotsbrig had passed to the Carlyles by 1826.
Other refs: Godsbrigge

Scotscraig
Fife: About 1 mile west of Tayport, on minor roads west of B945 or south of B946, at Scotscraig.
Private NO 445283 OS: 59 * Map: 7, no: 118
Site of castle or old house. The present substantial mansion dates from 1817, although there are gate piers of 1620.

The lands belonged to the Bishops of St Andrews, but passed to the Scotts of Balwearie in the 13th century. Scotscraig was sold to the Duries, who in turn sold it to the Ramsays. It was later held by the Buchanans, then the Erskines, then the Sharps. One of the family, Archbishop Sharp, was murdered on Magus Muir in 1679. It was later sold to the Colvilles, then the Dalgleish family, who built the present house, then the Maitlands.

Scotstarvit Tower
Fife: About 2 miles south of Cupar, on minor road west of the A916, about 0.5 miles north of Craigrothie, at Scotstarvit.
NTS NO 370113 OS: 59 ** Map: 7, no: 98**
A well-preserved building, Scotstarvit Tower is a 16th-century L-plan tower house of six storeys and a garret. It has a corbelled-out parapet without rounds, and the walls are pierced by shot-holes. The small stair-wing is crowned by a caphouse with a conical roof.

The arched entrance, in the re-entrant angle, leads through a lobby to the vaulted basement and to the turnpike stair, in the wing, which climbs to all floors. The hall, on the first floor, has a fireplace, and windows with stone seats. The second storey is vaulted.

Scotstarvit was originally a property of the Inglis family, but was sold to the Scotts in 1611. Sir John Scott of Scotstarvit was an eminent historian. The property was sold to the Gourlays of Craigrothie about 1780, then to the Wemyss family, then to the Sharps in 1904. It was given to The National Trust for Scotland in 1949.

The tower stands near to Hill of Tarvit (see separate entry).
Other refs: Tarvit Castle
OPEN: Administered by Historic Scotland. Key available at Hill of Tarvit, which is open Easter, May to September, weekends in October.
See Hill of Tarvit.
Tel: 01334 653127
Email: hs.explore@scotland.gov.uk Web: www.historic-scotland.gov.uk

Scrabster Castle
Sutherland & Caithness: About 0.5 miles north-west of Thurso, just north of A882, 0.5 miles south of Scrabster, just south of sea at Thurso Bay.
Ruin or site ND 107692 OS: 12 * Map: 12, no: 41
Virtually nothing remains of a 12th- or 13th-century castle of enclosure and keep of the Bishops of Caithness, which was later a royal castle, then a property of the Sinclairs. The Sinclairs seized it in 1544, but the Earl of Sutherland was made constable in 1557. A pillbox is built within the remains.

Harald Maddadson, Earl of Orkney, seized and destroyed a stronghold here in 1201, capturing the Bishop and other lords. William the Lyon brought the area under the control of the Kings of Scots, and had Maddadson blinded and castrated.

The Protestant bishops had a residence at Scrabster [ND 099699] until 1688. Scrabster House, a 19th-century mansion, may be built on the site.
Other refs: Bishop's Castle, Scrabster; Scrabstoun Castle

Scrabstoun Castle *see* Scrabster Castle

Scrogbank
Borders: About 3.5 miles east of Innerleithen, on minor roads south of A72, on south bank of the Tweed, at or near Scrogbank.
Ruin or site NT 383374 [?] OS: 73 * Map: 2, no: 99
Site of tower house.

Seacliff Tower

Lothians: About 3.5 miles east and south of North Berwick, on minor road east of A198, east of Seacliff, on cliffs above beach.
Ruin or site   NT 613844   OS: 67   *   Map: 4, no: 214
Not much survives of a small 16th-century tower house.
Nearby is the ruin of Seacliff House, built in 1841, but later burned out.

Seafield Tower

Fife: About 1.5 miles north of Kinghorn, east of the A921, east of the main railway line, on footpath on shore.
Ruin or site   NT 280885   OS: 66   **   Map: 7, no: 65
Standing on a rocky outcrop close to the shore, Seafield Tower is a ruined 16th-century tower house of four storeys, to which a small stair-tower was added. There was a courtyard, parts of which remain, with a round corner tower known as the 'Devil's Tower'. A nearby harbour remained in use until the 19th century.
It was a property of the Moultray family, and probably continued in use until the last laird was killed in the Jacobite Rising of 1715, after which the lands passed to the Melville Earl of Melville.

Seaforth Castle *see* Chanonry

Seagate Castle

Ayrshire: In Irvine, just south of Main Street in Seagate, south of A737, west of the River Irvine.
Ruin or site   NS 320392   OS: 70   **   Map: 3, no: 90
Probably on the site of the original 12th-century castle of Irvine, Seagate Castle is a ruined 16th-century tower and town house. It consists of a main block of three storeys with three projecting towers, two round and one triangular. Corbelling for a parapet survives, although this has been overbuilt. One round tower, containing a stair, is corbelled out to square and crowned by a ruined watch-chamber. There has been a courtyard and wall, enclosing other ranges of buildings.
The moulded entrance leads to a ribbed-vaulted pend, through the main block of the castle to the courtyard, and is defended by vaulted guardrooms. The kitchen, in the basement, has a deep-arched fireplace. The hall, on the first floor, has been a fine chamber. The private chambers, occupying the upper floors, were reached by the turnpike stair in the round tower. There is a pit-prison, in the thickness of the wall, which was reached by a trapdoor from the chamber above the kitchen.
The Treaty of Irvine may have been signed here in 1297, which brought peace for a while between the Scots and English during the Wars of Independence. The existing castle was built by the Montgomery Earl of Eglinton, who held the property from around 1361. Mary, Queen of Scots, visited the castle in 1563. The castle was occupied until about 1746, when the 10th Earl had the roof removed, and the timbers used for a church in Ardrossan.
Other refs: Irvine Castle

Sealskerry Bay

Orkney: South-west of Eday, on minor road and foot west of B9063, west of Sealskerry Bay.
Ruin or site   HY 530320 [?]   OS: 6   *   Map: 11, no: 54
A mound is said to mark the site of a castle.

Seatown Castle *see* Cullen Castle

Selkirk Castle

Borders: About 0.5 miles south of Selkirk, on minor roads south of A708, on Peel hill just north of The Haining.
Ruin or site   NT 470281   OS: 73   *   Map: 2, no: 137
Site of 12th-century castle of enclosure with a motte and bailey.
The motte and bailey are mentioned in the foundation charter of Selkirk Abbey of 1119. There was a royal castle here in the 12th and 13th centuries, which was visited by William the Lyon, Alexander II and Alexander III. It was rebuilt and held by the English in 1302, taken by the Scots, recaptured by the English in 1311, but then finally retaken by the Scots, who demolished it. The castle was not rebuilt.
Other refs: Peel Hill, Selkirk

Selvage

Fife: To west of Inverkeithing, on minor roads west of B981, on Selvage Hill.
Ruin or site   NT 125827   OS: 65   *   Map: 7, no: 19
Selvage Manor House, which dates from the middle of the 17th century, has been converted into a garage for a modern house.
The house was built in the 1630s or 40s by John Bairdie.
Other refs: Salvage

Semple Castle *see* Castle Semple

Semple House *see* Northbar

Sersly *see* Swinlees

Seton House

Lothians: About 1.5 miles north-east of Tranent, on minor road north of A198, just east of Seton.
Private   NT 418751   OS: 66   *   Map: 4, no: 165
Site of castle, which was apparently a splendid palace after being rebuilt in the 16th century.
The lands were acquired by the Setons in the 12th century, and the family were made Lords Seton in 1448. George, 3rd Lord Seton, was killed at the Battle of Flodden in 1513.
An older castle was destroyed by the English in 1544, and a new house – the Palace – was built on the site. George, 5th Lord Seton, was a supporter of Mary, Queen of Scots, and she fled here after the murder of David Rizzio in 1566. She also visited with Bothwell after the assassination of Darnley, her second husband. The following year her army camped at the castle the night before defeat at Carberry Hill. The Setons helped to rescue Mary from imprisonment in Lochleven Castle,

after which she stayed at another of their properties, Niddry Castle.
The family were made Earls of Winton in 1600. The house was damaged during the 1715 Jacobite Rising – having been held for three days by Highlanders against Hanoverian forces – after which the Setons were forfeited. The house was left a ruin and demolished in 1790, and a new mansion, designed by Robert Adam, built on the site.
A fine collegiate church stands near the house. It was founded in 1490, although it was looted and burned by the English in 1544. The church is in the care of Historic Scotland and open to the public.

Shandon *see* Faslane Castle

Shandwick Castle

Ross & Cromarty: About 1 mile south of Balintore, on minor roads south of B9166, at Old Shandwick.
Ruin or site   NH 858745   OS: 21   *   Map: 9, no: 131
Site of 15th-century castle of the Ross family, nothing of which survives. It was replaced Old Shandwick House, a derelict 18th-century house.
Clach a' Charridh [NH 855747], 'stone of the monument', is an impressive nine-foot-high Pictish cross-slab.

Shanno

Angus & Dundee: About 7.5 miles west and north of Fettercairn, on minor road west of B966, probably east of River North Esk, east of Craig of Shanno hill.
Ruin or site   NO 572764   OS: 44   *   Map: 8, no: 239
Site of 17th-century tower house.

Sheriffhall

Lothians: About 1.5 miles south-east of Dalkeith, on minor road east of A68, just south of junction with A720, just north of Park Burn.
Private   NT 320680   OS: 66   *   Map: 4, no: 133
Not much remains of a castle of the Scotts of Buccleuch, except a stair-turret with a gunloop. Most of it was demolished because of subsidence caused by mining.

Shethin

Aberdeen & Gordon: About 4.5 miles west and north of Ellon, on minor roads south of B9005 or east of B999, at or near Shethin.
Ruin or site   NJ 886326 [?]   OS: 30   *   Map: 10, no: 305
Site of castle of the Setons, which was demolished in 1644 by Covenanters.

Shian Castle *see* Cloak Castle

Shiel

Dumfriesshire: About 5.5 miles north-west of Langholm, on minor road just east of B709, east of River Esk, at or near Shiel.
Ruin or site   NY 283916   OS: 79   *   Map: 1, no: 287
Site of tower house, a property of the Beatties in the 16th century.

Shieldgreen Tower

Borders: About 2 miles north-east of Peebles, on forest tracks north of A72, in Glentress forest, near Shieldgreen.
Ruin or site   NT 274432   OS: 73   *   Map: 2, no: 69
Very little remains of a 16th-century tower house except for a mound covering the basement.
   It was a property of the Stoddart family in the 16th century, but passed in 1656 to the Hay Earl of Tweeddale, then in 1666 to Peebles Town Council, who held it until about 1850.

Shieldhill

Lanarkshire & Glasgow area: About 3 miles north-west of Biggar, on minor road west of B7016, at Shieldhill.
Private   NT 008407   OS: 72   **   Map: 3, no: 441
Set in rolling hills and six acres of wooded park land, Shieldhill incorporates a massive square keep, said to date from as early as 1199. The castle was extended and altered in the 16th and 17th centuries, again in 1820. The keep is now the entrance hall to the house.
   It was a property of the Chancellor family. The family supported Mary, Queen of Scots, and fought for her at the Battle of Langside. As a result their house at Quothquan was burned by the forces of Regent Moray. Shieldhill was occupied by the family until the 20th century, and since 1959 has been a hotel.
   The building is said to be haunted by a 'Grey Lady', the ghost of the young and good-looking daughter of one of the Chancellor lords. She is said to be seen wrapped in a grey cloak.
   There are several versions of the tragic story associated with her. Her ghost has apparently been seen in recent times, walking towards the burial place in the grounds of the hotel and especially in one of the rooms. She is mostly seen in the old keep and uses the original stone stair to move from floor to floor. Unexplained footsteps and thumps during the night have also been reported, as have chairs moving by themselves and television channels changing independently.
   It was at a nearby fort that William Wallace is said to have rallied his men before going on to victory over the English at the Battle of Biggar in 1297.
OPEN: Hotel – open all year and to non-residents.
16 rooms with ensuite facilities. Two Rosette restaurant. Facilities for weddings, conferences, private parties and meetings. Parking.
Tel: 01899 220035   Fax: 01899 221092
Email: enquiries@shieldhill.co.uk   Web: www.shieldhill.co.uk

Shielhill

Angus & Dundee: About 4.5 miles north of Forfar, on minor roads north of B957 or east of B955, just south of River South Esk, at Shielhill.
Private   NO 428574   OS: 54   *   Map: 8, no: 185
Shielhill, a later mansion, is built the on site of a castle of the Ogilvies. The property later passed to the Lyles.

Shielhill *see* Quiech Castle

Shiels

Aberdeen & Gordon: About 8 miles south and east of Alford, on minor road just east of B993, at or near Mains of Shiels.
Private   NJ 656094   OS: 38   *   Map: 10, no: 179
Site of castle or old house. The present T-plan two-storey house dates from 1742, although an outbuilding with a large fireplace may be older. The chambers on the first floor are panelled, and there is a walled garden.
   It was a property of the Mackays of Shiels. Charles Mackay of Shiels, who died in 1794, was a captain of a merchant ship which traded with the West Indies.

Shillinglaw Castle

Borders: About 1.5 miles south of Innerleithen, by foot east of B709, about 0.5 miles south of Traquair, near Curly Burn, at Shillinglaw.
Ruin or site   NT 326335   OS: 73   *   Map: 2, no: 83
Probable site of castle or old house, a property of the Stewarts of Shillinglaw.

Shillochan *see* Inverallan

Shine Castle *see* Cloak Castle

Shirmers Castle

Galloway: About 3 miles south-east of New Galloway, on minor road just south of A713, just east of Loch Ken, at Shirmers.
Ruin or site   NX 657743   OS: 77   *   Map: 1, no: 108
Little survives of a 16th-century castle of the Gordons of Kenmure. The house is said to have been torched in 1568 after Mary, Queen of Scots, was defeated at the Battle of Langside, because the family had supported her. It was probably still occupied in the 18th century.

Shivas *see* House of Schivas

Shuna Castle *see* Castle Shuna

Side *see* Syde Tower

Silvertonhill Castle *see* Tweedie Castle

Sinniness Castle

Galloway: About 2.5 miles south of Glenluce, on minor roads west of A747, at Castle Sinniness, about 0.25 miles from the sea.
Ruin or site   NX 215532   OS: 82   **   Map: 1, no: 34
Not much remains of a tower house, except the vaulted basement and one corner.
   It was built by Archibald Kennedy around the end of the 16th century, but passed to the Dalrymple Earl of Stair. The tower house was still in use by 1684, but probably abandoned soon afterwards.
Other refs: Castle Sinniness; Synniness

Skaill House

Orkney: About 5 miles north of Stromness, on minor road west of B9056, on south side of Bay of Skaill, 0.25 miles east of Skara Brae, at Skaill House.
Private   HY 234186   OS: 6   ***   Map: 11, no: 31
Standing near the important Neolithic village of Skara Brae, Skaill House is the most complete 17th-century mansion house in Orkney. The earliest part is a two-storey block and courtyard, which was extended over the following centuries into a large complex of buildings.

Skaill was built for Bishop George Graham in the 1620s. Captain Cook's dinner service is kept at the house, and the building is surrounded by spacious gardens.

The buildings is reputedly haunted. Manifestations have included the sound of feet from unoccupied areas, and the apparition of an old woman.

OPEN: Skaill House open Apr-Sep, daily 9.30-18.30; last ticket sold 18.00. (Skara Brae also Oct-Mar Mon-Sat 9.30-16.30, Sun 2.00-4.30; last ticket sold 16.00; closed 25/26 Dec &1-3 Jan).

Guided tours. Explanatory displays. Gift shop. WC. Disabled access. Garden. Car and coach parking. Group concessions. ££. Joint entry ticket for all Orkney monuments (£££).

Tel: 01856 841501   Fax: 01856 841668

Email: janette@skaillhouse.freeserve.co.uk   Web: www.skaillhouse.com

Skaithmore Tower

Stirlingshire & Clackmannan: About 2 miles north of Falkirk, on minor roads east of B902, between Stenhousemuir and Carronshore.

Ruin or site   NS 888834   OS: 65   **   Map: 6, no: 92

Site of 17th-century tower house of four storeys. It was dated 1607.

It was built by Alexander, 4th Lord Elphinstone, a judge of the Supreme Court of Scotland in 1599, and later Lord Treasurer of Scotland. The tower was adapted for use as a coal-pit pumping station, but then gutted and abandoned to be demolished in the 1960s. The site was grassed over.

Other refs: Skaithmuir Tower

Skaithmuir Tower *see* Skaithmore Tower

Skeith *see* House of Skeith

Skelbo Castle

Sutherland & Caithness: About 3.5 miles north of Dornoch, on minor roads east of A9, just south of shore of Loch Fleet, at Skelbo.

Ruin or site   NH 792952   OS: 21   **   Map: 12, no: 24

Skelbo Castle is a ruined much-altered 14th-century keep and castle, consisting of a rectangular block of two storeys and a garret. A triangular courtyard had a curtain-wall.

The basement was vaulted.

It was a property of the Sutherlands of Skelbo. A castle here was captured by Robert the Bruce in 1308, during the Wars of Independence. This branch of the Sutherlands acquired the Lordship of Duffus in the 14th century. William Sutherland, Lord Duffus, was slain by the Gunns at Thurso in 1530. Alexander, his son, sacked and burned the cathedral and town of Dornoch in 1567, and again in 1570. The family was forfeited for their part in the Jacobite Rising of 1715. The property was acquired by the Gordon Earls of Sutherland. The castle may be in a dangerous condition.

Old Skelbo House is a long two-storey house with a vaulted basement, and dates from about 1600. The basement contained a byre while the living chamber, on the first floor, was reached by a removable ladder.

Other refs: Old Skelbo House

Skeldon Castle

Ayrshire: About 5.5 miles north-east of Maybole, on minor roads south of B7034, near Skeldon House, north of the River Doon, at Castle Cottage.

Ruin or site   NS 378138   OS: 70   *   Map: 3, no: 131

The remains of the castle are built into a cottage on the site. The walls are very thick, and there are also the remains of a small square tower, which is not connected to the other building. Skeldon House dates from the end of the 18th century, and is a small classical mansion in a wooded park.

Skellater House

Aberdeen & Gordon: About 3 miles south and west of Strathdon, on minor road north of A944, north of River Don, at Skellater House.

Private   NJ 315108   OS: 37   **   Map: 10, no: 61

Skellater House is a 17th-century T-plan house.

It was a property of the Forbes family. George Forbes of Skellater was a Jacobite,

and fought at the Battle of Culloden in 1746. John Forbes of Skellater married a Portuguese princess, and became a Field Marshal in the Portuguese army. He died in Brazil in 1809.

Skelmorlie Castle

Ayrshire: About 4.5 miles north of Largs, on minor road east of A78, about 1.5 miles south of Skelmorlie, not far from the shore of the Firth of Clyde.

Private   NS 195658   OS: 63   *   Map: 3, no: 24**

Standing on the edge of a cliff, Skelmorlie Castle is a 16th-century tower house, rectangular in plan, of three storeys and an attic. Bartizans, with conical roofs, crown two corners. The walls are harled, and the gables are corbiestepped.

The original entrance was in the middle of one wall, but the present entrance is

modern. The basement is vaulted. The hall, on the first floor, had one end screened off for the kitchen. A turnpike stair climbs from the hall to the second floor.

Skelmorlie was a property of the Cunninghams of Kilmaurs in the 14th and 15th centuries, but passed to the Montgomerys in 1461. It was restored and extended in 1852 for the Graham family, but burned in 1959 and the 19th-century baronial extension was mostly demolished. The old part of the castle has been restored, and is still occupied.

The Montgomerys of Skelmorlie had a burial aisle and loft in Largs Old Kirk [NS 200594] from 1646, which is rather handily known as the Skelmorlie Aisle. There are a number of burial monuments, as well as a painted ceiling, and the key holder is Largs Museum, which is nearby.

Skene House

Aberdeen & Gordon: About 4 miles north-west of Westhill, on minor roads north of A944, south of B9126 or B977, south of Mains of Skene, at Skene House.

Private   NJ 768097   OS: 38   **   Map: 10, no: 249

Skene House, an extensive castellated mansion, incorporates a large 14th-century keep, which had three vaulted storeys. It was greatly altered in 1680, a wing was added in 1745, and the whole building was extended and remodelled about 1850.

It was a property of the Skene family from 1318. Adam Skene was killed at the Battle of Harlaw in 1411, Alexander Skene was killed at the Battle of Flodden in 1513, and another Skene laird died at the Battle of Pinkie in 1547. In 1827 the property passed to the Duff Earl of Fife, but was sold to the Hamiltons in 1880, and is still occupied.

One of the family Alexander Skene of Skene, an 18th-century laird, was said to be a warlock. A phantom carriage, occupied by himself and the devil, reputedly rides across the Loch of Skene at midnight on New Year's Eve.

Skibo Castle

Sutherland & Caithness: About 4 miles west of Dornoch, on minor roads south of A9, north of Loch Ospisdale, 1.5 miles east of Ospisdale, at Skibo Castle.

Private   NH 735891   OS: 21   *   Map: 12, no: 20

Site of castle, which was mentioned around the beginning of the 13th century. The present Skibo Castle is a massive 19th-century castellated mansion which was extended in 1899-1901.

The castle was a property of the Bishops of Caithness until 1565. It had been captured in 1544 by the Mackays, and later passed to the Grays. The Marquis of Montrose was imprisoned here after being betrayed at Ardvreck Castle. Robert Gray was fined after his wife, Jean Seton, hit one of Montrose's guards with a leg of meat. The property passed in 1776 to the Dowalls, then in 1786 to the Dempsters of Dunnichen. The building was remodelled for the Sutherland family in 1872, but was purchased by Andrew Carnegie in 1895. Carnegie was born in Dunfermline in 1835 but emigrated to America in 1848, and made a fortune through railways, and iron and steel. He was one of the richest men of his time, but gave away most of his money, Dunfermline particularly benefiting. The castle is now an exclusive country club.

The old castle was reputedly haunted by the ghost of a young woman. She was a village girl, who was entertained here by a servant of the castle, but afterwards never seen again. She was probably murdered, and the ghost of a partially dressed young woman had reportedly been seen in the castle. A skeleton was later found, sealed behind a wall in the castle, and, when it was buried, the hauntings stopped.

Skipness Castle

Argyll & Dunbartonshire: About 7 miles south of Tarbert, on minor road east of end of B8001 at Skipness, just north of the sea at Skipness Bay, at Skipness
His Scot NR 907577 OS: 62 *** Map: 5, no: 78
Skipness Castle is a 13th-century castle of enclosure, later consisting of a courtyard with a curtain wall surrounding a tower house and ranges of buildings. The wall has three ruined towers. The main entrance was from the sea, which was defended by a gatetower, with a portcullis and machiolation.

The 16th-century tower house rises to four storeys and a garret, and incorporates the late 13th-century keep or earlier hall house. The parapet has open rounds at three corners, and a gabled caphouse at the other. The basement is vaulted, and has no access to the floors above. The hall was reached by an external stone stair. A mural stair climbs to the second floor.

The first castle was probably built by the MacSweens around 1247, and it was strengthened against the Norsemen about 1262. It was held by the MacDonald Lords of the Isles until 1493, when they were forfeited. The castle was then granted to the Forresters, but was acquired by the Campbell Earl of Argyll in 1499. It was besieged unsuccessfully by Alaisdair Colkitto MacDonald in the 1640s, but abandoned at the end of the 17th century, then being used as a farm with the demolishing of the early courtyard buildings. In 1898 the farm was removed, and the ruins consolidated.

The ruins of a 13th-century chapel Kilbrannan, dedicated to St Brendan, lie to the south-east of the castle. There are fine grave slabs.

OPEN: Access at all reasonable times.
Car parking.
Tel: 0131 668 8800 Fax: 0131 668 8888
Email: hs.explore@scotland.gov.uk Web: www.historic-scotland.gov.uk

Skirling Castle

Borders: About 2 miles north-east of Biggar, on minor road north of A72 at Skirling, at moat site.
Ruin or site NT 072398 OS: 72 * Map: 2, no: 2
Not much remains of Skirling Castle, except the moat, although it probably had a 15th-century keep within a walled courtyard.

It was a property of the Cockburns from the late 14th century until the beginning of the 18th century. Sir James Cockburn was a supporter of Mary, Queen of Scots, who visited in 1563. The castle was blown up by the Regent Moray in 1568. The site has been excavated.

Slacks Peel

Borders: About 7 miles south and west of Jedburgh, on minor road south of A6088, just west of Southdean.
Ruin or site NT 628091 [?] OS: 80 ** Map: 2, no: 244
Slacks Peel is a small ruined 16th-century tower house of three storeys of the Oliver family. The basement was not vaulted, and it probably had a courtyard with outbuildings. This is probably the same site which is recorded as Lustruther [NT 624092], believed to have been destroyed at the same time.
Other refs: Lustruther

Slaidhills Tower

Borders: About 6 miles south-west of Hawick, on minor road and foot north of A7, near Slaidhill, east of Swanstead Hill.
Ruin or site NT 425090 [?] OS: 79 * Map: 2, no: 107
Not much survives of a 16th-century tower house.

Slains Castle

Banff & Buchan: About 1 mile east of Cruden Bay, on minor roads and foot east of A975, on cliffs above sea, at Slains.
Ruin or site NK 102362 OS: 30 *** Map: 10, no: 365
The huge ruin of Slains Castle, standing on precipitous cliffs above the sea, incorporates part of the basement of the 16th-century tower house of Bowness. The castle now consists of buildings around a central courtyard, with adjoining ranges. The building was greatly altered in 1664, when a corridor was inserted within the

courtyard, and was substantially rebuilt and granite faced in 1836. There were extensive gardens.

It was built by the 9th Hay Earl of Errol after James VI had destroyed his castle at Old Slains [NK 053300], 4.5 miles south-west of Cruden Bay, after the Hays had taken part in the rebellion of 1594. Dr Johnson and Boswell visited in 1773. Bram Stoker had the inspiration for writing Dracula here, although it was not a ruin at the time as some have suggested. It was sold by the Hays in 1916, and unroofed in 1925.

The castle is in a dangerous location near cliffs, and great care should be taken, particularly with children, if it is to be visited.
Other refs: Tower of Bowness; Bowness

Slains Castle *see* Old Slains Castle

Sleismenane *see* Invergarry Castle

Smailholm Tower

Borders: About 5 miles west of Kelso, on minor road south of B6397 west of Smailholm village, car park just west of Sandyknowe.
His Scot NT 637346 OS: 74 *** Map: 2, no: 252
Smailholm Tower is a plain 15th-century tower house, rectangular in plan, of four storeys and a garret. It has a parapet on the two longer sides. The tower is roofed with stone slabs, supported on a vaulted top storey, and stood in a small walled courtyard enclosing ranges of buildings, including a chapel and kitchen.

The arched entrance to the tower leads, through a lobby, to the vaulted basement, and to a turnpike stair in one corner. The hall, on the first floor, has a fireplace and two recessed window seats.

It was a property of the Pringle family from 1408. The family had been squires of the Black Douglas family before the Douglases were overthrown by James II in 1455. David Pringle of Smailholm was killed, together with his four sons, at the

Battle of Flodden in 1513. The tower was attacked by the English in 1543, and again in 1546, when the garrison of Wark made off with 60 cattle and four prisoners. The property was sold to the Scotts of Harden in 1645, but the tower was abandoned about 1700 for nearby Sandyknowe. Walter Scott came here as a boy – as his grandfather held Sandyknowe. The tower houses an exhibition of dolls illustrating some of the Border ballads.

OPEN: Open Apr-Sep, daily 9.30-18.30; open Oct-Mar wknds only, Sat 9.30-16.30, Sun 14.40-16.30; last ticket 30 mins before closing; closed 25/26 Dec and 1/2 Jan.

Explanatory displays. Sales area. Car and coach parking. £.
Tel: 01573 460365 Fax: 0131 668 8888
Email: hs.explore@scotland.gov.uk Web: www.historic-scotland.gov.uk

Smeaton Castle

Lothians: About 2 miles north of Dalkeith and 1 mile south of Inveresk, on minor road west of A6094, on east bank of River Esk.
Private NT 347699 OS: 66 ** Map: 4, no: 142
Smeaton Castle consists of a much-altered 15th-century courtyard castle, with round corner towers, only two of which remain. One range of buildings survives, as does the curtain wall between the two towers, but little remains of the rest of the castle, except traces of a ditch. One round tower, rising to four storeys, has an adjoining square stair-tower, while the other tower has been reduced in height. The walls have been pierced by gunloops.

The surviving range has been very altered, but the basement is vaulted, as is one of the towers. The main turnpike, in the square tower, climbs to all floors.

The lands belonged to the Abbey of Dunfermline in 1450, but had passed to the Richardsons by the time of the Reformation. The buildings are now part of a farm.
Other refs: Dalkeith Home Farm; Home

Smerby *see* Island Muller Castle

Smithfield Castle

Borders: To north of Peebles, on minor road east of A703, to north-west of Ven Law.
Private NT 253412 [?] OS: 73 * Map: 2, no: 62
Site of 14th-century castle of the Hays of Smithfield in the 16th and 17th centuries, which was also held by the Dicksons. Venlaw Castle, dating from around 1782 although mostly 19th century, is built on the site, and was a property of the Elphinstones in the 19th century. It is now used as a hotel.
Other refs: Venlaw Castle

Smithston Castle

Ayrshire: About 2.5 miles north-east of Maybole, east of A77, west of River Doon, at or near Laigh Smithston.
Ruin or site NS 323123 OS: 70 * Map: 3, no: 91
Site of castle, some remains of which survived in the 19th century.

Smithwood

Lanarkshire & Glasgow: About 4 miles south of Elvanfoot, on minor roads south of A702, 0.5 miles south of Wintercleugh, at Smithwood.
Ruin or site NS 959093 OS: 78 * Map: 3, no: 427
Probable site of tower or bastle house.

Snade *see* Place of Snade

Snadon

Kincardine & Deeside: About 1 mile north-west of St Cyrus, on minor roads west of A92, at or near Snadon.
Ruin or site NO 731655 OS: 45 * Map: 10, no: 229
Site of castle or old house.

Snaid *see* Place of Snade

Snair Castle *see* Snar Castle

Snar Castle

Lanarkshire & Glasgow area: About 3 miles south and west of Crawfordjohn, on minor road and track south of B740, on the east bank of Snar Water, near Snar Farm.
Ruin or site NS 863200 OS: 71 * Map: 3, no: 400
Little remains of a 16th-century tower house and courtyard. Two vaults of the castle were still inhabited in 1813.

It was a property of the Douglases of Snar, who made their living from mining lead and gold.
Other refs: Snair Castle

Snusgar *see* Castle of Snusgar

Solwaybank *see* Auchinbetrig

Somerville House *see* Drum House

Sorbie Castle

Galloway: About 2 miles west of Garlieston, on minor road north of B7052, about 1 mile east of village of Sorbie, just north of Whitehills.
Ruin or site NX 451471 OS: 83 * Map: 1, no: 74**
Once a strong and comfortable fortress, Sorbie Castle is a ruined 16th-century L-plan tower house of three storeys and an attic. It consists of a main block and stair-wing, which rises a storey higher to be crowned in a caphouse. There is a stair-turret in the re-entrant angle. The tower had 'pepperbox' turrets, but these have gone.

The entrance, in the re-entrant angle, leads to the vaulted basement, containing cellars and the kitchen. A scale-and-platt stair climbs to the first floor, beneath which may be a pit-prison. The hall, on the first floor, has a large fireplace. The floors above were reached by a turnpike stair in the stair-turret.

The lands belonged to Whithorn Abbey, but had passed to the Hannays by 1529, or earlier, who built the castle. The family feuded with the Murrays of Broughton, and were involved in fighting between the Stewarts of Garlies, the Kennedys, and Dunbars. In 1640 John Hannay was killed in a quarrel, and in the 1670s the property was sold to the Stewarts of Garlies, Earls of Galloway. The castle was inhabited until 1748. The castle became ruined, but the remains have been consolidated for visitors by members of the Hannay clan.
Other refs: Old Place of Sorbie
OPEN: Open all year.

Sorline

Sutherland & Caithness: Just west of Helmsdale, near A9, west of River Helmsdale, just north of sea, in West Helmsdale.
Ruin or site   ND 024153   OS: 17   *   Map: 12, no: 37
Site of castle.

Sorn Castle

Ayrshire: About 3 miles east of Mauchline, on B743, just north of River Ayr, at Sorn.
Private   NS 548269   OS: 70   **   Map: 3, no: 247
Sorn Castle consists of a much-altered 14th-century keep of three storeys and an attic, which was extended in the 16th and 18th centuries, restored in the mid 19th century, then further extended when a large wing was added in the 20th century. The old part has a corbelled-out parapet with open rounds.

The 16th-century extension contains a kitchen and cellars in the basement, with a hall on the first floor, and private chambers on the floors above. The interior of the old part of the house has been greatly altered.

The lands belonged to the Keiths of Galston, but passed by marriage to the Hamiltons of Cadzow in 1406, then to the Setons of Winton. James VI visited the castle, and it was garrisoned against Covenanters in the reign of Charles II. It was sold to the Campbell Earl of Loudoun about 1680, then to the Somervilles at the end of the 18th century, and finally to the McIntyre family in 1900, who still occupy the house.
OPEN: Guided tours. By appointment only.
Disabled access to grounds.
Tel: 01505 613304   Fax: 01505 612124

Sornhill

Ayrshire: About 1.5 miles south of Galston, on minor road west of B7037, 0.5 miles south and west of hamlet of Sornhill, at Sornhill.
Ruin or site   NS 509342   OS: 70   **   Map: 3, no: 219
Sornhill is a 17th-century L-plan tower house of three storeys and a garret, with a stair tower in the re-entrant angle. The stair tower is crowned by a watch-chamber, and the gables are corbiestepped. Some of the windows are small, while others have been enlarged. The tower may incorporate older work, but there appear to be few defensive features.

The property was held by the Nisbet family, but sold to the Campbells in 1553. The building was used as a farmhouse, but is apparently now derelict.

Sorrowlessfield *see* Cowdenknowes

Sound *see* Balfour Castle

South Synton *see* Synton

Southannan Castle

Ayrshire: About 3 miles south of Largs, on minor roads east of A78, 1 mile south of Fairlie, at Southannan.
Ruin or site   NS 209538   OS: 63   **   Map: 3, no: 32
Southannan Castle or Underbank consists of the ruinous remains of a castle and courtyard with an enclosing wall. There are some remains of vaults, and the walls were pierced by shot-holes.

Southannan was long a property of the Semples, and visited by Mary, Queen of Scots, in 1563. The castle was rebuilt around the turn of the 17th century, but

dismantled towards the end of the 18th century. The property had passed to the Montgomerys of Eglinton by the 19th century.
Other refs: Underbank

Southsyde Castle

Lothians: About 3 miles south-east of Dalkeith, on minor roads north of B6372, at Southside.
Private   NT 369638 [?]   OS: 66   *   Map: 4, no: 147**
Southsyde is a 17th-century L-plan tower house, originally of four storeys, crowned with bartizans at the corners. It was altered in the mid 19th century, and there are bartizans crowning two of the corners.

The entrance is at the foot of the stair-wing. The basement of the main block is vaulted, and contained the kitchen. The hall was on the first floor of the main block.

The lands originally belonged to Newbattle Abbey, but had passed to the Ellis family by 1640. The house was partly ruinous in the 19th century, but restored and the floor levels altered. It is still occupied.

Sparrow Castle *see* Cockburnspath House

Spedlins Tower

Dumfriesshire: About 3 miles north and east of Lochmaben, on minor roads east of B7020 and west of A74, just west of the River Annan.
Private   NY 098877   OS: 78   **   Map: 1, no: 226**
Spedlins Tower is a tower house, which incorporates two vaulted storeys from a 15th century keep, although the upper storeys date from about 1602. The main block rises to three storeys, and there are two further storeys in the garret. Corbelled-out bartizans crown the corners, and the gables are corbiestepped. The walls are pierced by shot-holes.

The entrance is in the basement, but would have been at first-floor level by an external stair. The basement is vaulted, and a mural stair climbs to the first-floor hall. The vaulted hall has a fine decorated Renaissance fireplace, and windows with stone seats. There was a pit-prison, in the thickness of the walls, and there were many private chambers on the floors above.

The lands were held by the Jardines from the 12th century. The tower was abandoned for nearby Jardine Hall, a 19th-century house, but was restored in the 1970s and is still occupied.

It was reportedly haunted by the ghost of a miller, called Porteous, who had the misfortune to be imprisoned here after trying to burn down his own mill. The laird,

forgetting about his prisoner, was called away to Edinburgh and took the key to the dungeon with him. Porteous gnawed at his feet and hands before eventually dying of hunger.

His ghost is then said to have manifested itself with all sorts of activity, until contained in the dungeon by a bible. Once when the bible was removed for repair, the ghost is said to have followed the family to nearby Jardine Hall.

Spey Tower, Perth *see* Perth Castle

Spittal Castle
Inverness & Nairn: About 6 miles south-west of Inverness, on minor roads west of B862, on east side at northern tip of Loch Ness, at or near Ballindarroch.
Ruin or site NH 613393 [?] OS: 26 * Map: 9, no: 81
Site of 15th-century castle.

Spittal Tower
Borders: About 4 miles west and south of Jedburgh, on minor roads south of A698, west of Rule Water, 1 mile south-east of Denholm, at Spittal Tower.
Ruin or site NT 585175 [?] OS: 80 * Map: 2, no: 222
Site of tower house, probably of the Turnbulls, marked as 'Tour' on Blaeu's Atlas Novus map of Teviotdale.

Spott House
Lothians: About 2.5 miles south of Dunbar, on minor road south of A1, just east of Spott hamlet, at Spott House.
Private NT 679752 OS: 67 * Map: 4, no: 223
Spott House, designed by William Burn in 1830, incorporates a much-modified castle.

The property originally belonged to the Cospatrick Earls of Dunbar, but passed to the Homes. George Home of Spott was made Earl of Dunbar in 1605. David Leslie, general of the Scottish army, stayed here in 1650 before going on to defeat at the Battle of Dunbar, Cromwell – the victor – staying here afterwards. The property passed from the Homes, and was later held by the Douglases, Murray, Hays, Sprot family, and the Watts.

The parish of Spott had an unusually large number of witchcraft accusations, and reputed witches were burned, even as late as 1705, on Spott Loan.

Spottiswoode House
Borders: About 5.5 miles east of Lauder, on minor roads north of A697 or north of B6456, south of Brunta Burn, 2 miles west of Westruther, at Spottiswoode.
Private NT 603499 OS: 74 * Map: 2, no: 235
Site of tower house, on the site of which, in the 1830s, was built Spottiswoode House, although the house apparently incorporated a substantial part of the castle. The new house, an imposing pile, was designed by William Burn, but demolished in 1928.

The property was held by the Spottiswoode family from the 13th century. William Spottiswoode of Spottiswoode was killed at the Battle of Flodden in 1513. One of the family was John Spottiswoode, Archbishop of St Andrews, who crowned Charles I; while another was Sir Robert Spottiswoode, Lord President of the Court of Session, who was executed in 1646. The property had been sold to the Bells in 1620, but was bought back by the family in 1700. In 1836 the property passed by marriage to Lord John Douglas-Montagu-Scott.

Springfield *see* Bonhard House

Sprouston
Borders: About 1.5 miles north-east of Kelso, at or near B6350, south of River Tweed, at or near Sprouston.
Ruin or site NT 755352 OS: 74 * Map: 2, no: 301
Site of tower house.

Spynie Castle *see* Castle Spynie

Spynie Palace
Moray: About 2.5 miles north of Elgin, on minor roads east of A941, west of Spynie Loch, south of the Terchick Burn (Spynie Canal), at Spynie.
His Scot NJ 231658 OS: 28 ** Map: 10, no: 43**
One of the finest fortresses in Scotland, Spynie Palace consists of a massive 15th-century keep at one corner of a large courtyard, enclosed by a wall, with square corner towers. In one wall is a gatehouse, and there were ranges of buildings, including a chapel, within the courtyard walls.

The keep, David's Tower, rises six storeys to the parapet, and has very thick walls. The garret and upper works have gone, although the corbels for the parapet survive. The walls are pierced by gunloops.

There were two entrances at basement level, one from the courtyard into the basement, and one, a postern, from outside the walls, which opens onto a stair to the first floor. The courtyard entrance led to the vaulted basement, which contains a large round vaulted chamber, formerly the basement of an older tower. Also housed in the basement of David's Tower, and reached by a passageway, is a wine-cellar, which was only reached from above by a hatch from the hall.

The main entrance, on the first floor, is approached by a stair up a mound. It leads, through a lobby, to a turnpike stair in one corner, and to a guardroom in the thickness of the wall. The hall, on the first floor, was a fine chamber with a large moulded fireplace and windows with stone seats. Five vaulted chambers, one above another, are built into the thickness of one wall, although these have been rebuilt. The top floor was vaulted, but this has collapsed, and has been replaced by a modern roof of a 'unique' design.

One corner tower of five storeys survives, as does a section of curtain wall and the gatehouse, but the rest of the courtyard is ruined. The elaborate gatehouse was defended by a portcullis.

In 1200 Bishop Richard moved the cathedral of Moray to Spynie, where it stayed for 24 years. Later Bishops fortified a promontory in Spynie Loch, once a sea loch with its own port, and although the cathedral was moved back to Elgin, they kept their residence and stronghold here. Over the next two centuries they built the grandest surviving Bishop's Palace in Scotland.

The palace was probably built by Bishop Innes, just after Elgin Cathedral had been torched by Alexander Stewart, the Wolf of Badenoch. Bishop David Stewart, who died in 1475, excommunicated the Gordon Earl of Huntly, and built the great keep, David's Tower, to defend himself against retribution by Huntly. James IV visited the palace in 1493 and 1505, as did Mary, Queen of Scots in 1562. James Hepburn,

Earl of Bothwell and third husband of Mary sheltered here after defeat at the Battle of Carberry Hill in 1567, but soon fled north to Orkney and the Continent.

After the Reformation the lands were sold to the Lindsays, but the castle was subsequently used by Protestant Bishops. James VI stayed here in 1589. General Munro besieged the castle in 1640, and compelled Bishop Guthrie to surrender it, and the Bishop was imprisoned. The castle was held by Innes of Innes and Grant of Ballindalloch – who were Covenanters – against the Gordon Earl of Huntly, who besieged the palace unsuccessfully in 1645, while acting for the Marquis of Montrose. The last resident Bishop was Colin Falconer, who died here in 1686, and Bishop Hay, the last Bishop, was removed from office in 1688. The building then became ruinous, and was stripped. It passed into care of the State in 1973.

Other refs: Palace of Spynie

OPEN: Open Apr-Sep, daily 9.30-18.30; Oct-Mar wknds only, Sat 9.30-16.30, Sun 14.00-16.30; last ticket sold 30 mins before closing; closed 25/25 Dec and 1/2 Jan.

Explanatory panels. Gift shop. WC. Picnic area. Car and coach parking. £. Joint ticket with Elgin Cathedral available (£).

Tel: 01343 546358 Fax: 0131 668 8888

Email: hs.explore@scotland.gov.uk Web: www.historic-scotland.gov.uk

St Andrews Castle

Fife: In St Andrews, to the north of the town on the sea, north of the A91, west of the Cathedral.

His Scot NO 513169 OS: 59 * Map: 7, no: 132**

Standing close to the remains of the cathedral, St Andrews Castle is a ruined courtyard castle, enclosed by a wall. There was a gatehouse and towers at the corners, one of which contained a bottle dungeon dug out of the rock. Much of the castle is very ruined.

The first castle here was built by Bishop Roger, but dismantled by Robert the Bruce around 1310. It was rebuilt in 1336 by the English in support of Edward Balliol, but captured by Sir Andrew Moray in 1337, and slighted again. At the end of the 14th century Bishop Trail rebuilt the castle. Patrick Graham, the first Archbishop, was deposed and imprisoned here in 1478. Archbishop Alexander Stewart was killed at the Battle of Flodden in 1513.

Cardinal David Beaton strengthened the castle by adding two round blockhouses, now destroyed. In 1546 a band of Protestants murdered Beaton in the castle, and hung his naked body from one of the towers. Reinforced by others, including John Knox, they held the castle for a year. The besiegers tunnelled towards the walls, and the defenders countermined and captured their tunnel. Both tunnels still survive. It was only with the arrival of a French fleet that the garrison surrendered and became galley slaves, John Knox among them.

The castle was annexed to the Crown in 1587, and given to the Home Earl of Dunbar in 1606, but was restored to the new Protestant bishops in 1612. However, the castle had lost its importance, and by 1654 the town council had stone removed from the castle to repair the harbour.

The ghost of Archbishop Hamilton, who was hanged at Stirling, is said to haunt the castle.

OPEN: Open all year: Apr-Sep, daily 9.30-18.30; Oct-Mar, daily 9.30-16.30; last ticket sold 30 mins before closing; closed 25/26 Dec and 1/2 Jan.

Visitor centre with exhibition. Explanatory panels. Gift shop. WC. Disabled access and WC. Car parking nearby. Group concessions. £. Combined ticket for cathedral & castle is available (£).

Tel: 01334 477196 Fax: 0131 668 8888

Email: hs.explore@scotland.gov.uk Web: www.historic-scotland.gov.uk

St David's Castle

Fife: About 1 mile east of Inverkeithing, on minor roads south of A921, at St David's.

Ruin or site NT 148825 OS: 65 * Map: 7, no: 22

Site of castle.

St Enoch's Hall *see* Tannochside House

St Gordians *see* Kirkhope Tower

St Serf's Church, Dysart

Fife: To east of Kirkcaldy, on minor roads south of A955, north of sea, Shore Road, Dysart.

Ruin or site NT 304930 OS: 59 ** Map: 7, no: 74

Not much remains of a old church, dedicated to St Serf, except the some of the nave arcade and the fortified tower. The tower has a corbelled-out parapet and a corbiestepped caphouse.

A cave at Dysart [NT 303930] was believed to be a retreat of St Serf, and was a place of pilgrimage.

Stac a' Chaisteal

Western Isles: About 6.5 miles north of Callanish, by minor road and foot north of A858, Garenin, on coast, Lewis.

Ruin or site NB 202454 OS: 8 ** Map: 11, no: 24

A small ruinous castle or dun stands on a small inaccessible promontory northwest of Garenin. The wall survives to a height of six feet, and the entrance passageway, with lintels in place, pierces the wall.

Stac Dhomhnuill Chaim

Western Isles: About 11 miles west of Callanish, on minor roads and foot west of B8011, Mangersta, on coast, Lewis.

Ruin or site NB 002315 OS: 13 ** Map: 11, no: 19

Standing on an inaccessible promontory – due to cliff falls – and defended by the remains of a wall, this is said to be the castle-refuge of Donald Cam MacAuley, the Uig hero of the first quarter of the 17th century.

Stackel Brae *see* Castle of Stackel Brae

Stair

Ayrshire: About 3 miles south of Tarbolton, on minor road east of B730, just south of the River of Ayr at Stair.

Private NS 442239 OS: 70 * Map: 3, no: 177**

Stair is a fine 16th-century L-plan tower house of three storeys, to which has been

added later wings, which were in turn extended in the 17th century. A square tower projects at one corner, and a round tower at another. An extension of two storeys, with a round tower, dates from the late 17th century, as does a three-storey extension with another round stair-tower. The walls are pierced by shot-holes.

The entrance has been moved.

The lands belonged to the Montgomerys, but passed by marriage to Sir John Kennedy of Dunure in the 14th century, then to the Dalrymples of Stair in 1450. The Dalrymples fought against Mary, Queen of Scots, at the Battle of Langside in 1568. They had to flee Scotland in the 1660s after supporting Cromwell, but returned with William of Orange, and were made Viscounts Stair in 1690. One of the family, John Dalrymple, Master of Stair, was responsible for the Massacre of Glencoe in 1692, and made Earl of Stair in 1703.

The property passed from the family in the 18th century, but was recovered about 1826. Stair was visited several times by Robert Burns, and the house has been restored and is still occupied.

Stakeheugh Tower *see* Auchenrivock Tower

Stalker Castle *see* Castle Stalker

Stane Castle

Ayrshire: About 1 mile east of Irvine, just east of A78 at junction with B769, at
Stane Castle in outskirts of Irvine.

Ruin or site NS 338399 OS: 70 ** Map: 3, no: 103

Standing among trees, Stane Castle is a small ruined 16th-century tower house,
square in plan. It rises four storeys to a corbelled-out parapet, with open rounds at
the corners, formerly with a garret storey above.

The basement has been vaulted, and a turnpike stair, in one corner, climbed to
the upper floors.

In 1417 the lands were held by the Francis family, but passed by marriage to Montgomerys of Greenfield, who built the tower. The castle was turned into a folly in
the 1750s, when large Gothic windows were inserted. It still belongs to the Montgomery Earls of Eglinton, but was made safe by the local council when nobody
could be found to restore it.

Stanely Castle

Renfrewshire: About 1 mile south and west of Paisley, on minor roads west of
B775, in Stanely reservoir.

Ruin or site NS 464616 OS: 64 * Map: 3, no: 192**

Originally surrounded by a marsh, Stanely Castle is a ruined 15th-century keep,
now L-plan, of four storeys and formerly a garret floor within the parapet. The
entrance, in the re-entrant angle, is defended by a machiolation at parapet level.

The lands were held in the 14th century by the Dennistouns or Danieltouns, but
passed by marriage to the Maxwells of Newark, who built the present castle. Stanely was sold to the Rosses of Hawkhead in 1629, then passed by marriage to the
Boyle Earl of Glasgow around 1750. It was abandoned in the early 19th century,
and since 1837 stands in Paisley Waterworks, the basement being flooded.

Staneyhill Tower

Lothians: About 2 miles west of South Queensferry, on minor road north of
A904, about 0.3 miles south of Hopetoun House.

Ruin or site NT 092784 OS: 65 ** Map: 4, no: 39

Once a fine building, Staneyhill Tower is a ruined 17th-century L-plan tower house,
with a stair-tower in the re-entrant angle. Only the octagonal stair-tower now stands
above the vaults.

The entrance, in the stair-tower, led to a wide turnpike stair. The basement is
vaulted, and contained cellars and the kitchen, while the hall was on the first floor.

The castle belonged to the Sharps (or Shairps) of Staneyhill.

Stanhope Tower

Borders: About 3 miles south and west of Drumelzier, on minor road east of
A702, west of the Tweed, near Stanhope Burn, at or near Stanhope.

Private NT 123297 [?] OS: 72 * Map: 2, no: 16

Site of tower house, mentioned in 1645. Stanhope was a property of the Murrays,
but sold in 1767 to the Montgomerys.

Easter Stanhope, with corbiestepped gable and harled walls, dates from the 18th
century.

Other refs: Wester Stanhope; Easter Stanhope

Stanley House *see* Inchbervie Castle

Staplegordon *see* Barntalloch Tower

Stapleton Tower

Dumfriesshire: About 3 miles north-east of Annan, on minor roads north of
B6357, about 0.3 miles south of Scotsfield, at Stapleton.

Ruin or site NY 234688 OS: 85 ** Map: 1, no: 270

Stapleton Tower is a ruined 16th-century tower house of three storeys, to which
had been added a mansion, but this was demolished in the 1950s.

The basement is vaulted, and a turnpike stair, in one corner, climbed to the upper
floors.

It was a property of the Irvines, but passed to the Grahams. There was some
dispute over ownership, however, and in 1626 a Christie Irvine captured the castle
in a surprise attack.

Stenhope's *see* Stenhouse

Stenhouse

Lothians: About 2.5 miles south-west of Edinburgh Castle, on minor road south
of A71, east of Water of Leith bridge, in Stenhouse Mill Crescent.

NTS NT 215717 OS: 66 ** Map: 4, no: 72

Stenhouse is an altered 16th-century L-plan tower house, consisting of a long main
block of three storeys and a garret, with two small projecting wings.

A wide turnpike stair climbs to the first floor, while the upper floors are reached
by a narrow turnpike stair, partly within the walling. A second-floor chamber has an
ornamental 17th-century plaster ceiling.

It was a property of Patrick Ellis, a prosperous merchant of Edinburgh, who extended an existing building in 1623. It was restored from dereliction in the 1930s,
and again in the 1960s, and is now a Conservation Centre.

Other refs: Stenhope's; Saughton Mills

OPEN: View from exterior.

Stenhouse

Stirlingshire & Clackmannan: About 2 miles north of Falkirk, on minor roads
west of B902, in Stenhousemuir, near Carron Iron Works.

Ruin or site NS 879829 OS: 65 * Map: 6, no: 91

Site of a 17th-century L-plan tower house of four storeys and an attic, which was
later altered and extended, but was demolished in the 1960s.

In the 15th century the lands were held by the Watsons, but they passed to the

Bruces of Stenhouse in 1611, who built the tower in 1622. One of the family, Sir William Bruce, was active in the Jacobite Risings of 1715 and 1719, while his grandson took part in the Rising of 1745. The property passed to the Sheriffs of Carronvale in the 19th century. The house was demolished in the 1960s by the Carron Ironworks Company, and the site is now occupied by a housing estate.

Steuarthall

Stirlingshire & Clackmannan: About 2 miles east of Stirling, on minor roads north of A905 and east of A91, just north of the Bannock Burn, at Steuarthall.
Private   NS 826927   OS: 57   **   Map: 6, no: 78
Steuarthall was a 17th-century tower house, square in plan, of four storeys, to which had been added a large wing in the 18th century. A semi-circular stair-turret climbed at one corner. The building has been demolished.

The lands were a property of the Murrays of Touchadam, but sold to the Cowans early in the 17th century. The property passed by marriage to the Stirlings of Garden. The ill-fated Lady Grange was probably imprisoned here by her husband, James Erskine, to stop her disclosing his Jacobite plotting. She was moved to the Hebrides from 1732, and is believed to have died on Skye, and buried in Trumpan graveyard.

The site was completely flattened by the owner in the 1980s.
Other refs: Wester Polmaise; Stewarthall

Stevenson

Borders: About 7 miles north-west of Peebles, on minor road east of A72, east of Lyne Water, at or near Stevenson.
Private   NT 170430 [?]   OS: 72   *   Map: 2, no: 33
Site of tower house.
Other refs: Stevenston

Stevenson House

Lothians: About 2 miles east and north of Haddington, on minor roads south of A1 or east of A6093 in Haddington, south of River Tyne, at Stevenson House.
Private   NT 544748   OS: 66   **   Map: 4, no: 196
Although the house was remodelled and extended in the 18th century, it incorporates a 16th-century castle. Part of the building may date from the 13th century, when it was held by the Cistercian Nunnery in Haddington. It was destroyed in 1544, but restored in 1560.

It was a property of the Sinclairs from the 16th century or earlier, and the Sinclairs of Stevenson were patrons of the Holy Blood altar in St Mary's in Haddington. The property passed to the Dunbars in the 20th century, and the house is still occupied.

Stevenston *see* Stevenson

Stewart Castle *see* Castle Stewart

Stewart Tower

Perth & Kinross: About 1.5 miles south of Murthly, on minor road east of A9 and west of B9099, about 0.5 miles north-west of Airntully, at Stewart Tower.
Private   NO 091362   OS: 53   *   Map: 8, no: 75
Site of castle of the Stewart family, who were descended from an illegitimate son of Robert II. In 1560 the Regent Moray ordered Stewart of Airntully to destroy any idolatrous images in Dunkeld Cathedral.
Other refs: Airntully Castle

Stewarthall *see* Steuarthall

Stewarton

Dumfriesshire: About 3.5 miles east of Moniaive, on minor roads south of B729, south of Cairn Water, at or near Stewarton.
Ruin or site   NX 828883   OS: 78   *   Map: 1, no: 150
Possible site of tower house.

Stewart's Rais *see* Tower Rais

Stirches

Borders: About 1 mile north of Hawick, on minor road north of A7, just south of Stirches Mains.
Private   NT 498162   OS: 79   *   Map: 2, no: 162
Stirches or Stirkshaw consists of a much-altered and extended 16th-century tower house of the Scotts. It was sold to the Chisholms in 1650. Since 1926 it has been used as a Roman Catholic Home for Ladies, called St Andrew's Convent.

Stirling Castle

Stirlingshire & Clackmannan: In Stirling, on minor roads west of A872, south of A84, at Stirling Castle.
His Scot   NS 790940   OS: 57   ***   Map: 6, no: 70**
One of the most important and powerful castles in Scotland, Stirling Castle stands on a high rock, and consists of a courtyard castle, which dates in part from the 12th century.

The castle is entered through the 18th-century outer defences and 16th-century forework of which the Prince's Tower and the gatehouse survive, but the Elphinstone Tower has been reduced to its base. The gatehouse leads to the Lower Square, which is bordered on one side by the King's Old Building, and on another by the gable of the Great Hall.

The King's Old Building contained royal chambers over a vaulted basement, reached by a turnpike stair. The entrance, through a porch, led to the King's halls and bedchamber.

A road leads between the King's Old Buildings and the hall to the Upper Square. The Chapel Royal is built on one side of the square, as is the Great Hall, which was completed during the reign of James IV. The Hall has five fireplaces, and had a magnificent hammer-beam ceiling – which had not survived, but has been replaced. The chamber has been restored from an 18th-century barrack conversion.

Other features of interest are the kitchens, the wall walk and the nearby 'King's Knot', an ornamental garden, which once had a pleasure canal.

The earliest recorded castle at Stirling was used by Malcolm Canmore in the 11th century. Alexander I died here in 1124, as did William the Lyon in 1214. Edward I of England captured the castle in 1304 when he used – after the garrison had surrendered – a siege engine called the 'War Wolf': he wanted to see if it would have worked. William Wallace took the castle for the Scots, but it was retaken by the English until the Battle of Bannockburn in 1314 when it was surrendered.

Robert the Bruce had the castle slighted, but it was rebuilt by Edward III of England, after his victory of Halidon Hill in 1333, in support of Edward Balliol. The English garrison was besieged in 1337 by Andrew Moray, but it was not until 1342 that the Scots recovered the castle.

James I had Murdoch Duke of Albany and his sons executed at the castle in 1425, James II was born here in 1430, as was James III in 1451. James II lured the 8th Earl of Douglas to it in 1452, murdered him, and had his body tossed out of one of the windows, despite promising him safe conduct. Mary, Queen of Scots, was crowned in the old chapel in 1533, and James VI was baptised here in 1566. He also stayed here in 1617, as did Charles I in 1633, and Charles II in 1650. In 1651 the castle was besieged by Monck for Cromwell, but it surrendered after a few days because of a

mutiny in the garrison.

It was in a poor state of repair in the 18th century, but the garrison harried the Jacobites during both the 1715 and 1745 Risings, and the Jacobites besieged the castle after the Battle of Falkirk in 1746, although not very successfully. After 1745 the castle was subdivided to be used as a barracks. In 1964 the army left.

Features include the royal chapel, exhibition of life in the royal palace, introductory display, medieval kitchen display. Museum of Argyll and Sutherland Highlanders, telling the story of the regiment from 1794 to the present day, and including uniforms, silver, paintings, colours, pipe banners and commentaries.

The 'Pink Lady', the apparition of a beautiful woman, has reputedly been seen at the castle, and may be the ghost of Mary, Queen of Scots. Another story is that she is the ghost of a woman searching for her husband, who was killed when the castle was captured by Edward I of England in 1303. The 'Green Lady's' appearance is a harbinger of ill news, often associated with fire. She may have been one of the ladies of Mary, Queen of Scots, and has reportedly been seen in recent times.

There are also many reports of ghostly footsteps in more than one area of the castle. They are said to have been heard in an upstairs chamber of the Governor's Block. In 1946 and 1956 the footsteps are said to have been heard by soldiers occupying the room. The manifestations may be connected with the death of a sentry in the 1820s. Even more recently, footsteps were also reported by workmen who were renovating the Great Hall, in one case frightening a man so much he would not return to work.

OPEN: Open all year: Apr-Sep daily 9.30-17.15 (last ticket sold); Oct-Mar daily 9.30-16.15 (last ticket sold); castle closes 45 mins after last ticket sold – joint ticket with Argyll's Lodging; closed 25/26 Dec and 1/2 Jan.

Guided tours are available and can be booked in advance. Exhibition of life in the royal palace, introductory display, medieval kitchen display. Museum of the Argyll and Sutherland Highlanders. Gift shop. Restaurant. WC. Disabled access and WC. Car and coach parking. Group concessions. ££.

Tel: 01786 450000 Fax: 01786 464678
Email: hs.explore@scotland.gov.uk Web: www.historic-scotland.gov.uk

Stirling Tower *see* Edzell Castle

Stobcross

Lanarkshire & Glasgow: About 2 miles west of Glasgow Cathedral, near A814, north side of Clyde, Stobcross.
Ruin or site NS 570655 [?] OS: 64 * Map: 3, no: 257
Site of castle or old house, dating from the 17th century or earlier. The house consisted of a main block and two wings at right-angles with stair-towers in the re-entrant angles. There was a courtyard

Stobcross was a property of the Andersons in the 16th century, but passed to the Orrs of Barrowfield in 1735. The estate was encroached upon by Glasgow, the house was demolished around 1850, and there are no remains.

Stobhall

Perth & Kinross: About 7 miles north of Perth, on minor road just west of A93, 1.5 miles north of Guildtown, just east of River Tay, at Stobhall.
Private NO 132344 OS: 53 * Map: 8, no: 92**
Stobhall is a 16th-century castle, consisting of ranges of buildings, one a tower house, within a courtyard.

The entrance is through a pend, beside a 17th-century two-storey range with corbiestepped gables. A straight stair climbs to the upper floor.

The L-plan 16th-century block, in the middle of the courtyard, rises to three storeys and attic, with a two-storey tower, crowned by a conical roof, projecting from one corner. It contains a 14th-century chapel, which has a tempera painted ceiling of 1630-40. The later building is dated 1578.

Next to this is a another two-storey range of the same date, containing a laundry, brewery and bakery. A library was built on the site of early cottages in 1965.

Stobhall passed to the Drummonds by marriage in 1360, although there may have been a chapel here as early as the 12th century. It was the main Drummond stronghold until 1487, when they moved to Drummond Castle. The property was forfeited for the family's part in 1745 Jacobite Rising. It passed to the Willoughbys,

later to the Earls of Ancaster, before returning to the Drummonds. It is now the home of the present Earl of Perth.
Other refs: Stobshaw

OPEN: Gardens and chapel open 22 May-19 Jun, daily 13.00-17.00; also 24 and 31 Oct 14.00-17.00; castle not open.
WC. Partial disabled access and WC. Limited parking. £.
Tel: 01821 640332

Stobo Castle

Borders: About 2.5 miles north-east of Drumelzier, on minor roads west of B712, west of River Tweed, at Stobo Castle.
Private NT 173367 OS: 72 * Map: 2, no: 35
Site of tower house, although the present Stobo Castle, consisting of a castellated square block and round corner towers, was first built at the beginning of the 19th century, then altered in 1849 and 1907. The building is now used as a health farm.

Stobo was originally a property of the Murrays, but sold in 1767 to the Montgomerys.
Other refs: Hillhouse

Stobs Castle

Borders: About 4 miles south of Hawick, on minor road south of B6399, east of Slitrig Water, at Stobs.
Ruin or site NT 510084 [?] OS: 79 * Map: 2, no: 173
Site of castle, which was burned in 1712, and the final vestiges removed in 1797. Stobs was a property of the Cranstons from 1370 or earlier, but passed to the Elliots of Stobs, who held the property until the 20th century.

The present castellated mansion was built in 1792-3 for the Elliots, and designed by Robert Adam, although it was completed after his death.

Stobshaw *see* Stobhall

Stone Hill, Jedburgh

Borders: To north of Jedburgh, on minor roads east of A68, east of Jed Water, at Stone Hill.
Ruin or site NT 654208 OS: 74 * Map: 2, no: 267
Site of castle, the last vestige of which was removed in the 1850s, apparently a property of the Kerrs of Ferniehirst.
Other refs: Jedburgh

Stonebyres House

Lanarkshire & Glasgow area: About 2.5 miles west of Lanark, on minor roads north of B7018, south of A744, just south of Stonebyres Holdings.
Ruin or site NS 838433 [?] OS: 72 * Map: 3, no: 387
Stonebyres House incorporated an altered 14th- or 15th-century keep, to which had been added a large castellated mansion, but the whole building was demolished in the mid 20th century. The house consisted of a strong rectangular keep, with bartizans crowning the corners. The walls of the basement were pierced by gunloops. The hall was said to have been one of the finest in the country. There are apparently slight remains of the keep foundations.

Stonebyres was a property of the Weir family from as early as the 13th century until 1845, when it was sold to the Monteiths. It was remodelled and extended in 1840 and 1906-14, demolished in 1934, and only foundations remain.

Stonefield Castle

Argyll & Dunbartonshire: About 2 miles north of Tarbert, on A83, on west side of Loch Fyne, at Stonefield Castle Hotel.
Private NR 864717 OS: 62 * Map: 5, no: 70**
Stonefield Castle is a modern mansion, and was held by the Campbells at the end of the 19th century. It is now used as a hotel, and the gardens are open to the public.

OPEN: Hotel: accommodation available. Gardens open all year, dawn to dusk.
Hotel. Gardens. Parking.
Tel: 01880 820836 Fax: 01880 820929

Stonehouse Tower

Dumfriesshire: About 1 mile west of Gretna, on minor road north of A75, east of Kirtle Water, at or near Stonehouse.
Ruin or site NY 296682 [?] OS: 85 * Map: 1, no: 292
Site of tower house, nothing of which remains.

Stonelaw Tower

Lanarkshire & Glasgow: In Rutherglen, on minor roads east of A730 or west of A749, south of Greystone Avenue, off Stonelaw Road.
Ruin or site NS 619609 OS: 64 * Map: 3, no: 290
Little remains of a castle except part of the enclosing wall and a doorway with gunloops. It consisted of an L-plan tower house of four storeys, which dated from the 15th century. The tower had a corbelled-out parapet with machiolations. To the tower had been added a T-plan mansion of one storey.
  Stonelaw was a property of the Spence family, several of whom were Provosts of Rutherglen. It was last occupied in 1963, then vandalised and demolished in 1965. Part of the site is occupied by a block of flats and a petrol station.

Stoneypath Tower

Lothians: About 3.5 miles south of East Linton, on minor road south of B6370, about 0.5 miles north of Nunraw Abbey, east of the Whittinghame Water.
Ruin or site NT 596713 OS: 67 ** Map: 4, no: 208
Standing on a promontory above a river with three steep sides, Stoneypath Tower is a 16th-century L-plan tower house, which may incorporate part of a 15th-century keep. The original entrance was reached by an external stair, but this was sealed and replaced by a new entrance. The hall was on the second floor, and a turnpike stair climbed to all floors. There was a prison in the thickness of the wall.
  It was a property of the Lyles, but later held by the Hamiltons of Innerwick, the Douglases of Whittinghame, then the Setons. The tower may have been blown up at some time.

Stormont

Perthshire: About 2 miles south of Blairgowrie, on minor roads west of A923, on an island in Stormont Loch.
Ruin or site NO 190421 OS: 53 * Map: 8, no: 116
Possible site of castle or refuge, remains of which survived in 1843.

Stornoway Castle

Western Isles: In Stornoway on island of Lewis, west of A857, under ferry pier in Stornoway Harbour.
Ruin or site NB 423327 OS: 8 * Map: 11, no: 27
Site of castle of the MacLeods of Lewis, some of which remained in the 19th century.
  An early castle here, possibly dating from the 11th century, is said to have been seized from the MacNicol family by a Norsemen called Leod, from whom the MacLeods were descended. The castle was captured by the Gordon Earl of Huntly in 1506, but successfully held out against the Campbell Earl of Argyll in 1554. It was destroyed by Cromwell's forces in 1653, although the garrison of his nearby small fort are said to have been massacred by the islanders. The last vestiges of the castle were removed in 1852, and Lews Castle, a 19th-century mansion, is not built on the site.
Other refs: Castle Macnicol

Stow

Borders: About 5 miles west of Lauder, near junction of B6362 with A7, east of Gala Water, at Stow.
Ruin or site NT 460445 OS: 73 * Map: 2, no: 126
There are some remains of a 15th- or early 16th-century bishop's palace or residence, the property of the Bishop and later Archbishops of St Andrews. It was demolished at the beginning of the 19th century.
Other refs: Bishop's Palace, Stow; Stow of Wedale

Stow of Wedale *see* Stow

Stoy Castle *see* MacLeod's Castle

Strachan

Kincardine & Deeside: About 3.5 miles south-west of Banchory, south of B976 at Castle Hill, north of Water of Feugh, at motte.
Ruin or site NO 657921 OS: 45 ** Map: 10, no: 181
Strachan consisted of a castle, on a large motte defended by a ditch, and was occupied until about 1310.
  It was a property of the of the Giffords in 1200, then the Durwards.
Other refs: Castlehill of Strachan

Strachbroch *see* Strathbrock Castle

Straiton

Lothians: About 4.5 miles south of Edinburgh Castle, near A701 junction with A720, at Straiton.
Ruin or site NT 273667 [?] OS: 66 * Map: 4, no: 114
Site of hall house, granted by Lady Christian Straiton to an Alexander Frog in 1447. In 1534 David Straiton was burned for heresy on Calton Hill.

Straloch House

Aberdeen & Gordon: About 2 miles north-west of New Machar, on minor roads west of A947, at Straloch.
Private NJ 860210 OS: 38 * Map: 10, no: 292
Site of castle or old house. Straloch House is a classical mansion of two storeys and an attic, and dates from 1780.
  The lands were a property of the Cheynes, but sold to the Gordons of Pitlurg in 1600. Robert Gordon of Straloch was a map maker and historian, and another Robert, his grandson, founded Robert Gordon's College. It was sold to the Ramsays in 1758, then passed by marriage to the Irvines of Drum.
Other refs: Old House of Straloch; Strathloch

Stranraer Castle

Galloway: In Stranraer, short distance south-west of junction of A77 with A75, in centre of town.
Private NX 061608 OS: 82 * Map: 1, no: 10**
Stranraer Castle is a much-altered 16th-century L-plan tower house of three storeys within a corbelled-out parapet, and has a 17th-century storey above parapet level.
  The building has been much added to and altered internally, but the basement is vaulted, and the large hall was on the first floor.
  The castle was probably built by Adair of Kilhilt around 1511, although it may be older, but had passed to the Kennedys of Chappel by 1596, then to the Dalrymples of Stair in 1680. John Graham of Claverhouse, 'Bonnie Dundee' or 'Bloody Clavers', stayed here while suppressing Covenanters from 1682-5 as one of his duties as the Sheriff of Galloway. The ground around the castle was cleared of 19th-century buildings in the 1970s. The castle is now a museum, with exhibitions telling the history from its building, through Covenanting times, to its use as a town jail in the 19th century.
Other refs: Kennedy's Castle; Castle of St John
OPEN: Open Easter-mid Sep, Mon-Sat 10.00-13.00 and 14.00-17.00; closed Sun.
Explanatory displays and videos. Gift shop. Family activities. Parking nearby. £.
Tel: 01776 705088/705544 Fax: 01776 705835
Email: JohnPic@dumgal.gov.uk Web: www.dumfriesmuseum.demon.co.uk

Strathallan Castle

Perth & Kinross: About 2 miles north-west of Auchterarder, on minor roads east of A823 or west of B8062, just south of Machany Water, at Strathallan Castle.
Private NN 919155 OS: 58 ** Map: 8, no: 35
Strathallan Castle, a castellated mansion, incorporates some of an old stronghold, although the exterior is more modern.
  It belonged to the Drummonds, who were made Viscounts Strathallan in 1686. The 4th Viscount was mortally wounded at the Battle of Culloden in 1746, during the Jacobite Rising. The family was forfeited, but recovered their titles in 1824.

Strathaven Castle

Lanarkshire & Glasgow area: In Strathaven, just south of the A71, just east of the junction with A726.

Ruin or site NS 703445 OS: 71 ** Map: 3, no: 326

Standing on a rocky mound, Strathaven Castle consists of a ruined 15th-century keep and castle, with the remains of 16th-century square range and a round tower.

The basement of the round tower is vaulted, but the castle is very ruined.

The property was held by the Bairds, then the Sinclairs, then the Douglases. The castle was surrendered to James II, and sacked and probably destroyed following

the fall of the Black Douglases in 1455. It then passed to the Stewart Lord Avondale in 1457, who built, or rebuilt, the castle. In the 16th century it was acquired by Sir James Hamilton of Finnart, and occupied by the Hamiltons until 1717, after which it was abandoned and fell into ruin. The building has been consolidated in a less than sympathetic way.

A skeleton, sealed up in one of the walls, is said to have been found when part of the castle was demolished.

Other refs: Avondale Castle

OPEN: Access at all reasonable times.

Explanatory board. Parking nearby.

Strathblane Castle *see* Ballagan Castle

Strathbogie Castle *see* Huntly Castle

Strathbrock Castle

Lothians: About 1 mile west of Uphall, on minor road north of A899, north of the Brox Burn.

Private NT 044717 [?] OS: 65 * Map: 4, no: 22

Little or nothing remains of a 12th-century castle, possibly of the Erskines. The remains may be built into Middleton Hall, which dates from around 1700, and is now a residential home for the elderly.

Other refs: Strachbroch; East Bangour

Strathcashell

Stirling & Clackmannanshire: About 2.5 miles north-west of Balmaha, on minor roads and foot off B837, on east bank of Loch Lomond, on Strathcashell Point.

Ruin or site NS 393932 OS: 56 * Map: 6, no: 3

Possible site of castle, although it may be the remains of a hill fort.

Strathendry Castle

Fife: About 4 miles north of Cardenden, on minor road north of A911, north of the River Avon, near Strathenry House.

Private NO 226020 OS: 58 * Map: 7, no: 43**

Strathendry Castle is a rectangular keep of three storeys and an attic with a project-

ing round stair tower. A corbelled-out parapet, with open rounds at each end, crowns one side. Many windows have been enlarged, and others have been sealed. In the courtyard is a round well, and 19th-century ranges of buildings.

The original entrance is in the foot of the stair-tower, but there is also a later doorway. The basement has been vaulted, and contained the kitchen with a wide fireplace. The first and second floors have two chambers, each with moulded fireplaces.

It was a property of the Strathendry family until it passed by marriage to the Forresters of Carden and Skipinch in 1496. It was visited by Mary, Queen of Scots, then in the 1650s by Cromwell. Strathendry passed by marriage to the Douglases of Kirkness around 1700, then to the Clephanes of Carslogie in 1882. It was altered and extended by William Burn in 1824, and David Bryce in 1845. It is the home of the MacIver Society.

The young Adam Smith, later author of 'The Wealth of Nations', was kidnapped from here by a party of gypsies.

Strathloch *see* Straloch House

Strathmartine Castle

Angus & Dundee: About 4 miles north and east of Dundee, on minor roads north of A923, about 1 mile north of Bridgefoot, at or near Strathmartine Castle.

Private NO 372363 [?] OS: 54 ** Map: 8, no: 167

Site of castle. The present mansion probably dates from no earlier than 1785.

Strathmiglo Castle *see* Cairneyflappet Castle

Stravithie Castle

Fife: About 3.5 miles south of St Andrews, on minor road west of B9131, just north of Kenly Water, near Stravithie House.

Ruin or site NO 531118 [?] OS: 59 * Map: 7, no: 139

Site of castle of the Lumsdens, located in a bog, with a ditch and drawbridge, which was surrounded by trees and ornamental walks. Nothing remains.

In the 16th century the property was held by Lady Margaret Erskine of Lochleven, jailer of Mary, Queen of Scots. Lady Margaret gave the estate to Lord James Stewart, Regent Moray – her illegitimate son by James V. Moray was shot and killed at Linlithgow in 1570 by the Hamiltons. The castle was entire in 1710, but there is now no trace.

Strichen

Aberdeen & Gordon: To the north of Strichen, on minor roads east of A981 north of junction with B9093, west of Brans Bog.

Private NJ 944549 [?] OS: 30 * Map: 10, no: 336

Site of 16th-century castle, which was replaced by Strichen House [NJ 935542], a three-storey building dating from 1821.

It was a property of the Frasers, and one of the family, Alexander Fraser of Strichen, became a judge of the Court of Session in 1730. Dr Johnson and Boswell visited Strichen. This branch of the family became Lords Lovat in 1837, but the property was sold to the Bairds in 1855. Strichen House is now roofless.

Other refs: Mormond

Strom Castle

Shetland: About 8 miles north and west of Lerwick on Shetland, on minor road and boat east of A971, on island, Castle Holm, in Loch Strom.

Ruin or site HU 395475 OS: 2 * Map: 11, no: 59

Not much remains of a castle on an islet, except part of a wall. It formerly had a causeway, and dated from the 12th century.

It was a property of the Sinclairs.

Other refs: Loch Strom Castle; Castle of Strom

Strome Castle

Ross & Cromarty: About 4 miles south-west of Lochcarron, on minor road south of A896, south of Stromemore, on north bank of Loch Carron, at Strome.

NTS NG 862354 OS: 24 ** Map: 9, no: 32

On a rock by the sea, Strome Castle is a very ruined 15th-century keep and courtyard, although it has also been described as a hall house. Part of the courtyard wall

stands to some height, but little remains of the keep, except a mound.

It was built by the Camerons of Lochiel or the MacDonald Lord of the Isles, and existed before 1472. It was besieged and captured in 1503 by the Gordon Earl of Huntly, who was granted the property in 1546. It passed to the MacDonalds of Glengarry. It was besieged, sacked and blown-up with gunpowder in 1602, after a long siege, by Kenneth Mackenzie of Kintail.

The castle is in the 'care' of The National Trust for Scotland, although more could be done to present the remains. (There is no ferry at Strome Ferry.)

OPEN: Access at all reasonable times.

Parking nearby.

Stronmilchan

Argyll & Dunbartonshire: About 1 mile north-west of Dalmally, north of B8077, at or near Stronmilchan.

Ruin or site NN 153278 OS: 50 * Map: 5, no: 118

Site of castle, which has a moat and drawbridge. It was a property of the MacGregors of Glenstrae. The last remains were apparently demolished early in the 19th century.

This may also have been known as Tigh Mor, or this may refer to another building close by [NN 154288]. The MacGregors also had a castle in Glenstrae [NN 138296].

Other refs: Bothan na Dige, Stronmilchan; Tigh Mor, Stronmilchan

Struie Castle

Perth & Kinross: About 7.5 miles south of Perth, on minor roads 4 miles south of B935 or 3.5 miles west of B995, just south of Pathstruie, at Mains of Struie.

Ruin or site NO 079114 OS: 58 * Map: 8, no: 69

Not much remains of a 17th-century castle, except a stair turret with a shot-hole.

Struthers Castle

Fife: About 4 miles south of Cupar, on minor road west of the A916, about 1 mile south of Craigrothie, at Struthers.

Ruin or site NO 377097 OS: 59 ** Map: 7, no: 102

Struthers Castle is a ruined 16th-century L-plan tower house of four storeys, which probably incorporates earlier work, but much altered in the 18th century with the insertion of large windows. The castle had a large park of some 200 acres, enclosed by a stone wall.

It was originally a property of the Keiths, but exchanged for Dunnottar in 1392. Struthers became the main stronghold of the Lindsays of The Byres, who later succeeded to the Earldom of Crawford. Mary, Queen of Scots, visited Struthers in 1565. Charles II stayed at the castle in 1651, and it was occupied by Cromwell's forces in 1653.

Stuart Castle *see* Castle Stuart

Sundaywell Tower

Dumfriesshire: About 5 miles south-east of Moniaive, on minor road 4 miles west of Dunscore on the B729, north of the Glenesslin Burn, just south of Bogrie.

Ruin or site NX 811845 OS: 78 ** Map: 1, no: 137

The remains of a 17th-century tower house, square in plan, are built into a modern farmhouse. There is a stone, dated 1651, set over the doorway.

It was a property of the Kirk or Kirko family, and a place of refuge for Covenanters.

Sunderland Hall

Borders: About 2 miles north of Selkirk, on minor roads east of A707, near meeting of River Tweed with Ettrick Water, at Sunderland Hall.

Private NT 479319 OS: 73 * Map: 2, no: 144

Sunderland Hall, built in 1850 and designed by David Bryce, incorporates or is built on the site of an old house or stronghold. The house, a castellated mansion, was enlarged in 1885, and is still occupied.

Sundrum Castle

Ayrshire: About 4.5 miles east of Ayr, on minor roads north of A70, about 1 mile north of Colyton, just south of the Water of Coyle.

Private NS 410213 OS: 70 ** Map: 3, no: 153

Sundrum Castle, a Georgian mansion of 1793, incorporates a much-altered 14th-century keep, with ten-feet thick walls. The keep rose to at least three storeys, and the basement was vaulted, as was the third floor. A straight stair led from the hall on the first floor to the basement, and the entrance was probably at first-floor level.

It was a property of the Wallaces of Sundrum from 1373 or earlier, but passed to the Cathcarts, then to the Hamiltons by 1750. It was used as a hotel, but was later divided, and bungalows built in the grounds.

The old part of the building, particularly the vaulted dining room, was reputedly haunted by a 'Green Lady', said to have been the wife of one of the Hamilton lairds. The disturbances have apparently stopped since the building was renovated.

Sunlaws House

Borders: About 3 miles south and west of Kelso, on minor roads west of A698, east of River Teviot, 0.5 miles south-west of Heiton, at Sunlaws House.

Private NT 705295 OS: 74 ** Map: 2, no: 288

Situated in 200 acres of gardens and wooded park land, Sunlaws House – which is now known as Roxburghe House – dates mostly from 1853 after the previous house was destroyed by fire. This old house may have dated from the 15th century. It was a property of the Kerrs of Chatto, and Bonnie Prince Charlie was entertained here in November 1745. The house was used to hold German prisoners of war during World War II, acquired by the Duke of Roxburghe in 1969, and is now an exclusive hotel.

The building is said to be haunted by the apparition of a woman, a 'Green Lady', seen late at night crossing the entrance hall of the house from the stair, through the lounge and conservatory up to the Chinese bridge. The story goes that she is searching for her baby, but there is no clue to her identity.

Another ghost is reputedly that of a soldier, possibly one of those imprisoned here during the war, which has been witnessed on the top floor of the house. This floor is currently only used as storage space.

The administration offices, housed in the old laundry in the oldest part of the building, are also said to be haunted.

Other refs: Roxburghe House

OPEN: Hotel - open all year.

22 bedrooms. Restaurant. Conferences and wedding receptions. Championship golf course, fishing and other sports facilities. Parking.

Tel: 01573 450331 Fax: 01573 450611

Sween Castle *see* Castle Sween

Swiney Castle

Sutherland & Caithness: About 5.5 miles north-east of Dunbeath, on minor road south of A9 at Swiney, 0.5 miles north of the sea, at or near Swiney.
Ruin or site   ND 232345 [?]   OS: 11   *   Map: 12, no: 55
Site of castle, a property of the Sutherlands of Forse.
  Swiney House, a mansion with a central stair-tower, dates from about 1730 and replaced the castle. It was restored in 1992, and is still occupied.
Other refs: Achastle

Swinlees

Ayrshire: About 2 miles north of Dalry, just east of B784, west of Pitcon Burn, at or near Swinlees.
Ruin or site   NS 295527 [?]   OS: 63   *   Map: 3, no: 72
Site of castle, although the location may be approximate.
Other refs: Sersly

Swinton

Borders: About 4.5 miles north of Coldstream, on minor roads north of B6461, 1 mile west of village of Swinton, north of Leet Water, at or near Swinton House.
Private   NT 819471 [?]   OS: 74   *   Map: 2, no: 334
Site of castle or old house, which was burned in 1797, and replaced by Swinton House, a two-storey classical mansion.
  The lands were held by the Swinton family, from the time of Malcolm Canmore in the 11th century, after having cleared the area of wild boar or swine, hence their family name. Sir John Swinton was one of those responsible for winning the Battle of Otterburn in 1388, although he was killed fighting the English at the Battle of Homildon Hill in 1402. Sir John, his son, slew the Duke of Clarence, the brother of Henry V, at the Battle of Bauge in 1421, but was himself slain at the Battle of Verneuil three years later. By the 19th century the property had passed to the Mac-Nabs.

Syde Tower

Borders: About 0.5 miles south of Newcastleton, near B6357, on west side of Liddel Water, north-west of Mangerton.
Ruin or site   NY 473865 [?]   OS: 79   *   Map: 2, no: 139
Site of tower house of the Armstrongs. This may have been the tower of Jock o' the Side, a character in old Border ballads. There was also a hamlet here, but all traces have apparently gone.
Other refs: Side

Sydserf

Lothians: About 2 miles south of North Berwick, on minor road just south of B1347, south and west of Fenton Tower, at Sydserf.
Private   NT 542818   OS: 66   **   Map: 4, no: 194
Sydserf consists of a much-altered L-plan house, now of two storeys, probably dating from the 17th century. The basement is not vaulted, the roof has been altered and the house probably lowered, but there are two shot-holes in one wall. The house now forms part of a farm.
  Sydserf was a property of the Sydserf family in 1600

Synniness *see* Sinniness Castle

Synton

Borders: About 4 miles south of Selkirk, on minor roads east of A7, south of Ale Water, 1 mile east of Ashkirk, at Synton.
Ruin or site   NT 487223   OS: 73   *   Map: 2, no: 149
Site of 16th century tower house of the Scotts, incorporated or demolished when Synton House was built in the 18th century.
Other refs: South Synton

T

Tain Castle

Ross & Cromarty: In Tain, near B9174, probably at Railway Hotel.
Ruin or site   NH 781281 [?]   OS: 21   *   Map: 9, no: 122
Site of 16th-century castle, the last vestige of which was removed in 1820. There is said to have been a tunnel from the castle to the collegiate church.
  Tain was a place of pilgrimage in medieval times to the chapel of St Duthac, and was visited by James IV and James V.
  Elizabeth de Burgh and other womenfolk of Robert the Bruce were seized here in 1306 by the Earl of Ross and delivered into the hands of Edward I of England. In 1427 MacNeil of Creich burned Mowat of Freswick and his men in the chapel.

Talla

Borders: About 2.5 miles south and east of Tweedsmuir, on minor road south of A701, east side of Talla Reservoir, at or near Talla Shiels.
Ruin or site   NT 124214   OS: 72   *   Map: 2, no: 17
Possible site of castle.

Talla Castle *see* Inchtalla Castle

Tangy Loch

Argyll & Dunbartonshire: About 4.5 miles north-west of Campbeltown, on minor roads, foot and boat north of A83, on island in Tangy Loch.
Ruin or site   NR 695279   OS: 68   *   Map: 5, no: 31
Site of a castle or fortified house, formerly reached by a causeway. The level of the loch has been raised, but there are some remains of two buildings.
  It was a property of the Bishops of the Isles, but granted to the Campbells in 1576, and the MacEachan family are said to have lived here in the 17th century.
  Tangy Mill [NR 662277], an early 19th-century mill used until 1961, is in good condition.

Tankerness House, Kirkwall

Orkney: Broad Street, Kirkwall, Orkney
Private   HY 446109   OS: 6   *   Map: 11, no: 47**
One of the finest town houses in Scotland, this 16th-century building with courtyard and gardens now houses the Museum of Orkney, which covers the islands' archaeology and history.
  The house was built as a deanery for the nearby cathedral, and is dated 1574. It passed to the Baikies of Tankerness in the 17th century, who were successful merchants in Kirkwall. Arthur Baikie was Provost of the town.
OPEN: Open all year: Oct-Apr, Mon-Sat 10.30-12.30 & 13.30-17.00; May-Sep, Mon-Sat 10.30-17.00, also Sun 14.00-17.00.
Guided tours by arrangement. Explanatory displays. Gift shop. Garden. WC. Disabled access. Parking nearby.
Tel: 01856 873191   Fax: 01856 874616

Tanlawhill Tower

Dumfriesshire: About 9 miles north-west of Langholm, on minor roads south of B709, south of Black Esk, south of Tanlawhill.
Ruin or site   NY 237910   OS: 79   *   Map: 1, no: 271
Very little remains of a tower house and outbuildings. There is a stone dated 1659 built into the later farm, and there were remains in the 18th century.
  It was a property of the Beatties of Tanlawhill at the end of the 16th century.

Tannochside House

Lanarkshire & Glasgow: About 2 miles south of Coatbridge, on minor roads east of A752 or north of A721, south of North Calder Water, Viewpark.

Ruin or site NS 716620 OS: 64 * Map: 3, no: 331

Site of castle or old house, which dated from the beginning of the 17th century. The mansion was a property of the Hosier family in about 1840, but demolished around 1950 and the site is occupied by housing.

Other refs: St Enoch's Hall

Tantallon Castle

Lothians: About 3 miles east of North Berwick, north on minor road from A198, on cliffs on southern shore of Firth of Forth.

His Scot NT 596851 OS: 67 ** Map: 4, no: 209**

One of the most impressive castles in southern Scotland, Tantallon Castle is a large and once strong 14th-century courtyard castle. It consists of a massively thick 50-foot-high curtain wall, blocking off a high promontory, the sea and the height of the cliffs defending the three other sides. In front of the wall is a deep ditch, and at each end are ruined towers: one round, one D-shaped. The shell of a massive keep-gatehouse stands at the middle of the wall, and rises to six storeys. Within the castle walls are the remains of a range of buildings, which contained a hall and private chambers. There is also a deep well, and the foundations of a sea gate.

Further earthworks form the outer bailey, which has a small stone gatehouse and a 17th-century doocot. A ravelin, a triangular artillery earthwork, was constructed beyond the outer bailey.

The castle was built by William Douglas, 1st Earl of Douglas, about 1350. William waylaid and slew his godfather, another William Douglas, the infamous 'Knight of Liddesdale', and secured his position as the most powerful lord in the Borders.

George Douglas, his son, became the 1st Earl of Angus, the first of the 'Red Douglases', and married Mary, second daughter of Robert II. He was captured at the Battle of Homildon Hill in 1402, and died the next year. James, the 3rd Earl, used Tantallon to pursue a vendetta against the rival branch of the family the 'Black

Douglases'. His brother, George, later 4th Earl, and James II's army routed Black Douglas forces at Arkinholm in 1455, and he was rewarded with the lordship of Douglas. He died in 1463.

Archibald, the 5th Earl, better known as 'Bell-the-Cat', hanged James III's favourites, including Cochrane, from the bridge at Lauder. He entered into a treasonable pact with Henry VII of England, which led to James IV besieging Tantallon. In 1513 Archibald died, and his two sons were killed at the Battle of Flodden the same year.

His grandson, another Archibald, succeeded as the 6th Earl of Angus. In 1514 he married Margaret Tudor, widow of James IV and sister of Henry VIII. In 1528, after many dubious ventures, Archibald had to flee, and James V besieged Tantallon with artillery. After 20 days the King was forced to abandon the attack. Douglas retired to England, and the castle passed into the hands of the king. When James V died in 1542, Angus returned, and again took possession of Tantallon. By 1543 England and Scotland were at war, and Archibald offered to surrender the castle to the English. However, during the invasion, the English desecrated the Douglas tombs at Melrose Abbey, and Archibald changed sides and led the Scots to victory at the Battle of Ancrum Moor in 1545. He also led the Scots, along with the Earl of Hamilton, to defeat at the much more decisive Battle of Pinkie in 1547. Cannons at Tantallon took part in a naval battle between an English and French fleet. Archibald died at the castle in 1556 .

Mary, Queen of Scots, visited in 1566. Archibald, the 8th Earl, entered into more treasonable negotiations with the English, and had to go into exile in 1581. He died in England in 1588, as a result – it was said – of a spell cast by Agnes Simpson, who was later condemned as a witch and burned. The 9th Earl died in 1591, and the 10th Earl, William, was a staunch Catholic, who was also forced into exile to die in France in 1611. His son, William, the 11th Earl also became Marquis of Douglas. Tantallon was seized by Covenanters in 1639.

In 1650 moss troopers, based at the castle, did so much damage to Cromwell's lines of communication that in 1651 he sent an army to attack the castle. The bombardment lasted 12 days and destroyed so much of the castle that the garrison surrendered.

The castle was then abandoned as a fortress and residence, and the property sold to the Dalrymples in 1699. It was taken into the care of the State in 1924.

OPEN: Open Apr-Sep, daily 9.30-18.30; Oct-Mar, Mon-Wed and Fri 9.30-16.30, Thu 9.30-12.00, Sun 14.00-16.30, closed Fri; ; last ticket 30 mins before closing; closed 25/26 Dec and 1/2 Jan.

Short walk to castle. Explanatory boards and exhibitions. Gift shop. WC. Limited disabled access. Car and coach parking. £.

Tel: 01620 892727   Fax: 0131 668 8888

Email: hs.explore@scotland.gov.uk   Web: www.historic-scotland.gov.uk

Tarbat Castle *see* Ballone Castle

Tarbat House

Ross & Cromarty: About 7.5 miles north-east of Alness on minor roads south of B817, north of shore of Nigg Bay, south of Milton, just north and east of Tarbat House.

Ruin or site NH 772737 [?] OS: 21 ** Map: 9, no: 119

Site of a house, built in the mid 17th century, once a stately, turreted edifice, which in turn stood near the site of a castle. It was replaced by nearby Tarbat House [NH 770736], a classical mansion of 1787.

The castle was built by the Munros, but sacked in 1745 by Jacobites, as the Munros fought against Bonnie Prince Charlie. It passed to the Mackenzie Viscounts Tarbat and Earls of Cromartie. The present house was occupied until the 1960s, but has been burned out and is a shell. Some consolidation work has been carried out.

Other refs: Milnton; Old Tarbat House

Tarbert Castle

Argyll & Dunbartonshire: To east of Tarbert, on minor road and foot opposite the Fish Quay south of A8015, south of East Loch Tarbert, in Knapdale, at Tarbert Castle.

Ruin or site NR 867687 OS: 62 ** Map: 5, no: 71

Tarbert Castle is a ruined 13th-century royal castle of enclosure, which was extended in the 14th century, by the addition of an outer bailey with towers. In the 16th century a tower house was built within the walls, but this is also ruinous. There were said to be two other castles near Tarbert: one at the head of West Loch Tarbert; and the other at the centre of the isthmus.

There was a stronghold here of the Dalriadan Scots, which was taken and torched at least once. Around 1098 Magnus Barelegs, King of Norway, had his longship taken across the isthmus here to symbolise his possession of the Isles and of the peninsula of Kintyre. Robert the Bruce strengthened the castle, and James IV extended it again, after capturing it from the MacDonalds, during his campaign to destroy the power of the Lord of the Isles. Walter Campbell of Skipness seized it from its hereditary keeper, the Campbell Earl of Argyll, in 1685 during a rebellion by Argyll. Beware of adders!

OPEN: Access by footpath beside old police station, opposite Fish Quay.

Parking in Tarbert.

Tarbert Castle – see previous page

Tarbert Castle *see* **Tarbet Castle**

Tarbet Castle

Argyll & Dunbartonshire: At Tarbet, north of junction of A82 and A83, at the north end of Loch Lomond.
Ruin or site   NN 320047 [?]   OS: 56   *   Map: 5, no: 132
Site of 14th-century castle, also known as Claddach Castle, which may be occupied by the manse.

It is said to have been built by Robert the Bruce, and it was a property of the MacFarlanes, becoming their seat along with Eilean Vhow after the destruction of Inveruglas in the middle of the 17th century. The MacFarlanes moved to a new house at Arrochar in 1697.

Another site has been given as Tarbet Island [NN 329055], and although there are remains on the island, this is believed not to have been a stronghold.
Other refs: Claddach Castle

Tarbet Castle

Ayrshire: About 1 mile south-east of West Kilbride, on minor roads east of B7047, south-west of Tarbert Hill, near Meadowhead.
Ruin or site   NS 215470 [?]   OS: 63   *   Map: 3, no: 38
Site of 15th-century castle, nothing of which remains.

It was a property of the Rosses of Tarbet. It was demolished about 1790, materials being used to build Meadowhead, and has been previously described as 'an old ruinous keep, with narrow, thick walls and small slits for windows'.
Other refs: Tarbert Castle

Tarbolton Motte

Ayrshire: About 4.5 miles east of Prestwick, just north of B744, south of Water of Fail, north side of Tarbolton.
Ruin or site   NS 432273   OS: 70   *   Map: 3, no: 171
The remains of a motte and bailey castle consists of a reduced mound with a larger bailey which was defended by a ditch.

Tarbolton was a property of Gilbert, son of Richard de Boyville, in the 12th century, and in 1671 was granted to the Cunninghams of Enterkine.

Tarbrax Castle *see* **Torbrex Castle**

Taringzean Castle *see* **Terringzean Castle**

Tarradale Castle

Ross & Cromarty: About 2.5 miles north-east of Beauly, on minor roads south of A832, on north shore of mouth of River Beauly, at or near Tarradale House.
Ruin or site   NH 553488   OS: 26   *   Map: 9, no: 67
Site of 13th-century castle of the Comyns. It was captured, probably from the English, by Robert the Bruce in 1308. It may then have been destroyed and never reused. The present Tarradale House is a field studies centre for Aberdeen University.

Tartraven Castle

Lothians: About 3 miles south of Linlithgow, on minor roads between A803 and A89 about 1.5 miles east of Cairnpapple Hill, at or near Mid Tartraven.
Ruin or site   NT 005726   OS: 65   *   Map: 4, no: 13
Site of castle, a vestige of which remains in the 19th century. It is believed to have been held by the Ross family in the mid 17th century.
Other refs: Tortrium

Tarvit Castle *see* **Scotstarvit Tower**

Taymouth Castle

Perth & Kinross: About 5 miles west of Aberfeldy, on minor roads north of A827 or south of B846, 1 mile north-east of Kenmore, just south of River Tay, at Taymouth.
Private   NN 785466   OS: 52   *   Map: 8, no: 14
Taymouth Castle, a large mansion built between 1801 and 1842, incorporates cellars from an altered and extended 16th-century Z-plan tower house, built by Sir Colin Campbell of Glenorchy around 1580.

It was a property of the Campbells, who were made Earls of Breadalbane in 1681, then Marquises in 1831. The existing mansion was built between 1801-42, but by 1920 had become a hotel, and in the 1980s was being used as a school for the children of Americans in Europe, although it is now empty. The castle and estate were put up for sale in 1997 for offers over £5,500,000.

The castle is reputedly haunted, and ghostly footsteps have been heard here.
Other refs: Balloch Castle; Castle of Balloch

Tayport Castle

Fife: To west of Tayport, near B945.
Ruin or site   NO 457291   OS: 59   *   Map: 7, no: 121
Nothing remains of a strong 15th-century castle, which had been completely demolished by 1855. It consisted of a main block with round towers at opposite corners. There were two cellars in the main block, a round chamber in one tower, and two rooms in the other.

The property was held by the Melvilles, but by 1599 had passed to the Duries, and was later acquired by the Douglases of Glenbervie.

Ferryport-on-Craig was the old name of the town which was changed to Tayport in 1824 when the North British Railway Company purchased the right to the ferry.
Other refs: Ferryport-on-Craig Castle; Castle Tayport

Tealing House

Angus & Dundee: About 5 miles north of Dundee, on minor roads west of A929 just north of Balmuir, to south-west of village of Tealing.
Private   NO 413380   OS: 54   **   Map: 8, no: 181
Tealing House, an altered 17th-century mansion remodelled by William Burn, may be built on the site of a castle, although it may have been nearby [NO 408308] as there is a hill known as Castle Hill.

Nearby is the fine 16th-century doocot [NO 412381], and there is also the remains of an Iron Age souterrain.

It was originally a property of the Fotheringhams.
Other refs: Castle Hill, Tealing
OPEN: Doocot and souterrain: access at all reasonable times.
Tel: 0131 668 8800   Fax: 0131 668 8888

Temple Preceptory

Lothians: About 3 miles south-west of Gorebridge, on minor roads south of B6372, near River South Esk, at or near Temple.
Ruin or site   NT 315588 [?]   OS: 66   ***   Map: 4, no: 130
Temple Preceptory was the main seat in Scotland of the Knights Templar. They were founded to protect pilgrims in the Holy Land, but became very powerful throughout Europe, and their order was suppressed in 1312. The property was given to the Order of St John, who had their base at Torphichen Preceptory. Little or nothing of the Preceptory remains, except the ruined parish church, dating at

least from the mid 14th century, which may incorporate, or be built on the site of, the Templar church. The church was repaired in the 1980s, and stands in an interesting burial ground.

Other refs: Balantradoch

OPEN: Access at all reasonable times.

Templehouse

Ayrshire: About 3 miles east of Prestwick, on minor roads north of B743, north of Mossblown, at or near Drumley House.

Ruin or site   NS 405253   OS: 70   *   Map: 3, no: 147

Site of castle or old house, occupied by a Marion Sawers in 1591.

Tenandry House *see* Greenlaw Castle

Terpersie Castle

Aberdeen & Gordon: About 3.5 miles north-west of Alford, on minor roads north of A944, south of Correen Hills, just north of the Backlatch Burn, at Terpersie.

Private   NJ 547202   OS: 37   *   Map: 10, no: 133**

Terpersie Castle is late 16th-century Z-plan tower house of three storeys and a garret. It consists of a main block with round towers projecting at opposite corners. The walls are pierced by shot-holes. A stair-turret is corbelled out above first-floor level in one re-entrant angle. The castle is dated 1581 (or 1561?).

The entrance leads to the original kitchen in the basement. Small octagonally vaulted chambers occupy the foot of each tower. A straight stair, in the walls, climbs to the first floor, while the upper floors are reached by the turret stair. A 17th-century addition contains a wider turnpike stair. The hall is on the first floor, and there have been private chambers in the towers and on the floors above.

The tower was built by William Gordon, 4th son of Gordon of Lesmoir. He fought at the Battle of Corrichie, when the Gordons were defeated in 1562, but in 1572 was at the Battle of Tillyangus, and killed the champion of the Forbes clan, Black Arthur. He also fought in the Battle of Craibstone and Battle of Brechin.

The castle was torched in 1645 by Covenanters following the Battle of Auldearn. George Gordon of Terpersie was involved in the murder of Alexander Clerihew of Dubston in 1707. One of the lairds fought at Culloden in 1746 during the Jacobite Rising, and after the defeat hid in the castle. However, his children unwittingly recognised and betrayed him, and he was executed and the family forfeited. The castle was used as a farmhouse, but ruinous by 1885. It was restored in the 1980s.

Other refs: Dalpersie Castle

Terregles *see* Penicuik Tower

Terregles Castle

Dumfriesshire: About 3.5 miles west of Dumfries, on minor roads west of A76 or north of A75, at or near Terregles.

Ruin or site   NX 928775   OS: 84   *   Map: 1, no: 179

Site of castle, on the site of which a mansion was built about 1789.

The property was held by the Herries family from the 13th century, who were made Lord Herries in 1489. Andrew, the 2nd Lord, was killed at the Battle of Flodden in 1513, and in 1543 the male line died out, and the property passed by marriage to the Maxwells in 1547. Mary, Queen of Scots, stayed here for a few days in 1568 before travelling on to Dundrennan Abbey and England after being defeated at the Battle of Langside. The castle may have been destroyed soon afterwards, because of the Maxwell's support for Mary, although mementoes of Mary's visit were kept at the later house.

The family became Earls of Nithsdale in 1667 after another branch of the family died out. The Maxwells were forfeited in 1716 for their part in the Jacobite Rising, after defeat at the Battle of Preston, and the 5th Earl only escaped execution when his wife had a Mrs Mills swap places with him, allowing him to flee from the Tower of London, dressed as a woman. The couple fled to the Continent, then to Rome, where the Countess became governess to Henry Benedict, younger brother of Bonnie Prince Charlie.

The burial vault or choir of the 4th Lord Herries, built in 1583, survives in the nearby parish church.

Other refs: Torregills Castle

Terringzean Castle

Ayrshire: About 1 mile west of Cumnock, on minor road and foot north of A70, just west of the Lugar Water, about 1 mile south of Auchinleck.

Ruin or site   NS 556205   OS: 71   **   Map: 3, no: 250

Not much remains of a 14th-century keep and courtyard with a ditch except the remains of an octagonal tower.

It was held by the Loudoun family, but later a property of the Crawfords.

Other refs: Taringzean Castle

Tertowie House

Aberdeen & Gordon: About 2 miles north of Westhill, on minor roads north or west of B979, at or near Tertowie House.

Private   NJ 822102 [?]   OS: 38   *   Map: 10, no: 275

Site of castle or old house. Tertowie House is a baronial mansion, dating from 1867 and extended in 1905, but incorporating parts of an earlier building. It is now used as student accommodation.

Thainstone House

Aberdeen & Gordon: About 2 miles south of Inverurie, on minor roads west of A96 or east of B993, Thainstone.

Private   NJ 759186   OS: 38   *   Map: 10, no: 242

Possible site of castle.

Set in acres of meadow land, Thainstone House, a classical mansion which dates from the 18th century, was extended in 1840 by the architect Archibald Simpson and again in 1992. An older house here was sacked by Jacobites in 1745, and home to James Wilson, who signed the American Declaration of Independence, and Sir Andrew Mitchell, who was ambassador to the Court of Prussia in the time of Frederick the Great.

The building is said to be haunted by a 'Green Lady', daughter of a former owner of the house. She was killed in a riding accident, and sightings of her apparition describe her as wearing a green cloak. Manifestations reported include objects moving by themselves, and pets will not enter one of the bedrooms.

OPEN: Hotel – open all year.

48 bedrooms. Restaurant and bar. Conferences, meetings and seminars. Country club with swimming pool, jacuzzi, and sports. Parking.

Tel: 01467 621643   Fax: 01467 625084

Email: info@thainstone.macdonald-hotels.co.uk

Web: www.macdonaldhotels.co.uk

Thanes Castle *see* Tinnis Castle

The Ard, Port Ellen

Argyll & Dunbartonshire: South of Port Ellen, on minor roads and foot south of A846, on coast, The Ard, Islay.

Ruin or site   NR 365447   OS: 60   *   Map: 5, no: 8

Little survives of ruins on a fortified knoll, possibly the remains of either a castle or a dun.

The Bass *see* Bass Rock

The Binns

Lothians: About 3 miles east and north of Linlithgow, on minor road north of A904, west of B9109, at The Binns.

NTS   NT 051785   OS: 65   **   Map: 4, no: 27

The Binns was built between 1612 and 1630, with additions later in the 17th century, in the 1740s, and the 1820s. It has fine plaster ceilings from the 17th century; and stands on the site of a 15th-century castle.

It was a property of the Livingstones of Kilsyth, but sold to the Dalziels in 1612. General Tom Dalyell of The Binns was taken prisoner in 1651 at the Battle of Worcester – when an army under Charles II was defeated by Cromwell – but escaped from the Tower of London, and joined the Royalist rising of 1654. He went into exile when the rising collapsed, and served in the Russian army with the Tsar's cossacks, when he is reputed to have roasted prisoners. Returning after the Restoration, Dalziel was made commander of forces in Scotland from 1666 to 1685. He led the force that defeated the Covenanters at the Battle of Rullion Green in 1666. Musket ball are said to have bounced off Tam.

The house was presented to The National Trust for Scotland in 1944. Collections of portraits, furniture and china. Grounds.

The house and grounds are reputedly haunted by the ghost of Tam Dalyell, which is said to sometimes be seen on a white horse riding up to the castle. Another ghost, said to haunt the grounds, is that of an old man gathering firewood.

Other refs: Binns, The; House of The Binns

OPEN: Open May-Sep, daily except Fri 13.30-17.30; last admission 17.00. Parkland open all year: Apr-Oct, daily 9.30-19.00; Nov-Mar, daily 9.30-16.00; last admission 30 mins before closing.

Collections of portraits, furniture and china. Guided tours. Explanatory displays. WC. Park land. Disabled access to ground floor and grounds and WC. Car parking. ££.

Tel: 01506 834255 Email: information@nts.org.uk Web: nts.org.uk

The Blair *see* Blairlogie Castle

The Byres *see* Byres

The Chapel, Wemyss *see* West Wemyss

The Drum *see* Drum House

The Hirsel

Borders: About 1 mile north of Coldstream, on minor roads from A697, north of the River Tweed, west of the Leet Water.

Private NT 829407 OS: 74 * Map: 2, no: 338

The Hirsel, a 19th-century mansion of the Earl of Home, includes work from the 16th century and possibly earlier.

The Homes moved here after their castle of Hume was destroyed by Cromwell's forces in 1650. The house was greatly altered and enlarged several times in the 19th century, by William Burn about 1815, and David Bryce about 1858, and is still owned by the Earl of Home.

While the house is closed to the public, the garden is open and there is a museum and craft shop

Other refs: Hirsel, The

OPEN: House not open. Gardens and craft workshops open all year daylight hours; museum and craft centre Mon-Fri 10.00-17.00, wknds 12.00-17.00.

Woodland walks. Gift shop. Craft centre. Tearooms. Picnic areas. Play area. WC. Partial disabled access and WC. Car and coach parking. Parties please book. £ (parking).

Tel: 01890 882965/834 Fax: 01890 882834

The Inch *see* Inch House

The Lee

Lanarkshire & Glasgow area: About 2.5 miles north-west of Lanark, on minor roads south of A73, north of the Auchenglen Burn, at Lee Castle.

Private NS 854465 OS: 72 * Map: 3, no: 398

The Lee, a 19th-century mansion, may include some of a castle of the Lockharts.

The lands were held by the family from the 12th century. One story is that the Lockharts were so named because Simon Lockhart helped bring back the heart of Robert the Bruce from Granada where it had been taken on a crusade – although they were actually called 'Loccard' before then. The 'Lee Penny', a healing amulet consisting of a dark red gem set in a silver setting, was acquired by the family on crusade, and could heal bleeding, fever, illnesses of animals and the bites of mad dogs when dipped in water. Alan Lockhart of the Lee was killed at the Battle of Pinkie in 1547, and George Lockhart of The Lee was an ardent Jacobite. The Lee was held by the Lockharts until the 20th century.

Other refs: Lee Castle; Lee, The

The Lour *see* Lour Tower

The Orchard, Hamilton *see* Hamilton Palace

The Peel, Busby

Lanarkshire & Glasgow area: About 2.5 miles north-east of East Kilbride, on minor road just west of B766, just north of junction with A726, just east of Busby.

Private NS 594561 OS: 64 ** Map: 3, no: 272

The Peel consists of a much-altered 16th-century L-plan tower house of four storeys, to which has been added later wings. The tower has a corbelled-out parapet with open rounds, and the walls are harled.

It was a property of the Douglases, but passed to the Hamiltons in 1455, then through many hands, including the Semples. It was acquired by the Houstons of Jordanhill in 1793, and is still occupied.

Other refs: Busby Peel; Peel, The

The Peel, Galashiels *see* Hunter's Hall, Galashiels

The Peel, Lochwinnoch *see* Belltrees Peel

The Steeple, Peebles *see* Peebles Castle

The Vault, Downfield *see* Downfield

The Vaults *see* Barnes Castle

The Wirk

Orkney: To west of Rousay, on minor road and foot north of B9064, 1 mile north-west of Westness Farm, near sea.

Ruin or site HY 374302 [?] OS: 6 ** Map: 11, no: 40

The remains of a small stone tower and hall with the traces of other buildings. It is believed to date from the 12th century. The property was held by Sigurd of Westness about 1150.

Other refs: Wirk

Thinacres Castle *see* Plotcock Castle

Thirdpart House

Fife: About 1.5 miles west of Crail, on minor roads north of A917, west of Old Barns, at Thirdpart.

Ruin or site NO 589067 [?] OS: 59 * Map: 7, no: 155

Possible site of castle or old house.

It was long held by the Scotts of Scotstarvit.

Thirlestane *see* Old Thirlestane Castle

Thirlestane Castle

Borders: Just north-east of Lauder, off A68, just south-west of meeting of Leader Water and Earnscleugh Water, Thirlestane Castle.

Private NT 540473 OS: 73 * Map: 2, no: 195**

Thirlestane Castle is a 16th-century castle, the oldest part of which is a rectangular tower house or block of three storeys, which had a large round tower at each corner. It was considerably enlarged in the 1670s with the rebuilding of the main block, heightening it to six storeys, and the addition of round turrets. Three semi-circular towers along each side contain stairs, as do many of the turrets. Parapets are supported on arches running along each side. A symmetrical forecourt was also added, with three-storey wings, which were extended in the 19th century.

The interior has been much altered. A fine 17th-century plaster ceiling survives on the second floor, as do Baroque plaster ceilings elsewhere.

The original castle of the Maitlands stood two miles away at Old Thirlestane. The present castle was built by Sir John Maitland, James VI's chancellor, but it was John Maitland, Duke of Lauderdale, a very powerful man in Scotland in the 17th century, who had the house remodelled in 1670 by William Bruce. Lauderdale was Secretary of State for Scotland from 1661-80, but eventually replaced after the Covenanter uprising which ended with their defeat at the Battle of Bothwell Brig. His ghost is

said to haunt Thirlestane, as well as St Mary's in Haddington. Bonnie Prince Charlie stayed here in 1745 on his way south. The 19th-century extensions were designed by David Bryce. The castle is still occupied by the same family.

OPEN: Open Apr- Oct, Sun-Fri 10.30-17.00, closed Sat; last admission 16.15.

Fine 17th-century plasterwork ceilings. Collection of portraits, furniture and china. Exhibition of historical toys and Border country life. Audio-visual presentation. Gift shop. Tea room. WC. Picnic tables. Adventure playground. Woodland walks. Car parking. Coaches by arrangement. Group concessions. £££.

Tel: 01578 722430 Fax: 01578 722761
Email: admin@thirlestanecastle.co.uk Web: www.thirlestanecastle.co.uk

Thirlestane Tower

Borders: About 5 miles south-east of Kelso, on minor road north of B6352, 1 mile west and north of Town Yetholm, at or near Thirlestane.
Ruin or site NT 803287 [?] OS: 74 * Map: 2, no: 326
Site of tower house of the Scotts, nothing of which survives, demolished around 1800. The tower was said to have a 'warlock's room', probably the laboratory of Dr Scott, a well-known chemist and physician to Charles II.

Thirlestane Tower

Borders: About 0.5 miles north-west of Ettrick, on minor road north of B709, west of the Ettrick Water, south of Thirlestane Hill.
Ruin or site NT 281154 OS: 79 * Map: 2, no: 70
Thirlestane Tower is a very ruined 16th-century L-plan tower house of the Scotts of Thirlestane. The basement was vaulted, and the tower rose to at least three storeys. There was a thinly-walled wing.

The property passed by marriage to the Napiers of Merchiston in 1699. They built a later adjoining mansion in 1820, but this was demolished in 1965.

The third son of Robert Scott of Thirlestane is said to have been treacherously slain by his brother-in-law, John Scott of Tushielaw, the story told in the old ballad 'The Dowie Dens of Yarrow'.

'She kissed his cheek, she kaimed his hair,
She searched his wounds all thorough;
She kissed them, till her lips grew red,
On the dowie houms of Yarrow.'

Thomaston Castle

Ayrshire: About 3.5 miles west of Maybole, just north of the A719 at Thomaston, about 1 mile south-east of Culzean Castle.
Ruin or site NS 240096 OS: 70 * Map: 3, no: 50**
Thomaston Castle is a ruined 13th-century courtyard castle, which enclosed a 16th-century L-plan tower house of three-storeys and formerly a garret. The tower con-

sists of a long main block and short wing, with a square stair-tower in the re-entrant angle. It has a corbelled-out parapet. An arched pend has been inserted through the wing basement, which led to the walled courtyard.

The entrance, at the foot of the stair-tower, leads to the vaulted basement. The basement contains four chambers, including a kitchen and a wine-cellar with a small stair up to the hall above. The hall, on the first floor, had a private chamber adjoining, as well as another chamber in the wing. The upper floors were occupied by private rooms.

The original castle was probably built by Thomas Bruce, nephew of Robert the Bruce. The property had passed to the Corries of Kelwood by 1507, who built the tower house. Thomaston passed by marriage to the MacIlvaines of Grimmet around 1632, and was occupied until about 1800.

Thorlieshope Tower

Borders: About 9 miles south of Bonchester Bridge, on minor road east of B6357, south of Liddel Water, about 0.5 miles east of Saughtree, at Thorlieshope.
Ruin or site NY 571965 OS: 80 * Map: 2, no: 214
Site of tower house of the Elliots in the garden of a late 17th-century house, itself now a ruin.

Thorniewhats

Dumfriesshire: About 1.5 miles north of Canonbie, on minor roads east of A7 or south of B6318, east of River Esk, at or near Thorniewhats.
Ruin or site NY 389784 [?] OS: 85 * Map: 1, no: 327
Site of tower house.

Thornton Castle

Kincardine & Deeside: About 1.5 miles north-west of Laurencekirk, on minor roads south of B9120, south of Black Burn, just east of Mains of Thornton, at Thornton.
Private NO 688718 OS: 45 ** Map: 10, no: 197**
Thornton Castle is a 16th-century L-plan tower house, although part is said to be from the 14th century, to which a modern mansion has been added. The tower consists of a main block and stair-wing, rising to four storeys, and has a corbelled-out crenellated parapet with open rounds at the corners. The oldest extension has a projecting round tower at one corner, also with a crenellated parapet. The castle is dated 1531 and 1662.

The basement is vaulted. A wide turnpike stair climbs to the hall, on the first floor, which is now panelled, and remains of tempera painting survive.

The property originally belonged to the Thorntons, but in 1309 passed by marriage to the Strachans. The family were Protestants, and in 1590 were appointed to act against Jesuits and seminary priests. In 1616 Strachan of Thornton had to pay 10,000 merks to keep the peace with Sir Robert Arbuthnott during a feud. The property passed by marriage to Robert Forbes of Newton in 1683, then to the Fullertons, to Lord Gardenstone, then in the 19th century to the Crombies. It was repaired about 1822, 'improved' in 1846, and sold in 1893 to Sir Thomas Thornton, and the house is still occupied.

Thornton Castle

Angus & Dundee: About 4.5 miles west and south of Forfar, on minor roads south of A94, 0.5 miles east of Glamis, at or near Thornton.
Ruin or site NO 397465 [?] OS: 54 * Map: 8, no: 173
Site of small castle or old mansion, dated 1531 and 1662, probably a property of the Lyon family.
Other refs: Castle of Thornton

Thornton Tower

Lothians: About 5 miles south-east of Dunbar, on minor roads south of A1, north of the Thornton Burn, at or near Thornton.
Ruin or site NT 739735 [?] OS: 67 * Map: 4, no: 227
Site of tower house of the Homes, which was held against the English by 16 men in 1540.

Thorril Castle

Lanarkshire & Glasgow area: About 2 miles east of Douglas, on east side of M74, near Parkhall Burn, east of Parkhead, at Thorril.
Ruin or site NS 864309 OS: 72 ** Map: 3, no: 402
Not much remains of a small two-storey rectangular tower or bastle house and courtyard, dating from the 16th century, which were unearthed during the M74 fieldwork project in 1990.
 It was probably a property of the Douglases of Parkhead.

Threave Castle

Galloway: About 1.5 miles west of Castle Douglas, on minor road north of A75, then foot and short boat trip to Threave Island in the River Dee.
NTS NX 739623 OS: 84 **** Map: 1, no: 118
Threave Castle consists of a massive 14th-century keep, rectangular in plan, of five storeys and formerly a garret. It stood within a courtyard, enclosed by a wall and ditch, with drum towers at each corner, only one of which survives. An impressive gateway remains in the curtain-wall.
 The entrance to the keep, at entresol level, was by a bridge from the gatehouse in

the curtain wall. A kitchen, with a fireplace, occupied the upper part of the vaulted basement. The chamber beneath contains a well and a deep pit-prison entered by a trapdoor.
 A turnpike stair climbs up to the hall, where there was a second entrance from a bridge from the upper floor of the gatehouse and parapet wall.
 An earlier castle here was burned by Edward Bruce in 1308. The present castle was started by Archibald the Grim – so named because his face was terrible to look upon in battle – 3rd Earl of Douglas, and Lord of Galloway from 1369 until 1390. He died at Threave in 1400. His son, Archibald, married James I's sister and was created Duke of Tourraine in France after winning the Battle of Bauge against the English. He was killed at the Battle of Verneuil in 1424.
 It was from Threave that the young 6th Earl and his brother rode to Edinburgh Castle in 1440 for the Black Dinner, where they were taken out and summarily executed.
 The 8th Earl was murdered in 1452 by James II at Stirling, after being invited there as an act of reconciliation. James, the 9th Earl, was rather hostile to the King after the murder of the 8th Earl and plotted with the English. In 1455, following the defeat of Douglas and his family the 'Black Douglases', James II besieged Threave with artillery, but not with Mons Meg, although this is a matter of dispute. The King was helped by the MacLellans: Sir Patrick MacLellan of Bombie, was murdered by beheading at Threave in 1452 by the Earl of Douglas. The garrison surrendered, however, but this seems to have been achieved as much by bribery as ordinance.
 Threave then became a Royal fortress. In 1513 the Maxwells were made keepers,

and in 1525 the post was made hereditary. After being captured at the Battle of Solway Moss in 1542, the Maxwell keeper was obliged to turn the castle over to the English, but it was retrieved by the Earl of Arran in 1545. In 1640 the castle was besieged by an army of Covenanters for 13 weeks until the Maxwell keeper, now Earl of Nithsdale, was forced to surrender it. The castle was slighted and partly dismantled.
 Threave was used as a prison for French troops during the Napoleonic wars. It was given to The National Trust of Scotland in 1948.
OPEN: Open Apr-Sep, daily 9.30-18.30; last ticket 18.00. Administered by Historic Scotland – includes long walk and short ferry trip.
Guided tours on request. Sales area. Picnic area. WC. Parking. £.
Tel: 01831 168512 Fax: 0131 668 8888
Email: hs.explore@scotland.gov.uk Web: www.historic-scotland.gov.uk

Threave House

Dumfries and Galloway: Off A75, 1 mile W of Castle Douglas, Galloway.
NTS NX 752605 OS: 84 *** Map: 1, no: 121
Threave House, a castellated mansion, was built in 1873 by the Gordon family, who acquired the estate in 1870. The garden has peat and woodland plants, a rock garden, some 200 varieties of daffodil, and herbaceous borders. There is also a walled garden and glasshouses. The house is The National Trust for Scotland's School of Horticulture.
OPEN: Garden and estate open all year, daily 9.30-sunset; walled garden and glasshouses 9.30-17.00; visitor centre, shop and exhibition Mar-23 Dec, daily 10.00-16.00, Apr-Oct, daily 9.30-17.30.
Visitor centre and exhibition. Gift shop. Restaurant. WC. Disabled access and WC. Parking. ££.
Tel: 01556 502575 Fax: 01556 502683

Thunderton House, Elgin

Moray: In Elgin, on minor roads south of A96, south of River Lossie, in Thunderton Place, at Thunderton House.
Private NJ 215615 OS: 28 ** Map: 10, no: 39
Thunderton House may incorporate part of a 14th-century royal castle, built to replace the old castle on Ladyhill. It was later a property of the Sutherland Lord Duffus, but passed to the Dunbars of Thunderton, and was greatly remodelled in the 17th century. It was altered in later years, and is now a public house.
 The building is said to be haunted by Bonnie Prince Charlie, who stayed here for 11 days before going on to defeat at the Battle of Culloden in 1746, although an alternative identity has been given as Lady Arradoul, his host on this occasion. Disturbances include the faint sounds of bagpipes and voices coming from the second floor, and the movement of objects.
Other refs: Elgin
OPEN: Public house.
Tel: 01343 554921 Fax: 01343 554922

Thurso Castle

Sutherland & Caithness: To east of Thurso, on minor roads north of A836, north of Thurso East, east of River Thurso at sea, near manse of St Andrew's Church.
Ruin or site ND 125689 OS: 12 * Map: 12, no: 45
Thurso Castle, a property of the Norse Earls, was destroyed in the late 12th cen-

tury, but a later stronghold on the site was a property of the Sinclairs of Greenland and Rattar in 1612. A tower house, dating from about 1640 (or 1664) and extended in 1806 and 1835, was replaced by a baronial mansion of 1872-8, which is itself now ruinous after being gutted by a fire and then partly demolished in 1952.

Thurso Castle was the home of Sir John Sinclair of Ulbster, who died in 1835 and compiled the Statistical Account of Scotland.

Tibbers Castle

Dumfriesshire: About 2 miles north and west of Thornhill, on minor roads south of A76, north of A702, in the Drumlanrig Estate, west of the River Nith.
Ruin or site NX 863982 OS: 78 ** Map: 1, no: 160
Not much remains, except foundations, of a 13th-century castle of enclosure with a rampart and ditch. The walls enclosed a hall block and other ranges, and round towers stood at each corner of the courtyard. There are remains of a barbican.

The castle was built by the Siwards, Sheriffs of Dumfries, although one story is that the Romans used the site and it is named after 'Tiberius Caesar'. The family sided with Edward I of England, who visited here in 1298, during the Wars of Independence, although the castle is said to have been captured by William Wallace. The castle was again seized by the Scots in 1306, but quickly retaken by the English, who hanged the garrison. It was again retaken by the Scots by 1314, and may have been dismantled. The lands passed to the Dunbar Earls of March, then to the Maitlands of Auchen in 1489, then in 1592 to the Douglases of Drumlanrig. It is recorded that Tibbers was torched in 1547.

The castle now stands in the park surrounding Drumlanrig Castle.
OPEN: *see* **Drumlanrig Castle, Thornhill.**

Tigh Dige *see* Flowerdale

Tigh Mor, Stronmilchan *see* Stronmilchan

Tighvechtichan

Argyll & Dunbartonshire: To west of Tarbet, on minor road north of A83, near railway station, at Tighvechtichan.
Ruin or site NN 312045 OS: 56 * Map: 5, no: 130
Site of old house or tower of the MacFarlanes, which was used to exact 'tolls' from those using the drove road.

Tillery

Aberdeen & Gordon: About 4 miles south and east of Pitmedden, on minor roads north of B999, at or near Tillery.
Private NJ 915229 [?] OS: 38 * Map: 10, no: 318
Site of castle or old house. Tillery House, which dates from 1788, is a Greek-Revival mansion of 1826, designed by Archibald Simpson. It was burned out in the 1950s, and most of it remains a gutted shell.

The lands were a property of the Udnys of Udny, but sold in 1788 to a John Chambers or Chalmers who had been a plantation owner in the southern USA.

Tillicoultry Castle

Stirlingshire & Clackmannan: Just north-west of Tillicoultry, on minor roads north of A91, Castle Mills.
Ruin or site NS 913975 OS: 58 * Map: 6, no: 101
Site of castle, some remains of which survived at the beginning of the 19th century. Tillicoultry House, which was a plain classical mansion dating from 1806, was demolished around 1938.

The lands were a property of the Erskines from 1236, but passed to the Colvilles of Culross in 1483, and the family were made Lords Colville in 1609. In 1634 the property was sold to the Alexanders of Menstrie, then passed through several families until it was held by the Wardlaw-Ramsays of Whitehill at the end of the 19th century.

Tillicoultry became a centre of weaving, and at one time there were eight woollen mills here.

Tilliefour *see* Place of Tillyfour

Tillycairn Castle

Aberdeen & Gordon: About 5.5 miles south-west of Kemnay, on minor road north of A944 at junction with B993, about 2.5 miles south of Monymusk, at Tillycairn.
Private NJ 664114 OS: 38 *** Map: 10, no: 185
Tillycairn Castle is a fine, but strong, 16th-century L-plan tower house of four storeys and an attic. The corners of the building are rounded, and crowned by corbelled-out bartizans. A semi-circular stair-tower stands in the re-entrant angle. The walls are pierced by gunloops.

The vaulted basement contained a kitchen, with a wide arched fireplace, and two cellars. The hall, on the first floor of the main block, has a fine fireplace. Private chambers occupied the wing and the floors above.

The lands were held by the Gordons, but passed to the Forbes family in 1444, who built the castle. The property was acquired by the Lumsdens in 1580, then the Burnets of Sauchen, then the Gordons again. The castle was ruinous by 1772, but was restored in 1980 by the Lumsdens.

Tillycorthie Castle

Aberdeen & Gordon: 3 miles south and east of Pitmedden, on minor roads east of B999, 0.5 miles south of Udny Station, at or near Tillycorthie Mansion House.
Ruin or site NJ 907234 [?] OS: 38 * Map: 10, no: 315
Probable site of tower house. Tillycorthie Mansion House, built in 1911, is a rather strange looking house, which has been divided into three homes.

Tillydown

Banff & Buchan: About 3.5 miles south-west of Aberchirder, on minor road west of B9117, west of River Deveron, at or near Tillydown.
Ruin or site NJ 578500 [?] OS: 29 * Map: 10, no: 147
Site of castle.

Tillyfour Castle *see* Place of Tillyfour

Tillyfruskie

Kincardine & Deeside: About 5 miles west and south of Banchory, on minor road north of B976, at or near Tillyfruskie.
Ruin or site NO 622929 OS: 45 * Map: 10, no: 167
Site of castle or old house.

Tillyhilt Castle

Aberdeen & Gordon: About 6.5 miles west of Ellon, on minor road west of B999, 1 mile north-west of Tarves, just south of Nethermill of Tillyhilt.
Ruin or site NJ 854318 [?] OS: 30 * Map: 10, no: 287
Not much remains of a 16th-century tower house of the Gordons.

Tilquhillie Castle

Kincardine & Deeside: About 1.5 miles south-east of Banchory, on minor roads west of A957 or east of B974, 1 mile south of River Dee, just south of Waulkmill, at Tilquhillie.
Private NO 722941 OS: 45 **** Map: 10, no: 220
Standing on high ground, Tilquhillie Castle is a tall 16th-century Z-plan tower house of three storeys and a garret. A semi-circular stair-tower rises in one re-entrant angle, and a corbelled-out stair-turret in another. The walls are rounded at the corners, and are pierced by small windows and shot-holes.

The entrance is at the foot of the semi-circular stair-tower. The basement is vaulted, and contains the kitchen and the wine-cellar, with a small stair to the hall above. The hall, on the first floor of the main block, has a private chamber adjoining it in one tower. The upper floors have been much altered.

Tilquhillie was a property of the Abbey of Arbroath, but acquired by the Ogston family after the Reformation. It passed by marriage to the Douglases of Lochleven, who built the castle. The family supported the Gordon Earl of Huntly against Mary, Queen of Scots, at the Battle of Corrichie, but were later pardoned. In 1665 the property passed by marriage to George Crichton of Cluny. The castle has been restored and is occupied.

Tilquhillie Castle – see previous page

Timpendean Tower

Borders: About 2 miles north-west of Jedburgh, near minor road south of A698 at Timpendean, about 1 mile north of Lanton.
Ruin or site   NT 636226 OS: 74   **   Map: 2, no: 251
Timpendean Tower is a ruined 16th-century tower house of four storeys, which stands within an earlier courtyard. The walls were pierced by gunloops.

The entrance led to a turnpike stair, in one corner, which climbed to all floors. Both this and a later entrance retain their original doors. The basement was vaulted, and contained a kitchen with a fireplace. The hall was on the first floor, with private chambers above.

It was a property of the Douglases.

Tinnis Castle

Borders: About 3 miles south-east of Broughton, south of the B712, about 0.3 miles north-east of Drumelzier.
Ruin or site   NT 141344 OS: 72   *   Map: 2, no: 22
Standing on a steep rocky hill, Tinnis Castle comprises a very ruined 15th-century keep and courtyard with round towers at two corners.

Tinnis may have been the stronghold of Dunthalamo, a warrior who Ossian, the legendary hero, slew at the gates. The castle stands within the ramparts of an Iron Age fort, and was built by the Tweedies of Drumelzier. John, 2nd Lord Fleming, was murdered by Tweedie of Drumelzier in 1524, and the castle may have been blown up with powder soon afterwards – although it is also recorded that it was to be destroyed on the orders of James VI in 1592 – this later mention may refer to a another site near Selkirk.
Other refs: Thanes Castle

Tinwald Place

Dumfriesshire: About 3 miles north of Dumfries, on minor roads east of A701, 0.3 miles west of Tinwald House.
Ruin or site   NY 006800 OS: 78   *   Map: 1, no: 195
Site of castle, said to have dated from the 14th century, and to have risen to three storeys. Some of the ditch could still be traced in 1856. It was demolished about 1830, and replaced by Tinwald House.

Tinwald was a property of the Maxwells, but passed to the Douglas Marquis of Queensberry, then in 1884 was sold to the Jardines.

Tioram Castle *see* Castle Tioram

Tirefour Broch

Argyll & Dunbartonshire: About 8 miles north of Oban, on south side of island of Lismore, on minor road and foot south of B8045, just north of Lynn of Lorn, at Tirefour Castle.
Ruin or site   NM 867429 OS: 49   *   Map: 5, no: 72**
Standing on a rocky outcrop, Tirefour Broch is a well-preserved broch. The wall

rises to over ten feet for most of its length, and in one place survives to a height of sixteen feet. The inside of the broch is partly filled with debris, but a doorway in one interior face survives. The entrance and the remains of an intramural gallery can be seen, and outside the broch are two ruinous outworks defending the approach.
Other refs: Broch of Tirefour

Tirfergus

Argyll & Dunbartonshire: About 4.5 miles west and south of Campbeltown, on minor road south of B843, 1 mile south of Drumlemble, at or near Low Tirfergus.
Ruin or site   NR 664184 OS: 68   *   Map: 5, no: 25
Site of castle or old house, nothing of which remains except some stones, one dated 1677. It was a property of the MacNeils of Tirfergus and Lossit.

Todholes Castle

Lanarkshire & Glasgow area: About 4 miles east of Carnwath, on minor roads north of A721, 1 mile south of Weston, north of South Medwin, at or near Todholes.
Ruin or site   NT 038461 OS: 72   *   Map: 3, no: 448
Site of tower house, with a vaulted basement, which was finally demolished about 1810 and no trace remains.

It was a property of the Douglases in 1572, but had passed to the Baillies by 1649.

Todrig Tower

Borders: About 5.5 miles north-west of Hawick, on minor road south from A7, just west of meeting of Todrig and Langhope Burns.
Private   NT 430197 OS: 79   *   Map: 2, no: 111
Todrig, now used as a farmhouse, consists of an altered 17th-century tower house of three storeys. It was extended in the 19th century.

It was held by the Scotts of Todrig.

Tofts *see* Purves Hall

Tolbooth Museum, Stonehaven

Kincardineshire: Old Pier, Stonehaven.
Private   NO 875858 OS: 45   *   Map: 10, no: 299**
Tolbooth Museum, which is housed in a building used in the 16th century as a storehouse for the Keith Earls Marischal at Dunnottar Castle, was the Kincardineshire County Tolbooth from 1600 until 1767. The museum features displays on local history and fishing, as well as imprisoned priests.
OPEN: Open Jun-Sep, Mon & Thu-Sat 10.00-12.00 and 14.00-17.00; Wed & Sun 14.00-17.00.
Guided tours. Explanatory displays. Gift shop. Disabled access. Car parking.
Tel: 01771 622906   Fax: 01771 622884
Email: general@abheritage.demon.co.uk
Web: www.aberdeenshire.gov.uk/ahc.htm

Tolbooth, Aberdeen *see* Aberdeen Tolbooth

Tollcross

Lanarkshire & Glasgow area: About 2.5 miles east and south of Glasgow Cathedral, on minor roads south of A89 and north of A74, off Wellshot Road, Tollcross Park.
Ruin or site   NS 637637 OS: 64   *   Map: 3, no: 299
Site of castle or old house of the Corbett family, who held the lands from 1242 until 1810, when they were sold to the Dunlops. The present mansion, built in 1848, was designed by David Bryce, and converted into special needs housing in 1992, having passed to the authority of Glasgow in 1896.

Tolquhon Castle

Aberdeen & Gordon: About 4 miles east of Oldmeldrum, on minor road west of B999 1 mile north of junction with A920, south of Newseat of Tolquhon, at Tolquhon.
His Scot   NJ 873286 OS: 38   *   Map: 10, no: 298**
Once a strong but comfortable fortress, Tolquhon Castle consists of a strong ru-

ined 15th-century keep in one corner of a courtyard enclosed by ranges of buildings, including a drum-towered gatehouse. A large round tower stands at one corner of the courtyard, with a square tower at the opposite side. The walls are pierced by gunloops.

The rectangular keep had a vaulted basement, but is very ruinous.

The main three-storey block, opposite the keep, has a projecting semi-circular stair-tower crowned by a square caphouse.

The entrance leads into a long vaulted passage. It opens into three vaulted cellars, one the wine-cellar; the kitchen, with a wide arched fireplace; and a bakehouse. Both kitchen and wine-cellar have small stairs to the hall above. There is also a pit-prison.

The first floor was reached by a wide curved stair. The hall, at this level, has a large moulded fireplace and is paved by hexagonal flagstones. An adjoining secret chamber was reached by a trapdoor from above. A turnpike stair in the central stair-tower led up to the private chambers on the upper floors.

The gatehouse range has two round towers and an arched pend, which was defended by shot-holes. The original iron yetts survive.

The original keep was built by the Prestons of Craigmillar, but the property passed by marriage to the Forbes family in 1420, who built the rest of the castle. The 6th Laird died at the Battle of Pinkie in 1547, while William Forbes, 7th Laird, built the castle as it now is – his carved tomb survives at Tarves. James VI visited in 1589, during his campaign against the Gordon Earl of Huntly. The 10th laird saved Charles II's life at the Battle of Worcester in 1651.

The Forbeses sold the property to the Farquhars in 1716 because of debts from involvement in the Darien Scheme, although the 11th Forbes laird had to be forcibly removed from the castle in 1718 by a detachment of soldiers. The property later passed to the Gordon Earl of Aberdeen, and part was used as a farmhouse for a while. It was abandoned around the end of the 19th century and became (more) ruinous. It was put into the care of the State in 1929.

OPEN: Open Apr-Sep, daily 9.30-18.30; open Oct-Mar wknds only, Sat 9.30-16.30; Sun 14.00-16.30; last ticket sold 30 mins before closing; closed 25/26 Dec and 1/2 Jan.
Sales area. Picnic area. WC. Disabled limited access and WC. Parking. £.
Tel: 01651 851286 Fax: 0131 668 8888
Email: hs.explore@scotland.gov.uk Web: www.historic-scotland.gov.uk

Tom a' Chaisteal, Kirkton

South Highland: About 4.5 miles west of Inverness, on minor road and foot south of A862, south of Kirkton, at Tom a' Chaisteal.
Ruin or site NH 604449 OS: 26 * Map: 9, no: 78
Site of castle, on the summit of a rocky knoll.

It was a property of a Baron Thomason in 1206, but by 1220 had passed to the Corbetts, who held it until 1498.

Tom a' Chaisteal, Trowan

Perth & Kinross: About 3 miles west of Crieff, on minor roads and foot south of A85, just east of River Earn, just north of Trowan, at fort site with monument.
Ruin or site NN 824216 OS: 52 * Map: 8, no: 19
Site of a castle, standing on a rocky eminence within an earlier fort, of the Celtic Earls of Strathearn. The last remains were removed in 1832 when an obelisk to Sir David Baird, who fought in India against Tippoo Sahib and won the Battle of Seringapatam – which may once have seemed worth remembering, no doubt – was built.

In 1511, at the nearby church of Monzievaird, a party of Drummonds massacred many men, women and children, by setting fire to the thatch of the church, during a feud with the Murrays of Ochtertyre.

Tom Bigla *see* Tom Pitlac

Tom Pitlac

South Highland: About 0.25 miles north-east of Boat of Garten, by minor road and foot west of B970, just east of River Spey, at Tom Pitlac.
Ruin or site NH 947196 OS: 36 * Map: 9, no: 151
Site of castle which was defended by a ditch and possibly a tower.

It was a property of the Cummings or Comyns in the 15th century, and is associated with Matilda or Bigla Cumming, daughter of Gilbert Cumming, Lord of Glenchearnach. Matilda is a character in a number of stories, and other places associated with her are Bigla's Chair [NH 932204], where she is believed to have received the rents for her lands, and Bigla's Key Stone [NH 945225?] where she hid her keys before going to the church at Duthil.
Other refs: Tom Bigla; Bigla Cumming's Castle

Tongue *see* House of Tongue

Tor Castle

Moray: About 8 miles south-west of Elgin, on minor road just south of Hatton, west of River Lossie, north of Dallas, at Tor Castle.
Ruin or site NJ 125530 OS: 28 * Map: 10, no: 20
Not much survives of a keep and castle of the Cummings – or Comyns – of Altyre, which was built about 1419. It was rebuilt in 1450 by Robert Cochrane, the royal architect, and occupied until the middle of the 17th century.
Other refs: Castle of Dallas

Tor Castle

South Highland: About 3 miles north-east of Fort William, on minor roads south of B8004, just west of River Lochy, east of the Caledonian Canal, at Torcastle.
Ruin or site NN 133786 OS: 41 ** Map: 9, no: 41
Tor Castle consists of a massive, but very ruinous, tower house or keep which had a courtyard. It was probably built, or strengthened, at the end of the 14th century, although there had been a castle here since the 11th century.

This is said to have been the stronghold of Banquo, of Macbeth fame. The lands were originally a property of the Macintoshes, who built a castle. Tor was seized by the Camerons around 1380, and in the early 16th century it was rebuilt to protect them from the MacDonalds of Keppoch. It was used until after the Jacobite Rising of 1745, when the last Cameron owner went into exile.

Torbain Tower

Fife: About 2 miles west of Kirkcaldy, on minor roads south of A92 or south of A910, at or near Torbrain Farm.
Ruin or site NT 243929 OS: 59 * Map: 7, no: 48
Site of castle.

Torbrex Castle

Lanarkshire & Glasgow: About 7 miles north of Carnwath, on minor roads west of A70, east of Greenfield Burn, at or near Tarbrax.
Ruin or site NT 027552 [?] OS: 72 * Map: 3, no: 445
Site of castle, a property of the Somervilles. It had passed to the Lockharts of Cleghorn by 1649.
Other refs: Tarbrax Castle

Tordarroch Castle

Inverness & Nairn: About 7 miles south of Inverness, on minor roads west of B851 or south of B861, east of River Nairn, north Milton of Farr, just west of Tordarroch.

Ruin or site NH 677335 [?] OS: 26 * Map: 9, no: 95
Site of castle.
  It was a property of the Shaws, from the 15th century, and the family fought for the Jacobites in the 1715 Rising. The castle was replaced by Tordarroch House.

Torduff

Dumfriesshire: About 3.5 miles east and south of Annan, on minor roads south of B721, 1 mile south and east of Eastriggs, north shore of Solway Firth, north-west of Torduff Point.

Ruin or site NY 258646 [?] OS: 85 * Map: 1, no: 280
Site of tower house. Torduff is marked both on Blaeu's Atlas Novus map of Annandale and on John Speed's map of Scotland.

Torhouse Castle

Galloway: About 3 miles west of Wigtown, on minor road north of B733, just north of River Bladnoch, at Torhouse.

Ruin or site NX 396554 OS: 83 ** Map: 1, no: 54
Torhouse Castle is a ruined 17th-century tower house of three storeys and an attic, rectangular in plan, although it may incorporate earlier work. The house has been much altered, and does not appear to have been vaulted. The entrance is in the middle of one side, and there are no surviving defensive features except a drawbar slot.
  Torhouse was a property of the MacCullochs

Torosay Castle

Argyll & Dunbartonshire: About 1.5 miles south-east of Craignure on island of Mull, on A849, at Torosay.

Private NM 729353 OS: 49 * Map: 5, no: 40**
Torosay Castle, a castellated mansion of 1858 designed by David Bryce for the Campbells of Possel, has no older origins. The gardens, laid out by Sir Robert Lorimer in 1899, include formal terraces, an Italian statue walk, and woodland. There is a miniature steam railway from Craignure.
OPEN: House open April-mid-Oct, daily 10.30-17.30; last admission 17.00; gardens open all year, daily 9.00-19.00 or daylight hours in winter.
Guided tours by arrangement. Gift shop. Tearoom. WC. Disabled access. Car and coach parking. Group concessions. ££.
Tel: 01680 812421 Fax: 01680 812470
Email: torosay@aol.com Web: www.holidaymull.org/members/torosay

Torphichen Preceptory

Lothians: About 4 miles south and west of Linlithgow, on minor roads east of B792, in village of Torphichen.

His Scot NS 972727 OS: 65 ** Map: 4, no: 7
A rather unusual and somewhat eerie place, all that remains of Torphichen Preceptory are the crossing and the transepts of the church, and traces of the nave, cloister and other domestic buildings. Parts of the building date from the 12th century, but it was much altered in the 15th century. The parish church was built on the site of the nave.
  Torphichen Preceptory was the main seat of the Knights Hospitallers from the 12th century. William Wallace held a convention of barons here in 1298, and Edward I of England stayed here after winning the Battle of Falkirk against Wallace the same year. The last Preceptor of the Order in Scotland was Sir James Sandilands, and the property was made into a temporal lordship for him in 1564. The Sandilands family moved to Calder House, and the Preceptory was probably abandoned.
  A stone in the churchyard is thought to mark the centre of the sanctuary land

afforded by the Preceptory – where criminals and debtors could shelter – while other stones, about one mile from the church, defined the limits.
OPEN: Open Apr-Sep, Sat 11.00-17.00, Sun and Bank Hols 14.00-17.00.
Parking nearby.
Tel: 0131 668 8800 Fax: 0131 668 8888
Email: hs.explore@scotland.gov.uk Web: www.historic-scotland.gov.uk

Torr Iain Ghairbh *see* Raasay House

Torran

Argyll & Dunbartonshire: About 4 miles north and east of Kilmartin, on minor roads north of B840 at Ford, on northern shore at west end of Loch Awe, at Torran.

Ruin or site NM 878048 OS: 55 ** Map: 5, no: 74
Site of 16th-century castle or fortified house and courtyard.
  It was a property of the Campbells of Inverliever from 1529.

Torrance Castle

Lanarkshire & Glasgow area: About 1.5 miles south-east of East Kilbride, off A726 East Kilbride to Strathaven Road, in Calderglen Country Park.

Private NS 654526 OS: 64 * Map: 3, no: 307**
Torrance Castle, a large rambling mansion, incorporates a plain 16th-century L-plan tower house of four storeys and a garret, part of which may date from the 14th century. A large square tower, in the re-entrant angle, contains the turnpike stair and a series of small chambers. Some of the windows have been enlarged.
  The original entrance, covered by a modern porch, was at the foot of the stair-tower. The castle, currently in private ownership, is in the process of being refurbished.
  The property was held by the Hamiltons, but passed in the mid 18th century to the Stewarts of Castlemilk. An outbuilding is now used as a visitor centre.
Other refs: Calderglen Country Park
OPEN: Country park open all year; visitor centre open summer, Mon-Fri 10.30-17.00, wknds & public hols 11.30-18.30; winter months daily 11.30-16.00.
Guided tours by arrangement. Explanatory displays. Gift shop. Courtyard cafe. Snack bar. Picnic areas. Ornamental gardens. Disabled access. Car and coach parking.
Tel: 01355 236644 Fax: 01355 247618

Torregills Castle *see* Terregles Castle

Torrie Castle

Fife: About 5 miles west and south of Dunfermline, on minor road south of A985, just east of Valleyfield, at or near Torrie House.
Ruin or site   NT 015867 [?]   OS: 65   *   Map: 7, no: 6
Site of castle of the Wardlaws of Torrie. Torrie House probably stands on the site, and in the 19th-century was held by the Erskine-Wemyss family.

Torriesoul *see* Carvichen

Torrisdale Castle

Argyll & Dunbartonshire: About 2 miles south-west of Carradale on Kintyre, on minor roads west of B842, south of Torrisdale Water, at Torrisdale Castle.
Private   NR 793361   OS: 68   *   Map: 5, no: 53
Torrisdale Castle, a 19th-century mansion, has no earlier origins.

Torrish Castle

Sutherland & Caithness: About 4 miles north-west of Helmsdale, on minor road south of A897, north of River Helmsdale, at or near Torrish.
Ruin or site   NC 975185 [?]   OS: 17   *   Map: 12, no: 35
Site of castle, a property of the Gordons in 1621.

Torsa Castle *see* Caisteal nan Con

Torsance Castle

Borders: About 1 mile south of Stow, on minor road east of A7 at Torsonce, east of the Gala Water.
Ruin or site   NT 456424 [?]   OS: 73   *   Map: 2, no: 124
Site of castle of the Pringle family, which is occupied by a house dating from 1830 with later additions.

Torthorwald Castle

Dumfriesshire: About 4 miles north-east of Dumfries, on minor road just south of A709, just south of Torthorwald village.
Ruin or site   NY 033783   OS: 84   **   Map: 1, no: 202
Torthorwald is a ruined altered 14th-century keep, which stands on a motte with earthworks and a ditch. The keep, which is rectangular in plan, had a vaulted basement and hall. A turnpike stair, in one corner, climbed to the upper floors, while another rose to the garret. The original entrance was probably at first-floor level.

It was a property of the Torthorwald family in the 13th century, but passed by marriage later that century to the Kirkpatricks, then again by marriage to the Carlyles in 1418. In 1544 Lord Carlyle sacked the castle in a raid against his sister-in-law. In 1590 an illegitimate son of the Regent Morton was created Lord Torthorwald by James VI. The property passed by marriage to the Douglases of Parkhead in 1609. James, Lord Torthorwald, was murdered, probably by Andro, Lord Ochiltree. In 1621 the property passed to the Douglases of Drumlanrig, who were later made Dukes of Queensberry. The castle was occupied until about 1715.

Tortrium *see* Tartraven Castle

Torwood Castle

Stirlingshire & Clackmannan: About 4 miles north west of Falkirk, on minor roads west of A9, about 0.5 miles south of Torwood, near course of Roman road.
Ruin or site   NS 836844   OS: 65   *   Map: 6, no: 83**
Torwood Castle, also recorded as Torwoodhead, is a ruined 16th-century L-plan tower house, which formerly had a courtyard enclosing 17th-century outbuildings. The tower consists of a main block of three storeys and a projecting wing, which rises two storeys higher. A square stair-tower, in the re-entrant angle, is a storey lower than the wing. The walls are pierced by shot-holes and gunloops.

The moulded entrance, in the re-entrant angle, leads through a lobby to the main turnpike stair. The basement is vaulted and contains three cellars, one the wine-

Torwood Castle – see above

cellar, with a stair climbing to the hall above; and another the kitchen, with an arched fireplace. The hall, on the first floor, has a decorated fireplace and an adjoining private chamber. The upper floors are now ruinous.

It was a property of the Forresters of Garden, keepers of the nearby royal forest of Torwood, in the 15th century. Sir Duncan Forrester was killed at the Battle of Pinkie in 1547. The present castle was built after the property had passed to the Baillies of Castlecary, but it returned to the Forresters of Corstorphine in 1653.

Other refs: Torwoodhead Castle

Torwoodhead Castle *see* Torwood Castle

Torwoodlee Tower

Borders: About 2 miles west and north of Galashiels, on minor roads north of A72, at Torwoodlee, about 1.5 miles north-east of Clovenfords.

Ruin or site NT 467378 OS: 73 ** Map: 2, no: 134

Torwoodlee Tower consists of a large ruined 16th-century tower house of two storeys and an attic, rectangular in plan, within a courtyard. The entrance is in a round tower, which is corbelled out to square and crowned by a watch-chamber. The courtyard enclosed ranges of buildings.

The basement was vaulted.

It was a property of the Pringles from 1509 or earlier. It was sacked by the Elliots in 1568, but rebuilt then to be abandoned in 1783 for nearby Torwoodlee House.

Touch Fraser *see* Touch House

Touch House

Stirlingshire & Clackmannan: About 2.5 miles west of Stirling, on minor roads south of A811, about 1 mile west of Cambusbarron, at Touch House.

Private NS 753928 OS: 57 *** Map: 6, no: 61

Nestling in the Touch Hills, Touch House is an altered 15th-century keep of four storeys and a garret, possibly later modified to a Z-plan with the addition of rectangular towers at opposite corners. To this a large mansion was added in the late 16th or early 17th century, and this was later remodelled with a classical front, possibly designed by William Adam. The keep has a crenellated parapet, around two sides, and a caphouse crowns the stair.

The original entrance, now built over, lay at the foot of the stairway. The basement is vaulted.

The property was held in 1234 by the Frasers, but by 1426 had passed to the Stewart Earls of Buchan, then was acquired by the Setons around the end of the 15th century. In 1708 the Laird of Touch was one of five lords involved in an unsuccessful attempt to put James VII on the throne, a venture in which Rob Roy MacGregor was implicated. The property passed by marriage to the Seton-Stewarts of Allanton and Touch around 1750, who held it until 1930.

The castle was later used as a hospital, but is now occupied as a private home.

Other refs: Touch Fraser

Toward Castle

Argyll & Dunbartonshire: About 7 miles south-west of Dunoon, on minor roads north of A815 at the southern tip of Cowal, east of Castle Toward School.

Ruin or site NS 119678 OS: 63 ** Map: 5, no: 113

Toward Castle consists of a ruined 15th-century keep, one wall standing to the height of the parapet, and a 16th-century courtyard, with a decorated arched gateway. The basement of the keep was vaulted, as was the first-floor hall. The stair, in the thickness of the walls, led up to the first floor, and the main entrance appears to have been at first-floor level.

The courtyard contained a range of buildings, housing a hall and kitchen, and there was also a gatehouse and bakehouse.

It was a property of the Lamonts, who had held lands in Cowal from 1200 or earlier. Mary, Queen of Scots, visited in 1563. The Lamonts were Royalists, and in 1646 the Campbells captured, looted and torched the castle. Although the Campbells had promised that the Lamonts could go free, they massacred and mistreated any Lamonts they found, including old folk, women and children. They took many of the captives back to Dunoon where they hanged 36 from one tree. Many Lamonts changed their name to Black after the slaughter. A hoard of more than 200 silver coins was found here in 1821.

In the 1820s, a new mansion, Castle Toward, was built nearby, and is now a residential school; the old castle stands within the grounds. The old castle was excavated and consolidated in 1970, and is in the care of the Clan Lamont Society.

The Campbells may have had a house nearby [NS 116682], known as Auchavoulin House, some remains of which survive.

Other refs: Auchavoulin; Castle Toward

OPEN: Accessible with care.

Tower

Ayrshire: About 3.5 miles north and west of Kilwinning, on minor roads west of A737, 1 mile south-west of Dalry, at or near Tower.

Ruin or site NS 277477 OS: 63 * Map: 3, no: 61

Possible site of tower.

Tower

Dumfriesshire: About 2.5 miles north-west of Sanquhar, on minor road north of A76, east of Tower Burn, at Tower.

Ruin or site NS 756119 OS: 71 * Map: 1, no: 122

Site of tower house, which was held by the McCalls of Guffockland towards the end of the 16th century.

Tower Lindsay *see* Crawford Castle

Tower of Benholm *see* Benholm Castle

Tower of Bowness *see* Slains Castle

Tower of Carnock *see* Bruce's Castle

Tower of Fintrie *see* Fintry Castle

Tower of Garden

Stirlingshire & Clackmannan: About 3.5 miles west of Kippen, on minor road just north of A811, about 0.5 miles west of Arnprior, at or near Garden.

Ruin or site NS 593948 OS: 57 * Map: 6, no: 31

Nothing remains of a tower house, except a mound. There were significant remains in 1878.

The Forresters of Garden were hereditary keepers of the Torwood for the kings of Scots, and they probably built the castle. It was later held by the Stirlings.

Garden is a two-storey classical mansion of 1824, incorporating work from 1724. It is likely that the tower was abandoned at this time.

Other refs: Garden Tower

Tower of Glen Ogilvie *see* Claverhouse Castle

Tower of Kilbride *see* Law Castle

Tower of Lethendy

Perth & Kinross: About 3.5 miles south-west of Blairgowrie, on minor road south of B947, about 0.5 miles east of Kirkton of Lethendy, at Tower of Lethendy.

Private NO 140417 OS: 53 ** Map: 8, no: 94

Tower of Lethendy is a much-altered and extended 16th- or 17th-century L-plan tower house of three storeys and a garret, to which has been added a 19th-century mansion.

The entrance, now enclosed by a modern building, is defended by a gunloop. The basement is vaulted, and contains a kitchen. A turnpike stair, above a pit-prison, climbs in the wing. The tower has been completely altered inside.

It was a property of the Herons. John Graham of Claverhouse, 'Bonnie Dundee' or 'Bloody Clavers', was descended from a daughter of the family. Nearby is a later castellated mansion.

A carved Pictish stone has been used as a lintel.

Other refs: Lethendy Tower

Tower of Mausonly *see* Moss Castle

Tower of Rule *see* Hallrule

Tower of Strathisla *see* Davoch of Grange

Tower of Torrey *see* Turriff Castle

Tower Rais
Renfrewshire: About 0.5 miles north of Barrhead, east of B773 (Darnley Road) junction with A736, east of Levern Water, near Dovecothall, at Tower Rais.
Ruin or site   NS 511594   OS: 64   *   Map: 3, no: 223
Site of castle.
  It was built by the Stewarts of Darnley before 1449 to guard the ford over the Levern, and was later used as a hunting lodge. It was ruined by the late 18th century, and demolished in 1932 as it was in a dangerous condition.
Other refs: Rais Tower; Stewart's Rais

Tower, Torrance *see* Broken Tower

Towie Barclay Castle
Aberdeen & Gordon: About 4 miles south of Turriff, on minor road just west of A947, north of River Ythan, south of Mains of Towie, at Towie Barclay.
Private   NJ 744439   OS: 29   *   Map: 10, no: 238**
Towie Barclay is an altered L-plan 16th-century tower house. It consists of a main block of three storeys and a garret and attic, and a projecting 17th-century wing. The walls are harled and pink-washed.
  The entrance, through a groin-vaulted lobby, leads to the vaulted basement containing four chambers, one of which is the wine-cellar with a small stair to the hall above. The main stair, to the first floor, starts straight but curves around inside the corner of the tower. The hall, on the first floor, is a magnificent chamber with a groin-vaulted ceiling and a wide fireplace with four stone seats.
  The castle was built by the Barclays of Towie, possibly in 1593, although there may have been an earlier castle here as the family held the lands from the 12th century. In 1639 the castle was attacked by Royalists supporting Charles I – as Walter Barclay of Towie was a Covenanter – the first action in the Civil War. One of the family, Prince Michael Barclay of Tolly was a Russian general during the Napoleonic Wars, and is a character in Tolstoy's 'War and Peace'.
  In 1792 the upper two storeys were demolished, and the parapet and rounds removed, although it was reroofed in 1874, and restored in the 1970s. The castle is occupied.

Towie Castle
Aberdeen & Gordon: About 3.5 miles south and west of Kildrummy, on minor road south of A97 at Glenkindie or east of A97, south of River Don, at Towie.
Ruin or site   NJ 440129   OS: 37   *   Map: 10, no: 94
Site of 17th-century L-plan tower house of three storeys, with corbelled-out bartizans, although there was probably an earlier castle here. The final remains of the castle were cleared away in the 1980s.
  It was a property of the Forbes of Towie. This may have been the place torched by Sir Adam Gordon of Auchindoun – rather than Corgarff Castle – when Margaret Campbell, wife of Forbes of Towie, and 27 of her household were burned to death, after she had shot one of Gordon's men in the knee with a pistol. The tale is related in the old ballad 'Edom o' Gordon'. The castle was rebuilt by 1618, remodelled in 1788, but very ruinous by 1968.

Trabboch Castle
Ayrshire: About 3.5 miles south of Mauchline, on minor roads north of A70, east of B730, or south of B743, just east of Trabboch Mains, south of Trabboch Burn.
Ruin or site   NS 458222   OS: 70   *   Map: 3, no: 189
Very little remains of a strong 14th-century castle which was defended by a ditch. Material from the castle was used to build Trabboch Mains.
  The property was given to the Boyds of Kilmarnock by Robert the Bruce, but had passed to the Douglases by about 1450. The lands were later acquired by the Boswells.

Tranent Tower
Lothians: On the north side of Tranent, on minor road east of B6414 between A199 and A1, in Church Street.
Ruin or site   NT 404729   OS: 66   **   Map: 4, no: 162
Tranent Tower is a ruined 16th-century L-plan tower house. It consists of a main block of three storeys and a square stair-wing, which rises a storey higher. The roof is pantiled.
  The basement contains two vaulted chambers. A narrow turnpike stair climbs to the upper floors. The hall was on the first floor, but the storeys above have lost their floors.
  The lands belonged to the Setons in 1542, but were acquired by the Valance family in the 17th century. The building may have been used as a barracks at one time. It is not in a good state of repair.

Traquair House
Borders: About 1 mile south of Innerleithen, on minor road between B709 and B7062, south of the River Tweed, at Traquair.
Private   NT 330354   OS: 73   **   Map: 2, no: 86**
Reputedly the oldest continuously inhabited house in Scotland, Traquair House is an altered and extended tower house, which incorporates work from as early as the 12th century. The oldest identifiable part, dating from 1492, is incorporated at the end of the main block. About the middle of the 16th century, a new wing was added with a projecting rectangular stair-tower. Lower late 17th-century wings were also added to the main house.
  The main part of the house rises to four storeys and a garret. The later extensions were reached by a round stair-tower at one corner. There is a priest's cell, on the

top floor, complete with secret stair.
  Alexander I had a hunting lodge here, and Traquair was visited by many of the kings of Scots, and some of England: Edward I and Edward II in the 14th century. The lands had passed to the Douglases by the 13th century, then through several families until sold to the Stewart Earls of Buchan in 1478. The laird of Traquair was killed at the Battle of Flodden in 1513. Mary, Queen of Scots, visited with Lord Darnley in 1566. She left behind a quilt, possibly embroidered by herself and her Four Marys, and the 4th Laird helped her escape from Lochleven Castle after her abdication in 1568. The bed where she slept some of her last nights on Scottish soil was rescued from Terregles and is at Traquair.
  The Marquis of Montrose fled here after the Battle of Philiphaugh in 1645, but was refused entry by the then laird.
  Bonnie Prince Charlie visited the house on his way south in 1745 to invade England. He entered Traquair through the famous Bear Gates. One story is that the 5th Earl closed and locked them after Charlie's departure, swearing they would not be unlocked until a Stewart once more sat on the throne of the country. They are still locked.
  Traquair is not believed to be haunted, and this is apparently not one of the places

that the spirit of Bonnie Prince Charlie frequents. The grounds, however, are believed to be. The apparition of Lady Louisa Stewart, sister of the 8th and last Earl of Traquair, is reported to have been sighted in the grounds around the house, going on her favourite walk by the Quair. She lived to a fine old age, dying in 1875 when she was nearly 100 years old. Her photograph hangs in the house.

OPEN: Open Easter-Oct, daily 12.30-17.30, Jun-Aug, daily 10.30-17.30.
Working 18th-century brewery. Guided tours by arrangement. Explanatory displays. 1745 Cottage Restaurant. W.C. Gardens, woodland walks and maze. Craft workshops. Gift, antique and the Brewery shop. Brewery. Car and coach parking (coaches please book). Group concessions. £££. Accommodation available: contact house.
Tel: 01896 830323 Fax: 01896 830639
Email: enquiries@traquair.co.uk Web: www.traquair.co.uk

Treesbanks

Ayrshire: About 2 miles south of Kilmarnock, on minor roads east of B7038, just south of Simon's Burn, at Treesbanks.
Private NS 420346 OS: 70 * Map: 3, no: 162
Treesbanks, a house of 1672, extended in 1838, incorporated a 16th-century tower house, but has been demolished. The present house on the site dates from no later than 1926.

It was a property of the Campbells of Cessnock.

Tresmass

Argyll & Dunbartonshire: About 2 miles east of Dumbarton, on minor roads north of A82, north of Milton, east of Loch Bowie, at or near Middleton.
Ruin or site NS 428753 [?] OS: 64 * Map: 5, no: 161
Site of castle of the Colquhouns, before they moved to Barnhills House in 1543. It was later occupied by the Lorane family. There were some remains at the beginning of the 19th century, but nothing now survives.
Other refs: Milton of Colquhoun; Middleton of Colquhoun

Trochrague

Ayrshire: About 2.5 miles north-east of Girvan, on minor road west of B741, at Trochrague.
Private NS 213004 OS: 76 * Map: 3, no: 35
Trochrague, an 18th-century house, is built on the site of an earlier castle.

Trochrie Castle

Perth & Kinross: About 3.5 miles west of Dunkeld station, on minor road just north of A822 at Trochry, just east of River Braan, just north of Trochry hamlet.
Ruin or site NN 978402 OS: 52 * Map: 8, no: 46
Little remains of a 16th-century Z-plan tower house, except for the lower part of a turret from a tower.

It was held by the Ruthvens of Gowrie, and the tower was torched in 1545.
Other refs: Trochry Castle

Trochry Castle *see* Trochrie Castle

Tronach Castle

Moray: About 0.5 miles east of Portnockie, north of A942, near shore, at or near Tronach.
Ruin or site NJ 475685 [?] OS: 28 * Map: 10, no: 105
Site of castle.

Another castle, Green Castle, also stood near Portnockie.
Other refs: Green Castle

Troup *see* Castle of Troup

Truill Castle *see* Castle Truill

Tulliallan Castle

Fife: About 0.5 miles north of Kincardine, on minor roads west of the A977, north of Kincardine Generating Station, just north-west of Harkhill.
Private NS 927888 OS: 65 * Map: 7, no: 1**
An unusual hall house stronghold, Tulliallan Castle consists of a 14th-century keep

or hall house, surrounded by a ditch. The entrance is in a projecting semi-octagonal stair-tower, and was defended by a drawbridge and portcullis. A similar stair-tower also projects from the other end.

The hall, a fine chamber in the basement, is vaulted with a central pier, and contains a moulded fireplace.

Edward I of England ordered a castle here to be strengthened in 1304. The lands were held by the Douglas family in the 14th century, then by the Edmonstones from 1410 or earlier, then passed by marriage to the Blackadders in 1486, who built much of the existing castle. Sir John Blackadder of Tulliallan was executed in 1531 for the murder of the Abbot of Culross. Patrick Blackadder was probably murdered

by the Homes of Wedderburn in Edinburgh, after the Homes had seized the Blackadder's lands in the Borders. Tulliallan was acquired by the Bruces of Carnock in 1605, and was inhabited until 1662. About 1820 a new castellated mansion was built about 0.5 miles away, which is now used by the police as a training college.

In 1619 five men were accused of imprisoning another man in the dungeon of Tulliallan and starving him to death.

The old castle is currently being restored for the Mitchell Trust.
Other refs: Hawkhill; Tulliallan Old Castle
OPEN: Open strictly by arrangement.

Tulliallan Old Castle *see* Tulliallan Castle

Tullibardine Castle

Perth & Kinross: About 2.5 miles west and north of Auchterarder, on minor road north of A823, probably near Tullibardine Chapel, at or near Mains of Tullibardine.
Ruin or site NN 910139 [?] OS: 58 * Map: 8, no: 33
Site of castle, which was completely demolished in 1833.

It was a property of the Murrays, created Earls of Tullibardine in 1606 and Marquises in 1707, who eventually became Dukes of Atholl.

The nearby chapel was founded by Sir David Murray of Tullibardine in 1446, and has been used as a burial place by the Murrays since the Reformation.
OPEN: Chapel: open May-Sep.
Chapel: Explanatory displays. Parking nearby.

Tullibody

Stirlingshire & Clackmannan: About 1.5 miles north-west of Alloa, on minor roads north of A907 or south of B9096, at Tullibody.
Ruin or site NS 865945 [?] OS: 58 * Map: 6, no: 89
Edward I intended to build a castle here around 1305, and although some work was carried out the following year, it does not appear to have been completed.

Tullibody House, which was set in fine wooded grounds, dated from the middle of the 17th century, or earlier, and was a property of the Meldrums. It passed to the Abercrombies about 1655, and they remodelled or rebuilt the house in 1710. The family moved to Airthrey Castle. Tullibody House was eventually abandoned and vandalised, then finally demolished in the 1960s.

Tullibole Castle

Perth & Kinross: About 0.5 miles east of Crook of Devon, on minor road north from B9097 1 mile east of junction with A977, east of Drum, at Tullibole.
Private NO 053006 OS: 58 *** Map: 8, no: 62
Tullibole Castle is a 17th-century L-plan tower house of three storeys and a garret,

which has later been extended. A stair-wing has two bartizans, and a machiolation defends the entrance. A stair-turret, in the re-entrant angle, is corbelled out at first-floor level. The walls are pierced by shot-holes.

The interior has been much altered.

A 13th-century castle here was a property of the Bishop of St Andrews. It was sold to the Hallidays in 1598, but passed by marriage to the Moncrieffe family in 1705. The house is still occupied by the Moncrieffes.

Tullichewan Castle

Argyll & Dunbartonshire: Just west of Alexandria, west of the A82, at or near Tullichewan Farm.
Ruin or site NS 380811 [?] OS: 63 * Map: 5, no: 150
The castellated mansion, designed by Robert Lugar in 1792, with towers and turrets, was completely demolished in 1954. It was a property of the Campbells at the end of the 19th century.

Tulloch Castle

Ross & Cromarty: About 1 mile north of Dingwall, on minor roads west of A862, on north side of the Cromarty Firth, at Tulloch Castle.
Private NH 547605 OS: 21 *** Map: 9, no: 65
Tulloch Castle incorporates an altered keep or tower, possibly from the early 16th century, square in plan, with a round stair-tower at one corner. It may include some work from the 12th or 13th century. The parapet and corbelling of the keep are modern, as is the caphouse. Windows have been enlarged. The walls are pierced by gunloops, and are harled.

There is a large gabled extension of the 17th century.

The basement of the keep is vaulted and the hall, on the first floor, has the original fireplace and a secret stair in one corner which leads to a stair down to another entrance . The first-floor chambers have ornate plaster ceilings.

The Norsemen may have had a stronghold here. Tulloch was a property of one Farquhar Oure in 1500, but passed in 1526 to the Innes family, then to the Bains from 1542 until 1762. It was sold to the Davidsons, who were related by marriage, and they held it until 1945. Part of the castle was destroyed by fire in 1845. The house was extended in 1891, and in 1920-3 by Sir Robert Lorimer, then passed to the Vickers. The building was used as a school, but has been a hotel since 1996.

It is said to be haunted by a 'Green Lady'. The story goes that a child surprised her father with another woman. The child was so startled that she fled the room and fell down a flight of stairs, killing herself.

There is a tunnel from the basement of the castle which is believed to have led across the town to Dingwall Castle. It has collapsed but part of it can be seen from the middle of the front lawn.
Other refs: Garoch Castle; Oulch Castle
OPEN: Hotel.
19 bedrooms with private facilities. Restaurant and Green Lady Lounge Bar. Celebrations, dinners and weddings. Conferences and meetings.
Tel: 01349 861325 Fax: 01349 863993

Tullochcarron Castle

Banff & Buchan: About 8 miles south-west of Charlestown of Aberlour, on minor roads south of A95, west of River Avon, at or near Castletown.
Ruin or site NJ 180350 OS: 28 * Map: 10, no: 28
Site of 15th-century castle. The lands originally belonged to the Ballindalloch family, but passed to the Grants.
Other refs: Ballindalloch

Tullos House

Aberdeen & Gordon: About 3 miles west of Inverurie, on minor roads west of A96 or north of B993, 2 miles south and west of Chapel of Garioch, east of Bennachie Forest, at Tullos.
Ruin or site NJ 703218 OS: 38 ** Map: 10, no: 211
Tullos House consists of the ruinous remains of an L-plan castle or old house, which dates from the 16th century. It was a property of the Leslies of Balquhain, and occupied until the end of the 18th century.

Tundergarth Castle

Dumfriesshire: About 3 miles east of Lockerbie, on minor road south of B7068, south of Water of Mill, at or near Tundergarth.
Ruin or site NY 176807 [?] OS: 79 * Map: 1, no: 257
Site of castle, a property of the Johnstones.

Turin House

Angus & Dundee: About 5.5 miles east and north of Forfar, on minor roads north of B9113, 2 miles east of Turin Hill, at Turin House.
Private NO 545527 OS: 54 * Map: 8, no: 229
Turin House may incorporate part of an old castle.

Turing's Tower *see* Foveran Castle

Turnberry Castle

Ayrshire: About 7 miles west of Maybole, on minor roads across airfield west from A77, on cliffs near Turnberry Lighthouse on the shore of the Firth of Clyde.
Ruin or site NS 196073 OS: 70 * Map: 3, no: 26
Standing on a promontory, not much remains of a 13th-century castle, although there was an earlier fortress here. A curtain wall enclosed the stronghold and there was a keep, which may have been partly round. There are some remains of vaults.

It was a property of the Earls of Carrick, and may be the birthplace of Robert the Bruce, Robert I, King of Scots. His mother, Marjorie, the widowed Countess of Carrick, had kidnapped Robert Bruce of Annandale, and forced him to marry her in 1271. Bruce, their son, was crowned in 1306, but his small army was quickly defeated and he fled Scotland. On his return, he landed at Turnberry in 1307 and led the Scots to victory at Bannockburn in 1314. The castle had been dismantled on his orders in 1310, and probably never rebuilt.
OPEN: Access at all reasonable times.
Parking nearby.

Turriff Castle

Banff & Buchan: In Turriff, near A947, north of Idoch Water, on Castlegate.
Ruin or site NJ 722500 [?] OS: 29 * Map: 10, no: 221
Site of castle, of which the vaulted basement, probably from a tower house, survived until the end of the 19th century. Robert the Bruce endowed a chapel so that masses would be said for his brother, Nigel, who was executed after being captured at the fall of Kildrummy Castle.

A 16th-century town house of the Hay Earls of Errol was only recently demolished

by road widening.
Other refs: Castle Rainy; Tower of Torrey

Tushielaw Tower

Borders: About 2.5 miles east and north of Ettrick, just north of the B709, about
0.3 miles south of junction with B711, west of the Ettrick Water.
Ruin or site   NT 300172   OS: 79   **   Map: 2, no: 75
Little survives of Tushielaw Tower, a 16th-century tower house, except part of the
basement, with a ruined outbuilding, and the scant remains of a courtyard.

It was built in 1507 by Adam Scott, known as 'The King of the Borders' and 'The
King of Thieves'. In 1530 he was executed by beheading in Edinburgh by James V.
John Scott of Tushielaw is said to have been responsible for the treacherous murder of Walter Scott, 3rd son of Robert Scott of Thirlestane – the story being related
in one version of the old ballad: 'The Dowie Dens of Yarrow'. The castle would
appear to have been ruined by 1630.

Tweedie Castle

Lanarkshire & Glasgow: About 1.5 miles south-east of Strathaven, on minor roads
north of A726, 0.5 miles east of Sandford, north of Kyle Water, at or near
Tweediehill.
Ruin or site   NS 727427   OS: 71   *   Map: 3, no: 338
Site of castle, which is said to be occupied by the present farm.

It was a property of the Hamiltons of Silvertonhill, and they built Newton House
at Cambuslang in 1602. The property had passed to the Lockharts of Castlehill by
1900.
Other refs: Tweedyhill; Silvertonhill Castle

Tweedyhill *see* Tweedie Castle

Tyninghame House

Lothians: About 3 miles west and north of Dunbar, on minor roads east of A198,
north of River Tyne, at Tyninghame House.
Private   NT 619798   OS: 67   **   Map: 4, no: 215
Set in picturesque wooded grounds, Tyninghame House incorporates part of a
building or castle from the 16th century or earlier. It was extended in 1617 and was
built around three sides of a courtyard, and remodelled in the castellated style and
added to in 1829 by William Burn.

Tyninghame is associated with St Baldred, and there are some remains of an old
church [NT 619797] to the south of the house, reputedly one of the three places
the saint was interred around 756 – the others being Auldhame and Preston – and
the Earls of Haddington are also buried here. There may have been a monastery
here, and Tyninghame was sacked by the Norseman Olaf Godfreysson in 941. The
lands remained with the church, and were held by the Bishopric, and later Arch-
bishopric, of St Andrews. It was leased to the Lauders of the Bass, who lived on the
Bass Rock in summer and here in the winter. The property was purchased by the
Hamilton Earls of Haddington in 1628, and is still occupied by the same family.
OPEN: Grounds: access at all reasonable times.
Parking.

Tynron Doon

Galloway: About 3.5 miles north-east of Moniaive, on minor roads and foot west
or north of A702, about 1 mile north-east of Tynron, north of Clonrae, at Tynron
Doon.
Ruin or site   NX 819939   OS: 78   **   Map: 1, no: 144
Site of castle, within the ramparts of an Iron Age fort. Robert the Bruce is said to
have sheltered here, with Kirkpatrick of Closeburn, in 1306 after stabbing the Red
Comyn at Dumfries. There was a later 16th-century L-plan tower house.

The ramparts of Tynron Doon which defend the western slopes can be seen clearly
from the approach to the hill. There are three ramparts separated by deep ditches
and a drystane wall around the summit. The outlines of a number of hut circles can
be made out within the enclosure. Finds from the site show that the fort was used
from the Iron Age until relatively recently.
Other refs: Doon of Tynron

Tyrie House *see* House of Tyrie

Udny Castle

Aberdeen & Gordon: About 4.5 miles east of Oldmeldrum, on minor roads south
A920 at junction with B9000, west of B999, just south of Pitmedden, at Udny.
Private   NJ 882268   OS: 38   **   Map: 10, no: 302**
Once a strong fortress, Udny Castle consists of a large altered 15th-century keep,
which may incorporate older work, to which 19th-century wings had been added –
although these were demolished in the 1960s. The keep was heightened, and corbelled-out bartizans and a parapet were added in the 17th century. The walls are
harled, rounded at corners, and pierced by gunloops and shot-holes.

The arched entrance leads to the vaulted basement, which contains the kitchen
and wine-cellar. A wide turnpike stair climbs to the vaulted hall on the first floor.
The windows of the hall have stone seats. A turnpike stair, in one corner of the hall,
leads up to the private chambers on the floors above.

The property was held by the Udnys from the 14th century. In 1634 the family
moved to Knockhall Castle, which was burned down in 1734. Udny was abandoned
about 1775, but later restored and extended. It is in good condition, and occupied
by descendants of the Udny family.

Uisdean *see* Caisteal Uisdein

Ulva House *see* Dun Ban, Ulva

Underbank *see* Southannan Castle

Underwood Castle

Ayrshire: About 3 miles north-east of Prestwick, on minor roads south of A77 or
north of A719, 1.5 miles south of Symington, Underwood.
Ruin or site   NS 390292   OS: 70   *   Map: 3, no: 138
Site of castle, with a moat. Nothing remains, and the site is occupied by Underwood, a mansion dating from 1792 but later extended.

Upper Wemyss *see* Hill of Tarvit Mansion House

Urie House

Kincardine & Deeside: About 1 mile north and west of Stonehaven, on minor
roads west of B979 or north of A957, north of Cowie Water, at Urie House.
Ruin or site   NO 860877   OS: 45   **   Map: 10, no: 291
Urie House, a large mansion of 1885 with additions of 1883-4, incorporates part of
a Z-plan tower house dating from the 16th and 17th centuries, which was demolished in 1854. The house is derelict.

It was a property of the Frasers, but passed by marriage to the Keith Earls Marischal. It was sold in 1415 to the Hays of Errol, who held it until 1647 when it was sold
back to the Keiths, then a year later to Barclay of Mathers. The Barclays were Quakers. Urie was sold in the 19th century to the Baird family.
Other refs: Ury House; Craghouse

Urquhart Castle

Inverness & Nairn: About 1.5 miles east of Drumnadrochit, on foot just east of
A82, on Strone Point on west shore of Loch Ness, south-east of Strone, at
Urquhart Castle.
His Scot   NH 531286   OS: 26   *   Map: 9, no: 61**
Standing on the shore of Loch Ness, Urquhart Castle consists of a 13th-century
castle of enclosure with a curtain wall and gatehouse. The courtyard encloses ranges
of buildings, including a hall and chapel, and has a 16th-century tower house at one
end. The lower storeys of the gatehouse survive, as well as parts of the curtain wall
and traces of the ranges within the courtyard. The tower house, part of which blew
down in a storm, had a vaulted basement, and a hall on the first floor, with private

chambers on the floors above.

The Picts had a fort here in the 6th century, which St Columba may have visited when he converted a Pictish chief Bridei or Brude – and where he may have confronted a kelpie or beastie in the loch. The first castle was built by the Durwards in the mid 13th century, and the large main courtyard was added in the late 13th and 14th centuries, probably by the Comyns. It was held in 1296 by forces of Edward I of England, but after two attacks was taken by the Scots, only to be recaptured by the English in 1303 after a long siege. In 1308 it was taken again by the Scots, led by Robert the Bruce.

The castle held out for David II in 1333 against Edward Balliol and Edward III of England. It was captured in 1437 by the Earl of Ross, but in 1476 was given to the Gordon Earl of Huntly. In 1509 James IV gave the castle to John Grant of Freuchie, on condition that he strengthen it, and the Grants built the tower house, gatehouse and present courtyard walls. The MacDonalds, however, captured the castle about 1515, after the death of their enemy, James IV, at the Battle of Flodden; and in 1545, with their allies the Camerons of Lochiel, devastated it and the surrounding area. In 1644 the castle was sacked by Covenanters. The castle held out against the Jacobites in 1689, but was later dismantled in 1691 to prevent them using it.

There have been many sightings of the Loch Ness Monster from near the castle – and there are two monster exhibition centres in nearby Drumnadrochit.

OPEN: Open all year: Apr-Sep, daily 9.30-18.30; Oct-Mar, daily 9.30-16.30; last ticket 45 mins before closing; closed 25/26 Dec and 1/2 Jan.

Walk to castle. Gift shop. WC. Car and coach parking. Group concessions. ££.
Tel: 01456 450551   Fax: 0131 668 8800
Email: hs.explore@scotland.gov.uk   Web: www.historic-scotland.gov.uk

Ury House *see* Urie House

Usan House

Angus & Dundee: About 2.5 miles south of Montrose, on minor roads east of A92, east of railway line, just north of hamlet of Usan, at Usan House.
Private   NO 723553   OS: 54   **   Map: 8, no: 273
Usan House, a mansion, may incorporate part of a castle.

The lands were held by the Leighton family, who built a castle on the site as early as the 13th century. The castle was rebuilt several times, including in 1608. The property later passed to the Scotts, then the Keiths, and is now held by the Alstons.

Uttershill Castle

Lothians: About 0.5 miles south of Penicuik, east of A701, south of River North Esk, just west of the Black Burn.
Ruin or site   NT 235594   OS: 66   **   Map: 4, no: 83
Uttershill Castle is a ruined altered 16th-century tower house, formerly of three storeys or more, which may have had a courtyard. The basement was vaulted, and the hall was on the first floor. It was extended, with the addition of an unvaulted kitchen and private chamber above, in the 17th century. The first floor was reached by a straight stair.

It was a property of the Prestons of Craigmillar. The Countess of Eglinton lived here in 1646. The property was sold in 1702 to the Clerks of Penicuik, who lived at Penicuik House, itself a ruin since a fire in 1899. Uttershill was ruined by the beginning of the 19th century, but used as a gunpowder store. It is about to be rebuilt or has been for several years.

Urquhart Castle – see above

V

W

Valence Castle *see* Bothwell Castle

Varrich *see* Caisteal Bharraich

Vaults, The *see* Windgate House

Vayne Castle
Angus & Dundee: About 7 miles west of Brechin, on minor roads and foot north and east of B957 at Tannadice, just south of Vayne, just north of the Noran Water.
Ruin or site NO 493599 OS: 54 ** Map: 8, no: 209
Vayne Castle is a ruined 16th-century Z-plan tower house. It consists of a main block, with a projecting square tower and round stair-tower at opposite corners. The tower probably rose to three storeys and an attic, although little remains above the basement except one gable. It was greatly enlarged in the 17th century, but materials were removed to build the nearby farmhouse.
  It was a property of the Mowats, who held the property from around the end of 12th century until 1450 (their castle was at Brandy Den [NO 478610]), when it passed to the Lindsay Earls of Crawford. It was acquired by the Carnegie Earl of Southesk in 1594, who sold it in 1766 to the Mills. They built an elegant new house at Noranside [NO 472609], which is apparently now a prison.
  The castle ruins are said to be haunted.
Other refs: Fearn

Vellore *see* Almond Castle

Venlaw Castle *see* Smithfield Castle

Vow *see* Eilean Vhow Castle

Walkinshaw
Renfrewshire: About 2 miles east of Renfrew, on minor roads west of A726, south of Black Cart Water, north of West Walkinshaw Farm.
Ruin or site NS 464667 OS: 64 * Map: 3, no: 193
Site of 16th-century tower house, which was replaced by a mansion, designed by Robert Adam in 1791 and extended in 1825, itself demolished in 1927.
  It was a property of the Walkinshaw family from 1235.
Other refs: Walkingshaw

Wall Tower *see* Ayton Castle

Wallace Tower *see* Auchterhouse

Wallace Tower *see* Benholm's Lodging

Wallace Tower, Ayr *see* Ayr Castle

Wallace's Buildings
Renfrewshire: In Elderslie, near A737, about 1 mile east of the Black Cart Water, on Main Street of the town.
Ruin or site NS 442630 OS: 63 * Map: 3, no: 179
Reputedly the site of the birthplace of William Wallace, this 17th-century house was demolished in the 1970s along with the farm of which it was part. The basement was vaulted, and contained a kitchen. All that remains are grassy mounds, and a monument.
  Elderslie was a property of the Wallaces in the 13th century until about 1850. William Wallace was a leader of the resistance against the English during the Wars of Independence. He led the Scots to victory at Stirling Bridge in 1296, but in 1298 was defeated at Falkirk by Edward I of England. He then travelled to Rome and France, to seek help from the Pope, but on his return was betrayed and captured by Edward I. He was hanged, drawn and quartered in London, and parts of his body were displayed at different towns in Scotland. However, it was his resistance which eventually put Robert the Bruce on the throne, and led to Scotland regaining her independence.
Other refs: Elderslie; Moat House, Elderslie
OPEN: Monument: access at all reasonable times.

Wallace's Castle *see* Pitgair Castle

Wallace's Tower
Borders: About 3 miles south and west of Kelso, in Roxburgh village, on minor roads south of A699, just west of the River Teviot.
Ruin or site NT 700304 OS: 74 ** Map: 2, no: 286
Wallace's Tower is a ruined 16th-century L-plan tower house. It consists of a main block and stair-wing, to which a tower had been added at one corner. The tower is ruined, above the basement, and very overgrown.
  The basement of the main block was vaulted.
  It was a property of the Kerrs of Cessford.

Wallace's Tower *see* Airth Castle

Wallans
Lanarkshire & Glasgow area: About 3 miles south-west of Carluke, near A72, near the River Clyde, near Overton.
Ruin or site NS 814490 [?] OS: 72 * Map: 3, no: 378
Site of castle, which is said to have stood on an islet and to have provided refuge to William Wallace.
Other refs: Overton; Castle Wallans

Walls *see* Old Walls

Walston

Lanarkshire & Glasgow: About 4 miles east of Carnwath, on minor roads north of A721, 1.5 miles north of Elsrickle, at or near Walston.
Ruin or site NT 060455 OS: 72 * Map: 3, no: 455
Site of a tower or fortified house, which was a property of the Hepburns in the 15th century, but had passed to the Baillies by 1650.

Wamphray Tower

Dumfriesshire: About 5 miles south and east of Moffat, on minor roads east of M74, just north of Wamphray Water, at Wamphray, near or at earthworks.
Ruin or site NY 128965 OS: 78 * Map: 1, no: 240
Site of castle, once a strong tower, which was altered and extended in later centuries. Little remains except some low walls.
  It was a property of the Corrie family, but passed to the Kirkpatricks in 1357, then to the Johnstones in 1476. In the second half of the 16th century it was home to William Johnstone, the 'Galliard'. His horse-stealing raid and death, and Willie o' Kirkhill's subsequent revenge, are recorded in the old ballad 'The Lads of Wamphray'. John Johnstone of Wamphray was imprisoned in his own home for his part in the Jacobite Rising of 1745, and only escaped execution by changing places with a kinsman. The property was sold to the Hope Earl of Hopetoun in 1747, and the castle was abandoned at this time and became ruinous.
Other refs: Leithenhall; Wamphray Place

Wandel Tower *see* Bower of Wandel

Ward of Lochnorris

Ayrshire: About 5.5 miles west of Cumnock, on minor road north of A70, south of Lugar Water, west of Dumfries House, Ward of Lochnorris.
Ruin or site NS 539205 OS: 70 * Map: 3, no: 244
Site of castle, nothing of which remains.
  It was a property of the Crawford family in 1440, but the property passed to the Dalrymple Earls of Dumfries. They built Dumfries House [NS 541204] in 1757, the building being designed by John and Robert Adam for William Dalrymple, 4th Earl of Dumfries. The house is a classical mansion with a central block and pavilions. The property later passed to the Stewart Marquis of Bute.
Other refs: Lesnoreis; Dumfries House

Ward, The *see* Clunie Castle

Warden's Tower, Cavers *see* Cavers House

Warder *see* Wardhouse

Wardhouse

Aberdeen & Gordon: About 2.5 miles west of Insch, on minor roads north of B9002, just south of Mains of Wardhouse.
Ruin or site NJ 593289 OS: 37 * Map: 10, no: 155
Nothing remains of a 13th-century castle of enclosure, except ditches and earthworks.
  It was a property of the Leslies in the 16th century, but passed to the Gordons.
Other refs: Warder

Wardhouse Tower *see* Woodhouse Tower

Warmanbie

Dumfriesshire: About 2 miles north of Annan, on minor roads east of B722, east of River Annan, at or near Warmanbie.
Ruin or site NY 196689 OS: 85 * Map: 1, no: 262
Site of tower house, which has a park. Warmanbie is a modern mansion, and now used as a hotel.
Other refs: Wormonby

Warthill House

Aberdeen & Gordon: About 2.5 miles south of Rothienorman, on minor roads south of A920, 1 mile east of North Rayne, 0.5 miles north-west of Meikle Wartle, at Warthill.
Private NJ 710315 OS: 29 * Map: 10, no: 216
Site of a castle. It was replaced by or is incorporated into a 17th-century L-plan house with bartizans, which was altered and extended in 1801, 1850 and 1891, but part of which has since been demolished.
  It was a property of the Leslies, and is still owned and occupied by their descendants.

Waterhead Castle

Ayrshire: About 5 miles east and north of Dalmellington, on minor road 5.5 miles south and west of A76, north of B741, just south of Beoch Lane, at Waterhead.
Private NS 543115 [?] OS: 70 * Map: 3, no: 245
Site of castle of the MacAdam family, also recorded as Waterheid.
  This castle, or another one nearby, was also known as Little Rigend and is recorded as being a property of the Cathcarts. Nothing remained of this building by the middle of the 19th century.
Other refs: Waterheid; Little Rigend Castle

Waterheid *see* Waterhead Castle

Waterton Castle

Aberdeen & Gordon: About 1 mile east of Ellon, on minor road south of A920 or north of A92, just north of River Ythan, at Waterton.
Ruin or site NJ 972305 OS: 30 * Map: 10, no: 343
Site of 17th-century tower house, little of which remains, except the vaulted basement. It formerly rose to four storeys, and consisted of a main block and wings. The basement was vaulted.
  The lands were originally held by Kinloss Abbey, but passed to the Knights Templars, then to the Bannermans about 1560, then to the Forbeses of Waterton, who held the property until at least 1770. John Forbes of Waterton was murdered by the Kennedys of Kermuck in 1652.
Other refs: Castle of Waterton

Wauchope Castle

Dumfriesshire: About 0.5 miles south-west of Langholm, on B7068, north of the Wauchope Water.
Ruin or site NY 354840 [?] OS: 79 * Map: 1, no: 311
Site of castle of enclosure, built on the site of a motte and bailey castle.
  Wauchope was a property of the Lindsays from 1285, and they built the castle. It was ruinous by 1580, and a manse built on the site, itself now gone.

Wauchope Tower

Borders: About 2.5 miles south of Bonchester Bridge, south of A6088 on minor road east of B6357, at Wauchope.
Ruin or site NT 580084 [?] OS: 80 * Map: 2, no: 219
Site of tower house, a property of the Turnbulls, which was completely demolished by the beginning of the 19th century.

Waughton Castle

Lothians: About 3 miles north-west of East Linton, on minor roads north of B1377, about 2 miles west of Whitekirk, about 0.5 miles north of Waughton.
Ruin or site NT 567809 OS: 67 ** Map: 4, no: 203
Waughton Castle is a ruined 14th-century castle and courtyard, of which only part of one wing survives.
  It was a property of the Hepburns. In 1475 a David Hepburn of Waughton was 'interdicted from interfering with the carting of goods dispatched from Haddington', and in 1536 Patrick Hepburn of Waughton had to pay a share of £1000 to build Blackness Castle as a punishment for a misdemeanour. In 1547 the castle here was sacked by the English. A dispossessed Hepburn raided the castle in 1569, when it was being kept by the Laird of Carmichael.

Waygateshaw House

Lanarkshire & Glasgow area: About 4.5 miles north-west of Lanark, on minor road north between B7056 and A73, on the east side of the River Clyde, at Waygateshaw.

Private NS 825484 OS: 72 *** Map: 3, no: 381

Waygateshaw House is a 16th-century courtyard castle. It consists of a 16th-century tower house, a 17th-century wing, and a modern block enclosing a small courtyard, the last side being completed by a wall. The entrance to the courtyard is through a moulded arched doorway, which is defended by gunloops.

The tower house, now of three storeys, has a small stair-wing. The walls are pierced by small windows and gunloops. The basement is vaulted. A steep turnpike stair climbs to all floors, including the vaulted hall on the first floor.

The 17th-century extension is three storeys and a garret in height.

Waygateshaw was a property of the Murrays of Touchadam, but in 1539 passed by marriage to the Lockharts. One of the family, Stephen Lockhart, was included in the indictment for the murder of Lord Darnley in 1572. The family were forfeited for their share in the Pentland Rising of 1666, but they later recovered the property. It was sold to the Weirs in 1720, and later passed to the Steel family. The house is still occupied, and has been restored.

Weaver's Castle

Western Isles: To south of island of Eriskay, about 8 miles south of Lochboisdale, by boat on southern tip of Stack Islands, on Eilean Leathan, at Weaver's Castle.

Ruin or site NF 787072 OS: 31 * Map: 11, no: 10

Built on an almost inaccessible site, Weaver's Castle or Stack consists of a small square ruined tower. The castle is also known as Castle Stalker and Caisteal a' Bhrebider.

Other refs: Castle Stalker; Caisteal a' Bhrebider

Wedderburn Castle

Borders: About 1.5 miles south-east of Duns, on minor roads south of A6105, just north of the Langton Burn, at or near Wedderburn Castle.

Private NT 809529 OS: 74 * Map: 2, no: 331

Site of castle, although the present house dates from 1771-5 and was designed by Robert and James Adam. The old castle stood within the courtyard of the newer house, but it was demolished in the 19th century.

The lands were originally held by the Wedderburns, but passed to the Homes. The Homes of Wedderburn gained the lands of Blackadder by murdering the last of the Blackadder male line, and forcing the remaining daughters to marry sons of the Homes, after besieging them in Blackadder Castle. The present house was built for unlucky Patrick Home of Billie who – having built one house for a girl he was unable to marry – built Wedderburn for his new bride only to catch her in bed with another man on their honeymoon in Venice.

Wedderburn Castle

Angus & Dundee: About 3.5 miles north-east of Dundee, on minor roads east of A929, north of B961, west of B978, west of Fithie Burn, near Barns of Wedderburn.

Ruin or site NO 435352 [?] OS: 54 * Map: 8, no: 186

Site of castle, which was mostly complete in 1704 but had been completely demolished before 1885. A doocot was built in the site.

It was a property of the Douglas Earls of Angus, passed to the Ogilvies, then to the Wedderburn family. It was later acquired by the Scrimgeours.

Other refs: Easter Powrie

Wedderlie House

Borders: About 1 mile north of Westruther, on minor roads north of B6456, south of the Blackadder Water.

Private NT 640515 OS: 74 *** Map: 2, no: 255

Wedderlie House, a mansion of 1680, incorporates a 16th-century L-plan tower house of three storeys.

The basement of one part is vaulted, and the hall was on the first floor.

Wedderlie was a property of the Polwarth family in the 13th century, but passed to the Edgars in 1327, and remained with them for 400 years. There was probably an earlier castle here, part of which may be incorporated into the tower house. In

1733 Wedderlie was acquired by the Stewart Lord Blantyre. Although ruined by the later part of the 19th century, it has since been restored and is still occupied.

Weems *see* Wemyss Castle

Well Tower, Cupar *see* Cupar Castle

Wellpark *see* Easter Greenock Castle

Wellwood House

Ayrshire: About 2 miles west of Muirkirk, on minor roads south of A70, just north of River Ayr, west of Midwellwood Farm.

Ruin or site NS 665263 OS: 71 * Map: 3, no: 313

Wellwood House, a mansion of 1878, incorporated a house or tower of the Campbells of about 1600. The new house was built by the Bairds, who bought the estate in 1863. The house was demolished in 1926.

The house was said to be haunted by the apparition of a young woman, called 'Beanie'. She appears to have been murdered, perhaps on the stairs of the house, for it was said a blood stain here could not be removed. Her ghost was reportedly seen walking from her room in the older part of the house out to the grounds, where she wept.

Wemyss Castle

Fife: About 3 miles north and east of Kirkcaldy, on minor roads south of A955, near the shore of the Firth of Forth, south of Coaltown of Wemyss.

Private NT 329951 OS: 59 **** Map: 7, no: 82

Wemyss Castle originally consisted of a 15th-century rectangular keep and a large irregularly shaped courtyard, with a round tower at one corner, which may date from the 13th century or earlier. Ranges of buildings were built within the courtyard in the 16th century, and about 1699 a large L-plan block was also added. The castle was extended again, and the courtyard was finally filled in during the 19th century. Most of the Victorian additions were demolished in the 1930s, and the castle was restored back to its original appearance.

The building has been much altered, but the original curtain wall can be traced, and the basements of some of the buildings are vaulted. A fine 17th-century scale-

and-platt stair survives, as does much panelling.

It was a property of the Wemyss family. Sir Michael Wemyss was one of the ambassadors sent to bring Margaret, Maid of Norway, to Scotland at the end of the 13th century, and a silver basin, preserved at the castle, is said to have been given to Sir Michael by the King of Norway. The castle was sacked by the English during the Wars of Independence. Sir David Wemyss was killed at the Battle of Flodden in 1513. Mary, Queen of Scots, first met Lord Darnley here in 1565.

The family were made Earls of Wemyss in 1633, and Charles II visited in 1650 and 1657. They were forfeited for their part in the Jacobite Rising of 1745, although the title was restored in 1826. The Wemyss family still occupy the castle.

A 'Green Lady' – Green Jean – reputedly haunts the castle, and is said to have been seen in all parts of the building, both by family and servants. In the 1890s she was described as 'tall and slim and entirely clad in green, with her visage hidden by the hood of her mantle'.

Wemyss Castle

Angus & Dundee: About 2.5 miles east and north of Forfar, on minor road just north of B9113, 1 mile east of Restenneth, at or near Wemyss.
Ruin or site NO 497524 [?] OS: 54 * Map: 8, no: 210
Site of castle of the Lindsay family.

The castle may have been at West Mains of Turin [NO 518532].
Other refs: Weems

Wemyss Chapel *see* West Wemyss

Wemyss Hall *see* Hill of Tarvit Mansion House

West Barcloy *see* Castlehill of Barcloy

West Barcloy

Galloway: About 6 miles south of Dalbeattie, on minor roads west of A710, 1 mile south of Rockcliffe, at or near West Barcloy.
Ruin or site NX 855532 [?] OS: 84 * Map: 1, no: 158
Site of tower house, which may have replaced the castle at nearby Castlehill of Barcloy NX 854524].
Other refs: Barcloy

West Barns *see* Barns

West Gellet *see* Broomhall

West Hall *see* Westhall

West Lilliesleaf *see* Riddell Tower

West Lilsly *see* Riddell Tower

West Linnbridgeford *see* Linnbridgeford

West Linton

Borders: In West Linton, near junction of A702 and B7059.
Private NT 149519 OS: 72 * Map: 2, no: 23
A small 16th-century L-plan tower house was extended in the 18th century, and altered more recently. It consists of a main block and stair-wing, which formerly contained a turnpike stair.

It was a property of the Melrose family.

West Mathers Castle *see* Kaim of Mathers Castle

West Port House, Linlithgow

Lothians: In Linlithgow, near A803, just south of Linlithgow Loch, at the west end of the High Street.
Private NT 002770 [?] OS: 65 ** Map: 4, no: 11
West Port House incorporates part of a 16th-century tower house. It consists of a plain three-storey L-plan tower house, which has been reduced in height and much altered in the 17th century. Gunloops and shot-holes have been sealed.

The interior has also been altered.

It was a property of the Hamiltons. Hamilton of Bothwellhaugh shot and killed the Regent Moray in 1570 from a house nearby, after Moray had turned his wife and baby out from their home at Old Woodhouselee.

West Preston *see* Preston

West Printonan *see* Bite-About Pele

West Quarter *see* Westquarter

West Reston *see* Reston

West Shield *see* Westshield

West Wemyss

Fife: About 2 miles north-east of Kirkcaldy, in West Wemyss, on minor roads south of A965, near the shore.
Ruin or site NT 319947 OS: 59 ** Map: 7, no: 79
West Wemyss consists of a tower house, built in 1589 and restored around 1965, which has a four-storey stair-tower.

In nearby Chapel Garden, where the Wemyss burial ground is located, is the ruin of another 16th-century house. It rises to four storeys and attic, with a round projecting stair-tower, and is crowned by a corbelled-out rectangular caphouse.

The basement is below ground, and contains a kitchen.

It was a property of the Wemyss family.
Other refs: The Chapel, Wemyss; Wemyss Chapel

Westburn House *see* Drumsargad Castle

Westburnflat Tower

Borders: About 1.5 miles north and east of Newcastleton, south of B6357 near junction with B6399, south of Liddel Water, east of Sandholm.
Ruin or site NY 497894 [?] OS: 79 * Map: 2, no: 159
Site of tower house, a property of the Armstrongs. It was still in use at the beginning of the 18th century by one Willie of Westburnflat, who was hanged for thieving cattle.

Wester Alemoor *see* Alemoor Tower

Wester Braikie *see* Braikie Castle

Wester Elchies

Moray: About 1 mile west of Charlestown of Aberlour, on minor roads south of B9102, north of River Spey, at Wester Elchies.
Ruin or site NJ 256431 OS: 28 * Map: 10, no: 47
Wester Elchies, which has been demolished, consisted of a 17th-century L-plan tower house, which was later extended to Z-plan, as well as many other alterations. The original part rose to three storeys, and had a round stair-tower. The gables were corbiestepped, and the roofline had been altered. The walls were pierced by shot-holes.

The basement was vaulted, the hall was on the first floor, and private chambers occupied the floors above.

It was a property of the Grants, but demolished in 1970.

Wester Greenock Castle *see* Greenock Castle

Wester Happrew

Borders: About 6 miles north-west of Peebles, on minor roads just west of A72, west of Lyne Water, at Wester Happrew.
Private NT 171418 OS: 72 * Map: 2, no: 34
Site of tower house.

Wester Kames Castle

Argyll & Dunbartonshire: On island of Bute, about 3 miles north-west of Rothesay, on minor road west of A886 at Kames Bay, 1 mile west of Port Bannatyne, at Wester Kames.
Private NS 062680 OS: 63 * Map: 5, no: 102**
Standing close to Kames Castle, Wester Kames Castle is a small 16th-century tower house. It consists of a rectangular main block with a projecting wing. A round stair-turret, in the re-entrant angle, is crowned by a corbelled-out square watch-chamber. One corner is topped by a bartizan, with a conical roof, and a machiolation, at parapet level, defends the entrance below.

The basement is vaulted, and contained a kitchen and wine-cellar. A turnpike stair leads up to the hall, on the first floor, while the upper floors were reached by the turret stair.

The lands were originally held by the MacKinlays, but the Crown took them after a squabble over an archery contest, and granted them to the royal butler, a MacDonald, who took the name Spence. In 1670 the property passed by marriage to the Grahams. The castle became ruinous, but was restored by the Stewart Marquis of Bute.
Other refs: Edinbeg Tower

Wester Keillor *see* Keillor Castle

Wester Moniack *see* Moniack Castle

Wester Ochiltree *see* Ochiltree Castle

Wester Polmaise *see* Steuarthall

Wester Powrie Castle *see* Powrie Castle

Wester Shian

Perth & Kinross: About 6 miles south of Aberfeldy, on minor road between A827 at Kenmore and A822 at Amulree, north of River Quaich, at Wester Shian.
Ruin or site NN 842400 [?] OS: 52 * Map: 8, no: 22
Site of castle, the last vestige of which was removed in 1820.

Wester Stanhope *see* Stanhope Tower

Wester Wormiston *see* Cringletie House

Westerhall Tower

Dumfriesshire: About 4 miles north-west of Langholm, on minor roads north of B709, just east of River Esk, at Westerhall.
Private NY 320893 OS: 79 ** Map: 1, no: 300
Westerhall Tower is a much-altered 16th-century tower house of three storeys, to which has been added a later mansion. The old part has a round stair-tower. The roof has been altered, but the windows are small.

An adjacent wing has a vaulted basement, and contained a kitchen.

It was a property of Johnstones of Westerhall, who held the lands for over 400 years. The house has been much altered, partly as a result of two fires, one in 1873, and is still occupied.

Westerkirk

Dumfriesshire: About 6 miles north-west of Langholm, on minor roads north of B709, between Megget Water and River Esk, at or near Westerkirk Mains.
Ruin or site NY 294916 OS: 79 * Map: 1, no: 291
Site of castle, a property of the Beatties.

Westhall

Aberdeen & Gordon: About 7 miles north-west of Inverurie, on minor roads north of B9002, south River Urie, north of Old Westhall, at Westhall House.
Private NJ 673266 OS: 38 * Map: 10, no: 191**
Westhall consists of a small 16th-century L-plan tower house of three storeys and a garret. To this has been added a gabled block, with a round stair-tower, probably in the 17th century. A stair-turret projects on corbelling in the re-entrant angle of the tower. A crenellated parapet has open rounds at all corners. The original windows are small.

The basement is vaulted, the hall is on the first floor, and private chambers occupied the floors above.

The lands were held by the Bishop of Aberdeen from the 13th century, but passed to the Gordons during the Reformation. The property was sold to the Hornes in 1681, then passed by marriage to the Elphinstones. The house is in good condition, and still occupied.
Other refs: West Hall

Westhall Tower

Lanarkshire & Glasgow area: About 5 miles east of Carnwath, on minor roads north of A721 at Newbigging and A702, north of the South Medwin, just south of Westhall.
Ruin or site NT 048473 OS: 72 ** Map: 3, no: 453
Little survives of a 16th-century L-plan tower house, except the vaulted basement with the scant remains of a turnpike stair. The property was held by the Grahams from 1477, then the Hepburns, the Douglases, and the Lockharts. The remains of the tower were cleared and excavated in the 1980s.

There may have been another tower nearby.

Westhills

Dumfriesshire: About 2.5 miles west of Gretna, on minor roads south of B721, 1.5 miles east and south of Eastriggs, north side of Solway Firth, at or near Westhills.
Ruin or site NY 272654 [?] OS: 85 * Map: 1, no: 284
Site of tower house, some remains of which survived in 1858. What appears to be a tower is marked on Blaeu's Atlas Novus map of Annandale round about Westhill, although it stands by the edge of a park with the name 'Blastwood'.
Other refs: Blastwood

Westhouses

Borders: About 0.75 miles north-west of Melrose, on minor roads north of A7, north of River Tweed, at or near Pavilion.
Ruin or site NT 527354 OS: 73 * Map: 2, no: 183
Site of strong tower house, square in plan, with gunloops, which was demolished at the beginning of the 19th century. The tower dated from the 15th century.

It was a property of the Ormistons, and there was a village nearby, all traces of which have gone.

This is possibly the same tower which is known as Allanhaugh or Allanmouth, although this property was apparently latterly held by the Scotts of Buccleuch. This is likely to be a confusion with Allanmouth Tower, south of Hawick, however.
Other refs: Pavilion; Allanhaugh

Weston

Lanarkshire & Glasgow: About 4 miles east of Carnwath, on minor roads north and east of A721, at or near Weston.
Ruin or site NT 043476 [?] OS: 72 * Map: 3, no: 452
Site of tower house.

Westquarter *see* Glassford

Westquarter

Falkirk: About 2 miles east of Falkirk, just north of B805, Westquarter.
His Scot NS 913787 [?] OS: 65 ** Map: 6, no: 100
Possible site of castle. West Quarter is marked on Blaeu's Atlas Novus map of Stirlingshire, and Westquarter House was held by the Jacksons of Halhill about 1890.
  A doocot, which is a fine rectangular building, has a heraldic panel over the doorway which is dated 1647.
Other refs: West Quarter
OPEN: Doocot: access at all reasonable times.
Parking nearby.
Tel: 0131 668 8800   Fax: 0131 668 8888
Email: hs.explore@scotland.gov.uk   Web: www.historic-scotland.gov.uk

Westraw

Lanarkshire & Glasgow: About 3 miles east of Lanark, on minor roads north of A73, 2 miles south of Carstairs, at Westraw Mains.
Ruin or site NS 947429 OS: 72 * Map: 3, no: 422
The present house dates from the 15th century, but there are no longer any defensive features. It was a property of the Carmichaels.

Westshield

Lanarkshire & Glasgow area: About 5 miles north-east of Lanark, on minor roads north of A70, east of A706, west of B7016, just north of the Mouse Water, at Westshield.
Ruin or site NS 946494 OS: 72 * Map: 3, no: 420**
Westshield incorporated a 16th-century tower house, rectangular in plan, of four storeys and a garret. Two gabled wings were added in the 17th century. A small square stair-tower stood in the re-entrant angle. Lower later wings were also added, but part had been demolished. Most of the windows had been enlarged. The building was demolished in the 1980s after a fire.
  The entrance was at the foot of the stair-tower. The basement was vaulted, and contained three chambers. A turnpike stair climbed as far as the third floor. The hall was on the first floor, with private chambers on the floors above.
  It was a property of the Denholm family, but passed to the Lockharts of The Lee in the 17th century.
Other refs: West Shield

Westside Tower *see* Black Esk Tower

Whistleberry Castle

Kincardine & Deeside: About 2.5 miles north-east of Inverbervie, on minor road and foot east of A92, just west of the sea on cliffs, east of Whistleberry.
Ruin or site NO 862753 OS: 45 * Map: 10, no: 293
Not much remains of a keep or tower house and courtyard with a gatehouse and drawbridge on a promontory above the sea.
  It may have been a property of the Allardice family.
  There are four castles here very close by: Whistleberry, Adam's, Kinneff and Caddan, as well as another on the coast, all in the parish known as Herbertshiel. This latter stronghold was held by the Lindsays but the location is not known.
Other refs: Herbertshiel Castle

Whitchesters

Borders: About 2 miles south-west of Hawick, on minor roads east of A7, east of River Teviot, at or near Whitchesters.
Ruin or site NT 469110 OS: 79 * Map: 2, no: 135
There is believed to have been a tower house here, a property of the Scotts.

Whitclaugh *see* Whithaugh Tower

White Castle

Lanarkshire & Glasgow area: About 4 miles south-east of Carnwath, just south of B7016, at Whitecastle.
Ruin or site NT 018417 [?] OS: 72 * Map: 3, no: 444
Site of castle.

White House, Calda *see* Calda House

White Walls, Kinnell *see* Kinnell Castle

Whitecastle *see* Nunraw Castle

Whitefield Castle

Perth & Kinross: About 13 miles north of Rattray, on minor road and track east of A924 at Dalnagairn, 1 mile north-west of Kirkmichael, at Whitefield.
Ruin or site NO 089617 OS: 43 ** Map: 8, no: 74
Whitefield Castle is a ruined 16th-century L-plan tower house, consisting of a main block of two storeys and a garret and stair-wing. The building was altered in the 18th century, and many windows were enlarged.
  The basement of the main block was vaulted and contained a kitchen and cellar, the hall was on the first floor, with private chambers on the floors above.
  It was a property of the Spalding family. The upper part of the castle was demolished in the early 19th century to build the nearby farm.

Whiteford Tower

Renfrewshire: About 1.5 miles south-east of Paisley Abbey, on minor roads east of A726, at Whiteford.
Ruin or site NS 505625 [?] OS: 64 * Map: 3, no: 215
Site of castle, a property of the Whiteford or Whitefoord family.
Other refs: Whitefoord

Whitehall of Perth *see* Gowrie House, Perth

Whitehaugh Castle

Ayrshire: About 5 miles west of Muirkirk, on minor road north of B743, west of Whitehaugh Water, at Nether Whitehaugh.
Ruin or site NS 616291 OS: 71 * Map: 3, no: 287
Little remains of a tower house and other buildings.
Other refs: Nether Whitehaugh Castle

Whitehills Castle *see* Kinnell Castle

Whitehouse

Lothians: About 4 miles west and north of Edinburgh Castle, in Cramond, on minor road south of A90, on Whitehouse Road.
Private NT 187766 [?] OS: 66 ** Map: 4, no: 59
Whitehouse is a much-altered 16th-century L-plan tower house, dated 1615 and much extended in 1901.

Whitehouse

Ayrshire: In Lamlash, on minor road just off A841, near Benlister Burn, at Whitehouse, Arran.
Ruin or site NS 024308 OS: 69 * Map: 3, no: 4
There is believed to have been a small square tower house here which, along with another on the Holy Island, defended Lamlash Bay. The towers are mentioned in 1543, but there are no apparent remains.

Whitekirk

Lothians: At Whitekirk, on A198 between A1 and North Berwick, about 2.5 miles north of East Linton.
Ruin or site NT 595816 OS: 67 ** Map: 4, no: 207
A much-altered 16th-century tower house is built into the barn behind the church.
  Whitekirk was a place of pilgrimage in the Middle Ages and was visited by Aeneas Sylvius Piccolomini (later Pope Pious II) who, after being saved from a storm, walked

barefoot to Whitekirk from Dunbar, and suffered from rheumatism for the rest of his life. A fresco in the chapter house of Sienna Cathedral records his visit.

Whitekirk may have been founded around 1295 after Agnes, Countess of Dunbar, was healed at a nearby well [NT 598817]. The number of miracles which occurred at the well was so great that a shrine was built in 1309 and dedicated to St Mary. This well apparently dried up around 1830, and its location is not certain.

The existing church [NT 596815] is largely 15th century, although parts date from the 12th. Although it survived attacks by English armies and restoration in 1885, it was burned by suffragettes in 1914. It was restored, and is a fine building, cruciform in plan with a large central tower.

There were so many pilgrims around the beginning of the 15th century that James I placed it under his personal protection and had pilgrims' hostels built to house visitors.

James IV also visited Whitekirk, but in 1537 James V granted the hostels to his favourite, Oliver Sinclair, who demolished them and built a tower house with the stone. Sinclair went on to lead the Scottish army to humiliating defeat at the Battle of Solway Moss in 1542 – soon after which James V died, reputedly of a broken heart. The tower was torched by the Earl of Hertford in 1544, and again in 1548. The building has been restored as a dwelling.

OPEN: Church: open all year.
Parking nearby.

Whiteside Peel

Borders: About 3.5 miles south of Gordon, on minor roads between B6397 and A6089, about 0.5 miles south of Mellerstain House.
Ruin or site NT 644384 OS: 74 ** Map: 2, no: 258
Not much remains of Whiteside Peel, except the basement. It was probably a property of the Homes.

Whiteside Tower

Borders: About 3.5 miles south of West Linton, on minor road and foot east of B7059, 1 mile south of Romanno Bridge, east of Lyne Water, at Whiteside.
Ruin or site NT 164462 OS: 72 * Map: 2, no: 29
Site of tower house, built with materials from an earlier castle nearby, which was known as Grahams Walls.

Whiteslade Tower *see* Whitslaid Tower

Whitesside *see* Whitlawside

Whithaugh Tower

Borders: About 0.5 miles north-east of Newcastleton, on minor roads east of B6357, east of Liddel Water, at Whithaugh.
Ruin or site NY 489880 OS: 79 * Map: 2, no: 152
Little survives of a 16th-century tower house of the Armstrongs, second in importance only to Mangerton, except the unvaulted basement built into the southern wing of a modern mansion. An armorial panel is also built into the mansion. The tower was burned by the English in 1582 and again in 1599. Simon Armstrong of Whithaugh was hanged for reiving in 1535. The tower had been demolished by 1770 and little was left by 1795.
Other refs: Hillhouse Tower; Whitclaugh

Whitlawside

Dumfriesshire: About 4 miles north-east of Canonbie, on minor road south of B6357, north of Liddel Water, near Whitlawside Burn, at or near Whitlawside.
Ruin or site NY 444800 [?] OS: 79 * Map: 1, no: 333
Site of tower house, a property of Simon [Armstrong?] of Whitesside.
Other refs: Whitesside

Whitmuir Hall

Borders: About 1.5 miles south-east of Selkirk, on minor roads south of A699, south of Whitmuir Hall.
Ruin or site NT 503271 OS: 73 * Map: 2, no: 169
Site of tower house, a property of Kelso Abbey. The present Whitmuir Hall dates from the 19th century, although date stones of 1250 and 1775 are said to survive.

Whitslade Tower *see* Whitslaid Tower

Whitslade Tower

Borders: About 2 miles south of Broughton, on minor road west of A701, near Whitslade House.
Ruin or site NT 112350 OS: 72 ** Map: 2, no: 10
Little survives of a 16th-century tower house with a small wing, except the vaulted basement, which is used as a store.

It was a property of the Porteous family, but later passed to the Murrays of Stanhope, then the Dicksons.

Whitslade Tower

Borders: About 5 miles west and north of Hawick, on minor roads north of B711, just north of Ale Water, 1 mile south of Todrig, at Whitslade.
Ruin or site NT 429180 OS: 79 * Map: 2, no: 110
Little or nothing remains of a tower house, located south of the farmhouse. It was a property of the Scotts of Whitslade, and a tower here was torched in 1502 by a Hector Lauder and the Armstrongs.
Other refs: Whitslaid

Whitslaid *see* Whitslade Tower

Whitslaid Tower

Borders: About 3 miles south-east of Lauder, on minor road east of A68, just east of the Leader Water.
Ruin or site NT 557446 OS: 73 * Map: 2, no: 208
Whitslaid Tower is a very ruined rectangular 16th-century tower house, formerly of three storeys. The basement was vaulted.

It was a property of the Lauders or the Maitlands, but in the mid 17th century was held by the Montgomerys of Macbiehill.
Other refs: Whitslade Tower; Whiteslade Tower

Whittinghame Castle

Lothians: About 2.5 miles south of East Linton, north of B6370 on minor road 1.5 miles south west of Stenton, on west bank of Whittinghame Water.
Private NT 602733 OS: 67 * Map: 4, no: 211**
Whittinghame Castle is an altered 15th-century L-plan keep, consisting of a main block and small stair-wing. The corbelled-out parapet is rounded at the corners.

Some of the windows have been enlarged.

The entrance is in the stair-wing, and the basement is vaulted. The hall, on the first floor, now housing a collection of old prints and documents, is panelled, and has a fine painted ceiling.

The lands originally belonged to the Cospatrick Earls of March, but were acquired by the Douglases in the 14th century. James Douglas, Regent Morton, held the castle during the reign of Mary, Queen of Scots. It is supposed to be where the plot to murder Lord Darnley, husband of Mary, was hatched with Morton, Maitland of Lethington and James Hepburn, Earl of Bothwell, later Mary's third husband. The property passed to the Setons, then to the Hays, and in 1818 to the Balfours of Balbirnie. One of the family was Arthur James Balfour, Prime Minister of Great Britain and the 1st Earl Balfour. The castle is still occupied by the Balfours.

Whitton Tower

Borders: About 2 miles south of Morebattle, on minor road south of B6401, at Whitton.
Ruin or site   NT 759222   OS: 74   **   Map: 2, no: 304
Whitton Tower is a ruined 16th-century tower house, one wall of which has been demolished. The basement was probably vaulted.

The property was held by the Bennetts in 1523, when their castle was sacked by the English. It was burned by the Earl of Hertford in 1545. The property had passed to the Riddels by 1602, who probably built, or rebuilt, the tower.

Whytbank Tower

Borders: About 3 miles west of Galashiels, west of B710 between A72 at Clovenfords and A7, south east side of Knowes Hill.
Private   NT 442377   OS: 73   **   Map: 2, no: 116
Whytbank Tower consists of a ruined 16th-century tower house, formerly of four storeys, with a later stair-tower. The tower had a courtyard, enclosing ranges of buildings, and a terraced garden and orchard.

Part of the basement is vaulted, the hall was on the first floor, with a private chamber above.

It was a property of the Pringles. The tower was occupied until 1790 or perhaps later, but roofless by 1823. It was restored, with considerable rebuilding, around 1990.
Other refs: Whytebank Tower

Whytebank Tower *see* Whytbank Tower

Wigg Castle *see* Castlewigg

Wigtown Castle

Galloway: Just south-east of Wigtown, on minor roads east of A714, just east of dismantled railway, just north of the mouth of the River Bladnoch.
Ruin or site   NX 437550   OS: 83   *   Map: 1, no: 70
Site of 13th-century castle of enclosure. It was round in shape, enclosed by stone walls, and the sea defended the stronghold and provided water for the moat. Nothing remains except slight traces of the ditch.

The castle was probably built by Alexander III in the 1280s. It was held for the English from 1291, although William Wallace is said to have captured it in 1297. It was demolished by the Bruces, after it had been recovered from the English around 1310, during the Wars of Independence. Foundations could still be seen in 1830.

The Flemings were made Earls of Wigtown in 1341, but the title passed to the Douglases in 1372. The title was renewed in 1606, again for the Flemings, and the last of the of the line, the 7th Earl, died in 1747.

Nothing has survived of the tower house William Hannay was licensed to build in 1549, on High Gate, in Wigtown.

At Wigtown in 1685, James Graham of Claverhouse, 'Bonnie Dundee' or 'Bloody Clavers', Sheriff of Wigtown, sentenced two women to death. Margaret MacLachlan and Margaret Wilson were ordered to be drowned by the incoming tide for refusing to renounce the Cameronian repudiation of the King. They became known as the 'Wigtown Martyrs', but there is some debate as to whether they were actually drowned.

Williamston

Perth & Kinross: About 9 miles west of Perth, on minor roads south of A85, about 0.5 miles south of Pow Water, 1 mile east of Madderty, at Williamstoun.
Private   NN 972220   OS: 58   **   Map: 8, no: 42
Williamstoun is an altered 17th-century tower house, which was built about 1655. It has a main block of two storeys and an attic, with a round stair-tower corbelled out to a square and crowned by a caphouse.

The lands were held by the Blairs of Kinfauns, who sold the property to the Oliphants. The house was built for Oliphant of Gask, after he was disinherited, because instead of marrying the 45-year-old sister of the Marquis of Douglas – as his family wished – he married a daughter of the Minister of Gask.
Other refs: Williamstoun

Williamstoun *see* Williamston

Williamwood *see* Lee Castle

Windgate House

Lanarkshire & Glasgow area: About 5 miles south and west of Biggar, on minor roads south of A702 at Coulter, near Cow Gill (Burn), south side Lamington Hill, at or near Cowgill.
Ruin or site   NT 016271   OS: 72   **   Map: 3, no: 442
Known locally as 'The Vaults', Windgate House is a small ruined tower house of the Baillies of Lamington, dating from the 16th century, with a vaulted basement.

An apparition of a couple in Victorian dress have reportedly been witnessed here, and the story goes that they only appear when something significant is going to happen to the Lamington family.
Other refs: Vaults, The

Windshiel

Borders: About 4 miles north-west of Duns, north of B6355, west of Windshiel.
Ruin or site   NT 739591   OS: 74   *   Map: 2, no: 298
The remains of a small tower house are incorporated into a farm, which is itself now ruinous.
Other refs: Windy Windshiel

Windy Hills *see* Milton Brodie House

Windy Windshiel *see* Windshiel

Windydoors Tower

Borders: About 4.5 miles north-west of Galashiels, on minor roads west of A7, just north of Stantling Craig Reservoir.
Ruin or site   NT 432398   OS: 73   **   Map: 2, no: 113
Not much remains of a 16th-century tower house, except the vaulted basement, which is incorporated into a farm. It was a property of the Kerrs.

Wine Tower, Fraserburgh *see* Kinnaird Head Castle

Winkston Tower

Borders: About 1.5 miles north of Peebles, on minor road east of A703 at Winkston, east of the Eddleston Water.
Ruin or site   NT 245430   OS: 73   **   Map: 2, no: 58
Winkston Tower is a much-altered 16th-century tower house, rectangular in plan, reduced in height and altered inside. A gunloop defends the original entrance. The tower is dated 1545 and 1734, and stands behind the 19th-century farmhouse.

The basement has been vaulted.

Winkston was a property of the Dicksons, one of whom was assassinated in 1572 while Provost of Peebles.

Wintercleuch Castle

Lanarkshire & Glasgow area: About 4 miles south and east of Elvanfoot, on minor road and track south of A702, near Wintercleuch Burn, 1 mile north-east of Wintercleuch, east of Mid Height.

Ruin or site NS 980114 OS: 78 * Map: 3, no: 434

Not much remains of a small tower or bastle house, except the basement. The lower part of a turnpike stair survives in one corner. The tower appears to have been burned at one time, and was abandoned by the middle of the 17th century, although buildings on the site were occupied into the 18th century. The site has been excavated.

Winton House

Lothians: About 3 miles south-east of Tranent, off A1 at Tranent, about 0.75 miles north of Pencaitland, north of the Tyne Water, at Winton.

Private NT 439696 OS: 66 * Map: 4, no: 169**

Winton House, a Renaissance mansion dating from 1620 with later additions, incorporates a 15th-century castle. There are some fine 17th-century plaster ceilings, decorated in honour of Charles I, as well as unique stone twisted chimneys, both added by William Wallace, the king's Master Mason.

The lands were originally held by the de Quincy family, but were granted to the

Setons after the de Quincys were forfeited by Robert the Bruce. Lord Seton built a castle here about 1480, which was later sacked by the English. The Setons were made Earls of Winton in 1600, and much of the present house dates from 1620. Charles I visited in 1633.

George, the 5th Earl, was forfeited for his part in the Jacobite Rising of 1715 and imprisoned in the Tower of London after being captured at Preston, although he managed to escape and went to Rome. The property was sold to the York Building Company, then to the Hamilton Lords Pencaitland in 1779, then passed to the Nisbet Hamiltons in 1885, then the Ogilvies in 1920. The house is still occupied.

OPEN: 2001: Open 2/3 Jun, 7/8 Jul, 4/5 Aug, 12.30-16.30; other times by prior arrangement.

Guided tours. Collections of pictures, furniture, and family exhibitions of costumes and photographs. Tearoom. WC. Picnic area. Terraced gardens and specimen trees. Woodland walks. WC. Limited disabled access, WC. Car and coach parking. Group concessions. ££. Corporate and private hospitality.

Tel: 01620 824986 Fax: 01620 823961

Email: enquiries@wintonhouse.co.uk Web: www.wintonhouse.co.uk

Wirk *see* The Wirk

Wishaw House

Lanarkshire & Glasgow: About 1 mile north-west of Wishaw, on minor roads north of A721, south of South Calder Water.

Ruin or site NS 786565 OS: 64 * Map: 3, no: 371

Site of castle, which may have been incorporated into a castellated mansion, itself remodelled and extended by James Gillespie Graham before 1839. The central portion of the house is said to have dated from 1665.

The lands were a property of the Hamilton Lords Belhaven, but the mansion was completely demolished about 1950.

Wiston Place

Lanarkshire & Glasgow: About 3 miles south-west of Symington, near B7055, at or near Wiston.

Ruin or site NS 956320 OS: 72 * Map: 3, no: 426

Site of castle or old house, the residence of the barony of Wiston. It was held by one Wice, probably a Fleming, around the middle of the 12th century.

Wolfclyde *see* Coulter Motte

Wolfelee *see* Wolflee

Wolfhopelee *see* Wolflee

Wolflee

Borders: About 2 miles south of Bonchester Bridge, on minor roads just west of B6357, at Wolflee.

Private NT 589093 OS: 80 ** Map: 2, no: 224

Probable site of castle. An old house here, incorporating a vaulted cellar from the 17th century or earlier, was rebuilt in 1698, again in 1825-7, and finally in 1862 by the architect David Bryce. The building was burned down in 1977.

Other refs: Wolfelee; Wolfhopelee

Wolf's Crag *see* Fast Castle

Woll

Borders: About 4 miles south of Selkirk, on minor roads west of A7 at Ashkirk, west of Ale Water, near manse in village of Woll.

Ruin or site NT 465218 [?] OS: 73 * Map: 2, no: 131

Site of a residence of the Archbishops of Glasgow, known as 'Palace Walls'.

Other refs: Palace Walls

Wooden Hill

Borders: About 5.5 miles south of Kelso, on minor roads east of A698, at or near Wooden Hill.

Ruin or site NT 715245 [?] OS: 74 * Map: 2, no: 293

Site of tower house.

Woodhall

Lothians: About 0.75 miles south of Pencaitland, on minor road south of A6093, at Woodhall.

Private NT 433680 OS: 66 ** Map: 4, no: 168

Woodhall, a small mansion, incorporates a rectangular 16th-century tower house. The tower has a corbiestepped gabled roof and a projecting turret. There was a courtyard.

The basement was vaulted, and contained the kitchen. The house has been modernised internally.

Woodhall was a property of the Seton family, but in 1488 passed to the Sinclairs of Herdmanston, who held it until the 18th century. The castle was ruined by 1799, and the property passed to the Lauders. Woodhall was restored in 1884, and is still occupied.

Woodhead *see* Penkaet Castle

Woodhead Castle

Lanarkshire & Glasgow area: About 3.5 miles north-east of Milngavie, south of the A891, about 1 mile west of Lennox Town, in the grounds of Lennox Castle Hospital.

Ruin or site   NS 606783   OS: 64   **   Map: 3, no: 279

Woodhead Castle is a ruinous 16th-century L-plan tower house of three storeys and an attic, consisting of a main block and small stair-tower.

It was built by Lennox of Balcorrach in 1572. The Lennoxes of Woodhead feuded with the Kincaids until the families were united by marriage. The castle was left a picturesque ruin when nearby Lennox Castle was built about 1840.

Woodhill *see* Loch Ronald

Woodhouse Hill

Borders: About 3 miles south-west of Peebles, on minor roads south of A72, west of Manor Water, near Woodhouse.

Ruin or site   NT 211370   OS: 73   *   Map: 2, no: 46

Site of tower house, also recorded as Woodhouse Manor. The property originally belonged to the Inglis of Manor family, but in 1522 passed to the Pringles, or Hoppringles, of Smailholm, and in the late 16th century to the Burnets of Barns. The property was split, and part was held by the Naesmiths of Posso in the 17th and 18th centuries.

Other refs: Woodhouse Manor

Woodhouse Tower

Dumfriesshire: About 5 miles north-east of Annan, on minor road just south of A74, just north of the Kirtle Water, just south of the railway line, at Woodhouse.

Ruin or site   NY 251715   OS: 85   **   Map: 1, no: 277

Woodhouse Tower is a ruined 16th-century tower house of the Irvines, much of which collapsed in the 19th century, although part was restored in 1877. The remaining fragment contains a stair and survives to parapet height, formerly of three storeys and an attic. The vaulted basement has two gunloops, and the castle had a courtyard, traces of which remain.

Other refs: Wardhouse Tower

Woodhouselee *see* Old Woodhouselee Castle

Woodhouselee *see* Fulford Tower

Woodhouselees Tower *see* Woodslee Tower

Woodmill House

Fife: About 3 miles south-east of Newburgh, on minor road west of B937, at or near Woodmill Mains.

Ruin or site   NO 272153   OS: 59   *   Map: 7, no: 60

Site of castle adjacent to modern farm buildings.

Other refs: Woodmylne

Woodmylne *see* Woodmill House

Woodrae Castle

Angus & Dundee: About 6 miles west and south of Brechin, on minor roads north of B9134, south of River South Esk, 1 mile north of Aberlemno, at or near Woodrae.

Ruin or site   NO 518566   OS: 54   *   Map: 8, no: 220

Site of castle, the last remains of which were removed in 1819.

The property was originally held by the Vellum family, but passed to the Lindsays. In the late 17th century Sir James Lindsay of Woodrae killed an Ogilvie of Ballinshoe. The castle later passed to the Fletchers, but was very ruined by the 19th century.

Two sculpted Pictish stones were found at the site, one of which was given to Sir Walter Scott, and by his family to what is now the Museum of Scotland. This panel has an interlaced cross surrounded by beasts, while the back has horsemen, and a double-disc, monsters and beasts. It is similar to the Aberlemno stones.

Other refs: Castle of Woodrae; Woodwray

Woodside House

Ayrshire: About 1 mile north-east of Beith, on minor road west of A737, just south of the Roebank Burn, at Woodside.

Private   NS 352553   OS: 63   **   Map: 3, no: 112

Woodside House incorporates a 16th-century tower house, square in plan, which was extended and altered in 1640 and 1759. It was remodelled in 1848 and 1890, when the house was given corbiestepped gables and bartizans. The tower is dated 1551.

It was built by the Ralston family, who held the property from 1551 until 1772, but in 1834 was sold to the Patrick family.

Woodslee Tower

Dumfriesshire: About 1.5 miles south of Canonbie, near B7201, west of River Esk, at or near Woodslee.

Ruin or site   NY 389741 [?]   OS: 85   *   Map: 1, no: 326

Site of tower house, a property of the Armstrongs of Woodslee. There may have been another tower to the north, listed as 'Dauy of Canobu'.

Other refs: Woodhouselees Tower; Kinmont Tower

Woodwray *see* Woodrae Castle

Woody Castle *see* Cockie's Field

Woolandslee Tower

Borders: About 5 miles north-east of Peebles, on minor road west of B709 north of Innerleithen, east of the Williamslee Burn.

Ruin or site   NT 318448   OS: 73   **   Map: 2, no: 82

Woolandslee Tower is a ruined 16th-century tower house, of which only the vaulted basement survives, along with the scant remains of outbuildings.

Woolmet House

Lothians: About 4 miles south-east of Edinburgh Castle, on minor roads west of A6106, just north of Danderhall, at or near Woolmet.

Ruin or site   NT 309701 [?]   OS: 66   *   Map: 4, no: 128

Woolmet House, a large gabled L-plan house with two round and one square tower and bartizans, was dated 1686, but parts appeared to date from the 16th century.

It was a property of the Biggar family, but had passed to the Wallaces by 1686. It was completely demolished in 1950, apart from the gateway, to allow mining work.

Wormiston *see* Hopeton Tower

Wormiston House

Fife: About 1.5 miles north of Crail, on minor road east of A917, just north of junction with B9171, at Wormiston.
Private   NO 612095   OS: 59   **   Map: 7, no: 161
Wormiston House is a 17th-century L-plan tower house, which had been greatly extended, although these extensions were demolished in 1988 during rebuilding.

It was a property of the Spence family of Wormiston, Constables of Crail. They supported Mary, Queen of Scots, during the 1570s. In 1612 Wormiston passed to the Balfours, who probably built most of the existing castle, but in 1621 it was acquired by the Lindsays. The house was rebuilt in the 1980s, and is occupied.

Wormonby *see* Warmanbie

Wrae Tower

Borders: About 3 miles south of Broughton, west of the A701, south-west of Wrae Farm, on the north side of Wrae Hill.
Ruin or site   NT 115332   OS: 72   **   Map: 2, no: 13
Not much survives of a 16th-century tower house, except part of the stair-tower. It was a property of the Tweedies of Wrae in the 16th and 17th centuries.

Wreaths Tower

Dumfriesshire: About 6.5 miles south of New Abbey, on minor road south of A710, just south-east of Mainsriddle, about 1 mile north of the Solway Firth.
Ruin or site   NX 953565   OS: 84   **   Map: 1, no: 184
Little remains of an early 16th-century tower house, except part of the vaulted basement and a turnpike stair.

The tower was a property of the Douglases, and held by the Regent Morton at the time of his execution in 1581. It passed to the Maxwells, but probably returned to the Douglases.
Other refs: Castle of Wraiths; Wreath's Tower

Wreaths Tower

Dumfriesshire: About 6 miles north and east of Locharbiggs, about 0.25 miles west of A701 at Kirkland, near Wreaths Burn.
Ruin or site   NY 031897   OS: 78   *   Map: 1, no: 201
Site of 16th-century tower house, nothing of which remains except a stony mound.

Wreath's Tower *see* Wreaths Tower

Wrightshouses *see* Wrychtishousis

Wrychtishousis

Lothians: About 0.5 miles south and west of Edinburgh Castle, on minor roads west of A702, Gillespie Crescent, Edinburgh.
Ruin or site   NT 247724   OS: 66   *   Map: 4, no: 90
Site of old house or castle, part of which may have dated from the 14th century, described as 'a curious old pile' and a picturesque mansion. It was demolished in 1802 to build James Gillespie's school, on the site of which was built the Blind Asylum – Gillespie's was moved to Bruntsfield House. Wrychtishousis was also known as Burgh Muir Castle and Barganie House.

It was a property of the Napiers, passed to the Clerks in 1664, but by the end of the 18th century was occupied by a Lieutenant General Robertson of Lawers. During his occupancy, a servant reported the apparition of a decapitated woman, with an infant in its arms, appearing from the hearth in his bedroom. The building was demolished a few years later, and under the hearth the remains of a woman and child were found. The woman's head had been removed, possibly to fit the rest of her into the space.

The story goes that after 1664 the house was occupied by a James Clerk, his wife and child. Clerk was killed in battle, and his younger brother murdered his wife and child so that he would inherit the property.
Other refs: Wrightshouses; Burgh Muir Castle

Yair House

Borders: About 2 miles north of Selkirk, on minor roads south of A707, just west of River Tweed, at or near Yair.
Ruin or site   NT 452328   OS: 73   *   Map: 2, no: 121
Standing in a scenic location by the River Tweed, Yair House, which dates from 1788, is a symmetrical three-storey mansion with later extensions. It was built by the Pringles of Whytbank. It may stand on the site of a tower house or castle, and the property was held by the Kerrs of Yair in 1588.

Yester Castle

Lothians: About 5.5 miles south-east of Haddington, on footpath south of B6355, about 1.5 miles south-east of Gifford, in Castle Wood, west of Hopes Water.
Ruin or site   NT 556667   OS: 66   **   Map: 4, no: 200
Standing on a promontory at the meeting place of two rivers, Yester Castle is a ruined 13th-century castle and keep. The original castle was triangular in plan, and defended by a ditch on the 'landward' side. A ruined gatehouse survives, as do parts of the curtain wall. A fine vaulted underground chamber, known as the 'Gob-

lin Hall', is reached by a flight of steps.

The lands were a property of the Giffords in the 12th century. Sir Hugo Gifford, who was reputedly a wizard, built the Goblin (or Hobgoblin of Bo') Hall, according to one story with the help of magic, spirits or goblins. The castle was occupied by the English during the Wars of Independence until recaptured by the Scots in 1311. It changed hands between the Scots and English in the late 1540s, the last castle in this part of Scotland to be surrendered. The castle passed by marriage to the Hays early in the 15th century, and was probably abandoned in the 17th or 18th century. The family were made Lords Yester in 1488, Earl of Tweeddale in 1646, then Marquis of Tweeddale and Earl of Gifford in 1694.

Nearby is the collegiate church, founded by William Hay in 1421, although access is difficult. Yester House [NT 543672], dating from the 18th century, replaced the castle, and was designed by William and Robert Adam, although it has since been altered. It is still occupied.
Other refs: Goblin Ha' (Hall), Yester

Yetholm Loch *see* Lochtower

Ghosts *and* Bogles Index

Abbotsford
Abergeldie Castle
Ackergill Tower
Airlie Castle
Airth Castle
Aldourie Castle
Allanbank House
Arbigland House
Ardachy
Ardblair Castle
Ardchattan Priory
Ardincaple Castle
Ardrossan Castle
Ardvreck Castle
Arrochar House
Ashintully Castle
Auchinvole House
Balcomie Castle
Baldoon Castle
Balfour House
Balgonie Castle
Ballindalloch Castle
Balnagown Castle
Balvenie Castle
Balwearie Castle
Barcaldine Castle
Barnbougle Castle
Bedlay Castle
Benholm Castle
Biel
Blantyre Priory
Borthwick Castle
Braco Castle
Braemar Castle
Brahan Castle
Brodick Castle
Brodie Castle
Broomhill Castle
Buchanan Castle
Buckholm Tower
Busta House
Caisteal Camus
Cameron House
Carleton Castle
Caroline Park House
Castle Cary

Castle Coeffin
Castle Fraser
Castle Grant
Castle Lachlan
Castle Levan
Castle Loch Heylipol
Castle of Mey
Castle Spioradain
Castle Stuart
Castlehill, Cambusnethan
Castlemilk
Cawdor Castle
Cessnock Castle
Claypotts Castle
Cloncaird Castle
Closeburn Castle
Colquhonnie Castle
Comlongon Castle
Corgarff Castle
Coroghon Castle
Corstorphine Castle
Cortachy Castle
Coull Castle
County Hotel, Peebles
Craigcrook Castle
Craighouse
Craigievar Castle
Craignethan Castle
Crathes Castle
Crichton Castle
Cromarty Castle
Culcreuch Castle
Cullen House
Culloden House
Culzean Castle
Dalhousie Castle
Dalkeith House
Dalmahoy
Dalpeddar
Dalry House, Edinburgh
Dalzell House
Dean Castle
Delgatie Castle
Dolphinston Tower
Douglas Castle
Drumlanrig Castle

Dryburgh Abbey
Duchal Castle
Dunnottar Castle
Dunphail Castle
Dunrobin Castle
Dunskey Castle
Dunstaffnage Castle
Duntrune Castle
Duntulm Castle
Dunure Castle
Durris House
Earlshall
Edinample Castle
Edinburgh Castle
Edzell Castle
Eilean Donan Castle
Ethie Castle
Fairburn Tower
Falkland Palace
Fasque
Fedderate Castle
Fernie Castle
Ferniehirst Castle
Fetteresso Castle
Finavon Castle
Floors Castle
Fort George
Frendraught Castle
Fulford Tower
Fyvie Castle
Galdenoch Castle
Garleton Castle
Garth Castle
Gight Castle
Glamis Castle
Gorrenberry Tower
Grandtully Castle
Grange House
Greenlaw House
Haddo House
Hallgreen Castle
Hermitage Castle
Holyroodhouse
Hopetoun House
Houndwood House
Huntingtower Castle

Inchdrewer Castle
Inveraray Castle
Inverawe House
Inverey Castle
Invergarry Castle
Inverquharity Castle
Jedburgh Castle
Kellie Castle
Kindrochit Castle
Kingcausie
Kinnaird Castle
Kinnaird Head Castle
Kinneil House
Knockderry Castle
Largie Castle
Lauriston Castle
Leith Hall
Liberton House
Linlithgow Palace
Littledean Tower
Loch of Leys
Lochleven Castle
Lochnell House
Lordscairnie Castle
Loudoun Castle
MacDuff's Castle
Mains Castle
Mantle House
Marlfield House
Maryculter House
Meggernie Castle
Meldrum House
Melgund Castle
Menie House
Monymusk Castle
Moy Castle
Muchalls Castle
Neidpath Castle
Newark Castle
Newbattle Abbey
Newton Castle
Noltland Castle
Old Woodhouselee Castle
Park
Penkaet Castle
Pinkie House

Pitcaple Castle
Pitfodels Castle
Pittodrie House
Place of Bonhill
Provan Hall
Rait Castle
Rockhall
Rosslyn Castle
Rothesay Castle
Rothiemurchus
Roxburgh Castle
Ruthven Barracks
Saddell Castle
Saltoun Hall
Sanquhar Castle
Scone Palace
Shieldhill
Skaill House
Skene House
Skibo Castle
Spedlins Tower
Spynie Palace
St Andrews Castle
Stirling Castle
Sundrum Castle
Sunlaws House
Taymouth Castle
Thainstone House
The Binns
Thirlestane Castle
Thunderton House, Elgin
Traquair House
Tulloch Castle
Vayne Castle
Wellwood House
Wemyss Castle
Windgate House
Wrychtishousis

Family Names Index

Abercrombie
Abercrombie Castle
Airthrey Castle
Birkenbog House
Carriden House
Colinton Castle
Fetternear House
Forglen House
Glassaugh House
Inchdrewer Castle
Manor Castle
Menstrie Castle
Murthly Castle
Tullibody
Abernethy
Dunlappie
Hawthornden Castle
Mains of Mayen
Pitcairlie House
Rothiemay Castle
Saltoun Hall
Adair
Drummore Castle
Dunskey Castle
Kilhilt
Morton Castle
Stranraer Castle
Adamson
Craigcrook Castle
Affleck
Affleck Castle
Auchinleck Castle
Balmanno Castle
Gillbank House
Glenbervie House
Agnew
Cruggleton Castle
Galdenoch Castle
Innermessan Castle
Lochnaw Castle
Aikman
Ross House
Ainslie
Delgatie Castle
Dolphingstone Castle
Dolphinston Tower
Airth
Airth Castle
Bruce's Castle
Fordell Castle
Aitchison
Airdrie House

Rochsolloch
Aitken
Dalmoak Castle
Aitkenhead
Ranfurly Castle
Aiton *see* **Ayton**
Alexander
Airdrie House
Argyll's Lodging
Menstrie Castle
Peffermill House
Rochsolloch
Tillicoultry Castle
Allan
Lauriston Castle
Allardice
Allardice Castle
Whistleberry Castle
Allardyce*see* **Allardice**
Alston
Usan House
Anderson
Boreland Tower
Candacraig
Curriehill Castle
Stobcross
Annan
Sauchie Tower
Anstruther
Airdrie House
Ardross Castle
Balcaskie House
Barns
Carmichael House
Dreel Castle
Elie House
Newark Castle
Arbuthnott
Arbuthnott House
Castle of Fiddes
Findrowie Castle
Keith Inch Tower
Ardrossan
Ardrossan Castle
Arklay
Dunninald Castle
Armstrong
Arkleton Tower
Burnfoot
Bush
Calfield Tower
Gilnockie Tower

Glendivan
Glenvorann
Greena Tower
Harelaw Tower
Hollows Tower
Kirkton Tower
Langholm Tower
Langholm Tower
Mangerton Tower
Muirburnhead
Puddingburn Tower
Roan Tower
Sark Tower
Syde Tower
Westburnflat Tower
Whithaugh Tower
Whitlawside
Woodslee Tower
Arnot
Arnot Castle
Fast Castle
Fernie Castle
Auchinleck *see* **Affleck**
Avenel
Abercorn Castle
Ayton
Ayton
Ayton Castle
Kinaldy Castle
Baikie
Tankerness House, Kirkwall
Baillie
Carnbroe House
Castle Cary
Castlehill Tower
Edmonston Castle
Hills Tower
Jerviston
Jerviswood House
Lamington Tower
Mantle House
Mellerstain
Monkton House
Penston
Pittillock House
Polkemmet House
Provan Hall
Red Castle
Todholes Castle
Torwood Castle
Walston
Windgate House

Bain
Docharty
Tulloch Castle
Baird
Auchmeddan Castle
Broomhill House
Castlehill, Cambusnethan
Closeburn Castle
Elie House
Gartsherrie House
Kilhenzie Castle
Langhaugh Tower
Lennoxlove
Newark Castle
Posso Tower
Selvage
Strathaven Castle
Strichen
Urie House
Wellwood House
Balcanquhal
Balcanquhal Tower
Balcomie
Balcomie Castle
Randerston
Balfour
Balfour Castle
Balfour House
Balgarvie Castle
Balgonie Castle
Bandon Tower
Burleigh Castle
Cairneyflappet Castle
Collairnie Castle
Dawyck House
Denmylne Castle
Fernie Castle
Isle of May
Kinnaird House
Kirkton
Melville House
Monimail Tower
Mountquhanie Castle
Noltland Castle
Pilrig House
Pitcullo Castle
Pittillock House
Randerston
Whittinghame Castle
Wormiston House
Ballindalloch
Ballindalloch Castle

Castle Stripe
Tullochcarron Castle
Balliol
Buittle Castle
Buittle Place
Cavers House
Dean Castle
Dunnideer Castle
Heston Island
Kenmure Castle
Kirkcudbright Castle
Lochinvar Castle
Motte of Urr
Penston
Balmanno
Balmanno Castle
Bannatyne
Bannatyne House
Corehouse Castle
Holylee
Kames Castle
Kelly House
Bannerman
Belmont Castle
Pitmedden House
Waterton Castle
Barbour
Gryffe Castle
Barclay
Allardice Castle
Ardrossan Castle
Balvaird Castle
Caddam Castle
Castle of Cullen of Buchan
Collairnie Castle
Gartly Castle
Innergellie Castle
Kaim of Mathers Castle
Kilbirnie House
Ladyland Castle
Monboddo House
Mondynes Castle
Perceton House
Towie Barclay Castle
Urie House
Barton
Kirkhill Castle
Bason
Boquhan Castle
Baxter
Kilmaron Castle

Beaton
Balfour Castle
Balfour House
Bandon Tower
Creich Castle
Dunbog Castle
Ethie Castle
Ethiebeaton
Innergellie House
Melgund Castle
Naughton Castle
Beattie
Black Esk Tower
Raeburnfoot
Shiel
Tanlawhill Tower
Westerkirk
Bell
Albie
Antermony Castle
Blacket House
Cowholm
Kirkconnel Tower
Nucke
Poldean
Scotsbrig
Spottiswoode House
Bellenden
Kilconquhar Castle
Belshe
Balmanno Tower
Fettercairn House
Invermay Tower
Purves Hall
Bennett
Whitton Tower
Bentinck
Crosbie House
Sandside House
Beresford
Macbiehill
Berkley
Red Castle
Beveridge
Pitreavie Castle
Biggar
Woolmet House
Birnie
Broomhill Castle
Bisset
Aboyne Castle
Beaufort Castle
Kilravock Castle
Knock Castle
Lessendrum House
Lovat Castle
Maryculter House
Red Castle
Black
Largo Castle

Blackadder
Blackadder Castle
Tulliallan Castle
Blackett
Arbigland House
McCulloch's Castle
Blackwood
Pittreavie
Blair
Ardblair Castle
Balthayock Castle
Blair Castle
Blairquhan
Bogton Castle
Borgue
Carberry Tower
Cowden Hall
Dunimarle Castle
Dunskey Castle
Glasclune Castle
Kinfauns Castle
Milton
Rossie Ochil
Williamston
Bonkyl
Bunkle Castle
Bonnar
Invermay Tower
Keltie Castle
Bontine
Balglass Castle
Law Castle
Borthwick
Borthwick Castle
Catcune Tower
Colmslie Tower
Crookston Old House
Dundarg Castle
Langshaw Tower
Newbyres Tower
Pilmuir House
Pittarthie Castle
Ravenstone Castle
Boswell
Auchinleck Castle
Balmuto Tower
Blackadder Castle
Milliken
Ochiltree Castle
Pitteadie Castle
Trabboch Castle
Boyd
Badenheath Castle
Ballochtoul Castle
Bedlay Castle
Brodick Castle
Callendar House
Dean Castle
Kipps Castle
Law Castle
Penkill Castle

Pitcon
Portencross Castle
Trabboch Castle
Boyle
Craigends House
Fairlie Castle
Kelburn Castle
Kilbirnie House
Rowallan Castle
Stanely Castle
Braid
Bavelaw Castle
Brisbane
Ballanreoch Castle
Bishopton House
Brisbane House
Brodie
Asliesk Castle
Brodie Castle
Castle Hill, Pluscarden
Lethen House
Milton Brodie House
Brook
Hoddom Castle
Brotherton
Brotherton Castle
Brown
Abbot's Tower
Bruntsfield House
Carsluith Castle
Colstoun House
Cunningar
Edmonston Castle
Greenhead Tower
Hartree Tower
Houndwood House
Midmar Castle
Newhall Castle
Bruce
Airth Castle
Annan Castle
Arkendeith Tower
Auchenbowie House
Balcaskie House
Broomhall
Bruce's Castle
Carnock House
Castlemilk
Clackmannan Tower
Culross Palace
Earlshall
Fingask Castle
Hallguards Castle
Hartshaw Tower
Kinross House
Loch Doon Castle
Lochleven Castle
Lochmaben Castle
Muness Castle
Myres Castle
Pittarthie Castle

Pitillock House
Stenhouse
Thomaston Castle
Tulliallan Castle
Turnberry Castle
Buchan
Auchmacoy House
Beldorney Castle
Kelloe Bastle
Buchanan
Arnprior Castle
Auchenreoch Castle
Auchleshie
Balfour Castle
Balgair Castle
Bardowie Castle
Blairvadach Castle
Boturich Castle
Buchanan Castle
Carbeth House
Carrick House
Catter Castle
Craigend Castle
Craigievern Castle
Dunglass Castle
Grandhome House
Leny House
Northbar
Ross Priory
Scotscraig
Bulmer
Glengonnar Castle
Glenochar Castle
Burnet
Barns Tower
Castlehill Tower
Cobairdy
Crathes Castle
Fairnington House
Gadgirth Castle
Glenbervie House
Kemnay House
Loch of Leys
Monboddo House
Muchalls Castle
Old Kendal
Tillycairn Castle
Woodhouse Hill
Burns
Cumbernauld Castle
Kilmahew Castle
Byres
Byres
East Coates House
Caddell
Grange House
Caird
Mains Castle
Cairncross
Colmslie Tower
Hillslap Tower

Cairns
Carsluith Castle
Orchardton Tower
Pilmuir House
Rusko Castle
Calder
Asloun Castle
Aswanley House
Cawdor Castle
Nairn Castle
Calderwood
Pitteadie Castle
Callendar
Balcastle
Callendar House
Colzium Castle
Drumry Castle
Manor Castle
Cambo
Baledgarno Castle
Cambo House
Cameron
Achnacarry
Baledgarno Castle
Eilean nan Craobh
Strome Castle
Tor Castle
Campbell
Aberuchill Castle
Achallader Castle
Ardchattan Priory
Ardincaple Castle
Ardkinglas House
Ardmaddy Castle
Ardpatrick Castle
Argyll's Lodging
Aros Castle
Asgog Castle
Asknish House
Auchenbreck Castle
Ballimore
Barcaldine Castle
Barr Castle
Bedlay Castle
Black Castle of Moulin
Caisteal na Nighinn Ruaidhe
Caisteal nan Con
Camis Eskan
Carnasserie Castle
Carnbane Castle
Caroline Park House
Carrick Castle
Castle Campbell
Castle Coeffin
Castle Ewen
Castle Loch Heylipol
Castle Stalker
Castle Sween
Cawdor Castle
Cessnock Castle
Corranmore

Corsewall Castle
Craignish Castle
Duart Castle
Dun an Garbh-Sroine
Dunderave Castle
Dundonald Castle
Dunstaffnage Castle
Duntrune Castle
Dunyvaig Castle
Edinample Castle
Eilean Dearg Castle
Eilean Ran Castle
Farnell Castle
Finlarig Castle
Fraoch Eilean Castle
Gargunnock House
Garvie Castle
Glenstrae Castle
Glentirran
Gorm Castle
Granton Castle
Inchinnan Castle
Innis Chonnel Castle
Inveraray Castle
Inverawe House
Kenmore Castle
Kilberry Castle
Kilbryde Castle
Kilchurn Castle
Kilkerran Castle
Kilmartin Castle
Kilmory Castle
Kilmun Church
Kingencleugh Castle
Kinnell House
Knockamillie Castle
Langton Castle
Loch Dochart Castle
Loch an Sgoltaire Castle
Lochhead Castle
Lochindorb Castle
Lochnell House
Lochranza Castle
Loudoun
Loudoun Castle
Lunga
Mains Castle
Mauchline Castle
Meggernie Castle
Minard Castle
Mingary Castle
Monzie Castle
Mugdock Castle
Newmilns Tower
Newton Castle
Rait Castle
Rarey
Renfield
Rosneath Castle
Rowallan Castle
Saddell Castle

Skipness Castle
Sorn Castle
Sornhill
Stonefield Castle
Tangy Loch
Taymouth Castle
Torosay Castle
Torran
Toward Castle
Treesbanks
Tullichewan Castle
Wellwood House
Cant
Comiston House
Grange House
Carlyle
Birrens
Dornock
Scotsbrig
Torthorwald Castle
Carmichael
Aithernie Castle
Carmichael House
Crawford Castle
Eastend
Ecclesiamagirdle House
Fenton Tower
Harehead Castle
Waughton Castle
Westraw
Carnegie
Arbigland House
Balnamoon
Bolshan Castle
Boysack
Brandy Den
Careston Castle
Carnegie Castle
Colluthie House
Craig Castle
Craig House
Cruivie Castle
Ethie Castle
Farnell Castle
Finavon Castle
Fithie
Hoddom Castle
Inglismaldie Castle
Invergowrie House
Kinblethmont
Kinfauns Castle
Kinnaird Castle
McCulloch's Castle
Pittarrow Castle
Pittencrieff House
Skibo Castle
Vayne Castle
Carruthers
Cornal Tower
Dormont
Dornock

Hallguards Castle
Hoddom Castle
Holmains Castle
Mouswald Tower
Raffles Tower
Carswell
Carnasserie Castle
Kilmartin Castle
Carstairs
Kilconquhar Castle
Cathcart
Auchencruive Castle
Auchendrane Castle
Camregan Castle
Carleton Castle
Carnell
Cathcart Castle
Dalmellington Castle
Easter Greenock Castle
Greenock Castle
Killochan Castle
Kisimul Castle
Pitcairlie House
Sauchie Tower
Sundrum Castle
Waterhead Castle
Caverhill
Caverhill Tower
Foulitch Tower
Chalmers
Aldbar Castle
Balbithan House
Gadgirth House
Tillery
Chambers
Ormiston Tower
Chancellor
Quothquan
Shieldhill
Chaplin
Colliston Castle
Charteris
Amisfield Tower
Eliock House
Kinfauns Castle
Cheyne
Ackergill Tower
Arnage Castle
Berriedale Castle
Caisteal Morar na Shein
Castle of Esslemont
Castle of Old Wick
Dirlot Castle
Duffus Castle
Dundarg Castle
Forse Castle
Inverugie Castle
Ravenscraig Castle
Straloch House
Chiesly
Dalry House, Edinburgh

Chirnside
Balintore Castle
Chisholm
Erchless Castle
Glassingall
Pitcur Castle
Stirches
Christie
Bedlay Castle
Cowden Castle
Durie House
Claverhouse
Claverhouse Castle
Clayhills
Invergowrie House
Cleland
Airdrie House
Cleland Castle
Knownoble
Monkland House
Clephane
Carslogie House
Strathendry Castle
Clerk
Dumcrieff
Penicuik Tower
Pittencrieff House
Ravensneuk Castle
Uttershill Castle
Wrychtishousis
Coat
Auchendrane Castle
Cochrane
Auchans
Auchindoun Castle
Cochrane Castle
Cowden Hall
Dundonald Castle
Gallowhill
Johnstone Castle
Kildrummy Castle
Kilmaronock Castle
Lee Castle
Lochnell House
Ochiltree Castle
Ralston
Ranfurly Castle
Rochsoles House
Cockburn
Bonaly Tower
Borthwick Castle
Carriden House
Cockburn Tower
Cockburn's Tower
Duns Castle
Langhaugh Tower
Langton Castle
Mayshiel
Ormiston Castle
Penkaet Castle
Skirling Castle

Colebrooke
Crawford Castle
Collace
Balnamoon
Colquhoun
Ardincaple Castle
Arrochar House
Balloch Castle
Bannachra Castle
Barnhill House
Camstraddan Castle
Corston Tower
Dunglass Castle
Faslane Castle
Fincastle House
Garscadden Castle
Inchgalbraith Castle
Rossdhu Castle
Tresmass
Colt
Gartsherrie House
Colville
Cleish Castle
Killernie Castle
Kinnaird Castle
MacDuff's Castle
Ochiltree Castle
Scotscraig
Tillicoultry Castle
Comyn
Altyre House
Auchry Castle
Balvenie Castle
Banff Castle
Bedrule Castle
Blair Castle
Blervie Castle
Cadzow Castle
Cairnbulg Castle
Castle of King Edward
Castle of Troup
Castle Roy
Castlemilk
Cluggy Castle
Comyn's Castle
Craig Castle
Craig of Boyne Castle
Craigmill
Cruggleton Castle
Cumbernauld Castle
Dalswinton Castle
Delgatie Castle
Dores Castle
Dundarg Castle
Dunphail Castle
Dunrod Castle
Ellon Castle
Gordonstoun
House of Tyrie
Inchtalla Castle
Inverallochy Castle

Inverlochy Castle
Kininmonth House
Kirkintilloch Peel
Leask House
Lochindorb Castle
Logie House
Mains Castle
Old Slains Castle
Quiech Castle
Rait Castle
Raploch Castle
Rattray Castle
Rowallan Castle
Ruthven
Ruthven Barracks
Tarradale Castle
Tom Pitlac
Tor Castle
Urquhart Castle
Coningsburgh
Barntalloch Tower
Constable
Craigcrook Castle
Cook
Balcaskie House
Cookson
Houndwood House
Cooper
Ballindalloch Castle
Corbett
Rowallan Castle
Tollcross
Tom a' Chaisteal, Kirkton
Cornwall
Bonhard House
Carriden House
Corrie
Lunelly Tower
Thomaston Castle
Wamphray Tower
Cospatrick
Black Bog Castle
Cockburnspath Castle
Dolphinston Tower
Dunbar Castle
Fast Castle
Hailes Castle
Longformacus
Luffness House
Morton Castle
Old Greenlaw Castle
Old Place of Mochrum
Peelhill
Polwarth Castle
Spott House
Whittinghame Castle
Coulson
Houndwood House
Couper
Badenheath Castle
Castle Gogar

Cowan
Logan House
Steuarthall
Cox
Clunie Castle
Glendoick House
Coxwell
Myres Castle
Craig
Riccarton
Craigie
Glendoick House
Langskaill House
Craik
Arbigland House
McCulloch's Castle
Crammond
Aldbar Castle
Cranston
Corehouse Castle
Corsbie Tower
Lanton Tower
Stobs Castle
Craw
Heugh Head
Crawford
Almond Castle
Ardmillan Castle
Auchinames Castle
Cartsdyke
Cloberhill
Craufurdland Castle
Crawfordjohn Castle
Crosbie Castle
Crosbie House
Douglaston House
Drongan Castle
Drumry Castle
Drumsoy Castle
Farme Castle
Fedderate Castle
Gartlea
Glendevon Castle
Jordanhill
Kilbirnie House
Laight Castle
Lauriston Castle
Lochcote Tower
Loch Doon Castle
Loudoun Castle
Mountquhanie Castle
Newark Castle
Possil
Rochsoles House
Rochsolloch
Terringzean Castle
Ward of Lochnorris
Creich
Comiston House
Crichton
Auchenskeoch Castle

Barnton Tower
Black Bog Castle
Blackness Castle
Bothwell Castle
Braal Castle
Brunstane Castle
Brunstane House
Cairns Tower
Carco Castle
Catslack Tower
Clunie Castle
Cluny Crichton Castle
Crichton Castle
Dunbeath Castle
Eliock House
Frendraught Castle
Kinnairdy Castle
Monzie Castle
Naughton Castle
Newhall Castle
Old Crawfordton
Ruthven Castle
Ryehill Castle
Sanquhar Castle
Tilquhillie Castle
Crombie
Kemnay House
Thornton Castle
Crozier
Adderston
Brighouse Tower
Hudshouse Tower
Riccarton Tower
Cruickshank
Aswanley House
Cumming *see* **Comyn**
Cunningham
Aiket Castle
Auchenbowie House
Auchenharvie Castle
Balgair Castle
Ballindalloch Castle
Barns
Belton House
Bonnington House
Caprington Castle
Castle of Park
Clonbeith Castle
Coilsfield Castle
Comiston House
Corsehill Castle
Craigends House
Dean Castle
Drumquhassle Castle
Dunragit House
Finlaystone House
Glengarnock Castle
Hill of Beith
Isle of May
Kerelaw Castle
Kilmaronock Castle

Kilmaurs Place
Kyle Castle
Lainshaw Castle
Livingston Peel
Logie House
Maxwelton House
Monkredding House
Montgreenan Castle
North Synton
Pittarthie Castle
Polmaise Castle
Robertland Castle
Skelmorlie Castle
Tarbolton Motte
Currie
Dumcrieff
Curror
Inchdrewer Castle
Cushnie
Cushnie Castle
Dacre
Hermitage Castle
Dalgleish
Lauriston Castle
Pitfirrane Castle
Scotscraig
Dalmahoy
Dalmahoy
Liberton Tower
Dalrymple
Balneil
Barbieston
Bargany Castle
Carscreugh Castle
Castle Kennedy
Cousland Tower
Craigcaffie Tower
Dalmahoy
Greenknowe Tower
Hailes Castle
Innermessan Castle
Nunraw Castle
Oxenfoord Castle
Sinniness Castle
Stair
Stranraer Castle
Tantallon Castle
Ward of Lochnorris
Dalziel
Amisfield Tower
Caldwell Tower
Carnwath House
Dalzell House
Eliock House
Glenae Tower
The Binns
Danielstoun *see* **Dennis-
toun**
Darleith
Darleith House

Darling
Ladhope Tower
Darroch
Gourock Castle
Davidson
Greenan Castle
Hatton House
Tulloch Castle
Dayell *see* **Dalziel**
De Bosco
Ogilface Castle
De Quincy
Leuchars Castle
Winton House
De Soulis *see* **Soulis**
Delgarno
Dean Castle
Garnieston Castle
Dempster
Careston Castle
Skibo Castle
Denholm
Hills Tower
Westshield
Dennistoun
Camis Eskan
Dennistoun Castle
Finlaystone House
Kilmaronock Castle
Maxwelton House
Newark Castle
Stanely Castle
Dewar
Deuchar Tower
Dupplin Castle
Dick
Cessnock Castle
Craighouse
Grange House
Pitkerro House
Dickson
Carberry Tower
Hartree Tower
Kilbucho Place
Ormiston Tower
Smithfield Castle
Whitslade Tower
Winkston Tower
Dingwall
Dingwall Castle, Edinburgh
Dishington
Ardross Castle
Flemington Tower
Douglas
Abercorn Castle
Aberdour Castle
Auchen Castle
Baads Castle
Balvenie Castle
Barjarg Tower
Bedrule Castle

Belstane Castle
Billie Castle
Blackhouse Tower
Blacklaw Tower
Bothwell Castle
Buittle Castle
Buittle Place
Bunkle Castle
Calder House
Castle of King Edward
Castlehill Tower
Castlemilk
Cavers House
Claypotts Castle
Cluny Crichton Castle
Cockburnspath Castle
Cockburnspath House
Cornal Tower
Coshogle Castle
Craig Douglas Castle
Craignethan Castle
Cramond Tower
Cranshaws Castle
Crawford Castle
Crawfordjohn Castle
Cruggleton Castle
Dalkeith House
Dalmahoy
Dalveen Castle
Darnaway Castle
Denholm
Douglas Castle
Drochil Castle
Drumlanrig Castle
Drumlanrig's Tower,
 Hawick
Drumsargad Castle
Dunbar Castle
Dundarg Castle
Dunglass Castle
Dunsyre Castle
Dupplin Castle
Edmonston Castle
Enoch Castle
Evelaw Tower
Farme Castle
Fast Castle
Gelston Castle
Glenbervie House
Glendevon Castle
Gourock Castle
Grange
Grey Peel
Hallbar Tower
Hatton House
Hawthornden Castle
Hermitage Castle
House of Mergie
Inveravon Castle
Kemnay House
Kilbucho Place

Kildrummy Castle
Killiewarren
Kilspindie Castle
Kinnordy
Kinross House
Kirkcudbright Castle
Kirkhope Tower
Knockdavie Castle
Langholm Tower
Lanton Tower
Lincluden Collegiate Church
Lochindorb Castle
Lochleven Castle
Longniddry House
Lugton
MacLellan's Castle
Mains Castle
Mains Castle
Melrose Abbey
Mordington House
Morton Castle
Mouswald Tower
Nairn Castle
Neidpath Castle
Newark Castle
Old Gala House
Ormond Castle
Red Castle
Redhouse Castle
Sanquhar Castle
Snar Castle
Spott House
Stoneypath Tower
Strathaven Castle
Strathendry Castle
Tantallon Castle
Tayport Castle
The Peel, Busby
Thorril Castle
Threave Castle
Tibbers Castle
Tilquhillie Castle
Timpendean Tower
Tinwald Place
Todholes Castle
Torthorwald Castle
Trabboch Castle
Traquair House
Tulliallan Castle
Wedderburn Castle
Westhall Tower
Whitslade Tower
Whittinghame Castle
Wreaths Tower

Dow
Arnhall Castle

Dowall
Skibo Castle

Dowane
Auchtyfardle Castle
Dowane

Drummond
Auchterarder Castle
Balmoral Castle
Bruce's Castle
Carnock House
Drummond Castle
Hawthornden Castle
Innergellie House
Innerpeffray Castle
Keltie Castle
Kincardine Castle
Kindrochit Castle
Logie-Almond House
Lundin Tower
Megginch Castle
Midhope Castle
Newton Castle
Stobhall
Strathallan Castle

Duff
Aswanley House
Auchintoul
Balvenie Castle
Blervie Castle
Cairneyflappet Castle
Castle Hill, Pluscarden
Corsindae House
Coxton Tower
Crombie Castle
Delgatie Castle
Drummuir
Duff House, Banff
Eden Castle
Fetteresso Castle
Fisherie
Gask House
Glassaugh House
Glenbuchat Castle
Hatton Castle
House of Mergie
Innes House
Invermarkie Castle
Lickleyhead Castle
Mains of Mayen
Park
Rothiemay Castle
Skene House

Duguid
Auchenhove Castle

Dumbreck
Dumbreck Castle

Dun
Benholm's Lodging

Dunbar
Ackergill Tower
Airyolland
Auchen Castle
Auldearn Castle
Baldoon Castle
Ballone Castle
Billie Castle

Black Bog Castle
Blervie Castle
Burgie Castle
Castle Cary
Castle Loch Castle
Castle of Old Wick
Conzie Castle
Crailloch
Cumstoun Castle
Dalvey Castle
Dunphail Castle
Forres Castle
Girnigoe Castle
Halhill Castle
Hempriggs Castle
Hempriggs House
Kilbulack Castle
Machermore Castle
Mindork Castle
Morton Castle
Old Place of Mochrum
Stevenson House
Thunderton House, Elgin
Tibbers Castle

Duncan
Fordell Castle
Gleneagles Castle
Lundie Castle

Dundas
Airth Castle
Arniston House
Ballinbreich Castle
Bavelaw Castle
Blairlogie Castle
Brunstane House
Dunbog Castle
Dundas Castle
Inchgarvie
Kersie
Manor Castle
Melville Castle
Newbyres Tower

Dundemore
Airdrie House

Dunlop
Aiket Castle
Bishopton House
Corsock Castle
Dunlop House
Tollcross

Dunmore
Ballindalloch Castle

Dunnet
Hallgreen Castle

Durham
Bonnington House
Duntarvie Castle
Duntervy Castle
Grange of Monifieth
Largo Castle
Pitkerro House

Durie
Durie House
Killernie Castle
Rossend Castle
Scotscraig
Tayport Castle

Durward
Castle Maud
Coull Castle
Peel Ring of Lumphanan
Peel of Fichlie
Peel of Lintrathen
Strachan
Urquhart Castle

Edgar
Peffermill House
Wedderlie House

Edmonstone
Boyne Castle
Colzium Castle
Craig of Boyne Castle
Dunglass Castle
Duntreath Castle
Edmonston Castle
Newton
Newton Castle
Tulliallan Castle

Eglinton
Eglinton Castle

Elder
Knock Castle

Elliot
Arkleton Tower
Baholm Tower
Breaken Tower
Brugh
Burnhead Tower
Clintwood Castle
Copshaw Tower
Copshaws Tower
Dinlabyre
Fatlips Castle
Foulshiels Tower
Gorrenberry Tower
Haggishaugh
Hartsgarth Tower
Kellie Castle
Larriston Tower
Melgund Castle
Minto House
Parck
Redheugh Castle
Riccarton Tower
Stobs Castle
Thorlieshope Tower
Torwoodlee Tower

Ellis
Illieston House
Mortonhall
Saughton House
Southsyde Castle

Stenhouse
Elphinstone
Airdrie House
Airth Castle
Airth Tower
Barnton Tower
Baronial Hall, Gorbals
Carberry Tower
Craighouse
Cumbernauld Castle
Elphinstone Tower
Haystoun
Herbertshire Castle
Kildrummy Castle
Lochend House
Logie House
Plean Castle
Renfield
Skaithmore Tower
Smithfield Castle
Westhall
Erskine
Airdrie House
Alloa Tower
Alva Castle
Balcomie Castle
Barjarg Tower
Board
Bonnington House
Braemar Castle
Brechin Castle
Cambo House
Cardross House
Corgarff Castle
Culross Palace
Dirleton Castle
Dryburgh Abbey
Dunimarle Castle
Erskine Castle
Gargunnock House
Garscadden Castle
Hallyards
Harthill Castle
House of Dun
Inveramsay
Kellie Castle
Kildrummy Castle
Linlathen House
Mains Castle
Mar's Castle, Aberdeen
Mar's Work, Stirling
Newhall Tower
Old Sauchie
Pittodrie House
Ravenscraig Castle
Rosslyn Castle
Scotscraig
Strathbrock Castle
Stravithie Castle
Tillicoultry Castle
Torrie Castle

Eviot
Balhousie Castle
Ewing
Keppoch House
Fairlie
Ascog House
Bruntsfield House
Comiston House
Fairlie Castle
Myres Castle
Falconer
Glenfarquhar Castle
Haulkerton Castle
Inglismaldie Castle
Lauriston Castle
Monkton House
Faries
Farme Castle
Farquhar
Gilmilnscroft
Mounie Castle
Tolquhon Castle
Farquharson
Abergairn Castle
Balfluig Castle
Balfour Castle
Balmoral Castle
Braemar Castle
Haughton House
Invercauld House
Inverey Castle
Fea
Carrick House
Fenton
Baikie Castle
Fenton Tower
Ferguson
Barclanachan
Dunfallandy
Foumerkland Tower
Hallyards
Inverugie Castle
Isle Tower
Kilkerran Castle
Raith Tower
Fernie
Fernie Castle
Findlay
Ardoch
Boturich Castle
Fisher
Darnick
Fithie
Fithie
Fleming
Antermony Castle
Barochan House
Bield Tower
Biggar Castle
Board
Boghall Castle

Cumbernauld Castle
Farme Castle
Garscadden Castle
Kilmaronock Castle
Kirkintilloch Peel
Oliver Castle
Palacerigg
Fletcher
Achallader Castle
Ballinshoe Tower
Saltoun Hall
Woodrae Castle
Folkerton
Folkerton Castle
Poneil
Forbes
Asloun Castle
Auchernach
Balfluig Castle
Boyndlie House
Brux Castle
Bunchrew House
Byth House
Callendar House
Castle Forbes
Castle Newe
Castle of King Edward
Castlehill, Druminnor
Colinton Castle
Colquhonnie Castle
Corgarff Castle
Corse Castle
Corsindae House
Craigievar Castle
Culloden House
Cunningar
Dounreay Castle
Druminnor Castle
Fettercairn House
Foveran Castle
Gask House
Herbertshire Castle
House of Schivas
Leslie Castle
Lickleyhead Castle
Menie House
Midmar Castle
Monymusk Castle
Newhall Castle
Pitfichie Castle
Pitsligo Castle
Pittencrieff House
Rothiemay Castle
Skellater House
Thornton Castle
Tillycairn Castle
Tolquhon Castle
Towie Castle
Waterton Castle
Fordyce
Ayton Castle

Brucklay Castle
Orrock House
Forest
Garrion Tower
Nemphlar
Forrester
Bavelaw Castle
Bedlormie
Comiston House
Corstorphine Castle
Skipness Castle
Strathendry Castle
Torwood Castle
Tower of Garden
Forsyth
Ethie Castle
Inchnock Castle
Fotheringham
Balfour Castle
Finzean House
Fotheringham Castle
Murroes Castle
Murthly Castle
Powrie Castle
Tealing House
Foulis
Bonnington House
Colinton Castle
Comiston House
Glendorch Castle
Ravelston House
Francis
Stane Castle
Fraser
Aboyne Castle
Aldourie Castle
Ardachy
Beaufort Castle
Braelangwell
Braikie Castle
Bunchrew House
Cairnbulg Castle
Castle Fraser
Cowie Castle
Cowie House
Dalcross Castle
Dores Castle
Durris House
Erchless Castle
Ford House
Fort Augustus
Fruid Castle
House of Tyrie
Inverallochy Castle
Kinnaird Head Castle
Knock Castle
Lonmay Castle
Lovat Castle
Moniack Castle
Muchalls Castle
Neidpath Castle

Oliver Castle
Overton Tower
Philorth Castle
Pitsligo Castle
Pittulie Castle
Red Castle
Strichen
Touch House
Urie House
French
Frenchland Tower
Fullerton
Carberry Tower
Crosbie House
Fullarton Castle
Portencross Castle
Thornton Castle
Furde
Purves Hall
Galbraith
Balgair Castle
Bannachra Castle
Bardowie Castle
Craigmaddie Castle
Culcreuch Castle
Garscadden Castle
Gartconnel Castle
Inchgalbraith Castle
Kincaid House
Mains Castle
Garden
Findon Castle
Pitsligo Castle
Gardyne
Delgatie Castle
Finavon Castle
Gardyne Castle
Middleton House
Garrioch
House of Mergie
Gartshore
Gartshore House
Gavin
Langton Castle
Geddes
Kittlehall
Geil
Ardmore
Gerard
Rochsoles House
Gibb
Carriber Castle
Gibson
Balhouffie
Boreland Tower
Durie House
Largo Castle
Riccarton
Gifford
Busta House
Lennoxlove

Strachan
Yester Castle
Gilchrist
Ospisdale House
Gillespie
Kirkton
Gilmour
Craigmillar Castle
Inch House
Gladstone
Cocklaw Castle
Fasque
Gladstone Castle
Gladstone's Land,
  Edinburgh
Glass
Ascog House
Glen
Balmuto Tower
Barr Castle
Glendowyn
Parton Place
Gordon
Abbot House, Dunfermline
Abergeldie Castle
Aboyne Castle
Aitkenhead Castle
Aswanley House
Auchanachie Castle
Auchindoun Castle
Auchintoul
Auchmeddan Castle
Auchoynanie
Avochie Castle
Badenyon Castle
Balbithan House
Balmoral Castle
Beldorney Castle
Birse Castle
Blairfindy Castle
Bogrie Tower
Brackley Castle
Buck o' Bield
Cairnbulg Castle
Cairston Castle
Cardoness Castle
Carnousie Castle
Castle of Esslemont
Clanyard Castle
Cluny Castle
Colliston Castle
Craig Castle
Craighlaw Castle
Culsalmond
Cunningar
Cunningar
Cyderhall
Davidston House
Dee Castle
Delnabo
Dornoch Palace

Drimnin Castle
Drumin Castle
Dundeugh Castle
Dunrobin Castle
Earlstoun Castle
Edinglassie Castle
Ellon Castle
Fedderate Castle
Finavon Castle
Findlater Castle
Findochty Castle
Fyvie Castle
Gight Castle
Glenbuchat Castle
Golspie Tower
Gordon Castle
Gordon Castle
Gordonstoun
Grandhome House
Greenknowe Tower
Haddo House
Hall of Tolophin
Hallhead
Halmyre House
Helmsdale Castle
House of Tongue
House of Schivas
Huntly
Huntly Castle
Huntly House, Edinburgh
Invergordon Castle
Inverlochy Castle
Invermarkie Castle
Kenmure Castle
Kildrummy Castle
Kisimul Castle
Knock Castle
Knockespock House
Leask House
Lesmoir Castle
Letterfourie
Lickleyhead Castle
Lincluden Collegiate Church
Little Tarrel
Loch an Eilean Castle
Lochinvar Castle
Lynturk Castle
Mains of Mayen
Melgund Castle
Midmar Castle
Migvie Castle
Muirfad Castle
Old House of Embo
Park
Pitlurg Castle
Place of Tillyfour
Poyntzfield
Proncy Castle
Rothiemay Castle
Rusko Castle
Ruthven

Ruthven Barracks
Shirmers Castle
Skelbo Castle
Straloch House
Strome Castle
Terpersie Castle
Threave House
Tillycairn Castle
Tillyhilt Castle
Tolquhon Castle
Torrish Castle
Urquhart Castle
Wardhouse
Westhall
Gourlay
Elie Castle
Hailes Castle
Kincraig Castle
Scotstarvit Tower
Govan
Cardrona Tower
Graham
Abercorn Castle
Airth Castle
Ardoch Tower
Auchterarder Castle
Ballanreoch Castle
Ballochtoul Castle
Boquhan Castle
Braco Castle
Buchanan Castle
Burleigh Castle
Carbeth House
Cardross Manor House
Catter Castle
Claverhouse Castle
Claypotts Castle
Coldoch
Craigcrook Castle
Crookston Castle
Dalkeith House
Darnley Castle
Douglaston House
Duchray Castle
Dudhope Castle
Finlaystone House
Fintry Castle
Gartartan Castle
Gillesbie Tower
Grahams Walls
Graham's Castle
Ha' Tower
Hermitage Castle
Inchbrackie Castle
Inchmurrin Castle
Inchtalla Castle
Inversnaid
Kilbryde Castle
Kilbucho Place
Kincardine Castle
Knockdolian Castle

Largie Castle
Linlathen House
Lochleven Castle
Mains Castle
Maryton
Morphie Castle
Mugdock Castle
Ogilvie Castle
Old Downie
Old Montrose Castle
Rednock Castle
Skelmorlie Castle
Stapleton Tower
Wester Kames Castle
Westhall
Westhall Tower
Grainger
Ayton Castle
Grant
Aldourie Castle
Ballindalloch Castle
Balnabreich
Beldorney Castle
Bishop's House, Elgin
Blairfindy Castle
Castle Grant
Castle Hill, Pluscarden
Castle Stripe
Cunningar
Dalvey Castle
Delnabo
Easter Elchies
Forres Castle
Inverlaidnan
Kilnmaichlie House
Lesmoir Castle
Lethendry Castle
Loch an Eilean Castle
Mains of Mulben
Midmar Castle
Monymusk Castle
Moy House
Muckrach Castle
Prestongrange House
Rothes Castle
Rothiemurchus
Tullochcarron Castle
Urquhart Castle
Wester Elchies
Gray
Abbot House, Dunfermline
Black Jack's Castle
Braikie Castle
Broughty Castle
Carntyne
Carse Gray
Castle Huntly
Dunninald Castle
Fowlis Castle
House of Schivas
Invergowrie House
Kinfauns Castle

Pittencrieff House
Skibo Castle
Greenock
Broadstone Castle
Gregory
Kinnairdy Castle
Grey *see* **Gray**
Grierson
Barjarg Tower
Lagg Tower
Rockhall
Grimond
Carbet Castle
Gunn
Dirlot Castle
Gunn's Castle
Halberry Castle
Latheron Castle
Guthrie
Balgavies Castle
Colliston Castle
Dysart
Gagie House
Guthrie Castle
Kirkbuddo
Red Castle
Hacket *see* **Halkett**
Hackston
Rathillet House
Haig
Bemersyde House
Haldane
Airthrey Castle
Boturich Castle
Gleneagles Castle
Lanrick Castle
Manor Castle
Halkett
Mains of Mayen
Pitfirrane Castle
Hall
Craigcrook Castle
Fast Castle
Halliday
Tullibole Castle
Halyburton
Castle Gogar
Dirleton Castle
Eaglescairnie
Ecclesiamagirdle House
Hatton Castle
Lintrose House
Mertoun House
Pitcur Castle
Hamilton
Airdrie House
Aitkenhead Castle
Auldton
Bardowie Castle
Barnbougle Castle
Barncluith Castle

Baronial Hall, Gorbals
Barr Castle
Biel
Blair Castle
Boghouse Castle
Brodick Castle
Broomhill Castle
Cadzow Castle
Calderwood Castle
Carnbroe House
Carnell
Carriden House
Carstairs Castle
Castle Kennedy
Castlemilk
Chatelherault Hunting
  Lodge
Cochno Castle
Cot Castle
Couston Castle
Cowden Hall
Craighlaw Castle
Craigmaddie Castle
Craignethan Castle
Crawfordjohn Castle
Dalmeny House
Dalzell House
Darngaber Castle
Drumry Castle
Drumsargad Castle
Easter Greenock Castle
Eddlewood Castle
Erskine Castle
Falside Castle
Farme Castle
Ferguslie Castle
Fingalton
Gallowhill
Garrion Tower
Gartshore House
Gilbertfield Castle
Gilkerscleugh House
Grange House
Greenock Castle
Hamilton House
Hamilton Palace
Harlawhill
Hills Tower
Inchnock Castle
Innerwick Castle
Karig Lion Castle
Kildonan Castle
Kingscavil
Kinkell
Kinneil House
Kirkhope Tower
Langton Castle
Law Tower
Lennoxlove
Loch Laggan Castle
Lochranza Castle

Malleny House
Mannerston
Mellerstain
Monk Castle
Monkland House
Monkton House
Murdostoun Castle
Newton Castle
Newton House
Northfield House
Ochiltree Castle
Ochiltree Castle
Old Woodhouselee Castle
Orbiston House
Pardovan Castle
Patrickholm
Penshiel Grange
Pinmore
Pitlessie Castle
Polmont House
Preston Tower
Provan Hall
Ralston
Ranfurly Castle
Raploch Castle
Redhouse Castle
Ridford
Ross House
Rutherglen Castle
Saltcoats Castle
Skene House
Sorn Castle
Stoneypath Tower
Strathaven Castle
Sundrum Castle
The Peel, Busby
Torrance Castle
Tweedie Castle
Tyninghame House
West Port House,
  Linlithgow
Winton House
Wishaw House
Hannay
  Kirkdale Tower
  Sorbie Castle
  Wigtown Castle
Harvey
  Castle Semple
Hatton
  Hatton House
Hay
  Balbithan House
  Balhousie Castle
  Belton House
  Benholm's Lodging
  Bield Tower
  Castle of Esslemont
  Castle of Park
  Craigenveoch Castle
  Craignethan Castle

Cramalt Tower
Delgatie Castle
Drumelzier Castle
Duns Castle
Dupplin Castle
Errol Park
Flemington Tower
Gowrie House, Perth
Haystoun
Inchnock Castle
Inshoch Castle
Kilspindie Castle
Kininmonth House
Kinnoull Castle
Lickleyhead Castle
Lochloy Castle
Logie-Almond House
Megginch Castle
Monkton House
Mounie Castle
Moyness Castle
Muchalls Castle
Naughton Castle
Neidpath Castle
Nunraw Castle
Old Slains Castle
Oliver Castle
Pinkie House
Pitfour Castle
Place of Snade
Rannas Castle
Renfield
Shieldgreen Tower
Slains Castle
Smithfield Castle
Spott House
Turriff Castle
Urie House
Whittinghame Castle
Yester Castle
Hebden
  Carrick House
Heiton
  Darnick Tower
Henderson
  Broomhill House
  Fordell Castle
  Otterston Tower
Henry
  Geilston House
Hepburn
  Alemoor Tower
  Athelstaneford
  Beanston
  Black Castle
  Bothwell Castle
  Bruce's Castle
  Crichton Castle
  Dolphinton
  Dunbar Castle
  Dunsyre Castle

Earlstoun Castle
Elsrickle
Fairnington House
Hailes Castle
Hermitage Castle
Humbie Old Place
Luffness House
Morham Castle
Moss Tower
Nunraw Castle
Walston
Waughton Castle
Westhall Tower
Heriot
  Hoddom Castle
  Lennox Castle
Heron
  Drumcoltran Tower
  Drumlochy Castle
  Tower of Lethendy
Herries
  Blacklaw Tower
  Drumcoltran Tower
  Hallguards Castle
  Terregles Castle
Holbourne
  Menstrie Castle
  Penkaet Castle
Home
  Ayton Castle
  Bassendean House
  Bastleridge
  Blackadder Castle
  Bothwell Castle
  Broxmouth House
  Bunkle Castle
  Claypotts Castle
  Cockburnspath Castle
  Cowdenknowes
  Deuchar Tower
  Douglas Castle
  Dreghorn Castle
  Dunglass Castle
  Duns Castle
  Fast Castle
  Fulton Tower
  Greenlaw Castle
  Harden
  Houndwood House
  Howliston Tower
  Hume Castle
  Hutton Castle
  Lee Tower
  Linthill House
  Manderston
  North Berwick Priory
  Old Greenlaw Castle
  Paxton House
  Peelwalls
  Polwarth Castle
  Preston Tower

Purves Hall
Redbraes Castle
Spott House
The Hirsel
Thornton Tower
Wedderburn Castle
Whiteside Peel
Hope
  Balcomie Castle
  Bridge Castle
  Carriden House
  Craighall
  Hopetoun House
  Illieston House
  Kersie
  Luffness House
  Midhope Castle
  Monkton House
  Niddry Castle
  Ormiston Castle
  Pinkie House
  Rankeilour Castle
  Rosyth Castle
  Wamphray Tower
Hoppringle *see* **Pringle**
Horne
  Langwell Castle
  Westhall
Horsburgh
  Horsburgh Tower
  Hutchinfield Tower
  Manorhead Tower
  Nether Horsburgh Castle
  Purvishill Tower
Hosier
  Tannochside House
Houston
  Houston House
  Isle of Whithorn Castle
  Johnstone Castle
  Milliken
  Park
  The Peel, Busby
Howieson
  Craufurdland Castle
Hume *see* **Home**
Hunt
  Pittencrieff House
Hunter
  Barjarg Tower
  Glenapp Castle
  Hunterston Castle
  Little Cumbrae Castle
  Polmood
Hutchinson
  Carlowrie Castle
  Partick Castle
Hynd
  Drumcoltran Tower
Inglis
  Aithernie Castle

Colluthie House
Cramond Tower
Eastshield Tower
Manorhead Tower
Murdostoun Castle
Newmore Castle
Scotstarvit Tower
Woodhouse Hill

Innes
Asliesk Castle
Ayton Castle
Balvenie Castle
Cowie Castle
Cowie House
Coxton Tower
Crombie Castle
Dunbeath Castle
Durris House
Edingight House
Gordonstoun
Innes House
Invermarkie Castle
Kinnairdy Castle
Leuchars House
Raemoir
Tulloch Castle

Irvine
Auchenrivock Tower
Barra Castle
Bonshaw Tower
Drum Castle
Drumcoltran Tower
Kellie Castle
Kingcausie
Kirkconnel Tower
Lynturk Castle
Monboddo House
Robgill Tower
Stapleton Tower
Straloch House
Woodhouse Tower

Irving *see* **Irvine**

Irwin
Burleigh Castle

Jaffray
Grandhome House

Jamieson
Kilallan House
Kilmory Castle

Jardine
Bower of Wandel
Castlemilk
Haggishaugh
Lanrick Castle
Spedlins Tower
Tinwald Place

Jeffrey
Craigcrook Castle

Johnstone
Alva Castle
Blacklaw Tower

Breconside Tower
Cochrane Castle
Corehead
Cornal Tower
Curriehill Castle
Elphinstone Tower
Elshieshields Tower
Glendinning Castle
Keith Hall
Kinnelhead Tower
Kirkton Tower
Knockhill
Lathrisk House
Lochhouse Tower
Lochwood Tower
Lockerbie Tower
Lunelly Tower
Mellingshaw Tower
Monzie Castle
Muirhead
Netherplace
Newbie Castle
Old Graitney
Raecleugh Tower
Sarkbridge
Tundergarth Castle
Wamphray Tower
Westerhall Tower

Kay
Edinbellie Castle

Keith
Aboyne Castle
Ackergill Tower
Aden House
Badenheath Castle
Balbithan House
Barmagachan
Benholm Castle
Benholm's Lodging
Boddam Castle
Clackriach Castle
Covington Castle
Dunnottar Castle
Fetteresso Castle
Forse Castle
Grandhome House
Hallforest Castle
House of Auchiries
Inverugie Castle
Keith Hall
Keith Inch Tower
Keith Marischal
Kinmuck Castle
Kintore Castle
Ludquharn
Old Maud
Pitmedden House
Ravenscraig Castle
Sorn Castle
Struthers Castle
Urie House

Usan House

Kelso
Brisbane House

Kemp
Durie House

Kennedy
Ailsa Craig Castle
Ardmillan Castle
Ardstinchar Castle
Auchtyfardle Castle
Balneil
Baltersan Castle
Barbieston
Bargany Castle
Blairquhan
Brockloch Castle
Brunston Castle
Cassillis House
Castle Kennedy
Craigneil Castle
Crossraguel Abbey
Cruggleton Castle
Culzean Castle
Cumstoun Castle
Dalquharran Castle
Drummellan Castle
Dunduff Castle
Dunure Castle
Ellon Castle
Fergus Loch
Glenays Castle
Greenan Castle
Inch Crindil
Kilhenzie Castle
Kirkhill Castle
Kirkintilloch Peel
Kirkmichael House
Knockdaw Castle
Loch Doon Castle
Maybole Castle
Newark Castle
Pinwherry Castle
Romanno Tower
Sinniness Castle
Stair
Stranraer Castle

Kerr
Ancrum House
Broxmouth House
Castle of Holydean
Cavers Carre
Cessford Castle
Colquhar Tower
Corbet Tower
Dolphinston Tower
Douglaston House
Fairnilee
Ferniehirst Castle
Floors Castle
Graden Tower
Harviestoun Castle

Hirendean Castle
Kersland
Lee Tower
Littledean Tower
Lochtower
Malleny House
Masterton House
Mersington Tower
Monkland House
Morriston Tower
Newbattle Abbey
Nisbet House
Prestongrange House
Stone Hill, Jedburgh
Sunlaws House
Wallace's Tower
Windydoors Tower
Yair House

Kilpatrick
Kirkmichael House

Kincaid
Auchenreoch Castle
Craiglockhart Castle
Kincaid House

King
Barra Castle
Dudwick Castle

Kinloch
Alderstone House
Cruivie Castle
Kinloch
Logie House
Newark Castle
Pitlochie Castle

Kinnaird
Kinnaird Castle

Kinnear
Easter Kinnear Castle

Kinninmond
Craighall
Kinkell
Melgund Castle

Kirk
Bogrie Tower
Sundaywell Tower

Kirkcaldy
Grange
Hallyards Castle

Kirkconnel
Kirkconnel House

Kirkpatrick
Closeburn Castle
Rockhall
Torthorwald Castle
Tynron Doon
Wamphray Tower

Kirkwood
Pilrig House

Knox
Craigends House
Ranfurly Castle

Laing
Carrick House
Redhouse Castle

Lamb
Lamb's House, Leith

Lamont
Ardlamont House
Asgog Castle
Carrick Castle
Knockamillie Castle
Toward Castle

Lauder
Bass Rock
Bruntsfield House
Grange House
Hatton House
Johnscleugh
Lauder Tower
Penkaet Castle
Quarrelwood Castle
Tyninghame House
Whitslaid Tower
Woodhall

Laurie
Blackwood House
Maxwelton House
Polmont House

Law
Clatto Castle
Lauriston Castle

Lawson
Baddingsgill House
Balthayock Castle

Lawtie
Inaltrie Castle

Learmonth
Balcomie Castle
Clatto Castle
Dairsie Castle
Isle of May
Rhymer's Tower

Leckie
Old Leckie House

Leighton
Usan House

Leith
Castle Croft
Freefield House
Fyvie Castle
Glenkindie House
Harthill Castle
Leith Hall
Leslie Castle
Lickleyhead Castle

Lennox
Antermony Castle
Balcastle
Balcorrach Castle
Ballagan Castle
Balloch Castle
Bencloich Castle

Boturich Castle
Cally Castle
Cameron House
Catter Castle
Duntreath Castle
Faslane Castle
Gordon Castle
Inchmurrin Castle
Kilmaronock Castle
Maiden Castle
Place of Bonhill
Plunton Castle
Rosneath Castle
Woodhead Castle

Leny
Leny House

Leslie
Aikenway Castle
Balgonie Castle
Ballinbreich Castle
Balquhain Castle
Castle Croft
Chanonry
Cushnie Castle
Drumdollo Castle
Drummuir
Eden Castle
Fetternear House
Findrassie Castle
Keir House
Keith Hall
Kininvie House
Leslie Castle
Leslie House
Letterfourie
Lickleyhead Castle
Newark Castle
Newton House
Pitcairlie House
Pitcaple Castle
Place of Tillyfour
Rothes Castle
Tullos House
Wardhouse
Warthill House

Lestalric
Lochend House

Lickprivick
Lickprivick Castle

Liddel
Broadstone Castle
Creich Castle
Elibank Castle

Lindsay
Alyth Castle
Auchenskeoch Castle
Auchmull Castle
Balcarres House
Balgavies Castle
Ballinshoe Tower
Barntalloch Tower

Barnyards
Belstane Castle
Blacklaw Tower
Brandy Den
Byres
Careston Castle
Carsluith Castle
Comyn's Castle
Corb Castle
Covington Castle
Craigie Castle
Crawford Castle
Crossbasket Castle
Daviot Castle
Dowhill Castle
Dunnottar Castle
Dunrod Castle
Edzell Castle
Evelick Castle
Farnell Castle
Finavon Castle
Fyvie Castle
Garleton Castle
Invermark Castle
Inverquiech Castle
Kilbirnie House
Kilspindie Castle
Kinblethmont
Kingask
Kirkbuddo
Lordscairnie Castle
Luffness House
Mains Castle
Monikie Castle
Ormiston Castle
Pitairlie Castle
Pitcruvie Castle
Pitfour Castle
Pitroddie
Place of Bonhill
Ruthven Castle
Spynie Palace
Struthers Castle
Vayne Castle
Wauchope Castle
Wemyss Castle
Whistleberry Castle
Woodrae Castle
Wormiston House

Lipp
House of Schivas

Little
Foulitch Tower
Liberton House
Liberton Tower

Livingstone
Almond Castle
Balcastle
Bedlormie
Belstane Castle
Bencloich Castle

Biggar Castle
Bridge Castle
Callander Castle
Callendar House
Castle Cary
Castle Hill, Slamannan
Colzium Castle
Drumry Castle
Glentirran
Inglismaldie Castle
Jerviswood House
Kersie
Kilsyth Castle
Law Tower
Livingston Peel
MacDuff's Castle
Midhope Castle
Ogilface Castle
Old Place
Saltcoats Castle
The Binns

Lloyd
Minard Castle

Lockhart
Barr Castle
Carnwath House
Carstairs Castle
Castlehill, Cambusnethan
Cleghorn House
Covington Castle
Craiglockhart Castle
Craiglockhart Castle
Dean Castle
Dunsyre Castle
Hallbar Tower
Hills Tower
Kerelaw Castle
Kirkton
Kirkton of Carluke
The Lee
Torbrex Castle
Tweedie Castle
Waygateshaw House
Westhall Tower
Westshield

Logan
Burncastle
Caroline Park House
Coltness Castle
Couston Castle
Fast Castle
Houndwood House
Lochend House
Pittarthie Castle
Preston
Renton Peel
Reston

Lorane
Tresmass

Lorimer
Craigieburn

Kellie Castle
Loudoun
Terringzean Castle
Lovell
Ballumbie Castle
Fernie Castle
Lovells' Castle, Hawick
Lowis
Castlehill Tower
Plora Tower
Lumsden
Airdrie House
Auchry Castle
Blanerne Castle
Cushnie Castle
Innergellie House
Lathallan Castle
Lumsdaine
Mountquhanie Castle
Pitcaple Castle
Pittillock House
Tillycairn Castle
Lundie
Balgonie Castle
Benholm Castle
Pitlochie Castle
Lundin
Aithernie Castle
Lundin Tower
Lyle
Duchal Castle
Dysart
Gardyne Castle
Gartartan Castle
Kinnordy
Shielhill
Stoneypath Tower
Lynn
Kinghorn Castle
Larg Castle
Lyon
Aldbar Castle
Baikie Castle
Balintore Castle
Beldorney Castle
Castle Huntly
Cossans Castle
Fletcherfield Castle
Glamis Castle
Karig Lion Castle
Thornton Castle
MacAdam
Banck Castle
Dumcrieff
Waterhead Castle
MacAlister
Glenbarr Abbey
MacAskill
Dun Sgathaich
MacAuley
Ardincaple Castle

Blairvadach Castle
Faslane Castle
MacBeth
Eilean Ghruididh
Macbeth's Castle
MacCall
Tower
MacCombie
Lynturk Castle
MacConnel
Craigneil Castle
Knockdolian Castle
MacCorquodales
Loch Tromlee
MacCubbin
Kilmaronock Castle
Knockdolian Castle
MacCulloch
Arbigland House
Ardwall
Ardwell House
Auchneight
Barholm Castle
Cardoness Castle
Druchtag Motte
Hills Tower
Killaser Castle
McCulloch's Castle
Myrton Castle
Torhouse Castle
MacDonald
Airds Castle
Ardtornish Castle
Armadale Castle
Aros Castle
A' Chrannog
Balloan Castle
Borve Castle
Breachacha Castle
Cairnburgh Castle
Caisteal Bheagram
Caisteal Camus
Caisteal Mhic Cneacail
Caisteal Uisdein
Castle Loch Heylipol
Castle of King Edward
Castle Sween
Castle Tioram
Claig Castle
Coroghon Castle
Delny Castle
Dun Aonais
Dun Athad
Dun Bhoraraic
Dun Chonnuill
Dun Sgathaich
Dun an Sticar
Dunaverty Castle
Dundonald Castle
Duntulm Castle
Dunyvaig Castle

Finlaggan
Gorm Castle
Invergarry Castle
Island Muller Castle
Keppoch Castle
Kildonan Castle
Kilkerran Castle
Largie Castle
Loch Kinellan
Loch an Sgoltaire Castle
Lochranza Castle
Moil Castle
Nairn Castle
Ormacleit Castle
Rammerscales House
Saddell Castle
Skipness Castle
Strome Castle
MacDonnel *see* **MacDonald**
MacDougall
Ardfad Castle
Ardmaddy Castle
Aros Castle
Caisteal nan Con
Castle Coeffin
Dun Chonnuill
Dunollie Castle
Dunstaffnage Castle
Fincharn Castle
Gallanach Castle
Gylen Castle
Lunga
Makerstoun House
Rarey
MacDowall
Auchness Castle
Balgreggan
Castle Semple
Freugh Tower
Garthland Castle
Heston Island
Logan House
Longcastle
Machermore Castle
Old Place of Mochrum
Ravenstone Castle
MacDuff
Airdit House
Barnslee
Castle Hill, North Berwick
Cupar Castle
Falkland Palace
Fernie Castle
Huntly Castle
Lindores Castle
MacDuff's Castle
Maiden Castle
Pittillock House
MacDuffie
Dun Eibhinn
Loch an Sgoltaire Castle

MacEachen
Tangy Loch
MacEwen
Ballimore
Bardrochat
Castle Ewen
MacFarlane
Arrochar House
Ballanreoch Castle
Eilean Vhow Castle
Gartartan Castle
Inveruglas Castle
Tarbet Castle
Tighvechtichan
MacGie
Balmaghie
Plunton Castle
MacGilchrist
Northbar
MacGill
Cousland Tower
Old Lindores Castle
Oxenfoord Castle
Rumgally House
MacGoune
Kilmaronock Castle
MacGregor
Aberuchill Castle
Edinample Castle
Eilean Molach
Glengyle Castle
Glenstrae Castle
Inversnaid
Kilchurn Castle
Lanrick Castle
Stronmilchan
MacIan
Dunyvaig Castle
Mingary Castle
MacIlvaine
Thomaston Castle
MacInnes
Kinlochaline Castle
MacIntyre
Sorn Castle
MacIver
Glendarroch
Mackay
Balnakeil House
Borve Castle
Dirlot Castle
Dounreay Castle
House of Tongue
Loch Stack Castle
Sandside House
Shiels
Skibo Castle
Mackenzie
Ardvreck Castle
Auchenskeoch Castle
Balloan Castle

Ballone Castle
Belmont Castle
Brahan Castle
Calda House
Caroline Park House
Castle Hill, Pluscarden
Castle Leod
Chanonry
Coul House
Dochmaluag Castle
Earlshall
Eilean Donan Castle
Fairburn Tower
Flowerdale
Granton Castle
Hatton Castle
Kilcoy Castle
Kinkell Castle
Loch Kinellan
Loch Slin Castle
Milliken
Newmore Castle
Ord House
Red Castle
Tarbat House
Mackie
Larg Tower
MacKinlay
Wester Kames Castle
MacKinnon
Caisteal Maol
Dun Ara
Dun Ringill
Mackintosh
Aldourie Castle
Blervie Castle
Castle Stuart
Cluny Castle
Culloden House
Dalcross Castle
Daviot Castle
Dunachton Castle
Halhill Castle
Keppoch Castle
Loch an Eilean Castle
Moy Castle
Rait Castle
Tor Castle
MacLachlan
Castle Lachlan
Dun Chonnuill
MacLaine
Loch Sguabain Castle
Moy Castle
MacLaurin
Dreghorn Castle
MacLean
Ardtornish Castle
Aros Castle
Breachacha Castle
Caisteal nan Con

Castle Loch Heylipol
Castle Spioradain
Drimnin Castle
Duart Castle
Dun Chonnuill
Eilean Amalaig Castle
Glensanda Castle
Gorm Castle
Kinlochaline Castle
MacLellan
Auchlane Castle
Barmagachan
Barscobe Castle
Bombie Castle
Cumstoun Castle
Lochfergus
MacLellan's Castle
Raeberry Castle
Ravenstone Castle
MacLeod
Ardvreck Castle
Assynt Castle
Bearasay
Brochel Castle
Cadboll Castle
Caisteal Camus
Caisteal MhicLeod
Calda House
Dolphingstone Castle
Dun Sgathaich
Duntulm Castle
Dunvegan Castle
Eilean Ghruididh
Geanies Castle
Gunnery of MacLeod
Invergordon Castle
MacLeod's Castle
Raasay House
Stornoway Castle
MacMaster
Glensanda Castle
MacMillan
Castle Sween
Finlaystone House
MacNab
Bovain
Eilean Ran Castle
Kinnell House
Swinton
MacNaughton
Dubh Loch Castle
Dunderave Castle
Fraoch Eilean Castle
MacNeil
Breachacha Castle
Caisteal Calvay
Castle Sinclair
Castle Sween
Kisimul Castle
Loch an Sgoltaire
Lossit House

Castle Loch Heylipol
Northfield House
Tirfergus
MacNeish
Loch Earn Castle
MacNicol
Stornoway Castle
MacNiven
Dunachton Castle
Macpherson
Ballindalloch Castle
Cluny Castle
Loch Laggan Castle
Loch a' Phearsain
Mains of Mulben
Newton Castle
MacQuarrie
Dun Ban, Ulva
MacQueen
Broughton Place
MacQuillan
Dunaverty Castle
MacRae
Eilean Donan Castle
Ochiltree Castle
MacSween
Castle Sween
Skipness Castle
MacThomas
Forter Castle
MacTire
Durris House
MacTire Castle
MacWhurter
Blairquhan
Main
Bishop's House, Lochwood
Maitland
Auchen Castle
Balgreggan
Brunstane Castle
Cumstoun Castle
Hallbar Tower
Hatton House
House of Schivas
Inveresk Lodge
Lennoxlove
Old Sauchie
Old Thirlestane Castle
Scotscraig
Thirlestane Castle
Tibbers Castle
Whitslaid Tower
Malcolm
Duntrune Castle
Lochore Castle
Marjoribanks
Bathgate Castle
Hallyards
Northfield House
Marshall
Castle of Esslemont

Curriehill Castle
Kittlehall

Martin
Carden Tower

Mathers
Provan Hall

Mathieson
Ardross Castle

Maule
Ardestie Castle
Auchterhouse
Balmossie
Brechin Castle
Carmyllie Castle
Edzell Castle
Fowlis Castle
Kellie Castle
Melgund Castle
Panmure Castle
Pitairlie Castle

Maxwell
Aitkenhead Castle
Annan Castle
Arkleton Tower
Auldhouse
Barclosh Castle
Belstane Castle
Bishopton House
Blackcraig Castle
Blacklaw Tower
Blawarthill
Breckonside Tower
Buittle Place
Caerlaverock Castle
Calderwood Castle
Cardoness Castle
Castlemilk
Cowhill Tower
Crookston Castle
Dalswinton Castle
Dargavel House
Darnley Castle
Dowies
Druchtag Motte
Drumcoltran Tower
Dubs
Dumfries Castle
Foumerkland Tower
Haggs Castle
Hills Tower
Hoddom Castle
Isle Tower
Kenmure Castle
Kirkconnel House
Langholm Tower
Langrig
Lee Castle
Lickprivick Castle
MacLellan's Castle
Mearns Castle
Moure Castle

Myrton Castle
Newark Castle
Newton Mearns
Orchardton Tower
Penkaet Castle
Pollok House
Portrack Castle
Repentance Tower
Stanely Castle
Terregles Castle
Threave Castle
Tinwald Place
Wreaths Tower

McCubbin *see* **MacCubbin**

Mein
Comiston House
Craigcrook Castle

Meldrum
Crombie Castle
Dumbreck Castle
Eden Castle
Fyvie Castle
Meldrum House
Newhall Tower
Tullibody

Melrose
West Linton

Melville
Balwearie Castle
Dysart
Glenbervie House
Grange
Granton Castle
Halhill Tower
Melville Castle
Melville House
Monimail Tower
Old Manse
Raith Tower
Rossend Castle
Seafield Tower
Tayport Castle

Menteith
Alva Castle
Carse Castle
Carstairs Castle
Closeburn Castle
Hill House
Kersie
Rednock Castle
Rusky Castle
Stonebyres House

Menzies
Arnprior Castle
Castle Menzies
Comrie Castle
Durisdeer Castle
Enoch Castle
Finlarig Castle
Fordyce Castle
Maryculter House

Meggernie Castle
Pitcur Castle
Pitfodels Castle
Pitfodel's Lodging

Mercer
Aldie Castle
Balhousie Castle
Inchbrackie Castle
Meikleour House

Merry
Belladrum

Middlemast
Grieston Tower

Middleton
Balbegno Castle
Fettercairn House

Mill
Vayne Castle

Millar
Manderston
Rossie Castle

Milliken
Milliken

Mitchell
Alderstone House
Dudwick Castle
Howliston Tower
Orrock House
Thainstone House

Moir
Old Leckie House

Moncrieffe
Balcaskie House
Hallyards Castle
Moredun Hall
Myres Castle
Randerston
Reedie
Tullibole Castle

Moncur
Moncur Castle

Monteith *see* **Menteith**

Montgomery
Ardrossan Castle
Auchans
Ballikillet Castle
Brigend Castle
Broadstone Castle
Cassillis House
Cloak Castle
Clonbeith Castle
Coilsfield Castle
Corslie Castle
Cumstoun Castle
Duchal Castle
Dunskey Castle
Eaglesham Castle
Eglinton Castle
Giffen Castle
Glenays Castle
Hessilhead Castle

Knock Castle
Lainshaw Castle
Little Cumbrae Castle
Lochleven Castle
Lochranza Castle
Macbiehill
Montfode Castle
Polnoon Castle
Saltcoats
Seagate Castle
Skelmorlie Castle
Southannan Castle
Stair
Stane Castle
Stanhope Tower
Stobo Castle
Whitslaid Tower

Monypenny
Kinaldy Castle
Kinkell
Pilrig House
Pitmilly House
Pittarthie Castle

Mordington
Mordington House

Morehead
Herbertshire Castle

Morham
Rankine Castle

Morrison
Colquhar Tower
Conzie Castle
Dairsie Castle
Dun Carloway
Frendraught Castle
Naughton Castle
Prestongrange House

Mortimer
Aberdour Castle
Craigievar Castle
Fowlis Castle
Inverugie Castle

Morton
Cambo House
Castle Levan
Randerston

Morville
Borgue
Glengarnock Castle
Saltoun Hall

Moultray
Seafield Tower

Mounsey
Rammerscales House

Mowat
Brandy Den
Bucholly Castle
Busbie Tower
Freswick House
Hatton Castle
Vayne Castle

Mowbray
Barnbougle Castle
Bavelaw Castle
Dalmeny House
Kellie Castle
Methven Castle
Otterston Tower

Muirhead
Lauchope House
Linnhouse

Mundeville
Moure Castle

Munro
Allan
Ardross Castle
Auchenbowie House
Contullich Castle
Delny Castle
Docharty
Foulis Castle
Fyrish House
Little Tarrel
Loch Slin Castle
Meikle Daan
Meikle Tarrel
Newmore Castle
Novar House
Pitcalnie
Poyntzfield
Tarbat House

Mure
Abercorn Castle
Auchendrane Castle
Barmagachan
Caldwell Tower
Cassencarie House
Cloncaird Castle
Cowden Hall
Craighlaw Castle
Glanderston Castle
Nether Auchendrane
Perceton House
Rowallan Castle

Murray
Abercairny
Aberscross
Airth Tower
Aldie Castle
Amhuinnsuidhe Castle
Auchencruive Castle
Baberton House
Ballencrieff House
Balmanno Castle
Balvaird Castle
Black Barony Castle
Blair Castle
Bothwell Castle
Broughton Place
Callands House
Cally Castle
Carrick Castle

Cluggy Castle
Cobairdy
Cockpool Castle
Comlongon Castle
Couston Castle
Cringletie House
Cromarty Castle
Culbin
Darnaway Castle
Deuchar Tower
Dreghorn Castle
Drumsargad Castle
Dumcrieff
Dunkeld House
Elibank Castle
Forres Castle
Fowlis Castle
Gauldwell Castle
Geanies Castle
Glendoick House
Hangingshaw
Hoddom Castle
Hopeton Tower
Huntingtower Castle
Inchbervie Castle
Invergowrie House
Invershin Castle
Kildrummy Castle
Langshaw Tower
Lintrose House
Livingston Peel
Logie-Almond House
Logierait Castle
Luthrie
Malleny House
McCulloch's Castle
Meikleour House
Melgund Castle
Moss Castle
Old Place of Broughton
Ormond Castle
Parton Place
Pittarthie Castle
Polmaise Castle
Romanno Tower
Scone Palace
Spott House
Stanhope Tower
Steuarthall
Stobo Castle
Tullibardine Castle
Waygateshaw House
Whitslade Tower
Muschett
Burnbank
Kincardine Castle
Naesmith
Dawyck House
Lour Tower
Posso Tower
Woodhouse Hill

Nairn
Belmont Castle
Inchbervie Castle
Napier
Balgair Castle
Culcreuch Castle
Edinbellie Castle
Gartness Castle
Kilmahew Castle
Lauriston Castle
Merchiston Castle
Old Ballikinrain
Thirlestane Tower
Wrychtishousis
Neilson
Craigcaffie Tower
Nelson
Corsock Castle
Nevan
Monkredding House
Newbigging
Dunsyre Castle
Newton
Newton
Nicholson
Balcaskie House
Carnock House
Glenbervie House
Niddrie
Niddrie Marischal
Nisbet
Cairnhill House
Craigentinny House
Dean House
Dirleton Castle
Drum House
Nisbet House
Northfield House
Sornhill
Winton House
Noble
Ardardan Castle
Ardkinglas House
Dunderave Castle
Ochterlony
Balgavies Castle
Flemington Tower
Kellie Castle
Ogilvie
Airlie Castle
Alyth Castle
Auchindoun Castle
Auchterhouse
Balbegno Castle
Balfour Castle
Barras Castle
Beldorney Castle
Benholm Castle
Bolshan Castle
Boyne Castle
Braikie Castle

Buchragie House
Carnousie Castle
Claverhouse Castle
Clova Castle
Clunie Castle
Cortachy Castle
Coull
Craig Castle
Craig of Boyne Castle
Cullen House
Deskford Castle
Findlater Castle
Findochty Castle
Forglen House
Forter Castle
Grandhome House
Halhill Castle
House of Auchiries
House of Skeith
Inaltrie Castle
Inchdrewer Castle
Inglismaldie Castle
Inshewan
Inverquharity Castle
Keltie Castle
Kinnell Castle
Kinnordy
Lochindorb Castle
Milton Keith Tower
Newton Castle
Peel of Lintrathen
Pittulie Castle
Portsoy Castle
Powrie Castle
Rothes Castle
Ruthven Castle
Shielhill
Wedderburn Castle
Winton House
Ogstoun
Gordonstoun
Pitfodels Castle
Pitfodel's Lodging
Tilquhillie Castle
Oliphant
Ackergill Tower
Ardblair Castle
Berriedale Castle
Castle of Old Wick
Condie
Drumsargad Castle
Dupplin Castle
Gascon Hall
Hatton Castle
Kellie Castle
Milton Keith Tower
Orbiston House
Pittheavlis Castle
Rossie Ochil
Williamston

Oliver
Dinlabyre
Gagie House
Mervinslaw Pele
Northbank Peel
Slacks Peel
Ord
Findochty Castle
Ormiston
Westhouses
Orr
Castle Campbell
Harviestoun Castle
Ralston
Stobcross
Orrock
Orrock House
Osborne
Peffermill House
Oswald
Auchencruive Castle
Otterburn
Auldhame
Redhall Castle
Palmer
Cavers House
Paxton House
Panton
Pitmedden House
Park
Park
Paterson
Bannockburn House
Castle Huntly
Caverhill Tower
Myres Castle
Robgill Tower
Paton
Grandhome House
Patrick
Woodside House
Pearson
Old Kippencross
Penicuik
Newhall Castle
Romanno Tower
Perrin
Ardross Castle
Phin
Pittencrieff House
Pierson
Auchtermeggities
Pitcairn
Abbot House, Dunfermline
Dreghorn Castle
Pollock
Arthurlie House
Lee Castle
Mearns Castle
Netherplace
Pinwherry Castle

Pollok Castle
Rothes Castle
Pollok *see* **Pollock**
Polwarth
Polwarth Castle
Wedderlie House
Porteous
Hawkshaw Castle
Whitslade Tower
Porterfield
Comiston House
Duchal Castle
Kilmacolm Castle
Preston
Airdrie House
Balgavies Castle
Craigmillar Castle
Fyvie Castle
Peffermill House
Tolquhon Castle
Uttershill Castle
Primrose
Barnbougle Castle
Dalmeny House
Livingston Peel
Malleny House
Pitreavie Castle
Rosebery House
Rosyth Castle
Pringle
Blackhouse Tower
Buckholm Tower
Chapelhill
Colmslie Tower
Craigcrook Castle
Greenknowe Tower
Hoppringle Castle
Old Gala House
Penkaet Castle
Smailholm Tower
Torsance Castle
Torwoodlee Tower
Whytbank Tower
Woodhouse Hill
Yair House
Purves
Fulford Tower
Purves Hall
Purvishill Tower
Rhymer's Tower
Purvis *see* **Purves**
Quincy *see* **De Quincy**
Rait
Hallgreen Castle
Rait Castle
Red Castle
Ralston
Ralston
Woodside House
Ramsay
Auchterhouse

Balbegno Castle
Bamff House
Barnton Tower
Barra Castle
Bothwell Castle
Brechin Castle
Clatto Castle
Colluthie House
Corston Tower
Cruivie Castle
Dalhousie Castle
Easter Deans
Fasque
Foulden Bastle
Old Sauchie
Scotscraig
Straloch House
Tillicoultry Castle

Randolph
Auchen Castle
Boyne Castle
Darnaway Castle
Duns Castle
Morton Castle
Nairn Castle

Rankeilour
Rankeilour Castle

Rattray
Corb Castle
Craighall
Rattray Castle

Reid
Affleck Castle
Airds Castle
Barra Castle
Colliston Castle
Daldilling
Isle of Whithorn Castle
Lauriston Castle

Rennie
Melville Castle

Renton
Billie Castle
Lamberton
Mordington House

Richardson
Broomhall
Pitfour Castle
Smeaton Castle

Riddel
Glengarnock Castle
Lilliesleaf Tower
Oxenfoord Castle
Preston Tower
Riddell Tower
Whitton Tower

Riddle *see* **Riddel**

Rigg
Carberry Tower

Riggs
Aithernie Castle

Robertson
Bedlay Castle
Dunalastair
Eilean nam Faoileag
Pitcastle
Wrychtishousis

Rollo
Balloch Castle
Bannockburn House
Dumcrieff
Duncrub
Inverquiech Castle
Keltie Castle

Rose
Balblair
Kilravock Castle

Ross
Arnage Castle
Arthurlie House
Auchlossan House
Balgone House
Balnagown Castle
Balneil
Carscreugh Castle
Castle of King Edward
Cromarty Castle
Hawkhead Castle
Inch Castle
Melville Castle
Pitcalnie
Pittheavlis Castle
Portencross Castle
Provost Ross's House,
  Aberdeen
Sanquhar Castle
Shandwick Castle
Stanely Castle
Tarbet Castle
Tartraven Castle

Rossie
Rossie Castle

Russell
Aden House
Ashiesteel House

Rutherford
Ashintully Castle
Buck o' Bield
Fairnilee
Fairnington House
Glendevon Castle
Hunthill
Lauriston Castle
Migvie Castle
Purves Hall

Ruthven
Carse Gray
Dirleton Castle
Gowrie House, Perth
Huntingtower Castle
Rohallion Castle
Scone Palace

Trochrie Castle

Rynd
Carse Gray

Sandilands
Alderstone House
Calder House
Couston Castle
Cruivie Castle
Newark Castle
Niddrie Marischal
Pitlochie Castle
Pitteadie Castle
Torphichen Preceptory

Schaws *see* **Shaw**

Schivas
House of Schivas

Scott
Abbotsford
Aikwood Tower
Allanmouth Tower
Ancrum House
Ardross Castle
Ashiesteel House
Balcomie Castle
Balwearie Castle
Bavelaw Castle
Benholm Castle
Bowhill
Branxholme Castle
Broadhaugh
Brotherton Castle
Brugh
Buccleuch Castle
Burnhead Tower
Cairneyflappet Castle
Caroline Park House
Cash Tower
Cessnock Castle
Craighall
Curriehill Castle
Dairsie Castle
Dalkeith House
Dean Castle
Drumlanrig Castle
Drumlanrig's Tower,
  Hawick
Dryburgh Abbey
Dryhope Tower
Eldinhope Tower
Elie House
Enoch Castle
Ettrick House
Gamescleuch Tower
Goldielands Tower
Hallyards
Harden
Hassendean Castle
Hermitage Castle
Horsleyhill
Humbie Old Place
Inveresk Lodge

Isle of May
Killernie Castle
Kirkhope Tower
Lessudden House
Lugton
Makerstoun House
Malleny House
Mangerton Tower
Mertoun House
Minto House
Moss Tower
Murdostoun Castle
Newark Castle
Old Gala House
Old Howpasley
Pitlour
Polwarth Castle
Queen Mary's House,
  Jedburgh
Rossie Castle
Rumgally House
Scotscraig
Scotstarvit Tower
Sheriffhall
Smailholm Tower
Spottiswoode House
Stirches
Synton
Thirdpart House
Thirlestane Tower
Thirlestane Tower
Todrig Tower
Tushielaw Tower
Usan House
Westhouses
Whitchesters
Whitslade Tower

Scrimgeour
Dudhope Castle
Fincharn Castle
Myres Castle
Wedderburn Castle

Scrymgeour *see* **Scrimgeour**

Sempill *see* **Semple**

Semple
Balgone House
Barochan House
Belltrees Peel
Bishopton House
Castle Hill, Busby
Castle Levan
Castle Semple
Cathcart Castle
Drumry Castle
Elliston Castle
Northbar
Southannan Castle
The Peel, Busby

Seton
Abercorn Castle

Barnes Castle
Barra Castle
Bishop's House, Elgin
Carriden House
Castle Gogar
Castle Hill, Pluscarden
Culcreuch Castle
Dalgety
Falside Castle
Fyvie Castle
Gargunnock House
Garleton Castle
Gordon Castle
Greenknowe Tower
Hailes Castle
Meldrum House
Mounie Castle
Niddry Castle
Parbroath Castle
Pinkie House
Pitmedden House
Pittencrieff House
Preston Tower
Seton House
Shethin
Sorn Castle
Stoneypath Tower
Touch House
Tranent Tower
Whittinghame Castle
Winton House
Woodhall

Sharp
Allanbank House
Banff Castle
Hill of Tarvit Mansion
  House
Hoddom Castle
Houston House
Scotscraig
Scotstarvit Tower
Staneyhill Tower

Shaw
Brisbane House
Carnock House
Easter Greenock Castle
Greenock Castle
Hindhaughead
Nether Horsburgh Castle
Polkemmet House
Sauchie Tower
Tordarroch Castle

Sherriff
Stenhouse

Sibbald
Arnage Castle
Balgonie Castle
Kipps Castle
Pitcullo Castle
Rankeilour Castle

Sinclair
Ackergill Tower
Aldbar Castle
Berriedale Castle
Bishop Sinclair's Tower
Braal Castle
Brabster Castle
Brims Castle
Bucholly Castle
Cadboll Castle
Carfrae Peel
Castle Hill, Pluscarden
Castle of Mey
Castle of Old Wick
Catcune Tower
Cessford Castle
Cockburnspath Castle
Cousland Tower
Cullen House
Deskford Castle
Dounreay Castle
Dunbeath Castle
Earlstoun Castle
Evelaw Tower
Findlater Castle
Freswick House
Geanies Castle
Girnigoe Castle
Haimer Castle
Hempriggs House
Herbertshire Castle
Herdmanston
Keiss Castle
Kirkwall Castle
Knockhall Castle
Knockinnan Castle
Langwell Castle
Logan House
Longformacus
Morton House
Mortonhall
Nisbet House
Old Woodhouselee Castle
Peelhill
Pitteadie Castle
Polwarth Castle
Ravenscraig Castle
Ravensneuk Castle
Rosslyn Castle
Scrabster Castle
Stevenson House
Strathaven Castle
Strom Castle
Thurso Castle
Whitekirk
Woodhall
Siward
Kellie Castle
Tibbers Castle
Skene
Cairneyflappet Castle

Curriehill Castle
Hallyards
Hallyards Castle
Leask House
Lethenty Castle
Mains of Dyce
Parkhill House
Provost Skene's House,
  Aberdeen
Skene House
Smith
Evelaw Tower
Glassingall
Mugdock Castle
Smollet
Cameron House
Place of Bonhill
Smythe
Braco Castle
Methven Castle
Somerville
Carnock House
Carnwath House
Castlehill, Cambusnethan
Coltness Castle
Corehouse Castle
Couthalley Castle
Drum House
Linton Tower
Plean Castle
Sorn Castle
Torbrex Castle
Soulis
Clintwood Castle
Dean Castle
Hermitage Castle
Liddel Castle
Spalding
Ashintully Castle
Kilgarie
Whitefield Castle
Speirs
Culcreuch Castle
Houston House
Inch Castle
Spence
Crail Castle
Lathallan Castle
Stonelaw Tower
Wester Kames Castle
Wormiston House
Spens *see* **Spence**
Spittal
Blairlogie Castle
Coldoch
Spottiswoode
Dairsie Castle
Spottiswoode House
Spreull
Cowden Hall

Sprot
Riddell Tower
Spott House
Stark
Auchinvole House
Gartshore House
Steel
Aikwood Tower
Inchnock Castle
Waygateshaw House
Stephen
Kelly House
Stewart
Abbot House, Dunfermline
Airdit House
Aitkenhead Castle
Allanbank House
Allanton House
Ardvorlich
Arthurlie House
Ascog House
Auchterhouse
Balcaskie House
Balloch Castle
Balravie Castle
Balvenie Castle
Bar Castle
Bathgate Castle
Belltrees Peel
Bishopton House
Bishop's Palace, Kirkwall
Blackhall Manor
Blackhouse Tower
Blair Castle
Blantyre Priory
Bothan an Lochain
Braal Castle
Breachacha Castle
Bridge Castle
Brodick Castle
Bunkle Castle
Caberston Tower
Cally Castle
Cardney House
Cardonald Castle
Careston Castle
Cardney House
Carrick House
Carstairs Castle
Castle Campbell
Castle Hill, Busby
Castle Levan
Castle of King Edward
Castle Shuna
Castle Stalker
Castle Stewart
Castle Stuart
Castle Sween
Castlehill, Cambusnethan
Castlemilk
Clachary

Coltness Castle
Corsewall Castle
Cortachy Castle
Crichton Castle
Croft an Righ House
Crookston Castle
Cruggleton Castle
Dalswinton Castle
Darnaway Castle
Darnley Castle
Deskie Castle
Donibristle Castle
Doune Castle
Drumin Castle
Duchal Castle
Duke Murdoch's Castle
Dunbar Castle
Dundas Castle
Dundonald Castle
Dunoon Castle
Dunrod Castle
Earl's Palace, Birsay
Earl's Palace, Kirkwall
Easter Greenock Castle
Eilean Dearg Castle
Eliock House
Erskine Castle
Fairnington House
Falkland Palace
Farme Castle
Fatlips Castle
Feddal
Fincastle House
Galloway House Gardens,
  Garlieston
Garlies Castle
Garth Castle
Gauldwell Castle
Glanderston Castle
Glasserton House
Gourock Castle
Grandtully Castle
Grange
Hailes Castle
Hallbar Tower
Hartshaw Tower
Hermitage Castle
Hillside
Houston House
Inch Castle
Inchcolm Abbey
Inchinnan Castle
Inchmurrin Castle
Inchtalla Castle
Innerwick Castle
Inverkip Castle
Invermay Tower
Jarlshof
Kames Castle
Kellie Castle
Kilbucho Place

Kildonan Castle
Kildrummy Castle
Kilmory Castle
Kilnmaichlie House
Kindrochit Castle
Kinfauns Castle
Kirkhill House
Kirkwall Castle
Kyle Castle
Lainshaw Castle
Lennox Castle
Lennoxlove
Lincluden Collegiate
  Church
Loch an Eilean Castle
Lochindorb Castle
Lochranza Castle
Mains Castle
Mar's Castle, Aberdeen
Mayshiel
Mearns Castle
Meggernie Castle
Methven Castle
Mount Stuart House
Murdostoun Castle
Murthly Castle
Northbar
Ochiltree Castle
Ochiltree Castle
Old Place of Mochrum
Old Place, Blantyre
Ormiston Tower
Pittenweem Priory
Pittheavlis Castle
Ravenstone Castle
Red Castle
Renfield
Renfrew Castle
Riccarton
Rosyth Castle
Rothesay Castle
Ruthven Barracks
Scalloway Castle
Shillinglaw Castle
Sorbie Castle
Stewart Tower
Strathaven Castle
Stravithie Castle
Torrance Castle
Touch House
Tower Rais
Traquair House
Ward of Lochnorris
Wedderlie House
Wester Kames Castle
Stirling
Alva Castle
Balglass Castle
Ballagan Castle
Cadder Castle
Craigbarnet Castle

Edzell Castle
Gargunnock House
Glorat House
Herbertshire Castle
Keir House
Keppoch House
Lauriston Castle
Law Tower
Moat
Old Kippencross
Steuarthall
Tower of Garden
Stoddart
Shieldgreen Tower
Strachan
Claypotts Castle
Craigcrook Castle
Fetteresso Castle
Glenkindie House
Lynturk Castle
Monboddo House
Thornton Castle
Straiton *see* **Stratton**
Strang
Balcaskie House
Strathendry
Strathendry Castle
Stratton
Kirkside Castle
Lauriston Castle
Straiton
Stuart *see* **Stewart**
Sutherland
Ardvreck Castle
Berriedale Castle
Castle of Old Wick
Cnoc Chaisteal
Dirlot Castle
Duffus Castle
Dunrobin Castle
Forse Castle
Golspie Tower
Helmsdale Castle
Langwell Castle
Loch Brora
Proncy Castle
Quarrelwood Castle
Skelbo Castle
Skibo Castle
Swiney Castle
Thunderton House, Elgin
Suttie
Balgone House
Prestongrange House
Swinton
Cranshaws Castle
Little Swinton
Mersington Tower
Swinton
Sydserf
Sydserf

Syme
Northfield House
Symmer
House of Mergie
Symson
Craighouse
Tait
Castle Campbell
Harviestoun Castle
Tennant
Cairns Tower
Innes House
Linnhouse
Thomson
Castle of Fiddes
Dunino Den
Thorburn
Ormiston Tower
Thornton
Thornton Castle
Threipland
Fingask Castle
Kinnaird Castle
Torthorwald
Torthorwald Castle
Tower
Garleton Castle
Trent
Pitcullo Castle
Trentham
Dunrobin Castle
Trotter
Broomhill House
Dreghorn Castle
Mortonhall
Troup
Castle of Troup
Findon Castle
Tulloch
Noltland Castle
Turing
Foveran Castle
Turnbull
Airdrie House
Barnhills Tower
Bedrule Castle
Fast Castle
Fatlips Castle
Fulton Tower
Hallrule
Houndwood House
Minto House
Newton Tower
Spittal Tower
Wauchope Tower
Tweedie
Bield Tower
Castlehill Tower
Dreva Tower
Drumelzier Castle
Halmyre House

Kittlehall
Oliver Castle
Quarter House
Tinnis Castle
Wrae Tower
Tyrie
Dunnideer Castle
Tytler
Fulford Tower
Udny
Knockhall Castle
Tillery
Udny Castle
Urie
Pitfichie Castle
Urquhart
Braelangwell
Castle Craig
Craigston Castle
Cromarty Castle
Crombie Castle
Kinbeachie Castle
Meldrum House
Valance
Lochore Castle
Pitteadie Castle
Tranent Tower
Vaux
Airyolland
Balneil
Barnbarroch Castle
Carscreugh Castle
Castle Loch Castle
Castlewigg
Dirleton Castle
Larg Castle
Longcastle
Veitch
Castlehill Tower
Dawyck House
Easter Dawyck
Eliock House
Flemington Tower
Lour Tower
North Synton
Vellum
Woodrae Castle
Vickers
Tulloch Castle
Vipont
Blackness Castle
Langton Castle
Walker
Crawfordton Tower
Walkinshaw
Bishopton House
Walkinshaw
Wallace
Auchans
Auchenbathie Castle
Auchencruive Castle

Auchinvole House
Candacraig
Caprington Castle
Carnell
Cessnock Castle
Craigie Castle
Crosbie Castle
Glassingall
Kelly House
Kildonan
Milliken
Newton Castle
Riccarton Castle
Sundrum Castle
Wallace's Buildings
Woolmet House
Wardlaw
Grange House
Lochore Castle
Pitreavie Castle
Torrie Castle
Warrender
Bruntsfield House
Watson
Aberdour Castle
Aithernie Castle
Pitcruvie Castle
Rothes Castle
Saughton House
Stenhouse
Watt
Spott House
Wauchope
Cakemuir Castle
Edmonstone Castle
Niddrie Marischal
Wedderburn
Kingennie
Wedderburn Castle
Weir
Auchtyfardle Castle
Blackwood House
Dowane
Glenane
Kirkton of Carluke
Stonebyres House
Waygateshaw House
Wellwood
Garvock Hill
Welsh
Mossfennan
Wemyss
Dura House
Elcho Castle
Logie House
MacDuff's Castle
Neidpath Castle
Pittencrieff House
Rires Castle
Rossend Castle
Rumgally House

Scotstarvit Tower
Torrie Castle
Wemyss Castle
West Wemyss
Wharncliffe
Belmont Castle
White
Overtoun Castle
Whitefoord
Blairquhan
Whiteford Tower
Whitelaw
Fenton Tower
Gartsherrie House
Gartshore House
Wilkie
Bonnington House
William
Kilbucho Place
Williamson
Cardrona Tower
Castle Robert
Chapelhill
Foulitch Tower
Hutchinfield Tower
Willougby
Drummond Castle
Stobhall
Wilson
Airdrie House
Thainstone House
Winram
Inch House
Wishart
Logie House
Pittarrow Castle
Wodropp
Edmonston Castle
Elsrickle
Wood
Balbegno Castle
Bonnyton Castle
Craig House
Geilston House
Largo Castle
Young
Aldbar Castle
Inverugie Castle
Kelly House
Kirkton
Younger
Auchen Castle
Yuille
Darleith House

435

Further Reading

Black, G F *The Surnames of Scotland,* (Edinburgh, 1993).

Council for Scottish Archeology, *Discovery and Excavation in Scotland*, yearly publications.

Coventry, M *The Haunted Places of Scotland,* (Musselburgh, 1999).

Donaldson, G and Morpeth, R S *A Dictionary of Scottish History*, (Edinburgh, 1988).

Groome, F *Ordnance Gazetter of Scotland*, 6 vols, (Glasgow, c1890).

Keay, J and Keay, J (eds) *Collins Encyclopedia of Scotland* (London, 1994).

Lindsay, M *The Castles of Scotland*, (London, 1986).

MacGibbon, D and Ross, T *The Castellated and Domestic Architecture of Scotland*, 5 vols, (Edinburgh, 1887-92).

Mason, G W *The Castles of Glasgow and the Clyde,* (Musselburgh, 2000).

McKean, C (series editor) *The Illustrated Architectural Guides to Scotland*, (Edinburgh, from 1985).

Salter, M *The Castles of South-West Scotland*, (Worcs, 1993).

Salter, M *The Castles of the Heartland of Scotland*, (Worcs, 1994).

Salter, M *The Castles of Lothian and the Borders*, (Worcs, 1994).

Salter, M *The Castles of Western and Northern Scotland*, (Worcs, 1995).

Salter, M *The Castles of Grampian and Angus*, (Worcs, 1995).

Stone, J *Illustrated Maps of Scotland from Blaeu's Atlas Novus of the 17th century*, (London, 1991).

Tabraham, C *Scotland's Castles*, (London, 1997).

Tranter, N *The Fortified House in Scotland*, 5 vols, (Edinburgh, 1962).

Way, G and Squire, R *Scottish Clan & Family Encyclopedia*, (Glasgow, 1994).